Lecture Notes in Computer Science   11014

Commenced Publication in 1973
Founding and Former Series Editors:
Gerhard Goos, Juris Hartmanis, and Jan van Leeuwen

Advanced Research in Computing and Software Science
Subline of Lecture Notes in Computer Science

More information about this series at http://www.springer.com/series/7407

Marco Aldinucci · Luca Padovani
Massimo Torquati (Eds.)

Euro-Par 2018: Parallel Processing

24th International Conference
on Parallel and Distributed Computing
Turin, Italy, August 27–31, 2018
Proceedings

 Springer

Editors
Marco Aldinucci 🔟
Department of Computer Science
University of Torino
Torino
Italy

Massimo Torquati 🔟
Department of Computer Science
University of Pisa
Pisa
Italy

Luca Padovani 🔟
Department of Computer Science
University of Torino
Torino
Italy

ISSN 0302-9743 ISSN 1611-3349 (electronic)
Lecture Notes in Computer Science
ISBN 978-3-319-96982-4 ISBN 978-3-319-96983-1 (eBook)
https://doi.org/10.1007/978-3-319-96983-1

Library of Congress Control Number: 2018949144

LNCS Sublibrary: SL1 – Theoretical Computer Science and General Issues

This Springer imprint is published by the registered company Springer Nature Switzerland AG
The registered company address is: Gewerbestrasse 11, 6330 Cham, Switzerland

Preface

This volume contains the papers presented at Euro-Par 2018, the 24th International European Conference on Parallel and Distributed Computing, held during August 27–31, 2018, in Turin, Italy. The whole computer hardware industry has embraced parallel computing. Today it is clear that in the long term, writing efficient, portable, and correct parallel programs must be no more challenging than writing the same programs for sequential computers. Euro-Par envisioned this challenge 24 years ago. It gracefully evolved from pioneering efforts to the mainstream of parallel computing maintaining its broad-spectrum coverage on parallel computing topics, from software to hardware to their co-design. Its adaptability and capability to frame emerging topics in an independent, consolidated structure is still the key to its success.

The main audience of Euro-Par comprises researchers in academia, public and private laboratories, and industrial organizations. Euro-Par's main objective is to be the primary choice of such professionals for the presentation of new results in the field.

Previous Euro-Par conferences took place in Stockholm, Lyon, Passau, Southampton, Toulouse, Munich, Manchester, Paderborn, Klagenfurt, Pisa, Lisbon, Dresden, Rennes, Las Palmas, Delft, Ischia, Bordeaux, Rhodes, Aachen, Porto, Vienna, Grenoble, and Santiago de Compostela. The 24th edition of Euro-Par was organized by the Computer Science Department of the University of Turin. The topics were organized into 12 tracks, namely: Support Tools and Environments; Performance and Power Modeling, Prediction, and Evaluation; Scheduling and Load Balancing; High-Performance Architectures and Compilers; Parallel and Distributed Data Management and Analytics; Cluster and Cloud Computing; Distributed Systems and Algorithms; Parallel and Distributed Programming, Interfaces, and Languages; Multicore and Manycore Methods and Tools; Theory and Algorithms for Parallel Computation and Networking; Parallel Numerical Methods and Applications; and Accelerator Computing for Advanced Applications. Overall, 194 papers were submitted from 39 countries. The number of submitted papers, the wide topic coverage and the aim of obtaining high-quality reviews resulted in a difficult selection process involving a large number of experts. The join effort of the members of the Scientific Committee and of the 306 external reviewers resulted in 787 reviews: five papers received three reviews, 173 received four reviews and 16 received five, that is, on average, 4.06 reviews per paper. The accepted papers were chosen after lengthy discussions and finalized during the physical selection meeting, which took place on April 27, 2018 in Turin. All local chairs and three members of the Steering Committee participated in the meeting. In the end, 57 papers were selected to be presented at the conference and published in the proceedings, resulting in a 29.4% acceptance rate. The following three papers were nominated as "distinguished" and presented in a plenary session: "Resource-Efficient Execution of Conditional Parallel Real-Time Tasks," "VIoLET: A Large-Scale Virtual Environment for Internet of Things," "Design Principles for Sparse Matrix Multiplication on the GPU."

Apart the presentation sessions of accepted papers, we were honored to host three keynote talks given by esteemed colleagues, namely: "ALGORAND: A Better Distributed Ledger" by Silvio Micali, "Algorithmic Adaptations to Extreme Scale Computing" by David E. Keyes, and "Datacenters for the Post-Moore Era" by Babak Falsafi. The conference program was complemented by two days of workshops and tutorials on specialized topics. Dora B. Heras and Gabriele Mencagli deserve recognition for managing them efficiently and effectively. A selection of the papers presented at the workshops will be published in separated proceedings volumes after the conference.

With respect to previous editions of Euro-Par, the 2018 edition introduced two novelties both aimed at improving the relevance and impact of the scientific works presented at the conference. For the first time in the history of Euro-Par, authors of accepted papers were encouraged to submit an *artifact* (e.g., source code, tools, benchmarks, datasets, models) to assess the reproducibility of the experimental results presented in the paper. Overall, 13 artifacts were submitted and all of them were positively evaluated by a separate Artifact Evaluation Committee. Papers with an associated artifact received a seal of approval in the proceedings and Springer kindly agreed to permanently host all artifacts on their servers. Although the practice of evaluating artifacts is becoming commonplace in other computer science conferences, it should be mentioned that it poses substantial challenges in a conference like Euro-Par, in which artifacts may require large and dedicated hardware infrastructures and may involve the processing of gigabytes of data for long periods of time. The resulting additional effort required of the organizers and the members of the Artifact Evaluation Committee was largely compensated by the enthusiasm of the authors who decided to submit an artifact. In the end, nearly one quarter of the papers had an associated artifact. The second novelty experimented with in Euro-Par 2018 was a session of *chess-timer talks*, in which the audience was encouraged to interact with the speakers, and the session chair balanced solo presentation and discussions using a chess timer. We got the idea of proposing chess-timer talks from the successful CurryOn conference as an "unusual solution to making tech conferences a more interactive, more fun, and better place for learning and discussions."

The Euro-Par conference in Turin would not have been possible without the support of many individuals and organizations. We owe special thanks to the authors of all the submitted papers, the members of the topic committees, in particular, the global and local chairs, as well as the reviewers for their contributions to the success of the conference. We would also like to express our gratitude to the members of the Organizing Committee and the local staff who helped us. We are indebted to the members of the Euro-Par Steering Committee, especially Christian Lengauer, Luc Bougé, and Fernando Silva, for their trust, constant guidance, and support. We are grateful to the staff of Springer, particularly Anna Kramer, Alfred Hofmann, and Graham Smith, for their support in the preparation of the proceedings and the management of artifacts. Finally, a number of institutional and industrial sponsors contributed to the organization of the conference. Their names appear on the Euro-Par 2018 website.

It was a pleasure and an honor to organize and host Euro-Par 2018 in Turin.

June 2018

Marco Aldinucci
Luca Padovani
Massimo Torquati

Organization

Steering Committee

Full Members

Luc Bougé (Chair)	ENS Rennes, France
Fernando Silva (Vice-Chair)	University of Porto, Portugal
Dora B. Heras (Workshops Chair)	CiTIUS, Santiago de Compostela, Spain
Emmanuel Jeannot	LaBRI-Inria, Bordeaux, France
Christos Kaklamanis	Computer Technology Institute, Patras, Greece
Paul Kelly	Imperial College, London, UK
Thomas Ludwig	University of Hamburg, Germany
Tomàs Margalef	University Autonoma of Barcelona, Spain
Wolfgang Nagel	Dresden University of Technology, Germany
Francisco Fernández Rivera	CiTIUS, Santiago de Compostela, Spain
Rizos Sakellariou	University of Manchester, UK
Henk Sips	Delft University of Technology, The Netherlands
Domenico Talia	University of Calabria, Italy
Jesper Larsson Träff	TU Wien, Austria
Denis Trystram	Grenoble Institute of Technology, France
Felix Wolf	TU Darmstadt, Germany

Honorary Members

Christian Lengauer	University of Passau, Germany
Ron Perrott	Oxford e-Research Centre, UK
Karl Dieter Reinartz	University of Erlangen-Nürnberg, Germany

Observers

Marco Aldinucci	University of Turin, Italy
Ramin Yahyapour	GWDG/University of Göttingen, Germany

Euro-Par 2018 Organization

Co-chairs

Marco Aldinucci	University of Turin, Italy
Luca Padovani	University of Turin, Italy
Massimo Torquati	University of Pisa, Italy

Workshops

Dora B. Heras   University of Santiago de Compostela, Spain
Gabriele Mencagli   University of Pisa, Italy

Tutorials and Industry

Peter Kilpatrick   Queen's University Belfast, UK
Claudia Misale   IBM T.J. Watson Research Center, USA

Publicity

Javier Garcia Blas   Universidad Carlos III de Madrid, Spain
Dalvan Griebler   Pontifical Catholic University of Rio Grande do Sul,
                               Brazil
Ivan Merelli   CNR-ITB, Italy
Fabio Tordini   University of Turin, Italy

Submission and Reviewing Process

Daniele D'Agostino   CNR-IMATI, Italy
Massimo Torquati   University of Pisa, Italy

Artifact Evaluation Process

Gabriele Mencagli   University of Pisa, Italy
Luca Padovani   University of Turin, Italy
Massimo Torquati   University of Pisa, Italy

Web and Social Media

Claudio Mattutino   University of Turin, Italy
Sergio Rabellino   University of Turin, Italy

Logistics

Katia Lupo   University of Turin, Italy
Claudio Mattutino   University of Turin, Italy
Sergio Rabellino   University of Turin, Italy

Program Committee

Topic 1: Support Tools and Environments

Global Chair
Siegfried Benkner   Universität Wien, Austria

Local Chair
Massimo Coppola   CNR-ISTI, Italy

Chairs

Franz Franchetti	Carnegie Mellon University, USA
Michael Gerndt	Technische Universität München, Germany
Erwin Laure	Royal Institute of Technology, Sweden
Nikos Parlavantzas	INSA Rennes and IRISA, France

Topic 2: Performance and Power Modeling, Prediction and Evaluation

Global Chair

Leonel Sousa	Universidade de Lisboa, Portugal

Local Chair

Daniele De Sensi	University of Pisa, Italy

Chairs

Giorgis Georgakoudis	Queen's University Belfast, UK
Aleksandar Ilic	Universidade de Lisboa, Portugal
Piotr Luszczek	University of Tennessee, USA
Federico Silla	Universitat Politecnica de Valencia, Spain
Guangming Tan	Chinese Academy of Sciences, China
Pedro Trancoso	Chalmers University of Technology, Sweden

Topic 3: Scheduling and Load Balancing

Global Chair

Anne Benoitć	ENS Lyon, France

Local Chair

Enrico Bini	University of Turin, Italy

Chairs

Maciej Drozdowski	Poznan University of Technology, Poland
Lionel Eyraud-Dubois	LaBRI-inria, Bordeaux, France
José Gracia	HLRS, Stuttgart, Germany
Nan Guan	Hong Kong Polytechnic University, Hong Kong, SAR China
Sascha Hunold	TU Wien, Austria
Krzysztof Rzadca	University of Warsaw, Poland

Topic 4: High-Performance Architectures and Compilers

Global Chair

Florian Brandner	Télécom ParisTech, Université Paris-Saclay, France

Local Chair

Fabio Luporini	Imperial College London, UK

Chairs

Alexandra Jimborean	Uppsala University, Sweden
Frank Hannig	University of Erlangen-Nürnberg, Germany
Gihan Mudalige	University of Warwick, UK

Topic 5: Parallel and Distributed Data Management and Analytics

Global Chair

K. Selçuk Candan	Arizona State University, USA

Local Chair

Ruggero Pensa	University of Turin, Italy

Chairs

Lei Chen	Hong Kong University of Science and Technology, SAR China
Gianmarco De Francisci Morales	Qatar Computing Research Institute, Qatar
Ming Zhao	Arizona State University, USA

Topic 6: Cluster and Cloud Computing

Global Chair

Ivona Brandić	Vienna University of Technology, Austria

Local Chair

Domenico Talia	Università della Calabria, Italy

Chairs

Toni Mastelic	Vienna University of Technology, Austria
Raffaele Montella	Università degli Studi di Napoli Parthenope, Italy
Anne-Cécile Orgerie	CNRS, Rennes, France
Thomas Renner	Technische Universität Berlin, Germany
Rafael Brundo Uriarte	IMT School for Advanced Studies, Lucca, Italy

Topic 7: Distributed Systems and Algorithms

Global Chair

Sonia Ben-Mokhtar	LIRIS, INSA de Lyon, France

Local Chair

Alberto Montresor	University of Trento, Italy

Chairs

Christof Fetzer	TU Dresden, Germany
Indranil Gupta	University of Illinois, Urbana-Champaign, USA

Topic 8: Parallel and Distributed Programming, Interfaces, and Languages

Global Chair
J. Daniel García   University Carlos III of Madrid, Spain

Local Chair
Patrizio Dazzi   CNR-ISTI, Italy

Chairs
Bryce Adelstein-Lelbach   NVIDIA, USA
Marcelo Pasin   Université de Neuchâtel, Switzerland
Mitsuhisa Sato   Riken and University of Tsukuba, Japan
Paolo Trunfio   DIMES, University of Calabria, Italy
Chan-Hyun Youn   KAIST, South Korea

Topic 9: Multicore and Manycore Methods and Tools

Global Chair
Christoph Kessler   Linköping University, Sweden

Local Chair
Marco Danelutto   University of Pisa, Italy

Chairs
Rudolf Eigenmann   University of Delaware, USA
Arturo González Escribano   Universidad de Valladolid, Spain
Kevin Hammond   University of St. Andrews, UK
Jesper Larsson Träff   TU Wien, Austria
Ana Lucia Varbanescu   University of Amsterdam, The Netherlands

Topic 10: Theory and Algorithms for Parallel Computation and Networking

Global Chair
Christos Zaroliagis   University of Patras, Greece

Local Chair
Tiziano De Matteis   University of Pisa, Italy

Chairs
Leszek Gąsieniec   University of Liverpool, UK
Ulrich Meyer   Goethe-Universität Frankfurt am Main, Germany
Henning Meyerhenke   Universität zu Köln, Germany

Topic 11: Parallel Numerical Methods and Applications

Global Chair

Elisabeth Larsson	Uppsala University, Sweden

Local Chair

Pasqua D'Ambra	CNR-IAC, Naples, Italy

Chairs

Aneta Karaivanova	Institute of Information and Communication Technology (IICT-BAS), Bulgaria
Ángeles Martínez Calomardo	University of Padova, Italy
Ulrike Meier Yang	CASC-LLNL, USA

Topic 12: Accelerator Computing for Advanced Applications

Global Chair

Angeles Navarro	Universidad de Málaga, Spain

Local Chair

Maurizio Drocco	University of Turin, Italy

Chairs

Raphael de Camargo	Federal University of ABC, Brazil
Jaejin Lee	Seoul National University, South Korea
Jose Luis Nunez-Yanez	University of Bristol, UK

Artifact Evaluation Committee

Javier Garcia Blas	University Carlos III of Madrid, Spain
Massimo Coppola	CNR-ISTI Pisa, Italy
Tiziano De Matteis	University of Pisa, Italy
Daniele De Sensi	University of Pisa, Italy
Manuel F. Dolz	University Carlos III of Madrid, Spain
Maurizio Drocco	University of Turin, Italy
Javier Fernandez Munoz	University Carlos III of Madrid, Spain
Salvatore Filippone	Cranfield University, UK
Dalvan Griebler	Pontifical Catholic University of Rio Grande do Sul, Brazil
Lu Li	University of Edinburgh, UK
Fabrizio Marozzo	DIMES, University of Calabria, Italy
Matteo Nardelli	University of Rome Tor Vergata, Italy
Mauricio Pilla	Federal University of Pelotas, Brazil
Paolo Viviani	University of Turin, Italy

Euro-Par 2018 Additional Reviewers

Aguilar, Xavier
Ahmed, Laeeq
Ahvar, Ehsan
Alguwaifli, Yasir
Amarís González, Marcos
Ancourt, Corinne
Angriman, Eugenio
Aral, Atakan
Areias, Miguel
Atalar, Aras
Atanassov, Emanouil
Aublin, Pierre-Louis
Aupy, Guillaume
Aurangzeb
Bacciu, Davide
Bachstein, Matthew
Bajic, Fani
Bajrovic, Enes
Balouek-Thomert, Daniel
Barker, Andrew
Baroli, Davide
Barwell, Adam
Basumallik, Ayon
Beaumont, Olivier
Behrens, Hans
Belcastro, Loris
Beltran, Vicenç
Benedict, Shajulin
Bergamaschi, Luca
Berlinska, Joanna
Bernaschi, Massimo
Bigot, Julien
Bolten, Matthias
Bourgoin, Mathias
Brandes, Thomas
Brown, Christopher
Brown, Dominic
Buesing, Henrik
Buttari, Alfredo
Cardellini, Valeria
Carlini, Emanuele
Caron, Eddy
Carpentieri, Bruno

Carretero, Jesus
Carribault, Patrick
Catena, Matteo
Cavalheiro, Gerson
Caíno-Lores, Silvina
Cecilia, José M.
Cesario, Eugenio
Chen, Yitao
Chester, Dean
Chester, Dean G.
Collange, Sylvain
Comito, Carmela
Corbera, Francisco
Coullon, Helene
Danelutto, Marco
Dao, Than Tuan
De Maio, Vincenzo
De Simone, Valentina
de Souza, Diego F.
Decouchant, Jérémie
Del Río Astorga, David
Denoyelle, Nicolas
Di Girolamo, Salvatore
Dickson, James
Do, Youngdong
Dobrev, Veselin
Dokulil, Jiri
Dolz, Manuel
Dreuning, Henk
Drocco, Maurizio
Du, He
Durastante, Fabio
Dutot, Pierre-François
Dutta, Hritam
Engblom, Stefan
Falcao, Gabriel
Faqeh, Rasha
Fernandez Fabeiro, Jorge
Fernandez, Javier
Fey, Dietmar
Fey, Florian
Filippone, Salvatore
Flores, Paulo

Folino, Francesco
Folino, Gianluigi
Forestiero, Agostino
Gadkari, Ashish
Gante, João
Garcia Blas, Javier
Gardner, David
Garg, Yash
Gaspar, Francisco
Gendron, Bernard
Geronimo, Guilherme
Gorlatch, Sergei
Gracia, José
Grahn, Håkan
Grelck, Clemens
Grubel, Patricia
Gu, Chuancai
Guermouche, Abdou
Guerreiro, João
Gurov, Todor
Guyon, David
Ha, Phuong
Herlihy, Maurice
Hiraishi, Tasuku
Hoefer, Martin
Hugo, Andra
Hückelheim, Jan
Ienco, Dino
Ivanovska, Sofiya
Janna, Carlo
Jeong, Chang-Sung
Jiang, Xu
Jo, Gangwon
Jung, Wookeun
Kallimanis, Nikolaos
Kang, Dong-Ki
Karlsson, Sven
Keller, Jörg
Kim, Heehoon
Kim, Hyngmo
Kim, Jungwook
Kim, Seong-Hwan
Kim, Woojoong

Kirk, Richard
Kontogiannis, Spyros
Koslovski, Guilherme
Kosta, Sokol
Krall, Andreas
Kritikos, Kyriakos
Kronbichler, Martin
Kukreja, Navjot
Kumar, Rakesh
Kumaraswamy, Madhura
Kunji, Khalid
Lambert, Thomas
Larsson, Elisabeth
Le Quoc, Do
Lee, Jinpil
Lee, Yongjun
Legrand, Arnaud
Li, Ruipeng
Li, Xueqi
Lin, Yuhan
Lirkov, Ivan
Liu, Jun
Liu, Sicong
Liu, Songran
Liu, Weifeng
Low, Tze Meng
Lujic, Ivan
Lulli, Alessandro
Madi-Wamba, Gilles
Maier, Tobias
Mao, Bo
Maouche, Mohamed
Marozzo, Fabrizio
Marques, Diogo
Martin, André
Martins, Paulo
Matsuda, Motohiko
Mazzia, Francesca
McKenney, Paul
Mehofer, Eduard
Mele, Valeria
Melot, Nicolas
Mendes, Rafael
Meng, Ke
Mijaković, Robert
Misale, Claudia

Morais, Mayuri
Mordacchini, Matteo
Mounié, Grégory
Nagarkar, Parth
Nakao, Masahiro
Netzer, Gilbert
Neves, Nuno
Nidito, Francesco
Oh, Pyeongseok
Ohshima, Satoshi
Oleksenko, Oleksii
Osborn, Sarah
Owen, Herbert
Owenson, Andrew
Padoin, Edson Luiz
Palkowski, Marek
Park, Sangdon
Pascual, Fanny
Penschuck, Manuel
Perarnau, Swann
Pereira, Fernando
Petri, Matthias
Pham, Linh Manh
Pllana, Sabri
Poccia, Silvestro
Poke, Marius
Ponce, Colin
Popov, Mihail
Popovici, Doru Thom
Prokopec, Aleksandar
Qiao, Bo
Qiu, Sheng
Raca, Valon
Rais, Issam
Raoofy, Amir
Rauchwerger, Lawrence
Rebonatto, M. Trindade
Reguly, Istvan
Rehn-Sonigo, Veronika
Reiche, Oliver
Reis, Valentin
Rezaei, Mohamad
Ricketson, Lee
Rivas-Gomez, Sergio
Romano, Diego
Ros, Alberto

Rupp, Karl
Sabne, Amit
Sadi, Fazle
Sakdhnagool, Putt
Sampathirao, Ajay Kumar
Sandrieser, Martin
Santana, Luis
Santander-Jiménez, Sergio
Santos, Danilo
Sarkar, Subhadeep
Sarkar, Susmit
Sato, Yukinori
Saveski, Martin
Schickedanz, Alexander
Schmitt, Christian
Schroder, Jacob
Schuchart, Joseph
Serafini, Marco
Serrano, Estefania
Shin, Dong-Jae
Shun, Julian
Sjogreen, Bjorn
Skowron, Piotr
Soliman, Amira
Spampinato, Daniele
Spataro, William
Spiga, Filippo
Stramondo, Giulio
Sun, Jinghao
Sun, Tianjiao
Sutra, Pierre
Tairum, Miguel
Tanase, Alexandru
Tang, Yue
Teabe, Boris
Terboven, Christian
Thamsen, Lauritz
Tomas, Andres
Tomov, Vladimir
Torres de La Sierra,
    Yuri
Trach, Bohdan
Trinitis, Carsten
Trunfio, Paolo
Träff, Jesper Larsson
Tsai, Yaohung

Tsigas, Philippas
Tsuji, Miwako
Ujaldon, Manuel
Utrera, Gladys
Vaddina, Kameswar
Vasiloudis, Theodore
Vaumourin, Gregory
Veiga, Luís
Veith, David
Venetis, Ioannis
Verbitskiy, Ilya
Verdoolaege, Sven
Vespa, Emanuele
Villegas, Alejandro
Vinci, Andrea

Viviani, Paolo
von Looz, Moritz
Voronin, Kirill
Wacrenier, Pierre-André
Wagner, Martin
Wallschläger, Marcel
Walulya, Ivan
Wang, Zhan
Weidendorfer, Josef
Wilhelm, Andreas
Wong, Michael
Wu, Meng-Ju
Xie, Zhen
Xu, Guanglin
Yang, Dai

Yang, Eunju
Yang, Qirui
Yao, Erlin
Yarkhan, Asim
Yasugi, Masahiro
Yeh, Tsung Tai
Zamani, Ali Reza
Zang, Dawei
Zhang, Fa
Zhang, Jiyuan
Zilic, Josip
Zlatev, Zahari
Zounon, Mawussi
Żuk, Paweł

Euro-Par 2018 Invited Talks

ALGORAND: A Better Distributed Ledger

Silvio Micali

CSAIL, MIT, USA

A distributed ledger is a tamperproof sequence of data that can be read and augmented by everyone. Distributed ledgers stand to revolutionize the way a democratic society operates. They secure all kinds of traditional transactions – such as payments, asset transfers, titling – in the exact order in which they occur; and enable totally new transactions – such as cryptocurrencies and smart contracts. They can remove intermediaries and usher in a new paradigm for trust. As currently implemented, however, distributed ledgers cannot achieve their enormous potential. Algorand is an alternative, democratic, and efficient distributed ledger. Unlike prior ledgers based on "proof of work", it dispenses with "miners". Indeed, Algorand requires only a negligible amount of computation. Moreover, its transaction history does not "fork" with overwhelming probability: i.e., Algorand guarantees the finality of all transactions.

Algorithmic Adaptations to Extreme Scale Computing

David E. Keyes

King Abdullah University, Saudi Arabia

Algorithmic adaptations to use next-generation computers close to their potential are underway. Instead of squeezing out flops – the traditional goal of algorithmic optimality, which once served as a reasonable proxy for all associated costs – algorithms must now squeeze synchronizations, memory, and data transfers, while extra flops on locally cached data represent only small costs in time and energy. After decades of programming model stability with bulk synchronous processing, new programming models and new algorithmic capabilities (to make forays into, e.g., data assimilation, inverse problems, and uncertainty quantification) must be co-designed with the hardware. We briefly recap the architectural constraints and application opportunities. We then concentrate on two types of tasks each of occupies a large portion of all scientific computing cycles: large dense symmetric/Hermitian linear systems (covariances, Hamiltonians, Hessians, Schur complements) and large sparse Poisson/Helmholtz systems (solids, fluids, electromagnetism, radiation diffusion, gravitation). We examine progress in porting "exact" and hierarchically rank-reduced solvers for these tasks to the hybrid distributed-shared programming environment, including the GPU and the MIC architectures that make up the cores of the top scientific computers "on the floor" and "on the books."

Datacenters for the Post-Moore Era

Babak Falsafi

EPFL, Switzerland

Datacenters are growing at unprecedented speeds fueled by the demand on global IT services, investments in massive data analytics and economies of scale. Worldwide data by some accounts (e.g., IDC) grows at much higher rates than server capability and capacity. Conventional silicon technologies laying the foundation for server platforms, however, have dramatically slowed down in efficiency and density scaling in recent years. The latter, now referred to as the post-Moore era, has given rise to a plethora of emerging logic and memory technologies presenting exciting new challenges and abundant opportunities from algorithms to platforms for server designers. In this talk, I will first motivate the post-Moore era for server architecture and present avenues to pave the path forward for server design.

Euro-Par 2018 Topics Overview

Topic 1: Support Tools and Environments

Siegfried Benkner, Massimo Coppola, Franz Franchetti,
Michael Gerndt, Erwin Laure, and Nikos Parlavantzas

Despite an impressive body of research over the last decades, parallel and distributed programming remains a complex task, a process that is prone to subtle software issues that can affect both the correctness and the performance of an application. The amount of implementation details and their hidden connections are getting harder and harder to manage as multilevel parallel hierarchical and hybrid architectures become more and more commonplace along the path to Exascale computing systems.

The Euro-Par Support Tools and Environments track focuses on tools, techniques and environments that help tackling that complexity by addressing the many challenges related to programmability, portability, correctness, reliability, scalability, efficiency, performance and energy consumption.

The papers submitted and accepted for this track do well represent the community that this topic brings together, gathering tool designers, developers, and users to share their ideas, solutions, products, and concerns for a wide range of parallel platforms. Key points of the evaluation were solid theoretical foundations and strong experimental validations on production-level parallel and distributed systems, as well as the novelty of program development tools and environments that tackle the daunting complexity of current and future parallel systems.

The track received 14 submissions, which were thoroughly reviewed by the members of the track program committee with the help of 27 external reviewers delivering in total 55 distinct reviews. Out of all the submissions and after a careful and detailed discussion among committee members, we finally decided to accept 5 papers, resulting in a per-topic acceptance ratio of 36%.

We would like to thank all the authors who submitted papers for their contribution to the success of this track, as well as all the external reviewers for their high-quality reviews and their valuable feedback.

Topic 2: Performance and Power Modeling, Prediction and Evaluation

Leonel Sousa, Daniele De Sensi, Giorgis Georgakoudis,
Aleksandar Ilic, Piotr Luszczek, Federico Silla, Guangming Tan,
and Pedro Trancoso

Power consumption is becoming a major factor to consider when designing hardware and applications. Due to the tight correlation to performance, these two goals need to be addressed together in a synergistic way. This topic covers different aspects of performance and power consumption modeling, prediction and evaluation on different types of computing architectures and for a wide variety of applications.

This year we received 24 submissions and each paper received 4 reviews, either from the nine program committee members and/or from external reviewers. After discussion, we accepted 6 papers (25% acceptance rate). The papers cover different aspects of performance optimization, power and energy efficiency, addressing the problem at different levels, from low-level optimizations to visualization tools and considering different platforms, from mobile devices to large-scale HPC systems.

We would like to thank the authors for their submissions, the Euro-Par 2018 Organizing Committee for their help throughout all the process, and the PC members and the reviewers for providing timely and detailed reviews, and for participating in the discussion we carried on after the reviews were received.

Topic 3: Scheduling and Load Balancing

Anne Benoit, Enrico Bini, Maciej Drozdowski,
Lionel Eyraud-Dubois, José Gracia, Nan Guan, Sascha Hunold,
and Krzysztof Rzadca

New computing systems offer the opportunity to reduce the response times and the energy consumption of the applications by exploiting the levels of parallelism. Heterogeneity and complexity are the distinguishing characteristics of modern architectures. Thereby, the optimal exploitation of modern platforms is challenging. Scheduling and load balancing techniques are key instruments to achieve higher performance, lower energy consumption, reduced resource usage, and predictability of applications.

This topic invites papers on all aspects related to scheduling and load balancing on parallel and distributed machines, from theoretical foundations for modeling and designing efficient and robust scheduling policies to experimental studies, applications and practical tools and solutions. It applies to multi-/manycore processors, embedded systems, servers, heterogeneous and accelerated systems, HPC clusters as well as distributed systems such as clouds and global computing platforms.

A total of 23 full-length submissions were received in this track, each of which received at least four reviews, from the eight chairs and/or from 21 additional experts. Following the thorough discussion of the reviews, five submissions have been accepted, including one that was nominated as distinguished paper.

The chair and local chair sincerely thank all the authors for their submissions, the Euro-Par 2018 Organizing Committee for all their valuable help, and the reviewers for their excellent work. They all have contributed to making this topic and Euro-Par an excellent forum to discuss scheduling and load balancing challenges.

Topic 4: High Performance Architectures and Compilers

Florian Brandner, Fabio Luporini, Alexandra Jimborean,
Frank Hannig, and Gihan Mudalige

This topic deals with architecture design, programming languages, and compilation for parallel high-performance systems. The areas of interest range from microprocessors to large-scale parallel machines (including multi-/many-core, possibly heterogeneous, architectures); from general-purpose to specialized hardware platforms (e.g., graphic coprocessors, low-power embedded systems); and from architecture design to compiler technology and programming language design.

On the compilation side, topics of interest include programmer productivity issues, concurrent and/or sequential language aspects, vectorization, program analysis, program transformation, automatic discovery and/or management of parallelism at all levels, autotuning and feedback directed compilation, and the interaction between the compiler and the system at large. On the architecture side, the scope spans system architectures, processor micro-architecture, memory hierarchy, multi-threading, architectural support for parallelism, and the impact of emerging hardware technologies.

This year the topic received 11 submissions, covering a wide range of topics ranging from hardware designs over compilation techniques to programming models. The five topic co-chairs solicited at least four experts in the respective fields to review each paper. A lively online discussion followed the reviewing phase, during which the various co-chairs frequently solicited additional input from the expert reviewers. Based on the online discussions, 3 papers were proposed for acceptance, which were ultimately confirmed during the final selection meeting held in Turin.

Topic 5: Parallel and Distributed Data Management and Analytics

K. Selçuk Candan, Ruggero Pensa, Lei Chen,
Gianmarco De Francisci Morales, and Ming Zhao

Many areas of science, industry, and commerce are producing extreme-scale data that must be processed – stored, managed, analyzed – in order to extract useful knowledge. This topic seeks papers in all aspects of distributed and parallel data management and data analysis. For example, HPC in situ data analytics, cloud and grid data-intensive processing, parallel storage systems, IoT data management and analytics, and scalable data processing workflows are all in the scope of this topic. Privacy and trust issues in parallel and distributed data management and analytics systems are also aspects of interest for this conference topic.

Seven full-length papers were submitted to this topic, and each paper received at least four reviews, mostly performed by track chairs. After discussion with the reviewers and track chairs, two papers were selected for publication, one related to the minimization of network traffic for distributed joins, the second one to privacy-preserving top-k query processing in distributed systems.

Topic 6: Cluster and Cloud Computing

Ivona Brandić, Domenico Talia, Toni Mastelic, Raffaele Montella,
Anne-Cécile Orgerie, Thomas Renner, and Rafael Brundo Uriarte

Cloud Computing evolved from Cluster Computing and Grid Computing as a new parallel and scalable architecture. Cloud Computing is a paradigm and a technology that today is largely used. Together with Grid and Cluster computing, Cloud Computing is a reality with many providers around the world. The use of massive storage and computing resources accessible remotely in a seamless way has become essential for many applications in various areas, in all these cases Clusters, Grids and Clouds are useful tools.

Beyond the scene, most of Cloud Computing solutions rely on federations of large-scale clusters where well-known but still unsolved challenges related to performance, reliability and energy efficiency of the infrastructures should be addressed by research. Moreover, Cloud Computing emphasized the importance of fundamental capabilities and services that are required to achieve the goal of user-friendly, security and service guarantees. Our community should also investigate these aspects.

Finally, there are important trends as going from large centralized infrastructures to smaller ones massively distributed at the edge of the network, and also to execute High Performance Computing applications on Clouds. The first referred as "fog/edge" computing, such a dawning paradigm is attracting growing interests as it brings computing resources closer to end-users, tackling the network overhead issues that prevent the use of the UC paradigm by latency-aware applications. The second still needs a large research effort, to allow the use of compute and network intensive applications without loss of performance on Clouds.

Topic 6 sought papers covering many aspects of Cluster and Cloud Computing dealing with infrastructure layer challenges, such as performance/energy optimizations, and security enhancements, as well as cloud-enabled applications, workflow management and High Performance Computing on Clouds. This year, 24 papers have been submitted to Topic 6. There were authors from several countries from all the continents. Four expert reviewers analyzed each submission. Overall, many specialists were involved into the reviewing process and, despite the high quality of the submitted papers, only 8 papers were accepted for publication. We would like to thank all the authors for their submissions, the PC members and the reviewers for providing us with constructive and informative reviews, and the Euro-Par 2018 Organizing committee for all the help that allows us to smoothly take over the whole process.

Topic 7: Distributed Systems and Algorithms

Sonia Ben-Mokhtar, Alberto Montresor, Christof Fetzer,
and Indranil Gupta

Parallel computing is heavily dependent on and interacts with the developments and challenges concerning distributed systems, such as load balancing, asynchrony, failures, malicious and selfish behavior, high latencies, network partitions, disconnected operations and heterogeneity. This track of Euro-Par provides a forum for both theoretical and practical research, of interest to both academia and industry, on distributed computing, distributed algorithms, distributed systems, distributed computing models, distributed data structures, and parallel processing on distributed systems, in particular in relation to efficient high performance computing.

This year the track received 10 submissions on various topics of the call and accepted 3 papers. Each paper had a minimum of four reviews and was discussed within the track PC meeting. A subset of papers was then proposed to the PC chairs for final discussions and decisions.

The track chairs would like to warmly thank the track members Indranil Gupta (University of Illinois Urbana-Champaign, USA) and Christof Fetzer (TU Dresden, Germany) for their work as well as the 12 external reviewers that greatly helped in the reviewing process.

Topic 8: Parallel and Distributed Programming, Interfaces, and Languages

J. Daniel García, Patrizio Dazzi, Bryce Adelstein-Lelbach,
Marcelo Pasin, Mitsuhisa Sato, Paolo Trunfio, and Chan-Hyun Youn

Parallel and distributed applications requires adequate programming abstractions and models, efficient design tools, parallelization techniques and practices. This topic was open for submissions of new results and practical experience in this domain: Efficient and effective parallel languages, interfaces, libraries and frameworks, as well as solid practical and experimental validation.

The topic emphasizes research on high-performance, correct, portable, and scalable parallel programs via adequate parallel and distributed programming model, interface and language support. Contributions that assess programming abstractions, models and methods for usability, performance prediction, scalability, self-adaptation, rapid prototyping and fault-tolerance, as needed, for instance, in dynamic heterogeneous parallel and distributed infrastructures, were welcome.

We received nineteen submissions on this topic that went through four independent reviews. Those reviews where further discussed among the PC members. As a result eight paper were accepted.

We would like to express our gratitude to all author for submitting their work. We received very good submissions and the selection of accepted paper was quite hard. We also would like to thank all the reviewers for their detailed reviews and their participation in discussions following the reviews. Finally we would like to also thank the organizing and steering committees for all their help, support and hard work.

Topic 9: Multicore and Manycore Methods and Tools

Christoph Kessler, Marco Danelutto, Rudolf Eigenmann,
Arturo González Escribano, Kevin Hammond, Jesper L. Träff,
and Ana L. Varbanescu

Modern homogeneous and heterogeneous multi-core and many-core architectures are now part of the high-end, embedded, and mainstream computing scene and can offer impressive performance for many applications. This architecture trend has been driven by the need to reduce power consumption, increase processor utilization, and deal with the memory-processor speed gap. However, the complexity of these new architectures has created several programming challenges, and achieving performance on these systems is often a difficult task. This topic seeks to explore productive programming of multi- and many-core systems, as well as stand-alone systems with large numbers of cores like GPUs and various types of accelerators. This can also include hybrid and heterogeneous systems with different types of multi-core processors. It focuses on novel research and solutions in the form of programming models, algorithms, languages, compilers, libraries, runtime and analysis tools to increase the programmability of multi-core, many-core, and heterogeneous systems, in the context of general-purpose, high-performance, and embedded parallel computing. It also covers issues such as lock-free algorithms and data structures, transactional memory, static and dynamic analysis and optimization techniques and tools, performance and power trade-offs, scalability aspects, and hardware support for programming models and runtime systems.

This year, 25 papers discussing some of these issues were submitted to this topic. Each paper was reviewed by four reviewers. Eventually, 6 regular papers were selected.

The accepted papers discuss the following issues: load balancing for parallel graph traversal algorithms on GPUs, energy-efficient stencil computations on clustered many-core processors, optimizing the thread placement for overlapping MPI-3 non-blocking collective communication operations on many-core processors, a lock-free cache-trie data structure, improving performance of multi-program workloads by cache-criticality aware last-level cache partitioning, and NUMA optimizations for algorithmic skeletons.

The topic chairs wish to thank all authors contributing their work to the topic, the PC members and the additional reviewers for their highly useful comments, as well as the Euro-Par Organizing Committee for creating a smooth process.

Topic 10: Theory and Algorithms for Parallel Computation and Networking

Christos Zaroliagis, Tiziano De Matteis, Leszek Gąsieniec,
Ulrich Meyer, and Henning Meyerhenke

Parallel computing is everywhere, on smartphones, laptops; at online shopping sites, universities, computing centres; behind the search engines. Efficiency and productivity at these scales and contexts are only possible by scalable parallel algorithms using efficient communication schemes, routing and networks. Theoretical tools enabling scalability, modelling and understanding parallel algorithms, and data structures for exploiting parallelism are more important than ever. Topic 10 solicits high quality, original papers on the general topic of theory and algorithms for parallel computation including communication and network algorithms.

Topic 10 received 9 submissions, all of which received 4 reviews. The papers and their reviews were discussed extensively, and 3 submissions were eventually accepted. We thank all authors for their valuable contributions, as well as the PC Committee members and external reviewers for investing their time in reviewing the papers, for providing constructive feedback and sharing their expertise, and for keeping the high scientific level of the Euro-Par conference.

Topic 11: Parallel Numerical Methods and Applications

Elisabeth Larsson, Pasqua D'Ambra, Aneta Karaivanova,
Ángeles Martínez Calomardo, and Ulrike Meier Yang

The need for high performance computing is driven by the need for predictive simulations in science and engineering, as well as in areas such as finance, life sciences, and humanities, where computational needs have more recently been increasing. This requires the development of highly scalable numerical methods and algorithms that are able to efficiently exploit modern, and in general heterogeneous, computer architectures. Another need that is currently arising with the increasing size of computer systems is fault tolerance, which puts additional demands on algorithms, run-time systems, and tools such as MPI.

This conference topic aims at providing a forum for presenting and discussing recent developments in parallel numerical algorithms and their implementation on current parallel architectures, including many-core and hybrid architectures. We encouraged submissions addressing algorithmic design, implementation details, performance analysis, as well as integration of parallel numerical methods in large-scale science and engineering applications.

The program committee for this topic consisted of five women with different specializations in high-performance parallel computing for numerical applications. We received 17 submissions on a broad variety of topics. Fourty-one additional experts were involved in the review process. Each submission received at least four reviews. After the paper selection meeting at the University of Turin, four high quality papers were accepted for presentation at EuroPar 2018. The topics of the papers cover application areas in plasma physics, quantum physics, seismic wave propagation, and matrix factorizations. Algorithmic aspects of the Particle-in-cell method and Cholesky factorization for dense matrices with compressed blocks are considered. Implementations are performed using task based parallel programming models as well as explicit programming models using MPI+threads.

We thank all the authors for their contributions, the reviewers for their careful reading of the papers, and the organizing committee members for their smooth operation of the whole process.

Topic 12: Accelerator Computing
for Advanced Applications

Angeles Navarro, Maurizio Drocco, Raphael de Camargo, Jaejin Lee,
and Jose Luis Nunez-Yanez

The need for high-performance computing is constantly growing in all kind of scenarios, from high-end scientific applications, to consumer electronics software. Hardware manufactures are involved in a race to develop specialized hardware to cover these critical demands.

Nowadays, hardware accelerators of various kinds offer a potential for achieving massive performance in applications that can leverage their high degree of parallelism and customization. Examples include graphics processors (GPUs), manycore coprocessors, as well as more customizable devices, such as FPGA-based systems, and streaming data-flow architectures. The research challenge for this topic is to explore new directions for actually realizing this potential. Significant advances in all areas related to accelerators are considered with special focus on architectures, algorithms, languages, compilers, libraries, runtime systems, coordination of accelerators and CPU, debugging and profiling tools, as well as application-related contributions that provide new insights into fundamental problems or solution approaches in this domain.

The program committee of this topic was formed by five members of different backgrounds and specializations in the accelerators field, with the collaboration of several other sub-reviewers. We received 11 contributions from researchers in many different countries. After the review process and the general PC meeting, three high-quality papers were selected for presentation in Euro-Par 2018 at Turin. They are focused on important hot-topics: exploiting the GPUs potential towards advanced hierarchical matrix computations in large-scale sparse applications, proposing runtime systems for dynamically adapting the state on heterogeneous systems to enhance its energy efficiency, or introducing stream processing frameworks that enable easily programmable and high-performance computations on hybrid CPU/Xeon Phi systems.

The committee members want to thank all the authors that submitted their work to this track, the reviewers for their timely and constructive comments, and the organization committee for the efforts to easy our task, and to provide a nice conference environment in Turin for a high-quality discussion of research results in this emerging topic.

Contents

Cluster and Cloud Computing

Distributed Systems and Algorithms

Theory and Algorithms for Parallel Computation and Networking

Parallel Numerical Methods and Applications

Accelerator Computing for Advanced Applications

Support Tools and Environments

Automatic Detection of Synchronization Errors in Codes that Target the Open Community Runtime

Jiri Dokulil[1(✉)] and Jana Katreniakova[2]

[1] Faculty of Computer Science, University of Vienna, Vienna, Austria
`jiri.dokulil@univie.ac.at`
[2] Comenius University, Bratislava, Slovakia
`katreniakova@dcs.fmph.uniba.sk`

Abstract. The complexity of writing and debugging parallel programs makes tools that can support this effort very important. In the case of the Open Community Runtime, one major problem is ensuring that the program manages runtime objects correctly. For example, when one task uses an object and another task is responsible for deleting the object, the tasks need to be synchronized to ensure that the object is only destroyed once it is no longer being used. In this paper, we present a tool which observes program execution and analyzes it in order to find cases where the required synchronization is missing.

1 Introduction

Task-based runtime systems, including StarPU [1], HPX [7], UPC++ [15], or PaRSEC [2] have received a lot of interest given the increased complexity, performance variability, and heterogeneity of emerging architectures. The Open Community Runtime (OCR, [9]) is a recent specification [10] for an event-driven task-based runtime system developed within the US XStack targeting next generation extreme scale architectures. The basic idea of OCR is to use tasks to decouple computation from compute units and data blocks to decouple application data from specific memory. Synchronization is also abstracted by dependences among tasks. Events can be used to build more complex dependence patterns. The responsibility for work scheduling and data placement is moved to the runtime. The application issues tasks to the runtime, along with their dependences. The runtime examines this task graph (which should be a DAG) and decides when and where to execute the tasks.

Writing parallel programs is a difficult task [8]. This is especially true when writing programs directly at the level of a task-based runtime system like OCR. When the work is split into tasks, which are scheduled and executed by the runtime, the global execution-time context normally available as the stack trace is lost. Debuggers are not able to map a running task to the place where it was created, like they do with a function and the corresponding call site. This makes debugging task-based applications tricky. Tools that can support the developers' effort to write and debug such programs are therefore important.

M. Aldinucci et al. (Eds.): Euro-Par 2018, LNCS 11014, pp. 3–15, 2018.
https://doi.org/10.1007/978-3-319-96983-1_1

To support our research on OCR [3–5], we created a single-threaded implementation of OCR, called OCR-V1, which can be used to aid the development of new OCR applications[1]. When an application is run with OCR-V1, the runtime checks that the OCR API is used correctly by the application, for example by testing that data blocks are not used after being released or destroyed. Many problems can be discovered this way, but because OCR-V1 uses a deterministic serial task schedule, its ability to detect synchronization errors is limited. Therefore, we have also extended OCR-V1 to collect execution traces, which can be analyzed to find synchronization errors. An unmodified OCR application is compiled and linked with the modified OCR-V1 runtime. When executed, the application generates an execution trace, which is then analyzed by a new tool that we developed to find errors. Due to the way synchronization is done in OCR, it is sufficient to use the instrumented runtime and the unmodified application.

Based on the OCR specification, we have defined a set of rules that a correct OCR application must follow. We detect errors by looking for violations of these rules. The rules (and errors) share one basic principle. Some operations on OCR objects (performed by the application via OCR API calls) need to happen in a certain order. For example, any object must not be used before it is created and it may not be used after it is destroyed. So, if one task accesses a data block and another task destroys the data block, the application must ensure that the access done by the first task happens before the delete operation in the second task. Dependences among the tasks have to be set up in such a way that there is causal relation (*happens-before*) among the operations. Our trace analyzer finds and reports instances where the synchronization is missing.

Existing tools like Valgrind/Helgrind [12] may not be able to detect these errors, as synchronization that is done internally by the runtime (for example, to ensure atomicity of concurrent operations) may appear as sufficient on the low level where Helgrind works. Naturally, we can only detect errors in the way the program interacts with the OCR runtime system, not application errors. If the desired algorithm is implemented incorrectly, but properly synchronized, no errors will be detected.

Our main contributions are: (1) the error-checking OCR-V1 runtime, which also generates execution traces of OCR programs; (2) definition of rules that a correct OCR application has to observe when dealing with OCR runtime objects; (3) trace analyzer, which finds violations of the rules in execution traces; (4) during our work, we have identified one problem where the OCR specification does not sufficiently specify how certain tasks should be synchronized.

The rest of the paper is organized as follows. First, related work is discussed in Sect. 2. In Sect. 3, we briefly describe key OCR concepts and explain how OCR programs are synchronized. Section 4 explains how we analyze OCR programs and find problems in them. Section 5 provides concrete examples of programs and the detected errors. The final section concludes the paper and discusses future work.

---

[1] OCR-V1 is available at: http://www.univie.ac.at/ocr-vx/.

2   Related Work

There are existing tools that try to find errors in parallel programs. One type are tools that observe execution of the parallel program and check for various error conditions. Probably the best know example is Valgrind [12], which is mostly used to look for incorrect use of memory, but it also includes two modules that detect threading errors (Helgrind and DRD). Clang ThreadSanitizer performs similar function. Intel Inspector is an example of a similar commercial tool.

There are also tools which use static code analysis. For example, there are tools like FindBugs that analyze either source or bytecode of Java and try to find concurrency problems [13].

Another option is too look at the way operations are ordered in threads. The `rr` tool saves program execution and allows it to be deterministically replayed. This solves at least two problems: concurrency problems are often non-deterministic (two subsequent executions of the same program on the same data may not encounter the same failure) and running the parallel program in the debugger changes timing, potentially preventing the problem from occurring at all. An alternative approach is taken by CHESS [11] and Maple [14], which influence the execution of a multi-threaded program in order to systematically explore possible thread schedules.

The architecture of our system is similar to the first category (e.g., Valgrind and its modules), where the parallel execution of the program is analyzed and the analyzer looks for known error "patterns". One pattern that Helgind, DRD, and ThreadSanitizer check are data races where access to a shared variable from multiple threads is not properly synchronized – they check the presence of the happens-before relation among the operations. Our solution uses a similar approach, but as data in OCR is handled differently from plain C/C++ and data races are generally not an issue, we focus on the correct use of OCR objects. But the basic principle is the same: observe the behavior of the program and then check that concurrent operations have been properly synchronized.

Our approach could be also applied to similar programming models. The key requirement for such model is that synchronization is done on the task level using dependences. Examples of such models are OpenCL (kernels correspond to tasks), CUDA (with multiple streams and events), and StarPU. In TBB and UPC++, where fine-grained synchronization (locks, atomic operations, ...) can be used in tasks or if there can be malicious data races caused by individual read and write operations, Valgrind and ThreadSanitizer are better starting points.

It would also be possible to apply those fine-grained techniques to data accesses made by OCR tasks. Although data in OCR is stored in data blocks which are acquired and released as whole, there are two different pairs of access modes that can be used. The first pair are the constant and exclusive-write access modes, where the runtime is responsible for ensuring that all data access is consistent (there are no data races). The second pair are read-only and read-write access modes, which permit data races (both read-write and write-write). We do not consider these. There is however ongoing work done at Georgia Tech, attempting to also find such data races.

3   OCR and Synchronization

In OCR, all work (all application code) should run inside tasks, which are scheduled by the runtime. Similarly, all application data is stored in data blocks, which are relocatable blocks of data also managed by the runtime. The tasks are non-blocking, which means that once a task starts, it is expected to run to completion without waiting for any other work to be done. The only way tasks can synchronize is using dependences with the help of events. The application defines what the dependences are, but they are evaluated by the runtime, which figures out when a task is ready to start.

3.1   Event Driven Synchronization

Events are used to synchronize tasks in OCR, hence the name used for tasks in OCR – Event Driven Tasks (EDTs). Events and tasks in OCR can be connected using dependences. Tasks and events have slots that can be used as sources (post-slots) and destinations (pre-slots) of a dependence. A task has to wait for all of its pre-slots to be *satisfied* before it can start. Slots can either be satisfied directly using an OCR API call or they are satisfied automatically when they are connected to a post-slot of an event and the event itself is satisfied.

There are different types of events that have different rules that determine when the event is satisfied. The simplest one, the *once* event, gets satisfied as soon as its single pre-slot is satisfied. In other words, it directly propagates the satisfaction signal. We also say that the event has been *triggered* to distinguish satisfaction of the event from satisfaction of its pre-slot. Another interesting type of event is the *latch* event. It has two pre-slots and maintains an internal counter. The counter is incremented when the first of the two slots gets satisfied and decremented when the second slot gets satisfied. When the counter reaches zero, the event itself is satisfied and forwards the satisfaction signal – satisfies all pre-slots that are connected to its post-slot. Another important kind of events are *output* events. These are not a specific type of event (they are in fact *once* or *latch* events), but events used in a specific situation. For every task, there is a matching output event, which is satisfied after the task finishes.

3.2   State of OCR Objects

We have already introduced three types of OCR objects: tasks, events, and data blocks. All OCR objects carry some state. For example, a *latch* event needs to store the value of its counter. A data block needs to know the size of the corresponding buffer and it may also track which tasks have acquired it. However, the actual data stored in a data block is not considered to belong to the state of the data block object. The data plays a special role in the OCR specification and cannot be modified by OCR API calls, but only directly by reading and writing memory via a pointer. Note that dependences are generally not considered to be OCR objects. Therefore, adding a dependence is considered to be a change of state of the two connected objects (event and task/event).

3.3   The *happens-before* Relation

Events and dependences are used to define the *happens-before* relation among the operations performed inside tasks. If operation *A* *happens-before* operation *B*, it means that they are synchronized in a way that ensures that operation *B* sees the results of operation *A*. A simple example is when an output event of a task is used as a source of a dependence connected to a second task. In that case, the satisfaction of the event happens after the first task finishes and the second task can only start after the event is satisfied. Therefore, all operations done by the first task *happen-before* all operations done by the second task. The OCR memory model guarantees that all changes made by the first task are visible in the second task. This is true not only for changes to the application data (in data blocks), but also to state changes of runtime objects. For example, a newly created event is valid in the second task. Also, if the counter of a latch event is incremented from 0 to 2 by the first task and the second task decrements it, it is a valid operation which changes the value from 2 to 1. If the second task was not synchronized after the first task, it could run in parallel and try to decrement the counter while it is still zero, which is illegal.

There are only two types of operations that may change the state of OCR objects. First, the OCR API calls made inside the tasks (e.g., `ocrDbCreate` creates a new data block). Second, the runtime may modify the state automatically. For example, after a task finishes, the associated output event is satisfied. This also causes tasks and events connected (via dependences) to this event's post-slot to be also satisfied. Additionally, the finished task and its output event are automatically destroyed by the runtime. The only exception are data blocks, whose data is modified by memory reads and writes done inside tasks. But the state of the data block object itself (the size of the buffer, etc.) is still managed purely by OCR API calls. Because we only focus on the state of the OCR objects and not the application data and since all synchronization has to be done using OCR objects (tasks, events, and dependences), we only need to observe OCR API calls being made by the application and implicit operations done by the runtime. Since the runtime processes all the OCR API calls, we only need to instrument the runtime to collect the relevant data, not the application itself.

Consider the following example in OCR pseudo-code:

```
running tasks: t1
available tasks: t2
events: e1, e2
t1 {
   ocrAddDependence(NULL,t2); //allow t2 to start
   ocrAddDependence(e1,e2);//set up dependence e1->e2
}
t2 {
   ocrEventSatisfy(e1); //satisfy event e1
}
```

Here, t2 has only one pre-slot, so when t1 sets up a dependence from a NULL object to the pre-slot, it effectively satisfies, allowing t2 to start. Then, t1 goes on to set up a dependence between events e1 and e2. For correct execution, the dependence should be set up before e1 is satisfied. Most of the time, the runtime will manage to set up the dependence before t2 starts and satisfies e1, resulting in correct execution. However, it's also possible that after t2 is allowed to start, t1 gets suspended. This could for example be due to the OS scheduler suspending the thread. So, t2 starts and satisfies e1. There is not yet a dependence connecting e1 and e2, therefore e2 is not satisfied and e1 gets destroyed. Then, t1 resumes and tries to add a dependence from the destroyed e1, resulting in an undefined behavior (e.g., a crash). There is a race condition among the two operations on the event. The error may be very hard to reproduce, especially if t2 performs other work before satisfying e1. Although OCR-V1 attempts to detect application errors, this error would never be detected, because t1 would always finish before t2 can start due to the sequential task execution.

Using *happens-before*, we can clearly see the problem. To make sure that the dependence is set up in time, we need ocrAddDependence(e1,e2) *happens-before* ocrEventSatisfy(e1). This is not the case here, only these hold: ocrAddDependence(NULL,t2) *happens-before* ocrAddDependence(e1,e2) and ocrAddDependence(NULL,t2) *happens-before* ocrEventSatisfy(e1).

4   Automatic Checking of OCR Programs

Our approach for checking of OCR programs is based on a OCR-V1, a single-threaded implementation of OCR. OCR-V1 was specifically designed to help debugging by exposing errors through explicit checks (using the standard C asserts). There are almost 100 checks like this in OCR-V1. Although they are very useful, these checks are only one of two parts of our system, which is complemented by the tracing functionality of OCR-V1 and the trace analyzer.

4.1   OCR Application Tracing and Trace Analyzer

As we have already shown with the example in the previous section, there are errors that cannot be detected by OCR-V1, since they only manifest when multiple tasks are executed concurrently. To cover these cases, we have extended OCR-V1 to export the list of operations (OCR API calls and implicit operations) performed by the OCR program. Only the operations relevant to synchronization are exported. Furthermore, OCR-V1 exports a subset of the *happens-before* graph that connects the operations. As the *happens-before* relation is transitive, we don't need to export the full graph, but only edges that are sufficient to construct it by transitive closure. The trace is loaded by the trace analyzer, which builds the full *happens-before* relation by performing a transitive closure. Then, it iterates through all OCR objects and checks that they are used correctly (the actual rules to check are described in Sect. 4.3). Rule violations are reported, along with the relevant context, like the file name and the line number of the location where the API call that violated the rule was made.

4.2   The *happens-before* Graph

To make checking the rules easier, the graph exported from OCR-V1 is not directly the graph of OCR API calls and *happens-before* relations among them. We modify the graph by introducing additional nodes and edges. For every operation performed by a task (*cause* node), there is also another node (*effect*) where the changed mandated by the operation is applied to the affected object. For example, when an OCR task invokes `ocrEventSatisfy(e1)`, the effect is the actual satisfaction of the event, which can be denoted as `e1.satisfied()`. The *happens-before* relation is also modified (extended) to ensure that the cause *happens-before* the effect, but also that if there is a *happens-before* relation among two causes, their effects also have this relation. This is achieved by *back edges*, which are edges connecting the effect of a cause to the operation that comes right after the cause. One cause can have multiple effects, for example connecting two events by dependence (`ocrAddDependence(e1,e2)`) changes both events (`e1.connectPostSlot(e2)` and `e2.connectPreSlot(e1)`). This format makes it easier to check if an event `e` is being used properly, as it is enough to check all actions applied to the event – `e.*`.

Furthermore, helper nodes (virtual operations) are added to objects. For example, we add `e.triggered()` to each event, signifying the point in time where the event is triggered. In the *happens-before* relation, this operation follows all satisfactions of the event and precedes satisfaction of all pre-slots connected to the event's post-slot. Also, a `x.destroyed()` node added to all objects that are automatically destroyed. This further simplifies checking of the rules.

Figure 1 shows an example of a graph of operations and their synchronization. The visualized graph corresponds to the example in Sect. 3.3.

4.3   Error Detection Rules

A set of rules are applied to the graph by the trace analyzer, in order to check for errors. We've already shown one example of such rule. For any *once* event, any `ocrAddDependence` call must *happens-before* satisfaction of the event. When viewed as by the effects of the operations, we require that `e.connectPostSlot(x)` *happens-before* `e.satisfy()`. The full list of rules is as follows:

1. Any use of an object must be (as per *happens-before*) between its creation and its destruction.
2. All dependences that start with a post-slot of a *once* or *latch* event have to be set up before the event is satisfied.
3. A *once* event can only be satisfied once.
4. ocrShutdown should be called from a task that comes after all other tasks.
5. Any valid (per *happens-before*) order of increments and decrements of a *latch* event must be correct – it must start with an increment, only reach zero once, and only reach zero at the end.

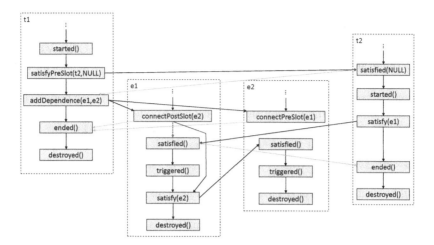

Fig. 1. The trace of the example in Sect. 3.3. Operations performed on two tasks (t1 and t2) and two events (e1 and e2). The black arrows are normal *happens-before* edges, the gray arrows are the back edges, which also contribute to *happens-before*. The red dotted arrow is the missing *happens-before* that would ensure that the event is used correctly. Note that *happens-before* is formed by transitive closure, so the shown arrows are only a subset. But even if transitivity is applied, it would not add the missing arrow. (Color figure online)

The first rule is probably the most important one, as it covers all types of objects and different possible error scenarios. The last rule, which checks *latch* events, is difficult to verify with a large number of increment and decrement operations, as we need to check all permutations of the operations.

5   Examples

To demonstrate the functionality of our tool, we have tried it on several OCR applications[2]. There are not many OCR applications and most of the existing ones have already been extensively debugged, so only very few errors were detected. Our tools are more useful when used by the application developer while the application is still being created, to identify problems as soon as possible.

5.1   Late Dependence Definition

The following code fragment is taken from an OCR tutorial. It is similar to the example given in Sect. 3.3. Two tasks fill and print are created and the output event of the fill task is used as a dependence for print, to make sure that print runs after fill. However, the dependence is added too late, after the print task is allowed to start. The task may run in parallel and destroy its output event before the dependence can be set up.

---

[2] https://xstack.exascale-tech.com/git/public?p=apps.git.

```
//create templates, fill has 1 pre-slot, print has 2
ocrEdtTemplateCreate(&fillTML, fill, 0, 1);
ocrEdtTemplateCreate(&printTML, print, 0, 2);
//create startEVT - an event which launches the computation
ocrEventCreate(&startEVT, OCR_EVENT_ONCE_T);
//create one instance of fill and print each
ocrEdtCreate(&fillEDT, fillTML, 0, 0, 1, NULL, &fillEVT);
ocrEdtCreate(&printEDT, printTML, 0, 0, 2, NULL, NULL);
//set up startEVT as predecessor of both tasks
ocrAddDependence(startEVT, fillEDT, 0, DB_MODE_EW);
ocrAddDependence(startEVT, printEDT, 1, DB_MODE_CONST);
//trigger the computation
ocrEventSatisfy(startEVT, NULL_GUID);
//set up a dependence from the output of fill to print
ocrAddDependence(fillEVT, printEDT, 0, DB_DEFAULT_MODE);
```

The trace analyzer reports the following error message:

```
ERROR: ONC.EVT may be satisfied before all post-slot are added
       Event 18:EVT.ONC-output-of(17:fill)
                   satisfied by 73 in epilogue of 17:fill
       Missing happens-before from 52 in 10:mainEdt
             invoked from ocr\apps\app_lab.cpp:75
```

The error message tells us that there is a problem with the event with ID 18. The event is the output event of task 17, which is the `fill` task. The event is satisfied by operation 73, which is one of the operations executed automatically by the runtime after `fill` finished. In the main task (ID 10), the event is used to perform operation 52, which is at the specified line in the source code. This happens to be the last line of the example, where `ocrAddDependence` is called.

5.2 Conflicting Operations in Parallel Tasks

The following program was created specifically to demonstrate our tools. It shows a scenario where multiple tasks contribute to the error. The code shows the whole program, except for includes, function argument lists, and some unimportant arguments in function calls. Besides the `mainEdt` task, which is the entry point of any OCR program, there are three other tasks. Tasks `task1` and `task2` run in parallel. The `mainEdt` task creates a data block (called `data`) and passes it to both tasks. While `task1` only accesses the data block, `task2` destroys it. Task `task3` shuts down the runtime after `task1` and `task2` finish. A task graph for this example is shown in Fig. 2. This figure is generated as a side-effect by the trace analyzer tool (it generates a DOT file for GraphViz [6]).

```
void task1(/*arguments omitted for brevity*/){
  int i = *(int*)depv[0].ptr; //access the data block
}
void task2(/*arguments omitted for brevity*/) {
  ocrDbDestroy(depv[0].guid);//line 10 in the actual file
```

```
}
void task3(/*arguments omitted for brevity*/) {
  ocrShutdown();
}
void mainEdt(/*arguments omitted for brevity*/) {
  ocrGuid_t data,tml1,tml2,tml3,edt1,edt2,edt3,evt1,evt2;
  void* ptr;
  ocrDbCreate(&data, &ptr, 8);
  ocrEdtTemplateCreate(&tml1, task1, 0, 1);
  ocrEdtTemplateCreate(&tml2, task2, 0, 1);
  ocrEdtTemplateCreate(&tml3, task3, 0, 2);
  ocrEdtCreate(&edt1, tml1, 0, 0, 1, 0, &evt1);
  ocrEdtCreate(&edt2, tml2, 0, 0, 1, 0, &evt2);
  ocrEdtCreate(&edt3, tml3, 0, 0, 2, 0, 0);
  ocrAddDependence(evt1, edt3, 0, DB_MODE_NULL);
  ocrAddDependence(evt2, edt3, 1, DB_MODE_NULL);
  ocrAddDependence(data, edt1, 0, DB_MODE_RW);
  ocrAddDependence(data, edt2, 0, DB_MODE_RW);
}
```

When the program is executed and analyzed, the following error is reported:

```
ERROR: operation may be after destruction
       data block 13 destroyed by 78 in 19:task2
             invoked from ocr\src\src\apps\app_lab.cpp:10
       61: acquire in 17:task1 may be after destruction
```

The error message tells us that when the data block 13 (the `data`) is acquired by task 17 (type `task1`), it may already have been destroyed by `ocrDbDestroy` (line 10 of the actual source code), which is in task 19 (type `task2`).

Note that the identifiers of tasks and events are their actual IDs used by the runtime, so when the program was running, the `data` variable in the main task actually contained 13, `edt1` contained 17, etc. However, the identifiers of the operations, like 61 used for the acquire operation, are only internal identifiers of OCR-V1 and cannot be accessed from the application code. As is often the

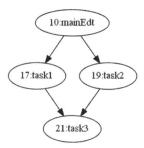

Fig. 2. Tasks and their dependences from the second example. The number is the ID of the task, the text label is the name of the C function which implements the task.

case when debugging programs based on logs, the developer therefore needs to carefully interpret the output to figure out what the operation is. In the case of 78, it is clear from the reference to the source code. To identify operation 61, one has to realize that the data block `data` is acquired by `task1` automatically before it starts, so there is no direct counterpart in the code.

5.3   SPMD Application – Synchronization Using Data Blocks

When we tested our tools on existing OCR applications, it reported a large number of errors in one of them. The application is an SPMD (single program multiple data) code which mimics the way MPI programs work[3]. There are virtual processes which are assigned numerical ranks and they can exchange data by send and receive calls using the rank numbers. Internally, the communication is handled by writing an identifier of the sent data into a so called *channel* data block, which is then read by the recipient. As part of the exchange, the sender creates an event which is satisfied by the recipient when the data is received. The tool reported that the event is being used but there is no guarantee that it's not used before it is created. There is no *happens-before* relation between the code that performs the send and the code that handles the received data.

This is not an error inside our tool. The relation really does not exist. The problem is that if two tasks acquire the same data block in exclusive write mode, no *happens-before* is established among them. However, looking from the outside, it seems it should not be detected as an error. The sender creates the event and then stores it in the channel data block. If the recipient initiates the receive operation (and acquires the channel data block) before the channel is updated by the sender, it does not see the event (it is not there yet), so it does not satisfy it. If the recipient acquires the channel data block after it has been modified, it means that the event has already been created and it can be satisfied. Because both sides acquire the data block in exclusive write mode, the recipient has to see one of the two consistent states.

On the other hand, it is conceivable to implement OCR so that the recipient sees the modified data block but the event is not yet valid. The specification [10] either needs to be updated to require the relation to be established in such cases or developers need to be very careful and avoid such scenarios.

5.4   Performance

As OCR-V1 was designed with safety and not performance in mind, the extra overhead introduced by exporting the graph is noticeable but not a game changer. On a machine equipped with dual core (4 threads) Intel i7-7500U CPU, a highly tuned native OCR seismic simulation code, which executes 768517 tasks, takes 105 s to complete with OCR-V1. The graph data size is around 3.5 GB. Without the graph export, it takes 22 s, almost 5x faster. However, on the same

---

[3] https://xstack.exascale-tech.com/git/public?p=apps.git;a=tree;f=apps/libs/src/ spmd.

machine, a shared-memory OCR implementation takes 2.4 s, improving the performance by another 9x, to a total speedup of around 44x. So, even though the graph export slows the execution down, it is still manageable for an application with hundreds of thousands of tasks.

The trace analyzer needs to explore the transitive closure of the exported *happens-before* subset. We store the closure as a dense adjacency matrix, which results in significant memory usage. The matrix is dense, because the existing OCR applications are often iterative algorithms and a task in iteration i is likely to be synchronized with all tasks from previous and subsequent iterations. The complexity of searching all permutations of n operations on a *latch* event is $n!$. For most other rules, the execution should be roughly n^2 for n operations.

The example from the first paragraph of this section cannot be analyzed in a reasonable amount of time. If we reduce it to just one thousand tasks (this version takes a quarter of a second to finish in OCR-V1), it produces around 48k operations and 77k edges. These can be analyzed in 10 s. However, if we double the number of tasks, the time goes up to over 40 s, following the predicted quadratic time complexity. This makes searching large graphs impractical.

In applications with some regular structure, it is possible to take a small workload and use that to check for errors. For example, the seismic simulation only has three different kinds of iterations (first, last, and all iterations in between) and in each iterations, there are 3 kinds of tasks (top, bottom, in between), so even a small run with 49 tasks in total is sufficient to test all these cases. As we are detecting all potential synchronization errors, increasing the number of tasks will not increase the chance of finding an error, as the process is not at all probabilistic. However, not all applications have a regular structure like this and it may not always be possible to test all cases with such a small sample.

6   Conclusion and Future Work

We have created a tool which can automatically detect synchronization errors in OCR applications, in cases where OCR objects are being used by the application without proper synchronization. While no automatic tool may detect all errors in such applications, any programmer aid is important for the difficult task of writing such programs.

In the future plan to use more sophisticated graph processing techniques to reduce overall memory footprint and processing time. We would also like to be able to efficiently handle common cases of very large *latch* events, without having to search all permutations.

Acknowledgment. The work was supported in part by the Austrian Science Fund (FWF) project P 29783 (Dynamic Runtime System for Future Parallel Architectures) and by VEGA 1/0684/16.

References

1. Augonnet, C., Thibault, S., Namyst, R., Wacrenier, P.-A.: STARPU: a unified platform for task scheduling on heterogeneous multicore architectures. In: Sips, H., Epema, D., Lin, H.-X. (eds.) Euro-Par 2009. LNCS, vol. 5704, pp. 863–874. Springer, Heidelberg (2009). https://doi.org/10.1007/978-3-642-03869-3_80
2. Bosilca, G., et al.: PaRSEC: exploiting heterogeneity to enhance scalability. IEEE Comput. Sci. Eng. **15**(6), 36–45 (2013)
3. Dokulil, J., Sandrieser, M., Benkner, S.: Implementing the open community runtime for shared-memory and distributed-memory systems. In: 2016 24th Euromicro International Conference on Parallel, Distributed, and Network-Based Processing (PDP), pp. 364–368, February 2016
4. Dokulil, J., Benkner, S.: OCR extensions - local identifiers, labeled GUIDs, file IO, and data block partitioning. CoRR abs/1509.03161 (2015). http://arxiv.org/abs/1509.03161
5. Dokulil, J., Sandrieser, M., Benkner, S.: OCR-Vx - an alternative implementation of the open community runtime. In: International Workshop on Runtime Systems for Extreme Scale Programming Models and Architectures, in conjunction with SC15, Austin, Texas (2015)
6. Ellson, J., Gansner, E., Koutsofios, L., North, S.C., Woodhull, G.: Graphviz— open source graph drawing tools. In: Mutzel, P., Jünger, M., Leipert, S. (eds.) GD 2001. LNCS, vol. 2265, pp. 483–484. Springer, Heidelberg (2002). https://doi.org/10.1007/3-540-45848-4_57
7. Kaiser, H., Heller, T., Adelstein-Lelbach, B., Serio, A., Fey, D.: HPX - a task based programming model in a global address space. In: The 8th International Conference on Partitioned Global Address Space Programming Models (PGAS) (2014)
8. Lee, E.A.: The problem with threads. Computer **39**(5), 33–42 (2006). https://doi.org/10.1109/MC.2006.180
9. Mattson, T.G., et al.: The open community runtime: a runtime system for extreme scale computing. In: 2016 IEEE High Performance Extreme Computing Conference (HPEC), pp. 1–7 (2016)
10. Mattson, T., Cledat, R. (eds.): The Open Community Runtime Interface, April 2016. https://xstack.exascale-tech.com/git/public?p=ocr.git;a=blob;f=ocr/spec/ocr-1.1.0.pdf
11. Musuvathi, M.: Systematic concurrency testing using CHESS. In: Proceedings of the 6th Workshop on Parallel and Distributed Systems: Testing, Analysis, and Debugging, PADTAD 2008, p. 10:1. ACM, New York (2008)
12. Nethercote, N., Seward, J.: Valgrind: a framework for heavyweight dynamic binary instrumentation. In: SIGPLAN Notices, vol. 42, no. 6, pp. 89–100 (2007)
13. Rutar, N., Almazan, C.B., Foster, J.S.: A comparison of bug finding tools for Java. In: 15th International Symposium on Software Reliability Engineering, pp. 245–256, November 2004
14. Yu, J., Narayanasamy, S., Pereira, C., Pokam, G.: Maple: a coverage-driven testing tool for multithreaded programs. In: SIGPLAN Notices, vol. 47, no. 10, pp. 485–502 (2012)
15. Zheng, Y., Kamil, A., Driscoll, M.B., Shan, H., Yelick, K.: UPC++: a PGAS extension for C++. In: 2014 IEEE 28th International Parallel and Distributed Processing Symposium, pp. 1105–1114, May 2014

A Methodology for Performance Analysis of Applications Using Multi-layer I/O

Ronny Tschüter[(✉)], Christian Herold, Bert Wesarg, and Matthias Weber

Center for Information Services and High
Performance Computing, Technische Universität
Dresden, Dresden, Germany
`ronny.tschueter@tu-dresden.de`

Abstract. Efficient usage of file systems poses a major challenge for highly scalable parallel applications. The performance of even the most sophisticated I/O subsystems lags behind the compute capabilities of current processors. To improve the utilization of I/O subsystems, several libraries, such as HDF5, facilitate the implementation of parallel I/O operations. These libraries abstract from low-level I/O interfaces (for instance, Posix I/O) and may internally interact with additional I/O libraries. While improving usability, I/O libraries also add complexity and impede the analysis and optimization of application I/O performance. In this work, we present a methodology to investigate application I/O behavior in detail. In contrast to current methods, our approach explicitly captures interactions between multiple I/O libraries. This allows to identify inefficiencies at individual layers of the I/O stack as well as to detect possible conflicts in the interplay between layers. We implement our methodology in an established performance monitoring infrastructure and demonstrate its effectiveness with an I/O analysis study of a cloud model simulation code. In summary, this work provides the foundation for application I/O tuning by exposing inefficiency patterns in the usage of I/O routines.

Keywords: I/O · Performance analysis · Monitoring
Instrumentation

1 Introduction

Modern HPC systems provide powerful storage hardware equipped with high bandwidth interconnects and parallel file systems. Nevertheless, input and output (I/O) operations still present a major limitation factor for the performance of scientific applications. Current research topics, such as *big data* and *machine learning*, further increase the trend of processing large data volumes.

Highly-scalable applications transfer data in parallel to cope with large data volumes and efficiently utilize available I/O resources. A wide range of I/O libraries, such as HDF5 [24], NetCDF [26], and MPI I/O [18, Chap. 13] support developers in implementing parallel I/O operations by abstracting from

© Springer International Publishing AG, part of Springer Nature 2018
M. Aldinucci et al. (Eds.): Euro-Par 2018, LNCS 11014, pp. 16–30, 2018.
https://doi.org/10.1007/978-3-319-96983-1_2

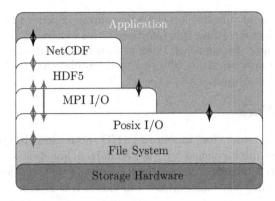

Fig. 1. Software layers of an application using three I/O interfaces concurrently.

low-level I/O interfaces. Often, these libraries provide features for storing meta-data to describe the data format and units along with specific data values. This further increases the data volume in addition to the actual raw data.

Hiding the complexity of implementing low-level parallel I/O operations is a major benefit of I/O libraries. Yet, using I/O libraries does not necessarily guarantee efficient I/O resource utilization [10]. Improved usability gained by abstraction also implies a more challenging I/O performance analysis. This is especially true for applications using multiple I/O interfaces concurrently. Figure 1 shows an example application that uses multiple I/O libraries independently. The application itself calls NetCDF, MPI I/O, and Posix I/O functions directly. The NetCDF library issues HDF5 function calls. HDF5 in turn contains MPI I/O and Posix I/O in its software stack. Complex interactions between I/O libraries and user code impact each other. It is essential to gather information from all involved I/O layers to evaluate the effectiveness of resulting I/O operations. This allows detailed understanding of the actual I/O behavior and enables the identification of underlying root causes of I/O problems. For example, I/O operations are propagated through the I/O software stack. An **open** call at the top level will also cause **open** operations in lower levels. Hence, each layer of the I/O software stack maintains own file descriptors to manage I/O resources. In case of writing data, each I/O layer may rearrange operations or add additional meta-information to the actual raw data. Thus, to correctly assign and evaluate specific operations, we need to capture information at each individual I/O layer.

Monitoring of multi-level I/O operations poses two challenges: (a) recording I/O operations arising from multiple I/O libraries and (b) recording of interactions between individual I/O libraries. This work addresses both challenges. Thereby, we support users in investigating and improving the I/O performance of parallel applications. Our contributions are:

– An approach to record information about I/O resources used by applications as well as performance relevant data of I/O operations including the interactions of multiple I/O libraries.

- Tracking the mount information of I/O resources in order to determine their generic scope and recording this information for enhanced analyses.
- Implementation of the approach in an established monitoring infrastructure.
- A detailed I/O analysis study of a real-world application to demonstrate the applicability of our approach.

2   Related Work

Several techniques exist for monitoring I/O activities. In principle these approaches can be distinguished by: (a) the data acquisition scope (system or application) (b) the recorded data format (statistics or event log) and (c) the ability for monitoring relations between individual I/O layers.

Statistics on System-Level: The tools iotop [15], iostat [14], blktrace [5], and sar [20] monitor system performance with special focus on I/O resource usage. These tools collect statistics and report measurement values per device, partition, or network filesystem as well as a global view of the whole system.

Statistics on Application-Level: Arm MAP [4], Darshan [8], and TAU [22] monitor individual applications. Among other runtime events, like function entry and exit, they can record information about I/O operations. With respect to I/O, Arm MAP focuses on Posix I/O and captures Lustre [16] counters, whereas Darshan and TAU record Posix I/O and MPI I/O activities. HPCToolkit [1] intercepts selected I/O operations and records their number of bytes read or written to mark I/O intensive application phases. In contrast to our work, all of the previously mentioned tools collect statistics.

Event Logs on Application-Level: VampirTrace [19] records I/O activities and writes the collected information to event logs. However, it only records calls to I/O functions of the standard C library and is no longer supported. Its successor Score-P [11] does not support I/O recording yet. ScalaIOTrace [28] generates compressed event logs of MPI I/O and Posix I/O function calls. None of the mentioned tools explicitly correlates individual layers of the I/O software stack.

Visualization: Vampir [2] visualizes event logs generated by VampirTrace and Score-P in timeline and statistical charts. Event logs retain temporal information of each individual event. This enables detection of performance problems with changing characteristics over application runtime. The Virtual Institute for I/O (VI4IO) [27] is a collaboration platform for research groups in the field of HPC I/O. It provides an overview about I/O middleware, benchmarks, and tools.

3   Methodology

This section describes our approach for analyzing applications using multiple I/O libraries. We cover both I/O resources (e.g., files and file descriptors) as well as I/O activities (e.g., reading and writing). Therefore, we distinguish between **definitions** and **events**. *Definitions* provide detailed information about I/O resources, whereas *events* represent I/O activities during application runtime.

3.1   Definitions

Definitions describe resources of I/O operations. Posix I/O operations do not
directly work on input/output resources, but use file descriptors as an abstract
handle. This allows multiple processes/threads to access the same file independently. Consequently, our definitions, Fig. 2, distinguish between I/O resources
and file descriptors. The following paragraphs introduce each definition in detail.

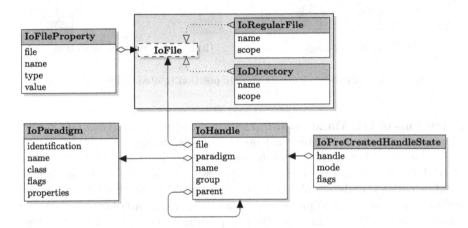

Fig. 2. Overview of definitions to reflect I/O resources and their relationships.

Definitions of I/O Resources: According to the *"Everything is a file"* philosophy Unix and its derivatives treat a wide range of I/O resources as a file,
e.g., files, directories, and sockets. This is reflected by the polymorph **IoFile** definition that provides a common namespace for objects used by I/O operations.
Currently, definitions for files (**IoRegularFile**) and directories (**IoDirectory**)
are available within this namespace. However, it is possible to add further definitions to this namespace.

IoRegularFile and *IoDirectory* definitions store the name of a file or directory.
HPC machines mount several file systems concurrently. Thus, name or path alone
do not represent unique identifiers for I/O resources. In principle, two categories
of file systems can be distinguished: (a) local file systems available only on a
single compute node (b) global file systems shared via network on the whole
machine. Figure 3 depicts an example. The illustrated compute nodes $node_a$ and
$node_b$ use two different file systems—a shared network file system fs_{global} and
a local scratch file system fs_{local}. The file $file_x$ in fs_{global} is accessible on the
whole machine. In contrast $file_y$ represents two distinct physical files, because
they reside in separate file systems fs_{local}. Therefore, the scope attribute marks
the physical scope with regard to the system topology.

The **IoFileProperty** definition attaches user-defined attributes (e.g., mount
point information or Lustre strip policy) to an *IoFile* definition.

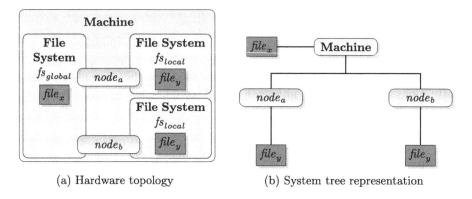

(a) Hardware topology   (b) System tree representation

Fig. 3. A file's scope depends on its storage position (global or local file system).

Definitions of I/O Handles: IoParadigm describes an available I/O library. The `identification` attribute categorizes an *IoParadigm* (e.g., "MPI I/O"), while the `name` distinguishes specific implementations (e.g., "OMPIO" [9] or "ROMIO" [23]). The `class` attribute specifies whether the I/O paradigm is serial or parallel. Only parallel I/O paradigms enable collective I/O operations within a group of multiple processes/threads. The `flags` attribute allows to set further boolean characteristics for the I/O paradigm (e.g., mark if the paradigm either directly accesses the operating system or maps its functionality to other I/O paradigms such as HDF5 or NetCDF). In addition, *IoParadigm* provides an extensible mechanism to specify further `properties` such as version information.

An **IoHandle** definition reflects a file descriptor based on a prior I/O resource definition specified by the `file` attribute. The `parent` attribute of an *IoHandle* models hierarchical relations between I/O handles. This mechanism enables correlation of operations between individual layers of the I/O software stack. If the `paradigm` supports collective I/O operations, the `group` attribute specifies the set of participating processes/threads.

The **IoPreCreatedHandleState** definition marks a `handle` that is standardly created (e.g., `stdin`, `stdout`, `stderr`) or inherited from a parent process/thread. The definition holds the access `mode` (e.g., read or write) and status `flags` of this default I/O handle.

3.2 Events

Events represent I/O activities at application runtime. In this work, we focus on events required for performance analysis. Therefore, we assume that I/O operations finish successfully, otherwise performance analysis is not reasonable. However, our approach is not limited to performance analysis and we plan to support the handling of unsuccessful I/O operations (see Sect. 7). We distinguish events into meta data (e.g., `open`/`create`, `close`) and data transfer (e.g., `read`/`write`) operations. All events store an accurate timestamp and information about the issuing process/thread. Additional information depend on the specific event type.

Meta Data Operations: Events of this category indicate the creation and the destruction of file descriptors. The **IoCreateHandle** event marks the creation of a new `handle` (e.g., after opening a file). The `mode` attribute determines the access mode to the file descriptor (e.g., read-only, write-only, or read-write). According to the Posix I/O API, *IoCreateHandle* stores optional `creationFlags` (e.g., create if the file does not exist) and `statusFlags` (e.g., open file in append mode). An **IoDestroyHandle** marks the end of an active I/O `handle`'s lifetime. Thus, a pair of consecutive *IoCreateHandle* and *IoDestroyHandle* events defines the time in which the handle is active and can be used by other events. The **IoDuplicateHandle** event represents the duplication of an existing file descriptor. This event references the original file descriptor (`oldHandle`) as well as the newly created one (`newHandle`). The *IoDuplicateHandle* activates the `newHandle` and the `oldHandle` remains active. In our event design, the new handle does not inherit the status flags. Instead, the `statusFlags` attribute explicitly records this information. This option releases analysis tools from the need of tracking the inheritance. Figure 4 illustrates the life cycle of tracked I/O handles.

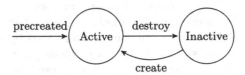

Fig. 4. Events create and destroy I/O handles at runtime. Commands to duplicate handles build a special case: the original handle remains in active state, the newly created handle changes from inactive to active state.

The following events track the status of active I/O handles. The **IoSeek** event records changes of the position within a file. The event stores the offset requested by the user (`offsetRequest`), the position to which the offset should be applied (`whence`), e.g., absolute from the start or end, relative to the current position, and the resulting offset relative to the beginning of the file (`offsetResult`). An **IoChangeStatusFlags** event tracks changes to the status flags of an active `handle`. The `statusFlags` attribute holds the updated status.

The **IoDeleteFile** event marks the deletion of an I/O resource. Similar to deletion functions, such as `unlink`, `rename`, or `remove`, this event operates on I/O resources instead of I/O handles. In addition to the affected `file`, this record stores the `paradigm` that issued the deletion.

Data Transfer Operations: Events of this category record data transfer operations. One complete transfer operation might be split into basic events. Further, we distinguish between blocking and non-blocking operations. For example, a blocking Posix I/O `read` operation consists of two events—one for its start and

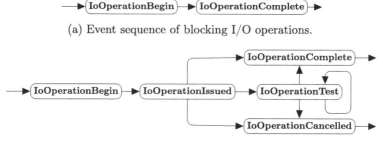

(a) Event sequence of blocking I/O operations.

(b) Event sequence of non-blocking I/O operations.

Fig. 5. Sequence of generated events for different I/O operation types.

one for its completion. Consequently, both events need an identifier to relate all parts composing an I/O operation. Therefore, these events contain a `matchingId` attribute, identifying an I/O operation in-flight. The attribute is valid for a process including all its threads. The **IoOperationBegin** event lists the affected `handle`, the operation `mode` (e.g., reading or writing), and `operationFlags` providing additional semantic information. In particular, the `operationFlags` attribute defines two distinct characteristics of an operation: (a) collective or non-collective, and (b) blocking or non-blocking. The `bytesRequest` attribute reflects the user defined maximum number of transferred bytes. An **IoOperationComplete** event marks the end of a data transfer operation. It references the affected `handle`. The `bytesResult` attribute stores the actual number of transferred bytes. Corresponding *IoOperationComplete-IoOperationBegin* event time stamps define the transfer operation duration. Figure 5a shows the event sequence generated by blocking I/O data transfer operations. The "blocking" bit in the `operationFlags` of the *IoOperationBegin* event is set accordingly. The semantic of blocking operations ensures that a pair of matching *IoOperationBegin* and *IoOperationComplete* events occurs within the event stream of the same thread. In contrast, Fig. 5b illustrates the event sequence of a non-blocking I/O data transfer operation (e.g., `aio_write`). Typical for non-blocking operations is the decoupling of issuing and completing operation, i.e., started on one thread but completed on another thread of the same process. Non-blocking data transfer operations also start with *IoOperationBegin* events. In case of a successful initiation an **IoOperationIssued** event follows. *IoOperationBegin* and its corresponding *IoOperationIssued* event must occur on the same thread. Users can test active non-blocking operations to ensure their completion. **IoOperationTest** events represent unsuccessful tests (I/O operation not finished yet), *IoOperationComplete* events indicate finished operations. The **IoOperationCancelled** event represents the successful cancellation of a non-blocking operation. Any thread of the same process can test, cancel, or complete a non-blocking I/O operation in-flight.

Collective I/O operations are executed by all processes/threads of the respective I/O handle. The "collective" bit in the `operationFlags` attribute of the *IoOperationBegin* event marks the special semantic of such operations.

4   Implementation

In the previous Sect. 3, we presented our approach for recording I/O operation information, whereas we focus on the implementation details in this section. We implement our design in OTF2 (Open Trace Format Version 2) [12]. Many analysis tools, such as Vampir and Scalasca [13], process OTF2 event traces. The OTF2 library provides an API for reading and writing event traces. It already supports events for function entry and exit, parallelization constructs, and communication. In this work, we extend OTF2 with definitions and events implementing the I/O operations presented in Sect. 3. OTF2 maintains a list of parallelization paradigms (e.g., MPI, OpenMP, Pthreads) as a C-enumeration in its application programming interface[1]. Adding support for new parallelization paradigms would require to extend this enumeration as well. However, this could result in inconsistencies due to unknown enumeration members, when older OTF2 versions read event logs written by a newer OTF2 version. Considering the wide range of available I/O interfaces, we conclude that this approach is unsuitable. Therefore, we abstain from providing a fixed list of supported I/O paradigms in our implementation. Instead, we implement the *IoParadigm* definition record using a self-describing mechanism. For the sake of convenience, the OTF2 library maintains a list of known I/O paradigms in its documentation[2]. Users are encouraged to follow these suggestions when generating their own event logs.

Besides OTF2, we require a software component that monitors the application behavior at runtime. For this purpose, we select the Score-P measurement infrastructure and add components for intercepting calls to specific I/O libraries. In order to intercept calls to MPI, we utilize the existing MPI profiling interface (PMPI) [18, Sect. 14.2]. For all remaining I/O interfaces we use a generic interception method [6]. Each time an application issues an I/O function, we intercept this call. The control flow passes to the Score-P measurement system which has access to all function parameters and can record performance relevant data. Then, the measurement system calls the original function. After the original function returns, the control flow passes back to the application and the program execution continues.

We strive to support a flexible list of I/O paradigms in Score-P. Therefore, Score-P must handle the interactions of I/O paradigms in a generic way. Especially, the mapping of I/O operations to an a priori known lower-level I/O paradigm requires a paradigm agnostic implementation. We achieve this by implementing a shared per-thread I/O management stack. Individual paradigms

---

[1] https://silc.zih.tu-dresden.de/otf2-2.1.1/OTF2_GeneralDefinitions_8h.html#aa14d0751354081d258913145a80e79a9.

[2] https://silc.zih.tu-dresden.de/otf2-2.1.1/group__io.html.

can communicate via this stack. The following describes this approach using the example case of MPI I/O implemented on-top of ISO-C. If the MPI I/O component from Score-P intercepts a call to `MPI_File_open`, it creates a new *IoHandle* ($handle_1$) and pushes it to the I/O management stack. Then, the `PMPI_File_open` function is called via the MPI profiling interface. The MPI implementation may than call `fopen`, which is subsequently intercepted by Score-P as well. The ISO-C component inspects the top element of the I/O management stack to determine whether a potential higher-level I/O paradigm is active. If a handle is available on the stack ($handle_1$ in this example), this handle is used as parent for the newly created *IoHandle* ($handle_2$). After leaving `fopen` and `MPI_File_open`, the top element from the I/O management stack is removed for each involved paradigm. In summary, whether lower-level paradigms will create new *IoHandle*s is unknown a priori. Therefore, each I/O component must push and pop its current active handle onto the I/O management stack. This ensures proper references to controlling higher-level I/O paradigms in individual handles. As a result, all occurring *IoHandle*s create a root-directed tree.

5   Case Study

We evaluate our methodology and implementation in an analysis of the Met Office NERC Cloud model (MONC) simulator. Our study checks MONC for I/O performance penalties and exposes insights of operations using multiple I/O layers. MONC, a Fortran+MPI code, utilizes NetCDF to write results to disk. The cloud simulator has two kinds of processes: (a) simulation processes for computing the cloud model and (b) I/O server processes for storing results to disk. Users can individually set the number of I/O server processes. At runtime, the I/O servers keep simulation results in main memory. After N simulation steps or at program termination, the I/O servers flush the results to disk [7].

We record the I/O behavior of MONC using our Score-P prototype. Score-P instruments the source code and intercepts library calls to Posix I/O, MPI I/O, and NetCDF. We conduct our experiments on ARCHER [3]. This Cray XC30 system consists of 4920 compute nodes, each containing two 12-core E5-2697 v2 (Ivy Bridge) processors running at 2.7 GHz. Our experiments use a 4.4 PB Lustre file system (stripe count 1, stripe size 1 GiB) to store simulation results and collected event logs. We run MONC on 112 processes, distributed over 8 nodes. Each node hosts one I/O server process with a pool of 10 additional threads. The remaining 104 simulation processes compute the cloud model. In our experiment setup, MONC simulates 100 timesteps. At the end of the application run, the I/O server processes write the data to disk via calls to NetCDF. Using our approach, we can inspect internal function invocations of MPI I/O and Posix I/O. In order to avoid interference with the I/O behavior of the observed application, we keep all collected performance data in main memory during application runtime. After the application has finished, event logs are written to disk. In our experiments the recording of performance data caused an increase in application runtime of about six percent. We visualize the resulting event logs using the tool

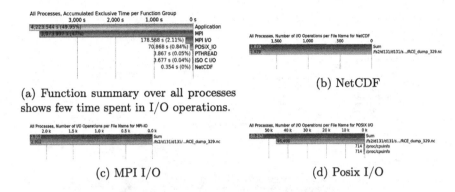

(a) Function summary over all processes shows few time spent in I/O operations.

(b) NetCDF

(c) MPI I/O

(d) Posix I/O

Fig. 6. Function and I/O statistics of the MONC experiment run.

Vampir. Since version 9.4 Vampir features new displays with special focus on the visualization of I/O behavior of applications. The paper "Visualization of Multi-layer I/O Performance in Vampir" [17] presents a detailed description of these sophisticated visualization techniques using I/O related performance data.

Figure 6a depicts the overall exclusive time spent in particular function groups. The event log contains 7 groups, while most of the time is spent in application code (about 50%). Furthermore, the simulator spends more time in MPI communication routines than in I/O operations. Although this first analysis suggests that MONC does not exhibit poor I/O performance it is worth taking a closer look at I/O operations.

To investigate I/O performance in detail, Fig. 6 depicts three I/O summary charts for NetCDF (Fig. 6b), MPI I/O (Fig. 6c), and Posix I/O (Fig. 6d), respectively. All three layers utilize the same RCE_dump_329.nc file. The number of accesses to this file increases while traversing the NetCDF, MPI I/O, and Posix I/O layer. This statistic reflects how each library abstracts functionality in order to hide complex operations. Furthermore, the figure shows that Posix I/O also utilizes additional files. In further analyses we will identify the origin of these file accesses.

Figure 7 depicts the I/O timeline (top) and the process summary (bottom) for Thread 7 of Rank 0. The I/O timeline displays the performed type of I/O operations (Read (orange), Write (yellow), Open (blue), Close (green)) on the x-axis and the accessed files as well as associated handles on the y-axis. If an I/O library (e.g., NetCDF) utilizes another I/O library, the individual handles of each library are attached to each other, as represented in a tree-like hierarchy to the left of the upper chart. The top chart in Fig. 7 depicts all handles used to access the NetCDF file RCE_dump_329.nc. Thereby, NetCDF internally utilizes MPI I/O (see handle MPI-IO #0) which in turn performs Posix I/O operations (see POSIX I/O #20) on RCE_dump_329.nc. This view also shows that MPI I/O opens (blue bars) maps-files from the /proc filesystem through the ISO-C API. Each I/O server process reads (red boxes) its maps-file before transferring simulation data to the NetCDF file.

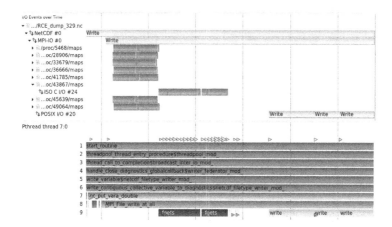

Fig. 7. The I/O timeline (top) shows individual I/O operations of Thread 7 from Rank 0 on specific files. The process summary (bottom) depicts the call stack. (Color figure online)

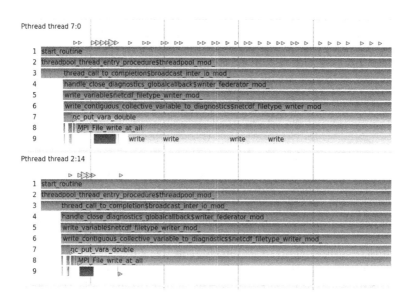

Fig. 8. Call stack comparison of two different I/O server processes. (Color figure online)

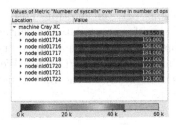

Fig. 9. Number of syscalls in MPI I/O mapped to the system tree topology.

The bottom chart in Fig. 7 depicts the process timeline for Thread 7 of Rank 0 and provides details about the calling context of I/O operations in this time slice. For example, the execution of nc_put_vara_double (bottom chart, level 7) creates an I/O write event of the NetCDF #0 handle (top chart). This operation in turn calls MPI_File_Write_at_all (bottom chart, level 8) which generates the I/O write event of the MPI-IO #0 handle (top chart). Level 9 in the bottom chart shows internal details of this collective MPI I/O routine. It depicts the fgets call to access the maps-file (/proc/43867/maps). write calls to store the final data which correspond to the write events of the POSIX I/O #20 handle (top chart). Interestingly, NetCDF executes MPI communication operations (bottom chart, level 8, red bars) within the nc_put_vara_double routine. In this time slice, these operations are small compared to the MPI_File_Write_at_all routine and do not impede performance. However, in a different scenario, these functions may lead to a communication bottleneck or undesirable wait states.

So far we investigated only one I/O server process. In the next analysis we will compare different I/O server processes. Figure 8 shows the process timelines of I/O server Rank 0/Thread 7 (top) and Rank 14/Thread 2 (bottom). Both servers call identical functions with similar durations until call level 9. On this level, both servers perform ISO-C I/O operations (brown bars) at the beginning of MPI_File_Write_at_all. Then, one server process (top) executes write functions. It seems that only one I/O server process accesses the RCE_dump_329.nc file through the collective I/O operation. The collective operation appears to synchronizes all processes (causing waiting time) except process Rank 0/Thread 7, that performs the actual I/O operations. Figure 9 depicts the number of syscalls within MPI I/O routines aggregated per compute node. Node nid01713 performs the most syscalls within MPI. This confirms, that only one I/O server transfers data to the RCE_dump_329.nc file. Reasons could be the (small) data size or missing support for parallel accesses in the current implementation. For MONC, our analysis suggests optimization potential by switching from collective operations to individual accesses per I/O server process.

6   Conclusions

This work presents a methodology for recording calls to I/O libraries on multiple layers of the software stack. In contrast to current approaches, our methodology explicitly correlates operations between multiple I/O libraries. This enhanced level of detail in the recorded performance data is essential for understanding the overall I/O behavior of applications. Consequently, users can now identify root causes of I/O bottlenecks inside a complex I/O stack. We prove the applicability of our approach in an analysis study of the Met Office/NERC Cloud Model (MONC) code.

7   Future Work

In this work, we show that our approach records valuable information about the I/O behavior of applications. With an intuitive presentation of this information, we support application developers in optimizing I/O-intensive applications. Currently, we are working on integrating our approach into the Score-P open-source measurement infrastructure and OTF2 trace format. Consequently, it will be available in one of the next official Score-P releases. Meanwhile, we provide a prototype implementation [25].

Automatic analysis as a complementary technique to visualization directly guides users to performance bottlenecks. Tools like Scalasca or Casita [21] apply detection mechanisms to identify inefficiency patterns in MPI message transfers or computation offloading to accelerator devices. Similar analysis techniques can be applied to our I/O performance data recordings.

This work focuses on performance analysis of file I/O operations. However, it can be easily extended to monitor I/O operations on sockets. This use case would only require new definitions for representing sockets as an I/O resource (besides files and directories). Furthermore, we plan to add information about failed operations to the current records. This would extend their usability from performance analysis to debugging and correctness checking applications.

Data Availability Statement and Acknowledgments. This research was undertaken as part of the NEXTGenIO project, which is funded through the European Union's Horizon 2020 Research and Innovation programme under Grant Agreement no. 671951. The datasets and code generated during and/or analysed during the current study are available in the figshare repository: https://doi.org/10.6084/m9.figshare. 6384164 [25].

References

1. Adhianto, L., et al.: HPCTOOLKIT: tools for performance analysis of optimized parallel programs. In: Concurrency and Computation: Practice and Experience (2010). https://doi.org/10.1002/cpe.1553
2. Knüpfer, A., et al.: The vampir performance analysis tool-set. In: Resch, M., Keller, R., Himmler, V., Krammer, B., Schulz, A. (eds.) Tools for High Performance Computing. Springer, Heidelberg (2008). https://doi.org/10.1007/978-3-540-68564-7_9
3. Archer Hardware Specification, February 2018. https://www.archer.ac.uk/about-archer/hardware

4. Arm MAP - Low-Overhead Profiling to Optimize C, C++, Fortran and F90 Codes, February 2018. https://www.arm.com/products/development-tools/hpc-tools/cross-platform/forge/map

5. blktrace(8) - Linux man page, February 2018. https://linux.die.net/man/8/blktrace

6. Brendel, R., Wesarg, B., Tschüter, R., Weber, M., Ilsche, T., Oeste, S.: Generic library interception for improved performance measurement and insight. In: Proceedings of the 6th Workshop on Extreme Scale Programming Tools, ESPT 2017, November 2017

7. Brown, N., et al.: A highly scalable met office NERC cloud model. In: Proceedings of the 3rd International Conference on Exascale Applications and Software, EASC 2015, pp. 132–137 (2015)

8. Carns, P., et al.: Understanding and improving computational science storage access through continuous characterization. Trans. Storage **7**(3), 8:1–8:26 (2011). https://doi.org/10.1145/2027066.2027068

9. Chaarawi, M., Gabriel, E., Keller, R., Graham, R.L., Bosilca, G., Dongarra, J.J.: OMPIO: a modular software architecture for MPI I/O. In: Cotronis, Y., Danalis, A., Nikolopoulos, D.S., Dongarra, J. (eds.) EuroMPI 2011. LNCS, vol. 6960, pp. 81–89. Springer, Heidelberg (2011). https://doi.org/10.1007/978-3-642-24449-0_11

10. Cyrille Rossant: Should you use HDF5? February 2018. http://cyrille.rossant.net/should-you-use-hdf5/

11. Dieter An Mey and others: Score-P: A Unified Performance Measurement System for Petascale Applications. In: Competence in High Performance Computing (2012)

12. Eschweiler, D., et al.: Open trace format 2 - the next generation of scalable trace formats and support libraries. In: Proceedings of the 14th Biennial ParCo Conference on Applications, Tools and Techniques on the Road to Exascale Computing. Advances in Parallel Computing, vol. 22, pp. 481–490 (2012)

13. Geimer, M., Wolf, F., Wylie, B.J.N., Ábrahám, E., Becker, D., Mohr, B.: The scalasca performance toolset architecture. Concurr. Comput.: Pract. Exp. **22**(6), 702–719 (2010). https://doi.org/10.1002/cpe.v22:6

14. iostat, February 2018. https://github.com/sysstat/sysstat

15. iotop, February 2018. http://guichaz.free.fr/iotop/

16. Lustre, February 2018. http://lustre.org/

17. Mix, H., Herold, C., Weber, M.: Visualization of multi-layer I/O performance in vampir. In: 2018 IEEE International Parallel and Distributed Processing Symposium Workshops (IPDPSW), May 2018

18. MPI Forum: MPI: A Message-Passing Interface Standard, Version 3.1, 14 June 2015. https://www.mpi-forum.org/docs/mpi-3.1/. Accessed May 2018

19. Müller, M., et al.: Developing scalable applications with Vampir, VampirServer and VampirTrace. In: Parallel Computing: Architectures, Algorithms and Applications. Advances in Parallel Computing, January 2007

20. sar(1) - Linux man page, February 2018. https://linux.die.net/man/1/sar

21. Schmitt, F., Stolle, J., Dietrich, R.: CASITA: a tool for identifying critical optimization targets in distributed heterogeneous applications. In: 43rd International Conference on Parallel Processing Workshops, pp. 186–195, September 2014. https://doi.org/10.1109/ICPPW.2014.35

22. Shende, S., Malony, A.D., Spear, W., Schuchardt, K.: Characterizing I/O performance using the TAU performance system. In: PARCO, pp. 647–655 (2011)

23. Thakur, R., Gropp, W., Lusk, E.: On implementing MPI-IO portably and with high performance. In: Proceedings of the 6th Workshop on I/O in Parallel and Distributed Systems, IOPADS 1999, pp. 23–32 (1999). https://doi.org/10.1145/301816.301826
24. The HDF Group: Hierarchical Data Format, version 5, February 1997–2018. http://www.hdfgroup.org/HDF5/
25. Tschueter, R., Herold, C., Wesarg, B., Weber, M.: Score-P measurement system code and event logs for Euro-Par 2018 paper: a methodology for performance analysis of applications using multi-layer I/O. figshare. Fileset (2018). https://doi.org/10.6084/m9.figshare.6384164
26. Unidata: Network Common Data Form (NetCDF) [software] (2018). https://doi.org/10.5065/D6H70CW6,https://doi.org/10.5065/D6H70CW6
27. Virtual Institute for I/O, February 2018. https://www.vi4io.org/start
28. Vijayakumar, K., Mueller, F., Ma, X., Roth, P.C.: Scalable I/O tracing and analysis. In: Proceedings of the 4th Petascale Data Storage Workshop, PDSW 2009 (2009). https://doi.org/10.1145/1713072.1713080

Runtime Determinacy Race Detection for OpenMP Tasks

Hassan Salehe Matar$^{(\boxtimes)}$ and Didem Unat

Koç University, Istanbul, Turkey
{hmatar,dunat}@ku.edu.tr

Abstract. One potential problem when writing parallel programs with OpenMP is to introduce determinacy races where for a given input, the program may unexpectedly produce different final outputs at different runs. Such startling behavior can result from incorrect ordering of OpenMP tasks. We present a method to detect determinacy races in OpenMP tasks at runtime. Based on OpenMP program semantics, our proposed solution models an OpenMP program as a collection of tasks with inferred dependencies among them where a task is implicitly created with a *parallel* region construct or explicitly created with a *task* construct. We define happens-before relation among tasks based on such dependencies for determining an execution order when detecting determinacy races. Based on this formalization, we developed a tool, TaskSanitizer, which detects and reports concurrent memory accesses whose tasks do not have common dependencies. Finally, TaskSanitizer works at runtime, has been able to find bugs in micro-benchmarks and it is reasonably efficient to be utilized in a working environment.

1 Introduction

OpenMP 3.0 introduced shared memory task execution model [1] in which programmers specify computations in units called *tasks*, which can be executed by concurrent threads. In OpenMP 4.0 [2], a programmer can specify execution order between tasks through *in* and *out* data dependencies, where a succeeding task waits for the completion of the preceding task's execution. Even though programmers have more flexibility to express various types of parallelism with the new tasking attributes, these new features can introduce subtle bugs if the operational semantics and scheduling policy of the OpenMP runtime are not reasoned about. One of such concurrency bugs is a *determinacy race* which occurs when concurrently executing entities access the same memory location without specified ordering between them and at least one access is a write to that memory location [8,16,21,22]. As a result, a program with determinacy races may produce different final output results at different runs on the same input [18]. Determinacy races are possible if the programmer does not specify necessary dependency between concurrent tasks which access the same memory locations. Since there is no specific order defined by the programmer, the scheduler is free to execute the tasks in any order or concurrently.

© Springer International Publishing AG, part of Springer Nature 2018
M. Aldinucci et al. (Eds.): Euro-Par 2018, LNCS 11014, pp. 31–45, 2018.
https://doi.org/10.1007/978-3-319-96983-1_3

The existing state-of-the-art runtime race detection tools for OpenMP such as Archer [3] – and general race detectors [11] – check for proper locking in programs which protects shared memory objects but can fail to detect determinacy races which stem from improper ordering of executions. Protecting memory accesses with critical sections or other explicit locking is not sufficient to avoid determinacy races. Rather, proper ordering of the executing entities is essential to avoid undesirable nondeterminism in OpenMP programs for correctness.

We present an algorithm to detect determinacy races in OpenMP programs by utilizing the concept of OpenMP tasks and their dependencies. Unlike the state-of-the-art race detection tools [3] that rely on *happens-before* model at thread level, we apply *happens-before* model at task level, which provides the advantage of reducing randomness due to scheduling. We implement our algorithm as an open source tool based on compile-time instrumentation through LLVM [15] compiler pass to instrument shared memory accesses in the program. The tool uses the OpenMP Performance Tools API (OMPT) [7] to monitor OpenMP-related events such as task creation, scheduling, and execution. In summary, the main contributions of this paper are:

- A formal definition of the determinacy races and a technique for detecting such races in OpenMP tasks. To our knowledge, no prior work has been done for detecting determinacy races in OpenMP tasks with mixed structures of critical and non-critical sections.
- Determinacy race detection tool for OpenMP called *TaskSanitizer* [20].
- Evaluation of our method using micro-benchmark applications and comparison of results against a race detection tool for OpenMP programs.

2   Background in OpenMP Tasks

Explicit tasks in OpenMP can be created with the construct *omp task*, which is readily available since OpenMP 3.0 [1]. For each task, OpenMP creates a work block which includes a sequence of program statements and the data environment. This block is set aside to be executed by a thread until the runtime schedules it. Starting with OpenMP 4.0 [2], it is possible to specify execution order among explicit tasks using the *depend* clause, where a programmer specifies input and output data dependencies between tasks. A collection of tasks through dependencies forms an implicit task dependency graph in which a task is not runnable until all its dependencies are satisfied. The runnable tasks can then be scheduled by the OpenMP runtime. If two or more tasks are simultaneously runnable at a given point in time, they can execute in any order or concurrently.

Every part of an OpenMP program executes in a task assigned to one or more threads. For example, implicit tasks can be generated at parallel regions with the OpenMP *parallel* construct and each implicit task is executed to completion by one thread in the thread group of the parallel region [1]. Figure 1 shows a simple OpenMP program, where a default implicit task is created as part of the main program. This task then creates two implicit tasks through the parallel region at line 3. One of these tasks executes the *single* region at line 4, which creates two explicit tasks *t* and *u* at lines 6 and 10, respectively. Both of these tasks have critical sections, in which they set different values to a shared variable *i*. This example has a determinacy race which is explained in detail in Sect. 3.

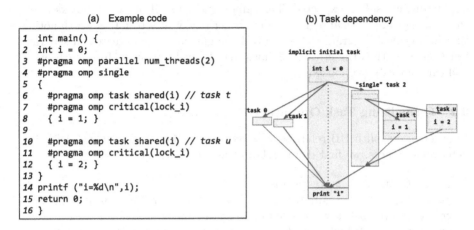

(a) Example code

```
1  int main() {
2  int i = 0;
3  #pragma omp parallel num_threads(2)
4  #pragma omp single
5  {
6    #pragma omp task shared(i) // task t
7    #pragma omp critical(lock_i)
8    { i = 1; }
9
10   #pragma omp task shared(i) // task u
11   #pragma omp critical(lock_i)
12   { i = 2; }
13 }
14 printf ("i=%d\n",i);
15 return 0;
16 }
```

(b) Task dependency

Fig. 1. OpenMP example illustrates explicit and implicit tasks and their logical flow dependency between tasks. The code example has a determinacy race.

3   Determinacy Race Detection

In this section, we first define determinacy races and present motivation on detecting them with the help of an OpenMP example. Then, we formally define a task with its operations and we devise happens-before (HB) relations between these operations for capturing partial ordering among them. Finally we use the defined HB relations to present our algorithm for detecting determinacy races.

3.1   Definition and Motivating Example

Determinacy race occurs between two tasks if the following two conditions are satisfied: *(i)* there is no ordering between these tasks enforced by task dependency, and *(ii)* both tasks access a common shared memory location and at least one access is a write. If simultaneously runnable tasks modify the same memory locations, different scheduling (i.e; order of execution) of these tasks may result in nondeterministic final values on these memory locations.

Many runtime race detection algorithms [9,23,24] do not take the notion of dependency into account. They monitor proper synchronization of threads on memory accesses to detect races. In this work, we monitor the proper ordering of tasks and critical sections to ensure that different possible ordering of critical sections in these tasks always generate a single, deterministic final program state. This helps the programmer to notice if nondeterminisim was not intentional.

We have provided a simple OpenMP program in Fig. 1, where there is no specified dependency between tasks *t* and *u*. As a result, their critical sections can execute in any order and thus the final result for *i* can either be 1 or 2 despite the fact that accesses to the shared variable are protected by a common lock. Unless the developer intends the program to behave as such, only one deterministic result is expected. The same issue arises if one of the tasks reads the value of *i* in a critical region and the other task writes to *i*. It is worth noting that in a typical program these two tasks might have been created in separate function calls, thus the critical sections may be well far apart from each other and can be easily overlooked.

3.2 Formalizing Task Operations

In order to establish HB relations and set up rules between tasks for detecting determinacy races, we first define relevant task operations:

- create(t,u): task *t* creates task *u*.
- wait(t,u): task *t* awaits termination of task *u* at *taskwait* or at a barrier.
- read(t,mem): task *t* reads value from shared memory location *mem*.
- write(t,mem,v): task *t* writes value v to shared memory location *mem*.
- out(t,u,x): signifies dependency from task *t* to task *u* through storage location *x*. Task *t* is the predecessor and *u* is the dependent task.
- in(u,t,x): signifies dependency from task *t* to task *u* through storage location *x*. Task *u* becomes runnable once *t* completes its execution.

Having defined task operations, we elaborate on shared memory accesses and associate them to segments of a task, rather than the task itself. We define a task as an enclosed sequence of unique *tasksegments* and *synchronization* operations executed together, as shown in Fig. 2. A tasksegment is a sequence of consecutive shared memory accesses between two synchronization operations in a task. Therefore, a synchronization operation in a task ends the current tasksegment and a new tasksegment starts at the next shared memory access operation in the task after the synchronization operation. We define synchronization operations as operations which trigger execution among tasks and are create, wait, out, and in. For example, Fig. 3 shows three tasks (a parent and two child tasks) but contains four tasksegments. In other words, in our formal task operations we differentiate the code bodies (e.g. tasksegment *s1* and tasksegment *s4*) that result from imperfectly nested tasks. Since this is necessary to establish HB relations, we revise the shared memory access operations as follows:

- read(t,s,mem) shared memory access that appears in tasksegment *s* where task *t* reads a value from shared memory location *mem*.
- write(t,s,mem,v) shared memory access that appears in tasksegment *s* where task *t* writes value v to shared memory location *mem*.

$$\textbf{task}_\textbf{t} \equiv \left[\begin{array}{c} \texttt{create(t,u), wait(t,u), out(t,u,x),} \\ \texttt{in(u,t,x), taskseg(t,s)} \end{array} \right]^+$$

$$\textbf{taskseg}_{\textbf{(t,s)}} \equiv \left[\begin{array}{c} \texttt{read(t,s,mem), write(t,s,mem,v)} \end{array} \right]^+$$

Fig. 2. Defining a task as a sequence of tasksegments (taskseg) and synchronizations

3.3   Happens-Before Relations Between Task Operations

For partial ordering of operations in an OpenMP program, we use happens-before (HB) ordering of events [14] by employing dependency among synchronization operations. Happens-before relation is a transitive-closure relation. For given three operations a, b, and c if there is an HB relation from a to b and from b to c, then there is an HB relation from a to c. We will infer this relation while categorizing HB relations between tasks operations. We use symbol $\prec$ to refer to an HB relation in general and use $<_\pi$ to refer to an inferred HB relation due to transitive-closure property.

$$a \prec b \wedge b \prec c \rightarrow a <_\pi c$$

We identify four types of HB edges among operations between tasks. These are (i) an HB relation among memory operations performed within a tasksegment; (ii) between a task and its child task through *create*; (iii) relation between *out* and *in* dependency operations; and (iv) relation at *wait* operation. We then use these HB relations to infer HB relations among tasksegments in tasks.

1. HB by program order: This is the basic type of HB relation where program operations within a tasksegment are ordered according to their execution sequence. Similarly, tasksegments within a task are ordered by program order.

2. HB relation by task dependency: If tasks t and u have a commonly specified data dependency such that u has an input dependency from t, then all tasksegments – as well as their enclosing memory operations – in t happen-before all tasksegments in u.

$$\frac{out(t, u, x) \prec in(u, t, x)}{\forall_{taskseg_{(t,a)}} \forall_{taskseg_{(u,b)}} taskseg_{(t,a)} <_\pi taskseg_{(u,b)}}$$

3. HB relation between a task and its child task: tasksegments of a task which execute before creating a child task happens-before the tasksegments executed in the created child task. For two tasks t and u:

$$\frac{create(t, u)}{\forall_{taskseg_{(t,a)}} taskseg_{(t,a)} <_\pi create(t, u) \rightarrow \forall_{taskseg_{(u,b)}} taskseg_{(t,a)} <_\pi taskseg_{(u,b)}}$$

4. HB relation at taskwait and barrier synchronizations: The last operation of a child task happens before the *taskwait* or implicit barrier synchronization operation of the parent task. Therefore, all tasksegments of such task

have HB relation with subsequent tasksegments of the parent task after the wait
operation is completed.

$$wait(t, u)$$
$$\forall_{taskseg_{(t,a)}} wait(t,u) <_\pi taskseg_{(t,a)} \rightarrow \forall_{taskseg_{(u,b)}} taskseg_{(u,b)} <_\pi taskseg_{(t,a)}$$

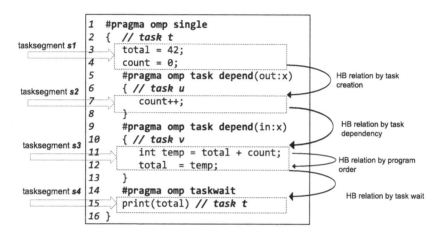

Fig. 3. Example with four categories of HB relation among operations of tasks

We use example Fig. 3 to illustrate the four categories of HB relations. The
memory operations at lines 11 and 12 belong to the same tasksegment *s3* and
thus are ordered by program order. Moreover, there is an HB relation between
memory operations at lines 4 and 7 because their corresponding tasksegments
have an HB relation through task creation synchronization operation as task *t*
executing the single region creates an explicit task *u* at line 5. Moreover, all operations in tasksegment *s2* happen-before all operations in tasksegment *s3* because
of specified dependency between tasks *u* and *v*. Finally, memory operations in
tasksegments *s3* and *s4* happen before the print statement in tasksegment *s4*
because of the *wait* synchronization operation at line 14. Without *taskwait*, we
would not be able to establish an HB relation between *s4* with *s2* or *s3*.

3.4 Determinacy Race Detection Algorithm

Algorithm 1 provides pseudo-code for determinacy race detection between any
two memory operations (α and β) in an OpenMP program. Between lines 4
and 9, it retrieves information of the operations: their task identifiers (IDs),
tasksegment IDs as well as the memory addresses they accessed. Then at line
10, the algorithm checks if the operations access the same memory location

and belong to two different tasks and tasksegments. At line 11, it checks if the corresponding tasksegments do not have an HB relation as inferred using the four HB types from Sect. 3.3. If there is no HB, then it reports a determinacy race bug if one operation is a *write* and the other a *read* at lines 12 and 13. In the case that they both are *write* actions, it reports a determinacy race if they are not commutative (lines 14–16).

Algorithm 1. Detecting determinacy race between two shared memory operations

---

1: **procedure** CHECKDETERMINACYRACE(α, β)
2:    **Input:** α ▷ *a shared memory operation*
3:    **Input:** β ▷ *another shared memory operation*
4:    t ← getTaskID(α)
5:    u ← getTaskID(β)
6:    seg_1 ← getTasksegmentID(α)
7:    seg_2 ← getTasksegmentID(β)
8:    mem_1 ← getMemoryAddress(α)
9:    mem_2 ← getMemoryAddress(β)
10:   **if** $mem_1 = mem_2$ **and** t ≠ u **and** $seg_1 \neq seg_2$ **then**   ▷ *on different tasks*
11:     **if not** *HappensBefore(seg₁, seg₂)* **then**   ▷ *check if no HB*
12:       **if** isWrite(α) ≠ isWrite(β) **then**   ▷ *one write, one read*
13:         REPORTBUG*(α, β)*
14:       **else if** *isWrite(α)* **and** *isWrite(β)* **then**   ▷ *both write*
15:         **if not** isCommutative(α, β) **then**   ▷ *check commutativity*
16:           REPORTBUG*(α, β)*
17:       **end if**
18:     **end if**
19:    **end if**
20:   **end if**
21: **end procedure**

Detecting Commutative Operations: Shared memory accesses can result in falsely detected determinacy races if these accesses involve in commutative arithmetic operations between same-lock critical sections. Two concurrent arithmetic operations on a shared memory location are commutative if their order of execution does not alter the final value produced. For example, if *var += temp1* and *var -= temp2* are in two different same-lock critical sections, then re-ordering them does not affect the final value of *var*. Thus in line 16 of Algorithm 1, we use the formalization of commutativity operation detection proposed in [18] to identify such memory actions and do not report determinacy races on them.

4   Implementation

As shown in Fig. 4, we implement our method as a tool that has three main parts (i) instrumentation; (ii) inferring happens-before relation between program operations; and (iii) determinacy race detection at runtime.

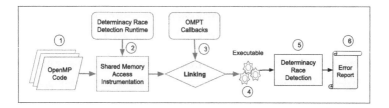

Fig. 4. Showing implementations of TaskSanitizer: architecture and tool flow

1. **Instrumentation:** We instrument an OpenMP program source code at compile-time through LLVM/Clang infrastructure [15]. The instrumentation injects our determinacy race detection runtime callbacks, which implement Algorithm 1, in step ②. We customize the shared memory instrumentation module of ThreadSanitizer [24] to identify shared memory operations and associated source code line numbers and functions for traceability in case of determinacy races. Moreover, we identify and store program statements which are in critical sections. These are later used by our algorithm to detect commutative operations on potential determinacy races where our tool does not report them if the ordering of those critical sections does not alter the final output.

2. **Constructing HB relations:** To capture HB ordering between tasks and operations, we implemented a module that uses the OMPT interface [7] in step ③ of Fig. 4 to register callbacks which capture synchronization operations. First, we locate the implicit tasks as well as explicit tasks defined using the tasking clause for specifying the ordering of program events. Second, task dependencies through *depend* clause as well as custom synchronization idioms such as locks and barriers are located to reason about the happens-before ordering. Finally, we use these operations to infer HB relations between task operations. Moreover, we assign a unique identification to each task and tasksegment at creation, during program execution. This has three advantages (a) Unique ID differentiates different instances of the same task code block or tasksegment executed at different times. (b) A task may run to completion by a single thread or its parts may be scheduled to different threads. Similarly two concurrent tasks may be executed by the same thread. Our approach is transparent from threads, hence regardless which thread(s) execute a task, a unique ID preserves its dependencies with other tasks and avoids false determinacy race alarms. (c) Each tasksegment has the same set of HB meta-data, as opposed to each memory operation, thus unique ID of the tasksegment is used to retrieve HB metadata for each of its memory operations.

3. **Runtime determinacy race detection:** As shown in Fig. 4, we link the library we implemented at step ③ to produce the instrumented executable binary, which executes at step ④. At step ⑤ relevant program events are captured at runtime and detection is performed and a bug report is generated in step ⑥. The tool reports a pair of line numbers where a common shared memory location was accessed by concurrent tasks. This pair is helpful for

the developer to revisit the source code and eliminate determinacy races. This module also implements the technique proposed in [18] to check if operations with determinacy races are commutative as they execute in critical sections of the same lock given that their execution order does not affect final output of the program to reduce false positives.

5   Results

We evaluate our tool on nine micro-benchmarks on three categories: (a) the number and nature of determinacy races reported as well as no determinacy races reported in correct programs, (b) detection comparison with Archer [3], (c) the runtime overhead with respect to input size. We first provide a brief summary of the applications before discussing evaluation results. The first five applications are custom implementations with races, accessible through TaskSanitizer[1].

- ***RacyBackgroundExample:*** implements the example in Fig. 1. There are two tasks each containing a critical section associated with the same lock. One task sets 1 to shared variable i while the other sets 2 without enforced dependency thus exhibiting a determinacy race as these operations do not commute even though they are in critical sections.
- ***RacyBanking:*** We mimic the motivating banking example in [18]. An initial task sets the account balance to 1000. Then three concurrent tasks access the account balance without specified dependency among them, thus causing three determinacy races and the updates on the account do not commute.
- ***RacyFibonacci:*** This program computes Fibonacci of a given number n using *memoization* technique of caching intermediate results in a shared integer array. A task for n creates two concurrent child tasks to compute Fibonacci of n-1 and n-2, respectively, and each stores its result in the *memoization* array. The task then sums the results from the array after a synchronization barrier with the child tasks. There are determinacy races in this example on five program locations between two concurrent sibling tasks as they access the memoization array without inferred dependency between them.
- ***RacyMapReduce:*** constructs histogram of words from a text file. It splits the input text into four chunks. Then each chunk is processed by *map* tasks. The partial results are merged into a final histogram by *reduce* tasks which are concurrent to each other, exhibiting four determinacy races while inserting new words into the final histogram and updating word counts.
- ***RacyPointerChasing:*** traverses a singly-linked list and creates an explicit task for each node to insert a number to the node for the purpose of forming an arithmetic sequence in the linked-list. In this program, two random nodes in the list mistakenly contain common memory address for storing their terms which breaks the arithmetic sequence. As a result, their corresponding tasks concurrently write values to the memory, causing a determinacy race.

---

[1] https://github.com/hassansalehe/TaskSanitizer/tree/master/src/benchmarks.

- *sectionslock1-orig-no:* As part of the DataRaceBench micro-benchmark suite [17], this program creates two parallel sections, which have critical sections in which one section increases a shared variable by 1 and other section increases it by 2. There are no determinacy races because these operations in critical sections commute and our tool does not report a bug.
- *taskdep1-orig-no:* As part of DataRaceBench, the program creates two explicit tasks with the first task setting 1 to a shared variable and the succeeding sibling task setting 2. These tasks have specified dependency between them and thus no determinacy races.
- *taskdep3-orig-no:* As part of DataRaceBench, this program creates two explicit tasks. The first task has dependency with each of the other sibling tasks which are concurrent to each other. Since the concurrent tasks only read from a shared variable, there is no determinacy race.
- *taskdependmissing-orig-yes:* As part of DataRaceBench, this program creates two concurrent explicit tasks which have no dependency in between. They modify a shared variable and thus constitute a determinacy race.

Table 1. Comparing detection results of TaskSanitizer against Archer

Application	Input size	Number of tasks	Known races	TaskSanitizer Races found	Archer Races found
RacyBackgroundExample	-	6	1	1	0
RacyBanking	-	11	3	3	2
RacyFibonacci	5	137	8	8	11
RacyMapReduce	-	17	4	4	1
RacyPointerChasing	14	34	1	1	0
sectionslock1-orig-no	-	2	0	0	0
taskdep1-orig-no	-	6	0	0	0
taskdep3-orig-no	-	8	0	0	0
taskdependmissing-orig-yes	-	6	1	1	0 or 1

5.1 Precision Evaluation of TaskSanitizer

Table 1 lists the reported bugs by our tool, TaskSanitizer and number of determinacy races known in advance for micro-benchmarks. In **RacyBackgroundExample** two concurrent tasks execute two critical sections which each sets different value to a shared memory location. This exhibits a determinacy race since the tasks do not have HB relation and their memory operations do not *commute* in critical sections. Our tool does not check for commutativity in remaining buggy programs as their operations happen outside critical sections. Even though tasks with critical sections in **sectionslock1-orig-no** do have dependency, there is no determinacy race reported because increment operation in these sections *commute*. Finally, our tool does not report false positives in the remaining programs.

5.2 Comparing Detection with Archer

We compare our determinacy race detection results with data race detection
results of Archer [3], which is an efficient tool based on ThreadSanitizer for
detecting data races. Data race detection in Archer differs from determinacy race
detection in our approach on two essences: (i) It relies on thread-level concurrency and thus it fails to detect races in concurrent tasks scheduled to execute by
the same thread. (ii) It aims at detecting violations of locking critical sections
which have shared memory accesses whereas our method focuses on different
ordering of events leading to determinacy races.

As shown on Table 1, Archer failed to detect races in *RacyBackgroundExample* and *RacyPointerChasing* despite multiple runs. Archer fails to detect
the race in *RacyBackgroundExample* because memory operations are protected by a common lock. However, our tool detects determinacy races because
the locks do not enforce deterministic ordering and thus the program can produce
different results at different runs.

Archer does not detect a race in *taskdependmissing-orig-yes* and other
buggy programs when concurrent tasks in the program are scheduled to execute with one thread. Therefore, Archer detects the race only if two tasks are
executed by different threads whereas our tool detects the determinacy race in
the program at all runs. This is because Archer depends on program threads
to infer concurrency whereas our approach abstracts away threads and detects
determinacy races at task level. Moreover, the number of races it reported on
the remaining buggy programs varied from zero to the expected depending on
scheduling of concurrent tasks to different threads. However it detected two races
in *RacyBanking* and did not produce false alarms in correct programs.

5.3 Overhead Evaluation

Even though the focus of this work is the method for detecting determinacy
races, we also measured the slowdown of determinacy race detection in the
micro-benchmark applications which accept varying input sizes, namely *Racy-
Fibonacci* and *RacyPointerChasing* as shown in Fig. 5. By increasing input

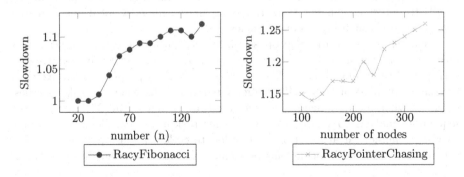

Fig. 5. Slowdown of determinacy race detection in programs as input size increases

size, we calculated execution times of the application without determinacy race detection as well as with detection. We calculated slowdown by dividing detection time by execution time without detection. The determinacy race detection slowdown from this experimental setting ranges from 1.0 to 1.26X, but we plan to evaluate with larger applications in our future work.

6 Related Work

Archer is an efficient tool for detecting data races in OpenMP programs between concurrent threads [3]. Through LLVM, it uses static analysis polyhedral techniques to ignore sequential code and instrument concurrent portion of the program. Then it uses runtime analysis to detect races in those parts by employing *ThreadSanitizer* [24] race detector in the background. In contrast, we detect determinacy races where ordering between concurrent components is missing. Archer may fail to detect such cases and it also misses concurrent tasks executed by the same thread. By building the happen-before relations on tasks rather than threads, we can catch these situations.

Determinacy race detection in [25] targets task-based programming models with *async, finish* and *future* constructs. There are works on detecting determinacy races in a very strict two-dimensional pipeline parallel program structures which restrict task dependency to at most two [6,27]. Other works target determinacy races [8,16,21,22] for structured parallelism programming models like X10 and Habanero. Most work targets data race detection [9,12,19,23,24] which manifest as a result of improper synchronization in programs.

DFinspec [18] proposes a technique for detecting output nondeterminism for Atomic Dataflow (ADF) [10] programs due to missing or improper ordering among tasks. It assumes that all concurrent portions of the program execute in atomic tasks. Unlike ADF, in OpenMP tasks are not atomic, thus the proposed solution in DFinspec would not work on OpenMP programs. The Starsscheck tool [5] identifies inconsistencies in *pragma* annotations for programs written in Starss programs [13]. The tool verifies that the programmer correctly annotates the application by checking the input and output dependencies of tasks. By assuming that a task accesses shared memory through only input dependencies, it fails to detect concurrent tasks accessing shared memory locations that are not specified through input dependencies.

A closely related work [8] proposes an algorithm for detecting *determinacy* races for Cilk programs [4] in which a spawned thread may execute concurrently with parent or sibling threads. These threads may need proper synchronization for shared memory accesses. We target OpenMP tasks where a task becomes runnable when all its dependencies are satisfied. Vechev et. al [26] uses a static sequential analysis to verify determinism for task-based parallel programs by leveraging numerical abstractions. They locate code sections that can execute concurrently and check for dependent memory accesses between those sections.

7 Conclusion

We propose a method to detect determinacy races in OpenMP tasks where unintended missing dependency between tasks can result in nondeterministic execution. We define happens-before relation among tasks based on their dependencies for determining an execution order when detecting determinacy races and implement our algorithm as a tool on top of ThreadSanitizer. We evaluated our solution with a set of small applications in terms of bug detection and overhead. The tool successfully finds bugs in benchmarks and its efficiency is reasonable.

Acknowledgments. This work has been funded under the Affordable Safe & Secure Mobility Evolution (ASSUME) project for smart mobility.

Data Availability Statement and Acknowledgments: The datasets and code generated during and/or analysed during the current study are available in the Figshare repository: https://doi.org/10.6084/m9.figshare.6392252

References

1. Openmp 3.0 api. www.openmp.org/wp-content/uploads/spec30.pdf
2. Openmp 4.0. http://www.openmp.org/wp-content/uploads/OpenMP4.0.0.pdf
3. Atzeni, S., et al.: ARCHER: effectively spotting data races in large OpenMP applications. In: 2016 IEEE International Parallel and Distributed Processing Symposium (IPDPS), pp. 53–62, May 2016
4. Blumofe, R.D., Joerg, C.F., Kuszmaul, B.C., Leiserson, C.E., Randall, K.H., Zhou, Y.: Cilk: an efficient multithreaded runtime system. SIGPLAN Not. **30**(8), 207–216 (1995)
5. Carpenter, P.M., Ramirez, A., Ayguade, E.: Starsscheck: a tool to find errors in task-based parallel programs. In: D'Ambra, P., Guarracino, M., Talia, D. (eds.) Euro-Par 2010. LNCS, vol. 6271, pp. 2–13. Springer, Heidelberg (2010). https://doi.org/10.1007/978-3-642-15277-1_2
6. Dimitrov, D., Vechev, M., Sarkar, V.: Race detection in two dimensions. In: Proceedings of the 27th ACM Symposium on Parallelism in Algorithms and Architectures, SPAA 2015, pp. 101–110. ACM, New York (2015)
7. Eichenberger, A.E., et al.: OMPT: an OpenMP tools application programming interface for performance analysis. In: Rendell, A.P., Chapman, B.M., Müller, M.S. (eds.) IWOMP 2013. LNCS, vol. 8122, pp. 171–185. Springer, Heidelberg (2013). https://doi.org/10.1007/978-3-642-40698-0_13
8. Feng, M., Leiserson, C.E.: Efficient detection of determinacy races in cilk programs. Theory Comput. Syst. **32**(3), 301–326 (1999)
9. Flanagan, C., Freund, S.N.: FastTrack: efficient and precise dynamic race detection. In: Proceedings of the 30th ACM SIGPLAN Conference on Programming Language Design and Implementation, PLDI 2009, pp. 121–133. ACM, New York (2009)
10. Gajinov, V., Stipic, S., Unsal, O., Harris, T., Ayguade, E., Cristal, A.: Integrating dataflow abstractions into the shared memory model. In: 2012 IEEE 24th International Symposium on Computer Architecture and High Performance Computing (SBAC-PAD), pp. 243–251, October 2012

44   H. S. Matar and D. Unat

11. Hong, S., Kim, M.: A survey of race bug detection techniques for multithreaded programmes. Softw. Test. Verif. Reliab. **25**(3), 191–217 (2015)
12. Kuru, I., Matar, H.S., Cristal, A., Kestor, G., Unsal, O.: PaRV: parallelizing runtime detection and prevention of concurrency errors. In: Qadeer, S., Tasiran, S. (eds.) RV 2012. LNCS, vol. 7687, pp. 42–47. Springer, Heidelberg (2013). https://doi.org/10.1007/978-3-642-35632-2_6
13. Labarta, J.: StarSs: a programming model for the multicore era. In: PRACE Workshop "New Languages & Future Technology Prototypes" at the Leibniz Supercomputing Centre in Garching (Germany) (2010)
14. Lamport, L.: Time, clocks, and the ordering of events in a distributed system. Commun. ACM **21**(7), 558–565 (1978)
15. Lattner, C., Adve, V.: LLVM: a compilation framework for lifelong program analysis & transformation. In: Proceedings of the 2004 International Symposium on Code Generation and Optimization (CGO 2004), Palo Alto, California, March 2004
16. Lee, I.T.A., Schardl, T.B.: Efficiently detecting races in cilk programs that use reducer hyperobjects. In: Proceedings of the 27th ACM Symposium on Parallelism in Algorithms and Architectures, SPAA 2015, pp. 111–122. ACM, New York (2015)
17. Liao, C., Lin, P.H., Asplund, J., Schordan, M., Karlin, I.: DataRaceBench: a benchmark suite for systematic evaluation of data race detection tools. In: Proceedings of the International Conference for HPC, Networking, Storage and Analysis, SC 2017, pp. 11:1–11:14. ACM, New York (2017)
18. Matar, H.S., Mutlu, E., Tasiran, S., Unat, D.: Output nondeterminism detection for programming models combining dataflow with shared memory. Parallel Comput. **71**, 42–57 (2018)
19. Matar, H.S., Tasiran, S., Unat, D.: EmbedSanitizer: runtime race detection tool for 32-bit embedded ARM. In: Lahiri, S., Reger, G. (eds.) RV 2017. LNCS, vol. 10548, pp. 380–389. Springer, Cham (2017). https://doi.org/10.1007/978-3-319-67531-2_24
20. Matar, H.S., Unat, D.: Source code and user guide for euro-par 2018 paper: runtime determinacy race detection for OpenMP tasks. Figshare (2018). https://doi.org/10.6084/m9.figshare.6392252
21. Raman, R., Zhao, J., Sarkar, V., Vechev, M., Yahav, E.: Efficient data race detection for async-finish parallelism. In: Barringer, H., et al. (eds.) RV 2010. LNCS, vol. 6418, pp. 368–383. Springer, Heidelberg (2010). https://doi.org/10.1007/978-3-642-16612-9_28
22. Raman, R., Zhao, J., Sarkar, V., Vechev, M., Yahav, E.: Scalable and precise dynamic datarace detection for structured parallelism. In: Proceedings of the 33rd ACM SIGPLAN Conference on Programming Language Design and Implementation, PLDI 2012, pp. 531–542. ACM, New York (2012)
23. Savage, S., Burrows, M., Nelson, G., Sobalvarro, P., Anderson, T.: Eraser: a dynamic data race detector for multi-threaded programs. In: Proceedings of the 16th ACM Symposium on Operating Systems Principles, SOSP 1997, pp. 27–37. ACM, New York (1997)
24. Serebryany, K., Iskhodzhanov, T.: ThreadSanitizer: data race detection in practice. In: Proceedings of the Workshop on Binary Instrumentation and Applications, WBIA 2009, pp. 62–71. ACM, New York (2009)
25. Surendran, R., Sarkar, V.: Dynamic determinacy race detection for task parallelism with futures. In: Falcone, Y., Sánchez, C. (eds.) RV 2016. LNCS, vol. 10012, pp. 368–385. Springer, Cham (2016). https://doi.org/10.1007/978-3-319-46982-9_23

26. Vechev, M., Yahav, E., Raman, R., Sarkar, V.: Automatic verification of determinism for structured parallel programs. In: Cousot, R., Martel, M. (eds.) SAS 2010. LNCS, vol. 6337, pp. 455–471. Springer, Heidelberg (2010). https://doi.org/10.1007/978-3-642-15769-1_28
27. Xu, Y., Lee, I.T.A., Agrawal, K.: Efficient parallel determinacy race detection for two-dimensional dags. In: Proceedings of the 23rd ACM SIGPLAN Symposium on Principles and Practice of Parallel Programming, PPoPP 2018, pp. 368–380. ACM, New York (2018)

Estimating the Impact of External Interference on Application Performance

Aamer Shah[1], Matthias Müller[1], and Felix Wolf[2(✉)]

[1] IT Center, RWTH Aachen University, Aachen, Germany
{shah,mueller}@itc.rwth-aachen.de
[2] Laboratory for Parallel Programming, TU Darmstadt, Darmstadt, Germany
wolf@cs.tu-darmstadt.de

Abstract. The wall-clock execution time of applications on HPC clusters is commonly subject to run-to-run variation, often caused by external interference from concurrently running jobs. Because of the irregularity of this interference from the perspective of the affected job, performance analysts do not consider it an intrinsic part of application execution, which is why they wish to factor it out when measuring execution time. However, if chances are high enough that at least one interference event strikes while the job is running, merely repeating runs several times and picking the fastest run does not guarantee a measurement free of external influence. In this paper, we present a novel approach to estimate the impact of sporadic and high-impact interference on bulk-synchronous MPI applications. An evaluation with several realistic benchmarks shows that the impact of interference can be estimated already based on a single run.

1 Introduction

On many HPC systems, the execution time of applications varies considerably between runs, which makes performance measurements hard to reproduce and challenges their validity. Possible sources of variation include operating system jitter, different process-to-node mappings, or contention on shared resources. While modern operating systems reduced their noise footprint [16], contention on heavily loaded centralized file systems and communication interconnects, such as torus and dragonfly networks, are still contributing to performance variation [3,21]. Because such external interference occurs randomly, benchmarking has become complicated.

Usually, performance analysts prefer measurements that are as close as possible to an application's *intrinsic* behavior, that is, without external influence beyond their control. To achieve this on a system with strong performance interference among jobs, one could take multiple measurements and pick the run with the shortest execution time or the average or median if a certain degree of interference is considered natural. No matter how, this strategy is both expensive and unreliable because neither may the minimum be free of interference nor the

© Springer International Publishing AG, part of Springer Nature 2018
M. Aldinucci et al. (Eds.): Euro-Par 2018, LNCS 11014, pp. 46–58, 2018.
https://doi.org/10.1007/978-3-319-96983-1_4

average or median representative. After all, the system load also changes along macroscopic time scales (e.g., daytime or season).

To help performance analysts decide how much they can "trust" their benchmarking results and whether they need to repeat measurements, we present a novel approach to estimate the impact of external interference on the execution time of a common class of MPI applications. As a distinctive feature, our method can deliver such an estimate with negligible overhead based on a single run. Moreover, it is agnostic to the source of interference. Instead, it exploits the properties of bulk-synchronous MPI applications that perform frequent global all-to-all operations. Such applications not only make up a significant portion of HPC workload (almost two-thirds of unique benchmarks in the SPEC MPI suite fall in this category), they are also most sensitive to external interference [1, 7, 10].

The remainder of the paper is structured as follows. While Sect. 2 provides the details of our approach, Sect. 3 demonstrates the accuracy of our estimates in a series of experiments. After presenting related work in Sect. 4, we review our results in Sect. 5.

2 Approach

Most HPC applications are iterative in nature. After a brief initialization, they go through different phases that are repeated over and over. Similar phases have similar execution times unless a phase instance is struck by external interference. The stronger the impact, the greater the elongation of the execution time.

Figure 1a shows a trace snippet of a typical HPC application. The application performs several iterations, whose execution times are, however, not uniform. The execution-time histogram in Fig. 1 illustrates two sources of variation – one intrinsic and one extrinsic. Intrinsic variation arises from programmatic differences because, for example, some iterations may calculate some extra physics every once in a while or store checkpoints. The example shows two classes of iterations, A and B, distinguished by their programmatic characteristics and visible as two peaks in Fig. 1b. The variation that remains after separating these two classes, as shown in Fig. 1c and 1d, is extrinsic and the result of noise such as interference from other jobs that happen to run at the same time.

The key idea of our approach is to divide the execution of a program into segments and classify them according to their intrinsic characteristics. In a noise-free environment, segments within each class are then expected to consume the same amount of time. Conversely, variations that occur within each class are likely caused by noise. Because execution time is subject to such noise, we have found hardware and software counters that reflect computation, communication, and file I/O features to be suitable metrics for our programmatic classification of execution segments.

To identify segments, we take advantage of the bulk-synchronous nature of many HPC applications, specifically we exploit periodic (blocking) all-to-all communication. Although this practically restricts our method to such applications, we claim that we can still cover major portions of today's HPC workloads. After

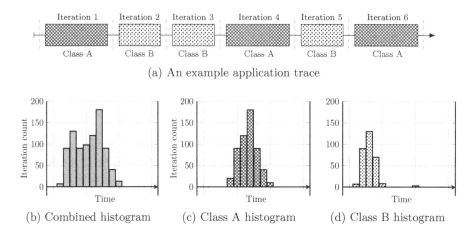

(a) An example application trace

(b) Combined histogram   (c) Class A histogram   (d) Class B histogram

Fig. 1. Application iterations and their histograms.

all, this is not an uncommon feature. For example, almost two-thirds of unique benchmarks in the SPEC MPI suite fall into this category. At the same time, applications with frequent all-to-all communication suffer more than others from external interference because every delay of a process will likely induce waiting time in all others.

We use global all-to-all communication operations as a boundary between execution segments. These might not exactly match programmatically specified iterations, but are expected to divide the execution into repeatedly executed pieces. For example, an all-to-all operation will likely appear at least once in every iteration of the core loop. Furthermore, such all-to-all operations constitute global synchronization points among processes. Although the MPI standard does not explicitly require it, the nature of all-to-all operations implies it. This makes the execution segments between them independent with respect to the propagation of wait states that occur in response to external interference. A wait state whose root cause lies within a segment will not propagate across a global synchronization point [4]. For applications using non-blocking collectives, the wait operation of the collective call could be used as a boundary indicator, while for non-bulk-synchronous applications recurring MPI calls may serve this purpose. However, in both cases, adjacent execution segments may not be fully independent, with wait states and interference-induced delays potentially propagating across segment boundaries. We therefore concentrate on blocking collectives in this study and consider the remaining cases as future work.

Profiling Methodology. To classify segments, we count computation, communication, and file I/O operations or volumes per segment and process using LWM^2 [18], a low-overhead profiler, which leverages the PMPI interface to find segment boundaries and collect metrics related to MPI. The specific metrics we capture are discussed further below. At the end of each all-to-all collective call, the profiler stores information pertaining to the completed segment in memory.

To reduce storage requirements, the values for each metric are quantized into 256 unique bins. When the number of unique values exceeds the number of bins, the two bins with the least distance between them are merged. Instead of actual values, a segment profile stores the indices of the corresponding bins. Whenever bins are merged, the indices in the segment profiles are updated accordingly. After the program has ended, we merge per-process bins into 512 unique program-wide bins. To keep computation diversity among segments manageable, a segment is always represented by the median of the computation feature metric across processes. For communication and file I/O, such aggregation is only performed if the diversity among segments exceeds a threshold.

Grouping Segments Based on Computation Features. To classify segments, we first compare them in terms of the amount of computation they are supposed to complete. To measure the amount of work, we count the number of floating-point instructions using hardware counters. When the floating-point counter is not available, as on some generations of modern processors, we use the total number of completed instructions as a proxy. To shield them from noise, we only count them outside communication or I/O operations. While the captured values are still perturbed by OS jitter, we have found floating-point operations to be most stable. The total instruction count shows still less than 1% variability.

We establish similarity among segments by clustering them based on the above instruction counts as features. As the duration of segments in an application can vary widely, the possible range of feature values can be quite large. Furthermore, OS jitter and inaccuracies introduced when reading and storing hardware counters [6] cause variation among hardware-counter values from similar segments. Therefore, the most appropriate clustering algorithm for our task needs to handle a large range of values, and at the same time be tolerant to variations inside a cluster.

Common clustering algorithms such as k-means require the number of clusters to be known *a priori*. If such information is not available, such algorithms are executed for a range of cluster counts and an internal cluster criterion, such as the Calinski and Harabasz (CH) criterion, is applied to identify the most appropriate number of clusters. Even for a particular number of clusters, these clustering algorithms require several iterations to find the optimum centroids. These factors result in algorithms that, overall, are complex to implement and can take a significant amount of time for large numbers of data points.

Clustering with Relative Distance. Density-based algorithms such as DBScan seem to present an alternative. They can identify the appropriate number of clusters in a single pass. Such algorithms use a distance threshold to split the data points into clusters. However, relying on a fixed distance for a large range of values results in either merging distinct clusters with lower values if the threshold is too large, or splitting a single cluster with a modest range of higher values into multiple clusters if the threshold is too small.

To overcome these difficulties, we designed a simple clustering algorithm that can identify clusters in one-dimensional data even with a large value range in a single pass. The algorithm requires the data type to have a total order and a threshold for the maximum *relative* distance between any two data points in a cluster. We define the relative distance between two points as their distance divided by the smaller of the distances of the two points from the origin. As the algorithm relies on relative distance, it can identify clusters with a modest degree of internal variance both at the lower and higher end of the value range. Our algorithm first sorts all the values in ascending order and then assigns the smallest element to the first cluster. After that, it iterates through the remaining sequence and, at each step, picks the value at position i from the sorted list that was assigned to a cluster in the previous step and determines the relative distance to the next value at $i + 1$. If the relative distance is less than the threshold, the value at $i + 1$ is placed in the same cluster as the value at i. Otherwise, a new cluster is created for the value at $i + 1$.

Using SPEC MPI benchmarks, we compared our new algorithm with k-means and an expectation-maximization (EM) algorithm that assumes the data to exhibit a mixed Gaussian distribution. Specifically, we analyzed the mean normalized standard deviation of the created clusters and the percentage of segments that ended up in clusters of less than five elements, which is the minimum size below which clusters are not considered for interference estimation. K-means identified tightly fitting clusters but left a larger portion of segments unclustered (up to 8%). EM, on the other hand, clustered almost all segments, but created clusters of high internal variance. We tried our new algorithm with several relative-distance thresholds, including 0.2, 0.1, and 0.05. With a relative-distance threshold of 0.1, the threshold we use in the remainder of this study, our customized algorithm identified clusters with slightly higher variance than k-means, but left only half the number of segments unclustered.

Grouping Segments Based on Communication and File I/O Features. As communication and I/O features of a segment we consider the number and accumulated volume of communication and I/O operations, including the number of point-to-point send/receive calls broken down by their blocking semantics, the number of collective calls broken down by their number of senders vs. recipients, and the number of bytes sent or received through them. Similarly, as file-I/O features we capture the number of open/close operations, the number of read/write operations and the accumulated number of bytes read or written. Since there is no clear relationship between these metrics and the execution time of a segment, we consider the corresponding values as nominal data. For example, a segment may run longer than another segment, although its number of sends is smaller. At the same time, these metrics are fairly stable and usually not subject to any jitter. Thus, we consider all segments that share the same unique combination of communication and file I/O metrics a separate group.

Estimating Interference. We estimate the impact of interference based on the segment profile of a single run. First, we cluster the segments according to their computation features, as described earlier. After that we split each cluster into groups according to the communication and file-I/O features of its elements. The segments in each of the resulting groups are assumed to exhibit similar behavioral characteristics and consume about the same intrinsic execution time.

Any segment in a group that has a significantly higher execution time is considered to be affected by interference. More precisely, we classify a segment as interfered if its execution time is four MAD greater than the median of the group, with MAD (Median Absolute Deviation) being $MAD = \text{median}(|X_i - \text{median}(X)|)$. Median and MAD are known for their robustness to variability. The threshold of four MAD greater than median gives a confidence interval of more than 99.5%. The impact of interference on a segment is estimated as the portion of execution time of the segment in excess of the threshold. Adding the interference impact computed for all segments yields the interference impact for the entire program and is provided as a percentage of the (interfered) execution time.

Separating Instantaneous Interference from Continuous Interference. Execution time variation can arise from either high-frequency but usually low-impact interference such as certain types of OS jitter or from low-frequency but often high-impact interference such as sudden I/O contention. We call the former kind continuous interference, and the latter kind instantaneous interference. Continuous interference affects almost all segments of a profile, and as a result also affects the median in a group. In contrast, instantaneous interference only affects selected segments, and the median remains largely unaffected. While both kinds of interference prolong execution time, instantaneous interference is more likely to create undesirable artifacts in performance measurements a performance analyst may wish to remove. In contrast, continuous interference is often seen as an unavoidable evil one has to live with on a given system. Our approach only reports instantaneous interference. The median displacement caused by continuous interference ensures that it leaves no imprint on our estimates.

Tool Workflow. LWM^2 profiles the target application during execution, capturing the required metrics separately for each segment. At the end of the execution, LWM^2 writes a segmented profile to disk. Later, the profile is subjected to automatic interference estimation in Matlab. First, we classify the segments into different groups based on their features. Later, we estimate the impact of interference first for each segment group, and then aggregate the results for the whole application.

3   Evaluation

To evaluate our approach, we use the following benchmarks: (i) those seven codes from the SPEC MPI 2007 suite V2.0 that are bulk-synchronous according to our definition and that have a large data set available; (ii) Sweep3D, a time-independent 3D neutron transport simulation; and (iii) HACC, an application that simulates the formation of collision-less fluids and whose regular checkpointing behavior makes it a popular I/O benchmark. We test our method both in a controlled environment with artificially injected interference, and on a production system with real interference.

Experimental Setup. Because of its low OS jitter, we chose JUQUEEN, an IBM BlueGene/Q system, as our controlled environment. Each of its 28,672 compute nodes consist of a 16 core IBM PowerPC®A2 processor and 16 GB of memory. JUQUEEN has a 5D Torus communication interconnect and minimizes network interference by making node boards with 512 cores the smallest allocation unit. Since its GPFS file system is shared, JUQUEEN cannot be considered controlled for I/O intensive workloads though, which, however, among our benchmarks only affects HACC. For our tests under production conditions, we use Hazel Hen, a Cray XC40 system with 7712 compute nodes, each of them featuring two 12-core Intel Haswell E5-2680v3 processors and 128 GB of memory. Applications running on Hazel Hen are known to experience significant run-to-run variation, majorly due to cache misses in the Aries chip under heavy network load from multiple applications [9].

Evaluation Methodology. With the exception of the file system, our controlled environment is without any significant natural interference. This is why the runtime of a job is usually close to its intrinsic execution time, providing us with a ground truth for interference-free execution. To test our method, we inject artificial interference into application runs using a tool called intM (interference Modeler), which we have developed for this purpose. intM sits as an interposition wrapper between an application and the runtime, and mimics network and file I/O interference by introducing delays in function calls. intM supports interference injection in MPI communication and I/O functions, as well as in POSIX I/O. The interference added to the regular execution time follows a Gaussian distribution, with configurable mean and standard deviation. The probability of when an interference event strikes a communication or file I/O operation is also configurable.

Specifically, we inject gradually increasing interference into multiple runs of a benchmark. Figure 2 shows such runs for the SPEC MPI benchmark tera_tf as an example. We compare the *estimated* with the *measured* impact of interference on each run. Measured interference is the execution-time difference between a run and the fastest run in percent of the (interfered) runtime. Estimated interference is calculated individually for each run as percentage of its runtime using our approach without considering any other run. To clean the measured interference from effects of continuous interference and other influences that are largely constant across the entire duration of a run but may vary between runs, such as different process-to-node mappings, we reduce the measured interference by the amount of time the medians are displaced. We observe the median displacement during clustering, and attribute it to continuous interference.

We categorize the impact of interference into the classes low, medium, and high, as shown in Fig. 2. A low-interference run is perturbed to a negligible degree

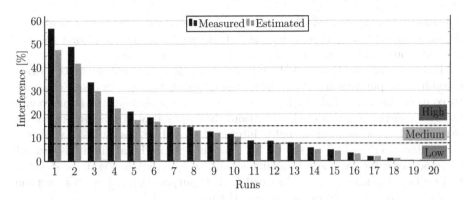

Fig. 2. Multiple runs of tera_tf on JUQUEEN, with measured and estimated interference classified as low, medium, or high. Runs are sorted by execution time in descending order.

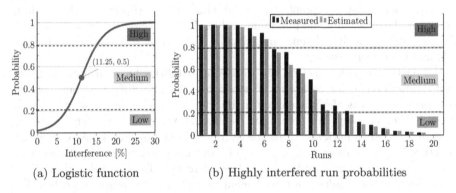

(a) Logistic function   (b) Highly interfered run probabilities

Fig. 3. Logistic function and the highly interfered run probabilities, when the function is applied on the tera_tf runs.

and can be used for performance analysis, whereas a high-interference run is heavily perturbed and should be discarded. The medium category is between these extremes: It might be worthwhile to invest in a new performance measurement, while, at the same time, the run can be used to gauge performance at large. Using the analogy of a traffic light, low means green light for performance analysis, medium means yellow light, and high red light. We have set the threshold for low interference to below 7.5%, for high interference to above 15%, and classify everything in-between as medium. While such categorization is useful to distinguish runs in practice, accuracy evaluation via *hard* classification into these three categories can run into pitfalls. For example, even if the difference between measured and estimated interference of a run is small, the two interference values can still fall into different classes, as it happened for runs 12 and 13 in Fig. 2. An alternative way of aggregating our results is calculating the percentage-point difference between measured and estimated interference. The downside of this approach is that for highly interfered runs, the percentage-point difference is not that critical as long as both agree on the judgment that the run is highly interfered. Runs 1 and 2 in the figure are such cases.

Based on the intuition that the impact of interference is a measure of a run's suitability for performance analysis, we use a logistic function as a *soft* classifier to convert the magnitude of interference into the probability of a run being highly interfered. Using soft classification, the probability that a run previously categorized as low is actually highly interfered should be close to zero, while for runs categorized as high it should be near one. Similarly, at the mid-point of the medium category, the probability should be exactly 0.5. Figure 3a shows a logistic function that we have designed for this purpose, while Fig. 3b shows the corresponding probabilities for the tera_tf runs.

Formally, a logistic function is an "S" shaped function that maps values from $(-\infty, \infty)$ onto $(0, L)$. It is defined as $f(x) = \frac{L}{1 + \exp^{-k(x - x_0)}}$, where k is the steepness, x_0 is the inflection point, and L is the maximum. As explained before, we define the inflection point, x_0, to be 11.25, the mid-point of the medium class. Similarly, setting the maximum value, L, to 1, and steepness, k to 0.35, the probabilities at interference magnitudes of 7.5%, 11.25%, and 15% are 0.21, 0.5, and 0.79, respectively.

Using this logistic function, we derive probabilities for measured and estimated interference for each run of a benchmark. The difference between the two probabilities is the inaccuracy of interference prediction, and its compliment is the accuracy. We determine the accuracy of our approach for all the runs of each benchmark and draw the results as boxplots (Fig. 4). As the logistic function in Fig. 3a shows, an accuracy of less than 0.5 means a significant deviation between measured and estimated interferences. To also give a more direct impression of the results, we complement probability differences with boxplots of the percentage-point difference between measured and estimated interference.

Results. On JUQUEEN, our controlled environment, each benchmark was executed at least 15 times with a gradually increasing amount of artificial interference injected. Figure 2 shows the series for tera_tf as an example. The interference was adjusted in such a way that multiple runs were produced for each interference class. We executed each benchmark on 256 nodes, with 4 processes running on each node. Figure 4a presents on the left how accurately we predict the interference probabilities and on the right the percentage-point difference between measured and estimated interference. Except for GAPgeofem, the median accuracy for all the benchmarks on JUQUEEN is above 0.9. Similarly, for most benchmarks, the minimum accuracy is above 0.8. This shows that in most cases estimated and measured interference leads to the same conclusion. That the accuracy of our predictions for certain runs of GAPgeofem was low can be attributed to its high collective-call rate of around 300 Hz. At such a high frequency, large numbers of small execution segments are created, easily leading to measurement artifacts that disturb our analysis.

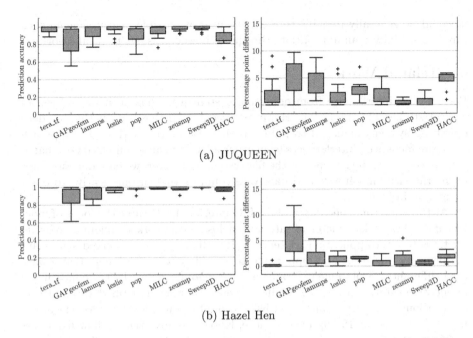

Fig. 4. Prediction accuracy as difference of soft classification probability (left) and percentage-point difference (right) between measured and estimated interference.

Because of its low run-to-run variation, we also used JUQUEEN to evaluate the overhead of our profiler. Using the same set of benchmarks, we executed each benchmark on 128 nodes, with 4 processes running on each node. For each benchmark, we executed two series of experiments, one instrumented and one uninstrumented. To avoid bias caused by daytime differences, we interleaved the execution of the two series, alternating between the instrumented and the uninstrumented version. Each series consisted of nine experiments. Measured by comparing execution time medians of the two series of experiments, the maximum dilation of execution time induced by our profiler was around 4%, but stayed below 1% for the majority of benchmarks.

On Hazel Hen, our production environment, we executed the benchmarks using 16 nodes, with 24 processes on each node. Each benchmark was executed 12 times. Due to the relative small scale of the runs and the sporadic nature of interference, many benchmarks were affected by interference to a smaller degree. Nonetheless, highly interfered runs were encountered and were accurately classified. On the left, Fig. 4b shows the prediction accuracy of benchmark runs, complemented by the percentage-point difference between measured and estimated interference on the right. The figures show that, except for GAPgeofem, the impact of interference was estimated with a high degree of accuracy. GAPgeofem shows again low accuracy, which may again be attributable to its high collective-call frequency. Since the call frequency is measurable, we believe that it would be generally possible to warn the user of possible inaccuracies in such rare cases. Finding an appropriate threshold, however, is left to future work.

4   Related Work

Performance interference from operating system jitter has been the subject of several studies [2,5,11,17,20]. However, recent work has shown that modern operating systems managed to reduce their noise footprint [16]. Our approach therefore focuses on interferences from other jobs that cause contention on shared resources such as the network or the file system. Moreover, we base our estimates of interference on software and hardware counters that are insensitive to operating system jitter.

At the same time, network and file I/O interference became the focus of more recent studies: Jokanovic et al. attributed loss in network throughput on slim fat trees to inter-application contention [12]. Bhatele et al. observed significant performance variation on Hopper due to neighbor jobs [3]. Yang et al. evaluated different job placement strategies on dragonfly networks to reduce inter-application interference [21]. Similarly, several studies identified variability in applications I/O performance and listed simultaneous file access as one of the possible reasons [14,15,19]. Furthermore, Kuo et. al. investigated how file access patterns influence the degree of I/O contention [13]. All these studies show that simultaneous access to shared resources is a major source of interference, which our method now allows users of HPC systems to quantify.

Mondragon et al. applied extreme value theory to create interference models that predict the execution times of bulk-synchronous applications under interference from OS noise, asynchronous checkpointing, and *in situ* analytics [16]. Our approach estimates the amount of low-frequency but high-impact interference such applications suffer in actual runs with the goal of obtaining performance data with low degrees of interference.

To identify similarity among execution phases of an application for the purpose of performance analysis, Gonzalez et. al. used the density-based clustering algorithm DBScan [8]. To estimate interference impact, we designed a 1D-clustering algorithm based on relative distance.

5   Conclusion

We have demonstrated that we can estimate the impact of interference with high accuracy based on a single run. Our tool chain now provides a warning light to performance analysts that tells them when they need to rerun their experiments because the data they have just collected was subject to interference. It can be integrated with other performance-analysis tools using the P^nMPI interface. In the future, we plan to create composite performance profiles free of performance artifacts from multiple interfered measurements. This will allow judging the intrinsic performance of applications in environments where interference is random but due to its frequency unavoidable, making performance measurements (e.g., of different code versions) easier to compare.

Acknowledgment. This work has been supported by the German Research Foundation (DFG) through the Program Performance Engineering for Scientific Software and the ExtraPeak project, by the German Federal Ministry of Education and Research (BMBF) under Grant No. 01IH16008D, and by the US Department of Energy under Grant No. DE-SC0015524. Additional funding was provided through the Hessian LOEWE initiative within the Software-Factory 4.0 project. Finally, we would like to express our gratitude to Jülich Supercomputing Centre and High Performance Computing Center Stuttgart for giving us access to their supercomputers JUQUEEN and Hazel Hen, respectively.

References

1. Agarwal, S., Garg, R., Vishnoi, N.K.: The impact of noise on the scaling of collectives: a theoretical approach. In: Bader, D.A., Parashar, M., Sridhar, V., Prasanna, V.K. (eds.) HiPC 2005. LNCS, vol. 3769, pp. 280–289. Springer, Heidelberg (2005). https://doi.org/10.1007/11602569_31

2. Beckman, P., Iskra, K., Yoshii, K., Coghlan, S., Nataraj, A.: Benchmarking the effects of operating system interference on extreme-scale parallel machines. Cluster Computing 11(1), 3–16 (2008)

3. Bhatele, A., Mohror, K., Langer, S.H., Isaacs, K.E.: There goes the neighborhood: performance degradation due to nearby jobs. In: Proceedings of the ACM/IEEE Conference on Supercomputing (SC 2013). IEEE Computer Society, November 2013

4. Böhme, D., Geimer, M., Wolf, F., Arnold, L.: Identifying the root causes of wait states in large-scale parallel applications. In: Proceedings of the 39th International Conference on Parallel Processing (ICPP), San Diego, CA, USA, pp. 90–100. IEEE Computer Society, September 2010. https://doi.org/10.1109/ICPP.2010.18

5. De, P., Kothari, R., Mann, V.: Identifying sources of operating system jitter through fine-grained kernel instrumentation. In: Proceedings of the IEEE International Conference on Cluster Computing (CLUSTER), pp. 331–340, September 2007

6. Dongarra, J., London, K., Moore, S., Mucci, P., Terpstra, D., You, H., Zhou, M.: Experiences and lessons learned with a portable interface to hardware performance counters. In: Proceedings of the International Parallel and Distributed Processing Symposium (IPDPS), pp. 1–6, April 2003

7. Garg, R., De, P.: Impact of noise on scaling of collectives: an empirical evaluation. In: Robert, Y., Parashar, M., Badrinath, R., Prasanna, V.K. (eds.) HiPC 2006. LNCS, vol. 4297, pp. 460–471. Springer, Heidelberg (2006). https://doi.org/10.1007/11945918_45

8. Gonzalez, J., Gimenez, J., Labarta, J.: Automatic detection of parallel applications computation phases. In: Proceedings of IEEE International Symposium on Parallel Distributed Processing (IPDPS), pp. 1–11, May 2009

9. HLRS: Communication on Cray XC40 Aries network, May 2017. wickie.hlrs.de/platforms/index.php/Communication_on_Cray_XC40_Aries_network

10. Hoefler, T., Schneider, T., Lumsdaine, A.: The impact of network noise at large-scale communication performance. In: Proceedings of the IEEE International Parallel and Distributed Processing Symposium (IPDPS), pp. 1–8, May 2009

11. Hoefler, T., Schneider, T., Lumsdaine, A.: Characterizing the influence of system noise on large-scale applications by simulation. In: Proceedings of the ACM/IEEE Conference on Supercomputing (SC 2010), pp. 1–11. IEEE Computer Society, Washington, DC, USA (2010)

12. Jokanovic, A., Rodriguez, G., Sancho, J.C., Labarta, J.: Impact of inter-application contention in current and future HPC systems. In: Proceedings of the IEEE Symposium on High Performance Interconnects, pp. 15–24, August 2010

13. Kuo, C.S., Shah, A., Nomura, A., Matsouka, S., Wolf, F.: How file access patterns influence interference among cluster applications. In: Proceedings of the IEEE International Conference on Cluster Computing (CLUSTER), pp. 1–8 (2014)

14. Lang, S., Carns, P., Latham, R., Ross, R., Harms, K., Allcock, W.: I/O performance challenges at leadership scale. In: Proceedings of the ACM/IEEE Conference on Supercomputing (SC 2009), pp. 40:1–40:12. ACM, New York (2009)

15. Lofstead, J., Zheng, F., Liu, Q., Klasky, S., Oldfield, R., Kordenbrock, T., Schwan, K., Wolf, M.: Managing variability in the IO performance of petascale storage systems. In: Proceedings of the ACM/IEEE Conference on Supercomputing (SC 2010), pp. 1–12. IEEE Computer Society, Washington, DC, USA (2010)

16. Mondragon, O.H., Bridges, P.G., Levy, S., Ferreira, K.B., Widener, P.: Understanding performance interference in next-generation HPC systems. In: Proceedings of the ACM/IEEE Conference on Supercomputing (SC 2016), pp. 384–395, November 2016

17. Petrini, F., Kerbyson, D., Pakin, S.: The case of the missing supercomputer performance: achieving optimal performance on the 8,192 processors of ASCI Q. In: Proceedings of the ACM/IEEE Conference on Supercomputing (SC 2003) (2003)

18. Shah, A., Wolf, F., Zhumatiy, S., Voevodin, V.: Capturing inter-application interference on clusters. In: Proceedings of IEEE International Conference on Cluster Computing (CLUSTER), pp. 1–5, September 2013

19. Shan, H., Shalf, J.: Using IOR to analyze the I/O performance for HPC platforms. In: Cray User Group Conference (2007)

20. Tsafrir, D., Etsion, Y., Feitelson, D.G., Kirkpatrick, S.: System noise, OS clock ticks, and fine-grained parallel applications. In: Proceedings of the 19th annual International Conference on Supercomputing (ICS 2005), pp. 303–312. ACM, New York (2005)

21. Yang, X., Jenkins, J., Mubarak, M., Ross, R.B., Lan, Z.: Watch out for the bully! job interference study on dragonfly network. In: Proceedings of the ACM/IEEE Conference on Supercomputing (SC 2016), pp. 750–760, November 2016

GT-Race: Graph Traversal Based Data Race Detection for Asynchronous Many-Task Parallelism

Lechen Yu and Vivek Sarkar[✉]

College of Computing, Georgia Institute of Technology, Atlanta, GA, USA
{lechen.yu,vsarkar}@gatech.edu

Abstract. *Asynchronous Many-Task* (AMT) parallelism is growing in popularity because of its promise to support future platforms with new heterogeneity and resiliency requirements. It supports the construction of parallel programs with fine-grained tasks, thereby enabling portability across a wide range of platforms. However, applications written for AMT parallelism still remain vulnerable to data races, and existing data race detection tools are unsuitable for AMT programs because they either incur intractably large overheads or are limited to restricted task structures such as fork-join parallelism.

In this paper, we propose GT-Race, a new graph-traversal based data race detector for AMT parallelism. It leverages the computation graph data structure, which encodes the general happens-before structures in AMT programs. After introducing a baseline algorithm for data race detection, we propose key optimizations to reduce its time and space complexity, including the *epoch adjacency list* to compress the computation graph representation, the *reachability cache* combined with *depth filtering* to reduce the number of unnecessary traversals, and *bounded race detection* to limit the range of data that is monitored. The impact of these optimizations is demonstrated for nine benchmark programs written for the Open Community Runtime (OCR), an open source AMT runtime that supports point-to-point synchronization and disjoint data blocks.

Keywords: Debugging and correctness tools · Data race detection
Asynchronous many-task parallelism

1 Introduction

With the ever-increasing complexity of modern computing architectures (e.g., large numbers of heterogeneous processing units, multi-level hierarchical memories, and high-bandwidth interconnect networks), applications on these machines must leverage the architectural complexity to perform efficiently. Although widely used high-performance parallel runtimes (e.g., PThreads, MPI, and OpenMP) provide comprehensive low-level interfaces to help programmers

© Springer International Publishing AG, part of Springer Nature 2018
M. Aldinucci et al. (Eds.): Euro-Par 2018, LNCS 11014, pp. 59–73, 2018.
https://doi.org/10.1007/978-3-319-96983-1_5

leverage the underlying architecture, the programmers have to tune the application to select the best granularity manually. In addition, manually tuned applications are not performance-portable. In order to mitigate these two problems, Asynchronous Many-Task (AMT) runtimes [1] (e.g., Cilk [2], Habanero-C (HC) [3], Realm [4] and Open Community Runtime (OCR) [5]) become a new trend in HPC area. AMT runtimes hide low-level details of architecture from programmers. When writing a parallel program executing on top of AMT runtimes (we refer to it as AMT program in this paper), programmers only need to split the program logic into *tasks*, a hardware agnostic abstraction of code snippets that can execute independently on any process unit, and specify the dependences among tasks. AMT programs can achieve higher performance with less programming and tuning efforts, compared to MPI implementations [4].

Although AMT parallelism alleviates the difficulty of writing efficient and portable parallel programs, AMT programs are still prone to data races, a notorious error in parallel programs. A data race occurs when a parallel program issues two unordered memory accesses to the same location, such that at least one of the accesses is a write.

There has been a lot of past work on detecting data race automatically at runtime [6–11]. But all of them suffer from at least one of the following four limitations:

- Incurring a space overhead that is proportional to the square of the number of dynamic tasks.
- Leveraging a locking scheme to detect data races, which introduces false positives for parallel programs that use synchronization primitives other than locks.
- Forcing the parallel program to execute in sequential order, which wastes the available hardware parallelism.
- Detecting data races based on restricted parallel structures.

Currently, there does not exist any data race detection algorithm with tractable overhead that can support the general AMT parallelism.

In this paper, we propose GT-Race, a new graph-traversal based data race detector for AMT parallelism. It leverages the computation graph data structure [12], which encodes the general happens-before structures in AMT programs. After introducing a baseline algorithm for data race detection, we propose key optimizations to reduce its time and space complexity, including the *epoch adjacency list* to compress the computation graph representation, the *reachability cache* combined with *depth filtering* to reduce the number of unnecessary traversals, and *bounded race detection* to limit the range of data that is monitored. The impact of these optimizations is demonstrated for nine benchmark programs written for the Open Community Runtime (OCR), an open source AMT runtime that supports point-to-point synchronization and disjoint data blocks.

The rest of this paper is organized as follows: In Sect. 2 we discuss a case study to show how an AMT program can encounter data races. Based on the clarified notion of data race, we illustrate the graph traversal based race detection algorithm and several optimizations. We discuss the implementation of GT-Race in Sect. 3. We evaluate the performance of GT-Race in Sect. 4. Section 5 summarizes some related works about data race detection, and finally in Sect. 6 we briefly conclude with some possible directions for future works.

2   GT-Race

In this section, we introduce GT-Race, an on-the-fly dynamic data race detector for AMT programs. First, we illustrate the architecture of GT-Race, and then we present several optimizations applied by GT-Race, which reduce the space overhead and improve the efficiency of data race detection.

2.1   Computation Graph and Data Races

The constructs in an AMT program can be divided into three classes according to their semantics:

- *spawn constructs*: They submit a new task to the underlying AMT runtime. The new task may execute in parallel with the caller.
- *synchronization constructs*: They specify dependences among tasks that can impact task scheduling in the AMT runtime. A task will be ready for execution after all its specified dependences are satisfied [13].
- *computation constructs*: All other constructs not related to task management belong to this class.

In a computation graph for a dynamic AMT program execution, each node denotes a *step* [12], an arbitrary sequential computation belonging to a task, which ends with a spawn construct or a synchronization construct, and each edge denotes an ordering constraint among the involved tasks. For any two steps in the computation graph, the happens-before relation holds if and only if there exists a directed path between the two steps. When two unrelated steps issue memory accesses to the same shared variable, and at least one step writes to that variable, the two memory accesses create a data race. Figure 1 shows how data races can occur in an AMT program. Figure 1a is a buggy implementation of parallel summation, and Fig. 1b is the corresponding computation graph. To fix the program, we need to link $t3$ to $t4$ by a join edge to guarantee that $t4$ will observe $t3$'s result.

2.2   Overview

Figure 2 shows GT-Race's architecture. It comprises three components: computation graph, shadow memory, and data race checker. The computation graph and shadow memory update dynamically according to the AMT program's runtime behaviors. These two components record happens-before relations and historical memory accesses respectively. Our implementation of shadow memory is similar

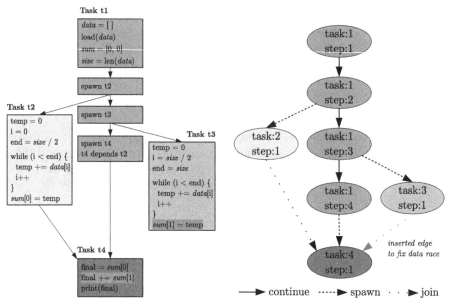

(a) A problematic implementation of parallel summation containing a data race

(b) Corresponding computation graph for the AMT program in Figure 1a

Fig. 1. Case study

to [14]. In order not to miss potential data races, the shadow memory records the latest write and all reads after the write for each shared memory location. The key module of GT-Race is the data race checker, which leverages the data in the computation graph and shadow memory to analyze the order of memory accesses. For each read (write) to a shared variable, the data race checker carries out a graph traversal on the computation graph to verify the read is causally ordered after the concurrent write(concurrent write and all concurrent reads). If the graph traversal fails to find any paths between the concurrent memory accesses, GT-Race will output the associated debug information of the conflicting memory accesses and the computation graph to help programmers figure out the cause of the detected race.

2.3 Epoch Adjacency List: A Compressed Representation for Computation Graph

Since the computation graph is a sparse graph, a straightforward way to store it is by using an adjacency list. Due to the large number of steps a task may contain, it is not memory efficient to allocate a list for each step. Further, explicitly storing all steps and edges may also slow down the graph traversal because of the redundant continue edges.

Since all steps in the same task execute sequentially, we can determine their execution order in constant time by numbering steps belonging to the same task (we refer to these numbers as *epochs*). Inspired by this idea, we propose the *epoch adjacency list*, a compressed storage for computation graphs. In an epoch adjacency list, each task occupies an edge list that records incoming spawn and join edges. For each edge in the edge list, the associated cell marks its source step using the source task ID and epoch.

2.4   Optimization: Reachability Cache

The original graph traversal algorithm is a breadth-first search that loops through the computation graph to find out directed paths between the two memory accesses. It is inefficient due to failing to utilize the locality in the AMT program. For two tasks that both access a shared variable, it is highly possible they have other common variables so that the race checker will check their causal ordering multiple times during the program execution.

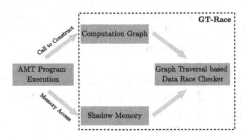

Fig. 2. GT-Race architecture

In order to reuse the results of previous graph traversal, we store them in a reachability cache and look up the cache during graph traversal to avoid redundant explorations. This can be implemented by adding cache lookup and cache update operations to the graph traversal algorithm. If there exists a record in the cache, the graph traversal terminates immediately. Otherwise, the graph traversal proceeds to check the next enqueued step. This optimized graph traversal algorithm is shown in Algorithm 1.

2.5   Optimization: Depth Filtering

Since the time overhead of graph traversal is dominated by the number of nodes and edges it accessed, traversing a large computation graph in a brute-force manner is always time-consuming. Every time after accessing a task, the algorithm will loop through all incoming edges and enqueue connected dependent tasks to avoid omitting any potential path to the expected destination, which leads to the inefficiency of graph traversal. In order to mitigate the time overhead, we introduce a guidance *depth* to help prune irrelevant tasks when looping through incoming edges. For any task t, its *depth* is defined by these two formulas:

- $depth(t_0) = 0$, where t_0 is the entry point of the whole program.
- $depth(t) = Max(depth(t_i)) + 1$, where t_i is a dependent task of t.

Data: Computation Graph CG, Reachability Cache $cache$, Operation $op1, op2$

Result: If $op1$ happens before $op2$, return $true$, otherwise return $false$

```
1  // Bounded Race Detection
2  if !isBoundedMemory(op2.getMemoryAddress()) then
3  │    return true
4  end
5  dst ← CG.getStep(op1), src ← CG.getStep(op2), queue ← ∅
6  queue.push_back(src)
7  while !queue.empty() do
8  │    curr ← queue.next(), queue.findNext()
9  │    if curr.task = dst.task ∧ curr.epoch ≥ dst.epoch then
10 │    │    cache.update(src, dst)
11 │    │    return true
12 │    end
13 │    // Reachability Cache
14 │    if cache.reachable(curr, dst) then
15 │    │    cache.update(src, dst)
16 │    │    return true
17 │    end
18 │    for prev in curr.incomingEdges do
19 │    │    if !queue.contain(prev) then
20 │    │    │    // Depth Filtering
21 │    │    │    if prev.depth >= dst.depth then
22 │    │    │    │    queue.push_back(prev)
23 │    │    │    end
24 │    │    end
25 │    end
26 end
27 return false
```

Algorithm 1. Revised Graph Traversal

The calculation of depth executes along with the computation graph construction and it does not increase the time complexity. According to the definition, we can deduce Theorem 1 (Depth-Reachability Theorem) and apply it to filter tasks.

First we introduce Lemma 1 and prove its correctness. Then we derive Theorem 1 on the basis of Lemma 1. For simplicity, we assume that all tasks in an AMT program are indivisible, so that each node in the corresponding computation graph represents a single task. It is straightforward to extend the theorem to the step level.

Lemma 1. *For two tasks a, b, if these exists a directed edge in the computation graph from a to b (we denote the edge as $a \rightarrow b$), then $depth(a) < depth(b)$.*

Proof. We need to consider two cases:

- Suppose b is the entry point of the program, then b has no preceding tasks, which is contrary to the assumption of Lemma 1.
- Suppose b is not the entry point of the program. Then $depth(b) = Max(depth(t_i)) + 1$, for all predecessors, t_i of b (with edges $t_i \rightarrow b$). So $depth(b) \geq depth(a) + 1$. Hence, the lemma statement is true.

Theorem 1 (Depth-Reachability Theorem). *For two tasks t_i, t_j, if $depth(t_i) \geq depth(t_j)$, then there exists no directed path from t_i to t_j in the computation graph.*

Proof. We prove Theorem 1 by contradiction. Suppose there exists two tasks a, b such that $depth(a) \geq depth(b)$ and there is a path $a \rightarrow t_1 \rightarrow t_2 \ldots t_n \rightarrow b$ in the computation graph. By Lemma 1, we know $depth(a) < depth(t_1)$, $depth(t_1) < depth(t_2) \ldots depth(t_n) < depth(b)$. So $depth(a) < depth(b)$, which contradicts the assumption. Theorem 1 is thus proved by contradiction.

2.6 Optimization: Bounded Race Detection

Apart from the graph traversal, the majority of time and space overhead comes from the shadow memory. Since GT-Race allows the AMT program to execute in parallel, all threads have to access shadow memory with proper synchronizations when they try to record a memory access or get previous memory accesses. These synchronizations are indispensable for the correctness, but they slow down GT-Race's execution.

For better performance and higher accuracy, in GT-Race, we bound the range of data race detection by programmers' knowledge. Since programmers have a full understanding of the AMT program, they are eligible to point out error-prone shared variables. We add an additional option for GT-Race which allows programmers to mark these variables before launching GT-Race. GT-Race will only record memory accesses and carry out data race detection for marked shared variables and ignore the accesses to other variables.

Line 2 in Algorithm 1 shows how bounded race detection works after capturing a memory access. Before starting a graph traversal, the algorithm first checks the desired address of the memory access to see whether it falls in the range of marked variables. If the memory access is to an outside memory location, the algorithm returns true immediately since programmers assume the accessed memory location will not be involved in any data race. The memory address check in line 2 avoids needless graph traversal during the program execution, which is beneficial for efficiency.

3 Implementation

We have developed a prototype implementation of GT-Race (see Fig. 3 for the architecture), based on the algorithm in Sect. 2. GT-Race works as a back-end tool of Intel Pin[1], a dynamic instrumentation framework that monitors the program execution and inserts callbacks for certain operations such as *construct calls* and *memory accesses*. These callbacks record parameters of operations at runtime and pass them to GT-Race. GT-Race will call corresponding modules to analyze the collected data.

The prototype is designed for Open Community Runtime (OCR) [5], an open-source AMT runtime that supports point-to-point synchronizations. An OCR program consists of three basic objects: (a) Event Driven Task (EDT) (b) data block (c) event.

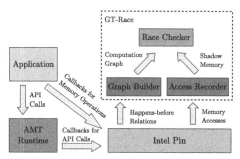

Fig. 3. Prototype architecture

An EDT is the basic execution unit that performs its computation asynchronously. It may have dependences on other EDTs and events. Once all its dependences are satisfied, an EDT can run non-preemptively without being interrupted by other EDTs. A data block is a chunk of consecutive memory managed by the OCR runtime automatically. It is the only way to share data among EDTs and may have various access modes (e.g. read-only, read-write, exclusive write, constant). Although data blocks in read-only and constant modes are supposed to be data race free, it is still possible to introduce data races for these blocks since the OCR runtime will not prevent EDTs from issuing write operations to these data blocks. In order not to miss any data race, we take all data blocks into consideration when detecting data races. However, it is also possible to constrain GT-Race so that it only performs data race detection for a specified subset of data blocks. Event is a synchronization object used to coordinate the activity of EDTs. The semantics is similar to that of a semaphore or latch. An EDT linking to an event, e, through its outgoing edges must wait for the termination of all EDTs linking through e's incoming edges.

As shown in Fig. 3, the inserted callbacks hide the internal details of OCR objects from GT-Race. They instead record operations on OCR objects as general happens-before relations and memory accesses that GT-Race can handle. Callbacks tackling API calls are injected into the OCR runtime. They treat both EDTs and events as tasks (an event can be viewed as a no-op task created solely for the purpose of synchronization) and dependences as directed edges among corresponding tasks. Callbacks for memory operations are weaved into the OCR application. When the application executes memory operations on data blocks, associated callbacks will convert them into equivalent memory read/write operations on shared memory locations. The separation of data collection and data race detection avoids unnecessary modifications to GT-Race when applying it to a new AMT runtime.

---

[1] https://software.intel.com/en-us/articles/pin-a-dynamic-binary-instrumentation-tool.

4 Performance Evaluation

4.1 Environment and Benchmarks

To evaluate the performance of GT-Race, we carried out several experiments using the OCR benchmarks. All experiments were conducted on an Intel workstation with a 24-core Intel Xeon E5-2667 processor and 125 GB of memory, running 64-bit Ubuntu 15.04. We performed experiments on nine OCR benchmarks from the OCR app repository[2]. These benchmarks are either scientific computing programs or mini-apps derived from real-world applications. All nine OCR benchmarks were compiled using GCC 4.9.2 with -O3 optimization level, and executed on top of a customized OCR v1.1 runtime with 24 threads. No data races were detected in these benchmarks used for performance evaluation, but we separately tested our tool for correctness with synthetically introduced data races. Note that the performance of our algorithm is not impacted by the absence or presence of data races.

Though we compare the technical aspects of our approach with related work in Sect. 5, we did not find any implementation of related work that could be used to obtain useful performance comparisons with GT-Race. For example, direct use of the vector clock approach is not practical for AMT parallelism because it would require that each task have its own entry in every vector clock.

4.2 Space Overhead of GT-Race

Table 1 contains dynamic statistics for each benchmark, when executed with a standard input from the OCR repository. Furthermore, the "Memory Usage of CG" columns show the space overhead of the computation graph with different storage strategies. We see that the memory space used by the optimized epoch adjacency list is only 29.20%–37.85% of that used by the unoptimized adjacency list representation. The improvement in memory usage is due to the implicit storage of steps and continue edges in the epoch adjacency list. *UTS* generates the largest computation graph, which spawns more than 400,000 tasks with millions of dependences at runtime. The corresponding computation graph is around 32 MB, which demonstrates the memory efficiency of epoch adjacency list.

4.3 Performance of GT-Race

Summary of Results. Table 2 lists the uninstrumented execution time and overhead of data race detection for each benchmark. All timing measurements are the geometric mean of 10 runs. We use separate columns in Table 2 to analyze the performance and the effectiveness of different optimizations in GT-Race. All listed slowdowns are relative to the uninstrumented running times in the "Base Time" column.

---

[2] https://xstack.exascale-tech.com/git/public/apps.git.

Table 1. Dynamic benchmark statistics. The first four columns contain the benchmark name, along with the numbers of tasks, events, and dependences created when executing the benchmark on a standard input in the OCR repository. The next two columns give the computation graph size in bytes for the unoptimized case, and the optimized case using epoch adjacency lists. The last column shows the ratio of the optimized size to the unoptimized size.

Benchmark	Tasks	Events	Dependences	Memory usage of CG (bytes)		
				Original	Epoch adjacency list	Ratio
Cholesky	222	605	1,101	81,504	30,848	37.85%
FFT	9	9	38	2,560	896	35.00%
Fibonacci	364,179	242,785	1,213,925	82,546,936	29,134,224	35.29%
QuickSort	3,937	7,871	19,678	1,385,360	503,776	36.36%
SmithWaterman	6,401	19,683	51,521	3,511,192	1,241,680	35.36%
UTS	302,014	111,116	1,692,399	104,689,464	33,688,464	32.18%
RSBench	30,033	50	766,540	43,648,232	12,745,968	29.20%
XSBench	36,835	52	898,874	51,222,232	14,972,176	29.23%
LCS	9,817	24,578	74,505	4,997,760	1,742,400	34.86%

Performance of Computation Graph Construction. The "CG" column reports the overhead of GT-Race when only constructing the computation graph. The geometric mean overhead is $1.11\times$ which is not significant. Since we utilize a lock-free data structure to store the computation graph in GT-Race, it reduces overhead due to unnecessary synchronizations and can also handle a large computation graph efficiently.

Performance of Shadow Memory. The "CG + SM" column shows the overhead of GT-Race when tracking shadow memory but performing no graph traversals for data race detection. Although the geometric mean overhead is $4.95\times$, *RSBench* has an overhead greater than $10\times$. Since each instance of shadow memory has to synchronize concurrent accesses from multiple threads to maintain a consistent historical record, GT-Race sacrifices some performance for correctness. But the slowdown is acceptable compared to existing work.

Performance of Data Race Detection. The last two "Slowdown" columns compare the effectiveness of optimizations for graph traversal. With the help of the reachability cache, GT-Race completed every benchmark's test in 4 min and incurred $7.77\times$ slowdown on cache usage. We also list the statistics on the cache usage in Table 3. The cache miss ratio is less than 2% for all benchmarks except *Fibonacci* and *UTS*. Besides, reachability cache also helps reduce the number of accessed steps during graph traversal. For all benchmarks except *RSBench* and *XSBench*, the average (arithmetic mean)[3] number of accessed steps is much smaller compared to the size of computation graph.

---

[3] We use geometric mean for ratios, and arithmetic mean for absolute counts such as accessed steps.

Depth filtering further reduces the slowdown of data race detection. For *UTS* and *RSBench*, it reduces the slowdown from 10.22× to 5.50× and 83.19× to 80.86×. For other benchmarks, the improvement is not substantial. Although *FFT* sees an increased overhead, the slowdown is close to the version without depth filtering. The reason for the performance for depth filtering in FFT is that its computation graph is not large and reachability cache already improves the performance of graph traversal, which causes the overhead of calculating depths to overshadow the performance gain.

Table 2. Benchmark results. Columns 4–6 contain slowdowns relative to the base time.

Benchmark	Base time (sec)	Slowdown			
		CG	CG + SM	Race detection (cache only)	Race detection (cache + depth filtering)
Cholesky	1.66	1.01	1.86	1.88	1.83
FFT	1.58	1.00	2.94	3.08	3.01
Fibonacci	5.54	1.05	1.22	1.31	1.29
QuickSort	1.46	1.02	7.58	7.62	7.73
SmithWaterman	1.59	1.05	8.39	8.89	8.43
UTS	6.29	1.45	3.88	10.22	5.50
RSBench	2.07	1.25	28.10	34.68	34.22
XSBench	2.68	1.20	7.03	83.19	80.86
LCS	1.62	1.03	5.50	6.81	6.71
Geometric mean		1.11	4.95	7.77	7.12

Performance of Bounded Race Detection. We performed another experiment on *RSBench* and *XSBench* (the two benchmarks with the largest overheads) to evaluate the impact of bounded race detection. During the experiment, GT-Race only monitored memory accesses and executed data race detection for a subset of data blocks whose size is smaller than a predefined threshold. For

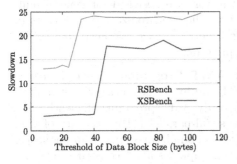

Fig. 4. Bounded race detection result

Table 3. Cache usage

Benchmark	Cache miss	Cache hit	Arith. mean steps
Cholesky	550	224,510	4
FFT	6	262,144	6
Fibonacci	653,329	849,746	4
Quicksort	19,431	283,366	4
SmithWaterman	25,281	1,452,800	5
UTS	549,166	2,629,321	48
RSBench	30,029	14,876,544	1,743
XSBench	73,632	3,128,693	3,204
LCS	20,480	2,329,707	144

each threshold, GT-Race tested 10 runs for each benchmark. We utilize this experiment to roughly evaluate the impact of the number of monitored data blocks on the slowdown of data race detection.

We list the data in Fig. 4. For both *RSBench* and *XSBench*, the slowdown is small when GT-Race carried out data race detection with a low threshold. At a certain point, the slowdown increases significantly then stays constant for a long period. This scenario is because the workload of data race detection is irregular on different data blocks and the slowdown is dominated by a few shared variables that are frequently accessed. These results show that input from the programmer, or perhaps a smart debugger, on which data blocks to monitor can have a significant impact on the overhead of data race detection.

5   Related Work

Since GT-Race is a graph traversal based dynamic data race detector, we relate our work to the state-of-art studies in the following areas.

Dynamic Data Race Detection for Multithreaded Programs: Most dynamic data race detectors are based on vector clock or lockset. FastTrack [6] is the state-of-art vector clock based race detector. It applies a concise representation of vector clock to compress the timestamps of concurrent operations. Although FastTrack reduces the time overhead of vector clock comparison and the space overhead of shadow memory, the size of each vector clock is still proportional to the number of threads. Furthermore, FastTrack can only report data races in the executed thread interleaving.

Eraser [7] is a lockset based lightweight race detector which finds out data races by the locking discipline. It incurs less runtime overhead to the program and can predict data races in other possible interleavings, but it may generate a large amount of false positive. Some work [8] combine lockset with vector clock to achieve both high accuracy and low overhead. They use lockset to replace the expensive vector clock when the program issues lock operations, and report data races when both vector clock and lockset do not prove the correctness of a memory access. These hybrid race detectors can achieve a good trade-off between accuracy and performance.

Because the above-mentioned race detectors are designed for general multithreaded programs, They either cannot handle synchronization constructs in AMT parallelism, or incur unacceptable time and space overhead due to the neglect of structural properties in AMT programs.

Dynamic Data Race Detection for AMT Programs: Some data race detectors are only targeting specific AMT runtimes and utilize the structural properties of the computation graph to verify AMT programs efficiently. SP-bags [9] and ALL-SETS [15] utilize the serial-parallel (SP) structure of Cilk programs to detect data races in amortized bound time and constant space. ESP-bags [16] is an extension to SP-bags that supports *finish* construct in async-finish AMT runtimes. The determinacy race detector in [10] leverages dynamic task reachability graph to handle async-finish AMT runtimes with futures. However, all these approaches require the program to execute in depth-first order, which wastes the available hardware parallelism in the underlying platform. PTRacer [11] is a parallel on-the-fly data race detector for async-finish AMT runtimes that support locks. It combines SPD3 and ALL-SETS to detect data races with constant memory space. PTRacer also adds a symbolic diagnosis phase after the dynamic analysis to predict hidden races at schedule sensitive branches of the not-taken paths. But PTRacer does not provide any support to point-to-point synchronization constructs.

Reachability Query for DAGs: GT-Race can be abstracted as conducting reachability queries on the computation graph to verify the causal ordering between concurrent memory accesses. Although reachability query has been comprehensively studied over decades, existing work is not suitable for GT-Race. According to the survey presented by [17], state-of-art reachability query algorithms [18–20] compute a label for every node when preprocessing the graph, and return the reachability between any two nodes by comparing assigned labels. These algorithms can answer reachability queries efficiently, but they require an expensive labeling process in advance, which is too time-consuming for large graphs. In addition, the space overhead of each label is proportional, or even square to the number of nodes, which will deplete available memory space quickly. The unacceptable time and space overhead of the labeling process restrict the usage of reachability query algorithms in GT-Race.

6   Conclusion and Future Work

In this paper, we propose GT-Race, a new graph-traversal based data race detector for AMT parallelism. It leverages the computation graph data structure, which encodes the general happens-before structures in AMT programs. GT-Race executes a graph-traversal based data race detection algorithm for each pair of concurrent memory accesses. After one execution, GT-Race can report data races in all possible thread interleavings for the same input. In order to reduce the time and space complexity for race detection, we also apply a few optimizations in GT-Race, such as *epoch adjacency list* to compress the representation of computation graph, *reachability cache* and *depth filtering* to avoid unnecessary explorations, and *bounded race detection* to reduce the range of monitored memory space. Based on our race detection techniques, we have implemented a prototype of GT-Race for OCR. The evaluation on a set of open source OCR benchmarks shows that our tool handles all OCR constructs and incurs acceptable time and space overhead to the program execution.

GT-Race addresses the challenges of data race detection for AMT programs mentioned in Sect. 1 as follows (a) The space complexity of the computation graph is linearly proportional to the number of tasks and dependences, which makes GT-Race scalable to AMT programs (b) GT-Race detects data races by using the happens-before relations among tasks, which incurs no false positives (c) When detecting data races, GT-Race doesn't require the AMT program to execute in sequential order. GT-Race works in parallel, thereby fully utilizing hardware parallelism for debugging executions as well (d) Since the computation graph is a general representation of happens-before relations, GT-Race can be applied to other AMT runtimes beyond OCR.

For future research, we plan to combine some static analysis techniques with GT-Race to filter out race-free shared variables during dynamic data race detection. We also plan to further improve the efficiency of graph traversal by learning the structural properties in the computation graph more comprehensively.

References

1. Pebay, P., Bennett, J.C., et al.: Towards asynchronous many-task in situ data analysis using legion. In: 2016 IEEE International Parallel and Distributed Processing Symposium Workshops. IEEE, pp. 1033–1037 (2016)
2. Blumofe, R.D., Joerg, C.F., Kuszmaul, B.C., Leiserson, C.E., Randall, K.H., Zhou, Y.: Cilk: an efficient multithreaded runtime system. J. Parallel Distrib. Comput. **37**(1), 55–69 (1996)
3. Chatterjee, S., Tasirlar, S., et al.: Integrating asynchronous task parallelism with MPI. In: 2013 IEEE 27th International Symposium on Parallel & Distributed Processing (IPDPS), pp. 712–725. IEEE (2013)
4. Treichler, S., Bauer, M., Aiken, A.: Realm: an event-based low-level runtime for distributed memory architectures. In: Proceedings of the 23rd International Conference on Parallel Architectures and Compilation, pp. 263–276. ACM (2014)
5. Mattson, T.G., Cledat, R., et al.: The open community runtime: a runtime system for extreme scale computing. In: 2016 IEEE High Performance Extreme Computing Conference (HPEC), pp. 1–7. IEEE (2016)
6. Stenzel, O.: The Physics of Thin Film Optical Spectra. SSSS, vol. 44, pp. 163–180. Springer, Cham (2016). https://doi.org/10.1007/978-3-319-21602-7_8
7. Savage, S., Burrows, M., et al.: Eraser: a dynamic data race detector for multithreaded programs. ACM Trans. Comput. Syst. (TOCS) **15**(4), 391–411 (1997)
8. O'Callahan, R., Choi, J.D.: Hybrid dynamic data race detection. In: ACM Sigplan Notices, vol. 38, pp. 167–178. ACM (2003)
9. Feng, M., Leiserson, C.E.: Efficient detection of determinacy races in cilk programs. Theory Comput. Syst. **32**(3), 301–326 (1999)
10. Surendran, R., Sarkar, V.: Dynamic determinacy race detection for task parallelism with futures. In: Falcone, Y., Sánchez, C. (eds.) RV 2016. LNCS, vol. 10012, pp. 368–385. Springer, Cham (2016). https://doi.org/10.1007/978-3-319-46982-9_23
11. Yoga, A., Nagarakatte, S., Gupta, A.: Parallel data race detection for task parallel programs with locks. In: Proceedings of the 2016 24th ACM SIGSOFT International Symposium on Foundations of Software Engineering, pp. 833–845. ACM (2016)
12. Sarkar, V.: Comp 322: fundamentals of parallel programming module 1: parallelism (2017). https://wiki.rice.edu/confluence/download/attachments/4435861/module1.pdf?version=5&modificationDate=1519055242728&api=v2
13. Tasirlar, S., Sarkar, V.: Data-driven tasks and their implementation. In: Proceedings of the 2011 International Conference on Parallel Processing, ICPP 2011, pp. 652–661, Washington, DC, USA. IEEE Computer Society (2011)

14. Nethercote, N., Seward, J.: How to shadow every byte of memory used by a program. In: Proceedings of the 3rd International Conference on Virtual Execution Environments, pp. 65–74. ACM (2007)
15. Cheng, G.I., Feng, M., Leiserson, C.E., Randall, K.H., Stark, A.F.: Detecting data races in Cilk programs that use locks. In: Proceedings of the Tenth Annual ACM Symposium on Parallel Algorithms and Architectures, pp. 298–309. ACM (1998)
16. Raman, R., Zhao, J., et al.: Efficient data race detection for async-finish parallelism. Form. Methods Syst. Des. **41**(3), 321–347 (2012)
17. Wei, H., Yu, J.X., Lu, C., Jin, R.: Reachability querying: an independent permutation labeling approach. Proceed. VLDB Endow. **7**(12), 1192–1202 (2014)
18. Wang, H., He, H., Yang, J., Yu, P.S., Yu, J.X.: Dual labeling: answering graph reachability queries in constant time. In: 2006 Proceedings of the 22nd International Conference on Data Engineering, p. 75, ICDE 2006. IEEE (2006)
19. Cheng, J., Huang, S., et al.: TF-label: a topological-folding labeling scheme for reachability querying in a large graph. In: Proceedings of the 2013 ACM SIGMOD International Conference on Management of Data, pp. 193–204. ACM (2013)
20. Trißl, S., Leser, U.: Fast and practical indexing and querying of very large graphs. In: Proceedings of the 2007 ACM SIGMOD International Conference on Management of Data, pp. 845–856. ACM (2007)

Performance and Power Modeling, Prediction and Evaluation

Reducing GPU Register File Energy

Vishwesh Jatala[1](✉)[iD], Jayvant Anantpur[2](✉)[iD], and Amey Karkare[1](✉)[iD]

[1] Indian Institute of Technology Kanpur, Kanpur, India
{vjatala,karkare}@cse.iitk.ac.in
[2] Mentor Graphics India Pvt. Ltd., Bangalore, India
jayvant.anantpur@gmail.com

Abstract. Graphics Processing Units (GPUs) maintain a large register file to increase the thread level parallelism (TLP). To increase the TLP further, recent GPUs have increased the number of on-chip registers in every generation. However, with the increase in the register file size, the leakage power increases. Also, with the technology advances, the leakage power component has increased and has become an important consideration for the manufacturing process. The leakage power of a register file can be reduced by turning infrequently used registers into low power (drowsy or off) state after accessing them. A major challenge in doing so is the lack of runtime register access information.

To address this, we propose a system called **GREENER**. It employs a compiler analysis that determines the power state of the registers, i.e., which registers can be switched off or placed in drowsy state at each program point and encodes this information in program instructions. Further, it uses a runtime optimization that increases the accuracy of power state of registers. We implemented the proposed ideas using GPGPU-Sim simulator and evaluated them on 21 kernels from several benchmarks suites. We observe that when compared to the baseline without any power optimizations, **GREENER** shows an average reduction of register leakage energy by 69.04% with a negligible number of simulation cycles overhead (0.53%).

Keywords: Register file · Power · Energy · Performance

1 Introduction

Graphics Processing Unit (GPU) achieves high throughput by utilizing thread level parallelism (TLP). Typically, GPUs maintain a large register file in each streaming multiprocessor (SM) to improve the TLP. GPUs allow a large number of resident threads [2] in each SM, and the resident threads can store their thread context in the register file, which facilitates faster context switching of the threads. The threads that are launched in each SM are grouped into sets of 32

Vishwesh Jatala is supported by Tata Consultancy Services (TCS) Research Scholarship Program. Amey Karkare acknowledges the travel fund received from TCS.

© Springer International Publishing AG, part of Springer Nature 2018
M. Aldinucci et al. (Eds.): Euro-Par 2018, LNCS 11014, pp. 77–91, 2018.
https://doi.org/10.1007/978-3-319-96983-1_6

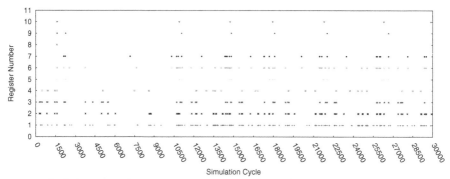

Each data point shows the access of a register (Y-axis) during a cycle (X-axis).

Fig. 1. Register access pattern for MUM [5]

threads (called warps), and they execute the instructions in a single instruction, multiple threaded (SIMT) manner. To keep improving the TLP of the GPUs, GPU architects increase the maximum number of resident threads and register file sizes in every generation.

Earlier studies [12,17] show that register files in GPUs consume around 15% of the total power. With the technology advances, the leakage power component has increased and has become an important consideration for the manufacturing process [16]. Moreover, registers in a GPU continue to dissipate leakage power throughout the entire execution of its warp even when they are not accessed by the warp.

1.1 Motivation

To understand the severity of leakage power dissipation by register file, consider Fig. 1 which shows the access patterns of some registers of warp 0 during the execution of *MUM* application (The experimental methodology has been discussed in Sect. 4). We use the access patterns of the registers of a single warp as a representative since all the warps of a kernel typically show similar behavior during execution [4]. We make the following observations:

- Register 10 is accessed very infrequently—it is accessed for only 7 cycles during the complete execution (life time) of the warp (29614 cycles).
- Register 1 is the most frequently accessed register during the warp execution. However, it is accessed for only 330 cycles (~1.11%) during the life time of the warp.

This shows that registers are accessed for a very short duration during the warp life time. However, they continue to dissipate leakage power for the entire life time of the warp. Figure 2 shows that the behavior is not specific to *MUM*, but is seen across a wide range of applications. The figure shows the percentage of simulation cycles spent in register accesses (averaged over all the registers in all

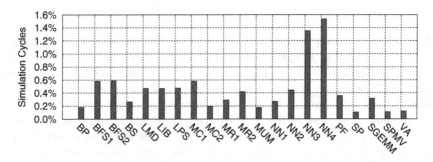

Fig. 2. Percentage of simulation cycles spent by a register (average of all the registers)

the warps) for several applications. We observe that registers on an average spend $< 2\%$ of the simulation cycles during the warp execution while leaking power during the entire execution. This behavior is expected since GPU allows large number of resident warps in each SM and these warps get executed according to a pre-defined scheduling policy. If a warp gets scheduled less frequently, then its registers leak power for a longer duration.

One solution [3] to reduce the leakage power of the registers is by putting the registers into drowsy or SLEEP[1] state *immediately* after the registers of an instruction are accessed. However, this can have run-time overhead whenever there are frequent wake up signals to the sleeping register. Consider Fig. 1 again:

- Putting register 10 to SLEEP state immediately after its accesses saves significant power due to the gaps of several thousands of cycles between consecutive accesses.
- In contrast, register 1 is accessed very frequently. If it is put to SLEEP after every access, it will have a high overhead of wake up signals.
- The access pattern of register 7 changes during the warp execution. It is accessed frequently for some duration (for example, between cycles 10500–11250), and not accessed frequently for other duration (between cycles 3000–7500). To optimize energy as well as run-time, the register needs to be kept ON whenever it is frequently accessed, and put to SLEEP otherwise.
- The last access to register 8 is at cycle 1602. The register can be turned OFF after its last access to save more power.

In summary, the knowledge of registers' access patterns helps improve energy efficiency without impacting the run-time adversely. Our proposed solution **GReEneR** statically estimates the run-time usage patterns of registers to reduce GPU register file leakage power.

---

[1] Drowsy [3,9] and SLEEP [14,18,19] states refer to the same low power data preserving states. In this paper, we use the term SLEEP. Also, the techniques [14,18] to reduce leakage power using low power states address the subthreshold leakage power. Hence, in this paper the savings on leakage energy refer to savings on subthreshold leakage energy.

1.2   Contributions

GREENER uses a compile-time analysis to determine the power state of the registers (OFF, SLEEP, or ON) for each instruction by estimating the register usage information. Further, it transforms an input assembly language by encoding the power state information at each instruction to make it energy efficient. The static analysis makes safe approximations while computing power state of the registers, therefore, the choice of the state can be suboptimal at run-time. Hence, to improve the accuracy and energy efficiency, it provides a run-time optimization that dynamically corrects the power state of registers of each instruction. We make the following contributions:

1. We introduce a new instruction format that supports the power states for the instruction registers (Sect. 3.2). We propose a compile-time analysis that determines the power state of the registers at each program point and transforms an input assembly language into a power optimized assembly language (Sects. 3.1 and 3.2).
2. We propose a run-time optimization to reduce the penalty of suboptimal (but safe) choices made by static analysis (Sect. 3.3).
3. We implemented the proposed compile-time and run-time optimizations using GPGPU-Sim simulator [10]. We integrated GPUWattch [17] with CACT-P [18] version to enable power saving mechanism (Sect. 4).
4. We evaluated our implementation on wide range of kernels from different benchmark suites: CUDASDK [8], GPGPU-SIM [5], Parboil [1], and Rodinia [7]. We observe a reduction in the register leakage energy by an average of 69.04% and maximum of 87.95% (Sect. 4) when compared to the baseline approach, which does not have any power optimizations.

In the paper, Sect. 2 briefs the background required for **GREENER**, while the system itself is described in Sect. 3. Section 4 gives the experimental evaluation. Section 5 describes related work, and Sect. 6 concludes the paper.

2   Background

GPUs consist of a set of streaming multiprocessors (SMs). Each SM contains a large number of execution units such as ALUs, SPs, SFUs, and Load/Store units. GPUs achieve high throughput because they can hide long memory execution latencies with massive thread level parallelism. Each SM has a large register file, which allows the resident threads to maintain their contexts, and hence can have faster context switching.

NVIDIA provides a programming language CUDA [8] to parallelize applications on GPU. A program written in CUDA is translated to an intermediate representation (PTX), which is finally translated to an executable code. NVIDIA provides tools such as *cuobjdump* to disassemble the executable into SASS assembly language. GPGPU-Sim converts SASS code to PTXPlus code for simulation.

GPUWattch [17] framework uses the simulation statistics of GPGPU-Sim to measure the power of each component in the GPUs. The framework is built on McPAT [19], which internally uses CACTI [6]. McPAT models the register files as memory arrays to measure the register power. **GREENER** inserts power state information of registers in the PTXPlus code to enable reduction in the leakage power of the register files.

3   GREENER

To understand the working of **GREENER**, we need to understand the different access patterns of a register and their effect on the wake up penalty incurred. Let W (threshold) denotes the minimum number of program instructions that are required to offset the wake-up penalty incurred when a register state is switched from OFF or SLEEP state to ON state. Consider a program that accesses some register R in a statement S during execution. The future accesses of R in this execution govern its power state. The following scenarios exist:

1. The next access (either read or write) to R is by an instruction S' and there are no more than W instructions between S and S'. In this case, since the two accesses to R are very close, it should be kept ON to avoid any wake-up penalty associated with SLEEP or OFF state.
2. The next access to R is a read access by an instruction S' and there are more than W instructions between S and S'. In this case, since the value stored in R is used by S', we can not switch R to OFF state as it will cause the loss of its value. However, we can put R in SLEEP state.
3. The next access to R is a write access by an instruction S' and there are more than W instructions between S and S'. In this case, since the value stored in R is being overwritten by S', we can put R in OFF state.
4. There is no further access to R in the program. In this case also, R can be safely turned OFF.

We now describe the compiler analysis used by **GREENER** to capture these scenarios.

3.1   Compiler Analysis

To compute power state of registers at each instruction, we perform compiler analysis at the instruction level. Determining the power state of each register requires knowing the life time of registers as well as the distance between the consecutive accesses to the registers. We use the following notations.

- IN(S) denotes the program point before the instruction S. OUT(S) denotes the program point after the instruction S.
- SUCC(S) denotes the set of successors of the instruction S. An instruction I is said to be successor of S if the control may transfer to I after executing the instruction S.
- isLive(π, R) is true if there is some path from program point π to Exit that contains a use of R not preceded by its definition.
- Dist(π, R) denotes the distance in terms of number of instructions from program point π till the next access to R. Dist(π, R) is set to ∞ when it exceeds the threshold W.

$$\mathsf{Dist}(\mathsf{IN}(S), R) = \begin{cases} 1, \text{ if } S \text{ accesses } R \\ \mathsf{INC}(\mathsf{Dist}(\mathsf{OUT}(S), R)), \text{otherwise} \end{cases}$$

$$\mathsf{INC}(x) = \begin{cases} \infty, \text{ if } x \text{ is } W \text{ or } \infty \\ x + 1, \text{otherwise} \end{cases}$$

$$\mathsf{Dist}(\mathsf{OUT}(S), R) = \begin{cases} \infty, \text{ if } S \text{ is Exit} \\ \max_{SS \in \mathsf{SUCC}(S)} \mathsf{Dist}(\mathsf{IN}(SS), R), \text{ otherwise} \end{cases}$$

Fig. 3. Data flow equations. Note that $\mathsf{INC}(x)$ is a saturating increment operator.

Table 1. Computing power state of a register R at a program point π

isLive(π, R)	SleepOff(π, R)	Power(π, R)
True	True	SLEEP
True	False	ON
False	True	OFF
False	False	ON

- SleepOff(π, R) is true if the register R can be put into SLEEP or OFF state at π.
- Power(π, R) denotes the power state of the register R at program point π.

The liveness information of each register, isLive(π, R), can be computed using traditional liveness analysis [15]. The data flow equations to compute the $\mathsf{Dist}(\mathsf{IN}(S), R)$ and $\mathsf{Dist}(\mathsf{OUT}(S), R)$ are given in Fig. 3. Since our analysis aims to reduce the power consumption, we compute $\mathsf{Dist}(\mathsf{OUT}(S), R)$ as the maximum value of $\mathsf{Dist}(\mathsf{IN}(SS), R)$ over the successors SS of S. A register R can potentially be put into SLEEP or OFF state at a program point π if it is not accessed within the distance window W on some path, i.e., $\mathsf{SleepOff}(\pi, R) = (\mathsf{Dist}(\pi, R) == \infty)$.

The power state of each register at each program point can be computed according to Table 1. Note that in GPUs, all the 32 threads of a warp execute the same instruction in SIMT manner, hence power state computed by the analysis is applicable to 32 registers corresponding to the 32 threads of a warp.

3.2 Encoding Power States

The power state (*Power_State*) of a register can be one of the three states: **OFF**, **SLEEP**, or **ON**. Thus, it requires two bits to represent *Power_State* of one register. Since the power state can change after every instruction at run-time, we need to encode the *Power_State* of the operand registers of an instruction in the instruction itself.

PTXPlus instructions [10] can support up to 4 source and 4 destination registers. Encoding *Power_State* of all the registers will require 16 bits. We observed that in our benchmarks, most instructions use only up to 2 source registers and 1 destination register. Therefore, to reduce the number of bits required to encode *Power_State* in each instruction, we encode information only for 2 source registers and 1 destination register. For instructions having more registers, *Power_State* of the remaining registers is assumed to be **SLEEP** to enable power saving. The modified instructions format is:

\<Opcode\> \<Options\> \<Operand_List\> *\<Power_State_List \>*

where Power$(\mathsf{OUT}(S), R)$ is *Power_State* encoded for a register R for an instruction S.

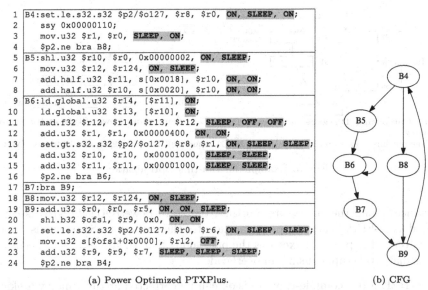

```
1  B4:set.le.s32.s32 $p2/$o127, $r8, $r0, ON, SLEEP, ON;
2      ssy 0x00000110;
3      mov.u32 $r1, $r0, SLEEP, ON;
4      $p2.ne bra B8;
5  B5:shl.u32 $r10, $r0, 0x00000002, ON, SLEEP;
6      mov.u32 $r12, $r124, ON, SLEEP;
7      add.half.u32 $r11, s[0x0018], $r10, ON, ON;
8      add.half.u32 $r10, s[0x0020], $r10, ON, ON;
9  B6:ld.global.u32 $r14, [$r11], ON;
10     ld.global.u32 $r13, [$r10], ON;
11     mad.f32 $r12, $r14, $r13, $r12, SLEEP, OFF, OFF;
12     add.u32 $r1, $r1, 0x00000400, ON, ON;
13     set.gt.s32.s32 $p2/$o127, $r8, $r1, ON, SLEEP, SLEEP;
14     add.u32 $r10, $r10, 0x00001000, SLEEP, SLEEP;
15     add.u32 $r11, $r11, 0x00001000, SLEEP, SLEEP;
16     $p2.ne bra B6;
17 B7:bra B9;
18 B8:mov.u32 $r12, $r124, ON, SLEEP;
19 B9:add.u32 $r0, $r0, $r5, ON, ON, SLEEP;
20     shl.b32 $ofs1, $r9, 0x0, ON, ON;
21     set.le.s32.s32 $p2/$o127, $r0, $r6, ON, SLEEP, SLEEP;
22     mov.u32 s[$ofs1+0x0000], $r12, OFF;
23     add.u32 $r9, $r9, $r7, SLEEP, SLEEP, SLEEP;
24     $p2.ne bra B4;
```

(a) Power Optimized PTXPlus.   (b) CFG

The shaded text in part (a) denotes the power states inserted by **GREENER**. The first power state corresponds to power state of the destination register and the subsequent two power states correspond to that of two source registers.

Fig. 4. A Snippet of the program and its CFG for *SP* benchmark [8]

Example 1. Figure 4(a) shows a snippet of power optimized PTXPlus code, which is generated for *SP* benchmark using a threshold value (W) 7. The control flow graph (CFG) corresponding to the snippet is shown in Fig. 4(b). Note that the CFG is shown with respect to traditional basic block level to show it in compact. In Fig. 4(a), explicit branch addresses have been replaced by block labels for ease of understanding.   □

At run-time, power state of the source registers are set after the register contents have been read, i.e., in the read operands phase in the GPU pipeline, and the power state of the destination registers are set after the register contents have been written, i.e., in the write back stage of the pipeline.

3.3   Run-Time Optimization

Recall that the compiler analysis described in Sect. 3.1 computes $\mathsf{Dist}(\mathsf{OUT}(S), R)$ as the maximum distance value over all successors when $\mathsf{OUT}(S)$ is a branch point. This decision increases the chances of power savings, but it can be suboptimal at run-time as shown by the following example.

Example 2. Consider the CFG in Fig. 5(a) for a hypothetical benchmark. Assume the threshold value of 7 for **GREENER**. Instruction S0 defines a register r0. The next access to r0 occurs along two paths: the path along S10 has a use at a distance of 2, and the other (along S1) has a use in S9 at a distance of ∞ (>7). **GREENER** computes $\mathsf{Dist}(\mathsf{OUT}(S0), r0)$ as ∞, the maximum of the

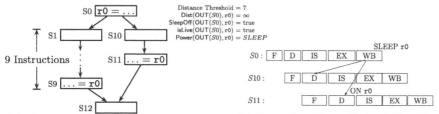

(a) **Computing Distance at Branch Diver-** (b) **Correcting Power State at Run-time**
gence

The pipeline phases are: Fetch (F), Decode (D), Issue (IS), Execute (EX), and Writeback (WB)

Fig. 5. Example for run-time optimization

distances along the successors. Further, the state $\mathsf{Power}(\mathsf{OUT}(S0), r0)$ is computed as SLEEP. When the program executes the path along S1, power is saved. However, if the program executes the path along S10, then the register needs an immediate wake up, causing an overhead.   □

GREENER's compile-time decision can be corrected at run-time by looking at near future accesses of a register in the pipeline. The hardware is modified to check in the pipeline if any decoded instruction from the same warp accesses a register whose power state is being changed to SLEEP or OFF. If so, then the register power is kept ON. This avoids the wake up latencies for instructions that access the same register within a short duration, thereby avoiding the performance penalty.

Example 3. Figure 5(b) shows a possible execution sequence of a program whose CFG is shown in Fig. 5(a). The instruction $S0$ writes to register r0. After writing the register value in write back stage (WB), the register needs to be put into SLEEP state. Assume that the program takes the path along S10 and decodes the instruction $S11$ before the write back stage of $S0$. Our run-time optimization detects the future access to r0 by $S11$, and keeps the register in ON state instead of putting it into SLEEP state to avoid additional wake up latencies. On the other hand, if the program takes the path along S1, then the instruction present in the S9 would appear much later in the pipeline (after WB stage of $S0$). The register r0 will be set to SLEEP state.   □

4   Experimental Analysis

Implementing **GREENER** requires to modify the GPU pipeline. We implemented the proposed hardware changes and compiler optimizations in GPGPU-Sim V3.x [10]. The details of the modified GPU architecture and the corresponding overheads (negligible) are discussed in [11] and ignored for brevity. The GPGPU-Sim configuration used for the experiments is shown in Table 2. We also evaluated **GREENER** on various other GPU configurations, whose results are reported in our technical report [11]. We measured the power consumption of register file using GPUWattch [17].

Note that GPUWattch internally uses CACTI [6], which does not support leakage power saving mechanism. Therefore, we modified GPUWattch to use CACTI-P version [18], which supports the leakage power saving mechanism. CACTI-P uses minimum data retention voltage to enable the SRAM cells to enter into SLEEP state without losing their data. We chose SRAM$_{vccmin}$ to be the default value (provided by CACTI-P depending on the technology node, 22 nm in this case). To put SRAM cells in OFF state, we configured SRAM$_{vccmin}$ to 0 V. After running several experiments, we chose the threshold value (W) as 3, which achieves lowest energy for maximum number of kernels. We used the latency to change a register state from SLEEP to ON to be 1 cycle, and the latency to change a register state from OFF to ON to be 2 cycles. We report these latency and energy overheads in our results and also include these overheads throughout our results. We evaluated **GREENER** on 21 kernels from the benchmark suites CUDA-SDK [8], GPGPU-SIM [5], Parboil [1], and Rodinia [7] as shown in Table 3.

Table 2. GPGPU-Sim configuration

Resource	Configuration
Architecture	NVIDIA Tesla K20x
Number of SMs	14
Shader core clock	732 MHz
Technology node	22 nm
Register file size per SM	256 KB
Number of register banks	32
Max number of TBs per SM	16
Max number of Threads per SM	2048
Warp scheduling	LRR
Number of schedulers per SM	4

Table 3. Benchmarks used for evaluation

#	Benchmark	Application	Notation	Kernel	#	Benchmark	Application	Notation	Kernel
1	RODINIA	backprop	BP	bpnn_adjustweights_cuda	12	GPGPU-SIM	MUM	MUM	mummergpuKernel
2	RODINIA	bfs	BFS1	Kernel	13	GPGPU-SIM	NN	NN1	executeFirstLayer
3	RODINIA	bfs	BFS2	Kernel2	14	GPGPU-SIM	NN	NN2	executeSecondLayer
4	CUDA-SDK	Blackscholes	BS	BlackScholesGPU	15	GPGPU-SIM	NN	NN3	executeThirdLayer
5	RODINIA	lavaMD	LMD	kernel_gpu_cuda	16	GPGPU-SIM	NN	NN4	executeFourthLayer
6	GPGPU-SIM	LIB	LIB	Pathcalc_Portfolio_KernelGPU	17	RODINIA	pathfinder	PF	dynproc_kernel
7	GPGPU-SIM	LPS	LPS	GPU_laplace3d	18	CUDA-SDK	scalarProd	SP	scalarProdGPU
8	CUDA-SDK	MonteCarlo	MC1	inverseCNDKernel	19	PARBOIL	sgemm	SGEMM	mysgemmNT
9	CUDA-SDK	MonteCarlo	MC2	MonteCarloOneBlockPerOption	20	PARBOIL	spmv	SPMV	spmv_jds
10	PARBOIL	mri-q	MR1	ComputePhiMag_GPU	21	CUDA-SDK	vectorAdd	VA	VecAdd
11	PARBOIL	mri-q	MR2	ComputeQ_GPU					

We use *Baseline* to denote the default GPGPU-Sim implementation that does not use any leakage power saving mechanisms. *Sleep-Reg* denotes the approach that optimizes the baseline approach by (1) turning OFF the unallocated registers and (2) turning the allocated registers into SLEEP state immediately after the registers are accessed [3].

Comparing Register Leakage Power: Figure 6 shows the effectiveness of **GREENER** and *Sleep-Reg* by measuring the reduction in leakage power with respect to *Baseline*. From the figure, we observe that **GREENER** shows an average (Geometric Mean denoted as *G.Mean*) reduction of leakage power by 69.21% when compared to the *Baseline*. It shows the **GREENER** is effective in turning the instruction registers into lower power state, such as SLEEP or OFF state depending on the behavior of the registers. The *Baseline* does not

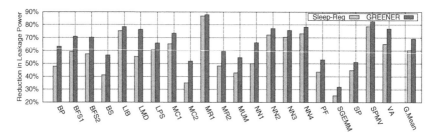

Fig. 6. Comparing register leakage power

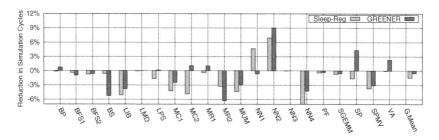

Fig. 7. Comparing performance in terms of simulation cycles

provide any mechanism to save the leakage power, as a result, the registers of a warp continue to consume leakage power throughout the warp execution. Figure 6 also shows that *Sleep-Reg* approach reduces the register leakage power by 60.23% when compared to *Baseline*, however, **GReEneR** is more power efficient than *Sleep-Reg*. It is because *Sleep-Reg* approach reduces the leakage power by turning the instruction registers into SLEEP state immediately after the instruction operands are accessed, without considering the access pattern of the registers. If a register needs an immediate access, then keeping the register into SLEEP instead of ON state requires additional latency cycles to wake up the register, and during these additional cycles, the registers consume power.

Performance Overhead Using Simulation Cycles: Figure 7 shows the performance overheads of **GReEneR** and *Sleep-Reg* approaches in terms of the number of simulation cycles with respect to *Baseline*. On an average, the applications show a negligible performance overhead of 0.53% with respect to *Baseline*. A slowdown is expected because **GReEneR** turns the registers into SLEEP or OFF states to enable power savings, and these registers are turned back to ON state (woken up) when they need to be accessed. This wake up process takes few additional latency cycles which leads to increase in the number of simulation cycles. Interestingly, some applications (*BP, LPS, MC2, MR1, NN2, SP,* and *VA*) show improvement in their performance. This occurs due to the change in the issuing order of the instructions. The warps that require their registers to be woken up can not be issued in its current cycle, instead other resident warps that are ready can be issued. This change in the issue order leads to

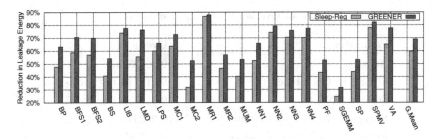

Fig. 8. Comparing register leakage energy

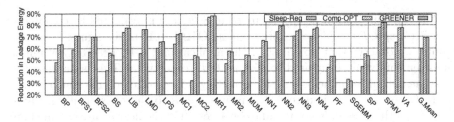

Fig. 9. Comparing effectiveness of individual optimizations

change in the memory access patterns, which in turns changes L1 and L2 cache misses etc. For instance, in case of *BP, LPS, MC2,* and *NN1* applications, we observe an improvement in the performance due to less number of pipeline stall cycles with **GREEN**ER when compared to *Baseline.* Figure 7 also shows that *Sleep-Reg* has an average performance degradation of 1.48% when compared to the *Baseline* approach. This degradation is more when compared to **GREEN**ER because *Sleep-Reg* turns all the instruction registers into SLEEP state after the instruction operands are accessed, irrespective of their usage pattern.

Comparing Register Leakage Energy: Figure 8 compares the total energy savings of **GREEN**ER and *Sleep-Reg* w.r.t. *Baseline.* The results show that **GREEN**ER achieves an average reduction of register leakage energy by 69.04% and 23.29% when compared to *Baseline* and *Sleep-Reg* respectively. From Figs. 6 and 7, we see that **GREEN**ER shows more leakage power saving, also has negligible performance overhead with respect to the *Baseline,* hence we achieve a significant reduction in leakage energy.

Effectiveness of Optimizations: We show the effectiveness of the proposed optimizations in Fig. 9. We observe that the compiler optimization (discussed in Sect. 3.1, and denoted as *Comp-OPT*) saves more energy (average 69.09%) when compared to *Sleep-Reg* (59.65%). This shows that turning the registers into low power states (SLEEP or OFF state) with the knowledge of register access pattern is more effective than turning the registers into SLEEP state after accessing them.

Table 4. Overheads of sleep transistors

Parameter	Overhead
Area	$0.00875\,\text{mm}^2$
SLEEP to ON latency	$0.0197\,\text{ns}$ ($\lhd 1$ cycle)
OFF to ON latency	$0.0551\,\text{ns}$ ($\lhd 1$ cycle)
Energy for SLEEP to ON and vice versa	$0.0633\,\text{nJ}$
Energy for OFF to ON and vice versa	$0.198\,\text{nJ}$

The run-time optimization (discussed in Sect. 3.3) is evaluated by combining it with *Comp-OPT*, and we denote them as **GREENER** in the figure. From the results, we observe that, for most of the applications, **GREENER** show minor improvements when compared to *Comp-OPT* respectively. This is because the run-time optimization helps only in correcting power state of a register by turning to ON state when it detects the future access to the register at run-time. However, if the register is not found to be accessed in the near future at run-time, it does not modify and retains the power state as directed by the *Comp-OPT*. For some applications (e.g. *NN3*), **GREENER** is less efficient when compared to *Comp-OPT*. It occurs when a register that is determined to be accessed in the near future does not get accessed due to reasons such as scheduling order, scoreboard stalls, or the unavailability of the corresponding execution unit. Note that the effectiveness of run-time optimization depends on the application behavior at the branch divergence points.

Analyzing Hardware Overheads: To support leakage power saving, CACTI-P [18] introduces additional sleep transistors into the SRAM structures. These transistors enable us to put the registers into low power states (SLEEP or OFF) after accessing the operands. For the configuration used in our experiments, Table 4 shows the additional area, latency, and energy associated with the additional sleep transistors circuitry. Note that in our experiments, we conservatively consider the latency overhead to change the power state from OFF to ON state to be 2 cycles. We also evaluated **GREENER** by varying the wake up latency cycle overhead (the results are reported in [11]). We observed that even with varying the wake up latency, the applications show significant reduction in the leakage energy when compared to *Baseline*.

5 Related Work

Leakage power has become a major source of power dissipation in CMOS technology. Reducing the leakage power has been well studied in the context of CPUs when compared to GPUs. Though **GREENER** is only for saving leakage power consumption of GPU register files, we describe briefly the techniques to save leakage power in the context of both CPUs as well as GPUs. A comprehensive list of architectural techniques to reduce leakage power of CPUs are described in [14]. A survey of methods to reduce GPU power is presented in [20].

CPU Leakage Power Saving Techniques: Powell et al. [22] proposed a state destroying technique, Gated-V_{dd}, to minimize the leakage power of SRAM cells by gating supply voltage. Several methods [13,23] leverage Gated-V_{dd} technique to reduce the leakage power of cache memory by turning off the inactive cache lines. However, these techniques cannot preserve the state of the cache lines. To maintain the state, Flautner et al. [9] proposed an architectural technique that reduces the leakage power by putting the cache lines into a drowsy state. Other approaches [21] exploit this by using cache access patterns to put cache lines in the drowsy state. As expected, the leakage power savings in this (drowsy) approach are less when compared to Gated-V_{dd} approach.

GPU Leakage Power Saving Techniques: Warped register file [3] leverages this drowsy approach to reduce leakage power of register files by putting the registers into the drowsy state immediately after accessing them. However, it does not take into account the register access pattern while turning the registers into low power states. Their approach is closest to **GREENER** and has been quantitatively compared in our results. Register file virtualization [12] reduces the register leakage power by reallocating unused registers to another warp. Pilot register file [4] partitions the register file into fast and slow register files, and it allocates the registers into these parts depending on the frequency of the register usage. The partition of the registers is done statically. Therefore, if a register is accessed more frequently for some duration, and less frequently for other duration, then allocating the register to either of the partitions can make it less energy efficient. **GREENER** changes power state during the execution, so it does not have this drawback.

6 Conclusions and Future Work

This paper focuses on reducing the leakage power of the register file in GPUs. We discuss various opportunities to save leakage power of the registers by analyzing the access patterns of the registers. We propose a system called **GREENER** that employs compiler analysis to determine the power state of each register at each program point. To improve the effectiveness further, we introduce a run-time optimization that dynamically corrects the power states determined by the static analysis. On evaluating **GREENER** using several applications, we observed that the knowledge of register access patterns and the compiler optimizations help in improving the energy efficiency of register file with a negligible number of simulation cycles overhead.

In future, we plan to explore several hardware and software strategies to reduce the register leakage energy further. For instance, we can study the effect of various register allocation mechanisms, scheduling polices and propose algorithms that minimize leakage energy by leveraging **GREENER**.

The register leakage power constitutes a part of the total leakage power. Similarly, other resources in the GPU such as shared memory, cache, and DRAM, dissipate leakage power during a kernel execution. In future, we plan to work on reducing the power consumption of the other GPU resources by analyzing the application behavior and the resource access patterns.

References

1. Parboil Benchmarks. http://impact.crhc.illinois.edu/Parboil/parboil.aspx
2. Kepler Architecture (2014). http://www.nvidia.com/object/nvidia-kepler.html
3. Abdel-Majeed, M., Annavaram, M.: Warped register file: a power efficient register file for GPGPUs. In: HPCA (2013). https://doi.org/10.1109/HPCA.2013.6522337
4. Abdel-Majeed, M., Shafaei, A., Jeon, H., Pedram, M., Annavaram, M.: Pilot register file: energy efficient partitioned register file for GPUs. In: HPCA (2017). https://doi.org/10.1109/HPCA.2017.47
5. Bakhoda, A., Yuan, G., Fung, W., Wong, H., Aamodt, T.: Analyzing CUDA workloads using a detailed GPU simulator. In: ISPASS (2009). https://doi.org/10.1109/ISPASS.2009.4919648
6. CACTI. http://www.hpl.hp.com/research/cacti
7. Che, S., et al.: Rodinia: a benchmark suite for heterogeneous computing. In: IISWC (2009). https://doi.org/10.1109/IISWC.2009.5306797
8. CUDA-SDK (2014). http://docs.nvidia.com/cuda/cuda-samples
9. Flautner, K., Kim, N.S., Martin, S., Blaauw, D., Mudge, T.: Drowsy caches: simple techniques for reducing leakage power. SIGARCH Comput. Archit. News **30**(2) (2002). https://doi.org/10.1145/545214.545232
10. GPGPU-Sim Simulator (2014). http://www.gpgpu-sim.org
11. Jatala, V., Anantpur, J., Karkare, A.: GREENER: a tool for improving energy efficiency of register files. CoRR abs/1709.04697 (2017)
12. Jeon, H., Ravi, G.S., Kim, N.S., Annavaram, M.: GPU register file virtualization. In: MICRO (2015). https://doi.org/10.1145/2830772.2830784
13. Kaxiras, S., Hu, Z., Martonosi, M.: Cache decay: exploiting generational behavior to reduce cache leakage power. In: ISCA (2001). https://doi.org/10.1145/379240.379268
14. Kaxiras, S., Martonosi, M.: Computer Architecture Techniques for Power-Efficiency, 1st edn. Morgan and Claypool Publishers (2008)
15. Khedker, U., Sanyal, A., Karkare, B.: Data Flow Analysis: Theory and Practice, 1st edn. CRC Press Inc., Boca Raton (2009)
16. Kim, N.S., et al.: Leakage current: Moore's law meets static power. Computer **36**(12) (2003). https://doi.org/10.1109/MC.2003.1250885
17. Leng, J., et al.: GPUWattch: enabling energy optimizations in GPGPUs. In: ISCA (2013). https://doi.org/10.1145/2485922.2485964
18. Li, S., Chen, K., Ahn, J.H., Brockman, J.B., Jouppi, N.P.: CACTI-P: architecture-level modeling for sram-based structures with advanced leakage reduction techniques. In: ICCAD (2011). https://doi.org/10.1109/ICCAD.2011.6105405
19. Li, S., Ahn, J.H., Strong, R.D., Brockman, J.B., Tullsen, D.M., Jouppi, N.P.: The McPAT Framework for multicore and manycore architectures: simultaneously modeling power, area, and timing. TACO **10**(1) (2013). https://doi.org/10.1145/2445572.2445577
20. Mittal, S., Vetter, J.S.: A survey of methods for analyzing and improving GPU energy efficiency. ACM Comput. Surv. **47**(2) (2014). https://doi.org/10.1145/2636342

21. Petit, S., Sahuquillo, J., Such, J.M., Kaeli, D.: Exploiting temporal locality in drowsy cache policies. In: CF (2005). https://doi.org/10.1145/1062261.1062321
22. Powell, M., Yang, S.H., Falsafi, B., Roy, K., Vijaykumar, T.N.: Gated-Vdd: a circuit technique to reduce leakage in deep-submicron cache memories. In: ISLPED (2000). https://doi.org/10.1145/344166.344526
23. Zhang, M., Asanović, K.: Fine-grain CAM-tag cache resizing using miss tags. In: ISLPED (2002). https://doi.org/10.1145/566408.566444

Taxonomist: Application Detection Through Rich Monitoring Data

Emre Ates[1]([✉])[iD], Ozan Tuncer[1], Ata Turk[1],
Vitus J. Leung[2], Jim Brandt[2],
Manuel Egele[1], and Ayse K. Coskun[1]

[1] Boston University, Boston, MA 02215, USA
{ates,otuncer,ataturk,megele,acoskun}@bu.edu
[2] Sandia National Laboratories,
Albuquerque, NM 87185, USA
{vjleung,brandt}@sandia.gov

Abstract. Modern supercomputers are shared among thousands of users running a variety of applications. Knowing which applications are running in the system can bring substantial benefits: knowledge of applications that intensively use shared resources can aid scheduling; unwanted applications such as cryptocurrency mining or password cracking can be blocked; system architects can make design decisions based on system usage. However, identifying applications on supercomputers is challenging because applications are executed using esoteric scripts along with binaries that are compiled and named by users.

This paper introduces a novel technique to identify applications running on supercomputers. Our technique, Taxonomist, is based on the empirical evidence that applications have different and characteristic resource utilization patterns. Taxonomist uses machine learning to classify known applications and also detect unknown applications. We test our technique with a variety of benchmarks and cryptocurrency miners, and also with applications that users of a production supercomputer ran during a 6 month period. We show that our technique achieves nearly perfect classification for this challenging data set.

Keywords: Supercomputing · HPC · Application detection
Monitoring · Security · Cryptocurrency

1 Introduction

Resource utilization and efficiency of supercomputers are top concerns for both system operators and users. It is typical to use figures of merit such as occupation of compute nodes or total CPU usage to assess utilization and efficiency; however, these metrics do not measure if the compute capacity is used meaningfully.

In fact, fraud, waste, and abuse of resources have been major concerns in high performance computing (HPC) [1]. Wasted resources in supercomputing

© Springer International Publishing AG, part of Springer Nature 2018
M. Aldinucci et al. (Eds.): Euro-Par 2018, LNCS 11014, pp. 92–105, 2018.
https://doi.org/10.1007/978-3-319-96983-1_7

stem from a variety of sources such as application hangs due to software and hardware faults, contention in shared resources (such as high speed networks, shared parallel file systems or memory), and fraudulent use (e.g., bitcoin mining, password cracking). Bitcoin mining in supercomputing environments has recently been gaining media attention [20, 23]. Knowing which applications are running on the system is a strong aid in addressing fraud, waste, and abuse problems.

Knowledge of applications running on the system can also be used for various system-level optimizations. Bhatele et al. have shown that network-intensive applications can slow down other applications significantly [7]. Similarly, Auweter et al. presented a scheduling method that leverages application-specific energy consumption models to reduce overall power consumption [5]. Knowing the most common applications and their characteristics is also useful to system architects who make design decisions, or to the supercomputer procurers who can make better funding and procurement decisions based on knowledge of typical application requirements.

Typically, supercomputer operators and system management software running on these large computers have no knowledge of which applications are executing in the supercomputer at a given time. A supercomputer is shared by many users and runs hundreds to thousands of applications concurrently per day [19]. These applications are compiled by users using different compiler settings, which result in vastly different executables even if compiled from the same source. It has been shown that static analysis of the binaries is not enough to detect the same application compiled with different compilers or flags [13]. Furthermore, users tend to use non-descriptive names for the binaries and scripts used in their job submission (e.g., `submit128.sh`, `a.out`, `app_runner.sh`). Therefore, naive methods for detecting applications such as looking at the names of the processes and scripts are not useful.

To address these challenges, we present *Taxonomist*, an automated technique for identifying applications running in supercomputers. To identify applications, Taxonomist leverages *monitoring data* that is periodically collected at runtime from a supercomputer's compute nodes. Monitoring data includes detailed resource usage information (e.g., CPU utilization, network events, etc.), and is typically used for application tuning [2], gaining information on system usage to aid procurement [12], or for anomaly detection [26]. Each application has (often non-obvious) resource utilization patterns that can be observed in the monitored data. Taxonomist uses machine learning techniques to learn these patterns in the data. Taxonomist can then identify known applications, even when they are running with new input configurations, and also new (unknown) applications. Specifically, our contributions in this paper are as follows:

- We present Taxonomist: a novel technique that uses machine learning to identify known and unknown applications running in a supercomputer based on readily available system monitoring data (Sect. 4). Taxonomist is able to detect applications that are new to the system, as well as previously unseen input configurations of known applications.

– We demonstrate the effectiveness of Taxonomist on a production supercomputer using over 50,000 production HPC application runs collected over 6 months of cluster usage, a wide selection of benchmarks, and cryptocurrency miners (Sect. 5). We report greater than 95% *F-score* with this data set (Sect. 6).

2   Related Work

Several prior approaches have explored identifying applications. Peisert has identified application detection as a problem in supercomputers [21]. He focused on using MPI calls through Integrated Performance Monitoring (IPM) [24] to identify application communication patterns. Further work by Whalen et al. refined the method to classify applications based on their communication graphs [28], and DeMasi et al. used system utilization data collected by IPM to identify applications [11]. These works are based on IPM, which is a tool that monitors the MPI calls in HPC applications. IPM needs to be linked with the applications and introduces up to 5% performance overhead [11].

Combs et al. have studied the applicability of using power signatures to identify applications [8]. As Combs et al. observed, power traces from different servers are not consistently comparable, so such a method is not scalable for large-scale systems. Our evaluation confirms that using only power signatures is insufficient to identify a diverse set of applications in large-scale systems.

Monitoring data has traditionally been used for analyses other than application detection. One of the earlier examples of data analysis in supercomputers was presented by Florez et al., who monitored system calls and library function calls for anomaly detection in applications [14]. Similarly, Tuncer et al. used monitoring data to detect node-level anomalies [26]. Agelastos et al. leveraged monitoring data for troubleshooting and application optimization in a 1200-node supercomputer [3].

In contrast to related work, Taxonomist uses a monitoring system with negligible overhead [2] that is capable of monitoring every application regardless of MPI use, and does not need to be linked with the applications. Taxonomist can be trained with a selection of applications of interest, and can reliably distinguish these applications from the remaining applications. Our method can also detect unknown applications it has not been trained with, which is very important for practical real-world scenarios.

Another line of work aims at blocking unwanted applications. One way to block cryptocurrency mining in supercomputers is to prevent miners from getting the most recent blockchain additions using firewalls [22]. However, many unwanted applications such as password crackers do not need to be connected to the Internet. Furthermore, firewalls may result in packet losses, and it has been shown that even very small packet loss is unacceptable for scientific computing because of the high bandwidth requirements [10]. Another approach to prevent waste might be to whitelist only applications compiled by the system administrators. However, availability is considered to be an important aspect of HPC

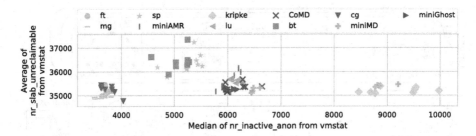

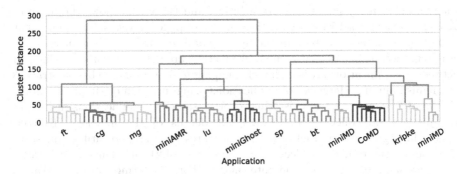

Fig. 1. Two example metrics from `/proc/vmstat` for 11 applications with two different input configurations, where each application is running on 4 nodes. These two metrics can be used to distinguish among some applications, but cannot be used to reliably detect each of the 11 applications.

Fig. 2. Clustering of 11 different applications, where each application is running on 4 nodes with two different input configurations. We manually assign different colors to represent different applications. (Color figure online)

systems, and limiting the users to use only specific applications would harm the user experience and limit the flexibility and usability of the systems. Therefore, knowledge of the applications running on the system can be a very important aid in blocking unwanted applications.

3   Motivation

Taxonomist uses monitoring data to identify applications. Modern monitoring systems are able to continuously collect hundreds of metrics per second from every compute node in an HPC system [2]. It is infeasible to manually inspect this data and identify applications relying on rules of thumb and expert knowledge; therefore, we design an automated approach to systematically discover the differences between the applications.

Figure 1 shows two example metrics for a set of 11 applications we run on a supercomputer (see Sect. 5 for details on experimental setup). The x-axis shows the median of `nr_inactive_anon`, which represents the number of

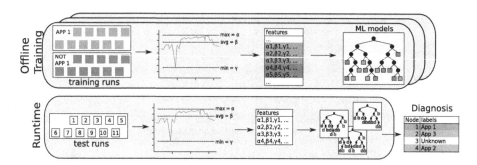

Fig. 3. Overview of Taxonomist.

anonymous memory pages that are inactive, and the y-axis shows the mean of nr_slab_unreclaimable, which is the number of pages in the slab memory that cannot be reclaimed. As seen in the figure, applications have different resource usage characteristics. However, these two metrics are not sufficient to distinguish between all applications. It is rather challenging to determine the best metrics to distinguish among a large set of applications using intuition or simple methods.

Figure 2 demonstrates clustering of the same 11 applications using all 721 metrics we collect (see Sect. 4.1 for details of the metrics). To construct this figure, we extract statistical features such as percentiles and standard deviation from the collected data (see Sect. 4.2), and cluster the statistics corresponding to the compute nodes. For clustering, we use Ward's method and standardized Euclidean distance (our implementation uses Python scipy.cluster.hierarchy.linkage). The results indicate that nodes running the same application are close to each other in the feature space, but the clustering is not perfect (e.g., miniMD is clustered incorrectly).

Manually finding which metrics are important to distinguish each application among hundreds of monitored metrics requires extensive knowledge on the metrics and applications. With supervised learning, the most relevant features can be automatically selected, and applications can be reliably identified. Thus, Taxonomist uses supervised learning techniques.

4 Taxonomist: A Technique for Identifying Applications

Taxonomist, outlined in Fig. 3, is a technique for identifying applications in large-scale systems using monitoring data collected from the machine. The monitoring data is collected from every compute node in a timeseries format. We then generate statistical features that reduce our storage and computation overhead, while enabling us to retain meaningful information in the timeseries. Finally, we train a classifier for each application to separate that application from the rest of the applications using labeled historical data. At runtime, Taxonomist analyzes monitoring data and labels each node's application according to the predictions from the classifiers. We also mark applications as *unknown*, based on the confidence of each classifier.

4.1 Monitoring

The first step of our technique is data collection. Typically some form of monitoring is in place in supercomputers. These systems collect numeric information about the usage of the network, memory, CPUs and other subsystems.

We monitor individual nodes and consider data from all nodes that are running a specific application separately. This enables us to recognize a known application that possibly runs on a different number of nodes than the number of nodes in that application's training runs.

4.2 Statistical Feature Extraction

After collecting monitoring data, Taxonomist removes a segment (40 s in our implementation) from each end of the timeseries to account for the transient initialization and finalization phases from the applications. We have observed 40 seconds to be sufficient for all applications in this study; however, this duration is application dependent. We also remove any constant metrics and convert metrics that represent counter values to their deltas.

We generate statistics from the timeseries data gathered from the compute nodes. The statistics used are the minimum, maximum, mean, standard deviation, skew, kurtosis and the 5th, 25th, 50th, 75th and 95th percentiles. Each metric's timeseries is distilled into these 11 features. These statistics have been shown to be useful in analyzing timeseries from supercomputers [26, 27]. They are also easy to calculate, reduce storage requirements, and enable us to compare applications that have different durations. We scale each feature to the $[0, 1]$ range according to the values observed in the training set. The same scaling factors are used at runtime.

4.3 Classification

To distinguish a set of given applications, we train a machine learning model using a training set of these labeled applications. Taxonomist labels each run with the corresponding application or it can also label new runs as *unknown*.

For each classifier, we use a *one-versus-rest* version of that classifier: i.e., for each application in the training set, we train a separate classifier that differentiates the application. This approach makes it easy to add a new application to the ensemble of classifiers and to get information about the nature of each application. This approach also enables us to train for only applications of interest, and we do not have to re-train every classifier when a new application is added.

For evaluation purposes, we compare the following classification algorithms: random forests, forests of extremely randomized trees (ExtraTrees), decision trees and the support vector machine classifier (SVC) with linear and radial basis function kernels. In practice, the best performing one for our data is the random forest (Sect. 6).

From every classifier, we obtain confidence values on whether a new observation belongs to one of the existing training classes. For example, the confidence threshold for the random forest is the percentage of trees in the forest that agree with the final classification. If none of the confidence values are above a predetermined *confidence threshold*, we mark this new observation as *unknown*.

Confidence Threshold Selection. A very high threshold would result in conservatively labeling new inputs of known applications as unknown, while too low values would result in unknown applications being labeled as a similar known application. To select the confidence threshold we first remove each application from the training set and perform testing with examples of that application in the training set while changing the confidence threshold. Then, we remove one input of each application and perform the same test. We select the threshold that results in the highest average F-score for both scenarios.

Hyperparameter Selection. Most classifiers have hyperparameters that describe the configuration of the algorithm. We find the best hyperparameters by splitting the training set into 5 cross validation folds. With 4/5 of the training data we train classifiers with different hyperparameters, and pick the best performing one using 1/5 of the training set. We choose the important hyperparameters for each classifier and over a certain range we train all combinations of hyperparameters, i.e., grid search. We find the best hyperparameter separately for each application's classifier. Note that we never use any test data during training or hyperparameter selection.

4.4   Operation of Taxonomist

During normal operation, Taxonomist uses the monitoring data to label each node of each application after a job finishes. These labels can be used to raise alarms in the case of cryptocurrency mining and to generate system usage reports or other summaries. They can also be used in further research and development on application-specific system optimizations. Furthermore, identifying fraud, waste, and abuse after application completion is still valuable.

As Taxonomist relies on machine learning, it requires a labeled training data set as input. This data set can be collected by a collaboration of users, operations staff, and analysts. After the applications of interest are determined, data can be collected by running them with different input configurations. This training is a one-time effort unless the applications of interest change.

In our current implementation, the application needs to finish before we identify it; however, Taxonomist can be modified to work with only the first few minutes of application data. The strategy proposed by Thebe et al. [25], which executes applications for a short time before the main run is scheduled, can be used with Taxonomist.

5   Experimental Methodology

We run our experiments on a production supercomputer, using the Lightweight Distributed Metric System (LDMS) [2] already in place. We evaluate our system with 11 benchmarks, 5 different *unwanted* applications, and also with 6 months of typical supercomputer usage.

Table 1. Applications used.

	Application	# of inputs	# of ranks	Description
	BT [6]	3	169	Block tri-diagonal solver
	CG [6]	3	128	Conjugate gradient
	FT [6]	3	128	Fourier transform
	LU [6]	3	192	Gauss-Seidel solver
	MG [6]	3	128	Multi-grid on meshes
Representative	SP [6]	3	169	Scalar penta-diagonal solver
applications	miniAMR [15]	4	192/1536	Adaptive mesh refinement
	miniMD [15]	4	192/1536	Molecular dynamics
	CoMD [15]	3	192	Molecular dynamics
	miniGhost [15]	4	192/1536	Structured PDE solver
	Kripke [17]	4	192/1536	S_N transport
	minerd	10	2/4	CPU cryptocurrency miner
	BFGminer	2	2/4	Cryptocurrency miner
Unwanted	xenon	2	96/192	Zcash competition [29] winner
applications[a]	davidjaenson	1	2/4	Zcash competitor
	tromp	1	2/4	Zcash competitor
	John the Ripper	194	96/192	Password cracker

[a]minerd: www.github.com/pooler/cpuminer, BFGminer: www.github.com/luke-jr/bfgminer, xenon: www.github.com/xenoncat/equihash-xenon,   davidjaenson: www.github.com/ davidjaenson/equihash, tromp: www.github.com/tromp/equihash, John the Ripper: www. openwall.com/john

5.1   Platform

We run all of our experiments on Volta, a Cray XC30m supercomputer located at Sandia National Laboratories. Volta is composed of 13 fully-connected routers, with 4 nodes each, leading to a total of 52 compute nodes. The operating system used is SLES 11 (SUSE Linux Enterprise Server) with kernel version 3.0.101. Each node has 64 GB of memory and two Intel Xeon E5–2695 v2 CPUs with 12 2-way hyper-threaded cores.

LDMS is a scalable monitoring system deployed on Volta. We use the memory metrics collected from /proc/meminfo and /proc/vmstat, CPU usage information from /proc/stat, and network usage information from Cray network interface card (NIC) counters. 721 metrics from every node every second in total.

5.2   Applications

Representative Applications. We pick a collection of 11 benchmarks and proxy applications, described in the upper section of Table 1. We choose these applications to be representative of characteristic HPC workloads. All representative applications use MPI, and are compiled with the Cray compilers. For each application, we use 3 different input configurations, and we run the applications on 4 nodes. We also run miniAMR, miniMD, miniGhost and Kripke on 32 nodes with an additional input. We run each application on the maximum number of hardware threads available that the application can utilize.

Unwanted Applications. These are applications that are usually not allowed on supercomputers such as cryptocurrency miners and password crackers. The tromp, davidjacnson, and xenon miners are from an open source miner competition [29]; BFGminer and minerd are popular miners for mining with CPUs. Xenon is single-threaded, so we execute 48 copies per node. Other cryptocurrency miners are multi-threaded, so we execute them one copy per node, using 48 threads. John the Ripper is a popular password cracking application which supports MPI; we execute it one rank per hardware thread. The inputs for John the Ripper are various password formats; and for the cryptocurrency miners, the inputs are the different types of cryptocurrencies. Due to ethical considerations, we ran all of the unwanted applications in benchmark mode to ensure that none of the cryptocurrency mined was connected to the main blockchains.

Typical Volta Usage. This data includes unlabeled applications run by 28 unique Volta users, consisting of 58,366 jobs, from August 2016 until January 2017. Our controlled experiments are removed from these runs.

5.3   Baseline Technique

Combs et al. [8] have proposed a technique (referred to as *Combs*) for application detection using power data instead of performance monitoring data. Combs uses a similar feature extraction approach, but in contrast to our method, it extracts serial correlation, non-linearity, self-similarity, chaos, and trend from the timeseries, as well as skew, kurtosis, serial correlation and non-linearity from the timeseries with the trend component removed. Furthermore, Combs et al. normalized maximum and median with the minimum for each timeseries to generate two additional features. Their method uses a random forest classifier and does not have a method for labeling unknown applications, so we do not implement any thresholding for Combs' method.

6   Evaluation

We evaluate the capability of Taxonomist in detecting applications with a variety of workloads and scenarios. First, we examine the classification performance in identifying known applications with new input configurations. Then, we evaluate the performance in labeling unknown applications.

For all tests, we first perform 5-fold cross validation, where we split the whole data into five sets with equal distributions of applications with the original data set. We then train five different Taxonomist instances using four of the sets. For testing, we use the fifth set that was removed from training data. For the normalization and hyperparameter selection steps, Taxonomist performs another 5-fold cross-validation on the training set.

For the results, we report the *F-Score*, which is a widely used measure of classifier performance. For binary classification, F-Score is defined as the harmonic mean of *precision* and *recall*. Precision is the ratio of true positives to

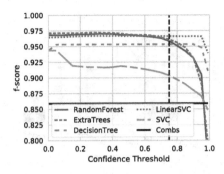
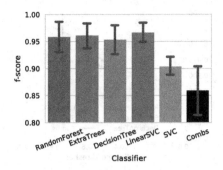

(a) F-scores for classifiers, vertical dashed (b) F-scores for classifiers at the chosen line indicates the chosen confidence thresh- confidence threshold, 0.75. Error bars in-old.   dicate the 95% confidence interval.

Fig. 4. F-scores with one input configuration removed from training. In most cases, the applications are correctly identified in spite of the unknown input configuration.

the number of all positive predictions, and recall is the ratio of true positives to the number of all actual positives in the data set. F-Score ranges between 1 (best) and 0 (worst). All of our results are multi-class; therefore we calculate the average precision and recall for each class, and take the harmonic mean to calculate the overall F-score.

Full Data Set. Table 2 shows the 5-fold cross validation results on the 11 representative applications. All of the results except the baseline technique (Combs) have an F-Score of over 0.99. However, this scenario where the training data contains all applications and all input configurations is unrealistic. SVM with the

Table 2. Five-fold cross validation results with the full data set.

Classifier	Precision	Recall	F-score
RandomForest	1.000	1.000	1.000
ExtraTrees	1.000	1.000	1.000
DecisionTree	0.998	0.998	0.998
LinearSVC	0.999	0.999	0.999
SVC	0.994	0.994	0.994
Combs	0.932	0.931	0.931

linear kernel (LinearSVC) performs better than the rbf kernel (SVC). This is likely due to the large data set with many features and datapoints, and this behavior is consistent with the literature [16].

Detecting Applications with Unknown Input Configurations. Applications' resource usage is affected by their input configurations. To evaluate Taxonomist's robustness against input configurations that are not in the training set, we remove one of the input sets from the training set. For the test set, we keep the cross validation folds the same. Figure 4 shows that the classification is successful unless the confidence threshold is over 0.9, in which case the unknown input configurations are marked as unknown applications.

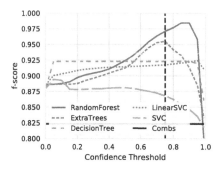
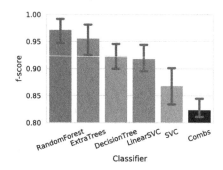

(a) F-scores for classifiers, vertical dashed line indicates the chosen confidence threshold.

(b) F-scores for classifiers at the chosen confidence threshold, 0.75. Error bars indicate the 95% confidence interval.

Fig. 5. F-scores with one application removed from the training set. With the correct confidence threshold choice, the unknown application can be correctly identified.

Detecting Unknown Applications. Figure 5 shows classification results with one application removed from the training set. If the removed application is labeled as unknown, we mark it as a correct prediction. In the majority of the cases, the unknown application is correctly identified as such. The lowest F-Scores are for the BT and SP applications, which are both partial differential equation solvers and they have been shown to have similar behavior [18]. Hence, the classifiers tend to mispredict SP and BT.

The confidence threshold that gives the maximum value for the average F-scores of the unknown input and unknown application cases is 0.75, and Random Forest is the classifier that gives the best average F-score.

Unwanted Applications and Typical Volta Usage. We show Taxonomist's ability to identify unknown applications from different domains by testing with unwanted applications such as bitcoin miners, shown in Fig. 6a, and with 6 months of Volta usage data, shown in Fig. 6b. In both of these tests, we train Taxonomist with the 11 representative applications, and consider the unknown label to be correct. Random Forest, Extra Trees and SVC have an almost perfect F-score for identifying any of these applications as unknown. Combs is not shown, because it is unable to identify unknown applications.

Feature Importance. In order to present the importance of different statistical features and metrics, we train a decision tree for each application, using all of the data from the 11 applications. To compare feature importances, we use *Gini reduction*, which is used to measure the reduction of heterogeneity in the data. A feature that can divide the data set well has a high Gini reduction, which means the resulting divided data sets are more homogeneous. We use the implementation in Python `scikit-learn` library (`sklearn.DecisionTreeClassifier.feature_importances_`).

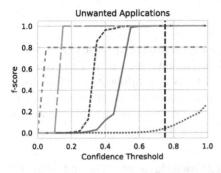
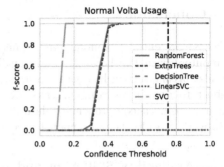

(a) F-scores when tested with bitcoin min- (b) F-scores when tested with HPC appli-
ers and password crackers. cations that are not known to the classifiers.

Fig. 6. The classifiers can correctly identify unknown applications, whether they are
HPC applications or bitcoin miners and password crackers.

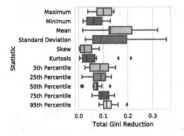
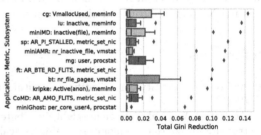

(a) The importance of each statis- (b) The most important metric for each 11 applica-
tical measure. tions and the metric's source subsystem.

Fig. 7. The importance of different metrics and statistics. Box-plots are constructed
using the different decision trees for each application. The box shows the quartiles
while the whiskers show the rest of the distribution except outliers, which are points
away from the low and high quartiles by more than $1.5 \times IQR$.

In the decision trees corresponding to our 11 applications, we calculate the
total Gini reduction of features extracted using the 11 statistics (Sect. 4.2), and
report it in Fig. 7a. The box-plots are constructed using the data from the decision trees, and the individual importance values from the trees are summed up.
Figure 7b shows the most important metric from each decision tree. The important metric and subsystem[1] are highly application specific.

---

[1] metric-set-nic: Cray network counters [9], vmstat: `/proc/vmstat`, meminfo: `/proc/`
`meminfo`, procstat: `/proc/stat`, AR stands for AR-NIC-RSPMON-PARB-EVENT-
CNTR.

7   Conclusion

We have presented Taxonomist, a technique for classifying applications in super-computers with the help of readily available monitoring data. The technique builds classifiers from historical data, and detects new applications while being robust to new input configurations of applications. We have evaluated Taxonomist using a comprehensive data set including controlled experiments and real-world workloads and demonstrated F-scores of over 95%.

Data Availability Statement and Acknowledgment. The datasets generated during and/or analyzed during the current study are available in the Figshare repository: https://doi.org/10.6084/m9.figshare.6384248 [4].

This work has been partially funded by Sandia National Laboratories. Sandia National Laboratories is a multimission laboratory managed and operated by National Technology and Engineering Solutions of Sandia, LLC., a wholly owned subsidiary of Honeywell International, Inc., for the U.S. Department of Energy's National Nuclear Security Administration under Contract DE-NA0003525.

References

1. ASCR cybersecurity for scientific computing integrity. DOE Workshop Report (2015)
2. Agelastos, A., et al.: The lightweight distributed metric service: a scalable infrastructure for continuous monitoring of large scale computing systems and applications. In: International Conference for High Performance Computing, Networking, Storage and Analysis (SC), pp. 154–165 (2014)
3. Agelastos, A., et al.: Toward rapid understanding of production HPC applications and systems. In: IEEE International Conference on Cluster Computing, pp. 464–473 (2015)
4. Ates, E., et al.: Artifact for taxonomist: application detection through rich monitoring data (2018). https://doi.org/10.6084/m9.figshare.6384248
5. Auweter, A., et al.: A case study of energy aware scheduling on SuperMUC. In: Kunkel, J.M., Ludwig, T., Meuer, H.W. (eds.) ISC 2014. LNCS, vol. 8488, pp. 394–409. Springer, Cham (2014). https://doi.org/10.1007/978-3-319-07518-1_25
6. Bailey, D., et al.: The NAS parallel benchmarks. Int. J. Supercomput. Appl. **5**(3), 63–73 (1991)
7. Bhatele, A., Mohror, K., Langer, S.H., Isaacs, K.E.: There goes the neighborhood: performance degradation due to nearby jobs. In: SC 2013, pp. 41:1–41:12. ACM, New York (2013)
8. Combs, J., et al.: Power signatures of high-performance computing workloads. In: Proceedings of the 2nd International Workshop on Energy Efficient Supercomputing, E2SC 2014, pp. 70–78. IEEE Press, Piscataway (2014)
9. Cray: Aries hardware counters (s-0045-20). Technical report (2015). http://docs.cray.com/books/S-0045-20/S-0045-20.pdf
10. Dart, E., Rotman, L., Tierney, B., Hester, M., Zurawski, J.: The science DMZ: a network design pattern for data-intensive science. In: SC 2013, pp. 1–10 (2013)

11. DeMasi, O., Samak, T., Bailey, D.H.: Identifying HPC codes via performance logs and machine learning. In: Proceedings of the First Workshop on Changing Landscapes in HPC Security, pp. 23–30. ACM, New York (2013)

12. Dongarra, J., et al.: The international exascale software project roadmap. Int. J. High Perform. Comput. Appl. **25**(1), 3–60 (2011)

13. Egele, M., Woo, M., Chapman, P., Brumley, D.: Blanket execution: dynamic similarity testing for program binaries and components. In: 23rd USENIX Security Symposium, pp. 303–317. USENIX Association, San Diego (2014)

14. Florez, G., Liu, Z., Bridges, S.M., Skjellum, A., Vaughn, R.B.: Lightweight monitoring of MPI programs in real time: research articles. Concurr. Comput.: Pract. Exp. **17**(13), 1547–1578 (2005)

15. Heroux, M.A., et al.: Improving performance via mini-applications. Technical report SAND2009-5574, Sandia National Laboratories (2009)

16. Hsu, C.W., Chang, C.C., Lin, C.J., et al.: A practical guide to support vector classification. Technical report (2003). https://www.csie.ntu.edu.tw/~cjlin/papers/guide/guide.pdf

17. Kunen, A., Bailey, T., Brown, P.: KRIPKE-a massively parallel transport mini-app. Technical report, Lawrence Livermore National Laboratory, Livermore (2015)

18. Ma, C., et al.: An approach for matching communication patterns in parallel applications. In: IEEE International Symposium on Parallel Distributed Processing, pp. 1–12 (2009)

19. NERSC: Number of NERSC users and projects through the years (2016). www.nersc.gov/about/nersc-usage-and-user-demographics/number-of-nersc-users-and-projects-through-the-years/

20. Office of Inspector General: Semiannual report to congress (2014). https://www.nsf.gov/pubs/2014/oig14002/oig14002.pdf

21. Peisert, S.: Fingerprinting communication and computation on HPC machines. Technical report, Lawrence Berkeley National Laboratory (2010). https://doi.org/10.2172/983323

22. RedLock CSI Team: Lessons from the cryptojacking attack at Tesla. Technical report (2018). https://blog.redlock.io/cryptojacking-tesla

23. Rosenberg, E.: Nuclear scientists logged on to one of Russias most secure computers to mine bitcoin. The Washington Post (2018)

24. Skinner, D., Wright, N., Fuerlinger, K., Yelick, K., Snavely, A.: Integrated performance monitoring IPM (2009). http://ipm-hpc.sourceforge.net/

25. Thebe, O., Bunde, D.P., Leung, V.J.: Scheduling restartable jobs with short test runs. In: Frachtenberg, E., Schwiegelshohn, U. (eds.) JSSPP 2009. LNCS, vol. 5798, pp. 116–137. Springer, Heidelberg (2009). https://doi.org/10.1007/978-3-642-04633-9_7

26. Tuncer, O., et al.: Diagnosing performance variations in HPC applications using machine learning. In: Kunkel, J.M., Yokota, R., Balaji, P., Keyes, D. (eds.) ISC 2017. LNCS, vol. 10266, pp. 355–373. Springer, Cham (2017). https://doi.org/10.1007/978-3-319-58667-0_19

27. Wang, X., Smith, K., Hyndman, R.: Characteristic-based clustering for time series data. Data Min. Knowl. Disc. **13**(3), 335–364 (2006)

28. Whalen, S., Peisert, S., Bishop, M.: Multiclass classification of distributed memory parallel computations. Pattern Recogn. Lett. **34**(3), 322–329 (2013)

29. Zcash Electric Coin Company: Zcash open source miner challenge (2016). www.zcashminers.org

Diagnosing Highly-Parallel OpenMP Programs with Aggregated Grain Graphs

Nico Reissmann and Ananya Muddukrishna[(✉)]

Norwegian University of Science and Technology, Trondheim, Norway
{nico.reissmann,ananya.muddukrishna}@ntnu.no

Abstract. Grain graphs simplify OpenMP performance analysis by visualizing performance problems from a fork-join perspective that is familiar to programmers. However, when programmers decide to expose a high amount of parallelism by creating thousands of task and parallel for-loop chunk instances, the resulting grain graph becomes large and tedious to understand. We present an aggregation method that hierarchically groups related nodes together to reduce grain graphs of any size to one single node. This aggregated graph is then navigated by progressively uncovering groups and following visual clues that guide programmers towards problems while hiding non-problematic regions. Our approach enhances productivity by enabling programmers to understand problems in highly-parallel OpenMP programs with less effort than before.

1 Introduction

The *grain graph* [1] is a recent visualization method that simplifies OpenMP performance analysis by highlighting problems from a fork-join perspective. Task and parallel for-loop chunk instances are collectively termed *grains* in the grain graph method. Grains that suffer performance problems such as work inflation, inadequate parallelism, and low parallelization benefit are pinpointed on the grain graph along with precise links to the problematic source code. This enables programmers to perform optimizations productively without relying on experts or trial-and-error tuning.

Programmers optimize OpenMP programs for large machines with hundreds of cores by exposing a high amount of parallelism during execution. This is achieved by adjusting special program inputs called *cutoffs* and *chunk sizes* such that a large number of fine-grained tasks and for-loop chunks are created. Scalability problems invariably occur when the runtime system is unable to efficiently handle the parallelism exposed [2–4]. These problems are pinpointed on the grain graph using metrics that isolate low parallelization benefit, work inflation, and poor memory hierarchy utilization to specific grains.

However, the large grain graphs resulting from highly-parallel OpenMP execution make problem diagnosis tedious (Fig. 1). Programmers have to zoom and pan to different sections while remembering characteristics of visited sections. Problems that are spread out become difficult to locate. Non-problematic grains

© Springer International Publishing AG, part of Springer Nature 2018
M. Aldinucci et al. (Eds.): Euro-Par 2018, LNCS 11014, pp. 106–119, 2018.
https://doi.org/10.1007/978-3-319-96983-1_8

that are shown dimmed to increase focus on problems combine at lower zoom levels and become pronounced. Programmers can perceive the dimming effect and spot problematic grains only when zoomed into higher levels. A powerful workstation with a large screen and copious amount of memory is required to render large grain graphs responsively. In light of these demands, programmers prefer to pore over text summaries and tabular formats of large graphs and reserve the visual approach only for small graphs.

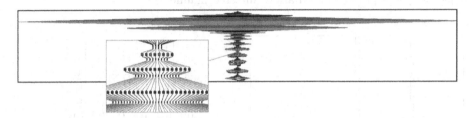

Fig. 1. The grain graph of the task-recursive sort program from the Barcelona OpenMP Task Suite (BOTS) for a high-parallelism input ($n = 20971520$, cutoffs = {65536, 8192, 128}) is dense with 11059 grains. Inset (blue box) zooms into a section at magnification 40X. (Color figure online)

This paper contributes with a new aggregation method that makes visual analysis of large grain graphs practical. The aggregation method (Sect. 3) groups related nodes by matching recurrent patterns in the grain graph, ultimately resulting in an aggregated graph with a single group node. Programmers navigate the aggregated graph by progressively opening and closing groups. Groups with problems are highlighted and non-problematic sections are removed from sight for distraction-free diagnosis. Navigation is further sped up through new group-based metrics that enable programmers to traverse the critical path and compare groups for structural similarity. Using highly-parallel executions of standard OpenMP programs, we demonstrate (Sects. 3 and 4) that aggregated grain graphs enhance the state-of-the-art in OpenMP problem diagnosis.

2   Background on Grain Graphs

The grain graph [1] is a visualization for OpenMP that connects performance problems to the fork-join program structure at the resolution of *grains* – task and parallel for-loop chunk instances created during execution. This simplifies problem diagnosis as programmers can readily identify with the fork-join program structure. In contrast, existing visualizations based on timeliness and call graphs complicate diagnosis by connecting performance problems to scheduling events that are unfamiliar and unpredictable to programmers [1,5]. Experts who understand scheduling internals nevertheless find it tiring to follow timelines and call graphs that depict recursive task-based execution – a popular style of using OpenMP.

2.1 Structure

The grain graph is a directed acyclic graph whose nodes denote grains and run-time system operations, and edges denote control-flow. Parent and child grains are shown in close proximity on the graph using *logical-time* placement [5,6] to maintain familiarity with the fork-join perspective (Fig. 2a[1]). The grain graph is laid out using the *Sugiyama* layout [7,8]. This layout places nodes in layers, removes cycles, and prevents edge crossings. These features are essential to depict fork-join progression in an uncluttered manner.

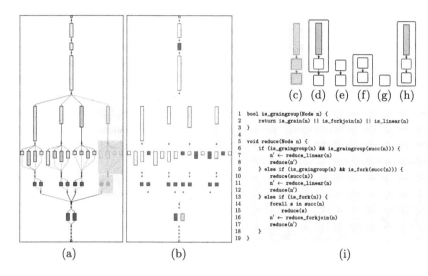

(c) (d) (e) (f) (g) (h)

```
1   bool is_graingroup(Node n) {
2       return is_grain(n) || is_forkjoin(n) || is_linear(n)
3   }
4
5   void reduce(Node n) {
6       if (is_graingroup(n) && is_graingroup(succ(n))) {
7           n' ← reduce_linear(n)
8           reduce(n')
9       } else if (is_graingroup(n) && is_fork(succ(n))) {
10          reduce(succ(n))
11          n' ← reduce_linear(n)
12          reduce(n')
13      } else if (is_fork(n)) {
14          forall s in succ(n)
15              reduce(s)
16          n' ← reduce_forkjoin(n)
17          reduce(n')
18      }
19  }
```

(a)   (b)   (i)

Fig. 2. Grain graph of the task-based Sort program from BOTS for small input ($n = 512$, $cutoffs = \{256, 64, 16\}$). (a) Structural view (b) problem view highlighting low parallel benefit in red (c) after two fork-join pattern reductions of the highlighted subgraph (d–g) linear pattern reductions leading to a single group node (h) after normalization (i) reduction pseudocode (Color figure online)

2.2 Diagnosing Problems

Grains are annotated with unique schedule-independent identifiers, links to source code locations, as well as performance metrics measured during profiling and derived post profiling. Profiled metrics include execution time, cache miss ratio, memory latency, and timestamps of control-flow events such as grain creation and synchronization. These metrics are used to compute derived metrics such as critical path, work deviation, instantaneous parallelism, memory hierarchy utilization, scatter, load balance, and parallel benefit.

Parallel benefit is a custom metric used in several discussions of this paper. It is computed by dividing a grain's execution time by its parallelization cost

---

[1] Readers should print in color as they are crucial to appreciate grains graphs.

including creation time. This metric aids inlining and cutoff decisions as grains with low parallel benefit should be executed sequentially to reduce overhead.

Commonly sought out metrics are encoded visually for quick identification on the graph (Fig. 2a). The length of a grain is set proportional to its execution time. Grain colors denote source code locations by default. Edges are colored by type and highlighted red if they are on the critical path.

Grains with metric values that cross programmer-defined thresholds are inferred as problematic. The thresholds have sensible values by default. Problematic grains are highlighted with a color that encodes problem severity in a separate view while non-problematic grains are dimmed (Fig. 2b). Additionally, problems are summarized in a separate text file and highlighted in a tabular form of the grain graph shown on a separate visualization widget.

Grain graphs have multiple conceptual views with colors encoding a single problem or property per view. Programmers shift between these views to understand properties or tackle problems. Problematic grains are highlighted and non-problematic grains are dimmed, and clicking on a grain opens a separate window that shows the grain's properties and performance metrics. Figure 2a–b show the programmer cycling between the low parallel benefit problem view and the structural view where no problems are highlighted.

3   Grain Graph Aggregation Method

Our aggregation method for grain graphs conceptually consists of four phases:

1. **Reduction** matches and replaces subgraph patterns with group nodes to construct an *aggregation tree*. This tree captures the graph structure and serves as a basis for further processing. After aggregation is complete, the tree is converted back to an aggregated grain graph with problematic grains exposed and non-problematic grains hidden.
2. **Normalization** transforms the aggregation tree into a canonical form, simplifying further processing.
3. **Propagation** propagates grain metrics at the leaves of the tree to upper levels in a sensible manner.
4. **Separation** transforms the aggregation tree to separate problematic nodes. This enables grouping and hiding of non-problematic grains in the resulting aggregated graph.

The algorithmic complexity of all four phases is linear in the number of graph nodes plus edges. The rest of this section explains the phases in detail and discusses the navigation of the resulting aggregated graph at the end.

3.1   Reduction

The reduction phase matches a *fork-join* and *linear* pattern, and replaces them with group nodes to construct an *aggregation tree*. The fork-join pattern consists of a single fork node connected to child grains or groups, which in turn are connected to a join node (Fig. 2c). The linear pattern has two nodes, either a grain or a group node, that are connected to each other (Fig. 2d). Both patterns are repeatedly matched, and replaced by a single group node until the entire grain graph is reduced to a single node (Fig. 2d–g).

The pseudocode of the reduction algorithm is shown in (Fig. 2i). The key steps in the pseudocode are explained next:

- Line 6 matches the linear pattern (Fig. 2d–g). It uses the helper function *is_graingroup* to detect whether a node and its successor is a grain or a group, and reduces the pattern to a linear group node. Reduction continues with the newly-created group node.
- Line 9 matches a grain or group node with a fork node as successor. The matched fork node is recursively aggregated to a fork-join group node (Fig. 2c). The resulting linear pattern is then reduced to a linear group node. Reduction continues with the linear group node.
- Line 13 matches a fork node (Fig. 2a) and recursively aggregates all successors of the fork node. The resulting fork-join pattern is then reduced to a fork-join group node. Reduction continues with the fork-join group node.

The grain graph is reduced greedily by the reduction algorithm. It always continues with the newly-created group node after a pattern match and never traverses past a join node. This ensures that the innermost fork-join in a nesting is reduced first.

The aggregation tree consisting of group and grain nodes explicitly captures the grain graph's nesting and fork-join structure. The leaves of the tree are grains and its intermediate nodes are the newly-created group nodes. Linear group nodes have the two matched nodes from the pattern as children, whereas fork-join group nodes have the children of the matched fork node as children.

The reduction algorithm is applicable to grain graphs where parents synchronize with all their children before completion. This essential property ensures that fork-join patterns are properly nested, permitting their reduction in a hierarchy of group nodes. While this property holds for well-behaved OpenMP 3.X programs, the *taskgroup* construct in OpenMP 4.0 violates this property. The construct permits parents to synchronize with their children and descendants in one step. This impedes reduction unless the grain graph is restructured so that all descendants are placed as immediate children of the root parent.

3.2   Normalization

Normalization transforms the aggregation tree into a canonical form by flattening nested linear group nodes. In the reduction phase, linear group nodes are always created for a pair of grain or group nodes, even if more nodes are chained together. This constructs nested linear subtrees where linear group nodes are the children of other linear group nodes as exemplified in Fig. 2d–g. Normalization flattens these subtrees to a single linear group node with all non-linear group nodes from the subtree as its children (Fig. 2h). In practice, this phase can be incorporated into the previous phase to speedup aggregation.

3.3 Propagation

This phase propagates leaf node metrics to the enclosing groups all the way up to the root node. It traverses the aggregation tree in post-order and attributes group nodes with metrics sensibly-derived from their children. For example, the *work* metric of a group node is the sum of the execution times of its children, while the schedule-independent identifiers of children are concatenated with the group node's depth to derive a schedule-independent identifier.

Metrics are attributed such that problems propagate to the root group. If a child is problematic, then its parent is marked as problematic as well. The minimum of the memory hierarchy utilization, parallel benefit, and instantaneous parallelism as well as the maximum of the load balance, work deviation, and scatter metrics of children are attributed to the parent group. Programmers can refine existing propagation metrics and define new ones. Given this ability, the range of values and other summary statistics of a group can be easily captured (for example, as string attributes). One useful custom metric that programmers could define is the percentage of time spent by a group on the critical path.

3.4 Separation

The separation phase groups non-problematic nodes to separate them from problematic nodes. This enables programmers to focus on problems and reduces graph viewer load. For example, consider a fork-join group that encloses a thousand grains among which only a single grain is problematic. An unseparated graph would require all grains to be rendered, while a separated graph requires only the rendering of one problematic grain and a non-problematic group node.

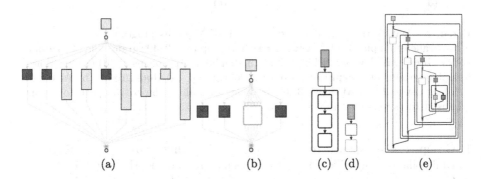

Fig. 3. Separation of problematic from non-problematic nodes. (a–b) Fork-join node separation. (c–d) Linear node separation. (e) Local (blue) and global (red) critical paths (Color figure online)

Separation traverses the aggregation tree in post-order and separates subtrees rooted at fork-join and linear nodes. In a fork-join separation, all non-problematic children of a fork-join node are grouped under a newly-created group node (Fig. 3a–b), while in a linear node separation, all consecutive non-problematic children of a linear group node are grouped under a new linear group node (Fig. 3c–d). After the separation phase, the aggregation tree is converted back to a grain graph where non-problematic subgraphs are hidden.

3.5   Navigation

The navigation of an aggregated graph starts at the root and continues by progressively opening/closing group nodes to understand graph structure and problems (Fig. 4). In contrast to the navigation in unaggregated graphs, the cognitive load on programmers and the graph viewer's resources are reduced as only a subset of the grains are laid out. Navigation is sped up using several optimizations:

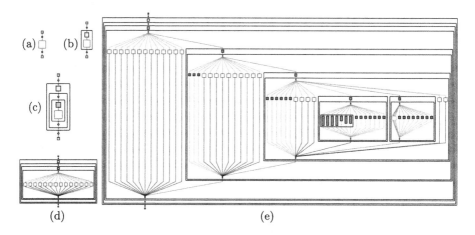

Fig. 4. Navigating the aggregated grain graph of NQueens program from BOTS for high-parallelism input ($n = 14$, $cutoff = 4$). The graph has 21492 grains and 3073 group nodes. Grains with low parallel benefit are highlighted as problems. (a–d) Drilling down to sibling groups at a depth of 3 from the root group. (a) Root group. (b) At depth 1. (c) At depth 2. (d) At depth 3. (e) Drilling down along the critical path to sibling groups at the lowest depth.

1. Groups can be opened to show all grains including those inside subgroups (full collapse), or drilled down to a specific group or depth level (Fig. 4).
2. Group nodes are drawn as rounded rectangles with no filling to differentiate them from grains. Group metrics are shown in a separate property window, similar to grains. Opened groups grow as large as required to envelop members whereas closed group nodes have a constant size. The borders of problematic closed groups are colored red to draw programmer attention, while the borders of non-problematic groups are colored green for quick identification. Our choices of group colors and sizes allow programmers already familiar with grain graphs to smoothly transit to the aggregation feature.

3. Once a group's structure is known, other similarly structured groups can be navigated confidently or skipped if problem-free. For example, twelve groups in Fig. 4d have the same structure. Group similarity is computed on-demand using a Weisfeiler-Lehman graph kernel [9].

4. Groups on the *global critical path* (gcb) are inspected first since they are good optimization candidates (Fig. 4e). The local critical path of groups not on the gcb can be computed on-demand and used for prioritized inspection (Fig. 3e). If off-gcb grains are optimized to reduce the total amount of work, the resulting slack can be used to execute grains on the gcb.

4   Prototype Implementation

The grain graph visualization is implemented in a prototype [10] that produces grain graphs in GRAPHML by processing profiling data from OMPT extensions [11] or the MIR runtime system [4,12,13]. We extended the prototype to produce aggregated graphs upon programmer request [14]. The aggregation method was implemented in C++, leveraging support for nested groups [15] in GRAPHML and using the igraph [16] library for basic graph processing.

We used the graph viewer yEd [17] to visualize aggregated grain graphs since it has sufficiently mature support for GRAPHML files with nested aggregations. For example, it has features to interactively open and close groups, and jump to groups at any hierarchy level. Its property editor dialog shows the annotations of group nodes. Switching between problem views was achieved by cycling through tabs that highlighted different problems.

External programs parameterized by group identifiers were used to compute local critical path and similarity. These programs do not update the visualization and programmers are required to manually load their output into yEd. Similarity was computed using a third-party implementation [18] of the Weisfeiler-Lehman graph kernel.

We recognize that interactions with aggregated graphs in yED have quite some room for improvement. Our plan is to incorporate improvements in a dedicated grain graph viewer as yEd is closed-source. The dedicated viewer will also enable programmers to define custom metrics derived from basic grain and group metrics in a GUI. This improves over the prototype where programmers customize metrics by editing source-code in convenient locations.

5   Evaluation

We tested our prototype on C/C++ benchmarks from SPEC OMP 2012 (SPEC-OMP12), Barcelona OpenMP Task Suite v2.1.2 (BOTS) and Parsec v3.0 (Parsec). The benchmarks were compiled with MIR-linked GCC v4.4.7 and profiled on a 48-core machine with 64 GB memory and four AMD Opteron 6172 processors running at 2.1 GHz with frequency scaling disabled. We provided input values that exposed abundant, fine-grained parallelism to standard OpenMP programs to obtain large grain graphs (Table 1).

5.1   Visible Node Count

We use the metric *visible node count* (θ) to judge the ability of our aggregation method to reduce programmer effort in navigating and diagnosing problems. θ is defined as the minimum number of visible nodes in a grain graph while diagnosing a problematic grain. If it is small, the cognitive load on programmers and the resource requirements of viewers are reduced.

The visible node count for a problematic grain in an aggregated graph is the number of nodes exposed by opening groups in the path leading to the grain. In contrast, the visible node count in an unaggregated graph is equal to the number of nodes in the entire graph irrespective of the position of the problematic grain, assuming programmers do not pan and zoom to the vicinity of the problematic grain manually.

Table 1 shows the maximum θ for two cases. The first is a conservative case (θ_c^{max}) that assumes all grains in the graph are problematic, while the second (θ_{pb}^{max}) considers graphs with low parallel benefit. For both cases, the reduction in maximum θ compared to the total size of the graph, *i.e.*, the maximum θ for the unaggregated graph, is reported as *Savings*.

Table 1. Benefit of aggregation for standard OpenMP benchmarks.

Benchmark	Input	#Nodes	#Grains	θ_c^{max}	Savings (%)	Low parallel benefit		
						#Prbl. Grains	θ_{pb}^{max}	Savings (%)
Strassen[a]	8192, 128, 2000	176480	137258	60	99.97	157	49	99.97
Bodytrack[b]	B261, 4, 261, 4000, 5, 3, 48, 0	126615	69061	5767	95.45	24627	5757	95.45
Floorplan[a]	15, 7	117960	82490	149	99.87	31125	148	99.87
376.kdtree[c]	200000, 10, 2	32808	16400	58	99.82	2055	57	99.83
NQueens[a]	14, 4	24565	21492	70	99.71	10540	66	99.73
359.botsspar[c]	64, 64	24161	23905	1154	95.22	2	9	99.96
358.botsalgn[c]	prot.200.aa	20505	20101	406	98.02	7	17	99.92
Sort[a]	20971520, 65536, 8192, 128	20293	11509	55	99.73	288	51	99.75
FFT[a]	16777216, 8192, 2	9240	4592	53	99.43	414	49	99.47
367.imagick[c]	See caption of Fig. 5	3935	3801	405	89.71	649	182	95.37
Blackscholes[b]	4M	2205	1201	112	94.92	400	112	94.92
Freqmine[b]	kosarak_990k.dat, 790	2111	2017	389	81.57	66	30	98.58

[a] BOTS
[b] Parsec
[c] SPEC-OMP12

For the conservative case, we see a large reduction in θ. The biggest saving is 99.97% for the Strassen benchmark and the smallest saving is 81.57% for Freqmine, with an average saving of 95.98%. This shows that aggregation can significantly reduce θ for any problematic grain in our evaluation setup.

For the second case, we see a further reduction in θ since non-problematic grains are grouped during the separation phase (Sect. 3). Benchmarks Freqmine, 367.imagick, 358.botsalgn, 359.botsspar, show large savings from aggregation since they contain a small number of problematic grains. On the other hand,

Bodytrack and Floorplan show barely any improvement over the conservative case due to a higher concentration of problematic grains that are clustered as siblings. Problematic siblings are ignored during separation by design.

5.2 Reducing Distractions

We further illustrate the benefit of aggregation using the 367.imagick benchmark from SPEC-OMP12 for an input that SPEC programmers noticed as poorly scaling. The unaggregated grain graph shows a chain of nine dense for-loops (Fig. 5a). The sixth loop contains several chunks that suffer from low parallel benefit since several instances of the parallelization-throttling macro *omp_throttle* are missing in the source. Diagnosing these problematic chunks requires programmers to sweep attentively across the graph ignoring the abundance of non-problematic grains and the frequent non-responsive rendering of the graph. The aggregated graph enables programmers to diagnose problematic chunks group by group (Fig. 5b), keeping only those groups with problematic chunks open, while uninteresting loops and non-problematic chunks are hidden from sight. This results in a more responsive graph viewer since fewer nodes need to be rendered.

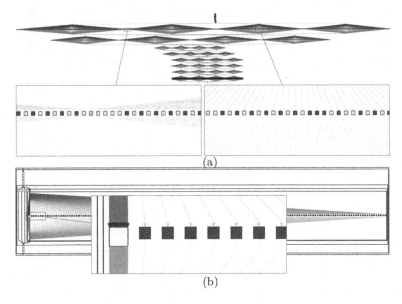

Fig. 5. Diagnosing problems with grains of 367.imagick from SPEC-OMP12 for input -shear 31 -resize 1280 x 960 -negate -edge 14 -implode 1.2 -flop -convolve 1,2,1,4,3,4,1,2,1 -edge 100 ref/input/input1.tga. (a) Sweeping across the entire unaggregated graph with 3801 grains to spot problems. (b) Aggregated grain graph enables programmers to diagnose problematic grains group-wise. Non-problematic grains are separated to promote focus (inset).

5.3 Similarity Across Runs

Grain graphs produced from two independent executions of a given program can be different in shape due to unpredictable inlining decisions taken by the runtime system or if the program adapts its behavior sensitive to available execution resources. Understanding such changes can provide vital clues for problem diagnosis. However, detecting the dissimilar sections by manually inspecting a pair of large grain graphs is extremely tiring and akin to finding matches between fingerprints using a magnifying lens.

Similarity is a powerful metric that not just helps to skip over structurally similar groups within the same graph (as demonstrated in Sect. 3.5), but can also compare groups across runs to detect structural differences. Programmers can gradually open two graphs side-by-side and compute the similarity metric for visible groups using their schedule-independent identifiers. Those groups

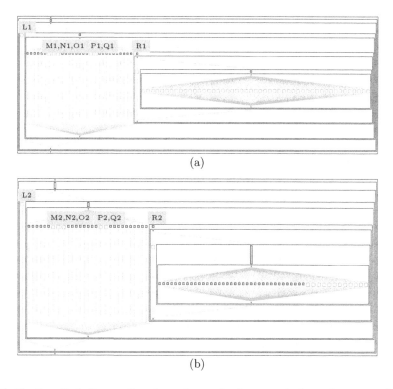

(a)

(b)

Fig. 6. Finding dissimilar sections in grain graphs from two independent executions of the non-deterministic Floorplan program from BOTS for input `cell-file = input.5`, `cutoff = 5`. (a) Graph produced from execution on 4 cores has 7974 grains. (b) Graph produced from execution on 48 cores has 3190 grains. The similarity metric allows programmers to understand without inspection that groups L1-2, M1-2, N1-2, and O1-2 have the same structure but P1-2, Q1-2, and R1-2 do not. Groups R1-2 are opened to show the dissimilarity. R2 encloses fewer subgroups than R1.

that have the same identifier but different similarity metrics are the sections that have changed between the graphs. We demonstrate this for the Floorplan program from BOTS in Fig. 6. Floorplan is a search-based program whose pruning behavior changes non-deterministically when more cores are allotted for execution.

6 Related Work

Aggregation is a standard approach to scale visualizations with increasing data [19, 20]. Sensible dimensions for aggregation include the program structure (e.g. tasks), middleware stack (worker threads), physical processing components (processors), and the visualization (node-links). However, aggregation can remove vital diagnosis data when applied aggressively across several dimensions. Isaacs et al. [19] recognize the balance between aggregation aggressiveness and information preservation as an important challenge. Our method strives to maintain this balance by reducing the size of the rendered graph and focusing it on problematic sections, while keeping the expected fork-join perspective.

For space reasons, we restrict the discussion to abstraction-centric, logical-time aggregated visualizations similar to grain graphs, and refer readers for other visualizations to recent surveys [19, 20] and a visualization explorer [21].

The dominant aggregation scheme in visualizations is statistical rather than visual, *i.e.*, metrics of selected elements in the main visualization are aggregated statistically and reported separately, typically as a property table [22–27]. The cognitive load of the main visualization is only reduced by zooming out to focus on large elements, while support for visual aggregation at the same zoom level is absent. Consequently, such visualizations suffer similar navigation and diagnosis difficulties as large unaggregated grain graphs.

The aggregation method for task graphs in *DAGViz* [28] resembles our work. It presents programmers with a single aggregated node that can be interactively opened to reveal subgraphs as well as a dedicated viewer. However, our approach is tailored to grain graphs and is unique in tracing the critical path and identifying the similarity of subgraphs. Unaggregated grain graphs are more effective in pinpointing problems than unaggregated DAGViz graphs due to more derived metrics. The expansion of DAGViz graphs results also in the rendering of more nodes as they show a fork-node per grain. Grain graphs avoid this thanks to fork-node reductions that produce a fork-node per set of siblings. DAGViz combats the scaling problem by using an elegant aggregation method that reduces subgraphs that executed wholly on a single worker-thread into a single, non-collapsible node.

ThreadScope [29] visualizes the logical-time structure of task-parallel programs. Its memory operations nodes can be grouped to improve clarity, but it is unclear whether programmers can interact with groups to uncover members.

The *causality graph* [30] visualization permits programmers to manually select and repeatedly aggregate nodes into *supernodes*, while special care must be taken to avoid graph cycles on their creation. Supernode metrics include the local critical path and metrics computed using user-defined combinators. The causality graph presents an unaggregated graph by default, while we present a fully aggregated graph and use sensible aggregation metrics to guide programmers.

7   Conclusion

This paper contributes an aggregation method for grain graphs that enables programmers to easily understand problems in highly-parallel OpenMP programs. Our method groups nodes arranged in recurring patterns to produce an aggregated graph that programmers can navigate by progressively opening and closing groups. Problematic groups are highlighted and non-problematic sections are cleared from sight, enabling focus without compromising the fork-join perspective expected by programmers. Using standard OpenMP programs as examples, we demonstrate a significant reduction of visible nodes throughout problem diagnosis. For future work, we plan to implement a dedicated grain graph viewer that smoothly and precisely guides programmers towards OpenMP problems and hints at solutions.

Acknowledgment. The paper was funded by the TULIPP project (grant number 688403) and the READEX project (grant number 671657) from the EU Horizon 2020 Research and Innovation programme. The authors thank NTNU colleagues Peder Voldnes Langdal, Magnus Själander, Jan Christian Meyer, and Magnus Jahre for constructive comments and KTH Royal Institute of Technology for providing test machinery.

References

1. Muddukrishna, A., et al.: Grain graphs: OpenMP performance analysis made easy. In: PPoPP (2016)
2. Olivier, S.L., et al.: Characterizing and mitigating work time inflation in task parallel programs. In: SC (2012)
3. Yoo, R.M., et al.: Locality-aware task management for unstructured parallelism: a quantitative limit study. In: SPAA (2013)
4. Muddukrishna, A., et al.: Locality-aware task scheduling and data distribution for OpenMP programs on NUMA systems and manycore processors. Sci. Program. **2015** (2015). https://doi.org/10.1155/2015/981759. Article no. 5
5. Isaacs, K.E., et al.: Combing the communication hairball: visualizing large-scale parallel execution traces using logical time. In: InfoVis (2014)
6. Cuny, J.E., et al.: Logical time in visualizations produced by parallel programs. In: IEEE Conference on Visualization (1992)
7. Sugiyama, K., et al.: Methods for visual understanding of hierarchical system structures. SMC **11**, 109–125 (1981)
8. Eiglsperger, M., et al.: An efficient implementation of Sugiyama's algorithm for layered graph drawing. In: International Symposium on Graph Drawing (2004)
9. Shervashidze, N., et al.: Weisfeiler-Lehman graph kernels. JMLR **12**, 2539–2561 (2011)

10. Muddukrishna, A., et al.: anamud/grain-graphs: Grain Graphs v1.0.0 (2017). https://doi.org/10.5281/zenodo.439355
11. Langdal, P.V., Jahre, M., Muddukrishna, A.: Extending OMPT to support grain graphs. In: de Supinski, B.R., Olivier, S.L., Terboven, C., Chapman, B.M., Müller, M.S. (eds.) IWOMP 2017. LNCS, vol. 10468, pp. 141–155. Springer, Cham (2017). https://doi.org/10.1007/978-3-319-65578-9_10
12. Muddukrishna, A., et al.: anamud/mir-dev: MIR v1.0.0 (2017). https://doi.org/10.5281/zenodo.439351
13. Muddukrishna, A., et al.: Characterizing task-based OpenMP programs. PLoS ONE 10(4), e0123545 (2015). https://doi.org/10.1371/journal.pone.0123545
14. Reissmann, N.: phate/ggraph: VPA17 (2017). https://doi.org/10.5281/zenodo.836838
15. Brandes, U., et al.: GRAPHML primer (2017). http://graphml.graphdrawing.org/primer/graphml-primer.html. Accessed 27 July 2017
16. Csardi, G., et al.: The igraph software package for complex network research. Inter-Journal 1695, 1–9 (2006)
17. yWorks GmBh: yEd Graph Editor (2015). http://www.yworks.com/en/products_yed_about.html. Accessed 10 Apr 2015
18. Sugiyama, M., et al.: GraphKernels: R and python packages for graph comparison. Bioinformatics 34, 530–532 (2017)
19. Isaacs, K.E., et al.: State of the art of performance visualization. In: EuroVis (2014)
20. Von Landesberger, T., et al.: Visual analysis of large graphs: state-of-the-art and future research challenges. In: Computer Graphics Forum (2011)
21. Katherine I.: Performance visualization: living digital library of state of the art of performance visualization (2017). http://cgi.cs.arizona.edu/~kisaacs/STAR/. Accessed 31 July 2017
22. Brinkmann, S., Gracia, J., Niethammer, C.: Task debugging with TEMANEJO. In: Cheptsov, A., Brinkmann, S., Gracia, J., Resch, M., Nagel, W. (eds.) Tools for High Performance Computing 2012, pp. 13–21. Springer, Heidelberg (2013). https://doi.org/10.1007/978-3-642-37349-7_2
23. Barcelona Supercomputing Center: OmpSs task dependency graph (2013). http://pm.bsc.es/ompss-docs/user-guide/run-programs-plugin-instrument-tdg.html. Accessed 10 Apr 2015
24. Subotic, V., et al.: Programmability and portability for exascale: top down programming methodology and tools with StarSs. J. Comput. Sci. 4, 450–456 (2013)
25. Blochinger, W., et al.: Visualizing structural properties of irregular parallel computations. In: VISSOFT (2005)
26. Haugen, B., et al.: Visualizing execution traces with task dependencies. In: VPA (2015)
27. Drebes, A., Bréjon, J.-B., Pop, A., Heydemann, K., Cohen, A.: Language-centric performance analysis of OpenMP programs with aftermath. In: Maruyama, N., de Supinski, B.R., Wahib, M. (eds.) IWOMP 2016. LNCS, vol. 9903, pp. 237–250. Springer, Cham (2016). https://doi.org/10.1007/978-3-319-45550-1_17
28. Huynh, A., et al.: DAGViz: a DAG visualization tool for analyzing task-parallel program traces. In: VPA (2015)
29. Wheeler, K.B.: Visualizing massively multithreaded applications with Thread-Scope. Concurr. Comput.: Pract. Exp. 22, 45–67 (2010)
30. Zernik, D., et al.: Using visualization tools to understand concurrency. IEEE Softw. 9, 87–92 (1992)

Characterization of Smartphone Governor Strategies

Sarbartha Banerjee[(✉)] and Lizy Kurian John

University of Texas at Austin, Austin, TX 78705, USA
{sarbartha,ljohn}@utexas.edu

Abstract. The voltage and frequency of the various components of a smartphone processor such as CPU cores, graphics, multimedia and display units can be independently controlled by their own dynamic voltage and frequency (DVFS) governors to fit the requirement of the workload. The dynamic change of the voltage and frequency performed by governors is targeted either towards achieving the optimal performance with the minimum energy consumption or choosing a mode which requires minimum supervision of workload and minimal change of DVFS modes (since changes in modes are accompanied by overheads of switching).

This paper explores the behaviour of different governors run on a wide variety of workloads and enlists the best strategy for different scenarios exemplifying the need for workload characterization. We also analyze the performance and power efficiency of workloads in a system having a common power source and study their behavior when multiple such blocks are operating together pushing the power source to its limit. Our results show that choosing the correct CPU governor alone is not sufficient but tuning the DVFS of different resources is necessary to achieve the best performance with minimum energy expenditure. We observe that the *powersave* governor does not always give the best energy efficiency. It was found to be sub-optimal for CPU intensive workloads due to increased execution time. Moreover, the *race-to-idle* strategy was found to be optimal for workloads in which one component is utilized for majority of the time. These results demonstrate the necessity for characterizing workloads and tuning the DVFS while distributing the power between the various components based on the workload's characteristics.

Keywords: SoC · Governor · Power budget · Race-to-idle · Pace-to-idle

1 Introduction

Getting desirable performance with optimum energy efficiency have become the major design criteria for modern smartphones. This is primarily because battery technology development has been much slower than processor development, with the form factor of the phones limiting the battery capacity and the stringent thermal limit of the device. To address this issue, all modern smartphones have multiple DVFS (Dynamic Voltage Frequency Scaling) modes to run different components in the most efficient mode. In typical DVFS, the frequency and the voltage of the processor is modified based on the component utilization. Tuning the frequency of the essential component not only saves

© Springer International Publishing AG, part of Springer Nature 2018
M. Aldinucci et al. (Eds.): Euro-Par 2018, LNCS 11014, pp. 120–134, 2018.
https://doi.org/10.1007/978-3-319-96983-1_9

power but also increases performance in certain scenarios. In smartphones, sometimes a single power source is shared among various components. There is a peak power limit of the power source in addition to thermal constraints. These constraints led to the development of new governor strategies which are not only focused on increasing performance but also tackling the workload in the most energy efficient way.

The availability of DVFS in different components and a high number of DVFS modes within a component makes the optimal choice very difficult. Moreover, providing the user with a satisfactory performance for prolonged period with high energy and thermal efficiency has become a new paradigm.

One simple heuristic for power management using DVFS is to run the job on the target system at the maximum possible frequency (maximum performance mode) and then throttle down to minimum or deep-sleep state as quickly as possible. This method is termed as *race-to-idle*. This method is simple, reduces latency and saves energy in certain use cases. The energy saving comes from the fact that the processing unit is active for the minimum amount of time and leakage power is saved in inactive modes. But, its validity and usefulness is yet to be conclusively established for smartphones as workloads tend to use different resources intermittently sometimes using multiple processing units at the same time. More complex methods can optimally switch the processor frequently to the optimum DVFS mode based on the workload performance requirement by polling the resource usage and trying to finish it in the most energy efficient manner. This is termed as *pace-to-idle*. But in such cases, some energy is wasted monitoring the workload continuously. Moreover, mapping a workload dynamically into heterogeneous clusters of multicore processors and various accelerators like the GPU cannot be done without efficient workload behavior characterization.

Furthermore, there are situations when the smartphone is running on low battery. Normally, the frequency of all the blocks are toned down to consume less energy. But the increasing leakage current raises the question if it really increases the energy efficiency when we need to run an application on the system at lower frequency?

Thus, understanding the workload behavior is essential while choosing the governor. At least if one can classify the workload and figure out the functional units needed, it will greatly help in choosing an appropriate governor for each resource. Also, most of the governors are designed for the CPU. But global decision of the various DVFS modes in an energy constrained system based on the workload improves the power efficiency and less temperature rise of the smartphone system-on-chip (SoC).

Our study encompasses the analysis of various categories of governors for different kind of workloads to explain the optimal strategy in a mobile platform. The race-to-idle strategy has been shown to be effective for servers where the quality of service and latency of the requests are important. But for mobile devices, an acceptable quality of service is desirable within the bounds of power limit of the source must be provided while respecting the thermal limits making it an optimization problem.

Some power-hungry governors are good for performance while some relaxed governors might be power saving. With the availability of multiple DVFS modes, finite DVFS switching time and workload detection, researchers are coming up with improved governors that predict the pattern of the workload and choose the appropriate DVFS point. The analysis shown in the paper is a start point for any governor designer to make reasonable decisions for a governor.

The rest of the paper is organized in the following format: Sect. 2 provides background about the DVFS modes, the governors and their characteristics. Section 3 elaborates on the experimental setup. Section 4 explains the workloads and benchmarks used. Section 5 shows results of our experiments. Section 6 explains the benchmark characteristics and their behavior with different governors. Section 7 provides our observations from the experiments conducted and conclusion in Sect. 8.

2 Background

The smartphone system on a chip (SoC) comprises of multi-core CPUs, a GPU and multimedia units running on a separate DVFS point while sharing the same current source. With the demand for new aggressive power saving techniques, designers have added more voltage-frequency (VF) points to individual units and added governors for independent control of different units. Power can be saved if one enables the desired unit at the appropriate frequency. But switching the DVFS modes consumes energy and has non-zero latency. Too much switching is also not desirable. In addition, every unit can also be separately put in the different idle power modes like clock gating, retention or deep sleep. All these low power modes have different wake up latency and leakage current consumed.

2.1 Governors

In this section, we will first give a brief overview of the types of CPU governors present in the Linux kernel of an android smartphone today and then go over some of the common governors and frequency scaling points of other units in the SoC.

Performance Governor. This governor is a constant frequency governor which keeps the system in highest possible voltage and frequency irrespective of the workload. This is highly power hungry and the core latches itself to maximum frequency. Worth noting is that this governor works best when a series of compute intensive job is run in the system. Moreover, it also keeps the bus to DDR at its peak frequency. It doesn't waste extra time and power in DVFS switching. But keeping the processor in this frequency can cause thermal throttling and unnecessarily running it near the peak current of the supply. But once the processor run queue is empty, it goes back to the sleep state. It is considered as a 'race' governor which finishes the job as quickly and goes to idle.

Interactive and Ondemand Governor. The ondemand governor [2] switches the system in highest possible voltage and frequency whenever a job is scheduled and immediately ramps down to lower frequency when the resource utilization fades. The interactive governor find the optimal frequency based on the load average of the system. If the load average is more than a pre-specified value, it switches to higher frequencies. Similarly, if the load average is low, the ondemand ramps down immediately while the interactive waits for a certain hysteresis time. This works well when we have a sequence of compute intensive jobs interspersed with long delays. The immediate return to low frequency ensures that it spends minimum time in the highest DVFS mode. However, if the idle time between jobs is very low, this governor hops between frequencies repeatedly. The Interactive governor adds a hysteresis timer on top of the ondemand governor to filter some of the switching. This governor can be considered as a pace' governor which will adapt the frequency based on the workload requirement.

Powersave Governor. Powersave governor is designed to save energy by running the CPU at the lowest possible operating frequency. This gives slow response but reduces average power in many situations and is often used when battery is low or during thermal throttling. It also gives good performance when the application is using another component of the SoC like the GPU with minimal CPU utilization but might falter in certain cases as the overall energy consumption may exceed others due to significantly higher runtime. It also fails to attain desirable QoS and provide poor user experience.

GPU Governors. Most of the chips have GPU as a proprietary unit, so the governors supported are specific to the hardware used in the experiment. Since our test setup had a Qualcomm Snapdragon processor, we will list down a couple of GPU governors.

Most of the fancy governors are largely pacing governors whose performance lie between the performance and the powersave governors. *Msm-adreno-tz* is one such governor which works like the interactive governor and tunes based on the GPUbusy data stating GPU utilization. It also has *performance* and *powersave* governors which are like the CPU counterparts working of GPU frequencies.

The optimization of the GPU governors can improve energy efficiency of the overall system as it is a high-power resource. Thus, the above options do tell us that battery power saving is not only limited to the CPUs but in every units of the SoC. Similar changes can be done to the DDR frequency and multimedia components.

2.2 DVFS Points

Owing to the need to save power and to provide flexibility to choose the appropriate mode to perform a task, hardware designers provide several DVFS points for different resources. Our testing platform is a Dragonboard 410c [14] platform consisting of a Qualcomm Snapdragon 410 processor having Quad-core ARM A53 processor with all four cores running at the same voltage & frequency. The cores can be independently put into low power mode but they cannot be run at different frequency. This Snapdragon processor supports the following eight different frequency points each having a different voltage.

• 1209 MHz	• 800 MHz
• 1152 MHz	• 533 MHz
• 1094 MHz	• 400 MHz
• 998 MHz	• 200 MHz

Apart from that the DDR memory also has different frequencies of 533, 400 or 200 MHz. Either it can be scaled independently or in tandem with the CPU frequency. Similarly, the GPU has its own independent DVFS modes but shares the same power rail as the CPU and others.

Choosing wrong DVFS points for individual components may prevent providing enough budget to the crucial component adversely affect performance. For instance, if there are a lot of I/O operation or if a multimedia application is running, keeping the CPU in performance mode will allocate a larger power budget from the current source to the CPU and the multimedia unit will simply perform poorer due to lack of power budget for this unit. In our test setup, we have observed a similar scenario by running Geekbench 3 by keeping the CPU at different frequencies. It is observed that the memory intensive tests that perform occasional computation perform poorly when the CPU is in its highest frequency as simple computations can be performed in lower frequency with same latency but without reaching the power limit of the device. Moreover, there can be thermal throttling forcing all units to tone down its activity. It is unique in smartphones as a lot of blocks share a single power source. Not only does it show poor performance but also consumes higher leakage and clock tree power when the processor fails to shut down when it is not required. Thus, choosing the correct DVFS point for each resource is essential for efficient power budget distribution for maximizing performance of the highest used resource.

2.3   Quality of Service

A governor should not only work towards energy efficiency but also provide user acceptable performance. The performance need not be the best but needs to comply to some standard. Researchers have collected user surveys to determine the level of user satisfaction for mobile devices. We compiled QoS data from prior research [7–10] and enlist them in the result section. Furthermore, we specify that the benchmark scores should be within 95% of the maximum possible score attained by the device.

3   Experimental Setup

We used Dragonboard 410c [14] for the analysis of energy consumption across various workloads and benchmarks. It contains a Qualcomm Snapdragon 410 consisting of Quad-core ARM Cortex A53 processors running Android 5.1.1. There are shunt registers provided on board [15] to check the incoming current to the processor. The reason of choice for this processor is its prevalence in value-tier market and the fact that it has a shared power source. Below are some of the specifications of this processor are listed in Table 1.

Table 1. Snapdragon 410c specification

CPU	4 x ARM Cortex A53 1.2 GHz
CPU arch	64 bit ARM V8 architecture
GPU	Qualcomm Adreno 306 400 MHz
DSP	Qualcomm Hexagon DSP
Memory	1 GB LPDDR3 533 MHz

The points across the shunt resistor (R77) on the board are tapped and a INA219 current sensor is connected to measure the current. The output of the current sensor is sampled using a microcontroller to get the data. A block diagram of the setup is shown in Fig. 1.

Some of the parameters of the hardware are tuned during the study of governor behavior. It includes *CPU governor, Governor tuning, DDR frequency, GPU frequency, Thermal throttler, Hotplugging setting.* All the parameters are tuned for every run and then the workload is run in the system. The android debug bridge [14] (ADB) is used for the measurements and various comparisons are performed.

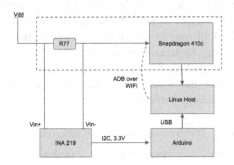

Fig. 1. Block diagram of the experimental setup

4 Applications and Benchmarks

A brief analysis of some of the experiments performed are described in this section. The results in term of scores and the normalized energy consumed in reported in Table 2. Linaro workload Automation suite [16] is used to run a host of applications explained in the Table 2 and standard benchmarks which includes the following:

- Antutu
- Geekbench
- BBench
- Nenamark

- Ebizzy
- Dhrystone
- Linpack
- Memcpy

Table 2. A description of the applications

Applaunch	Launches either the calculator, browser or google Maps application when no other application is running in the system
Multi_applaunch	Launches calculator, browser and maps application in a sequence on top of one another
Video	Playing a 720p video file in the native android video player
Audio	Plays an audio file in the native android audio player
Maps	Open google maps and perform a navigation task
Adobereader	Scrolls, zooms and searches a word after opening a pdf file
Facebook	Performs a series of tasks after logging in a facebook account including scrolling through the wall, like a friend's photo, post a status and comment on an existing post
Iozone	Performs a series of IO performance tasks

5   Results

First, we provide a distinction between *race-to-idle* and *pace-to-idle* governor strategies. The *performance* and *powersave* governors keep the CPU frequency at the max and the min operating point. This accounts for the least governor software overhead and no time wasted on voltage and frequency modulation. However, they cannot adapt to phase changes. Performance governor is a *race-to-idle* governor. On the other hand, the *pace-to-idle* strategies like the *interactive* and *ondemand* frequently changes DVFS points based on CPU utilization. These works better in the application workloads which interleaves different resources. A view of the number of switching is shown in Table 3. Antutu shows frequency toggles in performance mode because of thermal throttling pointing out the drawback of *race-to-idle* strategy in mobile devices. Interactive filters out some modulation using hysteresis as compared to ondemand governor and performs better in terms of performance and energy efficiency in most applications. Moreover, the performance must meet minimum standards which we compile from prior research and is enlisted in Table 4.

Table 3. DVFS mode switching of different governors

Benchmarks	Performance governor	Interactive governor	Ondemand governor	Powersave governor
Antutu	18	842	3809	0
Applaunch	0	1897	7463	0
Audio	0	43	112	0
Dhrystone	0	8	12	0
Geekbench	0	229	887	0
Homescreen	0	44	51	0
Linpack	0	31	83	0
Memcpy	0	10	12	0
Nenamark	0	1178	8383	0

Table 4. Quality of service of different user actions

Behavior	Quality	Application
Webpage load time	4 s	BBench, firefox
Online video loading time	2–10 s	Stream, Youtube
Facebook comment post	3 s	Facebook
Interactive tasks	100 ms	Applaunch, Adobereader
Video playback	30 fps–60 fps	Video/Game rendering
PDF rendering	1–10 s	Adobereader

Some of these are benchmarks like the Antutu, Geekbench, Dhrystone and Nenamark whose scores are directly reported in Table 5 when run with different governors. Antutu and Dhrystone primarily stresses the CPU. The interactive governor gives similar performance as performance governor but consumes more power because it unnecessarily toggles the frequency. Nenamark is a graphics benchmark running OpenGL-ES 2.0. The powersave governor gives best frame rate as the GPU governor is tweaked to performance and bus frequency is changed while the CPU is in powersave mode. This shows that changing the DVFS modes for the critical component not only increases performance but also consumes less power. Applaunch of both single and multiple application works best when the CPU is in performance mode as the QoS is for the quickest application load time. Moreover, there is not much difference in response time whenever we are launching light application like the calculator. The effect is more pronounced when heavier or multiple applications are launched. Table 5 shows the performance of different applications and benchmarks. The values are marked in green for the acceptable QoS and red for unacceptable ones.

Table 5. Performance comparison among different CPU governors and green ones have acceptable QoS.

Workload	metric	Governors			
		performance	*interactive*	*ondemand*	*powersave*
Antutu	Score	19246	19038	19027	12201
Dhrystone	DMIPS	4053	4053	4052	2679
Applaunch calculator	Launch time (s)	0.71	0.74	0.79	0.89
Applaunch Browser	Launch time (s)	1.007	1.02	1.07	1.46
BBench	Runtime(s)	190.9	184.17	187.2	246.24
Adobereader	Runtime(s)	77.14	79.14	79.95	103.61
ebizzy	Total records/sec	2017	2011	1757	472
Nenamark	Frames per second	35.6	35.2	34.9	37.4
Memcpy	Bandwidth (in MB/s)	3114	3060	2970	588

6   Benchmark and Application Classification

A host of benchmarks and user workloads were run with different governors. The workloads are classified in this section into the following categories:

6.1   CPU Intensive Workloads

These are the workloads that are compute intensive and works best when the processors are at peak frequency. Race-to-idle scheme gives better performance and is often energy efficient as well by reducing the number of DVFS switches and also keeping the SoC active for the minimum amount of time. The pace-to-idle governors on the other hand, suffer from too many unnecessary DVFS modulations. Interactive and ondemand governor works good if the workload is continuously CPU demanding and behaves like performance in Dhrystone [1]. This can be viewed in the minimal number of DVFS modulations in Table 3. Figure 2 shows the average current of CPU intensive benchmarks. Applaunch of calculator (simple application) and firefox works fastest in performance governor. Antutu benchmark shows that the performance has the highest power efficiency while meeting QoS. Powersave consumes the least power as its frequency is clipped to the lowest operating mode but it gives drastically poor performance. Thus, if we can categorize a phase of a workload as compute intensive, we can move to performance mode until the phase completes to get the maximum performance and minimal DVFS switching overhead.

6.2   Intermittent CPU Workloads with I/O Operation

Some of the workload we tested like the BBench which loads saved webpages by I/O operation and scrolls through the webpages which is CPU intensive works best in pace-to-idle type of governors. Since the CPU is only used intermittently, interactive governor is the most efficient as it lowers the frequency of the CPU while doing I/O operation. The lowering of CPU frequency also provides more power budget to the I/O unit and it can provide better response. Figure 3 shows that BBench is a heavy benchmark and consumes good amount of current throughout its execution. Facebook, Adobereader also are I/O intensive and saves CPU power during user interactions. Geekbench also has a lot of memory operations where interactive aces out. Performance governor scores better in the CPU intensive workloads of the Geekbench suite.

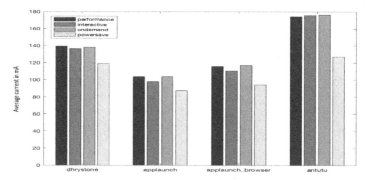

Fig. 2. Power comparison of CPU intensive benchmarks of different governors.

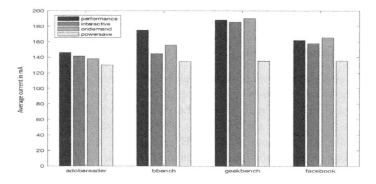

Fig. 3. Power comparison of user interactive applications of different governors.

We went in deeper into the Geekbench 3 workload and compared the *race-to-idle (performance)* and *pace-to-idle(interactive)* strategies closely. The performance governor aced in the compute intensive integer and floating point benchmarks. But due to constrained power budget, it performs poorly in most of the memory benchmarks. Since it clocked the CPU continuously at the highest frequency, it failed to provide enough power to the memory bus degrading performance. On the other hand, the interactive governor clocked the CPU at minimum operating point for simple operations and redirected the entire power to the memory bus giving better bandwidth as shown in Fig. 4(a).

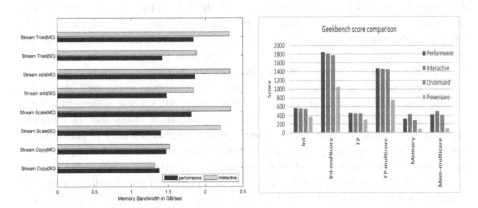

Fig. 4. (a) Geekbench 3 memory perf comparison between performance and interactive governor (b) Geekbench 3 score comparison of different types of workloads.

6.3 Application Requiring Other Blocks in the SoC

There are other applications like playing a video which requires the multimedia unit to be active. The CPU can stay in the powersave mode while providing power budget to the DDR and the multimedia unit to perform. Moreover, playing games require the GPU to be in higher performance mode to render better user experience.

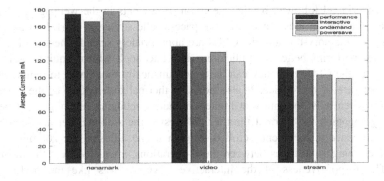

Fig. 5. Power comparison of governors running applications using other resource

In Fig. 5, the GPU is in performance mode in the Nenamark benchmark and the powersave not only consumes least power but also provides the highest fps as more power budget is allocated to the accelerator. Thus, application-wise characterization is useful to provide better power efficiency. Running in powersave ensures that the device remains cooler for a longer period which is the normal usage pattern of video and audio playback applications.

7 Observations

After running various types of workloads on all the different kinds of governors, it is seen that choosing the correct governor in a battery-operated system-on-a-chip is a multi-variable problem where one should consider the balance of activities in the various units. Governors should also minimize thermal throttling hardware to attain best efficiency and performance in addition to better chip life.

As mentioned in the introduction that a race-to-idle scheme works well for servers because more importance is given on the performance, this scheme is thought to be a poor fit for battery-operated devices. But our observation states that in compute intensive workloads, the race-to-idle scheme performs better not only in performance but also it gives better energy efficiency in some cases. In multicore devices, normally there is provision of switching off each core into several idle low power states. So, if a governor finishes the pending work in the minimum time and goes to idle, it will save operating power. This strategy will work even better with technology shrinking as the leakage current becomes comparable with the dynamic current. With more application-specific units are put in the SoC, having a global governor controlling the DVFS modes of every component based on workload characterization will be the desired solution as we observe by classifying the workload and showing that CPU powersave coupled with resource *race-to-idle* works better in scenarios which use accelerators. The race-to-idle scheme also makes sharing of power source easier as the units are active for the minimum amount of time. Last but not the least is the fact that race-to-idle schemes give better performance most of the time.

The pace-to-idle strategy also performs well in multiple scenarios where multiple resources are used together or in a sequential manner. For instance, the BBench workload loads a set of heavy webpages from the memory making it a memory intensive workload followed by the execution of contents in the webpages, which is compute-intensive. In these scenarios, the pace-to-idle strategies work best as all the units like the memory-bus and the CPUs are appropriately scaled whenever it is needed. It also performs better in applications like Facebook which requires user interaction where the CPU frequency can be opportunistically modulated to reduce power and temperature of the device. It also helps in thermal distribution as the cores get heated up when it is constantly at higher frequency reducing reliability and performance by engaging the thermal throttler. We tested the Adobereader applications in which we opened a document, scrolled through it and adjusted the zooming. Since there were enough idle times between these operations, interactive was the most efficient. The responsiveness of the interactive governor was like the performance governor but it performed poorly while searching a word in the file ending up consuming more power. But mere scrolling through the text would have been more efficient in the interactive governor.

Moreover, for video playback or a GPU-intensive game, the multimedia or GPU is used and changing the CPU governor doesn't make any difference in performance. But changing the governor of the corresponding block improves both performance and energy efficiency. Based on the above trends, we conclude that characterization of workload would help design a high performing energy efficient governor.

8 Related Work

There has been considerable amount of research performed to enhance the native interactive(default) governor of the system. The related works are grouped into the following categories:

8.1 Race-to-Idle vs Pace-to-Idle Schemes

Some works suggested pace-to-idle strategy is the better strategy [3] due to the intermittent CPU usage pattern of the workloads and waiting for I/O interrupts. With the constrained system power/thermal budget, it is not feasible to make all resources available simultaneously. But on the other hand, transistors are shrinking in size and leakage is comparable to the dynamic current. The reduction in resource active time by race-to-idle schemes are making it attractive. Moreover, Race-to-idle schemes give better performance. Coupled with all these benefits, the race-to-idle is becoming popular. Albers and Antoniadis [4] have proposed that the race-to-idle strategies provide better energy efficiency provided the system has multi-level and deep sleep states which is common in smartphones. It causes the minimum DVFS transitions causing less halts and power wastage. While Hoffman [3] claims that pace-to-idle betters than race-to-idle in smartphones due to the intermittent use of a specific resource diluting the effectiveness and energy efficiency of the resource. But workload characterization can help improve the effectiveness of the resource by deploying race-to-idle strategy for the required resource making it fully available when necessary thereby improving energy efficiency.

8.2 Governor Design Based on Runtime Phase Behavior and QoS Deadline

Isci et al. and others [5, 22] has used runtime phase behavior to perform dynamic DVFS management of a device. The phase behavior was identified from the branch predictor. On the other hand, some of the DVFS governors were designed keeping in mind the idea of meeting a quality-of-service(QoS) deadline while running the processor at the optimum frequency to achieve the highest energy efficiency [19, 20]. These policies explore the search space to figure out the most energy efficient DVFS mode. Though these works [6, 11] are promising but their applicability is restricted to limited applications like web browsing and video playback. Moreover, it doesn't consider system-wide power budget. A single power source can be shared among multiple resources like multi-core CPUs, GPUs and other accelerators. Redirecting the power to the most useful resource is important when the current consumed is near the limit of the source.

8.3   Power Sharing Among Different Resources

Paul et al. and others [18, 21] has evaluated the need of cooperative boosting between CPUs and GPUs in a AMD APU processor. This is critical in smartphones when multiple resources are sharing a power source or when the device is thermally limited. However, this work is focused on desktop CPUs. A smartphone CPU like the one used in this work has more resources sharing a current source and the QoS metrics are quite different. We evaluated the different smartphone governors on similar lines with higher granularity in the type of resource.

8.4   Reducing DVFS Switch Time

Another line of radically different effort is put to reduce the DVFS switch time. The pace-to-idle can be made even more aggressive in the switching time is reduced. New PLLs and voltage regulators have better response time to quickly switch the modes with minimum current spikes which improves the overall energy efficiency. Several researchers have proposed elegant methods [12, 13] to reduce the switch time. But still the DVFS switching time is of the order of several micro-seconds as it involves changing the voltage. Workload characterization and identification of phases based on usage pattern can reduce the number of DVFS mode changes and will increase efficiency but the algorithms can be made more aggressive when the DVFS switching time reduces.

9   Conclusion

In this paper, we studied various governor strategies and their impact on performance and energy consumption while running various workloads for a smartphone. We conclude that a good governor must wisely choose the DVFS mode of not only the CPU, but also the various non-CPU components when the workload demands varied utilization of multiple blocks sharing a current source. System wide governors tuning the DVFS modes of different units of SoC will provide efficient utilization of the available current. Since, smartphone applications mostly use a specific component of the SoC, characterization of workloads to boost the frequency of the corresponding component to the required level gives better performance with increased energy efficiency. Analyzing phase behavior and usage pattern of the program can further help in selection of the optimum DVFS mode. It was observed that turning on the powersave mode does not necessarily save battery in many scenarios. The powersave governor led to increased energy consumption for CPU intensive workloads because of higher run time causing more leakage energy consumption. Hence, characterization of a workload and wise current distribution to the critical components is imperative in designing a governor giving it desirable performance but also yields high energy and thermal efficiency.

Acknowledgement. This work was partially supported by National Science Foundation (NSF) under grant numbers 1725743 and 1745813. Any opinions, findings, conclusions or recommendations expressed in this material are those of the authors and do not necessarily reflect the views of NSF or other sponsors.

References

1. Weicker, R.P.: Dhrystone: a synthetic systems programming benchmark. Commun. ACM **27** (10), 1013–1030 (1984)
2. Pallipadi, V., Starikovskiy, A.: The ondemand governor. In: Proceedings of the Linux Symposium, vol. 2, pp. 215–230 (2006)
3. Hoffmann, H.: Racing and pacing to idle: an evaluation of heuristics for energy-aware resource allocation. In: Proceedings of the Workshop on Power-Aware Computing and Systems, p. 13. ACM (2013)
4. Albers, S., Antoniadis, A.: Race to idle: new algorithms for speed scaling with a sleep state. ACM Trans. Algorithms (TALG) **10**(2), 9 (2014)
5. Isci, C., Contreras, G., Martonosi, M.: Live, runtime phase monitoring and prediction on real systems with application to dynamic power management. In: Proceedings of the 39th Annual IEEE/ACM International Symposium on Microarchitecture. IEEE Computer Society (2006)
6. Rao, K., Wang, J., Yalamanchili, S., Wardi, Y., Handong, Y.: Application-specific performance-aware energy optimization on android mobile devices. In: 2017 IEEE International Symposium on High Performance Computer Architecture (HPCA), pp. 169–180 (2017)
7. Halpern, M., Zhu, Y., Reddi, V.J.: Mobile CPU's rise to power: quantifying the impact of generational mobile cpu design trends on performance, energy, and user satisfaction. In: 2016 IEEE International Symposium on High Performance Computer Architecture (HPCA). IEEE (2016)
8. Shneiderman, B.: Designing the User Interface. Addison-Wesley, Boston (1992)
9. Zhu, Y., Halpern, M., Reddi, V.J.: Event-based scheduling for energy-efficient QoS (eQoS) in mobile web applications. In: 2015 IEEE 21st International Symposium on High Performance Computer Architecture (HPCA). IEEE (2015)
10. https://blog.kissmetrics.com/speed-is-a-killer/
11. Zhu, Y., Reddi, V.J.: Optimizing general-purpose cpus for energy-efficient mobile web computing. ACM Trans. Comput. Syst. **35**, 1 (2017)
12. Eyerman, S., Eeckhout, L.: Fine-grained DVFS using on-chip regulators. ACM Trans. Archit. Code Optim. (TACO) **8**(1), 1 (2011)
13. Kim, W., Gupta, M.S., Wei, G.Y., Brooks, D.: System level analysis of fast, per-core DVFS using on-chip switching regulators. In: 2008 IEEE 14th International Symposium on High Performance Computer Architecture, HPCA 2008, pp. 123–134. IEEE (2008)
14. Dragonboard 410c. https://developer.qualcomm.com/hardware/dragonboard-410c
15. Measuring power consumption for Dragonboard 410c. https://developer.qualcomm.com/download/db410c/power-measurement-appnote.pdf
16. Linaro workload automation. https://media.readthedocs.org/pdf/workload-automation/latest/workload-automation.pdf
17. Android debug bridge. https://developer.android.com/studio/command-line/adb.html
18. Paul, I., et al.: Cooperative boosting: needy versus greedy power management. In: ACM SIGARCH Computer Architecture News, vol. 41, no. 3. ACM (2013)

19. Shingari, D., et al.: DORA: optimizing smartphone energy efficiency and web browser performance under interference. In: 2018 IEEE International Symposium on Performance Analysis of Systems and Software (ISPASS). IEEE (2018)
20. Gaudette, B., Wu, C.J., Vrudhula, S.: Improving smartphone user experience by balancing performance and energy with probabilistic QoS guarantee. In: 2016 IEEE International Symposium on High Performance Computer Architecture (HPCA). IEEE (2016)
21. Kim, Y., John, L., Paul, I., Manne, S., Schulte, M.: Performance boosting under reliability and power constraints. In: International Conference on Computer Aided Design (ICCAD), November 2013
22. Bircher, W.L., John, L.: Predictive power management for multi-core processors. In: Varbanescu, A.L., Molnos, A., van Nieuwpoort, R. (eds.) ISCA 2010. LNCS, vol. 6161, pp. 243–255. Springer, Heidelberg (2011). https://doi.org/10.1007/978-3-642-24322-6_21

HPC Benchmarking: Scaling Right and Looking Beyond the Average

Milan Radulović[1,2]([✉]), Kazi Asifuzzaman[1,2], Paul Carpenter[1],
Petar Radojković[1], and Eduard Ayguadé[1,2]

[1] Barcelona Supercomputing Center (BSC), Barcelona, Spain
{milan.radulovic,kazi.asifuzzaman,paul.carpenter,
petar.radojkovic}@bsc.es
[2] Universitat Politècnica de Catalunya (UPC), Barcelona, Spain
eduard@ac.upc.edu

Abstract. Designing a balanced HPC system requires an understanding of the dominant performance bottlenecks. There is as yet no well established methodology for a unified evaluation of HPC systems and workloads that quantifies the main performance bottlenecks. In this paper, we execute seven production HPC applications on a production HPC platform, and analyse the key performance bottlenecks: FLOPS performance and memory bandwidth congestion, and the implications on scaling out. We show that the results depend significantly on the number of execution processes and granularity of measurements. We therefore advocate for guidance in the application suites, on selecting the representative scale of the experiments. Also, we propose that the FLOPS performance and memory bandwidth should be represented in terms of the proportions of time with low, moderate and severe utilization. We show that this gives much more precise and actionable evidence than the average.

Keywords: HPC applications · Bottlenecks · FLOPS
Memory bandwidth · Scaling-out

1 Introduction

Deploying an HPC infrastructure is a substantial investment in time and money, so it is extremely important to make the right procurement decision. Unfortunately, evaluating HPC systems and workloads and quantifying their bottlenecks is hard. There are currently three main approaches. The approach taken by TOP500 and Green500 is to evaluate systems using a prominent HPC benchmark, such as High-Performance Linpack (HPL) [20] or High Performance Conjugate Gradients (HPCG) [5]. Another approach is to measure the sustained performance of the various components in the system using specialized kernel benchmarks, such as HPC Challenge [13]. By design, kernel benchmarks quantify only the sustainable performance of individual system components, so they lack the capability to determine how a real-world production HPC application will behave on the same platform.

© Springer International Publishing AG, part of Springer Nature 2018
M. Aldinucci et al. (Eds.): Euro-Par 2018, LNCS 11014, pp. 135–146, 2018.
https://doi.org/10.1007/978-3-319-96983-1_10

The final approach, which is the one taken in this paper, is to mimic production use by running a set of real HPC applications from diverse scientific fields [23]. We execute seven production HPC applications, together with HPL and HPCG, on a production x86 platform, and we reach two main conclusions. Firstly, we find that HPC application performance and CPU/memory system bottlenecks are strongly dependent on the **number of application processes**. This is typically overlooked in benchmark suites, which seldom define how many processes should be used. We argue that it is essential that HPC application suites specify narrow ranges on the number of processes, so that the results are representative of real world application use, or that they at least provide some guidelines. Secondly, we find that **average values of bytes/FLOP, bytes/s and FLOPs/s can be highly misleading**. Our results show that the applications under study have low average FLOPs/s utilization and moderate pressure on the memory bandwidth. However, we identified several applications, such as ALYA and GENE, with a moderate *average* memory bandwidth that spend more than 50% of their computation time in phases where the memory bandwidth bottleneck is severe. We therefore recommend that rather than thinking in terms of average figures, one measures the percentage of time that the utilization of memory bandwidth or FLOPs/s is low (below 40% of sustainable maximum), moderate (40% to 80%) and severe (above 80%). These three figures give a much more precise picture of the application behavior than the average.

In summary, given the substantial investment of time and money to deploy an HPC system, it is important to carefully evaluate HPC architectures. Compared with benchmarks or kernels, system evaluation with HPC application suites can give a more complete picture of the HPC system behavior. However, our results show that it is very important that HPC application suites specify narrow ranges for the number of processes that are representative of real-life application behavior, or at least provide some guidelines so users themselves could determine these ranges for their target platforms. In addition, reporting key application measurements using the average values may conceal bursty behavior, and give a misleading impression of how performance would be affected by changes in the platform's memory bandwidth. We suggest to avoid average figures when evaluating performance or bottlenecks, and instead measure the percentage of time that these figures are low, moderate and severe, with respect to their sustained peak, which gives a more precise picture of the application's or system's behavior.

We hope our study will stimulate awareness and dialogue on the subject among the community, and lead to improved standards of evaluating and reporting performance results in HPC.

2   Experimental Environment

In this section, we explain the experimental platform, workloads, methodology and tools we used in our analysis.

2.1 Experimental Platform

The experiments are executed on the MareNostrum 3 supercomputer [3], the third version of one of the six Tier-0 (largest) HPC systems in Europe [21]. It comprises dual-socket Intel Sandy Bridge-EP E5-2670 nodes. Each socket comprises eight cores operating at 3.0 GHz. As in most HPC systems, hyperthreading is disabled. The processors connect to main memory through four channels, each with a single DDR3-1600 DIMM. Regular MareNostrum compute nodes include 32 GB of DRAM memory, i.e., 2 GB per core. The nodes are connected with an InfiniBand FDR-10 (40 Gb/s) interconnect, as a non-blocking two-level fat-tree topology.

2.2 Workloads

High-Performance Linpack
For a long time, the High-Performance Linpack (HPL) [20] benchmark has been the de facto metric for ranking HPC systems. It measures the sustained floating-point rate (GFLOPs/s) for solving a dense system of linear equations using double-precision floating-point arithmetic. The linear system is randomly generated, with a user-specified size, so the user can scale the problem to achieve the best performance on a given system. HPL stresses only the system's floating point performance, without stressing other important contributors to overall performance, such as the memory subsystem. The most prominent evaluation of HPC systems constitutes the TOP500 list [24], which has been criticized for assessing system performance using only HPL [12]. The community has pointed out the weaknesses of HPL and advocated for a way to evaluate HPC systems that is better correlated with the needs of production HPC applications [6].

High-Performance Conjugate Gradients
High Performance Conjugate Gradients (HPCG) [5], has been released as a complement to the FLOPs-bound HPL. It is based on an iterative sparse-matrix conjugate gradient kernel with double-precision floating-point values. While HPL can exploit data locality and thus cope with relatively low memory bandwidth, HPCG performance is largely proportional to the available memory bandwidth. HPCG is a good representative of HPC applications governed by differential equations, which tend to have much stronger needs for high memory bandwidth and low latency, and tend to access data using irregular patterns.

HPC Applications
Evaluating HPC systems using benchmarks that target specific performance metrics is not enough to determine the performance of a real-world application. It is therefore essential to execute production applications on an HPC system to better understand the bottlenecks and constraints experienced by a production HPC application. There are efforts in making suites of HPC applications that could be used in benchmarking purposes, such as NSF [17], NCAR [15] and NERSC Trinity benchmarks [16] in USA, and EuroBen [8], ARCHER [25] and Unified European Application Benchmark Suite (UEABS) [18] in Europe.

Table 1. Scientific HPC applications used in the study

Name	Area	Selected no. of processes
ALYA	Computational mechanics	16–1024
BQCD[a]	Particle physics	64–1024
CP2K	Computational chemistry	128–1024
GADGET	Astronomy and cosmology	512–1024
GENE	Plasma physics	128–1024
NEMO	Ocean modeling	512–1024
QE[b]	Computational chemistry	16–256

[a]Quantum Chromo-Dynamics (QCD) is a set of five kernels. We study Kernel A, also called Berlin Quantum Chromo-Dynamics (BQCD), which is commonly used in QCD simulations.
[b]QE stands for Quantum Espresso application. QE does not scale on more than 256 processes.

In our evaluation, we used a set of UEABS applications. UEABS represents a set of production applications and datasets, from various scientific domains, designed for benchmarking the European HPC systems, included in the Partnership for Advanced Computing in Europe (PRACE) [21], for procurement and comparison purposes. Parallelized using the Message Passing Interface (MPI), these applications are regularly executed on hundreds to thousands of cores. We study 7 of 12 applications from UEABS [18], listed in Table 1.[1]

Tools and Methodology

The applications come with input datasets and a recommended range of CPU cores for the experiments. We use the *Test Case A* datasets, which are deemed suitable for Tier-1 systems up to about 1,000 cores [18]. In all experiments, we execute one application process per CPU core. The number of processes starts from 16 (a single MareNostrum node) and it increases by powers of two until 1,024 processes. Some of the applications have memory capacity requirements that exceed the available node memory, which limits the lowest number of processes in the experiments, e.g., BQCD cannot be executed with fewer than 64 processes (four nodes). The presented analysis keeps constant the input dataset and varies the number of application processes, which refers to a strong scaling case.[2]

---

[1] We could not finalize the installations of Code_Saturne and GPAW. The errors have been reported to the application developers. The remaining three applications had problems once the measurement infrastructure was included.

[2] The alternative would be a weak scaling analysis, in which the problem size scales with the number of nodes. Unlike HPL and HPCG, for which the problem size is defined by the user and the input data is generated algorithmically, application benchmark suites include specific input problem data. We are not aware of a production application benchmark suite that has problems suitable for weak scaling analysis. Although some of the UEABS benchmarks are distributed with two input datasets, small and large, they are not comparable so are insufficient for weak scaling analysis [26].

The application's computation bursts were instrumented with Limpio [19] and Extrae [4]. We used core performance counters [10] to measure FLOPS performance (scalar and vector FLOPS counters) and uncore performance counters [9] to measure memory bandwidth (read and write CAS commands counters).

We analyze the application behavior at two levels of granularity. First, we plot mean FLOPs and memory bandwidth utilization using end-to-end measurements and averaging the values of all application processes. Second, we analyze the fine-granularity measurements done at the computational burst level. For each computational burst, we measure the FLOPs, bandwidth utilization and the burst execution time. Afterwards, we analyze the cumulative distribution function of the measurements.[3] As we show in this paper, these two levels of the analysis can, and often do, actually lead to different conclusions.

3 Results

In this section, we analyze the stress of the production HPC applications on the CPU and memory resources, and pay special attention to understand how this stress may change during execution and as the application scales.

3.1 Floating-Point Performance Analysis

Figure 1a plots the average FLOPs/s utilization for different numbers of application processes. The results show that the average FLOPs/s utilization of production HPC applications is fairly low: for most applications it is below 30%, and in the best case it reaches only 51% (CP2K-128 experiment). Figure 1b summarizes the distribution of measurements done at computational burst level. We divide the computational burst measurements into five clusters: 0–20%, 20–40%, 40–60%, 60–80% and 80–100% of sustained FLOPs/s, and then plot the portion of execution time represented by each cluster. For example, in the BQCD-64 experiment, 72% of the time the FLOPs/s utilization is between 0 and 20%, while for the remaining 28% of the time it is between 20% and 40%.

Our results show that detailed measurements are indeed needed, and that plotting only average values may hide important information. The most obvious case would be the QE-16 experiment. Although the average FLOP utilization is only 24% (Fig. 1a), the application actually puts extremely high pressure on CPU FLOPs for around 18% of its computation time (Fig. 1b).

We also analyze changes in the application behavior when executing them using different numbers of processes. Both, average and per-burst measurements indicate significant changes in the application behavior as the applications scale-out[4].

---

[3] The cumulative distribution function, $y = F(x)$, in this case presents the fraction of samples y that are less or equal to a certain value x.

[4] We remind the reader that we used the official input datasets, and followed the recommendations about the range of CPU processes that should be used in the experiments (see Sect. 2.2).

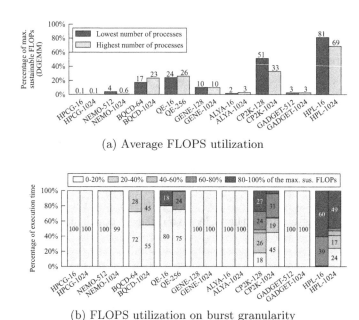

(a) Average FLOPS utilization

(b) FLOPS utilization on burst granularity

Fig. 1. Production HPC applications show fairly low FLOPS utilization, both on lowest and highest number of processes.

This opens a very important question: Which application behavior is the correct/representative one, i.e. which number should we report?

3.2 Memory Bandwidth Analysis

Memory bandwidth has become increasingly important in recent years. Keeping the memory bandwidth balanced with the CPU's compute capabilities, within affordable costs and power constraints, has become a key technological challenge. The increasing awareness of this challenge also resulted in the introduction of the HPCG benchmark, as an alternative to HPL. The industry also responded to the growing need for more memory bandwidth, and high-bandwidth 3D-stacked DRAM products are hitting the market. Their manufacturers promise significant performance boosts over standard DDRx DIMMs, although some independent studies doubt whether and to what extent high-bandwidth memory will benefit HPC applications [22].

Memory bandwidth collision can indeed have the strong negative performance impact. When a workload uses more than 40% of maximum sustainable bandwidth, concurrent memory accesses start to collide, which increases memory latency causing performance penalties. Using more than 80% of maximum sustainable bandwidth causes severe collisions among concurrent memory requests; thus memory latency increases exponentially and memory bandwidth becomes a serious performance bottleneck [11].

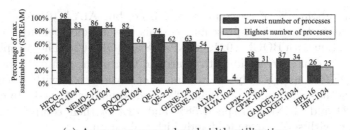

(a) Average memory bandwidth utilization

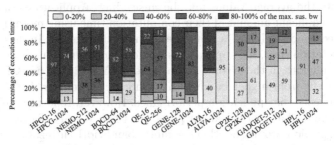

(b) Memory bandwidth utilization on burst granularity

Fig. 2. Contrary to FLOPS, memory bandwidth utilization of production HPC applications is substantial.

Figure 2 plots the memory bandwidth usage of UEABS applications. The memory bandwidth values are plotted relative to the maximum sustained memory bandwidth measured by the STREAM benchmark. Again, we plot the results at two levels of granularity: Fig. 2a plots average utilization over computation time and for different numbers of application processes, while Fig. 2b shows fine-granularity measurements at the computational burst level. The applications under study show higher utilization of memory bandwidth, than FLOPs performance, even for the average values.

Next we analyze the computational bursts measurements, presented in Fig. 2b. The chart shows moderate to high memory bandwidth utilization. All the applications under study have segments in which memory bandwidth utilization exceeds 40%, and all but two of them, CP2K and GADGET, spend a significant portion of time with bandwidth utilization above 60% or even 80%.

The computational burst measurements reveal some interesting scenarios, which are more apparent in Fig. 3. In this figure, the x-axis is the *average* memory bandwidth utilization, as in Fig. 2a. The y-axis is the proportion of time for which the memory bandwidth utilization is severe; i.e. more than 80% of the sustainable maximum, which corresponds to the darkest shade parts of the bars in Fig. 2b. Figure 3 shows that considering the average memory bandwidth on the x-axis, ALYA-16 and CP2K-128 may seem to be bandwidth insensitive, as their average bandwidths are around 50% and 40% of the sustained bandwidth. However, detailed in-time measurements show that they spent significantly different proportions of the time with severe memory bandwidth utilization: CP2K-128 spends only about 4% of its computation time, but ALYA-16 spends 55% of its computation time, which presents a serious performance penalty. We find a similar situation with BQCD-1024, GENE-128 and QE-1024. These applications all have average memory bandwidth of around 60% of the sustained maximum. Even so, QE-256 spends only 12% of its computation time with severe memory bandwidth utilization (more than 80% of maximum sustained). In contrast, BQCD-1024 and GENE-128 spend 58% and 72% of their computation time, respectively, with severe memory bandwidth utilization.

This is another confirmation that detailed measurements are needed, and that plotting only the average values may be misleading. Applications under study that spend significant amount of their computation time using more than 80% of the sustained bandwidth have a severe performance bottleneck. In these phases of their computation time, the applications would benefit out of increased available memory bandwidth in the system. In our case, ALYA-16, but not CP2K-128, is likely to benefit from higher bandwidth memories. It would reduce the bottleneck and increase the application performance. However, reporting only average values of memory bandwidth cannot point out the necessary details.

Our suggestion would be that memory bandwidth utilization should be defined at least with three numbers—as the percentage of execution time that applications use 0–40%, 40–80% and 80–100% of the maximum sustained bandwidth. This would correspond the portion of the execution time in which the application experiences negligible, moderate and severe performance penalties due to collision on concurrent memory requests.

3.3 Discussion

Our analysis emphasizes that HPC application behavior is tightly coupled with the number of application processes. There are two main reasons for this. First, application scaling-out increases the inter-process communication time. To illustrate this, in Fig. 4 we plot the portion of overall execution time that applications under study spend in inter-process communication.

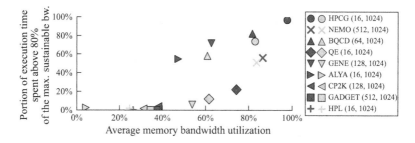

Fig. 3. Average memory bandwidth can mislead and hide potential bottlenecks. BQCD-1024, GENE-128 and QE-256 have similar average memory bandwidths, however BQCD-1024 and GENE-128 spend significantly more time utilizing more than 80% of max. sustainable bandwidth, which is a serious bottleneck.

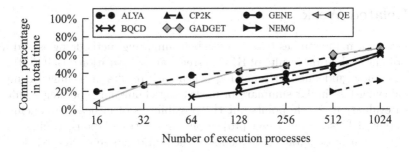

Fig. 4. Portion of total execution time spent in the inter-process communication for UEABS applications, strong scaling.

Even for the low number of application processes, the communication is non-negligible, and as the number of processes increases, it becomes the dominant part of the overall execution time. The higher the portion of time that is spent in communication, the lower the average utilization of FLOPs and memory bandwidth (as detected in Figs. 1a and 2a). Also, in general, the higher the number of processes, the smaller the portion of the input data handled by each process, which changes the effectiveness of cache memory and the overall process behavior (as detected in Figs. 1b and 2b).

HPC application behavior may be known by the application developers, but it is often overlooked in all HPC application suites for benchmarking purposes. State-of-the-art HPC application suites do not strictly define the number of processes to use in experiments. For example, UEABS recommends running the applications with corresponding input datasets on up to approximately 1,000 processes, but the minimum number of processes is not specified. Similarly, other HPC application suites either provide loose recommendations about the number of processes [15–17, 25] or do not discuss this issue at all [8]. However, it is not surprising that HPC application suites overlooked the problem that application behavior is tightly-coupled with number of application processes. After all, this problem does not exist for single-threaded benchmarks, and it was not detected for HPC benchmarks that put high stress to a single resource, such as HPCG, HPL or HPCC suite.

The essence of benchmarking is to provide representative use cases for characterization and valid comparison of different systems. If the application suite does not provide it, then the results are misleading. Our results show that it is very important that HPC application suites specify narrow ranges for the number of processes that are representative of real-life application behavior, or at least provide some guidelines so users themselves could determine these ranges for their target platforms.

4   Related Work

There are not many studies that analyse benchmarking methodologies and how to represent evaluation results of HPC systems and applications. Bailey [1] provides common guidelines for reporting benchmark results in technical computing, following his similar summary of misleading claims for reporting results in system evaluation [2]. He points out the possibilities of misleading conclusions and potential biases from using projections and extrapolations, tuning levels, evaluating non-representative segments of the workloads, etc. Nevertheless, he presents several rules and advocates the community to pay attention and avoid the biased results.

Hoefler and Belli [7] attempt to define ground rules and guidelines for the interpretation of HPC benchmarking. The authors propose statistical analysis and reporting techniques in order to improve the quality of reporting research results in HPC and ensure interpretability and reproducibility. In their study, they identify several frequent problems and propose rules to avoid them. Their analysis covers methods for reporting the results of speed-up, usage of various means, summarizing ratios, confidence intervals, normalization, usage of various chart techniques, and others.

Sayeed et al. [23] advocate the use of real applications for benchmarking in HPC, and that small benchmarks cannot predict the behavior of the real HPC applications. They discuss important questions, challenges, tools and metrics in evaluating performance using HPC applications. Afterwards, they evaluate the performance of four application benchmarks on three different parallel architectures, and measure the runtime, inter-process communication overhead, I/O characteristics and memory footprint. This way, they show the importance of reporting various metrics, in order to have a better representation of application and system performance. Since they measure these metrics on several numbers of execution processes, the results differ from one execution to another. It is clear from their results that on different numbers of execution processes, different platforms perform better or worse, which can significantly bias the analysis on certain scale of the experiments.

Marjanović et al. [14] explore the impact of input data-set for three representative benchmarks: HPL, HPCG and High-performance Geometric Multigrid (HPGMG). They perform an analysis on six distinct HPC platforms at the node level, and perform scale-out analysis on one of the platforms. Their results show that exploring multiple problem sizes gives a more complete picture of the underlying system performance, than a single number representing the best performance, which is the usual way of reporting the results. They advocate for the community to discuss and propose a method for aggregating these values into a representative result of the system performance.

In our study, we focus on two important aspects of benchmarking with HPC applications: the importance of defining the representative scale of the experiments and measurement granularity in quantifying performance bottlenecks, which are often overlooked by the community. To our knowledge, this is the first study that analyses the importance of a deterministic range for the number of execution processes. We also suggest a simple way to show several values for portions of time spent in different utilizations of certain metric. It does not require additional executions or special evaluation infrastructure, yet it gives much better representation of application behavior and clearer focus on its bottlenecks.

5   Conclusions

A clear understanding of HPC system performance factors and bottlenecks is essential for designing an HPC infrastructure with the best features and a reasonable cost. Such a perception can only be achieved by closely analysing existing HPC systems and execution of their workloads.

When executing production HPC applications, our findings show that HPC application performance metrics strongly depend on the number of execution processes. We argue that it is essential that HPC application suites specify narrow ranges on the number of processes, for the results to be representative of a real-world application use. Also, we find that average measurements of performance metrics and bottlenecks can be highly misleading. Instead, we suggest that performance measurements should be defined as the percentage of execution time in which applications use certain portions of maximum sustained values.

Overall, we believe this study offers new guidelines for accurately measuring key performance factors and their impact on overall HPC performance.

Acknowledgements. This work was supported by the Spanish Ministry of Science and Technology (project TIN2015-65316-P), Generalitat de Catalunya (contracts 2014-SGR-1051 and 2014-SGR-1272), Severo Ochoa Programme (SEV-2015-0493) of the Spanish Government; and the European Union's Horizon 2020 research and innovation programme under ExaNoDe project (grant agreement No 671578).

References

1. Bailey, D.H.: Misleading performance claims in parallel computations. In: 2009 46th ACM/IEEE Design Automation Conference, pp. 528–533, July 2009. https://doi.org/10.1145/1629911.1630049
2. Bailey, D.H.: Twelve ways to fool the masses when giving performance results on parallel computers. In: Supercomputing Review, pp. 54–55, August 1991
3. Barcelona Supercomputing Center: MareNostrum III System Architecture (2013). http://www.bsc.es/marenostrum-support-services/mn3
4. Barcelona Supercomputing Center: Extrae User guide manual for version 3.1.0, May 2015
5. Dongarra, J., Heroux, M., Luszczek, P.: The HPCG Benchmark (2016). http://www.hpcg-benchmark.org
6. Heroux, M., Dongarra, J.: Toward a New Metric for Ranking High Performance Computing Systems. Technical report SAND2013-4744, UTK EECS and Sandia National Labs, June 2013
7. Hoefler, T., Belli, R.: Scientific benchmarking of parallel computing systems: twelve ways to tell the masses when reporting performance results. In: Proceedings of the International Conference for High Performance Computing, Networking, Storage and Analysis, pp. 73:1–73:12, November 2015

8. Home page of the EuroBen Benchmark. http://www.euroben.nl
9. Intel Corporation: Intel® Xeon® Processor E5–2600 Product Family Uncore Performance Monitoring Guide. Technical report, March 2012
10. Intel Corporation: Intel® 64 and IA-32 Architectures Software Developer's Manual. Technical report, July 2017
11. Jacob, B.L.: The memory system: you can't avoid it, you can't ignore it, you can't fake it. Synth. Lect. Comput. Archit. 4(1), 1–77 (2009)
12. Kramer, W.T.: Top500 versus sustained performance: the top problems with the Top500 list - and what to do about them. In: Proceedings of the 21st International Conference on Parallel Architectures and Compilation Techniques, pp. 223–230, September 2012
13. Luszczek, P.R., et al.: The HPC Challenge (HPCC) Benchmark Suite. In: Proceedings of the ACM/IEEE Conference on Supercomputing (2006)
14. Marjanović, V., Gracia, J., Glass, C.W.: HPC benchmarking: problem size matters. In: Proceedings of the 7th International Workshop on Performance Modeling, Benchmarking and Simulation of High Performance Computing Systems, pp. 1–10, November 2016
15. National Center for Atmospheric Research: CISL High Performance Computing Benchmarks. http://www2.cisl.ucar.edu/resources/computational-systems/cisl-high-performance-computing-benchmarks
16. National Energy Research Scientific Computing Center: NERSC-8 / Trinity Benchmarks. http://www.nersc.gov/users/computational-systems/cori/nersc-8-procurement/trinity-nersc-8-rfp/nersc-8-trinity-benchmarks
17. National Science Foundation: Benchmarking Information Referenced in the NSF 11–511 High Performance Computing System Acquisition: Towards a Petascale Computing Environment for Science and Engineering. https://www.nsf.gov/pubs/2006/nsf0605/nsf0605.pdf
18. Partnership for Advanced Computing in Europe (PRACE): Unified european applications benchmark suite (2013). www.prace-ri.eu/ueabs/
19. Pavlovic, M., Radulovic, M., Ramirez, A., Radojković, P.: Limpio: LIghtweight MPI instrumentatiOn. In: Proceedings of the 23rd IEEE International Conference on Program Comprehension, pp. 303–306 (2015)
20. Petitet, A., Whaley, R.C., Dongarra, J., Cleary, A.: HPL - A Portable Implementation of the High-Performance Linpack Benchmark for Distributed-Memory Computers, September 2008. http://www.netlib.org/benchmark/hpl/
21. PRACE Research Infrastructure. www.prace-ri.eu
22. Radulovic, M., et al.: Another trip to the wall: how much will stacked DRAM benefit HPC? In: Proceedings of the International Symposium on Memory Systems, pp. 31–36 (2015)
23. Sayeed, M., Bae, H., Zheng, Y., Armstrong, B., Eigenmann, R., Saied, F.: Measuring high-performance computing with real applications. Comput. Sci. Eng. 10(4), 60–70 (2008). https://doi.org/10.1109/MCSE.2008.98
24. TOP500 List, November 2014. http://www.top500.org/
25. Turner, A.: UK National HPC Benchmarks. Technical report, UK National Supercomputing Service ARCHER (2016). http://www.archer.ac.uk/documentation/white-papers/benchmarks/UK_National_HPC_Benchmarks.pdf
26. Zivanovic, D., et al.: Main memory in HPC: do we need more or could we live with less? ACM Trans. Archit. Code Optim. 14(1), 3:1–3:26 (2017)

Combined Vertical and Horizontal Autoscaling Through Model Predictive Control

Emilio Incerto[1]([⊠]), Mirco Tribastone[1], and Catia Trubiani[2]

[1] IMT School for Advanced Studies, Piazza San Francesco 19, Lucca, Italy
{emilio.incerto,mirco.tribastone}@imtlucca.it
[2] Gran Sasso Science Institute, Viale Francesco Crispi 7, L'Aquila, Italy
catia.trubiani@gssi.it

Abstract. Meeting performance targets of co-located distributed applications in virtualized environments is a challenging goal. In this context, vertical and horizontal scaling are promising techniques; the former varies the resource sharing on each individual machine, whereas the latter deals with choosing the number of virtual machines employed. State-of-the-art approaches mainly apply vertical and horizontal scaling in an isolated fashion, in particular assuming a fixed and symmetric load balancing across replicas. Unfortunately this may result unsatisfactory when replicas execute in environments with different computational resources.

To overcome this limitation, we propose a novel combined runtime technique to determine the resource sharing quota and the horizontal load balancing policy in order to fulfill performance goals such as response time and throughput of co-located applications. Starting from a performance model as a multi-class queuing network, we formulate a model-predictive control problem which can be efficiently solved by linear programming. A validation performed on a shared virtualized environment hosting two real applications shows that only a combined vertical and horizontal load balancing adaptation can efficiently achieve desired performance targets in the presence of heterogeneous computational resources.

Keywords: Performance · Queuing networks · Control
Resource sharing · Load balancing

1 Introduction

Performance adaptation of co-located distributed applications consists in satisfying quality-of-service agreements expressed as response-time or throughput requirements for multiple applications that share common resources. It is considered a challenging activity [12]. Indeed, current resource schedulers blindly operate in a *performance unaware* fashion, both at the level of the hypervisor of virtual machines (VMs) or of the operating system [19,20]. As a consequence, the

© Springer International Publishing AG, part of Springer Nature 2018
M. Aldinucci et al. (Eds.): Euro-Par 2018, LNCS 11014, pp. 147–159, 2018.
https://doi.org/10.1007/978-3-319-96983-1_11

expected *performance isolation*, i.e., the behavior of one VM should not nega-tively impact performance of other running VMs (e.g., [11]), must be guaranteed by the computing platform providers [1,17,18].

Here we focus on CPU-intensive applications running on a virtualized envi-ronment. To effectively allocate resources at runtime and in an adaptive manner, *vertical* and *horizontal* scaling are promising techniques; the former varies the resource shares on each individual machine, whereas the latter deals with choos-ing the number of virtual machines employed [23]. Unfortunately, state-of-the-art approaches mainly apply vertical and horizontal scaling in an isolated fashion. According to a recent survey on this topic [23], among the 87 surveyed approaches only two have explored optimization techniques to search for combined vertical and horizontal scaling [8,9]. However, in both cases horizontal scaling assumes a fixed symmetric load balancing toward all the horizontal replicas. This may not be appropriate when machines have different hardware characteristics (i.e., due to uncertain runtime disruptive events such as software ageing or hardware degradation), since a symmetric load distribution may worsen performance.

To overcome this limitation, we propose a novel technique combining hori-zontal and vertical scaling that can efficiently determine the load distribution policy to continuously fulfill performance goals of distributed co-located appli-cations (Sect. 2). We consider a model-based approach using queuing networks (QNs) [3]. In particular, we employ multi-class QNs, where each class represents an application with its own demand on the CPU and specific performance tar-gets. Our analysis is based on a compact, approximate representation of QNs based on ordinary differential equations (ODEs) [5,16]. This avoids the state space explosion problem arising from the exact transient analysis of the Markov chain underlying the QN, thus enabling an effective runtime adaptation.

We formulate the question of finding a combined horizontal and vertical scal-ing strategy as a Model Predictive Control (MPC) problem [10]. MPC performs runtime optimization which uses the ODE model to predict the future evolution of the system given the currently measured state; the output is an allocation of the resource-sharing quotas on each machine and the routing probabilities across replicas that steer the model toward the reference set points for each application.

The use of MPC with an ODE model to control performance-related indices of a distributed application has been studied in [13], but for queuing models with a single class of users only. In this paper we present two significant extensions:

1. A multi-class model that enables an accurate representation of the *capped allocation* paradigm [4]. This is a CPU-sharing mechanism available in most modern off-the-shelf hypervisors (e.g., [2,22]), which defines the maximum share that a VM can receive from the CPU.
2. The specification of latency-based response-time requirements, enriching [13], which was limited to queue-length and throughput requirements only.

A positively surprising side effect of our new multi-class MPC formulation is the reduced computational cost, since the whole control problem is now encoded as a linear programming problem (LP, see e.g., [6]) as opposed to the mixed-integer program of the single class formulation of [13]. This is due to the fact that in [13] the control was acting on an integer variable representing the number of CPUs in each machine, whereas here we control a continuous variable that represents the CPU share allocated to each application.

We conducted the evaluation of the proposed approach on a real shared virtualized environment hosting two load-balanced applications (Sect. 3) by showing that only a combined vertical and horizontal load balancing adaptation can efficiently achieve desired performance targets when heterogeneous computational resources are considered.

2   Combined Vertical and Horizontal Autoscaling

A Running Example: Figure 1 shows a QN model of a prototypal system on which to perform combined autoscaling. There are two processing nodes represented by the queuing stations N_1 and N_2. Each node serves two application classes; each class may have different service demands and performance requirements. The demands are expressed as exponential distributions; for instance, $1/\mu_{1,2}$ is

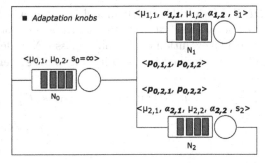

Fig. 1. Sample QN model.

the average service time of class-2 application on node 1. Node N_0 represents a dispatcher that submits user's requests (the *jobs* circulating in the QN) to either computational node. Horizontal scaling is achieved by choosing the routing probability with which the dispatcher selects the actual processing node. For example, setting $p_{0,1,1} = p_{0,2,1} = p_{0,1,2} = p_{0,2,2} = 0.5$ induces a symmetric load balancing policy according to which requests are evenly distributed across all the processing nodes. Vertical scaling is achieved by choosing the CPU quotas assigned to the applications in each machine. For example, fixing $\alpha_{1,2} = 0.3$ assigns a share of 30% of computational resources to class-2 jobs. The parameter s_1 indicates the total number of CPU cores available in node 1. We note that the shares need not to sum up to one at a node—in which case the computation resources are not fully utilized. The *adaptation knobs*, i.e., the values that can be changed at runtime are indicated in red. In the following we formally define all the different components of the proposed approach.

Multi Class Parametric QN: Formally, let us consider a set of stations S and a set of service classes C. A *Multi-class parametric QN* is described by a set of parameters, denoted by P, as follows:

- $s_i \in P$ is the concurrency level of station i, with $i \in S$;
- $\mu_{i,c} \in P$ is the service rate of station i for the jobs of service class c, with $i \in S, c \in C$;

- $p_{i,j,c} \in P$ is the *routing probability*, i.e., the probability that a request of class c from station i goes to j, with $i, j \in S$ and $c \in C$;
- $\alpha_{i,c}$ is the processing share assigned to jobs of class c at station i such that $\sum_{c \in C} \alpha_{i,c} \leq 1$ and $\alpha_{i,c} \geq 0$, with $i \in S, c \in C$.

Finally, to formally justify the ODE approximation, the service rates $\mu_{i,c}$ are assumed to be exponentially distributed. However, using [15] our framework can be extended to the nonexponential case with phase-type distributions [3].

Moreover in order to formally define the adaptation, we denote by $V \subseteq P$ the subset of adaptation knobs. For each parameter that is fixed, i.e., $p \in P - V$, $\hat{p}$ is its given value. Finally we denote by $x_{i,c}(0), i \in S$ the initial condition, i.e., the initial number of jobs of class c assigned to station i.

ODE Model: The ODE model is systematically derived from the parametric QN and it gives estimate of the average queue lengths $x_{i,c}(t)$ as a function of time. The evolution of the multi-class QN under a cap share resource allocation policy is described by the following ODE system:

$$\frac{dx_{i,c}(t)}{dt} = -\mu_{i,c}(t) \min\{x_{i,c}(t), \alpha_{i,c}(t)s_i(t)\}$$
$$+ \sum_{j \in S} p_{j,i,c}(t)\mu_{j,c}(t) \min\{x_{j,c}(t), \alpha_{j,c}s_j(t)\} \quad (1)$$

with initial condition $x_{i,c}(0)$, for all $i \in S, c \in C$.

Here the term $\mathcal{T}_{i,c}(t) = \mu_{i,c}(t) \min\{x_{i,c}(t), \alpha_{i,c}(t)s_i(t)\}$ represents the overall *nonlinear* instantaneous average throughput of station i for jobs of class c: when the queue length $x_{i,c}(t)$ in station i is less than the reserved fraction of servers $\alpha_{i,c}(t)s_i(t)$, then the $x_{i,c}(t)$ jobs are served in parallel; otherwise some of the jobs are enqueued and only $\alpha_{i,c}(t)s_i(t)$ of them are processed at once. The throughputs may be weighted by the class-dependent routing probabilities $p_{j,i,c}(t)$, because a station may receive only a fraction of the jobs elsewhere. Using the instantaneous average queue length $x_{i,c}(t)$ and the throughput $\mathcal{T}_{i,c}(t)$, we define $\mathcal{R}_{i,c}(t) = x_{i,c}(t)/\mathcal{T}_{i,c}(t)$ as the instantaneous average response time for jobs of class c at station i; this is the time spent by the last job of class c while competing for service at station i.

Basically, assuming a cap share resource allocation policy is equivalent to assuming that $s_{i,c} = \alpha_{i,c}(t)s_i(t)$ is the fraction of the original physical station capacity $s_i(t)$ assigned to the service class c, scaled by the sharing factor $\alpha_{i,c}$, such that $\sum_{c \in C} \alpha_{i,c}(t)s_i(t) \leq s_i(t)$. In Sect. 3 we validate this ODE model by comparing prediction results against real measurements taken from a multi-class system hosted in a shared virtualized environment.

LP Performance Adaptation Formulation: In [13] we showed how employing MPC for performance runtime adaptation of single class queuing network could be reduced to the solution of a mixed-integer program (MIP). This formulation relies on a linear time-varying system with auxiliary, "virtual" adaptation knobs which will be then related to the original ones. Here we extend this formulation for controlling the multi-class QN under the cap allocation sharing. The linear time-varying system that we consider is defined as:

$$\frac{dx_{i,c}(t)}{dt} = \gamma_{i,c}(t) + \sum_{j \in S}(-\gamma_{j,c}(t) + \zeta_{j,i,c}(t)), \quad i \in S, c \in C \tag{2}$$

where $\gamma_{i,c}(t)$ represents the virtual throughput of station i of class c and $\zeta_{j,i,c}(t)$ is a virtual routing probability (which will be related to $p_{j,i,c}$).

We show how (2), augmented with appropriate constraints, can be used for building an LP problem suitable for controlling systems whose performance dynamics can be described by the discrete time version of (1).

Discrete Time Model: In order to employ MPC, we rely on a time discretization of the ODE model with a finite step size Δt. MPC finds the optimal values of the adaptation knobs over a time horizon of H steps. Simple algebraic manipulations of (2) yield a formulation that reads:

$$x_{i,c}(k+1) = x_{i,c}(k) + \gamma_{i,c}(k) + \sum_{j \in S}(-\gamma_{j,c}(k) + \zeta_{j,i,c}(k)), \quad i \in S, c \in C. \tag{3}$$

Unfolding (3) over H time steps allows us to embed the dynamics of the model as a discrete set of constraints in the optimization problem:

$$x_{i,c}(1) = x_{i,c}(0) + \gamma_{i,c}(0) + \sum_{j \in S}(-\gamma_{j,c}(0) + \zeta_{j,i,c}(0))$$

$$x_{i,c}(2) = x_{i,c}(1) + \gamma_{i,c}(1) + \sum_{j \in S}(-\gamma_{j,c}(1) + \zeta_{j,i,c}(1))$$

$$\dots$$

$$x_{i,c}(H) = x_{i,c}(H-1) + \gamma_{i,c}(H-1) + \sum_{j \in S}(-\gamma_{j,c}(H-1) + \zeta_{j,i,c}(H-1))$$

for all $i \in S, c \in C$.

Virtual Knobs Constraints: In order to relate the virtual adaptation knobs, i.e., $\gamma_{i,c}(k), \zeta_{i,j,c}(k)$, to the original ones, i.e., $\alpha_{i,c}(k), p_{j,i,c}(k)$, respectively, we add specific constraints to the optimization problem. Hereafter we focus only on establishing a formal correspondence between the $\gamma_{i,c}(k)$ and the actual shares since the equivalence between the virtual routing probabilities and the actual ones is analogous to what discussed in [13].

The term $-\gamma_{i,c}(k)$ represents the throughput of station i for service of class c at discrete time step k, i.e., $\mu_{i,c}(k) \min\{x_{i,c}(k), \alpha_{i,c}(k)s_i(k)\}$. Since the shares can be chosen as close to 0 as desired, this consistency is given by adding the following constraints to the optimization problem:

$$-\gamma_{i,c}(k) \geq 0, \qquad\qquad -\gamma_{i,c}(k) \leq \mu_{i,c}s_i\Delta t \tag{4}$$

$$-\gamma_{i,c}(k) \leq \mu_{i,c}x_{i,c}(k)\Delta t, \qquad -\sum_{c \in C}\frac{\gamma_{i,c}(k)}{\mu_{i,c}} \leq s_i\Delta t \tag{5}$$

with $i \in S, c \in C$. In (4),(5) we consider a time invariant service rate $\mu_{i,c}(k) = \mu_{i,c}$ for each station i of service class c and a time invariant parallelism level $s_i(k) = s_i$. Indeed differently from [13] in the new LP control formulation the number of cores assigned to each machine is statically determined and only the share parameters are used to control the runtime performance of the system. However we remark that this formulation can be easily extended to those cases in which the number of virtual machines need to be computed at runtime (i.e., by considering a time variant s_i).

Objective Function: We define the objective function of the optimization problem. We consider R performance metrics to be optimized. For each time step $k = 0, 1, \ldots, H - 1$, in the vector $m(k) = \big(m_1(k), \ldots, m_R(k)\big)$ each component $m_r(k)$ represents the variable associated with the r-th performance metric, with $1 \leq r \leq R$. We specify the values that this can take according to the type of instantaneous average index to optimize: throughput, queue length, or response time. For all k we set:

$$m_r(k) = \begin{cases} -\dfrac{\gamma_{i,c}(k)}{\Delta t} & \text{if the } r\text{-th metric is the class-}c \text{ throughput at station } i, \\ x_{i,c}(k) & \text{if the } r\text{-th metric is the class-}c \text{ queue length at station } i. \end{cases}$$

For the encoding of response time, the treatment is different because we need to handle the nonlinear expression $\mathcal{R}_{i,c}(k) = \frac{x_{i,c}(k)}{T_{i,c}(k)} = \frac{x_{i,c}(k)\Delta t}{-\gamma_{i,c}(k)}$. We linearize this problem as follows. We let $\beta_{i,c}$ denote the desired response time requirement for class c in station i at time step k. Then, the idea is to minimize the quantity $|x_{i,c}(k)\Delta t + \beta_{i,c}(k)\gamma_{i,c}(k)|$. In order to do so, we consider auxiliary variables $\tilde{x}_{i,c}(k)$ and let $m_r(k) = \tilde{x}_{i,c}(k)$ if the r-th metric is the class-c response time at station i. Then, we can observe that by adding the following constraints to the LP problem

$$\tilde{x}_{i,c}(k) \geq 0 \tag{6}$$

$$\tilde{x}_{i,c}(k) \geq x_{i,c}(k)\Delta t + \beta_{i,c}\gamma_{i,c}(k) \tag{7}$$

$$-\tilde{x}_{i,c}(k) \leq x_{i,c}(k)\Delta t + \beta_{i,c}\gamma_{i,c}(k) \tag{8}$$

minimizing $\tilde{x}_{i,c}(k)$ results in finding the value for the adaptation knobs such that the response time at time k for station i and class c is as close as possible to the desired value $\beta_{i,c}(k)$.

Thus, overall we can collect the set points in vectors $o(k) = (o_1(k), \ldots, o_R(k))$. Each component of this vector, $o_r(k)$, is equal to the desired set point if the r-th requirement is throughput or a queue length, or 0 if the r-th requirement is a response time.

Our goal is to minimize the error between the performance indices and their reference values, i.e., $e(k) = m(k) - o(k)$, across all time steps in the horizon $k = 0, 1, \ldots, H - 1$. Thus, overall the LP formulation can be specified as follows:

$$\text{minimize}_{\{\gamma_{i,c}(k), \zeta_{i,j,c}(k), \tilde{x}_{i,c}(k)\}} \sum_{k=0}^{H-1} e(k)^T e(k) \tag{9}$$

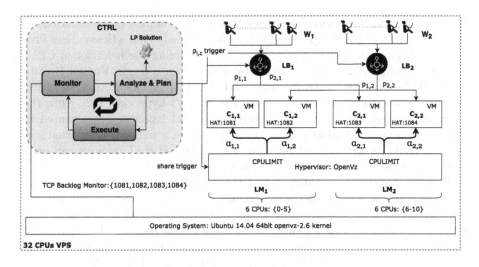

Fig. 2. Experiment system architecture.

subject to constraints Eqs. (3), (4), (6), (7), (8)

$$\zeta_{i,j,c}(k) \geq \gamma_{i,c}(k) \qquad\qquad \text{if } p_{i,j,c} \in V$$

$$\sum_{j \in S} \zeta_{i,j,c}(k) = \gamma_{i,c}(k)(|S| - 1),$$

$$\zeta_{i,j,c}(k) = \gamma_{i,c}(k)(1 - \hat{p}_{i,j,c}) \qquad \text{if } p_{i,j,c} \in P - V \qquad (10)$$

for all $k = 0, \ldots, H - 1$, $i \in S$, $c \in C$, where with (10) we set the values for all the parameters of the QN that are fixed.

Following [13], it is possible to define a *nonlinear MPC* formulation built on a discrete-time representation of the model (1). With the following result, we can recover the shares and routing probabilities for the original nonlinear model from the LP formulation above.

Theorem 1. *Denoting by* $\mathcal{S} = \{\alpha_{i,c}^*(k), p_{i,j,c}^*(k)\}$ *an optimal solution to the nonlinear MPC formulation built on (1) based on [13], there exists an MPC problem based on an LP formulation with dynamics (3) such that its optimal solution* $\mathcal{S}' = \{\gamma'_{i,c}(k), x'_{i,c}(k), \zeta'_{i,j,c}(k)\}$ *satisfies:*

$$\alpha_{i,c}^*(k) = \frac{\gamma'_{i,c}(k)}{s_i \Delta t}, \quad p_{i,j,c}^*(k) = \frac{\gamma'_{i,c}(k) - \zeta'_{i,j,c}(k)}{\gamma'_{i,c}(k)}$$

for all $k = 0, \ldots, H - 1$.

3   Numerical Evaluation

In this section we evaluate the effectiveness of the proposed adaptation approach on a real multi class load-balanced system. The code needed for setting up the experimental infrastructure is publicly available at https://goo.gl/6bNR23.

System Description and Implementation: For running our evaluation we relied on an in-house developed web application, namely HAT (Heavy Task Processing application), specifically designed for resembling the behavior of CPU-intensive systems [7,21]. We conducted our study on a single Virtual Private Server (VPS) equipped with 32 cores and 6 GB of memory. As a vertically scalable virtualized environment we used the *OpenVz* hypervisor [22], while the horizontal scaling has been enabled through a load balancer implemented in NodeJS. In order to validate our control approach in a resource contention scenario, we ran two instances of the same load balanced HAT deployment, each consisting of two OpenVz virtual machines.

Figure 2 depicts the architecture of the considered system. There are two classes of applications and two processing nodes. We emulated a distributed scenario by partitioning the available CPU cores into two Logical Machines **LM** with 6 cores each. The remaining cores are used for running the monitoring infrastructure and the controller. Component $\mathbf{C}_{i,j}$ is the instance of the computational service for class j running on logical machine $\mathbf{LM}_i$; $\mathbf{LB}_j$ is the dispatcher for class j; **CTRL** is the runtime controller. Component $\mathbf{W}_j$ represents the workload generator which injects requests of class-j service into the system. With these settings, $\mathbf{LB}_j$ dispatches user requests for class j to processing node i with routing probability $p_{i,j}$, while the resource share of class j executing at node i is $\alpha_{i,j}$. These values are adapted at runtime by the **CTRL** component, in a MAPE-K [14] fashion, through operating system signals (see Fig. 2) and the OpenVz interface.

CTRL ran the LP optimizations using the academic version of CPLEX tool. We implemented each $\mathbf{W}_j$ as a multi-process Python based workload generator running independent concurrent users that iteratively issue requests, waiting an exponentially distributed delay (i.e., the *think time* given by $1/\mu_{0,i} \geq 0$) between successive requests. Components $\mathbf{C}_{i,j}$ and $\mathbf{LB}_j$ have been implemented as multi-threaded NodeJs servers using the NAPA library.

Model Parametrization and Validation: We modeled the system under study with a multi-class QN as depicted in Fig. 1. The QN processing node N_0 represents the $\mathbf{W}_1$ and $\mathbf{W}_2$ workload generators, while nodes N_1 and N_2 model the logical machines $\mathbf{LM}_1$ and $\mathbf{LM}_2$.

For model validation, we set think times $1/\mu_{0,1} = 1/\mu_{0,2} = 1\,\mathrm{s}$, and population levels $X_1 = X_2 = 200$ users (i.e., we assumed a closed workload). We assigned $s_1 = s_2 = 2$ cores to each processing node and service rates $\mu_{i,j} = 20.5\,\mathrm{s}^{-1}$ for $i,j = 1,2$. These rates were estimated by measuring the maximum throughput on the actual hardware platform. Finally we deployed the system in its symmetric configuration, i.e., $p_{i,j} = 0.5$ for $i,j = 1,2$. To exercise the system under different conditions we considered 10 different resource share allocations.

Table 1 reports the validation results in terms of the measured and predicted throughputs for class-j application, denoted by $\mathcal{T}_{mj}$ and $\mathcal{T}_{pj}$, respectively, as well as their relative percentage errors $\mathcal{E}_{rj}$. For each resource share assignment, the throughputs were measured by averaging 10 independent executions, each

Table 1. Model validation results. The errors $\mathcal{E}_{r1}$ and $\mathcal{E}_{r2}$ between the measured and predicted throughputs for class 1 and class 2, respectively, are measured as absolute relative percentage errors.

$\alpha_{1,1}, \alpha_{2,1}$	0.15	0.30	0.40	0.50	0.60	0.65	0.70	0.75	0.80	0.85
$\alpha_{1,2}, \alpha_{2,2}$	0.85	0.70	0.60	0.50	0.40	0.35	0.30	0.25	0.20	0.15
$\mathcal{T}_{m1}$	10.85	22.47	29.85	40.85	45.90	50.10	54.57	57.73	62.50	65.06
$\mathcal{T}_{p1}$	12.00	24.00	32.00	39.99	48.00	52.00	56.00	60.00	63.99	67.97
$\mathcal{E}_{r1}$	10.53	6.78	7.21	2.12	4.56	3.80	2.61	3.93	2.39	4.48
$\mathcal{T}_{m2}$	65.94	53.40	44.54	40.80	30.67	26.83	22.90	18.72	14.79	10.84
$\mathcal{T}_{p2}$	67.97	56.00	48.00	39.99	32.00	28.00	24.00	20.00	16.00	12.00
$\mathcal{E}_{r2}$	3.08	4.87	7.75	2.00	4.34	4.34	4.79	6.82	8.18	10.62

lasting 2 min. The results show that the model can predict the trends of the real system adequately. We consider the errors acceptable, since a simple deterministic model omits many low-level interactions between the operating system and the virtualization environment.

Adaptation Evaluation: We evaluate the effectiveness of our approach by showing that the combined vertical and horizontal load balancing adaptation can efficiently meet performance targets when either of the two techniques alone cannot. We focus on a scenario of *hardware degradation*. Starting from a symmetric set-up where the service rates of nodes $\mathbf{C}_{i,j}$ are identical and equal to 20.5 (as in the validation set-up), we inject a degradation event where the service rate at node $\mathbf{LM}_1$ becomes 3 times smaller.

For both the symmetric and the degraded case, the objective of the adaptation was to maintain the following set points: instantaneous average response time of the class-1 application equal to 2 s; and class-2 instantaneous average throughput equal to 50 requests per second.

We controlled the performance of the system under a workload of $X_1 = X_2 = 200$ concurrent users with a think rate $\mu_{0,1} = \mu_{0,2} = 1\,\mathrm{s}^{-1}$. According to the system description (see Fig. 2), we assigned $s_1 = s_2 = 6$ to each logical machine. For the vertical scaling control we fixed the symmetric distribution $p_{i,j} = 0.5$, with $i, j = 1, 2$, while the controller could change all resource shares $\alpha_{i,j}$ in an isolated fashion. When the combined control approach is applied also the routing probabilities are changed at runtime.

We evaluated both the control approaches, i.e., vertical and combined, in two separated sessions, i.e., symmetric and degraded, each of which was 20-minutes long. We fixed an ODE sampling interval $\Delta t = 0.1\,\mathrm{s}$, an activation loop rate $= 0.1\,\mathrm{s}$, and control horizon $H = 10$.

Figure 3a and 3b report the class-1 instantaneous average response time distributions in the symmetric set-up (i.e., no degradation) when vertical scaling only and the combined approaches are applied, respectively. In this case both the control approaches are able to fulfill the requirements. This is due to the fact that

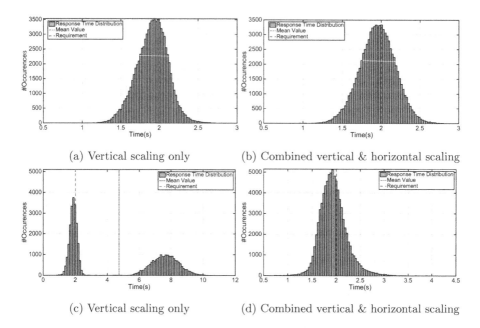

(a) Vertical scaling only   (b) Combined vertical & horizontal scaling

(c) Vertical scaling only   (d) Combined vertical & horizontal scaling

Fig. 3. Class-1 instantaneous average response time distribution without degradation (a-b) and with degradation (c-d).

the performance target is locally achievable on each logical machine by varying the allocation shares only. Under degradation, the advantage of the combined control (i.e., vertical plus dynamic load distribution policy) becomes evident. Indeed, Fig. 3c depicts the class-1 response time distribution when the vertical scaling is applied under the degradation scenario. Since the joint requirements for class-1 and class-2 are no longer satisfiable locally, all the users sent to LM_2 will still experience the intended response time, while the ones sent to LM_1 will be served by a saturated system characterized by poor performance. Figure 3d, instead, depicts the class-1 response time distribution when the combined vertical and horizontal load balancing autoscaling is applied. In this case the routing probabilities of both classes are properly adjusted, steering the system toward the requirements fulfillment regardless of the differences in the service rates. We remark how, under the same scenario, applying a state-of-the-art horizontal scaling technique (i.e., [8,9]) would lead to a system with a larger number of provisioned virtual machines, thus incurring higher costs and adaptation delays.

Regarding class-2 throughput adaptation, when the system works in the symmetric case both the control approaches are able to fulfill the requirements (see Fig. 4a and 4b). With degradation, only the combined approach is able to steer the system toward the desired set points (see Fig. 4c and 4d).

Table 2 reports the average values for the control signals used during each adaptation trace. We can observe that during the degradation case LM_1 is saturated since $\alpha_{1,1} + \alpha_{1,2} \simeq 1$. In this case the only way to satisfy the requirements

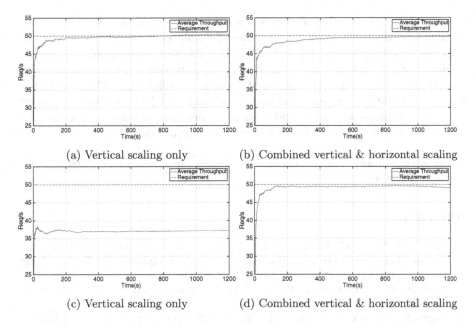

Fig. 4. Class-2 instantaneous average throughput without degradation (a-b) and with degradation (c-d).

Table 2. Optimal control signals.

Scenario	Ctrl type	$\alpha_{1,1}$	$\alpha_{2,1}$	$\alpha_{1,2}$	$\alpha_{2,2}$	$p_{1,1}$	$p_{2,1}$	$p_{1,2}$	$p_{2,2}$
No degradation	Vertical	0.26	0.26	0.25	0.27	0.50	0.50	0.50	0.50
	Combined	0.25	0.28	0.29	0.25	0.50	0.50	0.62	0.38
Degradation	Vertical	0.46	0.13	0.53	0.28	0.50	0.50	0.50	0.50
	Combined	0.46	0.37	0.32	0.38	0.27	0.73	0.24	0.76

of both classes is to operate at the load distribution level redirecting the majority of the user requests on the faster machine $\mathbf{LM_2}$ while properly varying the CPU shares, i.e., in a combined vertical and horizontal autoscaling fashion.

4   Conclusion

In this paper we have presented an efficient approach for the performance adaptation of distributed co-located applications using fluid multi class queuing network (QN) and model predictive control (MPC). The main novelties lay in the combined usage of vertical and horizontal load balancing autoscaling techniques and the extension of the fluid model presented in [13] for modeling multiclass distributed systems under a capped resources allocation scheduler. At each time step during system evolution a linear programming problem is solved for computing the adaptation knobs (i.e., routing probability and allocation shares) suitable to steer the system to throughput or response time set points. As future work we aim to extend our adaptation problem formulation to explicitly model the response time distribution instead of its instantaneous average only. Moreover, we also plan to: *(i)* study the scalability of the approach while varying the system size, e.g., increasing the number of VMs; *(ii)* extend our method to include resource contention policies for network, memory, and I/O; *(iii)* consider more expressive resource schedulers and system performance interactions such as the completely fair scheduler [20] and layered queuing networks [24].

Acknowledgement. Mirco Tribastone is partially funded by a DFG Mercator Fellowship (SPP 1593, DAPS2 Project).

References

1. Adam, O., Lee, Y.C., Zomaya, A.Y.: Ctrlcloud: performance-aware adaptive control for shared resources in clouds. In: International Symposium on Cluster, Cloud and Grid Computing (CCGRID), pp. 110–119 (2017)
2. Barham, P., et al.: Xen and the art of virtualization. ACM SIGOPS Oper. Syst. Rev. **37**, 164–177 (2003)
3. Bolch, G., Greiner, S., De Meer, H., Trivedi, K.S.: Queueing Networks and Markov Chains: Modeling and Performance Evaluation with Computer Science Applications. Wiley, Hoboken (2006)
4. Bolker, E., Ding, Y.: On the performance impact of fair share scheduling. In: International CMG Conference, pp. 71–82 (2000)
5. Bortolussi, L., Hillston, J., Latella, D., Massink, M.: Continuous approximation of collective system behaviour: a tutorial. Perform. Eval. **70**, 317–349 (2013)
6. Boyd, S., Vandenberghe, L.: Convex Optimization. Cambridge University Press, Cambridge (2004)
7. Corp., I.: Linpack. https://software.intel.com/en-us/articles/intel-math-kernel-library-linpack-download
8. Dutta, S., Gera, S., Verma, A., Viswanathan, B.: Smartscale: automatic application scaling in enterprise clouds. In: International Conference on Cloud Computing (CLOUD), pp. 221–228 (2012)
9. Gandhi, A., Dube, P., Karve, A., Kochut, A., Zhang, L.: Modeling the impact of workload on cloud resource scaling. In: International Symposium on Computer Architecture and High Performance Computing (SBAC-PAD), pp. 310–317 (2014)
10. Garcia, C.E., Prett, D.M., Morari, M.: Model predictive control: theory and practice–a survey. Automatica **25**, 335–348 (1989)
11. Gupta, D., Cherkasova, L., Gardner, R., Vahdat, A.: Enforcing performance isolation across virtual machines in Xen. In: van Steen, M., Henning, M. (eds.) Middleware 2006. LNCS, vol. 4290, pp. 342–362. Springer, Heidelberg (2006). https://doi.org/10.1007/11925071_18
12. Huang, D., He, B., Miao, C.: A survey of resource management in multi-tier web applications. IEEE Commun. Surv. Tutor. **16**, 1574–1590 (2014)
13. Incerto, E., Tribastone, M., Trubiani, C.: Software performance self-adaptation through efficient model predictive control. In: International Conference on Automated Software Engineering (ASE), pp. 485–496 (2017)
14. Kephart, J.O., Chess, D.M.: The vision of autonomic computing. Computer **36**, 41–50 (2003)

15. Kowal, M., Tschaikowski, M., Tribastone, M., Schaefer, I.: Scaling size and parameter spaces in variability-aware software performance models. In: International Conference on Automated Software Engineering (ASE), pp. 407–417 (2015)
16. Kurtz, T.G.: Solutions of ordinary differential equations as limits of pure Markov processes. J. Appl. Prob. **7**, 49–58 (1970)
17. Lakew, E.B., Klein, C., Hernandez-Rodriguez, F., Elmroth, E.: Performance-based service differentiation in clouds. In: International Symposium on Cluster, Cloud and Grid Computing (CCGRID), pp. 505–514 (2015)
18. Lakew, E.B., Papadopoulos, A.V., Maggio, M., Klein, C., Elmroth, E.: KPI-agnostic control for fine-grained vertical elasticity. In: International Symposium on Cluster, Cloud and Grid Computing (CCGRID), pp. 589–598 (2017)
19. Li, L., Franks, G.: Performance modeling of systems using fair share scheduling with layered queueing networks. In: International Symposium on Modeling, Analysis & Simulation of Computer and Telecommunication Systems (MASCOTS), pp. 1–10 (2009)
20. Molnar, I.: This is the CFS scheduler (1999). https://www.kernel.org/doc/Documentation/scheduler/sched-design-CFS.txt
21. NASA: Nas parallel benchmarks. http://www.nas.nasa.gov/Resources/Software/npb.html
22. Parallels: OpenVz user guide (2016). https://docs.openvz.org/openvz_users_guide.webhelp/
23. Qu, C., Calheiros, R.N., Buyya, R.: Auto-scaling web applications in clouds: a taxonomy and survey. ACM Computing Surveys **9**(4), 34 p (2017)
24. Tribastone, M.: A fluid model for layered queueing networks. IEEE Trans. Softw. Eng. **39**, 744–756 (2013)

Scheduling and Load Balancing

Early Termination of Failed HPC Jobs Through Machine and Deep Learning

Michał Zasadziński[1]([⊠]), Victor Muntés-Mulero[1], Marc Solé[1], David Carrera[2], and Thomas Ludwig[3]

[1] CA Technologies, Barcelona, Spain
{michal.zasadzinski,victor.muntes,marc.solesimo}@ca.com
[2] Universitat Politecnica de Catalunya, Barcelona, Spain
dcarrera@ac.upc.edu
[3] Deutsches Klimarechenzentrum GmbH, Hamburg, Germany
ludwig@dkrz.de

Abstract. Failed jobs in a supercomputer cause not only waste in CPU time or energy consumption but also decrease work efficiency of users. Mining data collected during the operation of data centers helps to find patterns explaining failures and can be used to predict them. Automating system reactions, e.g., early termination of jobs, when software failures are predicted does not only increase availability and reduce operating cost, but it also frees administrators' and users' time. In this paper, we explore a unique dataset containing the topology, operation metrics, and job scheduler history from the petascale Mistral supercomputer. We extract the most relevant system features deciding on the final state of a job through decision trees. Then, we successfully train a neural net to predict job evolution based on power time series of nodes. Finally, we evaluate the effect on CPU time saving for static and dynamic job termination policies.

Keywords: HPC · Slurm · Failure prediction · Failure prevention Deep learning · Data center

1 Introduction

Data centers are a core element in most IT systems, hosting cloud applications, enabling HPC or performing intensive Big Data analytics. Although the optimal architecture of a data center may be different for each of these applications, general maintenance problems remain the same. Failures in hardware and infrastructure can both cause software failures or may be the result of such software failures. Software errors are the most common cause of failures [4]. Also, many jobs produce large network and storage system loads which degrade the system performance [3].

The original version of this chapter was revised: For detailed information please see correction chapter. The correction to this chapter is available at https://doi.org/10.1007/978-3-319-96983-1_58

© Springer International Publishing AG, part of Springer Nature 2018
M. Aldinucci et al. (Eds.): Euro-Par 2018, LNCS 11014, pp. 163–177, 2018.
https://doi.org/10.1007/978-3-319-96983-1_12

Data presenting the state of a system is usually so complex that administrators might not take the best decision to recover a system efficiently. Moreover, in many cloud-oriented services, system monitoring information is limited to hardware metrics, and do not include user application logs. Thus, it is even more challenging to predict job failures and take proper action. Evaluating jobs in run-time augments administrative metrics and increases the confidence of taken decisions. Therefore, jobs which are likely to fail or decrease the performance of a system can be terminated in advance, saving resources, computing and human time, and lowering operational costs. According to the dataset used in this paper, completed jobs in the petascale Mistral[1] supercomputer consume about 45 million CPU hours per month and they are 91.3% of all submitted jobs. Predicting the final job state at the time of job submission and during run-time allows for forcing job termination before a failure occurs, enabling savings. However, deciding when it is necessary to terminate a job is a nontrivial task.

In this paper, we analyze the impact of both **static** and **dynamic** job termination **policies** using different data center metrics. We propose new job state prediction algorithms based on Decision Trees (DT) and Convolutional Neural Networks (CNN). We use data extracted from the Mistral supercomputer that includes system metrics, job scheduler history, and system topology information. We augment datasets during the exploration to show how knowledge coming from job scheduler, monitoring system, and topology and structure, can increase prediction capabilities and uncover new patterns. We discriminate among job submission features these that explain the termination status of jobs based on job traces. We use power series of nodes to build a model used for failure prediction at run-time. For this task, we use machine learning (ML) and a CNN. The trained CNN achieves 85% of precision in the classification of failed jobs by power series. The CNN predicts failures for more than 40% of failed jobs in the 20th percentile of their duration.

The remainder of this paper is divided into six sections. Work related to failure prediction and prevention in HPC is discussed in Sect. 2. In Sect. 3, we provide description of Mistral supercomputer (42nd most powerful computer in November 2017 (See footnote 1)) and data exported from this environment. Section 4 presents extraction of important features and their discovery by means of DTs that are created using these data. Then, in Sect. 5, we describe the training and use of a CNN for job state prediction. At the end of Sect. 5, we show savings applying different policies for early job termination. We discuss results, the usefulness of the proposed policies and include plans for future research in Sect. 6.

2   Related Work

Authors in [18] describe the role of software in failures occurring in data centers. Software problems in an OS, middleware, application, or the wrong configuration, e.g., underestimated resources cause the majority of job failures in HPC

---

[1] https://www.top500.org/system/178567.

workload [1,22]. The authors of [5] discover the correlation between failures, and different characteristics of supercomputer operations, such as node usage, last state of a job, and hardware metrics. This research explores state sequences from the perspective of a node. The authors perform job-oriented analysis only to point users with a high failure rate. Analysis of logs and the rate of failed jobs allows detecting slow-downs and targeted failures [4]. Recently, the authors in [10] characterized workload in an HPC environment with the primary goals to find patterns across different applications and disciplines. Latest work presented in [9] analyzes failures of the Oak Ridge supercomputer. The authors describe hardware reliability, correlate failure types, and investigate failure trends in the time and spatial distribution. However, leveraging user history for prediction of failed jobs and learning application workload patterns is not a primary focus area in the prior publications. Also, there are not many publications addressing the separate analysis of jobs and job steps.

There is many research on ML in data center maintenance for either prediction or classification problems [6,7,17,20]. For instance, research in [8] uses dynamic association rules to predict failures in the Blue Gene. The authors of [15] focus on predicting failures in computing nodes, and as a reaction, redirecting a job to another set of nodes. Another possible action is checkpointing, and the authors of [2] investigate the optimal policy to reduce trade-off between checkpoints frequency and MTBF. The authors in [13] use power and temperature metrics to predict errors in GPU clusters via neural network (NN) model. Recently, decision trees are implemented for failure prediction in HPC domain [12]. The proposed algorithm identifies the causes of failures, performing better comparing to other SoA techniques.

Despite the popularity and progress in ML algorithms and software, the area of prediction of the final HPC job states through accurate modeling of power series seems to be unexplored. The focus of most of the work is put on predicting failures per hardware unit, rather than learning workload patterns of failed jobs. The complexity of IT systems and their dynamic structure are one of the main obstacles to create accurate models. The authors in [21] propose power modeling techniques via Petri networks, to estimate power consumption. Also, work presented in [19] reports research on power profiling in HPC environments. The authors discuss application network architecture, performance, and scalability in the dimension of power consumption, and they propose a system for accurate power monitoring. However, in our work, we aim to use as little information as possible – power metrics representing the load of nodes.

3   Mistral Supercomputer Dataset

DKRZ Mistral supercomputer contains 3336 computing nodes, about 90 special nodes dedicated to other activities, and a separate 54 PiB Lustre file system. Applications for climate science generate the production workload. Slurm[2] maintains node reservations, resource allocation, and accounting.

---

[2] https://slurm.schedmd.com/.

3.1 Job Scheduler History

Through analysis of historical data from the scheduler, we investigate which features are important, thus deciding on a final job state. This goal motivates our strategy, which is oriented to jobs rather than nodes. We use states from the scheduler to determine an output of a job. In the dataset, each job finishes with one of the following states, defined by Slurm documentation.

- **Cancelled** – A user or administrator cancelled a job. The job may or may not have been initiated. In the following analysis, we take into account only cancelled jobs longer than 0 s.
- **Completed** – Job has terminated all processes on all nodes with an exit code of zero.
- **Failed** – Job terminated with non-zero exit code or another failure condition. According to Mistral, another failure condition includes failures caused by any external factor to an allocated node, e.g., failures of Lustre FS, IB.
- **Node fail** – Job terminated due to a failure of one or more allocated nodes. This state includes only hardware related problems of a computational node.
- **Timeout** – Job terminated upon reaching its time limit.

Each job consists of one or more steps. A job submission script defines the execution order of steps; also the order can be read from Slurm history. The order can be sequential, parallel, or mixed, see example script in Listing 1.1.

Listing 1.1. Example Slurm batch script. Two steps run sequentially on 80 nodes.

```
#SBATCH --nodes 80
#SBATCH --tasks-per-node 10
# First step
srun --nodes 80 --tasks 10 mkdir /home/$USER/$SLURM_JOBID
# Second step
srun app.mpi in.csv out.csv
```

Most steps in Mistral dataset are executed sequentially. In the Slurm database, there are 76 columns. They contain information about jobs: (1) job configuration specified by a user, and (2) statistics known at the end of a job. We give more details about these data in Subsect. 3.3. In this paper, we consider all above **job** states. For **steps**, the dataset includes: Completed, Failed and Cancelled.

3.2 Time Series Data Analysis

Mistral metrics are acquired every 60 s into an Open Time Series Database (OTSDB) instance that is installed on the top of HBase cluster. For this research, the data from the cluster are exported using the HBase ExportSnapshot tool. Then, we import a snapshot with the size of 0.5 TB from a regular continuous period of 10 months of system executions to our analysis environment containing 8 machines with 120 physical cores, 672 GB of RAM. We use Apache Spark for data processing. For training of a CNN, we need job scheduler data merged with power metrics. We merge Slurm steps with data from OTSDB representing power metrics of nodes used by a step during its run-time. That merged steps should contain at least two power measurements. In the worst case, for steps shorter than 120 s, it is possible to merge only one timestamp with node power metrics. So, in the evaluation, we consider a subset of steps longer than 120 s. Discarding short jobs, we do not lose a lot of data: about 1.2M of all steps from the set run for more than 60 s and 1.1M more than 120 s.

3.3 Dataset Split

We show how different knowledge sources: software – job scheduler, hardware – monitoring system, and platform – topology and structure, impact prediction and classification accuracy. Also, we detect which part of the data increases the prediction capabilities of a model when the only used information is the one known at the time of a job submission; and which part of the data improves classification capabilities, when we use statistics of finished jobs. Datasets are divided into the following sets - named with a capital letter for later reference:

- **Slurm job configuration data:** information of either jobs or steps, which is known at the time of submission e.g., reserved time, allocated nodes, required CPU frequency, start time.   [we call it *dataset C* in the experiments]
- **Slurm user data:** columns with information about prior user allocations. Also, this dataset contains aggregated user data. The set includes factors of jobs terminated with each of 5 possible states to a number of all submissions in different windows. We aggregate the data by user and windows with different sizes: last N submissions ($N = 1$, 100, 1k, 10k).   [*dataset U*]
- **Slurm job summary data:** information is known at the **end of a job**, e.g., duration, disk read/write (R/W) – the sum of local storage and Lustre operations done by a job, virtual memory (VM) size, other hardware usage.
  [*dataset S*]
- **Power metrics of nodes (OTSDB data):** power metrics of computing nodes (blades).   [*dataset P*]
- **Data center topology:** topology and localization of nodes.   [*dataset T*]
- **Hardware profiles of nodes:** types of nodes, number and types of CPUs, amount of RAM.   [*dataset H*]

4 Failed Job Analysis

According to the data from the job scheduler, more than 1.3M jobs, and more than 270k different job names are submitted in the 10-month period that is represented by the dataset extracted from the Mistral production environment. These submissions, which are mainly executed in batch mode (98.8%), result in over 4.8M steps. For detailed statistics, see Mistral technical report [23]. One of the observations from the statistics is coherent with usual state of the art reports - failed steps are usually more complex [22]. These statistics represent a convincing motivation for generating savings with the early termination of jobs that are predicted to fail. An average failed job consumes many more CPU hours than completed one and it also decreases resources availability.

4.1 Most Meaningful Features for Prediction of Job States

Extraction of Features. We generate DTs [14] to reveal job and step features explaining a job state. These ML models learn *if-then-else* rules, for either classification or regression task. An advantage of using a DT is the fact that it is a white-box model so that a human can easily understand a trained tree. We use all the features from each dataset for generation of a DT. To decide the optimal size of DTs, we consider (1) over-fitting and (2) readability of a model to a human. Firstly, we split our set into three sets using random stratified sampling. We create the training set containing 70% of jobs (samples), the validation set that has 10% of jobs (samples), and the test set with 20% of jobs. During the training, we measure accuracy on the validation set, while increasing depth of a tree. We set 100 as the minimum number of instances each node's child must have after a split. Trees with depth 5 obtain satisfactory performance. For larger DTs, the accuracy increase is low (0.03%), and the increase of the number of nodes is high. For instance, a tree with depth 9 has 275 nodes, and it is 84 nodes more than a DT with depth 8. Thus, we choose the optimal depth of the DT to be 5, which has 63 nodes. To check if models are not over-fitting, we evaluate random forests (RF) for each dataset. RF create DTs and train them with different training sets that are subsets of the main training set. Then, results from each DT are combined. Created RFs improve neither classification nor prediction quality when compared to the above DTs.

The test evaluations shows the fitness of generated models of either classification (having all information about a finished job), or prediction (having only information at the time of submission). We present the results of evaluations in Tables 1 and 2, including only features with importance over 3%.

Table 1. Decision trees – evaluation of different combinations of data sets - **jobs**

Data set	Important features		Job state	Completed	Failed	Cancelled	Timeout	Node fail
Configuration (C)	Time limit (74%)		Precision	0.91	0.0	0.0	0.0	0.0
	Daytime (24%)		Recall	**1.0**	0.0	0.0	0.0	0.0
			F1-score	0.96	0.0	0.0	0.0	0.0
Configuration + user's history (C + U)	Previous job state for a user (96%) Number of allocated nodes (3%)		Precision	**0.97**	0.75	0.52	0.68	0.0
			Recall	0.98	0.70	**0.44**	0.30	0.0
			F1-score	0.98	0.72	**0.48**	0.42	0.0
Statistics + configuration + user's history (S + C + U)	Previous job state (87%) Duration (9%) Number of allocated nodes (4%)		Precision	**0.97**	0.77	**0.63**	**0.81**	0.0
			Recall	0.99	**0.74**	0.36	**0.35**	0.0
			F1-score	**0.98**	0.75	0.46	**0.49**	0.0
Duration > 120 s statistics, configuration, user's history (S + C + U)	Previous job state (85%) Duration (8%) Number of allocated nodes (6%)		Precision	**0.97**	**0.81**	0.62	0.80	0.0
			Recall	0.99	**0.74**	0.31	0.33	0.0
			F1-score	**0.98**	**0.77**	0.41	0.47	0.0

Jobs. The above results show that the size of resource reservation is a principal factor determining the final state of a job. Also, the results expose that final

Table 2. Decision trees – evaluation of different combinations of data sets - **steps**

Data set	Important features	Job state	Completed	Failed	Cancelled
Configuration (C)	Number of allocated nodes (98%)	Precision	0.95	0.50	0
		Recall	**0.99**	0.07	0
		F1-score	0.97	0.12	0
Configuration, statistics (C + S)	Number of allocated nodes (47%) Average disk W (40%) Duration (4%)	Precision	**0.98**	0.83	0.58
		Recall	**0.99**	0.76	0.04
		F1-score	**0.99**	0.79	0.79
Duration > 120 s configuration, statistics (C + S)	Average disk W (47%) Number of allocated nodes (36%) Average CPU frequency (9%); Duration (4%)	Precision	0.95	0.59	**0.89**
		Recall	0.98	0.23	**0.83**
		F1-score	0.97	0.33	**0.86**
Configuration, topology, hardware information (C + T + H)	Number of allocated nodes (79%) Number of nodes 36C 64 GB RAM (15%) Number of nodes 36C 128 GB RAM (3%)	Precision	0.97	0.75	0.49
		Recall	0.98	0.41	0.01
		F1-score	0.98	0.53	0.01
Configuration, statistics, topology, hardware information, power statistics (C + S + T + H + P)	Number of allocated nodes (46%) Average disk W (41%); Average disk R (5%) Average VM size (4%)	Precision	**0.98**	0.85	0.52
		Recall	**0.99**	0.75	0.10
		F1-score	0.98	0.80	0.17
Duration > 120 s, (C + S + T + H + P)	Average disk W (49%) Number of allocated nodes (35%) Average CPU frequency (10%)	Precision	0.94	**0.93**	0.81
		Recall	**0.99**	**0.79**	0.13
		F1-score	0.97	**0.85**	0.22

states are highly correlated with a user's history. In general, this correlation is weaker for longer jobs.

Steps. Generated DTs reveal that the sum of *disk RW* is often higher for completed jobs than failed ones. Since the mean duration of failed steps is much higher than completed ones [23], higher storage usage can be explained by less active nodes in failed steps. We can state a hypothesis, that some nodes in failed steps stay in idle state, see Sect. 4.2. The evaluation shows the high importance of a number of allocated nodes with 36 cores. An investment done in DKRZ explains this phenomenon. The dataset includes the period when Broadwell nodes started their service in the production environment. That time, users were translating their software and scripts to the recently installed hardware. It is the primary cause of many job failures.

Conclusions. The evaluation of DT classification tasks shows that a DT model is unable to learn and recognize cancelled, node failed, or timeout jobs based only on configuration data. These data are the only information known to the scheduler after a job is submitted. The f1-score is 0 for all of the mentioned states. Augmenting this set with past user's submissions improves recall of failed jobs to 72% and lifts precision of predicting cancellations to 52% and timeouts to 68%. This result shows a strong correlation inside a sequence of final job states. Adding to the training dataset metrics which are known after a job is finished increases the precision of a classifier. The recall does not change for any of the states. Regarding steps, precision and recall are lower than those for job submissions. It is a reasonable result considering that steps have a lower number of features available for these evaluations. The number of allocated nodes is an important feature to predict the final state of a job even when used with hardware metrics features. Other important features are knowledge on past submissions and their states. According to the hardware statistics, average *disk W* is a highly important feature in the classification task of final job states, while general power statistics are features with low importance.

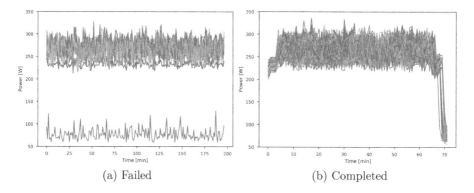

(a) Failed   (b) Completed

Fig. 1. Plots presenting power series of 198 nodes running in parallel a job from the same, user, project, and application. Two jobs were run in different points of time. First one is failed, the next one is completed.

4.2   Node-Power Analysis

We want to investigate the power statistics of failed jobs in comparison with completed ones, to detect idle states. Each computing blade is controlled and monitored by an isolated blade management controller which delivers power metrics. A controller is an external unit, and acquiring measurements does not infer with the workload of a blade. Power metrics of these blades perfectly depict their CPU load. Although in Subsect. 4.1 we evaluate the usefulness of power statistics in prediction, we might also evaluate whether these series can improve job state prediction during the run-time. We correlate power series of nodes allocated for a step with this step's final state and types of nodes. We analyze power statistics for steps longer than 1000 s, grouped by hardware profile to extract average values of power metrics in the last 300 s of the duration of a job. This value is at least 10% lower than for completed ones, when considering all hardware groups, and failed steps. The most probable explanation can be the fact that once a software failure occurs some of the nodes go to an idle state. For instance, Fig. 1 presents power series of 1-step jobs, both executed with the same configuration by the same user. This scenario represents a typical case where one node is in an idle state, and the rest are executing some workload. On the contrary, power series of nodes executing a completed step do not show any node in an idle state. This phenomenon appears in other cases in the dataset and suggests that using power metrics would be relevant for classification of a job state. Moreover, this observation matches with the expert knowledge at DKRZ. In words of one of its system engineers: "We check the idle state of a node during a problematic job, looking at InfiniBand traffic of nodes. If it is low, a job is likely to fail".

5   Prevention of Failures

Prior data exploration and evaluation of DTs show that power metrics and DTs can be used for prediction of final job state. Predictions contain probabilities for each step state. During prediction, we classify a step as failed, when the probability of failure is higher than a defined threshold and all other probabilities associated with other classes. Therefore, we propose two types of policies to be taken: a **static** and **dynamic** one. A static policy uses predictions based on a step configuration data, topology, and hardware information ($C + T + H$) through DTs. A dynamic policy uses predictions during run-time which are produced by a convolutional neural network (CNN), introduced in Sect. 5.1. The inputs to this model are power metrics, which are analyzed in Sect. 4.2. While using a dynamic policy, a job is killed when it is classified as failed for the first time – the earliest prediction over the given threshold.

The use of different types of models, one as a white-box and the other as a black-box has several advantages over, for instance, one complex NN model trained with both static and dynamic data. Firstly, the use of DTs enables to easily explain phenomena observed in a data center to system administrators. Since a model can evolve by repeating the training, changes in trends and user behavior occurred in a data center are observed as results of the comparison of models. Also, a failure prevention system gains performance during the run-time because of splitting evaluation to offline (time of submission only) and online (evaluation of a job during its runtime) one.

5.1   Convolutional Neural Networks

CNNs are a type of deep neural network following a design of biological vision systems [11]. They are widely used for image classification, natural language processing, and recommendation systems, and they have also been successfully used for time series classification and prediction. We propose to use a CNN for classification and prediction of multivariate time series, which are the power metrics of nodes (overall energy consumption of a computing blade) used in a step. Therefore, CNN learns "how a multivariate time series of nodes executing a step look like". A major advantage of using CNNs over neural nets with fully connected (dense) layers only, is that they need much fewer neurons and parameters to solve a particular classification or prediction problem.

In Fig. 3, we present the best CNN model trained for this task. We create the final model after a few iterations, through dropping layers from more complex models which over-fit during the training and do not increase the accuracy. The model presented in Fig. 3 comprises a few types of layers. Each convolutional layer comprises filters with size 3×3, and during the training, each filter learns weights. This layer is used to extract specific features, in this case from 2D matrices. Another important layer type used is a drop-out, which regularizes weights and through dropping neurons and connections, prevent overfitting [16]. A max pooling layer and dense layer are used to aggregate extracted features and classify them into defined classes and give probabilities. The input data are 2D matrices of size $M = 512$ (number of nodes) $\times T = 120$ (length of time series). For steps with matrices which shape is less than $M \times T$, we pad a sample with zeros - which are ignored by CNN during the training. For these matrices which are larger than that size, we downsample a matrix by averaging power metrics. The value for T is chosen so that it is large enough to represent the complete series of most of the steps (only 1.3% of steps are longer than 120 min) and at the same time it is small enough for the NN training to be practical. The dataset with steps is split randomly (the same split as in Sect. 4) into three sets: training (70% of the data), validation (10%), and test (20%) respectively.

The CNN is trained using tensorflow[3] and keras[4] libraries by means of 2x GPU GeForce 1080 Ti. Also, after a few trails and examining a shape of the loss curve, the learning rate is set to 0.001, and we choose a stochastic gradient descent optimizer. The final model, which contains 32261 parameters to train, is trained in 67 epochs with approximately 1 h per epoch. We stop training after lack of significant improvement in the loss curve, and when the model does not improve more than 1% in 5 epochs. We show results of the trained CNN in Table 3.

Table 3. CNN test results - classification. Data set: steps – power metrics, duration $> 120\,$s

	Completed	Failed	Cancelled
Precision	0.93	0.85	0.79
Recall	0.98	0.66	0.15
F1-score	0.96	0.74	0.25
test set	168875	28605	4457

5.2   Evaluation – Static and Dynamic Job-Killing Policies

The primary goal of the evaluation is to explore possible savings and losses depending on the aggressiveness of job-killing policy. We measure the aggres-

---

[3] https://www.tensorflow.org/.
[4] https://keras.io/.

siveness of a policy as the *threshold of class prediction probability*. For instance, a threshold of 60% means that a job is classified as failed when the probability of predicting failed is higher than 60%. An aggressive policy is the one with a low threshold, and the less aggressive one is the one with a high threshold, e.g., greater than 90%. We evaluate the trained CNN model and DT to predict the final states of steps. We use a test set which contains jobs with total CPU time of 84.7M h. CNN predicts a final job state and outputs probabilities for each timestamp during the run of a job. We evaluate proposed policies by depicting lost and gained CPU time, expressed in hours. Lost CPU time stands for the resources consumed by a step that is labeled as completed, but it is killed (false positive). Saved CPU time represents resources that would be used until a step ends but are saved due to a decision of early step termination. Approximate performance of CNN evaluation is 5000 samples/s which is considered sufficient for these experiments.

Table 4. Summary of the dynamic policy evaluation over a test set containing 11M CPU hours of failed jobs

Dynamic policy metric	CPU h	Probability threshold
Maximum savings achievable	7.9M	From 0 to 0.42
Maximum loss (false positive)	4.1M	0.52
Global maximum (savings - loss)	4.0M	From 0 to 0.42
Local maximum of (savings - loss) with the highest value of threshold	0.7M	0.82

Considering the dynamic policy, the maximum value of true positives is 0.9, and for false positives, the maximum value is 0.45. Both metrics decrease smoothly when the threshold grows. Figure 2 shows true and false positive rates depending on the probability threshold for failure prediction with the CNN. On the other hand, the static policy is characterized by the maximum value of the true positive rate of 0.47 and a small value of 0.02 for the false positive rate. The static policy is more accurate in predictions comparing to the dynamic one, but the maximum number of predicted steps to fail are almost two times lower.

Wastes. When it comes to the CPU time, the static policy allows for maximum savings of 0.8M CPU h, and the dynamic one of 8M CPU h. In Table 4, we present a summary of the evaluation of the dynamic policy taking into account CPU hours of jobs. Note, that the earlier we kill a failed job, the bigger savings are. On the other hand, the confidence of prediction increases with time a job is running as we gather more data. Regarding this trade-offs, there is a global maximum of losses for threshold 0.52. For instance, applying a dynamic policy with a threshold of 0.82 (local maximum with the highest threshold value) to the test dataset saves 1.6M CPU h with 0.9M CPU h lost and the total profit of 0.7M CPU h. For instance, a less aggressive policy would be the application of a threshold equal to 0.96. In this case, we save 210k CPU h, and we lose 24k CPU h, with the total profit of 190k CPU h. In contrast, executing static policy allows for maximum savings of 870k CPU h by killing 13k failed jobs with a side effect of killing 3.8k completed ones. Also, the application of the static policy, which is more conservative, does not cause a loss in CPU time, because it reacts after job submission.

Figure 4 presents the distribution of job time at which the dynamic policy will react and terminate a job. We can see that most of the jobs are killed during the first 30% of their total execution time (the time they take if they are not killed earlier). Then, for the remaining steps, prediction abilities increase after 60th percentile of their duration. Figure 4 shows that the dynamic policy can predict failures early.

Users and system administrators may use policies with different aggressiveness levels. For instance, a user might choose a very aggressive policy, both static and dynamic with a very low threshold, when the project budget is highly limited. On the other hand, a less aggressive policy, e.g., a dynamic policy with a high threshold, above 0.9, can be appropriate for long jobs, where user time is the most expensive factor to consider. Also, such a policy can maximize savings comparing to use of a static policy. A static policy used by system administrators can help eliminating problematic jobs, which may be causing the overload of a system. However, use of dynamic policy can cause dissatisfaction of users, since this policy can unexpectedly terminate their jobs without a known reason.

Also, supervised learning through interaction with a user can help improving the proposed policies. Firstly, users should receive a notification when their jobs are repeatedly killed after re-submissions. A user or a system administrator could label such a problematic job. This action provides a model with additional information for incremental improvement. Also, system administrators can decide to perform supervised learning, to set up the optimal aggressiveness of the policy (threshold).

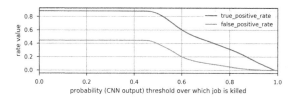

Fig. 2. Plot presents the evaluation of CNN model for different values of prediction probability threshold. The lower is the threshold, the more aggressive is the job terminating policy, greater savings, but we kill more good jobs as a consequence of inaccurate predictions. Total CPU Hours of failed jobs in a set: 11M

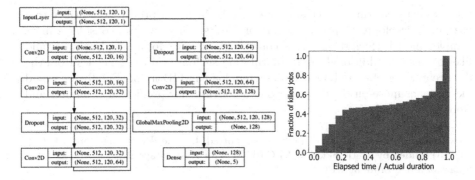

Fig. 3. Graph presenting a trained CNN with layers type and shape of the data

Fig. 4. Cumulative plot presenting the time when the probability of failure exceeds defined threshold 0.82. Number of samples N = 7300

6   Conclusions and Future Work

In this paper, we analyzed a dataset containing metrics, topology and job scheduler data for the Mistral supercomputer. We showed important features in a classification and prediction task of a job state. The number of allocated nodes, the state of a previous job submitted by a user, average storage writes are the most important ones. DTs detect specific node types as an important feature due to migration process from the old to the new computing nodes. DTs perform well as a classifier, with a recall nearly 80% and a precision of 93% for failed steps. As a predictor, DTs can point failed steps, using configuration and allocated hardware data exclusively, with a recall of 41% and a precision of 75%. In the case of CNNs, these scores increase to 66% and 85% respectively. This paper shows that one of the biggest influence on the next state of a job in a supercomputer like Mistral lies in the diversity and spatial distribution of allocated nodes, place of a job in a user sequence and number of disk operations.

We evaluated dynamic and static job-killing policies, pointing out possible savings related to the aggressiveness of both policies. For instance, using medium-aggressive approach, we can kill more than 28% of failed jobs. Through CNN predictions, the proposed dynamic policy kills 40% of jobs in the first 20% of their duration. These effects can be improved by utilizing feedback from users and system administrators and adjusting weights of CNN by supervised learning.

As future work, we would like to improve prediction capabilities of the created solution and focus on Lustre FS. Firstly, we can achieve more accurate analysis of final job states by adding OS logs to the analyzed dataset. Also, this would help to build prediction algorithm of final job states, which is not limited by Slurm job state but uses the utility of a job. For instance, the utility can be measured by analyzing users' actions after a job finishes, e.g., a user copied output data, re-run the same code with different parameters, changed the code. Therefore, this approach can differentiate jobs with a non-zero return code from these which were run unnecessary and these which can provide any utility to a user, e.g., development progress, part of results. Then, we can consider a more complex model which takes into account step sequence for a job. Also, we would like to consider additional input information such as real-time metrics from the data center, e.g., Lustre I/O, overall system load and IB traffic. Finally, we would like to focus more on the deep learning algorithms for prediction of failures and Root Cause Analysis.

Acknowledgments. This research is supported by the BigStorage project (ref. 642963) funded by Marie Skłodowska-Curie ITN for Early Stage Researchers, and it is a part of a doctorate at UPC.

References

1. Barroso, L.A., Clidaras, J., Hölzle, U.: The datacenter as a computer: an introduction to the design of warehouse-scale machines. Synth. Lect. Comput. Archit. **8**(3), 1–154 (2013)
2. Bautista-Gomez, L., Gainaru, A., Perarnau, S., et al.: Reducing waste in extreme scale systems through introspective analysis. In: 2016 IEEE International Parallel and Distributed Processing Symposium (IPDPS), pp. 212–221 (2016)
3. Casas, M., Bronevetsky, G.: Prediction of the impact of network switch utilization on application performance via active measurement. Parallel Comput. **67**(Suppl. C), 38–56 (2017)
4. Clark, A.D., Tellez, L.M., Besse, S., et al.: Dynamic prediction and estimation of intentional failures in HPCs. In: International Conference on Advances in Social Networks Analysis and Mining, pp. 1244–1250 (2016)
5. El-Sayed, N., Schroeder, B.: Reading between the lines of failure logs: understanding how HPC systems fail. In: 43rd Annual IEEE/IFIP International Conference on Dependable Systems and Networks (DSN), pp. 1–12 (2013)
6. Fu, S., Xu, C.Z.: Exploring event correlation for failure prediction in coalitions of clusters. In: Proceedings of the Conference on Supercomputing, pp. 41:1–41:12 (2007)
7. Gao, J.: Machine learning applications for data center optimization. Google White Paper (2014). https://research.google.com/pubs/archive/42542.pdf
8. Gu, J., Zheng, Z., Lan, Z., et al.: Dynamic meta-learning for failure prediction in large-scale systems: a case study. In: 37th International Conference on Parallel Processing (2008)
9. Gupta, S., Patel, T., Engelmann, C., et al.: Failures in large scale systems: long-term measurement, analysis, and implications. In: SC 2017, pp. 1–12 (2017)
10. Jones, M.D., White, J.P., Innus, M., et al.: Workload analysis of blue waters. CoRR abs/1703.00924 (2017). http://arxiv.org/abs/1703.00924
11. LeCun, Y., Bengio, Y., Hinton, G.: Deep learning. Nature **521**(7553), 436–444 (2015)
12. Nakka, N., Agrawal, A., Choudhary, A.: Predicting node failure in high performance computing systems from failure and usage logs. In: 2011 IEEE International Symposium on Parallel and Distributed Processing Workshops and PhD Forum, pp. 1557–1566, May 2011

13. Nie, B., Xue, J., Gupta, S., et al.: Characterizing temperature, power, and soft-error behaviors in data center systems: insights, challenges, and opportunities. In: IEEE 25th MASCOTS, pp. 22–31 (2017)
14. Safavian, S.R., Landgrebe, D.: A survey of decision tree classifier methodology. IEEE Trans. Syst. Man Cybern. Syst. **21**(3), 660–674 (1991)
15. Sîrbu, A., Babaoglu, O.: Towards operator-less data centers through data-driven, predictive, proactive autonomics. J. Cluster Comput. **19**(2), 865–878 (2016)
16. Srivastava, N., Hinton, G.E., Krizhevsky, A., et al.: Dropout: a simple way to prevent neural networks from overfitting. J. Mach. Learn. Res. **15**(1), 1929–1958 (2014)
17. Tuncer, O., et al.: Diagnosing performance variations in HPC applications using machine learning. In: Kunkel, J.M., Yokota, R., Balaji, P., Keyes, D. (eds.) ISC 2017. LNCS, vol. 10266, pp. 355–373. Springer, Cham (2017). https://doi.org/10.1007/978-3-319-58667-0_19
18. Vishwanath, K.V., Nagappan, N.: Characterizing cloud computing hardware reliability. In: Proceedings of the 1st ACM Symposium on Cloud Computing, pp. 193–204. ACM (2010)
19. Wallace, S., Zhou, Z., Vishwanath, V., et al.: Application power profiling on IBM Blue Gene/Q. Parallel Comput. **57**, 73–86 (2016)
20. Xie, B., Huang, Y., Chase, J.S., et al.: Predicting output performance of a petascale supercomputer. In: Proceedings of the 26th International Symposium on High-Performance Parallel and Distributed Computing, pp. 181–192 (2017)
21. Yu, L., Zhou, Z., Wallace, S., et al.: Quantitative modeling of power performance tradeoffs on extreme scale systems. J. Parallel Distrib. Comput. **84**(Suppl. C), 1–14 (2015)
22. Yuan, Y., Wu, Y., Wang, Q., et al.: Job failures in high performance computing systems: a large-scale empirical study. Comput. Math. Appl. **63**(2), 365–377 (2012)
23. Zasadziński, M., Muntés-Mulero, V., Sóle, M., Ludwig, T.: Mistral supercomputer job history analysis (2018). https://arxiv.org/abs/1801.07624

Peacock: Probe-Based Scheduling of Jobs by Rotating Between Elastic Queues

Mansour Khelghatdoust[✉] and Vincent Gramoli[✉]

The University of Sydney, Data61/CSIRO, Sydney, Australia
{mansour.khelghatdoust,vincent.gramoli}@sydney.edu.au

Abstract. In this paper, we propose Peacock, a new distributed probe-based scheduler which handles heterogeneous workloads in data analytics frameworks with low latency. Peacock mitigates the *Head-of-Line blocking* problem, i.e., shorter tasks are enqueued behind the longer tasks, better than the state-of-the-art. To this end, we introduce a novel probe rotation technique. Workers form a ring overlay network and rotate probes using elastic queues. It is augmented by a novel probe reordering algorithm executed in workers. We evaluate the performance of Peacock against two state-of-the-art probe-based solutions through both trace-driven simulation and distributed experiment in Spark under various loads and cluster sizes. Our large-scale performance results indicate that Peacock outperforms the state-of-the-art in all cluster sizes and loads. Our distributed experiments confirm our simulation results.

Keywords: Scheduling · Distributed system · Load balancing
Big data

1 Introduction

Data analytics frameworks increase the level of parallelism by breaking jobs into a large number of short tasks operating on different partitions of data to achieve low latency. Centralized techniques schedule jobs optimally by having near-perfect visibility of workers. However, with the growth of cluster sizes and workloads, scheduling time becomes too long to reach this optimality. To solve this problem, probe-based distributed techniques have been proposed [3–5] to reduce the scheduling time by tolerating a suboptimal result. These solutions typically sample two workers per probe and place the probe into the queue of the least loaded worker. Additionally, they are augmented with amelioration techniques such as re-sampling, work stealing or queue reordering to likely improve the initial placement of probes. However, the existing algorithms are not able to improve scheduling decisions continuously and deterministically to mitigate the *Head-of-Line blocking*, i.e., placing shorter tasks behind longer tasks in queues, efficiently. Moreover, the overall completion time of a job is equal to the finish time of its last task. Due to the distributed and stateless nature of probe-based schedulers, the existing solutions are not able to reduce the variance of tasks

© Springer International Publishing AG, part of Springer Nature 2018
M. Aldinucci et al. (Eds.): Euro-Par 2018, LNCS 11014, pp. 178–191, 2018.
https://doi.org/10.1007/978-3-319-96983-1_13

completion time of each job that are scheduled on various workers to reduce job completion time.

We propose Peacock, a fully distributed probe-based scheduler, which replaces the probe sampling and the unbounded or fixed-length worker-end queues with a deterministic probe rotation and elastic queues. This leads to better scheduling decisions while preserving fast scheduling of jobs. This probe rotation approach finds an underloaded worker better than probe sampling because probes traverse a higher number of workers. Workers are organized into a ring and send probes to their neighbors at fixed intervals. A probe rotation lets a loaded worker delegates the execution of a probe to its successor on the ring. *Elastic queues* regulate the motion of probes between workers and lets a worker dynamically adjust its queue size to balance load between workers. By decreasing the queue size, workers are forced to move some of their probes and increase the queue size to avoid unnecessary motion of probes. More interestingly, a probe in its journey, from when it is submitted to the scheduler until it runs on any arbitrary worker, moves between workers, stays in some worker and then continue rotating until eventually executing on a worker. Furthermore, Peacock is augmented with a probes reordering to handle the *Head-of-Line blocking* more effectively. The probes of one job are annotated with an identical threshold time equals to the cluster average load at the time of scheduling. This threshold determines a soft maximum waiting time for probes that are scattered independently between workers to reduce the variance of job completion time.

We evaluate Peacock through both simulation and distributed experiments. We use trace from Google [2]. We compare Peacock against Sparrow [3] and Eagle [4], two state-of-the-art probe-based schedulers. The results show Peacock outperforms Eagle and Sparrow in various cluster sizes and under different loads. We evaluate the sensitivity of Peacock to probe rotation and probe reordering. Section 2 describes Peacock in details. Section 3 explains the evaluation methodology. Section 4 describes simulation and implementation results. Section 5 discusses related work. Section 6 concludes the paper.

2 The Peacock Scheduler

Peacock comprises a large number of workers and a few schedulers. Workers shape a ring overlay network in that each worker connects to its successor and additionally stores descriptors to a few successors for fault tolerance purpose. Each scheduler connects to all workers. Schedulers manage the life cycle of each job without the need for expensive algorithms. Jobs are represented as a directed acyclic graph (DAG), with tasks as vertices and data flow between tasks as edges. This DAG is divided into stages and actually Peacock considers each stage as a job and hence a DAG consists of a number of dependent jobs. Similar to other approaches [4,5,7,11], Peacock needs to know the estimated task runtime of incoming jobs which is measured by methods explained elsewhere [11,18]. Jobs can be scheduled by any of the schedulers, however, all tasks of a job are scheduled by the same scheduler. When a scheduler has received a job, it submits probe messages to a set of random workers equals to the number of tasks. Each worker has a queue. According to the Fig. 1, once a worker has received the probe, (a) if the worker is idle (1.1), it requests the corresponding task of the probe from the scheduler (1.2) and the scheduler sends back the corresponding task data (source code) (1.3) and then the worker executes the task (1.4), (b) if the worker is executing a task and its queue consists of a number of waiting probes like (2.1) and (3.1), the worker may enqueue the probe for the future execution or rotation (2.2), or (c) the worker may either rotate the incoming probe instantly or enqueue the probe and rotate other existing waiting probes (3.2).

2.1 Probe Rotation

There are three important design questions that should be answered:

(i) How should probes move between workers?
(ii) When should each worker rotate probes?
(iii) Which probes should each worker choose to rotate?

Ring Overlay Network. The challenging design decision is how probes move between workers. The easiest solution is that workers maintain a complete list of workers and send probe to a sampled worker. However, it undermines the scalability and burdens some workers while some others might remain mostly idle. The efficient approach should be symmetric, balance load between workers and maximize resource utilization. To this end, Peacock exploits a ring overlay network as depicted in Fig. 1. We discuss whether exploiting a ring overlay network adversely impacts the scalability of Peacock. Peer-to-Peer overlay networks are

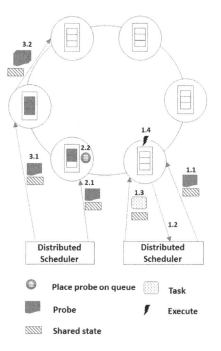

Fig. 1. Different scenarios workers handle probes.

extensively used to implement routing and lookup services [19]. In this respect, applying a ring overlay network with 1 in-out degree (i.e., 1 for in-degree and 1 for out-degree) in which lookup time grows linearly with the increment of ring size ruins scalability. However, there is no routing or lookup service in Peacock. It only rotates probes through a ring and typically probes are able to execute on any arbitrary worker node. Schedulers submit probes to sampled workers and probes are either rotated or stores at workers. Therefore, we can conclude that exploiting a ring overlay network does not undermine the scalability of the algorithm.

The Significance of Elastic Queues. Workers should decide when and which probes to rotate. Each worker utilizes one *elastic* queue, i.e., the size is adjusted dynamically and hence is resilient. This elasticity is crucial for queues because it enables workers to rotate probes between themselves in order to distribute the probes uniformly. If queues are too short, the resources get under-utilized due to the existence of idle resources between allocations. If the queues are too long, then the load among workers gets imbalanced and job completion gets delayed. Determining a static queue size might lead to an excessive number of probe rotations when the cluster is heavily loaded and an inefficient reduction in the number of probe rotations when the cluster is lightly loaded. Peacock bounds queues using a pair (*<size, average load>*) which is called *shared state*. The size is calculated as the average number of current probes on cluster. The average load is calculated as the average estimation execution time of current probes on workers. This pair is adjusted dynamically to make queues resilient.

Shared State. *Shared state* is a pair of information that consists of the queue size and the average load of cluster (*<queue size, average load>*) and is changing from time to time since the cluster has dynamic workload. Workers require to get the most recent *shared state*. However, it is challenging to update the *shared state* of workers continuously in a decentralized manner. Peacock is designed in such a way that workers and schedulers are not strictly required to have an identical *shared state* all the time and hence workers may have different values of *shared state* at times. Now, we describe how the *shared state* is calculated and through what ways workers can get the latest value of *shared state*. Each scheduler calculates the *shared state* continuously based on the messages it receives. These messages are when a scheduler receives a job arrival event, receives a task finish event or receives an update message from other schedulers. For example, suppose the current aggregation load of cluster is <1500, 25000> (the number of probes, aggregation load) and a task finished event is received for a task with 20 s estimated execution time. The scheduler updates the aggregation value to <1499, 24980> and sends asynchronously the message <−, 1, 20> to the other schedulers. Upon receiving this message, the other schedulers update their aggregation value. Similarly, receiving a new job with 10 tasks and 15s estimated execution time changes the aggregation value to <1510, 25150>, with update message <+, 10, 150> to the other schedulers. As an alternative solution, schedulers can manage *shared state* through coordination services such as ZooKeeper. It eliminates direct communication between schedulers. Each scheduler calculates the value of *shared state* through dividing aggregation value by the number of workers. Peacock does not impose extra messages to update the *shared state* of workers. The latest *shared state* is piggybacked by messages that workers and schedulers exchange for scheduling purposes. Figure 1 shows workers get *shared state* through three ways.

(i)   When schedulers submit a probe message to workers
(ii)   When schedulers send task data as a response of getting task by worker
(iii) When workers rotate probes to their neighbors.

Rotation Intervals. In ring, workers rotate probes to their successor. Peacock rotates probes periodically in rounds. Once a probe has been chosen to be rotated, it is marked for rotation until the next round. In the next round, workers send all the marked probes in one message to their neighbors. Such design reduces the number of messages that workers exchange. Most jobs consist of a large number of probes and it is common that in each round more than one probe of the same job are marked by the same worker to rotate. Peacock leverages this observation to remove the redundant information of such subset of probes to reduce the size of messages. To reduce the number of messages, workers send rotation message to their neighbor only if either there is/are probe(s) marked for rotation or when the *shared state* is updated from the last round. The interval between rounds is configurable from milliseconds to few seconds and it does not impact the job completion time since one probe is marked for rotation. This avoids having to wait in a long queue.

2.2   Probes Reordering

It is crucial to reduce the variance of probes queuing time of one job since job completion time is affected by the last executed task of the job. It is challenging since probes of a job are distributed on different workers. However, the addition of the probes to queues in FIFO order (i.e., in the order in which they are arrived) does not decrease the queuing time variance in the presence of heterogeneous jobs and workloads. Probe reordering is a solution to this problem [4,11]. Reordering algorithms should ideally be starvation-free, i.e., no probe should starve due to existence of infinite sequence of probes with higher priority. To this end, we propose a novel probe reordering algorithm. It performs collaboratively along with probe rotation algorithm to mitigate the *Head-of-Line blocking*. Since probes rotate between workers, the algorithm cannot rely on FIFO ordering of queues. Assume a scheduler submits probe p_1 to worker n_1 at time t_1 and probe p_2 to worker n_2 at time t_2. Then, n_1 rotates p_1 and reaches n_2 at time t_3. The problem is that p_1 is placed after p_2 in the queue of n_2 while it has been scheduled earlier. To overcome this problem, schedulers label job arrival time on probe messages so that workers place incoming probes into queues w.r.t the job arrival time. Then, schedulers attach task runtime estimation to probe messages. Once a worker has received a probe, it orders probes by giving priority to the probe with the shortest estimated runtime. While it reduces the *Head-of-Line blocking*, it may ends in starvation of long probes. To avoid this issue, schedulers attach a threshold value to all the probes of a job at arrival time. The value is the summation of the current time and the average execution time extracted from the current *shared state*. For example, if one job arrives at $t1$ and the *shared state* value is 10 s threshold, the value is $t1 + 10$ for all probes of that job. This threshold acts as a soft upper-bound to reduce tail latency and hence to reduce job completion time. It avoids starvation since probes do not allow other probes to bypass them after exceeding the threshold time and hence they eventually move to the head of queue and execute on worker.

We now present the algorithm. Workers receive a probe either because their predecessor rotates it along the ring or because the probe is submitted by a scheduler. Algorithm 1 depicts the procedure of enqueuing a probe and Table 1 explains the associated notations. Peacock maintains a sorted queue of waiting probes. Once a new probe has arrived, it is treated as the lowest priority among all waiting probes (Line 2) and tries to improve its place in the queue by passing other probes. It starts comparing its arrival time with the lowest existing probe (Line 4). If the new probe has been scheduled later than the existing probe, bypassing is not allowed unless it reduces head-of-line blocking without leading to starvation of the comparing probe. Bypassing the new probe can mitigate the *Head-of-Line blocking* if the execution time of the new probe is less than the existing probe. Such bypassing should not lead to the starvation of the passed probe which is checked through threshold. If the threshold of the existing probe has not exceeded in advance or will not exceed due to bypassing, then the new probe can bypass the existing probe. Otherwise, it is either simply enqueued or rotated to the neighbor worker on the ring (Lines 4–10). If the new probe has been scheduled earlier, it cannot bypass if the existing probe has less execution time. The new probe does not exceed the threshold if it does not bypass (Lines 11–16). Then, the new probe waits in the queue if it does not violate the starvation conditions, otherwise it is marked to be rotated in the next coming round (Lines 25–31). Once the process of enqueuing the probe has finished, Peacock checks the shared state of the worker and may rotate one or more probes if needed (Lines 21–23).

Table 1. List of notations

Symbol	Description	Symbol	Description
ϕ	Queue size	ω	Max threshold waiting probes
τ	Current time	μ	Max threshold waiting time for p
λ	Job arrival time	θ	runtime estimation of probe p
α	Total runtime of waiting probes	β	Arrival time probe p
γ	Waiting time estimation probe p	δ	Relict runtime of running task

3   Evaluation Methodology

Comparison. We compare Peacock against Sparrow [3] and Eagle [4], two probe-based schedulers which use probe sampling. We evaluate the sensitivity of Peacock to probe rotation and probe reordering. We use both simulation for large clusters of 10k, 15k, and 20k workers and real implementation for 100 workers.

Environment. We implemented an event-driven simulator and also all three algorithms within it to fairly compare them for large scale cluster sizes. In addition, we implemented Peacock as an independent component using Java and also a plug-in for Spark [1] written in Scala. We used Sparrow and Eagle source codes for the distributed experiments.

Workload. We utilize traces of Google [2,17]. Invalid jobs are removed from the Google traces and Table 2 gives the specification of the pruned traces. To generate *average* cluster workloads, job arrival time follows a Poisson process with a mean job inter-arrival time that is calculated based on expected average workload percentage, mean jobs execution time, and mean number of tasks per job. Since jobs are heterogeneous, the workload and expected average percentage vary over time. We consider 20%, 50%, and 80% as light and 100%, 200%, and 300% as heavy cluster workloads.

Table 2. Workloads general properties

Workloads	Jobs count	Tasks count	Avg task duration
Google	504882	17800843	68

Parameters. The estimated task runtime is computed as the average of job task durations. Each worker runs one task at a time, which is analogous to having multi-slot workers, each is served by a separate queue. The results are the average of a number of runs. Error bars are ignored due to stable results of different runs. We set rotation interval to 1s and network delay to 5ms for simulation experiments. Eagle relies on several static parameters. For fair comparison, we use the values used in the paper [4] even though any algorithm relying on static values may not be appropriate under dynamic workloads.

Performance Metrics. We measure the average job completion times, cumulative distribution function of job completion times, and the fraction of jobs that each algorithm completes in less time comparatively, to appraise how efficiently Peacock mitigates the *Head-of-Line blocking*.

4   Experimental Results

We deploy our algorithm within an event-driven simulator and a real distributed experiment to evaluate Peacock in different loads and cluster sizes.

Algorithm 1. Enqueue Probe submitted by scheduler or rotated by predecessor

```
 1: procedure ENQUEUEPROBE(p)
 2:     γ_p ← δ + α
 3:     for q in reversed waitingProbes do
 4:         if λ_p ≥ λ_q then
 5:             if θ_p ≤ θ_q AND λ_q + μ_q + θ_p ≤ τ then
 6:                 γ_p = γ_p - θ_q
 7:             else
 8:                 PLACEORROTATE(p); decided = true; break;
 9:             end if
10:         else
11:             if θ_q ≤ θ_p AND τ + γ_p ≤ λ_p + μ_p then
12:                 PLACEORROTATE(p); decided = true; break;
13:             else
14:                 γ_p = γ_p - θ_q
15:             end if
16:         end if
17:     end for
18:     if Not decided then
19:         waitingProbes.add(P, 0); α = α + θ_p
20:     end if
21:     while waitingProbes.size() ≥ φ OR α ≥ ω do
22:         q = waitingProbes.removeLast(); α = α - θ_q; rotatingProbes.add(q)
23:     end while
24: end procedure
25: procedure PLACEORROTATE(p)
26:     if τ + γ_p ≤ λ_p + μ_p OR λ_p + μ_p ≤ τ then
27:         waitingProbes.add(P); α = α + θ_p
28:     else
29:         rotatingProbes.add(p)
30:     end if
31: end procedure
```

Comparing Peacock Against Sparrow. Figure 2 shows that Peacock achieves better average jobs completion times than Sparrow under all loads and with all cluster sizes. Peacock outperforms the alternatives under heavy loads. The reason is that *Head-of-Line blocking* is reduced (i) locally in each worker by our reordering and (ii) collaboratively between workers by balancing the distribution of probes through both probe rotation and reordering. In light loads, the improvement is mostly due to probe rotation and rarely due to the reordering. Furthermore, Sparrow only uses batch sampling that does not handle workload heterogeneity. Figure 3 shows that Peacock, unlike Sparrow, is job-aware in the sense that it reduces the variance of task completion times for each job. Beside probes rotation and reordering, the way that Peacock assigns threshold value for jobs appears effective. Figure 4 shows that Peacock significantly outperforms Sparrow when comparing jobs individually. Under a 20% load, Sparrow shows better percentage than other loads because two samplings in Sparrow get empty slots faster than one sampling of Peacock even though probe rotation helps Peacock outperform Sparrow under other loads. We now provide some more detailed information. Figure 2 shows Peacock executes jobs in average between 13% to 77% faster than Sparrow in all settings. Figure 3(b) shows in 50% load, Sparrow only completes 2.2% jobs in less than 100 seconds while Peacock completes 21.6% jobs at the same time. In Fig. 3(a) and under the 300% load, Sparrow executes 0.3% jobs less than 100 seconds while it is 31.8% for Peacock. Figure 4 shows that Peacock executes between 66% to 91% of jobs faster than Sparrow.

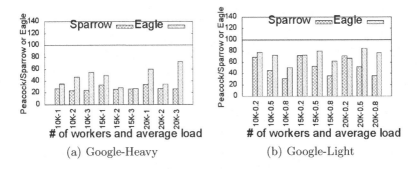

(a) Google-Heavy   (b) Google-Light

Fig. 2. Average job completion times for heavy and light load scenarios.

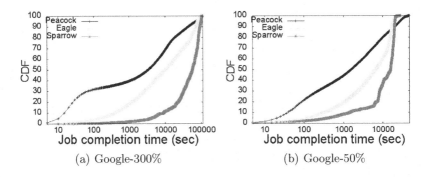

(a) Google-300%   (b) Google-50%

Fig. 3. Cumulative distribution function of jobs completion times. 10000 workers.

Comparing Peacock Against Eagle. Eagle is a hybrid probe-based sampling scheduler which divides jobs statically into two sets of long and short jobs. A centralized node schedules long jobs and a set of independent schedulers using batch sampling to schedule short jobs. The cluster is divided into two partitions, one is dedicated to short jobs and the other is shared for all jobs. Eagle mitigates *Head-of-Line blocking* using re-sampling technique and a static threshold-based queue reordering. Figure 2 shows that Peacock outperforms Eagle in average jobs completion times in all loads. It is because the continuous and deterministic probe

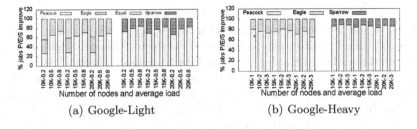

(a) Google-Light   (b) Google-Heavy

Fig. 4. Fraction of jobs with shorter completion time.

rotations through elastic queues along with the workload-aware probe reordering in Peacock outperforms a randomized re-sampling along with a static probe reordering through unbounded queues in Eagle. In Fig. 3, we see that Peacock executes jobs in lower latency than Eagle. Figures 2 shows, Peacock completes execution of jobs in average 16% to 73% faster than Eagle. Figure 4 shows Peacock executes between 54% to 82% of jobs faster than Eagle. Interestingly, we see that under 20% load, the percentage of jobs have identical completion time in both Eagle and Peacock. Figure 3 shows that Peacock executes however a high percentage of jobs with lower latency than Eagle.

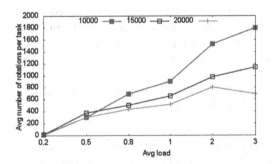

Fig. 5. Avg number of rotations per probe

How Much Is the Number of Probe Rotations per Task Influenced by Cluster Sizes and Loads? We investigate the average number of probe rotations per task for Google trace. We observe by increasing the cluster size that the number of rotations decreases. For example, for 80% load, the number of rotations for 10K, 15K, and 20K nodes are 901, 656, and 513 respectively. Also, for higher loads, at 300%, the number of rotations are 1791, 1140, and 692 for 10K, 15K, and 20K, respectively. The larger the cluster size, the lower the number of redundant rotations. It indicates that probe rotation does not hurt the scalability and hence Peacock can be deployed on large scale clusters. In addition, by increasing the load, there is a reduction in the number of rotations for all 3 cluster sizes. The heavier loads trigger a higher number of rotations than lighter loads. For 10K the number of rotations are 17, 299, 689, 901, 1523, and 1791 for 20%, 50%, 80%, 100%, 200% and 300% loads respectively (Fig. 5).

Sensitivity to Probe Rotation. We analyze the effectiveness of probe rotation on the performance of Peacock. Figures 6(a) and (b) reveal that the performance of Peacock stems from probe rotation technique on all loads. From Fig. 6(a), we see the average job completion time is negatively increased between 70% to 95% in all loads in comparison with complete Peacock version because probe rotation mitigates *Head-of-Line blocking*. Specifically, in light loads, probe rotation balances load between workers which result in increasing the cluster utilization and greatly reducing the formation of long-length queues. In heavy loads, due to the existence of long-length queues, Besides balancing the load between workers through probe reordering, Peacock uses probe rotation to mitigate *Head-of-Line blocking*. Figure 6(b) shows that 70% and 90% percentiles in the high loads perform better than the same percentiles for the light loads. It indicates that under high load probe reordering and probe rotation collaboratively mitigates *Head-of-Line blocking* while under light load the performance of probes rotation is crucial as there is no long queues to apply probes reordering.

Sensitivity to Probe Reordering. Probe reordering is more influential when the cluster is under a high load since workers have long queues when they are at high load. Thanks to the novel starvation-free reordering algorithm in which it allows jobs to bypass longer jobs. The result in Fig. 6(c) approves this fact wherein average job completion time for Peacock without reordering component is close to the original Peacock for 20% load while by increasing load, we observe an increasing difference in average job completion time (the biggest difference is 81% for loads 200% and 300%). From Fig. 6(d) we can conclude that reordering causes most of jobs to be executed faster. It shows an improvement of 90% in 70% percentile for loads 100%, 200%, and 300% while load 50% with 76% and 74% improvements has the best percentiles in 90% and 99%. As expected there is no significant difference for load 20% as there is no waiting probes in queues most of the time. It is obvious that the elimination of this component significantly increases the chance of having *Head-of-Line blocking*.

Implementation Results. We implement Peacock as an independent component using Java and a plug-in for Spark [1] written in Scala. We run experiments on 110 nodes consisting of 100 workers and 10 schedulers. To keep it traceable, we sample 3200 jobs of Google trace and we convert task durations from seconds to milliseconds. We implement a Spark job called *sleep task*. The current thread sleeps for a duration equals to task duration to simulate the execution time that each task needs. The method for varying the load is the same as the simulation experiments described in Sect. 3. We run real implementations of Sparrow and Eagle with the same specifications to compare Peacock against them. Figure 7(a) presents average job completion time at both light and heavy loads. The result shows that Peacock significantly outperforms both the algorithms in all loads. Peacock outperforms Sparrow with an at most 80% improvement under the 80% load and at least a 69% improvement under the 20% load scenario. Moreover, compared to Eagle, the maximum improvement reaches 81% when the load is 50% and the least enhancement is 57% for the load 300%. Figure 7(b) shows the fraction of jobs that each algorithm runs in less time. Again we can see that Peacock runs higher percentage of jobs faster than both Sparrow and Eagle.

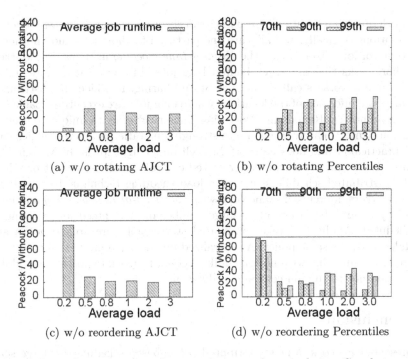

Fig. 6. Peacock versus w/o probes rotation or probes reordering. Google trace.

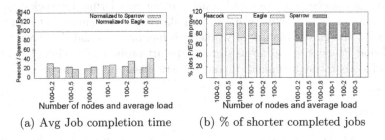

Fig. 7. Distributed experiments for heavy and light workloads.

5   Related Work

Original schedulers are usually designed in a centralized manner [9,12–16] and are a computationally expensive optimization problem. Such algorithms may increase scheduling times and lead to scalability problems. Distributed and hybrid schedulers are proposed to resolve the problem. Sparrow [3] is a distributed scheduler using batch sampling and late binding techniques to be scalable and offer low latency. However, it faces challenges in highly loaded clusters due to the lack of *Head-of-Line blocking* mitigation. Hawk [5] and Eagle [4] are hybrid schedulers that augment Sparrow to mitigate *Head-of-Line blocking*. A centralized scheduler schedules long jobs and distributed schedulers handles short jobs. Both divide jobs statically into long and short categories, splits workers into two partitions statically, and allocate one partition to short jobs and another to both types of jobs. To mitigate the *Head-of-Line blocking* in Hawk, idle workers steal short tasks that get stuck behind long jobs. Instead, Eagle shares information among workers called Succinct State Sharing, in which the distributed schedulers are informed of the locations where long jobs are executing. Eagle also proposes a Shortest Remaining Processing Time reordering technique to prevent starvation. Unfortunately, Eagle relies strongly on static parameters which limits its practicality and does not perform well under light loads. In Mercury [8], jobs are divided into two sets, either served centrally with best effort or scheduled by distributed schedulers. It uses a load shedding technique to re-balance load on workers. Mercury does no cope with the *Head-of-Line blocking* and faces scalability issues when there are a large number of guaranteed jobs waiting to be scheduled. Apollo [11] relies on shared states. Jobs are homogeneous and scheduled with the same policy. A centralized manager maintains a shared state updated by connecting with nodes. Unlike Apollo, Peacock imposes a tiny global information not relying on central coordination.

6   Conclusion

We presented Peacock, a new distributed probe-based scheduler for large scale clusters. Peacock mitigates the *Head-of-Line blocking* by combining probe rotation through the elastic queues with a novel probe reordering. Peacock organizes workers into a ring overlay network and regulates probes to move between workers through the elastic queues of workers to handle workload fluctuations. We showed that Peacock outperforms state-of-the-art probe-based schedulers in various workloads through simulation and realistic distributed experiments.

References

1. Zaharia, M., et al.: Resilient distributed datasets: a fault-tolerant abstraction for in-memory cluster computing. In: NSDI (2012)
2. GoogleTraceWebsite. Google cluster data. https://code.google.com/p/googleclusterdata/
3. Ousterhout, K., et al.: Sparrow: distributed, low latency scheduling. In: SOSP (2013)
4. Delgado, P., Didona, D., Dinu, F., Zwaenepoel, W.: Job-aware scheduling in eagle: divide and stick to your probes. In: SOCC, October 2016
5. Delgado, P., et al.: Hawk: hybrid datacenter scheduling. In: USENIX Annual Technical Conference (2015)
6. Tumanov, A., et al.: TetriSched: global rescheduling with adaptive plan-ahead in dynamic heterogeneous clusters. In: EuroSys (2016)
7. Rasley, J., et al.: Efficient queue management for cluster scheduling. In: Proceedings of the Eleventh European Conference on Computer Systems. ACM (2016)
8. Karanasos, K., et al.: Mercury: hybrid centralized and distributed scheduling in large shared clusters. In: USENIX Annual Technical Conference (2015)

 9. Isard, M., et al.: Quincy: fair scheduling for distributed computing clusters. In: SOSP (2009)
10. Hindman, B., et al.: Mesos: a platform for fine-grained resource sharing in the data center. In: NSDI, vol. 11, no 2011 (2011)
11. Boutin, E., et al.: Apollo: scalable and coordinated scheduling for cloud-scale computing. In: OSDI, vol. 14 (2014)
12. Ferguson, A.D., et al.: Jockey: guaranteed job latency in data parallel clusters. In: EuroSys (2012)
13. Zaharia, M., et al.: Delay scheduling: a simple technique for achieving locality and fairness in cluster scheduling. In: EuroSys (2010)
14. Curino, C., et al.: Reservation-based scheduling: if you're late don't blame us!. In: Proceedings of the ACM Symposium on Cloud Computing. ACM (2014)
15. Goder, A., Spiridonov, A., Wang, Y.: Bistro: scheduling data-parallel jobs against live production systems. In: USENIX ATC (2015)
16. Verma, A., et al.: Large-scale cluster management at Google with Borg. In: Proceedings of the Tenth European Conference on Computer Systems. ACM (2015)
17. Reiss, C., et al.: Heterogeneity and dynamicity of clouds at scale: Google trace analysis. In: SOCC (2012)
18. Zhou, J., et al.: SCOPE: parallel databases meet MapReduce. Int. J. Very Large Data Bases **21**(5), 611–636 (2012)
19. Stoica, I., et al.: Chord: a scalable peer-to-peer lookup service for internet applications. ACM SIGCOMM Comput. Commun. Rev. **31**(4), 149–160 (2001)
20. Chen, Y., et al.: The case for evaluating MapReduce performance using workload suites. In: MASCOTS (2011)

Online Scheduling of Task Graphs on Hybrid Platforms

Louis-Claude Canon[1,2], Loris Marchal[2],
Bertrand Simon[2(✉)], and Frédéric Vivien[2]

[1] FEMTO-ST Institute – Université de Bourgogne Franche-Comté,
16 route de Gray, 25 030 Besançon, France
louis-claude.canon@univ-fcomte.fr
[2] Univ Lyon, CNRS, ENS de Lyon, Inria, Université Claude-Bernard Lyon 1,
LIP UMR5668, 69342 Lyon Cedex 07, France
{loris.marchal,bertrand.simon}@ens-lyon.fr, frederic.vivien@inria.fr

Abstract. Modern computing platforms commonly include accelerators. We target the problem of scheduling applications modeled as task graphs on hybrid platforms made of two types of resources, such as CPUs and GPUs. We consider that task graphs are uncovered dynamically, and that the scheduler has information only on the available tasks, i.e., tasks whose predecessors have all been completed. Each task can be processed by either a CPU or a GPU, and the corresponding processing times are known. Our study extends a previous $4\sqrt{m/k}$-competitive online algorithm [2], where m is the number of CPUs and k the number of GPUs ($m \geq k$). We prove that no online algorithm can have a competitive ratio smaller than $\sqrt{m/k}$. We also study how adding flexibility on task processing, such as task migration or spoliation, or increasing the knowledge of the scheduler by providing it with information on the task graph, influences the lower bound. We provide a $(2\sqrt{m/k}+1)$-competitive algorithm as well as a tunable combination of a system-oriented heuristic and a competitive algorithm; this combination performs well in practice and has a competitive ratio in $\Theta(\sqrt{m/k})$. Finally, simulations on different sets of task graphs illustrate how the instance properties impact the performance of the studied algorithms and show that our proposed tunable algorithm performs the best among the online algorithms in almost all cases and has even performance close to an offline algorithm.

Keywords: Scheduling · Heterogeneous computing · Task graphs
Online algorithms

1 Introduction

Modern computing platforms increasingly use specialized hardware accelerators, such as GPUs or Xeon Phis: 102 of the supercomputers in the TOP500 list include such accelerators, while several of them include several accelerator types [24]. The increasing complexity of such computing platforms makes it hard to

© Springer International Publishing AG, part of Springer Nature 2018
M. Aldinucci et al. (Eds.): Euro-Par 2018, LNCS 11014, pp. 192–204, 2018.
https://doi.org/10.1007/978-3-319-96983-1_14

predict the exact execution time of computational tasks or of data movement. Thus, dynamic runtime schedulers are often preferred to static ones, as they are able to adapt to variable running times and to cope with inaccurate predictions. Indeed, with the widespread heterogeneity of computing platforms, many scientific applications now rely on runtime schedulers such as OmpSs [22], XKaapi [7], or StarPU [4]. Most of these frameworks model an application as a Directed Acyclic Graph (DAG) of tasks, where nodes represent tasks and edges represent dependences between tasks. While task graphs have been widely studied in the theoretical scheduling literature [14], most of the existing studies concentrate on static scheduling in the offline context: both the graph and the running times of the tasks are known beforehand.

We believe that there is a crucial need for online schedulers, that is, of scheduling algorithms that rely neither on the structure of the graph nor on the knowledge of tasks' running times. First, not all graphs are fully available at the beginning of the computation: sometimes the graph itself depends on the data being processed, different inputs may result in different task graphs. This is especially the case when the behavior of an iterative application depends on the accuracy of the output. Second, in most existing runtimes, even if the graph does not depend on the input data, it is not fully submitted at the beginning of the computation; instead, tasks are dynamically uncovered during the computation. Third, even if part of the graph is available, schedulers (such as StarPU [4]) usually avoid traversing large parts of the graph each time they take a decision in order to strongly limit the time needed to take decisions. Finally, tasks' processing times are not always known beforehand, and the occasionally available predictions may not be very accurate, as two successive executions of the same task may result in slightly different timings.

There has recently been an effort of the scheduling community to fill the gap between the assumptions used in theoretical studies and the information available to the underlying schedulers of runtime systems (see details in Sect. 2). Schedulers for independent tasks on hybrid platforms have first been proposed [5,8,11]. Some of them have been adapted for task graphs: [20] extends the algorithm of [5] to the (offline) scheduling of task graphs, while [2] adapts an online scheduler for independent tasks on hybrid platforms [17] to obtain a competitive online scheduler for task graphs.

In the present paper, we concentrate on the online scheduling of task graphs on a hybrid platform composed of 2 types of processors that we call CPU and GPU for convenience. There are m CPUs and k GPUs, where $m \geq k \geq 1$. Note that we do not make any assumptions on the CPUs and GPUs (i.e., on the processing times of each task), so that these results may be symmetrically applied to the converse case with more GPUs. The objective is to schedule a DAG G of tasks, so as to minimize the total completion time, or makespan. Each task can be assigned either to a single CPU or to a single GPU. We adopt the notations of [2]: the processing time of task T_i on a CPU is noted by $\overline{p_i}$ and on a GPU by $\underline{p_i}$.

We consider the following online problem. At the beginning, the algorithm is aware of all the input tasks of the graph, and can schedule each one on either a CPU or on a GPU. A task is released and becomes available to the scheduler only when all its predecessors are terminated. At any given point in the computation, the scheduler is totally unaware of tasks that have not yet been released, but it knows the processing times $\overline{p_i}$ and $\underline{p_i}$ of all available tasks: we assume that tasks correspond to well-known kernels whose processing times have been acquired through extensive benchmarking; this happens in particular in linear algebra applications. We do not take into account the time needed for moving data and assume that there is no delay between the release of a task and the start of its processing.

The closer related work considering the very same problem is [2], which provides a $4\sqrt{m/k}$-competitive algorithm for this problem. We recall that an online algorithm is x-competitive if the makespan returned by this algorithm on any instance is at most x times larger than the optimal makespan (which can be computed by an offline algorithm). The present paper brings the following contributions:

- We prove that the competitive ratio of any online algorithm is lower-bounded by $\sqrt{m/k}$. We study how the knowledge of the task graph and the flexibility of the tasks may influence the lower bound; we especially prove that knowing the bottom-level of any task (i.e., the critical path length from this task to the end of the graph) or having preemptive tasks does not help much, whereas the knowledge of the number of descendants allows to reduce the lower bound to $\frac{1}{2}(m/k)^{1/4}$ (Sect. 3).
- We propose a $(2\sqrt{m/k}+1)$-competitive algorithm, by refining both the algorithm and the analysis of [2] (Sect. 4.1).
- We propose a simple heuristic (Sect. 4.2) based on the system-oriented heuristic EFT, which is both a competitive algorithm and performs well in practice, as we show with a comprehensive simulation set (Sect. 5).

2   Related Work

We briefly position our contributions in comparison to the existing work, starting with the offline case where the whole scheduling problem (both task dependences and running times) is known beforehand.

Offline Algorithms. Several schedulers for independent tasks on hybrid platforms have been proposed. Bleuse et al. [8] designed a polynomial but expensive $\left(\frac{4}{3}+\frac{1}{3k}\right)$-approximation. Low complexity algorithms, which are closer to our work, have been studied in [5,11] and achieve approximation ratios respectively equal to 2 and $2+\sqrt{2}$. For tasks with precedence constraints, Kedad-Sidhoum et al. [18] provided a tight 6-approximation algorithm based on linear programming. In a different setting, Raravi et al. [21] also consider the same platform composed of two types of processors, on which the objective is to schedule a set of chains of tasks, with each task having a release date and a deadline. They design an algorithm that schedules the tasks of each chain on the same processor, under some assumptions such as the existence of a valid schedule on slightly slower processors.

Online Algorithms. When tasks with precedences are released over time, Graham's List Scheduling algorithm [16] is 2-competitive on homogeneous processors (note that this is also the best offline approximation for this problem). On our model with two sets of processors, Imreh [17] and Chen et al. [13] proposed an algorithm to schedule independent tasks with a competitive ratio smaller than 4. Based on this work, Amaris et al. [2] exhibited an online algorithm for precedence constraints, achieving a competitive ratio of $4\sqrt{m/k}$.

Runtime Strategies. Actual runtime schedulers usually rely on low-complexity scheduling policies to limit the time needed to allocate tasks. For instance, StarPU [4] builds a performance model of tasks that enables to predict their processing times. When a new task is submitted, it is allocated to the resource that will complete it the soonest (when using the **dm** policy, previously called **heft-tm** in [3]), which corresponds to the classical Earliest Finish Time (EFT) scheduling policy [19]. Other strategies have been proposed that take into account communication times, or precomputed task priorities, depending on the descendants of each task. We include similar information in the design of the lower bounds on competitive ratios (Sect. 3).

3   Lower Bound on Competitive Algorithms

In this section, we provide a lower bound on the competitive ratio of any online algorithm, as outlined in the following theorem. We also study how adding flexibility to task processing or giving some knowledge of the graph to the scheduler impacts this lower bound.

Theorem 1. *No online algorithm has a competitive ratio smaller than $\sqrt{m/k}$.*

Proof. We prove this result here only when $\tau = \sqrt{m/k}$ is an integer. The proof for the general case can be found in the corresponding research report [10]. Consider an online algorithm $\mathcal{A}$. We fix an integer n, which will later be made as large as we want for the competitive ratio to get closer to τ. We use an adversary proof: an adversary dynamically builds the graph depending on the current schedule produced by $\mathcal{A}$. This results in a graph composed of nm tasks denoted by T_i^j, with $j = 1, \ldots, n\tau$ and $i = 1, \ldots, k\tau$. Each task has a CPU processing time of τ and a GPU processing time of 1.

The procedure consists of $n\tau$ phases. During the jth phase, $k\tau$ tasks are released (tasks T_i^j for $i = 1, \ldots, k\tau$), without dependences between these tasks. The adversary selects the task that $\mathcal{A}$ completes the latest, breaking ties arbitrarily. Let T_*^j be this task. The $k\tau$ tasks of the next phase are then made successors of T_*^j. See Fig. 1a for an illustration of the resulting graph.

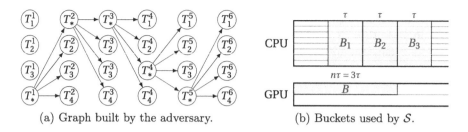

(a) Graph built by the adversary.   (b) Buckets used by $\mathcal{S}$.

Fig. 1. Illustration of the graph and the buckets for $\tau = 2$, $k = 2$, $n = 3$.

We now show how to build an efficient (offline) schedule $\mathcal{S}$ of the resulting graph. A *bucket* is defined as a set of processors, a starting time and a duration time. We use buckets to book some processors for an amount of time, and schedule a set of tasks in a given bucket. We consider $n + 1$ buckets, as illustrated in Fig. 1b. Each bucket B_i for $i = 1, \ldots, n$ contains all m CPUs, has a duration of τ, and starts at time $i\tau$. Note that m tasks fit into each of these buckets. The last bucket, B, contains one GPU, starts at time 0 and lasts for a time $n\tau$. $\mathcal{S}$ schedules the $n\tau$ tasks T_*^j successively on a single GPU, which fit into bucket B. In parallel, $\mathcal{S}$ schedules the remaining tasks on CPU. More precisely, it puts in bucket B_ℓ tasks T_i^j such that $(\ell - 1)\tau < j \leq \ell\tau$, except for tasks T_*^j. They all fit into the bucket as there are less than $\tau \times k\tau \leq m$ such tasks. Moreover, task $T_*^{\ell\tau}$ completes at time $\ell\tau$. Therefore, every task T_i^j with $(\ell - 1)\tau < j \leq \ell\tau$ can be started at time $\ell\tau$, and thus can be scheduled into bucket B_ℓ. Therefore, $\mathcal{S}$ achieves a makespan equal to $(n + 1)\tau$.

Now, we consider algorithm $\mathcal{A}$, and we show that the makespan obtained is at least $n\tau^2$. At each phase, the adversary reveals the next phase only when all the tasks of the current phase are completed. If one task of the phase is scheduled on CPU, it takes a time τ. Otherwise, all $k\tau$ tasks are scheduled on GPU, and the last one completes at time at least $k\tau/k = \tau$. Therefore, $\mathcal{A}$ completes each phase in time at least τ. As there are $n\tau$ phases, the whole graph cannot be scheduled in time smaller than $n\tau^2$. The competitive ratio of $\mathcal{A}$ is then at least:

$$\frac{n\tau^2}{(n + 1)\tau} \quad \xrightarrow[n \to \infty]{} \quad \tau.$$

$\square$

It seems from the above proof that the main difficulty for this problem arises from choosing on which type of resource (CPU or GPU) a given task should be processed, and not to come up with the final schedule. This is indeed proven in the following lemma, which states that given an allocation of the tasks to the two types of resources, scheduling them among the $m + k$ resources can be done with constant competitive ratio (for the proof, please refer to [10]).

Lemma 1. *If each task can be processed on a single type of resource, then any online list scheduling algorithm is $(3 - \frac{1}{m})$-competitive, and no online algorithm has a smaller competitive ratio.*

Table 1. Lower bounds for various combinations of flexibility in task processing and knowledge given to the scheduler (BL stands for bottom-level).

Flexibility	Knowledge	Lower bound	Special cases
None or spoliation	None or BL	$\sqrt{m/k}$	if BL and $k = 1$: $\frac{1}{2}\sqrt{m/k}$
	BL + descendants	$\frac{1}{2}(m/k)^{1/4}$	
Migration	None or BL	$\frac{1}{2}\sqrt{m/k}$	if BL and $k = 1$: $\frac{1}{4}\sqrt{m/k}$
	BL + descendants	$\frac{1}{4}(m/k)^{1/4}$	

The proof of Theorem 1 heavily relies on the fact that an online algorithm has no information on the successors of each task. In practice, it is sometimes possible to get some information on the task graph, for example by pre-computing some information offline before submitting the tasks. For instance, offline schedulers usually rank available tasks with priorities based on the dependences. On homogeneous platforms, the *bottom-level* of a task is commonly used, and is defined as the maximum length of a path from this task to an exit node, where nodes of the graphs are weighted with the processing time of the corresponding tasks. In the heterogeneous case, the priority scheme used in the standard HEFT algorithm [25] is to set the weight of each node as the average processing time of the corresponding task on all resources.

Knowing the bottom-level does not change the lower-bound of Theorem 1: it is possible to transform the above proof using an adversary that submits tasks with identical bottom-levels in each phase (see details in the corresponding research report [10]). When there is exactly one GPU, the lower bound is decreased to $\frac{1}{2}\sqrt{m/k}$. An interesting component of this proof is that all the tasks are equivalent (same CPU and GPU computing times) so other heterogeneous variants of the bottom-level result in the same lower bounds.

When the online scheduler is given the knowledge of the number of descendants of each submitted task in addition to their bottom-level, the lower bound of Theorem 1 is reduced to $\frac{1}{2}(m/k)^{1/4}$ when m/k is large enough, so no constant-factor competitive algorithm exists. Note that all the tasks are equivalent in this proof. The lower bound is thus also valid if the knowledge of the CPU and GPU computing times of all the descendants is given to the scheduler and only the pattern of precedence relations remains unknown. Note that, however, no algorithm has been proposed that reaches this bound.

Another interesting question is whether adding flexibility on how tasks are processed changes this bound. Allowing task spoliation (where tasks can be canceled and restarted on any resource, as done in [5]) does not help, and allowing task migration (where tasks can be preempted and resumed on any resource) only halves the bounds. Table 1 summarizes the lower bounds obtained for all combination of knowledge given to the scheduler and flexibility on the task processing (for proofs, please refer to [10]).

4   Competitive Algorithms

4.1   The Quick Allocation (QA) Algorithm

Amaris et al. [2] designed an online algorithm named ER-LS, which is proved to be $4\sqrt{m/k}$-competitive. The results of Sect. 3 show that this ratio can only be improved by a constant factor, as no online algorithm can be better than $\sqrt{m/k}$-competitive. ER-LS applies the following processing to each available task T_i:

1. (a) If T_i can be completed on a GPU before time $\overline{p_i}$, then assign it to GPUs.
   (b) Else, if $\overline{p_i}/p_i \leq \sqrt{m/k}$, then assign T_i to CPUs, else assign it to GPUs.
2. Schedule T_i as soon as possible on the allocated type of resource.

   The main objective of Step 1a is to avoid allocating the first tasks on a slow resource, which intuitively is desirable only on small graphs. Such a technique enables a similar online algorithm to be constant-factor competitive for independent tasks, see [13]. However, it actually increases the competitive factor with precedence constraints. We propose to simplify the allocation phase by suppressing Step 1a. The resulting algorithm QA (which stands for Quick Allocation) is then defined by Steps 1b and 2. Along with a rigorous analysis, this simplification allows us to reach a competitive ratio smaller than $2\sqrt{m/k} + 1$, which is almost tight, as outlined in the following theorems. The complete proofs of the following results are available in [10].

Theorem 2. QA is $\left(2\sqrt{m/k} + 1 - (mk)^{-1/2}\right)$ – competitive.

Proof Sketch. Consider a graph G and the schedule $\mathcal{S}$ obtained by QA, of makespan C_{max}. Let W_c (resp. W_g) be the sum of the processing times of the tasks scheduled on CPU (resp. GPU) by $\mathcal{S}$, and CP be the computing time of a critical path of G, given the allocation of $\mathcal{S}$. We first prove that:

$$C_{max} \leq \frac{W_c}{m} + \frac{W_g}{k} + \left(1 - \frac{1}{m}\right)CP.$$

Now, focusing first on the workload in the optimal solution, and then on the length of the critical path in the optimal solution, we can show the following inequalities and conclude:

$$\frac{W_c}{m} + \frac{W_g}{k} \leq \left(1 + \sqrt{\frac{m}{k}}\right)\text{OPT} \quad \text{and} \quad CP \leq \sqrt{\frac{m}{k}}\text{OPT}.$$

□

Theorem 3. *The competitive ratio of* QA *is at least* $\left(2\sqrt{m/k} + 1 - \frac{1}{k}\right)$.

Proof Sketch. Let ε be a small processing time. Consider the graph composed of the three groups of tasks below. The online instance will reveal the tasks in the same order. The only dependence is from task ε to task d.

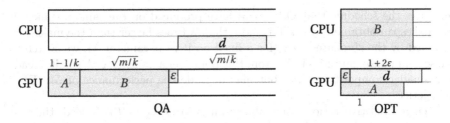

Fig. 2. Schedule obtained by QA (left) and the optimal one (right).

Group A. $k(k-1)$ tasks with $\overline{p_i} = \infty$ and $\underline{p_i} = 1/k$.
Group B. mk tasks with $\overline{p_i} = (1+\varepsilon)/k$ and $\underline{p_i} = 1/\sqrt{mk}$.
Group C. Task ε, with $\overline{p_\varepsilon} = \infty$ and $\underline{p_\varepsilon} = \varepsilon$, and task d, with $\overline{p_d} = \sqrt{m/k}$ and $\underline{p_d} = 1+\varepsilon$.

As depicted in Fig. 2, QA will schedule groups A and B and Task ε on GPU, then task d on CPU, for a total makespan equal to $2\sqrt{m/k} + 1 - \frac{1}{k} + \varepsilon$. The optimal solution schedules only group B on CPU, for a total makespan equal to $1 + 2\varepsilon$, hence the result.   □

The proofs of these two results give some intuition on why choosing a ratio equal to $\sqrt{m/k}$ is the best choice in Step 1b. With a smaller ratio (closer to 1), more tasks would be allocated to GPU. This would allow tasks on the critical path to be processed faster. However, the GPUs, which can be seen as a rare resource (since $m \geq k$), may be wasted on tasks that are not accelerated enough. For instance, if the GPU computing time of the tasks of group B in the proof of Theorem 3 were larger, such an algorithm would perform worse than QA. On the opposite, with a larger ratio (closer to m/k), the GPU would not be wasted on such tasks and the loads would be divided more equally on both types of resources. But computing the critical path, such as task d in the example graph, could be more expensive because such a task would be inefficiently executed on CPUs. Intuitively, the geometric mean between these two bounds (1 and m/k) is then the best solution.

4.2   A Competitive Algorithm that Performs Well in Practice

Although the QA algorithm has the best known competitive ratio, the greedy strategy EFT (see Sect. 2) actually leads to better schedules on most realistic instances because it balances the load among the resources. However, its performance can be $2 + (m-1)/k$ times worse than the optimal solution (see [10] for a proof of this result).

We propose a new tunable algorithm, named MIXEFT that benefits both from the performance of EFT on most instances, and from the robustness of QA on the hardest graphs. The idea is to improve EFT by switching to a guaranteed algorithm if EFT does not perform well enough. The algorithm is composed of two phases. In the first phase, it is equal to EFT except that it also simulates the schedule that QA would have produced on the same instance. If the makespan obtained by EFT is more than λ times larger than the makespan obtained by the simulated QA (for a fixed positive parameter λ), we switch to the second phase, and MIXEFT from this point behaves as QA. A small λ leads to a smaller competitive ratio, but may degrade the performance of MIXEFT in practice.

The competitive ratio of this algorithm is in $O(\lambda\sqrt{m/k})$. Indeed, the first phase cannot lead to a schedule more than λ times worse than QA, and the second phase has the competitive ratio of QA. Therefore, the algorithm is $(\lambda + 1)(2\sqrt{m/k}+1)$-competitive (see [10] for more details). Note that this competitive ratio is not tight. The worst performance observed so far is $\max(\lambda, 2\sqrt{m/k}+1)$.

5   Simulations

We now provide simulations to illustrate the performance of both competitive algorithms and simple heuristic strategies on various task graphs.

5.1   Baseline Heuristics

In addition to the four online algorithms discussed above (ER-LS from [2], QA, EFT, and MIXEFT, implemented with $\lambda = 2$ unless otherwise specified), we consider two simple strategies that follow the same scheme as QA, with a different allocation criteria: QUICKEST allocates each task to the resource type on which its computing time is smaller; RATIO allocates a task on GPUs if and only if its GPU computing time is at least m/k times smaller than its CPU computing time. Intuitively, QUICKEST should perform well on graphs on which the critical path is preponderant as it minimizes the execution time of each task. On the opposite, RATIO should perform well on graphs with a high parallelism throughout the execution, as it will execute more tasks concurrently on the CPUs. We also used the offline HEFT algorithm [25], which is known to perform well in practice, as a baseline to compare all online strategies.

5.2   Experimental Setup

We used three types of instances: realistic DAGs corresponding to a linear algebra application, namely the Cholesky factorization, random DAGs used in the literature, and ad hoc instances designed to be difficult for this problem and specifically for QA.

Cholesky factorization is a linear algebra application whose parallel implementation usually uses a blocked algorithm on a tiled matrix for performance issues. We consider matrix sizes ranging from 2×2 tiles to 15×15 tiles, which leads to DAGs with 4 to 680 tasks. Tasks correspond to four linear algebra kernels: GEMM, SYRK, TRSM, and POTRF. Their respective processing times on a CPU are set to 170ms, 95 ms, 88 ms, and 33 ms, and on a GPU to 5.95 ms, 3.65 ms, 8.11 ms, and 15.6 ms, which corresponds to measures [1,6] made using the Chameleon software [12].

The random instances come from the STG set [23], which is often used in the literature to compare the performance of scheduling strategies. We report here the simulations made with 180 graphs of 300 nodes each. We consider that the cost generated by the STG random generator is the processing time of the corresponding task on a GPU. Based on the previous measures for linear algebra kernels, we assume that the average speedup between CPU and GPU is around 15 with a large variance. Thus, to obtain the processing time of a task on CPU, we multiply its cost on GPU by a random value with expected value 15 and standard deviation 15. For that, we use a gamma distribution because it has been advocated for modeling job runtimes [15], it is positive and it is possible to specify its expected value and standard deviation by adjusting its parameters.

Finally, specific random instances have been designed to test the limitations of QA. These ad hoc instances consist of a chain of tasks together with a set of independent tasks, such that all cores are expected to finish simultaneously if a GPU is dedicated to the chain and all independent tasks are load-balanced on the other cores. The expected processing time of each task on a GPU is 1 (with a standard deviation of 0.1). Each instance is parameterized by a number μ, which represents the expected processing time on a CPU, and varies from $(m/k)^{-1/4}$ to $(m/k)^{5/4}$ (the standard deviation of the CPU processing times is equal to 10% of μ). For a given expected CPU cost μ, the number of tasks in the chain is equal to $\lceil \frac{n}{m/\mu+k} \rceil$, where $n = 300$ is the total number of tasks. Therefore, the larger μ, the longer the chain.

We have performed simulations for various platform sizes, whose results are available in [10]. As expected from the theoretical analysis, the behaviors of the heuristics mainly depend on the value m/k. For the sake of brevity, we only report here the results obtained for $m = 20$ CPUs and $k = 2$ GPUs, as it is representative of the results for relatively large values of m/k. The code and scripts used for the simulations and the data analysis are available online [9].

5.3   Results

Figure 3 depicts the performance of the six online scheduling algorithms. Except when varying its parameter (Fig. 3(d)), MixEFT performs exactly as EFT (and is thus omitted for better readability). On Cholesky DAGs (Fig. 3(a)), EFT (and thus MixEFT) is always the best strategy. The only difference between QA and ER-LS concerns the first tasks (as we removed Step 1a in QA), which explains why their behaviour is similar for large graphs. QA, ER-LS, and Ratio all put POTRF tasks on the CPU, which leads to performance loss when the graph is small because its parallelism is limited and the GPUs are often idle. However, it is acceptable for larger graphs in which many tasks may be executed in parallel on the GPUs. On the contrary, Quickest puts all tasks on the GPUs. This is efficient for small graphs with low parallelism but it becomes worse than Ratio for large graphs.

Figure 3(b) shows similar trends on the random graphs from STG set: EFT (and thus MixEFT) gives the best results, followed by QA and ER-LS.

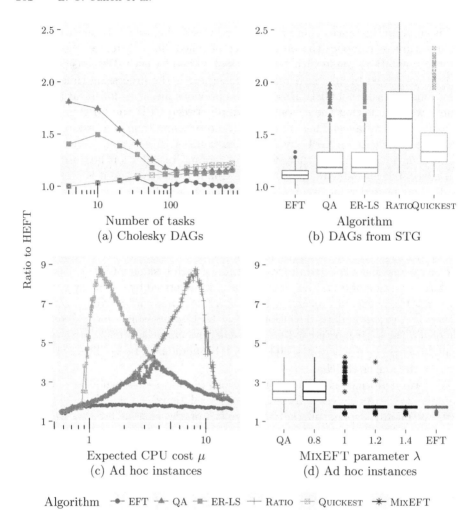

Fig. 3. Ratios of the makespan over HEFT for EFT, QA, ER-LS, Ratio, Quickest, and MixEFT with $m = 20$ CPUs and $k = 2$ GPUs. Except in Figure (d), MixEFT is not shown because it performs exactly as EFT. In Figure (d), ER-LS, Ratio, and Quickest are discarded.

Figure 3(c) first shows that EFT (and MixEFT) is almost always the best online heuristic for these ad hoc graphs. For extreme values of the expected CPU processing time μ (significantly smaller than 1 or larger than m/k), all four other heuristics are equivalent and perform well. Otherwise, when μ is slightly larger than 1, the instance contains many independent tasks and Quickest is almost m/k worst than HEFT because scheduling independent tasks on GPUs is not efficient. Symmetrically, when μ is slightly smaller than m/k, the instance contains a large critical path and Ratio shows poor performance, because it schedules the critical path on CPUs. QA and ER-LS take the best of these two strategies, and have a worst performance $\sqrt{m/k} \approx 3$ times larger than HEFT, when μ is close to $\sqrt{m/k}$.

Figure 3(d) shows that MIXEFT behaves like QA when its λ parameter is smaller than 1, and rapidly changes to mimic EFT when the parameter increases and exceeds 1. Note that in all studied instances, EFT was never far from HEFT and that there is no practical gain of using MIXEFT rather than EFT. The main advantage of MIXEFT lies in its competitive ratio whereas EFT can lead to very large makespans on specific instances.

6   Conclusion

In this paper, we have focused on the problem of scheduling task graphs on hybrid platforms made of two types of processors, such as CPUs and GPUs. We have studied the online case, when only the tasks whose predecessors are all completed are known to the scheduler, and the graph is thus gradually discovered. We proved that no scheduling algorithm can have a competitive ratio smaller than $\sqrt{m/k}$, and studied how this ratio varies when more knowledge on the graph is given to the scheduler and/or tasks may be migrated between processors. We have proposed a $(2\sqrt{m/k}+1)$-competitive algorithm as well as a mixed strategy, which is both $\Theta(\sqrt{m/k})$-competitive and performs as well as the best heuristics in practice. This is demonstrated through an extensive set of simulations. Our future work includes taking into account communication times when moving data from/to the GPUs, and coping with inaccurate processing time estimates.

Data Availability Statement and Acknowledgments. The datasets generated during and/or analyzed during the current study are available in the Figshare repository: https://doi.org/10.6084/m9.figshare.6353456.

This work was supported by the SOLHAR project (ANR-13-MONU-0007) which is operated by the French National Research Agency (ANR).

References

1. Agullo, E., Beaumont, O., Eyraud-Dubois, L., Kumar, S.: Are static schedules so bad? A case study on Cholesky factorization. In: IPDPS. IEEE (2016)
2. Amaris, M., Lucarelli, G., Mommessin, C., Trystram, D.: Generic algorithms for scheduling applications on hybrid multi-core machines. In: Rivera, F.F., Pena, T.F., Cabaleiro, J.C. (eds.) Euro-Par 2017. LNCS, vol. 10417, pp. 220–231. Springer, Cham (2017). https://doi.org/10.1007/978-3-319-64203-1_16
3. Augonnet, C., Clet-Ortega, J., Thibault, S., Namyst, R.: Data-aware task scheduling on multi-accelerator based platforms. In: ICPADS, pp. 291–298, December 2010
4. Augonnet, C., Thibault, S., Namyst, R., Wacrenier, P.A.: StarPU: a unified platform for task scheduling on heterogeneous multicore architectures. Concurr. Comput. Pract. Exp. **23**(2), 187–198 (2011)
5. Beaumont, O., Eyraud-Dubois, L., Kumar, S.: Approximation proofs of a fast and efficient list scheduling algorithm for task-based runtime systems on multicores and GPUs. In: IEEE IPDPS, pp. 768–777 (2017)

6. Beaumont, O., Cojean, T., Eyraud-Dubois, L., Guermouche, A., Kumar, S.: Scheduling of linear algebra kernels on multiple heterogeneous resources. In: HiPC (2016)

7. Bleuse, R., Gautier, T., Lima, J.V.F., Mounié, G., Trystram, D.: Scheduling data flow program in XKaapi: a new affinity based algorithm for heterogeneous architectures. In: Silva, F., Dutra, I., Santos Costa, V. (eds.) Euro-Par 2014. LNCS, vol. 8632, pp. 560–571. Springer, Cham (2014). https://doi.org/10.1007/978-3-319-09873-9_47

8. Bleuse, R., Kedad-Sidhoum, S., Monna, F., Mounié, G., Trystram, D.: Scheduling independent tasks on multi-cores with GPU accelerators. Concurr. Comput.: Pract. Exp. **27**(6), 1625–1638 (2015)

9. Canon, L.C., Marchal, L., Simon, B., Vivien, F.: Code for simulating online scheduling of task graphs on hybrid platforms, figshare, code (2018). https://doi.org/10.6084/m9.figshare.6353456

10. Canon, L.C., Marchal, L., Simon, B., Vivien, F.: Online scheduling of sequential task graphs on hybrid platforms. Research report 9150, INRIA, February 2018

11. Canon, L.-C., Marchal, L., Vivien, F.: Low-cost approximation algorithms for scheduling independent tasks on hybrid platforms. In: Rivera, F.F., Pena, T.F., Cabaleiro, J.C. (eds.) Euro-Par 2017. LNCS, vol. 10417, pp. 232–244. Springer, Cham (2017). https://doi.org/10.1007/978-3-319-64203-1_17

12. Chameleon, a dense linear algebra software for heterogeneous architectures. https://project.inria.fr/chameleon

13. Chen, L., Ye, D., Zhang, G.: Online scheduling of mixed CPU-GPU jobs. Int. J. Found. Comput. Sci. **25**(06), 745–761 (2014)

14. Drozdowski, M.: Scheduling parallel tasks – algorithms and complexity. In: Leung, J. (ed.) Handbook of Scheduling. Chapman and Hall/CRC, Boca Raton (2004)

15. Feitelson, D.: Workload Modeling for Computer Systems Performance Evaluation, pp. 1–601. Cambridge University Press, Cambridge (2014). Book Draft, Version 1.0.1

16. Graham, R.L.: Bounds on multiprocessing timing anomalies. SIAM J. Appl. Math. **17**(2), 416–429 (1969)

17. Imreh, C.: Scheduling problems on two sets of identical machines. Computing **70**(4), 277–294 (2003)

18. Kedad-Sidhoum, S., Monna, F., Trystram, D.: Scheduling tasks with precedence constraints on hybrid multi-core machines. In: IEEE IPDPS Workshops, pp. 27–33 (2015)

19. Leung, J.Y.: Handbook of Scheduling: Algorithms, Models, and Performance Analysis. CRC Press, Boca Raton (2004)

20. Beaumont, O., Eyraud-Dubois, L., Kumar, S.: Fast approximation algorithms for task-based runtime systems. Concurr. Comput.: Pract. Exper. https://onlinelibrary.wiley.com/doi/abs/10.1002/cpe.4502. Online version of record before inclusion in an issue

21. Raravi, G., Andersson, B., Nélis, V., Bletsas, K.: Task assignment algorithms for two-type heterogeneous multiprocessors. Real-Time Syst. **50**(1), 87–141 (2014)

22. Sainz, F., Mateo, S., Beltran, V., Bosque, J.L., Martorell, X., Ayguadé, E.: Leveraging OmpSs to exploit hardware accelerators. In: SBAC-PAD, pp. 112–119 (2014)

23. Tobita, T., Kasahara, H.: A standard task graph set for fair evaluation of multiprocessor scheduling algorithms. J. Sched. **5**(5), 379–394 (2002)

24. TOP500 Supercomputer Site. http://www.top500.org. List of November 2017

25. Topcuoglu, H., Hariri, S., Wu, M.: Performance-effective and low-complexity task scheduling for heterogeneous computing. IEEE TPDS **13**(3), 260–274 (2002)

Interference-Aware Scheduling Using Geometric Constraints

Raphaël Bleuse[1,2], Konstantinos Dogeas[1], Giorgio Lucarelli[1(✉)], Grégory Mounié[1], and Denis Trystram[1]

[1] Univ. Grenoble Alpes, CNRS, Inria, Grenoble INP, LIG, Grenoble, France
{konstantinos.dogeas,giorgio.lucarelli,gregory.mounie,
denis.trystram}@imag.fr
[2] FSTC/CSC, University of Luxembourg, Luxembourg City, Luxembourg
raphael.bleuse@uni.lu

Abstract. The large scale parallel and distributed platforms produce a continuously increasing amount of data which have to be stored, exchanged and used by various jobs allocated on different nodes of the platform. The management of this huge communication demand is crucial for the performance of the system. Meanwhile, we have to deal with more interferences as the trend is to use a single all-purpose interconnection network. In this paper, we consider two different types of communications: the flows induced by data exchanges during computations and the flows related to Input/Output operations. We propose a general model for interference-aware scheduling, where explicit communications are replaced by external topological constraints. Specifically, we limit the interferences of both communication types by adding geometric constraints on the allocation of jobs into machines. The proposed constraints reduce implicitly the data movements by restricting the set of possible allocations for each job. We present this methodology on the case study of simple network topologies, namely the line and the ring. We propose theoretical lower and upper bounds under different assumptions with respect to the platform and jobs characteristics. The obtained results illustrate well the difficulty of the problem even on simple topologies.

1 Introduction

In High Performance Computing, the demand for computational power is steadily increasing [16]. To meet up with the challenge of greater performance the architecture of supercomputers also grows in complexity at the whole machine scale. This complexity arises from various factors: (i) the size of the machines (supercomputers now integrates millions of cores); (ii) the heterogeneity of the resources (various architectures of computing nodes, nodes dedicated to I/O); (iii) the interconnection topology. The evolution in the interconnection networks faces two main challenges: first, the community is proposing new topologies [12]; and second, the interconnection network is now unique within the machine (the

© Springer International Publishing AG, part of Springer Nature 2018
M. Aldinucci et al. (Eds.): Euro-Par 2018, LNCS 11014, pp. 205–217, 2018.
https://doi.org/10.1007/978-3-319-96983-1_15

network is shared for various mixed data flows). Sharing such a single multi-purpose interconnection network creates complex interactions (e.g., network contention) between running applications, which have a strong impact on their performance [1,5], and limits the understanding of the system by the users [3]. As the volume of processed data increases, so does the impact of the network.

In this work, we introduce a generic framework for interference-aware scheduling. More precisely, we identify two main types of interleaved flows: the flows induced by data exchanges for computations and the flows related to I/O. Rather than explicitly taking into account these network flows, we address the issue of harmful interactions by constraining the shape of the allocations. Such an approach aims at taking into account the structure of the new platforms in a qualitative way that is more likely to scale properly. The scheduling problem is then defined as an optimization problem with the platform (nodes and topology) and the jobs' description as input. The objective is to minimize the maximum completion time while enforcing constraints on the allocations.

2   Problem Setting

In this work, we model a platform as a set $\mathcal{V}$ of m nodes divided in two groups: a set $\mathcal{V}^C$ of m^C nodes dedicated to computations, and a set $\mathcal{V}^{I/O}$ of $m^{I/O}$ nodes that are entry points to a high performance file system. As a consequence, we have $m = m^C + m^{I/O}$. We assume that the I/O nodes are exclusively used for communications with the file system and hence, there is no overlap between computing and I/O nodes, i.e., $\mathcal{V}^{I/O} \cap \mathcal{V}^C = \emptyset$. Moreover, a computing or an I/O node is exclusively allocated to a job for its lifespan, i.e., any node cannot be used at the same time by more than one job.

The nodes can communicate using an interconnection network with a given *topology*, while the localization of every node within the topology is known. In this direction, we study here the instantiation of this framework with unidimensional topologies, namely the line (Fig. 1(a)) and the ring (Fig. 1(b)). Studying topologies of one dimension is a first step towards the more complicated state-of-the-art platforms, while these basic topologies provide lower bounds for the later ones. The line may indeed be seen as a degenerate tree. Fat-tree topologies are a common interconnect, and are for example used in the Curie and Oakforest-PACS platforms. On the other hand, the torus topologies, such as the one of Blue Waters and Titan (3D torus) or the K computer (6D torus), may be studied from the ring with classical embedding techniques.

Batch schedulers are a critical part of the software stack managing HPC platforms: their goal is to efficiently allocate resources (nodes from $\mathcal{V}$ in our case) to the jobs submitted by the users of the platform. The jobs are queued in a set $\mathcal{J}$. The total number of jobs is n. Each job j requires q_j computing nodes and one I/O node. We distinguish two cases with respect to I/O requirements: in the *pinned* model each job asks for a specific I/O node, while in the *unpinned* model the jobs just need any arbitrary I/O node. The number of allocated computing nodes is fixed, i.e., the job is *rigid* [6]. We denote by $\mathcal{V}(j)$ the set of nodes

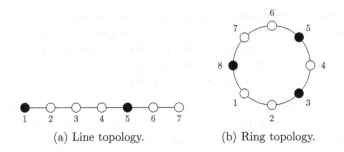

Fig. 1. Example of platforms with unidimensional topologies. The nodes are numbered using the natural order. White nodes represent computing nodes, and black nodes represent I/O nodes.

allocated to the job j. If needed, we use $\mathcal{V}^C(j)$ and $\mathcal{V}^{I/O}(j)$ to distinguish among the computing and the I/O nodes assigned in j, respectively. Each job j requires a certain time p_j to be processed, and it is *independent* of every other job. Once a job starts being executed, it runs until completion, i.e., it is *not preemptive*.

As stated above, the goal of this paper is not to finely model the full context of execution. Instead, we propose to model the platform in such a way that the network interactions are *implicitly* taken into account. In this direction, we augment the scheduling problem with geometric constraints on the allocations of the jobs in the resources based on the platform topology and the application requirements. Before presenting these constraints, we need to precisely define the network flows we target. We distinguish two types of flows, directly deriving from the fact that we are dealing with two kinds of nodes:

computational **communications** which are induced by data exchanges during computations. Such communications occur between two computing nodes allocated to the same application.

I/O **communications** which are induced by data exchanges between computing and I/O nodes. Such communications occur when computing nodes read input data, checkpoint the state of the application, or save output results.

In order to avoid computational communication interactions, we consider the following constraint.

Definition 1 (Contiguity [2,14]). *An allocation is said to be* contiguous *if and only if the nodes of the allocation form a contiguous range with respect to the nodes' ordering.*

Note that the contiguity constraint relies on the nodes' ordering. For topologies such as lines or rings this ordering is natural (see Fig. 1).

The contiguity constraint is well suited to take into account the computational communications, but not the I/O communications. Indeed, the former type of communications may occur between any pair of computing nodes within an allocation: we usually describe this pattern as all-to-all communication. On the other hand, I/O communications generate traffic towards few identified nodes in an all-to-one or one-to-all pattern. Hence, we propose the *locality* constraint, whose goal is to limit the impact of the I/O flows to the periphery of the job allocations. We must emphasize that the locality constraint proposed here is not related to the locality constraint described in [14].

Definition 2 (Locality). *A given allocation for a job j is said to be* local *iff it is contiguous, and the I/O node $\mathcal{V}^{I/O}(j)$ is adjacent to computing nodes from $\mathcal{V}^C(j)$, with respect to the underlying topology.*

In this paper, we are interested in minimizing the maximum completion time among all jobs (i.e., the *makespan* of the schedule) while enforcing the *contiguity* and the *locality* constraints. Specifically, we aim at developing algorithms with performance guarantees by adding geometric constraints on the allocations of jobs into nodes.

3 Related Work

Most actual implementations of schedulers allocate resources greedily without any topological constraint in the allocation of the computing nodes. However, this naive solution has a bad impact on performances [5]. Constraining the allocations to enhance performance is however not a new idea. For example, Lucarelli et al. studied the impact of enforcing contiguity or locality in backfilling scheduling [14] (for fat trees). They showed that enforcing these constraints can be done at a small cost, and has minimum negative impact on usual metrics such as makespan, flow-time, or stretch.

Tackling the interactions arising from the context of execution, or, more specifically, network contention, can be done either by preventing these interactions from happening or by mitigating them. Still, the approaches discussed above require some knowledge about the application communication patterns (either compute or I/O communications). We review briefly related work in the prevention/mitigation of interactions before discussing monitoring techniques.

Interactions Prevention. Some steps have been taken towards integrating more knowledge about the communication patterns of applications into batch schedulers. For instance, Georgiou et al. studied the integration of TREEMATCH into SLURM [9]. Given the communication matrix of an application, the scheduler minimizes the load of the network links by smartly mapping the application's processes on the resources. This approach however does not consider the temporality of communications. Targeting the mesh/torus topologies, the works of Tuncer et al. [18] and Pascual et al. [15] are noteworthy. Another way to prevent interactions is to force the scheduler to use only certain allocation shapes with good properties: this strategy has been implemented in the Blue Waters scheduler [5]. The administrators of Blue Waters let the scheduler pick a shape among 460 precomputed cuboids. Yet, the works proposed above only target compute communications. HPC applications usually rely on highly tuned libraries such as MPI-IO, parallel netCDF or HDF5 to perform their I/O. Tessier et al. propose to integrate topology awareness into these libraries [17]. They show that performing data aggregation while considering the topology allow to diminish the bandwidth required to perform I/O.

Interactions Mitigation. Given a set of applications, Gainaru et al. propose to schedule I/O flows of concurrent applications [7]. Their work aim at mitigating I/O congestion once applications have been allocated computation resources. To achieve such a goal, their algorithm relies on past I/O patterns of the applications to either maximize the global system utilization, or minimize the maximum slowdown induced by sharing bandwidth.

Application/Platform Instrumentation. A lot of effort have been put into developing tools to better understand the behavior of HPC applications. Characterizing I/O patterns is key as it allows the developers to identify performance bottlenecks, and allows the system administrator to better configure the platforms. A complementary path is to predict I/O performances during execution [4]. Such instrumentation efforts allow for a better use of the scarce communication resources. However, as they are application-centric, they fail to capture inter-application interactions. Monitoring of the platform is a way of getting insight on the inter-application interactions. We will not address this problem here.

4   Pinned I/O

In this section, we study the problem with respect to the *pinned* I/O model, according to which each job requests a specific I/O node. Such a model is representative of HPC platforms where the parallel file system is organized in stripes. For example, this is the case with the configuration of the Lustre file system in Blue Waters, where each I/O node is responsible for an address range (i.e., a stripe). Then, the jobs will request the I/O node corresponding to their data.

4.1   Complexity

We start by proving that the studied problem is $\mathcal{NP}$-complete even in the special case where all jobs require unit processing time to be executed, while the platform contains only three I/O nodes.

Theorem 1. *The problem of scheduling in the pinned model with respect to contiguity and locality constraints is strongly $\mathcal{NP}$-complete even in line topologies, with $m^{I/O} = 3$ and $p_j = 1$ for each job $j \in \mathcal{J}$.*

Proof. The problem clearly belongs to $\mathcal{NP}$. We give a reduction from a special case of the NUMERICAL 3-DIMENSIONAL MATCHING (N3DM) problem [8]. An instance of the classical N3DM problem consists of three disjoint sets W, X and Y, each containing M positive integers, and a bound $B \in \mathbb{Z}^+$. The objective is to decide whether $W \cup X \cup Y$ can be partitioned into M disjoint sets $A_1, A_2, \ldots, A_M$

such that each A_i contains exactly one element from each of W, X, and Y and $\sum_{a \in A_i} a = B$, for $1 \leq i \leq M$.

Consider now SN3DM be the special case of N3DM in which all integers that belong to the set X are at least $\frac{B}{2}$. It is not hard to see that SN3DM is also strongly $\mathcal{NP}$-complete. Indeed, it suffices to transform an instance of N3DM to an instance of SN3DM by setting $W' = W$, $Y' = Y$, $X' = \{x + B : \forall x \in X\}$ and $B' = 2B$. Then, any solution for N3DM corresponds to a solution for SN3DM, and vice versa.

We propose now a transformation from SN3DM to our problem as follows:

- $m^C = B$, $m^{I/O} = 3$;
- the topology is a line starting with an I/O node, followed by $\frac{B}{2}$ computing nodes, an I/O node, $\frac{B}{2}$ computing nodes, and finishing with a third I/O node;
- for each $a \in W \cup X \cup Y$, we create a job j with $q_j = a$, and $p_j = 1$. All jobs derived from sets W, X, and Y target the first, second, and third I/O node, respectively.

With respect to the ordering of the line topology, we refer to the computing nodes as $1, 2, \ldots, m^C$ and to the I/O nodes as $1, 2, \ldots, m^{I/O}$.

We will prove that a solution to SN3DM exists if and only if there is a schedule that satisfies all constraints and has a makespan at most M.

Assume that there is a solution for SN3DM. Then for each set $A_i, 1 \leq i \leq M$, we schedule the three jobs $j_1 \in W$, $j_2 \in X$ and $j_3 \in Y$ corresponding to this set at time interval $(i-1, i]$. Specifically, j_1 will use the computing nodes $1, \ldots, q_{j_1}$, j_2 the computing nodes $q_{j_1} + 1, \ldots, q_{j_1} + q_{j_2}$ and j_3 the computing nodes $q_{j_1} + q_{j_2} + 1, \ldots, m^C$. Note that each of these three jobs is adjacent to the targeted I/O node. Indeed, the j_1 and j_3 are adjacent to the leftmost and the rightmost I/O node, respectively, while j_2 is always adjacent to the middle I/O node, since $q_{j_2} \geq \frac{B}{2}$. The makespan of the created schedule is equal to M.

Assume now that there exists a schedule of makespan at most M. As the total work is $M \cdot B$, no computing node is idle during the time interval $(0, M]$. Hence, the partition is directly derived by assigning jobs that start at time $i-1$ to A_i, $1 \leq i \leq M$. □

4.2 Approximation Algorithm

In this section, we first propose a constant-factor approximation algorithm for line topologies and then we argue that it can be used even for ring topologies. The main idea of our algorithm is to first determine an allocation of each job to a specific set of computing nodes. We are interested in allocations that are simultaneously contiguous and local, while each job j requires a specific I/O node. As a consequence, there exist at most $q_j + 1 = O(m^C)$ valid allocations for each job j (see Fig. 2). Given an allocation of all jobs to computing nodes, our problem coincides with the well-studied DYNAMIC STORAGE ALLOCATION (DSA) problem [10]. Then, we use a known approximation algorithm for the latter problem.

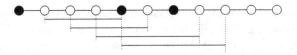

Fig. 2. Potential allocations for a job j requesting the middle I/O node with $q_j = 3$.

In order to decide the allocation of computing nodes we use an integer linear program. Let $\mathcal{A}_j$ be the set of all potential allocations for each job j, where $|\mathcal{A}_j| \leq q_j + 1$. Each allocation $a \in \mathcal{A}_j$ contains exactly q_j computing nodes as well as the required I/O node. Note that, an allocation may include more I/O nodes that will not be used during the execution of j neither by j nor by the other jobs due to the locality constraint. For example, in Fig. 2 the two rightmost allocations also cover the third I/O node in order to be able to include $q_j = 3$ computing nodes. For each job $j \in \mathcal{J}$ and allocation $a \in \mathcal{A}_j$, we introduce a binary indicator variable $x_{j,a}$ which is equal to one if j is executed according to the allocation a, and zero otherwise. Moreover, for each node $i \in \mathcal{V}$ we introduce a non-negative variable L_i which corresponds to the total load of jobs whose assigned allocation includes i. Finally, let Λ be the maximum load among all nodes. Then, we propose the following integer linear program which searches for the allocations that minimize the total load.

$$\text{minimize } \Lambda \qquad \qquad \text{(ILP)}$$

$$\Lambda \geq L_i \qquad \qquad \forall i \in \mathcal{V} \qquad (1)$$

$$L_i \geq \sum_{j \in \mathcal{J}} \sum_{a \in \mathcal{A}_j} \sum_{i \in a} x_{j,a} p_j \qquad \forall i \in \mathcal{V} \qquad (2)$$

$$\sum_{a \in \mathcal{A}_j} x_{j,a} = 1 \qquad \qquad \forall j \in \mathcal{J} \qquad (3)$$

$$x_{j,a} \in \{0,1\} \qquad \qquad \forall j \in \mathcal{J}, a \in \mathcal{A}_j \qquad (4)$$

Constraints (2) compute the total load for each node, while Constraints (3) ensure that each job is assigned an allocation. By relaxing the integrity Constraints (4), we can solve the corresponding linear program in polynomial time. Note that there are $O(mn)$ variables and $O(m+n)$ constraints. Moreover, an optimal solution to the above integer linear program is a lower bound to the makespan of an optimal solution for our problem, since it optimizes the maximum load without handling intersections of jobs in time, that is the scheduling phase.

Let $\tilde{\Lambda}$, $\tilde{L}_i$ and $\tilde{x}_{j,a}$ denote the values of the variables in an optimal solution of the relaxed linear program. Then, the solution of this linear program is rounded to an integral feasible solution whose variables are denoted by $\bar{\Lambda}$, $\bar{L}_i$ and $\bar{x}_{j,a}$. Specifically, we round the indicator variables independently for each job $j \in \mathcal{J}$

as follows: consider all possible allocations for the job j ordered with respect to the processors' ordering. The allocation chosen for j is the one with the smallest index k such that $\sum_{a=1}^{k} \tilde{x}_{j,a} \geq \frac{1}{2}$. Then, we set $\bar{x}_{j,k} = 1$ and $\bar{x}_{j,a} = 0$ for all $a \neq k$. Figure 3 gives an example of this rounding procedure.

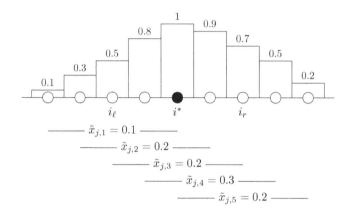

Fig. 3. Rounding procedure for the variables that correspond to job j: $\bar{x}_{j,3} = 1$ and $\bar{x}_{j,1} = \bar{x}_{j,2} = \bar{x}_{j,4} = \bar{x}_{j,5} = 0$.

The following lemma provides an upper bound to the integral solution $\bar{\Lambda}$ obtained after the rounding procedure.

Lemma 1. $\bar{\Lambda} \leq 2\tilde{\Lambda}$.

Proof. Consider a job j and let k_j be the index of the allocation of j in the rounded solution, i.e., $\bar{x}_{j,k_j} = 1$. Moreover, let $\mathcal{V}(j)$ be the set of nodes (both computing and I/O) that are included in this allocation. We will first prove the following statement:

$$\sum_{a \in \mathcal{A}_j:\ i \in a} \tilde{x}_{j,a} \geq \frac{1}{2} \text{ for every } i \in k_j$$

For example, in Fig. 3 we have that $k_j = 3$ and for each $i \in \{3, \ldots, 7\}$ the sum of the fractional variables that correspond to j and include i is at least 0.5. In order to prove the statement, let $k_j = \{i_\ell, \ldots, i_r\}$ be the set of nodes of the allocation k_j as these are ordered in the natural way. Recall that $\mathcal{V}^{I/O}(j) \in k_j$ is the I/O node required by j and assume that $\mathcal{V}^{I/O}(j)$ coincides with i^*, where $i_\ell \leq i^* \leq i_r$. By the definition of k_j, the statement is true for $i = i_\ell$. Moreover, the statement holds for each node $i \in \{i_\ell, \ldots, i^*\}$ since

$$\sum_{a \in \mathcal{A}_j:\ i \in a} \tilde{x}_{j,a} \geq \sum_{a \in \mathcal{A}_j:\ i_\ell \in a} \tilde{x}_{j,a} \geq \frac{1}{2}$$

It remains to prove it for $i \in \{i^* + 1, \ldots, i_r\}$. We focus first on i_r. Observe that by the definition of k_j it holds that $\sum_{a=1}^{k_j-1} \tilde{x}_{j,a} < \frac{1}{2}$. Then, we have that

$$\sum_{a \in \mathcal{A}_j:\ i_r \in a} \tilde{x}_{j,a} = \sum_{a \in \mathcal{A}_j} \tilde{x}_{j,a} - \sum_{a=1}^{k_j-1} \tilde{x}_{j,a} > 1 - \frac{1}{2} = \frac{1}{2}$$

Finally, the statement holds for each node $i \in \{i^* + 1, \ldots, i_r\}$ since

$$\sum_{a \in \mathcal{A}_j:\ i \in a} \tilde{x}_{j,a} \geq \sum_{a \in \mathcal{A}_j:\ i_r \in a} \tilde{x}_{j,a} \geq \frac{1}{2}$$

In order to finalize the proof of the lemma, consider the load $\bar{L}_i$ of a node i in the rounded solution. We have that

$$\bar{L}_i = \sum_{j \in \mathcal{J}} p_j \cdot \mathbf{1}_{\{\text{if } i \in k_j\}} = \sum_{j \in \mathcal{J}} p_j \sum_{a \in \mathcal{A}_j:\ i \in a} \bar{x}_{j,a} \leq \sum_{j \in \mathcal{J}} p_j 2 \sum_{a \in \mathcal{A}_j:\ i \in a} \tilde{x}_{j,a}$$

where the last inequality holds by the proven statement and since by Constraint (3) we have that $\sum_{a \in \mathcal{A}_j:\ i \in a} \bar{x}_{j,a} \leq 1$. Hence,

$$\bar{L}_i \leq 2 \sum_{j \in \mathcal{J}} p_j \sum_{a \in \mathcal{A}_j:\ i \in a} \tilde{x}_{j,a} = 2 \sum_{j \in \mathcal{J}} p_j \sum_{a \in \mathcal{A}_j} \sum_{i \in a} \tilde{x}_{j,a} = 2 \sum_{j \in \mathcal{J}} \sum_{a \in \mathcal{A}_j} \sum_{i \in a} \tilde{x}_{j,a} p_j = 2 \tilde{L}_i$$

The lemma follows by considering the node of maximum load in the rounded solution, i.e., $\bar{\Lambda} = \max_i \{\bar{L}_i\} \leq 2 \max_i \{\tilde{L}_i\} = 2\tilde{\Lambda}$. □

As mentioned before, given the allocations of all jobs, our problem coincides with the DSA problem [10]. An instance of the DSA problem consists of a set of n triples. Each triple (ℓ_j, r_j, s_j) corresponds to a rectangle parallel to x-axis of size $(r_j - \ell_j) \times s_j$. Specifically, ℓ_j and r_j are the projections of its leftmost and rightmost points, respectively, in the x-axis while s_j is its size projected in the y-axis. In other words, the position of the rectangle is fixed with respect to x-axis, but it can be shifted in any position in y-axis. The objective is to pack all rectangles without intersections in a strip of minimum height.

In our scheduling context, each job corresponds to a rectangle whose ℓ_j and r_j values are defined by a given allocation as the leftmost and the rightmost computing nodes respectively, while $p_j = s_j$. Moreover, the makespan coincides with the height of the strip.

Gergov [10] presented a greedy 3-approximation algorithm for the DSA problem. The important property of this algorithm is that it uses as lower bound the maximum load over all x-coordinates, which allows as to use it in our analysis. The following theorem describes this property in scheduling terms.

Theorem 2 [10]. *There is an algorithm which computes a feasible schedule whose makespan is at most three times the maximum load of every node.*

Algorithm 1.

---

1 Solve the relaxed version of (ILP)
2 **for** *each job* $j \in \mathcal{J}$ **do**
3   Find the smallest index k such that $\sum_{a=1}^{k} \tilde{x}_{j,a} \geq \frac{1}{2}$
4   Set $\bar{x}_{j,k} = 1$ and $\bar{x}_{j,a} = 0$ for all $a \neq k$

5 Create a feasible schedule by applying the algorithm proposed in Theorem 2
    using the allocations determined by the $\bar{x}_{j,a}$ variables

---

Due to the equivalence of our problem with DSA, we can apply the algorithm mentioned in Theorem 2 and get a final solution to our problem. A high-level description of the above described procedure is given in Algorithm 1.

Theorem 3. *Algorithm 1 achieves an approximation ratio of 6 for the line topology in the pinned I/O model.*

Proof. Consider a schedule created by Algorithm 1 and let $C_{\max}$ be the makespan of this schedule. Due to the allocation phase, we know that the maximum load over all nodes is equal to $\bar{\Lambda}$. Then, by Theorem 2 and Lemma 1, we have that $C_{\max} \leq 3\bar{\Lambda} \leq 6\tilde{\Lambda}$. Hence, the theorem follows by the fact that the optimal solution to (ILP) is a lower bound to the optimal solution for our problem. □

We observe that Gergov's algorithm remains a 3-approximation even in the case of rings. Moreover, the allocation procedure based on the rounding of (ILP) can be also applied for rings; we just need to define an ordering of the possible allocations of each job. Thus, by considering an clockwise ordering, we can apply Algorithm 1 and get the following theorem.

Theorem 4. *Algorithm 1 achieves an approximation ratio of 6 for the ring topology in the pinned I/O model.*

5 Unpinned I/O

In this section, we study the *unpinned* I/O model according to which each job requires any arbitrary I/O node.

5.1 Complexity

We start by proving that the studied problem is NP-complete even in the special case where all jobs require unit processing time to be executed, while the platform contains only three I/O nodes. The proof is similar with the proof of Theorem 1 with the difference that the reduction is done by the classical 3-PARTITION problem [8]. For this reason, it is omitted.

Theorem 5. *The problem of scheduling in the unpinned model with respect to contiguity and locality constraints is strongly $\mathcal{NP}$-complete even in line topologies, with $m^{I/O} = 3$ and $p_j = 1$ for each job $j \in \mathcal{J}$.*

5.2   An Approximation Algorithm for Equidistant I/O Nodes

In this section, we consider both line and ring topologies and we propose an approximation algorithm in the case where the I/O nodes are uniformly distributed. In other words, the I/O nodes are equidistant from each other. We denote by δ the distance separating two consecutive I/O nodes. Note that, given any instance, in line topologies δ can be either $\lfloor \frac{m^C}{m^{I/O}} \rfloor$ or $\lceil \frac{m^C}{m^{I/O}} \rceil$ while the first value is always the case in ring topologies.

We need some additional notation. We call a job *small* if it requires fewer computing nodes than the distance between two consecutive I/O nodes, i.e., $q_j^C < \delta$. In a similar way, we call a job *big* if $q_j^C \geq \delta$. Let $\mathcal{J}_{\leq \delta}$ and $\mathcal{J}_{\geq \delta}$ be the sets of small and big jobs, respectively. Our algorithm handles these sets separately.

A small job cannot be adjacent to more than one I/O nodes in any feasible schedule. Moreover, an I/O node along with δ consecutive computing nodes adjacent to it can be considered as a processing unit that can execute a small job. Based on this, we partition the set $\mathcal{V}^C$ into $\lfloor \frac{m^C}{\delta} \rfloor$ groups of consecutive computing units, each one of size at least δ. Assume that these groups as well as the I/O nodes are numbered from left to right and we consider the i-th such group and the i-th I/O node to compose a processing unit. Note that, by the definition of δ, $m^{I/O}$ can be either $\lfloor \frac{m^C}{\delta} \rfloor$ or $\lfloor \frac{m^C}{\delta} \rfloor + 1$. In the second case, which can happen only in line topologies, the last I/O node is not used. Then, we can transform our problem for small jobs to an instance of the classical $P \parallel C_{\max}$ problem with $\lfloor \frac{m^C}{\delta} \rfloor$ machines [11]. Specifically, each machine corresponds to one processing unit, while each small job has a processing time as in the initial instance and requires only one processing unit. Then, we solve the created instance of $P \parallel C_{\max}$ by using any known approximation algorithm for it. The following lemma, whose proof is omitted, summarizes the above procedure. The additional 2-factor in the line case is due to parity issues.

Lemma 2. *Any ρ_1-approximation algorithm for the $P \parallel C_{\max}$ scheduling problem, can be used to obtain a $2\rho_1$-approximation algorithm to schedule small jobs in a line and a ρ_1-approximation algorithm to schedule small jobs in a ring.*

Due to the contiguity constraint, the big jobs are structurally guaranteed to be adjacent to at least one I/O node, i.e., we can then ignore the existence of I/O nodes when scheduling big jobs. Hence, the objective is to pack the big jobs and our problem reduces to the strip-packing problem [13]. The following lemma, whose proof is omitted, summarizes the above reduction. The additional 2-factor in the ring case is due to the degeneration of the ring to a line.

Lemma 3. *Any ρ_2-approximation algorithm for the strip-packing problem, can be used to obtain a ρ_2-approximation algorithm to schedule big jobs in a line and a $2\rho_2$-approximation algorithm to schedule big jobs in a ring.*

By combining Lemmas 2 and 3 the following theorem follows.

Theorem 6. *For the unpinned model, there is a $(2\rho_1 + \rho_2)$-approximation algorithm for line topologies and a $(\rho_1 + 2\rho_2)$-approximation algorithm for ring topologies, where ρ_1 and ρ_2 are the approximation ratios for the $P \parallel C_{\max}$ and the strip-packing problems, respectively.*

Note that a PTAS exists for both $P \parallel C_{\max}$ and strip-packing problems [11, 13], leading for $(3 + \epsilon)$-approximation algorithms for line and ring topologies.

6   Conclusions

We studied the makespan minimization problem on line and ring topologies, when the allocations are constrained to be both contiguous and local. We proved that both the pinned and unpinned models are $\mathcal{NP}$-complete and we presented constant-factor approximation algorithms for them. The proposed algorithms can be also applied in different settings (the proofs will be developed in an extended version of this work). For example, in the case where the I/O nodes can be shared by more than one jobs, then the 6-approximation algorithm of Sect. 4.2 can be simply adapted by excluding the requested I/O node from the allocation of the job in the definition of the indicator variables of (ILP). Note that due to the locality constraint an I/O node cannot be shared by more than two jobs. Another example is the case where each job requires more than one I/O nodes. However, this assumption in conjunction with the locality constraint could lead to several unused nodes, limiting its interest.

As future steps, one could implement the proposed algorithms, and study their performances through simulation. From a theoretical point of view, the tightness results show the limits of the two-phase approach in Sect. 4.2. The approximation ratios might be improved by scheduling the problem in a single phase. Finally, the study of more enhanced topologies, like two-dimensional ones, is a very interesting direction. In this case, contiguity could be replaced by more general constraints implying the convexity of the shape of the allocations.

References

1. Bhatele, A., Mohror, K., Langer, S.H., Isaacs, K.E.: There goes the neighborhood: performance degradation due to nearby jobs. In: SC, pp. 41:1–41:12. ACM, November 2013
2. Błądek, I., Drozdowski, M., Guinand, F., Schepler, X.: On contiguous and non-contiguous parallel task scheduling. J. Sched. **18**(5), 487–495 (2015)
3. Chen, N.-C., Poon, S.S., Ramakrishnan, L., Aragon, C.R.: Considering time in designing large-scale systems for scientific computing. In: CSCW, pp. 1533–1545. ACM, February 2016
4. Dorier, M., Ibrahim, S., Antoniu, G., Ross, R.B.: Using formal grammars to predict I/O behaviors in HPC: the Omnisc'IO approach. IEEE Trans. Parallel Distrib. Syst. **27**(8), 2435–2449 (2016)
5. Enos, J., et al.: Topology-aware job scheduling strategies for torus networks. In: Cray User Group, May 2014

6. Feitelson, D.G., Rudolph, L., Schwiegelshohn, U., Sevcik, K.C., Wong, P.: Theory and practice in parallel job scheduling. In: Feitelson, D.G., Rudolph, L. (eds.) JSSPP 1997. LNCS, vol. 1291, pp. 1–34. Springer, Heidelberg (1997). https://doi.org/10.1007/3-540-63574-2_14

7. Gainaru, A., Aupy, G., Benoit, A., Cappello, F., Robert, Y., Snir, M.: Scheduling the I/O of HPC applications under congestion. In: IPDPS, pp. 1013–1022. IEEE, May 2015

8. Garey, M.R., Johnson, D.S.: Computers and Intractability: A Guide to the Theory of NP-Completeness. W. H. Freeman, New York (1979)

9. Georgiou, Y., Jeannot, E., Mercier, G. Villiermet, A.: Topology-aware resource management for HPC applications. In: ICDCN, pp. 17:1–17:10. ACM (2017)

10. Gergov, J.: Algorithms for compile-time memory optimization. In: SODA, pp. 907–908. ACM/SIAM, January 1999

11. Hochbaum, D.S., Shmoys, D.B.: Using dual approximation algorithms for scheduling problems: theoretical and practical results. J. ACM **34**(1), 144–162 (1987)

12. Kathareios, G., Minkenberg, C., Prisacari, B., Rodríguez, G., Hoefler, T.: Cost-effective diameter-two topologies: analysis and evaluation. In: SC, pp. 36:1–36:11. ACM, November 2015

13. Kenyon, C., Rémila, E.: Approximate strip packing. In: FOCS, pp. 31–36 (1996)

14. Lucarelli, G., Mendonça, F.M., Trystram, D., Wagner, F.: Contiguity and locality in backfilling scheduling. In: CCGRID, pp. 586–595. IEEE Computer Society, May 2015

15. Pascual, J.A., Miguel-Alonso, J., Antonio, L.J.: Application-aware metrics for partition selection in cube-shaped topologies. Parallel Comput. **40**(5), 129–139 (2014)

16. Strohmaier, E., Dongarra, J., Simon, H., Meuer, M.: TOP500 list, June 2018

17. Tessier, F., Malakar, P., Vishwanath, V., Jeannot, E., Isaila, F.: Topology-aware data aggregation for intensive I/O on large-scale supercomputers. In: COMHPC@SC, pp. 73–81. IEEE, November 2016

18. Tuncer, O., Leung, V.J., Coskun, A.K.: PaCMap: topology mapping of unstructured communication patterns onto non-contiguous allocations. In: ICS, pp. 37–46. ACM, June 2015

Resource-Efficient Execution
of Conditional Parallel Real-Time Tasks

Sanjoy Baruah[(✉)]

Washington University in St. Louis, St. Louis, MO, USA
baruah@wustl.edu

Abstract. Under the federated paradigm of multiprocessor scheduling, a set of processors is reserved for the exclusive use of each task. We consider the federated scheduling of parallel real-time tasks containing conditional (if-then-else) constructs, in which different executions of the task may result in workloads of substantially different magnitude and different character (e.g., degree of parallelism and critical path length). If the task is hard-real-time, then processors must be reserved for it under worst-case assumptions. However, it may be the case that most invocations of the task will have computational demand far below the worst-case characterization, and could have been scheduled correctly upon far fewer processors than had been assigned to it based upon the worst-case characterization of its run-time behavior. Provided we could safely determine during run-time if the worst-case characterization is likely to be realized during some execution and all the processors are therefore going to be needed, for the rest of the time the unneeded processors could be idled in low-energy "sleep" mode, or used for executing non-real time work in the background. In this paper we propose an algorithm for scheduling parallel conditional tasks that permits us to do so.

1 Introduction

This research is motivated by two trends in real-time computing: (i) the increasing use of multiprocessor and multicore platforms, and (ii) the increasingly complex control-flow that is to be found in real-time programs.

Modeling Parallelism. The models used in scheduling theory for representing real-time workloads that are implemented upon multicore platforms should be capable of exposing the parallelism that may exist within these workloads. Earlier models [1,2] that were developed in order to represent uniprocessor implementations of real-time systems, are not particularly suitable for this purpose; hence the *sporadic DAG task model* [3] was proposed as an appropriate candidate. A task in this model is specified as a 3-tuple (G, D, T), where G is a directed acyclic graph (DAG), and D and T are positive integers representing the relative deadline and period parameters of the sporadic DAG task respectively. The task repeatedly releases *dag-jobs*, each of which is a collection of (sequential) jobs. Successive dag-jobs are released a duration of at least T time

© Springer International Publishing AG, part of Springer Nature 2018
M. Aldinucci et al. (Eds.): Euro-Par 2018, LNCS 11014, pp. 218–231, 2018.
https://doi.org/10.1007/978-3-319-96983-1_16

units apart. The DAG G is specified as $G = (V, E)$, where V is a set of vertices and E a set of directed edges between these vertices. Each $v \in V$ represents the execution of a sequential piece of code (a "job"), and is characterized by a worst-case execution time (WCET). The edges represent dependencies between the jobs: if $(v_1, v_2) \in E$ then job v_1 must complete execution before job v_2 can begin execution. (Job v_1 is called a *predecessor* job of v_2, and job v_2 is called a *successor* job of v_1.) Jobs that are not predecessors or successors of each other, either directly or transitively, may execute simultaneously upon different processors. A release of a dag-job of the task at time-instant t means that all $|V|$ jobs $v \in V$ are released at time-instant t. If a dag-job is released at time-instant t then all $|V|$ jobs that were released at t must complete execution by time-instant $t + D$.

In this paper we restrict attention to *constrained-deadline* sporadic DAG tasks: these are sporadic DAG tasks satisfying the additional property that $D \leq T$ (and hence the duration of time during which successive dag-jobs are to be scheduled do not overlap). We focus upon the scheduling of a single such constrained-deadline sporadic DAG task upon a dedicated platform comprising a specified number m of identical processors (i.e., we restrict our attention to either systems comprising just a single task, or to multi-task systems scheduled under the *federated* paradigm of multiprocessor scheduling [4,5]). This problem is equivalent to the widely-studied problem of *makespan-minimization for precedence constrained tasks*: we seek to determine whether a single dag-job of the task can be scheduled to have a makespan[1] no larger than D upon the provided number of processors. We will discuss proposed solutions to this problem in Sect. 3.

Modeling Conditional Branching. As stated above, the sporadic DAG tasks model assumes that each release of a dag-job of the task causes the release of jobs corresponding to each and every vertex in V. It is thus successful in modeling intra-task parallelism: the workload generated by an individual task may comprise multiple jobs that are allowed to execute in parallel upon different processors. However, as we become more ambitious regarding the kinds of functionalities we attempt to implement in our real-time systems, these systems incorporate more complex control-flow than simply the straight-line code that characterized earlier systems. The presence of control structures such as conditional—*if-then-else*—constructs within the code that is being modeled by the task may mean that different activations of the task (i.e., different dag-jobs) cause different parts of the code to be executed. Assuming that jobs corresponding to all the vertices in V will execute during each such activation is pessimistic; there is a need to be able to model the fact that different dag-jobs of the same task may cause different collections of jobs to be executed. The *conditional sporadic DAG tasks* model [6,7] therefore further generalized the sporadic DAG tasks model by allowing for the representation of conditional execution of parts of a DAG. We will describe this model in detail in Sect. 2; for now, we

---

[1] The *makespan* of a schedule is the duration of it: the difference between the instants at which the first job begins execution and the last job completes.

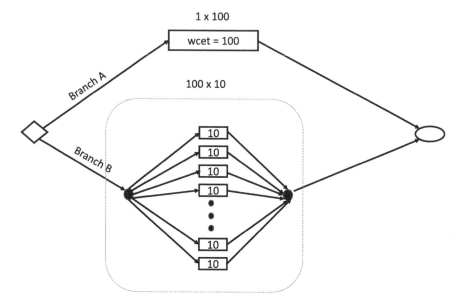

Fig. 1. Part of an example conditional DAG task. The diamond represents the start of a conditional (if-then-else) construct; the oval, the corresponding end. Each rectangle represents a sequential piece of code, and is labelled with its worst-case execution time (WCET).

illustrate its salient features via the example in Fig. 1. In this figure, the diamond-shaped vertex and the oval vertex respectively denote the beginning and end of an `if-then-else` construct. A conditional expression gets evaluated when flow of control reaches the diamond-shaped vertex: different executions of the task may result in the expression evaluating differently. Either the branch denoted "Branch A" or the one denoted "Branch B" is taken depending on whether this expression evaluates to true or false. Branch A leads to a single piece of sequential code of WCET 100, while Branch B leads to one hundred pieces of sequential code, each of WCET 10, that may execute in parallel.

The Problem Considered. We consider the scheduling of *hard-real-time* tasks: tasks for which it is imperative that they always meet their deadlines. For such tasks, computing resources must be provisioned under worst-case assumptions; for our conditional real-time tasks, this means that processors must be reserved for the task that enable it to meet its deadline regardless of which conditional expressions evaluate to true and which to false. The determination of how many processors should be assigned to a (regular, i.e., not conditional) DAG task in order to ensure that it always meets its deadlines is usually based upon computing the cumulative WCET of all the nodes in the DAG (this quantity is called the *work* parameter of the DAG) and the maximum cumulative WCET of any sequence of precedence-constrained nodes (called the *span* of the DAG). Algorithms are known for computing *work* and *span* of a regular DAG in time linear in the representation of the DAG. Techniques for computing *work* and *span* have been developed for conditional DAGs as well [6,7]. However, it may be the case that *work* and *span* for a conditional DAG as computed in this manner correspond to *mutually exclusive* branches in the conditional code. (E.g., in the example task segment of Fig. 1 *span* corresponds to the Branch A and is equal to 100, while *work* corresponds to Branch B and equals 1000. Clearly this worst-case *work* and this worst-case *span* cannot both occur during any individual execution of the task.) Assigning processors to the conditional task on the basis of such *work* and *span* parameters results in over-provisioning of computing resources to this task, and consequent resource under-utilization during run-time. Due to algorithm complexity considerations (see, e.g., [5] for a discussion), such under-utilization seems unavoidable in general. However, suppose that it is determined by extensive experimental *profiling* of the run-time behavior of this task that Branch A is taken the vast majority of the time. It may then be possible to carefully design a run-time scheduling strategy that reduces some of this inefficiency. Specifically, one could provision processors to the conditional task assuming the most conservative characterization (the *work* and *span* parameters as determined by the algorithms of [6,7]), but keeping some of the provisioned resource in "reserve", perhaps by placing some processors in sleep mode or having them execute background (non real-time) work, with the option of switching them to work upon executing the task if we are able to determine, during run-time, that the task's run-time behavior is in fact not likely to approach its most conservative estimates. In this paper, we derive an algorithm that adopts this approach to enhance run-time efficiency while continuing to ensure that deadlines are always met.

Organization. We describe the conditional sporadic DAG task model in Sect. 2, and briefly review some prior results on the scheduling of DAG tasks in Sect. 3. In Sect. 4 we describe, and prove the correctness of, our proposed approach for resource-efficient scheduling of hard-real-time sporadic DAG tasks. We conclude in Sect. 5 by placing this work within a larger context of research on the design and implementation of complex parallelizable real-time code upon multiprocessor platforms.

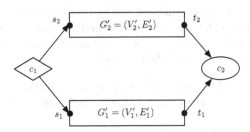

Fig. 2. A canonical conditional construct with branching factor 2. Vertices s_1 and t_1 (vertices s_2 and t_2, resp.) are the sole source vertex and sink vertex of G'_1 (G'_2, resp.).

2   Conditional Sporadic DAG tasks [6, 7]

Like a regular sporadic DAG task, each conditional sporadic DAG task τ is specified as a 3-tuple (G, D, T), where $G = (V, E)$ is a DAG, and D and T are positive
integers denoting (as with regular DAG tasks) the relative deadline and period
parameters of the task. We require that G have a single source vertex and a single sink vertex (of course any DAG with multiple sources and/or multiple sinks
is easily transformed in polynomial time to an equivalent conditional DAG satisfying this requirement, by perhaps adding an additional dummy source and/or
an additional dummy sink). *Conditional vertices* are special vertices in V that
are defined in pairs. Let (c_1, c_2) be such a pair in the DAG $G = (V, E)$—see
Fig. 2. Informally speaking, vertex c_1 can be thought of as representing a point
in the code where a conditional expression is evaluated and, depending upon the
outcome of this evaluation, control will subsequently flow along exactly one of
several different possible paths in the code. It is required that all these different
paths meet again at a common point in the code, represented by the vertex c_2.
More formally,

1. There are multiple outgoing edges from c_1 in E. Suppose that there are exactly
   k outgoing edges from c_1 to the vertices $s_1, s_2, \ldots, s_k$, for some $k > 1$. We
   call k the *branching factor* of this conditional. (The branching factor for an
   "if-then-else" condition is 2.) Then there are exactly k incoming edges into
   c_2 in E, from the vertices $t_1, t_2, \ldots, t_k$,
2. For each $\ell \in \{1, 2, \ldots, k\}$, let $V'_\ell \subseteq V$ and $E'_\ell \subseteq E$ denote all the vertices and
   edges on paths reachable from s_ℓ that do not include vertex c_2. By definition,
   s_ℓ is the sole source vertex of the DAG $G'_\ell \overset{\text{def}}{=} (V'_\ell, E'_\ell)$. It must hold that t_ℓ
   is the sole sink vertex of G'_ℓ.
3. It must hold that $V'_\ell \cap V'_j = \emptyset$ for all $\ell, j, \ell \neq j$. Additionally, with the exception
   of (c_1, s_ℓ) there should be no edges in E into vertices in V'_ℓ from vertices not
   in V'_ℓ, for each $\ell \in \{1, 2, \ldots, k\}$. I.e., $E \cap ((V \setminus V'_\ell) \times V'_\ell) = \{(c_1, s_\ell)\}$ should
   hold for all ℓ.

Edges (v_1, v_2) between pairs of vertices neither of which are conditional vertices represent precedence constraints exactly as in traditional sporadic DAG
tasks, while edges involving conditional vertices represent conditional execution
of code. More specifically, let (c_1, c_2) denote a defined pair of conditional vertices
(recall that conditional vertices are always defined in pairs). The semantics of
conditional DAG task execution mandate that

- After the job c_1 completes execution, exactly one of its successor jobs becomes
  eligible to execute; it is not known beforehand which successor job may execute.
- Job c_2 begins to execute upon the completion of exactly one of its predecessor
  jobs.

It is important to note that the conditional expressions may evaluate differently
during different executions of a conditional DAG task. Let $\mathcal{J}$ denote all possible

complete collections of jobs that comprise a single dag-job of the task, along with the precedence constraints amongst these jobs that are imposed by the edges of the DAG. Thus each $J \in \mathcal{J}$ denotes a collection of precedence-constrained jobs obtained by completely executing through the DAG once, taking into account the conditional branches within it. There may in general be exponentially many different flows through a graph: consider for example the following skeleton of code (here each (Ci) represents a boolean condition that may evaluate to either true or false, and each {Sij} a block of straight-line code):

```
if (C1) then {S11} else {S12}
if (C2) then {S21} else {S22}
. . . . . . . . . . . . . . .
. . . . . . . . . . . . . . .
if (Cn) then {Sn1} else {Sn2}
```

Depending upon whether the (Ci)'s evaluate to true or false, this code fragment may experience any of 2^n different execution flows through it; hence $|\mathcal{J}|$, the number of precedence-constrained collections of jobs in $\mathcal{J}$, may be exponential in the number of vertices in G. As a consequence, algorithms for the analysis of conditional DAG tasks that are based upon explicitly examining each $J \in \mathcal{J}$ will necessarily have exponential worst-case running time.

3   Some Prior Results on Scheduling DAG Tasks

As stated in Sect. 1 above, the workload of a DAG is often succinctly characterized via the *work* (the cumulative worst-case execution time) and *span* (the maximum cumulative worst-case execution time of any sequence of precedence-constrained jobs) parameters. The relevance of these two parameters arises from well-known results in scheduling theory concerning the multiprocessor scheduling of precedence-constrained jobs (i.e., DAGs) to minimize makespan—this is the widely-studied P | prec | $\mathcal{S}_{max}$ problem in the classic 3-field $\alpha \mid \beta \mid \gamma$ notation [8]. This problem has long been known to be NP-hard in the strong sense [9]; i.e., computationally highly intractable. However, Graham's *list scheduling* algorithm [10], which constructs a work-conserving schedule by executing at each instant in time an available job, if any are present, upon any available processor, performs fairly well in practice. It was shown [10] that list scheduling makes the following guarantee: if $\mathcal{S}_{max}$ denotes the minimum makespan with which a particular DAG can be scheduled upon m processors, then the schedule generated by list scheduling this DAG upon m processors will have a makespan no greater than $(2 - \frac{1}{m}) \times \mathcal{S}_{max}$. This result, in conjunction with a hardness result in [11] showing that determining a schedule for this DAG of makespan $\leq \frac{4}{3}\mathcal{S}_{max}$ remains NP-hard in the strong sense, suggests that list scheduling is a reasonable algorithm to use in practice, and in fact most run-time scheduling algorithms that are used for scheduling DAGs upon multiprocessors use some variant or the other of list scheduling. We will do so in this paper as well.

An upper bound on the makespan of a schedule generated by list scheduling is easily stated. Letting *work* and *span* denote the work and span parameters of the DAG being scheduled, it has been proved in [10] that the makespan of the schedule for a given DAG is guaranteed to be no larger than

$$\frac{work - span}{m} + span \qquad (1)$$

Computing *work* and *span* for Conditional DAGs. As in Sect. 2, let $\mathcal{J}$ denote all possible complete collections of jobs that comprise a single dag-job of the conditional DAG task under consideration, along with the precedence constraints amongst these jobs that are imposed by the edges in the DAG. Recall that the *work* of a regular (i.e., not conditional) DAG task denotes the sum of the WCETs of all the nodes, and *span* the maximum sum of WCETs of any precedence-constrained chain of nodes, in the DAG. These definitions have been extended to conditional DAGs [6]: for each $J \in \mathcal{J}$, let $work(J)$ denote the sum of the WCETs of all the jobs in J and $span(J)$, the maximum sum of WCETs of any precedence-constrained chain of jobs in J. If J is the collection of precedence-constrained jobs yielded during some execution of a dag-job of τ, the makespan of a schedule generated by the List Scheduling algorithm is, by Expression 1, guaranteed to be no larger than

$$\left(\frac{work(J) - span(J)}{m} + span(J) \right)$$

Letting

$$work \overset{\text{def}}{=} \max_{J \in \mathcal{J}} \left\{ work(J) \right\} \quad \text{and} \quad span \overset{\text{def}}{=} \max_{J \in \mathcal{J}} \left\{ span(J) \right\}, \qquad (2)$$

it has been shown in [5] that $\left(\frac{work-span}{m} + span \right)$ is a 2-approximation on the actual makespan if the conditional DAG is list-scheduled upon m processors. We therefore use the following sufficient condition for ensuring that conditional sporadic DAG task τ, with relative deadline parameter D, is correctly list-scheduled upon m unit-speed processors:

$$\frac{work - span}{m} + span \leq D \qquad (3)$$

It remains to specify how the *work* and *span* parameters of a conditional sporadic DAG task are to be computed. As mentioned above, an algorithm based on exhaustive enumeration of $\mathcal{J}$, and then computing $work(J)$ and $span(J)$ separately for each $J \in \mathcal{J}$ would yield an exponential-time algorithm; a recursive procedure for computing *span* and *work* for a given conditional DAG task is specified in [6,7] that has running time polynomial in the representation of the task.

4   Our Proposed Scheduling Approach

Given a conditional DAG task that is to be executed upon a platform comprising m identical processors, we will perform some analysis prior to run-time to compute the values of two parameters m_N and $\mathcal{S}_N$. These two parameters are then used during run-time by the run-time scheduler to ensure that the task always executes correctly (i.e., always meets its deadline) during runtime.

Pre-run-time analysis comprises three steps: given the conditional DAG task and the number m of processors that are available for its use,

1. Determine the *work* and *span* parameters of the conditional DAG task (as defined in Expression 2), using the algorithm of [6,7].
2. Check whether Inequality 3 holds. If it does not, our scheduling algorithm declares failure: it is unable to schedule this task in a manner that guarantees timing correctness.
3. Otherwise, it computes a pair of values m_N and $\mathcal{S}_N$—the manner in which these values are computed will be presented in Sect. 4.1; a property that they will satisfy is derived in Theorem 1.

Example 1. Consider the example task fragment in Fig. 1. Suppose this has a deadline $D = 300$, and that we have $m = 7$ processors available. Suppose, too, that upper branch (Branch A) is taken overwhelmingly more frequently than the lower branch (Branch B).

1. For this task, *work* $= 1000$ and *span* $= 100$
2. Inequality 3 evaluates as

$$\left(\frac{work - span}{m} + span \le D\right) \Leftrightarrow \left(\frac{1000 - 100}{7} + 100 \le 300\right) \Leftrightarrow \left(228.6 \le 300\right)$$

which is true. Hence, the task can be scheduled correctly upon the eight processors provided.
3. In Example 3, we will see that our pre-processing algorithm, using the technique for computing m_N and $\mathcal{S}_N$ derived in Sect. 4.1, would compute the values $m_N = 2$ and $\mathcal{S}_N = 100$ (these parameter values are used during run-time scheduling as discussed below).

□

Run-Time Scheduling. Suppose that the conditional sporadic DAG task releases a dag-job at some time-instant t_o during run-time.

1. Our run-time scheduler sets a timer to go off at time-instant $(t_o + \mathcal{S}_N)$, and begins executing the task upon m_N processors using the list-scheduling algorithm [10]. The remaining $(m - m_N)$ processors are placed/remain in sleep mode.
2. If the task has not completed execution when the timer goes off at time-instant $(t_o + \mathcal{S}_N)$, then the scheduler awakens the $(m - m_N)$ sleeping processors, and uses list-scheduling to execute the remainder of the task upon the entire bank of m processors.

We highlight that the run-time scheduler does not need to monitor the flow of control through the code – i.e., which branches are taken – during execution of the conditional DAG; in fact, no run-time monitoring is needed other than whether the DAG completes execution within $\mathcal{S}_N$ units of arrival or not. This enables far more efficient implementation than if it needs to actively examine the internal state (the program counter; the values of the conditional expressions that are evaluated; etc.) of the task.

Example 2. Returning to the task in Example 1, each time a dag- job of this task is released the run-time scheduler list-schedules it upon two processors. If the task does not complete execution within 100 time units of its arrival, the remaining $(7 - 2 =)$ five processors are awakened, and the task list-scheduled upon all seven processors for the remaining 200 time units until its deadline. □

In Theorem 1 below we derive sufficient conditions upon the values that are assigned to m_N and $\mathcal{S}_N$ in order to ensure that this run-time algorithm always meets the task deadline.

Theorem 1. *Suppose that we are given values of m_N and $\mathcal{S}_N$, with $0 < m_N \le m$ and $0 \le \mathcal{S}_N \le D$. If these given values satisfy*

$$\mathcal{S}_N \le \frac{D - span - (work - span)/m}{1 - (m_N/m)} \tag{4}$$

then the run-time scheduling algorithm described above is guaranteed correct.

Proof: If the task completes execution within $\mathcal{S}_N$ time units, correctness is preserved since $\mathcal{S}_N \le D$. Let us therefore consider the case when it does not complete execution by time-instant $\mathcal{S}_N$. Let $work'$ and $span'$ denote the work and span parameters of the remaining amount of computation, which will execute upon m processors. By Expression 1 the overall makespan is therefore bounded from above by

$$\mathcal{S}_N + \big((work' - span')/m + span'\big) \tag{5}$$

Since the remaining span at time-instant $\mathcal{S}_N$ is $span'$, an amount $(span - span')$ of the critical path of the task has executed during $[0, \mathcal{S}_N]$. At each instant when the critical path is not executing, all m_N processors must be busy executing tasks not on the critical path. Hence the total amount of execution occurring over $[0, \mathcal{S}_N)$ is at least $\big[(\mathcal{S}_N - (span - span')) \times m_N + (span - span')\big]$, from which it follows that

$$work' \le work - \mathcal{S}_N \times m_N + (span - span') \times m_N - (span - span')$$
$$= work - \mathcal{S}_N \times m_N + span \times (m_N - 1) - span' \times (m_N - 1) \tag{6}$$

Substituting Inequality 6 into the Expression 5, we obtain the following upper bound on the overall makespan:

$$\mathcal{S}_N + \left(\frac{work - \mathcal{S}_N \times m_N + span \times (m_N - 1) - span' \times (m_N - 1) - span'}{m} + span'\right)$$
$$= \mathcal{S}_N + \left(\frac{work - \mathcal{S}_N \times m_N + span \times (m_N - 1)}{m} + span' \times \left(1 - \frac{m_N}{m}\right)\right) \tag{7}$$

Since $m_N \leq m$, Expression 7 is maximized when $span'$ is as large as possible; i.e., $span' = span$. Substituting $span' = span$ into Expression 7, we get the following upper bound on the overall makespan:

$$S_N + \left(\frac{work - S_N \times m_N + span \times (m_N - 1)}{m} + span \times \left(1 - \frac{m_N}{m}\right) \right)$$

$$= S_N + \left(\frac{work - S_N \times m_N - span}{m} + span \right)$$

Correctness is guaranteed by having this upper bound on the makespan be $\leq D$:

$$\left(S_N + \left(\frac{work - S_N \times m_N - span}{m} + span \right) \right) \leq D$$

$$\Leftrightarrow \left(S_N - \frac{S_N \times m_N}{m} \right) \leq \left(D - \frac{work - span}{m} - span \right)$$

$$\Leftrightarrow S_N \left(1 - \frac{m_N}{m} \right) \leq \left(D - \frac{work - span}{m} - span \right)$$

$$\Leftrightarrow S_N \leq \frac{D - span - (work - span)/m}{1 - (m_N/m)}$$

which is the same as Expression 4, and the theorem is thus proved.   □

4.1   Computing m_N and S_N

We now describe how we assign values to the parameters m_N and S_N satisfying Expression 4. We reiterate that our objective here is to enhance *efficiency* while maintaining correctness – the guarantee that the deadline will be met. Our approach to this will be based on profiling the run-time behavior of the task, in order to obtain an estimate of the likelihood (i.e., probability) that the makespan on the m_N processors will exceed the threshold S_N, thus triggering the use of the remaining $(m - m_N)$ processors.

In somewhat greater detail, let us suppose that we seek to *minimize the expected number of processors that will be used during any given invocation of the task*[2]. We first observe that one strategy for guaranteeing correctness is to execute the task upon $\hat{m}$ processors that will be used during each invocation, where $\hat{m}$ satisfies

$$\left(\frac{work - span}{\hat{m}} + span \right) \leq D$$

$$\Leftrightarrow \hat{m} \geq \left\lceil \frac{work - span}{D - span} \right\rceil \tag{8}$$

This value of $\hat{m}$ represents an upper bound on the desired value of m_N: our run-time scheduler will never need to activate more than $\hat{m}$ processors upon the

---

[2] We point out that other optimization objectives could also reasonably be considered, such as *minimizing the cumulative expected duration that the processors will be active*, using an approach similar to the one we adopt here – see the discussion in the paragraphs immediately following displayed equation (10).

arrival of a dag-job. Below, we exhaustively consider each potential value of m_N in $[0, \hat{m}]$:

---

for $m' = 1$ **to** $\hat{m}$ **do**

1. Assign $\mathcal{S}_N(m')$ a value as follows:

$$\mathcal{S}_N(m') = \frac{D - span - (work - span)/\hat{m}}{1 - (m'/\hat{m})} \qquad (9)$$

so that Expression 4 of Theorem 1 is satisfied with $m_N = m'$ and $\mathcal{S}_N = \mathcal{S}_N(m')$.

2. Profile the run-time behavior of the task upon m' processors to determine the probability that the makespan of the task is $\leq \mathcal{S}_N(m')$. Let $p(m')$ denote this probability.

3. Compute $E(m')$, the expected number of processors that are used during any given invocation of the task if our run-time algorithm is implemented with $m_N = m'$, as follows:

$$E(m') = p(m') \times m' + (1 - p(m')) \times m \qquad (10)$$

This represents the fact that there is a probability $p(m')$ that just the m' processors will be used, and a probability $(1 - p(m'))$ that all m processors will be used.

If we were interested in optimizing the *duration* for which the processors are to be kept active, we would replace Expression 10 with

$$E(m') = m' \times \mathcal{S}_N(m') + (1 - p(m')) \times m \times (D - \mathcal{S}_N(m'))$$

Let $m_{\min}$ denote the value of m' for which $E(m')$, as computed in Expression 10 above, is the minimum. We assign m_N and $\mathcal{S}_N$ values as follows:

$$m_N \leftarrow m_{\min} \quad \text{and} \quad \mathcal{S} \leftarrow \mathcal{S}_N(m_{\min}).$$

Example 3. Let us revisit the example task fragment in Fig. 1, that was considered in Examples 1 and 2. Recall that this task had $work = 1000$, $span = 100$, and $D = 300$, and is to be scheduled upon $m = 7$ processors. Furthermore, we had assumed that the upper branch in Fig. 1 is taken far more frequently than the lower branch; let p_o denote the probability that the uper branch is taken upon any given execution.

We compute $\hat{m} = \lceil (1000 - 100)/(300 - 100) \rceil = \lceil 900/200 \rceil = 5$. From Expression 9, we have

$$\mathcal{S}(m') = \frac{300 - 100 - (1000 - 100)/7}{1 - m'/7} = \frac{200 - 900/7}{1 - m'/7} = \frac{500}{7 - m'}$$

Hence $\mathcal{S}(1) = 500/6 \approx 83.3$, while $\mathcal{S}(2)$–$\mathcal{S}(5)$ are all ≥ 100. Making the simplifying conservative assumption that each piece of sequential code executes for a duration equal to its WCET, it is clear from visual inspection of the task fragment in Fig. 1 that when the upper branch is taken, the makespan is 100; hence $p(1) = 0$ while $p(2)$–$p(5)$ are all equal to p_o (the probability that the upper branch is taken). Consequently, $m_{\min} = 2$ and our algorithm computes and returns

$$m_N \leftarrow 2 \text{ and } \mathcal{S}_N \leftarrow 100.$$

$\square$

5   Context and Summary

To our knowledge, the concept of representing a single parallelizable real-time task with multiple pairs of work and span parameters was first proposed by Li et al. [12], in the context of *mixed-criticality scheduling* [13]. Li et al. [12] were motivated by the fact that determining tight upper bounds on WCET's of even sequential pieces of code can be a very challenging problem upon the kinds of advanced computing platforms that are widely used today; additionally, upon such platforms the difference between typical-case and worst-case execution times may be very considerable. They hence proposed that two pairs of work and span parameters be estimated for each parallel task, one pair that is made under very conservative assumptions and therefore perhaps very large but trust-worthy to a very high level of assurance, and another pair made under less conservative assumptions and therefore considerably smaller than the conservative bounds, but also to be trusted to a lesser level of assurance. The appropriate pair of estimates—the more conservative pair, or the less conservative one, could then be used for validating the correctness of the run-time behavior of each task depending upon the criticality of the functionality that it is responsible for.

Integrating multiply-specified tasks of this kind with the approach of dynamically changing the number of processors assigned to an individual task during run-time was originally proposed in [14]. The principal motivation for the work in [14] was to explore whether ideas and techniques from the considerable body of prior research (e.g., [15–17]) on measurement-based techniques for estimating *probabilistic* worst-case execution time distributions (pWCET) are applicable to run-time scheduling of parallel real-time tasks.

The work presented in the current paper extends and generalizes these prior approaches: we have proposed here a method based upon combining worst-case characterization and experimental profiling of run-time behavior, for modeling complex parallelizable real-time code that may include conditional branching, that is to be implemented upon multiprocessor platforms. This model, and the scheduling algorithms we have derived for it, enables us to obtain implementations that combine correctness guarantees with improved efficiency. Correctness depends only upon the conservative worst-case characterization, while the sole effect of the experimental characterization is on efficiency; hence, system correctness is not compromised at all if the experimental profiling mis-characterizes, or fails to capture all subtleties of, actual run-time behavior. In this manner the correctness of safety properties may be validated under worst-case assumptions; a system so validated may be experimentally profiled to enhance the run-time efficiency of its implementation.

Acknowledgements. This research was supported in part by NSF Grants CNS 1409175, CPS 1446631, and CNS 1563845.

References

1. Liu, C., Layland, J.: Scheduling algorithms for multiprogramming in a hard real-time environment. J. ACM **20**(1), 46–61 (1973)
2. Baruah, S., Mok, A., Rosier, L.: Preemptively scheduling hard-real-time sporadic tasks on one processor. In: Proceedings of the 11th Real-Time Systems Symposium, Orlando, Florida, pp. 182–190. IEEE Computer Society Press (1990)
3. Baruah, S., Bonifaci, V., Marchetti-Spaccamela, A., Stougie, L., Wiese, A.: A generalized parallel task model for recurrent real-time processes. In: Proceedings of the IEEE Real-Time Systems Symposium, RTSS 2012, San Juan, Puerto Rico, pp. 63–72 (2012)
4. Li, J., Saifullah, A., Agrawal, K., Gill, C., Lu, C.: Analysis of federated and global scheduling for parallel real-time tasks. In: Proceedings of the 2012 26th Euromicro Conference on Real-Time Systems, ECRTS 2014, Madrid, Spain. IEEE Computer Society Press (2014)
5. Baruah, S.: The federated scheduling of systems of conditional sporadic DAG tasks. In: Proceedings of the 15th International Conference on Embedded Software (EMSOFT), Amsterdam, The Netherlands (2015)
6. Baruah, S., Bonifaci, V., Marchetti-Spaccamela, A.: The global EDF scheduling of systems of conditional sporadic DAG tasks. In: Proceedings of the 2014 26th Euromicro Conference on Real-Time Systems, ECRTS 2015, Lund, Sweden, pp. 222–231. IEEE Computer Society Press (2015)
7. Melani, A., Bertogna, M., Bonifaci, V., Marchetti-Spaccamela, A., Buttazzo, G.: Response-time analysis of conditional DAG tasks in multiprocessor systems. In: Proceedings of the 2014 26th Euromicro Conference on Real-Time Systems, ECRTS 2015, Lund, Sweden, pp. 222–231. IEEE Computer Society Press (2015)
8. Graham, R.L., Lawler, E.L., Lenstra, J.K., Kan, A.H.G.R.: Optimization and approximation in deterministic sequencing and scheduling: a survey. Ann. Discret. Math. **5**, 287–326 (1979)
9. Ullman, J.: NP-complete scheduling problems. J. Comput. Syst. Sci. **10**(3), 384–393 (1975)
10. Graham, R.: Bounds on multiprocessor timing anomalies. SIAM J. Appl. Math. **17**, 416–429 (1969)
11. Lenstra, J.K., Rinnooy Kan, A.H.G.: Complexity of scheduling under precedence constraints. Oper. Res. **26**(1), 22–35 (1978)
12. Li, J., Ferry, D., Ahuja, S., Agrawal, K., Gill, C., Lu, C.: Mixed-criticality federated scheduling for parallel real-time tasks. In: Proceedings of the 22nd IEEE Real-Time and Embedded Technology and Applications Symposium (RTAS), April 2016
13. Vestal, S.: Preemptive scheduling of multi-criticality systems with varying degrees of execution time assurance. In: Proceedings of the Real-Time Systems Symposium, Tucson, AZ, pp. 239–243. IEEE Computer Society Press, December 2007

14. Agrawal, K., Baruah, S.: A measurement-based model for parallel real-time tasks. In: 2018 30th Euromicro Conference on Real-Time Systems. Schloss Dagstuhl - Leibniz-Zentrum fuer Informatik, July 2018
15. Edgar, S., Burns, A.: Statistical analysis of WCET for scheduling. In: 2001 IEEE Real-Time Systems Symposium (RTSS), pp. 215–224, December 2001
16. Bernat, G., Colin, A., Petters, S.M.: WCET analysis of probabilistic hard real-time systems. In: 2002 IEEE Real-Time Systems Symposium (RTSS), pp. 279–288 (2002)
17. Bernat, G., Colin, A., Petters, S.: pWCET: a tool for probabilistic worst-case execution time analysis of real-time systems. Technical report, The University of York, England (2003)

High Performance Architectures and Compilers

Improving GPU Cache Hierarchy Performance with a Fetch and Replacement Cache

Francisco Candel[1](✉), Salvador Petit[1], Alejandro Valero[2],
and Julio Sahuquillo[1]

[1] Department of Computer Engineering, Universitat Politècnica de València,
46022 Valencia, Spain
fracanma@inf.upv.es, {spetit,jsahuqui}@disca.upv.es
[2] Departamento de Informática e Ingeniería de Sistemas,
Instituto Universitario de Investigación en Ingeniería de Aragón
Universidad de Zaragoza, 50018 Zaragoza, Spain
alvabre@unizar.es

Abstract. In the last few years, GPGPU computing has become one of the most popular computing paradigms in high-performance computers due to its excellent performance to power ratio. The memory requirements of GPGPU applications widely differ from the requirements of CPU counterparts. The amount of memory accesses is several orders of magnitude higher in GPU applications than in CPU applications, and they present disparate access patterns. Because of this fact, large and highly associative Last-Level Caches (LLCs) bring much lower performance gains in GPUs than in CPUs.

This paper presents a novel approach to manage LLC misses that efficiently improves LLC hit ratio, memory-level parallelism, and miss latencies in GPU systems. The proposed approach leverages a small additional Fetch and Replacement Cache (FRC) that stores control and coherence information of incoming blocks until they are fetched from main memory. Then, fetched blocks are swapped with victim blocks to be replaced in the LLC. After that, the eviction of victim blocks is performed from the FRC. This management approach improves performance due to three main reasons: (i) the lifetime of blocks being replaced is increased, (ii) the main memory path is unclogged on long bursts of LLC misses, and (iii) the average L2 miss delaying latency is reduced. Experimental results show that our proposal increases the performance (OPC) over 25% in most of the studied applications, reaching improvements up to 150% in some applications.

1 Introduction

In recent years, GPU (Graphics Processing Unit) architectures have acquired a great relevance in the field of high-performance computing. The main reason has been that GPUs are able to accelerate the execution of massively parallel

© Springer International Publishing AG, part of Springer Nature 2018
M. Aldinucci et al. (Eds.): Euro-Par 2018, LNCS 11014, pp. 235–248, 2018.
https://doi.org/10.1007/978-3-319-96983-1_17

applications, since they provide a much higher level of parallelism than CPU architectures. In addition, GPUs are energetically more efficient [1, 2] for a given performance, than its CPU counterparts. Because of these reasons, many super-computers in the top 500 list [3] rely on GPUs. For instance, the Piz Daint supercomputer, ranked in third place of the list in November 2017, was built with Nvidia Tesla P100 GPU devices.

GPU architectures are optimized to run applications composed of thousands of logical threads. In order to support the execution of such a high number of threads, the GPU core must be coupled with a memory subsystem able to support a high Memory-Level Parallelism (MLP). GPU memory subsystems are therefore designed to sustain a high memory bandwidth. Because of the poor data temporal locality of GPGPU applications or kernels, on a *very long* burst of L2 accesses many requests can miss, which cause subsequent main memory accesses.

In this scenario, the memory subsystem of GPUs poorly performs. In this paper, we look into the reasons explaining this behavior, and we find that one of the main sources of performance losses of the memory subsystem is the management of L2 cache misses. We find that conventional caches designed to address memory patterns of CPU applications do not properly meet the requirements of GPGPU applications, but they seriously penalize their performance since they can significantly slow down the management of L2 cache requests on long bursts of requests. The previous rationale means that improving the L2 cache management is a key design concern that should be tackled to improve the system performance. This paper proposes a novel L2 cache design aimed at boosting the memory level parallelism by adding a Fetch and Replacement Cache (FRC) that provides additional cache lines that help unclog the memory subsystem. The FRC approach uses these extra resources to prioritize the fetch of incoming L2 cache requests and to delay the eviction of the blocks to be replaced. The proposal has been evaluated considering an AMD GPU based architecture, although the results would also apply in almost all current GPU architectures as they implement a similar memory hierarchy.

The proposal has been modeled in the Multi2Sim simulation framework [4], a state-of-the-art GPU simulator widely used in both the academia and the industry. Experimental results show that FRC improves the Operations Per cycle (OPC) more than 25% in most applications by drastically reducing the Misses Per Kilo-Operation (MPKO) and L2 miss latency.

The remainder of this work is organized as follows. Section 2 describes the architecture of the AMD *Southern Islands* family of GPUs. Section 3 motivates this work by presenting the problems that FRC tackles in current GPU memory subsystems. In Sect. 4, the proposed approach is described in detail. Section 5 presents the experimental results. Section 6 summarizes related studies about GPU memory subsystems. Finally, in Sect. 7 some concluding remarks are drawn.

2   Background

This section provides some background about the architecture of modern GPUs. Since this paper focuses on the AMD *Southern Islands* [5] family of GPUs, AMD terminology is used throughout this work.

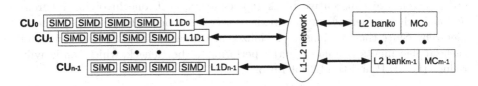

Fig. 1. Diagram of an AMD Southern Islands GPU.

Figure 1 depicts a block diagram of an AMD Southern Islands GPU. This GPU includes up to 32 *Compute Units* (CUs), each one implementing the *Graphics Core Next* (GCN) [6] microarchitecture. Internally, a GCN CU consists of 4 *Single Instruction Multiple Data* (SIMD) arithmetic logic units.

GPU applications or *kernels* are composed of a massive number of threads or *work-items*. These threads are organized in 64-thread bundles, named *wavefronts*, which are allocated to SIMD units. During most of the execution time of a kernel, the GPU ensures that each SIMD unit is assigned tens of wavefronts. In this way, SIMD units can switch among wavefronts in a fine-grain basis, which helps hide memory latencies.

A SIMD unit executes instructions from threads of a wavefront in a lockstep manner. That is, at a given point of the execution time a SIMD unit is performing the same arithmetic instruction in the 64 threads of the same wavefront. Memory reference instructions are also executed following the SIMD paradigm; that is, a wavefront can generate up to 64 memory requests at the same time. To reduce the overall amount of memory requests, those referencing the same 64-byte cache block are *coalesced* into a single memory request, which is issued to the memory subsystem.

As in a conventional processor, the memory subsystem is organized hierarchically. After being coalesced, memory requests access the L1 data cache of the corresponding CU. Those requests that miss the L1 cache are forwarded to a multi-banked L2 cache, acting as Last-Level Cache (LLC). L2 banks contain interleaved block addresses at a granularity of 256 bytes, and each bank is connected to a dual-channel memory controller that manages the corresponding off-chip GDDR5 main memory. This design reduces the number of channel conflicts and increases the memory bandwidth utilization.

3   Motivation

The coalesce mechanism reduces the number of requests to the memory subsystem. However, GPGPU applications generate enormous amounts of memory traffic; for instance, a typical GPU can issue thousands of memory requests in a given cycle. These amounts yield conventional cache organizations to significant performance losses. The main reason is that the massive number of threads is executing in parallel causes sudden bursts of memory transactions, which involve a high number of cache replacements. As a consequence, in a relatively short interval of time, a given cache line can suffer a long number (e.g. in the order of tens) of consecutive block replacements, each one involving different actions such as coherence invalidations or accesses to lower levels of the memory hierarchy. Since these actions are serialized at the cache line, the management of cache replacements becomes a major performance bottleneck, which can heavily reduce the MLP and the L2 hit ratio.

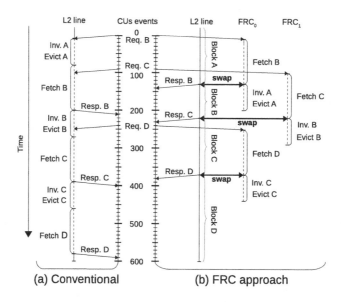

Fig. 2. Sequence of events involved in three consecutive replacements targeting the same L2 cache line for both the conventional and the proposed approaches.

To help understand the problem, Fig. 2 depicts a time diagram with the events involved in three consecutive replacements all targeting the same L2 victim line. The three requests causing these replacements have been labeled as *Req. B, C,* and *D,* and have been generated at cycles 0, 90, and 240, respectively, after the requests miss the L1 cache and are forwarded to the L2 cache.

As can be seen in Fig. 2a, which shows the behavior of a conventional replacement approach, *Req. B* triggers the replacement of the currently stored block (block *A*). From this moment, the victim line is in a transient state (represented by dashed lines), preventing other requests from accessing the line. To manage the replacement, depending on the state of *A*, an invalidation to the L1 cache and an L2 cache eviction must be performed. Once the victim line is freed, the requested incoming block (B), must be fetched from main memory and allocated to this line.

While block B is being fetched, *Req. C* arrives to L2, which triggers another replacement in the same victim line. However, because of the line is in a transient state, *Req. C* must be enqueued. Thus, *Req. C* cannot be attended until cycle 210, delaying its completion until cycle 400. This serialization also affects *Req. D* at cycle 240.

Moreover, the hit ratio is also reduced, since (i) the invalidation and eviction of the contents of a victim line are performed before fetching the requested block and (ii) the fetch operation is the longest one involved in a replacement due to the high main memory latencies. As an example, even if a complex protocol allows reading the contents of a cache line while it is in a transient state, a load requesting block A would only hit between cycles 0 and 90, and would miss afterwards.

Although theoretically possible, it is very rare that this situation occurs in a conventional CPU processor since there is likely a non-transient line in the same cache set that can be selected as a victim, which avoids the serialization of replacements. In contrast, in GPUs, it is often the case that a burst of misses triggers replacements in all the lines of the same cache set. Therefore, further misses targeting the same set cannot be served from memory, which impacts on the exploited memory parallelism.

A naive solution to this problem is blindly increasing cache associativity so that a set has more available lines. However, this approach incurs in high latencies and energy penalties since associative tag lookups do not scale well with the number of ways. Moreover, although such a solution may alleviate the problem, larger sets can also be blocked provided that bursts of misses affecting the same cache set are large enough.

4   FRC Approach

The proposed approach is aimed at increasing MLP and LLC hit ratio. With this aim, we introduce a Fetch and Replacement Cache (FRC) to each L2 cache bank. The FRC provides additional cache lines that allow (i) start fetching from memory as soon as an L2 miss rises, increasing MLP, and (ii) performing invalidation and eviction actions *after* fetching the requested block, which increases the lifetime of victim blocks and the overall hit ratio.

Figure 2b shows how the FRC can help improve the management of consecutive replacements affecting the same line. By cycle 10, when *Req. B* misses in L2, instead of immediately invalidating the victim line, a free FRC entry (FRC_0) is allocated and used to fetch block B. After this block is fetched, the contents of the victim line and FRC_0 are swapped. Then, the invalidation and eviction of block A are performed from FRC_0, which becomes free when the eviction is completed. In this way, fetch actions can be performed as long as there are free FRC entries (e.g. the fetch of block C can start in parallel at cycle 90). To ensure that there are free FRC entries, they are recycled. Thus, after block A

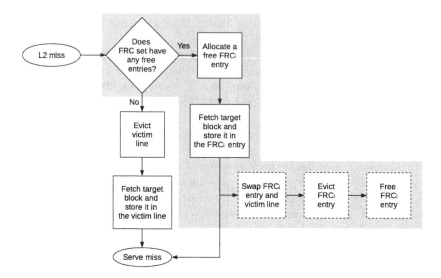

Fig. 3. Block diagram with the steps followed on an L2 miss. Those steps introduced with the FRC are highlighted in gray color.

has been replaced, FRC_0 is freed, which allows this entry to be used later by *Req. D*.

The swap operation guarantees that the victim line is never in a transient state (note that it is not represented with dashed lines in Fig. 2b), and that the invalidation and eviction of its contents are performed after the requested block is fetched. Consequently, FRC supports a higher cache level parallelism that allows responding to several requests at the same time. Furthermore, compared to the conventional approach, the lifetime of the victim block becomes longer when FRC is used.

Tags and control bits of blocks in transient state are stored in the FRC. Thus, to reduce tag lookup overhead, FRC is organized as a conventional cache, although its geometry (i.e. associativity and number of sets) can be different from that of the L2 cache. L2 accesses must search the requested block both in the target L2 bank and its associated FRC. A hit in the L2 bank is performed as in the conventional approach, while a hit in FRC for a block being fetched is enqueued until the fetch operation completes.

As shown in Fig. 3, the FRC approach modifies the classical miss management by adding the events highlighted in gray color. On an L2 miss (both in the L2 bank and the FRC), and if there are free entries in the FRC's set mapped to the missing block, the block is assigned to a FRC 's entry and the access is immediately propagated to the lower memory hierarchy level (early fetch). Once the fetch has been performed, the miss can be already served. In this way, the victim block eviction is taken out of the critical path. To manage the eviction without leaving L2 cache lines in a transient state, the data stored in the FRC's entry and the victim line are swapped. Thereby, the eviction is done from the

FRC's entry. Once the eviction has finished, the FRC's entry is set as free to handle subsequent L2 misses.

Finally, note that in case there is not any free entry in the FRC's set targeted by the missing block, the proposed approach operates like the conventional approach. In addition, FRC does not change the state of blocks stored in the cache, but only modifies the resources they are using. Thus, it does not affect the coherence protocol.

Overall, as experimental results will show, FRC has three main impacts on performance: (i) new requests do not wait (or wait much less) for cache block's evictions, which reduces the memory access latency, (ii) the lifetime of an L2 block becomes longer, decreasing the number of misses, and (iii) a higher MLP is achieved, since FRC allows immediate access to lower memory levels as long as there are free FRC entries.

5 Experimental Evaluation

To evaluate the proposal, we have modeled the FRC approach with the Multi2Sim [4] simulation framework. We focus on the Southern Islands GPU architecture from AMD, which is one of the most recent GPU architectures modeled on a detailed simulation framework. In particular, we model the characteristics of an HD7770 GPU [6], including CUs, L1 and L2 caches, memory controllers, and GDDR5 memory [7]. The L2 cache consists of two 16-way 128 KB banks, which is our baseline configuration. In addition, to evaluate the impact on performance of cache associativity and capacity, we evaluate two additional conventional L2 caches consisting of two 32-way 256 KB banks and two 32-way 512 KB banks. Both configurations are compared to the FRC one, which is composed of the baseline configuration plus two additional FRCs (1 per bank). We analyze the sensitivity our proposal to the number of FRC entries, which ranges between 4 and 512. All the evaluated FRC configurations, except the smallest one with 4 entries, are organized with 8-way sets.

Notice that the FRC approach represents a minor area increase over the baseline, since the area occupied by an additional FRC is much smaller than doubling or quadrupling the cache bank capacity, which would present roughly the same cost in area as adding 2048 and 6144 entries, respectively. Nevertheless, we conservatively assume that all the analyzed L2 cache configurations have the same access time.

For evaluation purposes, a subset of the OpenCL SDK 2.5 benchmarks [8] has been used, covering all the possible performance behaviors from the entire benchmark suite. These benchmarks are executed until completion.

5.1 Performance Analysis

System performance has been quantified in terms of Operations Per Cycle (OPC), which is analogous to its counterpart IPC used to evaluate CPU processors [7]. This metric accounts for the number of single scalar operations each

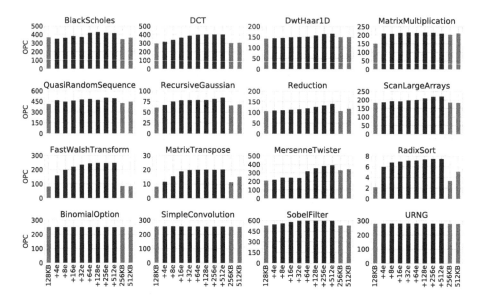

Fig. 4. Operations Per Cycle (OPC) across the studied applications. (Color figure online)

GPU instruction executes during the workload execution. For instance, if a given vector instruction is internally executed as 64 individual scalar operations, this metric accounts for 64 operations instead of only one instruction.

Figure 4 shows the OPC for the studied benchmarks. The red bar on the left side of each plot represents the 2×128 KB L2 baseline cache, and the two red bars on the right side represent the 2×256 KB L2 cache and the 2×512 KB L2 cache, respectively. The black bars show results of the FRC configuration varying the number of entries per FRC ranging from 4 to 512, labeled as $+Ne$, where N indicates the number of entries. The proposed approach achieves, across most of the studied applications, OPC improvements higher than 25% compared to the baseline, reaching improvements up to 150% in applications such as FastWalshTransform and MersenneTwister. In general, it can be observed that almost all the applications achieve their highest OPC with around 32 or 64 entries, which represents by 64× and 32× less area, respectively, than doubling the cache bank size to 256 KB. Moreover, in most applications, the performance achieved by FRC is much higher than that obtained by blindly increasing the L2 cache capacity with a higher associativity degree.

Three main behaviors can be appreciated:

- Smooth OPC increase. The OPC of applications exhibiting this behavior, which is the common one, increases in small steps with additional FRC entries until a given saturation point. This is the case of benchmarks such as FastWalshTransform, MersenneTwister, and DCT.
- Sharp OPC increase. Applications presenting this behavior show significant performance increase with just 4 FRC entries, but no remarkable

OPC improvement is observed with additional entries. This is the case of `MatrixMultiplication`.

– Similar OPC. Applications in this category experience the same performance across all the studied cache approaches. This is the case of `BinomialOption` and `URNG`, mainly due to their low number of memory accesses as discussed below. Obviously, the OPC of this type of applications is also not affected when enlarging the L2 cache size and associativity.

5.2   Analysis of Memory Subsystem Metrics

To provide insights into the OPC trend shown by the studied applications, we analyze the following metrics: number of misses measured in *Misses Per Kilo-Operation* (MPKO), percentage of misses served by FRC additional entries, and the L2 miss latency penalty.

Misses Per Kilo-Operation. We define the metric MPKO for GPUs with analogous meaning to the MPKI (Misses Per Kilo-Instruction), widely used when studying the cache hierarchy of the CPU counterparts. Figure 5 plots the results. It can be observed that the baseline configuration shows high MPKO values, which can be notably reduced by adding FRC entries. This fact confirms the benefits on performance brought by the FRC approach by keeping victim blocks in a non-transient state until fetch actions are completed. As a consequence, the hit ratio is improved compared to the conventional approach.

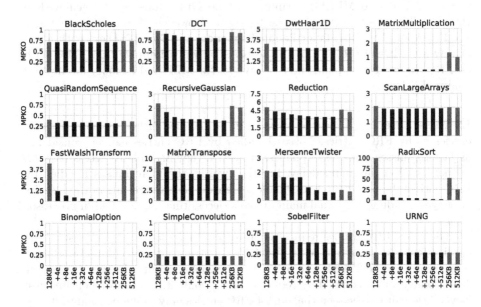

Fig. 5. Misses Per Kilo-Operation (MPKO) in the L2 cache.

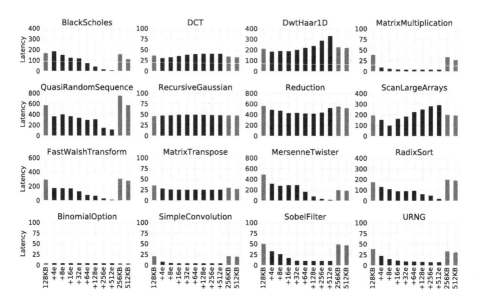

Fig. 6. Average L2 miss delaying latency quantified in processor cycles.

Overall, a clear inverse correlation between OPC and MPKO can be appreciated. However, in a few applications like DwtHaar1D and Reduction, a significant MPKO reduction over the baseline with a few FRC entries has a minimal effect on OPC. On the other hand, as observed, BinomialOption and URNG present a near-zero MPKO, meaning that no OPC gains can be achieved in these applications by acting on the L2 cache. However, there are applications like BlackScholes, DCT, QuasiRandomSequence, and SobelFilter, with a relatively low MPKO (below 1.5) in the baseline which improve their OPC with an FRC. In order to explain these behaviors, the MLP and memory latency are analyzed below.

L2 Miss Latency. L2 cache misses can be handled either by normal cache entries or by FRC entries. Misses handled by FRC entries can be considered as *fast* L2 misses since, as explained in Sect. 4, they are able to access to main memory with a minimum delay. In other words, the more misses handled by FRC entries the better the performance. Figure 6 plots the results of the L2 miss latency (excluding the actual main memory access time), quantified in processor cycles.

The use of FRC entries reduce the average L2 miss latency for almost all the applications. As observed, with just 4 FRC entries, latency is largely reduced with respect to the 256 KB and 512 KB cache configurations. In fact, the largest FRC configuration completely reduces the L2 contention in most benchmarks. Nevertheless, it can be seen that just 4 FRC entries only provide a slight latency improvement in some applications, thus large-sized FRCs are preferred. However,

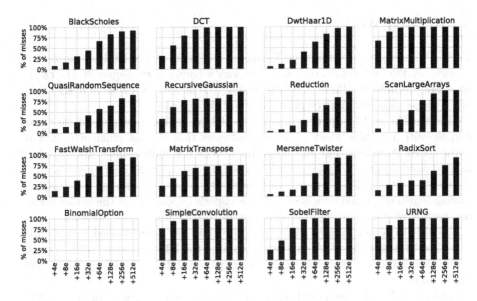

Fig. 7. Percentage of L2 misses handled by FRC entries.

DwtHaar1D and ScanLargeArrays suffer an increase in latency as the number of
FRC entries grows over around 8 entries. This is because the parallelism level is
higher than the baseline, which increases the memory contention. Notice that,
in spite of this increase, the higher MLP turns into OPC improvements.

Percentage of Misses Served by the FRC. Since the service of misses
is not stalled in case of consecutive replacements over the same victim line,
MLP is also improved. Figure 7 shows the percentage of misses served by the
FRC. As observed, FRC with only 64 entries handles by 75% of misses in most
applications. Moreover, this percentage significantly rises, even to almost 100%
in some benchmarks, for configurations smaller than the +512e configuration.

The applications Matrixtranspose and BinomialOption show an unexpected behavior as the percentage of misses handled by FRC entries saturate in
a relatively low number of entries, that is, this percentage does not increase even
if more entries are added. In other words, the L2 cache misses are mostly handled
by the cache itself instead of by FRC entries. This is due to two different reasons.
First, the kernel of Matrixtranspose presents bursts of accesses targeting the
same FRC set. This behavior can be improved by increasing FRC associativity
(8-way in these experiments). Second, BinomialOption makes important use of
the local memory of the CU, which significantly reduces the number of accesses
to main memory.

6 Related Work

The GPU memory subsystem performance has been widely analyzed in recent years from different angles, including memory scheduling strategies [9–11], cache bypassing techniques [12,13], and optimizing the memory subsystem design [14–18]. This section summarizes prior work in this regard.

Elastic-Cache [14] supports fine-grained L1 cache line management for those kernels with irregular memory access patterns that do not efficiently exploit cache space. Auxiliary tags for fine-grained cache line management are stored in unused shared memory space, which is not fully occupied in many kernels.

Gebhart et al. [15] propose to dynamically adjust the storage partitioning among registers, primary caches, and scratchpads depending on the kernel memory requirements, resulting in a reduction of the on-chip access latencies.

IBOM [16] is an integrated architecture that leverages unused register file entries with lightweight ISA support to enlarge the L1 cache size. With enough cache capacity, a set balancing technique exploits underutilized sets to improve cache usage.

Other works have proposed additional memory structures to improve GPU performance. Wang et al. [17] incorporate a victim cache between L1 and L2 that presents the same capacity and associativity as the L1 cache. Reused blocks are kept in the L1 cache by enabling swap operations with the victim cache. Since a victim cache so large would impact on energy and area, unused entries from the register file and shared memory are proposed as an alternative to holding data that otherwise would remain in the victim cache.

In [18], the authors propose to allocate *TinyCaches* between each lane in a CU and the L1 cache to filter out memory requests to lower memory levels for energy saving purposes. By leveraging intrinsic characteristics of CUDA and OpenCL programming models, these caches are kept non-coherent to avoid incurring additional overheads.

All the above works primarily focus on L1 caches. In contrast, our proposed FRC design targets LLCs where all accesses from L1 are merged and contention greatly limits MLP. Furthermore, the FRC approach can be easily implemented in different memory subsystem architectures, since it does not change the actions required to handle misses, but the locations where these actions are performed (i.e. FRC entries).

7 Conclusions

This paper has presented a novel GPU cache subsystem design that leverages a small Fetch and Replacement Cache (FRC) between the Last-Level Cache (LLC) and the main memory. The design provides additional cache lines that allow prioritizing the fetch of incoming LLC cache blocks over the replacement of victim blocks. The proposed design boosts the system performance by increasing the Memory-Level Parallelism (MLP) and enlarging the lifetime of the victimized blocks.

FRC attacks by design three main cache performance related events, which results in a much better L2 cache management: (i) it reduces the number of Misses Per Kilo-Operation (MPKO) by keeping victim blocks in cache until fetch actions are completed, (ii) it reduces the miss latency by starting the fetch actions from main memory as soon as a miss rises, and (iii) it increases the MLP by unclogging new block requests whose victim line is already being replaced.

Experimental results have shown that, compared to a conventional LLC design, FRC increases the Operations Per Cycle (OPC) over 25% in all the applications suffering contention in main memory.

Acknowledgments. This work was supported by the Spanish *Ministerio de Economía y Competitividad* (MINECO) and Plan E funds under Grant TIN2015-66972-C5-1-R and TIN2016-76635-C2-1-R (AEI/FEDER, UE), and by the *Programa de Ayudas de Investigación y Desarrollo* (PAID) *de la Universitat Politècnica de València*.

References

1. Huang, S., Xiao, S., Feng, W.: On the energy efficiency of graphics processing units for scientific computing. In: Proceedings of the IEEE International Symposium on Parallel and Distributed Processing, pp. 1–8 (2009)
2. Glenis, A., Petridis, S.: Performance and energy characterization of high-performance low-cost cornerness detection on GPUs and multicores. In: Proceedings of the 5th International Conference on Information, Intelligence, Systems and Applications, pp. 181–186 (2014)
3. Top500.org: Top500 Supercomputer Sites. http://top500.org
4. Ubal, R., Jang, B., Mistry, P., Schaa, D., Kaeli, D.: Multi2Sim: a simulation framework for CPU-GPU computing. In: Proceedings of the 21st International Conference on Parallel Architectures and Compilation Techniques, pp. 335–344 (2012)
5. AMD: Southern Islands Series Instruction Set Architecture (2012)
6. AMD: AMD Graphics Cores Next (GCN) Architecture White Paper (2012)
7. Candel, F., Petit, S., Sahuquillo, J., Duato, J.: Accurately modeling the on-chip and off-chip GPU memory subsystem. Future Gener. Comput. Syst. **82**, 510–519 (2018)
8. AMD: AMD Accelerated Parallel Processing (APP) Software Development Kit (SDK) (2012)
9. Mu, S., Deng, Y., Chen, Y., Li, H., Pan, J., Zhang, W., Wang, Z.: Orchestrating cache management and memory scheduling for GPGPU applications. IEEE Trans. Very Large Scale Integr. (VLSI) Syst. **22**(8), 1803–1814 (2014)
10. Jia, W., Shaw, K.A., Martonosi, M.: MRPB: memory request prioritization for massively parallel processors. In: Proceedings of the IEEE 20th International Symposium on High Performance Computer Architecture, pp. 272–283 (2014)
11. Sethia, A., Jamshidi, D.A., Mahlke, S.: Mascar: speeding up GPU warps by reducing memory pitstops. In: Proceedings of the IEEE 21st International Symposium on High Performance Computer Architecture, pp. 174–185 (2015)
12. Li, C., Song, S.L., Dai, H., Sidelnik, A., Hari, S.K.S., Zhou, H.: Locality-driven dynamic GPU cache bypassing. In: Proceedings of the 29th International ACM Conference on Supercomputing, pp. 67–77 (2015)

13. Liang, Y., Xie, X., Wang, Y., Sun, G., Wang, T.: Optimizing cache bypassing and warp scheduling for GPUs. IEEE Trans. Comput.-Aided Des. Integr. Circuits Syst. (2018, to appear)
14. Li, B., Sun, J., Annavaram, M., Kim, N.S.: Elastic-cache: GPU cache architecture for efficient fine- and coarse-grained cache-line management. In: Proceedings of the IEEE International Parallel and Distributed Processing Symposium, pp. 82–91 (2017)
15. Gebhart, M., Keckler, S.W., Khailany, B., Krashinsky, R., Dally, W.J.: Unifying primary cache, scratch, and register file memories in a throughput processor. In: Proceedings of the IEEE/ACM 45th Annual International Symposium on Microarchitecture, pp. 96–106 (2012)
16. Mu, S., Deng, Y., Chen, Y., Li, H., Pan, J., Zhang, W., Wang, Z.: IBOM: an integrated and balanced on-chip memory for high performance GPGPUs. IEEE Trans. Parallel Distrib. Syst. **29**(3), 586–599 (2018)
17. Wang, J., Fan, F., Jiang, L., Liang, X., Jing, N.: Incorporating selective victim cache into GPGPU for high-performance computing. Wiley Concurr. Comput.: Pract. Exp. **29**(24), 1–11 (2017)
18. Sankaranarayanan, A., Ardestani, E.K., Briz, J.L., Renau, J.: An energy efficient GPGPU memory hierarchy with tiny incoherent caches. In: Proceedings of the International Symposium on Low Power Electronics and Design, pp. 9–14 (2013)

Abelian: A Compiler for Graph Analytics on Distributed, Heterogeneous Platforms

Gurbinder Gill[✉], Roshan Dathathri, Loc Hoang, Andrew Lenharth, and Keshav Pingali

The University of Texas at Austin, Austin, TX 78712, USA
{gill,roshan,loc,pingali}@cs.utexas.edu, andrewl@lenharth.org

Abstract. The trend towards processor heterogeneity and distributed-memory has significantly increased the complexity of parallel programming. In addition, the mix of applications that need to run on parallel platforms today is very diverse, and includes graph applications that typically have irregular memory accesses and unpredictable control-flow. To simplify the programming of graph applications on such platforms, we have implemented a compiler called Abelian that translates shared-memory descriptions of graph algorithms written in the Galois programming model into efficient code for distributed-memory platforms with heterogeneous processors. The compiler manages inter-device synchronization and communication while leveraging state-of-the-art compilers for generating device-specific code. The experimental results show that the novel communication optimizations in the Abelian compiler reduce the volume of communication by 23×, enabling the code produced by Abelian to match the performance of handwritten distributed CPU and GPU programs that use the same runtime. The programs produced by Abelian for distributed CPUs are roughly 2.4× faster than those in the Gemini system, a third-party distributed CPU-only system, demonstrating that Abelian can manage heterogeneity and distributed-memory successfully while generating high-performance code.

Keywords: Graph analytics · Heterogeneous computing
Distributed computing · Compilers · High performance computing

1 Introduction

Graph analytics systems must handle very large data-sets with billions of nodes and trillions of edges [16]. Graphs of this size are too big to fit into the memory of a single machine, so one approach is to use distributed-memory clusters consisting of multicore processors. Writing efficient distributed-memory programs can be difficult, so a number of frameworks and libraries such as Pregel [18], PowerGraph [12], and Gemini [33], have been developed to ease the burden of writing graph analytics applications for such machines. New trends in processor architecture have made this programming problem much more difficult. To

© Springer International Publishing AG, part of Springer Nature 2018
M. Aldinucci et al. (Eds.): Euro-Par 2018, LNCS 11014, pp. 249–264, 2018.
https://doi.org/10.1007/978-3-319-96983-1_18

reduce energy consumption, computer manufacturers are turning to *heteroge-neous* processor architectures in which each machine has a multicore proces-sor and GPUs or FPGAs. To exploit such platforms, we must tackle the twin challenges of *processor heterogeneity* and *distributed-memory computing*. Frame-works like Lux [15] and Gluon [10] permit graph analytics applications writers to use distributed GPUs, but they require writing platform-specific programs that are not portable.

Ideally, we would have a compiler that takes single-source, high-level speci-fications of graph analytics algorithms and automatically translates them into distributed, heterogeneous implementations while optimizing them for diverse processor architectures. This paper describes such a compiler, called *Abelian*. Application programs are generalized vertex programs written in the Galois programming model, which provides programming patterns and data structures to support graph applications [20]. Section 2 describes this programming model in more detail. The Abelian compiler, described in Sect. 3, targets the Gluon runtime [10], which implements bulk-synchronous execution. Unlike other sys-tems in this space, this runtime supports a number of graph partitioning policies including edge-cuts and vertex-cuts, and the programmer can choose any of these policies. The compiler exploits domain-knowledge to generate distributed code, inserting optimized communication code. Back-end compilers generate optimized code for NUMA multi-cores and GPUs from the output of Abelian.

The experimental results presented in Sect. 4 show that the communica-tion optimizations in Abelian reduce communication volume by 23×, enabling Abelian-generated implementations to match the performance of hand-tuned distributed-CPU and distributed-GPU programs on the same platform. In addi-tion, the distributed-CPU implementations produced by Abelian yield a geomet-ric mean speedup of 2.4× over those in the stand-alone distributed-CPU system Gemini [33] on the same hardware. This shows that the flexibility of Abelian in compiling a high-level, shared-memory, single address space specification for heterogeneous and distributed-memory architectures does not come at the cost of performance, even when compared to integrated, homogeneous systems.

2   Programming Model

The Abelian compiler supports a generalized vertex programming model [12, 18,33] that is a restriction of the Galois programming model [20,24]. Nodes and edges of the graph have labels that are updated iteratively by the program until some quiescence condition is reached. Updating of labels is performed by applying *operators* to *active nodes* in the graph; this is called an *activity*. A push-style operator uses the label of the active node to conditionally update the labels of immediate neighbors of that node while a pull-style operator reads the labels of the immediate neighbors and conditionally updates the label of the active node.

Abelian supports more general operators than other systems in this space. In particular, an operator is allowed to update the labels of both the active node *and* its immediate neighbors, which is useful for applications like matrix completion using stochastic gradient descent. In addition, Abelian does not require updates to node labels to be reduction operations. For example, k-core decomposition evaluated in Sect. 4 uses subtraction on node labels.

In addition to the operator, the programmer must specify how active nodes are found in the graph [19]. The simplest approach is to execute the program in rounds and apply the operator to every node in each round. The order in which nodes are visited is unspecified, and the implementation is free to choose whatever order is convenient. These *topology-driven algorithms* [24] terminate when a global quiescence condition is reached. The Bellman-Ford algorithm for single-source shortest-path (sssp) is an example.

An alternative strategy is to track active nodes in the graph and apply the operator only to those nodes, which potentially creates new active nodes. These *data-driven algorithms* [24] terminate when there are no more active nodes in the graph. As before, the order in which active nodes are to be processed is left unspecified, and the implementation is free to choose whatever order is convenient. Chaotic relaxation sssp uses this style of execution. Tracking of active nodes can be implemented by maintaining a *work-list* of active nodes. Alternatively, this can be implemented by marking active nodes in the graph and making sweeps over the graph, applying the operator only to marked nodes; we call this approach *filtering*. Fine-grain synchronization in marking and unmarking nodes can be avoided by using Jacobi-style iteration with two flags, say *current* and *next*, on each node; in a round, active nodes whose *current* flag is set are processed, and if a node becomes active in that round, its *next* flag is set using an ordinary write operation. The roles of these flags are exchanged at the end of each round. In our programming model, data-driven algorithms are written using work-lists, but the compiler transforms the code to use a filtering implementation. The correctness of this transformation is ensured by the fact that active nodes can be processed in any order.

Implementation: This programming model is implemented in C++ using the Galois library [20]. Figure 1 shows a program for push-style data-driven algorithm of pagerank. A work-list is used to track active nodes. The **Galois::for_each** in line 30 populates the work-list initially with all nodes in the graph and then iterates over it until the work-list is empty. The operator computes the update to the pagerank of the active node, and it pushes this update to all neighbors of the active node. If the residual at a neighbor exceeds some user-specified threshold, that neighbor becomes active and is pushed to the work-list.

The semantics of the **Galois::for_each** iterator permit work-list elements to be processed in any order. In a parallel implementation of the iterator, each operator application must appear to have been executed atomically. To ensure this, the application programmer must use data structures provided in the Galois library which include graphs, work-lists, and accumulators. This permits the runtime to manage updates to distributed data structures on heterogeneous devices and allows the compiler to treat data structures as objects with known semantics, which enables program optimization and generation of parallel code from implicitly parallel programs as described in Sect. 3.

Restrictions on Operators: Like in other programming models for graph analytics [12,15,26,33] and compilers for data-parallel languages [3,27,30], operators cannot perform I/O operations. They also cannot perform explicit dynamic memory allocation since some devices (like GPUs) have limited support for this in their runtimes. The library data structures can perform dynamic storage allocation, but this is done transparently to the programmer.

3   Abelian Compiler

Figure 4 is an overview of how input programs are compiled for execution on distributed, heterogeneous architectures. The Abelian compiler (implemented as a source-to-source translation tool based on Clang's libTooling) analyzes the patterns of data accesses in operators, restructures programs for execution on distributed-memory architectures, and inserts code for optimized communication. The output of the Abelian compiler is a bulk-synchronous parallel C++ program with calls to the Gluon [10] communication runtime (Fig. 3). Gluon transparently handles the graph partitioning while loading the input graph. The generated code is independent of the partitioning policy, but the partitioning policy determines which portions of this code are executed. This permits Gluon's optimization that exploits structural invariants in partitioning without recompiling the program. The Abelian compiler also generates IrGL [22] intermediate representation kernels corresponding to each Galois::do_all call in the C++ program and inserts code in the C++ program to switch between calling the Galois::do_all and the corresponding IrGL kernel depending on the configuration chosen for the host (these are not shown in Fig. 3 for brevity). The C++ program and the IrGL intermediate code are then compiled using device-specific compilers. The output executable is parameterized by the graph input, the partitioning policy, and the number of hosts and their configuration (CPU or GPU). The user can thus experiment with a variety of partitioning strategies and heterogeneous devices with a single command-line switch.

```
1 struct NodeData{
2   // data on each node
3   unsigned int nout; // out-degree
4   float rank;
5   std::atomic<float> res; // residual
6 };
7
8 struct PageRank {
9   Graph* g;
10  PageRank(Graph* g) : g(g) {}
11  void operator()(GNode src,
12                  Worklist& wl) {
13    auto& sd = g->getData(src);
14    auto res_old=sd.res.exchange(0);
15    // apply residual to self
16    sd.rank += res_old;
17    auto delta=res_old*alpha/sd.nout;
18    for (auto e : g->getEdges(src)) {
19      GNode dst = g->getEdgeDst(e);
20      auto& dd = g->getData(dst);
21      // update residual of dest
22      dd.res += delta;
23      if (dd.res > tolerance) {
24        wl.push(dst);
25      }
26    }
27  }
28 };
29
30 Galois::for_each(g, PageRank{g});
```

Fig. 1. Pagerank source program

```
1 struct Add_contrib {
2   typedef float ValTy;
3   static ValTy extract(NodeData& node){
4     return node.contrib;
5   }
6   static bool reduce(NodeData& node,
7                      ValTy y) {
8     add(node.contrib, y);
9     return true;
10  }
11  static void reset(NodeData& node) {
12    node.contrib = 0;
13  }
14 };
15
16 struct Bcast_contrib {
17  typedef float ValTy;
18  static ValTy extract(NodeData& node){
19    return node.contrib;
20  }
21  static void setVal(NodeData& node,
22                     ValTy y) {
23    node.contrib = y;
24  }
25 };
```

Fig. 2. Compiler-generated synchronization structures for field contrib in pagerank

```
1 struct NodeData {
2   // data on each node
3   unsigned int nout; // out-degree
4   float rank;
5   float res; // residual
6   // compiler added field
7   std::atomic<float> contrib;
8 };
9 DistributedAccumulator work_done;
10 ... // field-specific bitvector, flags
11 ... // field-specific sync structures
12 struct PageRank {
13  Graph* g;
14  const float &l_alpha, &l_tolerance;
15  ... // copy constructor for members
16  void operator()(GNode src) {
17    auto& sd = g->getData(src);
18    if(sd.res > l_tolerance) {
19      work_done += 1; // do not terminate
20      auto res_old = sd.res;
21      sd.res = 0;
22      sd.rank += res_old;
23      Bitvec_rank.set(src);
24      auto delta=res_old*l_alpha/sd.nout;
25      for (auto e:g->getEdges(src)) {
26        GNode dst = g->getEdgeDst(e);
27        auto& dd = g->getData(dst);
28        dd.contrib += delta;
29        Bitvec_contrib.set(dst);
30      } } }
31 };
32 struct PageRank_splitOp {
33  Graph* g;
34  PageRank_splitOp(Graph* g) : g(g) {}
35  void operator()(GNode src) {
36    auto& sd = g->getData(src);
37    sd.res += sd.contrib;
38    Bitvec_res.set(src);
39    sd.contrib = 0;
40  }
41 };
42 ... // 1st round for all nodes in
          initial work-list
43 do { // subsequent rounds: predicate-
          based filter
44   work_done.reset(); // for termination
45
46   ... // sync res if required: readSrc
47   Galois::do_all(g.getSources(),
48                  PageRank{&g, alpha, tolerance});
49   Flag_rank.set_writeSrc();
50   Flag_contrib.set_reduceDst();
51
52   if (Flag_contrib.is_reduceDst()) {
53     graph.sync<reduceDst, readSrc,
54       Add_contrib, Bcast_contrib>
55       (Bitvec_contrib); // executed
56     Flag_contrib.reset_reduceDst();
57   }else if(Flag_contrib.is_reduceSrc()){
58     // sync contrib: reduceSrc, readSrc
59   } else {...} // sync contrib if required
60   Galois::do_all(g.getSources(),
61                  PageRank_splitOp{&g});
62   Flag_res.set_writeSrc();
63 } while(work_done.reduce());
```

Fig. 3. Compiler-generated pagerank program

3.1 Graph-Data Access Analysis

The access analysis pass analyzes the fields accessed in an operator. The results of this analysis are used to insert required communication code. Field accesses are classified as follows:

- *Reduction:* The field is read and updated using a reduction operation inside an edge iterator within the operator (e.g., addition to *residual* in line 22 in Fig. 1). This is a common and important pattern in graph analytics applications.
- *Read:* The field is read, and it is not part of a reduction (e.g., read from *nout* in line 17 in Fig. 1).
- *Write:* The field is written, and it is not part of a reduction (e.g., write to *rank* in line 16, Fig. 1).

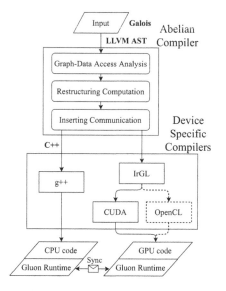

Fig. 4. System overview

In addition, it is useful to abstract the context in which a field access is made.

- *At source:* The field is accessed at the source node of an edge.
- *At destination:* The field is accessed at the destination node of an edge.
- *At any:* The field is accessed at a node independent of any edge or at both endpoints of an edge.

3.2 Restructuring Computation

The goal of computation restructuring is to bridge the semantic gap between the programming model, which has a single address space, and the execution model, which is distributed-memory and bulk-synchronous parallel. The semantics of Galois iterators permit iterations to be executed in parallel as long as each iteration appears to execute atomically. This fine-grain, iteration-level parallelism must be converted to round-based, bulk-synchronous parallelism by the Abelian compiler. This includes eliminating global variables (similar to *closure conversion* in functional languages) by adding them as members of the structure. This also requires two key transformations.

Splitting Operators. When active nodes are processed in parallel on a shared-memory machine, fine-grain synchronization may be needed for correct execution. This problem appears in a different guise on distributed-memory machines: if the two active nodes are on different hosts, proxies will be created on both hosts for the common neighbor, and it is necessary to reconcile the values pushed to these proxies so that the semantics of the program are respected. The bulk-synchronous execution model does not permit fine-grain synchronization, so these kinds of problems must be solved, in general, by breaking up the operator into phases if necessary and introducing sync calls between phases. There are a number of cases to consider depending on the type of field access as determined by the graph-data access analysis. We describe this for one such case.

In the PageRank source code in Fig. 1, the *residual* field is read (line 14) to update the *rank* field (line 16) and written (line 14 using *exchange(0)*) at the *source*, but it is also reduced (line 22) at the *destination*. Since different hosts could update the residual, the hosts reading it should have the reduced value. To handle this, the compiler splits any operator that has such a dependence into multiple operators (a form of *loop fission*): one with only Read and Write accesses to the field and another with only Reduction accesses, as shown in the PageRank and PageRank_splitOp operators (lines 12–41) respectively in Fig. 3. This may involve introducing new fields to store the intermediate values (e.g., contrib). The compiler also transforms some non-reduction read-after-write operations (e.g., subtraction) to equivalent reduction operations (e.g., addition) in a similar way. After this transformation, sync calls are introduced between the parallel phases, as described in Sect. 3.3.

Eliminating Work-Lists. The Abelian compiler eliminates work-lists by using *filtering*, as explained in Sect. 2: in a given round, all nodes in the graph are visited and the operator is applied to nodes whose *current* flag is set. This flag is reset, and if a node becomes active in that round, its *next* flag is set; the roles of the flags are exchanged at the end of each round.

In some algorithms, the predicate used in the source program to push an active node to the work-list can be used during filtering to check if the node is active. Extracting this predicate involves a form of *loop fission*, and it avoids introducing flags and synchronizing their accesses. For example, in Fig. 1, the code in lines 23–24 adds active nodes to the work-list. In the generated code, this is eliminated, and a new operator is created to conditionally activate nodes as shown in line 18 in Fig. 3. Another operator is created to execute all nodes that would have been on the initial work-list (line 42). Abelian can also directly take filter-based implementation of data-driven algorithms as an input, in which case this transformation is not required. Termination is detected using a distributed accumulator (lines 19 and 63) provided by Gluon.

3.3 Inserting Communication

The final pass of the Abelian compiler inserts code for communication and synchronization. A simple approach is the following: in each round, every mirror sends its value to its master where these values are combined, and the result is broadcast back to all the mirrors. This is essentially the gather-apply-scatter model used by most systems in this space, and it can be implemented by inserting a Gluon [10] sync call after each operator for every field that might be updated by that operator. Compilers for heterogeneous systems, such as Falcon [30], Dandelion [27], LiquidMetal [3], and DMLL [6], take a similar approach since their granularity of synchronization is an object or field. This coarse-grained approach can be seen as a more elaborate version of the write-broadcast cache coherence protocol used in systems with hardware cache-coherence. Abelian implements a different, fine-grained communication protocol to reduce the communication volume: a host sends the value of a field to other hosts only if that field has been updated in the previous rounds and if this value will be read in the current round. Static analysis is not adequate to determine these properties, so instrumentation code is inserted to track this dynamically. The actual communication is performed by the Gluon runtime, and it is invoked by inserting sync calls into the code.

Fine-Grained Communication. In graph analytics applications, each round typically updates the field of only a small subset of graph nodes. A device-local, field-specific bit-vector is used to track updates to nodes' fields that participate in communication. The analysis pass determines points in the operator where these fields might be updated, and the compiler inserts instrumentation code at those points to also update the node's bit in the bit-vector for that field (lines 23, 29, 38 in Fig. 3). The Gluon sync interface permits this bit-vector to be passed to the runtime system, which uses it to avoid sending node values that have not been updated in the current round.

On-Demand Communication. Using the bit-vector ensures only updated values are communicated, but it does not permit Gluon's communication optimization that exploits structural invariants in partitioning policies [10]. To do so, the domain-specific knowledge of abstract write and read locations for the last reduction access(es) and next read access of the field must be specified, respectively. If it is unspecified or imprecise, Gluon may conservatively perform some redundant synchronization. The Abelian compiler can only precisely identify the abstract locations of fields accessed within an operator and cannot be precise about the future accesses. Therefore, after an operator, it inserts code that sets or invalidates the sync-state invalidation flags for fields that could be written in the operator using its write location (lines 49, 50, 62 in Fig. 3). Before an operator, it inserts the synchronization structures, as shown in Fig. 2 (equivalent GPU functions generated for a vector of nodes are omitted for brevity), and the communication code for fields that could be read in the operator (lines 46, 52–59 in Fig. 3). The code checks the field-specific sync-state flags and calls the Gluon sync routine with the precise write and read locations if the flag is invalidated.

3.4 Device-Specific Compilers

The Abelian compiler outputs C++ code that can be compiled using existing compilers like g++ to execute on shared-memory NUMA multicores using the

Galois runtime [20]. A naive translation of this C++ code to CUDA or OpenCL is not likely to yield high-performance code because it will not exploit SIMD execution. We instead use the IrGL [22] compiler, which produces highly optimized CUDA and OpenCL code from an intermediate representation that is intended for graph applications. This compiler exploits nested parallelism, which is important when processing scale-free graphs. To interface with the IrGL compiler, the Abelian compiler generates IrGL intermediate code, translating data layout of fields from arrays of structures to structures of arrays.

4   Experimental Results

To evaluate the performance of programs generated by the Abelian compiler, we studied a number of graph analytical applications: betweenness centrality (bc), breadth-first search (bfs), connected components (cc), k-core decomposition (kcore), pagerank (pr), single-source shortest path (sssp), and matrix completion using stochastic gradient descent (sgd). We specify the programs in Galois C++: pull-style topology-driven algorithm for pr, push-and-pull-style topology-driven algorithm for sgd, and push-style work-list-driven algorithms for the rest. The Abelian compiler analyzes the program, restructures the operators, and synthesizes precise communication. Unless otherwise noted, all optimizations are applied in our evaluation, including eliminating work-lists. The programs work with different partitioning policies. In our evaluation, we choose incoming edge-cut for pr, cartesian vertex-cut for sgd, and outgoing edge-cut for all other benchmarks. We have empirically found these policies to work well in practice; an exhaustive search to find the best policy is outside the scope of this work.

Table 1 shows the input graphs we used along with their properties. All the CPU experiments were done on the Texas Advanced Computing Center's [2] Stampede [28] KNL

Table 1. Inputs and their key properties

	clueweb12 [25]	kron30 [17]	rmat28 [7]	amazon [13]
$|V|$	978M	1073M	268M	31M
$|E|$	42,574M	10,791M	4,295M	82.5M
$|E|/|V|$	44	16	16	2.7
max D_{out}	7,447	3.2M	4M	44557
max D_{in}	75M	3.2M	0.3M	25366

Cluster. For GPU experiments, the Bridges [21] supercomputer at the Pittsburgh Supercomputing Center [1,29] was used. Table 2 shows the configuration of these clusters used in our experiments. In all our experiments, we choose the max-degree node as the source for bc, bfs, and sssp. For kcore, we solve for $k = 100$. We present the mean execution time of 3 runs, excluding graph partitioning time. *We run pr and sgd for 100 and 50 iterations, respectively; all other algorithms are run until convergence.*

4.1   Comparison with the State-of-the-Art

We compare the with handwritten D-Galois programs for CPU-only systems [10] and handwritten D-IrGL programs for GPU-only systems [10]. D-Galois and

Table 2. Cluster configurations

	Stampede (CPU)	Bridges (GPU)
NIC	Omni-path	Omni-path
Machine	Intel Xeon Phi KNL	4 NVIDIA Tesla K80s
No. of hosts	32	16
Each host	272 threads	1 Tesla K80
Memory	96 GB DDR4	128 GB DDR5
Compiler	g++ 7.1	g++ 5.3

Table 3. Bridges: execution time (in seconds) on 16 GPUs for rmat28

	D-IrGL	Abelian
bc	9.6	9.6
bfs	1.1	1.2
cc	2.6	2.7
kcore	1.5	1.5
pr	32.9	30.5
sssp	2.5	2.5

D-IrGL programs have explicit synchronization specified by the programmer; in contrast, synchronization in programs produced by the Abelian compiler is introduced automatically by the compiler. However, all these programs use Gluon [10], a communication substrate that optimizes communication at runtime by exploiting structural and temporal invariants in partitioning (Gluon uses LCI [9] for message transport between hosts). In addition, D-Galois and Abelian use the same Galois [20] computation operators on the CPU while D-IrGL and Abelian use the same IrGL [22] computation kernels on the GPU. Therefore, differences in performance between Abelian-generated code and D-Galois/D-IrGL code arise mainly from differences in how synchronization code is inserted by the Abelian compiler.

We also compare Abelian-generated programs with distributed-CPU programs written in the Gemini framework [33] (Gemini does not have kcore and sgd; bc in Gemini uses bfs while that in Abelian uses sssp, so it is omitted). Gemini has explicit communication messages in the programming model, and it provides a third-party baseline for our study.

Table 4. Stampede: execution time (in seconds) (H: hosts)

		Gemini		D-Galois		Abelian	
		8H	32H	8H	32H	8H	32H
bc	clueweb12	-	–	OOM	430.4	OOM	437.6
	kron30	-	–	41.3	27.0	39.7	27.3
bfs	clueweb12	OOM	69.9	11.6	9.1	12.0	10.1
	kron30	5.1	7.1	5.1	4.0	5.2	4.2
cc	clueweb12	39.3	38.8	OOM	16.5	OOM	18.3
	kron30	15.8	14.8	7.6	4.6	7.7	4.0
kcore	clueweb12	-	–	OOM	290.4	OOM	289.1
	kron30	-	–	4.4	3.0	4.5	3.0
pr	clueweb12	OOM	257.9	395.1	248.0	402.1	277.4
	kron30	245.1	232.4	278.1	221.9	281.0	232.5
sssp	clueweb12	OOM	128.3	OOM	14.3	OOM	15.8
	kron30	14.0	14.9	9.4	8.2	9.3	8.2
sgd	amazon	-	–	1570.2	701.6	1570.2	696.2

Tables 3 and 4 show the distributed-GPU and distributed-CPU results. Abelian programs match the performance of D-Galois and D-IrGL programs; the difference is not more than 12%. Gemini is 15% faster than Abelian for pr with kron30 on 8 hosts. In all other cases, Abelian matches or outperforms Gemini. The geometric mean speedup of Abelian over Gemini on 32 KNL hosts is 2.4×. These results show that Abelian is able to compile a high-level, shared-memory, single address space specification into efficient implementations that either match or beat the state-of-the-art graph analytics platform. Although the Abelian compiler produces code for heterogeneous devices, we do not report numbers for distributed CPU+GPU execution because the 4 GPUs on a node on Bridges outperform the CPU by a significant margin.

4.2 Impact of Communication Optimizations

We analyze the performance impact of the communication optimizations in Abelian (Sect. 3.3) by comparing three levels of communication optimization.

1. *Unoptimized* (UO): the Gluon sync call is inserted for a field after an operator if it could be updated in that operator. The bit-vector as well as the abstract write and read locations are left unspecified, so all elements in the field are synchronized. Existing compilers for heterogeneous systems like Falcon [30], Dandelion [27], and Liquid Metal [3] do similar field-specific, coarse-grained synchronization.
2. *Fine-grained communication optimization* (FG): the compiler instruments the code to use a bit-vector that dynamically tracks updates to fields. The Gluon sync call used is the same as in UO, but it only synchronizes the elements in the field that have been updated using the bit-vector. This is similar to existing graph analytical frameworks [8,12,33] that synchronize only the updated elements.
3. *Fine-grained and on-demand communication optimization* (FO): this (default of Abelian compiler) uses on-demand communication along with fine-grained optimization. It instruments invalidation flags to track fields that have been updated and inserts Gluon sync calls before an operator for fields that could be read in the operator, thereby precisely identifying both the abstract write and read locations. This enables Gluon's communication optimization that exploits structural invariants in partitioning policies.

We compare these three communication optimization variants with hand-tuned (HT) programs written in D-Galois and D-IrGL on distributed CPUs and distributed GPUs respectively. In these programs, the programmer (with global control-flow knowledge) specified the precise communication using Gluon sync calls.

Figures 5 and 6 present the comparison results on 32 KNL hosts of Stampede and 16 GPU devices of Bridges respectively. Each bar in the figures shows the execution time (maximum across hosts). We measure the maximum computation time across hosts in each round and take their sum, which is the total computation time (top). The rest of the execution time is non-overlapped communication time (bottom). We also measure the total communication volume across all rounds, shown in text on the bars.

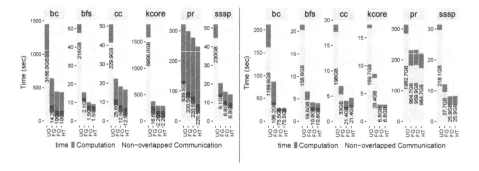

Fig. 5. 32 KNL hosts on Stampede: clueweb12 (left) and kron30 (right). Different variants are: UnOpt (UO), Fine-Grained opt (FG), Fine-grained+On-demand opt (FO), Hand-Tuned (HT)

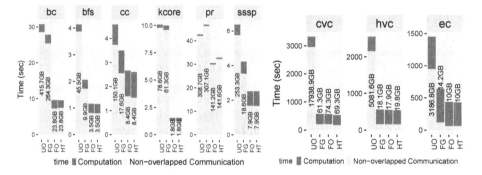

Fig. 6. 16 GPU devices on Bridges: rmat28   **Fig. 7.** 32 KNL hosts on Stampede: partitionings for bc on clueweb12

The trends are clear in the figure. Each optimization reduces communication volume and time, improving execution time further. FG significantly reduces communication volume and time over UO, with the exception of pr. FG performs atomic updates to the bit-vector, which could be overhead when the updates are dense, like in pr. FO optimizes the communication volume and time further to match the performance of HT. FO reduces communication volume by 23× over UO, yielding a geometric mean execution time speedup of 3.4×. Fine-grained and on-demand communication optimizations (FO) are thus essential to match the performance of HT on both CPUs and GPUs.

Abelian compiler-generated programs can support different partitioning policies, and we study whether they can fully exploit Gluon's partition-aware optimizations like HT. Figure 7 presents the comparison results for bc on clueweb12 using different partitioning policies namely, cartesian vertex cut [5] (cvc), hybrid vertex-cut [8] (hvc), and outgoing edge cut (ec). This shows that FO matches the performance of HT, although FG does not. This shows that the compiler can capture sufficient domain-specific knowledge to aid the Gluon runtime in performing partition-aware optimizations.

5 Related Work

Distributed Graph Processing Systems: Many frameworks [8,10,12,15,18,31,33] exist which provide a runtime to simplify writing distributed graph analytics algorithms. Like Abelian, these systems use a vertex programming model and bulk-synchronous parallel (BSP) execution. Abelian is the first compiler that synthesizes the required communication. Our evaluation shows that the programs generated by the Abelian compiler that use the Gluon [10] runtime match hand-tuned programs in the Gluon system and outperform those in the Gemini [33] system.

Single-Host Heterogeneous Graph Processing Systems: There are several frameworks for graph processing on a single GPU [22], multiple GPUs [4,23,32] and multiple GPUs with a CPU [11]. All of these are restricted to a single physical node that connects all devices unlike our system, and consequently, they cannot handle graphs as large as the ones our system can. Abelian leverages the throughput optimizations in the IrGL [22] compiler that are essential for performance on power-law graphs. Unlike IrGL, which compiles an intermediate-level program representation to CUDA, the Abelian compiler not only generates this from a high-level C++ program but also synthesizes synchronization code to execute the compiled code on multiple devices in multiple hosts.

Compilers for Distributed or Heterogeneous Architectures: Liquid Metal [3] compiles the Lime language to heterogeneous CPUs, GPUs, and FPGAs. Dandelion [27] compiles high-level LINQ programs to distributed heterogeneous systems. Green-Marl [14] is a DSL that is compiled to Pregel. Brown et al. [6] compile a data-parallel intermediate language DMLL to multicores, clusters, and GPUs. Upadhyay et al. [30] compile a domain-specific language, Falcon, to Giraph code for CPU clusters and MPI+OpenCL code for GPU clusters, but it does not do GPU-specific computation restructurings like nested parallelism which Abelian compiler does using IrGL. In all these compilers, the granularity of communication is an object or field, whereas Abelian identifies fine-grained elements of a label-array and communicates them precisely using the Gluon runtime. Moreover, none of the existing compilers use domain-specific analysis and computation restructurings for graph analytical applications like Abelian.

6 Conclusions

Abelian is the first graph analytics compiler that can produce high-performance, distributed, heterogeneous implementations from high-level, shared-memory, single address space specification of graph algorithms. It splits operators and eliminates work-lists to make the programs bulk-synchronous. The fine-grained, on-demand communication optimizations in Abelian yield a speedup of 3.4× over field-specific, coarse-grained communication code generated by existing compilers. This enables the generated implementations to match the performance of hand-tuned implementations for distributed CPUs and distributed GPUs in the state-of-the-art Gluon system using the same computation engines on the same hardware. The distributed-CPU implementations produced by Abelian also yield a geometric mean speedup of 2.4× over programs in the distributed CPU-only system Gemini on the same hardware. This shows that the Abelian compiler can manage heterogeneity and distributed-memory successfully while generating high-performance code, even in comparison to homogeneous systems.

Acknowledgments. This research was supported by NSF grants 1337217, 1337281, 1406355, 1618425, 1725322 and by DARPA contracts FA8750-16-2-0004 and FA8650-15-C-7563. This work used XSEDE grant ACI-1548562 through allocation TG-CIE170005. We used the Bridges system, supported by NSF award number ACI-1445606 at the Pittsburgh Supercomputing Center, and the Stampede system at the Texas Advanced Computing Center at The University of Texas at Austin.

References

1. Pittsburgh Supercomputing Center (PSC) (2018). https://www.psc.edu/
2. Texas Advanced Computing Center (TACC), The University of Texas at Austin (2018). https://www.tacc.utexas.edu/
3. Auerbach, J., et al.: A compiler and runtime for heterogeneous computing. In: DAC (2012). https://doi.org/10.1145/2228360.2228411
4. Ben-Nun, T., Sutton, M., Pai, S., Pingali, K.: Groute: An asynchronous multi-GPU programming model for irregular computations. In: PPoPP (2017). https://doi.org/10.1145/3018743.3018756
5. Boman, E.G., Devine, K.D., Rajamanickam, S.: Scalable matrix computations on large scale-free graphs using 2D graph partitioning. In: 2013 SC - International Conference for High Performance Computing, Networking, Storage and Analysis (SC), pp. 1–12, November 2013. https://doi.org/10.1145/2503210.2503293
6. Brown, K.J., et al.: Have abstraction and eat performance, too: optimized heterogeneous computing with parallel patterns. In: CGO (2016). https://doi.org/10.1145/2854038.2854042
7. Chakrabarti, D., Zhan, Y., Faloutsos, C.: R-MAT: a recursive model for graph mining, pp. 442–446 (2004). https://doi.org/10.1137/1.9781611972740.43
8. Chen, R., Shi, J., Chen, Y., Chen, H.: PowerLyra: differentiated graph computation and partitioning on skewed graphs. In: EuroSys (2015). https://doi.org/10.1145/2741948.2741970
9. Dang, H.V., et al.: A lightweight communication runtime for distributed graph analytics. In: IPDPS (2018)
10. Dathathri, R., et al.: Gluon: a communication optimizing framework for distributed heterogeneous graph analytics. In: PLDI (2018)
11. Gharaibeh, A., Beltrão Costa, L., Santos-Neto, E., Ripeanu, M.: A yoke of oxen and a thousand chickens for heavy lifting graph processing. In: PACT (2012)
12. Gonzalez, J.E., Low, Y., Gu, H., Bickson, D., Guestrin, C.: PowerGraph: distributed graph-parallel computation on natural graphs. In: OSDI (2012). http://dl.acm.org/citation.cfm?id=2387880.2387883

13. He, R., McAuley, J.: Ups and downs: modeling the visual evolution of fashion trends with one-class collaborative filtering. In: WWW (2016). https://doi.org/10.1145/2872427.2883037
14. Hong, S., Chafi, H., Sedlar, E., Olukotun, K.: Green-Marl: a DSL for easy and efficient graph analysis. In: ASPLOS (2012). https://doi.org/10.1145/2150976.2151013
15. Jia, Z., Kwon, Y., Shipman, G., McCormick, P., Erez, M., Aiken, A.: A distributed multi-GPU system for fast graph processing. In: Proceedings of VLDB Endowment, November 2017. https://doi.org/10.14778/3157794.3157799
16. Lenharth, A., Nguyen, D., Pingali, K.: Parallel graph analytics. Commun. ACM **59**(5), 78–87 (2016). https://doi.org/10.1145/2901919
17. Leskovec, J., Chakrabarti, D., Kleinberg, J., Faloutsos, C., Ghahramani, Z.: Kronecker graphs: an approach to modeling networks. J. Mach. Learn. Res. 11, 985–1042 (2010). http://dl.acm.org/citation.cfm?id=1756006.1756039
18. Malewicz, G., et al.: Pregel: a system for large-scale graph processing. In: SIGMOD (2010). https://doi.org/10.1145/1807167.1807184
19. Nasre, R., Burtscher, M., Pingali, K.: Data-driven versus topology-driven irregular computations on GPUs. In: Proceedings of the 27th IEEE International Parallel and Distributed Processing Symposium. IPDPS 2013. Springer, London (2013)
20. Nguyen, D., Lenharth, A., Pingali, K.: A lightweight infrastructure for graph analytics. In: SOSP (2013). https://doi.org/10.1145/2517349.2522739
21. Nystrom, N.A., Levine, M.J., Roskies, R.Z., Scott, J.R.: Bridges: a uniquely flexible HPC resource for new communities and data analytics. In: Proceedings of the 2015 XSEDE Conference: Scientific Advancements Enabled by Enhanced Cyberinfrastructure. XSEDE 2015, pp. 30:1–30:8. ACM, New York (2015). https://doi.org/10.1145/2792745.2792775
22. Pai, S., Pingali, K.: A compiler for throughput optimization of graph algorithms on GPUs. In: OOPSLA (2016)
23. Pan, Y., Wang, Y., Wu, Y., Yang, C., Owens, J.D.: Multi-GPU graph analytics. In: IPDPS, May 2017. https://doi.org/10.1109/IPDPS.2017.117
24. Pingali, K., et al.: The TAO of parallelism in algorithms. In: Proceedings of ACM SIGPLAN Conference on Programming Language Design and Implementation. PLDI 2011, pp. 12–25 (2011). https://doi.org/10.1145/1993498.1993501
25. The Lemur Project: The clueweb12 dataset (2013). http://lemurproject.org/clueweb12/
26. Prountzos, D., Manevich, R., Pingali, K.: Synthesizing parallel graph programs via automated planning. In: Programming Language Design and Implementation. PLDI 2015 (2015)
27. Rossbach, C.J., Yu, Y., Currey, J., Martin, J.P., Fetterly, D.: Dandelion: a compiler and runtime for heterogeneous systems. In: SOSP (2013). https://doi.org/10.1145/2517349.2522715
28. Stanzione, D., et al.: Stampede 2: the evolution of an XSEDE supercomputer. In: Proceedings of the Practice and Experience in Advanced Research Computing 2017 on Sustainability, Success and Impact, pp. 15:1–15:8. PEARC17. ACM, New York (2017). https://doi.org/10.1145/3093338.3093385
29. Towns, J., et al.: XSEDE: accelerating scientific discovery. Comput. Sci. Eng. **16**(5), 62–74 (2014)
30. Upadhyay, N., Patel, P., Cheramangalath, U., Srikant, Y.N.: Large scale graph processing in a distributed environment. In: Heras, D.B., Bougé, L. (eds.) Euro-Par 2017. LNCS, vol. 10659, pp. 465–477. Springer, Cham (2018). https://doi.org/10.1007/978-3-319-75178-8_38

31. Xin, R.S., Gonzalez, J.E., Franklin, M.J., Stoica, I.: GraphX: a resilient distributed graph system on spark. In: GRADES (2013)
32. Zhong, J., He, B.: Medusa: simplified graph processing on GPUs. IEEE TPDS (2014). https://doi.org/10.1109/TPDS.2013.111
33. Zhu, X., Chen, W., Zheng, W., Ma, X.: Gemini: a computation-centric distributed graph processing system. In: OSDI (2016). http://dl.acm.org/citation.cfm?id=3026877.3026901

Using Dynamic Compilation to Achieve Ninja Performance for CNN Training on Many-Core Processors

Ankush Mandal[1]([✉]), Rajkishore Barik[2], and Vivek Sarkar[1]

[1] Georgia Institute of Technology, Atlanta, GA 30332, USA
{ankush,vsarkar}@gatech.edu
[2] Uber Technologies Inc., San Francisco, USA
rajbarik@uber.com

Abstract. Convolutional Neural Networks (CNNs) represent a class of Deep Neural Networks that is growing in importance due to their state-of-the-art performance in pattern recognition tasks in various domains, including image recognition, speech recognition, and natural language processing. However, CNNs are very time consuming to train due to the computationally intensive nature of their convolution operations. Typically, a convolution operation is exposed as a library API that duplicates and reorganizes input tensors under-the-hood in order to leverage existing matrix-matrix multiplication (GEMM) BLAS routines. Unfortunately, this widely-used approach suffers not only from memory expansion but also from memory bandwidth limitations. Moreover, although there has been a significant amount of past work on optimizing CNNs on GPUs, those approaches are not directly applicable to many-core CPU platforms such as Intel Xeon Phi.

In this paper, we show how a novel dynamic code generation approach can be used to implement convolution on Intel Knights Landing systems with AVX-512 support, so as to obtain order-of-magnitude performance improvements compared to the GEMM-based approach. Moreover, our approach gives robust performance across different convolution layers of the state-of-the-art CNNs, such as AlexNet, GoogleNetV1, Overfeat, and Vgga. The methods in this paper should be applicable to future many-core CPU platforms with vector lengths of 512 bits or larger.

Keywords: Direct convolution · KNL · Dynamic code generation

1 Introduction

Concepts from the field of Machine Learning drive many aspects of modern society, from social networks to recommendations on e-commerce, and are powering

Rajkishore Barik contributed to this work when he was at Intel Labs, Santa Clara CA 95054, USA.

an increasing number of consumer products, including cameras, and self-driving cars. In particular, Deep Learning (DL) has become one of the most critical technologies, demonstrating equal or even better than human-level performance for tasks in domains such as object recognition, board games, and speech recognition. This became possible due to two reasons - (1) Deep Neural Networks (DNNs) can learn features automatically from large datasets and represent complex functions using multiple hidden layers, (2) recent advances in processor technologies made it possible to satisfy the huge computational requirement associated with DL.

Although different DNNs aim at different problems, one of the most critical DL applications today is image recognition [11], and currently, Convolution Neural Network (CNN) is the state-of-the-art DNN for image recognition. A CNN consists of multiple hidden layers, and among these layers, the core of a CNN is the convolution layer. It is also the most computationally expensive layer [1] of a CNN where it performs a large number of small convolutions. As an abundant amount of data parallelism is available in the computation of convolution through many images or mini-batch size and feature maps or channels, massively parallel architectures such as GPUs, in particular, have been used for training and inference on CNNs. As a consequence, all existing CNN frameworks [2,5,10,12] have GPU backends that implement convolution layers as libraries using cuDNN [4]. However, recent advancement in many-core CPUs, such as Intel Knights Landing (KNL) [16] with 68–72 cores and AVX-512 support, have made it potentially capable of delivering significantly high erformance (6TFLOPs for single precision). Still, many-core CPUs have not been explored much from the perspective of optimizing CNNs due to several challenges – (a) low-end cores have high penalties for branches and memory accesses, (b) although vectorization of regular apps is simple for AVX-512 on KNL, it is extremely difficult to extract peak performance due to the cores being two issue-wide and at the same time having two VPUs (it is practically impossible to saturate the issues only with vector floating point instructions), (b) it is harder to hide memory latency because of inherent latency oriented design, and (c) cache prefetching plays an important role in performance but it can be challenging to get right. In order to overcome these challenges and get near-peak performance, we require very high-quality code generation.

A widely used approach to implementing convolutions in CNNs is to flatten the corresponding input data (image2column or *im2col* operation [3]) and use standard matrix multiplications (GEMM) on the flattened data. One of the main reasons behind the popularity of this method is ample availability of optimized libraries for GEMM operations. While it is easier to implement, this method has severe drawbacks when aiming for high performance on CPUs. The image flattening step is a data copy and redistribution operation which is purely memory bandwidth bound. Even though the GEMM computation is highly optimized, the flattening step acts as a bottleneck and creates a huge performance penalty. On the other hand, the direct convolution method does not involve the *im2col* operation.

Even though CNNs provide state-of-the-art accuracy, training CNNs requires an enormous amount of time and can span several weeks. For example, it requires 21 days to train GoogleNetV1 [17] with the ImageNet dataset on a single Nvidia® K20 GPU [8]. Training on CNNs involves forward propagation and back-propagation phases. Although our method is applicable for convolutions in all phases, for the purpose of demonstration in this paper, we choose convolution in back-propagation as a focused candidate problem. We believe that it is a good candidate problem since it involves a more complex data reuse pattern than forward propagation. Due to this complex data reuse over the data it writes to, it is much harder to exploit data reuse in back-propagation, thereby posing a more challenging optimization problem than the forward propagation case.

In this work, we leverage the direct convolution approach to avoid the expensive memory operations associated with an *im2col* operation and to optimize the convolution in back-propagation. Another critical aspect to consider, when trying to optimize convolution in CNNs, is that the input parameters for convolution vary significantly across layers of a CNN and also across different CNNs. Thus, the parameter values are only known during runtime, making it hard to achieve good performance through static compilation. In this work, we instead explore runtime code specialization for optimizing CNNs on many-core CPUs with large vector lengths.

Our main contributions in this work are:

- For optimizing convolutions in state-of-the-art CNNs, we propose a novel dynamic code generation approach targeting high performance on Intel's Knights Landing architecture. Prior work has shown that it is a daunting task to extract peak performance on Xeon Phi processors even for regular matrix-matrix multiplication application [6]. Our research novelty lies in using a low overhead dynamic code generator to achieve close to possible peak performance for convolutions on Xeon Phi processors. This code generator not only performs standard compiler optimizations including register allocation, loop unrolling, tiling, vectorization, latency hiding, software pipelining, and software prefetching, but it also specializes generated code based on the parameters of the convolution operation, which vary widely across layers and networks.
- As another research contribution, our work debunks the claim that direct convolution is not a good method when aiming for high performance [4]. Almost all existing approaches in CNNs use GEMM formulation for convolutions, which has performance bottleneck due to a memory bandwidth bound step. We show that the direct convolution method, with our runtime code specialization, can achieve order-of-magnitude performance improvement by avoiding such overhead.
- We provide a thorough performance analysis of our implementation of direct convolution in back-propagation on KNL for several state-of-the-art CNNs. We further compare our performance with other leading approaches on KNL, such as Intel® MKL-DNN and ZNNPhi.

2   Background

As our work focuses on optimizing the costly convolution operation associated with the convolution layers, we start with a brief description of it. During a convolution operation, each output pixel is generated from the weighted sum of a spatially connected neighborhood of inputs. Specifically, the operation adds each element of the input image with elements from a defined region after multiplying all the elements with specific weights from filter data.

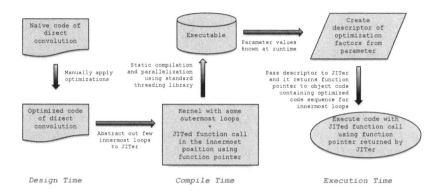

Fig. 1. Pipeline used in our approach

In case of CNNs, we usually perform convolution over a batch of images. This is termed as batched convolution [4]. A batched convolution deals with three four-dimensional tensors: $I \in \mathbf{R}^{NCHW}$ as input image data, $O \in \mathbf{R}^{NKPQ}$ as output data, and $F \in \mathbf{R}^{KCRS}$ as filter data. The input data ranges over N images in a mini-batch, C input image feature maps, H rows or image height, W columns or image width. The filter data ranges over K output feature maps, C input feature maps, R rows or filter height, and S columns or filter width. A mathematical definition of the convolution operation can be found in [4] and other references.

One interesting observation regarding the values of the parameters mentioned above is that they vary significantly across different convolution layers of a CNN and also across different CNNs. For example, in the case of GoogleNetV1 [17], the input feature map or channel (C) ranges from 16 to 832. For the same CNN, the image height (H) and width (W) vary from 224 to 7. Thus, even though the parallelism in a convolution operation may appear to be straightforward, efficient exploitation of this parallelism can be very challenging because of the substantial variation in loop lengths based on the input data. Due to these widely varying parameter values, it is almost impossible to propose a single optimized solution for computing the convolution that gives excellent performance in every scenario. We describe our approach to addressing this challenge in Sect. 3.

3   Overview of Our Approach

In this section, we present our novel code generation approach to optimize direct convolution for parallel execution on KNL. As mentioned in Sects. 1 and 2, the input parameters for the convolution operation in CNNs vary widely. Moreover, the dynamic values of these parameters are only known at execution time. Further, the computational pattern of the convolution kernel depends on the input parameter values. For example, when the filter height (R) and width (S) are 5, the density of arithmetic operations is almost 25 times for image tensors compared to the scenario when R and S are 1. The apparent dependence of the kernel runtime behavior on dynamic parameter values given at execution time indicates that achieving good performance through static compilation is very hard for our problem. So, as a more suitable alternative, we perform runtime code specialization and adopt a Just-In-Time (JIT) compilation approach[1]. We determine the optimization factors from the input parameter values at runtime and provide our dynamic code generator with such factors to produce highly optimized code for the kernel. We show in Sect. 6.2 that, from the performance perspective, our JIT-based method is highly adaptable to a wide range of input parameter values compared to other-state-of-the-art methods.

Figure 1 gives a high-level overview of our approach. First, we start with manually applying standard compiler optimizations to the naive code. Then we take the optimized code and abstract several innermost loops to the JITer. In the static code segment, we refer to the output of the JITer as a function pointer. During static compilation of the code, we leverage widely available threading libraries such as OpenMP for parallelization of the outermost loops. Now, at runtime, we create a descriptor of optimization factors from the parameter values. We pass this descriptor to the JITer to produce optimized code for the abstracted code at runtime. Then JITer creates an in-memory function and returns a pointer to it. We use this function pointer in the static code segment to execute the JITer generated code.

Parameter	Description	
N:	Number of images	
C:	Input feature map	
K:	Output feature map	
P:	Output image height	
Q:	Output image width	
R:	Filter/Weight height	
S:	Filter/Weight width	

```
1.#pragma omp for collapse(2)
2.for(img = 0; img < N; ++img) {
3. for(ifm = 0; ifm < C; ++ifm) {
4.  for(ofm = 0; ofm < K; ++ofm) {
5.   for(oj = 0; oj < P; ++oj) {
6.    ij = oj * stride_h;
7.    for(oi = 0; oi < Q; ++oi) {
8.     ii = oi * stride_w;
9.     for(kj = 0; kj < R; ++kj) {
10.     for(ki = 0; ki < S; ++ki) {
11.      grad_input(img, ifm, ij + kj, ii + ki) +=
              grad_output(img, ofm, oj, oi) *
              weight(ofm, ifm, kj, ki);
} } } } } } }
```

Fig. 2. Pseudo code of naive direct convolution for back-propagation

---

[1] For convenience, we will use "JIT" as a shorthand root in words such as "JITer" and "JITed".

4   Runtime Code Specialization

To start with, we show a "C" style pseudocode[2] of a straightforward, but naive, implementation of the kernel in Fig. 2. In this section, we discuss the runtime specialization of this code and separation of code blocks between dynamic code generation and static compilation.

During the design of our dynamic code generator, we exploit the fact that it is targeted for domain-specific JIT code generation (that is, it targets CNN computations). This enables us to design and implement a very low overhead JITer compared to traditional dynamic compilers. At a high level, our JITer can avoid all the steps of handling generic code in a traditional JITer, and directly proceed to the assembly code generation phase because we have manually applied all the high-level optimizations beforehand and know the exact computation sequence inside the JITer. So, we hardcode the register allocation, loads/stores of data, fused multiply-add computation, tiling, unrolling, and prefetching process inside our code generator while the associated factors still depend on the descriptor we pass to our JITer. For the conversion of the assembly code generated by our JITer to machine code, we have extended the dynamic assembler from LIBXSMM [7] which targeted matrix multiplication style applications. Section 5 discusses the optimizations that we consider for the implementation of our JITer on KNL architecture and how the input parameter values influence the factors associated with these optimizations.

After applying the optimizations described in Sect. 5 on the code in Fig. 2, we determine the partitioning of the kernel between the code that is statically compiled using standard compilers such as Intel® ICC and the code that we generate at runtime. Figure 3 depicts that partition. The idea here is to keep the overhead of JIT code generation as low as possible. We achieve this by leaving low-level optimizations and parallelization to a static compiler and amortizing the cost of JIT code generation over the outermost loops.

Figure 3 also depicts the interface for our dynamic code generator. First, we create a descriptor (bp_desc) of optimization factors depending on the runtime values of the input parameters. Then pass the descriptor to our JITer (bp_jit). The JITer generates optimized code using the descriptor and returns a function pointer ($conv\_bp$). We use this function pointer to execute the JITed code inside the innermost loop that we statically compile (in this case, the oi loop in line 9). During the descriptor creation, we derive several crucial optimization factors depending on the input parameter values, such as register blocking factor, cache blocking factor, which loops to unroll, and how much to prefetch in each iteration. Additionally, we ensure that the JITed code fits in L1 instruction cache and that the data footprint of JITed code fits in L1 data cache. This is important because the penalty for missing L1 caches are multiplied by the number of outermost loops and effectively becomes quite high.

---

[2] Array accesses appear within "( )" instead of "[ ]" due to the use of macros e.g., A(i, j, k, l) denotes location A [i*dim2*dim3*dim4 + j*dim3*dim4 + k*dim4 + l].

```
                    Statically Compiled

1.bp_desc = setup backward convolution descriptor using parameters
  N,C,H,W,K,R,S,stride_h,stride_w,pad_h,pad_w;
2.conv_bp = bp_jit(bp_desc); //Generate optimized code at Runtime
3.#pragma omp for collapse(2)
4. for(img = 0; img < N; ++img) {
5.   for(ifm = 0; ifm < C/B_I; ++ifm) { //blocked by B_I for vectorization
6.    for(ofm = 0; ofm < K/B_O; ++ofm) { //blocked by B_O for cache blocking
7.     for(oj = 0; oj < P; ++oj) {
8.      ij = oj * stride_h;
9.      for(oi = 0; oi < Q/B_Q; ++oi) { //blocked by B_Q for register blocking
10.       float *inp_ptr = &(grad_input[img][ifm][ij][oi*B_Q*stride_w][0]);
11.       const float *out_ptr = &(grad_output[img][ofm][oj][oi*B_Q][0]);
12.       const float *wt_ptr = &(weight[ofm][ifm][0][0][0][0]);
13.       conv_bp(input_ptr, wt_ptr, out_ptr); //Use JITed function

14.       for(kj = 0; kj < R; ++kj) {
15.        for(ki = 0; ki < S; ++ki) {                          JITed

               Vector code block
               ...

16.            Pattern repeated B_Q times
17.          Pattern repeated B_O times
18. } } } } } } } }
```

Fig. 3. Partition between static compilation and dynamic code generation

5   Optimizations for KNL Many-Core Architecture

5.1   Key Features to Consider for Code Optimization

The processor under discussion is the second generation Intel Xeon Phi many-core processor, codenamed Knights Landing (KNL). An architectural overview of the KNL chip can be found in [16]. The KNL chip features up to 72 out-of-order Silvermont Atom cores, each with 4 hardware-level hyper-threads. A key feature of this processor's microarchitecture is that each core includes two 512-bit vector processing units (VPUs) for increased SIMD level parallelism, i.e., each core can start the execution of two 16-wide single precision SIMD instructions in the same clock cycle. Another important feature of KNL is that it supports explicit instructions to prefetch data into L1 or L2 caches (via prefetcht0 and prefetcht2 instructions respectively).

5.2   Fine-Grain Parallelism and Related Optimizations

Data Layout - Needless to say, the large number of on-chip VPUs makes vectorization a critical optimization to consider for KNL. Keeping this in mind, we design the data layouts for the tensors to favor vectorization on x86 systems. From our domain knowledge, we find that the input feature map, C, and the output feature map, K, are typically multiples of vector length on x86 architectures. So, we block these dimensions by the vector length and bring the blocking factor to the innermost dimension to have contiguous SIMD access for the tensors. The resulting data layouts are as follows: (a) $Input : NCHW \longrightarrow NC_{B_I}HWB_I$, $B_I = VLEN$, (b) $Output : NKPQ \longrightarrow NK_{B_O}PQB_O$, $B_O = VLEN$, and (c) $Filter\ or\ Weight : KCRS \longrightarrow K_{B_O}C_{B_I}RSB_OB_I$.

Vectorization - Following the notations in Fig. 2, we block the *ifm* loop by a factor of vector length (B_I) and bring that blocking factor loop to the inner-most position, i.e., after *ki* loop. Then we vectorize the loop and perform the computation of the loop with a single fused multiply and add (**fmadd**) vector instruction.

Is Vectorization All We Need? - Let's consider where we are in the per-formance landscape after vectorization. To get some insight, we present perfor-mance for convolution layers from Overfeat [14] in Table 1. As we can see, we gain significant performance improvement over the naive code in Fig. 2 through vectorization. However, the theoretical peak performance of KNL is 6 TFLOPs and large HPC-style matrix-multiplication benchmarks (Top500 benchmark [13]) achieve roughly 4.5 TFLOPs on KNL for single precision. This means we are still a large distance away from the peak performance. So, how can we do better? The following describes other equally important optimizations for KNL which improve the performance beyond vectorization, and we finally show in Sect. 6 that we achieve an order-of-magnitude better performance and sometimes, even close to peak performance (>4 TFLOPs).

Table 1. Performance gain from vectorization (Using 64 threads)

Convolution layer	Performance from naive code (GFLOPs)	Performance from vectorized code (GFLOPs)
Overfeat_CONV2	22.618	267.22
Overfeat_CONV3	11.797	180.05
Overfeat_CONV4	11.948	169.38
Overfeat_CONV5	11.959	174.09

Exploiting Instruction-Level Parallelism - KNL has 32 vector registers per core. We use these registers for register blocking to increase both instruction-level parallelism and register reuse. Our input tensor layout is $NC_{B_I}HWB_I$, and we vectorize along the B_I dimension. Therefore, a good candidate for register block-ing would be the next innermost dimension, i.e., W dimension. Correspondingly, we perform register blocking along *oi* loop and bring the blocking factor(B_Q) loop inside *ki* loop.

Optimizing Vector Load and Stores - Vector loads and stores can be quite expensive in number of cycles, even when their data resides in L1 cache. It is therefore important to reduce the number of loads and stores as much as possible, so as to reduce their overhead, as well as to reduce the number of stalls in the instruction pipeline. One interesting observation regarding the input access pattern is that we have significant reuse for input values over ki loop when the stride is 1. We exploit this to gain register reuse for the input tensor. The strategy is outlined in Fig. 4. Basically, we rotate the logical register indices from one ki loop iteration to the next iteration. Thus we get significant reuse of physical registers and effectively reduce the number of loads and stores on input tensor. To hide load latencies, we use software pipelining to issue loads on the weight tensor ahead of its usage. The strategy is depicted in Fig. 5.

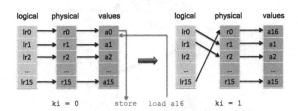

Fig. 4. Register reuse for input tensor

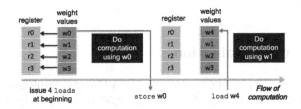

Fig. 5. Software pipelining for loads on weight tensor

5.3   Thread-Level Parallelism and Optimizations

We use the standard OpenMP® threading library for multi-threading. To ensure coarse granularity of work, we use the outermost loops, i.e., img and ifm loops to exploit thread-level parallelism. We collapse the iteration space of these two loops and issue a `parallel for` using the `#pragma omp for collapse(2)` directive. As the work inside each ifm iteration is similar, there is no problem of load imbalance here.

Cache Blocking - We consider improving thread performance through blocking for L1 Data cache. The output tensor layout is $NK_{B_O}PQB_O$. If we do cache blocking along B_O, we gain spatial locality for the output tensor. Furthermore, since the input tensor does not depend on B_O, we ensure temporal locality for the input tensor. So, we apply a cache blocking along the ofm loop by a factor of B_O and bring the tiled loop inside the ki loop.

Software Prefetching - KNL supports explicit L1 and L2 cache prefetch instructions (`prefetcht0` and `prefetcht2` respectively). We use these instructions in our dynamic code generator to hide load latencies by bringing data into cache before their actual usage, while also ensuring that the data are not prefetched too early so as to be evicted before their usage. Our software prefetch pipeline is presented in Fig. 6.

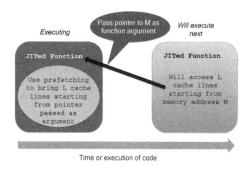

Fig. 6. Software prefetch pipeline to hide load latencies

6   Performance Evaluation

In this section, we evaluate the performance of a C-based implementation of our method on a single-socket Intel® Xeon Phi 7250 processor which is equipped with 68 cores and 16 GB MCDRAM. We used Turbo mode which set the processor frequency at 1.3 GHz. We also configured the processor with FLAT memory mode and QUADRANT cluster mode. We keep all the data on MCDRAM using `numactl -membind=1`. For multi-threading, we set the number of threads to 64 for all the experiments. We compiled our code with Intel® C++ Compiler (ICC) 2017 with the "-O2" flag.

For evaluating our approach, we chose four state-of-the-art CNNs, namely Alexnet [11], Overfeat [14], Vgga [15], and GoogleNet_V1 [17]. We get 67 convolution layers in total from these CNNs. However, to improve readability, we present performance results on 12 convolution layers from these CNNs. We tried to include as diverse parameter values as possible. The parameter values of the selected convolution layers are presented in Table 2.

6.1   Comparison with GEMM-Based Method

As we can see from Fig. 7, we get an order-of-magnitude performance improvement over GEMM-based method implemented with Intel® MKL 2018. Moreover, the figure also supports our hypothesis that the image flattening step (*im2col*) required by the GEMM-based methods incurs significant overhead. We see that

Table 2. Parameter values for convolution layers

Layers	W	H	N	C	K	R	S	Pad	Stride
Alexnet_CONV2	27	27	256	96	256	5	5	2	1
Alexnet_CONV4	13	13	256	384	384	3	3	1	1
Overfeat_CONV2	28	28	256	96	256	5	5	0	1
Overfeat_CONV3	12	12	256	256	512	3	3	1	1
Vgga_CONV2	112	112	128	64	128	3	3	1	1
Vgga_CONV3	56	56	128	128	256	3	3	1	1
Googlenetv1_CONV4	28	28	128	192	64	1	1	0	1
Googlenetv1_CONV17	14	14	128	96	208	3	3	1	1
Googlenetv1_CONV18	14	14	128	480	16	1	1	0	1
Googlenetv1_CONV25	14	14	128	32	64	5	5	2	1
Googlenetv1_CONV41	7	7	128	160	320	3	3	1	1
Googlenetv1_CONV49	7	7	128	48	128	5	5	2	1

the FLOPs measured for only the GEMM operation is much higher than the effective FLOPs for the method. Hence, our work shows that direct convolution method can achieve much higher performance over GEMM-based approach by avoiding memory bandwidth bound *im2col* operation. One thing to note here, the GEMM operation does not reach very high FLOPs (i.e. >4 TFLOPs) due to the irregular sizes of matrices.

6.2 Comparison with State-of-the-Art Libraries

To compare our method with other state-of-the-art methods, we present performance comparison with Intel® MKL-DNN [9] and ZNNPhi [18]. Both of them have optimized the convolution operation for KNL. Figure 8 presents the performance results. It shows that our method gives better performance for all the convolution layers except for Alexnet_CONV2 where MKL-DNN gives the best performance. It proves the importance of our adaptable runtime code specialization which decides the optimization factors depending on the execution time values of input parameters. We see that even MKL-DNN, a highly optimized manually tuned library by experts, fails to capture specific scenarios and gives quite poor performance, for example, Vgga_CONV2 and Googlenetv1_CONV18. On the other hand, ZNNPhi generates several kernels with different values of the optimization parameters. We only present the best performance achieved among those kernels. In general, our method gives much better performance than ZNNPhi except for convolution layers from Vgga where the performance is similar. Another important advantage of our method is that we do not incur the overhead of any benchmarking or auto-tuning step involving several kernels to choose the best one.

Performance Comparison with GEMM-based Method

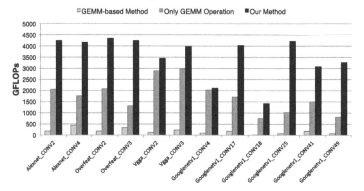

Fig. 7. Comparison of the performance in GFLOPS of our Back-Propagation method with the GEMM-based method implemented using Intel® MKL 2018. For completeness, we also show the performance of only the GEMM calls.

Performance Comparison with State-of-the-art Libraries

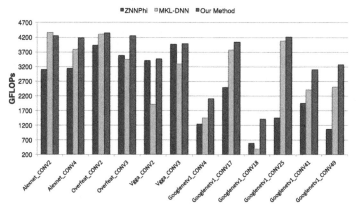

Fig. 8. Back-propagation: comparison with state-of-the-art libraries

6.3 Overhead of JIT Code Generation

Figure 9 shows an evaluation of the overhead of our dynamic code generation using the following metric: code generation time as a percentage of the total execution time for convolution over a mini-batch. In reality, the kernel is executed over several iterations during the training step, while JIT code generation is required only once. Hence, in practice, the cost of JIT code generation is amortized over multiple executions of the kernel with the same parameter values, which in most cases is well over 1,000. Nevertheless, even for a single execution, we see negligible overhead for many convolution layers, especially the ones with high iteration space. In case of kernels with comparatively low iteration space, such as Googlenetv1_CONV18 and Googlenetv1_CONV25, we see a discernible

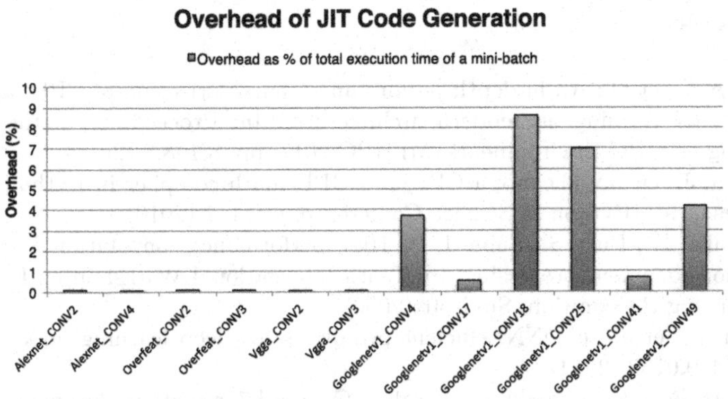

Overhead of JIT Code Generation

Fig. 9. Overhead of JIT code generation as a percentage of the total execution time of a mini-batch

overhead (but still under 10%) because they have significantly small execution times (9.6 ms for Googlenetv1_CONV18). However, with amortization from the number of iterations, this small overhead becomes negligible.

7   Conclusion

Convolution Neural Networks (CNN) are state-of-the-art Deep Neural Networks for image recognition applications today. The core of these CNNs is the convolution layer, which performs a large number of small convolutions with irregular dimensions. CNN training requires massive computing power, and it turns out that the convolution operation is the key performance enabler for CNNs. As a primary contribution of this work, we propose a novel low overhead dynamic code generation approach for runtime code specialization based on the input parameter values for convolution. We demonstrate that an efficient implementation of direct convolution in back-propagation using our approach can achieve close to peak performance in many cases on the Intel Knights Landing (KNL) processor. Furthermore, we debunk the claim that the direct convolution method is not suitable for high performance. We show that the direct convolution method, using our approach, can achieve a significant performance improvement over the GEMM based method on KNL. Finally, we compare our performance results with other cutting-edge approaches on KNL, such as MKL-DNN and ZNNPhi for several convolution layers of state-of-the-art CNNs. The comparison supports the robustness of our method on performance over a wide range of input parameter values. We have released our implementation at https://github.com/hfp/libxsmm, which is currently used by high-level frameworks such as TensorFlow.

References

1. Awan, A.A., et al.: An in-depth performance characterization of CPU- and GPU-based DNN training on modern architectures. In: Proceedings of the Machine Learning on HPC Environments. MLHPC 2017, pp. 8:1–8:8 (2017)
2. Bergstra, J., et al.: Theano: a CPU and GPU math compiler in Python. In: Proceedings of 9th Python in Science Conference, pp. 1–7 (2010)
3. Chellapilla, K., Puri, S., Simard, P.: High performance convolutional neural networks for document processing. In: Tenth International Workshop on Frontiers in Handwriting Recognition. Suvisoft (2006)
4. Chetlur, S., et al.: cuDNN: efficient primitives for deep learning. arXiv preprint arXiv:1410.0759 (2014)
5. Collobert, R., Kavukcuoglu, K., Farabet, C.: Torch7: a matlab-like environment for machine learning. In: BigLearn, NIPS Workshop, No. EPFL-CONF-192376 (2011)
6. Heinecke, A., et al.: Design and implementation of the linpack benchmark for single and multi-node systems based on intel® xeon phi coprocessor. In: Proceedings of the 2013 IEEE 27th International Symposium on Parallel and Distributed Processing. IPDPS 2013, pp. 126–137 (2013)
7. Heinecke, A., Pabst, H., Henry, G.: LIBXSMM: a high performance library for small matrix multiplications. In: Poster and Extended Abstract Presented at SC (2015)
8. Iandola, F.N., et al.: FireCaffe: near-linear acceleration of deep neural network training on compute clusters. In: Proceedings of the IEEE Conference on Computer Vision and Pattern Recognition, pp. 2592–2600 (2016)
9. Intel: MKL-DNN (2017). https://github.com/01org/mkl-dnn
10. Jia, Y., et al.: Caffe: convolutional architecture for fast feature embedding. In: Proceedings of the 22nd ACM International Conference on Multimedia, pp. 675–678 (2014)
11. Krizhevsky, A., et al.: Imagenet classification with deep convolutional neural networks. In: Advances in Neural Information Processing Systems, pp. 1097–1105 (2012)
12. Martin, A., et al.: TensorFlow: large-scale machine learning on heterogeneous systems (2015). tensorflow.org
13. Meur, H., et al.: Top500 list, June 2016. https://www.top500.org/
14. Sermanet, P., et al.: Overfeat: integrated recognition, localization and detection using convolutional networks. arXiv preprint arXiv:1312.6229 (2013)
15. Simonyan, K., Zisserman, A.: Very deep convolutional networks for large-scale image recognition. arXiv preprint arXiv:1409.1556 (2014)
16. Sodani, A., et al.: Knights landing: second-generation intel xeon phi product. IEEE Micro **36**(2), 34–46 (2016)
17. Szegedy, C., et al.: Going deeper with convolutions. In: Proceedings of the IEEE Conference on Computer Vision and Pattern Recognition, pp. 1–9 (2015)
18. Zlateski, A., Seung, H.S.: ZNNPhi (2017). https://github.com/seung-lab/znnphi-release

Parallel and Distributed Data Management and Analytics

Privacy-Preserving Top-k Query Processing in Distributed Systems

Sakina Mahboubi[✉], Reza Akbarinia, and Patrick Valduriez

INRIA & LIRMM, University of Montpellier, Montpellier, France
sakina.mahboubi@inria.fr

Abstract. We consider a distributed system that stores user sensitive data across multiple nodes. In this context, we address the problem of privacy-preserving top-k query processing. We propose a novel system, called SD-TOPK, that is able to evaluate top-k queries over encrypted distributed data without needing to decrypt the data in the nodes where they are stored. We implemented and evaluated our system over synthetic and real databases. The results show excellent performance for SD-TOPK compared to baseline approaches.

1 Introduction

We consider a distributed system where users can outsource their sensitive data and issue top-k queries. A top-k query is an important kind of query that allows the user to get the k data items that are most relevant to the query. The user data are encrypted (for privacy reasons) and distributed (for performance reasons) across multiple nodes. In this context, we address the problem of privacy-preserving top-k query processing.

Privacy preserving top-k query processing is critical for many applications that outsource sensitive data. For example, consider a university that outsources the students database in a public cloud, in Infrastructure-as-a-Service (IaaS) mode, with non-trusted nodes. The database is vertically partitioned (for performance reasons) and encrypted. Then, an interesting top-k query over the encrypted distributed data is the following: return the k students that have the worst averages in some given courses.

There are different approaches for processing top-k queries over *plaintext* (non encrypted) data. One of the best known approaches is TA [6] that works on sorted lists of attribute values. However, there is no efficient solution capable of evaluating efficiently top-k queries over encrypted data in distributed systems.

In this paper, we propose a system, called SD-TOPK (Secure Distributed TOPK), that encrypts and stores user data in a distributed system, and is able to evaluate top-k queries over the encrypted data. SD-TOPK comes with a novel top-k query processing algorithm that finds a set of encrypted data that is proven to contain the top-k data items. This is done without having to decrypt the data in the nodes where they are stored. In addition, we propose a powerful filtering

© Springer International Publishing AG, part of Springer Nature 2018
M. Aldinucci et al. (Eds.): Euro-Par 2018, LNCS 11014, pp. 281–292, 2018.
https://doi.org/10.1007/978-3-319-96983-1_20

algorithm that removes the false positives as much as possible without data decryption.

We implemented and evaluated the performance of our system over synthetic and real databases. The results show excellent performance for SD-TOPK compared to TA-based approaches. They show the efficiency of our filtering algorithm that eliminates almost all false positives in the distributed system, and reduces significantly the communication cost between the distributed system and the user.

The rest of this paper is organized as follows. Section 2 gives the problem definition. Section 3 describes SD-TOPK system. Section 4 presents the performance evaluation results. Section 5 discusses related work, and Sect. 6 concludes.

2 Problem Definition

In this section, we define the problem which we address.

2.1 Top-k Queries

By a top-k query, the user specifies a number k, and the system should return the k most relevant answers. The relevance degree of the answers to the query is determined by a *scoring function*. A common method for efficient top-k query processing is to run the algorithms over *sorted lists* (also called *inverted lists*) [6]. Let us define them formally.

Let D be a set of n data items, then the sorted lists are m lists $L_1, L_2, \ldots, L_m$, such that each list L_i contains every data item $d \in D$ in the form of a pair $(id(d), s_i(d))$ where $id(d)$ is the identification of d and $s_i(d)$ is a value that denotes the *local score* (attribute value) of d in L_i. The data items in each list L_i are sorted in descending order of their local scores. For example, in a relational table, each sorted list represents a sorted column of the table where the local score of a data item is its attribute value in that column.

Let f be a scoring function given by the user in the top-k query. For each data item $d \in D$ an *overall score*, denoted by $ov(d)$, is calculated by applying the function f on the local scores of d. Formally, we have $ov(d) = f(s_1(d), s_2(d), \ldots, s_m(d))$.

The result of a top-k query is the set of k elements that have the highest overall scores among all elements of the database. In this work, we assume that the scoring function is in the class of linear functions with positive coefficients (denoted by *LFPC*). Formally, a function f is LFPC if $f = a_1x_1 + a_2x_2 + \cdots + a_mx_m$ where each coefficient $a_i \geq 0$ for $1 \leq i \leq m$. Many functions such as SUM, COUNT, AVG and MAX are in the class of LFPC functions.

2.2 Distributed System and Adversary Model

We suppose that the sorted lists are stored in the nodes of a *distributed system*. We make no specific assumption about the distributed system architecture which can be very general, *e.g.*, a cluster of nodes. Formally, let P be the set of the nodes in the distributed system. Each sorted list L_i is kept in a node $p \in P$. We call p the *owner* of L_i.

We consider the *honest-but-curious* adversary model for the nodes of the distributed system. In this model, the adversary is inquisitive to learn the sensitive data without introducing any modification in the data or protocols. This model is widely used in many preserving processing solutions [10].

2.3   Problem Statement

The problem we attack in this paper is top-k query processing over encrypted data in distributed systems.

Let D be a database composed of n data items. We want to encrypt the data items contained in D, and store the encrypted data items in a distributed system. Then, our goal is to develop a distributed algorithm A that given any top-k query q (including a scoring function f) returns the k data items that have the highest overall scores with regard to f. This should be done without decrypting the data items in the nodes of the distributed system, while minimizing the response time and the communication cost of the query execution.

3   SD-TOPK System

In this section, we present our system, called SD-TOPK, that encrypts and outsources the user data in a distributed system, and is capable to efficiently evaluate top-k queries over the distributed encrypted data.

The rest of this section is organized as follows. We first describe the architecture of our outsourcing system. Then, we present our method for encrypting the data items and storing them in the distributed system. Afterwards, we propose our algorithm for processing top-k queries over the encrypted data.

3.1   System Architecture

The architecture of our outsourcing system has two main components:

- **Trusted client.** It is responsible for encrypting the user data, decrypting the results and controlling the user accesses. The security keys used for data encryption/decryption are managed by this part of the system. When a query is issued by a user, the trusted client checks the access rights of the user. If the user does not have the required rights to see the query results, then her demand is rejected. Otherwise, the query is transformed to a query that can be executed over the encrypted data. Note that the trusted client component should be installed in a trusted location, *e.g.*, the machine(s) of the person/organization that outsources the data.

– **Remote service.** It is installed in the nodes of the distributed system, and is responsible for storing the encrypted data, executing the queries provided by the trusted client, and returning the results. This component does not keep any security key, thus cannot decrypt the encrypted data in the distributed system.

3.2 Data Encryption and Outsourcing

Before outsourcing a database, SD-TOPK creates sorted lists for all important attributes, *i.e.*, those that may be used in the top-k queries. Then, each sorted list is partitioned into buckets. There are several methods for partitioning a sorted list, for example dividing the attribute domain of the list to almost equal intervals or creating buckets with equal sizes. In the current implementation of our system, we use the latter method, *i.e.*, we create buckets with almost the same size where the bucket size is configurable by the system administrator.

Let $b_1, b_2, \ldots, b_t$ be the created buckets for a sorted list L_j. Each bucket b_i has a lower bound, denoted by $min(b_i)$, and an upper bound, denoted by $max(b_i)$. A data item d is in the bucket b_i, if and only if its local score (attribute value) in the list L_j is between the lower and upper bounds of the bucket, *i.e.*, $min(b_i) \leq s_j(d) < max(b_i)$.

We use two types of encryption schemes (methods) for encrypting the data item ids and the local scores of the sorted lists: *deterministic* and *probabilistic*. With the *deterministic* scheme, for two equal inputs, the same ciphertexts (encrypted values) are generated. We use this scheme to encrypt the ID of the data items. This allows us to have the same encrypted ID for each data item in all sorted lists.

The *probabilistic* scheme is used to encrypt the local scores (attribute values) of data items. With the *probabilistic* encryption, for the same plaintexts different ciphertexts are generated, but the decryption function returns the same plaintext for them. Thus, for example if two data items have the same local scores in a sorted list, their encrypted scores may be different. The probabilistic encryption is the strongest type of encryption.

After encrypting the data IDs and local scores of each list L_i, the trusted client puts them in their bucket (chosen based on the local score). Then, the trusted client sends the buckets of each sorted list to one node in the distributed system. The buckets are stored in the nodes according to their lower bound order. However, there is no order for the data items inside each bucket, *i.e.*, *the place of the data items inside each bucket is chosen randomly*. This prevents the nodes to know the order of data items inside the buckets.

3.3 Top-k Query Processing Algorithm

The main idea behind top-k query processing in SD-TOPK is to use the bucket boundaries and a new technique to decide when to stop reading the encrypted data from the lists.

For each top-k query, one of the nodes of the distributed system performs the coordination between the nodes to execute the query. We call this node as *coordinator*. The coordinator may be the node that initially receives the user's query or be randomly chosen among the system nodes.

Let us describe our top-k query processing algorithm. Given a top-k query with a number k and a scoring function f that is linear with positive coefficients, i.e., it is in the form of $f = a_1x_1 + a_2x_2 + \cdots + a_mx_m$. SD-TOPK chooses a node as *coordinator*, and then the following steps are performed to answer the query:

1. The coordinator broadcasts the query in parallel to the nodes, and asks each node to return the buckets that contain the k first data items in its list. Each node returns the encrypted identifier of the first k data items, as well as the lower bound of their including buckets.
2. For each returned data item d, the coordinator calculates its *minimum overall score* defined as follows: $ov_{min}(d) = f(v_1(d), v_2(d), \ldots, v_m(d))$ where $v_i(d)$ is the lower bound of the bucket that contains d in the list L_i. If d has not been returned to the coordinator by the owner of a list L_j then $v_j(d) = 0$.
3. The coordinator sorts the received data items according to their minimum overall score, and chooses the data item d' that has the kth minimum overall score denoted by δ. Then, it uses the minimum overall score of d' to calculate a threshold θ as follows: $\theta = \frac{\delta}{\sum_{i=1}^{m} a_i}$ where $a_1, \ldots, a_m$ are the coefficients in the scoring function.
4. The coordinator broadcasts θ in parallel to the nodes. Each node returns to the coordinator the buckets that have upper bounds greater than or equal to θ.
5. Let Y be the set of all data items that are sent to the coordinator by at least one node. We call Y the set of *candidate items*. The coordinator sends the encrypted id of all data items contained in Y to the nodes, and they return the encrypted score of each data item contained in Y.
6. Finally, the coordinator returns to the trusted client the candidate items and their encrypted local scores.

When the trusted client receives the candidate items, it decrypts them using the secret keys. Then, it calculates for each candidate d its overall score, extracts the k data items that have the highest overall scores, and returns them to the user.

The following theorem shows that the output of the above algorithm contains the encrypted top-k data items.

Theorem 1. *Given a top-k query with a scoring function f that is linear with positive coefficients. Then, the output of the top-k algorithm of SD-TOPK contains the encrypted top-k results.*

Proof. Let the scoring function be $f = a_1x_1 + a_2x_2 + \cdots + a_mx_m$. Let Y be the output of the algorithm, i.e., the set of candidate items. To prove the theorem, it is sufficient to show that each data item d that has not been sent to the coordinator in the 4th step of the algorithm, has an overall score less than or equal to the overall score of at least k data items in Y. Let θ be the threshold value that is sent to the nodes in the 4th step of the algorithm. For each list L_i, let s_i be the local score of d in the list L_i. The overall score of d is computed as $ov(d) = a_1 s_1 + \cdots + a_m s_m$. Since d has not been sent to the coordinator, from the 4th step of the algorithm we know that $s_i < \theta$. Thus, we have $ov(d) < a_1 \times \theta + \cdots + a_m \times \theta = \sum_{i=1}^{m} a_i \times \theta$. From the 3rd step of the algorithm, we know that $\theta = \frac{\delta}{\sum_{i=1}^{m} a_i}$. Thus, we have $ov(d) < \delta$. In other words, the overall score of d is less than the minimum overall score of the data item d' that is the kth data item found in the 3rd step of the algorithm. Therefor, the overall score of d is less than at least k data items found by the top-k algorithm of SD-TOPK, so d cannot be among the top-k results.   □

In the set Y returned by the above algorithm, in addition to the top-k results there may be false positives. Below, we propose a filtering algorithm to eliminate most of them in the distributed system, without decrypting the data items.

Given the set of candidate data items Y, the filtering algorithm executed by the coordinator proceeds as follows:

1. Calculate the *minimum overall score* of all candidate data items, sort them according to their minimum overall score, and take the kth *minimum overall score* denoted by δ_2.
2. Calculate the *maximum overall score* of all candidate data items, and eliminate those with *maximum overall score* less than $< \delta_2$. The *maximum overall score* of a data item d is computed as follows: $ov_{max}(d) = f(v_1(d), v_2(d), ..., v_m(d))$ where $v_i(d)$ is the upper bound of the bucket that contains d in the list L_i. If d has not been returned to the coordinator by the node that keeps L_i then $v_i(d)$ is equal to the lower bound of the last bucket received from that node.

The above algorithm eliminates almost all false positives (see the experimental results on filtering rate in Sect. 4), and by doing that it improves significantly the response time of the queries because the eliminated false positives do not need to be communicated to the trusted client and should not be decrypted.

To strengthen the security of our system, we obfuscate the bucket boundaries as follows. We choose two random numbers a and c. These numbers are kept secret in the trusted client. Before sending the encrypted database to the nodes of the distributed system, the trusted client multiplies the lower (and upper) bounds of buckets by a secret number a, and then adds the secret number c to the result. These obfuscated bucket boundaries are sent to the nodes together with the encrypted IDs and scores.

4   Performance Evaluation

In this section, we first describe the experimental setup, and then report the results of our experiments.

4.1   Setup

We implemented SD-TOPK and performed experiments on real and synthetic datasets. As in some previous work on privacy (*e.g.*, [10]), we use the Gowalla database, which is a location-based social networking dataset collected from users locations. The database contains 6 million tuples where each tuple represents user number, time, user geographic position, etc. In our experiments, we are interested in the attribute time, which is the second value in each tuple. As in [10], we decomposed this attribute into 6 attributes (year, month, day, hour, minute, second), and then created a database with the values of those attributes. In addition to the real dataset, we have also generated random datasets using uniform and Gaussian distributions.

We compared SD-TOPK with two algorithms based on the TA algorithm [6]: *Remote-TA* and *Block-TA*. In Remote-TA, the trusted client retrieves the encrypted data from the sorted lists of the distributed system one by one using sorted access, and for each retrieved data d, it retrieves the encrypted local scores of d from the other lists, decrypts the read local scores, computes the TA threshold, and checks if it can stop or not (as in TA). Block-TA is like Remote-TA, except that the encrypted data items are read block by block. For the TA-based algorithms, we sort the encrypted data items in each list based on their initial order (*i.e.*, their order in plaintext).

In the experiments, the number of nodes is equal to the number of lists, *i.e.*, each node stores one of the lists. The coordinator of SD-TOPK is one of the nodes of the system (randomly chosen).

We study the effect of several parameters: (1) n: the number of data items in the database; (2) m: the number of lists; (3) k: the number of required top items; (4) $bsize$: the number of data items in the buckets (or blocks) in SD-TOPK and Block-TA. The default value for n is 2M items. Unless otherwise specified, m is 5, k is 50, and $bsize$ is 10. The default database is the synthetic uniform database, and the latency of the messages is around 50 ms.

To evaluate the performance of SD-TOPK, we measured the following metrics:

- **Response time:** includes top-k query processing time, communication time, filtering time, and the result post-processing time (*e.g.*, decryption).
- **Filtering rate:** the number of false positives eliminated by the filtering algorithm in the distributed system.
- **Communication cost:** we measure two metrics: (1) the number of messages communicated between the nodes to answer a top-k query; (2) the total number of bytes communicated to answer a top-k query.

4.2   Effect of Database Size

In this section, we compare the response time of SD-TOPK, Remote-TA and Block-TA, while varying the number of data items, *i.e.*, n.

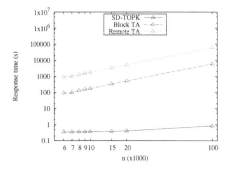

Fig. 1. Response time vs. number of database tuples

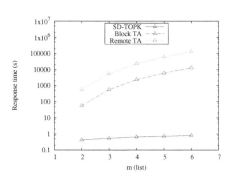

Fig. 2. Response time vs. number of lists

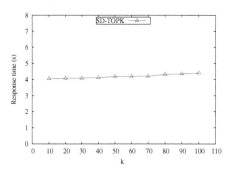

Fig. 3. Response time vs. k

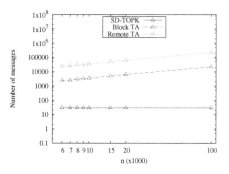

Fig. 4. Number of communicated messages vs. number of database tuples

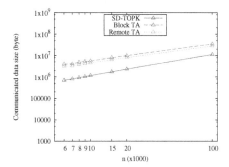

Fig. 5. Size of communicated data (in bytes) vs. number of database tuples

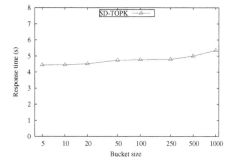

Fig. 6. Response time vs. bucket size

Figure 1 shows how response time evolves, with increasing n, while the other parameters are set as default values described in Sect. 4. Note that the results are shown in logarithmic scale. The response time of all approaches increases with increasing the database size. SD-TOPK is the best; its response time is at least two orders of magnitude better than the other algorithms. This high difference between SD-TOPK and TA-based algorithms is mainly due to the high number of encrypted data items that should be decrypted by TA-based algorithms in trusted client, and also the messages needed for communicating them. Block-TA performs better than Remote-TA, because of reading the lists in blocks, thus it needs less number of messages.

4.3 Effect of the Number of Lists

Figure 2 shows the response time of SD-TOPK and TA-based algorithms when varying m (i.e., the number of attributes in the scoring function), and the other parameters set as default values. We observe that the response time of SD-TOPK increases slightly comparing to Remote-TA and Block-TA when the number of lists increases. The reason is that when we increase the number of lists, more data (sent by the nodes) should be processed by the coordinator for finding the candidate items.

4.4 Effect of k

Figure 3 shows the response times of SD-TOPK with increasing k, and the other parameters set as default values. We observe that with increasing k the response time increases slightly. The reason is that when k increases, SD-TOPK needs to get more data items from the list owner nodes in each step. In addition, increasing k augments the number of data items that the trusted client needs to decrypt (because at least k data items are decrypted by the trusted client).

4.5 Effect of Bucket Size

Figure 6 reports the response time of SD-TOPK when varying the size of buckets, and the other parameters set as default values. We observe that the response time increases slightly when the bucket size increases. The reason is that increasing the bucket size increases the number of data items to be considered in the different steps of SD-TOP algorithm. It also increases the number of false positives to be removed by the filtering algorithm.

4.6 Communication Cost

We measure the communication cost of SD-TOPK, Remote-TA and Block-TA in terms of the total number of messages exchanged between the different nodes of the distributed system and the size of the exchanged data.

Figure 4 shows the number of communicated messages while increasing the number of tuples and fixing the other parameters to the default values. We observe that SD-TOPK needs to exchange a small number of messages comparing to the others approaches. The reason is that SD-TOPK runs in only some rounds of communication, and does not depend on the database size. But for the TA-based algorithms, the number of messages depends on the position where they stop in the lists, and that position depends on the database size.

Figure 5 illustrates the size of the communicated data in bytes, while increasing the number of tuples in the database and setting the other parameters to the default values. We note that the size of the communicated data increases with the database size. The amount of data transferred by SD-TOPK is less than that of Remote-TA and Block-TA. The reason is that SD-TOPK uses the obfuscated bucket boundaries to check the top-k data items and these boundaries have a size less than the encrypted scores used by other algorithms.

4.7   Filtering Rate

We study the efficiency of the filtering algorithm of SD-TOPK by using different datasets. The results are shown in Table 1. The results show that the filtering algorithm is very efficient over all the tested datasets. However, there is a little difference in the filtering rates because of the local score distributions. For example, in the Gaussian distribution, the local scores of many data items are very close to each other, thus the filtering rate decreases in this dataset.

Table 1. False positive elimination by the filtering algorithm of SD-TOPK over different databases

	Uniform dataset	Real dataset	Gaussian dataset
Filtering rate	100%	99.995%	99.991%

5   Related Work

In the literature, there has been some research work to process keyword queries over encrypted data, e.g., [2,13]. For example [2,13] propose matching techniques to search words in encrypted documents. However, the proposed techniques cannot be used to answer top-k queries. There have been also some solutions proposed for secure kNN similarity search, e.g., [3–5,11,15]. The problem is to find k points in the search space that are the nearest to a given point. This problem should not be confused with the top-k problem in which the given scoring function plays an important role, such that on the same database and with the same k, if the user changes the scoring function, then the output may change. Thus, the proposed solutions proposed for kNN cannot deal with the top-k problem.

The bucketization technique (i.e., creating buckets) has been used in the literature for answering range queries over encrypted data, e.g., [7,8]. For example, in [8], Hore et al. use this technique, and propose optimal solutions for distributing the encrypted data in the buckets in order to guarantee a good performance for range queries. In [9], Kim et al. propose an approach for preserving the privacy of data access patterns during top-k query processing. In [14], Vaidya et al. propose a privacy preserving method for top-k selection from the data shared by individuals in a distributed system. Their objective is to avoid disclosing the data of each node to other nodes. Thus their assumption about the nodes is different from ours, because they can trust the node that stores the data (this is why the data are not crypted), but in our system we trust no node of the distributed system.

CryptDB [12] is a system designed for processing SQL like queries over encrypted data. It is capable to execute several types of queries, *e.g.*, exact-match, join and range queries. However, top-k queries are not supported by CryptDB.

The Three Phase Uniform Threshold (TPUT) [1] is an efficient algorithm to answer top-k queries in distributed systems. Like our SD-TOPK algorithm, it is done in few round-trips between the nodes of the distributed system. However, TPUT can be used only with the queries in which the scoring function is SUM, whereas our algorithm can be used for a large range of scoring functions. In addition, our algorithm finds top-k results over encrypted data, while TPUT can be used only over plaintext data.

In [16], the authors propose an approach for top-k query processing over encrypted data. The proposed approach assumes the existence of two non-colluding nodes s_1 and s_2 in two different clouds. One of the nodes, say s_2, has the decryption keys, and the other one, say s_1, stores the data. Top-k query processing proceeds by using the TA algorithm and accessing the encrypted data in s_1, such that after reading each data in s_1, its encrypted local scores are sent to the node s_2 (using a special protocol) where they are decrypted and compared with the TA threshold. Our assumptions about the distributed system are different. In our solution, we do not need to trust any node, and during the top-k query processing, we do not decrypt the encrypted data in the nodes of the system. In addition, the solution in [16] needs a lot of communications between cloud nodes (*i.e.*, at least two messages for each sorted/random access, which is even more than the TA-based algorithms compared with SD-TOPK).

6 Conclusion

In this paper, we proposed SD-TOPK, an efficient system that encrypts and outsources user data in a distributed system, and is able to evaluate top-k queries over encrypted data, without decrypting them in the nodes of the system. We evaluated the performance of our solution over synthetic and real databases. The results show excellent response time and communication cost for SD-TOPK. They show that the response time of SD-TOPK can be several order of magnitude better than that of the TA-based algorithms. This is mainly due to its optimized top-k query processing and filtering algorithms. The results also show a significant gain in communication cost of SD-TOPK compared to the other algorithms. They also show the efficiency of the filtering algorithm that eliminates almost all false positives in the distributed system.

Acknowledgement. The research leading to these results has received funding from the European Union's Horizon 2020 - The EU Framework Programme for Research and Innovation 2014–2020, under grant agreement No. 732051.

References

1. Cao, P., Wang, Z.: Efficient top-k query calculation in distributed networks. In: Proceedings of ACM PODC, pp. 206–215 (2004)
2. Chang, Y.-C., Mitzenmacher, M.: Privacy preserving keyword searches on remote encrypted data. In: Ioannidis, J., Keromytis, A., Yung, M. (eds.) ACNS 2005. LNCS, vol. 3531, pp. 442–455. Springer, Heidelberg (2005). https://doi.org/10.1007/11496137_30
3. Choi, S., Ghinita, G., Lim, H.-S., Bertino, E.: Secure kNN query processing in untrusted cloud environments. IEEE TKDE **26**(11), 2818–2831 (2014)
4. Ding, X., Liu, P., Jin, H.: Privacy-preserving multi-keyword top-k similarity search over encrypted data. IEEE TDSC **99**, 1–14 (2017)
5. Elmehdwi, Y., Samanthula, B.K., Jiang, W.: Secure k-nearest neighbor query over encrypted data in outsourced environments. In: Proceedings of IEEE ICDE, pp. 664–675 (2014)
6. Fagin, R., Lotem, A., Naor, M.: Optimal aggregation algorithms for middleware. J. Comput. Syst. Sci. **66**(4), 614–656 (2003)
7. Hore, B., Mehrotra, S., Canim, M., Kantarcioglu, M.: Secure multidimensional range queries over outsourced data. J. VLDB **21**(3), 333–358 (2012)
8. Hore, B., Mehrotra, S., Tsudik, G.: A privacy-preserving index for range queries. In: VLDB, pp. 720–731 (2004)
9. Kim, H.-I., Kim, H.-J., Chang, J.-W.: A privacy-preserving top-k query processing algorithm in the cloud computing. In: Bañares, J.Á., Tserpes, K., Altmann, J. (eds.) GECON 2016. LNCS, vol. 10382, pp. 277–292. Springer, Cham (2017). https://doi.org/10.1007/978-3-319-61920-0_20
10. Li, R., Liu, A.X., Wang, A.L., Bruhadeshwar, B.: Fast range query processing with strong privacy protection for cloud computing. In: PVLDB, vol. 7, no. 14, pp. 1953–1964 (2014)
11. Liao, X., Li, J.: Privacy-preserving and secure top-k query in two-tier wireless sensor network. In: Global Communications Conference (GLOBECOM), pp. 335–341 (2012)
12. Popa, R.A., Redfield, C.M.S., Zeldovich, N., Balakrishnan, H.: CryptDB: processing queries on an encrypted database. Commun. ACM **55**(9), 103–111 (2012)
13. Song, D.X., Wagner, D., Perrig, A.: Practical techniques for searches on encrypted data. In: IEEE S&P, pp. 44–55 (2000)
14. Vaidya, J., Clifton, C.: Privacy-preserving top-k queries. In: 21st International Conference on Data Engineering. ICDE 2005, pp. 545–546 (2005)
15. Wong, W.K., Cheung, D.W.-L., Kao, B., Mamoulis, N.: Secure kNN computation on encrypted databases. In: ACM SIGMOD, pp. 139–152 (2009)
16. Zhu, H., Meng, X., Kollios, G.: Top-k query processing on encrypted databases with strong security guarantees. arXiv:1510.05175v2 (2016)

Minimizing Network Traffic
for Distributed Joins Using Lightweight
Locality-Aware Scheduling

Long Cheng[1,2](✉), John Murphy[1], Qingzhi Liu[2], Chunliang Hao[3],
and Georgios Theodoropoulos[4]

[1] PEL, University College Dublin, Dublin, Ireland
`long.cheng@ucd.ie`
[2] Eindhoven University of Technology, Eindhoven, The Netherlands
[3] Institute of Software, CAS, Beijing, China
[4] Southern University of Science and Technology, Shenzhen, China

Abstract. Large computing systems such as data centers are becoming the mainstream infrastructures for big data processing. As one of the key data operators in such scenarios, distributed joins is still challenging current techniques since it always incurs a significant cost on network communication. Various advanced approaches have been proposed to improve the performance, however, most of them just focus on data skew handling, and algorithms designed specifically for communication reduction have received less attention. Moreover, although the state-of-the-art technique can minimize network traffic, it provides fine-grained optimal schedules for all individual join keys, which could result in obvious overhead. In this paper, we propose a new approach called LAS (Lightweight Locality-Aware Scheduling), which targets reducing network communication for large distributed joins in an efficient and effective manner. We present the detailed design and implementation of LAS, and conduct an experimental evaluation using large data joins. Our results show that LAS can effectively reduce scheduling overhead and achieve comparable performance on network reduction compared to the state-of-the-art.

1 Introduction

To cope with the growing Big Data from various domains, large systems such as data centers have been built across the globe to support high-performance data processing. As one of the core tasks in such scenarios, efficient execution of distributed data operators such as joins is still challenging current techniques and systems. The main reason is that these operators are always expensive, in terms of both network resource consumption and network communication time. In fact, in recent years, the performance of CPUs has grown much faster than network bandwidth and, as such, the network becomes a performance bottleneck to computation [1,2]. Therefore, effective strategies on the execution of

© Springer International Publishing AG, part of Springer Nature 2018
M. Aldinucci et al. (Eds.): Euro-Par 2018, LNCS 11014, pp. 293–305, 2018.
https://doi.org/10.1007/978-3-319-96983-1_21

distributed data operators, which can reduce data communication time, becomes increasingly desirable.

In this work, we focus on one of the most challenging operators – distributed joins, which is used to facilitate combination of two relations based on a common key. More specifically, we focus on reducing its network traffic. The main reason is that any communication reduction in a distributed join will be directly translated to faster execution, for both low-end and high-end platforms [3]. Moreover, data systems would also benefit from our design in terms of energy consumption, since data centers could consume obvious energy on communication links, switching and aggregation elements.

A typical distributed join implementation contains a data redistribution process, which always incurs large amounts of data transferring over networks [4]. Various advanced join approaches have shown that they can effectively reduce network communication [4,5]. However, they mainly focus on data skew handling, i.e., communication reduction is only considered as a byproduct of their designs. In comparison, the state-of-the-art *track* approach [3] is designed specifically for minimizing network traffic. It provides a fine-grain granularity optimum on data locality for all input tuples, and thus minimal data communication can always be achieved. Moreover, the experiments have shown that the method can significant speed up conventional join approaches. However, the scheduling process of *track* is relatively complex, which would make the scheduling itself costly and thus bring in obvious overhead for the final joins, especially when the number of keys is large (details see Sect. 2).

To reduce network traffic for distributed joins in an efficient and effective manner, in this paper, we present a novel algorithm called LAS (**L**ightweight Locality-**A**ware **S**cheduling). We provide the detailed design and implementation of LAS in a distributed computing environment and conduct a performance evaluation using maximal 100 GB data over up to 128 computing cores (32 nodes). We summarize the contributions of this work as following:

- We introduce the state-of-the-art scheduling approach for distributed joins and analyze its possible performance issues in the presence of big datasets.
- We propose LAS, for minimizing network traffic in distributed joins, by incorporating efficient and effective strategies on data locality exploration.
- Our experimental results demonstrate that LAS is obviously lightweight and can achieve comparable performance on network reduction compared to the state-of-the-art. Moreover, join implementations based on LAS can significantly outperform the conventional approaches for large datasets.

The rest of this paper is organized as follows: In Sect. 2, we introduce some current distributed join approaches and analyze their possible performance issues. We describe our new method and its implementation in Sect. 3, and present the experimental evaluation in Sect. 4. We report on related work in Sect. 5 while we conclude the paper in Sect. 6.

2   Background

In this section, we briefly introduce two basic join approaches and two advanced techniques. Moreover, we also discuss about their possible performance issues in terms of network communication.

2.1   Basic Approaches

The redistribution-based and duplication-based joins are the two conventional distributed join methods. In the former approach, tuples on each node are firstly partitioned into distinct sets. Then, each set is transferred to a remote node for final local joins [4]. As the partitioning is usually based on the hash values of join keys, we refer the method to Hash in the following. An example of the scheme between two relations R and S is shown in Fig. 1(a). There, tuples are in the form of $\langle k, v \rangle$ pairs, where k is join key and v is payload. Assuming each hash value is calculated based on the modulus of 5, then all the tuples with key 3 will be transferred to node 3. If we quantify the cost of network traffic by the number of tuples transferred to remote nodes, then the cost of Hash is 13. Similarly, as shown in Fig. 1(b), for a duplication-based case, all the 4 tuples in the small relation R is duplicated to all the remote nodes, and thus its cost is 16.

From a scheduling perspective, the two approaches have not used any related techniques: the destination node(s) of a tuple only depends on the hash value of its join key or the size of the relation it belongs to. These kinds of straightforward processing make the two methods far from optimal in terms of network communication, because transferring all input tuples or broadcasting a relation over networks is always expensive. Additionally, as a well known issue, the performance of Hash will dramatically decrease in the presence of significant data skew [4]. We will focus on Hash in the following, as the approach is widely used in various data applications. In contrast, the duplication-based method is relatively seldom adopted, except for small-large joins [4].

2.2   Skew Handling Methods

To improve the performance of the conventional approaches, various advanced techniques have been proposed, and one of them is PRPD (partial redistribution & partial duplication) [5]. Its main idea is to distinguish skew and non-skew tuples and handle them in different ways: non-skew tuples are processed by Hash while the skew ones are based on duplication. As shown in Fig. 2(a), assume the tuples with key 3 are the skew ones, then the two tuples $\langle 3, 10 \rangle$ and $\langle 3, 11 \rangle$ of R at node 2 will be broadcast, and the tuples $\langle 5, 13 \rangle$ and $\langle 8, 12 \rangle$ will be redistributed. Then, the network cost of PRPD is 10, which is smaller than Hash. Moreover, it should be noticed that all the skew tuples in S are kept locally rather than being redistributed, and thus the data skew problem in Hash is well addressed.

In terms of data locality scheduling, PRPD only needs to identify the skew keys of input tuples. This process would be simple and can be done in a quick way, such as *sampling*, while the cost of which is always negligible for join time [5].

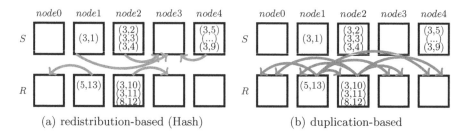

Fig. 1. Two basic data movement approaches in a distributed join.

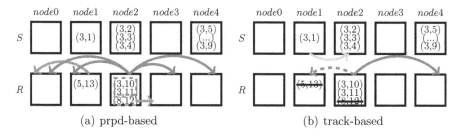

Fig. 2. Two advanced data movement approaches in a distributed join.

Because of the efficiency of PRPD, the method has been widely used and studied in various large data systems. However, if we look at the details of PRPD in Fig. 2(a), we can find that PRPD is not optimal in communication reduction in two perspectives: (1) part of data transferring is actually unnecessary. For example, the tuples ⟨5, 13⟩ and ⟨8, 12⟩ do not make any contributions to the join, i.e., their join results are actually empty, but they are scheduled to be transferred; and (2) some nodes may receive some tuples that they do not really need. For instance, S does not have any tuples on node 0 and 3, but the two tuples ⟨3, 10⟩ and ⟨3, 11⟩ are scheduled to be duplicated to the two nodes.

2.3 The State-of-the-art

Compared to PRPD, the *track* approach [3] (referred to Track) is able to minimize network traffic for a distributed join, which can be considered as the state-of-the-art. The method is based on the complete knowledge of occurrence frequency of each key on each node. As illustrated in Fig. 2(b), based on a global statistic, Track knows that none of the five nodes has tuples with keys 5 or 8 in S, thus the tuples with these two keys in R, i.e., ⟨5, 13⟩ and ⟨8, 12⟩, will be scheduled to keep locally (and be ignored in later join execution). Moreover, for the case with key 3, Track only broadcasts the two tuples ⟨3, 10⟩ and ⟨3, 11⟩ to the nodes with matching keys in S, i.e., node 1 and 4. This process is called as *select broadcast*, which is different from PRPD that broadcasting to all the nodes (i.e., *full broadcast*). After that, Track uses a very smart way, i.e., *migration*, to further explore the possibilities on reducing communication traffic. For example,

Track will check whether the cost is decreased, when moving $\langle 3, 1 \rangle$ from node 1 to node 2 with removing the duplication of $\langle 3, 10 \rangle$ and $\langle 3, 11 \rangle$ from node 2 to node 1. In this case, the traffic is indeed decreased, and consequently the schedule plan will be updated. Following this processing, the final network cost of Track is 3, which is much smaller than the above approaches.

Track is actually an approach which has extensively used the philosophy of moving *small* data chunks instead of *large* data chunks in a distributed environment to minimize network traffic. More specifically, it employs of a fine-grained multi-phase scheduling algorithm to explore data locality in a superlative way, i.e., *per distinct key*[1]. In fact, the global statistic of each key is done in a way which is very similar to a distributed join over all unique keys. This could be costly, when the number of unique keys is large. Moreover, different from a simple join, to record the frequency and location of each distinct key, the pre-join has to aggregate all the keys in the form of (key, (list[N_r], list[N_s]), the computing of which could be expensive. In addition to that, the scheduling using *select broadcast and migration* (SBM) has to be performed on all the aggregated (list[N_r], list[N_s]), which would be also time costly if the number of nodes is large. All of these could result in obvious overhead for the join execution of Track. In comparison, as we will show later that LAS is significantly lightweight and can achieve comparable performance to Track on network reduction.

3 Our Approach

In this section, we present LAS and its implementation in detail. Additionally, we also discuss about its advantages by the comparison with current techniques.

3.1 The LAS Method

Based on the analysis of the approaches described above, we can see that there is actually a trade-off between communication reduction and scheduling overhead. Namely, scheduling leading to less network traffic could have a heavier overhead in data locality exploration, and vice versa. To reduce network traffic as much as we can and also in a quick manner for big data joins, we have one core design principle for LAS: fine granularity optimal scheduling such as Track should only be applied to a small number of keys which can greatly reduce network traffic, rather than all the distinct keys.

Following the above principle, we can use a hybrid way to explore data locality for input tuples, i.e., applying Track on the skew tuples and Hash on the rest ones. The main motivation is that the number of skewed tuples could be huge, but the number of their unique keys is normally small, and thus they can be scheduled in a quick way. Moreover, although the number of non-skew keys is large, Hash can always handle them quickly. This means that such a hybrid

---

[1] Note that here *per distinct key* means that even though a key in R and a key in S have the same value, they will be distinguished, i.e., each of them is identified by a tag like R or S. Later, we will use the term *per join key* to remove this distinction.

scheduling will be very lightweight. However, since the communication reduction ability of Hash is weak, the network traffic brought by the hybrid scheduling could be still high. Taking the case in Fig. 2(b) for example, the non-skew tuples $\langle 5, 13 \rangle$ and $\langle 8, 12 \rangle$ will be transferred, which is actually not necessary.

To improve the above problem, we use a relatively fine-grained method for the non-skew data from the idea of Track: exploring data locality in a *per-key* level. The main difference is that we perform our scheduling based on *per join key* rather than *per distinct key*. Namely, when we count the key appearing frequency, a key in R and a key in S will be treated as a same key, if they have the same value (i.e., matching). For the detailed scheduling, we do not distinguish keys from R and S, thus we do not need to perform any SBM operations. Instead, for each join key, we just set its destination to a node, which contains the most number of tuples having the key. We call this processing as a *locality-aware* operation (LA). Obviously, LA can greatly simplify the statistic and data locality exploration operations on each node, compared to Track. In general, the proposed LAS can be divided into the following three main phases from a global point of view:

- *phase 1*: on the basis of identified skew keys, group all input tuples of R and S into two parts, the skew ones (R', S') and non-skew ones (R'', S'').
- *phase 2*: minimize the network traffic for (R', S') use Track [3], i.e., exploring data locality for *each distinct key* using *select broadcast and migration*.
- *phase 3*: minimize the network traffic for (R'', S'') by exploring data locality for *each join key* with a *locality-aware* way.

Based on LAS, the non-skew tuples $\langle 5, 13 \rangle$ and $\langle 8, 12 \rangle$ in Fig. 2(b) will not be transferred. The reason is that node 1 has the most number tuples with key 5 and node 2 with 8, and thus the destination nodes of the two tuples will be assigned to node 1 and node 2 respectively. In this case, the network cost of LAS is 3, which is much smaller than Hash and PRPD.

3.2   Comparison with Current Approaches

From a scheduling granularity viewpoint, we summarize the differences of the four techniques Hash, PRPD, Track and LAS, in Table 1. It can be seen that LAS is based on per-key level scheduling, thus it will be more powerful than Hash and PRPD on communication reduction. More specifically, LAS has inherited the advantages from Track so that it can avoid any redundant duplication for skew data, compared to PRPD. Moreover, for non-skew tuples, LAS also has tried to explore data locality, instead of just simply redistributing them.

Compared to Track, LAS does not distinguish keys with a same value in R and S for the non-skew inputs. The used LA operation is much simpler than SBM, and thus LAS will be more lightweight than Track, especially when the number of unique keys is large. We have an additional skew quantification process in LAS. Nevertheless, as we have described in Sect. 2.2, the cost (of sampling) will be very small. Moreover, although we have used a relatively coarse way to schedule the non-skew tuples, our approach is still based on per-key, and thus

Table 1. A general comparison of different approaches

Data/Alg.	Hash	PRPD [5]	Track [3]	LAS
Skew	Chunk, FR	Per join key, FB	Per distinct key, SBM	Per distinct key, SBM
Non-skew	Chunk, FR	Chunk, FR	Per distinct key, SBM	Per join key, LA

FR: *full redistribut.*, FB: *full broadcast*, SBM: *select broadcast & migration*, LA: *locality-aware*

Algorithm 1. Implementation of LAS, parallel processing on each node i

---

Input: R_i, S_i, $skew$
Output: schedule plan $L_i(key, src, des)$

step 1: key statistics
1: initialize dk and jk in Array[Map[int,int]](n)
2: **for** $key \in R_i, S_i$ **do**   //record frequency
3:     $h \leftarrow$ hash($|key|$)
4:     **if** $key \in skew$ **then**
5:         increase freq of key in $dk(h)$ by 1
6:     **else**
7:         increase freq of $|key|$ in $jk(h)$ by 1
8:     **end if**
9: **end for**
10: **for** $j \leftarrow 0..(n-1)$ **do**   //send to node j
11:     send $dk(j), jk(j)$ to $dk\_r(i), jk\_r(i)$ at node j
12: **end for**

step 2: locality exploration
13: initialize dk_aggr in Map[int,List[Triple]] and jk_aggr in Map[int,List[Pair]]

//aggregation on key
14: **for** $j \leftarrow 0..(n-1)$, $st \in dk\_r(j)$ **do**
15:     put $(|st.k|, (st.k, j, st.v))$ in dk_aggr
16: **end for**
17: **for** $j \leftarrow 0..(n-1)$, $st \in jk\_r(j)$ **do**
18:     put $(st.k, (j, st.v))$ in jk_aggr
19: **end for**
20: **for** $entry \in dk\_aggr$ **do**   //apply Track
21:     apply SBM on $entry.v$
22:     **for** $tr \in entry.v$ **do**
23:         put $(tr.1, tr.2, SBM(tr.1))$ in L_i
24:     **end for**
25: **end for**
26: **for** $entry \in jk\_aggr$ **do**   //apply LA
27:     get pair P with max. $pair.v$ in $entry.v$
28:     **for** $pair \in entry.v$ **do**
29:         put $(entry.k, pair.k, P.k)$ in L_i
30:     **end for**
31: **end for**

32: collect each L_j

---

network traffic can still be effectively reduced. In fact, as we will show in our later evaluation, LAS can achieve comparable performance on communication reduction to Track, and much better than other methods.

3.3 Parallel Implementation

LAS schedules each key independently, therefore it can be implemented in parallel in a distributed computing environment. The parallel implementation of LAS on each node i is given in Algorithm 1. We assume that we have obtained the skew keys. Then, the inputs of LAS are the two relations and the skew, and the output is a schedule plan including the source node and destination node(s) of each key. In the local statistic process, we count the appearing frequency of keys in skew and non-skew tuples in a separate way (lines 2–9). The recorded information is in the form of $\langle key, freq \rangle$ pairs, and each pair is collected by a specified bucket, based on the hash value of the key. We have to distinguish the keys with the same value but from different relations for the skew data (i.e., per distinct key). For simplicity, we have added a negative sign to each key from S, when we read the relation (assume all the input keys are positive integers). In this condition, when we count the appearing number for the non-skew keys, we just simply used their absolute values (lines 6–7). After that, similar to a hash redistribution, each bucket is pushed to the assigned remote node for further processing (lines 10–12).

Based on the received pairs from each node, the detailed scheduling of LAS is presented in lines 13–31 of Algorithm 1. All the keys are firstly aggregated, so that we can get the frequency information of each key on each node. Then, we perform the SBM operations over the skew data (lines 20–25). For each key in the non-skew part, we simply scan the aggregated entries and search the node with the maximal value on $freq$. Then, the found node will be added into schedule plan as the destination node for the key (lines 26–31). All the scheduling process will be ended when the destination(s) of each key from each node is assigned. For the latter join executions, input tuples will be partitioned based on their destination nodes and then transferred to remote nodes for local joins.

4 Experimental Evaluation

4.1 Experiment Setup

We evaluate our approach over a cluster located at SUSTech in Shenzhen City in China. We use 4 CPU cores running at 2.80 GHz for each computing node with 64 GB of RAM. The nodes are connected by Infiniband, and the operating system is Linux kernel version 2.6.32-431.

We compare LAS with the widely used Hash and the state-of-the-art Track, and have implemented the three methods using the programming language X10 [6], with version 2.3, compiling to C++ with gcc version 4.4.7. The evaluation is implemented on joins between two relations R and S. We fix the cardinality of R to 64 million and S to 1 billion records. Following a general way, we set the data format to $\langle key, payload \rangle$ pairs, where each key is an integer. We assume that R and S meet the foreign key relationship, and thus we only add skew to S, following the Zipf distribution. As listed in Table 2, besides a uniform distributed dataset, we have generated another three sets with different degrees of skew, by varying the Zipf factor from 0.8 to 1.1. It should be noted that joins with such characteristics and workloads are common in data warehouses [4].

Table 2. Details of test datasets and meanings of used parameters

Data set	Skew	# unique	Top1	Top10	Data set	Skew	# unique	Top1	Top10
DS1	0	250,000,000	0.0%	0.0%	DS3	1	46,947,295	4.7%	13.8%
DS2	0.8	136,137,483	0.3%	1.1%	DS4	1.1	19,966,276	10.7%	28.7%

X: *the number of selected top skew keys,* **Y**: *the size of the payload for each tuple*

In all our experiments, we set the system parameter X10_NPLACES to the number of cores. This lets us be able to focus on analyzing the performance of our approach in distributed computing environments rather than computing

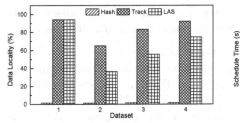
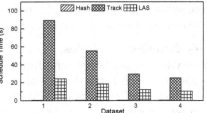

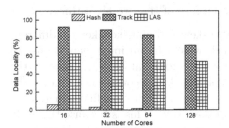
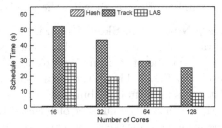

Fig. 3. Data locality and scheduling time by varying data skew over 64 cores (16 nodes).

Fig. 4. Data locality and scheduling time by varying number of cores over *skew=1*.

with multiple thread parallelism (as each *place* in X10 can be considered as a logical node). To capture the precise characteristics of LAS, we manually set the first top **X** keys as skewed keys and do not take the actually skew quantification time into account in our results. As a default, we set **X** to 4000, and we use 64 cores (16 nodes) and the data set DS3.

4.2 Experimental Results

We measure the efficiency and effectiveness based on three metrics: data locality, scheduling time and join runtime. The first metric indicates the volume of network traffic, a high data locality indicates a light traffic load on a network.

Vary Data Skew. We run our tests using 64 cores (16 nodes) over the four different datasets. Figure 3 shows the results of data locality and scheduling time of each algorithm. There, LAS and Track achieve much higher data locality than Hash in all the cases, demonstrating the effectiveness of the two approaches on reducing data communication. Specifically, their data locality is around 92% when the data is uniform distributed. This means the per-key level strategies can effectively explore data locality for non-skew tuples, and Hash or current skew handling techniques such as PRPD [5] have not considered such an optimization. Moreover, we can observe that the data locality of LAS is generally lower than Track. However, their results are still in a comparable range. In fact, as shown in our later results in Fig. 5, this kind of data locality difference can be decreased by increasing **X** in LAS. For scheduling time, it can be seen that LAS is always more lightweight than Track. Moreover, their scheduling time decreases with the increasing of data skew, the reason is that the number of unique keys decreases.

Vary Number of Nodes. We also test the three approaches over the system by varying the number of cores from 16 (4 nodes) to 128 over the default dataset. As shown in Fig. 4, the data locality of LAS and Track are always much higher than Hash. Although Track transfers less data than LAS, their difference is decreasing with increasing the number of cores. The possible reason is that the distribution of keys becomes sparse, and part of skew keys could become not so skew, and thus the LA operation in LAS starts to perform similarly to the SBM in Track. For scheduling time, both the LAS and Track decrease with increasing the number of cores, showing the good scalability of the two algorithms.

Vary Number of Skew Keys. LAS treats skew and non-skew keys in different ways. To show the impacts of the selected skew keys in our implementations, we vary the value of **X** from 1000 to 50000 over the four datasets and present the results in Fig. 5. There, the data locality for DS1 keeps consistence, due to the dataset is uniform distributed. For the skew cases, the data locality is increasing with increasing the number of selected top skew keys. This is because the SBM operation used for skew keys can provide a more fine-grained control on reducing network traffic than the LA. In this experiment, we find that the scheduling time over each data set has only slight changes (in 1 s) with increasing **X**. The reason is that the number of selected keys is still much smaller compared to the whole unique keys. This also means that we can actually set **X** to 50 K rather than 4 K as a default at least, to keep the data locality differences between LAS and Track smaller in the results presented in Figs. 3 and 4. For example, the data locality of LAS can be increased from 55% to 68% for DS3 by changing **X** from 4 K to 50K, without any increase on the scheduling time.

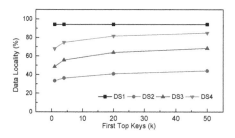

Fig. 5. Data locality with different **X**.

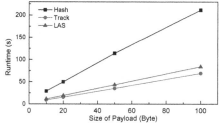

Fig. 6. Join comparison with different **Y**.

Join Performance. We finally compare the join performance of the three approaches by varying the size of payload **Y** for all tuples, from 10 Bytes to 100 Bytes. This means that the maximal dataset in size is around 100 GB. For local join execution, we select the commonly used hash joins, i.e., hash table building and probing [4]. For each join, we only count the number of matches rather than materializing the output. Additionally, to avoid the network congestion in data transferring, we use a simple and efficient round-robin communication pattern in the joins [4]. The results are shown in Fig. 6. There, joins using LAS and Track perform better than Hash. However, we notice that when the dataset is small (e.g., $Y = 10$), the runtime difference between Hash and LAS (and Track) is only 20 s. Considering the scheduling time of LAS is 12 s and Track is 29 s, we believe Hash could be the best choice for joins, when the number of keys is huge but the whole dataset in size is small. With the increase of Y, the advantages of LAS and Track become obviously, indicating that these two approaches would be more suitable for large datasets (in size). Moreover, we can see that LAS can always achieve similar performance with Track, and their difference is only 15 s when the data reaches 100 GB. Since LAS is around 17 s faster than Track on scheduling for the case, we believe that LAS would be a better solution for moderate size datasets (e.g., 100 GB or smaller). It should be noticed that, in real cases, a system optimizer will be able to get the possible cost of scheduling and network communication for each approach, and consequently to choose the best plan for executions. Nevertheless, detailed discussion on how to compute and compare the cost is outside the scope of this paper.

Brief Summary. In general, LAS has applied per-key strategies on communication reduction, thus it always transfers much less data over networks than Hash. Compared to the state-of-the-art Track, LAS has adopted a relatively coarse-grained operation (i.e., LA) to large number of non-skew keys, and thus its scheduling is more lightweight, especially when the number of unique keys is large. From above results, we can see the LAS can always achieve comparable performance to Track, in terms of data locality and join runtime. In such scenarios, we believe that LAS can be considered as a new and efficient solution for distributed joins in large-scale distributed scenarios.

5 Related Work

Research towards optimizing main-memory joins has already achieved significant performance speedups through optimizations over modern processors. Nevertheless, as applications grow, join performance would be limited by the available computing cores or system memory [4]. The two conventional Hash and duplication-based methods offer the potential scalability on processing big data. However, they are far from network-optimal, because transferring all input tuples or broadcasting a single relation would incur a heavy time-cost. Moreover, Hash could meet serious load balancing issues when input data is skew.

As data skew is quite common in data applications, various advanced algorithms have been proposed to against join skew [4,5]. The main idea of these approaches is keeping large number of skew tuples locally instead of transferring them over networks. This leads to obvious network traffic reduction in their join executions. However, all these methods focus on skew handling rather than reducing network traffic, and thus they are still not optimal. For example, although the work [4] proposes a *fetch on demand* method to process skew tuples, similar to PRPD [5], it has not explored data locality issues for non-skew data yet. In comparison, LAS provides a more fine-grained scheduling for all input tuples, and thus it can perform better on communication reduction.

To maximize data-locality, different data partitioning techniques have been proposed to avoid remote join operations for queries [7]. More generally, various advanced data placement and replication strategies have been proposed for data center storage systems to reduce the network overhead for particular workloads [8,9]. Different from them, we focus on exploring data locality using online scheduling rather than pre-processing. On the other hand, although the state-of-the-art Track [3] is able to minimize network traffic, it applies complex schedules to all join keys, which could lead to heavy overhead in the presence of big data. In comparison, LAS has used a simpler but effective way to handle input data, and thus LAS is more lightweight. More important, as we have shown in our experiments, LAS can reduce the network traffic significantly, and also can achieve comparable performance to Track.

Recent work has tried to optimize network time for distributed joins [10]. However, the optimization problem is NP-complete, making the technique can not be applied to per-key [3]. Although an efficient heuristic has been proposed for the optimization [11], its scheduling still performs based on data chunks (i.e., partitions) rather than individual keys. In contrast, LAS uses linear scheduling applied to each join key and thus it is more powerful on communication reduction. On the other hand, LAS can be used in conjunction with these techniques to optimize network communication time at a more fine-grained granularity.

6   Conclusions

In this paper, we focus on effective and efficient scheduling techniques to reduce network traffic for distributed joins. We have discussed the possible performance issues of current approaches and proposed the LAS algorithm on that basis. We have described the detailed design and implementation of LAS, and experimentally shown that LAS is lightweight and can achieve comparable performance on communication reduction, compared to the state-of-the-art. Moreover, we have also shown that LAS can obviously outperform the conventional approaches such as Hash in both communication reduction and join runtime. Our future work mainly lies in extending the proposed scheduling approach in more complex environments such as mobile and cloud computing systems [12,13].

Acknowledgments. Part of this work was supported by the European Union's Horizon 2020 research and innovation programme under the Marie Sklodowska-Curie grant agreement No 799066. The computations were performed on the Inspur TS10K Cluster at the High Performance Computing Center in SUSTech.

References

1. Greenberg, A., et al.: VL2: a scalable and flexible data center network. Commun. ACM **54**(3), 95–104 (2011)
2. Cheng, L., Wang, Y., Pei, Y., Epema, D.: A coflow-based co-optimization framework for high-performance data analytics. In: ICPP, pp. 392–401 (2017)
3. Polychroniou, O., Sen, R., Ross, K.A.: Track join: distributed joins with minimal network traffic. In: SIGMOD, pp. 1483–1494 (2014)
4. Cheng, L., Kotoulas, S., Ward, T.E., Theodoropoulos, G.: Improving the robustness and performance of parallel joins over distributed systems. J. Parallel Distrib. Comput. **109**, 310–323 (2017)
5. Xu, Y., Kostamaa, P., Zhou, X., Chen, L.: Handling data skew in parallel joins in shared-nothing systems. In: SIGMOD, pp. 1043–1052 (2008)
6. Charles, P., et al.: X10: an object-oriented approach to non-uniform cluster computing. ACM SIGPLAN Not. **40**(10), 519–538 (2005)
7. Zamanian, E., Binnig, C., Salama, A.: Locality-aware partitioning in parallel database systems. In: SIGMOD, pp. 17–30 (2015)
8. Yang, Z., et al.: AutoTiering: automatic data placement manager in multi-tier all-flash datacenter. In: IPCCC, pp. 1–8 (2017)
9. Yang, Z., Wang, J., Evans, D., Mi, N.: AutoReplica: automatic data replica manager in distributed caching and data processing systems. In: IPCCC, pp. 1–6 (2016)
10. Rödiger, W., Muhlbauer, T., Unterbrunner, P., Reiser, A., Kemper, A., Neumann, T.: Locality-sensitive operators for parallel main-memory database clusters. In: ICDE, pp. 592–603 (2014)
11. Cheng, L., Li, T.: Efficient data redistribution to speedup big data analytics in large systems. In: HiPC, pp. 91–100 (2016)
12. Mao, Y., Wang, J., Sheng, B.: Mobile message board: location-based message dissemination in wireless ad-hoc networks. In: ICNC, pp. 1–5 (2016)
13. Wang, J., Yao, Y., Mao, Y., Sheng, B., Mi, N.: Fresh: fair and efficient slot configuration and scheduling for hadoop clusters. In: CLOUD, pp. 761–768 (2014)

Cluster and Cloud Computing

VIoLET: A Large-Scale Virtual Environment for Internet of Things

Shreyas Badiger, Shrey Baheti, and Yogesh Simmhan[(⊠)]

Indian Institute of Science, Bangalore, India
{shreyasb,shreybaheti,simmhan}@IISc.ac.in

Abstract. IoT deployments have been growing manifold, encompassing sensors, networks, edge, fog and cloud resources. Despite the intense interest from researchers and practitioners, most do not have access to large-scale IoT testbeds for validation. Simulation environments that allow analytical modeling are a poor substitute for evaluating software platforms or application workloads in realistic computing environments. Here, we propose VIoLET, a virtual environment for defining and launching large-scale IoT deployments within cloud VMs. It offers a declarative model to specify container-based compute resources that match the performance of the native edge, fog and cloud devices using Docker. These can be inter-connected by complex topologies on which private/public networks, and bandwidth and latency rules are enforced. Users can configure synthetic sensors for data generation on these devices as well. We validate VIoLET for deployments with >400 devices and >1500 device-cores, and show that the virtual IoT environment closely matches the expected compute and network performance at modest costs. This fills an important gap between IoT simulators and real deployments.

1 Introduction

Internet of Things (IoT) is expanding rapidly as diverse domains deploy sensors, communication, and gateway infrastructure to support applications such as smart cities, personalized health, and autonomous vehicles. IoT is also accelerating the need for, and the use of edge, fog and cloud resources, in a coordinated manner. The need comes from the availability of large volumes of data streams that need to be analyzed closer to the edge to conserve bandwidth (e.g., video surveillance), or of fast data streams that need to be processed with low latency [16]. Edge gateway devices such as Raspberry Pi and Smart Phones have non-trivial resource capabilities, and can run a full Linux stack on 64-bit ARM processors. Fog devices such as NVidia's TX1 and Dell's Edge Gateways have power-efficient Atom processors or GPUs to support the needs of several edge devices [3,19]. At the same time, edge and even accelerated fog devices may not have the elastic and seemingly infinite on-demand resource capacity that is available in the cloud, and necessary for processing by certain IoT applications.

Besides production deployments of IoT, there is also active research at the intersection of IoT, and edge, fog and cloud computing that is investigating application scheduling, resiliency, big data platforms, and so on [8,9]. However, a key

© Springer International Publishing AG, part of Springer Nature 2018
M. Aldinucci et al. (Eds.): Euro-Par 2018, LNCS 11014, pp. 309–324, 2018.
https://doi.org/10.1007/978-3-319-96983-1_22

gap that exists is the ability to validate these research outcomes on real or realistic IoT environments. Research IoT testbeds may have just 10's of devices, and simulation environments make too many idealized assumptions and do not allow actual applications to be deployed. Manually launching and configuring containers is time consuming and error-prone. Even planning of production deployment of IoT, edge and fog resources are based on analytical models or simulations, which may not hold in practice [11,14,18].

What is lacking is a virtualized IoT environment that offers the computing and network ecosystem of a real deployment without the need to purchase, configure and deploy the edge, fog and networking devices. Here, we propose *VIoLET, a Large-scale Virtual Environment for Internet of Things*. VIoLET offers several essential features that make it valuable for researchers and planners. It is a virtualized environment that uses containers to offer comparable compute resources as edge, fog and cloud, and can run real applications. It allows the easy definition of diverse network topologies, and imposes bandwidth and latency limits between containers. VIoLET also allows the definition of virtual sensors that generate data with various distributions within the containers. It runs on top of cloud VMs or commodity clusters, allowing it to scale to hundreds or thousands of devices, provided cumulative compute capacity is available on the host machines. All of these help setup and validate an environment that mimics the behavior of city-scale IoT deployments in a fast, reproducible and cost-effective manner. *VIoLET v1.0* is available for download from https://github.com/dream-lab/VIoLET.

The rest of this paper is organized as follows. We motivate various requirements for VIoLET in Sect. 2, describe its architecture design that meets these requirements and its implementation in Sect. 3, present results on deploying and scaling VIoLET for different IoT topologies in Sect. 4, compare it with related literature and tools in Sect. 5, and finally present our conclusions and future work in Sect. 6.

2   Design Requirements

Here, we present high-level requirements for a *Virtual Environment (VE)* like VIoLET, based on the needs of researchers and developers of applications, platforms and runtime environments for IoT, edge, and fog resources.

Compute Environment. The VE should provide the ability to configure computing resources that capture the performance behavior of *heterogeneous IoT resources*, such as edge devices, gateways, fog and even cloud resources. Key resource capabilities to be controlled include CPU rating, memory and storage capacity, and network. Further, a *compute environment* that can host platforms and run applications should be provided within these resources. Virtual Machines (VM) have traditionally offered such capabilities, but are too heavy-weight for the often light-weight and plentiful IoT devices. *Containers* are much more lightweight and offer similar capabilities. One downside is the inability to change the underlying Operating System (OS) as it is coupled with the Linux kernel of the host machine. However, we expect most IoT devices to run a flavor of Linux.

Networking. Communication is central to IoT, and the networking layer is sensitive to various deployment limitations on the field. Wired, wireless and cellular networks are common, each with different *bandwidth and latency characteristics.* There is also a distinction between *local and wide area networks,* and *public and private networks* – the latter can limit the visibility of devices to each other. These affect the platforms and applications in the computing environment, and can decide who can connect to whom and if an indirection service is required. The VE needs to capture such diverse network topologies and behavior.

Sensing and Data Streams. Sensors (and actuators) form the third vital component of IoT. These are often connected to the edge computing devices by physical links, *ad hoc* wireless networks, or even on-board the device. These form the source of the distributed, fast data streams that are intrinsic to IoT deployments. The VE should provide the ability to simulate the generation of sensor event streams with various sampling rates and distributions at the compute devices for consumption by hosted applications.

Application Environment. IoT devices often ship with standard platforms and software pre-loaded so that potentially hundreds of devices do not have to be reconfigured across the wide area network. The VE should allow platforms and application environments to be pre-configured as part of the deployment, and the setup to be ready-to-use. Users should not be forced to individually configure each compute resources, though they should have the ability to do so if required.

Scalable. IoT deployments can be large in the number of devices and sensors – ranging in the 1000's – and with complex network topologies. A VE should be able to scale to such large deployments with minimal resource and human overheads. At the same time, these devices offer real computing environments that require underlying compute capacities to be available on the host machine(s). Hence, we require the VE to *weakly scale,* as long as the underlying infrastructure provides adequate cumulative compute and network capacity for all the devices. The use of elastic cloud resources as the host can enable this.

Reproducible. Simulators offer accurate reproducibility but limit the realism, or the ability to run real applications. Physical deployments are hard to get access to and may suffer from transient variability that affects reproducibility. A VE should offer a balance between running within a realistic deployment while being reproducible at a later point in time. This also allows easy sharing of deployment recipes for accurate comparisons.

Cost Effective. Clouds are able to offer a lower cost per compute unit due to economies of scale at data centers. But IoT devices while being commodity devices are costlier to purchase, deploy and manage. Having VEs offer comparable resource performance as the IoT deployment but for cheaper compute costs is essential. They should also make efficient use of the pay-as-you-go resources.

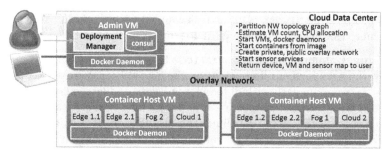

(a) Architecture Design

(b) JSON describing devices, sensors, VE deployment and host VMs.

Fig. 1. VIoLET architecture and deployment documents

Further, they should be deployable on-demand on elastic resources and release those resources after the experiments and validations are done.

Ease of Design and Deployment. Users should be able to configure large IoT deployments with ease, and have them deploy automatically and rapidly. It should be possible to mimic realistic real-world topologies or generate synthetic ones for testing purposes.

3   Architecture

We give the high-level overview architecture of VIoLET first, and then discuss individual components and design decisions subsequently. Figure 1a shows the high-level architecture of our framework. Users provide their IoT VE as *JSON deployment documents* (Fig. 1b) that declaratively capture their requirements. A `devices.json` document lists the devices, their types (e.g., Raspberry Pi 3B, NVidia TX1) and their CPU performance. Another, `sensors.json` document list the virtual sensors and their configurations available. Lastly, the actual deployment document, `deployment.json` lists the number of devices of various types, the network topology of the device inter-connects, including bandwidths and latencies, and optionally the virtual sensors and applications available on each device.

VIoLET takes these documents and determines the number of cloud VMs of a specified type that are required to host containers with resources equivalent to the device types. It also decides the mapping from devices to VMs while meeting the compute capacity, and network bandwidth and latency needs of the topology, relative to what is made available by the host VMs.

Then, containers are configured and launched for each device using *Docker*, and the containers are inter-connected through an overlay network. This allows different private and public networks to be created in the VE. Further, Traffic Control (TC) and Network Address Translation (NAT) rules are set in each container to ensure that the requested network topology, bandwidth and latency limits are enforced.

Virtual sensors, if specified, are then started on each device and their streams available on a local network port in the container. Application environments or startup scripts if specified are also configured or launched. After this, the user is provided with a mapping from the logical device names in their deployment document to the physical device IPs of the matching container, and the VMs on which the containers are placed on. Users can access these devices using the Docker `exec` command. Further, the port numbers at which various logical sensors streams are available on each device is also reported back to the user. Together, these give access to the deployed runtime environment to the user.

3.1   Compute Resources

Containers are emerging as a light-weight alternative to VMs for multi-tenancy within a single host. They use Linux kernel's `cgroups` feature to offer benefits of custom software environment (beyond the OS kernel) and resource allocation and isolation, while having trivial overheads compared to hypervisors. They are well-suited for fine-grained resource partitioning and software sand-boxing among trusted applications.

Computing devices in VIoLET are modeled as containers and managed using the *Docker* automation framework. There are two parts to this: the *resource allocation* and the *software configuration*. Docker allows containers to have resource constraints to be specified[1]. We use this to limit a container's capacity to match the CPU and Memory available on the native device. We use CPU benchmarks on the native device and the host machine to decide this allocation. The commonly used *CoreMark*[2] is currently supported for an integer-based workload, while *Whetstone*[3] has been attempted for floating-point operations. One subtlety is that while we use the multi-core benchmark rating of the device for the CPU scaling, this may map to fewer (faster) cores of the host machine.

---

[1] Docker Resource Constraints, docs.docker.com/config/containers/resource_constraints.

[2] y, Embedded Microprocessor Benchmark Consortium (EEMBC), coremark.org.

[3] Whetstone Benchmark History and Results, roylongbottom.org.uk/whetstone.htm.

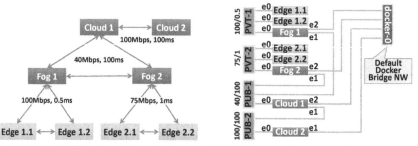

(a) Sample Topology Description   (b) Bridges in Overlay to Achieve Topology

Fig. 2. Network topology and Docker overlay network

A container's software environment is defined by the user as an image script (`Dockerfile`) that specify details like applications, startup services, and environment variables, and allow modular extensibility from other images. Public Docker repositories have existing images for common IoT platforms and applications (e.g., Eclipse Californium CoAP, Microsoft IoT Edge, RabbitMQ, Spark). VIoLET provides a base image that includes its framework configuration and allow users to extend their device images from this base with custom software configuration. This is similar to specifying a VM image, except that the users are limited to the host device's Linux kernel OS[4]. Hence, defining a compute device in VIoLET requires associating a device type for resources, and a device image for the software environment.

3.2   Network Topology

Users define the network topology for the devices based on three aspects: the public network or a private network the device is part of; the visibility of devices to each other as enforced by firewalls; and the bandwidth and latency between pairs of devices. IoT networks are usually composed of numerous private networks that interface with each other and the public Internet through gateways. We allow users to define logical private networks and assign devices to them. These exist in their own subnet. Each private network has a gateway device defined, and all traffic to the public network from other devices is routed through it. All gateway devices are part of one or more public networks, along with other devices that are on those public networks.

For simplicity, all devices in a private network by default can access each other, and have a common latency and bandwidth specified between pairs of devices by the user; and similarly for all devices connected to a public network. By default, devices on different public networks can reach each other. However,

---

[4] Docker recently introduced support for Windows and Linux containers hosted on Windows Server using the Hyper-V hypervisor. But this is more heavy-weight than Linux containers, and not used by us currently.

users can override this visibility between any pair of devices, and this is directional, i.e., $D1 \rightarrow D2$ need not imply $D1 \leftarrow D2$.

We implement the bandwidth and latency between devices using *Traffic Control (TC) rules* offered by Linux's `iproute2` utility, and the `network` service that we start on each container using `systemd`[5]. Here, every unique bandwidth and latency requirement gets mapped to a unique virtual Ethernet port, and the rules and enforced on it. This Ethernet port is also connected to the bridge corresponding to the (private or public) network that the device belongs to. The bridges physically group devices that are on the same network, and also logically assign a shared bandwidth and latency to them. All devices on public networks are also connected to a common `docker-0` bridge for the VM they are present on, and which allows all to all communication by default. Restricting the routing of traffic in a private network to/from the public network only through its gateway device is enacted through `ip` commands and *Network Address Translation (NAT) rules*. These rules redirect packets from the Ethernet port connected to the private network, to the Ethernet port connected to the public network.

Docker makes it easy to define connectivity rules and *IP addressing* of containers present in a single host machine using custom bridges defined on the Docker daemon running on the host. However, devices in VIoLET can be placed on disparate VMs and still be part of the same private network. Such communication between multiple Docker daemons requires custom Docker *overlay networks*. We create a standalone *Docker Swarm pool* which gives us the flexibility to set network and system parameters[6]. For this, the host machines must be able to access a shared key-value store that maintains the overlay networking information. In VIoLET, we use the *Consul* discovery service as our key-value store that is hosted in a separate container on an *admin VM*.

E.g., Fig. 2 shows a sample network topology, and the Ethernet ports and bridges to enact this in VIoLET. Here, the edge devices E1.1, E1.2 form a private network PVT-1 with the fog device F1 as a gateway, and likewise E2.1, E2.2 and F2 form another private network, PVT-2. Each device can have sensors enabled to simulate data streams with different distributions. The bandwidth and latency within these private networks is uniform: 100 Mbps/0.5 ms for PVT-1, and 75 Mbps/1 ms for PVT-2. F1 and F2 fog devices go on to form a public network PUB-1 along with the cloud device, C1, with 40 Mbps/100 ms. Similarly, the two cloud devices form another public network PUB-2, with 100 Mbps/100 ms. All these devices are on a single VM, and the public devices are also connected to the `docker-0` bridge for that VM. While the edge devices are connected to a single overlay network, the fog and cloud devices can be connected to multiple overlay networks, based on bandwidth and latency requirements.

As can be seen, configuring the required network topology is complex and time consuming – if done manually for each IoT deployment. Having a sim-

---

[5] Traffic Control in Linux, tldp.org/HOWTO/Traffic-Control-HOWTO.

[6] Multi-host networking with standalone swarms, docs.docker.com/network/over lay-standalone.swarm.

ple declarative document that captures the common network patterns in IoT deployments helps automate this.

3.3 Sensors and Virtual Observation Streams

Edge devices are frequently used to acquire IoT sensor data over hardware interfaces like serial, UART or I2C, and then make them available for applications to process and/or transfer. Experiments and validation of IoT deployments require access to such large-scale sensor data. To enable this, we allow users to define virtual sensors that are collocated with devices. These virtual sensors simulate the generation of sensed events and make them available at a local network port, which acts as a proxy for a hardware interface to the sensor. Applications can connect to this port, read observations and process them as required.

We support various configuration parameters for these sensors. The values for the sensor measurements themselves may be provided either as a text file with real data collected from the field, or as the properties of a statistical distribution, such as uniform random, Gaussian, and Poisson from which we sample and return synthetic values. In addition, the rate at which these values change or the events are generated is also specified by the user. Here too we can specify real relative timestamp or a distribution.

We implement each sensor as a Python script that is launched as part of the container startup. The script starts a *Flask* application server that listens on a local port. It takes the sensor's parameters, and internally starts generating observations corresponding to that. When a client connects to this port and requests a measurement, the service returns the *current* reading. For simplicity, this is reported as a CSV string consisting of a user-defined logical sensor ID, the observation timestamp and a sensed value, but can be easily modified.

3.4 Resource Mapping and Deployment

The *admin VM* runs a service that receives the user's deployment document as a REST request and enacts the deployment on cloud VMs in that data center. The default resource hosts are Amazon EC2 VMs but this can easily be extended to resources on other cloud providers or even a private cluster. All AWS EC2 VM instances belong to a same Virtual Private Cloud (VPC) and the same subnet. On receipt of the deployment request, VIoLET builds a graph of the network topology that is used to deploy the devices onto host resources. Here, the vertices of the graph are the devices and are labeled with the device's CPU requirement, given in the CPU benchmark metrics, e.g., iterations/sec for *CoreMark*, and MWIPS for *Whetstone*. An edge exists if a source device can connect to a sink device, and this is labeled by the bandwidth and latency for that network link. E.g., a private network where all devices can see each other will form a clique.

We then make a gross estimate of the number of underlying resources we require. This is done by adding the vertex weights, dividing by the benchmark metric for the host (cloud VM) and rounding it up. This is the least number of identical host resources, say n, needed to meet the compute needs of all devices.

Table 1. Device perf., device counts and host VM counts used in deployments

Deployment→			D105		D408	
Device	Cores	CMark	Count	$\sum$CMark (k)	Count	$\sum$CMark (k)
Pi 2B	4	8,910	50	445	200	1,782
Pi 3B	4	13,717	50	685	200	2,743
NVidia TX1	4	26,371	4	105	7	184
Softiron	8	76,223	1	76	1	76
Total				1,311		4,786
m4.10XL *(host)*	40	371,384	4	1,485	13	4,827

Then, we partition the graph across these n hosts using `gpmetis` such that the vertex weights are balanced across hosts and the sum of edge cuts between hosts, based on device bandwidths, is minimized. This tries to collocate devices with high bandwidth inter-connects on the same host. We then check if the sum of the bandwidth edge cuts between devices in each pair of hosts is less than the available bandwidth capacity between them, and if the sum of benchmark metrics of all devices in a host is smaller than its capacity. If not, we increment n by 1 and repeat the partitioning, and so on.

This greedy approach provides the least number of host resources and the mapping that will meet the CPU and bandwidth capacities of the deployment. For now, we do not optimize for memory capacity and latency, but these can be extended based on standard multi-parameter optimization techniques.

4   Evaluation

We evaluate VIoLET for two different IoT deployment configurations: **D105** with 105 edge and fog devices, and **D408** with 408 edge and fog devices. The configuration of each of the devices, their CoreMark CPU performance and the deployment counts are shown in Table 1, along with the number of AWS VMs required to support them. CoreMark v1.0 is run with multi-threading enabled.

We use two generations of *Raspberry Pis* as edge devices – *Pi 2B* with 4 × 900 MHz ARM32 cores and *Pi 3B* with 4×1.2 GHz ARM64 cores, and 1 GB RAM each. In addition, we have two fog resources – a *Softiron 3000 (SI)* with AMD A1100 CPU with 8 × 2 GHz ARM64 cores and 16 GB RAM, and an *NVidia TX1* device with 4 × 1.7 GHz ARM64 cores and 4 GB RAM (its GPU is not exposed). We use Amazon AWS *m4.10XL* VMs that have 40 × 2.4 *GHz* Intel Xeon E5-2676 cores, 160 GB RAM and 10 Gbps network bandwidth as the host. Each costs US\$2.00/hour in the US-East (Ohio) data center. As we see, the D105 deployment with 424 ARM cores requires 3 of these VMs with 120 Xeon cores, and D408 with 1,636 ARM cores requires 13 of these VMs with 390 Xeon cores. These deployments cost about US\$6/hour and US\$26/hour, respectively – these are cheaper than a single Raspberry Pi device, on an hourly basis.

Table 2. Configuration of private and public networks in D105, and deviation% between observed and expected bandwidth and latency per network.

Network	Expected		Obs. BW Dev.%		Obs. Lat. Dev.%	
	BW (Mbps)	Lat. (ms)	Median	Mean	Median	Mean
PVT-1	5	25	11.0	11.0	0.6	0.5
PVT-2	5	75	13.8	13.8	0.0	0.0
PVT-3	25	1	4.8	4.8	15.0	15.5
PVT-4	25	25	4.0	3.7	1.0	1.1
PVT-5	25	50	1.6	1.4	0.0	0.0
PUB-1	25	75	−3.6	−3.6	0.0	0.0
PUB-2	25	75	−3.6	−3.6	0.0	0.0
PUB-3	25	75	−3.6	−3.5	0.0	0.0
PUB-4	25	75	−3.6	−3.6	0.0	0.0

Table 3. Configuration of private and public networks in D408, and deviation% between observed and expected bandwidth and latency per network.

Network	Expected		Obs. BW Dev.%		Obs. Lat. Dev.%	
	BW (Mbps)	Lat. (ms)	Median	Mean	Median	Mean
PVT-1	100	5	−2.6	−2.4	6.0	5.2
PVT-2	75	5	−1.1	−1.3	3.0	4.9
PVT-3	75	25	−4.1	−4.0	0.6	1.0
PVT-4	50	5	0.0	0.1	4.0	4.9
PVT-5	50	25	−1.8	−2.0	0.6	0.8
PVT-6	25	25	−1.8	−2.0	0.6	0.8
PVT-7	25	5	2.8	3.2	0.6	0.8
PVT-8	25	50	4.8	5.0	0.6	0.8
PUB-1	25	75	−3.6	−3.6	0.0	0.0
PUB-2	25	100	−7.0	−7.0	0.0	0.0

4.1   Results for D105 and D408

The network topology for these two deployments is generated synthetically. D105 is defined with 5 private networks and 4 public networks, while D408 has 8 private networks and 2 public networks. A fog device serves as the gateway in each private network, and we randomly place an equal number of edge devices in each private network. Their respective network configurations are given in Tables 2 and 3. Each network has a fixed bandwidth and latency configuration, and this ranges from 5–100 Mbps bandwidth, and 1–100 ms latency, as specified. All devices in the public networks can see each other. Edge devices in the private network can access the public network, routed through their gateway, but devices

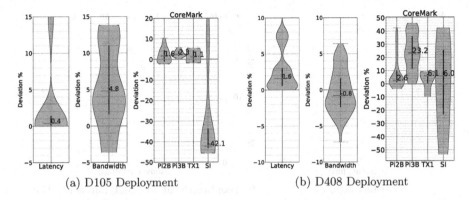

(a) D105 Deployment   (b) D408 Deployment

Fig. 3. Violin plot of *deviation%* for network latency, bandwidth and CoreMark CPU.

in the public network cannot access the devices in the private network. It takes about 8 mins and 24 mins to launch these two topologies on VIoLET.

Once deployed, we run four baseline benchmarks to validate them. The first does `fping` between $2n$ pairs of devices in each private and public network, where n is the number of devices in the network, and measures the observed latency on the defined links. Next, we sample a subset of $\frac{n}{2}$ links in each private and public network and run `iperf` on them to measure the observed bandwidth. Since `iperf` is costlier than `fping`, we limit ourselves to fewer samples. Third, we run `traceroute` to verify if the gateway device configured for each device matches the gateway of the private network, as a sanity check. These network sanity checks take ≈ 3 mins per network for D105, and run in parallel for all networks. Lastly, we run multi-core CoreMark concurrently on all devices.

Figures 3a and b show a violin plot of the *deviation%* of the observed network latency, bandwidth, and CoreMark performance from the expected metrics for the two deployments, where $deviation\% = \frac{(Observed - Expected)}{Expected}\%$. The median value is noted in purple text. We see that the median latency and bandwidth deviation% are within $\pm 5\%$ for both the D105 and D408 deployments, with latency of 0.4% and 1.6%, and bandwidth of 4.8% and -0.8%, respectively. This is within the margin of error for even real-world networks. The entire distribution in all these cases does not vary by more than 15%, showing a relatively tight grouping given the number of devices and VMs. We analyze these further for diverse network configurations in the next section.

We run the CoreMark CPU benchmark on all the devices concurrently and report the violin plot for the deviation% for each of the 4 device types. The median CoreMark value for each device is included in the violin, except for the SI fog where we report values from all the trials since there is just one such device in each deployment. We see that for the two Pis and TX1 – the three slowest devices – the median CoreMark deviation% is within $\pm 2.5\%$ for D105, and the most deviation is +10% for Pi2B. These indicate that the observed performance is marginally higher than expected, and there is little negative

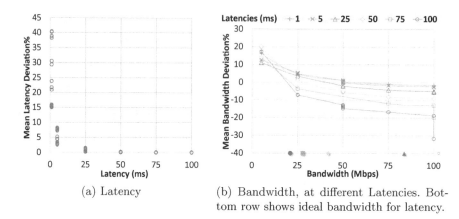

(a) Latency

(b) Bandwidth, at different Latencies. Bottom row shows ideal bandwidth for latency.

Fig. 4. Variation of *deviation%* for different latency and bandwidth configurations.

deviation for these three devices. However, we see that the single SI fog device, which is the largest device, has a median deviation% of -42.1% from 40 trials of CoreMark that were run on it. The distribution is also wide, ranging from -45% to $+21\%$. This indicates that the concurrent multi-threaded CoreMark runs on 10's of containers on the same VM is causing the largest device container to have variable performance. In fact, the sum of the observed CoreMarks for all the deployed devices in D105 is $1,319k$, which is close to the sum of the expected CoreMark from the devices of $1,311k$. So the small over-performance of many small devices is causing the under-performance of the large device. D408 shows a different behavior, with Pi3B showing higher positive deviations, with a median of 23.2%, while the other devices show a smaller positive deviation of $2.6\text{–}6\%$. SI however does show a wider distribution of the deviation% as before.

Besides these baseline network and CPU metrics, we also run two types of application workloads. One of them starts either an MQTT publisher or a subscriber on each device, and each connects to an *Eclipse Mosquitto MQTT broker* on its gateway. A publisher samples observations from a local sensor and publishes it to a unique topic at its gateway broker while a subscriber subscribes to it. This tests the network and process behavior for the common pub-sub pattern seen in IoT. While results are not plotted due to lack of space, we observe that the median end-to-end latency for each message is $\approx 50\,\text{ms}$, which loosely corresponds to the two network hops required from the publisher to the broker, and broker to subscriber.

Another workload that we evaluate is with the ECHO dataflow platform for edge and cloud [15]. Here, we incrementally launch 100 Extract-Transform-Load dataflows using the Apache NiFi engine on distributed devices and observe the latency time for deployment and the end to end latency for the dataflows. This is yet another use-case for VIoLET to help evaluate the efficacy of such edge, fog and cloud orchestration platforms and schedulers.

4.2 Analysis of Network Behavior

Being able to accurately model network behavior is essential for IoT VEs. Here, we perform more detailed experiments that evaluate the impact of specific bandwidth and latency values on the deviation%. Specifically, we try out 19 different network configurations of the D105 deployment while varying the pair of bandwidth and latency values on these networks. These together form 143 different networks. In Fig. 4b, we plot the deviation% of the mean bandwidth, as the bandwidth increases for different latency values, while in Fig. 4a, we plot the deviation% of the mean latency, as latency increases.

It is clear from Fig. 4a that the latency deviation is sensitive to the absolute latency value. For small latency values of 1 ms, the deviation% ranges between 15–40%, and this drops to 2.6–8% for 5 ms. The deviation% exponentially reduces for latencies higher than that, with latencies over 50 ms having just 0.1% deviation. The latency between VMs is measured at 0.4 ms, while between containers on the same VM is 0.06 ms. Hence, achieving a latency better these is not possible, and the achieved latency depends on the placement of containers on the same or different VMs. Since our network partitioning currently is based on bandwidth and compute capacity, and not latency limits, it is possible that two devices requiring low latency are on different VMs. As a result, the deviation% increases. Here, we see that the latency deviation is independent of the bandwidth of the network link.

We observe that the deviation in bandwidth is a function of both latency and bandwidth. In fact, it is also a function of the *TCP window size*, which by default is set to $262,144$ bytes in the containers. The *Bandwidth Delay Product (BDP)* is defined as the product of the bandwidth and latency. For efficient use of the network link, the TCP window size should be greater than this BDP, i.e., $Window \geq Bandwidth \times Latency$. In other words, given a fixed latency and TCP window size, the *Peak Bandwidth* $= \frac{Window}{Latency}$.

Figure 4b shows the bandwidth deviation% on the Y axis for different latencies, as the bandwidth increases on the X axis. It also shows the maximum possible bandwidth for a given latency (based on the window size) along the bottom X axis. We observe that for low latencies of 1–25 ms, the bandwidth deviation% is low and falls between −5.1–18% for all bandwidths from 5–100 Mbps. This is because with the default window size, even a latency of 25 ms supports a bandwidth of 83 Mbps, and lower latencies support an even higher peak bandwidth. The positive deviation% is also high for low bandwidth values and lower for high bandwidth values – even small changes in absolute bandwidth causes a larger change in the relative deviation% when the bandwidth is low.

We also see that as the latency increases, the negative deviation% increases as the bandwidth increases. In particular, as we cross the peak bandwidth value on the X axis, the deviation% becomes more negative. E.g., at 75 ms, the peak bandwidth supported is only 28 Mbps, and we see the bandwidth deviation% for this latency worsen from −3.6% to −11.9% when the bandwidth configuration increases from 25 Mbps to 75 Mbps. This is as expected, and indicates that the users of the container need to tune the TCP window size in the container to enforce bandwidths more accurately.

5   Related Work

The growing interest in IoT and edge/fog computing has given rise to several *simulation environments. iFogSim* [11] extends the prior work on CloudSim [5] to simulate the behavior of applications over fog devices, sensors and actuators that are connected by a network topology. Users define the compute, network and energy profiles of fog devices, and the properties and distributions of tuples from sensors. DAG-based applications with tasks consuming compute capacity and bandwidth can be defined by the user, and its execution over the fog network is simulated using an extensible resource manager. The goal is to evaluate different scheduling strategies synthetically. We similarly let devices, network and sensors to be defined, but actually instantiate the first two – only the sensor stream is simulated. This allows users to evaluate real applications and schedulers.

Edgecloudsim [18] offers similar capabilities, but also introduces mobility models for the edge into the mix. They simulate network characteristics like transmission delay for LAN and WAN, and also task failures due to mobility for a single use-case. *IOTSim*, despite its name, simulates the execution of Map Reduce and stream processing tasks on top of a cloud data center, and uses CloudSim as the base simulation engine. While IoT motivates the synthetic application workloads for their big data platform simulation, they do not actually simulate an IoT deployment.

In the commercial space, city-scale simulators for IoT deployments in smart cities are available [14]. These mimic the behavior of not just devices, sensors, actuators and the network, but also application services like MQTT broker and CoAP services that may be hosted. These offer a comprehensive simulation environment for city-planners to perform what-if analysis on the models. We go a step further and allow realistic devices and networks to be virtualized on elastic cloud VMs, and applications themselves to be executed, without physically deploying the field devices. Simulators are popular in other domains as well, such as cloud, network and SDN simulators [5, 12, 13].

There have been container-based solutions that are closer to our approach, and allow large-scale customized environments to be launched and applications to be run on them. Ceesay et al. [6], deploy container-based environments for Big Data platforms and workloads to test different benchmarks, ease deployment and reduce reporting costs. Others have also used such container-based approaches to inject faults into the containers, and evaluate the behavior of platforms and applications running on them [7].

Other have proposed IoT data stream and application workloads for evaluating big data platforms, particularly stream processing ones. Here, the sensor data is simulated at large-scales while maintaining realistic distributions [1,10]. These can be used in place of the synthetic sensor streams that we provide. Our prior work has proposed stream and stream processing application workloads for IoT domains [17]. These can potentially use VIoLET for evaluating execution on edge and fog, besides just cloud resources.

Google's Kubernetes [4] is a multi-node orchestration platform for container life-cycle management. It schedules containers across nodes to balance the load, but is not aware of network topologies that are overlaid on the containers. VIo-LET uses a simple graph-partitioning approach for placement of containers on VMs to balance the CPU capacity, as measure by CoreMark, and ensure that the required device bandwidths stay within bandwidth available between the hosts.

6   Conclusions and Future Work

In this paper, we have proposed the design requirements for a Virtual IoT Environment, and presented VIoLET to meet these needs. VIoLET allows users to declaratively create virtual edge, fog and cloud devices as containers that are connected through user-defined network topologies, and can run real IoT platforms and applications. This offers first-hand knowledge of the performance, scalability and metrics for the user's applications or scheduling algorithms, similar to a real IoT deployment, and at large-scales. It is as simple to deploy and run as a simulation environment, balancing ease and flexibility, with realism and reproducibility on-demand. It is also affordable, costing just US$26/hour to simulate over 400 devices on Amazon AWS Cloud. VIoLET serves as an essential tool for IoT researchers to validate their outcomes, and for IoT managers to virtually test various software stacks and network deployment models.

There are several extensions possible to this initial version of VIoLET. One of our limitations is that only devices for which container environments can be launched by Docker are feasible. While any device container that runs a standard Linux kernel using cgroups (or even a Windows device[7]) can be run, this limits the use of edge micro-controllers like Arduino, or wireless IoT motes that run real-time OS. Also, leveraging Docker's support for GPUs in future will help users make use of accelerators present in devices like NVidia TX1[8]. There is also the opportunity to pack containers more efficiently to reduce the cloud costs [2], including over-packing when devices will not be pushed to their full utilization.

Our network configurations focus on the visibility of public and private networks, and the bandwidth and latency of the links. However, it does not yet handle more fine-grained transport characteristics such as collision and packet loss that are present in wireless networks. Introducing variability in bandwidth, latency, link failures, and even CPU dynamism is part of future work. More rigorous evaluation using city-scale models and IoT applications are also planned using large private clusters to evaluate VIoLET's weak scaling.

Acknowledgments. This work is supported by research grants from VMWare, MHRD, IUSSTF and Cargill, and by cloud credits from Amazon AWS and Microsoft Azure. We also thank other DREAM:Lab members, Aakash Khochare and Abhilash Sharma, for design discussions and assistance with experiments. We also thank the reviewers of Euro-Par for their detailed comments that has helped us improve the quality of this paper.

---

[7] Docker for Windows, https://docs.docker.com/docker-for-windows/.

[8] GPU-enabled Docker Containers, https://github.com/NVIDIA/nvidia-docker.

References

1. Arlitt, M., Marwah, M., Bellala, G., Shah, A., Healey, J., Vandiver, B.: IoTAbench: an internet of things analytics benchmark. In: International Conference on Performance Engineering (ICPE) (2015)
2. Awada, U., Barker, A.: Improving resource efficiency of container-instance clusters on clouds. In: Cluster, Cloud and Grid Computing (CCGRID) (2017)
3. Bonomi, F., Milito, R., Zhu, J., Addepalli, S.: Fog computing and its role in the internet of things. In: ACM Workshop on Mobile Cloud Computing (MCC) (2012)
4. Burns, B., Grant, B., Oppenheimer, D., Brewer, E., Wilkes, J.: Borg, omega, and kubernetes. ACM Queue **14**(1), 10 (2016)
5. Calheiros, R.N., Ranjan, R., Beloglazov, A., De Rose, C.A.F., Buyya, R.: CloudSim: a toolkit for modeling and simulation of cloud computing environments and evaluation of resource provisioning algorithms. Softw.: Pract. Exp. (SPE) **41**(1), 23–50 (2011)
6. Ceesay, S., Barker, D., Varghese, D., et al.: Plug and play bench: simplifying big data benchmarking using containers. In: IEEE International Conference on Big Data (BigData) (2017)
7. Dabrowa, J.: Distributed system fault injection testing with Docker. In: JDD (2016)
8. Dastjerdi, A.V., Gupta, H., Calheiros, R.N., Ghosh, S.K., Buyya, R.: Internet of things: principles and paradigms. In: Fog Computing Principles, Architectures, and Applications. Morgan Kaufmann (2016)
9. Ghosh, R., Simmhan, Y.: Distributed scheduling of event analytics across edge and cloud. ACM Trans. Cyber Phys. Syst. (TCPS) (2018, to Appear)
10. Gu, L., Zhou, M., Zhang, Z., Shan, M.C., Zhou, A., Winslett, M.: Chronos: an elastic parallel framework for stream benchmark generation and simulation. In: IEEE International Conference on Data Engineering (ICDE) (2015)
11. Gupta, H., Vahid Dastjerdi, A., Ghosh, S.K., Buyya, R.: iFogSim: a toolkit for modeling and simulation of resource management techniques in the internet of things, edge and fog computing environments. Softw.: Pract. Exp. **47**(9), 1275–1296 (2017)
12. Henderson, T.R., Roy, S., Floyd, S., Riley, G.F.: Ns-3 project goals. In: Workshop on Ns-2: The IP Network Simulator (2006)
13. Lantz, B., Heller, B., McKeown, N.: A network in a laptop: rapid prototyping for software-defined networks. In: Workshop on Hot Topics in Networks (2010)
14. Leland, J.: Deploy scalable smart city architectures confidently with network simulation. Technical report, insight tech (2017)
15. Ravindra, P., Khochare, A., Reddy, S.P., Sharma, S., Varshney, P., Simmhan, Y.: Echo: an adaptive orchestration platform for hybrid dataflows across cloud and edge. In: International Conference on Service-Oriented Computing (ICSOC) (2017)
16. Satyanarayanan, M., et al.: Edge analytics in the internet of things. IEEE Pervasive Comput. **14**(2), 24–31 (2015)
17. Shukla, A., Chaturvedi, S., Simmhan, Y.: RIoTBench: a real-time IoT benchmark for distributed stream processing platforms. Concurr. Comput.: Pract. Exp. **29**(21), 1–22 (2017)
18. Sonmez, C., Ozgovde, A., Ersoy, C.: EdgeCloudSim: an environment for performance evaluation of edge computing systems. In: Fog and Mobile Edge Computing (FMEC) (2017)
19. Varshney, P., Simmhan, Y.: Demystifying fog computing: characterizing architectures, applications and abstractions. In: IEEE International Conference on Fog and Edge Computing (ICFEC) (2017)

Adaptive Bandwidth-Efficient Recovery Techniques in Erasure-Coded Cloud Storage

Rekha Nachiappan$^{(\boxtimes)}$, Bahman Javadi, Rodrigo N. Calheiros, and Kenan M. Matawie

School of Computing, Engineering and Mathematics, Western Sydney University, Sydney, Australia
{30045376,B.Javadi,R.Calheiros,K.Matawie}@westernsydney.edu.au

Abstract. In order to handle the dramatic growth of digital data, cloud storage systems demand novel techniques to improve data reliability. Replication and erasure codes are the most important data reliability techniques employed in cloud storage systems, but individually they have their own challenges. In this paper, we propose a hybrid technique employing proactive replication of data blocks in erasure-coded storage systems. The technique employs a set of erasure coding-agnostic bandwidth-efficient data recovery techniques that reduce the bandwidth used for recovery without compromising data reliability. Experiments show that our approach improves repair bandwidth efficiency and reduces network traffic in cloud storage systems with limited storage overhead compared to available recovery approaches.

1 Introduction

A recent trend in cloud storage systems is the adoption of erasure codes, as it provides excellent reliability with less storage overhead than replication [1]. For example, Facebook and Microsoft Azure replaced replication with erasure coding in parts of their data, resulting in significant cost savings in terms of storage overhead [2]. However, failure rates in large-scale cloud storage systems are high as such systems are composed of large number of hardware and software components. Repairing a single data block stored using Reed-Solomon(n,k) code requires k data blocks to be transferred over the network, while repairing a single data block in replication involves the transfer of one data block [3]. Hence, repair network traffic is increased by k times in Reed-Solomon(n,k) code compared to replication. The network traffic incurred by such data movement has also the extra drawback of increasing energy consumption significantly, resulting in extra costs for cloud service providers. Moreover, growing network traffic is regulated by network throttling, which affects read performance. All the above facts prevent cloud storage systems to adopt erasure codes in large scale.

Hardware failures (disk failures, machine failures, and latent sector errors) and temporary machine failures are the most common failures that affect durability and availability of data in cloud storage [2]. In order to avoid permanent

© Springer International Publishing AG, part of Springer Nature 2018
M. Aldinucci et al. (Eds.): Euro-Par 2018, LNCS 11014, pp. 325–338, 2018.
https://doi.org/10.1007/978-3-319-96983-1_23

data loss due to hardware failures, contents in failed nodes or disks have to be restored in another hardware devices, a process that is known as *data recovery*. Data stored in a machine that experiences temporary outage will cause temporary data loss. Temporary data loss in erasure code is handled by degraded read, i.e., data blocks in the failed node are reconstructed and served using the next available k blocks. In order to avoid unnecessary repairs of short term transient node failures, data recovery is delayed for a certain amount of time. Google File System (GFS) delays recovery of unavailable nodes for 15 min. However, this affects availability and degrades read performance [5]. In contrast, when replication is used, degraded read is handled by simply redirecting the request to the next available replica.

As both replication and erasure coding has its own advantages, cloud storage systems require hybrid approaches in order to leverage the advantages of both methods, which are the recovery performance of replication and the storage efficiency of erasure coding. In this paper, we propose several novel recovery techniques. These techniques follow a proactive replication method. They replicates erasure-coded data blocks which are predicted to fail, keeping down repair network bandwidth/traffic at the same time without much overhead. We also showed that the ProDisk method proposed by Li et al. [13], reduces repair network bandwidth/traffic. All the aforementioned methods use machine and disk failure prediction techniques to predict hardware failures and long-time temporary machine outage. When hardware failures (permanent machine/disk failures) are predicted, proposed storage system immediately starts the recovery of data and proactively replicates erasure-coded data fragments in to permanent storage. When long-term machine failures are predicted, proposed storage system starts proactive recovery with the goal of maintaining data availability. During proactive recovery of long-term machine failures, data is written into dedicated temporary storage rather than on recovered blocks.

The amount of dedicated temporary storage required in the proposed approach is linearly related to the number of long term machine failures predicted over the time period. In order to address this issue, we introduce a novel method to proactively replicate hot data in temporary storage and apply lazy recovery for cold data. This reduces the recovery bandwidth/traffic significantly without increasing the temporary storage needed for supporting transient node failures.

2 Background and Motivation

In a distributed storage system, a data file is dispersed into multitude of interconnected nodes, which serves any end user request by tapping data from multiple nodes. Improving the resilience of distributed storage system with limited storage overhead is desirable. Replication is the simplest mean of increasing resiliency of the distributed storage. In replication, a data file is divided into multiple data blocks which are replicated into several locations such that failure of any data block in one location enables the user to access it from different location. However, reliability is directly proportional to storage overhead in replication.

Erasure coding is an important option to increase reliability with less storage overhead. In erasure coding, data file is divided in to k data blocks and dispersed into n locations while adding n-k parity blocks. Upon any failure, a data block is reconstructed by downloading any k available data blocks. The data recovery in erasure coding increases recovery network bandwidth k times, compared to replication.

Facebook employed Reed-Solomon to only 8% of data in 3000 node production cluster and it has been estimated that if 50% of data were replaced with Reed-Solomon, repair network traffic would saturate their network links [4]. Increased repair network traffic is one of the major bottleneck to erasure coding becoming more pervasive in cloud storage systems. Novel blockchain-based cloud storage systems like Sia[1] and Storj[2] use consumer storage to serve their customer's storage needs. They suggest, as a means to improve reliability, the use of Reed-Solomon (60, 40) code. This means that, to reconstruct any missing data, 40 surviving data fragments have to be transferred to reconstruct any single failed data fragment. These novel storage systems demand more bandwidth-efficient recovery, which is the focus of this paper. The proactive recovery techniques proposed in this paper use several failure prediction methods. As these systems are running on end-users client, it may not be possible to apply existing hardware failures prediction techniques on the users computers. However, it is possible to predict the availability of user computers using availability logs. Hence it is possible to apply the proposed methods in blockchain-based cloud storage systems.

The main contribution of this paper is the definition of bandwidth-efficient recovery techniques based on client's needs without significant increase of permanent storage.

3 Related Work

A substantial amount of research concentrated on reducing repair bandwidth of erasure codes. Dimakis et al. [6] presented a theoretical framework for regeneration codes that can optimize recovery bandwidth for a given storage. However, exact repair of regeneration codes, matching information theoretic bound, remained unresolved. Following this, several works [2] showed that exact repair is possible for some parameters. Sathiamoorthy et al. [4], proposed Xorbas which reduces network traffic by half compared to Reed-Solomon codes with 14% additional storage overhead [4]. LRC in Windows Azure storage reduces repair network bandwidth significantly with the help of local parities, which have the side effect of increasing storage overhead by 1.33x compared to Reed-Solomon [1]. Hitchhiker code, built on top of Reed-Solomon code using "piggybacking" framework, reduces network traffic by 35% with some encoding time overhead incurred [7].

---

[1] https://sia.tech/.

[2] https://storj.io/.

Failure predictions in cloud storage systems offer cloud service providers an efficient proactive failure management in cloud storage. Various statistical and machine learning methods are used to predict failures in cloud storage systems. A few methods [8,9] are used to predict hard drive failures based on SMART attributes. Li et al. [9], achieved 95% predictions with False Alarm rate less than 0.1%. Many researches focused on predicting failures in distributed systems based on system logs. Javadi et al. [10], presented failure model as a predictive method of distributed systems availability and unavailability. Agrawal et al. [11], uses log messages to predict failures in Hadoop clusters.

Silberstein et al. [12], proposed lazy recovery to reduce recovery bandwidth in distributed storage by reducing the recovery rate. It reduces recovery bandwidth up to 76% compared to Reed-Solomon. However, applying this method on cloud storage affects read performance and data durability. Li et al. [13], used failure prediction techniques to implement proactive replication in erasure codes for reducing degraded read latency and improving read performance. Li et al. [14], defined a cost effective data reliability management mechanism to ensure reliability of massive data with minimum replication based on a generalized data reliability model. Wu et al. [15,16], used prediction tools to identify the upcoming events and proactively migrates the data blocks on the degraded device belonging to the hot data zones in the large-scale data centers.

4   The Proposed Cloud Storage System

The target system in this paper is an object storage that initially stores data with any appropriate erasure code to reduce storage overhead while maintaining reliability. Consider a distributed cloud storage system composed of a number of disks accommodated in a machine, group of machines in a rack, and several racks in a distributed storage. Data blocks stored in a disk can be determined as an *at-risk block* based on the machine and disks health status where it is stored. Machine and disk failure prediction algorithms run individually to predict disk/machine failure and machine unavailability. Since rack failures are transitory, the health of data blocks is determined with machine and disks health status. Data blocks that are marked as at-risk in this system are proactively replicated before the occurrence of failure based on the client's Service Level Agreement (SLA). Proactive replication reduces the number of blocks required for reconstructions in erasure coded cloud storage system. Hence, the system reduces network traffic with less storage overhead. This system utilizes various recovery schemes to reduce reconstruction bandwidth in erasure coded cloud storage systems.

4.1   Architecture and Design

An overview of the system architecture is depicted in Fig. 1. It is implemented as an extension of a regular object storage. Object storage manages data as objects where each object has both data and metadata. A dedicated proxy server

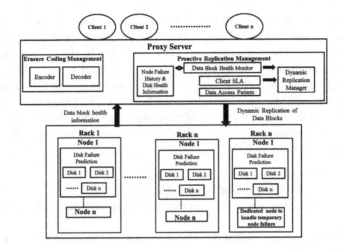

Fig. 1. Architecture of the proposed recovery techniques.

extends the support of encoding and decoding erasure codes. It also handles failures in storage systems. The object server stores and retrieves object data. Object server's availability status and disks health status are reported to the proxy server, which is responsible for increasing or decreasing the data object's replication factor. The system adjusts the replication factor of erasure coded objects when failures are predicted. The components of the architecture are discussed as follows.

Disk Failure Prediction. This module monitors the health status of individual disks and reports prediction results to the Node Failure History & Disk Health Information module in the proxy server. SMART is implemented on disks and it monitors, compares disk attributes and issues warnings. This SMART attributes are used to predict disk health status using various statistical and machine learning techniques [8,9]. Disk failures are calculated using classification and regression trees methods here [9].

Proactive Replication Management. Redundancy of data blocks are adjusted according to node/disk health status and client SLA.

Node Failure History and Disk Health Information. This module collects the information of disk health status and node failure history. Various statistical and machine learning techniques can be used to predict node's Mean Time To Failure (MTTF) and Mean Time To Repair (MTTR). Based on node's predicted MTTF and MTTR, node failures are classified as permanent, long time, or short time failures. Node's MTTF and MTTR are calculated using various statistics of availability and unavailability [10].

Data Block Health Monitor and Client SLA. Failure predicted nodes and disks information are collected from Node Failure History and Disk Health Information module. It identifies the disks that are predicted to fail in the underlying storage system. It also identifies permanent, long term, and short term machine failures by predicting machines MTTF and MTTR. Permanent machine failures are handled as disk failures. This module sends failure information to the Dynamic Replication module, which takes an action when necessary. Clients can request various recovery schemes based on their needs. The client can define several reconstruction requests as follows,

- High durability, normal availability (ProDisk).
- High durability, high availability (ProMachine).
- High durability, high availability for hot and normal availability for cold data (ProHot).
- High durability, high availability for hot and low availability for cold data (ProHot_LazyCold).

Based on the client SLA, the variable for different recovery scheme will be set.

Data Access Pattern. Data access patterns in a distributed storage can be used to identify the popularity of data blocks in real-time over a certain period of time. Based on their popularity, data blocks can be classified as hot, warm, or cold. As the access pattern changes, popularity of data blocks need to be updated. Various researches used popularity-based classification to improve durability, availability, and read performance of cloud storage systems [17]. Our approach combines both failure prediction and data access patterns to make the decisions. Data access pattern is used here to define hot data. We assume that data blocks with high access frequency have more chance to be accessed in the future and those are defined as hot. This module uses data access pattern to classified a block as hot data block and recorded as $H = \{b_1, b_2, ...\}$ where the block b_i is identified as hot.

Dynamic Replication Manager. This module collects information from Data Block Health Monitor, Client SLA, and Data Access Pattern module and activates various proposed recovery schemes, as follows:

- **ProDisk:** When disk failures/permanent machine failures are predicted, all the data blocks in the failure predicted disks (all disks in failure predicted machine) are proactively replicated permanently as described in [13]. In the occurrence of failure, the reference is made to the proactively replicated data instead of the typical reconstruction of erasure codes. This was originally proposed by Li et al. [13] but the early approach only considered the recovery performance not recovery bandwidth. The following ProMachine, ProHot, ProHot_LazyCold are the novel methods proposed in this research which are the main contribution of this paper.
- **ProMachine:** When temporary long term machine failures are predicted with MTTR greater than 15 min, data in failure predicted machines are

proactively replicated to a dedicated node allocated specifically to handle temporary machine failure. In case of any failure, data is accessed from the dedicated node.

- **ProHot:** When temporary long term machine failures are predicted with MTTR greater than 15 min, data identified as hot in failure predicted machine will be proactively replicated to the dedicated node which has been allocated to handle temporary machine failure. In case of any failure, hot data is accessed from the dedicated node and typical reconstruction is applied to recover cold data.

- **ProHot_LazyCold:** When temporary long term machine failures are predicted with MTTR greater then 15 min, data identified as hot in failure predicted machine is proactively replicated to a dedicated node that is allocated specifically to handle temporary machine failure. In case of any failure, hot data is accessed from the dedicated node and lazy recovery [12] is applied for cold data recovery.

This module is responsible for scaling up and down the number of dedicated temporary storage nodes, according to the failure predictions and amount of data need to be stored in temporary storage during a period of time. It is also responsible for allocating highly available node as a temporary storage such that any failure in this temporary storage node is minimal. Any failure prediction in this temporary storage will also lead to proactive replication. Any failure prediction in this temporary storage will also lead to proactive replication.

4.2   Recovery Approach

In our target scenario, a cloud storage system initially stores data with any (n,k) erasure code. With the help of disk/machine failure prediction methods employed in cloud storage systems, failure types and MTTR of node failures are predicted. Failures are also identified as disk, permanent machine, temporary long term machine (MTTR > 15 min), or temporary short term machine (MTTR < 15 min) failures. The set of data blocks $(b_1, b_2, ..., b_i)$ that is more likely to be accessed soon is defined as the hot data set H. Based on the failure types, hot data blocks, and client SLAs, one of the proposed recovery techniques ProDisk, ProMachine, ProHot, ProHot_LazyCold will be chosen.

When the disk/permanent machine failures are predicted (proDisk), all the data blocks in the failure predicted disk (all data blocks of each disk in a failure predicted machine) are proactively replicated into the permanent storage as described in Procode [13]. The counter variables of corresponding replicated data blocks are incremented. These counter variables are used to identify if the particular data blocks are replicated already or to delete data blocks against noisy prediction. A delay is applied while deleting data blocks against noisy prediction. Time In Advance (TIA) which is provided by failure prediction algorithm is used as a time delay to delete the data blocks that are replicated due to noisy prediction. Time delay larger than TIA is the better choice. However, this will result in extra storage. The choice of time delay varies and depends on the storage system where the system is utilized.

While temporary machine failures are predicted, proactive recovery is activated for either all (ProMachine) or some of the data blocks (ProHot, ProHot_LazyCold) in a failure predicated machine. Data are replicated into the dedicated temporary storage. The data blocks that are not replicated are recovered by typical reconstruction of erasure codes. While data blocks are proactively replicated into temporary storage, the corresponding data blocks counter variables are incremented. These variables are used to identify if the particular data blocks are replicated already or to delete blocks when the machine recovers from temporary machine failures. The dynamic replication module also provisions and adjusts the number of temporary dedicated nodes, based on long term temporary machine failure rate and client SLAs. When the failure predicted nodes recover from actual failure and if no further failures are predicted for the same nodes, the proactively replicated data blocks corresponds to those nodes are deleted. Also, any data fragments which have more than one copy in the system are also deleted periodically. In the occurrence of node/disk failure, the reference is made to proactively replicated blocks which reduces number of data reconstructions in erasure coded storage systems.

5   Performance Analysis

Since all the methods proposed in this paper use a combination of proactive and lazy recovery methods, we will carry out the performance analysis on those methods.

5.1   Bandwidth Analysis

The bandwidth required to reconstruct any missing data is directly proportional to the number of transfers required, which is k in (n,k) erasure coded storage system. The amount of data transfer required to recover any missing block is

$$TransferRequired = S * (k + NumberOfMissingBlocks - 1) \qquad (1)$$

where S is the chunk size and k is number of fragments needed to reconstruct data. k is 1 for replication. The recovery bandwidth is calculated as

$$RecoveryBandwidth = TransferRequired/RecoveryTime \qquad (2)$$

Equation 2 shows that the RecoveryBandwidth is directly proportional to TransferRequired. Let us consider (14, 10) Reed-Solomon code with the chunk size of 250 MB. From Eq. 1, TransferRequired can be calculated as 2500 MB for recovering a single missing data block. However, it is 250 MB if the data block is proactively replicated. From this, we can conclude that proactive replication reduces the recovery bandwidth significantly. Lazy recovery delays the recovery of the data fragments until certain amount of data fragments are unavailable.

In this paper, we use lazy recovery only for handling long term temporary machine failures such that it does not impact durability of data. Since all the predicted disk failures are proactively replicated, it does not affect durability. Furthermore, lazy recovery is activated based on client SLA. If the client needs good read performance only for data identified as hot, it activates lazy recovery only for cold data. It also activates proactive recovery for hot data.

5.2   Storage Overhead Analysis

Erasure coding offers excellent storage efficiency compared to replication. Proportional increase in storage of various reliability methods is defined as:

$$(systematicdata + originaldata)/systematicdata \qquad (3)$$

The method proposed in this paper proactively replicates data into a new hardware device when permanent node/disk failures are predicted. Once the failure predicted device fails, reference will be made to the proactively replicated device. Eventually, there will be wrong predictions about devices failing. When this occurs, it is expected that the storage overhead will suffer a slightly increase. False positive for disk failures are calculated as less than 0.1% using classification and regression trees [9]. Hence, the storage overhead will not be significantly increased by wrong predictions. Temporary nodes are dedicated to handle long term node failures. However, data in those temporary nodes are periodically evicted. Hence, temporary node failures will not increase storage overhead permanently.

6   Performance Evaluation

We use ds-sim simulator [12] to compare recovery bandwidth from replication and erasure coding to the various bandwidth efficient recovery technique proposed in this paper. We have simulated 3-tier storage components including disks, machines, and racks. We have modified ds-sim to add failure predictions, proactive replication, and hot data prediction. As output, ds-sim calculates repair bandwidth and number of degraded strips. The simulator models distributed storage systems of 3 Petabyte of storage for 10 years. Simulation parameters are 11 machines/rack, 20 disks/machine with each disk capacity of 750 GB and maximum recovery bandwidth capacity of 650 TB/day. Also 40% of random data blocks were considered as hot to evaluate ProHot and Pro-Hot_LazyCold recovery methods. For each result we run the simulation with number of iterations and calculated the result with 95% confidence interval.

6.1   Results and Discussions

In this section, we compare the bandwidth and reliability of replication, Reed-Solomon (14,10) and various recovery techniques proposed in this paper.

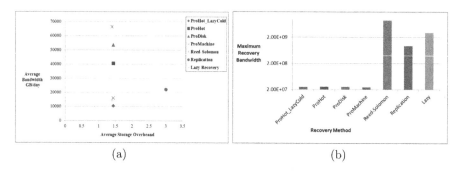

Fig. 2. (a) Average recovery bandwidth in GB per day and (b) Maximum instantaneous recovery bandwidth, in MB/hr, calculated over 10 years.

Recovery Bandwidth. We run simulations with the above configuration parameters with failure prediction rate 90%, false positive 0.1%, and time in advance 24 h which found reasonable in [9,11]. Recovery bandwidth is calculated for each failure event except for machine failures lasting less than 15 min. Figure 2 shows the comparison of average recovery bandwidth in GB/day versus storage overhead for replication, Reed-Solomon(14,10), Lazy [12], and the various recovery techniques proposed in this paper. The proposed recovery techniques are also applied on Reed-Solomon (14,10) erasure code in this comparison.

Replication reduces recovery bandwidth in up to 66% compared to Reed-Solomon (14,10). ProDisk reduces average repair bandwidth up to 19% compared to Reed-Solomon (14,10). ProHot reduces recovery bandwidth up to 38% whereas ProMachine reduces recovery bandwidth by 75% compared to the same approach. ProMachine and ProHot_LazyCold outperform replication.This is because in replication, data blocks are distributed among large number of hardware devices. Hence it experiences a large number of recovery events that increases recovery bandwidth. ProHot_LazyCold outperform lazy recovery. This is because the failure predicted hot data blocks are replicated proactively and it reduces number of lazy recoveries. However, ProMachine technique increases the temporary storage proportionally to the temporary long term machine failure rate.

Figure 2(b) shows the maximum instantaneous recovery bandwidth, in MB/hr (network traffic) in distributed storage systems over the simulation period. The simulation calculates network traffic as follows. Upon each recovery event, instantaneous total recovery bandwidth, in MB/hr is calculated and compared with the previous maximum recovery bandwidth. If the new recovery bandwidth is larger than maximum recovery bandwidth, the new recovery bandwidth becomes the maximum recovery bandwidth. The network traffic in (14,10) Reed-Solomon code is approximately 10 times higher than replication.

ProDisk, ProMachine, ProHot and ProHot_LazyCold reduces network traffic better than replication and lazy recovery. This is due to proactive replication in erasure coding, which reduces amount of data to be transferred while keeping number of recoveries less than replication.

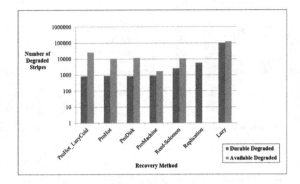

Fig. 3. Number of durable degraded and available degraded slices over 10 years.

Reliability. To evaluate reliability of different approaches, we use the number of durable degraded slices and available degraded slices to compare durability and availability over the mission time. In a distributed storage systems, disks are partitioned into units called strip. Set of corresponding strips from n disks that encode and decode together is called stripe [18]. A stripe is termed degraded if one or more systematic blocks is unavailable. The term durable degraded refers the degraded stripe due to permanent failures, whereas available degraded refers to transient failures.

Replication does not increase available degraded slice counts in the system as request to any temporary unavailable slices are redirected to next available replica. Smaller number of durable and available degraded stripes indicates smaller probability of data loss as the system has less number of failure and repair events. Moreover, smaller number of degraded slices reduces the access latency and increases the performance of the application running on it. From Fig. 3 ProHot and ProHot_LazyCold methods do not decrease number of available degraded stripes. However, available degraded slices are increased with respect to cold data. Also, the proposed system predicts and handles disk and node failures separately. ProHot and ProHot_LazyCold methods handle all failure predicted disk failures proactively. Hence, they do not affect durability, contrary to lazy recovery method [12].

Proactively replicated data blocks reduce the number of durable degraded and available degraded slices in cloud storage systems and hence reduce the number of reconstructions. Less reconstructions reduces the number of data loss events in distributed storage. Figure 3 shows that even 90% of disk failure prediction rate do not eliminate degraded slices.

6.2 Sensitivity Analysis

The proposed recovery techniques are influenced by various important factors such as TIA and Failure Detection Rate. In this section, we examine how disk failure prediction rate affects network traffic and how the recovery bandwidth is affected by TIA.

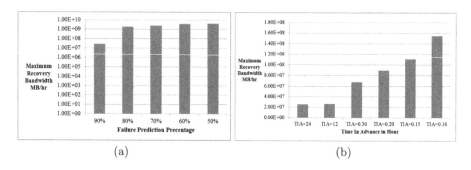

(a)   (b)

Fig. 4. Maximum instantaneous recovery bandwidth, in MB/hr, calculated over 10 years. (a) with varying failure prediction rates (b) for ProDisk with varying TIA.

Disk Failure Prediction Rate. For analyzing how the system is affected by the failure prediction rate, we measured network traffic with varying disk failure prediction rate. Li et al. [9], showed that more than 90% accuracy of disk failure prediction is possible. We run simulation with disk failure prediction accuracy varying from 50% to 90% and calculated recovery network traffic in ProDisk method, as shown in Fig. 4(a).

The proactive recovery in the storage systems will reduce network traffic (max instantaneous recovery bandwidth in MB/hr) associated with data reconstruction. As expected, network traffic decreases as the failure prediction rate increases. Accurate failure predictions proactively handle failures (transfer one data block instead of 10 data blocks in Reed-Solomon) in storage systems and hence reduce the recovery traffic. Moreover, only in the ProDisk the network traffic varies according to the prediction rate. The rest of the methods are accordance with machine failures. It transfers large amount of data while proactive recovery compared to ProDisk. Hence it is not showing much variations in network traffic with respective to prediction rates.

Time in Advance. We examine how the failure prediction's TIA affects recovery network traffic of storage systems. Figure 4(b) shows how the recovery network traffic changes with reduction of TIA of failure prediction in the ProDisk method. This will be similar for the rest of the methods. Since the maximum recovery bandwidth capacity in this experiments is set to 650 TB/day, reducing TIA from 24 h to 12 h does not change average recovery bandwidth drastically. However, reduction in TIA below 30 min increases network traffic in storage systems. Hence TIA will not affect the recovery bandwidth drastically.

Amount of Data Transferred. To evaluate resource savings from proactive replication only for hot data, we calculated the total amount of data transferred to the temporary dedicated storage to handle long term temporary machine failure. The amount of data transferred in ProHot/ProHot_LazyCold are directly proportional to the percentage of data determined as hot. Figure 5 shows that the

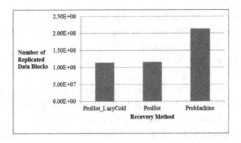

Fig. 5. Total number of proactively replicated slices due to long term temporary machine failures calculated over 10 years.

total amount of data transferred in ProMachine is approximately twice than in ProHot. The methods ProHot and ProHot_LazyCold reduces temporary storage needs.

7   Conclusions and Future Work

The two primary reliability mechanisms employed by cloud storage systems have its own drawbacks. Even though erasure code offers tremendous storage savings compared to replication, reconstructing lost or corrupted data blocks involves large communication overhead.

In this paper, we proposed an approach that applies failure prediction techniques to proactively replicate and handle failures in erasure coded storage systems. We defined various recovery techniques with the combination of replication, erasure codes, and lazy recovery methods in order to reduce network bandwidth/traffic in cloud storage systems. It uses data blocks hot data status and client SLAs to define an appropriate recovery technique in cloud storage systems.

In our future work, we plan to investigate scheduling of proactive replicas in distributed storage such that it reduces degraded read latency in cloud storage. The interactions of foreground running tasks during proposed recovery schemes could also be considered in future. Another interesting and promising area of future research is energy-efficient scheduling of proactive replicas in cloud storage.

References

1. Huang, C., et al.: Erasure coding in windows azure storage. In: Presented as part of the 2012 USENIX Annual Technical Conference (USENIX ATC 12), Boston, USA, pp. 15–26. USENIX, June 2012
2. Nachiappan, R., Javadi, B., Calheiros, R.N., Matawie, K.M.: Cloud storage reliability for big data applications: a state of the art survey. J. Netw. Comput. Appl. **97**, 35–47 (2017)

3. Plank, J.S.: T1: erasure codes for storage applications. In: Proceedings of the 4th USENIX Conference on File and Storage Technologies (FAST), San Francisco, USA, pp. 1–74. USENIX, December 2005

4. Sathiamoorthy, M., et al.: XORing elephants: novel erasure codes for big data. Proc. VLDB Endow. **6**(5), 325–336 (2013)

5. Ford, D., et al.: Availability in globally distributed storage systems. In: Proceedings of the 9th USENIX Symposium on Operating Systems Design and Implementation (OSDI), Vancouver, Canada. USENIX, October 2010

6. Dimakis, A.G., Godfrey, P.B., Wu, Y., Wainwright, M.J., Ramchandran, K.: Network coding for distributed storage systems. IEEE Trans. Inf. Theory **56**(9), 4539–4551 (2010)

7. Rashmi, K., Shah, N.B., Gu, D., Kuang, H., Borthakur, D., Ramchandran, K.: A hitchhiker's guide to fast and efficient data reconstruction in erasure-coded data centers. ACM SIGCOMM Comput. Commun. Rev. **44**(4), 331–342 (2015)

8. Li, J., Stones, R.J., Wang, G., Liu, X., Li, Z., Xu, M.: Hard drive failure prediction using decision trees. Reliab. Eng. Syst. Saf. **164**, 55–65 (2017)

9. Li, J., et al.: Hard drive failure prediction using classification and regression trees. In: Proceedings of the 44th Annual IEEE/IFIP International Conference on Dependable Systems and Networks (DSN), Atlanta, USA, pp. 383–394. IEEE, June 2014

10. Javadi, B., Kondo, D., Iosup, A., Epema, D.: The failure trace archive: enabling the comparison of failure measurements and models of distributed systems. J. Parallel Distrib. Comput. **73**(8), 1208–1223 (2013)

11. Agrawal, B., Wiktorski, T., Rong, C.: Analyzing and predicting failure in hadoop clusters using distributed hidden Markov model. In: Qiang, W., Zheng, X., Hsu, C.-H. (eds.) CloudCom-Asia 2015. LNCS, vol. 9106, pp. 232–246. Springer, Cham (2015). https://doi.org/10.1007/978-3-319-28430-9_18

12. Silberstein, M., Ganesh, L., Wang, Y., Alvisi, L., Dahlin, M.: Lazy means smart: reducing repair bandwidth costs in erasure-coded distributed storage. In: Proceedings of the International Conference on Systems and Storage (SYSTOR), Haifa, Israel, pp. 1–7. ACM, June 2014

13. Li, P., Li, J., Stones, R.J., Wang, G., Li, Z., Liu, X.: Procode: a proactive erasure coding scheme for cloud storage systems. In: Proceedings of the 2016 IEEE 35th Symposium on Reliable Distributed Systems (SRDS), Budapest, Hungary, pp. 219–228. IEEE, September 2016

14. Li, W., Yang, Y., Yuan, D.: Ensuring cloud data reliability with minimum replication by proactive replica checking. IEEE Trans. Comput. **65**(5), 1494–1506 (2016)

15. Wu, S., Jiang, H., Mao, B.: Proactive data migration for improved storage availability in large-scale data centers. IEEE Trans. Comput. **64**(9), 2637–2651 (2015)

16. Wu, S., Jiang, H., Feng, D., Tian, L., Mao, B.: Improving availability of raid-structured storage systems by workload outsourcing. IEEE Trans. Comput. **60**(1), 64–79 (2011)

17. Liu, J., Shen, H.: A popularity-aware cost-effective replication scheme for high data durability in cloud storage. In: Proceedings of the 2016 IEEE International Conference on Big Data (Big Data), Washington, DC, USA, pp. 384–389. IEEE December 2016

18. Plank, J.S., Luo, J., Schuman, C.D., Xu, L., Wilcox-O'Hearn, Z., et al.: A performance evaluation and examination of open-source erasure coding libraries for storage. In: FAST, vol. 9, pp. 253–265 (2009)

IT Optimization for Datacenters Under Renewable Power Constraint

Stephane Caux[1], Paul Renaud-Goud[2], Gustavo Rostirolla[1,2(✉)], and Patricia Stolf[2]

[1] LAPLACE, Université de Toulouse, CNRS, Toulouse, France
{caux,gustavo.rostirolla}@laplace.univ-tlse.fr
[2] IRIT, Université de Toulouse, 31062 Toulouse, France
{paul.renaud.goud,stolf}@irit.fr

Abstract. Nowadays, datacenters are one of the most energy consuming facilities due to the increase of cloud, web-services and high performance computing demands all over the world. To be clean and to be with no connection to the grid, datacenters projects try to feed electricity with renewable energy sources and storage elements. Nevertheless, due to the intermittent nature of these power sources, most of the works still rely on grid as a backup. This paper presents a model that considers the datacenter workload and the several moments where renewable energy could be engaged by the power side without grid. We propose to optimize the IT scheduling to execute tasks within a given power envelope of only renewable energy as a constraint.

Keywords: Cloud computing · Renewable energy · Scheduling

1 Introduction

Datacenters are now known to be one of the biggest actors when talking about energy consumption [1]. In 2006, particularly, datacenters were responsible for consuming 61.4 billion kWh in the United States [2]. In another study [3], datacenters are in charge of consuming about 1.3% of world's electricity consumption. Datacenters are currently consuming more energy than the entire United Kingdom, and our needs are increasing.

Supplying datacenters with clean-to-use renewable energy is therefore essential to help mitigate climate change. The vast majority of cloud provider companies that claim to use green energy supply on their datacenters consider the classical grid, and deploy the solar panels/wind turbines somewhere else and sell the energy to electricity companies [4], which incurs in energy losses when the electricity travels throughout the grid. Even though several efforts have been conducted at the computing level in datacenters partially powered by renewable energy sources, the scheduling considering the variations in the power production without the grid can still be widely explored. In this paper we consider a datacenter powered only with renewable energy.

© Springer International Publishing AG, part of Springer Nature 2018
M. Aldinucci et al. (Eds.): Euro-Par 2018, LNCS 11014, pp. 339–351, 2018.
https://doi.org/10.1007/978-3-319-96983-1_24

Since energy efficiency in datacenters is directly related to the resource consumption of a computing node [5], performance optimization and an efficient load scheduling is essential for energy saving. Today, we observe the use of cloud computing as the basis of datacenters, either in a public or private fashion. The task management is first optimized by Virtual Machine (VM) management [6], where a task should be placed considering an energy consumption model to describe the task's consumption, depending on the resource description (processor and memory power characteristics) and task's demand (resources usage) while respecting the Quality of Service (QoS - in our case their due dates).

To address the IT load scheduling while considering the renewable energy available we propose Renewable Energy Constrained Optimization (RECO). RECO is a module to schedule batch tasks, which are characterized by their release time, due date and resource demand, in a cloud datacenter while respecting a power envelope. This envelope represents an estimation which would be provided by a power decision module and is the expected power production based on weather forecasts, states of charge of storage elements and other power production characteristics. We also highlight that this RECO module is intended to be used as part of the ANR Datazero project[1]. RECO aims at maximizing the Quality of Service with a constraint on electrical power. There are several possible power envelopes which could be generated using only renewable energy sources and the different moments when storage elements can be engaged. This interaction between datacenter electrical consumption and electrical power sources part is fundamental to profit as much as possible from the renewable energy sources. We propose and evaluate this RECO module with a comparison between classical greedy algorithms and meta-heuristics constrained by power envelopes.

The remainder of this article will present the classical approaches on scheduling with and without renewable energy sources in Sect. 2. In Sect. 3 the problem formulation is presented in details, followed by the resolution in Sect. 4 and the evaluation methodology as well as the results obtained are presented in Sect. 5. Finally, Sect. 6 presents final remarks, highlights the contributions with quantitative data and also directions for future works.

2   Related Work

Several techniques exist to save energy [5, 7]. In this section some of these research initiatives are presented, mainly related to the energy aware task scheduling in datacenters. In this sense, several authors tackle this problem using heuristics to schedule tasks trying to reduce the energy consumption in a cloud datacenter, some of which consider also the use of renewable energy. Below we present some initiatives that utilizes green energy to the datacenter in order to maximize the green energy usage.

Goiri et al. proposes GreenSlot [8] which focus on batch jobs and Green-Hadoop [9] focused on MapReduce jobs scheduling for a datacenter powered

---

[1] http://www.datazero.org.

by photovoltaic panels and the electrical grid. The schedulers are based on a predicted amount of solar energy that will be available, and aims to maximize the green energy consumption while meeting the jobs constraints. If grid energy must be used to avoid due date violations, the scheduler finds the cheapest point. Aksanli et al. [10] proposes an adaptive datacenter job scheduler which also utilizes short term prediction but in the case of solar and wind energy production. The aim of the scheduler is to reduce the number of canceled or violated jobs, and improve the efficiency of the green energy usage. Liu et al. [11] investigates the feasibility of powering cloud datacenters using renewable energy. The study focus on geographical load balancing, and the optimal mix of renewable energy using a concept called "follow the renewables" in which the workload is migrated among datacenters to improve the renewable energy usage. Finally, Beldiceanu et al. [4] presents EpoCloud, a prototype aims at optimizing the energy consumption of mono-site cloud datacenters connected to the regular electrical grid and to renewable energy sources, aiming to find the best trade-off between energy cost and QoS degradation using application reconfiguration or jobs suspension along with Vary-On/Vary-Off (VOVO) policy which dynamically turn on/off the computing resources. Sharma et al. [12] presents Blink, a way to handle intermittent power constraints activating and deactivating servers. For example, a system that blinks every 30 seconds is on for 30 seconds and then off for 30 seconds. This approach can be useful for some web applications, but not realistic for the vast majority of applications running in cloud platforms.

As it can be observed, techniques are employed in order to reduce the brown energy consumption [5], such as node consolidation, DVFS (processor voltage and frequency variation) and some authors also take profit of heterogeneity in the datacenter. Nevertheless, with exception of Sharma et al. [12] the authors always consider the grid as a backup and not a datacenter powered only by renewable energy sources, and the fluctuations that could occur in the power production. The scheduling over several possible power profiles allow us to see the impact on metrics such as QoS and the usage of renewable energy. To do so, a module to schedule tasks in a cloud datacenter is proposed in this paper while respecting the several possible power envelopes, minimizing the number of due date violations. For comparison purposes we also explore classical greedy algorithms and meta-heuristics constrained by a provided power envelope.

3 Core Problem Formulation

3.1 The Principles of the RECO Module

IT scheduling problems consist in allocating tasks on the IT resources under constraints depending on the IT platform current state and on energy availability. Several levels of decision are concerned as IT resource management (server switch on/off, process migration, voltage and frequency scaling, etc.). On the other side, we have the power systems where several power profiles could be provided, depending on the moment when the renewable energy is produced and the batteries are engaged for instance.

RECO focuses on integrating both power and computing systems to provide a power constrained optimization using power envelopes, which is applicable in the context of projects such as Datazero. The power envelope is considered as an input of the IT scheduling problem. The objective is to optimize the tasks placement in a cloud datacenter respecting a power envelope provided by the Power Management while maximizing the QoS (in our case, minimizing the due date violations).

RECO can be triggered when a new task arrives or due to some changes in the power envelope. It decides which task will be executed on which resource, when and at which frequency (using DVFS), and also when each node will be turned on or off. RECO ensures that the placement will respect a power envelope engaged by a power module, while minimizing the number of tasks that will be violated (finishing after the due date).

In the next sections, the models for IT and power characteristics and the proposed scheduling approaches are exposed in details.

3.2   IT Management Model

In this work we focus mainly on batch tasks. The IT system receives a set of n tasks $\{T_j\}_{j \in \{1,...,n\}}$, characterized by the following information: et_j represents the execution time of task T_j running at a reference frequency $F_{1,1}^{(1)}$ (see later), mem_j is the requested memory, rt_j represents the release time of the task (the moment when T_j can start to be executed), and d_j represents the due date of this task (the moment when T_j must be finished).

M multi-processor hosts $\{\mathcal{H}_h\}_{h \in \{1,...,M\}}$ populate the datacenter, while each host $\mathcal{H}_h$ is composed of C_h processors equipped with DVFS, each of them exposing M_h memory. The power dissipated by $\mathcal{H}_h$ can be computed based on Mudge [13]:

$$
P_h = \begin{cases} P_h^{(\text{idle})} + \sum_{h=1}^{C_h} run_{h,p} \cdot P_h^{(\text{dyn})} \cdot (f_{h,p})^3 & \text{if } s_h = on \\ 0 & \text{otherwise} \end{cases} \tag{1}
$$

where s_h determines whether $\mathcal{H}_h$ is *on* or *off*, $P_h^{(\text{idle})}$ is the idle power, $run_{h,p}$ is a boolean describing whether there is a task running on the processor, $P_h^{(\text{dyn})}$ is a host-dependent coefficient, and $f_{h,p}$ is the clock frequency of processor p on host h.

Every processor have a set of available frequencies $\mathcal{F}_{h,p} = \{F_{h,p}^{(1)}, \ldots, F_{h,p}^{(FM_{h,p})}\}$, in such a way that at any instant, $f_{h,p} \in \mathcal{F}_{h,p}$. Finally, note that under any clock frequency, a power overhead of $P_h^{(on)}$ (resp. $P_h^{(off)}$) is paid during $t_h^{(on)}$ (resp. $t_h^{(off)}$) when $\mathcal{H}_h$ is turned *on* (resp. *off*).

We consider that an external Power Management module sends a set of piecewise power envelopes in a *time window* $[t_{i,\min}, t_{i,\max}]$ where each envelope i is described with time steps $\{t_{i,l}\}_{l \in \{0,...,N\}}$ (where $t_{i,0} = t_{i,\min}$ and $t_{i,N} = t_{i,\max}$)

and power values. The available electrical power, constant on each $[t_{i,l}, t_{i,l+1}]$, is given in Watts and N represents the granularity. Here we also loosely call these time intervals as *steps*.

3.3   Objective

The aim is to find when and at which frequency to run every task, *i.e.* to find assignment functions σ_{proc}, σ_{host} and σ_{freq} expressing that T_j runs on processor $\sigma_{\text{proc}}(j)$ of host $\sigma_{\text{host}}(j)$ at frequency $F^{(\sigma_{\text{freq}}(j))}_{\sigma_{\text{host}}(j),\sigma_{\text{proc}}(j)}$, and a starting point function st expressing that T_j starts at time $st(j)$. We denote by $ft(j)$ the finish time of T_j, hence, for all j:

$$ft(j) = st(j) + \frac{F^{(\sigma_{\text{freq}}(j))}_{\sigma_{\text{host}}(j),\sigma_{\text{proc}}(j)}}{F^{(1)}_{1,1}} \cdot et_j. \tag{2}$$

The problem can then be formulated as follows: minimize $\sum_j \max(0, ft(j) - d_j)$, while fulfilling memory and power constraints.

4   Core Problem Resolution

Finding a mapping of the tasks onto the processors such that no due date constraint is violated is an NP-complete problem, while DVFS is not enabled and memory is not taken into account, even with two processors. In this way, we focus on approximation methods. More specifically, we explore Greedy Heuristics (GH) and Genetic Algorithms (GA) as a way to validate our proposal. GH can provide locally optimal decisions, and in general have a short execution time. On the other hand, the combinations of choices locally optimal do not always lead to a global optimum. The second approach (GA), can provide a large number of adapted solutions and also makes possible to approach a local minimum starting from an existing solution. Nevertheless, the problem of GA methods can be the execution time on large scale problems. In this work we propose a time window approach. More specifically, an off-line resource allocation problem is considered with a fixed set of tasks that have constant resource needs.

The difference from regular scheduling algorithms is that in this case we need considering the power envelope as a constraint. To do so, the implemented algorithms use a power check function which is responsible for evaluating if a task can be scheduled in a given processing element on the desired time interval. It returns how much power would be consumed to schedule the task using a specific processor and frequency. Hereafter, two different approaches that provide scheduling possibilities are presented but this model is not limited to it and new approaches could be used as long as they rely on the presented function.

For GH, we considered three versions of the Best Fit, where we use different sort task functions. It tries to fit the tasks in the node that presents the smallest power consumption, respecting the power envelope and resource constraints, and three versions of the First Fit algorithm which schedules a task at the first

available node which can finish the task before the due date. The difference
among the three versions of each algorithm is the way that the tasks are sorted:
(i) Due date, closest task first; (ii) Arrival time, first task that arrives is the first
to be scheduled; and (iii) Task size, longest one first. Even though the changes
occur only in the task ordering, the impact on the results can be significant.
All considered GH algorithms must respect the power envelope, meaning that
if there is not enough power in a given time step to power a machine, this task
will be delayed until the next time step in which a possible solution is found
(increasing the start step).

Regarding the GA we propose two variations, the first one where the fitness
function consists only in reducing the number of due date violations, and the
second one uses a weight based approach, also trying to minimize the power
consumption in a Mixed Objective (hereafter called MPGA - MultiPhase Genetic
Algorithm and MPGA-MO - MultiPhase Genetic Algorithm Mixed Objective,
respectively). Equation 3 is used to normalize all metrics considered for each
chromosome C_k, described below, where $M^{(\max)}$ is the maximum value for a given
metric, $M^{(\min)}$ is the minimum, and M_k is the value of the kth chromosome. The
normalized values are then inputs in Eq. 4 where DD_k is the normalized due date
violations and E_k is the normalized energy consumption. The metrics should be
weighted using α, depending on the importance of the objective (for MPGA the
only metric considered is the number of due date violations, $i.e.$ α is equal to 1).

$$M_k^{(\text{norm})} = \frac{M^{(\max)} - M_k}{M^{(\max)} - M^{(\min)}} \tag{3}$$

$$fitness_k = \alpha \times DD_k + (1 - \alpha) \times E_k \tag{4}$$

In both cases each chromosome represents a scheduling possibility for the
given power profile. Figure 1 presents an example of crossover operation (Algorithm 1) where each gene represents a task and the value is the node where it
will be executed. For the crossover operation we consider two points crossover
since it allows the change of a higher number of genes in a single operation, and
the selection consists in tournament selection, which allows the best fitted genes
to survive. After that, the processor, frequency and time are assigned using a
greedy algorithm. To improve the execution time of both GAs (the verification
of the power available occurs for each step in the power envelope) we also use
two different power envelopes, the first one provides a rough scheduling based
on an aggregation of the initially provided envelope, reducing in this case the
number of *steps*. After obtaining an initial placement, a fine grained power envelope (smaller steps) is used to absorb power peaks and respect the given power
envelope.

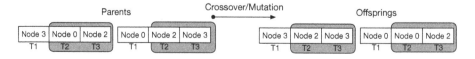

Fig. 1. Genetic algorithm chromosome representation and crossover example.

A pseudocode of the GA used is presented in Algorithm 1 where it can be seen the generation of the simplified envelope in line 2 (assigned to individuals in line 4), the first execution from line 6 to 11, and the execution with the detailed power envelope and the respective stopping criteria from line 12 to 19. The stopping criteria for the MPGA, since it only considers the number of due date violations, is when it has at least one chromosome that has no violation the execution can be stopped, or the maximum number of generations is reached. For the second algorithm (MPGA-MO) the stopping criteria is only the number of generations, since the minimum energy to schedule the tasks in advance cannot be defined easily.

Algorithm 1. Multiphase genetic algorithm pseudocode.

---

   input   : Set of tasks in queue, set of resources available, power envelope for the
                  window, selection method, population size, number of generations first phase,
                  number of generations second phase, number of simplified steps, mutation
                  probability, crossover probability
   output: Tasks scheduled, actions to be performed in nodes, QoS metrics, power
                  consumption estimation

1 **begin**
2   simplifiedPowerEnvelope = generateSimplifiedEnvelope(powerEnvelope,nSteps);
       /* First Phase - Simplified Power Envelope   */
3   **foreach** *Individual i in population* **do**
4 | i.setPowerEnvelope(simplifiedPowerEnvelope.copy);
5   **end**
6   generateInitialPopulation();
7   **for** *(g=0; g < generationsFirstPhase; g++)* **do**
8   scheduleAndCheckConstraints(individuals);
9   calculateFitness(individuals);
10   selectionMethod.select(individuals);
11   **end**
       /* Second Phase - Detailed Power Envelope   */
12   **foreach** *Individual i in population* **do**
13 | i.setPowerEnvelope(powerEnvelope.copy);
14   **end**
15   **while** *StopCriteriaNotReached* **do**
16   scheduleAndCheckConstraints(individuals);
17   calculateFitness(individuals);
18   selectionMethod.select(individuals);
19   **end**
20 **end**

When a set of individuals of a generation is computed, the greedy algorithms is used to perform the time schedule and DVFS adjustment (*scheduleAndCheckConstraints* called in lines 8 and 16). In a simplified manner, how the tasks would be allocated in a processor is presented in Fig. 2 where we illustrate a node with two processors. In (a) we present the scheduling after

the greedy algorithm that defines the time and processor inside a node is executed. The aim of this greedy algorithm is to align the execution of the processors
of the same node to be able to switch it off. First we populate an associative
array with all the tasks and the time intervals where they can be scheduled.
After, we get the first unscheduled task and compare if there is another task
which the time to be schedule intercepts this time interval. The algorithm evaluates then, what is the earliest start step in which the tasks can be allocated
and not violated. Finally, the algorithm finds a free processor inside the node
and schedule the tasks in parallel (as illustrated in (b) by T_1 in Processor 1 and
T_2 and T_3 in Processor 2. We also highlight that the algorithm always verifies
the power envelope and resources constraints.

In Fig. 2(c) we show a per processors DVFS where we reduce the frequency
of Processor 2 in this case, to reduce the power consumption, and consequently
increasing the execution time of tasks T_2, T_3. The frequency in this case is only
reduced if the due date is not violated. This DVFS control does not impact
the idle power consumption of a node, allowing an easy consolidation of nodes
where more energy saving can be obtained. In this sense, at the end of the
task placement and DVFS adjustment we also calculate when each node can
be turned off in order to reduce the power consumption without impacting the
system performance.

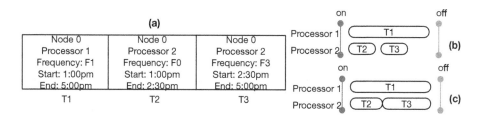

Fig. 2. Tasks allocation inside a node with two processing elements using greedy
scheduling inside GA (a), and DVFS adjustment where (b) is before DVFS and (c)
after DVFS adjustment.

5   Evaluation Methodology and Results

5.1   Methodology

To validate RECO we simulated an IT and Power production infrastructure
based on the prototype presented in the previous section. The DCWoRMS simulator and the other modules are executed on the same machine. The IT infrastructure inside the simulator is based on Villebonnet et al. [14], more specifically
we are using 30 hosts (15 of each kind) and the power consumption values of Paravance and Taurus clusters from Grid5000[2]. We consider $P^{(dyn)} = 4.725\,W \cdot s^3$

---

[2] https://www.grid5000.fr/.

(see Eq. 1) and $P^{(\mathrm{idle})} = 69.9\,W$ for Paravance and $P^{(\mathrm{dyn})} = 5.255\,W \cdot s^3$ and $P^{(\mathrm{idle})} = 95.8\,W$ for Taurus. For Paravance we considered $P^{(on)} = 112.91\,W$ over $t^{(on)} = 189\,s$ and for $P^{(off)} = 65.7\,W$ over $t^{(off)} = 10\,s$. For Taurus we considered $P^{(on)} = 125.78\,W$ over $t^{(on)} = 164\,s$ and for $P^{(off)} = 106.63\,W$ over $t^{(off)} = 11\,s$.

Regarding the GA, we bound the number of generations to 100 (resp. 400) with the simplified power envelope (resp. with the original power envelope) and the population size to 100 individuals. The probabilities for crossover and muta-tion are 0.9 and 0.3 respectively. For the MPGA-MO we consider $\alpha = 0.9$ where the main objective is minimize the due date violations. For the Google based workload [15] generator we use a two-day window (i.e. all the tasks have to be executed inside this interval) to generate 3 different workloads with 234, 569 and 1029 tasks. Each workload is scheduled with 3 different power profiles as observed in Fig. 3. PROFILE I with peak production of 7249 W and average of 2879W, PROFILE II peak production of 7249 W and average of 2893 W and PRO-FILE III with peak production of 6387 W and average of 2756W. Even though the values are similar, the moment in which the power is delivered is different, as observed in Fig. 3.

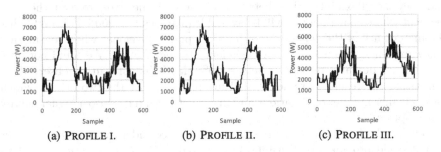

(a) PROFILE I.   (b) PROFILE II.   (c) PROFILE III.

Fig. 3. Graphical representation of the three power profiles.

5.2   Results Evaluation

In Fig. 4 we present the number of due date violations (a) the total time violated (b) and energy consumption (c) for all the proposed workloads for best fit and genetic algorithms (first fit is presented only in text for better visualization), considering the three different power profiles.

Considering the three power profiles with only 234 tasks, almost all algo-rithms, even with the power constraint, can reduce the number of violations to 0 and keep the energy consumption around 15 kWh. The exceptions in this case are the first fit algorithms which have a higher energy consumption (around 18 kWh) and one violation (198s of total time violated) with PROFILE II. As the number of tasks increases an expected degradation of performance of both first fit and best fit algorithms is observed when compared to the GA. When considering 1029 tasks we have in PROFILE I 18 due date violations (114046 s) for the best fit algorithm against 5 (545446 s) and 6 (30684 s) of the two genetic algorithms variations, which also obtained a reduction of 6.3% in the energy consumption. In PROFILE II we observed the same behavior, reducing from 19 (189892 s) to 12 (78471 s and 114845 s) due date violations with a reduction of 4.9% in the energy consumption. The same goes for PROFILE III which reduced from 22 (169612 s) to 11 (118092 s and 118477 s) due date violations with an economy of 5% in energy. The values for the total time violated of the tasks may seem high but we need to consider that the scheduling is constrained by a power envelope, and in this case the tasks need to be delayed for the next moment with enough power available (if we consider only solar energy for instance, this may take a whole day).

In Fig. 5 we present the power produced and consumed for PROFILE I. These results were obtained when using the Best Fit Due Date (a) and MPGA-MO (b) scheduling planners with PROFILE I and 1029 tasks. We can observe that in some points (such as in the first 100 samples) the power consumption can be similar for both algorithms due to the high number of tasks that needs to be scheduled and so reaching the maximum power available. This justifies why we have different number of due date violations with the same workload under different power profiles: at some points we have too many tasks to be scheduled, and they lack flexibility (time between release and due date) to wait the next moment where enough power will be available (samples 100–200). This highlights the importance of the generation of multiple power envelopes when considering renewable energy sources and storage elements engagement. We could not only save energy but also provide a better QoS; this behavior can be observed by comparing the results obtained with PROFILE I against the two others, which have a higher number of violations and in case of PROFILE II also a higher energy consumption.

The results become even more significant if we consider the long term impact that it could provide. For PROFILE I, displayed in Fig. 5, in a period of 2 days we could save 164.98 kWh using the MPGA-MO, instead of 155.35 kWh and 160.04 kWh for first fit and best fit due date respectively. This energy could be stored and used in the generation of the next scheduling windows improving the results, or sold to the grid power provider.

In Fig. 6 the average execution time of all the algorithms (with minimum and maximum values in the bars) is presented. Despite of the smaller number of due date violations and lower energy consumption, as expected, the Genetic Algorithm can have an execution time exponentially higher than the greedy ones. Nevertheless, if the scheduling requested is not a reactive action, this execution time is not prohibitive (around 12 min in the worst case for two days scheduling). We also highlight that it is possible to improve even more the execution time by improving the stopping criteria, but this will have an impact of the quality of the schedule.

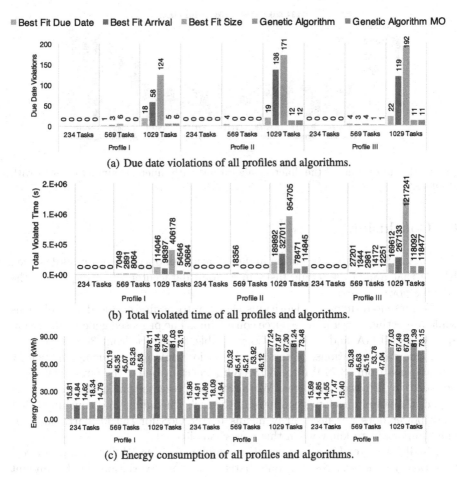

(a) Due date violations of all profiles and algorithms.

(b) Total violated time of all profiles and algorithms.

(c) Energy consumption of all profiles and algorithms.

Fig. 4. Power available and consumed in the power profiles using best fit and genetic algorithm scheduling plan.

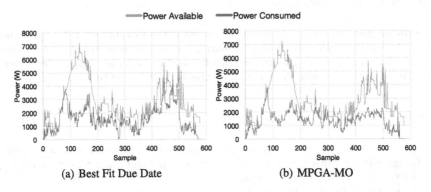

(a) Best Fit Due Date

(b) MPGA-MO

Fig. 5. Power available and consumed in the power PROFILE I considering two different algorithms and 1029 tasks.

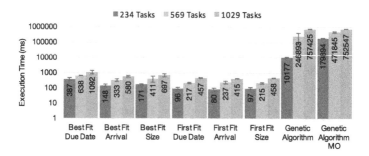

Fig. 6. Execution time of the different algorithms with different number of tasks with PROFILE I.

6   Conclusion

This article focused on presenting and evaluating an optimization module called RECO that aims to schedule tasks in a cloud datacenter while respecting the possible power envelopes.

We presented different algorithms that try to minimize due date violations while respecting power and resource constraints. The proposed genetic algorithm approach (MPGA and MPGA-MO) was able to reduce from 304 (First Fit) to 11 due date violations, in the best scenario, while also reducing the energy consumption from 78.7 kWh to 73.15 kWh respecting one of the power envelopes provided by a power manager. We have also presented an evaluation of the impact the power envelopes can have in the task scheduling, and concluded that more power does not necessarily means better QoS for the IT part, but it is more important to know when this power is delivered.

Finally, we intend to continue our research extending RECO to support real time task arrival, services (not only batch tasks), and variations in the amount of resources that are consumed by the applications. We also intend to connect RECO's generic interface through a message queue with an electrical middleware to receive the power envelopes.

Acknowledgments. The work presented in this paper was supported by the French ANR DATAZERO project ANR-15-CE25-0012. For source characterization, the experimental database has been obtained thanks to the financial support of several LAPLACE projects, France (leaders Christophe TURPIN, Eric BRU)

References

1. Khan, Z., Kiani, S.: A cloud-based architecture for citizen services in smart cities. In: 2012 IEEE Fifth International Conference on Utility and Cloud Computing (UCC), pp. 315–320, November 2012
2. Le, K., Bilgir, O., Bianchini, R., Martonosi, M., Nguyen, T.D.: Managing the cost, energy consumption, and carbon footprint of internet services. SIGMETRICS Perform. Eval. Rev. **38**(1), 357–358 (2010)

3. Koomey, J.: Growth in data center electricity use 2005 to 2010. In: A report by Analytical Press, completed at the request of The New York Times, p. 9 (2011)
4. Beldiceanu, N., et al.: Towards energy-proportional clouds partially powered by renewable energy. Computing **99**(1), 3–22 (2017)
5. Orgerie, A.-C., Assuncao, M.D.D., Lefevre, L.: A survey on techniques for improving the energy efficiency of large-scale distributed systems. ACM Comput. Surv. **46**(4), 1–31 (2014)
6. Borgetto, D., Stolf, P.: An energy efficient approach to virtual machines management in cloud computing. In: 2014 IEEE 3rd International Conference on Cloud Networking (CloudNet), pp. 229–235, October 2014
7. Deng, W., Liu, F., Jin, H., Li, B., Li, D.: Harnessing renewable energy in cloud datacenters: opportunities and challenges. IEEE Netw. **28**(1), 48–55 (2014)
8. Goiri, I., et al.: GreenSlot scheduling energy consumption in green datacenters. In: 2011 International Conference for High Performance Computing, Networking, Storage and Analysis (SC), pp. 1–11, November 2011
9. Goiri, I., Le, K., Nguyen, T.D., Guitart, J., Torres, J., Bianchini, R.: GreenHadoop: leveraging green energy in data-processing frameworks. In: Proceedings of the 7th ACM European Conference on Computer Systems, EuroSys 2012, pp. 57–70. ACM, New York (2012)
10. Aksanli, B., Venkatesh, J., Zhang, L., Rosing, T.: Utilizing green energy prediction to schedule mixed batch and service jobs in data centers. In: Proceedings of the 4th Workshop on Power-Aware Computing and Systems, HotPower 2011, pp. 5:1–5:5. ACM, New York (2011)
11. Liu, Z., Lin, M., Wierman, A., Low, S.H., Andrew, L.L.: Geographical load balancing with renewables. SIGMETRICS Perform. Eval. Rev. **39**(3), 62–66 (2011)
12. Sharma, N., Barker, S., Irwin, D., Shenoy, P.: Blink: managing server clusters on intermittent power. SIGARCH Comput. Archit. News **39**(1), 185–198 (2011)
13. Mudge, T.: Power: a first-class architectural design constraint. Computer **34**, 52–58 (2001)
14. Villebonnet, V., Costa, G.D., Lefevre, L., Pierson, J.M., Stolf, P.: Energy aware dynamic provisioning for heterogeneous data centers. In: 2016 28th International Symposium on Computer Architecture and High Performance Computing (SBAC-PAD), pp. 206–213, October 2016
15. Da Costa, G., Grange, L., Courchelle, I.D.: Modeling and generating large-scale Google-like workload. In: 2016 Seventh International Green and Sustainable Computing Conference (IGSC), pp. 1–7, November 2016

GPU Provisioning: The 80 − 20 Rule

Eleni Kanellou[1(✉)], Nikolaos Chrysos[1], Stelios Mavridis[1], Yannis Sfakianakis[1], and Angelos Bilas[1,2]

[1] ICS-FORTH, N. Plastira 100, 70013 Heraklion, Greece
{kanellou,chrysos,mavridis,jsfakian,bilas}@ics.forth.gr
[2] Computer Science Department, University of Crete,
Voutes Campus, 70013 Heraklion, Greece

Abstract. The use of accelerators, such as GPUs and FPGAs, in datacenters has been increasing in an effort to improve response time for user-facing tasks. Although accelerators offer performance improvements for certain types of applications, they contribute to total cost of ownership and need to be deployed thoughtfully. In addition, the complexity of modern applications and different accelerator types, makes this a challenging task. In this paper, we derive a generalized model of workload core performance in datacenters. We find that the sweet spot for cost/benefit is when deploying a relatively low number of GPU accelerators compared to the number of servers. We also quantify this effect in the presence of data transfers and verify our observations using performance simulations and experiments in a realistic testbed with multiple GPUs. Overall, we detect aspects of accelerator deployment that should be taken into account to achieve trade-offs for their use in datacenters.

1 Introduction

With the end of Dennard scaling [1], the evolution of general-purpose processors cannot benefit from technology improvements alone. Thus, modern datacenters actively pursue heterogeneity by including special-purpose accelerators. For instance, Microsoft, Google, and Amazon reportedly use FPGA, ASIC, and GPU accelerators in order to speedup the execution of user-facing tasks, such as web search, speech recognition, etc. [2,3]. The spreading integration of accelerators in datacenters raises a question that we address in this paper: *how many and what type of accelerators should we deploy in a functional datacenter?*

Deployment decisions may influence many datacenter cost and performance aspects, such as machine utilization, energy consumption, task latencies, cost of purchase and maintenance (as evidenced for instance in [4–7]). In addition, modifying a deployment paradigm can be a costly and time-consuming process. In this paper, we evaluate deployment compositions for heterogeneous datacenters. We use a model that approximates the performance of a datacenter when executing a given workload. We experiment with workloads that have a determined specific characteristics on some aspects (e.g. task duration and type) but we have also experimented with workloads that we designed so as to mimic the

© Springer International Publishing AG, part of Springer Nature 2018
M. Aldinucci et al. (Eds.): Euro-Par 2018, LNCS 11014, pp. 352–364, 2018.
https://doi.org/10.1007/978-3-319-96983-1_25

real-life traces available in literature that are representative for at least a class of datacenters. In summary, our main observation is the 80 − 20 *rule*, i.e. that under certain circumstances, building a deployment with more than 20% GPUs does not significantly improve performance. Experiments in small-scale systems validate this finding.

Our results can help and guide datacenter designers when they plan a deployment. The data transfer overhead can limit the performance gain from accelerators, challenging our key observations, especially considering deployments with *remote* accelerators (or GPUs). Nevertheless, we were able to partly validate our results in such deployments using simulations and realistic testbeds. Our main contributions in this paper are:

1. A model to evaluate workload core performance in datacenters.
2. A powerful rule-of-thumb that can help direct GPU provisioning.
3. Evaluation some of our results on a realistic testbed of 6 GPUs and 6 CPUs.

The remainder of this paper is organized as follows. In Sect. 2, we outline the conceptual model of the datacenter, on which we base our analysis. Then, Sect. 3 describes the theory behind the 80-20 rule. In Sect. 4, we elaborate further on this rule, by providing simulations results taking data transfer into account and by presenting our results from small scale testbed with a mix of CPUs and GPUs. Related efforts in literature are summarized in Sect. 5. Section 6 provides a discussion of further aspects of the work and a summary.

2   Conceptual Datacenter Model

In this section, we construct a model that will allow us to define and evaluate various datacenter deployments. We actively neglect processor architecture details, such as out-of-order execution, core number, memory hierarchy, etc. The performance variability of the heterogeneous nodes is not (re)constructed by the model itself, but comes as user input[1]. We consider heterogeneous *processing units*, such as CPUs, GPUs, FPGAs, and ASICs. Each processing unit, or accelerator, has coordinates that identify its position (rack and shelve IDs) inside the datacenter. In the following, we may abuse terminology and refer to processing units in general as *accelerators*. The processing units execute tasks (or kernels), which are pieces of computation. Tasks may have input and output data, both of which are characterized by size and rack/shelve coordinates. Similarly with processing units, tasks are also characterized by a type. To simplify things, we assume that all tasks can be executed on all processing units, an assumption that we expect to hold true in the near future.

A datacenter is used in order to execute *workloads*. A workload is a collection of tasks. Tasks arrive in different time slots, as can be defined by a time-series or trace. The tasks in a workload may be stand-alone or they may belong to

---

[1] In practice, we derive it by profiling applications or by using the raw capacity numbers advertized by device vendors.

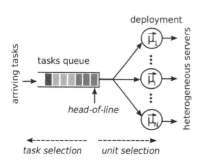
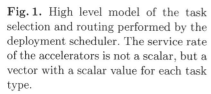

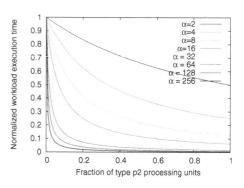

Fig. 1. High level model of the task selection and routing performed by the deployment scheduler. The service rate of the accelerators is not a scalar, but a vector with a scalar value for each task type.

Fig. 2. Total execution time normalized to that of a CPU-only deployment as a function of $f = \frac{n}{N}$, i.e. the fraction of GPUs in the deployment, for varying affinity ratios between CPUs and GPUs.

a *taskset* or *job*. Tasks belonging to a user-facing job are latency-critical tasks. Typically, they all have to complete fast in order for the job to terminate on time [8]. In our model, we vary the workload by using different mixes of task types and sizes. We consider that tasks arrive at the datacenter at a configurable arrival rate λ. At one extreme, tasks arrive slowly, and the datacenter is largely idle; at the other, many tasks arrive concurrently, in a burst, in which case they may have to spend some time in a task queue of infinite capacity.

Our model takes as input a 2D *affinity matrix* that defines the throughput of the processing units for each task type, measured in tasks per second. The affinity matrix expresses the heterogeneity of computation and hides the node-level intricacies of nodes, while nevertheless allowing the model to accurately model node-level performance. Any particular instance of a datacenter, i.e. a datacenter for which the specific numbers, types, and affinities of processing units is referred to as a datacenter *deployment*.

We may view the datacenter as an $M/M/c$ queuing system (multiple servers), where, however, not only the servers are heterogeneous in terms of service rate, but where the arriving "customers", i.e. tasks, also belong to several different classes. Effectively, as shown in Fig. 1, the mean service times of the N computing units/accelerators are vectors instead of scalar values. Arriving tasks enter the system task queue waiting for service. The task queue is controlled by a *task scheduler*, which assigns tasks to time processing units, scheduling their execution. Each task will be executed by a processing unit. We identify the following two decisions in task scheduling: (i) Task selection, which determines the order in which the scheduler visits the tasks in the task queue, and (ii) Unit selection (or task routing), which selects the processing unit that will execute the currently examined task. The task selection order can be *FIFO or non-FIFO*, but in either case, multiple tasks can be selected at the same time when multiple computing units are available. The tasks can be issued in parallel, as would happen in a Map-Reduce workload, and can complete out of order. The unit selection can be *work conserving*, when it always picks one of the available accelerators for the next task, or *non-work conserving*, when the scheduler may prefer to wait for a better match to become available. The unit selection may be aware of resources heterogeneity, or oblivious of affinity relationships of tasks to accelerators.

We could set out to find the performance of an examined deployment using optimal scheduling. For instance, the minimization of workload completion time can be formulated as a maximum-weight flow problem in directed graphs. However, in principle, the optimal task scheduling may depend on the workload and probably also on the deployment. For this reason, in this paper we chose to compare deployments for the following set of schedulers for heterogeneous datacenters: (i) the *oblivious scheduler* visits tasks in FIFO order, and assigns them to an available processing unit; and (ii) the *fastest server first* visits tasks in FIFO order and the next (head of line) task is assigned to the available processing unit with the highest affinity. In either case, the unit selection is work-conserving.

3 Deciding How Many Accelerators to Deploy

Suppose that we want to populate a rack with N machine slots using a mix of type p_1 and p_2 computing units. To improve the correspondence with a realistic (and popular nowadays) setup, assume that p_1 units are CPUs and p_2 units are GPUs. The workload of interest, W, consists of M number of tasks. We will first consider that all tasks are of the same type, t, and that, possibly belonging to a single job, they all arrive together, in a burst. Such workloads with a *predominant task-type* may be seen in dedicated clusters of production datacenters [9] working e.g. on web-search or deep learning. Furthermore, assume that it's a peak hour for the service provided by the cluster. In this work, we find that for a highly loaded system, i.e. $M >> N$, if the cluster is working on a single task type, any work-conserving scheduler performs optimally. Below we assume such a scheduler.

Assume that the affinity of CPUs on type t tasks is equal to 1 and that of GPUs is $\alpha > 0$. (Note that in general α is a function of task type t.) A starting deployment contains only CPUs (p_1 units), without any GPU (p_2 unit). The aggregate throughput (or service rate) in tasks per second of the deployment is $A_{CPU}^W = N$ tasks per time unit. Now consider the deployment that results if we substitute n out of N CPUs with GPUs. The aggregate service rate of the new deployment for this workload is $A_n^W = (N - n) + \alpha \cdot n$.

The system can be modeled as a queue of tasks drained by the heterogeneous processing units. Let T^W be the total time necessary to execute workload W. According to Little's law, the total drain time of the task queue is inversely proportional to the aggregate service rate of the deployment. Therefore, we can express the *speedup* obtained by a deployment containing n GPUs and $N - n$ CPUs relative to the CPU-only deployment as: $S_n = \frac{T_{CPU}^W}{T_n^W} = \frac{A_n^W}{N} = \frac{N + (\alpha - 1) \cdot n}{N}$,

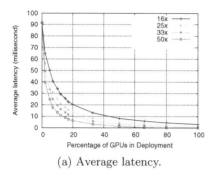
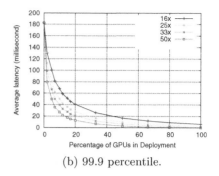

(a) Average latency.   (b) 99.9 percentile.

Fig. 3. Latency under high load of workload consisting of GPU-F task-type only, in deployments where α, the relative affinity of GPUs and CPUs, changes.

and if we set $f = n/N$, we obtain:

$$S_n^W = 1 + (\alpha - 1) \cdot f. \tag{1}$$

If $\alpha = 1$, changing the proportions of CPUs and GPUs does not affect the execution speed. If $\alpha > 1$, then adding GPUs speeds up the execution; reversely, if $0 < \alpha < 1$, adding GPUs slows it down.

Indicative curves of the execution time of the n-GPUs deployment relative to the CPUs-only one, i.e. $\frac{T_n^W}{T_{CPU}^W} = \frac{1}{S^W}$, are presented in Fig. 2 for various values of $\alpha > 1$. Because $\alpha > 1$, the latency is reduced as we add more GPUs. For each curve, the latency is minimized when all processing units are of GPUs, at the right end of graph. The figure shows clearly that, for large α, *the deployments with more than than around* 20% *GPUs, depending on α, provide diminishing benefits.* We refer to this observation as *the 80 − 20 rule.* At first, this may seem somewhat surprising because according to Eq. 1 (and normal intuition), the speedup is proportional to f. The catch is that the speedup is also proportional to α, which can outweigh the effect of f: a few but well customized accelerators may cut down sharply the workload execution time, masking out the benefits of bringing in more accelerators.

One can further show that, for $\alpha \gg 1$, we can have at least 75% of the latency reduction achieved by the N-GPUs system $(T_0^W - T_N^W)$ with a deployment containing $(f =) \frac{4+a}{3}$ times fewer GPUs. For example, if a GPU kernel achieves a speedup $\alpha \geq 12$ relative to CPUs, we need to replace just 20% of the processors to reach this performance point. To get the remaining 25% of latency reduction, we need to buy $5x$ more GPUs. Many accelerators with good affinity are reported in the literature [10]. For instance, GPUs contain thousands of cores and can greatly speedup traditional high-performance computing or deep-learning tasks.

Adding GPUs to a Fixed Deployment: Adding GPUs (accelerators) to servers *without removing CPUs* does not modify the aforementioned results.

One can easily show that the speedup obtained by a deployment with N CPUs and m GPUs is: $S_m^W = \frac{T_{CPU}^W}{T_m^W} = \frac{A_m^W}{N} = \frac{N+(\alpha+1)\cdot m}{N}$ therefore: $S_m^W = 1 + (\alpha+1) \cdot f$.

Bad Performing Accelerators: The hardware of accelerators is frequently built to match the requirements of certain tasks. Effectively, some tasks with a lot of branching activity may run faster on CPUs instead of GPUs. In order to account for such tasks in our model, allow for values of $\alpha < 1$. The results are analogous to those considered so far: adding GPUs in place of CPUs increases the workload execution time, along curves that are symmetrical to the ones shown in Fig. 2.

4   Exploring the $80 - 20$ Rule

In this section, we validate $80 - 20$ rule with experiments for the above analysis, both in a custom-made C++ simulator, as well as in a setup with real machines.

System Simulations. Our simulator essentially follows the abstract datacenter model described in Sect. 2 and outlined in Fig. 1. In our first experiment, we model a *single rack* consisting of $N = 40$ machines, each of which can be either CPU or GPU. We feed the simulator with a workload consisting of same-type tasks. A new job arrives in the system every 10 μs and consists of 30 tasks. We use an abstract task type *GPU-friendly* (GPU-F) that can be accelerated on GPUs. These tasks take 500 μs to execute on the simulated CPU. On a simulated GPU a task takes $\frac{500}{a}$ μs, i.e. a single GPU is α times faster than a CPU. Thus, α defines the relative affinity of GPUs and CPUs with respect to GPU-F tasks. Notice that we have based decision of considering a proportional relation of relative affinity between GPUs and CPUs, on real-life experiments that we have performed, where we measured individual execution time of tasks on GPUs and CPUs. In each of those experiments, our workload consisted of a single task of a different type for each experiment, focusing on making sure the execution times that we measured excluded any data transfer or queuing delays.

With respect to our simulated experiments, the small job inter-arrival that we use (10 μs) creates a high load for any deployment, thus resembling peak hours in a datacenter. In this experiment, we use the fastest-server first scheduler, described in Sect. 2. However, we have observed that for single-task workloads operating under high load, any work-conserving scheduling performs the same. In this experiment, we assume that no data transfers are needed in order to execute a task.

Figure 3 shows the results of a GPU-friendly workload, executed in configurations that contain a varying percentage of GPUs. It depicts multiple plots, representing deployments with a varying number of GPUs and a fixed affinity relationship (i.e. α) between CPUs and GPUs for tasks of type GPU-F. The x-axis shows a varying percentage of GPU contents. In Fig. 3a, the y-axis shows the average task latency in ms; in Fig. 3b, we depict the 99.9 percentile of task latency. Our simulation results match our theoretical expectations (cf. Sect. 3): the higher the affinity ratio between GPUs and CPUs, the greater the overall

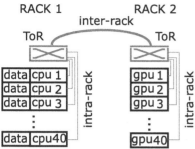

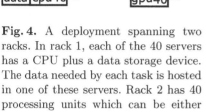

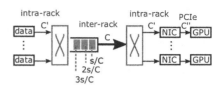

Fig. 4. A deployment spanning two racks. In rack 1, each of the 40 servers has a CPU plus a data storage device. The data needed by each task is hosted in one of these servers. Rack 2 has 40 processing units which can be either a CPU or a GPU. The hosts inside each rack are connected to a top-of-rack (ToR) switch using 10 Gb/s links. The two racks are connected with a link running at 200 Gb/s.

Fig. 5. Transfers between the host that holds the task data and a remote accelerator, which can be a CPU or a GPU. The GPUs are attached to the PCI interface in another rack. As multiple transfers of size s may be concurrently active between the two racks, they are necessarily serialized on the inter-rack link of capacity $C = 200$ Gb/s. The maximum rate of a *single transfer* is, however, always limited by the capacity of an intra-rack link which runs at 10 Gb/s.

performance improvement, *both in average and tail latency*. Currently, a usual practice is to over-provision datacenters, aiming at always ensuring resource availability. However, as we see in the plot, after 20% of GPUs, "throwing more hardware at the problem" does not significantly improve latency.

The Case of Remote Accelerators. In this experiment, we examine whether the effect of data transfers influences the observed trends. For this purpose, we simulate two racks, racks 1 and 2. We assume that all GPUs in the deployment are located in rack 2, as shown in Fig. 4. This models a deployment with remote (network-attached) accelerators, which highly stresses the network. All tasks must take their data from a server in rack 1. Therefore, whenever a processing unit in rack 2 is used to accelerate the execution, a data transfer over the inter-rack link is triggered.

As noted in Fig. 5, the intra-rack link runs at 200 Gb/s. In our model, the rate of a single transfer is limited by the minimum of the current fair share on inter-rack link and the 10 Gb/s rate of a single intra-rack link–assuming that the modern PCI can run faster than that. In this experiment, we assume a relative affinity between GPUs and CPUs equal to $\alpha = 16$. Interestingly, the $80 - 20$ rule still holds. Figure 6 contains multiple plots corresponding to different task data size. In our configuration, moderate data sizes correspond to up to 320K bytes. For larger transfers, the data transfers dominate and the use of accelerators does not improve the performance even at 100% GPUs in the deployment.

This effect is depicted in Fig. 7. The vertical blocks depict the delay incurred by task execution and the required data transfers over inter-rack links, assuming

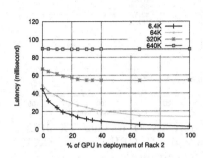

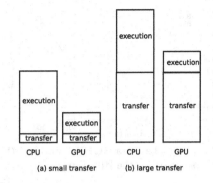

Fig. 6. Average latency, under high load, of workload consisting of same-size, GPU-F task-type only, with different data transfer sizes. X-axis indicates % of GPUs in the deployment of rack B.

Fig. 7. The effect of data transfers on accelerator speedup.

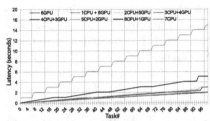

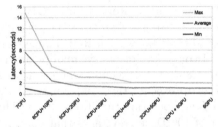

(a) Individual task latency with varying GPU/CPU ratio deployments.

(b) Average task latency with varying GPU/CPUs ratio deployments.

Fig. 8. Task latency behaviour for deployments with 6 (CPU/GPU) accelerator.

the data that the task needs has to be transferred to the CPU or the GPU from a remote rack. The higher the block, the longer the corresponding delay. Notice that in the case of GPUs, we assume that, once the data reaches the rack and node where the GPU is located, then the eventual PCI transfer delay is negligible, compared to the rack-to-rack transfer delay. The observed effect is reminiscent of Amdahl's law: the data transfer is the serial part of a computation that limits the speedup that can be obtained by any good accelerator. When the latency of the communication required to move the data to a remote accelerator approaches the computation time on the CPU, the maximum speedup that can be obtained is upper bounded by 2×. In this case, we might be better off if we avoid the data transfer and schedule the task to a processing unit that can access the data locally [11].

Validation with NVidia GPUs. We have tested our theoretical and simulation findings on a real machine setup. Specifically, we populated six (6) Gen

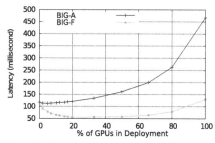
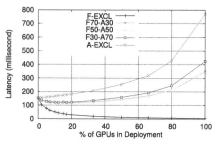

(a) BIG-A: Big jobs contain GPU-A tasks. The inverse holds for the BIG-F trace.

(b) A trace AX-FY contains X% GPU-A jobs and Y% GPU-F jobs. -EXCL stands for "exclusive".

Fig. 9. Realistic synthesized job size distribution. Average task latency during simulated peak hours.

PCIe (8x) slots of an Intel Xeon CPU E5 − 2630 processor with (6) P1000 GPUs from NVidia. We employ a custom middleware [12], which allows for the sharing of several accelerators, such as GPUs, among the processors residing on a single node. We use *DarkGrey* kernels as workload. DarkGrey is a custom-created kernel that converts an RGB image to grayscale and then darkens the result.

In our experiments, we manipulate a 62 MB image files. On a CPU, the kernel takes 895 ms to execute, whereas it takes only 7.26 ms on P1000. However, in order to execute the task on the GPU, we need to *transfer the data over the PCI*, an operation that takes 38 ms. The workload tested in our experiments is set of 100 DarkGrey tasks that enter a task queue. Tasks are scheduled across the available processing units, regardless of task affinity, using the oblivious work-conserving FIFO scheduler policy. In Fig. 8, we keep the total number of processing units constant to six (6), and we examine how the task latency is affected when vary the mix of GPUs and CPUs in the deployment.

Figure 8a depicts the individual latency of each one of the 100 tasks for each deployment. The latency of each task includes the queuing delay, i.e. the total execution time of the tasks that precede it in the queue. Tasks that can be executed concurrently from start to finish, incur the same queuing delay. This is most clearly shown in the plot depicting the task latency in the deployment with 6 CPUs. This deployment produces a stair-step-type graph, where task latency increases in every batch of 6 consecutive tasks, since 6 tasks can be executed in parallel on the 6 processing units. Figure 8b shows the average task latency for each of the deployments. As can be seen, we obtain a great reduction of average task latency after trading the first two CPUs for two GPUs. However, this trend does not continue so prominently after the inclusion of more GPUs. This is in accordance with our theoretical expectations outlined previously in Fig. 2. Note that this effect is still observable, despite the fact that executing on the GPU incurs an additional latency of 38 ms.

Mixed Workloads. We now turn our attention to workloads that may contain both GPU-F tasks, as well tasks that are not suitable for execution on GPU, meaning that the GPU cannot sufficiently accelerate them, possibly even harming their execution time with respect to the execution on CPU. We refer to this type of tasks as *GPU-averse* (GPU-A)[2]. The GPU-A type represents, for example, tasks with branching or memory access patterns ill-suited for GPUs.

We start by examining average task latency in Fig. 9. We have used the fastest-server-first scheduling policy and showcase various workloads in situations of high load. Given that information regarding the task length, exact type, distribution, etc., of a datacenter trace, is not readily available, we attempt to synthesize workloads that are as realistic as possible, basing our choice of values on datacenter trace analyses such as [13–17] and others. We use simple algorithms such as the ones used in [17] in order to create synthetic datacenter traces containing combinations of GPU-A and GPU-F tasks.

Figure 9a shows task traces with realistic taskset size distributions, where the task type depends on the job size; and Fig. 9b shows task traces with realistic taskset size distributions and different task type mixes. We observe that the highest gain in task latency occurs once more with the inclusion of already a few GPUs. However, this only occurs on those traces that are predominantly or exclusively composed of GPU-F tasks. On the contrary, when traces are exclusively of type GPU-A or when GPU-A tasks dominate, the inclusion of more GPUs than CPUs ceases to offer benefit and is instead even detrimental. But what is more, when GPU-F and GPU-A tasks are in equivalent numbers or when even GPU-A tasks are in the trace even though GPU-F tasks dominate, then again only the inclusion of the first few GPUs offers benefit.

5   Related Work

As an alternative to pure simulation, analytical modeling and analysis can be used. In [18], the performance of a given workload is expressed as a function of the CPU and GPU throughput and the data transfer time between them. Mathematical solvers are used to predict the optimal relative content of CPUs and GPUs. However, this method requires some partial profiling and is targeted at specific applications. While it remains to be seen whether such analysis could be applied to datacenters, in our paper we wished to eschew analytical solving and explore performance over a more generic variety of application types and deployment compositions. In [19], a queuing-theoretical approach is favored, in order to determine which deployment decisions lead to robustness, i.e. maintaining the minimum worst-case energy consumption in the face of a varying workload. In contrast, in this work, we are concerned with reducing task queuing time and execution latency. An exploratory approach is also followed in [20]. There, however, analytic workloads are modeled and used as workload inputs to

---

[2] We opt for these two categories because our model relies on expressing the suitability of an accelerator for a task instead of the nature of its computation.

a machine-learning system. After training on a variety of hardware configurations, the system predicts expected performance of a given workload on a given datacenter setup. We tackle the issue differently, striving to predict the hardware configuration that is sufficient, given expected workload characteristics.

6 Conclusion

In this paper, we studied what constitutes a good datacenter deployment in the face of heterogeneity. We focused on the use of GPUs in datacenters and developed a model in order to explore various deployment options, but our insights may prove useful in cases of ad hoc heterogeneity, as well. Our main finding shows that even including few GPUs significantly improves performance, while often, a few but powerful GPUs can outperform many, but less powerful ones. We proceed to discuss a number of assumptions made in obtaining these results, as well as some general trends worth noting.

All Tasks can be Executed on all Processing Units: We made the assumption that any task may be executed on any accelerator. While this was done for the sake of abstraction, it may gradually become a reality as people port their codes into accelerators. For instance, specialized, highly parallel applications, traditionally executed on dedicated grids, are now moved to datacenters for the sake of lowering energy consumption [21] and applications such as analytics are being actively rewritten to take advantage of new accelerator architectures [22].

Independent Tasks: Our model assumes that tasks in a taskset are not interdependent, and therefore, that they can be executed in parallel as long as accelerators are available. This assumption is valid for jobs belonging to Online Data-Intensive (OLDI) services and Map-Reduce-style computations.

Homogeneous Workloads: Datacenter workloads do not necessarily consist of a single task type. However, many high-performance datacenter clusters work on a predominant task type, e.g. web search, and many datacenters are deployed to run tasks that benefit from the presence of certain accelerators. For instance, one may deploy a set of physical machines, or of virtual machines in the cloud, in order to run machine learning algorithms. Both the learning and inference phases of neural networks can benefit from GPUs or ASIC accelerators [22]. Our work can help the user estimate the number of accelerators needed in order to obtain the targeted performance.

While our exploration is not exhaustive, we regard our findings as a step towards understanding the benefits offered by accelerators, considering as a plus that they were derived without being dependent on a specific datacenter configuration or a particular application. Besides datacenter planners, our results can be also used by users that deploy virtual machines and GPUs (or generally accelerators) in the cloud. Given that scarce FPGA resources are a constraint, our results may also prove useful when populating cluster of FPGAs [23,24]. In future work, we plan to deal with diversifying some of the aforementioned assumptions. For instance, our current efforts focus on workloads with interdependent tasksets, and we consider that heterogeneous workloads and the validation of the 80 − 20 rule under different scheduling techniques are interesting avenues of future research.

Acknowledgments. This work has received funding from the European Union's Horizon 2020 Research and Innovation program "VINEYARD: Versatile Integrated Accelerator-based Heterogeneous Data Centers", under grant agreement No 687628.

References

1. Esmaeilzadeh, H., Blem, E., Amant, R.S., Sankaralingam, K., Burger, D.: Dark silicon and the end of multicore scaling. In: Proceedings of the 38th Annual International Symposium on Computer Architecture (ISCA), pp. 365–376. ACM, New York (2011)
2. Jouppi, N.P., et al.: In-datacenter performance analysis of a tensor processing unit. arXiv preprint arXiv:1704.04760 (2017)
3. Putnam, A., et al.: A reconfigurable fabric for accelerating large-scale datacenter services. In: ACM/IEEE 41st International Symposium on Computer Architecture (ISCA), pp. 13–24. IEEE (2014)
4. Kindratenko, V.V., et al.: GPU clusters for high-performance computing. In: IEEE International Conference on Cluster Computing and Workshops (2009)
5. Wu, C., Buyya, R.: Cloud Data Centers and Cost Modeling: A Complete Guide To Planning, Designing and Building a Cloud Data Center, 1st edn. Morgan Kaufmann Publishers Inc., San Francisco (2015)
6. Koomey, J., Brill, K., Turner, P., Stanley, J., Taylor, B.: A simple model for determining true total cost of ownership for data centers. Technical report, Uptime Institute (2008)
7. Popa, L., Ratnasamy, S., Iannaccone, G., Krishnamurthy, A., Stoica, I.: A cost comparison of datacenter network architectures. In: Proceedings of the 6th International Conference on Emerging Networking Experiments and Technology, pp. 16:1–16:12. ACM, New York (2010)
8. Dean, J., Barroso, L.A.: The tail at scale. Commun. ACM **56**(2), 74–80 (2013)
9. Barroso, L.A., Dean, J., Hölzle, U.: Web search for a planet: the google cluster architecture. IEEE Micro **23**, 22–28 (2003)
10. Kachris, C., Soudris, D.: A survey on reconfigurable accelerators for cloud computing. In: 2016 26th International Conference on Field Programmable Logic and Applications (FPL), pp. 1–10. IEEE (2016)
11. Zaharia, M., Borthakur, D., Sen Sarma, J., Elmeleegy, K., Shenker, S., Stoica, I.: Delay scheduling: a simple technique for achieving locality and fairness in cluster scheduling. In: Proceedings of the 5th European conference on Computer systems, pp. 265–278. ACM (2010)
12. Mavridis, S., et al.: VineTalk: simplifying software access and sharing of FPGAs in datacenters. In: 2017 27th International Conference on Field Programmable Logic and Applications (FPL), pp. 1–4. IEEE (2017)
13. Chen, Y., Alspaugh, S., Katz, R.: Interactive analytical processing in big data systems: a cross-industry study of MapReduce workloads. Proc. VLDB Endow. **5**(12), 1802–1813 (2012)

14. Reiss, C., Tumanov, A., Ganger, G.R., Katz, R.H., Kozuch, M.A.: Heterogeneity and dynamicity of clouds at scale: Google trace analysis. In: Proceedings of the Third ACM Symposium on Cloud Computing. SoCC 2012, pp. 7:1–7:13. ACM, New York (2012)
15. Awasthi, M., Suri, T., Guz, Z., Shayesteh, A., Ghosh, M., Balakrishnan, V.: System-level characterization of datacenter applications. In: Proceedings of the 6th ACM/SPEC International Conference on Performance Engineering, pp. 27–38. ACM, New York (2015)
16. Moreno, I.S., Garraghan, P., Townend, P., Xu, J.: Analysis, modeling and simulation of workload patterns in a large-scale utility cloud. IEEE Trans. Cloud Comput. **2**(2), 208–221 (2014)
17. Wang, G., Butt, A.R., Monti, H., Gupta, K.: Towards synthesizing realistic workload traces for studying the hadoop ecosystem. In: 2011 IEEE 19th Annual International Symposium on Modelling, Analysis, and Simulation of Computer and Telecommunication Systems, pp. 400–408, July 2011
18. Shen, J., Varbanescu, A.L., Sips, H.: Look before you leap: using the right hardware resources to accelerate applications. In: Proceedings of 16th IEEE International Conference on High Performance Computing and Communications (HPCC 2014), pp. 383–391. IEEE, August 2014
19. Garg, S., Sundaram, S., Patel, H.D.: Robust heterogeneous data center design: a principled approach. SIGMETRICS Perform. Eval. Rev. **39**(3), 28–30 (2011)
20. Venkataraman, S., Yang, Z., Franklin, M., Recht, B., Stoica, I.: Ernest: efficient performance prediction for large-scale advanced analytics. In: Proceedings of the 13th Usenix Conference on Networked Systems Design and Implementation. NSDI 2016, Berkeley, CA, USA, pp. 363–378. USENIX Association (2016)
21. Li, K.: Power and performance management for parallel computations in clouds and data centers. J. Comput. Syst. Sci. **82**(2), 174–190 (2016)
22. Abadi, M., et al.: TensorFlow: large-scale machine learning on heterogeneous distributed systems. arXiv preprint arXiv:1603.04467 (2016)
23. Katevenis, M., et al.: The exanest project: interconnects, storage, and packaging for exascale systems. In: 2016 Euromicro Conference on Digital System Design (DSD), pp. 60–67. IEEE (2016)
24. Abel, F., Weerasinghe, J., Hagleitner, C., Weiss, B., Paredes, S.: An FPGA platform for hyperscalers. In: IEEE 25th Annual Symposium on High-Performance Interconnects (HOTI), pp. 29–32. IEEE (2017)

ECSched: Efficient Container Scheduling on Heterogeneous Clusters

Yang Hu[1,2]([envelope]), Huan Zhou[1], Cees de Laat[1], and Zhiming Zhao[1]

[1] University of Amsterdam, Amsterdam, The Netherlands
{Y.Hu,H.Zhou,delaat,Z.Zhao}@uva.nl
[2] National University of Defense Technology, Changsha, China

Abstract. Operating system (OS) containers are becoming increasingly popular in cloud computing for improving productivity and code portability. However, container scheduling on large heterogeneous cluster is quite challenging. Recent research on cluster scheduling focuses either on scheduling speed to quickly assign resources, or on scheduling quality to improve application performance and cluster utilization. In this paper, we propose ECSched, an efficient container scheduler that can make high-quality and fast placement decisions for concurrent deployment requests on heterogeneous clusters. We map the scheduling problem to a graphic data structure and model it as minimum cost flow problem (MCFP). We implement ECSched based on our cost model, which encodes the deployment requirements of requested containers. In the evaluation, we show that ECSched exceeds the placement quality of existing container schedulers with relatively small overheads, while providing 1.1× better resource efficiency and 1.3× lower average container completion time.

1 Introduction

Operating system (OS) containers are becoming increasingly popular in cloud computing for improving productivity and code portability. Major cloud providers have recently announced container-based cloud services to cater for this popularity [1,4]. Meanwhile, container orchestration platforms, such as Docker Swarm [2], Mesosphere Marathon [12], and Google Kubernetes [8], are emerging to provide container-based infrastructure for automating deployment, scaling, and management of containers on underlying clusters.

Typically, Infrastructure as a Service (IaaS) offered by the cloud providers (e.g., Amazon EC2, Microsoft Azure [1,4]) is based on Virtual Machines (VMs). Compared with VM-based infrastructure, container-based infrastructure (1) can be deployed on both physical and virtual machines, and the highly diverse configuration of VMs makes the clustered machines more heterogeneous; (2) can provide fine-grained resource allocation based on operating-system-level virtualization techniques, which is much more flexible than predefined VM types in VM-based infrastructure; and (3) can support users specifying affinities among containers (e.g., Affinity in Kubernetes) for a distributed application, which facilitates the coordination of containers.

© Springer International Publishing AG, part of Springer Nature 2018
M. Aldinucci et al. (Eds.): Euro-Par 2018, LNCS 11014, pp. 365–377, 2018.
https://doi.org/10.1007/978-3-319-96983-1_26

With these new features, container-based infrastructure imposes emerging and stringent requirements on the scheduling to provide performance guarantee for applications.

1. Multi-resource demands from each container are often specified as a combination of constraints of CPU, memory, network, etc., which have to be considered with the diverse capacity and capability of the underlying heterogeneous cluster.
2. Containers of a distributed application often have strong affinities with other containers (due to frequent data communication) or specific machines (due to data locality). Placing containers on the appropriate node can significantly reduce the latency of container communication and the volume of data transferred. Thus, affinity also has to take into account in the deployment scheduler.
3. Scheduling overheads in large clusters are relatively high, which may hurt the performance of quality critical applications [13, 24, 27, 28], especially for very short jobs like real-time analytics [19, 23]. Moreover, the scheduling algorithm is frequently invoked during the execution of an application when scaling out or recovering from failure, which often has critical time constraints. Thus, the scheduler should be fast to scale to large clusters.

During the past years, container orchestration and scheduling have attracted quite a lot research attention. In the containers orchestration platforms, such as Swarm [2] and Kubernetes [3], they typically adopt queue-based scheduler which process one container at a time (process one pod at a time in Kubernetes). The requested container first waits in a queue until the scheduler fetches it and performs the scheduling algorithm. Regarding the scheduling algorithms to the queue-based scheduler, variants of heuristic packing algorithms, such as Best-Fit Decreasing (BFD) and First-Fit Decreasing (FFD) [6, 16], are often used to achieve practical solutions.

Container-by-container scheduling has the advantage of being suitable for concurrent, parallel decisions in distributed scheduler [9, 19]. On the contrary, scheduling one container at a time also has a crucial disadvantage: the scheduler makes a decision early for a container and restricts its choices for the waiting containers, where it is difficult to make a high-quality placement. To schedule a batch of tasks concurrently, the most common method is using meta-heuristic algorithms [17, 25], which consider the scheduling problem as a whole and find an optimal solution offline. However, they often face difficulties online for a real-time response to dynamic requests [26].

In this paper, we propose ECSched, an efficient container scheduler that can make high-quality and fast placement decisions for concurrent deployment requests on heterogeneous clusters. We map the scheduling problem to a graphic data structure and model it as minimum cost flow problem (MCFP). In the model, edge weights and capacities encode the container demands of multiple resources and container/machine affinities. We implement ECSched based on classical MCFP algorithms and problem-specific optimizations, which can compute the optimal solution online according to our cost model. We evaluate

ECSched in a small-scale cluster and large-scale simulations. In the evaluation, we show that ECSched exceeds the placement quality of state-of-the-art container schedulers with relatively small overheads, while providing 1.1× better resource efficiency and 1.3× lower average container completion time.

2   Problem Formulation

In this section, we first formulate the containers scheduling problem with networked heterogeneous machines in the cluster. Then, we analyze different requirements for container deployment.

2.1   Model Description

In container-based infrastructure, the cluster is typically composed of a set of networked heterogeneous machines $\{\mathbb{M} = \{m_1, m_2, ..., m_M\}$ where $M = |\mathbb{M}|$ is the number of machines. We consider R types of resources $\mathbb{R} = \{r_1, r_2, ..., r_R\}$ (e.g., CPU, memory, or network bandwidth) in each machine. For machine m_i, let $\overrightarrow{V_i} = (V_i^1, V_i^2, ..., V_i^R)$ be the vector of its resource capacities where the element V_i^j denotes the total amount of resource r_j available on machine m_i.

We model the deployment request in the scheduler as a set of containers $\mathbb{C} = \{c_1, c_2, ..., c_N\}$ that are to be deployed on M machines, and $N = |\mathbb{C}|$ is the number of containers. For container c_i, let $\overrightarrow{D_i} = (D_i^1, D_i^2, ..., D_i^R)$ be the vector of its resource demands, where the element D_i^j denotes the amount of resource r_j that the container c_i demands. To affinity specification, let matrix $\mathbb{CA} = [CA_{ij}]_{N \times N}$ denote the container affinity. If $CA_{ij} = 1$, it means that the container c_i has a affinity with container c_j. Let matrix $\mathbb{MA} = [MA_{ij}]_{N \times M}$ denote the machine affinity. If $MA_{ij} = 1$, it means that the container c_i has a affinity with machine m_j.

Next, we model a placement solution of the scheduler. Note that a placement solution means a mapping of containers to machines on the cluster in this paper. Let matrix $\mathbb{X} = [X_{ij}]_{N \times M}$ denote a solution, where X_{ij} is 1 if container c_i is to be deployed on machine m_j, otherwise X_{ij} is 0.

2.2   Deployment Requirements

By analyzing the features of container-based infrastructure, we desire a placement solution that satisfies the following objectives.

Multi-resource Guarantee. Providing multi-resource guarantee for each container on the heterogeneous cluster is the primary requirement to the scheduler. Container-based infrastructure, which has the advantages and benefits of container techniques inherently, can allocate resources in a more fine-grained way than VM-based infrastructure, which facilitates the flexibility of resource allocation for applications. Given the constraints of Service Level Agreements (SLAs) with users, different types of resource demands should be at least guaranteed with a placement solution so that SLAs are not violated. Thus, the resource demands of the containers in the same machine should not exceed its capacity.

$$\sum_{c_i \in \mathbb{C}} X_{ij} D_i^k \leq V_j^k$$

$$\forall m_j \in \mathbb{M}, \ \forall r_k \in \mathbb{R}$$

(1)

Affinity Awareness. In container-based infrastructure, users can specify the affinity of containers in a deployment request, which represents the demands of data communication or data locality. As distributed applications, especially data-intensive applications, transfer data frequently, the network performance would directly affect the overall performance. Considering the influence of the network, the scheduler should be aware of the affinity requirements so that it can take advantage of this information to adjust container placement. The intuitive and effective solution is to co-locate the containers which have container affinities on the same machine,

$$\sum_{m_k \in \mathbb{M}} X_{ik} X_{jk} \geq CA_{ij}$$

$$\forall c_i, \forall c_j \in \mathbb{C}$$

(2)

and place the container on the affinity machine.

$$X_{ik} \geq MA_i^k$$

$$\forall c_i \in \mathbb{C}, \forall m_k \in \mathbb{M}$$

(3)

With these objectives, the challenge for a scheduler is how to make placement decisions fast to improve cluster resource utilization while maintaining container performance.

3   ECSched Approach

As existing queue-based schedulers process one container at a time, the entire workload cannot be considered in the decision-making phase. Consequently, it is hard for the scheduler to make a high-quality placement. In this paper, we choose a graph-based approach to achieve concurrent containers scheduling and model the scheduling problem as minimum cost flow problem (MCFP) [5]. In the rest of this section, we describe how to construct the graph of MCFP to solve the container scheduling problem and what MCFP algorithms to use.

3.1   Minimum Cost Flow Problem

The minimum cost flow problem is an optimization and decision problem to find the minimum-cost way of sending a certain amount of flow through a flow network. A flow network is a directed graph $G = (V, E)$ with a source node $s \in V$ and a sink node $t \in V$, where each edge $e_{u,v} \in E$ has capacity $c_{u,v} > 0$

and cost $a_{u,v}$. The edge $e_{u,v}$ can be assigned a flow $f_{u,v} \geq 0$, and the cost of sending this flow is $f_{u,v} \cdot a_{u,v}$. The problem requires an amount of flow K to be sent from source s to sink t, and the goal is to minimize the total cost of the flow over all edges:

$$\text{Minimize} \quad \sum_{e_{u,v} \in E} f_{u,v} \cdot a_{u,v} \tag{4}$$

$$\text{subject to:} \quad f_{u,v} \leq c_{u,v} \tag{5}$$

$$\sum_{w \in V} f_{w,u} = \sum_{w \in V} f_{u,w} \ (u \neq s, t) \tag{6}$$

$$\sum_{w \in V} f_{s,w} = \sum_{w \in V} f_{w,t} = K \tag{7}$$

3.2 Flow Network Structure

To map the container scheduling problem to MCFP, we represent it using a specific flow network. Figure 1 shows an example of the flow network, in which we only annotate the capacity on edges. This graph corresponds to an instantaneous status of the container cluster, encoding a set of requested containers and clustered machines. The overall structure of the graph can be described as follows.

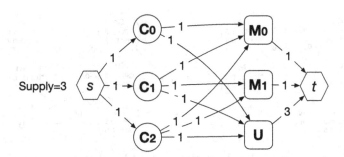

Fig. 1. An example of the flow network

- **Source Node:** The source node s on the left hand with a supply K, which represents how many containers can be scheduled at a time in our context. By default, the supply is set to the total number of requested containers in the scheduler ($K = N$).
- **Container Node:** Each requested container is represented as node C_i in the graph, and has an edge from source node s with capacity 1.
- **Machine Node:** Each clustered machine is represented as node M_i in the graph, and has an edge from the container node with capacity 1 if the machine is eligible to place the container.

- **Unscheduled Node:** Inspired by the work [14], we add a new node, called unscheduled node U. All container nodes have an outgoing edge to node U with capacity 1.
- **Sink Node:** The sink node t on the right hand is the place to drain off the flow. All machine nodes have an edge to sink with capacity 1, and the unscheduled node has an edge to sink with capacity N.

MCFP algorithms would optimally route the flow from the source to the sink without exceeding the capacity constraint on any edge. A path in the flow network first gets to a container node from the source, and then reaches the sink through a machine node or unscheduled node. Thus, if the path goes through a machine node, it corresponds to an assignment for the container. Otherwise, if the path goes through an unscheduled node, it does not schedule the container at this moment.

3.3 Encoding Deployment Requirements

As the goal of the MCFP problem is to minimize the total cost of the flow over all edges, we can flexibly assign the costs on the edges to make the MCFP algorithms return a solution which we desire for the container placement. Considering two deployment requirements from containers, we propose following methods to encode them on edges.

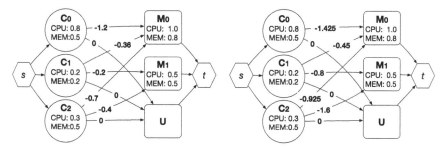

(a) Cost based on dot-product heuristic   (b) Cost based on most-loaded heuristic

Fig. 2. An example for encoding the multi-resource requirements

Multi-resource Guarantee. In order to make the values of different resources comparable to each other and easy to handle, we first normalize the resource number to be the fraction of the corresponding maximum capacity independently. After normalization, the scheduler checks which machines have sufficient resources to place the requested containers. If a machine is eligible for a container, it adds an edge from the container node to the machine node with capacity 1. The challenge here is how to assign the costs on the edges to differentiate the quality of different placements. We introduce two strategies which are inspired by vector bin packing algorithms [20]: dot-product heuristic and most-loaded heuristic.

In dot-product heuristic, dot product between the demand vector of container c_i and the capacity vector of machine m_j is defined as $dp_{ij} = \sum_{r_k \in \mathbb{R}} D_i^k V_j^k$. The higher dp_{ij} is, the better the placement is. The idea of this heuristic is that it takes into account not only the resource demands of containers but also how well its demands align with the resource capacities of machines. Nevertheless, the cost on the edge between them is assigned to $-dp_{ij}$, because the lower the cost is, the better the flow is in MCFP. For the edge from container node to unscheduled node, the cost is 0 which is the highest. An example is shown in Fig. 2(a).

In most-loaded heuristic, the container tends to be placed on the most loaded machine. In our cost model, it is also based on a scalar value $ml_{ij} = \sum_{r_k \in \mathbb{R}} \frac{D_i^k}{V_j^k}$ between the container c_i and the machine m_j to prioritize the placement. The higher ml_{ij} is, the more loaded the machine is. Similarly, the cost on the edge is assigned to $-ml_{ij}$. An example is shown in Fig. 2(b).

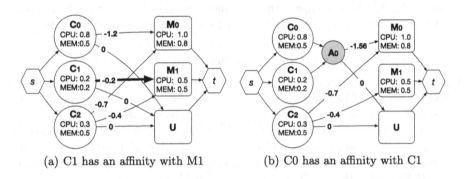

(a) C1 has an affinity with M1   (b) C0 has an affinity with C1

Fig. 3. An example for encoding the affinity requirements (dot-product heuristic)

Affinity Awareness. The location of containers is crucial for the overall performance. In the flow network, it is flexible to handle container affinity (co-located on the same machine) and machine affinity (located on specific machine). Figure 3(a) shows an example with machine affinity, where container c_1 has a machine affinity to machine m_1. In the example, container c_1 has only the edge to machine m_1 but no edge to machine m_0. Figure 3(b) shows an example with container affinity, where container c_0 and container c_1 have an affinity. In the flow network, we add a new node, called aggregator node A_i (A_0 in the example). Both container c_0 and container c_1 have an edge to aggregator node A_0. Hence, the scheduler can treat the two containers as one to handle container affinity.

3.4 MCFP Algorithms

After constructing the flow network, the scheduler will perform a MCFP algorithm to find the optimal placement solution with respect to the costs we have assigned. Known worst-case complexity bounds on the MCFP are $O(M \log(N)(M + N \log(N)))$ [18] and $O(NM \log(N) \log(NC))$ [11], Where N is the number nodes, M the number of edges and C the number of the largest edge capacity. In the container scheduling problem, it is the case as $M > N > C$. We currently implement the latter algorithm in our ECSched. However, MCFP algorithms have variable runtimes depending on the input graph. The comparison of different algorithms and the optimization of algorithms can be explored as future work. The design of ECSched is based on a heartbeat mechanism. On a heartbeat, ECSched fetches all the deployment requests to construct a flow network, and performs the MCFP algorithm to find a placement solution.

4   Evaluation

We implement ECSched with a container manager and the above MCFP algorithm in Python. In this section, we evaluate our ECSched on a 30-machine cluster in ExoGENI to compare the placement quality. To understand the overhead of ECSched, we do large-scale simulations using synthetic workloads.

4.1   Comparison of Placement Quality

Cluster. We create a container cluster with 30 virtual machines (VM) in Exo-GENI [7] testbed. Considering the heterogeneity, we choose three types of VM configurations in our experiments. Thus, the container cluster is composed of 10 VMs of "XOMedium" type (1 core, 3 GB of memory), 10 VMs of "XOLarge" type (2 core, 6 GB of memory) and 10 VMs of "XOXLarge" type (4 core, 12 GB of memory). After normalization, the capacity vectors are: (CPU: 0.25, MEM: 0.25), (CPU: 0.5, MEM: 0.5), and (CPU: 1, MEM: 1).

Workloads. To test our prototype, we constructed container deployment requests based on the Google cluster trace [21], which provides data from a 12,500-machine cluster over a month-long period. As we chose to spend 5 hours at each experiment, we analyzed the trace of the first five hours. There are 83,241 tasks completed, and the average duration of the tasks is 764 s. Considering the scale of our testbed cluster, we randomly sample 8,300 tasks (10%) from them at each experiment. The generator yields container requests according to following aspects from the trace: task submission times, task durations and task resource requirements. The resource requirements have been normalized in the trace. Additionally, we add the requirements of container affinity and machine affinity with 6% probability according to the percentage of task constraints in the trace [21].

Baselines. We compare ECSched to state-of-the-art scheduling algorithms implemented in Google Kubernetes [3] and Docker Swarm [2]. Under multi-resource requirements, the default scheduler of Kubernetes tends to distribute pods (smallest deployable units in Kubernetes) evenly across the cluster to balance the resources, while the scheduler of Swarm tends to place containers on the most loaded machines to improve resource utilization. Both are queue-based schedulers, which schedule one unit at a time.

Metrics. We consider two metrics: the average container completion time and average cluster resource utilization to compare the placement quality of different schedulers. The improvement of average container completion time is computed as:

$$\text{Factor of Improvement} = \frac{\text{Duration of a Baseline}}{\text{Duration of ECSched}} \tag{8}$$

Factor of Improvement greater than 1 means ECSched is performing better, and vice versa.

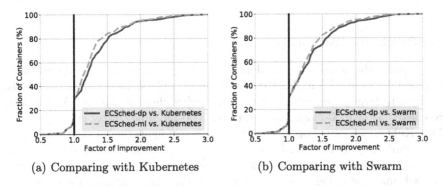

(a) Comparing with Kubernetes   (b) Comparing with Swarm

Fig. 4. CDF of factors of improvement in average container completion time

Figure 4 compares the performance of ECSched with baseline schemes to handle 8,300 container requests on the cluster. We use two strategies in our scheduler to do the comparisons, where ECSched-dp is based on dot-product heuristic, and ECSched-ml is based on most-loaded heuristic. In the figure, the results show that for more than 68% of the containers, ECSched performs better than the alternatives, and only 10% of the containers slow down. For two different strategies, ECSched-dp performs better than ECSched-ml in our evaluation. To the scheduler of Kubernetes, ECSched-dp speeds up containers by 1.2× at the median, 1.28× at the 60th percentile, and 1.5× at the 80th percentile. To the scheduler of Swarm, ECSched-dp speeds up containers by 1.21× at the median, 1.3× at the 60th percentile, and 1.57× at the 80th percentile. Overall, ECSched improves over the alternatives by up to 1.3× on average. The improvements accrue from the increase in the number of simultaneously running containers (less waiting time in the queue), as ECSched takes entire workloads into consideration to make placement decisions.

To evaluate the resource efficiency, we make some changes to the workloads. All the container requests are submitted at the beginning in the experiment.

Table 1 shows the average cluster resource utilization of the experiment. Due to the better placement (cause less resource fragmentation), ECSched sustains higher cluster resource utilization than the baselines. Overall, ECSched provides 1.1× better resource efficiency. Consequently, it demonstrates that the ECSched approach can achieve higher quality placements for deploying containers on heterogeneous clusters.

Table 1. Average cluster resource utilization in the experiment

Resource type	ECSched-dp	ECSched-ml	Kubernetes	Swarm
CPU	**76.57**%	75.80%	70.00%	69.98%
MEMORY	**76.71**%	75.93%	70.12%	70.10%

4.2   Overheads Evaluation

As we model the scheduling problem as a MCFP, the scheduling algorithm in our scheduler is more complex than existing schedulers. To estimate overheads, we simulate large-scale clusters to run our scheduling algorithm. We consider two cluster sizes: 1000-machine cluster and 5000-machine cluster (largest cluster which Kubernetes can support currently). The configuration of each machine is chosen uniformly at random from Amazon EC2 instances (19 kinds of general purpose instances) in order to make the simulated cluster more heterogeneous, and each machine is half loaded in the simulation. By analyzing the trace [21], the scheduler needs to make hundreds of task placement decisions per second in peak hours. Thus, we try to submit 100, 200 and 300 container deployment requests to the scheduler to evaluate the algorithm runtime. In order to fairly compare the algorithm runtime, we also implement the scheduling algorithm of Kubernetes and Swarm in Python. We conduct this experiment on a server with 48 cores and 128 GB memory.

Figure 5 shows the results of the experiment which we repeated ten times. We see that the algorithm runtime of ECSched is longest while Swarm is shortest. The algorithm of Swarm is a simple greedy search to place requested containers. Compared with Swarm, the algorithm of Kubernetes is complex, which has multiple predicated policies and priorities policies to filter and score machines. Obviously, our algorithm is the most complicated one. Nevertheless, ECSched can respond in sub-second time when the number of requested containers is less than 100. When processing 300 containers concurrently, the ECSched responds in about 1.8 s for 1000-machine cluster and about 3.4 s for 5000-machine cluster. Actually, compared to the average duration (764 s in our experiments) of the containers in the cluster [21], the overhead is relatively small and acceptable. We believe that our scheduler is effective and usable in practice.

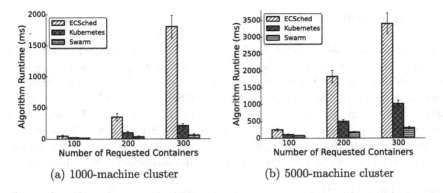

Fig. 5. Comparing algorithm runtime in large-scale simulation

5 Related Work

The problem investigated in this paper - container scheduling on heterogeneous clusters - is related to a variety of research topics as follows.

Bin Packing. The problem of VM placement or consolidation which is similar to our problem is often formulated as vector bin packing problem, and various heuristics have been proposed for this problem [15,16]. Mark Stillwell et al. [22] studied variants of FFD concluding that the algorithm that reasons on the sum of the resource needs of the tasks are the most effective. Panigrahy et al. [20] presented a generalization of the classical first fit decreasing (FFD) heuristic. In their experiments, it showed that the Dot-Product heuristic often outperforms FFD-based heuristics. These contributions focus on VM packing, and only consider each request independently.

Metaheuristics. In recent years, many metaheuristic techniques have become prevalent for the approximate solution of multi-objective optimization problems [25]. Mi et al. [17] proposed a genetic algorithm based approach, namely GABA, to adaptively self-reconfigure the VMs in virtualized large-scale data centers consisting of heterogeneous nodes. Xu et al. [25] presented a modified genetic algorithm with fuzzy multi-objective evaluation for efficiently searching the large solution space and conveniently combining possibly conflicting objectives. However, these approaches often take minutes or hours to generate a solution, which face difficulties for a online response.

Cluster Schedulers. Many cluster schedulers have been proposed for different purposes. Sparrow [19] and Tarcil [9] are distributed schedulers developed for clusters that achieve a high throughput for short tasks. Quincy [14], a cluster fair scheduler, models the fair scheduling problem as a minimum cost flow problem to schedule jobs into slots. Firmament [10], a centralized scheduler, achieves low latency via a min-cost max-flow (MCMF) optimization. Differently, ECSched shows that how to encode multi-resource requirements and affinity requirements in MCFP.

6 Conclusion

In this paper, we have presented ECSched, an efficient container scheduler to schedule concurrent containers on heterogeneous clusters. ECSched is a graph-based scheduler, which takes entire deployment requests into consideration for placement decisions. We demonstrate that ECSched can achieve better placement quality than state-of-the-art scheduler in the evaluation. The large-scale simulation shows there are small overheads of ECSched, but it is acceptable in practice. In the future work, we will consider container dependencies and resource dynamics for the scheduler to adopt more sophisticated situations.

Acknowledgments. This research has received funding from the European Union's Horizon 2020 research and innovation program under grant agreements 643963 (SWITCH project), 654182 (ENVRIPLUS project) and 676247 (VRE4EIC project). The research is also funded by Chinese Scholarship Council.

References

1. Amazon web services. https://aws.amazon.com/
2. Docker swarm. https://docs.docker.com/engine/swarm/
3. Google kubernetes. https://kubernetes.io/
4. Microsoft azure. https://azure.microsoft.com/
5. Ahuja, R.K., Magnanti, T.L., Orlin, J.B.: Network Flows. Elsevier, New York (2014)
6. Ajiro, Y., Tanaka, A.: Improving packing algorithms for server consolidation. In: International CMG Conference, vol. 253 (2007)
7. Baldin, I., et al.: ExoGENI: a multi-domain infrastructure-as-a-service testbed. In: McGeer, R., Berman, M., Elliott, C., Ricci, R. (eds.) The GENI Book, pp. 279–315. Springer, Cham (2016). https://doi.org/10.1007/978-3-319-33769-2_13
8. Burns, B., Grant, B., Oppenheimer, D., Brewer, E., Wilkes, J.: Borg, omega, and kubernetes. Commun. ACM **59**(5), 50–57 (2016)
9. Delimitrou, C., Sanchez, D., Kozyrakis, C.: Tarcil: reconciling scheduling speed and quality in large shared clusters. In: Proceedings of the Sixth ACM Symposium on Cloud Computing, pp. 97–110. ACM (2015)
10. Gog, I., Schwarzkopf, M., Gleave, A., Watson, R.N., Hand, S.: Firmament: fast, centralized cluster scheduling at scale. USENIX (2016)
11. Goldberg, A.V., Tarjan, R.E.: Finding minimum-cost circulations by canceling negative cycles. J. ACM (JACM) **36**(4), 873–886 (1989)
12. Hindman, B., et al.: Mesos: a platform for fine-grained resource sharing in the data center. In: NSDI, vol. 11, p. 22 (2011)
13. Hu, Y., et al.: Deadline-aware deployment for time critical applications in clouds. In: Rivera, F.F., Pena, T.F., Cabaleiro, J.C. (eds.) Euro-Par 2017. LNCS, vol. 10417, pp. 345–357. Springer, Cham (2017). https://doi.org/10.1007/978-3-319-64203-1_25
14. Isard, M., Prabhakaran, V., Currey, J., Wieder, U., Talwar, K., Goldberg, A.: Quincy: fair scheduling for distributed computing clusters. In: Proceedings of the ACM SIGOPS 22nd Symposium on Operating Systems Principles, pp. 261–276. ACM (2009)

15. Lee, S., et al.: Validating heuristics for virtual machines consolidation. Microsoft Research, MSR-TR-2011-9 pp. 1–14 (2011)
16. Lodi, A., Martello, S., Vigo, D.: Recent advances on two-dimensional bin packing problems. Discret. Appl. Math. **123**(1), 379–396 (2002)
17. Mi, H., Wang, H., Yin, G., Zhou, Y., Shi, D., Yuan, L.: Online self-reconfiguration with performance guarantee for energy-efficient large-scale cloud computing data centers. In: 2010 IEEE International Conference on Services Computing (SCC), pp. 514–521. IEEE (2010)
18. Orlin, J.B.: A faster strongly polynomial minimum cost flow algorithm. Oper. Res. **41**(2), 338–350 (1993)
19. Ousterhout, K., Wendell, P., Zaharia, M., Stoica, I.: Sparrow: distributed, low latency scheduling. In: Proceedings of the Twenty-Fourth ACM Symposium on Operating Systems Principles, pp. 69–84. ACM (2013)
20. Panigrahy, R., Talwar, K., Uyeda, L., Wieder, U.: Heuristics for vector bin packing (2011). research.microsoft.com
21. Reiss, C., Tumanov, A., Ganger, G.R., Katz, R.H., Kozuch, M.A.: Heterogeneity and dynamicity of clouds at scale: Google trace analysis. In: Proceedings of the Third ACM Symposium on Cloud Computing, p. 7. ACM (2012)
22. Stillwell, M., Schanzenbach, D., Vivien, F., Casanova, H.: Resource allocation algorithms for virtualized service hosting platforms. J. Parallel Distrib. Comput. **70**(9), 962–974 (2010)
23. Taherizadeh, S., Jones, A.C., Taylor, I., Zhao, Z., Stankovski, V.: Monitoring self-adaptive applications within edge computing frameworks: a state-of-the-art review. J. Syst. Softw. **136**, 19–38 (2018)
24. Wang, J., et al.: Planning virtual infrastructures for time critical applications with multiple deadline constraints. Future Gen. Comput. Syst. **75**, 365–375 (2017)
25. Xu, J., Fortes, J.A.: Multi-objective virtual machine placement in virtualized data center environments. In: Proceedings of the 2010 IEEE/ACM International Conference on Green Computing and Communications & International Conference on Cyber, Physical and Social Computing, pp. 179–188. IEEE Computer Society (2010)
26. Zhan, Z.H., Liu, X.F., Gong, Y.J., Zhang, J., Chung, H.S.H., Li, Y.: Cloud computing resource scheduling and a survey of its evolutionary approaches. ACM Comput. Surv. (CSUR) **47**(4), 63 (2015)
27. Zhao, Z., et al.: A software workbench for interactive, time critical and highly self-adaptive cloud applications (switch). In: 2015 15th IEEE/ACM International Symposium on Cluster, Cloud and Grid Computing (CCGrid), pp. 1181–1184. IEEE (2015)
28. Zhou, H., et al.: Fast resource co-provisioning for time critical applications based on networked infrastructures. In: 2016 IEEE 9th International Conference on Cloud Computing (CLOUD), pp. 802–805. IEEE (2016)

Combinatorial Auction Algorithm Selection for Cloud Resource Allocation Using Machine Learning

Diana Gudu$^{(\boxtimes)}$, Marcus Hardt, and Achim Streit

Karlsruhe Institute of Technology, Karlsruhe, Germany
{diana.gudu,marcus.hardt,achim.streit}@kit.edu

Abstract. Demands for flexibility, efficiency and fine-grained control for the allocation of cloud resources have steered the research in this field towards market-inspired approaches. Combinatorial auctions can fulfill these demands, but their inherent $\mathcal{NP}$-hardness makes them impractical if an optimal solution is desired in a reasonable time. Various heuristic algorithms that yield good allocations fast have been proposed, but their performance and solution quality are highly dependent on the input. In this paper, we investigate which features of a problem instance are predictive of algorithm performance and quality, and propose an algorithm selection method that uses machine learning to find the best heuristic for each given input. We introduce a new cost model for the trade-off between execution time and solution quality, which enables quantitative algorithm comparison. Using feature-based classification to train the algorithm selection model, we can show that our approach outperforms the single best algorithm, as well as a random algorithm selection.

Keywords: Cloud resource allocation · Combinatorial auction
Algorithm selection · Feature-based classification

1 Introduction

Cloud computing leverages economies of scale to provide resources as a utility. Therefore, market-oriented approaches are necessary to regulate the demand and supply of cloud resources, as well as provide economic incentives for both providers and customers [1].

The concept of dynamic pricing is gaining interest, as cloud providers such as Amazon use single-good auctions to sell their unused resources on the spot market [2]. Moreover, dynamic pricing is an essential part of smart contracts [3], an emerging alternative to broker-based matchmaking for cloud service selection, which support changes in agreements while offering quality and security guarantees through their self-executing nature.

Combinatorial auctions [4] can offer more flexibility and fine-grained control, by affording customers to request and pay only for the combination of

© Springer International Publishing AG, part of Springer Nature 2018
M. Aldinucci et al. (Eds.): Euro-Par 2018, LNCS 11014, pp. 378–391, 2018.
https://doi.org/10.1007/978-3-319-96983-1_27

resources that fits their requirements. However, their applicability to resource allocation has been limited to the realm of academic research [5], due to their $\mathcal{NP}$-hardness. The forecast growth of public cloud services market [6] will further impede their practical use due to scalability concerns – as long as optimal solutions are desired. Therefore, for real-world adoption, it is necessary to sacrifice optimality requirements by using heuristics.

Existing heuristic algorithms for combinatorial auctions [7–9] perform differently depending on the input characteristics, in terms of both runtime and solution quality [10]. A more robust usage is essential, since any performance gain can translate into high increases in revenue for cloud providers. Furthermore, the quality-speed trade-off of each algorithm needs to be reliably controlled, in order to fit any particular needs.

In this paper, we address these challenges by using machine learning to select the most suited heuristic for each individual auction instance, while introducing a quantitative definition for this suitability – based on a runtime and welfare-dependent cost model. Furthermore, we propose a feature set tailored to combinatorial auctions to aid the learning process. We perform an extensive evaluation and show that the proposed approach outperforms single algorithms, as well as a random algorithm selection.

2   Related Work

Various approaches for algorithm selection have been applied to combinatorial search problems, as summarized in [11]. The techniques are categorized according to the type of algorithm portfolio (static or dynamic), features (low or high-knowledge, static or dynamic), performance models, and prediction types. Their applicability is exemplified across a range of application domains: SAT, Mixed Integer Programming, machine learning, etc. However, these methods focus on a single optimization objective, usually runtime.

The only work where algorithm selection was applied to combinatorial auctions [12] is concerned with optimal algorithms and minimizing the execution time, whereas we look at heuristic algorithms and optimize both social welfare and execution time. Leyton-Brown et al. [12] studied the empirical hardness of combinatorial auctions and devised a methodology to understand this hardness using feature-based supervised learning. They identified certain structural features of the WDP that are predictive of running time, and used this runtime prediction to select the fastest algorithm for each problem instance, outperforming the best algorithm in the average case. We note that this work used regression-based learning techniques to predict the runtime of algorithms instead of classification, in order to penalize mispredictions differently.

Beck and Freuder [13] use algorithm selection for scheduling problems. They optimize the performance of a portfolio of optimal algorithms only based on low-knowledge information, obtained by running all the algorithms for a short time, recording their performance, and using this information to inform the prediction.

3   Formal Problem Definition

To model the cloud resource allocation using market-inspired concepts, we make the following assumptions:

1. there are multiple cloud providers offering computing resources and multiple customers requesting resources from any provider at a centralized market-place,
2. there is a fixed number of resource types on the market, known apriori by all market participants,
3. all resources requested by a customer need to come from the same provider,
4. all requests and offers are independent, and
5. no partial allocations or floating point quantities are allowed.

The problem can then be formalized as a multi-unit, double combinatorial auction, consisting of: a set of n bidders $U = \{1, \ldots, n\}$, a set of m providers $P = \{1, \ldots, m\}$, a set of l goods $G = \{1, \ldots, l\}$, and an auctioneer that decides the allocation and pricing of resources based on the bids and asks.

Each customer i submits a single bid for a bundle of resources, expressed as $(\langle r_{i1}, \ldots, r_{il} \rangle, b_i)$, where r_{ik} is the number of items of resource type k that the bidder i requests, and b_i is the maximum amount bidder i is willing to pay for the entire bundle. Similarly, a seller j submits its ask expressed as $(\langle s_{j1}, \ldots, s_{jl} \rangle, a_j)$, where s_{jk} are the quantities offered by seller j of each resource type k. Seller j offers its bundle of resources at a price a_j, which is the minimum acceptable.

In the context of cloud computing, a bundle represents a virtual machine (VM), consisting of resources such as CPU cores, memory, disk storage, GPU cores, etc. This model makes assumption 3 indispensable, since a VM cannot contain resources from different providers. Furthermore, we showed that the resource locality constraint makes the allocation problem harder in terms of time complexity [10], and thus requires the use of heuristic algorithms. Therefore, the algorithm selection approach is aimed at this specific use case.

The auctioneer collects the bids and asks, and finds the best allocation of resources that maximizes the social welfare of the system. To that end, it first determines which bidders will receive the requested bundles and which providers can sell their resources – also called the Winner Determination Problem (WDP) [14] – and then decides the trading prices – also called the payment scheme.

The social welfare is defined [15] as the sum of all the participants' utilities, where the utility is a measure of a trader's satisfaction. For example, a bidder i's utility for a requested bundle S is defined as $u_i(S) = v_i(S) - p_i$, if i wins the auction, and 0 otherwise, where $v_i(S)$ (valuation) is the true value bidder i is willing to pay for bundle S, and p_i is the actual price paid at the end of the auction. When a bidder is truthful, $v_i(S) = b_i$.

We assume that customers and providers are single-minded, which means that they are only interested in buying or selling the full bundle, and have 0 valuation for all the other bundles.

Then the WDP can be written as the following integer program:

$$\max_{x,y} \left(\sum_{i=1}^{n} b_i x_i - \sum_{j=1}^{m} \sum_{i=1}^{n} a_j y_{ij} \right) \tag{1}$$

subject to:

$$x_i, y_{ij} \in \{0, 1\}, \forall i \in U, \forall j \in P \tag{2}$$

$$\sum_{i=1}^{n} y_{ij} \leq 1, \forall j \in P \tag{3}$$

$$\sum_{j=1}^{m} y_{ij} = x_i, \forall i \in U \tag{4}$$

$$r_{ik} x_i \leq \sum_{j=1}^{m} s_{jk} y_{ij}, \forall i \in U, \forall k \in G \tag{5}$$

where constraint (2) expresses the single-mindedness of bidders and sellers, constraint (3) ensures that a seller can allocate its bundle to at most one bidder, and constraint (4) ensures that each customer receives the resources in its bundle from a single provider. Finally, constraint (5) ensures that a provider cannot sell more than the amount of resources it offered.

The auctioneer then uses a κ-pricing scheme [10] to set the bundle prices by distributing the trade surplus among the auction winners, thus ensuring budget-balance. The truthfulness requirement is relaxed, but it was shown that it can be achieved in practice, since non-truthful bidding increases the risk of no allocation [16].

4 Algorithm Selection

Combinatorial auctions are $\mathcal{NP}$-hard [4], hindering their wide adoption in real-world applications. Existing heuristic algorithms mitigate the scalability and efficiency issues posed by optimal algorithms, but their solution quality varies with the input [10]. For a more robust usage of heuristic algorithms for combinatorial auctions, we propose using an algorithm selection approach [11]: selecting the most suitable algorithm on a case-by-case basis. To predict which heuristic will perform best on each problem instance, we propose the use of supervised machine learning in conjunction with an algorithm portfolio.

The workflow for algorithm selection, based on similar approaches for runtime prediction [12], is depicted in Fig. 1. We first build an algorithm portfolio by assembling a collection of complementary heuristic algorithms for combinatorial auctions. The data are collected in two sub-steps: (1.a) generating a large number of auction instances (defined by a set of bids and asks) that covers a representative part of the input space, by using our artificial input generator for combinatorial auctions CAGE [10]; (1.b) running all the algorithms in the

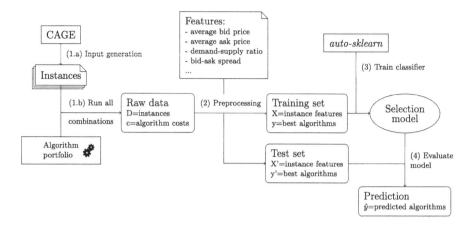

Fig. 1. Algorithm selection workflow

portfolio on all the generated instances to record their runtime and resulting social welfare. Since using the raw input for learning can be computationally expensive or even intractable, we propose to use domain knowledge to extract a set of features that contain sufficient information; the features are mainly statistics related to bid and ask values, quantities or demand-supply balance (see Sect. 4.2). The preprocessing step (2) includes feature extraction, labeling the data by selecting the best algorithm for each instance – the algorithm with the lowest cost, as defined in Sect. 4.3 – and splitting the dataset into training and test data for supervised learning. We formulate the algorithm selection problem as a multi-class classification problem: given observations (a set of instances defined by their features) whose class labels (best algorithm) are known, we (3) train a model that can predict the class label of any new observation. The model is then (4) tested on unseen data. At this step, several appropriate metrics to evaluate the quality of the prediction should be considered (see Sect. 4.4).

4.1   Algorithm Portfolio

In [10], we investigated and compared different algorithms for approximating the solutions of WDPs. We built an algorithm portfolio by either adapting various combinatorial auction algorithms [7–9], or applying well-known optimization methods [17,18] to combinatorial auctions. The experiments revealed that algorithm runtime and solution quality are highly dependent on the input, and no single algorithm outperformed the others in all test cases. This result was most pronounced when resource locality was a desired property – all resources requested by a customer being allocated on the same cloud provider. The problem formulation presented in this paper already includes the resource locality constraint, and the algorithms were adapted accordingly.

In the rest of this section, we briefly describe the 12 algorithms included in our portfolio. Based on the employed optimization approach, we can group the algorithms into four families: greedy, hill climbing, simulated annealing, and stochastic local search.

The greedy algorithms sort the bid and ask lists according to a certain criteria (e.g. bid density), and then traverse the list to greedily match bids with asks. Based on [7], we used three different sorting criteria to implement algorithms GREEDY1, GREEDY2 and GREEDY3. A greedy algorithm that gives priority to sellers was also implemented (we denote seller priority by a '-S' suffix: GREEDY1S).

Hill climbing algorithms perform a local search in the solution space, similar to gradient descent. We included two methods of exploring the neighborhood of a solution: first, by changing the ordering of bids or ask onto which a greedy allocation is performed [8] (algorithms HILL1 and HILL1S), and second, by toggling the allocation of a bid through the x_i variables [19] (HILL2 and HILL2S).

Simulated annealing algorithms (SA and SAS) use the same method of generating a neighboring solution as HILL2, but randomly accept worse solutions to escape from local optima.

Finally, to mitigate the same problem, stochastic local search algorithms (CASANOVA and CASANOVAS) use random walks with restarts, while exploring the solution neighborhood by adding bids based on their ranking and novelty [9].

The algorithms based on simulated annealing and stochastic local search techniques are stochastic, yielding different results for multiple runs on the same input. For reliable usage, the average welfare and execution time over 10 runs were used in our experiments.

The portfolio is easily extensible, and more algorithms can be added as they are developed. However, this affects the rest of the algorithm selection pipeline: the prediction models need to be retrained for every portfolio change.

4.2 Features

Using domain knowledge – insights into the inner workings of combinatorial auctions, as well as each individual algorithm – we defined a number of 75 features that can be extracted from any problem instance. The features are mainly statistics, and can be computed in $\mathcal{O}\left(l\left(m+n\right)\right)$, which is faster than any of the algorithms in the portfolio. The defined features can be grouped in four categories: price related, quantity related, quantity per resource related (as measures of heterogeneity of requests) and demand-supply balance related.

We give some examples of features in the following. First, statistics of the distribution of the asking price per unit over all asks were included (mean, standard deviation, skewness and kurtosis). Similarly, we looked at the distribution of the bid price per unit over all bids, as well as the corresponding quantity related features: the total bundle sizes of bids and asks. Moreover, we included economics concepts such as the bid-ask spread, defined as the difference between the minimum ask and maximum bid, and used as a measure of the market liquidity. Similarly, we defined a quantity spread per resource, as the difference between the maximum requested quantity and the minimum offered quantity per resource, and computed the first four central moments of the distribution of quantity spread over all the l resource types. Other features in the group of demand-supply balance related features deal with quantity surpluses, either total surplus (the difference between the total number of resources offered and requested), or a quantity surplus per resource type.

4.3   Cost Model

Since the algorithms in the portfolio are heuristic, they generally trade solution quality for speed. Thus, labeling the dataset requires, for each problem instance, a comparison of all algorithms with respect to both social welfare and execution time, which can then yield the best algorithm for both criteria. We propose modeling this as a multi-objective optimization problem [20], whose objectives are a maximum social welfare and a minimum execution time. In order to find a Pareto optimal solution, we use the idea of a compromise solution [21], which minimizes the distance between the potential optimal point and a utopia (or ideal) point.

As welfare and time are measured on different scales, they should first be normalized to obtain non-dimensional objective functions. We normalize the welfare objective function, and call it welfare cost $c_w(o, a)$, as defined in Eq. 6, where $w(o, a)$ is the welfare computed by algorithm a on instance o, while $w_{min}(o)$ and $w_{max}(o)$ are, respectively, the minimum and maximum welfare obtained for instance o by any algorithm in the portfolio. Thus, the best algorithm when only welfare objective is considered will have zero welfare cost.

$$c_w(o, a) = \frac{w_{max}(o) - w(o, a)}{w_{max}(o) - w_{min}(o)} \quad (6)$$

Similarly, in Eq. 7 we define the time cost $c_t(o, a)$ as the normalized time objective, where $t(o, a)$ is the execution time of algorithm a on instance o, and $t_{min}(o)$ and $t_{max}(o)$ are the execution times of the fastest and slowest algorithms in the portfolio on instance o. The best algorithm with respect to time will also have zero time cost.

$$c_t(o, a) = \frac{t(o, a) - t_{min}(o)}{t_{max}(o) - t_{min}(o)} \quad (7)$$

Then the multi-objective function is defined as a vector in the two-dimensional objective space, $C = \begin{bmatrix} c_w & c_t \end{bmatrix}^\top$. Furthermore, we introduce a user-defined preference parameter $\lambda \in [0, 1]$ that reflects the relative importance of the two objectives, in order to provide more control over the decision of selecting the best algorithm. This changes the multi-objective vector to $C_\lambda = \begin{bmatrix} \lambda & (1 - \lambda) \end{bmatrix} C$. A value of $\lambda = 1$ implies that solely the welfare objective should be considered, while $\lambda = 0.5$ places equal importance on welfare and time.

Finally, we find the optimal solution (best algorithm) by minimizing the distance to the utopian vector C°, whose components are the lower bounds of each objective function – in this case $\begin{bmatrix} 0 & 0 \end{bmatrix}^\top$. We use the Euclidean distance to compute the scalar cost metric that will ultimately be used to select the best algorithm, as defined in Eq. 8.

$$c_\lambda(o, a) = \|C_\lambda - C^\circ\| = \sqrt{(\lambda c_w(o, a))^2 + ((1 - \lambda) c_t(o, a))^2} \tag{8}$$

In Fig. 2, we exemplify the use of λ on a random problem instance. For different λ values, different algorithms have minimum cost and are thus selected as the best: when speed is more important ($\lambda = 0.1$), the CASANOVAS algorithm is selected, while an algorithm based on hill climbing (HILL2s) is best when welfare has a higher priority ($\lambda = 0.9$). A simulated annealing algorithm (SAS) is the best when time and welfare are weighted equally ($\lambda = 0.5$).

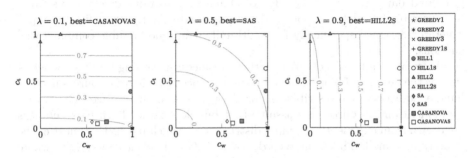

Fig. 2. Visualization of a problem instance in the two-dimensional objective space. Isolines represent scalar cost c_λ. Different algorithms emerge as best depending on λ.

4.4 Evaluation Metrics

There are several success measures when evaluating a classification model. The most intuitive measure is the accuracy, namely how often the model correctly predicts the algorithm with the lowest cost. More specifically, we define the accuracy in Eq. 9, for a given dataset O, as the fraction of the instances for which the predicted algorithm $\hat{y}_o$ is the same as the algorithm with the lowest cost y_o.

$$\text{accuracy}_\lambda(y, \hat{y}) = \frac{1}{|O|} \sum_{o \in O} 1(\hat{y}_o = y_o) \tag{9}$$

However, the accuracy does not give a quantitative evaluation of a model's mispredictions: it penalizes all misclassifications equally, irrespective of their associated costs. To that end, we introduce a metric that considers the cost of the predicted algorithm: the mean relative error (MRE), as defined in Eq. 10.

$$MRE_\lambda(y, \hat{y}) = \frac{1}{|O|} \sum_{o \in O} (c_\lambda(o, \hat{y}_o) - c_\lambda(o, y_o))^2 \tag{10}$$

For a meaningful evaluation, we also compare our portfolio-based algorithm selection against a single algorithm a^*. Therefore, we introduce the relative mean relative error (RMRE) metric, defined in Eq. 11 as the ratio between the MRE of the classification model and the MRE of using algorithm a^* on the entire dataset. The classification model can be similarly compared to a random selection model.

$$RMRE_\lambda(y, \hat{y}, a^*) = \frac{MRE_\lambda(y, \hat{y})}{MRE_\lambda(y, a^*)} \tag{11}$$

5   Evaluation

We evaluated our machine learning-based algorithm selection on an artificially generated dataset, as real data for combinatorial auctions of cloud resources (e.g. user bidding data) is not available. We used CAGE [10], a flexible input generator designed specifically for multi-unit, multi-good double combinatorial auctions.

We created a dataset of 5970 auction instances by varying input parameters such as the number of bids, asks and resource types, sparsity of resources inside a bundle, additivity, and distributions used for generating base prices. Given that we model cloud resources, we assume that bundle sizes for both bids and asks are drawn from exponential random distributions, which means that most of the bundles are small. This is in accordance with Google cloud traces [22], where most task are short, while only a few tasks are long running with high resource demands. Regarding bidding strategies, we assume a normal distribution around base prices, meaning that bidders are willing to pay, per unit, a price close to a resource's known market price.

5.1   Dataset Analysis

We analyze the dataset by evaluating the relevance of the defined features to the prediction, as well as the distribution of class labels. The dataset was labeled by selecting, for each problem instance, the algorithm that yielded the lowest cost. Since the cost is λ-dependent, so are the labels.

Figure 3 shows the support for each class, over 11 values of λ equidistantly distributed over $[0, 1]$. Note that the dataset is imbalanced for all λ. Furthermore, for small λ values, when time is more important than welfare, greedy algorithms were selected more frequently, as they are fast, but have poor quality, while at the other end hill climbing algorithms, although slower, were selected for their higher welfare. For $\lambda \in [0.1, 0.6]$, simulated annealing algorithms were often selected as best – not surprising, since they are similar to hill climbing, but randomly accept worse solutions to climb out of local optima and reach to a solution faster. An interesting result is the λ-independent number of instances for which the greedy algorithms are selected as best (e.g. 47 instances for GREEDY1). These are the infeasible instances, or the auctions where no match exists and the social welfare is 0—thus the fastest algorithm is always selected as best.

Figure 3 hence demonstrates the input-dependent performance of heuristic algorithms, and the potential for improvement by using algorithm selection.

Next, we investigated which features are more relevant to the prediction. The aim is to identify irrelevant or redundant features, and remove them to

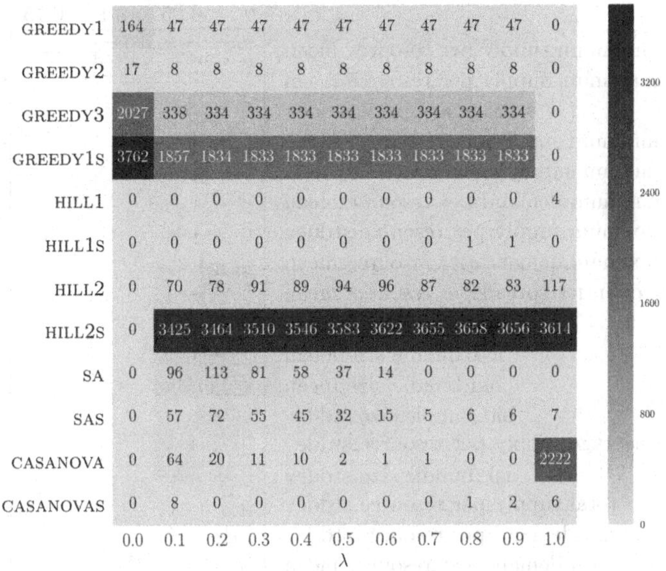

	0.0	0.1	0.2	0.3	0.4	0.5	0.6	0.7	0.8	0.9	1.0
GREEDY1	164	47	47	47	47	47	47	47	47	47	0
GREEDY2	17	8	8	8	8	8	8	8	8	8	0
GREEDY3	2027	338	334	334	334	334	334	334	334	334	0
GREEDY1S	3762	1857	1834	1833	1833	1833	1833	1833	1833	1833	0
HILL1	0	0	0	0	0	0	0	0	0	0	4
HILL1S	0	0	0	0	0	0	0	0	1	1	0
HILL2	0	70	78	91	89	94	96	87	82	83	117
HILL2S	0	3425	3464	3510	3546	3583	3622	3655	3658	3656	3614
SA	0	96	113	81	58	37	14	0	0	0	0
SAS	0	57	72	55	45	32	15	5	6	6	7
CASANOVA	0	64	20	11	10	2	1	1	0	0	2222
CASANOVAS	0	8	0	0	0	0	0	0	1	2	6

λ

Fig. 3. Algorithm selection dataset: breakdown by class labels for several λ values.

reduce the dimensionality of the input space and prevent over-fitting. We used tree-based estimators to compute relative feature importances to the model's performance.

In Fig. 4, all 75 features are sorted based on their importance and the first 20 are shown. Note that only a few are relevant, e.g. 16 features have an importance over 0.02. The most relevant features are related to the quantities per resource, demanded or supplied on the market – minimum, maximum, and average values – as well as the mean and standard deviation of bundle sizes. This can be explained by the fact that quantities per resource are instrumental in assessing the feasibility of a solution, as enforced by constraint (5), and influence the way algorithms move in the search space. From the price-related features, only the minimum and standard deviation of the asking price per unit have a certain effect on the prediction.

5.2   Classification Evaluation

The dataset was split into a training set (70%) and a test set (30%), used to test how the model generalizes on unseen data. Because of the imbalanced dataset, the splitting was performed using stratified sampling, to ensure that the train and test sets have the same percentage of samples of each class as the full set.

Using *auto-sklearn* [23], we trained a classification model for each λ value. The *auto-sklearn* library implements an automated machine learning approach, which relies on Bayesian optimization methods to construct an ensemble of classifiers and find their best hyperparameters and preprocessing steps. The preprocessing,

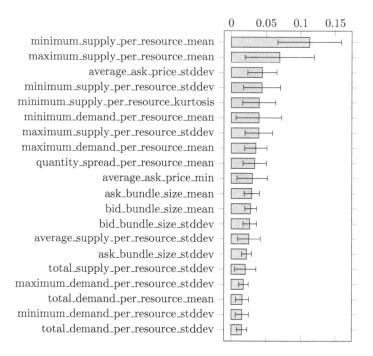

Fig. 4. Relative feature importances averaged over all λ values, computed using Extra-TreesClassifier in *scikit-learn* with 500 estimators. Only the first 20 most relevant features are shown.

in this case, includes feature scaling and feature selection for dimensionality reduction, based on their relevance as described in Sect. 5.1.

Figure 5 shows the accuracy of the models for each λ, on both training and test set. Good accuracies over 93% are obtained for most λ preferences, with higher accuracy for higher λ, suggesting that the selected features are more relevant to the welfare objective rather than the time objective.

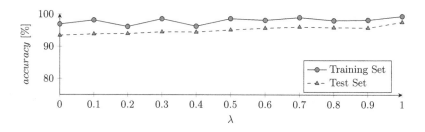

Fig. 5. Accuracy of ML-based algorithm selection for different λ values.

More importantly, a comparison between the trained models for each λ and random selection (see Fig. 6) shows that our algorithm selection approach is always 2 to 4 orders of magnitude better than a random selection approach. Note that an RMRE value below 1 implies that the algorithm selection using machine learning is better than its counterpart in the comparison.

Similarly, a comparison between our models and the best pure algorithm a^* for each λ, where a^* is defined as the algorithm selected most often as the best in the labeling phase (cf. Fig. 3), showed that our approach outperforms the best pure algorithm for all values of λ except 0.7 and 0.8 (see Fig. 6), with overall lower RMRE for smaller λ. The best pure algorithm method can also be seen as a rule-based system that uses domain knowledge to select an algorithm per λ value, e.g. when speed is the most important, greedy algorithms are always used.

Therefore, our machine learning approach yields higher welfare, but also higher cost error MRE with increasing λ, leading to worse performance than a single algorithm when only the welfare obective is considered. This can be explained by the fact that the algorithms' performances vary more in the welfare dimension than the runtime, but classification penalizes all mispredictions eaqually, ultimately leading to the paradox of 96% accuracy with $RMRE \geq 1$.

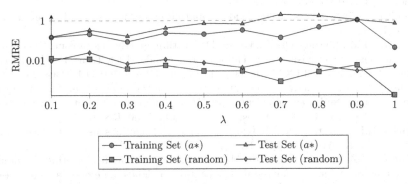

Fig. 6. RMRE comparison of ML-based algorithm selection to random selection and best pure algorithm for different λ values.

6   Conclusions

In this paper, we proposed an algorithm selection approach to improve the performance and solution quality of combinatorial auctions, applied to the problem of cloud resource allocation. We introduced a machine learning approach that selects the best heuristic algorithm for each problem instance, where the *best algorithm* is defined by our proposed multi-objective cost model. Another contribution of this paper is a feature set to aid in the learning process, engineered using domain knowledge. We showed that our proposed approach predicts the best algorithm per instance with an accuracy of up to 99%. This approach also outperforms a random algorithm selection approach, as well as the best pure algorithm, in most cases.

To further improve the prediction, in the future we will integrate low-knowledge, dynamic features, that can be obtained by running all the algorithms on a small sample of the problem instance.

References

1. Buyya, R., Yeo, C.S., Venugopal, S.: Market-oriented cloud computing: vision, hype, and reality for delivering IT services as computing utilities. In: 10th IEEE International Conference on High Performance Computing and Communications, 2008. HPCC 2008, pp. 5–13. IEEE (2008). https://doi.org/10.1109/HPCC.2008.172
2. Amazon: Amazon EC2 spot instances (2017). https://aws.amazon.com/ec2/spot/
3. Scoca, V., Uriarte, R.B., De Nicola, R.: Smart contract negotiation in cloud computing. In: 2017 IEEE 10th International Conference on Cloud Computing (CLOUD), pp. 592–599. IEEE (2017). https://doi.org/10.1109/CLOUD.2017.81
4. De Vries, S., Vohra, R.V.: Combinatorial auctions: a survey. INFORMS J. Comput. **15**(3), 284–309 (2003). https://doi.org/10.1287/ijoc.15.3.284.16077
5. Zaman, S., Grosu, D.: Combinatorial auction-based allocation of virtual machine instances in clouds. J. Parallel Distrib. Comput. **73**(4), 495–508 (2013). https://doi.org/10.1016/j.jpdc.2012.12.006
6. Smith, D.M.: Predicts 2017: cloud computing enters its second decade. Gartner Special report (2017)
7. Nejad, M.M., Mashayekhy, L., Grosu, D.: Truthful greedy mechanisms for dynamic virtual machine provisioning and allocation in clouds. IEEE Trans. Parallel Distrib. Syst. **26**(2), 594–603 (2015). https://doi.org/10.1109/TPDS.2014.2308224
8. Zurel, E., Nisan, N.: An efficient approximate allocation algorithm for combinatorial auctions. In: Proceedings of the 3rd ACM conference on Electronic Commerce, pp. 125–136. ACM (2001). https://doi.org/10.1145/501158.501172
9. Hoos, H.H., Boutilier, C.: Solving combinatorial auctions using stochastic local search. In: AAAI/IAAI, pp. 22–29 (2000)
10. Gudu, D., Zachmann, G., Hardt, M., Streit, A.: Approximate algorithms for double combinatorial auctions for resource allocation in clouds: an empirical comparison. In: Proceedings of the 10th International Conference on Agents and Artificial Intelligence, ICAART, pp. 58–69 (2018). https://doi.org/10.5220/0006593900580069
11. Kotthoff, L.: Algorithm selection for combinatorial search problems: a survey. In: Bessiere, C., De Raedt, L., Kotthoff, L., Nijssen, S., O'Sullivan, B., Pedreschi, D. (eds.) Data Mining and Constraint Programming. LNCS (LNAI), vol. 10101, pp. 149–190. Springer, Cham (2016). https://doi.org/10.1007/978-3-319-50137-6_7
12. Leyton-Brown, K., Nudelman, E., Shoham, Y.: Empirical hardness models: methodology and a case study on combinatorial auctions. J. ACM (JACM) **56**(4), 22 (2009). https://doi.org/10.1145/1538902.1538906
13. Beck, J.C., Freuder, E.C.: Simple rules for low-knowledge algorithm selection. In: Régin, J.-C., Rueher, M. (eds.) CPAIOR 2004. LNCS, vol. 3011, pp. 50–64. Springer, Heidelberg (2004). https://doi.org/10.1007/978-3-540-24664-0_4
14. Lehmann, D., Müller, R., Sandholm, T.: The winner determination problem. In: Combinatorial Auctions, pp. 297–318 (2006). https://doi.org/10.7551/mitpress/9780262033428.003.0013
15. Shoham, Y., Leyton-Brown, K.: Multiagent Systems: Algorithmic, Game-Theoretic, and Logical Foundations. Cambridge University Press, Cambridge (2008). https://doi.org/10.1145/1753171.1753181

16. Schnizler, B., Neumann, D., Veit, D., Weinhardt, C.: Trading grid services-a multi-attribute combinatorial approach. Eur. J. Oper. Res. **187**(3), 943–961 (2008). https://doi.org/10.1016/j.ejor.2006.05.049
17. Kirkpatrick, S., Gelatt, C.D., Vecchi, M.P., et al.: Optimization by simulated annealing. Science **220**(4598), 671–680 (1983). https://doi.org/10.1126/science.220.4598.671
18. Russell, S., Norvig, P.: Beyond classical search. In: Artificial Intelligence: A Modern Approach, pp. 125–128 (2010)
19. Bertocchi, M., Butti, A., Słomiń ski, L., Sobczynska, J.: Probabilistic and deterministic local search for solving the binary multiknapsack problem. Optimization **33**(2), 155–166 (1995). https://doi.org/10.1080/02331939508844072
20. Deb, K.: Multi-objective optimization. In: Burke, E., Kendall, G. (eds.) Search Methodologies, pp. 403–449. Springer, Boston (2014). https://doi.org/10.1007/978-1-4614-6940-7_15
21. Marler, R.T., Arora, J.S.: Survey of multi-objective optimization methods for engineering. Struct. Multidiscip. Optim. **26**(6), 369–395 (2004). https://doi.org/10.1007/s00158-003-0368-6
22. Mishra, A.K., Hellerstein, J.L., Cirne, W., Das, C.R.: Towards characterizing cloud backend workloads: insights from Google compute clusters. ACM SIGMETRICS Perform. Eval. Rev. **37**(4), 34–41 (2010)
23. Feurer, M., Klein, A., Eggensperger, K., Springenberg, J., Blum, M., Hutter, F.: Efficient and robust automated machine learning. In: Advances in Neural Information Processing Systems, pp. 2962–2970. Curran Associates, Inc. (2015)

Cloud Federation Formation
in Oligopolistic Markets

Yash Khandelwal[1], Karthik Ganti[1], Suresh Purini[1(✉)], and Puduru V. Reddy[2]

[1] International Institute of Information Technology, Hyderabad, India
suresh.purini@iiit.ac.in
[2] Indian Institute of Technology, Chennai, India

Abstract. In this paper, we study how an oligopolist influences the coalition structure in federated cloud markets. Specifically, we use cooperative game theory to model the circumstances under which a cloud provider prefers to join a cloud federation vis-a-vis consider taking a price offer made by an oligopolist.

Keywords: Federated clouds · Oligopoly · Linear production games

1 Introduction

The current cloud computing market structure is akin to *oligopoly* as few mega cloud providers completely own the market share. Each of them individually or in collusion has the power to affect the market prices leading to what is called an *imperfect competition*. Further, due to the large scale of operations in the data centers associated with these oligopolists, there is an acute stress on electricity and other natural resources. Many studies [1,2] indicated the resulting adverse impact on the environment due to carbon emissions and other pollutants.

Since computing has become a common commodity these days, it is easy to envisage a large number of micro cloud providers with small to medium scale data centers. With the presence of a large number of producers, an oligopolistic market leans towards *perfectly competitive market*. In a market with perfect competition, producers become price takers and it is not possible for one or few cloud providers to affect the market prices. Further, as these small data centers are geographically spread out, the stress on the local resources and the impact on the microclimate will be mitigated, especially by the usage of renewable energy resources and productive use of dissipated heat energy.

However, such micro cloud providers will be able to serve only moderate sized consumer requests due to the limited availability of resources in their data centers. In order to serve large consumer requests many micro cloud providers have to come together and form a coalition or a federation. The federation formation can happen in a peer-to-peer fashion leading to what is called an Peer-to-Peer Inter-Cloud Federation (refer Fig. 1(a)) [3]. The other option is to use the services of a broker as in Fig. 1(b) resulting in a Multi-Cloud federation model.

© Springer International Publishing AG, part of Springer Nature 2018
M. Aldinucci et al. (Eds.): Euro-Par 2018, LNCS 11014, pp. 392–403, 2018.
https://doi.org/10.1007/978-3-319-96983-1_28

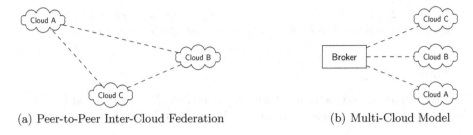

(a) Peer-to-Peer Inter-Cloud Federation   (b) Multi-Cloud Model

Fig. 1. Cloud federation models

Given a set of cloud providers and a broker, in this paper, we study the question whether it is beneficial for cloud providers to form a peer-to-peer federation or to subscribe to the services of a broker. We use cooperative game theory to address this interesting question. To the best of our knowledge, we did not find any prior work related to the proposed problem of study in this paper.

In Sect. 2, we provide the necessary background on cooperative game theory and linear production games; in Sect. 3, we formulate the cloud federation formation and payoff distribution using linear production games; in Sect. 4, we show the impact of an oligopolist on federation formation and how we can arrive at stable coalitional structures; in Sect. 5 we present our experimental analysis; Sect. 6 contains the related work; and finally we conclude with Sect. 7.

2 Background

We study the proposed problem in this paper using a special class of games called linear production games [4] from the cooperative game theory [5,6]. We provide the necessary game theoretic background in this section to understand the rest of the paper.

2.1 Cooperative Game Theory

Given a set of $N = \{1, \cdots, n\}$ players, a subset $S \subseteq N$ of them can pool their resources and form a coalition to generate an utility or value $v(S)$. We say that the utility is *transferable* if it can be split among the coalition partners in an arbitrary fashion.

Definition 1. *A cooperative n-person game in coalitional form is denoted by* $G = (N, v)$ *where* $N = \{1, \cdots, n\}$ *and* $v : 2^N \rightarrow \mathbb{R}^+$, *with* $v(\phi) = 0$. *The function v is called the characteristic function of the game and* $v(S)$ *is called the value of the coalition S.*

We say that a cooperative game is *super-additive* if $v(S \cup T) \geq v(S) + v(T)$ for all $S, T \in 2^N$ with $S \cap T = \phi$. When a game is super-additive, then the value $v(N)$ generated by the *grand coalition* N would be the maximum. However, the formation of a grand coalition or any other coalition depends on the payoff vector which determines the profit distribution among the coalition members.

Definition 2. *A payoff vector $x = (x_1, \cdots, x_n) \in \mathbb{R}^n$ is called an imputation if it satisfies the following individual rationality and efficiency conditions.*

1. *Individual rationality: $x_i \geq v(\{i\})$ $\forall i \in N$.*
2. *Efficiency: $\sum_{i=1}^{n} x_i = v(N)$.*

The set of imputations associated with a game $G = (N, v)$ is denoted by $I(G)$. For a payoff vector x and a coalition $S \subseteq N$, let $x(S)$ denote $\sum_{i \in S} x_i$.

Definition 3. *The core of a game $G = (N, v)$ denoted as $C(G)$ is defined as follows.*

$$C(G) = \{x \in I(G) \mid x(F) \geq v(F) \ \forall F \subseteq N\}$$

If the payoff vector is from the core, then there is no incentive for any sub-coalition $S \subset N$ to deviate from the grand coalition N, thus ensuring stability. However, the core of a game is not necessarily non-empty. Bondareva [7] and Shapley [8] gave independently a characterization of games with a non-empty core. The characteristic vector e^S associated with a coalition $S \subseteq N$ is defined as $e_i^S = 1$ if $i \in S$ and $e_i^S = 0$ if $i \in N \setminus S$.

Definition 4. *A map $\lambda : 2^N \setminus \{\phi\} \to \mathbb{R}^+$ is called a balanced map if*

$$\sum_{S \in 2^N \setminus \{\phi\}} \lambda(S) e^S = e^N$$

Definition 5. *A cooperative game $G = (N, v)$ is called a balanced game if for each balanced map $\lambda : 2^N \setminus \{\phi\} \to \mathbb{R}^+$ the following condition holds good.*

$$\sum_{S \in 2^N \setminus \{\phi\}} \lambda(S) v(S) \leq v(N)$$

A cooperative game $G = (N, v)$ can induce a subgame $G_S = (S, v_S)$ where $S \subseteq N$ and $v_S(T) = v(T)$ for all $T \subseteq S$.

Definition 6. *A cooperative game $G = (N, v)$ is called totally balanced if every induced subgame $G_S = (S, v_S)$ for all $S \in 2^N \setminus \{\phi\}$ is balanced.*

The following theorem due to Bondareva and Shapley characterizes the set of games with a non-empty core.

Theorem 1. *A cooperative game $G = (N, v)$ will have a non-empty core if and only if it is a balanced game.*

2.2   Linear Production Games

Consider a production situation where m different types of products $P_1, \ldots, P_m$ can be manufactured using q distinct kind of resources $G_1, \ldots, G_q$. Further, there is a *production matrix* $A_{m \times q}$ whose $(j, k)^{th}$ entry a_{jk} denotes the number of units of resource G_k required to manufacture an unit of product P_j. Overall, the jth row of the matrix denoted by a_j gives the overall resource requirements per unit of product P_j. The linearity of the production situation comes from the fact that to manufacture α units of product P_j the corresponding resource requirements scale-up linearly to αa_j. Let the jth entry of the price vector $c_{1 \times m} = (c_1, \cdots, c_m)$ denote the price per unit of product P_j. Given a resource bundle $b_{q \times 1} = (b_1, \cdots, b_q)^T$ with non-negative entries, the optimal production plan $x_{m \times 1} = (x_1, \cdots, x_m)^T$ is obtained by solving the following linear programming problem.

$$\begin{array}{ll} \underset{x}{\text{Maximize}} & c \cdot x \\ \text{subject to} & A^T \cdot x \leq b \\ & x \geq 0 \end{array}$$

Consider now an n-player game $G = (N, v)$ wherein the resource bundle owned by the ith player is denoted by b_i. The resource bundle owned by a coalition $S \subseteq N$ is defined as $b(S) = \sum_{i \in S} b_i$. The value $v(S)$ associated with the coalition S is obtained by solving the following linear programming problem.

$$\begin{array}{ll} \underset{x}{\text{Maximize}} & c \cdot x \\ \text{subject to} & A^T \cdot x \leq b(S) \\ & x \geq 0 \end{array}$$

The following is an important theorem which we use in this paper.

Theorem 2. *Every linear production game $G = (N, v)$ is totally balanced. Hence not only the core $C(G)$ is non-empty but also the core $C(G_S)$ of every induced subgame $G_S = (S, v_S)$ where $S \subseteq N$ is also non-empty.*

3   Federation Formation and Payoff Distribution Using Linear Production Games

In this section, we will present a model for peer-to-peer inter-cloud federation and an efficient payoff distribution scheme which gives a core allocation using linear production games.

3.1   Federation Formation Model

Let $\mathcal{I} = \{C_1, \cdots, C_n\}$ be a collection of cloud providers. A cloud provider C_i owns a resource bundle $b_i = (b_i^c, b_i^m, b_i^s)^T$ where b_i^c is the total number of available compute cores; b_i^m and b_i^s denotes the total available main memory and secondary storage respectively. The cloud providers can offer m types of virtual machines denoted by VM_j, $1 \leq j \leq m$. The core, main memory and storage requirements for each virtual machine type is given by the production matrix $A_{m \times 3}$ whose j^{th} row, $a_j = (a_j^c, a_j^m, a_j^s)$, corresponds to the resource configuration vector of a virtual machine of type VM_j. Table 2 gives example virtual machine types and the associated production matrix used in the experimental analysis section of this paper. The per unit market price of different types of virtual machines is denoted by the price vector $p = (p_1, \cdots, p_m)$. Table 2 also provides the hourly rental price for various types of virtual machines considered. Given this market scenario, the cloud providers have to decide upon a federation structure such that each of them maximize their respective payoffs.

It can be observed that we can model this problem by constructing a linear production game which is exactly similar to the game $G_{lp} = (N, v)$ described in the Sect. 2.2. We denote the total pooled cores, memory and storage from a federation S by $b^c(S)$, $b^m(S)$ and $b^s(S)$ respectively. The value $v(S)$ associated with a federation S is obtained by solving the following linear programming problem OPTLP(S).

$$\text{Maximize}_{x} \quad \sum_{j=1}^{m} x_j p_j \tag{1a}$$

$$\text{subject to} \quad \sum_{j=1}^{m} x_j a_j^c \leq b^c(S) \tag{1b}$$

$$\sum_{j=1}^{m} x_j a_j^m \leq b^m(S) \tag{1c}$$

$$\sum_{j=1}^{m} x_j a_j^s \leq b^s(S) \tag{1d}$$

$$x_j \geq 0 \ (1 \leq j \leq m) \tag{1e}$$

Constraints 1b, 1c and 1d denote the capacity constraints corresponding to core, memory and storage respectively. In fact, this game being super additive, we can infer that the grand coalition generates the maximum revenue, which is obtained by solving the linear programming problem OPTLP(N). Further, from Theorem 2, we know that there is a core allocation possible as it is a totally balanced game. In the next section, we show how we can do payoff distribution using a core allocation, thereby achieving the stability of the grand coalition.

3.2   Payoff Distribution

Owen [9] showed that we can compute a core allocation for a linear production game $G_{lp} = (N, v)$ by solving the following dual problem associated with the primal problem OPTLP(N).

$$\text{Minimize}_{y} \quad y_1 b^c(N) + y_2 b^m(N) + y_3 b^s(N) \tag{2a}$$

$$\text{subject to} \quad y_1 a_j^c + y_2 a_j^m + y_3 a_j^s \geq p_j \ (\forall j, 1 \leq j \leq m) \tag{2b}$$

$$y \geq 0 \tag{2c}$$

We interpret the optimal solution $y_* = (y_*^c, y_*^m, y_*^s)$ to the dual problem as the shadow prices for cores, memory and storage. Owen proved that we can obtain a core allocation vector by paying the ith player with the resource bundle $b_i = (b_i^c, b_i^m, b_i^s)^T$ as follows.

$$\alpha_i(N) = \sum_{j \in \{c,m,s\}} y_*^j b_i^j$$

We denote the payoff vector as $\alpha(N) = (\alpha_1(N), \cdots, \alpha_n(N))$ where the parameter N indicates that the payoff corresponds to the grand coalition. The subset of core allocations which are formed using optimal dual solutions is know as the Owen set. In the next section, we will present how a broker or an oligopolist can intervene in the formation of a grand coalition by offering higher payoff to individual cloud providers.

4   Intervention of an Oligopolist in Federation Formation

In order to maintain market control, the oligopolists may intervene in the peer-to-peer federation formation, refer Fig. 1(a), by offering incentives to the micro cloud providers to lend their resources to them. The oligopolists in turn use the lent resources to supply virtual machines to the end consumers potentially at a higher price due to their wider market reach. During this process, an oligopolist assumes the role of a broker leading to a multi-cloud architecture depicted in Fig. 1(b). In the rest of this section, we study how an oligopolist can affect the structure of cloud federation and the resulting impact on the payoff to individual cloud providers.

Let an oligopolist offers a price m_i to rent the entire resource bundle b_i from the cloud provider C_i. In this paper, we study the restricted problem of an interaction between a single oligopolist and a set of cloud providers[1]. One simple way of considering more than one oligopolist is to set the price offer m_i made to the cloud provider C_i to the maximum of the offers made by different oligopolists in the market, and the rest of the theory proposed in this section holds good.

4.1   Core Allocation for Subgames

In Sect. 3.2, we described how the payoff distribution vector $\alpha(N)$ can be computed for the game $G_{lp} = (N, v)$. Since, every subgame $G_S = (S, v_S)$ induced by G_{lp} is also a linear production game, we can analogously compute the payoff distribution vector $\alpha(S)$ by solving the dual problem for the primal problem OPTLP(S). Overall, we have to solve $2^n - 1$ linear programming problems to compute the payoff distribution vectors for all the induced subgames, which

---

[1] An alternate way to view this problem is to consider the single oligopolist as a monopolist by ignoring the market influences due to other oligopolists which is not the subject matter of this paper.

is computationally expensive. However, it can be noted from the constraints (2b) and (2c), the feasible region for the dual problem of OPTLP(S) is independent of the federation S and only the coefficients of the objective function change. Hence, for practical values of m, we can enumerate the basic feasible solutions, in other words, the extreme points of the polyhedra defined by the dual problem constraints. For different objective functions associated with different subgames, we can exhaustively check the list of extreme points and find the optimal solution.

4.2 Influence of the Oligopolist

Definition 7. *The marginal payoff for a cloud provider C_i with respect to a coalition S and a price offer m_i from an oligopolist is defined as*

$$\beta_i(S) = \alpha_i(S) - m_i.$$

A cloud provider has an incentive to deviate from a federation S and take up the offer of an oligopolist if and only if $\beta_i(S) < 0$. Thus the oligopolist may destabilize the grand coalition as all the cloud providers whose $\beta_i(N) < 0$ will break away from the coalition.

Definition 8. *For a cooperative game $G = (N, v)$ and a price offer vector $m = (m_1, \cdots, m_n)$, a coalition $S \subseteq N$ is called a feasible coalition if and only if $\beta_i(S) \geq 0$ for all $i \in S$.*

From the discussion in Sect. 4.1, we can enumerate the list of all feasible coalitions in 2^N by computing the respective payoff distribution vectors.

Definition 9. *Given price offer vector $m = (m_1, \cdots, m_n)$, we call a partition $CS = \{F_1, \cdots, F_{k-1}, F^*\}$ of the player set N as a stable coalition structure if*

1. *The coalitions $F_i, 1 \leq i \leq k - 1$ are feasible coalitions.*
2. *There exists no subset $S \subseteq F^*$ which is a feasible coalition. Thus all the cloud players from F^* take the price offer made by the monopolist.*

Note that if $m_i < v(\{i\})$, then cloud provider C_i is a feasible coalition by himself.

4.3 Finding a Stable Coalition Structure

There can be many possible stable coalition structures for a given price offer vector from the oligopolist. We may prefer one stable coalition structure to other based on certain criteria. For example, one criteria could be to minimize the number of cloud providers taking up oligopolist's offer, i.e., $|F^*|$. Another criteria could be to be maximize the sum of payoffs of all the cloud providers, i.e., $\sum_{i=1}^{k-1} \sum_{j \in F_i} \alpha_j(F_i) + \sum_{j \in F^*} m_j$.

Definition 10. *Associated with a feasible coalition F and a price offer vector $m = (m_1, \cdots, m_n)$, we define a goodness value $g(F)$ as follows.*

$$g(F) = \sum_{i \in F} (\alpha_i(F) - m_i)/|F|$$

In this paper, we propose the following simple greedy algorithm for stable coalition formation.

1. Let the initial coalition structure be $CS = \phi$. Repeat the following step until it terminates.
2. (i^{th} iteration)
   (a) Among all the feasible coalitions, choose a coalition F_i with a maximum goodness value $g(F_i)$ and $F \cap F_i = \phi$ for all $F \in CS$.
   (b) If there exists no feasible coalition which is disjoint with the already chosen feasible coalitions, then set

$$F^* = N - \cup_{F \in CS} F$$
$$CS = CS \cup \{F^*\}$$

   and exit the algorithm.

We can easily note from the above algorithm, that different goodness functions will yield different coalition structures. In the next section, we do an experimental analysis on the influence of the oligopolist on stable coalition formation and overall payoff distribution.

5   Experimental Results

In this section, we study how increasing price offers from the oligopolist to the individual cloud providers impact the structure of stable coalitions formed. We consider a set of 12 cloud providers $\mathcal{I} = \{C_1, \cdots, C_{12}\}$ whose resource capacities are given in the Table 1. These resource capacities are randomly chosen, first by choosing one of the three buckets: small, medium and large; and then choosing a capacity randomly within a range determined by that bucket type. Inspired from Microsoft Azure, we let each cloud provider offer four types of virtual machines: General Purpose (B2S), Storage Optimized (L4), Memory Optimized (E8 v3), and Compute Optimized (F16 v2). The resource requirements of each type of virtual machine is given in the Table 2. The same table also provides the hourly rental price for each type of virtual machine.

We consider $l = 45$ different market scenarios. In the ith market scenario, M_i, $1 \leq i \leq l$, the oligopolist makes a price offer $m = (m_1, \cdots, m_j, \cdots, m_{12})$ wherein

$$m_j = (1 + \frac{i}{100}) \times v(\{C_j\}). \tag{3}$$

That means the oligopolist is offering a price which is $i\%$ greater than the value a cloud provider can generate by working all alone. For small values of i, a cloud provider can potentially get better payoff by forming a coalition; whereas for larger values of i he may be better off taking up the oligopolist's offer. This can be observed from the Fig. 2 which depicts how the stable coalition structure evolves with the increasing price offers from the oligopolist.

Table 1. Resource capacity of cloud providers. vCPUs are expressed in 100s of cores, memory and storage in 100 GB units.

	vCPU	Memory	Storage
C_1	36	44	1845
C_2	55	74	1704
C_3	120	165	548
C_4	15	133	1906
C_5	61	490	2100
C_6	110	503	3164
C_7	119	900	3468
C_8	181	150	3900
C_9	182	986	6814
C_{10}	210	610	4654
C_{11}	166	531	13000
C_{12}	239	850	4100

Table 2. VM instance types, their resource configurations and hourly rental prices.

	vCPU	Memory (in GB)	Storage (in GB)	Price (per hour)
General Purpose	2	4	8	0.047$
Storage Optimized	4	32	678	0.312$
Memory Optimized	8	64	200	0.532$
Compute Optimized	16	32	128	0.716$

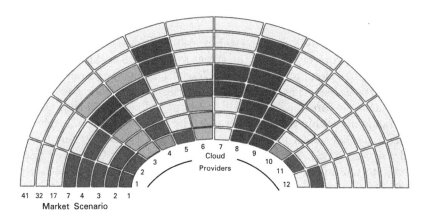

Fig. 2. Evolution of coalition structure with increasing price offers going from market scenario M_1 to M_{45} (refer Eq. (3)).

The stable coalition structures are computed using the greedy algorithm proposed in Sect. 4.3. Each track of the semi-circle represents the coalition structure for a given price offer. The purple colored cloud providers are those who take up the oligopolists offer. Similar colored cloud providers in a track belong to the same coalition. For example, at one percent price offer, the coalition structure is $CS = \{\{1, 2, 5, 11\}, \{3, 6\}, \{4, 10\}, \{8, 9\}, \{7, 12\}\}$. The members of the last set $F^* = \{7, 12\}$ are those who accepted the offer made by the oligopolist. Further, the semi-circle shows only those tracks where there is a change in the coalition structure from the previous market scenario. For example, since the coalition structure did not change from the market scenario M_7 till M_{17}, the intervening coalition structures are not represented. We can notice the increasing purple color as we move from inside to outside in the semi-circle indicating that with increasing price offers more cloud providers will lean towards the oligopolist. This is further illustrated by the graph in Fig. 3 which shows the size of F^*, $|F^*|$, with increasing price offers. Another interesting observation is that a cloud provider may take an oligopolist's offer in market scenario M_i but may change his mind in $M_{i'}$ where $i' > i$. This is due to the overall change in the coalition structure. This phenomenon can be observed by looking at the sector corresponding to the cloud provider 5 in Fig. 2.

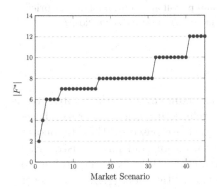

Fig. 3. Number of cloud providers taking up the offer made by the oligopolist with increasing price offers.

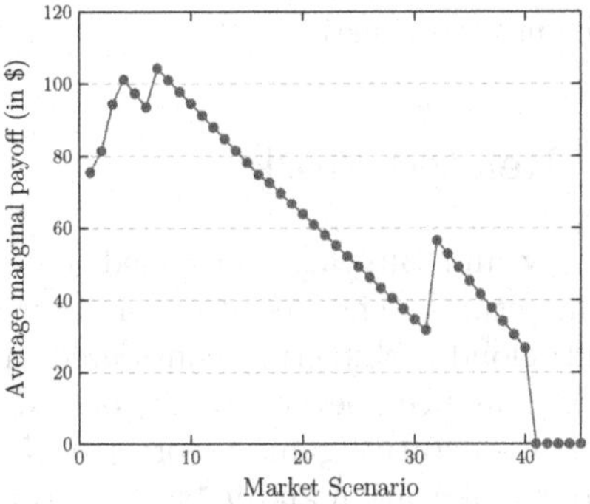

Fig. 4. Average marginal payoff with changing market scenarios.

Figure 4 shows the average marginal payoff of the cloud providers who preferred to form a peer-to-peer coalition. For a given market scenario, CS is a stable coalition structure (refer Definition (9)), then the average marginal payoff is defined as $\sum_{F_i \in CS \setminus F^*} \sum_{j \in F_i} \beta_j(F_i)/|N \setminus F^*|$. As expected, with the increasing price offer from the oligopolist, the marginal payoff goes down. However, it need not be monotic, as it may increase locally due to the changes in the stable coalition structure. Figure 5 shows the total time taken for the computation of the stable coalition structure for a given market scenario. It can be noted that overall it is in the order of milliseconds and hence computationally feasible problem to solve. Further, with the increasing price offers, the number of feasible coalitions go down, which makes the greedy algorithm converge faster.

For a coalition, we know that $v_S(S)$ is the total payoff available for the coalition S. The combined payoff from an oligopolist to a coalition S is $\sum_{i \in S} m_i$. Figure 6 compares the coalitional payoff and the combined broker payoff for all the coalitions in the market scenario M_1. For cloud providers 7 and 12, who take up the oligopolist's offer, these two values are almost the same (one percent difference).

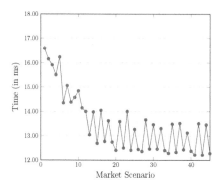
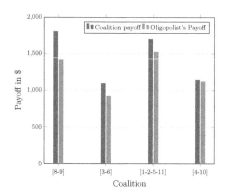

Fig. 5. Total time taken to compute the stable coalition structure for a given market scenario.

Fig. 6. Comparision between the coalitional payoff and combined broker price offer for the market scenario M_1.

6 Related Work

Grozev and Buyya [3] provided a systematic taxonomy of various inter-cloud architectures. The peer-to-peer inter-cloud architecture and the broker based multi-cloud architecture considered in this paper are based on their taxonomy. There has been several works on federation formation and payoff distribution using cooperative game theory [10–15]. Hassan et. al. [16] solved the problem of resource allocation and federation formation using Stackelberg games. However, none of these works consider the impact of an oligopolist or a monopolist on coalition formation which is the main focus of this paper. Niytao et al. [12] proposed the usage of stochastic linear programming games for payoff distribution among coalition members. The payoff distribution scheme we presented in this paper using linear production games is similar to their work. The closest work related to ours in literature is due to Fragnelli [17]. The author studied a market scenario which is very similar to that of ours but the specific problem addressed is the pricing strategy to be adopted by the players. Innes and Sexton [18] also studied very similar market scenario but the problem they studied is the pricing strategy to be adopted by the monopolist to deter coalition formation.

7 Conclusions

In this paper, we showed how we can model the influence of an oligopolist in a cloud market where multiple cloud providers can potentially come together to form a federation in order to increase their market reach. Further, we introduced the notion of stable coalition structures in the presence of oligopolists and a greedy algorithm for computing them. We believe that our work paves way for further research in this less studied facet of federated cloud computing.

References

1. Dai, X., Wang, J.M., Bensaou, B.: Energy-efficient virtual machines scheduling in multi-tenant data centers. IEEE Trans. Cloud Comput. **4**(2), 210–221 (2016)
2. Wajid, U., et al.: On achieving energy efficiency and reducing CO_2 footprint in cloud computing. IEEE Trans. Cloud Comput. **4**(2), 138–151 (2016)
3. Grozev, N., Buyya, R.: Inter-cloud architectures and application brokering: taxonomy and survey. Softw. Pract. Exp. **44**(3), 369–390 (2014)
4. Granot, D.: A generalized linear production model: a unifying model. Math. Program. **34**(2), 212–222 (1986)
5. Curiel, I.: Cooperative Game Theory and Applications. Springer, Boston (1997). https://doi.org/10.1007/978-1-4757-4871-0
6. Tijs, S.: Introduction to Game Theory. Hindustan Book Agency, Gurgaon (2003)
7. Bondareva, O.N.: Some applications of linear programming methods to the theory of cooperative games. Probl. Kibern. **10**, 119–139 (1963)
8. Shapley, L.S.: On balanced sets and cores. Nav. Res. Logist. Q. **14**(4), 453–460 (1967)
9. Owen, G.: On the core of linear production games. Math. Program. **9**(1), 358–370 (1975)
10. Mashayekhy, L., Nejad, M.M., Grosu, D.: Cloud federations in the sky: formation game and mechanism. IEEE Trans. Cloud Comput. **3**(1), 14–27 (2015)
11. Khandelwal, Y., Purini, S., Reddy, P.V.: Fast algorithms for optimal coalition formation in federated clouds. In: Proceedings of the 9th International Conference on Utility and Cloud Computing. UCC 2016, pp. 156–164. ACM, New York (2016)
12. Niyato, D., Vasilakos, A.V., Kun, Z.: Resource and revenue sharing with coalition formation of cloud providers: game theoretic approach. In: 2011 11th IEEE/ACM International Symposium on Cluster, Cloud and Grid Computing, pp. 215–224, May 2011
13. Romero Coronado, J.P., Altmann, J.: Model for incentivizing cloud service federation. In: Pham, C., Altmann, J., Bañares, J.Á. (eds.) GECON 2017. LNCS, vol. 10537, pp. 233–246. Springer, Cham (2017). https://doi.org/10.1007/978-3-319-68066-8_18
14. Samaan, N.: A novel economic sharing model in a federation of selfish cloud providers. IEEE Trans. Parallel Distrib. Syst. **25**(1), 12–21 (2014)
15. Guazzone, M., Anglano, C., Sereno, M.: A game-theoretic approach to coalition formation in green cloud federations. In: 14th IEEE/ACM International Symposium on Cluster, Cloud and Grid Computing (CCGrid), pp. 618–625, May 2014
16. Hassan, M.M., Hossain, M.S., Sarkar, A.M.J., Huh, E.N.: Cooperative game-based distributed resource allocation in horizontal dynamic cloud federation platform. Inf. Syst. Front. **16**(4), 523–542 (2014)
17. Fragnelli, V.: A note on the owen set of linear programming games and nash equilibria. In: Gambarelli, G. (ed.) Essays in Cooperative Games. TDLC, vol. 36, pp. 205–213. Springer, Boston (2004). https://doi.org/10.1007/978-1-4020-2936-3_16
18. Innes, R., Sexton, R.J.: Customer coalitions, monopoly price discrimination and generic entry deterrence. Eur. Econ. Rev. **37**(8), 1569–1597 (1993)

Improving Cloud Simulation Using the Monte-Carlo Method

Luke Bertot$^{(\boxtimes)}$ ⓘ, Stéphane Genaud ⓘ, and Julien Gossa

Icube-ICPS — UMR 7357, Université de Strasbourg, CNRS Pôle API,
300 Blvd S. Brant, 67400 Illkirch-Graffenstaden, France
{lbertot,genaud,gossa}@unistra.fr

Abstract. In the cloud computing model, cloud providers invoice clients for resource consumption. Hence, tools helping the client to budget the cost of running his application are of pre-eminent importance. However, the opaque and multi-tenant nature of clouds make task runtimes variable and hard to predict, and hamper the creation of reliable simulation tools. In this paper, we propose an improved simulation framework that takes into account this variability using the Monte-Carlo method.

We consider the execution of batch jobs on an actual platform, scheduled using typical heuristics based on the user estimates of task runtimes. We model the observed variability through simple random variables to use as inputs to the Monte-Carlo simulation. Based on this stochastic process, predictions are expressed as interval-based makespan and cost. We show that, our method can capture over 90% of the empirical observations of makespan while keeping the capture interval size below 5% of the average makespan.

1 Introduction

Over the last decade, the advancement of virtualization techniques has led to the emergence of new economic and exploitation approaches of computer resources in Infrastructure as a Service (IaaS), one form of cloud computing. In this model, all computing resources are made available on demand by third-party operators and paid based on usage. The ability to provision resources on demand is mainly used in two ways. First, it can serve for scaling purposes where new machines are brought online to face higher workloads and allows for a lower baseline cost. Second, it is useful for parallelizing tasks to achieve a shorter makespan (*i.e.* the time between the submission of the first task and the completion of the last task) at equal cost, this approach being often used for scientific and industrial workloads when runtime is heavily dependent on computing power. This approach is made possible by the pricing model of cloud infrastructures, as popularized by Amazon Web Services, in which payment for computing power provided as Virtual Machines (VMs), happens in increments of arbitrary lengths of time, billing time unit (BTU), usually of one hour. This model offers the client an almost complete freedom to start or stop new servers as long as it can be afforded. However, for distributed applications, it quickly becomes difficult to manually provision

© Springer International Publishing AG, part of Springer Nature 2018
M. Aldinucci et al. (Eds.): Euro-Par 2018, LNCS 11014, pp. 404–416, 2018.
https://doi.org/10.1007/978-3-319-96983-1_29

the resources in an efficient way. The use of a scheduler becomes unavoidable for such workloads. In this paper, we are interested in predicting the execution time and cost of such workloads, in which the scheduling plays an important role.

Independently of scheduling decisions, the accurate prediction of complex workload execution is hampered by the inherent variability of clouds, explained by multiple factors. Firstly IaaS operates in an opaque fashion: the exact nature of the underlying platforms is unknown, and their hardware are subject to evolution. Secondly cloud systems are multi-tenant by nature. This adds uncertainty due to contention on network and memory accesses. This variability, reported by a number of practitioners who evaluate parallel application performance on clouds (e.g. [13], who report an average 5%–6% variability on AWS cluster compute instances), has also been measured by one of the most comprehensive and recent surveys by Leitner and Cito [9]. We will see in this paper that our observations fit with the figures presented in this survey. This variability increases the difficulty of modeling task execution times. In this regard, the prediction is highly dependent on the underlying simulator of the system and on the phenomena it can capture. In our work, we rely on the SimGrid [4] simulation toolkit, enabling us to build discrete event simulators of distributed systems such as Grids, Clouds, or HPC systems. SimGrid has been chosen for its well-studied accuracy against reality (e.g. [18,20]). In particular, given a precise description of the hardware platform, its network model takes into account network contention in presence of multiple communication flows.

However, we may not be able to provide a fully accurate platform description, or be unable to estimate the network cross-traffic, yielding a distortion between simulation and reality. To deal with this problem, the standard approach is to consider task runtimes to be stochastic. Every task can be modeled by a random variable (RV) that models the whole spectrum of possible runtimes. These RVs are the basis required for a stochastic simulation. Such simulations output RVs of the observed phenomenon (*makespan* or *BTU*) which in turn can be used to create intervals of possible results with their assorted confidence. In this paper, we propose a stochastic method to enrich the classical prediction based on the discrete-event simulator SimGrid, and we study the conditions needed for this approach to be relevant. This study is carried out in a real setting, described in Sect. 3, where the applications, and the scheduler are presented. The stochastic framework we propose is then presented in Sect. 4 and is evaluated in Sect. 5. We discuss the limits of this approach in Sect. 6.

2   Related Work

Simulation. Most cloud simulators are based on discrete event simulation (DES). In discrete event simulation the simulation is a serie of events changing the state of the simulated system. For instance, events can be the start (or end) of computations or communications. The simulator will jump from one event to the next, updating the times of upcoming events to reflect the state change in the simulation. Such DES-based simulators require at least a platform specification and an application description. The available cloud DESs can be divided in two categories. In the first category are the simulators dedicated to study the clouds from the provider point-of-view, whose purpose is to help evaluating the design decisions of the datacenter. Examples of such simulators are MDCSim [11], which offers specific and precise models for low-level components including network (e.g. InfiniBand or Gigabit ethernet), operating system kernel and disks. It also offers a model for energy consumption. However, the cloud client activity that can be modeled is restricted to web-servers, application-servers, or data-base applications. GreenCloud [8] follows the same purpose with a strong focus on energy consumption of cloud's network apparatus using a packet-level simulation for network communications (NS2). In the second category (which we focus on) are the simulators targeting the whole cloud ecosystem including client activity. In this category, CloudSim [2] is the most broadly used simulator in academic research. It offers simplified models regarding network communications, CPU, or disks. However, it is easily extensible and serves as the underlying simulation engine in a number of projects. Simgrid [4] is the other long-standing project, which when used in conjunction with the SchIaaS cloud interface provides similar functionalities as CloudSim. Among the other related projects is iCanCloud [15] proposed to address scalability issues encountered with CloudSim (written in Java) for the simulation of large use-cases. Most recently, PICS [7] has been proposed to evaluate specifically the simulation of public clouds. The configuration of the simulator uses only parameters that can be measured by the cloud client, namely inbound and outbound network bandwidths, average CPU power, VM boot times, and scale-in/scale-out policies. The data center is therefore seen as a black box, for which no detailed description of the hardware setting is required. The validation study of PICS under a variety of use-cases has nonetheless shown accurate predictions.

However, when the simulated system is subject to variability, it is difficult to establish the validity of simulation results formally. Indeed, given some defined inputs, a DES outputs a single deterministic result, while a real system will output slightly different results at each repeated execution. Hence, in practice the simulation is informally regarded as valid if its results are "close" to one or some of the real observations.

Stochastic Simulation and Monte-Carlo Method. For more comprehensive predictions in such variable environments, the simulation must be *stochastic*. In stochastic simulations inputs become random variables (RVs) representing the distribution of possible values for the parameters. The result of one such simulation is itself an RV representing the distribution of the results.

Extensive work has been done on numerical methods for solving stochastic simulations of directed acyclic graph (DAG) [10,12]. In a DAG model the vertices represent the tasks comprising the application, and the edges represent the dependencies between those tasks. The numerical approach presented in [10,12] shows that, when tasks' runtimes are independent, the makespan distribution of two successive tasks is the convolution product of the tasks' probability density function, while the makespan of two parallel tasks joining is the product of the tasks' cumulative distribution function. This makes the numerical approach computationally intensive and its core constraint, the tasks RVs independence, can not be guaranteed in all cases. Moreover this DAG-based approach implies fixed scheduling, since the scheduling creates implicit dependencies between tasks scheduled one after another. In a cloud context where resources can be provisioned on the fly, dynamic scheduling is much more common.

Instead of numerically computing the resulting RV, a Monte-Carlo simulation (MCS) samples the possible results by testing multiple *realizations* in a deterministic fashion. A realization is obtained by drawing a runtime that follows their task's respective RV for every task in the application. This allows one to simulate each realization using traditional methods like DES. Eventually, given enough realizations, the distribution of the simulation results will tend towards the distribution of the equivalent stochastic simulation. Statistical fitting techniques can then be used to characterize this makespan RV. MCS's permits non-independent RV and dynamic scheduling. This approach was first suggested in [17] for stochastic PERT graphs. Later, in the context of grids, where the number of resources is fixed during one execution, Tang et al. [19] proposed, a modification of the well-known scheduling heuristic HEFT to compute a schedule yielding the shortest makespan given randomly variable task durations. Canon and Jeannot [3] have used MCS to evaluate the robustness of DAG schedules when task durations vary, and similarly, Zheng and Sakellariou [21] evaluated the impact of this variability on the makespan. More recently, ElasticSim [1] has been proposed as a simulator extending Cloudsim to integrate resource auto-scaling and stochastic task durations. Similarly to our work, ElasticSim computes a schedule whose objective is to minimize rental cost while meeting deadline constraints. For several generated workflows, the study compares the simulation results regarding rental cost and makespan, when varying the variability of task duration and deadline with arbitrary values. By contrast, our work focuses on how the MCS method, under some given variability assumptions, captures actual observations.

3   Work Context

The study conducted in this paper is built upon a real comparison between experiments run in actual environments and experimental results obtained by simulation. To strengthen the validity of the comparison, the experimental conditions for the real setup and the simulation should share as many commonalities as possible, as advocated in [16]. Our experimental setup described hereafter consists of two test applications which, on one hand, are run on a real platform with our scheduler Schlouder, and on the other hand are simulated with our simulator SimSchlouder based on SimGrid.

Test Applications. We carried out multiple executions of two broadly used scientific applications to evaluate Schlouder performance. The execution traces for those runs were collected in an archive. This backlog of real executions is the benchmark against which our simulation performance will be evaluated. Those applications are:

- Montage [6], the Montage Astronomical Image Mosaic Engine, is designed to splice astronomical images. This application is a data intensive fork-join type workflow with a *communication-to-computation* ratio greater than 90%.
- OMSSA [5], the Open Mass-Spectrometry Search Algorithm, is used to analyze mass-spectrometer results. The application is a computation intensive set of independent parallel tasks with a *communication-to-computation* ratio lower than 20%.

Real Execution Setup. Schlouder [14] is a client-side cloud broker for IaaS capable of executing the user's batch jobs, sets of independent tasks and workflows alike. The broker's main role is to schedule the tasks onto a set of cloud resources, which the broker can scale up or down. Technically, the broker connects to the cloud management system (for instance, OpenStack) to instruct how the infrastructure should be provisioned. It then assigns the tasks to the resources using the Slurm job management system. As in most batch scheduler systems, the task description includes its runtime estimation by the user called *user estimate*. In case of a workflow, the task dependencies are also provided. Schlouder uses just-in-time scheduling where tasks are assigned to VMs as soon as all their dependencies are satisfied. A task's real runtime, called *effective runtime*, usually differs from estimated runtimes, but this does not change previous scheduling decisions. The scheduling problem in IaaS clouds is a bi-objective optimization problem, taking into account the rental cost of resources and the execution makespan. Schlouder's requests users to choose a strategy that favors one objective or the other. The scheduling and provisioning decisions are then controlled accordingly by specific *heuristics*. In this paper, we used the two following heuristics:

- ASAP (*as soon as possible*) schedules each task onto an idle VM if one is available, or provisions a new VM otherwise. This heuristic minimizes the makespan.
- AFAP (*as full as possible*) schedules each task onto one VM if it does not increase the rental cost (*i.e.* the number of BTU), or provisions a new VM otherwise. This heuristic minimizes cost by minimizing the BTU count.

Simulated Execution Setup. As a follow-up to our work on Schlouder we developed SimSchlouder, a simulator mimicking the behaviour of Schlouder. It has the same interfaces and implements the same scheduling heuristics as Schlouder. It uses SimGrid as its core simulation engine. In practice, SimSchlouder is included as a plugin into Schlouder to allow the user to request an estimate of the makespan and cost before choosing an heuristic for a real run. SimSchlouder shares with Schlouder a common subset of inputs, including the same tasks description and heuristic. Whereas Schlouder operates on a real cloud controller, SimSchlouder provisions simulated VMs through SimGrid's cloud interface called SchIaaS. Additionally SimSchlouder requires a platform specification,

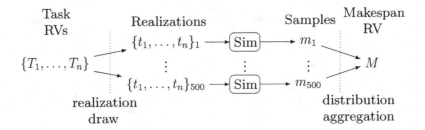

Fig. 1. Overview of a 500-iteration Monte-Carlo simulation.

which describe the physical nature of the cloud as well as the management rules, and the effective runtime of each task, that are used by the simulator to compute the tasks' end dates. Together, they allow the simulation to be accurately representative of reality.

4   Proposal: An Enriched Simulation Framework

To address the limited trustworthiness of DES in variable environments such as clouds, we propose a framework implementing the Monte-Carlo method using SimSchlouder as simulation engine. This solution combines the extensive results provided by stochastic simulations with correctness of scheduling and provisioning provided by SimSchlouder.

4.1   Simulation Process

The whole extended simulation process is referred to as MCS. For an application composed of n tasks (as depicted Fig. 1), MCS consists in applying successive MCS-iterations. Assuming we can provide a runtime distribution T_j for every task j, a MCS-iteration k consists in:

- drawing a runtime value, t_j, for each task from the associated RV, T_j;
- proceed to a simulation using all runtimes t_j to obtain a makespan m_k.

With enough makespans m_k, we can compute a statistical distribution of the makespan as a final RV noted M. We extend our simulation to two output variables: we will not only observe the makespan computed at every iteration but also the cost for each execution in number of BTU.

4.2   Real Observations

Using Schlouder (cf. Sect. 3), we performed numerous executions of the application of OMSSA and Montage. These executions were performed on a 96 cores Openstack cloud system set up on 4 identical dual 2.67 GHz Intel Xeon X5650 servers. We used the KVM hypervisor and Openstack version 2012.1 and 2014.4.

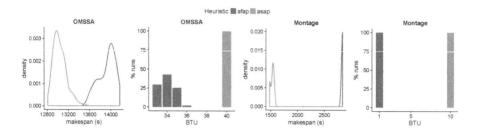

Fig. 2. Empirical observations for makespan distributions and #BTU.

The traces obtained from these experiments contain several useful metrics including, but not limited to, the VM start dates, boot time, shutdown times, and assigned tasks, as well as the task start date and effective runtimes. They were initially used all along the development of Schlouder and then to properly tune SimSchlouder in order to make the simulation as accurate as possible. As a result, for the execution used in this paper, simulations done with SimSchlouder are precise to the second on the makespan and systematically exact on the BTU count. Regarding variability, we find our platform variability to stand between 3% and 6% using the metrics described in the study [9] based on relative standard deviation of tasks runtimes. This variability is within the range reported in the study for platforms like Amazon's EC2 or Google Cloud Engine, with the exception of shared CPU instances.

In this paper these execution traces are used to generate our MCS input RVs using the method we will describe in Sect. 4.3 and we compare the makespan and BTU distributions of the MCS to the distribution observed in the corresponding traces. For this purpose, traces from comparable runs are grouped by application and heuristic. Figure 2 presents the distribution of resulting makespans and BTU counts. For OMSSA, ASAP yields a makespan variation in the range [12811s;13488s] (variability ≈5%) with a constant BTU count of 40, and AFAP yields [13564s;14172s] (4%) with a BTU count ranging [33;36]. For Montage, the makespans are in the range [1478s;1554s] ($\approx$ 4%) with 10 BTUs for ASAP and [2833s;2837s] (0.1%) with 1 BTU for AFAP.

4.3 Input Modeling

Using a MCS we can account for this variability and provide the user with a range of possible makespans. The MCS requires a runtime RV for every task in the application. These RVs form the input model. Although precise models will yield more exact results, creating such models would not be possible in more common use-cases where a backlog of real observations is not available. In this section we propose a simple model to represent the variability of the whole system using a single factor parameter to create a small range around every estimated runtime. We test this model against our backlog of real runs. The key finding detailed hereafter is that this simple model can be precise enough for the MCS to predict over 90% of real runs.

This model for the runtimes RV uses a single expected runtime per task and a global perturbation level for all tasks. This model uses uniform distributions ($\mathcal{U}$). These RVs are centered on the expected runtime of the task they represent. The relative spread of these distributions is defined by the *perturbation level P*, which is the same for every task. If we assume P can summarize the variability of the whole system, a central question is how should P and the expected runtimes be chosen to assess the validity of the MCS. To this end, we assume a good guess for an expected runtime is the average of all effective runtimes, $\bar{r}_j$ for a given task j. As such the runtime distribution's RV T_j for task j is:

$$T_j = \mathcal{U}[\bar{r}_j \times (1 - P), \bar{r}_j \times (1 + P)] \tag{1}$$

Since the global perturbation level P establishes the limit for the worst deviations from the estimated runtimes, the relative standard deviation metric used in [9] is not well suited. Instead we choose to build P using the average of the worst observed deviation for every task in the application. With r_j^n the nth runtime observation for task j, P is set to :

$$P = \underset{j}{\mathrm{mean}} \left(\underset{n}{\max} \left(\frac{|r_j^n - \bar{r}_j|}{\bar{r}_j} \right) \right) \tag{2}$$

For OMSSA, the perturbation level given by this model is $P \approx 10\%$ for both heuristics. For Montage our calculated perturbation level is $P \approx 20\%$ for ASAP and $P \approx 5\%$ for AFAP. Using a similar metric, [7] also observed most deviations to be within 10% of the average runtime when working on Amazon EC2 instances with dedicated CPUs.

Simulation Execution. The execution of an MCS is implemented through a series of scripts created to automate large numbers of simulations. The simulation driver first passes an application template, including dependencies and task expected runtimes, to a generator script. The generator creates the necessary number of simulation input files, with task runtimes randomised following the input model. The driver script can then execute an instance of SimSchlouder for every input file, sequentially or concurrently. Once all the instances of SimSchlouder have been executed, the result are aggregated in the MCS output file. This process is supple enough to accommodate other simulator and models as long as the user can provide a command to generate input files and another to parse simulation outputs.

5   Evaluation

We ran a 500-iteration MCS for every heuristic $\times$ application group using the task model described in the previous section. The resulting distributions are shown in Fig. 3. The makespan density graphs show the simulation result distribution as filled curves. The real observed executions, as in Fig. 2, are shown as non-filled curves. On the BTU count graphs, the left bar represents the empirical data, and the right bar the results from the simulation. These graphs show

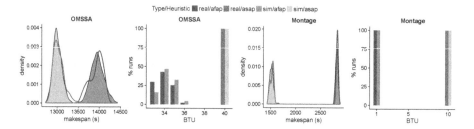

Fig. 3. Makespan and #BTU distributions for MCS compared to reality for $P = 10\%$.

the simulation results cover the same ranges as the real observation, but do not present the same distribution within those ranges. We quantify our simulation results correctness using statistical confidence intervals. Since the makespan is in essence the sum of the tasks' runtimes in the execution critical path and tasks are all distributed using the uniform distribution which has a finite variance, we consider the Central Limit Theorem applicable. Fitting to a normal distribution gives us an average makespan μ, and a standard deviation σ. These can be used to build confidence intervals (CIs). For the normal distribution the 95% CI, defined as $[\mu - 2\sigma, \mu + 2\sigma]$ and the 99% CI, $[\mu - 3\sigma, \mu + 3\sigma]$. The capture rate expresses the number of observed real makespans that fall within a given CI relative to the total number of real observations. Table 1 presents the capture rate obtained by each interval computed after normal fitting. Additionally we provide for each interval its size relative to the average makespan. Regarding OMSSA, the MCS captures at least 90% of real observed makespans. The divergence between the capture rate and the CI expected capture rate is due to the fact that the empirical makespan distribution does not follow a perfect normal distribution. Using a 99% CI improves the capture rate up to 98%, hence very close to the theoretical expectation. Regarding Montage the MCS achieves a capture rate of 100% for any CI.

Our MCS and a simple task model can capture 90% of reality all the while producing makespan intervals of limited size, a 3% relative size representing

Table 1. Makespan and BTU capture rate depending on CI for P = 10%.

Application	Heuristic	Makespan (size of CI)		BTU
		CI 95%	CI 99%	
OMSSA	ASAP	90% (3%)	98% (5%)	100%
	AFAP	92% (4%)	100% (6%)	100%
Montage	ASAP	100% (2%)	100% (4%)	100%
	AFAP	100% (1%)	100% (2%)	100%

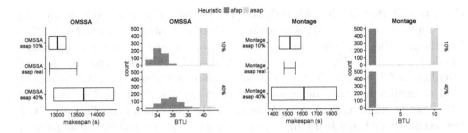

Fig. 4. Makespan intervals and #BTU distributions for OMSSA and Montage at different perturbation levels. In the makespan interval graph the boxes represent the 95% CI resulting from the normal fit of the MCS's results, and the bar the results of a single unperturbed simulation.

7 min on a 3 h 45 m long makespan. We consider this result a satisfactory trade-off between the simplicity of the input model and the accuracy with regards to the theoretical CI.

6   Perspectives

Outside of the realm of reproduction or predictions, we believe that MCS can have other more research oriented applications. In this section we will illustrate one such application. Then we will discuss limitations we have encountered in our work with MCS.

High Perturbation Simulations. We have so far set the perturbation level to a value that was relevant to the real system observed (see Sect. 4.3). A subsequent question is how does the prediction change when increasing this perturbation level. In this section we will focus on simulation of makespans using the ASAP heuristic. Figure 4 presents the 95% CIs obtained through the normal distribution fitting of simulations with both $P = 10\%$ and $P = 40\%$. Notice that a 40% perturbation level may be experienced in current cloud provider offers when renting shared instances ([9]). On the makespan interval graphs (first and third subfigures from left to right) the boxes represent the span of the CI interval. The mean simulated makespan (μ) is represented by the vertical bar inside the interval. The middle row shows the interval of real observed makespans. Simulation of OMSSA using $P = 40\%$ exhibits a clear drift upward of the ranges of simulated makespans and BTU. This drift is significant compared to the growth of the capture interval to the point that the capture rate of the simulation with $P = 40\%$ is of only 83% when the $P = 10\%$ simulation had a 90% capture rate. Montage simulations exhibit the upwards drift but not to the extent that it affects the simulation's capture rate. These results have two interesting implications. Firstly, the perturbation level can not be used as a trade-off variable to augment capture rate at the expense of CI compactness. The lower capture rate at $P = 40\%$ is a strong indication that our real platform exhibits a variability closer to 10% than to 40%. Misestimation of the perturbation level will have the same implication for the MCS as a wrong effective runtime given to DES. Users for whom higher capture rates are more important than interval compactness should use statistical methods to build higher rate CIs, like the 99% normal distribution CI used in Sect. 5. Secondly, this result shows that MCSs can be used to exhibit heuristic behaviours. This upwards shift of the CI shows that ASAP, an heuristic geared towards reducing the makespan regardless of cost, is not as effective when scheduling bag-of-tasks with task runtimes that might vary widely. However, the same observation on Montage shows that when scheduling workflows ASAP remains capable of low makespans. This can be explained by the scheduler's behaviour and the workflow's nature. In workflows the makespan depends only on execution of tasks in the critical path, and remains unaffected by variability of tasks outside the path. This is compounded by the just-in-time scheduling used in Schlouder, later scheduling decisions take into account the tasks' deviation from their expected runtimes. This kind of analysis can be used to gain insight in the strengths and weaknesses of any heuristic, regardless of complexity.

Limitations of the Enriched Simulation. In this paper all the MCS presented used 500 iterations. Such an MCS requires in average 15 min of CPU time, and iterations can be parallelized. We determined that this was enough in the context of our simulation as additional simulations did not change the results and only marginally increased the confidence of the fitting process. The number of simulations necessary in an MCS depends on the number of input variables and the distribution of these variables. A MCS works by sampling the possible scenarios to get a distribution of possible outcomes, hence when more scenarios are possible then more samples are required. The relative quick convergence (as compared to other scientific fields where MCS is used) is explained by the relatively low number of input variables found in batch job scheduling. In our case, there are respectively 223 and 184 tasks for OMSSA and Montage. As the perturbation level influences the input variable distribution, we are currently studying its relationship with the number of required MCS-iterations.

7   Conclusion

Predicting the execution behaviour of complex workloads in the cloud is an important challenge. While a number of works have proposed model-driven simulators, much remains to be done for their adoption in production-grade cloud settings. As advocated by Puchert et al. [16], the trust we can put in the prediction demands certainty and precision that only comes from validating simulation against empirical observation. This paper contributes to this effort in two ways. First, we propose a Monte-Carlo simulation extension to a discrete event simulator based on SimGrid. This extension provides stochastic predictions which are more informative than single values of billing cost and makespan produced by traditional discrete event simulators. The Monte-Carlo simulation must be parameterized to draw random values from relevant value spaces. In this work we show that the variability we seek to account for can be modeled by a single parameter, called perturbation level and applied to all task runtimes. Second, we apply our model in a real setting, on two different applications, for which we have collected execution traces. At the light of these empirical observations, our study shows that the proposed model could capture over 90% of the observed makespans for all combinations of application and scheduling heuristics given an appropriate perturbation level. We now aim to test our simulator on more use-cases and platforms. In particular as a number of studies on public clouds have reported variability levels similar to our platform [7,9], we intend to reproduce these results on public clouds.

References

1. Cai, Z., Li, Q., Li, X.: ElasticSim: a toolkit for simulating workflows with cloud resource runtime auto-scaling and stochastic task execution times. J. Grid Comput. **15**(2), 257–272 (2017). https://doi.org/10.1007/s10723-016-9390-y
2. Calheiros, R.N., Ranjan, R., Beloglazov, A., De Rose, C.A., Buyya, R.: CloudSim: a toolkit for modeling and simulation of cloud computing environments and evaluation of resource provisioning algorithms. Softw.: Pract. Exp. **41**(1), 23–50 (2011)
3. Canon, L., Jeannot, E.: Evaluation and optimization of the robustness of DAG schedules in heterogeneous environments. IEEE Trans. Parallel Distrib. Syst. **21**(4), 532–546 (2010). https://doi.org/10.1109/TPDS.2009.84
4. Casanova, H., Giersch, A., Legrand, A., Quinson, M., Suter, F.: Versatile, scalable, and accurate simulation of distributed applications and platforms. J. Parallel Distrib. Comput. **74**(10), 2899–2917 (2014). https://doi.org/10.1016/j.jpdc.2014.06.008
5. Geer, L.Y., et al.: Open mass spectrometry search algorithm. J. Proteome Res. **3**(5), 958–964 (2004)
6. Jacob, J.C., et al.: Montage: a grid portal and software toolkit for science-grade astronomical image mosaicking. Int. J. Comput. Sci. Eng. **4**(2), 73–87 (2009)
7. Kim, I.K., Wang, W., Humphrey, M.: PICS: a public IaaS cloud simulator. In: Pu, C., Mohindra, A. (eds.) 8th IEEE International Conference on Cloud Computing, CLOUD 2015, New York City, NY, USA, 27 June–2 July 2015, pp. 211–220. IEEE Computer Society (2015). https://doi.org/10.1109/CLOUD.2015.37
8. Kliazovich, D., Bouvry, P., Khan, S.U.: GreenCloud: a packet-level simulator of energy-aware cloud computing data centers. J. Supercomput. **62**(3), 1263–1283 (2012)
9. Leitner, P., Cito, J.: Patterns in the chaos - a study of performance variation and predictability in public IaaS clouds. ACM Trans. Internet Technol. **16**(3), 15:1–15:23 (2016). https://doi.org/10.1145/2885497
10. Li, Y.A., Antonio, J.K.: Estimating the execution time distribution for a task graph in a heterogeneous computing system. In: 6th Heterogeneous Computing Workshop, HCW 1997, Geneva, Switzerland, 1 April 1997, pp. 172–184. IEEE Computer Society (1997). https://doi.org/10.1109/HCW.1997.581419

11. Lim, S., Sharma, B., Nam, G., Kim, E., Das, C.R.: MDCSim: a multi-tier data center simulation, platform. In: Proceedings of the 2009 IEEE International Conference on Cluster Computing, 31 August–4 September 2009, New Orleans, Louisiana, USA, pp. 1–9. IEEE Computer Society (2009). https://doi.org/10.1109/CLUSTR.2009.5289159

12. Ludwig, A., Möhring, R.H., Stork, F.: A computational study on bounding the makespan distribution in stochastic project networks. Annals OR **102**(1–4), 49–64 (2001). https://doi.org/10.1023/A:1010945830113

13. Mehrotra, P., et al.: Performance evaluation of Amazon elastic compute cloud for NASA high-performance computing applications. Concurr. Comput.: Pract. Exp. **28**(4), 1041–1055 (2016). https://doi.org/10.1002/cpe.3029

14. Michon, E., Gossa, J., Genaud, S., Unbekandt, L., Kherbache, V.: Schlouder: a broker for IaaS clouds. Future Gener. Comput. Syst. **69**, 11–23 (2017). https://doi.org/10.1016/j.future.2016.09.010

15. Nuñez, A., Vázquez-Poletti, J.L., Caminero, A.C., Castañé, G.G., Carretero, J., Llorente, I.M.: iCanCloud: a flexible and scalable cloud infrastructure simulator. J. Grid Comput. **10**(1), 185–209 (2012). https://doi.org/10.1007/s10723-012-9208-5

16. Pucher, A., Gul, E., Wolski, R., Krintz, C.: Using trustworthy simulation to engineer cloud schedulers. In: 2015 IEEE International Conference on Cloud Engineering, IC2E 2015, Tempe, AZ, USA, 9–13 March 2015, pp. 256–265 (2015). https://doi.org/10.1109/IC2E.2015.14

17. van Slyke, R.M.: Monte carlo methods and the PERT problem. Oper. Res. **11**(5), 839–860 (1963). http://www.jstor.org/stable/167918

18. Stanisic, L., Thibault, S., Legrand, A., Videau, B., Méhaut, J.: Faithful performance prediction of a dynamic task-based runtime system for heterogeneous multi-core architectures. Concurr. Comput.: Pract. Exp. **27**(16), 4075–4090 (2015). https://doi.org/10.1002/cpe.3555

19. Tang, X., Li, K., Liao, G., Fang, K., Wu, F.: A stochastic scheduling algorithm for precedence constrained tasks on grid. Future Gener. Comput. Syst. **27**(8), 1083–1091 (2011). https://doi.org/10.1016/j.future.2011.04.007

20. Velho, P., Schnorr, L.M., Casanova, H., Legrand, A.: On the validity of flow-level tcp network models for grid and cloud simulations. ACM Trans. Model. Comput. Simul. **23**(4), 23:1–23:26 (2013). https://doi.org/10.1145/2517448

21. Zheng, W., Sakellariou, R.: Stochastic DAG scheduling using a monte carlo approach. J. Parallel Distrib. Comput. **73**(12), 1673–1689 (2013). https://doi.org/10.1016/j.jpdc.2013.07.019

Distributed Systems and Algorithms

Nobody Cares if You Liked Star Wars:
KNN Graph Construction on the Cheap

Anne-Marie Kermarrec[1,2], Olivier Ruas[3(✉)] [iD], and François Taïani[3] [iD]

[1] Mediego, Rennes, France
anne-marie.kermarrec@mediego.com
[2] EPFL, Lausanne, Switzerland
[3] Univ Rennes, Inria, CNRS, IRISA, Rennes, France
olivier.ruas@inria.fr, francois.taiani@irisa.fr

Abstract. K-Nearest-Neighbors (KNN) graphs play a key role in a large range of applications. A KNN graph typically connects entities characterized by a set of features so that each entity becomes linked to its k most similar counterparts according to some similarity function. As datasets grow, KNN graphs are unfortunately becoming increasingly costly to construct, and the general approach, which consists in reducing the number of comparisons between entities, seems to have reached its full potential. In this paper we propose to overcome this limit with a simple yet powerful strategy that samples the set of features of each entity and only keeps the least popular features. We show that this strategy outperforms other more straightforward policies on a range of four representative datasets: for instance, keeping the 25 least popular items reduces computational time by up to 63%, while producing a KNN graph close to the ideal one.

1 Introduction

K-Nearest-Neighbors (KNN) graphs play a crucial role in a large number of applications, ranging from classification [22] to recommender systems [4,15,17]. In a KNN graph, every entity (or node) is linked to its k closest counterparts, based on a given similarity metric. Despite being one of the simplest model of machine learning, computing an exact KNN graph[1] is unfortunately a highly time consuming task. A simple brute force approach for instance has a quadratic complexity in the number of entities. For applications for which data freshness is more valuable than the exactness of the results, such as news recommenders, such computation time is prohibitive. To overcome these costs, most applications therefore compute an approximate KNN graph by using pre-indexing mechanisms [5,11] or by exploiting greedy incremental strategies [4,10] to reduce the number of similarity computations. However, it seems hard to lower even further that number.

---

[1] We focus here on the computation of the whole graph, which is different from the related but distinct problem of answering KNN queries.

M. Aldinucci et al. (Eds.): Euro-Par 2018, LNCS 11014, pp. 419–431, 2018.
https://doi.org/10.1007/978-3-319-96983-1_30

In this paper we focus on an orthogonal approach, and leverage *sampling* as a preliminary pruning step to accelerate the time to compute similarities between two entities. Our proposal stems from the observation that many KNN graphs computations are performed on entities (users, documents, molecules) linked to items (e.g. the web pages an user has viewed, the terms of a document, the properties of a molecule). In these KNN graphs, the similarity function is expressed as a set similarity between bags of items (possibly weighted), such as Jaccard's coefficient or cosine similarity. The goal of sampling is to limit the size of these bags of items and thus the time to compute the similarity.

Sampling might however degrade the resulting approximated KNN graph to a point where it becomes unusable, and must therefore be performed with care. In this paper we propose to sample the bags of items associated with each entity to a common fixed size s, by keeping their s *least popular* items. Our intuition is that less popular items are more discriminant when comparing entities than more popular or random items. For instance, the fact that Alice enjoys the original 1977 *Star Wars* movie tells us less about her tastes than the fact she also loves the 9 hour version of Abel Gance's 1927 *Napoléon* movie.

We compare this policy against three other sampling policies: *(i)* keeping the s most popular items of each entity, *(ii)* keeping s random items of each entity, and *(iii)* sampling the universe of items, independently of the entities. We evaluate these four sampling policies on four representative datasets. As a case study, we finally assess the effects of these strategies on recommendation, an emblematic application of KNN graphs. Our evaluation shows that our sampling policy clearly outperforms the other policies in terms of computation time and resulting quality: keeping the 25 least popular items reduces the computational time by up to 63%, while producing a KNN graph close to the ideal one. The recommendations done by using the resulting KNN graphs are moreover as good as the one relying on the exact KNN graph on all datasets.

The rest of this paper is organized as follows. In Sect. 2 we formally define the context of our work and our approach. The evaluation procedure is described in Sect. 3. Section 4 presents our experimental results. The related work is discussed in Sect. 5 and we conclude in Sect. 6.

2   Problem Statement: Reduce KNN Computation Time

2.1   System Model and Problem

For ease of exposition, we will speak about *users* rather than *entities*, but our approach remains applicable to any entity-item dataset. We consider a set of users $U = \{u_1, \ldots, u_n\}$ in which each user u is associated with a set of items (the movies this user has liked, the pages she has viewed), termed her *profile*, and noted P_u. We note I the universe of all items: $I = \cup_{u \in U} P_u$.

A *k-nearest neighbor* (KNN) graph associates each user u with the set of k other users $knn(u) \subseteq U$ which are closest to u according to a given similarity metric on profiles:

$$sim : U \times U \to \mathbb{R}$$
$$(u, v) \quad sim(u, v) = f_{sim}(P_u, P_v).$$

Thus computing the KNN graph results in finding $knn(u)$ for each u such that

$$knn(u) \in \operatorname*{argmax}_{S \in \mathcal{P}(U \setminus \{u\}) : |S| = k} \sum_{v \in S} sim(u, v), \tag{1}$$

where $\mathcal{P}(X)$ is the powerset of a set X. We focus in this work on Jaccard similarity, a commonly used similarity metric, but our work can be applied to others. The Jaccard similarity between two users u and v is expressed as the size of the intersection of their profiles divided by the size of the union of their profiles:

$$f_{sim}(P_u, P_v) = J(P_u, P_v) = \frac{|P_u \cap P_v|}{|P_u \cup P_v|} \tag{2}$$

Since $|P_u \cup P_v| = |P_u| + |P_v| - |P_u \cap P_v|$, and since we can store $|P_u|$ for every user, computing the size of the intersection is the only non-trivial operation required to compute the Jaccard similarity.

2.2 Gance's Napoléon tells us more than Lucas's Star Wars

Computing the intersection $P_u \cap P_v$ is time consuming for large sets and is the main bottleneck of Jaccard's similarity. To reduce the complexity of this operation, we propose to sample each profile P_u into a subset $\widehat{P}_u$ in a preparatory phase applied when the dataset is loaded into memory, and to compute an approximated KNN graph on the sampled profiles.

Although simple, this idea has surprisingly never been applied to the computation of KNN graphs on entity-item datasets. Sampling carries however its own risks: if the items that are most characteristic of a user's profile get deleted, the KNN neighborhood of this user might become irremediably degraded. To avoid this situation, we adopt a *constant-size sampling* that strives to retain the *least popular items* in a profile.

The intuition is that unpopular items carry more information about a user's tastes than other items: if Alice and Bob have both enjoyed Abel Gance's *Napoléon*—a 1927 silent movie about Napoléon's early years—they are more likely to have similar tastes, than if they have both liked *Star Wars: A New Hope*—the 1977 first installment of the series, enjoyed by 96% of users[2].

2.3 Our Approach: Constant-Size Least Popular Sampling (LP)

More formally, if the size of the profile of an user u is larger than a parameter s, we only keep its s least popular items

$$\widehat{P}_u \in \operatorname*{argmin}_{S \in \mathcal{P}_u^s} \sum_{i \in S} pop(i), \tag{3}$$

---

[2] https://www.rottentomatoes.com/m/star_wars, accessed 21 Feb. 2018.

where $\mathcal{P}_u^s$ is the set of subsets of P_u of a given size s, i.e. $\mathcal{P}_u^s = \{S \in \mathcal{P}(I) : |S| = s \wedge S \subseteq P_u\}$, and $pop(i)$ is the popularity of item $i \in I$ over the entire dataset:

$$pop(i) = |\{u \in U : i \in P_u\}|. \tag{4}$$

If the profile's size is below s, the profile remains the same: $\widehat{P}_u = P_u$.

In terms of implementation, we compute the popularity of every item when reading the dataset from disk. We then use Eq. (3) to sample the profile of every user in a second iteration. The sampled profiles are finally used to estimate Jaccard's similarity between users when the KNN graph is constructed:

$$\widehat{J}(P_u, P_v) = J(\widehat{P}_u, \widehat{P}_v) = \frac{|\widehat{P}_u \cap \widehat{P}_v|}{|\widehat{P}_u| + |\widehat{P}_v| - |\widehat{P}_u \cap \widehat{P}_v|} \tag{5}$$

3 Experimental Setup

3.1 Baseline Algorithms and Competitors

Our Constant-Size Least Popular sampling policy (*LP* for short) can be applied to any KNN graph construction algorithm [4,5,10]. For simplicity, we apply it to a brute force approach that compares each pair of users and keeps the k most similar for each user. This choice helps focusing on the raw impact of sampling on the computation time and KNN quality, without any other interfering mechanism.

We use full profiles for our baseline, and compare our approach with three alternative sampling strategies: *constant-size most popular*, *constant-size random*, and *item sampling*.

Baseline: No Sampling. We use our brute force algorithm without sampling as our baseline. This approach yields an exact result, which we use to assess the approximation introduced by sampling, and provide a reference computing time.

Constant-Size Most Popular Sampling (MP). Similarly to LP, MP only keeps the s most popular items of each profile P_u:

$$\widehat{P}_u \in \underset{S \in \mathcal{P}_u^s}{\operatorname{argmax}} \sum_{i \in S} pop(i). \tag{6}$$

As with LP, we do not sample the profile if its size is lower than s.

Constant-Size Random Sampling (CS). This sampling policy randomly selects s items from P_u, with a uniform probability. As above, there is no sampling if the size of the profile is lower than s. In terms of implementation, this policy only requires one iteration over the data.

Table 1. The datasets used in our experiments

Dataset	Users	Items	Scale	Ratings > 3	$|P_u|$	$|P_i|$	Density
ml1M [13]	6,038	3,533	1–5	575,281	95.28	162.83	2.697%
ml10M [13]	69,816	10,472	0.5–5	5,885,448	84.30	562.02	0.805%
ml20M [13]	138,362	22,884	0.5–5	12,195,566	88.14	532.93	0.385%
AM [20]	57,430	171,356	1–5	3,263,050	56,82	19.04	0.033%

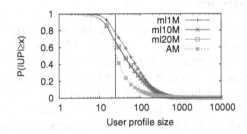

Fig. 1. CCDF of user profile sizes on the datasets used in the evaluation (positive ratings only). Between 77% (movielens1M) and 53% (AmazonMovies) of profiles are larger than the default cut-off value 25 (marked as a vertical bar).

Item Sampling (IS). This last policy uniformly removes items from the complete dataset. More precisely, each item $i \in I$ is kept with a uniform probability p to construct a reduced item universe $\hat{I}$ (i.e. $\forall i \in I : \mathbb{P}(i \in \hat{I}) = p$). The sampled profiles are then obtained by keeping the items of each profile that are also in $\hat{I}$: $\hat{P}_u = P_u \cap \hat{I}$. On average, the profile of all users is reduced by a factor of $\frac{1}{p}$, but this policy does not adapt to the characteristics of individual profiles: small profiles run the risk of losing too much of their content to maintain good quality results.

3.2 Datasets

We use four publicly available datasets containing movie ratings (Table 1): 3 datasets from the MovieLens project, and one from Amazon. Ratings range from disliking (0.5 or 1) to liking (5). To apply Jaccard similarity, we binarize the datasets by keeping only ratings that reflect a positive opinion (i.e. > 3), *before* performing any sampling. Figure 1 shows the resulting Complementary Cumulative Distribution Functions (CCDF) of profile sizes for each dataset. For instance, more than 66% of users have profiles larger than 25 in movielens10M (ml10M). This means that a constant-size sampling with $s = 25$ on movielens10M removes more than 3 millions ratings (−69.23%).

The Three Movielens Datasets. movielens1M (ml1M for short), movielens10M (ml10M) and movielens20M (ml20M) originate from GroupLens

Research [13]. They contain movie reviews by on-line users from 1995 to 2015, and only consider users with more than 20 ratings.

The AmazonMovies Dataset. (AM) [20] aggregates movie reviews received by Amazon from 1997 to 2012. To avoid users with very few ratings (the so-called *cold start problem*), we only consider users with at least 20 ratings.

3.3   Evaluation Metrics

We measure the effect of sampling along two main metrics: *(i)* their computation *time*, and *(ii)* the *quality* ratio of the resulting KNN graph.

The time is measured from the beginning of the execution of the algorithm, until the KNN graph is computed. It does not take into account the preprocessing of the dataset, which is evaluated separately in Sect. 4.2.

When applying sampling, the resulting KNN graph is an approximation of the exact one. In many applications such as recommender systems, this approximation should provide neighborhoods of high quality, even if those do not overlap with the exact KNN. To gauge this quality, we introduce the notion of *similarity ratio*, which measures how well the average similarity of an approximated graph compares against that of an exact KNN graph. Formally we define the *average similarity* of an approximate KNN graph $\widehat{G}_{\text{KNN}}$ as

$$avg\_sim(\widehat{G}_{\text{KNN}}) = \mathop{\mathbb{E}}_{(u,v)\in U^2 : v\in \widehat{knn}(u)} f_{sim}(P_u, P_v), \tag{7}$$

i.e. as the average similarity of the edges of $\widehat{G}_{\text{KNN}}$, and we define the *quality* of $\widehat{G}_{\text{KNN}}$ as its *normalized* average similarity

$$quality(\widehat{G}_{\text{KNN}}) = \frac{avg\_sim(\widehat{G}_{\text{KNN}})}{avg\_sim(G_{\text{KNN}})}, \tag{8}$$

where G_{KNN} is an ideal KNN graph, obtain without sampling.

A quality close to 1 indicates that the approximate neighborhoods of $\widehat{G}_{\text{KNN}}$ present a similarity that is very close to that of ideal neighborhoods, and can replace them with little loss in most applications, as we will show in the case of recommendations in our evaluation.

Throughout our experiments, we use a 5-fold cross-validation procedure which creates 5 training sets composed of 80% of the ratings. The remaining 20%, i.e. the training sets, are used for recommendations in Sect. 4.4. Our results are the average on the 5 resulting runs.

3.4   Experimental Setup

We have implemented the sampling policies in Java 1.8. We ran our experiments on a 64-bit Linux server with two Intel Xeon E5420@2.50GHz, totaling 8 hardware threads, 32 GB of memory, and a HHD of 750 GB. We use all 8 threads.

Table 2. Computation time (s) of the baseline and the 4 sampling policies. The parameters were chosen to have a quality equal to 0.9. LP reduces computation time by 40% (ml1M) to 63% (AM), and outperforms other sampling policies on all datasets.

Dataset	Base.	LP	Δ (%)	MP	Δ (%)	CS	Δ (%)	IS	Δ (%)
ml1M	19	**11**	**−40.5**	14.3	−24.7	14.2	−25.3	12.9	−32.1
ml10M	2028	**1131**	**−44.2**	1416.6	−30.1	1461.6	−27.9	1599.8	−21.1
ml20M	8393	**4865**	**−42.0**	5766.0	−31.3	5965.0	−28.9	6535.3	−22.1
AM	1862	**687**	**−63.1**	817.8	−56.1	748.1	−59.8	850.0	−54.4

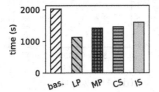

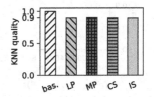

(a) Computation time (lower is better)   (b) KNN quality (higher is better)

Fig. 2. Computation time and KNN quality of the baseline and the sampling policies on movielens10M, when quality is set to 0.9. LP yields a reduction of 44.2% in computation time, outperforming other sampling policies.

Our code is available online[3]. In our experiments, we compute KNN graphs with k set to 30, which is a standard value.

4   Experimentations

4.1   Reduction in Computing Time, and Quality/Speed Trade-Off

The baseline algorithm (without sampling) produces an exact KNN graph, with a quality of 1. To compare the different sampling policies (LP, MP, CS and IS) on an equal footing, we configure each of them on each dataset to achieve a quality of 0.9. The resulting parameter s ranges from 15 (LP on AM) to 75 (MP on movielens1M), while p (for IS) varies between 0.35 (on AmazonMovies) and 0.68 (on movielens20M). Table 2 summarizes the computation times measured on the four datasets with the percentage time reduction obtained against the baseline (Δ columns), while Fig. 2 shows the results on movielens10M. LP outperforms all other policies on all datasets, reaching a reduction of up to 63%.

Because they reduce the size of profiles, sampling policies exchange quality for speed. To better understand this trade-off, Fig. 3 plots the evolution of the computation time and the resulting quality when s ranges from 5 to 200 for LP, MP, and CS ($s \in \{5, 10, 15, 20, 30, 40, 50, 75, 100, 200\}$), and p ranges from 0.1 to 1.0 for IS ($p \in \{0.1, 0.2, 0.4, 0.5, 0.75, 0.9, 1.0\}$).

---

[3] https://gitlab.inria.fr/oruas/SamplingKNN.

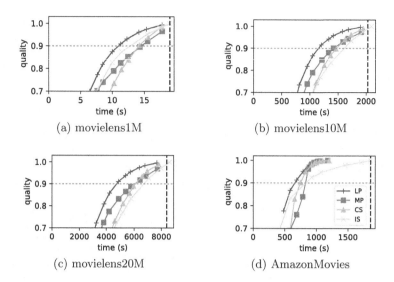

Fig. 3. Trade-off between computation time and quality. Closer to the top-left corner is better. LP clearly outperforms all other sampling policies on all datasets.

Table 3. Preprocessing time (seconds) for each dataset, and each sampling policy, with parameters set so that the resulting KNN quality is 0.9. The preprocessing times are negligible compared to the computation times.

Dataset	Base.	LP	Δ (s)	MP	Δ (s)	CS	Δ (s)	IS	Δ (s)
ml1M	0.36	0.50	+0.14	0.49	+0.13	0.46	+0.10	0.33	−0.03
ml10M	4.03	5.49	+1.46	5.67	+1.64	4.99	+0.96	3.98	−0.05
ml20M	8.55	11.95	+3.40	12.35	+3.80	11.05	+2.50	8.71	+0.16
AM	3.42	4.90	+1.48	4.70	+1.28	4.32	+0.90	2.41	−1.01

For clarity, we only display points with a quality above 0.7, corresponding to the upper values of s and p. The dashed vertical line on the right shows the computation time of the baseline (producing a quality of 1), while the dotted horizontal line shows the quality threshold of 0.9 used in Table 2 and Fig. 2.

Lines closer to the top-left corner are better. The figures confirm that our contribution, LP, outperforms other sampling policies on all datasets. There is however no clear winner among the remaining policies: IS performs well on movielens1M, but arrives last on the other datasets, and MP and CS show no clear order, which depends on the dataset and the quality considered.

4.2   Preprocessing Overhead

As is common with KNN graph algorithms [5,10], the previous measurements do not include the loading and preprocessing time of the datasets, which is typically dominated by I/O rather than CPU costs. Sampling adds some overhead to this preprocessing, but Table 3 shows that this extra cost (Δ columns) remains negligible compared to the computation times of Table 2. For instance, LP adds 3.4s to the preprocessing of movielens20M, which only represents 0.07% of the complete execution time of the algorithm (4865s + 11.95s = 4877s). IS even decreases the preprocessing time on 3 datasets out of 4, by starkly reducing the bookkeeping costs of profiles while introducing only a low extra complexity.

4.3   Influence of LP at the User's Level

Constant size sampling has a different influence on each user, depending on this user's profile's size. Profiles whose sizes are below the parameter s remain unchanged while larger profiles are truncated, thus losing information.

Figure 4 investigates the impact of this loss with our approach, LP, on movielens10M with $s = 25$ (corresponding to a quality of 0.9). Figure 4a plots the distribution of the similarity error $\epsilon = |J(P_u, P_v) - J(\widehat{P}_u, \widehat{P}_v)|$ introduced by sampling when ϵ is computed for each pair of users (u, v). The figure shows that 35% of pairs experience no error ($\epsilon = 0$), and that 96% have an error below 0.05 (dotted vertical line), confirming that our sampling only introduces a limited distortion of similarities.

Figure 4b represents the impact of LP on the quality of users' neighborhoods, according to the initial profile size of users. For every user u with an initial profile size of $|P_u|$, we compute the average similarity of u's approximated neighborhood $\widehat{knn}(u)$, and normalize this similarity with that of u's exact neighborhood $knn(u)$. The closest to 1 the better. We then average this normalized similarity for users with the same profile size $\{u \in U : |P_u| = P\}$. These points are displayed as a scatter plot (in black, note the log scale on the x axis), and using a moving average of width 50 (red curve). The first dashed vertical line is the value of the truncation parameter s ($x = 25$). The points after the second vertical line (at $x = 1553$) represent 24 users (out of 69816) and thus are not statistically significant. As expected, there is a clear threshold affect around the truncation value $s = 25$, yet even users with much larger profiles retain a high neighborhood quality, that remains on average above 0.75.

4.4   Recommendations

We want to evaluate the impact of the loss in quality on a practical use of the KNN graphs. To do so we perform item recommendations using the exact KNN graphs and the approximated graphs produced with LP. We recommend the items that an user u is more likely to like. This likelihood is expressed as a weighted average of the ratings the items received by the neighbors of u, weighted by the similarity of u with them. We use the real profiles, without sampling nor binarization, to compute these predicted ratings. After computing the score of every item, we recommend to u a set R_u composed by 30 items with the highest scores:

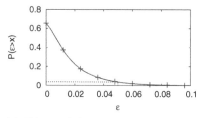
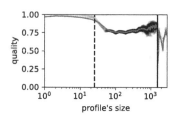

(a) CCDF of the similarity's error. Only 4% of the users have their similarities changed by more than 0.05.

(b) Quality per user as a function of a user's profile size (note the log scale for x).

Fig. 4. Influence on the similarity and the quality of sampling with LP with $s = 25$ on movielens10M (total KNN quality equal to 0.9) (Color figure online).

Table 4. Recommendation recall without sampling (*Base.*) and using the *Least Popular* (LP) policy (total KNN quality set to 0.9).

Dataset	Base.	LP	Δ
movielens1M	0.218	0.220	+0.002
movielens10M	0.273	0.275	+0.002
movielens20M	0.256	0.258	+0.002
AmazonMovies	0.595	0.596	+0.001

$$R_u \in \underset{R \subseteq I \setminus P_u : |R| = 30}{\mathrm{argmax}} \sum_{i \in S} \sum_{v \in knn_u} sim(u, v) * r_{v,i}, \tag{9}$$

where $r_{v,i}$ is the rating made by the user v on the item i. We use the same 5-fold cross-validation as used for the KNN graph computation. We consider a recommendation successful when a recommended item is found within the 20% removed ratings (the testing set) with a rating above 3 ($r_{u,i} > 3$). The quality of the recommendation is measured using *recall*, the proportion of successful recommendations among all recommendations.

Table 4 shows the recall we obtain by using the exact KNN graphs obtained with the baseline and with LP using when the KNN quality is set to 0.9. In spite of its approximation, LP introduces no loss in recall, and even achieves slightly better scores than the baseline, which shows that our sampling approach can be used with little impact in concrete applications.

5   Related Work

For small datasets, some specific data structures can be used to compute the KNN graphs very efficiently [3,18,21]. On the other hand, these solutions do not scale and computing efficiently exact KNN graphs with large datasets remains an open problem.

For large datasets, an approximation of the KNN graph, called approximate nearest-neighbor (ANN) graph, is computed instead, by decreasing the number of comparisons between users. Locally Sensitive Hashing [11,14] hashes users into buckets and only users within the same buckets are compared. Depending on the chosen similarity, different hashing functions are used [6–8]. Despite being very efficient for KNN queries, the preprocessing is too expensive to compete with other ANN graph algorithms. KIFF [5] first assigns to every user the users with which she shares at least one item. Since the Jaccard similarity is null if two users do not share any item, the neighbors research is limited to these ones. This algorithm performs particularly well on sparse datasets. Hyrec [4] and NNDescent [10] rely on the assumption that the neighbors of the neighbors are more likely to be also neighbors than random users to decrease drastically number of similarity computed.

However it seems that lowering even further the number of similarities is no longer possible. An orthogonal strategy is to speed-up the similarity computation itself by compacting the users' profiles. b-bit minwise hashing [2,16] relies on a similar approach than LSH to compact users' profiles in order to approximate the Jaccard similarity. It is space efficient but at the expense of a high preprocessing time. In [9] the profiles are compacted by using bit arrays: each bit represents a feature, which value has been rounded. This does not scale and cannot be used in our case where the items are the features. To avoid such a problem [12] uses constant-sized Bloom filters to encode the profiles. Then the Jaccard's similarity is approximated by a bitwise AND operation. Despite its privacy properties and its speed-up, there is a substantial loss in precision.

As far as we know, sampling has never been used to compact the users' profiles, even though it is used in information filtering systems such as collaborative filtering. It can be used to find association rules [1], to reduce the size of the items' universe to recommend [17] and to change the distribution of the training points [19,23]. The popularity is used to solve the cold-start problem [24] by finding items the new user is likely to rate, but not to represent its profile in a compact manner.

6 Conclusion

In this paper, we have proposed *Constant-Size Least Popular Sampling* (LP) to speed up the construction of KNN graphs on entity-item datasets. By keeping only the least popular items of users' profiles, we make them shorter and thus faster to compare. Our extensive evaluation on four realistic datasets shows that LP outperforms more straightforward sampling policies. More precisely, LP is able to decrease the computation time of KNN graphs by up to 63%, while providing a KNN graph close to the ideal one, with no observable loss when used to compute recommendations.

In the future, we plan to investigate more advanced sampling policies, and to explore how sampling could be combined with orthogonal greedy techniques to accelerate KNN graph computations [4,5,10].

Acknowledgments. This work was partially funded by the PAMELA project of the French National Research Agency (ANR-16-CE23-0016), the Web-Alter-Ego Google Focused Award, the ANR-DFG joint project DISCMAT (ANR-14-CE35-0010) and the DeSceNt project granted by the Labex CominLabs excellence laboratory of the French Agence Nationale de la Recherche (ANR-10-LABX-07-01).

References

1. Agrawal, R., Srikant, R.: Fast algorithms for mining association rules. In: VLDB 1994 (1994)
2. Bachrach, Y., Porat, E.: Sketching for big data recommender systems using fast pseudo-random fingerprints. In: Fomin, F.V., Freivalds, R., Kwiatkowska, M., Peleg, D. (eds.) ICALP 2013. LNCS, vol. 7966, pp. 459–471. Springer, Heidelberg (2013). https://doi.org/10.1007/978-3-642-39212-2_41
3. Beygelzimer, A., Kakade, S., Langford, J.: Cover trees for nearest neighbor. In: ICML (2006)
4. Boutet, A., Frey, D., Guerraoui, R., Kermarrec, A.-M., Patra, R.: Hyrec: leveraging browsers for scalable recommenders. In Middleware (2014)
5. Boutet, A., Kermarrec, A.-M., Mittal, N., Taïani, F.: Being prepared in a sparse world: the case of KNN graph construction. In: ICDE (2016)
6. Broder, A.Z.: On the resemblance and containment of documents. In: Compression and Complexity of Sequences 1997 (1997)
7. Broder, A.Z., Glassman, S.C., Manasse, M.S., Zweig, G.: Syntactic clustering of the web. In: Computer Networks and ISDN Systems (1997)
8. Charikar, M.S.: Similarity estimation techniques from rounding algorithms. In: STOC 2002 (2002)
9. Cui, B., Shen, H.T., Shen, J., Tan, K.-L.: Exploring bit-difference for approximate KNN search in high-dimensional databases. In: ADC (2005)
10. Dong, W., Moses, C., Li, K.: Efficient k-nearest neighbor graph construction for generic similarity measures. In: WWW (2011)
11. Gionis, A., Indyk, P., Motwani, R., et al.: Similarity search in high dimensions via hashing. In: VLDB (1999)
12. Gorai, M., Sridharan, K., Aditya, T., Mukkamala, R., Nukavarapu, S.: Employing bloom filters for privacy preserving distributed collaborative KNN classification. In: WICT (2011)
13. Harper, F.M., Konstan, J.A.: The movielens datasets: history and context. In: TIIS (2015)
14. Indyk, P., Motwani, R.: Approximate nearest neighbors: towards removing the curse of dimensionality. In: STOC (1998)
15. Levandoski, J.J., Sarwat, M., Eldawy, A., Mokbel, M.F.: LARS: a location-aware recommender system. In: ICDE (2012)
16. Li, P., König, A.C.: Theory and applications of b-bit minwise hashing. Commun. ACM **54**, 101–109 (2011)
17. Linden, G., Smith, B., York, J.: Amazon.com recommendations: item-to-item collaborative filtering. Internet Comput. **7**, 76–80 (2003)
18. Liu, T., Moore, A.W., Yang, K., Gray, A.G.: An investigation of practical approximate nearest neighbor algorithms. In: NIPS (2004)
19. Mani, I., Zhang, I.: KNN approach to unbalanced data distributions: a case study involving information extraction. In: Workshop on learning from imbalanced datasets, ICML (2003)

20. McAuley, J.J., Leskovec, J.: From amateurs to connoisseurs: modeling the evolution of user expertise through online reviews. In: WWW (2013)
21. Moore, A.W.: The anchors hierarchy: using the triangle inequality to survive high dimensional data. In: UAI (2000)
22. Nodarakis, N., Sioutas, S., Tsoumakos, D., Tzimas, G., Pitoura, E.: Rapid aknn query processing for fast classification of multidimensional data in the cloud. CoRR (2014)
23. Pan, R., et al.: One-class collaborative filtering. In: ICDM (2008)
24. Rashid, A.M., et al.: Getting to know you: learning new user preferences in recommender systems. In: IUI (2002)

One-Sided Communications for More Efficient Parallel State Space Exploration over RDMA Clusters

Camille Coti, Sami Evangelista$^{(\boxtimes)}$, and Laure Petrucci

LIPN, CNRS UMR 7030, Université Paris 13, Sorbonne Paris Cité,
99, Avenue J.-B. Clément, 93430 Villetaneuse, France
Sami.Evangelista@lipn.univ-paris13.fr

Abstract. This paper investigates the use of one-sided communications in the context of state space exploration. This operation is often the core component of model checking tools that explores a system state space to look for behaviours deviating from its specification. It basically consists in the exploration of a (usually huge) directed graph whose nodes and edges represent respectively system states and system changes. We revisit the state of the art distributed algorithm and adapt it to RDMA clusters with an implementation over the OpenSHMEM library and report on preliminary experiments conducted on the Grid'5000 cluster. This asynchronous approach thus reduces the significant communication costs induced by process synchronisation in two-sided communications.

1 Introduction

Model checking [2] based on state space exploration is a prominent approach used to prove that finite-state systems match behavioural specifications. In its most basic form, it is based on a systematic exhaustive exploration of all system states (the state space) in the search for illegal behaviours violating the specification. This state space can be viewed as a graph capturing the behaviour of the system. Its nodes represent system states (e.g., program counters and content of variables and channels in the case of a distributed system) and its edges represent system changes (e.g., variable assignments or synchronisations). Despite the simplicity of this technique, its practical application is subject to the well-known state explosion problem [17]: the state space may be far too large to be explored in reasonable time or to fit within the available memory. Distributed verification thus arose [16] as a natural means to push the limits of model checking: distributing state space search allows to benefit from the aggregate memory and computational power of a machine network and hence to analyse larger models and/or reduce exploration times.

Although distributed algorithms have been proposed for various classes of properties, e.g., LTL (Linear-time Temporal Logic) properties [4,18], we focus in this work on the verification of safety properties, i.e., system invariants that can be verified using a simple enumeration of system states. Many interesting properties can however be expressed as system invariants.

An important characteristic of graph-based algorithms used in verification is that the graph is not known *a priori*. The model checker is instead provided with an initial state describing the system's initial configuration and a successor function that, from one state, can generate its successors. Many verification algorithms are built upon this state space construction step. Therefore, the workload cannot be divided using traditional, static domain decomposition techniques. Moreover, the granularity of this step does not make it a good candidate for chunk-based approaches such as master-worker patterns.

The state-of-the-art algorithm that can be used for the verification of safety properties [16] distributes the search by partioning the state space among participating processes. A partition function maps state vectors (i.e., bit strings encoding states) to processes. Each process is then responsible of any state that is assigned to it: it stores it in a local state table, generates its successors and sends them to their owners that will later process these states in the same way.

To the best of our knowledge, all implementations of [16] are based on two-sided communications. In this distributed programming paradigm, two processes have to synchronise to exchange data. This means that, from a development perspective, the programmer has to explicitly mention in the code where processes have to wait for incoming data by invoking a receive statement. This constraint adds points of synchronisation in the code that makes each communication a big concern in terms of performance.

In this paper we redesign the algorithm of [16] to adapt it to one-sided communications. In such a model, a process can directly access remote memory segments of another process without the latter being aware of this access. The one-sided communication model is particularly interesting here, because when a process needs data located in another process's memory, the target process does not need to be aware that the source process needs it: the source process can get the remote data on its own.

In the more general context of model checking, [14] is the only work we are aware of, that proposes a distributed algorithm for Remote Direct Memory Access (RDMA) clusters. It can be used in the context of symbolic model checking, a different algorithmic approach than ours.

After an overview of the verification process by state space exploration considered in this work in Sect. 2 and a quick presentation of the communication and distributed memory model in Sect. 3, our new algorithm is described in Sect. 4. We present experiments conducted with this new implementation and compare it to the well known distributed model checker DiVinE [3] in Sect. 5.

2   Background

Model checking by state space exploration explores all the possible states of the system until it finds a counterexample of the property to be verified. If it can explore all possible states without finding a counterexample, it concludes that

---

Algorithm 1. Sequential state space exploration

1: **procedure** *exploreSequential* **is**
2:     $Q.init(s_0); R.init(s_0)$
3:     **while** $\neg Q.isEmpty()$ **do**
4:         $s := Q.remove()$
5:         **for** $s' \in succ(s)$ **do**
6:             **if** $\neg s'.checkInvariant()$ **then**
7:                 **halt and report error**
8:             **else if** $\neg R.isIn(s')$ **then**
9:                 $Q.insert(s'); R.insert(s')$

---

the property is always verified by the system. Therefore, it is of major importance to use an efficient algorithm for this state space exploration.

In this paper we assume a universe of system states S, an initial state $s_0 \in S$ and a mapping $succ : S \rightarrow 2^S$, that, from one state s, gives its set of successors. We want to explore the state space induced by these parameters, i.e., the smallest set $R \subseteq S$ of reachable states defined inductively as : $s_0 \in R \wedge (s \in R \Rightarrow succ(s) \in R)$.

Algorithm 1 is a sequential state space exploration algorithm usable for invariant checking. It operates on a queue Q of unexplored states and incrementally builds the reachability set R. Both initially contain the initial state. States are taken from Q (l. 4), their successors generated and put in R and Q (if not seen before) to be later processed (loop at ll. 5–9). The algorithm terminates when an erroneous state is found (ll. 6–7) or when the queue is empty, which is guaranteed to happen for finite-state systems.

The distributed algorithm of [16] that represents the core component of many distributed algorithms is given in Algorithm 2. P exploration processes are used (l. 2). Each process i owns a local portion of the queue and the reachable states. The state space is partitioned among processes using a state hash function. Each exploration process basically acts as the sequential algorithm presented above except that when a state s' is reached, the process checks if it is the owner of this state (condition at l. 8). In that case, it is processed as in the sequential scenario. Otherwise it is sent to its owner and discarded by the current process. Similarly, only the owner of the initial state puts it in its local data structures (ll. 13–14). Processes also have to check for incoming messages (ll. 16–19). A state received is handled as would be any other new state owned by the process (i.e., ll. 18–19 and ll. 10–11 match).

Termination detection (not shown in the algorithm) is triggered by a unique process (e.g., node 0) when this one has been idle (i.e., it does not receive any messages and its queue is empty) for some amount of time. It then asks it peers if they are in the same situation and if all channels are empty (check made by counting messages sent and received) before notifying termination to other nodes if both conditions are met.

Algorithm 2. Distributed state space exploration algorithm usable for invariant checking

1: **procedure** *exploreDistributed()* **is**	12: **procedure** *explore$_i$()* **is**
2: **launch** *explore$_0$* $\|$ ... $\|$ *explore$_{P-1}$*	13: **if** $s_0.hash()\%P = i$ **then**
3: **procedure** *processQueue$_i$()* **is**	14: $Q.insert(s_0); R.insert(s_0)$
4: $s := Q.remove()$	15: **while** $\neg termination()$ **do**
5: **for** $s' \in succ(s)$ **do**	16: **if** *stateReceived()* **then**
6: **if** $\neg s'.checkInvariant()$ **then**	17: $s := receiveState()$
7: **halt and report error**	18: **if** $\neg R.isIn(s)$ **then**
8: **else if** $s'.hash()\%P \neq i$ **then**	19: $Q.insert(s); R.insert(s)$
9: $s'.sendTo(s'.hash()\%P)$	20: **if** $\neg Q.isEmpty()$ **then**
10: **else if** $\neg R.isIn(s')$ **then**	21: $processQueue_i()$
11: $Q.insert(s'); R.insert(s')$	

3 RDMA Architectures and the OpenSHMEM Specification

This section gives a brief presentation of the one-sided communication model we are using in this paper, and its implementation in the OpenSHMEM shared heap and communication interface.

3.1 RDMA and One-Sided Communications

RDMA (Remote Direct Memory Access) is a communication mechanism that implements one-sided inter-process communication. It relies on two basic communication primitives: put() and get(). A process can read (get()) and write (put()) in another process's memory. In practice, not all the process's memory can be reached from other processes, but only a specific, *public* area.

An attractive feature of one-sided communications is that only the process that initiates the communication needs to take active part in it. The process that owns the memory area it is reading from or writing into is not participating to the communication, nor is it even aware that this communication is happening. This fact makes one-sided communication more tricky to use in parallel, distributed programs compared to two-sided communications, and more prone to race conditions.

Fast cluster interconnection networks such as InfiniBand implement RDMA communications with zero-copy, meaning that the NIC transfers data directly from one process's memory into the other process's memory, and, in particular, without involving the other process's operating system.

3.2 The OpenSHMEM Communication and Memory Model

OpenSHMEM is an API for parallel programs. It defines a set of one-sided, RDMA communication routines, designed specifically for clusters featuring low-latency networks [1]. The processes are called *Processing Elements* (PEs). Each

PE has its own (private) memory, and it exhibits a public heap. One particularity of OpenSHMEM is that this heap is *symmetric*: every PE has a shared heap of the same size and that contains the same allocated objects and static global objects (Fig. 1).

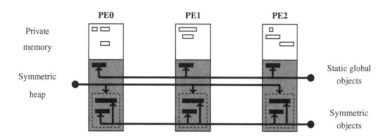

Fig. 1. OpenSHMEM memory model.

Symmetry is maintained between shared heaps through the use of dedicated memory management routines: shmem_malloc(), shmem_realloc(), shmem_align() and shmem_free() (or shmalloc(), shrealloc(), shmemalign() and shfree() until OpenSHMEM v1.2). The OpenSHMEM specification states that these routines are *collective* routines and must end by something semantically equivalent to a barrier. Hence, every object is allocated at the same offset from the beginning of the buffer on all the PEs [8]. Besides, global and static variables are also located in the shared heaps and therefore remotely accessible by other PEs.

The OpenSHMEM specification also defines interfaces for atomic accesses (such as fetch-and-add), collective operations, locks and synchronisation and ordering routines.

4   Distributed Reachability Analysis with One-Sided Communications

We now propose a distributed algorithm (see Algorithm 3) for state space exploration on RDMA clusters using one-sided communications. It assumes the following two procedures are provided by the communication layer:

– $getMem(i, o)$ returns the shared object o stored on PE i
– $putMem(i, o, data)$ stores *data* in the shared object o of PE i.

These correspond in the OpenSHMEM API to shmem_getmem and shmem_putmem.

Our algorithm acts basically as the distributed algorithm presented in Sect. 2. PEs exchange states on the basis of a state space partition induced by the state hash function. These states are communicated through the shared memory space using remote put operations. Hence, we focus next on the specificities of our implementation.

A PE shares two objects with its peers: *buf*, an array of buffers containing states sent by other PEs ; and *free*, a boolean array used to prevent the PE from erasing states it has previously put in the *buf* object of another PE and which have not been consumed yet. Basically, it is an invariant property of the algorithm that $getMem(i, free[j]) = true$ implies that the buffer $getMem(j, buf[i])$ does not contain states put by PE i for PE j but not consumed by PE j yet.

Besides its private queue Q of states to process and its reachable states R, a PE also owns an array *sbuf* containing buffers of states to be sent to their owner and grouped together to avoid sending individual states.

In the main procedure (ll. 3–12), each PE periodically processes incoming states (ll. 7–8). This is done (ll. 36–43) by inspecting the *buf* array of its local shared memory space. All the states put by remote PEs are put in the private queue and in the reachable states set (ll. 42–43). Each time a buffer has been retrieved, the remote PE that sent these states is notified via the *free* array (l. 40) located in the shared memory of this remote PE. The implementation of *checkForIncomingStates* used to decide if input buffers must be inspected is discussed in Sect. 5. As soon as its queue empties the process also has to flush its output buffers containing states destinated to remote PEs (ll. 9–10). This is mandatory to avoid a premature termination caused by all PEs being idle and ready to terminate whereas buffers still contain potentially new states to be processed. This is the purpose of procedures *flushOutBuffer*$_i$ described below and *flushOutBuffers*$_i$ (ll. 23–26) that simply flushes all non empty buffers.

Any state s belonging to another PE is processed by function *processOutState*$_i$ (ll. 13–16). The PE puts s in a private buffer containing states to be sent to their owner, i.e., the PE $j = s.hash\%PES$. This private buffer is *sbuf*[j]. If it becomes full, it has to be put in the shared space memory of PE j using procedure *flushOutBuffer*$_i$ (ll. 17–22). In this one, the PE first periodically polls its local shared memory to check whether the states it previously put in the shared memory of PE j have been consumed by this one. The condition at l. 18 evaluates to *false* as soon as PE j has completed its put statement at l. 40. Hence, we see that the purpose of the *free* shared array is to avoid communications when checking whether or not the states can be remotely put in the shared memory segment of its owner. Also note that, during polling, the process also has to process incoming states it may have received (l. 19). This is mandatory as, otherwise, a deadlock could occur. This would be the case, for instance, with two PEs, each PE waiting for the other to free its buffer, i.e., completing the put operation at l. 40, whereas it is blocked at ll. 18–19.

For termination detection (not shown in the algorithm to avoid overloading it) we adapted the algorithm of [16]. As soon as PE 0 has been idle for 100 ms it sends a token to PE 1. A PE receiving the token passes it to the next PE if it is idle, or destroys it otherwise. If PE 0 receives back the token, it asks all other PEs to participate to termination detection: a synchronisation barrier occurs, then all PEs process incoming states (if any) and publish in the shared memory their status (idle, i.e., without any state to process, or working). Termination occurs when all the processes are idle. The circulation of the token can be more efficient than a ring, for instance using Bruck's algorithm [6], which has a logarithmic number of steps. However, we have measured in the experimental evaluation of this algorithm that the termination phase is not significantly long with respect to the overall execution time. A more scalable algorithm can be used if this algorithm is meant to be executed on a large scale system.

Sketch of proof that all states in a buffer are indeed read. Let us assume a PE i has written states in the buffer of PE j. PE j can read them as long as they are not superseeded by other values, which could only be the result of PE i flushing a new version of the buffer. This operation is performed by $flushOutBuffer_i(j)$. Before PE i actually flushes the buffer at l. 21, it waits for $free[j]$ to become true (l. 18). This boolean value can only be set to true at l. 40 by PE j. This occurs after PE j reads the contents at l. 38. Note that PE i is also the only PE to set this variable to false, at l. 20, before writing the contents.

Therefore, it is not possible to write twice to a distant buffer without the corresponding process reading in between.

Sketch of proof that all states are processed. A state is created as the initial state s_0 at ll. 4–5, or as the successor of a state being processed. In this case, if it belongs to the same PE, it is inserted in the local queue at l. 35. Otherwise, *processOutState* is called, and the state is added to its PE buffer at l. 14, to be sent later. The buffer is sent when it is full (l. 16), or when the current PE has an empty queue (l. 10). In both cases, *flushOutBuffer* is eventually called, which puts the buffer in its associated PE memory. A PE checks its incoming states regularly, at l. 7 and l. 19. In both cases, the states read from the buffers are inserted in the local queue at l. 43.

Thus, all states are explored either processed locally or sent/received/ processed.

Sketch of proof that there is no livelock at l. 18. The only place where a PE could get stuck waiting forever is at l. 18. In this case, PE i is waiting for PE j to free the memory by reading it and setting the free boolean to true. This operation is done in $processInStates_j$, which reads all incoming buffers. Note that a PE cannot be stuck in *processInStates* nor calls any function from it. Function $processInStates_j$ is called either in the *while* loop at ll. 18–19 or from $explore_j$ at l. 8. PE j is thus handling its own states in the *while* loop at ll. 6–12, one by one, checking for any incoming state after processing one state. If it has no state to handle it flushes its buffers, and thus executes $processInStates_j$ at l. 19.

Hence no process gets stuck in the *while* loop of ll. 18–19.

5   Experiments

We have implemented the algorithm of the previous section in the Helena tool [9] (see http://www-lipn.univ-paris13.fr/evangelista/helena). We experimented with our algorithm on models of BEEM [15], a database of models written in the DVE modelling language and used to benchmark model checkers.

Algorithm 3. Distributed state space exploration based on one-sided communications

Constant	$PES : \mathbf{int} :=$ number of processing elements
Shared objects	$buf : \mathbf{state\_list}[PES] := \{\mathbf{empty}, \dots, \mathbf{empty}\};$
	$free : \mathbf{bool}[PES] := \{\mathbf{true}, \dots, \mathbf{true}\};$
Private objects	$Q, R : \mathbf{state\_set} := \mathbf{empty};$
	$sbuf : \mathbf{state\_list}[PES] := \{\mathbf{empty}, \dots, \mathbf{empty}\};$

```
 1: procedure exploreDistributed() is
 2:     launch explore_0 || ... || explore_{PES-1}
 3: procedure explore_i() is
 4:     if s_0.hash()%P = i then
 5:         Q.insert(s_0); R.insert(s_0)
 6:     while ¬termination() do
 7:         if checkForIncomingStates() then
 8:             processInStates_i()
 9:         if Q.isEmpty() then
10:             flushOutBuffers_i()
11:         else
12:             processQueue_i()
13: procedure processOutState_i(j, s) is
14:     sbuf[j].append(s)
15:     if sbuf[j].full() then
16:         flushOutBuffer_i(j)
17: procedure flushOutBuffer_i(j) is
18:     while ¬getMem(i, free[j]) do
19:         processInStates_i()
20:     putMem(i, free[j], false)
21:     putMem(j, buf[i], sbuf[j])
22:     sbuf[j].empty()

23: procedure flushOutBuffers_i() is
24:     for j ∈ {0, ..., |PES| − 1} with j ≠ i do
25:         if ¬sbuf[j].isEmpty() then
26:             flushOutBuffer_i(j)
27: procedure processQueue_i() is
28:     s := Q.remove()
29:     for s' ∈ succ(s) do
30:         if ¬s'.checkInvariant() then
31:             halt and report error
32:         else if s'.hash()%P ≠ i then
33:             processOutState_i(s'.hash()%P, s')
34:         else if ¬R.isIn(s') then
35:             Q.insert(s'); R.insert(s')
36: procedure processInStates_i() is
37:     for j ∈ {0, ..., |PES| − 1} with j ≠ i do
38:         buf := getMem(i, buf[j])
39:         if ¬buf.isEmpty() then
40:             putMem(j, free[i], true)
41:             for s ∈ buf do
42:                 if ¬R.isIn(s) then
43:                     Q.insert(s); R.insert(s)
```

Helena first compiles the model into a C library including state and transition definitions, the transition relation (successors computation), the initial state definition, and so on. This library is then linked with the model checking engine integrating search algorithms to produce a dedicated executable. This approach, adopted by many other model checkers, greatly speeds up the verification compared to model checkers that directly interpret the model without compiling it.

5.1 Experimental Environment

Experiments presented in this paper were carried out using the Grid'5000 [7] testbed, supported by a scientific interest group hosted by Inria and including CNRS, RENATER and several Universities as well as other organisations (see https://www.grid5000.fr). We used the Graphene cluster, which is made of 144 nodes (although we could not experiment with more than 127 nodes), each of which features a quad-core Intel Xeon X3440 running at 2.53 GHz, 16 GiB of RAM and a 20G InfiniBand network interconnection. The nodes were running a 64-bit Linux 4.9 kernel. All the code was compiled using the GNU gcc 6.3.0 compiler with -03 optimization flag. We used the OpenSHMEM implementation provided by OpenMPI 2.0.1 and the InfiniBand communication libraries libverbs 1.2.1 and librdmacm 1.1.0.

Since the machines feature four cores, we executed four processes per node. Each experiment was run 5 times and plots present the average and standard deviation of the set of measurements. Each run consisted of a complete state space exploration, i.e., no property was checked.

5.2   Implementation Details

We now address some implementation details that were left out in the description of the algorithm of the previous section.

First, at l. 7 in the main procedure, a process checks if it has received any new state to be processed. Such a check implies to look at all buffers of the shared memory space and must therefore not be done too frequently. The simple solution we adopted is to perform this check every 10 000th state processed. We experimented with other values and this one yielded the best performance on the average although we did not witness this parameter to have a large impact unless set to a too small value. It would however be relevant to experiment with a dynamic solution allowing this frequency to evolve during the search in order to try to maximise the state generation rate.

The SHMEM heap size was set to a number that allows buffers of 65 000 bytes which is close to the MTU of our network interfaces. Hence, a buffer becomes full (test at l. 15 of the algorithm) when it cannot store any more state (DVE states are encoded with a constant number of bytes). We did not intensively experiment with that parameter and leave this to future works.

5.3   Scalability

We evaluated the scalability of Helena on models of various sizes. The sizes (number of states and transitions) of these models are given in Table 1. The last column indicates the range of process numbers we experimented with on the model. Unless noted otherwise, the speed-up is computed as, by definition, the ratio between the execution time of the sequential implementation of Helena and the execution of the parallel implementation on a given set of processes, using one core per process.

As expected, small size models (see Fig. 2(a)) can be run on a small number of cores, but they do not scale well beyond a certain number of processes, i.e., about 100–150 processes. Then the runtime tends to slightly increase. Indeed, as the number of processes grows, the number of states owned by each process decreases, meaning that queues often become empty. This causes an excessive number of flushes of partially filled buffers (l. 16 of the algorithm), synonym of an inefficient network usage.

When the size of the input model increases, Helena cannot be run on a single node. For medium and large size models, we computed the speed-up by normalizing using the execution time on the smallest number of processes we could get.

Table 1. Model characteristics

	Name	States	Transitions	Processes used
Small size models (runnable on 1 node)	iprotocol.7	59 794 192	200 828 479	1–384
	peterson.5	131 064 750	565 877 635	1–384
	elevator.5	185 008 051	185 008 051	1–384
Medium size models ($< 10^9$ states)	lifts.9	266 445 936	846 144 885	16–384
	firewire_link.3	425 333 983	1 621 543 475	16–384
	leader_filters.8	431 401 020	1 725 604 080	32–384
	collision.5	431 965 993	1 644 101 878	32–384
	iprotocol.8	447 570 146	1 501 247 756	32–384
	anderson.8	538 699 029	2 972 732 133	32–384
Large size models ($\geq 10^9$ states)	public_subscribe.5	1 153 014 089	5 447 695 171	32–508
	lamport.9	1 436 848 880	7 025 053 020	48–508
	brp.8	1 526 547 707	3 207 513 490	32–508
	synapse.9	1 675 298 471	3 291 122 975	48-508
	szymanski.6	6 779 809 484	38 604 341 308	256–508

For medium size models (see Fig. 2(b)), the plots have the same shape, but the number of processes for which the execution time stagnates or increases is pushed to about 300 processes.

For four of the large models (see Fig. 2(c)) we did not observe any slow-down: they scale well on the full range of processes we were able to execute them on which is remarkable for a non-embarrassingly parallel application that communicates often.

For model brp.8, we faced some unexpected behaviour described in Sect. 5.4 that explains the relatively bad speed-up observed. But beyond this problem, we conjecture that the high depth of this graph makes this model less appropriate for distributed model checking. The parallel exploration of such graphs is known to be less efficient.

5.4   Process Workload

We also studied the process workload to further investigate some issues revealed by Fig. 2 and make sure the load is balanced evenly among processes. Indeed, for some configurations (same model and number of processes) we noticed significant variations in the execution times of the five runs performed. This is especially visible for model brp.8 through the error bars. We thus recorded during each run, the number of states visited by each process during each second. The heat maps of Fig. 3 reproduce this data for two problematic runs of models brp.8 and firewire_link.3 (with 320 and 304 processes respectively); and, for

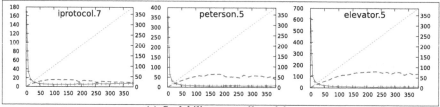

(a) Scalability on small models

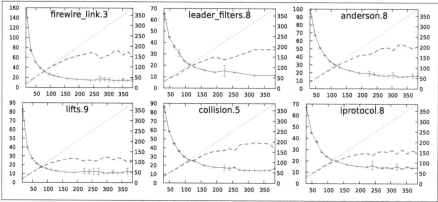

(b) Scalability on medium models

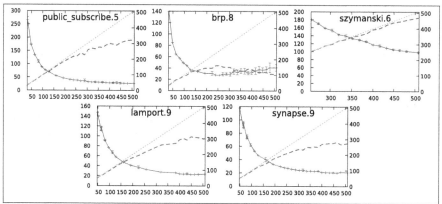

(c) Scalability on large models

Fig. 2. Scalability of Helena on the models of Table 1. On the X axis are the numbers of processes. On the left (resp. right) Y axis are execution times (speed-ups). The plain line with error bars gives execution times. The dashed one gives speed-ups. The dotted one gives the optimal theoretical speed-up (linear).

the sake of comparison, for two "friendly" runs of models leader_filters.8 and public_subscribe.5 (with 240 and 384 processes respectively).

We first observe in all cases a slow start during which all processes have very few states to visit and spend most of their time idle, waiting for states coming from processes. This scenario is actually common to all models although the duration of this phase can vary, depending on—we conjecture—the structural characteristics of the state space graph. More specifically, the shape of the graph might be such that little parallelism can be extracted. The hash function distributes the few states between the processes and therefore, processes need to access only remote states. In the case of model brp.8 the long idle time at startup could indeed be explained by the important depth of its graph and the fact that very few states are gathered around the initial state. To remedy this issue we will investigate in future works the use of a small state cache used by a process to explore states it does not own in order to accelerate the discovery of its states, rather than waiting for other processes to send these states.

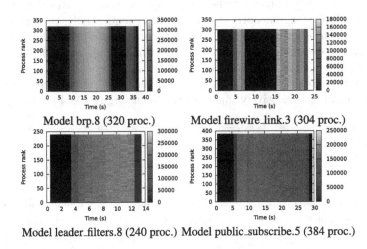

Model brp.8 (320 proc.)   Model firewire_link.3 (304 proc.)

Model leader_filters.8 (240 proc.) Model public_subscribe.5 (384 proc.)

Fig. 3. Workload (number of states processed by second) of processes for four runs

In the case of models brp.8 and firewire_link.3, the heat maps also reveal that, after this slow start, the algorithm enters again a phase during which all processes are completely idle. This represents approximatively 5 and 7 s of the whole execution times of these two runs. Unfortunately, we are currently unable to explain this phenomenon. We plan to profile the code to identify the source of this problem. Let us remark that this issue is actually the only source of the variations we observed during different runs with the same configuration. When the processes did not mysteriously halt this way during the search, we obtained remarkably stable performances.

Last, Fig. 3 also shows that the workload is well balanced among processes. This was however expected since all processes perform the same task and receive approximately the same amount of work, since states are distributed using the state hash function. Again, this observation can be generalised to all experiments we made.

5.5 Comparison with the DiVinE Model Checker

We also experimented with the DiVinE model checker [3], version 3.3, under the same conditions. DiVinE is a state-of-the-art verification tool that implements parallel algorithms for LTL model checking and reachability analysis using two-sided MPI communications [18]. Comparing these two tools can be viewed under two perspectives: speed, which depends highly on the speed of sequential computations, and parallel speed-up, which exhibits the efficiency of the parallel approach.

In this section, we are presenting both metrics. In their sequential implementation, Helena is slower than DiVinE, as we can see on the only models for which we were able to run sequential executions and presented Fig. 4 (top). We can see that, Helena has a higher speed-up and scales better than DiVinE. Although DiVinE is significantly faster when run sequentially, the two runtime curves cross each other quickly and Helena becomes faster. Therefore, our approach is efficient enough to make Helena faster when we use more than a handful of processes and the parallelism become non-trivial.

On very big models (public_subscribe.5, anderson.8), the difference between Helena and DiVinE is relatively small, especially at large scale. In our algorithm,

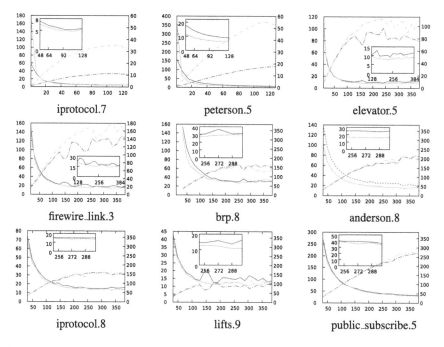

Fig. 4. Performance comparison between DiVinE and Helena on models of Table 1. On the X axis are the numbers of processes. On the left (resp. right) Y axis are execution times (speed-ups). Helena is represented by red lines, that are plain for the execution time and a pattern made of two dots and a dash for the speed-up. DiVinE is represented by blue lines, that are dashed for the execution time and a pattern made of a dot and a dash for the speed-up. Inside of each plot is a zoom on the execution time. (Color figure online)

the number of communication scales with the size of the model. Therefore, on large models, the parallel application performs a large number of communications. On DiVinE, we can expect that communicating often on all the processes reduces the penalty involved by the "forced" synchronisation between the processes and reduces the performance gap.

As explained in Sect. 5.3, when we cannot explore the state space with the sequential implementations, we normalize the speed-up using the execution time of the smallest possible parallel execution (using the same number of processes for DiVinE and Helena). Therefore, for larger models (Fig. 4, bottom), we normalize the speed-up beyond this cross-over between the execution time of DiVinE and Helena. But still, Helena scales better than DiVinE. We believe that the higher parallel efficiency of Helena is due to the less synchronous nature of the parallel algorithm for the state space exploration, which is made possible by the one-sided communication model.

6   Conclusion and Perspectives

This paper is a first step towards the use of one-sided based communications in the context of distributed state model checking. Our experiments revealed that our distributed state space exploration algorithm can compete with the DiVinE model checker which is, to the best of our knowledge, the reference tool in distributed automated verification.

An immediate perspective is to experiment more thoroughly with our algorithm. The experiments have revealed some undesired behaviour that has to be investigated and we need to gain better understanding of the impact of some parameters such as the SHMEM shared heap size.

Our algorithm currently is a direct adaptation of the state of the art distributed algorithm for the one-sided communication model and it does not fully benefit from the primitives provided by the OpenSHMEM library (or any other library that falls in that category, such as MPI 3.0), such as, e.g., remote atomic compare-and-swap. We therefore plan, in future works, to study how to take advantage of the specificities of OpenSHMEM to efficiently implement distributed versions of state space reduction techniques such as the state compression technique of [11] based on distributed hash tables or other distributed state space exploration algorithms like the one we designed for multi-core architectures [10].

The adaptation of various optimisations proposed by the model checking community, such as load balancing [5,12], to the context of one-sided communications, is another perspective. Such techniques are especially required in the case of heterogeneous networks, which we did not consider nor experiment with in this work.

Last, we will consider the design of a multi-threaded version of our algorithm as done in the Eddy_Murphi tool [13] that separates state operations (e.g., successor computation, insertion in the hash table) performed by a first thread from communications done by second thread.

References

1. OpenSHMEM Application Programming Interface version 1.4, December 2017. http://www.openshmem.org/site/sites/default/site_files/OpenSHMEM-1.4.pdf
2. Baier, C., Katoen, J.-P.: Principles of Model Checking. MIT Press, Cambridge (2008)
3. Baranová, Z., et al.: Model checking of C and C++ with DIVINE 4. In: D'Souza, D., Narayan Kumar, K. (eds.) ATVA 2017. LNCS, vol. 10482, pp. 201–207. Springer, Cham (2017). https://doi.org/10.1007/978-3-319-68167-2_14
4. Barnat, J., Brim, L., Stříbrná, J.: Distributed LTL model-checking in SPIN. In: Dwyer, M. (ed.) SPIN 2001. LNCS, vol. 2057, pp. 200–216. Springer, Heidelberg (2001). https://doi.org/10.1007/3-540-45139-0_13
5. Bingham, B., Bingham, J., de Paula, F.M., Erickson, J., Singh, G., Reitblatt, M.: Industrial strength distributed explicit state model checking. In: PDMC 2010 (2010)
6. Bruck, J., Ho, C.-T., Kipnis, S., Upfal, E., Weathersby, D.: Efficient algorithms for all-to-all communications in multiport message-passing systems. IEEE Trans. Parallel Distrib. Syst. **8**(11), 1143–1156 (1997)
7. Cappello, F., et al.: Grid'5000: a large scale and highly reconfigurable grid experimental testbed. In: SC 2005: Proc. The 6th IEEE/ACM International Workshop on Grid Computing CD, Seattle, Washington, USA, pp. 99–106. IEEE/ACM, November 2005
8. Coti, C.: POSH: Paris OpenSHMEM: a high-performance OpenSHMEM implementation for shared memory systems. In: Procedia Computer Science, Special Issue on the 2014 International Conference on Computational Science (ICCS 2014), vol. 29, pp. 2422–2431 (2014)
9. Evangelista, S.: High level petri nets analysis with Helena. In: Ciardo, G., Darondeau, P. (eds.) ICATPN 2005. LNCS, vol. 3536, pp. 455–464. Springer, Heidelberg (2005). https://doi.org/10.1007/11494744_26
10. Evangelista, S., Kristensen, L.M., Petrucci, L.: Multi-threaded explicit state space exploration with state reconstruction. In: Van Hung, D., Ogawa, M. (eds.) ATVA 2013. LNCS, vol. 8172, pp. 208–223. Springer, Cham (2013). https://doi.org/10.1007/978-3-319-02444-8_16
11. Holzmann, G.J.: Recursive indexing and compression training runs. In: SPIN 1997 (1997)
12. Kumar, R., Mercer, E.G.: Load balancing parallel explicit state model checking. ENTCS **128**(3), 19–34 (2005)
13. Melatti, I., Palmer, R., Sawaya, G., Yang, Y., Kirby, R.M., Gopalakrishnan, G.: Parallel and distributed model checking in Eddy. STTT **11**(1), 13–25 (2009)
14. Oortwijn, W., van Dijk, T., van de Pol, J.: Distributed binary decision diagrams for symbolic reachability. In: SPIN 2017, pp. 21–30. ACM (2017)
15. Pelánek, R.: BEEM: benchmarks for explicit model checkers. In: Bošnački, D., Edelkamp, S. (eds.) SPIN 2007. LNCS, vol. 4595, pp. 263–267. Springer, Heidelberg (2007). https://doi.org/10.1007/978-3-540-73370-6_17
16. Stern, U., Dill, D.L.: Parallelizing the Murφ verifier. In: Grumberg, O. (ed.) CAV 1997. LNCS, vol. 1254, pp. 256–267. Springer, Heidelberg (1997). https://doi.org/10.1007/3-540-63166-6_26
17. Valmari, A.: The state explosion problem. In: Reisig, W., Rozenberg, G. (eds.) ACPN 1996. LNCS, vol. 1491, pp. 429–528. Springer, Heidelberg (1998). https://doi.org/10.1007/3-540-65306-6_21
18. Verstoep, K., Bal, H., Barnat, J., Brim, L.: Efficient large-scale model checking. In: IPDPS 2009, pp. 1–12. IEEE (2009)

Robust Decentralized Mean Estimation with Limited Communication

Gábor Danner[1] and Márk Jelasity[2(✉)]

[1] University of Szeged, Szeged, Hungary
[2] MTA-SZTE Research Group on Artificial Intelligence, University of Szeged, Szeged, Hungary
jelasity@inf.u-szeged.hu

Abstract. Mean estimation, also known as average consensus, is an important computational primitive in decentralized systems. When the average of large vectors has to be computed, as in distributed data mining applications, reducing the communication cost becomes a key design goal. One way of reducing communication cost is to add dynamic stateful encoders and decoders to traditional mean estimation protocols. In this approach, each element of a vector message is encoded in a few bits (often only one bit) and decoded by the recipient node. However, due to this encoding and decoding mechanism, these protocols are much more sensitive to benign failure such as message drop and message delay. Properties such as mass conservation are harder to guarantee. Hence, known approaches are formulated under strong assumptions such as reliable communication, atomic non-overlapping transactions or even full synchrony. In this work, we propose a communication efficient algorithm that supports known codecs even if transactions overlap and the nodes are not synchronized. The algorithm is based on push-pull averaging, with novel features to support fault tolerance and compression. As an independent contribution, we also propose a novel codec, called the pivot codec. We demonstrate experimentally that our algorithm improves the performance of existing codecs and the novel pivot codec dominates the competing codecs in the scenarios we studied.

1 Introduction

Mean estimation has been studied in decentralized computing for a long time [1,6,8,19]. The applications of these algorithms include data fusion in sensor networks [20], distributed control [15] and distributed data mining [17]. A very interesting potential new application is federated learning, where a deep neural network (DNN) model is trained on each node and these models are then averaged centrally [11]. This average computation could be decentralized, allowing for a fully decentralized solution. However, since DNNs may contain millions

This research was supported by the Hungarian Government and the European Regional Development Fund under the grant number GINOP-2.3.2-15-2016-00037 ("Internet of Living Things").

© Springer International Publishing AG, part of Springer Nature 2018
M. Aldinucci et al. (Eds.): Euro-Par 2018, LNCS 11014, pp. 447–461, 2018.
https://doi.org/10.1007/978-3-319-96983-1_32

of floating-point parameters all of which have to be averaged simultaneously, optimizing the utilized bandwidth during decentralized averaging becomes the central problem.

Many approaches have been proposed for bandwidth-efficient average calculation. For example, floating point numbers can be compressed to a few bits using different quantization methods and these quantized values can then be averaged by a server [9,18]. This is a synchronized and centralized solution, and the approach also introduces an estimation error. Quantization has been studied also in decentralized gossip protocols where the communicated values are quantized onto a fixed discrete range (see, for example, [21]). Here, an approximation error is introduced again, even in reliable networks, and message exchanges cannot overlap in time between any pairs of nodes.

In control theory, more sophisticated dynamic quantization approaches have been proposed that can provide exact convergence at least in reliable systems by compensating for the quantization error. An example is the work of Li et al. [10]. Here, full synchronization and reliability are assumed, and the quantization range is scaled by a fixed scaling function. Dynamic quantization has also been proposed in the context of linear control in general, again, in a synchronized model [5]. Carli et al. [4] adopt the compensating idea in [10] and compare it with other static (non-adaptive) quantization techniques. The same authors also study adaptive quantization; that is, dynamically changing the sensitivity of the quantizer [3] (originally proposed in [2]), which is feasible over a fixed communication overlay. The system model in these studies assumes reliability and atomic communication as well.

A rather different kind of method involves compressing a stream of floating point values using prediction and leading zero count compression [16]. Although this method could be adapted to our application scenario with some modifications, in this study we focus only on the quantization-based compression methods.

Our contributions include a modified push-pull averaging algorithm and a novel codec. These two contributions are orthogonal: the codec can be used along with any algorithm and the push-pull algorithm can use any codec. The novel codec, called *pivot codec*, encodes every floating point value onto a single bit and it can adapt dynamically to the range of the encoded values. The novel push-pull protocol is robust against message drop failure, it does not require the synchronization of the clocks of the nodes, and it includes a smoothing feature based on recorded link-flows that improves the performance of our compression codec. Here, we evaluate our contributions in simulation. We compare our solutions with the competing codecs and algorithms from related work and show that we can improve both robustness and the compression rate significantly.

2   System Model

We model our system as a large set of nodes that communicate via message passing. The protocols we discuss here send very large messages, so the delay of successfully delivered messages is determined by the message size and the available network bandwidth (as opposed to network latency). Our protocols assume that the delay of most (but not necessarily all) of the messages that are delivered is less than an upper bound. This upper bound is at least half of the gossip period, or more, depending on the overlay network. The messages can be lost and their order of delivery is not guaranteed. We do not require time to be synchronized over the nodes but we do assume the existence of a local clock. Each node is assumed to have a small set of neighbors, with which the node can exchange messages. This neighbor set is assumed to be stable and in this study we do not consider node failure. The set of neighbors might be a uniform random sample from the network or it might be defined by any fixed overlay network, depending on the application.

3   Proposed Algorithms

We first discuss our novel codec and then present the modified push-pull averaging protocol in several steps, addressing its robustness, compression, and smoothing features.

3.1   Codec Basics

Central to our algorithms is the concept of encoding and decoding messages over a given directed link using a codec. A codec consists of an encoder and a decoder placed at the origin and the target of the link, respectively. We assume that the link is used to send a series of real valued messages during the execution of the protocol. We follow the notations used in [13]. First of all, the compression (or encoding) is based on quantization, that is, mapping real values to a typically small discrete space (an alphabet) denoted by S. The decoding maps an element of alphabet S back to a real value.

Codecs may also have state. This state might contain, for example, information about the current granularity or scale of the encoding, the previous value transmitted and elapsed time. The state space will be denoted by Ξ. Every codec implementation defines its own state space Ξ (if the implementation is stateful). Both the encoder and the decoder are assumed to share the same state space.

We now introduce a notation for the mapping functions mentioned above. Let $Q : \Xi \times \mathbb{R} \rightarrow S$ denote the encoder (or quantizer) function that maps a given real value to a quantized encoding based on the current local state of the encoder. Let $K : \Xi \times S \rightarrow \mathbb{R}$ denote the decoding function that maps the encoded value back to a real value based on the current local state of the decoder. Finally, let $F : \Xi \times S \rightarrow \Xi$ define the state transition function that determines the dynamics of the state of the encoder and the decoder. Note that in a given codec both the encoder and the decoder uses the same F. These three mappings are always executed in tandem, that is, an encoded message is decoded and then the state transition is computed.

Although the encoder and the decoder are two remote agents that communicate over a limited link, the algorithms we discuss will ensure that both of them maintain an identical state. In this sense, we can talk about the state of the codec. To achieve this, first we have to initialize the state using the same value ξ_0. Second, if the encoder and the decoder have identical states at some point in time, then an identical state can be maintained also after the next transmission, because the encoder can simulate the decoder locally, thus they can both execute the state transition function with identical inputs. Note that here we assumed that communication is reliable. If this is not the case, the algorithms using the codec must handle unreliability appropriately so as to maintain the identical states.

3.2   Pivot Codec

Here we describe our codec implementation that we coined the *pivot codec*, for reasons that will be explained below. The main goal in our implementation was aggressive compression, so we put only a single bit on the wire for each encoded value. This means $S_{pivot} = \{0, 1\}$.

The intuition behind the design is that we treat the encoder and the decoder as two agents, such that the encoder stores a constant value and the decoder has to guess this value based on a series of encoded messages. Obviously, in real applications the encoded value is rarely constant. However, the design is still efficient if the encoded values do not change much between two transmissions. In fact, this assumption holds in many applications, including decentralized mean approximation, which allows for an efficient compression. Many competing codecs, especially simple quantization techniques, do not make any assumptions about the correlation of subsequent encoded values, hence they are unable to take advantage of the strong positive correlation that is present in many applications.

The codec is stateful. The state is defined by a triple $(\widehat{x}, d, s_{last}) \in \Xi_{pivot} = \mathbb{R} \times \mathbb{R} \times S_{pivot}$. Here, $\widehat{x}$ is the approximation of the *pivotal value*, namely the actual (constant or slowly changing) real value stored by the encoder agent. The remaining values are d, the signed step size, and s_{last}, the last encoded value that was transmitted. The encoding function is given by

$$Q_{pivot}((\widehat{x}, d, s_{last}), x) = \begin{cases} 1, & \text{if } |\widehat{x} + d - x| < |\widehat{x} - x| \\ 0, & \text{otherwise}, \end{cases} \tag{1}$$

where x is the value to be encoded. In other words, the encoded value is 1 if and only if adding the current step size to the approximation makes the approximation better. Accordingly, the decoding function

$$K_{pivot}((\widehat{x}, d, s_{last}), s) = \begin{cases} \widehat{x} + d, & \text{if } s = 1 \\ \widehat{x}, & \text{otherwise} \end{cases} \tag{2}$$

will add the step size to the current approximation if and only if a 1 is received. Note that this design ensures that the approximation never gets worse. It can only get better or stay unchanged, assuming the encoded value is a constant. Note that both the encoder and the decoder share the same state. This is possible because the encoder can simulate the decoder locally, thus both the encoder and the decoder can compute the same state transition function given by

$$F_{pivot}((\widehat{x}, d, s_{last}), s) = \begin{cases} (\widehat{x} + d, 2d, s), & \text{if } s = 1 \wedge s_{last} = 1 \\ (\widehat{x} + d, d, s), & \text{if } s = 1 \wedge s_{last} = 0 \\ (\widehat{x}, -d/2, s), & \text{otherwise.} \end{cases} \quad (3)$$

Here, if d is added for the second time, we double it (assuming that the direction is good) and if we have $s = 0$ then we halve the step size and reverse its direction, assuming that adding d overshot the target. The step size is left unchanged after its first successful application (middle line).

In order for the encoder and the decoder to share their state, they also have to be initialized identically. The initial state ξ_0 might use prior knowledge, for example, prior information about the expected mean and the variance of the data are good starting points for $\widehat{x}$ and d, respectively, but a generic value like $\xi_0 = (0, 1, 0)$ can also be used.

3.3   Robust Push-Pull Averaging

As a first step towards the compressed algorithm, here we propose a variant of push-pull averaging (Algorithm 1) that is robust to message loss and delay and that also allows for the application of codecs later on. We assume that the links are directed. This means that if both $A \rightarrow B$ and $B \rightarrow A$ exist, they are independent links. Over a given directed link there is a series of attempted push-pull exchanges with push messages flowing along the link and the answers (pull messages) moving in the opposite direction. The algorithm ensures that both ends of each link will eventually agree on the flow over the link. This will ensure a sum preservation (also called mass conservation) property which we prove below.

The algorithm is similar to traditional push-pull averaging in that the nodes exchange their values first. However, as a generalization the new value will not be the average of the two values, but instead a difference δ is computed at both sides using a "learning rate" parameter $\eta \in (0, 1]$, where δ can be viewed as the amount of material being transferred by the given push-pull exchange. Note that both sides can compute the same δ (with opposite signs) independently as they both know the two raw values and they have the same parameter η. Here, $\eta = 1$ results in the traditional variant, and smaller values allow for stabilizing convergence when the push-pull exchanges are not atomic, in which case—despite sum-preservation—convergence is not guaranteed.

As for ensuring sum preservation, we assign an increasing unique ID to all push-pull exchanges. Using these IDs we simply drop out-of-order push messages. Dropping push messages has no effect on the update counters and the local approximations so no further repair action is needed. When the pull message arrives in time, the update is performed, and since the sender of the pull message

---

Algorithm 1. Robust push-pull

1: x is the local approximation of the average, initially the local value to be averaged.
2: $u_{i,in}$ and $u_{i,out}$ record the number of times the local value was updated as a result of an incoming push or pull message from i, respectively.
3: s_i is the value that was sent in the last push message to i.
4: $\delta_{i,out}, \delta_{i,in}$ are the last push, or pull transfers to i, respectively.
5: id_i is the current unique ID created when sending the latest push message to i, initially 0.
6: $id_{max,i}$ is the maximal unique ID received in any push message from i, initially $-\infty$.
7:
8: **procedure** ONNEXTCYCLE   ▷ called every Δ time units
9:     $i \leftarrow$ randomOutNeighbor()
10:     $s_i \leftarrow x$
11:     $id_i \leftarrow id_i + 1$
12:     send push message $(u_{i,out}, s_i, id_i)$ to node i
13:
14: **procedure** ONPUSHMESSAGE(u, s, id, i)   ▷ received from node i
15:     **if** $id_{max,i} < id$ **then**
16:         $id_{max,i} \leftarrow id$
17:         **if** $u < u_{i,in}$ **then**   ▷ last pull has not arrived, roll back corresponding update
18:             $x \leftarrow x + \delta_{i,in}$
19:             $u_{i,in} \leftarrow u_{i,in} - 1$
20:         send pull message (x, id) to node i
21:         update(i, in, x, s)
22:
23: **procedure** ONPULLMESSAGE(s, id, i)   ▷ received from node i
24:     **if** $id_i = id$ **then**
25:         update(i, out, s_i, s)
26:
27: **procedure** UPDATE(i, d, s_{loc}, s_{rem})
28:     $u_{i,d} \leftarrow u_{i,d} + 1$
29:     $\delta_{i,d} \leftarrow \eta \cdot \frac{1}{2}(s_{loc} - s_{rem})$
30:     $x \leftarrow x - \delta_{i,d}$

(say, node B) has already performed the same identical update (using the same δ), the state of the network is consistent. If, however, the pull message was dropped or delayed then the update performed by node B has to be rolled back. This is done when B receives the next push message and learns (with the help of the update counters) that its previous pull message had not been received in time. The update can be rolled back using δ, which ensures that the sum in the network is preserved.

After this intuitive explanation, let us describe the sum-preservation property in formal terms. For this, let us assume that there exists a time t after which there are no failures (message drop or delay). We will show that after time t the sum of the approximations will eventually be the same as the original sum of local values.

Definition 1. *We say that, over link $A \rightarrow B$, a* successful transaction *with ID j is completed when node A receives a pull message with $id = j$ from node B before sending the next push message with $id = j + 1$ to B.*

Let j_k be the ID of the kth successful transaction over link $A \to B$, and let $j_0 = 0$. For any variable v of Algorithm 1, let v^X denote the value of variable v at node X.

Theorem 1. *For any index $K \geq 0$, right after processing the pull message from B to A of a successful transaction j_K (or for $K = 0$ right after initialization), A and B agree on the total amount of mass transferred over the link $A \to B$, furthermore, $u_{B,out}^A = u_{A,in}^B = K$ holds.*

Proof. The theorem trivially holds for $K = 0$. Assume that the theorem holds for $K = k - 1$. We show that it holds for $K = k$ as well. First of all, line 25 is executed if and only if the transaction is successful. Then, $u_{B,out}^A$ is incremented by 1, therefore $u_{B,out}^A = k$ indeed holds right after the kth successful transaction. As for $u_{A,in}^B$, the inductive assumption states that $u_{A,in}^B = k - 1$ right after the $(k - 1)$-th successful transaction. After this point, there will be a series of incoming push messages that are not out of order with IDs $i_1, \ldots, i_n$ such that $j_{k-1} < i_1 < \cdots < i_n = j_k$, where j_k is the ID of the kth successful transaction. These incoming messages are assumed to be processed sequentially. In all of these push messages we will have $u = k - 1$. It follows that after processing i_1 we will have $u_{A,in}^B = k$ and after processing each new message $i_2, \ldots, i_n$ we will still have $u_{A,in}^B = k$. This means we have $u_{B,out}^A = u_{A,in}^B = k$ right after the successful transaction j_k.

Let us turn to the transferred mass, and show that after the kth successful transaction A and B will add or remove, respectively, the same δ mass from their current approximations. This is analogous to our previous reasoning about the counters $u_{B,out}^A$ and $u_{A,in}^B$, exploiting the observation that only at most one update has to be rolled back between consecutive updates (which can be done due to recording $\delta_{A,in}^B$) until the correct update occurs. Also, due to recording s_B^A both A and B can compute the same δ despite the delay at A between sending the push message and updating after receiving the pull message.

Corollary 1. *After time t push-pull exchanges become atomic transactions so after a new push message is sent on each link, each pair of nodes will agree on the transferred amount of mass, resulting in global mass conservation. Also, the algorithm will become equivalent to the atomic push-pull averaging (for $\eta = 1$), for which convergence has also been shown [6].*

Note that if the message delay is much longer than the gossip period Δ then progress becomes almost impossible, because sending a new push message over a link will often happen sooner than the arrival of the pull message (the reply to the previous push message), so the pull message will be dropped. Therefore, the gossip period should be longer than the average delay. In particular, if the gossip period is at least twice as large as the maximal message delay then no pull messages will be dropped due to delay.

Transactions over different links are allowed to overlap in time. When this happens, it is possible that the variance of the values will temporarily increase, although the sum of the values will remain constant. In networks where transactions overlap to a great degree, it is advisable to set the parameter η to a lower value to increase stability.

3.4 Compressed Push-Pull Averaging

Here, we describe the compressed variant of push-pull averaging, as shown in Algorithm 2. Although the algorithm is very similar to Algorithm 1, we still present the full pseudocode for clarity. Let us first ignore all the f variables. The algorithm is still correct without keeping track of the f values, these are needed to achieve a smoothing effect that we explain later on. Without the f values, the algorithm is best understood as a compressed variant of Algorithm 1 where values are encoded before sending and decoded after reception. There are some small but important additional details that we explain shortly.

Algorithm 2. Compressed smooth push-pull

1: $\xi_{i,in,loc}, \xi_{i,in,rem}, \xi_{i,out,loc}, \xi_{i,out,rem} \in \Xi$ are the states of the codecs for the local node and remote node i, initially ξ_0.

2: $f_{i,in}, f_{i,out}$ are the amounts of mass transferred so far to i, initially 0.

3: $\xi_{i,in',loc}, \xi_{i,in',rem}$, and $f_{i,in'}$ are the previous values of $\xi_{i,in,loc}, \xi_{i,in,rem}$, and $f_{i,in}$, initially ξ_0, ξ_0, and 0, respectively.

4:

5: **procedure** ONNEXTCYCLE $\triangleright$ called every Δ time units

6:     $i \leftarrow$ randomOutNeighbor()

7:     $s_i \leftarrow Q(\xi_{i,out,loc}, x + f_{i,out})$

8:     $id_i \leftarrow id_i + 1$

9:     send push message $(u_{i,out}, s_i, id_i)$ to node i

10:

11: **procedure** ONPUSHMESSAGE(u, s, id, i) $\triangleright$ received from node i

12:     **if** $id_{max,i} < id$ **then**

13:         $id_{max,i} \leftarrow id$

14:         **if** $u < u_{i,in}$ **then** $\triangleright$ last pull has not arrived, roll back corresponding update

15:             $x \leftarrow x + \delta_{i,in}$

16:             $u_{i,in} \leftarrow u_{i,in} - 1$

17:             $(\xi_{i,in,loc}, \xi_{i,in,rem}, f_{i,in}) \leftarrow (\xi_{i,in',loc}, \xi_{i,in',rem}, f_{i,in'})$

18:         $s_{pull} \leftarrow Q(\xi_{i,in,loc}, x + f_{i,in})$

19:         $(\xi_{i,in',loc}, \xi_{i,in',rem}, f_{i,in'}) \leftarrow (\xi_{i,in,loc}, \xi_{i,in,rem}, f_{i,in})$

20:         send pull message (s_{pull}, id) to node i

21:         update(i, in, s_{pull}, s)

22:

23: **procedure** ONPULLMESSAGE(s, id, i) $\triangleright$ received from node i

24:     **if** $id_i = id$ **then**

25:         update(i, out, s_i, s)

26:

27: **procedure** UPDATE(i, d, s_{loc}, s_{rem})

28:     $u_{i,d} \leftarrow u_{i,d} + 1$

29:     $\delta_{i,d} \leftarrow \eta \cdot \frac{1}{2}(K(\xi_{i,d,loc}, s_{loc}) - K(\xi_{i,d,rem}, s_{rem}) - 2f_{i,d})$

30:     $(\xi_{i,d,loc}, \xi_{i,d,rem}, f_{i,d}) \leftarrow (F(\xi_{i,d,loc}, s_{loc}), F(\xi_{i,d,rem}, s_{rem}), f_{i,d} + \delta_{i,d})$

31:     $x \leftarrow x - \delta_{i,d}$

In the messages, the value of x is compressed, but the u and id values are not. This is not an issue, however, because our main motivation is the application scenario where x is a large vector of real numbers. The amortized cost of transmitting two uncompressed integers can safely be ignored.

The algorithm works with any codec that is given by the definition of the state space Ξ, the alphabet S, and the functions Q, F and K, as described previously. We maintain a codec for every link and for every direction. That is, for every directed link (j, i) there is a codec for the direction $j \to i$ as well as $j \leftarrow i$. For the $j \to i$ direction, node j stores the codec state (used for encoding push messages) in $\xi_{i,out,loc}$ and for the $j \leftarrow i$ direction the codec (used for decoding pull messages) is stored in $\xi_{i,out,rem}$ at node j. In this notation, "out" means that the given codecs are associated with the outgoing link. The states for the incoming links are stored in a similar fashion.

Recall that codecs must have identical states at both ends of the link and this state is used for encoding and decoding as well. For example, the codec state $\xi_{i,out,loc}$ at node j for the direction $j \to i$ should be the same as $\xi_{j,in,rem}$ at node i. This requirement is implemented similarly to the calculation of δ in Algorithm 1. The codec state transitions, too, are calculated at both ends of each link independently, but based on shared information, so both nodes can follow the same state transition path, assuming also that the states have the same initial value ξ_0. This state transition is computed right after computing δ, in line 30.

Apart from δ, here we also need the previous codec states for rolling the last update back if a pull message was dropped or delayed. To this end, the codec states are backed up (line 19) and are rolled back when needed (line 17).

When calculating δ, we must take into account the fact that encoding and decoding typically introduces an error. Therefore, in order to make sure that both nodes compute the same δ, both nodes have to simulate the decoder at the other node, and work with the decoded value instead of the exact value that was sent (line 29). Fortunately, this can be done, since the state of the decoder at the other node can be tracked locally, as explained previously. However, since we are no longer working with the exact values, there is no guarantee that every update will actually reduce variance over the network, so it is advisable to set η to a value less than one.

3.5   Flow Compensation

So far we have ignored the f variables in Algorithm 2. The purpose of these variables is to make compression more efficient by making the transmitted values over the same link more similar to each other. This way, good stateful adaptive codecs can adjust their parameters to the right range achieving better compression.

The f values capture the flow over the given link. This approach was inspired by flow-based approaches to averaging to achieve robustness to message loss [7, 14]. However, our goal here is not to achieve robustness, but rather to reduce fluctuations in the transmitted values. The algorithm accumulates these flows for each link in both directions. In addition, the flow value is added to the transmitted value. This has a smoothing effect, because if a large δ value was computed over some link (that is, the value of x changed by a large amount), then the sum of x and the flow will still stay very similar the next time the link is used. The beneficial effect of this on compression will be demonstrated in our experimental study.

Clearly, both nodes can still compute the same δ locally, because the flow value is also known at both ends of a link, only the sign will differ. Hence we can apply the formula in line 29.

4   Simulation Results

We evaluate our algorithms in simulation using PeerSim [12]. Apart from the modified push-pull protocol presented here, we experiment with the synchronized version of average consensus, the most well-known algorithm in related work in connection with quantized communication. In addition, we study a set of codecs and combine these with the two algorithms (synchronized iteration and our push-pull gossip). This way, both the codecs and the algorithms can be compared, as well as their different combinations.

Synchronized average consensus is described, for example, in [1]. The idea in a nutshell is that—assuming the values of the nodes are stored in a vector $x(t)$ at time t—if the adjacency matrix A of the nodes is invertible and doubly stochastic then the iteration $x(t+1) = Ax(t)$ will converge to a vector in which all the elements are equal to the average of the original values. The distributed implementation of such an iteration requires strong synchronization. Quantized and compressed solutions in related work focus on such approaches, as well as slightly more relaxed versions where the adjacency matrix can be different in each iteration, but the different iterations can never overlap.

The codecs we test include simple *floating point quantization (F16, F32)* assuming a floating point representation of 16 and 32 bits (half and single precision, respectively). Here, the codec is stateless, and decoding is the identity mapping. Encoding involves finding the numerically closest floating point value.

We also include the *zoom in - zoom out codec (Zoom)* of Carli et al. [3]. We cannot present this codec in full detail due to lack of space, but the basic idea is that an m-level quantization is applied such that there is a quantizer mapping to $m-2$ equidistant points within the $[-1, 1]$ interval and the values -1 and 1 are also possible levels used for mapping values that are outside the interval. The codec state also includes a dynamically changing scaling factor that scales this interval according to the values being transferred. This codec resembles the pivot codec we proposed, and to the best of our knowledge this is the state of the art dynamic adaptive codec. Note that the minimal number of quantization levels (or alphabet size) is 3, when $m = 3$. The codec has two additional parameters: $z_{in} \in (0, 1)$ and $z_{out} > 1$. The first determines the zoom-in factor and the second is the zoom-out factor. We fix the setting $z_{out} = 2$ based on the recommendation of the authors and our own preliminary results.

4.1   Experimental Setup

The network size is $N = 5{,}000$, and the results are the average of 5 runs. We also simulated a select subset of algorithms with $N = 500{,}000$ (single run) in order to demonstrate scalability. The overlay network is defined by a k-out network, where $k = 5$ or $k = 20$. In the case of synchronized average consensus, we transform this network into a doubly stochastic adjacency matrix A by dropping directionality and setting the weights on the links using the well-known Metropolis-Hastings algorithm: $A_{ij} = 1/(1 + \max(d_i, d_j))$, where d_i is the degree of node i. Loop edges are also added with weight $A_{ii} = 1 - \sum_{j \neq i} A_{ij}$.

The initial distribution of values is given by the worst case scenario when one node has a value of 1, and all the other nodes have 0. This way, the true average is $1/N$ (where N is the network size). Our performance metric is the mean squared distance from the true average. We study the mean squared error as a function of the number of bits that are transferred by an average node to average a single value. Recall that we assume that many values are averaged simultaneously (we work with a large vector) so network latency can be ignored. This means that the number of transmitted bits can be converted into wall-clock time if one fixes a common bandwidth value for all the nodes.

We examine the value of the parameter η (see Algorithm 1) using a range depending on the actual codec (we determined the optimal value for each scenario and experimented with neighboring values). We also vary the cycle length Δ. We experiment with short and long cycles. When using short cycles, the round-trip time of a message is assumed to be 98% of the cycle length. With long cycles, the

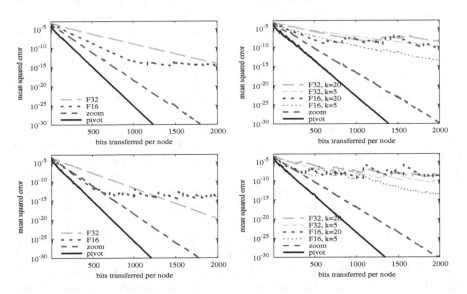

Fig. 1. Comparison of codecs in push-pull with no message drop (left) and a 5% message drop (right) with short cycles (top) and long cycles (bottom). The parameters of all of the codecs have been optimized.

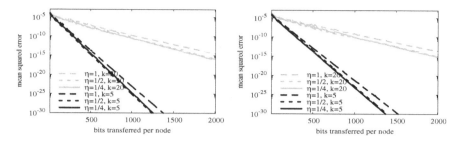

Fig. 2. The effect of parameters η and neighborhood size k on the pivot codec, with no message drop (left) and a 5% message drop (right).

round trip time is assumed to be only 2% of the cycle length. The motivation of looking at these two extreme scenarios is that in the latter case messages overlap to a much lesser extent than in the former case. Thus, we wish to demonstrate that our solutions are robust to short cycles. As for failures, we simulate message drop failure, where the message drop rate is either 0% or 5%.

4.2   Results

Figure 1 gives a comparison of the performance of different codecs when using our push-pull algorithm. The parameters were optimized for every codec using a grid search in the space $\eta \in \{2^0, 2^{-1}, \ldots, 2^{-4}\}$, $k \in \{5, 20\}$, $z_{in} \in \{0.35, 0.4, \ldots, 0.85\}$ and $m \in \{4, 8, 16\}$. In all the four scenarios shown on the plots, the best parameter settings were $\eta = 1/2$ and $k = 5$ for the pivot codec and $\eta = 1/4$, $k = 5$, $m = 4$, and $z_{in} = 0.55$ for the zooming codec. For the floating point codecs, $\eta = 1/2$ and $\eta = 1$ were the best for short and long cycles, respectively, and $k = 20$ was the best without message drop. With message drop, the floating point codecs are more stable with $k = 5$ but they converge slightly faster with $k = 20$, especially with short cycles. The pivot codec clearly dominates the other alternatives.

The difference between $k = 5$ and $k = 20$ is that in the former case more transactions are performed over a given fixed link. In the case of the stateless codecs, this means that $k = 5$ results in a more stable convergence because errors are corrected faster, but with $k = 20$ the correlation between consecutive updates over a fixed link are lower which results in a faster initial convergence. In the case of the pivot codec, Fig. 2 illustrates the effect of parameters η and k. It is clear that the algorithm is robust to η, however, parameter k has a significant effect. Unlike the stateless codecs, the pivot codec benefits from a somewhat larger correlation between updates as well as the higher frequency of the updates over a link since these allow for a better prediction of the value at the other end of the link. The zooming codec has a similar behavior (not shown), and we predict that every stateful codec prefers smaller neighborhoods.

Figure 3 presents a similar comparison using the synchronized average consensus algorithm. Note that here, the long and short cycle variants behave

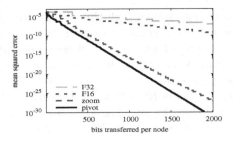

Fig. 3. Comparison of codecs in synchronized average consensus. The parameters of all of the codecs are optimized.

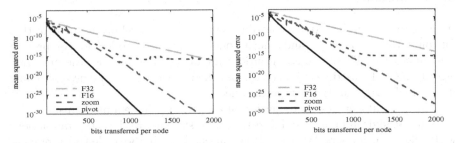

Fig. 4. Comparison of codecs with network size $N = 500{,}000$ (left) and without the flow compensation technique (with $N = 5{,}000$, right).

identically. Again, the parameters were optimized for every codec and the best parameter settings were $\eta = 1/2$ and $k = 5$ for the pivot codec, $\eta = 1$ and $k = 5$ for the floating point codecs, and $\eta = 1$, $k = 5$, $m = 8$, and $z_{in} = 0.45$ for the zooming codec. Again, the pivot codec dominates the other alternatives. Furthermore, note that, for the pivot codec, the optimal parameters are the same as those in the case of the push-pull algorithm. This suggests that these parameters are robust.

Figures 1 and 3 allow us to compare the push-pull algorithm with the synchronized algorithm. It is clear that all the codecs perform better with push-pull than with the synchronized algorithm. This implies that the push-pull algorithm is a better choice for compression, independently of the selected codec.

Figure 4 contains two remaining observations. First, it demonstrates that the mean squared error of push-pull gossip does not depend on network size as the results with $N = 500{,}000$ (left plot) are very similar to those with $N = 5{,}000$ (Fig. 1, top left). This is not surprising as this is predicted by theory when no compression is applied [6].

Second, Fig. 4 (right) shows the effect of the flow compensation technique introduced in Algorithm 2, where we used the f variables to smooth the stream of values over each link. As before, we optimized the parameters for all the codecs. The optimal parameter value for the pivot codec turned out to be $\eta = 1/8$ and $k = 5$. This means that if we drastically reduce η, thus smoothing the transactions much more aggressively with this alternative technique, the pivot codec still dominates the other codecs. However, we are not able to get the same compression rate we could achieve with flow compensation (Fig. 1) so the flow compensation technique is a valuable addition to the protocol. The other codecs have the same optimal parameters as with flow compensation. Note that the zooming codec also benefits from flow compensation, although to a lesser extent. We also observed that the zooming codec is very sensitive to z_{in} in this case, small deviations from the optimal value result in a dramatic performance loss (not shown).

5   Conclusions

In this paper we presented two contributions, namely a novel push-pull algorithm for computing the average, and a novel codec (called pivot codec) for compressed communication. These two contributions are orthogonal, because the push-pull algorithm can be used with any codec and the pivot codec can be used with any distributed algorithm that supports codecs.

The original features of the push pull algorithm include a mechanism to tolerate message drop failure, and a technique to support overlapping transactions with different neighbors. We also added a mechanism that we called flow compensation, which makes the stream of values over a given link smoother to improve compression. Another smoothing technique is a learning rate parameter η that controls the magnitude of each transaction. The pivot codec that we introduced is based on the intuition that in decentralized aggregation algorithms the values sent over a link are often correlated so compressing the stream is in fact similar to trying to guess a constant value on the other side of an overlay link.

We demonstrated experimentally that the novel codec is superior in the scenarios we studied in terms of the compression rate. We also demonstrated that the flow compensation mechanism indeed improves performance, although the pivot codec dominates the other codecs from related work even without the flow compensation mechanism. We saw that the push-pull protocol is highly robust to overlapping transactions as well, and in general outperforms the synchronized iteration algorithm independently of the codec used.

References

1. Boyd, S., Ghosh, A., Prabhakar, B., Shah, D.: Randomized gossip algorithms. IEEE Trans. Inf. Theory **52**(6), 2508–2530 (2006)
2. Brockett, R.W., Liberzon, D.: Quantized feedback stabilization of linear systems. IEEE Trans. Autom. Control **45**(7), 1279–1289 (2000)
3. Carli, R., Bullo, F., Zampieri, S.: Quantized average consensus via dynamic coding/decoding schemes. Int. J. Robust Nonlinear Control **20**(2), 156–175 (2010)
4. Carli, R., Fagnani, F., Frasca, P., Zampieri, S.: Gossip consensus algorithms via quantized communication. Automatica **46**(1), 70–80 (2010)
5. Fu, M., Xie, L.: Finite-level quantized feedback control for linear systems. IEEE Trans. Automatic Control **54**(5), 1165–1170 (2009)

6. Jelasity, M., Montresor, A., Babaoglu, O.: Gossip-based aggregation in large dynamic networks. ACM Trans. Comput. Syst. **23**(3), 219–252 (2005)
7. Jesus, P., Baquero, C., Almeida, P.S.: Fault-tolerant aggregation for dynamic networks. In: Proceedings of 29th IEEE Symposium on Reliable Distributed Systems (SRDS), pp. 37–43 (2010)
8. Kempe, D., Dobra, A., Gehrke, J.: Gossip-based computation of aggregate information. In: Proceedings of 44th Annual IEEE Symposium on Foundations of Computer Science (FOCS 2003) (2003)
9. Konecný, J., McMahan, H.B., Yu, F.X., Richtárik, P., Suresh, A.T., Bacon, D.: Federated learning: strategies for improving communication efficiency. In: Private Multi-Party Machine Learning (NIPS 2016 Workshop) (2016)
10. Li, T., Fu, M., Xie, L., Zhang, J.F.: Distributed consensus with limited communication data rate. IEEE Trans. Automatic Control **56**(2), 279–292 (2011)
11. McMahan, B., Moore, E., Ramage, D., Hampson, S., y Arcas, B.A.: Communication-efficient learning of deep networks from decentralized data. In: Singh, A., Zhu, J. (eds.) Proceedings of 20th International Conference on Artificial Intelligence and Statistics. Proceedings of Machine Learning Research, vol. 54, pp. 1273–1282 (2017)
12. Montresor, A., Jelasity, M.: Peersim: a scalable P2P simulator (extended abstract). In: Proceedings of 9th IEEE International Conference on Peer-to-Peer Computing (P2P 2009), pp. 99–100 (2009)
13. Nair, G.N., Fagnani, F., Zampieri, S., Evans, R.J.: Feedback control under data rate constraints: an overview. Proc. IEEE **95**(1), 108–137 (2007)
14. Niederbrucker, G., Gansterer, W.N.: Robust gossip-based aggregation: A practical point of view. In: Proceedings of Fifteenth Workshop on Algorithm Engineering and Experiments (ALENEX), pp. 133–147 (2013)
15. Olfati-Saber, R., Fax, J.A., Murray, R.M.: Consensus and cooperation in networked multi-agent systems. Proc. IEEE **95**(1), 215–233 (2007)
16. Ratanaworabhan, P., Ke, J., Burtscher, M.: Fast lossless compression of scientific floating-point data. In: Data Compression Conference (DCC 2006), pp. 133–142 (2006)
17. van Renesse, R., Birman, K.P., Vogels, W.: Astrolabe: a robust and scalable technology for distributed system monitoring, management, and data mining. ACM Trans. Comput. Syst. **21**(2), 164–206 (2003)
18. Suresh, A.T., Yu, F.X., Kumar, S., McMahan, H.B.: Distributed mean estimation with limited communication. In: Proceedings of 34th International Conference on Machine Learning, (ICML), pp. 3329–3337 (2017)
19. Xiao, L., Boyd, S.: Fast linear iterations for distributed averaging. Syst. Control Lett. **53**(1), 65–78 (2004)
20. Xiao, L., Boyd, S., Lall, S.: A scheme for robust distributed sensor fusion based on average consensus. In: IPSN 2005: Proceedings of 4th International Symposium on Information Processing in Sensor Networks, p. 9 (2005)
21. Zhu, M., Martinez, S.: On the convergence time of asynchronous distributed quantized averaging algorithms. IEEE Trans. Automatic Control **56**(2), 386–390 (2011)

Parallel and Distributed Programming, Interfaces, and Languages

Snapshot-Based Synchronization: A Fast Replacement for Hand-over-Hand Locking

Eran Gilad[1]($\boxtimes$), Trevor Brown[2], Mark Oskin[3], and Yoav Etsion[1]

[1] Technion – Israel Institute of Technology, Haifa, Israel
erangi@cs.technion.ac.il, yetsion@tce.technion.ac.il
[2] Institute of Science and Technology, Klosterneuburg, Austria
[3] University of Washington, Seattle, USA

Abstract. Concurrent accesses to shared data structures must be synchronized to avoid data races. Coarse-grained synchronization, which locks the entire data structure, is easy to implement but does not scale. Fine-grained synchronization can scale well, but can be hard to reason about. Hand-over-hand locking, in which operations are pipelined as they traverse the data structure, combines fine-grained synchronization with ease of use. However, the traditional implementation suffers from inherent overheads.

This paper introduces snapshot-based synchronization (SBS), a novel hand-over-hand locking mechanism. SBS decouples the synchronization state from the data, significantly improving cache utilization. Further, it relies on guarantees provided by pipelining to minimize synchronization that requires cross-thread communication. Snapshot-based synchronization thus scales much better than traditional hand-over-hand locking, while maintaining the same ease of use.

1 Introduction

Hand-over-hand locking[1] is a fine-grained synchronization technique that prevent data races among concurrent operations. Commonly applied to pointer-based data structures, operations lock nodes as they traverse the data structure. In order to prevent bypassing, a node's lock is released by the owning operation only after it acquires the next node's lock. Generally, operations that traverse the same path are *pipelined*. As the pattern guarantees a node will not be concurrently accessed by two threads, data races are avoided.

The fine nature of hand-over-hand locking exposes more parallelism. Given each thread locks at most two nodes at once, multiple threads can operate on a data structure concurrently. Threads are ordered, namely one is forced to wait for another, only when trying to access the same node. In a tree, ordering always applies to the root, as locks are associated with nodes. However, threads operating on different branches need not be ordered once their paths diverge.

---

[1] Also known as *lock coupling*, *chain locking*, *latch coupling*, *crabbing* etc.

© Springer International Publishing AG, part of Springer Nature 2018
M. Aldinucci et al. (Eds.): Euro-Par 2018, LNCS 11014, pp. 465–479, 2018.
https://doi.org/10.1007/978-3-319-96983-1_33

The concept of hand-over-hand locking is appealing: fine-grained locking exposes large amounts of parallelism, and ordering provides thread safety. Ordering also makes hand-over-hand locking easy to apply to sequential data structures (that have properties discussed later), providing a quick way to parallelize existing sequential code. Indeed, the popular textbook The Art of Multiprocessor Programming [1] uses hand-over-hand locking to demonstrate fine-grained locking. However, naïve hand-over-hand locking suffers from a few inherent limitations, causing it to be rarely used in the real world.

Poor Cache Utilization: Memory latencies are the most significant shortcoming of hand-over-hand locking. Acquiring and releasing per-node locks cause memory state modifications. As a thread makes its way to a certain node, it modifies the state of each node it passes. The modification is not performed on the data that the data structure is designed to hold (keys, values and pointers) but rather to the state of each node's lock. Consequently, even read-only accesses still require changes to memory for each node accessed. In the memory system, writes to a node that are performed on one core invalidate any cached copies of that node on other cores. Accessing nodes that are not in the cache can be two orders of magnitude slower than accessing cached nodes. Given a large enough number of threads operating on the same data structure, the overhead incurred by poor cache utilization can exceed the potential benefits of parallelism.

Entrance Bottleneck: Locking each node during traversal provides thread safety, but also turns the entrance to the data structure into a bottleneck. Consider operations on a tree: as every thread must go through the root, the root's lock effectively serializes all accesses. While parallelism increases as threads diverge in the tree, the serialized entrance caps potential speedup on parallel execution. The effect of the bottleneck is determined by the number of threads and the depth of the tree, which yield a ratio between threads actively traversing the tree and threads stalled at the entrance.

Extra Locking: As each node is associated with a different lock, moving from one node to the next requires both to be locked at the beginning of the transition. Albeit for a short while, the extra locking delays the divergence of threads that share an initial prefix of their paths. This initial prefix always includes the entrance of the data structure, which should be evacuated quickly.

1.1   Snapshot-Based Synchronization

Snapshot-based synchronization is designed to address the shortcomings of basic hand-over-hand locking while maintaining the same ease of use. The fundamental insights driving snapshot-based synchronization are: (1) the number of locations that must be locked at any given moment is bound by the number of threads, not the number of nodes; and (2) as long as nodes are locked in the correct order,

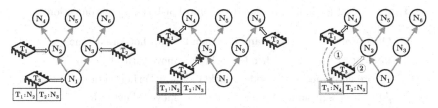

(a) T_3 enters. Snapshot: T_1 at N_2, T_2 at N_3

(b) T_3 can't access N_2 - snapshot indicates T_1 might be there

(c) After loading T_1's new location, T_3 can proceed

Fig. 1. (a) Thread T_3 creates a snapshot when entering tree; (b) uses it to detect potential collision; and (c) moves on after ensuring T_1 is no longer at N_2.

a thread cannot overtake (namely, race with) the thread in front of it, even if it somehow gets a delayed view of the first thread's traversal.

Building on those insights, snapshot-based synchronization decouples locks from nodes and associates them with threads. Each lock is then dynamically assigned to a single memory location, which represents the location of the node currently accessed by the thread. At any given moment, the set of locked locations can be considered to be a snapshot of all threads' locations. As depicted in Fig. 1, a thread that obtains such a snapshot when entering the data structure can query it throughout the traversal; as long as a node it wishes to access is not in the snapshot, the thread can freely access that node. If the node's location happens to exist in the snapshot, the current thread must wait until the thread at that location moves on.

Snapshot-based synchronization's main component is therefore the snapshot, which marks the locations of all other threads when taken. As threads move on, the snapshot quickly becomes outdated. However, observing outdated location can merely cause unnecessary waits; necessary waits to threads traversing the same path will never be missed. Crucially, since threads that complete an operation can reenter the data structure, a snapshot cannot be used indefinitely, and a thread must obtain a fresh snapshot at the beginning of each operation.

To facilitate location-based synchronization, threads must report their whereabout in a place that is visible to other threads. Reporting should take place often to reduce unnecessary stalls caused by false synchronization. However, the use of snapshots allows location reports to be seldom read – only when a snapshot indicates possible contention must a thread reload the locations of the others.

2 Snapshot-Based Synchronization Design

In this section we describe the basic design of snapshot-based synchronization and its core components. While the basic design overcomes most of the limitations of hand-over-hand locking, some are rooted deep in the pipelining pattern. Optimizations that address those limitations are discussed on the next section.

Hand-over-hand locking pipelines threads that traverse the same path. In other words, a thread can access a node that was locked by the thread in front

Table 1. API for hand-over-hand vs. snapshot-based synchronization

Operation	Hand-over-hand	Snapshot-based sync.
Lock head	head->lock()	moveToHead(head)
Before accessing node	node->lock()	waitForLoc(node)
After access granted	prev->unlock()	moveToLoc(node)

of it only once the leading thread moved on and unlocked the node. Bypassing within such a pipeline is impossible, so data races are avoided. Threads whose paths diverge are no longer synchronized, consequently hand-over-hand locking is only applicable to data structures that have no cycles (and algorithms that introduce no such cycles by, say, revisiting a node during a rebalancing phase). Snapshot-based synchronization is designed as a substitute for hand-over-hand locking, and its correctness is guaranteed only when the latter is safe. Graph data structures that have cycles, for instance, can neither be synchronized using hand-over-hand nor using snapshot-based synchronization.

The central component of snapshot-based synchronization is the snapshot. As depicted in Fig. 1, when a thread enters the data structure, it records the location of all other threads. Before the thread moves to another location, it checks if the snapshot recorded any other thread at that location. If so, it must not access the location until it verifies the other thread has moved. This verification is done by obtaining the latest location of the other thread (and possibly additional ones, as discussed later). Consequently, each thread must report its current location once it moves.

Snapshot-based synchronization manages two kinds of data: private (per thread) and public (shared). Snapshot-based synchronization reduces cross-thread communication by serving most reads from private data, falling back to reading public data only when encountering possible contention. Each thread stores the snapshot in private memory. The current location of each thread, on the other hand, is stored publicly and is available to all other threads. However, public data is read only when a snapshot must be created or updated.

Snapshot-based synchronization leverages modern hardware features to reduce overheads: loads from local caches are much faster than loads from main memory, and stores do not stall subsequent operations. The snapshot is read often but can be efficiently cached. Threads frequently report their locations publicly, but due to micro-architecture features such as out-of-order execution and store buffers, location reports do not stall subsequent instructions even if they incur a cache miss.

2.1   Interface and Algorithms

Snapshot-based synchronization's interface is similar to hand-over-hand locking's, and converting code using the latter to the former is straightforward. However, the underlying operations differ significantly, and the interface naming represents the actual semantics. Briefly, when using snapshot-based synchronization, operations must start with a call to moveToHead. Before accessing a location, waitForLoc must be called to make sure no other thread is present at that location. Lastly, moveToLoc is used to publish the new location of the thread, preventing others from accessing it. Table 1 compares the two interfaces.

moveToHead. Since most synchronization is done using the private snapshot, it is crucial that the snapshot is sufficiently up-to-date. In particular, a snapshot *must include the location of each thread that entered the data structure before the current thread and has not completed its operation yet.* Using a snapshot that does not include all threads ahead might yield a race.

The pipelining pattern must be maintained by snapshot creation as well. A snapshot is used to ensure a thread does not bypass (race with) threads in front of it. Given all threads enter the data structure via a single entry point, a snapshot must be created right before attempting to enter and must record all threads ahead. However, the snapshot needs not include threads that are behind in the pipeline – it is up to those threads behind to make sure they stay behind.

The moveToHead operation is implemented as follows:

1. Establish ordering among threads competing at the entrance.
2. Once the leading thread allows, create a snapshot by gathering the locations of all threads ahead.
3. Wait for the entrance to become available.
4. Move to the entrance and update current location.
5. Allow following thread to create a snapshot.

Two threads must not create a snapshot at the same time. Doing so will cause both to miss each other, and since one will eventually enter ahead of the other, the missing location will cause a race.

A significant part of entering the data structure requires serialization. Measures must therefore be taken to mitigate the bottleneck. Those measures are detailed in Sect. 3. moveToHead has no equivalent operation in hand-over-hand. Instead, in hand-over-hand the order in which threads lock the root of the data structure determines the order in which they will lock (and access) all other nodes, until their paths diverge.

waitForLoc. Before a thread can access a location, it must make sure no other thread will concurrently modify that location. To do so, the thread must:

1. Check if the snapshot contains any other thread at that location.
2. If no thread was observed at that location, waitForLoc can safely return.
3. Else, the current thread must wait until the thread ahead moves.
4. Update its snapshot.

The minimal update of the snapshot depends on the modifications done by the data structure algorithms. Consider a thread T_1, which executes an operation

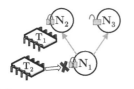
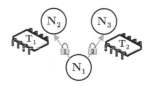

(a) T_1 locks all N_1, preventing T_2 from moving towards N_3

(b) T_1 locks the pointer to N_2, allowing T_2 to move to N_3

Fig. 2. Locking nodes vs. locking pointers. The latter allows more parallelism.

that does not modify the layout of the data structure (e.g., updates a value in a binary search tree), and a thread T_2 which is behind T_1. If T_2 waits for T_1 before accessing some location, only T_1's location must be updated in T_2's snapshot. However, if T_1 deletes a node, it might prevent T_2 from waiting to some T_0 that T_2 observed at the deleted node. In such cases, T_2's snapshot must be recreated.

moveToLoc. Moving to the next location is simple: a thread just updates its publicly visible location. This move is equivalent to locking the next node and unlocking the previous one in hand-over-hand. The overhead, however, is noticeably lower: the state of involved nodes is not changed, and only one location is locked at any given moment. Hand-over-hand's excessive locking is due to the lack of support for a single atomic modification of multiple memory locations in current hardware[2], which does not allow two locks to be modified at once.

2.2 Locking Granularity

Hand-over-hand relies on locks, and must therefore bind a lock to every object it wishes to protect. The most natural locking granularity is one lock per node[3]. Locking a node prevents all its fields from being accessed by other threads. Consider a tree in which node N_1 points to N_2 and N_3, depicted in Fig. 2a. Thread T_1 locks N_1, and is now considering whether it needs to delete N_2 (which will also involve modifying the pointer on N_1). Thread T_2 is heading towards N_3, but must pass through N_1. While neither N_2 nor the pointer to N_2 will be accessed by T_2, per-node locking will force T_2 to wait until T_1 unlocks N_1.

Snapshot-based synchronization does not use lock objects, and instead (semantically) locks memory locations. Consequently, locking can be done at any desired granularity. The one we had found most useful is per pointer. Consider the previous example; as depicted in Fig. 2b, on a per-pointer synchronization scheme, T_1 would have locked the pointer to N_2. T_2 could have then check N_1's key, determine it needs to go to N_3, and freely move on without being stalled by

---

[2] Hardware transactional memory does allow multiple modifications to happen effectively atomically, but is not ubiquitous. We discuss software TM in Sect. 4.

[3] A lock array can service any number of nodes using some hash function but might cause deadlocks, and in our experiments, not faster than storing locks as node fields.

T_1. On lower parts of the tree, threads usually diverge and locking granularity has little effect. However, contention is a major problem at the top of the tree, and locking pointers eliminates unneeded synchronizations.

3 Optimized Implementation

The basic snapshot-based synchronization scheme eliminates hand-over-hand's poor cache utilization and excessive locking overheads. However, the root of the data structure remains a bottleneck. Creating a snapshot involves reading the current locations of all threads. Since the locations are constantly being updated by the reporting threads, creating a snapshot incurs multiple cache misses. Given snapshots cannot be created in parallel, taking a snapshot before entering the data structure serializes execution for a large portion of the run. In this section, we discuss major optimizations that improve snapshot-based synchronization's efficiency, and in particular mitigate the entrance bottleneck.

3.1 Copying Snapshots

Creating a snapshot involves accessing data constantly updated, incurring multiple cache misses. To avoid creating a snapshot from scratch, a thread can copy the snapshot used by the immediate leading thread. If the complete snapshot resides on a single cache line, copying incurs a single cache miss.

Snapshots can only be copied from the thread that entered immediately before the thread that needs the snapshot. Consider threads T_1, T_2 and T_3 entering a data structure, in this order. T_1's snapshot is created first, thus does not include T_2's location. If T_3 copies from T_1, it might race with T_2. On the other hand, if T_3 copies T_2's snapshot it might obtain a somewhat stale view of T_1's location. However, the worst outcome would be the detection of false collisions. Importantly, care must be taken to avoid using snapshots after re-entrance into the data structure: if T_2 completes its operation, enters the data structure again and tries to copy T_3's snapshot before T_3 gets to copy T_2's, neither will have a valid snapshot. This is a variant of the ABA problem, which we solve using the conventional tool – timestamps. Once a thread detects it copied an invalid snapshot, it simply falls back to creating a new one from scratch.

3.2 Deferring Snapshot Creation by Trailing

A thread that immediately follows a previous thread does not need a snapshot; we call this state *trailing*. Due to the nature of pipelining, no thread can appear between two consecutive threads. As illustrated in Fig. 3, while T_2 trails T_1, it can rely on T_1 to resolve any collision with threads in front of them, allowing T_2 to merely ensure it does not bypass T_1. T_2 can thus defer obtaining a snapshot until trailing breaks. Trailing thus eliminates the need to create a snapshot before entering, significantly shortening the bottleneck. Further, trailing eliminates most contention points involving more than two threads, akin to MCS locks [2].

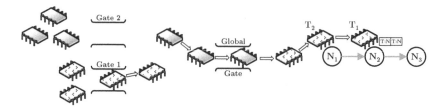

Fig. 3. Local gates order threads coming from the same NUMA node, creating *chains*. The global gate orders the entrance of chains into the data structure. While *trailing*, prev.'s position is examined directly without using a snapshot.

While T_2 trails T_1, T_2 examines the location of T_1 instead of checking the snapshot. As long as T_1 is still at the location T_2 wishes to move to, T_2 will spin; once T_1 moves, T_2 can immediately follow. While this cross-thread communication is more expensive than checking a private snapshot, it is cheaper than creating one. In the heavily-contended entrance, quickly evacuating the entrance reduces stalls. Trailing stops as soon as T_2 cannot be sure T_1 passed through the memory location it tries to access, whether because T_1 moved too fast to the next location or because T_1 turned another way. Once trailing stops, T_2 cannot rely on T_1 and must create (or copy) a snapshot before moving on.

3.3   NUMA Awareness

On NUMA systems, accessing remote memory (associated with another NUMA node) is significantly slower than accessing local memory. Keeping as much cross-thread communication within the same NUMA node can therefore reduce memory latencies. While snapshot-based synchronization is agnostic to the memory management of the hosting data structure, adding NUMA-awareness to the synchronization mechanism reduces its overhead.

Snapshot-based synchronization employs a technique that groups threads of the same NUMA node, orders them internally, and lets them enter the data structure in this exact order. The mechanism, depicted in Fig. 3, resembles the one used in cohort locks [3]: a per NUMA node gate is first used to create *chains* of threads belonging to that NUMA node. The *head* of each chain (namely the first thread) competes over the global gate only with other heads. Once acquired, the head closes its following chain and announces the last thread in the chain via the global gate. The head of the next chain (probably coming from another NUMA node) will trail the last thread in the chain in front of it.

Threads within the same chain all run on the same NUMA node. Trailing and snapshot copying among those threads are noticeably faster than across NUMA nodes. The ratio between local and remote communication is determined by the length of the chains. Interestingly, if entering the data structure becomes slow (e.g., due to some external interference) and threads accumulate at the entrance, longer chains will be created. This in turn will provide more local communication, allowing threads to leave the head quicker, reducing entrance time.

3.4   Reader Synchronization

Read-only operations such as lookups are usually easier to parallelize, as they need not synchronize with other readers (synchronization with write operations is required, of course). In a hand-over-hand algorithm, readers can thus safely bypass each other. This freedom could be of great use when threads enter the data structure. Unfortunately, the straightforward readers optimization breaks other optimizations. For instance, if writer W_1 trails reader R_1, and R_1 bypasses R_2, then W_1 will race with R_2. Similarly, writers cannot copy snapshots from readers as they might include stale locations of other readers. Our implementation includes a restricted set of reader optimizations. We do not elaborate on them due to lack of space, and leave further reader optimizations for future work.

3.5   Putting it All Together

The optimized snapshot-based synchronization overcomes inherent limitations of hand-over-hand: **Poor cache locality** is minimized by decoupling synchronization state from the data structure and using a snapshot to further reduce cross-thread communication. **The entrance bottleneck** is mitigated by using NUMA-aware algorithms, deferring snapshot creation and reusing snapshots. **Extra locking** is avoided by allowing an atomic move from one location to another and by locking pointers rather than nodes. **Reader synchronization** is reduced by allowing readers to bypass each other. The following section shows snapshot-based synchronization is indeed faster than hand-over-hand locking.

4   Evaluation

In this section we compare the actual performance of snapshot-based synchronization (*SBS*) to alternative synchronization mechanisms, revealing both strengths and weaknesses. The alternative mechanisms are (a) traditional hand-over-hand (*HOH*) and (b) software transactional memory (*STM*). Like SBS, STM is a synchronization mechanism external to the data structure, which can be used to parallelize sequential data structures. State-of-the-art concurrent data structures can be much faster, but synchronization is deeply integrated in the structures and associated algorithms. We therefore do not consider them comparable.

4.1   Experimental Setup

We perform a series of micro-benchmarks, running a mix of operations on binary trees. We consider both integers (*INT*) and strings (*STR*) as key types – while the former is more common in the literature, the latter is very common in real programs, and sometimes exhibits a different behavior. All evaluations execute a similar number of inserts and deletes, keeping the data structure size stable; we also study the effect of the initial size. Lastly, read-write ratio on all benchmarks

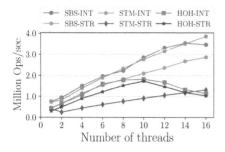

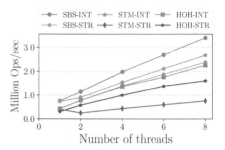

Fig. 4. Scalability using 2 NUMA nodes (init: 10^6)

Fig. 5. Scalability using 1 NUMA node (init: 10^6)

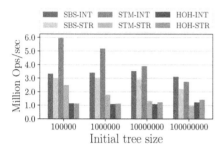

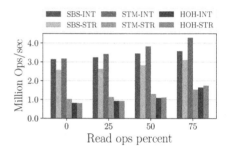

Fig. 6. Effect of initial size (16 threads)

Fig. 7. Effect of read-write ratio (16 threads, 10^6 init size)

is 50–50. We do not analyze other ratios due to space limitations; in short, our evaluation finds snapshot-based synchronization favors write-heavy workloads.

The server used has 2 NUMA nodes and Intel Xeon E5-2630 processors running at 2.4 Ghz. Hyperthreading, Turbo Boost and adjacent cache line prefetching were disabled. Each core has 32 KB L1 and 236 KB L2 caches; each processor has a 20 MB L3 cache; and the system has 62 GB of RAM. Code was written in C++ and compiled with GCC 7.2, which also provided the STM support.

4.2   Scalability

Figure 4 presents the throughput of all workloads running on a varying number of threads, evenly distributed between the 2 NUMA nodes. Evidently, HOH does not scale past 10 threads, and synchronization overhead overwhelms performance as the number of threads increases. On the INT workloads, SBS is slightly slower than STM. However, while STM's scalability is consistent, SBS reaches its peak at 14 threads. The STR workloads demonstrate different trends, as more work is performed during traversal (mostly string comparisons, involving multiple memory accesses in a loop). Extending traversals reduces contention at the entrance, allowing SBS to continue scaling past 16 threads. STM, however, suffers from enlarged read and write sets, causing throughputs to drop.

Figure 5 presents scalability when running on a single NUMA node. The results emphasize the effect of NUMA: as cross-core communication is much faster when running on the same NUMA node, HOH and SBS scale much better. Most of the gain comes from entering the tree faster due to reduced cross-thread communication latencies. STM, which does not require communication at that point, sees little gain in this scenario. In summary, HOH and SBS are more NUMA sensitive than STM. SBS performs best on most scenarios, but short traversal times (INT) with long communication (NUMA) cap scaling at 14 threads.

4.3   Effect of Data Structure Size

The size of the data structure affects the duration of the traversal. As indicated by the difference between INT and STR workloads, traversal time correlates to entrance contention, which in turn determines scalability. Figure 6 presents the throughput of the 6 benchmarks when running on trees of different sizes - 10^5, 10^6, 10^7 and 10^8; all using 16 threads. Accessing more memory locations as the tree grows causes STM throughput to decrease. SBS, however, has about the same throughput on the smaller 3 sizes. This somewhat unexpected behavior is clearer when examining the results in the opposite direction: SBS throughput does not increase as the tree size becomes smaller, indicating the size is not the dominant factor. For SBS, 16 threads is the scalability limit on 10^7 trees; on smaller trees, entrance is even more contended, canceling the benefit of shorter traversals. In summary, SBS is more appropriate for trees of size 10^7 and higher when using simple INT keys. When using STR keys that increase SBS traversal times and STM's read sets, SBS consistently performs best.

4.4   Effect of Read-Write Ratio

Since in our snapshot-based synchronization implementation readers enter the data structure one-by-one, entrance bottleneck has a similar effect on scalability regardless of reader-write ratio. Figure 7 shows that the write-only throughput of SBS is equivalent to STM, but STM becomes faster as the percent of read operations is increased. Further optimizing readers could make SBS scale better, but the implementation is non-trivial. Instead, snapshot-based synchronization can be integrated with mechanisms such as RCU [4], combining multiple concurrent writers with wait-free readers.

4.5   Entrance Bottleneck Analysis

Serialization at the entrance limits parallelism; we now dive deeper into this part of execution. In our implementation, execution can be divided into 3 parts: (1) initial ordering, (2) accessing the head, and (3) traversing the tree. The first and last parts are mostly parallel. Accessing the head, however, can be done by a single thread at a time. A thread can not access the head until it detected the

Table 2. Breakdown of overhead between accessing the head and allowing the following thread to access the head.

Operation	Overhead	Frequency
Evacuate global gate	Cache misses on local read and remote write	Once per chain
Create a snapshot	Varies	Rare, due to trailing
Await node after head	Varies	Always
Move to node after head	Sometimes cache miss on local write	Always
Arrival of updated location to next thread	Cache miss on read	Once per chain remote miss, otherwise local miss

previous thread moved to another node. Single-threaded execution thus takes place between the time one thread detects it can access the head to the time the following thread detects it can move on.

Before a thread can allow the following one to access the head, it needs to move to another node. If the thread is the first in a chain, it must first make the global gate available for the next chain once it accessed the head. It must then move to the other node and report its new location. Lastly, the following thread must read that report. The overheads of this sequence are detailed in Table 2. In our experiments, on a 16-thread write-only SBS execution the sequence took an average of 700 cycles. Multiplying this sequence latency by the throughput of 3M ops/s yields 2.1G cycles. The latency incurred by the traversal of the head is the execution's critical path, and matches our processors 2.4 GHz frequency. In summary, Scalability is limited by the rate in which threads access the head. Our implementation minimizes accesses to remote memory, but cache misses that involve communication with a core residing on the same NUMA node incur significant overhead. Serialized execution time can be reduced by either eliminating operations or using faster cross-core communication; x86 MONITOR and MWAIT, once available in user mode, are certainly of interest [5].

5 Related Work

The hand-over-hand locking scheme (also known as lock coupling, latch coupling, crabbing etc.) was first described by Bayer and Schkolnick [6] as a way to construct concurrent B-trees. It has since been used to parallelize various data structures. As the major synchronization mechanism, it was used in linked lists [1], B-trees [7], skip lists [8], relaxed red-black trees [9] and a Treap [10]. As a utility for a certain part of the algorithm, it was also used in priority queues [11], B+-trees [12,13], B^{link}-trees [14,15] and hash tables [16].

Data structures with properties allowing hand-over-hand synchronization have been defined as Unipath [17] and Dominance Locking [10]. Those properties allow serializability verification [18,19] and even automatic parallelization [10].

Locking individual memory locations has been supported in various forms. Lock-box [20] provided architectural support for SMT threads to lock particular addresses without using conventional synchronization mechanisms. The Synchronization State Buffer [21] extended this idea to a many-core system, while vLock [22] offered a software solution. TL2 [23] incorporated an array of locks in an STM library, allowing a fixed (yet large) set of locks to protect any number of locations. ROKO [24] synchronized accesses using versioning memory locations, and O-structures [25] added renaming to eliminate false dependencies.

6   Conclusions

Hand-over-hand locking is a widespread fine-grained synchronization technique. The simple interface makes hand-over-hand attractive, and it has been used to parallelize multiple data structures. Furthermore, the method is simple to reason about, allowing verification and automatic parallelization. However, fine-grained locking comes at a price: locking causes cache misses on every node access. As all threads enter at the same place, the top of the data structure becomes a bottleneck that disallows scaling past a small number of threads.

Snapshot-based synchronization is a drop-in replacement for hand-over-hand locking, but uses a very different synchronization mechanism under the hood. Leveraging the data structure layout, private snapshots allow threads to avoid data races without communicating with other threads. Leveraging modern hardware, communication minimally interferes with the surrounding algorithm. In our evaluation, on large data structures snapshot-based synchronization is on average 2.6× faster than hand-over-hand locking and 1.6× faster than STM.

While its interface is simple and easy to use, Snapshot-based synchronization's implementation is considerably more complex than simple per-node locks. Albeit undesired in general, complexity brings about many optimization opportunities. We consider the implementation described in this paper a baseline: other implementations, possibly using newer hardware features, can make snapshot-based synchronization scale even better. In particular, reducing data structure entrance time and relaxing reader-to-reader synchronization are of interest.

Acknowledgements. This research was funded, in part, by Google and the Israel Ministry of Science, Technology, and Space. Trevor Brown was supported in part by the ISF (grants 2005/17 & 1749/14) and by a NSERC post-doctoral fellowship. Eran Gilad was supported by the Hasso-Plattner Institute fellowship.

References

1. Herlihy, M., Shavit, N.: The Art of Multiprocessor Programming. Morgan Kaufmann Publishers Inc., Los Altos (2008)
2. Mellor-Crummey, J.M., Scott, M.L.: Algorithms for scalable synchronization on shared-memory multiprocessors. ACM Trans. Comput. Syst. **9**(1), 21–65 (1991)

3. Dice, D., Marathe, V.J., Shavit, N.: Lock cohorting: a general technique for designing NUMA locks. In: Symposium on Principles and Practices of Parallel Programming (PPoPP) (2012)
4. Desnoyers, M., McKenney, P.E., Stern, A.S., Dagenais, M.R., Walpole, J.: User-level implementations of read-copy update. IEEE Trans. Parallel Distrib. Syst. **23**(2), 375–382 (2012)
5. Akkan, H., Lang, M., Ionkov, L.: HPC runtime support for fast and power efficient locking and synchronization. In: International Conference on Cluster Computing (2013)
6. Bayer, R., Schkolnick, M.: Concurrency of operations on B-trees. Acta Inform. **9**, 1–21 (1977)
7. Rodeh, O.: B-trees, shadowing, and clones. ACM Trans. Storage **3**(4), 2:1–2:27 (2008)
8. Sánchez, A., Sánchez, C.: A theory of skiplists with applications to the verification of concurrent datatypes. In: Bobaru, M., Havelund, K., Holzmann, G.J., Joshi, R. (eds.) NFM 2011. LNCS, vol. 6617, pp. 343–358. Springer, Heidelberg (2011). https://doi.org/10.1007/978-3-642-20398-5_25
9. Ohene-Kwofie, D., Otoo, E.J., Nimako, G.: Concurrent operations of O2-tree on shared memory multicore architectures. In: Australasian DB Conference (ADC) (2013)
10. Golan-Gueta, G., Bronson, N., Aiken, A., Ramalingam, G., Sagiv, M., Yahav, E.: Automatic fine-grain locking using shape properties. In: Object-Oriented Programming, Systems, Languages, and Applications (OOPSLA) (2011)
11. Tamir, O., Morrison, A., Rinetzky, N.: A heap-based concurrent priority queue with mutable priorities for faster parallel algorithms. In: International Conference on Principles of Distributed Systems (OPODIS) (2016)
12. Srinivasan, V., Carey, M.J.: Performance of B+ tree concurrency control algorithms. Very Large Databases J. (JVLDB) **2**(4), 361–406 (1993)
13. Mao, Y., Kohler, E., Morris, R.T.: Cache craftiness for fast multicore key-value storage. In: European Conference on Computer Systems (EUROSYS) (2012)
14. Evangelidis, G., Lomet, D., Salzberg, B.: The hB$^{\Pi}$-tree: a multi-attribute index supporting concurrency, recovery and node consolidation. Very Large Databases J. (JVLDB) **6**(1), 1–25 (1997)
15. Jaluta, I., Sippu, S., Soisalon-Soininen, E.: Concurrency control and recovery for balanced B-link trees. Very Large Databases J. (JVLDB) **14**(2), 257–277 (2005)
16. Ellis, C.S.: Distributed data structures: a case study. IEEE Trans. Comput. **34**, 1178–1185 (1985)
17. Gilad, E., Mayzels, T., Raab, E., Oskin, M., Etsion, Y.: Towards a deterministic fine-grained task ordering using multi-versioned memory. In: Computer Architecture and High Performance Computing (SBAC-PAD) (2017)
18. Attiya, H., Ramalingam, G., Rinetzky, N.: Sequential verification of serializability. In: Symposium on Principles of Programming Languages (POPL) (2010)
19. Vafeiadis, V., Herlihy, M., Hoare, T., Shapiro, M.: Proving correctness of highly-concurrent linearisable objects. In: Symposium on Principles and Practices of Parallel Programming (PPoPP) (2006)
20. Tullsen, D.M., Lo, J.L., Eggers, S.J., Levy, H.M.: Supporting fine-grained synchronization on a simultaneous multithreading processor. In: Symposium on High-Performance Computer Architecture (HPCA) (1999)
21. Zhu, W., Sreedhar, V.C., Hu, Z., Gao, G.R.: Synchronization state buffer: supporting efficient fine-grain synchronization on many-core architectures. In: International Symposium on Computer Architecture (ISCA) (2007)

22. Yan, J., Tan, G., Zhang, X., Yao, E., Sun, N.: vLock: lock virtualization mechanism for exploiting fine-grained parallelism in graph traversal algorithms. In: International Symposium on Code Generation and Optimization (CGO) (2013)
23. Dice, D., Shalev, O., Shavit, N.: Transactional locking II. In: Dolev, S. (ed.) DISC 2006. LNCS, vol. 4167, pp. 194–208. Springer, Heidelberg (2006). https://doi.org/10.1007/11864219_14
24. Segulja, C., Abdelrahman, T.: Architectural support for synchronization-free deterministic parallel programming. In: Symposium on High-Performance Computer Architecture (HPCA) (2012)
25. Gilad, E., Mayzels, T., Raab, E., Oskin, M., Etsion, Y.: Architectural support for unlimited memory versioning and renaming. In: International Parallel and Distributed Processing Symposium (IPDPS) (2018)

Measuring Multithreaded Message Matching Misery

Whit Schonbein[1,2]([✉]), Matthew G. F. Dosanjh[1], Ryan E. Grant[1,2],
and Patrick G. Bridges[2]

[1] Sandia National Laboratories, Center for Computing Research,
Albuquerque, USA
{wwschon,mdosanj,regrant}@sandia.gov
[2] Department of Computer Science, University of New Mexico,
Albuquerque, USA
bridges@cs.unm.edu

Abstract. MPI usage patterns are changing as applications move towards fully-multithreaded runtimes. However, the impact of these patterns on MPI message matching is not well-studied. In particular, MPI's mechanic for receiver-side data placement, message matching, can be impacted by increased message volume and nondeterminism incurred by multithreading. While there has been significant developer interest and work to provide an efficient MPI interface for multithreaded access, there has not been a study showing how these patterns affect messaging patterns and matching behavior. In this paper, we present a framework for studying the effects of multithreading on MPI message matching. This framework allows us to explore the implications of different common communication patterns and thread-level decompositions. We present a study of these impacts on the architecture of two of the Top 10 supercomputers (NERSC's Cori and LANL's Trinity). This data provides a baseline to evaluate reasonable matching engine queue lengths, search depths, and queue drain times under the multithreaded model. Furthermore, the study highlights surprising results on the challenge posed by message matching for multithreaded application performance.

1 Introduction

As the number of cores per node increase, scientific codes are moving toward hybrid model of parallelism combining an inter-process communication model,

---

Sandia National Laboratories is a multimission laboratory managed and operated by National Technology and Engineering Solutions of Sandia LLC, a wholly owned subsidiary of Honeywell International Inc. for the U.S. Department of Energy's National Nuclear Security Administration under contract DE-NA0003525.

This research was supported by the Exascale Computing Project (17-SC-20-SC), a collaborative effort of the U.S. Department of Energy Office of Science and the National Nuclear Security Administration.

Under the terms of Contract DE-NA0003525, there is a non-exclusive license for use of this work by or on behalf of the U.S. Government.

© National Technology & Engineering Solutions of Sandia, LLC 2018
M. Aldinucci et al. (Eds.): Euro-Par 2018, LNCS 11014, pp. 480–491, 2018.
https://doi.org/10.1007/978-3-319-96983-1_34

such as MPI, with a threading model. Due to performance concerns with MPI implementations, most contemporary codes leverage a hybrid BSP model where computation phases fan out to use multiple threads and communication phases filter down to a single thread. However, there is significant developer interest in leveraging MPI in a multithreaded manner to increase communication and computation overlap, decrease thread fan in/out overheads, and reduce development overheads.

While some studies address improvements to MPI's multithreaded codepaths, few assess how multithreaded communication affects the behavior of MPI message processing. Specifically, in single-threaded contexts, determinism in communication patterns allows users to ensure performance by ordering receive requests to match the corresponding sends. In contrast, non-determinism introduced by multithreaded communication may undermine this optimization, leading to increased message processing times. Furthermore, since the common strategy of packing data into a few large messages is likely to be discarded in favor of having each thread send smaller messages, the issue may be exacerbated by the increased number of messages. Since the acceptable performance of many current scientific codes is based on the assumption MPI message processing overhead is small in comparison to time spent in computation phases, it is of critical importance we grasp the implications of multithreaded communication so that appropriate steps can be taken in advance of the exascale timeframe.

In this paper, we explore the impact of increased messaging and decreased determinism in message ordering on MPI message processing. This study explores this impact on widely-used, simple, and highly-scalable stencil communication patterns that limit communication to a minimal number of peers. We introduce a model for the number of threads engaged in inter-process communication, and messages exchanged, when these stencil patterns are converted to multithreaded messaging in straightforward ways. We then empirically assess the effects of these patterns on average search depths and times. The results of these tests are surprising to us as MPI experts, as the MPI queue search depths are worse than expected. This means that MPI multi-threaded message processing overhead will be unacceptable when compared to the current performance of scientific codes.

The contributions of this paper are:

- A theoretical analysis of the characteristics of different thread-level decompositions for common stencil communication patterns;
- A testing structure enabling experiments of the effect of different thread-level decompositions on MPI message matching;
- An empirical study of the effects of threading on average search depths and queue drain times for MPI message matching.

The rest of this paper is organized as follows: Sect. 2 explores the background of this work including MPI Matching and MPI thread multiple. Section 3 presents our analysis of thread decompositions of different stencil patterns that we explore in this paper. Section 4 presents our empirical study of multithreaded non-determinism on search depth, list length, and queue drain time. Section 5 presents the state-of-the-art related work to this study. Finally, Sect. 6 presents the conclusions and implications of this work.

2   Background

In this section we present relevant background on MPI message matching and multithreaded MPI.

2.1   Message Matching

Message matching is MPI's receiver-side data-placement mechanic, used primarily to support point-to-point communication. To send a message (e.g., MPI_Send or MPI_Isend), an MPI process specifies a buffer containing data to be sent, a destination ID ('rank'), and a placement identifier ('tag'). The receiving MPI process posts a corresponding receive (e.g., MPI_Recv or MPI_Irecv) specifying a buffer where data will be placed, the rank of the sender, and the tag of the expected message. The communication is completed when the receiver matches the sending rank and tag of an incoming message to that of a posted receive, and the payload delivered to the specified buffer.

The MPI specification imposes several constraints on receiver-side message matching. First, messages must be matched in the order their receives are posted. Second, the matching mechanism must allow wildcards for both rank and tag. To handle these requirements, traditional implementations use two linked lists: a list of outstanding receive requests in a posted receive queue (PRQ), and a list of unmatched messages in the unexpected message queue (UMQ). When an MPI process posts a receive, its UMQ is traversed to determine whether a message with the desired sending rank and tag has already arrived, and if not, the receive is appended to the PRQ. When a message arrives at that process, the PRQ is traversed to determine whether a receive with the required rank and tag has already been posted, and if not, the information is appended to the UMQ. MPI ordering and wildcard semantics are guaranteed by initiating searches from queue heads and appending to their tails.

For the purposes of this paper, we use a traditional model for message matching, based on the model used by MPICH [19] and its derivatives. Some other implementations have opted for different models. For example, Open MPI [20] utilizes an array of lists, indexed by sending rank, which can reduce average search depth at the cost of increased memory. The benchmark and results presented in this paper can provide a better understanding on how these optimized models will impact next-generation applications.

2.2   Multithreaded MPI

The MPI standard introduces four threading modes which can be chosen during initialization [15]. Three of these require the user to prevent simultaneous requests while the fourth provides thread-safety. This paper is concerned with

MPI's thread-safe mode, MPI_THREAD_MULTIPLE, which requires the underlying implementation be able to handle simultaneous requests from different threads.

While the prevalence of hybrid-parallel applications has risen, few have leveraged MPI_THREAD_MULTIPLE. This has been due to the community's perception of the performance implications of this mode [7]. These performance implications are not inherent in the MPI standard, but are often a result of the complexity of implementing that standard. Recently, there have been efforts to improve this performance through mechanisms such as fine grained locks [1,2], one sided communication [10], and software offloading [23]. These efforts have primarily looked at improving the mechanics of multithreaded MPI; there has been little work on the impact of multithreaded MPI access patterns on MPI processing such as message matching.

3   Analysis of Stencil Decomposition

In this section, we provide an analysis for several possible stencil communication patterns using thread-level decompositions. The analysis assumes, first, that the thread decomposition is uniform, and second, each thread is responsible for its own outgoing and incoming data. This has implications for number of messages received, but maintains memory management schemes used by current applications at the process level (Table 1).

Table 1. Notation

L_d	Length of decomposition along dimension d
T_r	Number of receiving threads
T_s	Number of sending threads
M_e	Number of messages across a 1d edge
M_s	Number of messages across a 2d surface
M_t	Total number of messages exchanged in BSP communication phase

Given these assumptions, the simplest pattern is a *naive* case, where each thread communicates with all of its neighbors. For example, if the problem domain allocated to an MPI process is decomposed into $L_x \times L_y$ threads, and the stencil is 9 point, then each thread posts 8 receives, and the MPI matching engine must handle $8L_xL_y$ total messages during each BSP communication phase, distributed across L_xL_y threads.

A more nuanced approach assumes threads need only communicate along a process' domain boundaries; intra-process communication is handled outside of the MPI message matching engine. This maps well to real-world applications, where shared memory is typically used for intra-process communication. Even if intra-process MPI calls are used, they often bypass internal data structures and processing.

In this scenario, the number of sending and receiving threads differ because of corners and edges of the decomposed domain, as well as the type of stencil. Here we provide analyses for the case of 2d, 9pt and 3d, 27pt stencil communication. The analyses of 5pt and 7pt stencils are omitted for space. Note these analyses make the additional assumption that the length of each dimension is ≥ 2 subdomains.

3.1   9 Point Stencil

$$M_e = 3L_e \tag{1}$$
$$M_t = 6L_x + 6L_y - 4 \tag{2}$$
$$T_r = 2L_x + 2L_y - 4 \tag{3}$$
$$T_s = 2L_x + 2L_y + 4 \tag{4}$$

A 9-point stencil is a communication pattern for a 2 dimensional split of the problem space based on a 2d, radius-1 Moore neighborhood. The pattern requires communication to each neighbor process, including the corners. Equation 1 shows the number of messages sent across a single edge of the domain. Under our assumptions, the number of messages crossing an edge is three times the number of subdomains along that edge. Equation 2 extends the previous equation, by summing the number messages across all four edges and removing overlap. Equation 3 counts the communicating internal threads by calculating the sum of all the subdomains touching an edge of the process's domain and subtracting the overlap. This formula is subject to the $L_d \geq 2$ limitation as the overlap at $L_d = 1$. Finally, Eq. 4 counts the external threads by calculating the sum of all the subdomains that touch an edge of the process's domain and accounting for the four corners that weren't previously counted.

3.2   27 Point Stencil

$$M_s = 9L_m L_n \tag{5}$$
$$M_t = 2(\sum_{m<n|m,n\in\{x,y,z\}} 9L_m L_n) - 4(\sum_{m\in x,y,z} 3L_m) + 8 \tag{6}$$
$$T_r = 2(\sum_{m<n|m,n\in\{x,y,z\}} L_m L_n) - 4(\sum_{m\in x,y,z} L_m) + 8 \tag{7}$$
$$T_s = 2(\sum_{m<n|m,n\in\{x,y,z\}} L_m L_n) + 4(\sum_{m\in x,y,z} L_m) + 8 \tag{8}$$

A 27-point stencil is a communication pattern for a 3 dimensional split of the the problem space, based on a 3d, radius-1 Moore neighborhood. The pattern requires communication to each neighbor process across edges and corners. Equation 5 shows the number of messages sent across a single surface of the domain. Under our assumptions, the number of messages crossing a surface is the number of subdomains on that surface times 9. Equation 6 extends the previous equation, by summing the number messages across all six surfaces and removing overlap. Note in these equations, the notation $m < n | m, n \in \{x, y, z\}$ can be thought of as nested loops generating the products xy, xz, and yz; an alternative notation is $N \in \{x, y, z\}^{(2)}$, where N is a metavariable ranging over the *set* formed by the 'n choose k' operator. Messages going diagonally from an edge are counted twice and are thus removed. Corner communication is counted three times but removed three times by accounting for the diagonal edge, and so are re-included. Equation 7 counts the internal threads by calculating the sum of all the subdomains touching an edge of the process' domain, subtracting the overlapped edges, and re-including corners. This formula is subject to the $L_d \geq 2$ limitation. Finally, Eq. 8 counts the external threads by calculating the sum of all the subdomains that touch an surface of the process's domain and accounting for the twelve edges and eight corners that weren't previously counted.

4   Experimental Results

4.1   Methods

To investigate the effects of multithreading on MPI matching, we (i) instrumented MPI to report average PRQ search depths and time spent searching, and (ii) designed a benchmark to utilize MPI point-to-point communication in thread-multiple mode, while varying the thread count and total messages exchanged. For the former, an Open MPI development branch[1] was modified to use a matching engine mimicking that of MPICH. Open source MPICH does not provide support for our high-speed network, but is the basis for the vendor optimized MPI library on our system, therefore we used an open-source instrumented Open MPI with a MPICH style match list to best represent a fully-optimized vendor MPI. Since all messages originate from the same sending process, the list length under Open MPI's native matching engine is the same, although lengths for Open MPI matching can be roughly estimated from the results given below, by dividing by the anticipated number of sending MPI processes.

The benchmark emulates the behavior of an MPI process participating in bulk synchronous parallel (BSP) application with multi-threaded communication. Two nodes are allocated, each hosting a single MPI process. One is designated the receiving process, while the other serves as a proxy for the sending processes in the communication pattern. In an openMP region utilizing T_r threads, the receiving process pre-posts M_t receives; each message is given a unique tag. The order in which receives are posted is thus determined by thread scheduling and lock contention. Both processes barrier to ensure that all receives are pre-posted. The sending process then issues M_t sends, distributed across T_s threads, also in a free-for-all ordering incurred by a multithreaded region. To ensure fairness, tags are strided across sending and receiving threads. This provides a tag-ordering to the messages as m_i will have higher priority than m_j given $i < j$.

---

[1] Open MPI git hash f56847542eace89512aa482b186012d43fed7d4d.

As recent work has shown that some applications have queue lengths in excess of 1000 messages [11], the naive results include the case where each thread posts 512 receives, in addition to 9 and 27 point stencils. For the two- and three-dimensional decompositions, two stencils are considered for each: 5 and 9 point for 2d, and 7 and 27 point for 3d.

Experiments were run on a Cray XC40 using KNL nodes with 68 cores and four hardware threads per core, for a total of 272 possible threads. This system uses the Aries Interconnect. In all experiments, the receiving process is never oversubscribed. Since we only model threads at the boundaries of the decomposition, in some cases we are able to present data that goes beyond the expected number of total receiving threads for the system. We allow for oversubscription of sending threads. For the data points where this occurs the oversubscription is noted in the figure captions. To avoid overhead incurred by thread start up costs, no data is collected during initial trials. Runs are distributed across different nodes as determined by the resource manager (SLURM), and all values given are averaged across ten runs.

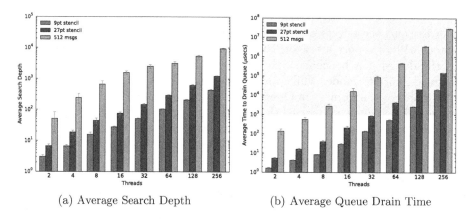

(a) Average Search Depth   (b) Average Queue Drain Time

Fig. 1. Naive decomposition. Oversubscription does not occur. Grey region highlights drain times ≥1 ms.

4.2   Results

Figure 1(a) shows the average search depths observed for the naive decomposition using 9 and 27 point stencils (8 and 26 messages per thread, respectively), and 512 messages per thread. Average search depths increase rapidly as the number of threads grow. For instance, at 64 threads the average search depth for 512 messages-per-thread is over 3000 list elements, and the 27 point stencil exceeds 1000 at 256 threads.

Unsurprisingly, these inflated search depths translate into onerous search times (Fig. 1(b)). In this and subsequent graphs, the grey region highlights the range where drain times extend beyond 1 ms, which is problematic for many

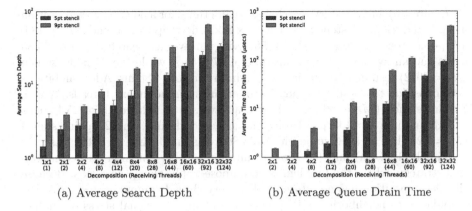

(a) Average Search Depth   (b) Average Queue Drain Time

Fig. 2. 2D square domain decomposition. Oversubscription does not occur. Queue drain times for both stencils in the 1×1 condition are under one μsec, so are not shown.

codes (see discussion in Sect. 4.3). For instance, at 64 threads, the 27 point case requires, on average, more than four milliseconds to drain the queue, and at 256 threads requires 147147 ms.

More reasonable decompositions reduce search depths and times, but these remain surprisingly large (Fig. 2(a) and (b)). For instance, a 32-by-32 decomposition using a 5 point stencil has 124 receiving threads and 128 total messages, yielding an average search depth of 35.512 items and an average queue drain time of 91.78 μs; the 9 point stencil increases these to 85.18 items searched and 486.54 μs to drain the queue.

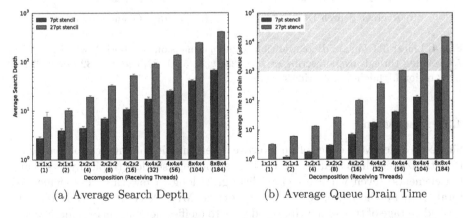

(a) Average Search Depth   (b) Average Queue Drain Time

Fig. 3. 3D domain decomposition. Sending threads for 7pt never oversubscribe; those for 27pt oversubscribe at $8 \times 8 \times 4$ ($T_s = 344$). Grey region highlights drain times ≥ 1 ms.

Figure 3(a) and (b) show search depths and times for a 3d cube decomposition using 7 and 27 point stencils. For an $8 \times 8 \times 4$ decomposition where $T_r = 184$, a 7 point stencil results in $M_t = 256$ giving an average search depth of 65.85 items and an average queue drain time of 479.15 μs, while the 27 point stencil ($M_t = 2072$) results in 410.02 items and drain time of 14.86 ms. A less-ambitious decomposition to $4 \times 4 \times 4$ yields 56 communicating boundary threads. With a 7 point stencil ($M_t = 96$), we observe an average search depth of 25.1 items and drain time of 41.02 μs. Under the same conditions, the 27 point stencil ($M_t = 728$) has an average depth of 135.86 items and a time of 1044.17 μs.

Finally, Fig. 4(a) and (b) show results for another common 3d decomposition strategy, where the problem is decomposed only along the z axis. Because this decomposition has no internal cells, every thread communicates across the boundaries to neighboring MPI processes, putting additional stress on matching. For example, a $1 \times 1 \times 256$ decomposition ($T_r = 256$) using a 7 point stencil ($M_t = 576$) has an average search depth of 114.81 and a drain time of 3.29 ms, while the 27 point counterpart has a depth of 967.27 and time of 163.05 ms.

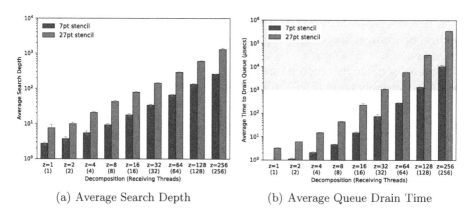

(a) Average Search Depth   (b) Average Queue Drain Time

Fig. 4. Linear 3D domain decomposition; x and y dimensions are both 1, while z varies. 7pt sending threads oversubscribe at $z = 128$ ($t_s = 514$), 27pt at $z = 32$ ($T_s = 274$). Grey region highlights drain times ≥ 1 ms.

4.3   Discussion

Single-threaded MPI codes often leverage deterministic communication patterns to optimize search so that search depths can be kept shallow (typically less than ten elements), even when matching lists grow long (a few thousand elements, total) [11]. Furthermore, contemporary hybrid MPI+X codes typically do not take advantage of thread multiple mode due to inefficiencies in current implementations. However, not only are these implementation issues being addressed for the exascale time frame (2020s), recent surveys show send/recv will remain the dominant programming model for exascale applications, and developers anticipate taking advantage of multi-threaded MPI communication [7]).

The results reported here suggest the matching overhead introduced by multi-threaded point-to-point MPI communication may be unacceptable for the future performance of some scientific codes. For example, molecular dynamics codes commonly use halo exchanges of the sorts investigated here. It is important to note that these halo-exchanges represent the highest scalability and lowest complexity of the communication patterns observed in scientific computing. From discussions with the developers of leading MD codes and comparative benchmarks [14,16], we observe the number of timesteps performed per second – where each step includes a halo exchange – ranges from tens to thousands (where each timestep simulates 1 femtosecond of time). This creates a total time budget per timestep of 100 ms to less than 1 ms. In the preceding timing graphs, this budget is highlighted in grey. This is the region where message matching overhead alone can exceed the iteration's time budget. Our results confirm this budget can be met for low thread-counts across all common communication patterns. However, as thread counts grow, and non-determinism increases, these same communication patterns can introduce more overhead than the entire current budget for completing a timestep at a competitive application speed. MPI matching overheads can take up to 30x to 300x the target iteration time for highly-scalable stencil communication patterns.

5   Related Work

Understanding MPI message matching has been a topic of interest that has been explored for single threaded MPI in the past. Initial work by Underwood and Brightwell [21] explored the performance impact of long lists. Further studies by Barrett et al. [3] showed the impact of match list length on a variety of system architectures.

A significant body of contemporary work exploring how to enhance the performance of MPI Message Matching exists, with some approaches looking to alter the matching list themselves to hash tables [12] or modifying the fundamental match list structures [24]. Other approaches have used a hybrid hash table approach, to accelerate common cases while providing long list performance [6]. Work using unique hardware features [17] and GPUs [13] has also been performed. Alternative solutions accelerate matching by not providing support for some MPI features [8]. MPI message matching hardware has also been explored [22] and specified/developed [4,9]. While hardware mitigates the long list matching performance concerns, it is limited in how many elements can be supported in the hardware match unit (typically 1K–4K). Despite this, recent work has shown that modern applications don't need these solutions: by leveraging programmer knowledge and sequential execution determinism, search depths can be kept low, even for long lists [11]. However, as noted above, many application developers expect to leverage communication libraries in ways that don't provide the same levels of ordering determinism that exist today [7]. To the best of the authors' knowledge there is no publicly available empirical data showing the effect of the lack of determinism on processes such as MPI message matching. While some new approaches with hybrid fine-grained over-decomposition of computation has been done that would create large amounts of non-determinism in some cases [5,18], this work did not introduce the effect, as it serialized the threaded access to MPI in order to avoid the issues we explore in this paper (with the penalty of not having concurrent network accesses). The goal of this paper is to explore the effects of multithreaded non-determinism on message matching to enable new techniques as well as support traditional multi-threaded MPI access.

6   Conclusions

As we move towards exascale, we expect developers to both retain common stencil communication patterns under a send/receive model, and to take advantage of improvements in fully multithreaded MPI runtimes [7]. However, the potential impact of the nondeterminism introduced by multithreading on MPI's mechanic for receiver-side data placement – message matching – is not well-understood.

In this paper, we addressed this gap by characterizing the number of threads engaged in inter-process communication, and the number of messages exchanged, when common stencil patterns are converted to multithreaded messaging. On this basis, we conducted an empirical study of the consequences of multithreading for average message matching search depths and queue drain times, assuming a BSP model. Results indicate that under some decompositions and stencils, search depths and times may become unacceptable given current performance expectations.

References

1. Amer, A., Lu, H., Wei, Y., Balaji, P., Matsuoka, S.: MPI+ threads: runtime contention and remedies. ACM SIGPLAN Not. **50**(8), 239–248 (2015)
2. Balaji, P., Buntinas, D., Goodell, D., Gropp, W.D., Thakur, R.: Fine-grained multithreading support for hybrid threaded MPI programming. Int. J. High Perform. Comput. Appl. **24**(1), 49–57 (2010)
3. Barrett, B.W., Brightwell, R., Grant, R.E., Hammond, S.D., Hemmert, K.S.: An evaluation of MPI message rate on hybrid-core processors. Int. J. High Perform. Comput. Appl. **28**(4), 415–424 (2014)
4. Barrett, B.W., et al.: The Portals 4.0.2 networking programming interface (2014)
5. Barrett, R.F., Stark, D.T., Vaughan, C.T., Grant, R.E., Olivier, S.L., Pedretti, K.T.: Toward an evolutionary task parallel integrated MPI+X programming model. In: Proceedings of the Sixth International Workshop on Programming Models and Applications for Multicores and Manycores, pp. 30–39. ACM (2015)
6. Bayatpour, M., Subramoni, H., Chakraborty, S., Panda, D.K.: Adaptive and dynamic design for MPI tag matching. In: 2016 IEEE International Conference on Cluster Computing (CLUSTER), pp. 1–10. IEEE (2016)
7. Bernholdt, D.E., et al.: A survey of MPI usage in the U.S. exascale computing project. Concurrency and Computation: Practice and Experience (2017, in Press)
8. Dang, H.-V., Snir, M., Gropp, W.: Towards millions of communicating threads. In: Proceedings of the 23rd European MPI Users' Group Meeting, pp. 1–14. ACM (2016)

9. Derradji, S., Palfer-Sollier, T., Panziera, J.-P., Poudes, A., Atos, F.W.: The BXI interconnect architecture. In: 2015 IEEE 23rd Annual Symposium on High-Performance Interconnects (HOTI), pp. 18–25. IEEE (2015)
10. Dosanjh, M.G., Groves, T., Grant, R.E., Brightwell, R., Bridges, P.G.: RMA-MT: a benchmark suite for assessing MPI multi-threaded RMA performance. In: 2016 16th IEEE/ACM International Symposium on Cluster, Cloud and Grid Computing (CCGrid), pp. 550–559. IEEE (2016)
11. Ferreira, K.B., Levy, S., Pedretti, K., Grant, R.E.: Characterizing MPI matching via trace-based simulation. In: Proceedings of the 24th European MPI Users' Group Meeting, p. 8. ACM (2017)
12. Flajslik, M., Dinan, J., Underwood, K.D.: Mitigating MPI message matching misery. In: Kunkel, J.M., Balaji, P., Dongarra, J. (eds.) ISC High Performance 2016. LNCS, vol. 9697, pp. 281–299. Springer, Cham (2016). https://doi.org/10.1007/978-3-319-41321-1_15
13. Klenk, B., Froning, H., Eberle, H., Dennison, L.: Relaxations for high-performance message passing on massively parallel SIMT processors. In: 31st International Parallel and Distributed Processing Symposium (IPDPS). IEEE (2017)
14. Lindahl, E., Hess, B., Páll, S., Metere, A.: GROMACS 5.0 benchmarks (2017)
15. MPI Forum: MPI: a message-passing interface standard version 3.0. Technical report, University of Tennessee, Knoxville (2012)
16. Plimpton, S., Crozier, P., Thompson, A.: LAMMPS-large-scale atomic/molecular massively parallel simulator, vol. 18. Sandia National Laboratories (2007)
17. Rodrigues, A., Murphy, R., Brightwell, R., Underwood, K.D.: Enhancing NIC performance for MPI using processing-in-memory. In: 19th IEEE International Parallel and Distributed Processing Symposium (IPDPS), p. 8-pp. IEEE (2005)
18. Stark, D.T., Barrett, R.F., Grant, R.E., Olivier, S.L., Pedretti, K.T., Vaughan, C.T.: Early experiences co-scheduling work and communication tasks for hybrid MPI+X applications. In: Proceedings of the 2014 Workshop on Exascale MPI, pp. 9–19. IEEE Press (2014)
19. MPICH Development Team: MPICH (2017). Accessed 30 Mar 2017
20. Open MPI Development Team: Open MPI (2017). Accessed 28 Mar 2017
21. Underwood, K.D., Brightwell, R.: The impact of MPI queue usage on message latency. In: International Conference on Parallel Processing (ICPP), pp. 152–160. IEEE (2004)
22. Underwood, K.D., Hemmert, K.S., Rodrigues, A., Murphy, R., Brightwell, R.: A hardware acceleration unit for MPI queue processing. In: 19th IEEE International Parallel and Distributed Processing Symposium (IPDPS), p. 10-pp. IEEE (2005)
23. Vaidyanathan, K., et al.: Improving concurrency and asynchrony in multithreaded MPI applications using software offloading. In: Proceedings of the International Conference for High Performance Computing, Networking, Storage and Analysis, p. 30. ACM (2015)
24. Zounmevo, J.A., Afsahi, A.: A fast and resource-conscious MPI message queue mechanism for large-scale jobs. Future Gener. Comput. Syst. 30, 265–290 (2014)

Global-Local View: Scalable Consistency for Concurrent Data Types

Deepthi Akkoorath[1(✉)], José Brandão[2],
Annette Bieniusa[1], and Carlos Baquero[2]

[1] Technical University of Kaiserslautern, Kaiserslautern, Germany
{akkoorath,bieniusa}@cs.uni-kl.de
[2] HASLab, Universidade do Minho and INESC TEC, Braga, Portugal
jose.brandao1994@gmail.com, cbm@di.uminho.pt

Abstract. Concurrent linearizable access to shared objects can be prohibitively expensive in a high contention workload. Many applications apply ad-hoc techniques to eliminate the need for synchronous atomic updates, which may result in non-linearizable implementations. We propose a new model which leverages such patterns for concurrent access to objects in a shared memory system. In this model, each thread maintains different views on the shared object: a thread-local view and a global view. As the thread-local view is not shared, it can be updated without incurring synchronization costs. These local updates become visible to other threads only after the thread-local view is merged with the global view. This enables better performance at the expense of linearizability. We discuss the design of several datatypes and evaluate their performance and scalability compared to linearizable implementations.

1 Introduction

As the number of cores increases in multi-core systems, the synchronization cost becomes more apparent [20]. While linearizability [14] is very useful for reasoning about the correctness of concurrent data structures, its implementation can be prohibitively expensive. As a consequence, programming patterns are emerging in practice, that attempt to limit the associated cost of the required synchronization on the memory accesses by relaxing the concurrent objects semantics. For example, in the widely used messaging library ZeroMQ, adding messages to the queue is performance-critical to the application. While lock-free linearizable queues are fast, the developers observed that the synchronous enqueue of each new messages was affecting the overall performance, especially in high contention workloads [21]. An analysis of the problem domain revealed that only the relative order of messages from a single thread is relevant for the semantics of the message queue; it is not necessary to maintain a strict order of enqueue operations when two independent threads try to insert messages. To overcome the linearizability penalty, the developers re-engineered their message queue such that multiple messages are added in batch, within a single atomic operation.

© Springer International Publishing AG, part of Springer Nature 2018
M. Aldinucci et al. (Eds.): Euro-Par 2018, LNCS 11014, pp. 492–504, 2018.
https://doi.org/10.1007/978-3-319-96983-1_35

For another example, consider a shared counter that is concurrently updated by several threads. The final value must include all increments performed, but the order of increments is not relevant since they are commutative. If each increment by each thread is an atomic operation made visible to all other threads, it can become a bottleneck [8]. In many cases, it is sufficient to execute the increment on a thread-local variable and to apply a combined update to the shared object.

In this paper, we propose a new model for shared objects that leverages the different views of an object, the *global-local view* model. In this model, each thread has a *local view* of the object which is private to it. Threads update and read primarily their local view. The local updates, though visible in a local view, are made visible on a *global view* only after an explicit two-way merge operation is performed. The other threads observe these changes once they synchronize, by merge, their local view with the global view. As the local view is non-shared, the local updates can be executed without requiring synchronization. Threads can execute many local updates without synchronizing with the global view, thus enabling better performance, albeit at the expense of linearizability.

In addition to the local operations, the model also provides synchronous operations on the global view. We call the operations that perform only on local view, *weak operations* and those on global view, *strong operations*. Combining operations on the global and the local views, we can build data types with customizable semantics on the spectrum between sequential and purely merge-able data types. *Mergeable data types* provide only weak and merge operations; *hybrid mergeable data types* offer both weak and strong operations. An application that uses a hybrid mergeable data type may use weak updates when a non-linearizable access is sufficient (e.g. weak enqueue on a local queue) and can switch to use only strong operations when stronger guarantees are required (e.g. strong dequeue to guarantee that item are dequeued only once).

In distributed systems, similar concerns led to the development of conflict-free replicated data types (CRDTs) [19]. CRDTs allow asynchronous updates to local replicas, while guaranteeing strong eventual consistency. In this distributed setting, each replica can be concurrently updated without requiring any synchronization. It can then later be merged with other replicas, while it is guaranteed that all nodes reach a convergent state once all updates are known. CRDTs play an essential role in partition tolerance and scalability [1,2]. However, the applicability of CRDTs as described in literature [19] is limited in a concurrent shared memory environment. For example, a CRDT counter is implemented as a map of replica id to integer. The merge operation iterates over the two maps to be merged and returns a map with the maximum for each entry. Thus, the relative cost in space and time of the merge is linear in the number of entries and as such unfeasibly high. In the global-local view model, the merge is executed synchronously on the global view. If the cost of merge is high, we lose the benefits of allowing parallel updates. While our work is inspired by them, the current CRDT designs are not suitable for relaxing consistency in concurrent shared-memory objects.

Contributions. This paper makes the following contributions:

1. We describe the global-local view model for multi-threaded applications with high contention that implements an adaptable trade-off between update visibility and synchronization cost (Sect. 3).
2. We discuss the implementation of a mergeable counter, a hybrid counter and queue (Sect. 4) and compare their performance with their linearizable counterparts under both low and high contention workloads (Sect. 6).

2   Related Work

Programming Models: Maintaining per-thread replicas and performing updates on them has been considered by different programming models in the literature. In Concurrent Revisions [9], a forked thread applies changes on its copy which is merged (using type-specific merge) to the parent thread when it is joined back. The focus of this work is on a fork-join model, where threads can communicate their state only when they join their parent. In contrast, we provide a generic model for the data types where a two-way merge and strong updates can share states among the threads at any point in the execution.

The Global Sequence Protocol (GSP) [10] is a model for replicated and distributed data systems that allows offline client updates. Since GSP addresses a distributed system model, with no bounds on message delays, there is much less control on replica divergence and liveness of the global sequence evolution. In contrast, we address a shared-memory concurrent architecture that allows bounds on divergence and stronger guarantees on the evolution of shared state.

Read-copy-update (RCU) [13] is a synchronization mechanism, suitable for a single-writer/multiple-readers scenario, that allows processes to read a shared object while a concurrent modification is in progress. Read-log-update (RLU) [16] is an improvement over RCU that allows concurrent writers. Unlike our model, concurrent writes are serialized using fine-grained locking.

Relaxed Consistency Models: Many models attempt to relax the strict semantics of linearizability [14] to achieve better performance. Quasilinearizability [3] allows each operation to be linearized at a different point at some bounded distance from its strict linearization point. Our work is complimentary to this model, allowing a combination of strong and weak updates to achieve different consistency semantics. Weak and medium future linearizability [15] is applicable to data types implemented using futures which allow reordering of the operations. Others models, such as k-linearizability [4] and quiescent consistency [22], also define the correctness based on some sequential history, possible reordered, of the operations. Local linearizability [12] requires that each *thread induced history* (a subset of each thread operations) is linearizable.

Mergeable Data Types: Conflict free Replicated Data Types (CRDTs) [19] provide deterministic merges and are now widely used in distributed replicated data systems. Here, we present implementations of mergeable data types that are tailored for shared memory concurrent programs. We benefit from a stronger system model, where idempotence and merging among arbitrary replicas are no longer required, as local state is merged atomically to a single global state.

Even though no consolidated theory on mergeable data types exists in the shared memory ecosystem, there have been systems that use such types with restricted properties. Doppel [18] is a multi-core database that uses a mechanism called phase reconciliation to parallelize conflicting transactions. When a high contention workload is detected, Doppel switches to a split phase where the transaction updates per-core copy of the objects. At the end of the split phase, per-core copies are merged. Only operations that are commutative are executed in the split phase, thus guaranteeing serializability.

3   Global-Local View Model

The system we consider is built upon a classical shared-memory architecture as supported by specifications such as the C++ or Java memory models. We assume that the system consists of a variable number of threads. Any thread can spawn new threads that may outlive their parent thread. The system distinguishes two types of memory: local memory is associated to a single thread and can only be accessed by this thread; shared memory can be accessed by any thread. Communication and coordination between the threads are done via shared-memory objects; we assume that there are no side channels. In particular, spawned threads do not inherit local objects from their parents.

Each shared object o has a global view that is accessible by all threads that obtained a reference to it. In addition, each thread has its own local view of o. A thread may update and read its local view, but the view is not accessible by any other thread. The local updates are incorporated into the global copy when a merge operation is executed. Conflicting (non-commutative) updates from concurrent threads are resolved through a type-specific merge operation. In addition to the local updates and reads, we also provide updates and reads performed directly on the global view. This gives us flexibility for the data type semantics and the implementation of the underlying data structure.

An object in the global-local view model consists of a global view g, and for each thread identified by t, a non-shared local view consisting of two components, s_t and l_t. s_t denotes a local snapshot of the shared object state g which gets updated upon synchronization, and l_t refers to the local updates not yet incorporated in the shared global state g. The state variables – g, s_t, l_t – are each modeled as a sequence of updates, initially empty; a sequence x can be concatenated with another sequence y (or a single update), denoted by $x \cdot y$.

An operation opKind on an object performed by thread t can be formalized as a function

$$\mathsf{opKind}_t(m, g, s_t, l_t) = (r, g', s_t', l_t')$$

where m comprises the (optional) type-specific update (u) or query (q) method applied on the object. The operation returns a tuple (r, g', s_t', l_t') where r is the return value of the method m and the other variables refer to the updated global g' and local state s_t', l_t'.

Following are the basic operations in the global-local view model; these are type-independent and mergeable data types typically implement only a subset of them:

$$\mathsf{pull}_t(\_, g, s_t, l_t) = (\bot, g, g, l_t)$$
$$\mathsf{weakRead}_t(q, g, s_t, l_t) = (q(s_t \cdot l_t), g, s_t, l_t)$$
$$\mathsf{strongRead}_t(q, g, s_t, l_t) = (q(g \cdot l_t), g, s_t, l_t)$$
$$\mathsf{weakUpdate}_t(u, g, s_t, l_t) = (s_t \cdot l_t \cdot u, g, s_t, l_t \cdot u)$$
$$\mathsf{strongUpdate}_t(u, g, s_t, l_t) = (g \cdot u, g \cdot u, s_t, l_t)$$
$$\mathsf{merge}_t(\_, g, s_t, l_t) = (\bot, g', g', \bot) \qquad \text{where } g' = merge(g, (s_t, l_t))$$

pull updates the local object snapshot with the global object state; local operations are not modified. weakRead returns the result of a type-specific read-only operation q on the state obtained by applying local updates on the local snapshot. strongRead returns the result of a type-specific read-only operation q on the state obtained by applying local updates on global state. Neither the global state nor the local snapshot are modified. weakUpdate applies the update method u on the local copy without any synchronization to the global state. strongUpdate applies the update method u on the global state atomically. The previous weak updates that are batched in l_t are not merged at this point. merge incorporates the local updates to the global states and updates the local snapshot, using the type-specific $merge(g, (s_t, l_t))$ operation.

A merge must incorporate all local updates into the global state in a meaningful way, so that conflicting concurrent updates lead to a deterministic state. For example, if the updates are commutative, they can be appended to the global sequence $g' = g \cdot l_t$. If they are not commutative, the data types offer a conflict resolving merge operation, modifying the sequence of updates merged to g.

While weakRead and weakUpdate act exclusively on the local copy, strongRead and strongUpdate act on the global state. The combination of these two operations supports flexible optimizations on each given data type. For example, a queue can guarantee that an element is dequeued only once by executing dequeues in strongUpdate. At the same time, enqueues can use weakUpdate and merged later for better performance. For counters, we may enforce a weak limit on the maximum value, i.e. values should not diverge arbitrarily from the defined maximum value. We can use a strongRead to check the global value to adapt the merge interval or switch to a fully synchronized version.

4   Data Types

Each mergeable type defines a subset of the basic operations from the global-local view model, depending on the semantics needed. In this section, we discuss the specification of several data types and their implementation.

4.1 Specification

Given a sequential counter with methods *inc* (increments the counter by 1), and *value* (returns the current value), a purely mergeable counter implements the following operations.

- $\mathsf{weakValue}_t() = \mathsf{weakRead}_t(value, \_, s_t, l_t)$
- $\mathsf{weakInc}_t() = \mathsf{weakUpdate}_t(inc, \_, \_, l_t)$
- $merge(g, (s_t, l_t)) = g \cdot l_t$

The merge appends the local increments to the global sequence g, because the increments are commutative. A hybrid mergeable counter defines the following operations in addition to the above ones. The applications may choose weak or strong operations dynamically based on different criteria.

- $\mathsf{strongInc}_t() = \mathsf{strongUpdate}_t(inc, g, \_, \_)$
- $\mathsf{strongValue}_t() = \mathsf{strongRead}_t(value, g, \_, l_t)$

The queue datatype has operations *enqueue*(*e*) and *dequeue*. A hybrid mergeable queue with mergeable enqueue and synchronized dequeue defines the following operations:

- $\mathsf{enqueue}_t(e) = \mathsf{weakUpdate}_t(enqueue(e), \_, \_, l_t)$
- $\mathsf{dequeue}_t() = \mathsf{strongUpdate}_t(dequeue, g, \_, \_)$
- $merge(g, (s_t, l_t)) = g \cdot l_t$

In the above semantics, if the global copy is empty, *dequeue* returns null even if there are local enqueue operations by the same thread which have not been merged yet. We can allow dequeue to include local enqueue operations by defining

$$\mathsf{dequeue}_t() = \mathsf{strongUpdate}_t(dequeue, g', \_, \_) \text{ with } (\_, g', \_) = \mathsf{merge}_t(g, s_t, l_t).$$

In this way we can combine the operations to give different semantics. For example, a queue with weak enqueue and weak dequeue may be useful if redundant dequeue is not a problem for the application. A queue with only strong enqueue and strong dequeue behaves as a linearizable queue.

A grow-only bag is a set that provides only an *add* operation, and allows duplicate elements. A purely mergeable bag implements weakAdd and merge [7].

4.2 Implementation

The implementation of (hybrid) mergeable data types consists of two parts – a reference to the local view and another one to the global view.

Counter. The global view of a mergeable counter is an integer g. The local view consists of a pair of integers (s,l). The weak increments are collected in the thread-local state l and added to g during the merge. This design is inspired on *sloppy counters* [8], while using a local counter per thread instead of per core. The following pseudocode shows the implementation of a counter. It is easy to extend this implementation to allow decrements, explicit arguments for increments/decrements, and generalize to other commutative monoids.

```
type Counter: {                        int weakValue(){
    int g,                                 return s+1;
    ThreadLocal int s,                 }
    ThreadLocal int l                  int strongValue(){
}                                          return g+1;
weakInc() {                            }
    l++;                               merge(){
}                                          atomic {
strongInc(){                                   g += l; s = g; l = 0;
    atomic {g++}                           }
}                                      }
```

A variable specified as ThreadLocal exists per thread in the thread's private storage. Many programming languages support some form of thread-local storage (TLS). A mergeable data type can also implement its own TLS by mapping thread ids to different instances of the local object. atomic refers to any synchronization mechanism such as mutex or lock-free techniques such as compare-and-swap or transactional memory that atomically executes the code block within.

For some data types, local views are isolated from each other and the global view, by maintaining a full copy of the object in each view. For large data structures, such as lists or trees, maintaining a full copy is not feasible. Thus, the local views may contain references to parts of the data structures that are shared by other local views and global view. The shared parts are not directly updated by the weak updates, but only read. For example, a *lookUp* on a list may first traverse the locally added items and then the shared parts of the list. The following are the designs of a few data types where this can be done efficiently and correctly without copying the entire data structure.

Grow-only Bag. A grow-only bag [7] is implemented using a multi-headed list as shown in Fig. 1. The thread local view consists of a pointer to the local head. A merge updates the global head of the list and does not change the local views of other threads. A lookup that traverses the list starting from the local head will never see an item that is concurrently added or merged.

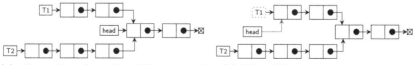

(a) Two threads with different local views.

(b) After T1's local view is merged.

Fig. 1. Mergeable grow-only bag.

Queue. A hybrid mergeable queue can be implemented using a single-linked list similar to a linearizable queue. The items enqueued are added to the tail of the list, while dequeue is performed from the head. A mergeable queue instance contains a global view – (`head, tail`), which points to the head and tail nodes respectively of the global list and local view – (`ThreadLocal lhead, ThreadLocal ltail`), which are the head and the tail of the local list of each thread. The local list collects the items enqueued by the thread that are not yet merged. The merge atomically appends the local list to the global list. The time needed to merge a group of nodes is the same as the time needed to enqueue a single node. By batching the enqueues, we can reduce the number of synchronization operations, thus improving the overall throughput.

The *dequeue* operation directly updates the shared part of the list. For some data types, an update on the shared part of the data structure should preserve the old version, because local views may be keeping reference to it. However, there is no weakRead, such as a weak lookup, defined on queue that must observe a version before a concurrent dequeue. Hence, there is no need to keep those versions, which simplifies the implementation.

5   Applications

In this section, we sketch some application scenarios that benefit from multi-view mergeable data types.

A *work-stealing queue* is used to distribute tasks among threads running in parallel. In Cilk runtime [11] each thread owns a queue with operations *pushTop*, *popTop*, and *popBottom*. There is no *pushBottom*. When a thread is devoid of tasks, it retrieves one from its queue using *popTop*, executes it and may generate new tasks that are added to its queue using *pushTop*. When a thread's task queue is empty, it steals from other threads' queue using *popBottom*. A work stealing queue with this semantics is a natural fit to the global-local view model. Instead of a queue per thread, we have a multi-view queue with a global view and a local-view per thread. *pushTop* and *popTop* executes on the thread-local views, and *popBottom* on the global view. One downside of this design is that it may prevent threads from stealing tasks when the global view is empty even if there are unmerged tasks in the local views. To avoid this, threads can be forced to merge when the global view drops below a threshold.

In-memory multi-core databases. In high contention workloads, we can achieve high performance by allowing concurrent conflicting transactions to proceed in parallel on different cores. Instead of serializing the access to the objects, the transactions can update a per core copy of the object and merge them later. In [18], authors describe a system that automatically parallelize high contention transactions. A multi-view data type implemented in the global-local view model is a natural fit to such scenario.

Message queues where multiple messages can be batched together and added to the shared queue is a direct application of the hybrid queue described in this paper. The applications that use aggregation counters that are computed by

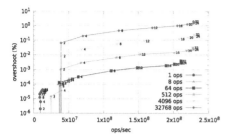
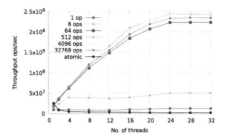
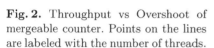

Fig. 2. Throughput vs Overshoot of mergeable counter. Points on the lines are labeled with the number of threads.

Fig. 3. Throughput of hybrid mergeable counter (overshoot free) vs atomic counter, labelled with merge-interval.

parallel threads can use our mergeable counter. Similarly, the objects that store statistical measures such as sums, min, max etc. that are computed by parallel threads will benefit from the global-local view model. In software transactional memory, we may use mergeable objects to avoid unnecessary aborts where the conflicting updates can be meaningfully merged [6].

6   Evaluation

We evaluated the performance and scalability of the mergeable counter and the hybrid mergeable queue using different micro-benchmarks. As an example of real applications, we employed the hybrid queue in a breadth-first traversal on graphs. We implemented the counter in C++ and the queue in Java. The evaluations are performed on a 12 core CPU (2 NUMA nodes) with 2-way hyper-threading.

Counter. We provide two variants of a mergeable counter and compare them with an atomic counter, implemented using the atomic compare and swap operation. In the first experiment, we allow threads to increment the shared purely mergeable counter until a *target* value is reached. Since threads might not know about non-merged increments from other threads, they typically end up overshooting the target. For this experiment, the *target* is set to 5×10^6 increments. We evaluated several merge-intervals, labelled with how many local increments are allowed between merges. Figure 2 shows that the throughput scales linearly with the number of threads and with the merge-intervals. At the same time, the overshoot increases. However, the percentage of the overshoot is small. (Notice that overshoot is upper bound by the number of threads times the merge-interval, as this reflects the amount of increments not yet accounted for.) The atomic counter never overshoots the *target*, but since threads are always competing on the increment, performance is very low and no speedup is obtained. In contrast, the mergeable counter can scale linearly up to a good fraction of the available concurrency, in particular with merge-interval of ≥ 4096.

While some applications could tolerate an overshoot, in general, applications will require to further bound the overshoot. To address this, we provide a variant of the mergeable counter that makes a hybrid use of initial weak local increments and later switches to atomic strong increments when approaching the target. The first thread that, upon the periodic merges, detects that it is close to the target, initiates a barrier synchronization to ensure that all threads have switched to strong operations. Figure 3 shows that under this approach, overshoot is eliminated while the performance is mostly identical to the mergeable counter.

Comparison to CRDT. In this experiment, we demonstrate that CRDT designs have significant overhead in performance when used in a shared memory program. We implemented a CRDT counter on the global-local view model, where each local view and global view are a CRDT replica. We implemented the G-counter [19] using (1) a HashMap that maps thread-id to an integer, (2)

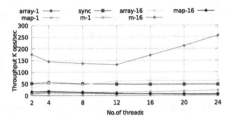

Fig. 4. CRDT counter using array and map, m-mergeable counter with merge-interval 1,16. sync-atomic counter.

an array where the array index corresponds to a thread id. Figure 4 shows that the array scales better when the merge-interval is large. However, the size of array must be fixed to the number of threads. The map implementation does not scale well because (1) there is an overhead in accessing the map entries, (2) merge requires an iteration over the entire map resulting in longer critical section. Thus, the cost of merge operation is negating the benefit achieved by the asynchronous local increment.

Queue. To evaluate the scalability of hybrid mergeable queue (referred to as mergeable queue) in comparison to classical algorithms, we implemented four different queues in Java – (1) a lock-based linearizable queue based on Michael and Scott's 2-lock queue [17] (LL), (2) a lock-based mergeable queue which uses similar 2-lock mechanism (ML), (3) a lock-free linearizable queue adapted from Michael and Scott's lock-free queue [17] (LF) and (4) a lock-free mergeable queue (MLF). Figure 5 shows the time to perform a total of 5×10^6 enqueues and dequeues. We evaluated mergeable queues with different merge intervals m (a merge is performed by a thread after m enqueues). In this experiment, we forced half of the threads to run on one NUMA node and the other half on the second NUMA node. For both lock-based and lock-free versions, the mergeable queue is faster than the linearizable counterpart. Since this is a high-contention workload, the lock-based version performs better than the lock-free version. Unlike the mergeable counter, increasing the merge interval from 8 to 64 does not improve the performance significantly because *dequeue* is always executed synchronously which shadows the performance gain from asynchronous *enqueues*.

Breadth-First Traversal. A standard breadth-first traversal algorithm using queues can be parallelized using concurrent queues. We evaluated four versions

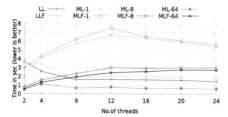
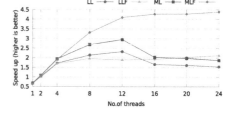

Fig. 5. Queue. linearizable lock based (LL), lock-free (LF). mergeable lock based (ML), lock-free (MLF) 1,8,64-merge interval.

Fig. 6. Breadth-first traversal. linearizable lock based (LL), lock free (LLF). mergeable lock-based (ML), lock-free (MLF).

of the algorithm using different queue implementations, that traversed randomly generated graphs of size of 2×10^6 vertices and 2×10^7 edges. Unlike the micro-benchmark for the queue, there is no fixed merge interval. The threads merge their local queue at the end of processing each level. Figure 6 shows the speedup of each version compared to a single-threaded implementation. Mergeable queues scale better than their linearizable counterparts. The speedup of the lock-free mergeable queue is significantly higher than that of the others, and scales almost linearly until 16 threads. Beyond 16 threads, the number of vertices processed by each thread at each level is reduced, as they are divided among the threads, leading to smaller merge frequencies. We believe the sudden drop in the speedup of lock-based queues after 12 threads is due to the additional cost in synchronization to the second NUMA core. This is a low-contention workload because a significant amount of time is spent in processing the nodes rather than updating the queue.

7   Conclusion

Incorporating more information about the respective datatype semantics is crucial for datatype designs that are more parsimonious regarding synchronization. CRDTs succeeded in capturing datatypes with clear concurrency semantics and are now common components in industry. However, they do not migrate trivially to shared-memory architectures due to high computational costs from merge functions, which becomes apparent once network communication is removed.

In this paper, we define the *global-local view* model as base for a framework that allows capturing the semantics of multi-view datatypes. The *global-local view* distinguishes between local fast state and distant shared state where operations need to be synchronized. This distinction allows the datatype designer to explore the trade-offs in the design when using weak or strong operations. Our approach enables speedups in order of magnitudes while preserving the datatypes' target behavior. It is quite possible that further increments of the number of components involved will lead to a hierarchical model with more levels than the current binary, local vs global, scheme.

Data Availability Statement and Acknowledgements. The work presented was partially supported by EU H2020 LightKone project (732505), and SMILES Research Line within project "TEC4Growth - Pervasive Intelligence, Enhancers and Proofs of Concept with Industrial Impact /NORTE-01- 0145-FEDER-000020" financed by the North Portugal Regional Operational Programme (NORTE 2020), under the PORTU-GAL 2020 Partnership Agreement, and through the European Regional Development Fund (ERDF).

The datasets and code generated during and/or analysed during the current study [5] are available in the figshare repository: https://doi.org/10.6084/m9.figshare.6383807

References

1. Antidotedb. http://syncfree.github.io/antidote/
2. Riak KV: a distributed key-value database. http://basho.com/products/riak-kv/
3. Afek, Y., Korland, G., Yanovsky, E.: Quasi-linearizability: relaxed consistency for improved concurrency. In: Lu, C., Masuzawa, T., Mosbah, M. (eds.) OPODIS 2010. LNCS, vol. 6490, pp. 395–410. Springer, Heidelberg (2010). https://doi.org/10. 1007/978-3-642-17653-1_29. http://dl.acm.org/citation.cfm?id=1940234.1940273
4. Aiyer, A., Alvisi, L., Bazzi, R.A.: On the availability of non-strict quorum systems. In: Fraigniaud, P. (ed.) DISC 2005. LNCS, vol. 3724, pp. 48–62. Springer, Heidelberg (2005). https://doi.org/10.1007/11561927_6
5. Akkoorath, D., Brando, J., Bieniusa, A., Baquero, C.: Code to run experiments for euro-par 2018 paper: Global-local view: Scalable consistency for concurrent data types (2018). https://doi.org/10.6084/m9.figshare.6383807
6. Akkoorath, D.D., Bieniusa, A.: Transactions on mergeable objects. In: Feng, X., Park, S. (eds.) APLAS 2015. LNCS, vol. 9458, pp. 427–444. Springer, Cham (2015). https://doi.org/10.1007/978-3-319-26529-2_23
7. Akkoorath, D.D., Bieniusa, A.: Highly-scalable concurrent objects. In: Proceedings of the 2nd Workshop on the Principles and Practice of Consistency for Distributed Data. PaPoC 2016, pp. 13:1–13:4. ACM, New York (2016). https://doi.org/10. 1145/2911151.2911158
8. Boyd-Wickizer, S., et al.: An analysis of linux scalability to many cores. In: Proceedings of the 9th USENIX Conference on Operating Systems Design and Implementation. OSDI 2010, pp. 1–16. USENIX Association, Berkeley (2010). http:// dl.acm.org/citation.cfm?id=1924943.1924944
9. Burckhardt, S., Baldassin, A., Leijen, D.: Concurrent programming with revisions and isolation types. In: Proceedings of the ACM International Conference on Object Oriented Programming Systems Languages and Applications. OOP-SLA 2010, pp. 691–707. ACM, New York (2010). https://doi.org/10.1145/1869459. 1869515
10. Burckhardt, S., Leijen, D., Protzenko, J., Fähndrich, M.: Global sequence protocol: a robust abstraction for replicated shared state. In: Boyland, J.T. (ed.) 29th European Conference on Object-Oriented Programming (ECOOP 2015). Leibniz International Proceedings in Informatics (LIPIcs), vol. 37, pp. 568–590. Schloss Dagstuhl-Leibniz-Zentrum fuer Informatik, Dagstuhl, Germany (2015). https:// doi.org/10.4230/LIPIcs.ECOOP.2015.568
11. Frigo, M., Leiserson, C.E., Randall, K.H.: The implementation of the Cilk-5 multithreaded language. In: Proceedings of the ACM SIGPLAN Conference on Programming Language Design and Implementation. PLDI 1998, pp. 212–223. ACM, New York (1998). https://doi.org/10.1145/277650.277725

12. Haas, A., et al.: Local Linearizability for Concurrent Container-Type Data Structures. In: 27th International Conference on Concurrency Theory (CONCUR 2016). Leibniz International Proceedings in Informatics (LIPIcs), vol. 59, pp. 6:1–6:15 (2016). https://doi.org/10.4230/LIPIcs.CONCUR.2016.6

13. Hart, T.E., McKenney, P.E., Brown, A.D.: Making lockless synchronization fast: performance implications of memory reclamation. In: Proceedings of the 20th International Conference on Parallel and Distributed Processing. IPDPS 2006, p. 21. IEEE Computer Society, Washington, D.C. (2006). http://dl.acm.org/citation.cfm?id=1898953.1898956

14. Herlihy, M.P., Wing, J.M.: Linearizability: a correctness condition for concurrent objects. ACM Trans. Program. Lang. Syst. **12**(3), 463–492 (1990). https://doi.org/10.1145/78969.78972

15. Kogan, A., Herlihy, M.: The future(s) of shared data structures. In: Proceedings of the 2014 ACM Symposium on Principles of Distributed Computing. PODC 2014, pp. 30–39. ACM, New York, (2014). https://doi.org/10.1145/2611462.2611496

16. Matveev, A., Shavit, N., Felber, P., Marlier, P.: Read-log-update: a lightweight synchronization mechanism for concurrent programming. In: Proceedings of the 25th Symposium on Operating Systems Principles. SOSP 2015, pp. 168–183. ACM, New York (2015). https://doi.org/10.1145/2815400.2815406

17. Michael, M.M., Scott, M.L.: Simple, fast, and practical non-blocking and blocking concurrent queue algorithms. In: Proceedings of the Fifteenth Annual ACM Symposium on Principles of Distributed Computing. PODC 1996, pp. 267–275. ACM, New York (1996). https://doi.org/10.1145/248052.248106

18. Narula, N., Cutler, C., Kohler, E., Morris, R.: Phase reconciliation for contended in-memory transactions. In: Proceedings of the 11th USENIX Conference on Operating Systems Design and Implementation. OSDI 2014, pp. 511–524. USENIX Association, Berkeley (2014). http://dl.acm.org/citation.cfm?id=2685048.2685088

19. Shapiro, M., Preguiça, N., Baquero, C., Zawirski, M.: Conflict-free replicated data types. In: Défago, X., Petit, F., Villain, V. (eds.) SSS 2011. LNCS, vol. 6976, pp. 386–400. Springer, Heidelberg (2011). https://doi.org/10.1007/978-3-642-24550-3_29. http://dl.acm.org/citation.cfm?id=2050613.2050642

20. Shavit, N.: Data structures in the multicore age. Commun. ACM **54**(3), 76–84 (2011). https://doi.org/10.1145/1897852.1897873

21. Sstrik, M.: ZeroMQ. In: The Architecture of Open Source Applications, vol. 2 (2012)

22. Viotti, P., Vukolić, M.: Consistency in non-transactional distributed storage systems. ACM Comput. Surv. **49**(1), 19:1–19:34 (2016). https://doi.org/10.1145/2926965

OpenABL: A Domain-Specific Language for Parallel and Distributed Agent-Based Simulations

Biagio Cosenza[1]([⊠]), Nikita Popov[1],
Ben Juurlink[1], Paul Richmond[2],
Mozhgan Kabiri Chimeh[2], Carmine Spagnuolo[3],
Gennaro Cordasco[3], and Vittorio Scarano[3]

[1] TU Berlin, Berlin, Germany
cosenza@tu-berlin.de
[2] University of Sheffield, Sheffield, UK
[3] University of Salerno, Fisciano, Salerno, Italy

Abstract. Agent-based simulations are becoming widespread among scientists from different areas, who use them to model increasingly complex problems. To cope with the growing computational complexity, parallel and distributed implementations have been developed for a wide range of platforms. However, it is difficult to have simulations that are portable to different platforms while still achieving high performance.

We present OPENABL, a domain-specific language for portable, high-performance, parallel agent modeling. It comprises an easy-to-program language that relies on high-level abstractions for programmability and explicitly exploits agent parallelism to deliver high performance. A source-to-source compiler translates the input code to a high-level intermediate representation exposing parallelism, locality and synchronization, and, thanks to an architecture based on pluggable backends, generates target code for multi-core CPUs, GPUs, large clusters and cloud systems.

OPENABL has been evaluated on six applications from various fields such as ecology, animation, and social sciences. The generated code scales to large clusters and performs similarly to hand-written target-specific code, while requiring significantly fewer lines of codes.

1 Introduction

Agent-based simulations (ABS) are a powerful instrument to study a wide range of scientific phenomena. According to Epstein [1], agent-based computational models are well-suited to the analysis of phenomena where agent populations are heterogeneous, there is no central control over individuals (autonomy), the space where the agents work is explicit (e.g., an n-dimensional grid), and agents only have local interactions with neighboring agents. Since SugarScape [2], computational models have been used to interpret society by translating social dynamics into a type of computation. Examples are voting behaviors [3], epidemics [2], and spatial unemployment patterns [4]. Applications go beyond social sciences,

© Springer International Publishing AG, part of Springer Nature 2018
M. Aldinucci et al. (Eds.): Euro-Par 2018, LNCS 11014, pp. 505–518, 2018.
https://doi.org/10.1007/978-3-319-96983-1_36

from ecologists studying the predator-prey equilibrium [5] to hazard prevention in evacuations [6].

With an increasing number of applications where agent modeling is used, there is also a growing demand for computational power, due to larger agent populations and increasingly complex models. For this purpose, parallel and distributed implementations targeting different platforms, such as desktop GPUs [7], HPC architectures [8], and distributed cloud systems [9] have been developed, each focusing on a specific class of simulations and particular parallelization issues. While the core concepts of all existing frameworks are fundamentally the same, the variety of both hardware platforms and application contexts has led to very different implementations. Ideally, ABS should be written in a portable environment that can target a variety of parallel and distributed systems without any program modifications.

The necessity of portable solutions to reproduce simulations on different parallel implementations and hardware platforms, has led to the OpenAB initiative[1], a community-driven collaborative project to provide models and procedures for the benchmarking of multi-agent simulations on parallel and distributed computing systems. This work aims at providing an effective and efficient tool to these communities through the design and implementation of a *domain-specific language* (DSL) for portable, parallel and high-performance ABS.

The contributions of this paper are:

1. The design of OPENABL, a novel domain-specific language for agent-based computational modeling and simulation. The language targets the core requirements of these simulations with tailored high-level semantics, and enables parallel processing by explicitly exposing agent-parallelism.
2. A source-to-source compiler implementing the OPENABL language and supporting five different parallel and distributed backends, which are capable of running on diverse platforms such as multi-core CPUs, GPUs, and distributed clouds.
3. A collection of six test simulations from different application fields including biology, ecology and social sciences, and an experimental evaluation and comparison across different platforms.

2 Background

Many frameworks and libraries for implementing parallel ABS have been proposed; however, each addresses quite different target architectures, with distinct solutions for locality and synchronization. REPAST [10] is an agent-based simulation toolkit written in C++, later extended and parallelized into the REPAST-HPC framework [11], and tested on a Blue Gene/P HPC cluster. Cosenza et al. [8] introduced a distributed load balancing schema for parallel ABS that scales a simulation with one million agents on a cluster with 64 processors. Mason [12] is a popular multi-agent simulation library written in Java. D-Mason [13,14]

---

[1] More information is available at http://www.openab.org.

provides an effective and efficient way of parallelizing Mason programs for distributed systems, handling communication strategies and load balancing [15], tested on Amazon Web Services [15], and used on several social science scenarios [16]. Flame [7] is an agent-based environment based on an underlying formal model, called the X-Machine, and used in various scenarios such as cell simulations [17] and immune system modeling [18]. FlameGPU [19] is an extension of Flame that executes agent-based models on GPU architectures. Other GPU implementations have focused on bio-inspired visual clustering [20] and on efficient compression of agent direction [21]. Several authors have performed a comparison among ABS toolkits, both sequential [22] and parallel [23].

The idea of assuring portability across parallel implementations through DSLs has been exploited in many application scenarios, in particular to target large-scale computing systems [24]. Liszt [25] is the most similar to our work, with a DSL for constructing mesh-based PDE solvers and capable of targeting clusters, SMPs and GPUs. Liszt applications perform within 12% of hand-written C++ code and scale to large clusters. Other DSL have been designed for stencil computations [26], graph algorithms [27], and image processing pipelines [28].

3   Language Design

The goal of the OPENABL language is to provide a portable, efficient and easy-to-use environment for agent-based modeling. This is achieved by a rich language supporting domain-specific constructs, allowing the users to quickly prototype, reproduce, and compare different models with different parameters. The language also provides implicit support for agent parallelism and locality, so that OPENABL codes can be efficiently mapped onto parallel and distributed implementations.

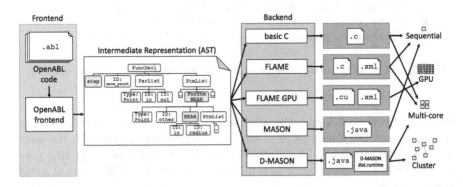

Fig. 1. OPENABL compilation workflow. The input code is translated to an AST-based intermediate representation, from which different backends generate code for specific platforms. The AST shows an excerpt of Listing 1.1.

Listing 1.1 shows a simple OPENABL code that demonstrates the general structure of a simulation. The program is subdivided into multiple top-level sections: agent declarations, simulation parameters, environment parameters, step functions and the main code. The language uses C-like syntax to maintain familiarity with mostly C and Java based ABS frameworks, and supports standard operators and control-flow statements, as well as vector types.

```
1   // Agent declarations
2   agent Point {
3     position float3 pos;
4   }
5   // Simulation parameters and environment def.
6   float radius = 5;
7   float env_size = 100;
8   param int num_agents = 1000;
9   param int num_timesteps = 100;
10  environment { max: float3(env_size) }
11  // Step function
12  step move_point(Point in -> out) {
13    // Move towards the average direction of the neighbors
14    float3 dir = float3(0);
15    int num_neighbors = 0;
16    for (Point other : near(in, radius)) {
17      dir += normalize(other.pos - in.pos);
18      num_neighbors += 1;
19    }
20    out.pos = clamp(in.pos + dir/num_neighbors, float3(
        env_size));
21  }
22  // Main code: Initialization and execution
23  void main() {
24    for (int i : 0..num_agents)
25      add(Point {pos: random(float3(env_size))});
26    simulate(num_timesteps) { move_point }
27    save("result.json");
28  }
```

Listing 1.1. An OpenABL code example implementing a simple agent motion.

Step Functions and Agent Parallelism. It is important to incorporate agent parallelism into the language in a way that can be supported with the same semantics by all backends. In OPENABL, this is accomplished using *step functions*, which take an input agent of some type and yield a modified output agent. For example, in

```
step move_point(Point in -> out) { ... }
```

the input agent in of type Point is the result of the last timestep, while the output agent out will be the result of the current timestep. The output will only become available once a step function has been called for all agents of that type. Conceptually, this corresponds to a double buffering mechanism: an input buffer of read-only agents and an output buffer of write-only agents, which are swapped at the end of a discrete simulation step. The strict in/out separation is required in order to produce deterministic, order-independent simulations. Surprisingly, we found that many sequential agent libraries such as Mason do not provide a native double-buffering mechanism. Therefore their results are not deterministic, as they depend on the updating order of the agents. OPENABL overcomes this limitation and always produces order-independent models.

The simulate statement invokes a simulation for a certain number of timesteps, during which a list of step functions will be executed in the given order. First one step function is executed for all agents (of the applicable type), before the next step function is run. Between step functions, the out parameter becomes the new in parameter. For instance, in the *Ants* model

```
simulate(num_timesteps) { ant_act1, pheromone_deposit,
    ant_act2 }
```

three step functions are called: the first on ant agents; the second on pheromone agents; the last again on ant agents.

The whole simulation starts at the main function, which is used to set up agents (typically from a file or randomly generated), to invoke the simulation and save the simulation results. Simulation parameters are declared as global constants. If a constant is prefixed with the param keyword it may also be over-ridden from the command line.

Locality. A fundamental concept of agent-based modeling is locality, because interactions are usually limited to nearby agents. In general, this may be governed by arbitrary topologies, but OPENABL is currently limited to the common case of two- and three-dimensional Euclidean topologies. Each agent declares a designated position member of type float2 or float3, which provides the position of the agent for spatial queries. The agent neighborhood can then be accessed through the combination of a for loop and a radius-based near() query:

```
for (AgentT neighbor : near(in, radius)) { ... }
```

The type of the input agent and the type of the neighboring agents that are fetched does not necessarily have to match. The query is performed using a backend-specific spatial acceleration data structure such as grid [19] and kd-tree [29].

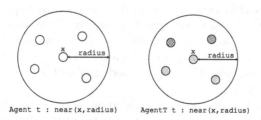

Fig. 2. near() queries with homogeneous and heterogeneous agent types.

Simulations with *heterogeneous* agents, i.e. with multiple agent types, are implemented with multiple step functions on different agent types, and by specifying different return types on near() queries, as shown in Fig. 2.

Environment properties are specified using an environment declaration which includes the environment dimensionality and bounds (min and max). Agent positions must stay within these bounds. For performance reasons, this is not automatically enforced by the language, but functions to perform the necessary clamping or wrap-around are provided. The radius used for spatial acceleration structures is usually determined automatically, but may also be explicitly given here. The standard library also provides commonly used functions for geometric and trigonometric operations.

Dynamic Agent Creation and Removal. Typically, the agents are created at the beginning of the simulation and are not removed until the end; however, some simulations require a dynamic mechanism for the creation and removal of agents. For example, in the *Predator-Prey* model, predators pursue and eat prey, who reproduce at a given rate. As a result, the agent populations periodically increase and decrease during the course of a simulation. The language enforces a number of additional constraints for backend compatibility: in a step function, each agent may add at most one new agent. This means that in a single step, the number of agents can at most double. The new agent position must be the same as the generating agent position (e.g., in.pos). An agent can remove itself by using the removeCurrent() function, but cannot remove a different agent.

4   Implementation

Compilation Process. OPENABL is a source-to-source compiler employing a classical three-stage pipeline: First, Flex and Bison are used to parse the source code into an *abstract syntax tree* (AST), which acts as our primary intermediate representation. Then, target-independent analysis is performed, which validates the code and enforces semantic constraints, while also annotating the AST with necessary type and dependency information. Finally, different backends emit source code (and other auxiliary files) for the target platform based on the annotated AST.

Backends. OPENABL currently supports five backend implementations targeting different agent models, acceleration data structures and platforms.

A *basic C* backend serves as a reference implementation and basis for other C-based backends. It does not use acceleration structures, implements double-buffering using two arrays of agents swapped after each step, and uses OpenMP for trivial parallelization.

Flame [7] models agents using X-Machines, which are state machines that support sending messages between agents. A step function can modify the memory of the current agent, send messages and iterate over messages sent in the previous step. To support neighborhood queries, we determine which members of neighboring agents are used inside a for-near loop and generate one step function that sends a message containing all the used members. A second step function processes the messages falling into the specified neighborhood. A side-effect of this process is that no explicit double buffering of the agent memory is necessary: because messages are generated in a previous step, changes to agents in the current timestep are not observable. The backend generates the three parts of a Flame model: an XML model specification, an XML initial agent state file, and the C step function definitions. Flame does not support adding or removing agents at runtime and does not use spatial acceleration structures.

FlameGPU [19] is based on Flame, but targets execution on the GPU using CUDA. Our FlameGPU backend is structurally similar to the Flame backend. It supports grid-based spatial acceleration, which requires a specification of the environment dimensions and partitioning radius in the XML model. The environment bounds must be adjusted upwards to be multiples of the radius. Runtime agent removal/addition is supported, but only the current agent may be removed and one added per step function. Both restrictions are enforced by the language.

Mason [12] is an ABS and visualization library written in Java. The two main components are an environment, which supports grid-based neighborhood queries, and a schedule, which executes the step functions. Mason does not have native support for double-buffering: simulations are fundamentally order-dependent, based on the assumption that for most models it does not make a significant difference if the state from the current (rather than previous) timestep is used for some agents. To support our execution semantics, agents hold two state objects, which are used alternately and swapped at the end of a step function. In Mason, each agent has only a single step function; however, our execution model may require multiple step functions, executed for all agents and in a specific order.[2] We solve this with a cyclic counter for each agent indicating which step function to execute. Mason supports both removal and addition of agents at runtime. This backend also produces code for the visualization of the simulation.

D-Mason [13,14] is a distributed extension of Mason that allows the distribution of the simulation across multiple, even heterogeneous machines. It is based on a Master/Workers paradigm where the master partitions the simulation environment into regions. All the agents in a region are assigned to a machine, which performs the simulation, handles the migration of agents, and manages the synchronization between neighboring regions. The D-Mason communication mechanism is based on the Publish/Subscribe pattern. Unlike Mason, D-Mason requires environments to use only positive coordinates. D-Mason supports agent removal/addition at runtime; however, new agents must be positioned in the current space partition.

Compiler flags are provided for further backend-specific configuration. For example, the `float` data-type used by OPENABL is mapped to double-precision

---

[2] While Mason itself supports multiple step functions in the form of anonymous Steppables, this is not supported by D-Mason, so a different solution is required.

floats by default, because this is the only type supported by all backends, but Flame and FlameGPU can switch to single-precision through a compiler flag.

5   Experimental Evaluation

OPENABL has been evaluated on six applications in terms of programmability of the language and the performance of the code generated for the five backends, including single-node performance on CPUs and GPUs, scalability on a cluster, and a comparison against hand-written target-specific code.

Reference Simulation Models. The evaluation uses six agent-based models from different domains, for which reference implementations were available for at least one of our targets. Table 1 lists general properties of these models.

Circle is a standardized benchmark part of the OpenAB initiative, for assessing the performance of fixed-radius near neighbor lookups, formally defined by Chisholm et al. [30]. *Boids* [31] is a steering behavior for autonomous characters in animation and games, which simulates the flocking behavior of birds. The agent motion is derived from three components: separation, alignment, and cohesion. Conway's *Game-of-life* is a cellular automaton model, implemented with one agent per cell and an `alive` boolean status variable. *Sugarscape* is a social science model where agents move on a grid of a regrowing resource (sugar), which they must consume to survive. We implement it using a stationary grid of agents. The *Ants Foraging* model simulates ants that, when they discover a food source, establish a trail of pheromones between the nest and the food source. The model uses two pheromones, which set up gradients and evaporate after some simulation steps, to the nest and to the food source respectively. We parallelized the original Mason model [32]: sequential access to global data structures, which is not suitable for parallelization, has been replaced by two step functions that handle the deposition and evaporation of (grid) pheromones, and one for the ant movement. *Predator-Prey* is our largest model, which involves three different agent types (prey, predator and grass), 13 step functions, and utilizes dynamic agent creation and removal. Both predators and prey implement short-range collision avoidance, a mid-range flocking, and can reproduce at different rates. Each predator follows the closest prey, which is eaten if it is too close. Conversely, prey avoids predators and eats grass, which regrows after a fixed time interval. All simulations have been executed with a different number of agents. The environment is scaled with the square root (for two-dimensional simulations) of the agent number, so that the agent density remains constant.

Programmability Evaluation. To evaluate the programmability and ease of use of OPENABL, we compare the eLOC (effective lines of code, ignoring comments and blank lines) of OPENABL models with available reference models

Table 1. Simulation benchmarks with the number of agent types, number of step functions, whether dynamic agent addition/removal is used (AR), effective lines of code (eLOC) of the implementations in OpenABL, FlameGPU and D-Mason.

Application	Area	Model properties			Implementation size in eLOC		
		Types	Steps	AR	OpenABL	FlameGPU	D-Mason
Circle	Micro-benchmark	1	1		36	184 (×5.1)	537 (×14.9)
Boids	Animation	1	1		82	240 (×2.9)	767 (×9.4)
Game of Life	Cellular automaton	1	1		48	133 (×2.8)	477 (×9.9)
Sugarscape	Social science	1	4		154	345 (×2.2)	n/a
Ants Foraging	Animal ecology	2	3		191	n/a	967 (×5.1)
Predator-Prey	Animal ecology	3	13	✓	248	858 (×3.5)	n/a

from FlameGPU and D-Mason.[3] As seen in Table 1, the FlameGPU implementations are 2–5 times larger, while the D-Mason models are 5–15 times larger. While eLOC is not a very reliable indicator of programmability, it is clear that OpenABL models tend to be significantly more compact than manual implementations.

Single-Node Performance Comparison. For single-node performance evaluation, we compared the performance of the code generated by the OpenABL compiler for the basic C, Mason, Flame and FlameGPU backends. The six test models were run for 100 timesteps with population sizes ranging from 250 to 10^6 agents. The *Predator-Prey* model was only evaluated on backends supporting dynamic addition/removal of agents. The benchmarks were performed on a system with an Intel Core i5-4690K CPU (4 cores at 3.50 GHz), 16 GB of memory, running on Ubuntu 16.04. For FlameGPU, we used an NVIDIA Titan Xp (Pascal architecture) with 12 GB of memory. The basic C backend was configured to use multiple threads using OpenMP.

The results in Fig. 3 show that Flame and basic C scale quadratically with the number of agents. This is expected, as they do not use any spatial acceleration structure. Mason is much faster than Flame, and is the best implementation for small-sized simulations. FlameGPU pays a high overhead for small-sized simulations, because of the data transfer from the host to the GPU; however, it is the best-performing solution for larger simulations with more than 10^4 agents. For most models, both Mason and FlameGPU scale approximately linearly at large population counts. One notable exception is *Ants*, where Mason degenerates to quadratic behavior, because of a very dense agent clustering at the start of the simulation.

---

[3] The used reference models are available at https://github.com/FLAMEGPU/FLAMEGPU, https://github.com/FLAMEGPU/Tutorial and https://github.com/isislab-unisa/dmason.

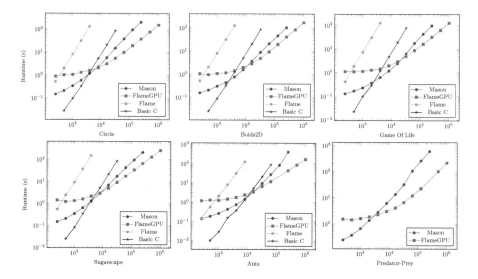

Fig. 3. Performance of generated Mason, FlameGPU, Flame and basic C code with a different number of agents (x-axis).

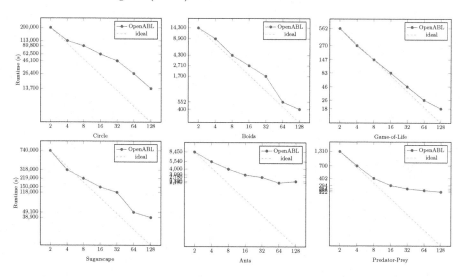

Fig. 4. OpenABL D-Mason strong scaling with different number of cores (x-axis).

Cluster Scaling. To evaluate the performance scaling of the OPENABL D-Mason backend, we use a cluster of 12 nodes equipped with two Intel Xeon E5-2430 (six cores) with hyper-threading disabled, connected by I350 Gigabit network adapters. One node is used for coordinating the simulation, while the others allocate one D-Mason logical processor for each core, running on Oracle JVM 1.8 and exploiting Apache ActiveMQ as message broker for communication/synchronization (the broker is allocated on the coordinating node). Figure 4 shows the strong scalability of the six applications, with each model simulating 10^6 agents for 1000 timesteps. The plots show the runtime in seconds for an increasing number of logical processors (cores).

The *Boids* model exhibits good scalability. Despite having similar behavior, *Circle*'s scaling is slightly worse due to different parametrization, e.g., a wider interaction radius. In *Game-of-Life* and *Sugarscape*, agents are distributed evenly in the space (on a grid) and are stationary, resulting in high scalability. *Ants* and *Predator-Prey* are the most complex simulations. The *Ants* model suffers from a dense concentration of the ant agents, especially at the start of the simulation, resulting in an uneven distribution of the workload. *Predator-Prey* is highly dynamic because of the addition/removal of agents, which drastically affects prey-crowded areas after the arrival of predators. This represents a challenge for distributed memory system, leading to bad scalability. We believe that more advanced load balancing strategies may substantially improve this aspect [33].

Performance Comparison Against Manually-Tuned Code. The potential overhead of the generated code has been evaluated against manual implementations of the *Boids* benchmark, because it is available for most libraries and is simple to validate. Results are summarized in Table 2. The generated code for Mason is 9% slower than the manual implementation; the reason is the double buffering mechanism introduced by OPENABL to ensure order-independent correctness, not supported in standard Mason. For FlameGPU, both generated code and manual implementation have similar performance: the semantics of the language map very well without any noticeable overhead. The overhead for D-Mason is 30%, motivated essentially by an improvement of the synchronization mechanism for each step function (agent buffer analysis may potentially reduce such overhead by avoiding unnecessary synchronizations). We omitted Flame from the comparison because of its very poor scalability (impractical with >5000 agents).

Table 2. Overhead of OPENABL generated code for *Boids* model compared to manually tuned code.

Backend	Overhead	Main reason
Mason	9%	Double-buffering
D-Mason	30%	Double-buffering and additional synchronization
Flame	n/a	(Too slow to compare)
FlameGPU	0%	Perfect programming model match

6   Conclusion

We present OPENABL, a domain-specific language designed for agent modeling on high-performance parallel and distributed architectures. It comprises an easy-to-program language that relies on high-level abstractions for programmability and explicitly exploits agent parallelism to deliver high-performance. It supports a wide range of context-specific semantics such as order-independent step functions, neighborhood queries, heterogeneous agents, and dynamic agent addition and removal. A source-to-source compiler translates the input OpenABL code into an AST-based intermediate representation exposing parallelism, locality and synchronization at the agent level. Subsequently, a collection of pluggable back-ends generate target codes for multi-core CPUs, massively parallel GPUs, large clusters and cloud systems. The OPENABL generated codes have been tested on a collection of six applications from various fields. While a program written in OPENABL is much smaller than one written for non-portable platform-specific libraries, its performance is very close to manual implementations.

OPENABL is an open source project available at https://github.com/OpenABL/OpenABL, with the goal of becoming an open research platform. The used code and instructions to reproduce our benchmarking results are available in a figshare repository [34].

This research has been partially funded by the DFG project *CELERITY* (CO 1544/1-1) and by the EPSRC fellowship *Accelerating Scientific Discovery with Accelerated Computing* (EP/N018869/1).

References

1. Epstein, J.M.: Agent-based computational models and generative social science. Complexity **4**(5), 41–60 (1999)
2. Epstein, J.M., Axtell, R.: Growing Artificial Societies: Social Science from the Bottom Up. The Brookings Institution, Washington, D.C. (1996)
3. Kollman, K., Miller, J.H., Page, S.E.: Adaptive parties in spatial elections. Am. Polit. Sci. Rev. **86**(4), 929–937 (1992)
4. Topa, G.: Social interactions, local spillovers and unemployment. Rev. Econ. Stud. **68**(2), 261–295 (2001)
5. Haynes, T., Sen, S.: Evolving behavioral strategies in predators and prey. In: Weiß, G., Sen, S. (eds.) IJCAI 1995. LNCS, vol. 1042, pp. 113–126. Springer, Heidelberg (1996). https://doi.org/10.1007/3-540-60923-7_22
6. Pelechano, N., Allbeck, J.M., Badler, N.I.: Controlling individual agents in high-density crowd simulation. In: EG Symposium on Computer Animation, pp. 99–108 (2007)
7. Kiran, M., Richmond, P., Holcombe, M., Chin, L.S., Worth, D., Greenough, C.: FLAME: simulating large populations of agents on parallel hardware architectures. In: Conference on Autonomous Agents and Multiagent Systems, pp. 1633–1636 (2010)
8. Cosenza, B., Cordasco, G., Chiara, R.D., Scarano, V.: Distributed load balancing for parallel agent-based simulations. In: International Euromicro Conference on Parallel, Distributed and Network-based Processing, PDP, pp. 62–69 (2011)

9. Carillo, M., Cordasco, G., Serrapica, F., Spagnuolo, C., Szufel, P., Vicidomini, L.: D-MASON on the cloud: an experience with amazon web services. In: Desprez, F., et al. (eds.) Euro-Par 2016. LNCS, vol. 10104, pp. 322–333. Springer, Cham (2017). https://doi.org/10.1007/978-3-319-58943-5_26

10. North, M.J., Collier, N.T., Vos, J.R.: Experiences creating three implementations of the repast agent modeling toolkit. Trans. Model. Comp. Sim. **16**(1), 1–25 (2006)

11. Collier, N., North, M.: Parallel agent-based simulation with repast for high performance computing. SIMULATION **89**(10), 1215–1235 (2013)

12. Luke, S., Cioffi-Revilla, C., Panait, L., Sullivan, K., Balan, G.: MASON: a multi-agent simulation environment. SIMULATION **81**(7), 517–527 (2005)

13. Cordasco, G., De Chiara, R., Mancuso, A., Mazzeo, D., Scarano, V., Spagnuolo, C.: A framework for distributing agent-based simulations. In: Alexander, M., et al. (eds.) Euro-Par 2011. LNCS, vol. 7155, pp. 460–470. Springer, Heidelberg (2012). https://doi.org/10.1007/978-3-642-29737-3_51

14. Cordasco, G., De Chiara, R., Mancuso, A., Mazzeo, D., Scarano, V., Spagnuolo, C.: Bringing together efficiency and effectiveness in distributed simulations: the experience with D-MASON. SIMULATION **89**(10), 1236–1253 (2013)

15. Cordasco, G., Chiara, R.D., Raia, F., Scarano, V., Spagnuolo, C., Vicidomini, L.: Designing computational steering facilities for distributed agent based simulations. In: SIGSIM Principles of Advanced Discrete Simulation, pp. 385–390 (2013)

16. Lettieri, N., Spagnuolo, C., Vicidomini, L.: Distributed agent-based simulation and GIS: an experiment with the dynamics of social norms. In: Hunold, S., et al. (eds.) Euro-Par 2015. LNCS, vol. 9523, pp. 379–391. Springer, Cham (2015). https://doi.org/10.1007/978-3-319-27308-2_31

17. Oliveira, A.P., Richmond, P.: Feasibility study of multi-agent simulation at the cellular level with FLAME GPU. In: FLAIRS Conference, pp. 398–403 (2016)

18. Tamrakar, S., Richmond, P., D'Souza, R.M.: PI-FLAME: a parallel immune system simulator using the FLAME graphic processing unit environment. SIMULATION **93**(1), 69–84 (2017)

19. Richmond, P., Walker, D., Coakley, S., Romano, D.: High performance cellular level agent-based simulation with FLAME for the GPU. Brief. Bioinform. **11**(3), 334 (2010)

20. Erra, U., Frola, B., Scarano, V.: A GPU-based interactive bio-inspired visual clustering. In: Symposium on Computational Intelligence and Data Mining, pp. 268–275 (2011)

21. Cosenza, B.: Behavioral spherical harmonics for long-range agents' interaction. In: Hunold, S., et al. (eds.) Euro-Par 2015. LNCS, vol. 9523, pp. 392–404. Springer, Cham (2015). https://doi.org/10.1007/978-3-319-27308-2_32

22. Macal, C.M., North, M.J.: Tutorial on agent-based modeling and simulation. In: 37th Conference on Winter Simulation, pp. 2–15 (2005)

23. Rousset, A., Herrmann, B., Lang, C., Philippe, L.: A survey on parallel and distributed multi-agent systems. In: Lopes, L., et al. (eds.) Euro-Par 2014. LNCS, vol. 8805, pp. 371–382. Springer, Cham (2014). https://doi.org/10.1007/978-3-319-14325-5_32

24. Grasso, I., Pellegrini, S., Cosenza, B., Fahringer, T.: A uniform approach for programming distributed heterogeneous computing systems. J. Parallel Distrib. Comput. **74**(12), 3228–3239 (2014)

25. DeVito, Z., et al.: Liszt: a domain specific language for building portable mesh-based PDE solvers. In: Conference on High Performance Computing Networking, Storage and Analysis, pp. 9:1–9:12 (2011)

26. Christen, M., Schenk, O., Cui, Y.: Patus for convenient high-performance stencils: evaluation in earthquake simulations. In: Conference on High Performance Computing, Networking, Storage and Analysis, SC, pp. 11:1–11:10 (2012)
27. Hong, S., Chafi, H., Sedlar, E., Olukotun, K.: Green-Marl: a DSL for easy and efficient graph analysis. In: ASPLOS, pp. 349–362 (2012)
28. Ragan-Kelley, J., Adams, A., Paris, S., Levoy, M., Amarasinghe, S.P., Durand, F.: Decoupling algorithms from schedules for easy optimization of image processing pipelines. ACM Trans. Graph. **31**(4), 32:1–32:12 (2012)
29. Kofler, K., Steinhauser, D., Cosenza, B., Grasso, I., Schindler, S., Fahringer, T.: Kd-tree based N-body simulations with volume-mass heuristic on the GPU. In: 2014 IEEE International Parallel and Distributed Processing Symposium Workshops, Phoenix, AZ, USA, 19–23 May 2014, pp. 1256–1265 (2014)
30. Chisholm, R., Richmond, P., Maddock, S.: A standardised benchmark for assessing the performance of fixed radius near neighbours. In: Desprez, F., et al. (eds.) Euro-Par 2016. LNCS, vol. 10104, pp. 311–321. Springer, Cham (2017). https://doi.org/10.1007/978-3-319-58943-5_25
31. Reynolds, C.W.: Flocks, herds and schools: a distributed behavioral model. ACM SIGGRAPH **21**(4), 25–34 (1987)
32. Panait, L., Luke, S.: A pheromone-based utility model for collaborative foraging. In: Conference on Autonomous Agents and Multiagent Systems, pp. 36–43 (2004)
33. Cordasco, G., Cosenza, B., De Chiara, R., Erra, U., Scarano, V.: Experiences with mesh-like computations using prediction binary trees. Scalable Comput.: Pract. Exp. Sci. Int. J. Parallel Distrib. Comput. (SCPE) **10**(2), 173–187 (2009)
34. Cosenza, B., et al.: OpenABL: a domain-specific language for parallel and distributed agent-based simulations, figshare. Fileset (2018). https://doi.org/10.6084/m9.figshare.6384413

Bulk: A Modern C++ Interface
for Bulk-Synchronous Parallel Programs

Jan-Willem Buurlage[1]([✉])[iD], Tom Bannink[1,2][iD], and Rob H. Bisseling[3][iD]

[1] Centrum Wiskunde & Informatica, Amsterdam, The Netherlands
{j.buurlage,bannink}@cwi.nl
[2] QuSoft, Amsterdam, The Netherlands
[3] Mathematical Institute, Utrecht University, Utrecht, The Netherlands
r.h.bisseling@uu.nl

Abstract. The bulk-synchronous parallel (BSP) programming model gives a powerful method for implementing and describing parallel programs. In this article we present Bulk, a novel interface for writing BSP programs in the C++ programming language that leverages modern C++ features to allow for the implementation of safe and generic parallel algorithms for shared-memory, distributed-memory, and hybrid systems. This interface targets the next generation of BSP programmers who want to write fast, safe, clear and portable parallel programs. We discuss two applications: regular sample sort and the fast Fourier transform, both in terms of performance, and ease of parallel implementation.

1 Introduction

The bulk-synchronous parallel (BSP) model was introduced as a bridging model for parallel programming by Valiant in 1989 [1]. It enables a way to structure parallel computations, which aids in the design and analysis of parallel programs.

The BSP model defines an abstract computer, the BSP computer, on which BSP algorithms can run. Such a computer consists of p identical processors, each having access to their own local memory. A communication network is available which can be used by the different processors to communicate data. During the execution of an algorithm, there are points at which bulk synchronizations are performed. The time of such a synchronization, the *latency*, is denoted by l. The communication cost per data word is denoted by g. The parameters l and g are usually expressed in number of floating-point operations (FLOPs). They can be related to *wall-clock time* by considering the computation rate r of the individual processors which is measured in floating-point operations per second (FLOP/s). A BSP computer is captured completely by the parameter tuple (p, g, l, r).

At a high level, a BSP algorithm is a series of supersteps that each consist of a *computation phase* and a *communication phase*. The processors of a BSP computer can simultaneously send and receive data, and they can do so independently. This means that the cost of communication is dominated by the maximum number of words sent or received by any processor. At the end of each superstep a bulk synchronization is performed ensuring that all outstanding

© Springer International Publishing AG, part of Springer Nature 2018
M. Aldinucci et al. (Eds.): Euro-Par 2018, LNCS 11014, pp. 519–532, 2018.
https://doi.org/10.1007/978-3-319-96983-1_37

communication has been resolved. Each processor runs the same program, but on different data, which means that BSP algorithms adhere to the Single Program Multiple Data (SPMD) paradigm.

The BSP cost of a BSP algorithm can predict the runtime of that algorithm when it is run on a BSP computer. This cost can be expressed completely in the parameters of a BSP computer. For each superstep, the cost depends on (1) $w_i^{(s)}$ the amount of work, measured in FLOPs, performed by processor s in the ith superstep, (2) $r_i^{(s)}$, the number of data words received, and (3) $t_i^{(s)}$ the number of data words transmitted (sent) by processor s in superstep i. The runtime of a parallel algorithm is dominated by the processor that takes the longest time, both for computation and communication. In the case of communication, we therefore require the concept of an h-relation, defined as the maximum number of words transmitted or received by any processor during the superstep, i.e., $h_i = \max_{0 \le s < p} \max\{t_i^{(s)}, r_i^{(s)}\}$. This leads naturally to the following cost, the BSP cost, of a BSP algorithm consisting of k supersteps:

$$T = \sum_{i=0}^{k-1} \left(\max_{0 \le s < p} w_i^{(s)} + g\, h_i + l \right).$$

The BSP model has inspired many parallel programming interfaces. BSPlib [2] describes a collection of a limited set of primitives which can be used for writing BSP programs in the C programming language. Libraries that implement the BSPlib standard include BSPonMPI [3] and MulticoreBSP for Java [4] and C [5]. Paderborn University BSP (PUB) [6] is an alternative BSP library that includes features not included in BSPlib such as subset synchronization and non-blocking collective operations. A functional BSP library is provided in BSML [7] for the multi-paradigm programming language Objective CAML. Big data methodologies based on the BSP model include the popular MapReduce [8] and Pregel [9] frameworks introduced by Google. These frameworks have open-source implementations in respectively Apache Hadoop and Apache Giraph, the latter of which is used for large scale graph computing by e.g. Facebook [10]. Apache Hama [11] is a recent BSPlib alternative for the Java programming language.

For the C++ programming language, high-level parallel programming libraries include HPX [12], whose current interface focuses on asynchronous and concurrent applications, UPC++ [13], which provides a generic and object-oriented partitioned global address space (PGAS) interface, and BSP++ [14] which targets hybrid SMP architectures and implements direct remote memory access but not bulk-synchronous message passing.

Modern hardware is increasingly hierarchical. In a typical HPC cluster there are many nodes, each consisting of (several) multi-core processors together with accelerators such as GPUs or many-core coprocessors. Furthermore, there are multiple layers of random-access memory and caches which all differ in e.g. size, latency, and read and write speed. In 2011, Valiant introduced Multi-BSP [15], a hierarchical execution model based on BSP. The nested execution of BSP programs is available in e.g. the PUB, MulticoreBSP, and NestStep [16] libraries.

In this article we introduce Bulk, a library for the C++ programming language. The current version is based on the C++17 standard [17]. By leveraging common idioms and features of modern C++ we increase memory safety and code reuse, and we are able to eliminate boilerplate code from BSP programs. Furthermore, the flexible backend architecture ensures that programs written on top of Bulk are able to simultaneously target systems with shared memory, distributed memory, or even hybrid systems. The remainder of this article is structured as follows. In Sect. 2, we introduce the Bulk library, and highlight the differences with previous BSP libraries. In Sect. 3, we discuss two applications, *regular sample sort* and the *fast Fourier transform (FFT)*. In Sect. 4, we provide experimental results for these applications. Finally, in Sect. 5, we present our conclusions and discuss possibilities for future work.

2   The Bulk Library

The Bulk library is a modern BSPlib replacement which focuses on the memory safety, portability, code reuse, and ease of implementation of BSP algorithms. Additionally, Bulk provides the possibility to program hybrid systems and it has several new features compared to existing BSP libraries. First, we present all the concepts of the library that are necessary to implement classic BSP algorithms.

Bulk Interface. Here, we give an overview of the Bulk C++ interface[1]. We use a `monospace` font in the running text for C++ code and symbols. A BSP computer is captured in an `environment`. This can be an object encapsulating e.g. an MPI cluster, a multi-core processor or a many-core coprocessor. Within this BSP computer, an SPMD block can be spawned. Collectively, the processors running this block form a *parallel world* that is captured in a `world` object. This object can be used to communicate, and for obtaining information about the local process, such as the processor identifier (PID, in Bulk denoted `rank`) and the number of active processors. In all the code examples, `s` refers to the local rank, and `t` to an arbitrary target rank.

A simple program written using Bulk first instantiates an environment object, which is then used to spawn an SPMD block (in the form of a C++ function) on each processor, to which the local world is passed. See Listing 1 for a code example, and Table 1 for a table with the relevant methods.

```
bulk::backend::environment env;
env.spawn(env.available_processors(), [](auto& world) {
    world.log("Hello world from %d / %d\n",
              world.rank(), world.active_processors());
});
```

Listing 1: The entry point for parallelism using Bulk. We create an environment, where `backend` is a placeholder for a concrete backend such as MPI or C++ threads. Next, we spawn an SPMD block using all the available processors.

---

[1] Although we try to be as complete as possible, we do not give a detailed and exhaustive list of all the methods and functions provided by the library. For such a list, together with all the function signatures and further examples we refer to the online documentation which can be found at https://jwbuurlage.github.com/Bulk/.

Table 1. Available methods for `environment` and `world` objects.

Class	Method	Description
environment	spawn	starts an SPMD block
	available_processors	returns maximum p
world	active_processors	returns chosen p
	rank	returns local processor ID s
	next_rank	returns $s + 1 \pmod{p}$
	prev_rank	returns $s - 1 \pmod{p}$
	sync	ends the current superstep
	log	logs a string message

The spawned SPMD section, which is a function that takes the world as a parameter, consists of a number of supersteps. These supersteps are delimited with a call to `world::sync`. The basic mechanism for communication revolves around the concept of a distributed variable, which is captured in a `var` object. These variables should be constructed in the same superstep by each processor. Although each processor defines this distributed variable, its value is generally different on each processor. The value contained in the distributed variable on the local processor is called the *local value*, while the concrete values on remote processors are called the *remote values*.

A distributed variable is of little use if it does not provide a way to access remote values of the variable. Bulk provides encapsulated references to the local and remote values of a distributed variable. We call these references *image* objects. Images of remote values can be used for reading, e.g. `auto y = x(t).get()` to read from processor `t`, and for writing, e.g. `x(t) = value`, both with the usual bulk-synchronous semantics. See Listing 2 for a more elaborate example. Since the value of a remote image is not immediately available upon getting it, it is contained in a `future` object. In the next superstep, its value can be obtained using `future::value`, e.g. `y.value()`.

```
auto x = bulk::var<int>(world);

auto t = world.next_rank();
x(t) = 2 * world.rank();
world.sync();
// x now contains two times the ID of the previous logical processor

auto b = x(t).get();
world.sync();
// b.value() now contains two times the local ID
```

Listing 2: The basic usage of a distributed variable. The variable is created on each processor running the SPMD block. Its images can then be written to by using the convenient syntax `x(processor) = value`. Remote values are obtained by using the syntax `x(processor).get()`.

In this simple example, we already see some major benefits of Bulk over existing BSP libraries: (1) we avoid accessing and manipulating raw memory locations in user code, making the code more memory safe and (2) the resulting code is shorter, more readable and therefore less prone to errors. Note that these benefits do not come at a performance cost, since it can be seen as syntactic sugar that resolves to calls to internal functions that resemble common BSP primitives.

When restricting ourselves to communication based on distributed variables, we lose the possibility of performing communication based on (sub)arrays. Distributed variables whose images are arrays have a special status in Bulk, and are captured in `coarray` objects. The functionality of these objects is inspired by Coarray Fortran [18]. Coarrays provide a convenient way to share data across processors. Instead of manually sending and receiving individual data elements, coarrays model distributed data as a 2D array, where the first dimension is over the processors, and the second dimension is over local 1D array indices. The local elements of a coarray can be accessed as if the coarray were a regular 1D array. Images to the remote arrays belonging to a coarray `xs` are obtained in the same way as for variables, by using the syntax `xs(t)`. These images can be used to access the remote array. For example, `xs(t)[5] = 3` puts the value 3 into the array element at index 5 of the local array at processor `t`. Furthermore, convenient syntax makes it easy to work with slices of coarrays. A basic slice for the element interval `[start, end)`, i.e., including `start` but excluding `end`, is obtained using `xs(t)[{start, end}]`. See Listing 3 for examples of common coarray operations. We summarize the most important put and get operations for distributed variables and coarrays in Table 2.

```
auto xs = bulk::coarray<int>(world, 4);

auto t = world.next_rank();
xs[0] = 1;
xs(t)[1] = 2 + world.rank();
xs(t)[{2, 4}] = {123, 321};

world.sync();
// xs is now [1, 2 + world.prev_rank(), 123, 321]
```

Listing 3: The basic syntax for dealing with coarrays.

Instead of using distributed variables, it is also possible to perform one-sided *mailbox communication* using message passing, which in Bulk is carried out using a `queue`. The message passing syntax is greatly simplified compared to previous BSP interfaces, without losing power or flexibility. This is possible for two reasons. First, it is possible to construct several queues, removing a common use case for *tags* to distinguish different kinds of messages. Second, messages consisting of multiple components can be constructed on demand using a syntax based on variadic templates. This gives us the possibility of *optionally*

Table 2. An overview of the syntax for puts and gets in Bulk. Here, x and xs are a distributed variable and a coarray, respectively, e.g. `auto x = bulk::var<int>(world)`, `auto xs = bulk::coarray<int>(world, 10)`

Object	Image	Description	Code
var	local [(*)]	set	`x = 5`
		use	`auto y = x + 3`
	remote	put	`x(t) = 5`
		get	`auto y = x(t).get()`
coarray	local [(*)]	set	`xs[idx] = 5`
		use	`auto y = xs[idx] + 3`
	remote	put	`xs(t)[idx] = 5`
		get	`auto y = xs(t)[idx].get()`
		put slice[(**)]	`xs(t)[{start, end}] = {values...}`
		get slice[(**)]	`auto ys = xs(t)[{start, end}].get()`

[(*)]: a local image of a value of type T gets implicitly cast to a T& reference to the underlying value.
[(**)]: subarrays corresponding to slices are represented using `std::vector` containers.

attaching tags to messages in a queue, or even denoting the message structure in the construction of the queue itself. For example, `queue<int, float[]>` is a queue with messages that consist of a single integer, and zero or more real numbers. See Listing 4 for the basic usage of these queues.

```
// queue containing simple data
auto numbers = bulk::queue<int>(world);
numbers(t).send(1);
numbers(t).send(2);
world.sync();
for (auto value : numbers)
    world.log("%d", value);

// queue containing multiple components
auto index_tuples = bulk::queue<int, int, float>(world);
index_tuples(t).send({1, 2, 3.0f});
index_tuples(t).send({3, 4, 5.0f});
world.sync();
for (auto [i, j, k] : index_tuples)
    world.log("(%d, %d, %f)", i, j, k);
```

Listing 4: The use of message passing queues. The local inbox acts as a regular container, so we can use a range-based for-loop. The messages can be accessed in a concise way using structured bindings.

In addition to distributed variables and queues, common communication patterns such as `gather_all`, `foldl`, and `broadcast` are also available. The Bulk library also has various utility features for e.g. logging and benchmarking. We note furthermore that it is straightforward to implement generic skeletons on top of Bulk, since all distributed objects are implemented in a generic manner.

Backends and Nested Execution. Bulk has a powerful backend mechanism. The initial release provides backends for *distributed memory* based on MPI [19], *shared memory* based on the standard C++ threading library, and *data streaming* for the Epiphany many-core coprocessor [20]. Note that for a shared-memory system, only standard C++ has to be used. This means that a parallel program written using Bulk can run on a variety of systems, simply by changing the environment that spawns the SPMD function. No other changes are required. In addition, libraries that build on top of Bulk can be written completely independently from the environment, and only have to manipulate the world object.

Different backends can be used together. For example, distinct compute nodes can communicate using MPI while locally performing shared-memory multi-threaded parallel computations, all using a single programming interface. Hybrid shared/distributed-memory programs can be written simply by nesting `environment` objects with different backends.

3 Applications

3.1 Parallel Regular Sample Sort

Here, we present our BSP variant of the parallel regular sample sort proposed by Shi and Schaeffer in 1992 [21]. Hill et al. [22] presented a BSP version, and Gerbessiotis [23] studied variants with regular oversampling. Our version reduces the required number of supersteps by performing a redundant mergesort of the samples on all processors.

Our BSP variant is summarized in Algorithm 1. Every processor first sorts its local block of size $b = n/p$ by a quicksort of the interval $[sb, (s+1)b - 1]$, where s is the local processor identity. The processor then takes p regular samples at distance b/p and broadcasts these to all processors. We assume for simplicity that p divides b, and, for the purpose of explanation, that there are no duplicates (which can be achieved by using the original ordering as a secondary criterion). All processors then synchronize, which ends the first superstep. In the second superstep, the samples are concatenated and sorted. A mergesort is used, since the samples originating in the same processor were already sorted. Thus, p parts have to be merged. The start of part t is given by $start[t]$ and the end by $start[t+1] - 1$. From these samples, p splitters are chosen at distance p, and are used to split the local block into p parts. At the end of the second superstep, a local contribution X_{st} is sent to processor $P(t)$. In the third and final superstep, the received parts are concatenated and sorted, again using a mergesort because each received part has already been sorted. See Listing 5 for an illustration of Bulk implementations of the two communication phases of Algorithm 1.

Shi and Schaeffer have proven that the block size at the end of the algorithm is at most twice the block size at the start, thus bounding the size by $b_s \leq 2b$. A small optimization made possible by our redundant computation of the samples is that not all samples need to be sorted, but only the ones relevant for the local processor. The other samples merely need to be counted, separately for those larger and for those smaller than the values in the current block.

The total BSP cost of the algorithm, assuming p is a power of two, is

$$T_{\text{sort}} \leq \frac{n}{p} \log_2 \frac{n}{p} + p^2 \log_2 p + \frac{2n}{p} \cdot \log_2 p + \left(p(p-1) + 2\frac{n}{p} \right) g + 2l. \quad (1)$$

This is efficient in the range $p \leq n^{1/3}$, since the sorting of the array data then dominates the redundant computation and sorting of the samples.

```
auto samples = bulk::coarray<T>(world, p * p); // Broadcast samples
for (int t = 0; t < p; ++t)
    samples(t)[{s * p, (s + 1) * p}] = local_samples;
world.sync();

auto q = bulk::queue<int, T[]>(world); // Contribution from P(s) to P(t)
for (int t = 0; t < p; ++t)
    q(t).send(block_sizes[t], blocks[t]);
world.sync();
```

Listing 5: Two communication phases in the regular sample sort algorithm.

3.2 Fast Fourier Transform

The discrete Fourier transform (DFT) of a complex vector x of length n is the complex vector y of length n defined by

$$y_k = \sum_{j=0}^{n-1} x_j e^{-2\pi ijk/n} = \sum_{j=0}^{n-1} x_j \omega_n^{jk}, \quad \text{for } 0 \leq k < n, \quad (2)$$

where we use the notation $\omega_n = e^{-2\pi i/n}$. The DFT can be computed in $5n \log_2 n$ floating-point operations by using a radix-2 Fast Fourier Transform (FFT) algorithm assuming that n is a power of two.

Our parallel algorithm for computing the DFT uses the *group-cyclic distribution* with cycle $c \leq p$, and is based on the algorithm presented in [24] and explained in detail in [25]. The group-cyclic distribution first assigns a block of the vector x to a group of c processors and then assigns the vector components within that block cyclically. The number of processor groups (and blocks) is p/c. The block size of a group is nc/p. Here, we assume that n, p, c are powers of two. For $c = 1$, we retrieve the regular block distribution, and for $c = p$ the cyclic distribution.

The parallel FFT algorithm starts and ends in a cyclic distribution. First, the algorithm permutes the local vector with components $x_s, x_{s+p}, x_{s+2p}, \ldots,$ x_{s+n-p}, by swapping pairs of components with bit-reversed local indices. The resulting storage format of the data can be viewed as a block distribution, but

---

Algorithm 1. Regular sample sort for processor $P(s)$, with $0 \leq s < p$.

---

input: x : vector of length n, $n \bmod p^2 = 0$, block distributed with block size $b = n/p$.
output: x sorted in increasing order, block distributed with variable block size $b_s \leq 2b$.

$\text{Quicksort}(x, sb, (s+1)b - 1);$ ▷ Sort local block and create samples
for $i := 0$ **to** $p - 1$ **do**
    $sample_s[i] := x[sb + i \cdot \frac{b}{p}];$

for $t := 0$ **to** $p - 1$ **do**   ▷ Broadcast samples
    put $sample_s$ in $P(t)$;
Sync;

for $t := 0$ **to** $p - 1$ **do**   ▷ Concatenate and sort samples
    $start[t] := tp;$
    for $i := 0$ **to** $p - 1$ **do**
       $sample[tp + i] := sample_t[i];$
$start[p] := p^2;$
$\text{Mergesort}(sample, start, p);$

for $t := 0$ **to** $p - 1$ **do**   ▷ Create splitters
    $splitter[t] := sample[tp];$
$splitter[p] := \infty;$

for $t := 0$ **to** $p - 1$ **do**   ▷ Split local block and send its parts
    $X_{st} := \{x_i \ : \ sb \leq i < (s+1)b \ \wedge \ splitter[t] \leq x_i < splitter[t + 1]\};$
    put X_{st} in $P(t)$;   ▷ Contribution from $P(s)$ to $P(t)$
Sync;

$x_s := \cup_{t=0}^{p-1} X_{ts};$ ▷ Concatenate received parts

$start_s[0] := 0;$ ▷ Sort local block
for $t := 1$ **to** p **do**
    $start_s[t] := start_s[t - 1] + |X_{t-1,s}|;$
$b_s := start_s[p];$
$\text{Mergesort}(x_s, start_s, p);$

---

with the processor identities bit-reversed. The processor numbering is reversed later, during the first data redistribution. After the local bit reversal, a sequence of butterfly operations is performed, just as in the sequential FFT, but with every processor performing the pairwise operations on its local vector components. In the common case $p \leq \sqrt{n}$, the BSP cost of this algorithm is given by

$$T_{\text{FFT}, \ p \leq \sqrt{n}} = \frac{5n \log_2 n}{p} + 2\frac{n}{p}g + l. \tag{3}$$

4 Results

We evaluate the performance of Bulk implementations of the BSP algorithms regular sample sort and FFT outlined in the previous section. The numbers presented are obtained on a single computer with two Intel Xeon Silver 4110 CPUs, each with 8 cores and 16 hardware threads for a total of 32 hardware threads, using the C++ threads backend. The benchmark programs are compiled with GCC 7.2.1. The results are shown in Table 3. The parallel sort implementation is a direct translation of Algorithm 1, except that we opt for a three-phase communication protocol instead of relying on bulk-synchronous message passing to avoid potentially superfluous buffer allocations. The parallel FFT implementation is as described in Sect. 3.2, where we use FFTW [26] as a sequential kernel[2]. The input arrays for both algorithms have size n, and the algorithms are run on p processors.

For the parallel sorting algorithm, the array contains uniformly distributed random integers between 0 and 2×10^5. We observe that good speedups are obtained compared to the sequential implementation. The maximum speedup seen is about $16\times$ with $p = 32$ and $n = 2^{23}$.

For the FFT results, we observe good scalability up to $p = 16$, where we seem to hit a limit presumably because of the shared floating-point unit (FPU) between two logical threads on the same physical core, and possibly also due to the memory requirements in the redistribution phase.

Various other algorithms and applications have been implemented on top of Bulk. The current library release includes a number of examples, such as simple implementations for the *inner product*, or the *word count* problem. Future releases of the library are planned to have additional features such as arbitrary data distributions, which is already available as an experimental feature. Fur-

Table 3. Speedups of parallel sort (top) and parallel FFT compared to `std::sort` from libstdc++, and the sequential algorithm from FFTW 3.3.7, respectively. Also given is the sequential time t_{seq}.

		$p = 1$	$p = 2$	$p = 4$	$p = 8$	$p = 16$	$p = 32$	$t_{seq}(s)$
Sort	$n = 2^{20}$	0.93	1.95	3.83	6.13	8.10	12.00	0.08
	$n = 2^{21}$	1.01	2.08	4.11	7.28	10.15	15.31	0.19
	$n = 2^{22}$	0.88	1.82	3.58	5.99	10.27	13.92	0.33
	$n = 2^{23}$	0.97	1.90	3.63	6.19	11.99	16.22	0.72
	$n = 2^{24}$	0.93	1.79	3.21	6.33	8.47	14.76	1.39
FFT	$n = 2^{23}$	0.99	1.07	2.08	2.77	5.60	5.51	0.20
	$n = 2^{24}$	1.00	1.26	2.14	3.07	5.68	6.08	0.45
	$n = 2^{25}$	1.00	1.23	2.22	3.09	5.80	6.05	0.96
	$n = 2^{26}$	0.99	1.24	2.01	3.28	5.48	5.97	1.93

---

[2] We use plans with the so-called planning-rigor flag `FFTW_MEASURE`.

thermore, an open-source application in computed tomography, Tomos, has been developed on top of Bulk, illustrating that the library can be used for the implementation of more complicated software.

4.1 Bulk vs. BSPlib

We believe the main goal of Bulk, which is to improve memory safety, portability, code reuse, and ease of implementation compared to BSPlib, has been largely achieved. In Listing 6, we show a Bulk and a BSPlib implementation of a common operation. The Bulk implementation avoids the use of raw pointers, uses generic objects, requires significantly fewer lines of code, and is more readable.

```
// BSPlib
int* xs = malloc(10 * sizeof(int));
bsp_push_reg(xs, 10 * sizeof(int));
bsp_sync();

int ys[3] = {2, 3, 4};
bsp_put((s + 1) % p, ys, xs, 2, 3 * sizeof(int));
bsp_sync();
...
bsp_pop_reg(xs);
free(xs);

// Bulk
auto xs = bulk::coarray<int>(world, 10);
xs(world.next_rank())[{2, 5}] = {2, 3, 4};
world.sync();
```

Listing 6: A comparison between Bulk and BSPlib for putting a subarray.

We compare the performance of Bulk to a state-of-the-art BSPlib implementation, MulticoreBSP for C (MCBSP) [5], version 2.0.3 released in May 2018. We use the implementations of BSPedupack [25], version 2.0.0-beta, as the basis of our BSPlib programs.

Table 4 shows the performance of Bulk compared to BSPlib. For sorting, the Bulk implementation is significantly faster, presumably because the internal sorting algorithm used is different. The Bulk implementation uses the sorting algorithm from the C++ standard library, whereas the BSPlib implementation uses the quicksort from the C standard library. The BSPedupack FFT implementation has been modified to use FFTW for the sequential kernel. For the FFT, MCBSP outperforms Bulk slightly on larger problem sizes.

In Table 5, the BSP parameters are measured for Bulk and MCBSP. The computation rate r is measured by applying a simple arithmetic transformation involving two multiplications, one addition and one subtraction, to an array of 2^{23} double-precision floating-point numbers. The latency l is measured by averaging over 100 bulk synchronizations without communication. The communication-to-computation ratio g is measured by communicating subarrays of various sizes,

Table 4. Comparing implementations of BSPedupack running on top of MCBSP, to our implementations on top of Bulk.

Sort			FFT		
Size	t_{MCBSP} (ms)	t_{Bulk} (ms)	Size	t_{MCBSP} (s)	t_{Bulk} (s)
$n = 2^{20}$	24.49	13.80	$n = 2^{22}$	0.153	0.144
$n = 2^{21}$	53.00	28.76	$n = 2^{23}$	0.305	0.320
$n = 2^{22}$	113.6	62.42	$n = 2^{24}$	0.629	0.694
$n = 2^{23}$	237.2	142.8			

consisting of up to 10^7 double-precision floating-point numbers, between various processor pairs.

The MCBSP library uses a barrier based on a spinlock mechanism by default. This barrier gives better performance, leading to a low value for l. Alternatively, a more energy-efficient barrier based on a mutex can be used, which is similar to the barrier that is implemented in the C++ backend for Bulk. With this choice, the latency of MCBSP and Bulk are comparable. MCBSP is able to obtain a better value for g. We plan to include a spinlock barrier in a future release of Bulk, and to improve the communication performance further.

Table 5. The BSP parameters for MCBSP and the C++ thread backend for Bulk.

Method	r (GFLOP/s)	g (FLOPs/word)	l (FLOPs)
MCBSP (spinlock)	0.44	2.93	326
MCBSP (mutex)	0.44	2.86	10484
Bulk	0.44	5.65	11702

5   Conclusion

We present Bulk, a modern BSP interface and library implementation with many desirable features such as memory safety, support for generic implementations of algorithms, portability, and encapsulated state, and show that it allows for clear and concise implementations of BSP algorithms. Furthermore, we show the scalability of two important applications implemented in Bulk by providing experimental results. Even though both algorithms have $\mathcal{O}(n \log n)$ complexity, and nearly all input data have to be communicated during the algorithm, we still are able to obtain good speedups with our straightforward implementations. The performance of Bulk is close to that of a state-of-the-art BSPlib implementation, except for the mutex-based barrier.

References

1. Valiant, L.G.: A bridging model for parallel computation. Comm. ACM **33**(8), 103–111 (1990)
2. Hill, J.M.D., et al.: BSPlib: the BSP programming library. Parallel Comput. **24**(14), 1947–1980 (1998)
3. Suijlen, W.: BSPonMPI v0.3. https://sourceforge.net/projects/bsponmpi/
4. Yzelman, A.N., Bisseling, R.H.: An object-oriented bulk synchronous parallel library for multicore programming. Concurr. Comput.: Pract. Exp. **24**(5), 533–553 (2012)
5. Yzelman, A.N., Bisseling, R.H., Roose, D., Meerbergen, K.: MulticoreBSP for C: a high-performance library for shared-memory parallel programming. Int. J. Parallel Programm. **42**(4), 619–642 (2014)
6. Bonorden, O., Juurlink, B., von Otte, I., Rieping, I.: The Paderborn University BSP (PUB) library. Parallel Comput. **29**(2), 187–207 (2003)
7. Loulergue, F., Gava, F., Billiet, D.: Bulk synchronous parallel ML: modular implementation and performance prediction. In: Sunderam, V.S., van Albada, G.D., Sloot, P.M.A., Dongarra, J.J. (eds.) ICCS 2005. LNCS, vol. 3515, pp. 1046–1054. Springer, Heidelberg (2005). https://doi.org/10.1007/11428848_132
8. Dean, J., Ghemawat, S.: MapReduce: simplified data processing on large clusters. In: Proceedings of OSDI, pp. 137–149 (2004)
9. Malewicz, G., et al.: Pregel: a system for large-scale graph processing. In: Proceedings of SIGMOD, pp. 135–145 (2010)
10. Ching, A., Edunov, S., Kabiljo, M., Logothetis, D., Muthukrishnan, S.: One trillion edges: graph processing at Facebook-scale. VLDB **8**(12), 1804–1815 (2015)
11. Siddique, K., Akhtar, Z., Yoon, E.J., Jeong, Y.S., Dasgupta, D., Kim, Y.: Apache Hama: an emerging bulk synchronous parallel computing framework for big data applications. IEEE Access **4**, 8879–8887 (2016)
12. Heller, T., Diehl, P., Byerly, Z., Biddiscombe, J., Kaiser, H.: HPX-An open source C++ standard library for parallelism and concurrency. In: Proceedings of Open-SuCo, p. 5 (2017)
13. Zheng, Y., Kamil, A., Driscoll, M.B., Shan, H., Yelick, K.: UPC++: a PGAS extension for C++. In: Proceedings of IEEE IPDPS, pp. 1105–1114 (2014)
14. Hamidouche, K., Falcou, J., Etiemble, D.: Hybrid bulk synchronous parallelism library for clustered SMP architectures. In: Proceedings of HLPP, pp. 55–62 (2010)
15. Valiant, L.G.: A bridging model for multi-core computing. J. Comput. Syst. Sci. **77**(1), 154–166 (2011)
16. Keßler, C.W.: NestStep: nested parallelism and virtual shared memory for the BSP model. J. Supercomput. **17**(3), 245–262 (2000)
17. ISO/IEC: 14882:2017(E) - Programming languages - C++ (2017)
18. Numrich, R.W., Reid, J.: Co-array Fortran for parallel programming. ACM SIGPLAN Fortran Forum **17**(2), 1–31 (1998)
19. MPI Forum: MPI: a message-passing interface standard. Int. J. Supercomput. Appl. High-Perform. Comput. **8**, 165–414 (1994)
20. Olofsson, A., Nordström, T., Ul-Abdin, Z.: Kickstarting high-performance energy-efficient manycore architectures with Epiphany. In: Proceedings of IEEE ACSSC, pp. 1719–1726 (2014)
21. Shi, H., Schaeffer, J.: Parallel sorting by regular sampling. J. Parallel Distrib. Comput. **14**(4), 361–372 (1992)

22. Hill, J.M.D., Donaldson, S.R., Skillicorn, D.B.: Portability of performance with the BSPLib communications library. In: Proceedings of MPPM, p. 33 (1997)
23. Gerbessiotis, A.V.: Extending the BSP model for multi-core and out-of-core computing: MBSP. Parallel Comput. **41**(Suppl. C), 90–102 (2015)
24. Inda, M.A., Bisseling, R.H.: A simple and efficient parallel FFT algorithm using the BSP model. Parallel Comput. **27**(14), 1847–1878 (2001)
25. Bisseling, R.H.: Parallel Scientific Computation: A Structured Approach using BSP and MPI. Oxford University Press, Oxford (2004)
26. Frigo, M., Johnson, S.G.: FFTW: an adaptive software architecture for the FFT. In: Proceedings of IEEE ICASSP, pp. 1381–1384 (1998)

SharP Unified Memory Allocator: An Intent-Based Memory Allocator for Extreme-Scale Systems

Ferrol Aderholdt[1]([✉]), Manjunath Gorentla Venkata[1],
and Zachary W. Parchman[2]

[1] Oak Ridge National Laboratory, Oak Ridge, TN 37831, USA
{aderholdtwf1,manjugv}@ornl.gov
[2] Tennessee Technological University, Cookeville, TN 38501, USA
zwparchman42@students.tntech.edu

Abstract. The pre-exascale systems will soon be deployed with a deep, complex memory hierarchy composed of many heterogeneous memories. This presents multiple challenges for users including: how to allocate data objects with locality between memories and devices for the various memories in these systems, which includes DRAM, High-bandwidth Memory (HBM), and non-volatile random access memory (NVRAM), and how to perform these allocations while providing portability for their application. Currently, the user can make use of multiple, disjoint libraries to allocate data objects on these memories. However, it is difficult to obtain locality between memories and devices when using libraries that are unaware of each other. This paper presents the *Unified Memory Allocator* (UMA) of the SHARed data-structure centric Programming abstraction (SharP) library, which provides a unified interface for memory allocations across DRAM, HBM, and NVRAM and is extensible to support future memory types. In addition, the SharP UMA allows for portability between systems by supporting both explicit and implicit, intent-based memory allocations. To demonstrate the ease of use of the SharP UMA, we have extended both *Open MPI* and *OpenSHMEM-X* to support SharP. We validate this work by evaluating the performance implications and intent-based approach with synthetic benchmarks as well as adaptations of the Graph500 benchmark.

F. Aderholdt—This manuscript has been authored by UT-Battelle, LLC under Contract No. DE-AC05-00OR22725 with the U.S. Department of Energy. The United States Government retains and the publisher, by accepting the article for publication, acknowledges that the United States Government retains a non-exclusive, paid-up, irrevocable, worldwide license to publish or reproduce the published form of this manuscript, or allow others to do so, for United States Government purposes. The Department of Energy will provide public access to these results of federally sponsored research in accordance with the DOE Public Access Plan (http://energy.gov/downloads/doe-public-access-plan).

1   Introduction

Many current extreme-scale systems have a deep, complex memory hierarchy composed of heterogeneous memories including DRAM and high-performance graphics DRAM. The memory hierarchy is becoming deeper with the inclusion of HBM and NVRAM in many current and soon to be deployed systems. With this trend of a deeper and more complex memory hierarchy continuing into the exascale era, it is important that users are able to achieve high-performance from each system executing their scientific or analytic applications.

Currently, for each memory and device in the system, there exists API calls and libraries capable of allocating data objects on their particular memories. These include libraries such as malloc in libc for DRAM, CudaMalloc in the CUDA library for HBM memory on Graphical Processing Units (GPUs), and the PMEM library for allocating memory on NVRAM. However, for each of these memories, the libraries are not knowledgeable of the other libraries in the system, which can create challenges for users who are attempting to obtain locality and affinity with their memory allocations.

These challenges and the deepening of the memory hierarchy have caused many in industry and the research community to develop new memory allocators capable of efficiently allocating memory on the newly included memories, such as the *memkind* allocator [3]. The memkind allocator is capable of allocating memory on both DRAM and HBM (i.e., MCDRAM on Intel KNL) and presents itself to the user as an extensible interface, which can support future heterogeneous memories. However, applications making use of *memkind* are not portable between systems as the allocations of data objects are completed in an explicit manner, which requires systems to have both identical memories and affinities between devices and memories.

To alleviate the *User* from needing architectural knowledge of the machine, with respect to allocating memory, the *User*'s intent could be captured and interpreted to perform the proper memory allocation. Capturing *User* intent is a challenging task. The question that needs to be answered is: *How do we abstract the system architecture from the user while still providing accurate memory allocations?* Abstracting the system while forcing the *User* to know latency and bandwidth characteristics of the underlying memory accomplishes little unless these are used as thresholds for acceptable performance.

This paper presents a higher-level approach to solving this challenge with the UMA of the SharP library [14]. The UMA is a unified memory allocator abstracting the memories of the system and the allocators for those memories. This is achieved through an internal, extensible interface that utilizes the excellent memory allocators for memories such as DRAM, HBM, and NVRAM including the memkind, CudaMalloc, and PMEM allocators. This allows the user to leverage existing allocators while having SharP coordinate memory allocations and provide data locality and affinity for the *User*.

The allocator is presented to the *User* through a single interface that abstracts the memories from the *User* such that the *User* can perform memory allocations with high-level *Hints* and *Constraints* that describe the user's intent, enabling intent-based memory allocations. In addition to high-level *Hints* and *Constraints*, users with expert knowledge of the system may explicitly declare the memory their data is to be allocated on as a constraint to the SharP UMA.

This work makes the following contributions:

- We classify and design higher-level abstractions for *Users* to perform memory allocations on multiple memory types in the system while enabling data locality and affinity, which will reduce data movement.
- We design and implement the SharP UMA based on these higher-level abstractions and demonstrate their ease of use by extending both Open MPI and OpenSHMEM-X [1] to make use of this memory allocator.
- We demonstrate the effectiveness of this allocator with synthetic micro-benchmarks on multiple systems, demonstrating the portability of the approach, as well as porting the Graph500 benchmark to make use of our extended Open MPI and OpenSHMEM-X.

2   Related Work

There are two main areas of research related to this work. The first is the area of memory allocation, which has been thoroughly studied over many years for both single node and distributed allocations. The second area focuses on programming models that also use similar abstractions to provide portable memory allocation across various memories within the system. We will first discuss the area of memory allocators and then the abstractions enabling portable memory allocations and memory usage.

There have been many memory allocators developed over the past several years focused on providing simple interfaces for users to allocate memory. The majority of the earlier memory allocators such as Doug Lea's dlmalloc [11], GNU's malloc (ptmalloc) [8], Jason Evans' malloc (jemalloc) [6], and others [2]. In each of these allocators, the primary focus is on allocation performance and the reduction of fragmentation, as well as the elimination of false-sharing, through interfaces that leveraged arenas or thread specific memory pools inside their implementations. This allowed for thread-based allocations that remained lock-free resulting in higher-performance within the critical paths of execution and a reduction in false-sharing. Because of jemalloc's ability to perform fast allocations, it has been leveraged by other allocators such as the memkind [3] and PMEM memory allocators [9]. The memkind allocator is an extensible memory allocator that is designed to provide memory allocations on DRAM and HBM for the Intel Xeon Phi Knights Landing. It accomplishes this by providing interfaces for the user to create allocators for each memory kind in the system. If there are memories other than DRAM and HBM, the user must manually implement the underlying functionality for those memories. The PMEM memory allocator focuses specifically on persistent memory and provides multiple methods of allocating on these memories including: (i) memory-mapping a file in NVRAM and using jemalloc to provide memory allocations of that memory, (ii) treating the memory as a data object allowing the user to modify the object as they see fit throughout execution, and (iii) giving the user a direct interface to treat the memory as if its virtual scratch memory with jemalloc.

With respect to abstracting the memories of the system and allowing a user to allocate memory in a portable fashion, there are multiple works focused on these areas including UNITY [10] and kokkos [5]. UNITY is a library that abstracts the memories of the system from the user allowing the user to consider only their data structures. The abstraction is done so the data objects allocated by the user are placed in memory and moved automatically based on usage and need. Kokkos similarly handles data placement for the user based on "traits" of memory, which are declared by the user in order to allocate memory appropriately.

Based on these works, the SharP UMA is different from the above works by not only abstracting the memories of the system like UNITY and kokkos, but also allow the user the place data in memories based on their intent. More clearly, the user can implicitly and explicitly allocate memory using the SharP UMA as well as being able to optimize their algorithms and data placement beyond the capabilities that are provided by our library.

3   Capturing User Intent

Many of the current extreme-scale systems are composed of CPUs, compute accelerators, and high-performing NICs. These architectures, while delivering high-performance, are often dissimilar to other systems with different affinities between devices, memories present, etc. With these differing architectures, it is difficult for research scientists to produce high-performing, portable implementations of their scientific algorithms because the implementation will have to be optimized for each system. With the increasing complexity of the memory hierarchy, the changes necessary to optimize an application will grow.

Capturing the user's intent could serve to lessen the changes required for an application moving from system to system and increase productivity for the application developer. The challenge of capturing user intent is determining the required granularity to provide a sufficient amount of performance portability. While the performance characteristics and programming of particular accelerators may require changes to an application when not using programming models such as OpenMP or OpenACC, we argue that users should not need to modify their application when moving from system to system due to architectural differences with respect to affinities and memory types. This is especially true as we move to systems with an increased heterogeneity of devices.

In general, there are two levels of granularity that could be used to capture user-intent. These levels include (i) lower-level characteristics and (ii) higher-level generalizations of the components of the system.

For (i), the lower-level characteristics of the memories used for the storage of data objects may include performance characteristics or device traits. This can be demonstrated by having the user specify that a particular data object should be allocated on a memory with a particular access latency or bandwidth. However, this requires the user to have a relatively high understanding of the memory technologies available in the system. Additionally, using specific constraints on the latency and bandwidth of memories makes the assumption that memory technologies and their performance will be relatively static. Improving the latency and bandwidth characteristics of memory types could cause previously assumed values to be incorrect, resulting in an incorrectly behaving application or a failure at runtime.

In (ii), a higher-level granularity further abstracts the system allowing the user to know little about the underlying memory other than its general properties. For example, the user may wish to use HBM on a GPU for their computation, but not know the specific latency and bandwidth measurements of the HBM. By using a high-level hint, the user would still be able to ensure an allocation on the proper memory. However, high-level abstractions of the memory types can produce incorrect results without the coupling of multiple hints to help describe affinities to devices or other memory types that may be used. Using the same example of HBM on a GPU, the user can specify that they wish to allocate memory on the GPU that is also close to the executing Processing Element (PE) by combining hints (i.e., a hint for HBM and locality to the PE).

4   SharP Unified Memory Allocator

Based on the discussion in Sect. 3 and to support the emerging architectures in extreme-scale systems while providing high-performance and portability, we have designed an interface to make use of high-level *Hints* and *Constraints* to capture user intent while providing support for memory allocations on various memories including DRAM, HBM, and NVRAM. In this section, we will discuss both the capturing of user intent by our unified interface as well as the mapping from the intent to the underlying allocators.

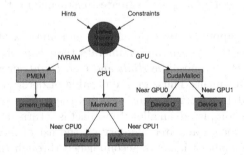

Fig. 1. Memory allocation with the SharP UMA.

4.1   Unified Memory Allocator's Interface

To provide a useful interface for the *User*, both the system and the allocators used for the system are abstracted. This abstraction is accomplished by capturing user intent at a high-level with *Hints* and *Constraints* and mapping these correctly to the memories that will use them. To abstract the system and represent many possible intents the user may have, we provide several *Hints* specific to areas such as data (i) usage, (ii) accessibility, and (iii) resilience.

1. **Usage:** To capture user intent for data usage, we provide various hints related to usage based on computation. This includes computation on the *Central Processing Unit* (CPU) and compute accelerators such as GPUs. In addition, locality is another aspect of usage that may be described such as allocation of data objects near the PE and near the NIC.
2. **Accessibility:** While providing usage hints allows us to narrow a mapping of intent to a memory, it does not complete it. Coupling usage with accessibility, which describes the properties of the memory with respect to its accessibility by PEs within a job, we are capable of better defining a mapping. Examples of accessibility include memories that are accessible only within a node, between nodes, and across jobs.
3. **Resilience:** Resilience is captured from the user and their intent based on persistence. This allows the user to declare specific data objects need to be allocated such that the data objects can persist through catastrophic failures.

The list of hints and constraints can be used individually, where a single hint is satisfactory for an accurate description of usage, access, or resilience, or the user can compose the hints and form more complex descriptions. For example, describing the level of resilience provided may be difficult for users. While only persistence may be used to describe the users intent, memory placement is important. For instance, if the user wished to describe that memory should be persistent but backed by the parallel filesystem rather than NVRAM, then the persistence hint is not satisfactory. However, when adding access hints, as the parallel filesystem will be accessible between jobs, it can be used for persistent data objects. This mapping is the greatest challenge for this type of unified interface.

To support the mapping between memories and hints, we first abstract the physical memories of the system and enumerate their capabilities to be stored internally. We similarly compose the *Hints* and *Constraints* provided by the user into an enumerated element. Thus, we are capable of determining mapping by creating a list of matching enumerations between the memories and user intent. After the mapping is completed, an allocator object is returned to the user, which allows the user to allocate and free memory on the list of memories satisfying their request. Explicit allocations are accomplished through the same interface with explicit *Hints* (e.g., HINT_DRAM0, HINT_HBM0, HINT_HBM1, etc.).

The resulting interface can be seen in Listing 1.1 and a demonstration of memory allocation with the SharP UMA in Fig. 1.

```
typedef struct sharp_allocator_info_params {
    sharp_hint_t        allocator_hints;
    sharp_constraints_t allocator_constraints;
} sharp_allocator_info_params_t;

sharp_allocator_obj_t * sharp_allocator_init_obj(sharp_allocator_info_params_t * params);

void * sharp_allocator_alloc(sharp_allocator_obj_t * allocator, size_t size);

void * sharp_allocator_alloc_memalign(sharp_allocator_obj_t * allocator,
                                      size_t size,
                                      int alignment);

int sharp_allocator_free(sharp_allocator_obj_t * allocator, void * buffer);
```

Listing 1.1: Intent-based Interface for SharP's UMA

5 Extending Existing Programming Model Implementations

To demonstrate the ease of leveraging SharP for allocating memory, we have extended two popular programming model implementations: (i) Open MPI and (ii) OpenSHMEM-X. In both cases, we extended the implementation to provide the functionality of SharP to the *User*. However, in the case of OpenSHMEM, the programming model, rather than just the implementation, had to be extended to support the memory allocator. In this section, we will describe the modifications we made to support SharP in both Open MPI and OpenSHMEM-X.

5.1 Extending Open MPI

In an effort to demonstrate the utility of the SharP UMA, we extended the Open MPI implementation to support intent-based memory allocations on hierarchical and heterogeneous memories. To do this, we leveraged the MPI_Alloc_mem functionality available in the Message Passing Interface (MPI) specification. From the specification, MPI_Alloc_mem allocates memory for the user with an effort in allocating efficient memory for *Remote Direct Memory Access* (RDMA) operations [7]. This allows the user to allocate data objects on memories regardless of whether the usage is purely local (i.e., local computation) or remote (i.e., point-to-point and one-sided communication).

To extend the functionality of MPI_Alloc_mem to support the SharP UMA, we made use of its *info objects*. The info object in MPI is an object containing key-value pairs, which are parsed by functions like MPI_Alloc_mem with the information contained in the object being used to provide extra functionality. This allowed us to extend the function to support the *Hints* and *Constraints* mentioned in Sect. 3. This allows Open MPI to allocate data objects based on user intent across heterogeneous memories.

Unfortunately, the interface for the SharP UMA will generate an allocator object based on the user's *Hints* and *Constraints*. This presents a challenge as only Open MPI will have access to the object, which means each call to MPI_Alloc_mem will generate a new allocator object and can increase overhead if placed in critical sections. In order to reduce this overhead, we added a caching mechanism that caches the most recent allocator objects for future memory allocations. This reduces the overhead as allocator objects only need to be generated if the *Hints* and *Constraints* change between allocations.

Freeing allocated memory is accomplished by making use of `MPI_Free_mem`, which only takes in a pointer to an allocated data object. In order to correctly free the memory, we keep track of allocated memories in a list that is traversed to determine if the memory is from SharP. If it is, then SharP will free the memory.

5.2   Extending OpenSHMEM-X

Unlike the extension of Open MPI, which leveraged interfaces already present in the MPI specification, OpenSHMEM uses a different memory model. In OpenSHMEM, memory is allocated on DRAM in the symmetric heap, which is a memory heap where all PEs allocate data objects with a symmetric address. This means, new interfaces must be created such that OpenSHMEM may support the heterogeneous memories present in many extreme-scale systems.

To provide the necessary support in OpenSHMEM, we created a set of new interfaces that both create a heap on a particular memory and allow future symmetric memory allocations on these memories. For simplicity, the addressing in these generated heaps are asymmetric. The new interfaces are as follows:

- `shmemx_hhm_create`: Creates a new heterogeneous memory region for future memory allocations. This interface takes the *Hints* and *Constraints* from the user along with a size parameter defining how large the heap should be. This will generate an allocator object, which is stored internally and associated with the memory region, which we refer to as a partition similar to Cray SHMEM [12].
- `shmemx_partition_malloc`: Allocates memory on the newly created partition, which interfaces with the allocator object from the SharP UMA. There are similar allocation interfaces for `realloc`, aligned memory allocations, and freeing memory, and, for brevity, they are not listed here.

6   Experimental Evaluation

To evaluate this work, we will validate both the performance characteristics of the allocator and the correctness of the allocator's ability to provide intent-based allocations. To show the performance characteristics of the allocator, we will only measure the overhead of performing allocations as the allocator's ability to handle fragmentation and other characteristics are already known as the SharP UMA is leveraging known allocators. To validate the correctness, we make use of micro-benchmarks to measure the bandwidth and message rate of one-sided *Put* operations. We also study the overhead of using the extended programming model implementations from Sect. 5 with applications by porting and evaluating the Graph500 benchmark.

The testbeds we used for the evaluation include multiple systems at ORNL and the *Oak Ridge Leadership Computing Facility* (OLCF). These include Turing, a small 16 node cluster comprised of two Intel Xeon processors, 128 GB of RAM, and a ConnectX-4 EDR interconnect per node, and Rhea, a 512 node cluster similarly comprised of two Intel Xeon processors, 128 GB of RAM, and a Connect-X 3 FDR interconnect per node. These two systems are very similar in composition but have separate affinities with respect to the NIC, which should give us a good understanding of the ability of intent-based memory allocation.

6.1 Performance

To determine the overhead of the SharP UMA interface for both Open MPI and OpenSHMEM-X, we will perform a series of memory allocations and frees with 70% of the operations being allocations and 30% being free operations. This is completed on increasing sizes of allocations from 8 byte allocations up to 2 MB huge page allocations with the evaluation of each size being comprised of 20,000 operations. For this benchmark, we made use of the Turing cluster. The results of this benchmark can be seen in Fig. 2.

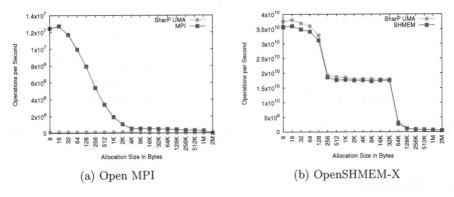

(a) Open MPI   (b) OpenSHMEM-X

Fig. 2. Memory allocations and frees using the extended (a) Open MPI and (b) OpenSHMEM-X versions with the SharP UMA with 70% of operations being memory allocations. Higher is better.

The results for both the extended Open MPI and OpenSHMEM-X versions were as expected. For Open MPI, the performance of the extension with SharP UMA is very poor due to the constant checking of *Hints* and *Constraints* to determine if an appropriate allocator object has been created yet. However, the average time per memory allocation of a page size (i.e., 4 KB) and lower is roughly 7 μs, which means the extension is still useful so long as it used outside of critical paths. On the other hand, the extension of OpenSHMEM-X is more favorable with many allocation times being within 5% of the unmodified shmem_malloc timings. This is because the extension for OpenSHMEM-X does not require a check to determine if a new allocator object needs to be created. Instead, memory can be allocated from an already allocated pool.

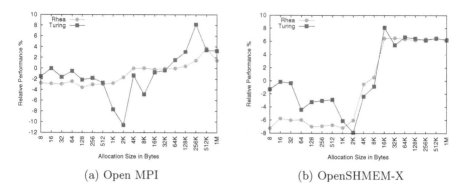

(a) Open MPI   (b) OpenSHMEM-X

Fig. 3. Bandwidth results on two systems with differing affinities to the NIC. Higher is better.

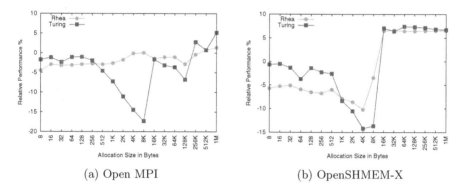

(a) Open MPI   (b) OpenSHMEM-X

Fig. 4. Message rate results on two systems with differing affinities to the NIC. Higher is better.

6.2   Correctness

To validate the correctness, we will perform a series of micro-benchmarks in which we measure the bandwidth and message rate of *Put* operations on two systems, Rhea and Turing, which have different affinities between DRAM and the NIC. Thus, if we attempted to allocate memory near the NIC on one system using the SharP UMA, then we would expect for the memory to be allocated near the NIC on the other system without any code changes as the memory should be allocated based on user intent.

For bandwidth and message rate, we increased the message size from 8 bytes to 1 MB with 10,000 operations being completed for each message size. For the evaluation of each size, we took the median result. For both systems and both Open MPI and OpenSHMEM-X, the Unified Communication X (UCX) communication library [13] was used with short messages used for message sizes up to 128 bytes, buffered messages used for sizes between 128 bytes and 8 KB, and zero-copy used afterwards. The relative results for each test can be seen in Figs. 3

and 4. In both, the relative performance is normalized based on memory allocated near the calling PE with both communicating PEs being located without affinity to the NIC. This particular configuration was chosen as PEs without affinity to the NIC suffer from lower network performance than PEs near the NIC.

As expected, the relative results for both systems under test follow a similar path, with an increased amount of similarity when messages are large enough to make use of zero-copy. For Open MPI, the similarity is less pronounced as the overhead of buffered messages is quite large on the Turing cluster as compared to the Rhea cluster. This suggests that as applications move large amounts of data, the allocation of memory near the NIC is beneficial for PEs without affinity to the NIC.

6.3   Graph500

For the Graph500 benchmark, we made use of the one-sided MPI implementation and the OpenSHMEM adaptation [4]. In each, we modified the implementations to make use of the interfaces described in Sect. 5 and allocate memory near the PE and near the NIC. We used a scale of 16 and evaluated the strong scaling of the application up to 256 PEs on the Turing cluster. The relative results can be seen in Fig. 5, with the results normalized based on memory allocated near the PE.

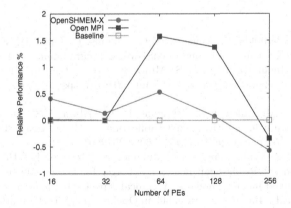

Fig. 5. Results of the Graph500 benchmark with results normalized based on memory allocated near the calling PE. Higher is better.

The results of this evaluation are relatively similar showing no significant improvement in performance by allocating memory near the NIC. However, the takeaway from these results is that we can now allocate the data objects used in Graph500 across any memory with affinities to different devices. In addition, the overhead of the allocator for Open MPI does not significantly impact the performance of the application, which is promising.

7 Conclusion

In this paper, we presented the SharP UMA, an intent-based memory allocator with a unified interface for allocating memory across DRAM, HBM, and NVRAM. We presented the interface of the SharP UMA in Sect. 4 and demonstrated its simplicity by extending well known programming model implementations, Open MPI and OpenSHMEM-X, to support the SharP UMA in Sect. 5. Additionally, we validated this work through an evaluation that examined the performance implications of the intent-based allocator and the correctness of the allocator while moving from system to system. We found the SharP UMA provides minimal overhead in OpenSHMEM-X, but does provide overhead for allocations of memory in Open MPI, which can be mitigated by not placing memory allocations in critical sections. We also showed the movement of our microbenchmarks between systems with differing device affinities without recompilation produced similar results, demonstrating the correctness of our implementation. In addition, we ported the Graph500 benchmark to make use of the extensions we made to Open MPI and OpenSHMEM-X and found relatively similar performance while having greater control of the allocated memory.

Acknowledgment. This research used resources of the Oak Ridge Leadership Computing Facility, which is a DOE Office of Science User Facility supported under Contract DE-AC05-00OR22725.

References

1. Baker, M., Aderholdt, F., Venkata, M.G., Shamis, P.: OpenSHMEM-UCX: evaluation of UCX for implementing openSHMEM programming model. In: Gorentla Venkata, M., Imam, N., Pophale, S., Mintz, T.M. (eds.) OpenSHMEM 2016. LNCS, vol. 10007, pp. 114–130. Springer, Cham (2016). https://doi.org/10.1007/978-3-319-50995-2_8

2. Berger, E.D., McKinley, K.S., Blumofe, R.D., Wilson, P.R.: Hoard: a scalable memory allocator for multithreaded applications. SIGPLAN Not. **35**(11), 117–128 (2000). http://doi.acm.org/10.1145/356989.357000

3. Cantalupo, C., Venkatesan, V., Hammond, J., Czurlyo, K., Hammond, S.D.: Memkind: an extensible heap memory manager for heterogeneous memory platforms and mixed memory policies. Technical report, March 2015

4. D'Azevedo, E.F., Imam, N.: Graph 500 in OpenSHMEM. In: Gorentla Venkata, M., Shamis, P., Imam, N., Lopez, M.G. (eds.) OpenSHMEM 2014. LNCS, vol. 9397, pp. 154–163. Springer, Cham (2015). https://doi.org/10.1007/978-3-319-26428-8_10

5. Edwards, H.C., Trott, C.R., Sunderland, D.: Kokkos: enabling many-core performance portability through polymorphic memory access patterns. J. Parallel Distrib. Comput. **74**(12), 3202–3216 (2014). Domain-Specific Languages and High-Level Frameworks for High-Performance Computing. http://www.sciencedirect.com/science/article/pii/S0743731514001257

6. Evans, J.: A scalable concurrent malloc (3) implementation for FreeBSD. In: Proceedings of the BSDCan Conference, Ottawa, Canada (2006)

7. Forum, M.P.: MPI: a message-passing interface standard. Technical report, Knoxville, TN, USA (1994)

8. Gloger, W.: Wolfram Gloger's malloc homepage. http://www.malloc.de/en
9. Intel: Intel NVM library. http://pmem.io/nvml/libpmem
10. Jones, T., et al.: Unity: unified memory and file space. In: Proceedings of the 7th International Workshop on Runtime and Operating Systems for Supercomputers ROSS 2017, pp. 6:1–6:8, ACM, New York (2017). http://doi.acm.org/10.1145/3095770.3095776
11. Lea, D., Gloger, W.: A memory allocator (1996)
12. Namashivayam, N., et al.: Symmetric memory partitions in openSHMEM: a case study with intel KNL. In: Gorentla Venkata, M., Imam, N., Pophale, S. (eds.) OpenSHMEM 2017. LNCS, vol. 10679, pp. 3–18. Springer, Cham (2018). https://doi.org/10.1007/978-3-319-73814-7_1
13. ORNL: UCX: Unified Communication X (2015). http://www.openucx.org
14. Venkata, M.G., Aderholdt, F., Parchman, Z.W.: Sharp: towards programming extreme-scale systems with hierarchical and heterogeneous memory. In: Proceedings of the 6th International Workshop on Heterogeneous and Unconventional Cluster Architectures and Applications, August 2017

Multi-granularity Locking in Hierarchies with Synergistic Hierarchical and Fine-Grained Locks

K. Ganesh, Saurabh Kalikar[(⊠)], and Rupesh Nasre

CSE, IIT Madras, Chennai, India
{cs16m006,saurabhk,rupesh}@cse.iitm.ac.in

Abstract. We propose a new locking mechanism for hierarchies wherein the locking requests can be a combination of coarse and fine. Existing protocols such as multiple-granularity locking (MGL) are efficient when all the requests are of the same granularity. MGL is either too coarse or too fine-grained when multiple threads request for various parts of the hierarchy with differing granularity requirements. Simultaneous handling of hierarchical and fine-grained requests poses new challenges in checking for racy requests. We propose a novel indexing technique for hierarchies which uniquely identifies every node as an interval value and effectively captures hierarchical dependencies between nodes even when the hierarchy is a tree, DAG or a cycle. Our experiments with real-world XML hierarchies and synthetic benchmarks show that the proposed locking technique provides a higher degree of concurrency with minimal locking cost resulting in overall performance improvement.

1 Introduction

One of the main challenges in developing a multi-threaded parallel application is the design of an efficient synchronization mechanism for shared data structures. *Lock* constructs are widely used for thread synchronization. The nature of data structures and their associated operations necessitate the use of various locking protocols. In the context of shared data structures, *hierarchies* are special linked structures, where each child node denotes a specialization or a part of its parents. For instance, a node representing a *department* in an academic hierarchy is a part of its parent *institute*. Conversely, a node representing an *institute* contains all its *departments*. In the concurrent setting, operating on different nodes in such a hierarchy is achieved using traditional fine-grained locking, which maintains a lock with each node. While fine-grained locks ensure consistency of the data structure, it also poses scalability challenges in the presence of a large number of threads and unpredictable locking request pattern. For instance, in fine-grained locking, an operation such as *calculate GPA for all the students in department*

M. Aldinucci et al. (Eds.): Euro-Par 2018, LNCS 11014, pp. 546–559, 2018.
https://doi.org/10.1007/978-3-319-96983-1_39

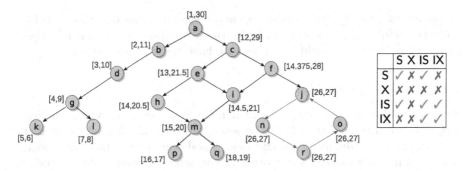

Fig. 1. (a) Example hierarchy along with its HiFi numbering (b) Compatibility matrix for intention locking protocol

CS needs to acquire a lock on *each student* separately. This is clearly inefficient and happens because locking cost is proportional to the number of students.

In this example, it seems logical to acquire a single lock on the department CS, and process all the student records. This is achieved using hierarchical locking or multi-granularity locking. Multi-granularity locking (MGL) protocols [7,9] ensure that if a node in a hierarchy (say, CS department) is locked, then every node reachable from the locked node (i.e., every student, faculty and staff member) is also implicitly locked.

On the other hand, there exist several operations that do not require hierarchical locks. For instance, a fine-grained operation such as *update class-room-count = 20 where department = CS* does not need the whole department (students, staff, faculty) to get locked. Existing approaches do not support co-existence of hierarchical and fine-grained locks. Thus, all the MGL locks are either purely hierarchical (e.g., even to update number of classrooms), or purely fine-grained (e.g., even to update GPA of all the students). The former is too conservative leading to reduced concurrency, while the latter is too precise leading to locking overheads.

To address these issues, this paper makes the following contributions:

1. We propose a novel indexing technique which allows quick checking of overlaps between two thread requests in a hierarchy. The indexing has useful properties which can be independently exploited for other applications.
2. We propose HiFi, a locking protocol that allows synergistic co-existence of fine-grained and hierarchical locks. The protocol crucially relies on the new indexing mechanism and offers more concurrency.
3. We illustrate that HiFi considerably improves the parallel performance of the underlying application. Using real-world XML hierarchies and synthetic datasets, we identify scenarios where HiFi is a better choice for locking.

2   Background and Motivation

In this section, we provide a brief background on a *de facto* hierarchical locking technique and highlight its limitations. To motivate HiFi, we use the example hierarchy from Fig. 1 which contains 18 nodes spread across six levels. The hierarchy is carefully crafted to contain paths, tree-like substructure, as well as DAGs and a cycle. Most real-world hierarchies we have come across are acyclic.

2.1   Hierarchical Locking

Hierarchical locking is a way to lock a node in a hierarchy which implicitly locks its descendants. This is useful because the whole sub-hierarchy rooted at a node can be protected using a single lock. A node could be hierarchically locked only if (i) it is not locked by any other thread, and (ii) none of its descendants are currently locked by any other thread, and (iii) none of its ancestors are currently locked by any other thread. For instance, in Fig. 1, hierarchical locking of node g requires that no other thread currently holds locks on (i) g itself, (ii) its descendant nodes k and l, and (iii) its ancestors a, b, and d. Clearly, the naïve mechanism of traversing through the descendants and ancestors for *every lock request* works, but is impractical. In practice, database management systems such as MySQL use an optimized traversal technique called *intention locking*.

Intention Locks. Traditionally, hierarchical locking is implemented using *intention locks* [7]. Unlike traversing sub-hierarchies, intention locking technique *marks* all the ancestors of the targeted node before acquiring a hierarchical lock. These markers serve as indicators to other concurrent threads, that there exists a node along this path on which a lock has been acquired. These markers are nothing but the intention locking modes, i.e., IS and IX of conventional *shared* (S) and *exclusive* (X) locks respectively. Thus, before locking any node in S or X mode, a thread has to lock all the ancestors (i.e., all the reference paths from root) in IS or IX modes respectively. For example, before locking node g in X mode, a thread must lock its ancestor nodes a, b and d in IX mode. Possible locking modes and their inter-operability are shown in the compatibility matrix 1. Intention locks is an effective way to achieve hierarchical locking for tree structures, as each tree node has a single reference path from the root. However, in case of directed graph structures (such as DAGs), a node may have multiple reference paths from the root necessitating intention locking across *each* reference path. For instance, for locking node i, we need to traverse the hierarchy to mark intention along each path a-c-e and a-c-f. For a large real-world hierarchy, such a traversal is costly, and increases the thread waiting time. In summary, intention locks are ill-suited for complex hierarchical structures.

Motivating Example. Consider a thread T_1 currently holding a hierarchical lock on node g for *exclusive access* and another thread T_2 which wants to perform a simple fine-grained update operation on node d. Intuitively, such a concurrent operation seems plausible. However, intention locking (IL) protocol does not support it, as MGLs support only hierarchical locking. Thus, locking node d using IL protocol also locks g. IL can be extended to support extra modes for fine-grained (shared and exclusive) locking. Thus, in this extension, a thread would also mark along the path whether it wants to lock the target node in fine-grained mode or hierarchical mode. Unfortunately, such an extension takes away the very benefits of fine-grained locking – although the update is local (fine-grained), the thread needs to traverse the hierarchy of ancestors. This poses several scalability challenges when both hierarchical and fine-grained locking modes are desired. To address this, we need a mechanism that (i) supports efficient co-existence of fine-grained and hierarchical locks, and (ii) allows quick checking of overlap between two lock requests (e.g., whether a node is already locked in a fine-grained manner within a sub-hierarchy which is to be locked in hierarchical mode).

In this paper, we propose a new locking protocol which supports efficient handling of fine-grained locks in presence of hierarchical (MGL) locks.

3   Our Proposal: HiFi

We design a new protocol that allows maximum concurrency; that is, if two lock requests do not overlap, they can be executed in parallel (assuming the availability of enough computing resources). Central to our method is a new interval numbering technique which converts the structural overlap between sub-hierarchies to interval overlap between numbers, which allows fast overlap check, retaining the benefits of fine-grained locking.

Overview. Our proposed numbering is shown for the example hierarchy in Fig. 1. Each node is assigned an interval [low, high] where low and high are floating-point numbers. The numbering of nodes in a hierarchy follows the following invariants:

$\mathcal{I}1$ The interval of each node is unique if the node is not part of a cycle. All the nodes in a cycle have the same interval.
$\mathcal{I}2$ The interval of every ancestor *strictly subsumes* the interval of each of its (transitive) descendants. Interval [a, b] *strictly subsumes* interval [c, d] iff $a < c$ and $b > d$.
$\mathcal{I}3$ Intervals of two nodes partially overlap if they have a common descendant.

For instance, in Fig. 1, each node has a unique interval value, except for the cycle nodes j, n, r, o, which all have the same interval [26, 27], validating Invariant $\mathcal{I}1$. Also, interval of node e, which is [13, 21.5], subsumes those of its descendants h, i, m, p, q, validating Invariant $\mathcal{I}2$. The root subsumes the intervals of all other nodes in the hierarchy (except when the root itself is part of a cycle). Similarly, each leaf node has a non-overlapping interval with other leaves. We can observe that nodes h and f have overlapping intervals that do not subsume one another. The overlap is justified by the common descendants m, p, q, thereby validating Invariant $\mathcal{I}3$. Note that although h and f do not subsume one another's intervals, they both individually subsume the intervals of m, p, and q, due to Invariant $\mathcal{I}2$.

Using such an interval numbering, HiFi can quickly check if two hierarchies overlap. Thus, the proposed numbering acts as an alternative to IL. In other words, if there are two *hierarchical* locking requests, HiFi can exploit the proposed numbering mechanism to identify if the two requests can be simultaneously satisfied. For instance, if thread T1 wants to lock the hierarchy rooted at

h, and thread T2 wants to lock the hierarchy rooted at j, then HiFi can check their intervals [14, 20.5] and [26, 27] which do not overlap, and permit access. In contrast, if thread T2 wants to lock the hierarchy rooted at node i, then HiFi can check the intervals [14, 20.5] and [14.5, 21] which overlap, and disallow one of the locking requests (the other thread needs to block or try again later). Note that, unlike in IL, HiFi protocol does not need to traverse the hierarchy to identify overlap. This considerably improves the performance of the underlying application – which usually has locking in its critical path. Once the hierarchy is numbered as a pre-processing step, all runtime locking requests can be quickly served.

3.1   Compatibility in HiFi

Assuming a numbering such as the previous subsection exists, we now describe how fine-grained and hierarchical locks can co-exist in HiFi. Note that the locking request could be shared or exclusive, and fine-grained or hierarchical.

Figure 2 shows the compatibility matrix for various locking scenarios in HiFi. Using this matrix, our locking methodology allows/disallows locking the input set of nodes in the given mode (S/X, fine/hierarchical). For instance, in our running example from Fig. 1, if thread T1 has locked descendant node g in f_x mode, and thread T2 requests node d in H_s mode, then the requests being incompatible according to the matrix, would be denied concurrent access. In contrast, if T1 has locked node g in H_x mode, and T2 requests node d in f_s mode, then the matrix deems these operations compatible with each other for concurrent execution. Compared to the original compatibility matrix from Fig. 1, clearly inter-operability of fine-grained and hierarchical locks allows more concurrent operations.

	Ancestor				Descendant			
	f_s	f_x	H_s	H_x	f_s	f_x	H_s	H_x
f_s	✓	✓	✓	✗	✓	✓	✓	✓
f_x	✓	✓	✗	✗	✓	✓	✓	✓
H_s	✓	✓	✓	✗	✓	✗	✓	✗
H_x	✓	✓	✗	✗	✗	✗	✗	✗

Lock held by (column group header above Ancestor/Descendant). Lock requested (row group label to the left).

Fig. 2. Lock compatibility matrix in HiFi (Legend: H = Hierarchical, f = Fine-grained, s = shared, x = exclusive)

3.2   Numbering Algorithm

We now describe our numbering algorithm in detail. We first attend to cyclic substructures in the hierarchy, if present. Unlike trees and DAGs, the nodes forming cycles in a hierarchy do not have well-defined ancestor-descendant relationship among themselves, that is, every node is an ancestor as well as a descendant of every other node. For instance, nodes j, n, r and o are part of a cycle and each of them is assigned the same interval [26, 27]. Therefore, it is logical to treat all the nodes forming a cycle as one entity, with a single interval value.

Our interval-numbering algorithm has two passes. In the first pass, we perform a conventional depth-first traversal (DFS) from the root node and track pre-visit and post-visit numbers of each node in the hierarchy. The advantage of DFS-based numbering is that the intervals obtained using the pre- and post-visit numbers [pre, post] satisfy *all* the three invariants when the underlying hierarchy is a tree. This can be validated from the left subtree of the root node a in our running example from Fig. 1. Such a numbering, however, does not satisfy the invariants in case of DAGs because DFS does not explore the already visited nodes. Due to this, the numbering may miss out on some descendants, essentially failing to satisfy invariants $I2$ and $I3$.

Meeting the invariants necessitates a bottom-up propagation of [pre, post] intervals from leaf nodes towards the root. Such a propagation re-adjusts the intervals of the ancestors to satisfy all the invariants.

Interval Propagation. Intervals are propagated in bottom-up fashion, therefore the intervals of leaf nodes remain unchanged to [pre, post] intervals according to DFS traversal. According to Invariant $I2$, a node's interval must *strictly* subsume those of all its descendants. Therefore, the smallest *integer* interval which subsumes the interval of the child nodes is assigned to the parent. For instance, with k [5, 6] and l [7, 8] as children, g's interval becomes[4, 9]. Similarly, the intervals of nodes d, b and m become [3, 10], [2, 11] and [15, 20] respectively.

Such a mechanism works well when the sub-hierarchy is a tree. When a node has more than one parent (e.g. node m), the subhierarchy is no longer a tree and it poses interesting challenge to the numbering algorithm. The interval assigned to each parent should be such that (i) it strictly subsumes the children's interval, and (ii) the parent intervals must overlap with each other but not subsume one another. Thus, intervals of nodes h and i must overlap with each other, but not subsume each other; however, they both should subsume m's interval. To satisfy these conditions, we exploit the range of floating point numbers. For instance, we assign intervals [14, 20.5] to h and [14.5, 21] to i which both subsume m's interval [15, 20] and also have partial overlap with each other.

The propagation faces another difficulty due to strict subsumption. Since the intervals of the ancestors are always larger than those of the children, it can happen that an ancestor's interval becomes so big that it subsumes that of another of its sibling! For instance, when i propagates its interval [14.5, 21] to its parent node f, strict subsumption property can assign interval [13, 22] to f. While this does satisfy Invariant $I2$ between i and f, it also falsely satisfies the invariant between h and f ([13, 22] subsumes [14, 20.5]). Note that f is not an ancestor of h, and hence their intervals should not subsume each other. This necessitates *limiting* the interval propagation to parents (as explained next).

Maintenance of Locks. To check if the new locking request overlaps with an existing one, HiFi needs to track the currently locked nodes (along with their type S/ X and fine-grained / hierarchical). We use the lock-pool imple-

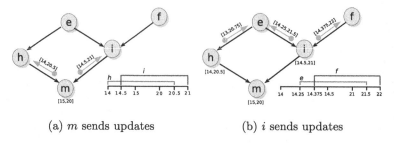

(a) m sends updates   (b) i sends updates

Fig. 3. Example of interval propagation

Algorithm 1. Bottom-up traversal (invoked with ROOT as the parameter)

```
1 Function bottomUp(root):
2     if root.isLeafNode() then  root.lowLimit = root.upLimit = −1  ;
3     else
4         forall the  c ∈ root.children do
5             if c.explored == false then  bottomUp(c);
6         root.mergeIntervals()
7     sendPartitionLimits(root.lowLimit, root.upLimit, root)
8     root.explored = true
```

---

mentation from DomLock [9], which maintains per-thread lock information in
a table. A thread needs to check the complete table before inserting its entry,
which requires heavy synchronization. To counter this inefficiency, the lock-pool
exploits sequence locks to make the reading synchronization-free.

3.3   Main Algorithm

We now present Algorithm 1 for interval numbering and explain it using our running example. After the first phase of DFS pre-post visit numbering for the leaf
nodes, we call Algorithm 1 with the root of the hierarchy as a parameter. Algorithm recursively traverses down to the leaf nodes and starts back-propagation
of intervals to respective parents (line 2). We use two flags lowLimit and upLimit
to indicate the restrictions placed on the interval updates that a node can send
to its parent(s). For instance, starting from the root node a in Fig. 1, the algorithm recursively descends to the leaf node k and assigns default limit of -1.
Node k with interval $[5, 6]$ invokes the method **sendPartitionLimits** to propagate the limits upward (line 7). The function **sendPartitionLimits** is presented
in Algorithm 2. It partitions an interval into np (number of parents) partially
overlapping intervals, each of which strictly subsumes the child's interval and is
within the range of lowLimit and upLimit. Thus, Algorithm 2 ensures that the
interval updates sent to the parents conform to the invariants $\mathcal{I}1 - \mathcal{I}3$.

For instance, When k invokes the method to partition and update its parents,
Case 1 (line 2) of the method is invoked. It sends the intervals $[4, 7]$ to g.

Similarly, g receives the interval [6, 9] from l, which is merged along with k's update to g (Algorithm 1, line 6), expanding g's interval to [4, 9]. Similarly, node m, as seen previously, has the default limits of -1 (line 2), and therefore splits the range [14, 21] among its parents. In this case, the offsets for the limit partitioning Δ_l and Δ_h are set to $\frac{1}{2}$ since m has two parents (line 5). As illustrated in Fig. 3a, the interval [14, 20.5] is updated to h while the interval [14.5, 21] is sent to i (lines 20–25). With the interval updates, m also sends the relevant upper and lower limits to its parents for interval expansion, to be used while they further propagate intervals towards the root of the hierarchy. In case of node i, it receives interval [14.5, 21] along with a lower limit of 14, and no upper limit from its child node m (Case 3, line 10). This indicates to i that the interval updates it sends to its parents must be bounded within the range [14.25, 22]. As illustrated in Fig. 3b, node i splits the interval [14.25, 22] into two equal partitions. Note that in this case Δ_l and Δ_h are $\frac{1}{4}$ and $\frac{1}{2}$ respectively (line 13). Therefore, via i nodes e and f's intervals are updated to [14.25, 21.5] and [14.375, 22] respectively. Node e also merges the interval updates from h and i and assigns the interval [13, 21.5] to itself. The backpropagation of intervals continues until the root receives all the updates.

4   Experimental Evaluation

All our experiments are carried out on an Intel Xeon E5-2640 v4 machine with 40 cores clocked at 2.40 GHz having 64 GB RAM running CentOS 7.4. To assess the effectiveness on real-world data, we use XML hierarchy from Treebank [16]. Further, to check scalability aspects and how HiFi works on various structures, we also use synthetically generated hierarchies. In our synthetic dataset, we generate k-ary trees with a million nodes, and arbitrary graphs with 0.1 million nodes. k-ary trees allow us to assess the effect of HiFi on *bushy* versus *skinny* structures by varying k, while graphs allow us to check for multiple path locking. Our test-driver creates multiple pthreads which operate concurrently on the underlying data structure. We note that the standard deviation in all our results is quite small (about 2%). We compare HiFi against state-of-the-art DomLock [9] and Intention Locking [7], under different values of critical section (CS) size, number of nodes locked, and the density of the hierarchy (k-ary trees). DomLock is an alternative to IL which locks the dominator of the requested nodes, and hence has a constant locking cost. Note that neither of the two protocols support co-existence of fine-grained and hierarchical locks.

4.1   Effect of Number of Nodes

Figure 4 describes the effect of varying locking request size. Figures 4a–c capture the performance of concurrent requests with increasing number of nodes on binary trees, while Figs. 4d–f show the same for arbitrary graphs. IL acquires intention locks on nodes lying on all the paths that lead to the requested set of nodes, while DomLock acquires a single lock on their dominator. With increasing

---

Algorithm 2. Procedure `sendPartitionLimits` to propagate interval limits

---

1 **Function** `sendPartitionLimits`(lowLimit, upLimit, root):
    // np is number of parents of the root node
2   **if** lowLimit $== -1$ AND upLimit $== -1$ **then**
        // Case 1: No Limits on interval expansion on either side
3   **if** np $== 1$ **then**
4   `updateParent`(lowLimit,upLimit,root.l -1,root.h $+1$)
5         $\Delta_l = \frac{1}{np}$; $\Delta_h = \frac{1}{np}$; l' $= root.l - 1$; h' $= root.h + 1$
6   **else if** lowLimit $== -1$ AND upLimit $\neq -1$ **then**
        // Case 2: Limited interval expansion only on right side
7   **if** np $== 1$ **then**
8   `updateParent`(lowLimit,upLimit,root.l -1,$\frac{root.h+upLimit}{2}$)
9         $\Delta_l = \frac{1}{np}$; $\Delta_h = \frac{upLimit-root.h}{2np}$; l' $= root.l - 1$; h' $= \frac{root.h+upLimit}{2}$
10   **else if** lowLimit $\neq -1$ AND upLimit $== -1$ **then**
        // Case 3: Limited interval expansion only on left side
11   **if** np $== 1$ **then**
12   `updateParent`(lowLimit,upLimit,$\frac{root.l+lowLimit}{2}$,root.h $+1$)
13         $\Delta_l = \frac{root.l-lowLimit}{2np}$; $\Delta_h = \frac{1}{np}$; l' $= \frac{root.l+lowLimit}{2}$; h' $= root.h + 1$
14   **else if** lowLimit $\neq -1$ AND upLimit $\neq -1$ **then**
        // Case 4: Limited interval expansion on both sides
15   **if** np $== 1$ **then**
16   `updateParent`(lowLimit,upLimit,$\frac{root.l+lowLimit}{2}$,$\frac{root.h+upLimit}{2}$)
17         $\Delta_l = \frac{root.l-lowLimit}{2np}$; $\Delta_h = \frac{upLimit-root.h}{2np}$;
18   l' $= \frac{root.l+lowLimit}{2}$; h' $= \frac{root.h+upLimit}{2}$
19   **for** i $= 1$ to np AND np $\neq 1$ **do**
20   **if** i $== 1$ **then**
21   `updateParent`(lowLimit,root.h$+2\Delta_h$,l',root.h$+\Delta_h$)
22   **else if** i $== 1$ to np -1 **then**
23   `updateParent`(l' $+(i-2)\Delta_l$,root.h$+(i-1)\Delta_h$,l' $+(i-1)\Delta_l$,root.h$+i$ Δ_h)
24   **else if** i $== np$ **then**
25   `updateParent`(l' $+(np-2)\Delta_l$,upLimit,l' $+(np-1)\Delta_l$,h')

---

locking request size, the cost of marking intention across paths also increases, making IL a less favorable choice until a certain threshold, as shown in Figs. 4a–c. We do not depict IL's performance in case of graphs as it is far worse compared to that of DomLock and HiFi. In comparison, HiFi acquires exactly n_r locks, where n_r is the number of nodes requested. In the cases shown in Figs. 4a, b, d and e HiFi and DomLock perform almost similarly when the number of nodes requested is less than 32, irrespective of the size of the critical section (small and medium here). Beyond a threshold number, the cost of individual fine-grained operations increases, and it is expected that hierarchical locking performs better, which is evident from better performance of DomLock. In summary, HiFi is better suited for operations with fewer node requests.

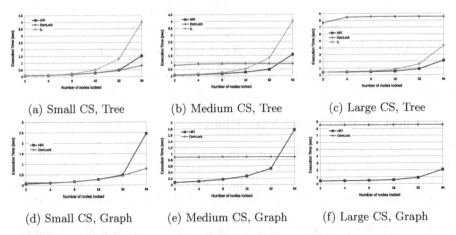

(a) Small CS, Tree   (b) Medium CS, Tree   (c) Large CS, Tree

(d) Small CS, Graph   (e) Medium CS, Graph   (f) Large CS, Graph

Fig. 4. Effect of the number of nodes locked, for varying critical section sizes (small CS = 6 μs, medium CS = 60 μs, large CS = 600 μs)

4.2 Effect of Critical Section Size

Critical section is critical in deciding the overall performance of an application. It can be observed from Fig. 4 that for large critical section (CS) size, the critical section quickly becomes the bottleneck compared to the rest of the processing. Thus, the importance of fine-grained locking is more imperative for large CS. This can be observed from Figs. 4c and f, wherein co-existence of fine-grained and hierarchical locks improves concurrency in case of HiFi. This suggests that HiFi is better suited for large critical sections. Figure 6 indicates that HiFi scales well with increasing the value of k in a k-ary tree.

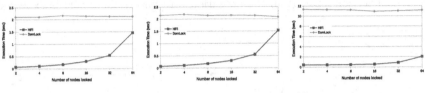

(a) Small critical section   (b) Medium critical section   (c) Large critical section

Fig. 5. Effect of the number of nodes in XML hierarchy, with varying CS size

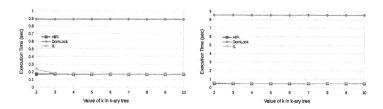

(a) 8 Nodes requested, Medium CS   (b) 8 Nodes requested, Large CS

Fig. 6. Effect of varying k in k-ary trees

4.3   Effect on Real-World XML Hierarchy

XML, since its inception has been used to transfer and store information. Its hierarchical method of organizing data provides us with a real-world use case to verify the effectiveness of our locking protocol. We use a real dataset, Treebank hierarchy, publicly available in XML format [16] as the input hierarchy. The XML hierarchy contains 2,437,666 nodes, over 57% of which are leaf nodes. Over 37% of all the nodes are at a height of one from the leaf nodes, and the maximum out-degree among the non-root nodes is 51. This indicates that the hierarchy is quite bushy towards the bottom. Figure 5 shows the performance of HiFi against DomLock for varying critical section sizes. We observe that HiFi performs consistently better than DomLock. Due to the bushy nature of the hierarchy, the dominator of the requested nodes occurs closer to the root, reducing concurrency in case of DomLock. DomLock acquires a lock on the dominator, in this case the root or a node close to the root, thereby blocking concurrent access to the underlying hierarchy. HiFi, however, acquires locks only on the requested nodes, improving the concurrency. To summarize, HiFi is better suited when the concurrent data structure accessed is irregular and has a large fanout.

4.4   Effect of Variation in Fine-Grain Operations

We now study the behavior of HiFi, DomLock and IL for different percentages of hierarchical versus fine-grained operations. Figure 7 shows the effect for different critical section sizes. If all the operations are fine-grained, HiFi is expected

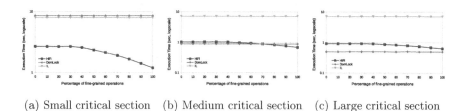

(a) Small critical section   (b) Medium critical section   (c) Large critical section

Fig. 7. Effect of varying the percentage of fine-grained locks

to perform better than IL and DomLock. On the other hand, if all the operations are hierarchical, then HiFi should ideally be comparable to DomLock, as both the approaches avoid traversal using intervals. However, a major difference between HiFi and DomLock is that DomLock acquires a lock on a single dominator node, while HiFi locks each interval separately. Therefore, for hierarchical-only operations, DomLock performs better than HiFi, as shown in Figs. 7a and b. Interestingly, however, for large critical section size (Fig. 7c), HiFi outperforms DomLock. This is primarily because of the imprecise nature of DomLock which internally restricts the degree of concurrency.

In a general case of mixed fine-grained and hierarchical operations, we observe that the performance of HiFi improves as we increase the percentage of fine-grained operations. IL and DomLock are unaffected by the percentage of fine-grained operations as all the operations are treated uniformly as hierarchical operations. We believe that HiFi would offer an attractive alternative for synchronization in hierarchies.

5 Related Work

The idea of MGL was introduced in database systems [7]. Ries and Stonebraker [14,15] report that there are cases where a coarse-grain-only approach may not be desired. In particular, if all the transactions requesting access to the database are randomly requesting small parts of it, then finer granularity is to be preferred. Their work also reported that transactions operating on more than one percent of the database must use few large locks rather than many locks of finer granularity. This indicates the need for co-existence of fine- and coarse-grained locks. Unrau et al. [1] describe a hybrid approach combining properties of both coarse and fine-grained for four types of access behaviors, namely, non-concurrent accesses, concurrent accesses to independent data structures, concurrent read-shared accesses, and concurrent write-shared accesses. Their method uses coarse-grained locks held for short duration to collectively lock multiple data structures, and fine-grained locks should the underlying data be held for longer duration. The method, however, locks one resource only in one type of mode and does not support co-existence. Golan-Gueta et al. [6] proposed automatic fine-grain locking for trees, while Chaudhri et al. [2] proposed locking for DAGs and trees. These methods perform sub-graph traversals to compute lock request intersections thereby giving rise to performance issues when large number of rows are queried. Liu and Zhang [10] presented fine-grain locking for hierarchies based on intention locks by applying fine-grain locks on fields of objects in the hierarchy. The hierarchy under access here is an abstract object graph which is statically constructed to approximate the runtime object graph. This method also suffers from the same issues as IL. Recent advances in automatic lock inferences [3,4,13] for parallel programs also adopted MGL for efficient lock placements. Cherem et al. [3] use static analysis for extracting points-to information of shared objects and apply MGL locking for avoiding deadlocks.

The idea of using logical intervals to capture structural subsumption property for hierarchical locking was originally proposed in DomLock [9]. However, the interval numbering in DomLock does not work with fine-grained locks, let alone together for fine-grained and hierarchical. HiFi proposes a new indexing mechanism to support this. The interval labels assigned unique intervals only to the leaf nodes in the hierarchy, otherwise leaving the internal nodes indistinguishable in case of chain like structures within the hierarchy.

The key-range locking [11,12] and predicate queries in semi-structured databases [5] also use locks as a range of keys in the databases community. In key-range locking, every lock protects the key value of a record as well as the keys which are absent during the transaction. The locks on absent keys restrict the insertion of any phantom record by other parallel transaction. However, the notion and the purpose of our interval locking is quite different from the key-range locking.

6   Conclusion

We proposed HiFi, a new locking protocol that allows simultaneous co-existence of fine-grained and hierarchical locks. The protocol devises a new indexing scheme for hierarchies, which ensures quick identification of concurrent, overlapping lock requests. We illustrated the effectiveness of our approach using real-world XML hierarchies, and the scalability using synthetic datasets of varying complexity. We believe HiFi would pave the way for newer locking protocols in future.

Data Availability Statement and Acknowledgments. We thank all the reviewers whose comments improved the quality of the paper substantially. The work is supported by IIT Madras Grants CSE/13- 14/812/NFIG/RUPS and CSE/13-14/636/NFSC/RUPS and the travel is supported by The Department of CSE, IIT Madras through Kris Gopalakrishnan Endowment – Student Travel Grant.

The datasets generated during and/or analyzed during the current study are available in the Figshare repository: https://doi.org/10.6084/m9.figshare.6390554 [8].

References

1. Unrau, R.C., Krieger, O., Gamsa, B., Stumm, M.: Experiences with locking in a NUMA multiprocessor operating system kernel, November 1994
2. Chaudhri, V.K., Hadzilacos, V.: Safe locking policies for dynamic databases. In: PODS, pp. 233–244. ACM, New York (1995)
3. Cherem, S., Chilimbi, T., Gulwani, S.: Inferring locks for atomic sections. In: Proceedings of the 2008 ACM SIGPLAN Conference on Programming Language Design and Implementation, PLDI 2008 (2008)
4. Emmi, M., Fischer, J.S., Jhala, R., Majumdar, R.: Lock allocation. In: POPL 2007, pp. 291–296. ACM (2007). https://doi.org/10.1145/1190216.1190260
5. Eswaran, K.P., Gray, J.N., Lorie, R.A., Traiger, I.L.: The notions of consistency and predicate locks in a database system. Commun. ACM **19**(11), 624–633 (1976). https://doi.org/10.1145/360363.360369

6. Golan-Gueta, G., Bronson, N., Aiken, A., Ramalingam, G., Sagiv, M., Yahav, E.: Automatic fine-grain locking using shape properties. In: OOPSLA, pp. 225–242. ACM, New York (2011)
7. Gray, J.N., Lorie, R.A., Putzolu, G.R.: Granularity of locks in a shared data base. In: VLDB, pp. 428–451. ACM, New York (1975)
8. Kalikar, S., Nasre, R.: Source code and experiment scripts for HiFi hierarchy locking technique: Euro-Par 2018 artifact (2018). https://doi.org/10.6084/m9.figshare.6390554
9. Kalikar, S., Nasre, R.: DomLock: a new multi-granularity locking technique for hierarchies. ACM Trans. Parallel Comput. 4(2), 7:1–7:29 (2017)
10. Liu, P., Zhang, C.: Unleashing concurrency for irregular data structures. In: ICSE, pp. 480–490. ACM, New York (2014)
11. Lomet, D., Mokbel, M.F.: Locking key ranges with unbundled transaction services. Proc. VLDB Endow. 2(1), 265–276 (2009)
12. Lomet, D.B.: Key range locking strategies for improved concurrency. In: Proceedings of the 19th International Conference on Very Large Data Bases, VLDB 1993, pp. 655–664. Morgan Kaufmann Publishers Inc., San Francisco, CA, USA (1993)
13. McCloskey, B., Zhou, F., Gay, D., Brewer, E.: Autolocker: synchronization inference for atomic sections. In: Conference Record of the 33rd ACM SIGPLAN-SIGACT Symposium on Principles of Programming Languages, POPL 2006, pp. 346–358. ACM, New York (2006). https://doi.org/10.1145/1111037.1111068
14. Ries, D.R., Stonebraker, M.: Effects of locking granularity in a database management system. ACM Trans. Datab. Syst. 2(3), 233–246 (1977)
15. Ries, D.R., Stonebraker, M.R.: Locking granularity revisited. ACM Trans. Datab. Syst. 4(2), 210–227 (1979)
16. Treebank: Xml data repository (2002). http://aiweb.cs.washington.edu/research/projects/xmltk/xmldata/www/repository.html

Efficient Communication/Computation Overlap with MPI+OpenMP Runtimes Collaboration

Marc Sergent[1(✉)], Mario Dagrada[1], Patrick Carribault[2], Julien Jaeger[2(✉)], Marc Pérache[2], and Guillaume Papauré[1]

[1] Atos Bull Technologies, 38130 Echirolles, France
{marc.sergent,mario.dagrada,guillaume.papaure}@atos.net
[2] CEA, DAM, DIF, 91297 Arpajon, France
{patrick.carribault,julien.jaeger,marc.perache}@cea.fr

Abstract. Overlap network communications and computations is a major requirement to ensure scalability of HPC applications on future exascale machines. To this purpose the *de-facto* MPI standard provides non-blocking routines for asynchronous communication progress. In various implementations, a dedicated progress thread (PT) is deployed on the host CPU to actually achieve this overlap. However, current PT solutions struggle to find a balance between efficient detection of network events and minimal impact on the application computations. In this paper we propose a solution inspired from the PT approach which benefits from idle time of compute threads to make MPI communication progress in background. We implement our idea in the context of MPI+OpenMP collaboration using the OpenMP Tools interface which will be part of the OpenMP 5.0 standard. Our solution shows an overall performance gain on unbalanced workloads such as the AMG CORAL benchmark.

Keywords: Parallel computing · Distributed computing · Runtime systems · Runtime collaboration

1 Introduction

The simultaneous use of networking and computing resources by overlapping communications with computations has become a major concern in the High Performance Computing (HPC) domain. This overlap is indeed crucial to achieve scalability on exascale machines [8]. To this purpose, the *de-facto* Message Passing Interface (MPI) standard [14] specifies non-blocking communication routines. They are meant to make network communications progress in background while the application continues its computations on local data.

An example of communication/computation overlap is shown in Fig. 1. In theory, if a process requests to asynchronously receive a piece of data and starts computations, the matching sender process should be able to actually send the data through the network without further intervention from the receiver side.

© Springer International Publishing AG, part of Springer Nature 2018
M. Aldinucci et al. (Eds.): Euro-Par 2018, LNCS 11014, pp. 560–572, 2018.
https://doi.org/10.1007/978-3-319-96983-1_40

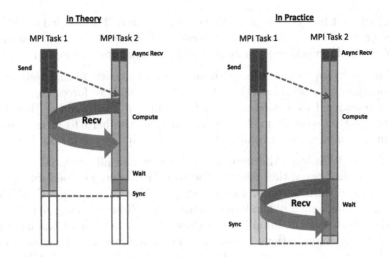

Fig. 1. Example of the communication/computation overlap problem. The left-hand side shows the ideal case of full overlap case whereas the right-hand side presents the practical case with almost no overlap.

In practice, with modern interconnect cards the actual reception occurs only when a call to `MPI_Wait()` or equivalent function is performed, usually at the end of the computation step. This invalidates any communication/computation overlap (right panel of Fig. 1). A common solution to this issue is to dedicate a thread on the host CPU, commonly known as progress thread (PT), to drive MPI communication progress in background.

In this paper we propose a novel PT method to achieve communication/computation overlap in hybrid MPI+X applications. Our method leverages the idle periods of computational threads to progress MPI communications with minimal overhead on the application execution. This is achieved through a collaboration between the thread-based runtime and MPI. We choose the OpenMP (OMP) model to illustrate our contribution. The paper is organized as follows: Section 2 details the asynchronous progress problem in MPI and discusses related work. Section 3 explains our contribution in the context of MPI+OMP applications and an implementation based on the OMP Tools interface (OMPT). Section 4 applies our tool on both a dedicated microbenchmark and on two CORAL proxy applications. Finally Sect. 5 concludes and exposes future work.

2 Related Work

An efficient way to achieve communication/computation overlap with MPI is by asynchronously progressing network communications. This raises two issues: (i) the actual progression of communications, and (ii) the completion detection. As discussed in [5], the MPI-2 standard only defines how the implementation should address the completion of non-blocking communications (*Progress Rules* section) and not how the progress should be performed. This has led to different implementations of asynchronous progress [6]. Brightwell *et al.* [5] distinguish several methods to perform this communication/computation overlap.

Application-Driven Progression. A simple solution consists in manually calling MPI routines (e.g., `MPI_Test()`) in the application code to force progress. This is often considered as a good solution for highly optimized codes. However it leads to error-prone code modifications and it is also hard to assess whether performance improvements come from actual overlap increase or not [19].

Third-Party Offloading. Alternatively, one can offload all communication progresses to a third party, thus allowing the host CPU to keep on performing computations. The third party is often a dedicated Network Interface Card (NIC) designed to independently handle communications. However commercially available NICs, such as EDR InfiniBand or Cray Aries, either cannot handle critical parts of the communications protocols, such as message matching, or provide only a blocking network programming interface [6] on top of which MPI can be implemented. The Bull eXascale Interconnect (BXI) [7] aims at tackling these issues by providing full hardware message matching and a non-blocking programming interface based on the Portals4 standard [4]. However BXI is still under development at the time of writing.

Thread-Based MPI. Another possibility is to consider MPI processes as threads, which enables the strengths of MPI+X implementations without tampering with application codes. These implementations are called *unified runtimes*. A typical representative example is the MPC framework [16,17]. Within MPC an MPI task can make communications progress for another task located on the same physical node.

Progress Threads. Last but not least, asynchronous communications can be orchestrated by the host CPU which drives NIC operations before going back to the application compute phase. At the MPI implementation level, the most popular solution of this kind is based on progress threads (PT) [10] on top of RDMA-capable networks such as InfiniBand [18]. A PT is a thread dedicated to make communications progress. PTs are usually spawned next to the compute threads such that the application programmer is unaware of their existence. However, to meet HPC performance requirements, PT methods must face two main issues. First, they need to detect network events as close as possible to actual communication completion. Second, the detection process should be as lightweight as possible to limit the impact on the application execution. The tradeoff between these requirements has led to two main PT implementations in literature:

– The first implementation favors *detection reactivity*. The thread actively polls the NIC, thus allowing an almost immediate treatment of new events. This can however lead to a huge disturbance of compute threads if a careful scheduling is not performed. Indeed, the Linux kernel scheduler tries not to favor the computational thread rather than the PT if they share a core during the execution, leading to relevant perturbation on the execution. That is why many

MPI+X applications prefer losing available resources by purposely leaving a free core per MPI process and binding the PT to that core. This often yields better overlap and better performance than oversubscribing [10].

- The other solution, which favors *lightweight detection,* is based on network interruptions. When a message lands on the NIC, an interruption is raised by the card to the kernel, which reschedules the PT. Since the kernel is involved, this breaks the OS bypass property of modern interconnects. Moreover, the PT is simply added to the Linux scheduler run queue. This can delay its execution up to a kernel time slice ($\sim$4 ms). In general this is hardly acceptable from an HPC application's perspective.

In conclusion, it is worth mentioning an alternative PT method implemented by the PIOMan progress engine [22]. PIOMan is devised to schedule MPI progress operations when the computing cores are in idle state. CPU idle times are obtained by querying the current topology mapping (thread binding) or the kernel (CPU occupation). However, on common HPC workloads retrieving this information turns out in a non acceptable overhead and practically limits the application of PIOMan to real-world use cases [21].

3   Contribution: Hybrid Progress

In this section we propose an original PT mechanism for achieving efficient communication/computation overlap in a hybrid MPI+threads context. We call our contribution *Hybrid Progress* (HP). In the first part we detail the general algorithmic choices and ideas behind our contribution. In the second part we expose an implementation in the context of MPI+OMP collaboration.

3.1   Hybrid Progress Method

Despite the longstanding efforts, available PT solutions are not yet completely satisfactory from the application's perspective. Our HP method aims at circumventing some drawbacks of current PT methods by tackling the progression problem from an alternative point of view: efficient communication/computation overlap is achieved by a dedicated scheduling of MPI progress on *existing* compute threads. Before detailing our idea it is important to recall that driving MPI progress to achieve this overlap is effective only if the underlying network protocol splits the messages in several fragments processed separately. In most MPI implementations this is performed by the *rendezvous* protocol, as opposed to the *eager* protocol which sends the whole data as soon as possible. The *rendezvous* protocol is usually employed for long messages (i.e., larger than a threshold).

The core idea behind HP method is to finely control the state of application compute threads. This control allows then to drive MPI communication progress at the right time thus avoiding perturbations in the computations and at the same time enabling efficient communication/computation overlap. The main difference from the PT solutions is that our method does not require to spawn a dedicated thread for progression. Instead it exploits the compute threads which have been already created by the application. Thus, it avoids kernel calls and therefore, it maintains the OS bypass feature of modern interconnects. On the other hand, similarly to interruption-based PT methods, our contribution aims at reducing the interference with computation phases. In fact if MPI progress calls are not performed at the right time, they can lead to strong perturbation in synchronizations, invalidate cache optimizations and load balancing choices made by the application developper, and so on. However, whereas interruption-based PTs identify the right timing by answering to specific network events, we followed here a different route: the best spot for communication progress is chosen at the runtime level, i.e., by selecting only the time intervals when the thread-based runtime is in a waiting state. Our contribution is generally applicable to any thread-based model stacked with MPI. However, the target runtime should make its idle time accessible to an external tool through a suitable interface.

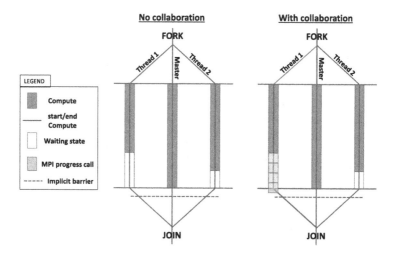

Fig. 2. Typical behavior of the OMP runtime within a parallel construct with (right) and without (left) our runtime collaboration.

3.2   Implementation in an MPI+OpenMP Context

In this section we implement our idea in the context of an MPI+OMP programming model. Our contribution needs to target OMP threads waiting times for progressing MPI communications. We identify these idle intervals within OMP compute parallel regions. A typical example of a parallel-region behavior is sketched on the left panel of Fig. 2. In particular, an implicit barrier is triggered by the runtime before each *join* operation. Because of *imbalance* acquired when performing computations, compute threads do not reach this barrier at the same time leading to idle periods. This spot nicely suits our purpose since it can be arbitrarily large depending on the thread imbalance generated by the application. In the worst case (i.e., when all threads are perfectly synchronized) the largest perturbation introduced by our solution is given by the duration of one MPI progress call (see right panel of Fig. 2). Therefore, even though perfect synchronization should not yield to any overlap increase with our method, we also expect it to introduce a negligible performance loss in this case.

Other approaches in the literature tried to identify idle times in the OMP runtime in a similar fashion than the one needed here, notably for parallelizing internal operations of the MPI runtime with OMP nested loop constructs. Due to lack of space, we refer the reader to [20] for a detailed discussion on how to characterize thread idle times in the OMP runtime. However, while the prerequisite is the same, we only need here to identify periods of time large enough to call the progress engine of the MPI runtime. Moreover, we observed in our experiments that calling the progress engine of the MPI runtime concurrently from multiple threads can be prohibitive if the implementation does not ensure a proper handling of concurrent calls to the progress.

To target the waiting times showed in Fig. 2 we need to access the internal states of the OMP runtime. To this purpose we use the OMP Tools (OMPT) interface. This API has been added to the most-recent OMP technical draft released in November 2017 [15] and is expected to be officially released with OMP 5.0. At the time of writing, only the LLVM OMP runtime provides a mature implementation of this tool interface [3]. All results presented in this paper are therefore obtained using this runtime. OMPT has been primarily designed for enabling OMP profiling in tools (e.g., HPCToolkit [13]). It is built upon a simple idea: each time a thread changes its state (e.g., it enters/exits a parallel region, waits on a lock or task construct...) a specific event is raised by OMPT and a corresponding callback function is triggered. An external tool can overload these functions and gather almost realtime information on the probed thread. An exhaustive list of thread states and events is provided in [15].

The sync_region_wait event is a perfect fit for our purpose. In fact it notifies that the probed thread is waiting for synchronization with other workers within a parallel region, for example before reaching an implicit barrier as shown in Fig. 2. We thus developed a tool which overloads the callback function of the sync_region_wait event, and calls the MPI progress function. Since the current MPI standard does not provide any function to invoke the message progression, our tool directly calls the opal_progress routine of the OpenMPI [9] implementation of MPI we used for our experiments. In our implementation only the first OMP thread entering the waiting state make MPI communication progress, as depicted in the right panel of Fig. 2. Message progression is then performed until the last thread encounters the *join* barrier. On one hand, this avoids concurrent calls to the MPI progress function and makes our tool compatible with MPI implementations not fully compliant with multithreaded communications. On the other hand, since only the first thread raising the callback is chosen, it allows exploiting the thread waiting regions at full length. Thanks to the simplicity of the OMPT interface, our tool is extremely lightweight, with only around two hundreds lines of C code. Furthermore our library only needs to be loaded via the LD_PRELOAD environment variable without any code recompilation.

4   Experimental Results

This section first presents an experimental study of our contribution against a naive PT implementation on a handwritten micro-benchmark. We then evaluate our approach against the state-of-the-art PT approach of the OpenMPI PML Yalla component, designed by Mellanox, on two CORAL [1] benchmarks.

All experiments have been conducted on the Bull Pluton cluster, located at Echirolles, France. Each node is composed of an Intel Xeon Phi Knights Landing (KNL) 7230 64-core processor with 16 GB of MCDRAM configured in flat mode, and 192 GB of main memory. They are linked together by an InfiniBand EDR @100 Gb/s 4X interconnect. We use the BTL OpenIB communication component of the OpenMPI 2.0.2 MPI implementation, and compiled with the Intel 17.0.0 compiler. For the OpenMP model, we use the open-source LLVM OMP runtime (revision 319448) providing the OMPT interface.

4.1   Micro-benchmark

To evaluate our contribution we implement a bulk-synchronous benchmark [23]. This programming scheme is representative of patterns used in industrial HPC codes and it can strongly benefit from communication/computation overlap. Figure 3 presents this benchmark: it is composed of pairs of processes (sender and receiver) executing 3 steps: initiate non-blocking communications, perform an OMP parallel region, and collect communications and synchronize.

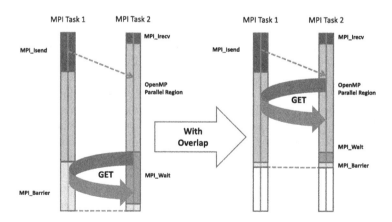

Fig. 3.   Micro-benchmark scenario without (left) and with communication/computation overlap (right): GET labels usually correspond to several RDMA Get operations.

This scenario is designed to force the reception of a communication buffer during an OMP parallel region, by explicitly delaying the sender MPI_Isend. We focus our attention on a situation where asynchronous progress is necessary to achieve communication/computation overlap. As aforementioned, this corresponds to a *rendezvous* protocol as implemented in OpenMPI. If no progress is performed, the reception happens at the end of the computation step (see left of Fig. 3). With asynchronous progress of the MPI runtime, we should instead observe the scenario on the right panel, where the progress happens inside the OMP parallel region and the time spent in MPI_Wait becomes negligible. We compare our HP approach with a naive PT implementation, built on top of OMPT – similarly to our contribution – in order to make the comparison as fair as possible. We name this approach *Progress Thread* (PT) in the following. For each experiment, we run 10 iterations of our micro-benchmark with 4 sender/receiver pairs of MPI tasks (i.e. 8 MPI processes). Each pair exchanges 10 buffers per iteration, each of 4 MB. All the experiments on this micro-benchmark are performed with 2 computing nodes, where all sender MPI processes are bound to one node and all receiver MPI processes to the other to force inter-node communications. Finally, each MPI process launches 64 OMP threads, for 512 threads in total.

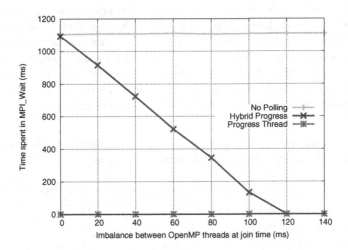

Fig. 4. Time spent in MPI_Wait in our micro-benchmark depending of the imbalance between OMP threads. 2 s of sleep per iteration, 10 iterations.

We first investigate how much imbalance between OMP threads is needed for our approach to achieve efficient communication/computation overlap. Indeed, since MPI progress is only called at *join* time of OMP parallel regions, one can argue that this interval might not be sufficient to achieve a level of overlap competitive with PT. To do so, we substitute real computations in OMP regions with a fixed amount of sleeping time – 2 s in the case of our micro-benchmark

– to ensure a perfect balance between OMP threads. We then introduce an imbalance by making some of the threads randomly sleep a certain amount of time more than others. In this way we are able to control the level of thread imbalance in our benchmark. Figure 4 presents the amount of time spent in MPI_Wait, measured with MPI_Wtime(), depending on the maximum amount of imbalance introduced among OMP threads, measured with omp_get_wtime() (lower is better). The top straight line is the time spent in MPI_Wait without any communication/computation overlap, and represent the lower bound of this overlap. The bottom straight line is the time spent in MPI_Wait with the PT approach, and represent the overlap upper bound. We observe that each time we introduce 20 more milliseconds of imbalance per iteration, the amount of time spent in MPI_Wait reduces of about 200 ms in total. This fits well with the behavior presented in Sect. 3.1, where the imbalance between OMP threads directly drives the amount of MPI progress calls, and thus the amount of time saved in MPI_Wait.

However, the cost of calling the MPI progress is often not negligible. As explained in Sect. 3.1, since our approach targets only overhead times of the OMP runtime to call the MPI progress, it less likely disturbs the application computations compared to PT. To prove our claim, we run the same micro-benchmark replacing sleeps with actual computations. We aim at observing the perturbation on computations introduced by each approach. The performed computations are hand-written General Matrix Multiplication (GEMM) kernels on small matrices (256×256), shared between OMP threads. We did not use any optimized version of GEMM kernels such as the Intel MKL library since our purpose is not to assess the GEMM performance. Instead we want to study the perturbation introduced by the PT on computations, i.e. how much time originally dedicated to the compute phase is assigned to the PT by the OS kernel.

Table 1. Execution time (in seconds) of our micro-benchmark with each approach. 200 GEMM kernel computations per iteration, 10 iterations.

	MPI_Wait time	Computation time	Total execution time
No polling	0.9411 s	16.92 s	17.97 s
Hybrid progress	0.0002 s	16.87 s	16.99 s
Progress thread	0.0002 s	27.27 s	27.54 s

Table 1 presents the average execution time of different approaching executing 200 GEMM kernel computations per iteration, on 10 iterations. The standard deviation of these runs is negligible on our setup, and thus omitted. We observe that, while the PT approach strongly disturbs the computation (with an overhead on computations of ∼63%) the overhead of our HP approach is negligible. Moreover, the MPI_Wait time column shows that common computational workloads such as GEMM kernels exhibit enough imbalance among OMP threads to allow an efficient communication/computation overlap with our contribution.

This translates in an effective gain in execution time, while the PT approach heavily slows down the application. This shows that our contribution achieves the best trade-off between communication/computation overlap and perturbation of computations in this case.

4.2   CORAL Benchmarks

We showed in the previous section that our contribution allows a competitive communication/computation overlap compared to PT approaches, while having a negligible overhead on computations. To assess the applicability of our contribution to real-life workloads, this section presents experiments on LULESH and AMG CORAL benchmarks.

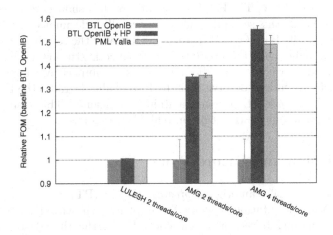

Fig. 5. Relative FOM of LULESH and AMG CORAL hybrid MPI+OMP benchmarks on 16 Intel KNL nodes. Baseline: BTL OpenIB setup.

As first benchmark we choose LULESH. While being a compute-bound stencil code for shock hydrodynamics, its numerous fine-grained compute loops allow us to better assess the overhead of our contribution than our micro-benchmark. The other benchmark, AMG2013, computes a Conjugate Gradient (CG) sparse linear solver. The distributed CG algorithm is known to be communication-bound because of the communication requirements coming from the Sparse Matrix Vector product (SpMV) [12], and seems to be a good candidate for communication/computation overlap improvements. We present in Fig. 5 the Figures of Merit (FOM) of each benchmark – higher is better – relative to the FOM of the BTL OpenIB standard approach. The PT approach is represented by the PML Yalla, which is an OpenMPI component maintained by Mellanox and the state-of-the-art reference of such approaches. We use for these experiments 16 nodes of the Bull Pluton cluster, previously described in Sect. 4.1. The two benchmarks are launched with the same MPI+OMP distribution, 5 times each.

32 MPI processes per node are used such that each process is bound to a L2 cache on the KNL memory hierarchy. Four OMP threads per MPI process are spawned, to bind two threads per KNL core and fully exploit their two pipelines.

We observe that the difference between all three approaches on LULESH is less than 1%. This means that, even with fine-grained OMP loops, the overhead of our approach is indeed negligible. On AMG2013, we observe a FOM improvement of 35% for both our approach and the PML Yalla PT approach. Indeed, Issacs *et al.* explain in [11] that a high differential lateness between MPI processes exists in AMG2013, especially in the MPI_Waitall routine. This makes the reduction of the time spent in this routine a critical factor for improving the performance of the solve phase, thus the FOM. To study more precisely the perturbation on computations of each approach, we run the AMG2013 benchmark with all the computing resources available, i.e. by using all four hyperthreads per KNL core instead of two. The FOM of each approach is shown on the right hand side of Fig. 5. While this setup degrades the overall performance of the application by ∼26% in the BTL OpenIB case – which is why the relative gain with PT approaches is higher, but the absolute performance is still lower than the case with two threads per core – this allows to assess the impact on computations of each approach. We indeed observe that the PML Yalla degrades the FOM of the application while our contribution maintain its efficiency. This result confirms the applicability of our contribution on real-life workloads.

5   Conclusion and Future Work

In this paper we propose an original *progress-threads* (PT) method for achieving communication/computation overlap. We implement it within an MPI+OMP programming model. Based on a fine control over the thread states, we are able to target thread waiting times within compute regions and use them to drive MPI communications progress. Our solution does not need any dedicated thread on the host CPU and it is designed to have minimal perturbation on the application execution. Through the OMPT interface we easily implement our idea with few hundreds lines of C code. We devise a micro-benchmark representative of a widely used parallel programming scheme for assessing the features of our solution. Results on real-world workloads are very encouraging with up to 35% of performance gain on the AMG CORAL application which strongly benefits from communication/computation overlap. Our results are comparable to the PML Yalla from Mellanox, a state-of-the-art PT-based implementation. Moreover, compute-bound workloads such as the LULESH benchmark are not impacted in terms of performance. This proves that our tool introduces a negligible overhead in the application compute phases.

In the short term we intend to extend our tool to target idle times outside parallel regions for MPI progress. This will greatly improve the applicability of our solution to generic HPC workloads. However OMP implementations usually keep the threads in an *active* waiting state outside parallel regions. This makes harder to efficiently target those idle times. In parallel we plan to test our tool on real-life industrial use cases. To this purpose an ongoing collaboration between Atos Bull and CEA aims at assessing performance and scalability of our solution up to exascale workloads on the Tera-1000 supercomputer [2].

Finally, while our HP approach can be applied to multiple runtimes, its concrete applicability is still an open question. As we show in this paper, runtimes currently lack an API exposing a minimal set of state information (such as idle periods and suitable progress functions) to allow generic and portable runtime collaborations. A standardization of such API would also pave the way to new kinds of collaborations. For instance thread waiting times can be used to prefetch data to GPU accelerators, other memory spaces or schedule tasks in advance when coupled with a task-based runtime.

References

1. Collaboration of Oak Ridge, Argonne, and Livermore benchmark codes. https:// asc.llnl.gov/CORAL-benchmarks
2. Tera-1000-2-Part 1 (2017). https://www.top500.org/system/179162
3. OpenMP Tools Interface (2018). https://github.com/OpenMPToolsInterface/ LLVM-openmp
4. Barrett, B.W., et al.: The Portals 4.0 network programming interface. Technical Report, Sandia National Laboratories, SAND2013-3181 (2013)
5. Brightwell, R., Riesen, R., Underwood, K.D.: Analyzing the impact of overlap, offload, and independent progress for message passing interface applications. HPCA J. **19**, 103–117 (2005)
6. Cardellini, V., Fanfarillo, A., Filippone, S.: Overlapping communication with computation in MPI applications. Technical Report, Universita di Roma Tor Vergata, DICII RR-16.09 (2016)
7. Derradji, S., Palfer-Sollier, T., Panziera, J.P., Poudes, A., Atos, F.W.: The BXI interconnect architecture. IEEE, August 2015
8. Dongarra, J., et al.: The international exascale software project roadmap. HPCA J. **25**, 3–60 (2011)
9. Gabriel, E., et al.: Open MPI: goals, concept, and design of a next generation MPI implementation. In: Kranzlmüller, D., Kacsuk, P., Dongarra, J. (eds.) EuroPVM/MPI 2004. LNCS, vol. 3241, pp. 97–104. Springer, Heidelberg (2004). https://doi.org/10.1007/978-3-540-30218-6_19
10. Hoefler, T., Lumsdaine, A.: Message progression in parallel computing - to thread or not to thread? In: IEEE CLUSTER (2008)
11. Isaacs, K.E., Gamblin, T., Bhatele, A., Schulz, M., Hamann, B., Bremer, P.T.: Ordering traces logically to identify lateness in message passing programs. IEEE Trans. Parallel Distrib. Syst. **27**, 829–840 (2016)
12. Lewis, J.G., Van de Geijn, R.A.: Distributed memory matrix-vector multiplication and conjugate gradient algorithms. In: Proceedings of the 1993 ACM/IEEE Conference on Supercomputing (1993)
13. Mellor-Crummey, J.: Performance Analysis of MPI+OpenMP Programs with HPCToolkit, March 2015
14. Message Passing Interface Forum: MPI: a message-passing interface standard, version 3.1, June 2015

15. OpenMP Language Working Group: OpenMP®RTechnical Report 4: Version 5.0 Preview 2. Technical report, The OpenMP Architecture Review Board, November 2017
16. Pérache, M., Carribault, P., Jourdren, H.: MPC-MPI: an MPI implementation reducing the overall memory consumption. In: Ropo, M., Westerholm, J., Dongarra, J. (eds.) EuroPVM/MPI 2009. LNCS, vol. 5759, pp. 94–103. Springer, Heidelberg (2009). https://doi.org/10.1007/978-3-642-03770-2_16
17. Pérache, M., Jourdren, H., Namyst, R.: MPC: a unified parallel runtime for clusters of NUMA machines. In: Luque, E., Margalef, T., Benítez, D. (eds.) Euro-Par 2008. LNCS, vol. 5168, pp. 78–88. Springer, Heidelberg (2008). https://doi.org/10.1007/978-3-540-85451-7_9
18. Pfister, G.F.: An introduction to the InfiniBand^{TM} architecture. In: High Performance Mass Storage and Parallel I/O (2001)
19. Rabenseifner, R.: Hybrid parallel programming on HPC platforms. In: Proceedings of the Fifth European Workshop on OpenMP, EWOMP (2003)
20. Si, M., Pea, A.J., Balaji, P., Takagi, M., Ishikawa, Y.: MT-MPI: multithreaded MPI for many-core environments. ACM Press (2014)
21. Trahay, F., Brunet, E., Denis, A.: An analysis of the impact of multi-threading on communication performance. In: IEEE IPDPS (2009)
22. Trahay, F., Denis, A.: A scalable and generic task scheduling system for communication libraries. In: IEEE CLUSTER (2009)
23. Valiant, L.G.: A bridging model for parallel computation. Commun. ACM **33**, 103–111 (1990)

Multicore and Manycore Methods and Tools

Efficient Lock-Free Removing and Compaction for the Cache-Trie Data Structure

Aleksandar Prokopec[(✉)]

Oracle Labs, Adliswil, Switzerland
aleksandar.prokopec@gmail.com

Abstract. The recently proposed cache-trie data structure improves the performance of lock-free Ctries by maintaining an auxiliary data structure called a cache. The cache allows basic operations to run in expected $O(1)$, instead of the previous $O(\log n)$ bound. While earlier work showed that cache-tries improve inserts and lookups by 1.5–5× on standard workloads, the remove operation was not previously examined. One of the main challenges of remove is to compact the trie – removing the elements should recycle the unused parts of the data structure.

In this paper, we describe a new non-compacting and two new compacting non-blocking variants of the remove operation for cache-tries. We ensure that each remove implementation runs in expected $O(1)$ time. Compared to standard Ctries, performance improvements range between 10% and 35%, depending on the size of the data structure, the parallelism level and the hardware architecture.

1 Introduction

Cache-tries [28] improve the running time of traditional lock-free hash tries [32] with a quiescently consistent auxiliary data structure called a *cache*. While cache-trie lookup and insert were shown to run in expected $O(1)$ time [26], original work on cache-tries gives almost no attention to removing elements.

This paper shows that the lock-free cache-trie remove operation also runs in expected $O(1)$ time. This operation takes care to *compact* the cache-trie – the memory management system is allowed to recycle the unused parts of the data structure. The main idea in compaction is to, after removing, speculatively detect if the affected node can be compacted, and then *freeze* it. Freezing facilitates compaction by atomically preventing subsequent updates to the candidate node.

After summarizing the earlier results and explaining how cache-tries work in Sect. 2, this paper brings forth the following contributions:

- A description and an implementation of a lock-free remove operation for cache-tries, both with and without compaction (Sect. 3).
- An optimization that brings a further 5–15% improvement on the expected execution time (Sect. 3.2).

© Springer International Publishing AG, part of Springer Nature 2018
M. Aldinucci et al. (Eds.): Euro-Par 2018, LNCS 11014, pp. 575–589, 2018.
https://doi.org/10.1007/978-3-319-96983-1_41

```
class SNode:                class FNode:              class CacheTrie:
    val key: KeyType            val frozen: Any           val root = new ANode(16)
    val value: ValueType                                  var cacheHead: Cache = nil
    var txn: Any             val NoTxn
                            val FVNode                  type Cache = Array<Any>
type ANode = Array<Any>     val FSNode
```

Fig. 1. Cache trie data types

– A performance evaluation on two architectures, against three similar concurrent data structures. We find that cache-trie removes improve the execution time of standard lock-free hash tries [34] by 10–35% and that, without compaction, removing can additionally be made 30–65% faster (Sect. 4).

Finally, Sect. 5 presents the related work, and Sect. 6 concludes.

2   Overview of Cache-Tries

A lock-free *cache-trie* [28] is a special type of a *hash trie* data structure [3,4,32]. A newly created cache-trie consists of a single empty array, which has the length 16, since nodes are 16-way in our implementation[1]. Inserting a key works similar to a hash table – the 4 lowest hash code bits are used to determine the position in the table. Consider the following figure:

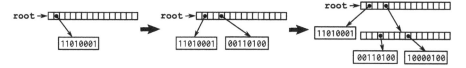

In the first figure above, a key with the hash code 11010001_2 occupies the index 1_{10}. The key with the hash code 00110100_2 occupies the index 4_{10} in the second figure. In the third figure, keys 00110100_2 and 10000100_2 collide at the index 4_{10}. The collision is resolved by creating another array, and using the higher hash code bits to map the keys to indices 3_{10} and 8_{10}. Collision resolution repeats recursively until running out of hash bits, and relies on a linked list thereafter.

Data Types. The aforementioned array nodes are modeled with the ANode type, shown in Fig. 1. ANode is defined as an array of pointers of Any type. The SNode type models the leaf nodes. Each leaf holds a key and the value it is mapped to. Additionally, SNode objects have a mutable field txn, which is used by the mutating threads to announce that they are about to replace the respective SNode.

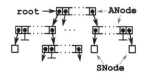

---

[1] Other arities are possible, but we found 16 to work well, because the node fits into a 64 byte cache-line when JVM's compressed object pointers are used.

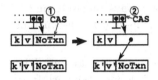

To insert a key into the cache-trie in a lock-free manner, a thread finds the appropriate ANode, and atomically replaces a nil array entry with a new SNode, using a compare-and-swap (CAS) instruction. A new SNode has the txn field set to a special value NoTxn. To replace an existing SNode, a mutation operation first announces the new value by CASing it into the txn field, as shown on the left. If the first CAS is successful, the corresponding array entry is replaced with a second CAS.

Freezing. Mutation operations must sometimes prevent all future modifications to specific subtries. This is achieved with *freezing* [6,23], which ensures that all subsequent CAS invocations on the frozen node fail.

In figure ① on the right, a thread selects an ANode that contains an SNode, a nil entry, and a child ANode. In figure ②, the thread CASed an FSNode value into the txn field of the SNode, and replaced nil with an FVNode value. To freeze the child ANode, the thread first writes an FNode value into the corresponding entry, as shown in Figure ③, and then recursively freezes

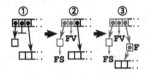

the child. Note that, once freezing starts, it eventually completes – the reason is that a thread that observes an ongoing freeze operation will cooperatively complete the freeze. In addition, any operation that starts after the freeze started will notice the freeze if it works on the respective subtrie, and ongoing operations do only finitely many changes. The linearization point is the CAS that freezes the last non-frozen node in the respective subtrie.

Invariants. All operations maintain the following invariants: (1) If an SNode with a hash code h is reachable from the cache-trie root, then it is only reachable with a chain of pointers $a_0 \xrightarrow{a_0[p_0]} [u_0 \longrightarrow] a_1 \xrightarrow{a_1[p_1]} [u_1 \longrightarrow] \ldots \xrightarrow{a_n[p_n]} [u_n \longrightarrow] s_{n+1}$ starting from the $a_0 = \text{root}$, such that $p_0 p_1 \ldots p_n$ is a prefix of h (and parts in the $[\cdot]$ brackets are optional). Here, each a_i is an ANode, s_i is an SNode, and u_i is any other type of node. (2) If a node is not reachable from the root, then it is frozen. (3) Once frozen, a node is not subsequently modified.

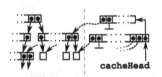

Cache. Most of the previous description applies to standard lock-free hash trie variants [1,2,31,32,34]. In these hash tries, the search time grows logarithmically with the number of keys in the hash trie. A cache-trie additionally maintains an auxiliary data structure called a *cache*, shown on the left, which speeds up the node searches. The cache is a list of C arrays, starting with the field cacheHead. Each array corresponds to a level ℓ, $0 \leq \ell < 4 \cdot C$, and is effectively a concatenation of the entries of the ANodes at level ℓ (including any missing ones). Levels are counted in multiples of 4, i.e. $0, 4, 8, 12, \ldots$ and so on. A special entry in each array contains a pointer to the next array in this list. The list is sorted, going from the largest arrays (i.e. deepest trie levels) to the smallest.

The cache entries are populated lazily, so they do not always precisely match the trie. However, when they are present, they allow skipping a non-constant number of cache-trie levels.

Slow Path and Fast Path. Consider how to implement a key lookup. The slow lookup relies on the aforementioned invariant (1) – it follows the path from the root to the unique leaf for that key. The fast path lookup attempts to first find the key in the cache, and then continues the search from some node deep in the cache-trie. If the cache entry is empty, the search reverts to the slow path from the root. Similarly, if the cache contains a frozen entry, then the respective node is potentially unreachable, and must be ignored (recall the invariants (2) and (3)). The precise pseudocode of lookup was shown in earlier work [28].

When the cache is appropriately positioned and populated, the slow path runs less frequently. When it does occasionally occur, the slow path updates the relevant cache entry, and records a *miss*. When sufficiently many misses occur, a sampling pass inspects the trie and updates the cache depth if necessary.

Performance. By analyzing the key distribution across levels [26], it was shown that the expected running time of the lookup and insert operations is $O(1)$. Performance evaluations on typical sizes ($\approx$1M elements) showed that cache-trie lookup performance is around 3× better when compared against other hash tries, and insertion is around 33% faster [28]. Compared to the JDK 8 `ConcurrentHashMap` [14], cache-tries have faster insertion, but 1.5–2× slower lookup.

3   Remove Operation

Depending on the implementation, a remove operation may or may not compact the cache-trie. Compaction recycles the unused parts of the data structure, and ensures that the memory footprint corresponds to the actual number of keys. For example, the JDK `ConcurrentHashMap` implementation [14] does not recycle memory, so its footprint corresponds to the maximum number of keys present at any point during its lifetime. As a benefit, removing without compaction is faster because no time is spent in housekeeping. Next, we will show one non-compacting lock-free remove operation, and two compacting variants.

3.1   Basic Implementation

The basic remove implementation does not compact the cache-trie. If the specified key exists, it is atomically removed. Otherwise, the remove operation leaves the trie intact.

Summary. We first consider the slow path version. At every step, the search is anchored at an array node `cur` at level `lev` (the parent node `prev` is at `lev-4`). The search calculates the index in `cur` and reads the respective child pointer. The child is either non-existing (`nil`), or another array node, or an `SNode`. For `nil`, the search

```
 1 def remove(k: KeyType, h: Int, lev: Int,     29 def remove(k: KeyType) =
 2   cur: ANode, prev: ANode, cLev: Int) =       30   val h = hash(k)
 3   val pos = (h >>> lev)⊙(cur.length-1)        31   if ¬remove(k,h,0,root,nil,0):
 4   val ch = READ(cur[pos])                     32     remove(k)
 5   if ch == nil: return false                  33
 6   else if ch ∈ ANode:                         34 def fastRemove(k: KeyType) =
 7     return remove(k,h,lev+4,ch,cur,cLev)      35   val h = hash(k)
 8   else if ch ∈ SNode:                         36   var cache = READ(cacheHead)
 9     if lev ≥ cLev + 8:                        37   if cache == nil:
10       recordMiss()                            38     return remove(k)
11     val txn = READ(ch.txn)                    39   val topLev =
12     if txn == NoTxn:                          40     trailingZeros(cache.length-1)
13       if ch.key == k:                         41   while cache ≠ nil:
14         if CAS(ch.txn,txn,nil):               42     val pos = 1+(h⊙(cache.length-2))
15           CAS(cur[pos],ch,nil)                43     val cur = READ(cache[pos])
16           return true                         44     val lev =
17         else:                                 45       trailingZeros(cache.length-1)
18           return                              46     cache = READ(cache[0])
19             remove(k,h,lev,cur,prev,cLev)     47     if cur ∈ ANode:
20       else: return true                       48       if lev < topLev-4:
21     else if txn == FSNode:                    49         recordMiss()
22       return false                            50       if remove(k,h,lev,cur,nil,lev):
23     else:                                     51         return true
24       CAS(cur[pos],ch,txn)                    52       else:
25       return                                  53         continue
26         remove(k,h,lev,cur,prev,cLev)         54     else:
27   else:                                       55       continue
28     return false                              56   return remove(k)
```

Fig. 2. Remove operations

terminates, since the key is not present, by invariant (1). For SNode, the search checks if the keys match, and then attempts to remove the SNode. Otherwise, the search resumes recursively. If the search sees a frozen node, it restarts by returning false.

The fast path version aims to start the search from an ANode within the trie, so it starts by reading the cacheHead field, which points to the deepest trie level. If the respective entry is not an ANode, this is retried at the next (higher) cache level, until reaching the root of the cache-trie.

Implementation. The remove subroutine, shown in Fig. 2, implements the slow path of the remove operation. The subroutine takes the key k, its hash code h, the current level lev, and the current and previous node cur and prev. The cLev is the cache level at which the search was entered. The subroutine returns true if successful, and false if it must be retried.

The array index pos is calculated in line 3, and the child ch is read in line 4. The nil and the ANode case are as described above. The SNode case first checks if the cache is misaligned – if the current trie level is sufficiently far away from cache level cLev (lines 9 and 10), it increments the cache miss counter by calling the recordMiss subroutine [28]. After that, the subroutine checks if the keys match, and performs the two-step SNode replacement described in Sect. 2.

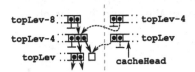

By convention, the cache level corresponds to the level of the nodes it points to. The figure on the left shows three trie levels topLev-8, topLev-4 and topLev. On the right, the deepest cache level is at topLev, and the one above is at `topLev-4`. Under this convention, the level ℓ of a cache node is the number of trailing zeros of $S - 1$, where S is the cache length (note: the zeroth entry in the cache is a pointer to the next cache level). For example, the cache with $S = 17$ elements is at level 4 – note that its pointees are likewise at level 4. Separately, the index in the cache for the hash code h is determined by the ℓ lowest bits, i.e. with the expression $h \odot (S - 2)$, where $\odot$ is the bitwise-and operation.

The `fastRemove` subroutine in Fig. 2 iteratively traverses the cache levels until a call to `remove` in line 50 is successful. If the current cache level `lev` is less than `topLev-4`, where `topLev` is the deepest cache level, a cache miss is recorded in line 49. Note that using the cache level `topLev-4` is not a miss, because the deepest cache node can point to an `SNode`, indicating that the corresponding `ANode` must be looked up one level above, as shown in the previous figure.

```
 1 def remove(k: KeyType, h: Int, lev: Int,    34 def fastRemove(k: KeyType) =
 2   cur: ANode, prev: ANode, cLev: Int) =      35   val h = hash(k)
   ...                                          36   var cache = READ(cacheHead)
 6   else if old ∈ ANode:                       37   if cache == nil:
 7     val status =                             38     return remove(k)
 8       remove(k,h,lev+4,old,cur,cLev)         39   val topLev =
 9     if status ∧ prev ≠ nil:                  40     trailingZeros(cache.length-1)
10       if isCompactible(cur):                 41   while cache ≠ nil:
11         compactNode(cur,prev,h,lev)          42     val pos = 1+(h⊙(cache.length-2))
12     return status                            43     val cur = READ(cache[pos])
   ...                                          44     val lev =
14         if CAS(ch.txn,txn,nil):              45       trailingZeros(cache.length-1)
15           CAS(cur[pos],ch,nil)                  ...
16         if isCompactible(cur):               50     if remove(k,h,lev,cur,nil,lev):
17           compactNode(cur,prev,h,lev)        51       if isCompactible(cur):
18         return true                          52         compactUp(h,lev)
   ...                                          53       return true
26         remove(k,h,lev,cur,prev,cLev)        54     else:
27   else if old ∈ XNode:                       55       continue
28     completeCompaction(xn)                   56   else:
29     return false                             57     continue
   ...                                             ...
```

Fig. 3. Adding compaction to remove operations

3.2 Cache-Trie Compaction

Summary. To compact the cache-trie, the remove operation must ensure that there is no `ANode` that has at most one `SNode` child. In the figure ① on the right, the rightmost `SNode` must be removed. Removing it in ② 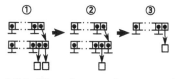 produces an `ANode` that has a single `SNode` child. The slow path remove has the parent pointer `prev`, so it can compact the `ANode` into its parent, as shown in ③.

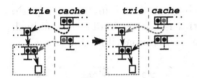

However, the fast path version does not track the current node's parent, preventing it from immediately compacting. To discover the parent, the `fastRemove` operation must read the parent `ANode` from the cache nodes at the higher levels if it detects that the current node is compactible.

Consider the first figure on the left, in which the `remove` subroutine produced an `ANode` with a single remaining `SNode`. This `ANode` must be compacted, but the `prev` parameter is `nil`, so `remove` only "sees" the part in the green frame. In the second figure, the `fastRemove` operation reads the parent from the next level of the cache, which allows it to perform the compaction.

Implementation. Figure 3 shows the difference between the non-compacting and the compacting remove implementation. In the slow path `remove` subroutine, after successfully announcing that the `SNode` will be removed in line 14, the `isCompactible` call checks the current `ANode`, and calls `compactNode` to compact the current node if necessary. As we show briefly, compaction introduces a new node type `XNode` to mark the compact regions. If any operation observes an `XNode`, then it must first help complete the compaction, as shown in line 27.

The `fastRemove` subroutine checks if the current node is compactible as soon as its call to `remove` returns `true`. If so, the `compactUp` call in line 52 iteratively compacts the path to the root until no further compaction is possible.

Figure 4 shows the pseudocode of the different compaction operations. Compaction of a single node is done in `compactNode`, which starts by replacing the candidate node with a special `XNode` value. The `XNode` contains the pointer to the parent node `prev`, the current node `cur`, the

```
class XNode:
  val prev: Anode
  val ppos: Int
  val cur: ANode
  val hash: Int
  val lev: Int
```

position `ppos` of the current node in its parent, and the respective hash code and the current level. Threads that observe this node are obliged to help compaction. The `compactNode` then calls `freeze` on the candidate node to prevent further updates (freezing is described in Sect. 2). Finally, the current `ANode` can be replaced in its parent with the compacted version.

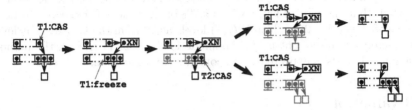

Example. In the preceding figure, the thread T1 inserts the `XNode` and starts freezing the candidate. Before freezing completes, another thread T2 attempts to modify the candidate by inserting another `SNode`. In the first outcome, T1 succeeds in freezing the node before T2 manages to complete its update, and compaction succeeds. In the second outcome, T2 inserts the key. After freezing, T1 sees two keys in the candidate node, so it just swaps in a copy of the node.

The `compactUp` and `compactDown` subroutines are used in the fast path. These operations ascend the cache-trie on a path that corresponds to some hash code h, and invoke compaction until reaching a non-compactible node.

Counter Optimization. Every successful remove operation invokes `isCompactible` to traverse all the entries in the candidate node, and check if the node can be potentially compacted. This check can be made more efficient 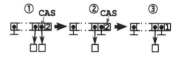 by adding a counter into each `ANode`, which tracks the number of non-`nil` entries. This counter is updated after the linearization point, as shown in the figure above, and it is quiescently consistent – its value is guaranteed to be correct after the operations complete.

3.3 Correctness Discussion

For space reasons, we omit the precise proofs. Instead, we refer to the existing analysis with a similar structure [26], and we briefly discuss the main points.

Linearizability. To show that the remove is correct and linearizable, we identify the linearization points, and show that they preserve the invariants. Concretely, the CAS instruction in line 14 of `remove` is the linearization point. Other CASes do not change the state, and neither of them violates the invariants.

Lock-Freedom. We must show that, for any failed CAS, the trie state changes in a finite number of steps. Consider, for example, the CAS in line 6 of `freeze`. Failure implies either a successful CAS *in line 14 of remove*, indicating concurrent success, or that another thread froze the entry, indicating local progress.

Complexity. When there is no contention among threads, we claim that the fast path runs in expected $O(1)$. We note that the expected time spent searching for the node with the specified key is $O(1)$, by the same arguments as for the cache-trie lookup operation [26]. The only variable amount of time could be spent in the `compactUp` subroutine, whose worst-case is indeed $O(\log n)$. However, it was shown that the pair of levels with $\approx 87\%$ or more keys is expected to be at the level of the cache [26], which is $O(1)$ levels away from the key. At that level, the expected number of entries in the `ANode` is above 2. Therefore, the number of compacted levels is expected to be constant, and `fastRemove` is $O(1)$.

4   Evaluation

We implemented cache-tries in Scala, and compared different remove implementations against similar data structures: JDK `ConcurrentHashMap` [14], Scala standard library Ctries [34], and the concurrent skip list from the JDK [43]. The single threaded benchmark takes an existing cache-trie and removes all of its N keys, where N is $100k$, $250k$, $500k$, and $4M$. The multithreaded benchmark alternates the number of concurrent threads that are removing the elements.

```
 1 def freeze(cur: ANode) =
 2   var i = 0
 3   while i < cur.length:
 4     val ch = READ(cur[i])
 5     if ch == nil:
 6       if ¬CAS(cur[i],ch,FVNode):
 7         continue
 8     else if ch ∈ SNode:
 9       val txn = READ(ch.txn)
10       if txn == NoTxn:
11         if ¬CAS(ch.txn,NoTxn,FSNode):
12           continue
13       else if txn ≠ FSNode:
14         CAS(cur[i],ch,txn)
15         continue
16     else if ch ∈ ANode:
17       val fn = new FNode(ch)
18       CAS(cur[i],ch,fn)
19       continue
20     else if ch ∈ FNode:
21       freeze(ch.frozen)
22     else if ch ∈ XNode:
23       completeCompaction(ch)
24       continue
25     i += 1
26
27 def isCompactible(cur: ANode) =
28   var found = nil
29   var i = 0
30   while i < cur.length:
31     val ch = READ(cur[i])
32     if ch ∈ SNode ∧ found == nil:
33       found = ch
34     else:
35       return false
36     i += 1
37   return true
38
39 def compactNode(cur: ANode,
40   prev: ANode, h: Int, lev: Int) =
41   val pmask = prev.length-1
42   val ppos = (h >>> (lev-4))⊙pmask
43   val xn =
44     new XNode(prev,ppos,cur,h,lev)
45   if CAS(prev[ppos],cur,xn):
46     return completeCompaction(xn)
47   else:
48     return false
```

```
49 def completeCompaction(xn: XNode) =
50   freeze(xn.cur)
51   var compact = nil
52   var i = 0
53   while i < xn.cur.length:
54     val ch = READ(xn.cur[i])
55     if ch ∈ SNode ∧ compact == nil:
56       compact = ch
57     else:
58       compact = createANode(xn.cur)
59       break
60     i += 1
61   if compact ∈ SNode:
62     compact = createSNode(compact)
63   CAS(xn.prev[xn.ppos],xn,compact)
64   return compact == nil ∨
65     compact ∈ SNode
66
67 def compactUp(h: Int, from: Int) =
68   var cache = READ(cacheHead)
69   while cache ≠ nil:
70     val ppos = 1+(h⊙(cache.length-2))
71     val prev = READ(cache[ppos])
72     val lev =
73       trailingZeros(cache.length-1)
74     cache = READ(cache[0])
75     if lev ≥ from ∨ prev ∈ SNode:
76       continue
77     val pos =
78       (h >>> lev)⊙(prev.length-1)
79     val cur = READ(prev[pos])
80     if cur ∉ ANode:
81       continue
82     if ¬compactDown(h,lev+4,cur,prev):
83       return
84   compactDown(h,0,root,nil)
85
86 def compactDown(h: Int, lev: Int,
87   cur: ANode, prev: ANode) =
88   val pos = (h >>> lev)⊙(cur.length-1)
89   val ch = READ(cur[pos])
90   if ch ∈ ANode:
91     if ¬compactDown(h,lev+4,ch,cur):
92       return false
93   if isCompactible(cur) ∧ prev ≠ nil:
94     if compactNode(cur,prev,h,lev):
95       return true
96   return false
```

Fig. 4. Compaction operations

The benchmarks were executed on two machines. The first is an Intel i7-4900MQ 3.80 GHz quad-core CPU with hyperthreading, dual-channel memory and 32GB RAM. The second machine is a dual-socket with 2 Intel Xeon E5-2683 3.00 GHz tetradeca-core CPUs with hyperthreading, quad-channel memory and 32 GB RAM. We used the ScalaMeter tool to run the benchmarks [22], and we followed the standard performance evaluation techniques for the JVM [11]. We ran each benchmark 30 times, reporting the mean and the standard deviation. Our implementation is available online [30], and integrated into the Reactors framework [24,25,27,35,40].

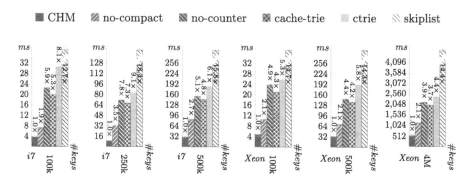

Fig. 5. Single threaded performance comparison between remove implementations

Single Threaded Performance. Figure 5 shows the results of the single threaded benchmarks on i7 and Xeon. The JDK `ConcurrentHashMap` does not compact the underlying hash table, which increases its performance at the cost of memory footprint. We therefore use the `ConcurrentHashMap` as a baseline, since it is unlikely that compacting removes can achieve better performance.

We test three different cache-trie remove variants: basic removes from Sect. 3.1 (*no-compact*), removes with compaction from Sect. 3.2 (*no-counter*), and the removes with the counter optimization (*cache-trie*). *CHM*, *ctrie* and *skiplist* represent JDK concurrent hash maps, Scala Ctries and JDK concurrent skip lists, respectively. Results show that the cache-trie without compaction is 2–3.5× slower than that `ConcurrentHashMap`. The reason for this is that the majority of keys are distributed across two consecutive levels of the cache [26], so the fast-path needs ≈2 pointer hops, and consequently up to ≈2 cache misses, to reach the leaf through the cache (unlike the hash table, which undergoes ≈1 pointer hop), and is consistent with earlier findings [28]. Compaction reduces performance by 1.5–3×, depending on the cache-trie size. The counter optimization from Sect. 3.2 improves compaction performance by only around 5–15%. This is not very surprising – the loop in the `isCompactible` subroutine (which the counters help avoid) is not particularly expensive, since (immediately after a remove) the respective node is usually already in the L1 cache.

Multi Threaded Performance. Figure 6 shows the results of the multi threaded benchmarks. On the i7, we vary the number of threads from 1 to 8. We test Xeon for 1, 2, 4, 8, 14, 28, 42 and 56 threads. The results are overall consistent with the single threaded benchmarks, although the performance gap is lowered at higher parallelism levels. The i7 processor, with is dual-channel memory, saturates the memory bandwidth before reaching 4 cores. The Xeon architecture saturates the bandwidth before reaching 14 cores, and exhibits a slight slowdown at higher parallelism levels. Notably, while skip lists are ≈7–13× slower in the single threaded benchmarks due to a larger number of pointer hops, they scale better, and are only ≈4.5× slower at 4 and 14 threads, respectively.

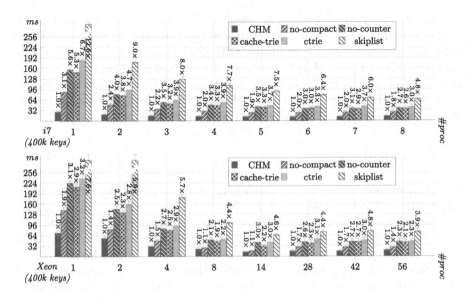

Fig. 6. Multi threaded performance comparison between remove implementations

5 Related Work

Tries were proposed by Briandais [8], and later named by Fredkin [10], as a string retrieval data structure. Several authors studied the use of tries as a dictionary for arbitrary data types [3,4,16]. In the recent years, a non-blocking concurrent hash trie called Ctrie, which supported lock-free insert, lookup and remove operations, was proposed by Prokopec [31,32]. An atomic two-keys replace operation was later proposed in the context of Patricia trees [45]. Ctries were extended with non-blocking snapshots, which, along with along with high-level compiler optimizations [36,48], enabled efficient data-parallel traversal [20,21,33,34,39,42]. Areias and Rocha studied how to improve performance of lock-free hash tries in the context of concurrent Prolog programs, by specializing hash tries for insert operations [1,2]. Separately, Joisha showed that non-blocking tries can be made more efficient when the delete operation is disallowed [13]. Steindorfer studied techniques for automatically deriving the hash trie with optimal tradeoffs for a given program [46,47]. Oshman and Shavit were the first to improve complexity of the trie operations from $O(\log n)$ to $O(\log \log n)$ with SkipTries [19], and cache-tries [26,28] were the first to lower the complexity for trie lookups and inserts to $O(1)$. The freezing technique used in cache-tries is similar to freezing used by SnapQueues [23,41], freezing in locality-conscious lists [5], and sealing in FlowPools [37,38,44] and future values [12].

There are other concurrent data structures that implement the non-blocking dictionaries. Lea's `ConcurrentHashMap` [14], available in the JDK, is loosely based on Michael's lock-free hash table description [18]. `ConcurrentHashMap` has a highly efficient wait-free lookup operation, it is a flat data structure, and it avoids compaction altogether. As such, it is a good baseline for comparison against tree-like and trie data structures, which generally do compaction and suffer cache misses due to indirections. Other concurrent hash maps are due to Liu et al. [17] and Li et al. [15]. The JDK `ConcurrentSkipListMap`, compared in Sect. 4, is based on Pugh's concurrent skip list [43]. Other notable concurrent trees include Bronson's SnapTree (a lock-based AVL tree) [7], lock-free binary trees from Ellen et al. [9], and Braginsky's lock-free B^+-trees [6].

6   Conclusion

We described several novel non-blocking implementations of the remove operation for the cache-trie data structure. We evaluated a compacting and a non-compacting variant, and found that the overhead of compaction is around 1.5–3×, depending on the workload. However, compared to the standard Ctrie implementation [34], the compacting remove on cache-tries is 10–35% faster.

Although the compacting remove operation exceeds the performance of Ctries, it does represent a considerable overhead. One way to alleviate these costs may be to compact lazily, i.e. trigger compaction only after removing a considerable subset of the keys. We leave these considerations for future work.

7   Data Availability Statement and Acknowledgments

The datasets and code generated during and/or analysed during the current study are available in the figshare repository [29]: https://doi.org/10.6084/m9.figshare.6369134

References

1. Areias, M., Rocha, R.: On the correctness and efficiency of lock-free expandable tries for tabled logic programs. In: Flatt, M., Guo, H.-F. (eds.) PADL 2014. LNCS, vol. 8324, pp. 168–183. Springer, Cham (2014). https://doi.org/10.1007/978-3-319-04132-2_12
2. Areias, M., Rocha, R.: A lock-free hash trie design for concurrent tabled logic programs. Int. J. Parallel Program. **44**(3), 386–406 (2016)
3. Bagwell, P.: Ideal hash trees (2001)
4. Baskins, D.: The Judy array implementation (2000). http://judy.sourceforge.net/
5. Braginsky, A., Petrank, E.: Locality-conscious lock-free linked lists. In: Aguilera, M.K., Yu, H., Vaidya, N.H., Srinivasan, V., Choudhury, R.R. (eds.) ICDCN 2011. LNCS, vol. 6522, pp. 107–118. Springer, Heidelberg (2011). https://doi.org/10.1007/978-3-642-17679-1_10. http://dl.acm.org/citation.cfm?id=1946143.1946153
6. Braginsky, A., Petrank, E.: A lock-free B+tree. In: Proceedings of the Twenty-Fourth Annual ACM Symposium on Parallelism in Algorithms and Architectures. SPAA 2012, pp. 58–67. ACM, New York (2012). https://doi.org/10.1145/2312005.2312016

7. Bronson, N.G., Casper, J., Chafi, H., Olukotun, K.: A practical concurrent binary search tree. In: SIGPLAN Not, vol. 45, no. 5, pp. 257–268, January 2010. https://doi.org/10.1145/1837853.1693488

8. De La Briandais, R.: File searching using variable length keys. In: Papers Presented at the the March 3–5, 1959, Western Joint Computer Conference. IRE-AIEE-ACM 1959 (Western), pp. 295–298. ACM, New York (1959). https://doi.org/10.1145/1457838.1457895

9. Ellen, F., Fatourou, P., Ruppert, E., van Breugel, F.: Non-blocking binary search trees. In: Proceedings of the 29th ACM SIGACT-SIGOPS Symposium on Principles of Distributed Computing. PODC 2010, pp. 131–140. ACM, New York (2010). https://doi.org/10.1145/1835698.1835736

10. Fredkin, E.: Trie memory. Commun. ACM 3(9), 490–499 (1960). https://doi.org/10.1145/367390.367400

11. Georges, A., Buytaert, D., Eeckhout, L.: Statistically rigorous java performance evaluation. SIGPLAN Not. 42(10), 57–76 (2007). https://doi.org/10.1145/1297105.1297033

12. Haller, P., Prokopec, A., Miller, H., Klang, V., Kuhn, R., Jovanovic, V.: Scala improvement proposal: futures and promises (SIP-14) (2012). http://docs.scala-lang.org/sips/pending/futures-promises.html

13. Joisha, P.G.: Sticky tries: fast insertions, fast lookups, no deletions for large key universes. In: Proceedings of the 2014 International Symposium on Memory Management. ISMM 2014, pp. 35–46. ACM, New York (2014). https://doi.org/10.1145/2602988.2602998

14. Lea, D.: Doug Lea's workstation (2014). http://g.oswego.edu/

15. Li, X., Andersen, D.G., Kaminsky, M., Freedman, M.J.: Algorithmic improvements for fast concurrent cuckoo hashing. In: Proceedings of the Ninth European Conference on Computer Systems. EuroSys 2014, pp. 27:1–27:14. ACM, New York (2014). https://doi.org/10.1145/2592798.2592820

16. Liang, F.M.: Word Hy-phen-a-tion by Com-pu-ter. Ph.D. thesis, Stanford University, Stanford, CA 94305, June 1983. also available as Stanford University, Department of Computer Science Report No. STAN-CS-83-977

17. Liu, Y., Zhang, K., Spear, M.: Dynamic-sized nonblocking hash tables. In: Proceedings of the 2014 ACM Symposium on Principles of Distributed Computing. PODC 2014, pp. 242–251. ACM, New York (2014). https://doi.org/10.1145/2611462.2611495

18. Michael, M.M.: High performance dynamic lock-free hash tables and list-based sets. In: Proceedings of the Fourteenth Annual ACM Symposium on Parallel Algorithms and Architectures. SPAA 2002, pp. 73–82. ACM, New York (2002). https://doi.org/10.1145/564870.564881

19. Oshman, R., Shavit, N.: The skipTrie: low-depth concurrent search without rebalancing. In: Proceedings of the 2013 ACM Symposium on Principles of Distributed Computing. PODC 2013, pp. 23–32. ACM, New York (2013). https://doi.org/10.1145/2484239.2484270

20. Prokopec, A., Petrashko, D., Odersky, M.: Efficient lock-free work-stealing iterators for data-parallel collections. In: 2015 23rd Euromicro International Conference on Parallel, Distributed, and Network-Based Processing, pp. 248–252, March 2015

21. Prokopec, A.: Data structures and algorithms for data-parallel computing in a managed runtime. Ph.D. thesis, IC, Lausanne (2014)

22. Prokopec, A.: Scalameter website (2014). http://scalameter.github.io

23. Prokopec, A.: SnapQueue: lock-free queue with constant time snapshots. In: Proceedings of the 6th ACM SIGPLAN Symposium on Scala. SCALA 2015, pp. 1–12. ACM, New York (2015). https://doi.org/10.1145/2774975.2774976

24. Prokopec, A.: Pluggable scheduling for the reactor programming model. In: Proceedings of the 6th International Workshop on Programming Based on Actors, Agents, and Decentralized Control. AGERE 2016, pp. 41–50. ACM, New York (2016). https://doi.org/10.1145/3001886.3001891

25. Prokopec, A.: Accelerating by idling: how speculative delays improve performance of message-oriented systems. In: Rivera, F.F., Pena, T.F., Cabaleiro, J.C. (eds.) Euro-Par 2017. LNCS, vol. 10417, pp. 177–191. Springer, Cham (2017). https://doi.org/10.1007/978-3-319-64203-1_13

26. Prokopec, A.: Analysis of Concurrent Lock-Free Hash Tries with Constant-Time Operations. ArXiv e-prints, December 2017

27. Prokopec, A.: Encoding the building blocks of communication. In: Proceedings of the 2017 ACM SIGPLAN International Symposium on New Ideas, New Paradigms, and Reflections on Programming and Software. Onward! 2017, pp. 104–118. ACM, New York (2017). https://doi.org/10.1145/3133850.3133865

28. Prokopec, A.: Cache-tries: concurrent lock-free hash tries with constant-time operations. In: Proceedings of the 23rd ACM SIGPLAN Symposium on Principles and Practice of Parallel Programming. PPoPP 2018. ACM, New York (2018). https://doi.org/10.1145/3178487.3178498

29. Prokopec, A.: Efficient lock-free removing and compaction for the cache-trie data structure (2018). https://doi.org/10.6084/m9.figshare.6369134

30. Prokopec, A.: Reactors.io website (2018). http://reactors.io

31. Prokopec, A., Bagwell, P., Odersky, M.: Cache-aware lock-free concurrent hash tries. Technical report (2011)

32. Prokopec, A., Bagwell, P., Odersky, M.: Lock-free resizeable concurrent tries. In: Rajopadhye, S., Mills Strout, M. (eds.) LCPC 2011. LNCS, vol. 7146, pp. 156–170. Springer, Heidelberg (2013). https://doi.org/10.1007/978-3-642-36036-7_11

33. Prokopec, A., Bagwell, P., Rompf, T., Odersky, M.: A generic parallel collection framework. In: Jeannot, E., Namyst, R., Roman, J. (eds.) Euro-Par 2011. LNCS, vol. 6853, pp. 136–147. Springer, Heidelberg (2011). https://doi.org/10.1007/978-3-642-23397-5_14. http://dl.acm.org/citation.cfm?id=2033408.2033425

34. Prokopec, A., Bronson, N.G., Bagwell, P., Odersky, M.: Concurrent tries with efficient non-blocking snapshots. In: Proceedings of the 17th ACM SIGPLAN Symposium on Principles and Practice of Parallel Programming. PPoPP 2012, pp. 151–160. ACM, New York (2012). https://doi.org/10.1145/2145816.2145836

35. Prokopec, A., Haller, P., Odersky, M.: Containers and aggregates, mutators and isolates for reactive programming. In: Proceedings of the Fifth Annual Scala Workshop. SCALA 2014, pp. 51–61. ACM, New York (2014). https://doi.org/10.1145/2637647.2637656

36. Prokopec, A., Leopoldseder, D., Duboscq, G., Würthinger, T.: Making collection operations optimal with aggressive JIT compilation. In: Proceedings of the 8th ACM SIGPLAN International Symposium on Scala. SCALA 2017, pp. 29–40. ACM, New York (2017). https://doi.org/10.1145/3136000.3136002

37. Prokopec, A., Miller, H., Haller, P., Schlatter, T., Odersky, M.: FlowPools: a lock-free deterministic concurrent dataflow abstraction, proofs. Technical report (2012)

38. Prokopec, A., Miller, H., Schlatter, T., Haller, P., Odersky, M.: Flowpools: a lock-free deterministic concurrent dataflow abstraction. In: LCPC, pp. 158–173 (2012)

39. Prokopec, A., Odersky, M.: Near optimal work-stealing tree scheduler for highly irregular data-parallel workloads. In: Cascaval, C., Montesinos, P. (eds.) Languages and Compilers for Parallel Computing, pp. 55–86. Springer International Publishing, Cham (2014). https://doi.org/10.1007/978-3-319-09967-5_4

40. Prokopec, A., Odersky, M.: Isolates, channels, and event streams for composable distributed programming. In: 2015 ACM International Symposium on New Ideas, New Paradigms, and Reflections on Programming and Software (Onward!), pp. 171–182. Onward! 2015. ACM, New York (2015). https://doi.org/10.1145/2814228.2814245

41. Prokopec, A., Odersky, M.: Conc-trees for functional and parallel programming. In: Shen, X., Mueller, F., Tuck, J. (eds.) LCPC 2015. LNCS, vol. 9519, pp. 254–268. Springer, Cham (2016). https://doi.org/10.1007/978-3-319-29778-1_16

42. Prokopec, A., Petrashko, D., Odersky, M.: On lock-free work-stealing iterators for parallel data structures, p. 10 (2014)

43. Pugh, W.: Concurrent maintenance of skip lists. Technical report, College Park, MD, USA (1990)

44. Schlatter, T., Prokopec, A., Miller, H., Haller, P., Odersky, M.: Multi-lane flow-pools: a detailed look, p. 13 (2012)

45. Shafiei, N.: Non-blocking patricia tries with replace operations. In: 2013 IEEE 33rd International Conference on Distributed Computing Systems, pp. 216–225, July 2013

46. Steindorfer, M.J., Vinju, J.J.: Optimizing hash-array mapped tries for fast and lean immutable JVM collections. In: SIGPLAN Not, vol. 50, no. 10, pp. 783–800, October 2015. https://doi.org/10.1145/2858965.2814312

47. Steindorfer, M.J., Vinju, J.J.: Towards a software product line of trie-based collections. In: Proceedings of the 2016 ACM SIGPLAN International Conference on Generative Programming: Concepts and Experiences. GPCE 2016, pp. 168–172. ACM, New York (2016). https://doi.org/10.1145/2993236.2993251

48. Sujeeth, A.K., et al.: Composition and reuse with compiled domain-specific languages. In: Castagna, G. (ed.) ECOOP 2013. LNCS, vol. 7920, pp. 52–78. Springer, Heidelberg (2013). https://doi.org/10.1007/978-3-642-39038-8_3

NUMA Optimizations for Algorithmic Skeletons

Paul Metzger[1]([✉]), Murray Cole[1], and Christian Fensch[2]

[1] School of Informatics, University of Edinburgh, Edinburgh EH8 9AB, UK
{paul.metzger,m.cole}@inf.ed.ac.uk
[2] MACS, Heriot-Watt University, Edinburgh EH14 4AS, UK
c.fensch@hw.ac.uk

Abstract. To address NUMA performance anomalies, programmers often resort to application specific optimizations that are not transferable to other programs, or to generic optimizations that do not perform well in all cases. Skeleton based programming models allow NUMA optimizations to be abstracted on a pattern-by-pattern basis, freeing programmers from this complexity. As a case study, we investigate computations that can be implemented with stencil skeletons. We present an analysis of the behavior of a range of simple and complex stencil programs from the NAS and Rodinia benchmark suites, under state-of-the-art NUMA aware page placement (PP) schemes. We show that even though an application (or skeleton) may have implemented the correct, intuitive scheduling of data and work to threads, the resulting performance can be disrupted by an inappropriate PP scheme. In contrast, we show that a NUMA PP-aware stencil implementation scheme can achieve speed ups of up to 2x over a similar scheme which uses the Linux default PP, and that this works across a set of complex stencil applications. Furthermore, we show that a supposed PP performance optimization in the Linux kernel never improves and in some cases degrades stencil performance by up to 0.27x and should therefore be deactivated by stencil skeleton implementations. Finally, we show that further speed ups of up to 1.1x can be achieved by addressing a work imbalance issue caused by poor conventional understanding of NUMA PP.

1 Introduction

Modern systems have complex and non-uniform memory organizations to meet the high bandwidth requirements of increasing core counts. For example, multi-socket systems feature multiple memory controllers that are spread over sockets (see Fig. 1). CPUs can access memory that is attached to a remote memory controller via interconnects. The downside of this is that memory accesses are non-uniform in terms of latency and bandwidth. Thus, great care must be taken when choosing the right location for a memory page at a given time during program execution. These complexities in memory systems of NUMA machines cause hard to predict performance anomalies [1,2].

© Springer International Publishing AG, part of Springer Nature 2018
M. Aldinucci et al. (Eds.): Euro-Par 2018, LNCS 11014, pp. 590–602, 2018.
https://doi.org/10.1007/978-3-319-96983-1_42

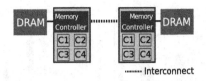

Fig. 1. Illustration of a NUMA system with two NUMA nodes.

NUMA aware program optimizations that address this problem are at the extremes of a spectrum. At one end are generic NUMA page placement (PP) schemes, such as First-Touch, Interleaved, and the Linux automatic NUMA Balancing feature which are known to exhibit pathological behavior in hard to predict situations [3,4]. At the other end of the spectrum are application specific memory optimizations such as shared variable privatization. However, transferring these to other applications is a labor-intensive process. Skeleton-based programming systems [5–7] have the potential to support a compromise position: NUMA aware optimizations that are transparently applicable across the class of computations captured by each skeleton. In support of this hypothesis, we present a case study for *stencil* computations. NUMA aware PP optimizations for other skeletons will be investigated in the future. We conduct an analysis of the behavior of stencil applications from the NAS-PB and Rodinia benchmark suites, comparing their performance under state-of-the-art NUMA PP schemes with performance under a stencil-skeleton-aware NUMA PP scheme, and its extension with a novel work distribution heuristic. We show that

- the stencil-skeleton-aware NUMA PP scheme has good applicability across a wide range of stencil computations, well beyond the simple Jacobi-style stencils which motivate it, offering speed-ups of up to 2x over similar state-of-the-art schemes.
- automatic NUMA Balancing, a generic optimization in the Linux kernel, is actively disruptive of stencil performance, diminishing performance by up to 0.27x, and so should be disabled by stencil skeletons.
- our novel work distribution approach further speeds up applications by 1.1x.

The remainder of this paper is structured as follows: Section 2 provides a motivating example that demonstrates the possible performance benefits of stencil aware PP. Section 3 introduces stencil computations and standard NUMA PP schemes. Section 4 motivates and describes our stencil aware PP and work distribution scheme, and provides an overview of the experimental program which informs and evaluates it. Section 5 describes the experimental set up and Sect. 6 presents experimental results. Finally, Sects. 7 and 8 discuss related work and conclusions.

2   Motivating Example

As has previously been demonstrated for individual applications [8–11], this section provides an example which confirms that performance improvements

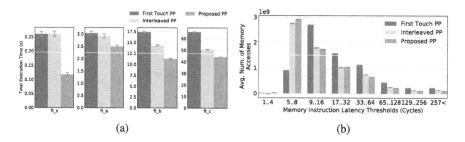

(a)   (b)

Fig. 2. (a) Execution times of the NAS-PB ft benchmark with different page placement (PP) schemes. The letters *s, a, b, c* indicate the standard problem set sizes in ascending order. (b) Access latency histogram of ft with the largest input data set.

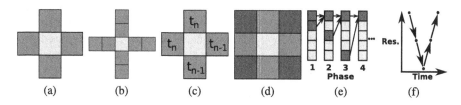

(a)   (b)   (c)   (d)   (e)   (f)

Fig. 3. Jacobi stencils (a + b), a Gauss-Seidel stencil (c), a stencil with a dynamic neighborhood (d), a butterfly divide-and-conquer stencil (e) and the multigrid method (f). (Color figure online)

over state of the art schemes can be achieved by adding application awareness to the page placement (PP) process. We use the NAS-PB Fourier Transformation (ft) benchmark as a case-study. Figure 2a shows execution times of ft with different PP schemes. Stencil Aware PP performs significantly better than the other schemes in all cases and the maximum speed up is 57%. We sampled the number of memory accesses that fall into set latency ranges to better understand the performance benefits (see Fig. 2b). The results indicate that Stencil Aware and Interleaved PP take pressure from interconnects and memory controllers compared to First-Touch PP as they use all interconnects and memory controllers evenly (see Sect. 3 for explanations of the state of the art PP schemes). Stencil Aware PP also minimizes the number of high latency remote memory accesses and, therefore, performs better than Interleaved PP.

3   Background

3.1   Stencil Computations

Stencil computations update elements in a buffer based on the values in the elements' neighborhoods. The neighborhoods are regular and predictable. Figure 3a illustrates this for a single element (grey) and its neigborhood (green). Updates are performed in a single sweep or multiple iterations. The remainder of this subsection discusses different types of stencil computations.

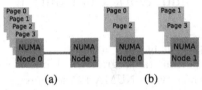
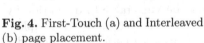
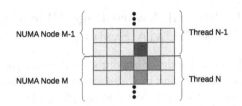

(a)   (b)

Fig. 4. First-Touch (a) and Interleaved (b) page placement.

Fig. 5. Illustration of parallelization, collocation and remote memory access (red) when stencil aware PP is used. Elements above the red line are placed on NUMA node M-1 and elements below are placed on node M. (Color figure online)

Jacobi stencil computations are conceptually the simplest stencils as their neighbourhood and input grid have a fixed size and shape. Shape and dimensionality of the neighborhood can vary across Jacobi stencils (see, for example, Fig. 3a and b). *Gauss-Seidel* stencils use values from the current and the previous iteration. In Fig. 3c elements at the top and the left-hand side are from the current and the elements at the bottom and right-hand side are from the previous iteration. Some stencils have a *variable* neighborhood that changes depending on the input data. The stencil in Fig. 3d uses either the green or the green and the dark red elements as input. The *red black* method arranges the elements in the input buffer like a checker board. Black elements are updated based on values of neighboring red elements and vice versa. The *Butterfly divide-and-conquer* method works in phases and changes the size of the stencil in each phase. Figure 3e illustrates this based on the computation of one element. Arrows indicate which elements of the input buffer are read in each phase. The *multigrid method* changes the resolution of the in- and output data dynamically (see Fig. 3f).

3.2 Page Placement Schemes

This section presents state of the art PP schemes. *First-Touch Page Placement* allocates pages on the same NUMA node as cores that first access them and is the default scheme of Linux. Figure 4a illustrates this PP policy. All pages are placed on node zero if the thread that runs on this node accesses them first. First-Touch PP optimises for data locality if pages are mostly accessed by threads that access them first. *Interleaved Page Placement* places pages on NUMA nodes in a round robin fashion and can be used as an alternative to First-Touch PP (see Fig. 4b). This scheme distributes memory accesses equally across memory controllers and interconnects but fails to optimise for data locality. *Automatic NUMA Balancing* migrates pages and threads across NUMA nodes, informed by run-time memory access statistics, to increase data locality. This is known to cause page thrashing and an extension called *Pseudo-Interleaving* has been proposed to address this [3]. Automatic NUMA Balancing is activated by default on Linux systems (i.e. in addition to First-Touch).

4   Stencil Aware Page Placement and Work Distribution for NUMA Systems

This section describes our stencil aware page placement (PP) and work distribution scheme and provides an overview of the experimental program which informs and evaluates it. We first describe a basic stencil aware NUMA PP scheme, as motivated in Sect. 2 and explain how this may be vulnerable to disruption by LinuxNUMA, a phenomenon which we will evaluate in Sect. 6. We then explain why the basic stencil aware PP scheme may experience performance degradation due to uneven distribution of remote accesses, and propose a novel work distribution technique which addresses this. The new PP and work distribution scheme are evaluated in Sect. 6.

A Basic Stencil Aware Page Placement Scheme. Motivated by previously reported ad-hoc PP experiments, this scheme places pages on NUMA nodes that access them most frequently to improve data locality prior to a computation. Figure 5 illustrates this with a simple 2D Jacobi stencil. Stencil aware PP collocates thread N with the Nth memory block on NUMA node M, and so on. Note that in doing so we are going beyond conventional stencil-skeleton wisdom of simply associating threads with specific data partitions (and hence work), in order to ensure that this allocation is also respected by the underlying PP scheme. We also investigate whether this can be achieved for more complex types of stencil computations than simple Jacobi stencils (see Sect. 3.1).

Performance Degradation Through Automatic NUMA Balancing. NUMA Balancing is known to cause page thrashing if multiple NUMA nodes access the same pages in an alternating fashion [4]. NUMA Balancing then migrates pages back and forth between these nodes. The stencil access pattern causes some pages to be shared between two NUMA nodes in each iteration of the stencil computation. In our experiments we investigate whether this effect degrades performance predictably for stencil computations.

Bad Work Distribution and Our NUMA Aware Scheme. The intuitive work distribution scheme for stencils allocates an equal share of grid points to each thread. However, this fails to consider the potential for unequal NUMA memory accesses to impact upon the time it takes to complete the corresponding work. Figure 5 illustrates this for one element with a simple 2D Jacobi stencil. Meanwhile, some threads are not penalized by remote memory accesses and so complete their iteration sooner. These threads must wait on a barrier after each iteration, potentially creating a significant imbalance in waiting time and signifying a wasted resource. Our experiments investigate the extent to which this phenomenon occurs.

We propose and evaluate a novel work distribution scheme which aims to reduce the idle waiting time of threads that do not access remote memory. This work distribution reflects the different access latencies in NUMA systems. Threads that are penalized by high latency remote memory accesses are assigned smaller chunks of input data than threads that access only local memory. Our experiments evaluate the impact of this new scheme.

5   Experimental Setup

To reduce the complexity of our experiments, we did not use a skeleton library but implemented the Stencil Aware PP and work distribution schemes, which could be implemented by a skeleton library, by hand. To enact the basic PP policy on top of the default OS First-Touch policy we introduce OpenMP code that creates and fills the stencil buffers with initial values. This parallel code imitates the memory access patterns of subsequent stencil computations, and so places pages on NUMA nodes that subsequently access them. In the srad benchmarks, buffers for precalculated indices are interleaved when Stencil Aware PP is used as the entire buffers are accessed by all threads. Stencil Aware PP can only work if the OS cannot migrate threads to another NUMA node, since otherwise, pages that these migrated threads access would then be on a remote NUMA node. Therefore, we use thread pinning to prevent this. Finally, the stencil iterations are implemented with an OpenMP parallel for region, using the static scheduling.

Table 1 lists details of the test systems. Machine A's kernel uses Pseudo-Interleaving (see Sect. 3.2) [3]. Benchmarks are taken from the Rodinia [12] and NPB-PB [13] suites (see Table 2) and are compiled with ICC 17.0.4 and the -O2 flag. The standard inputs of the benchmark applications are used except for the largest hotspot input due to very long execution time, and the iteration count that the Rodinia benchmarks perform are made higher to reduce noise. Five samples are taken in the access latency experiment in Sect. 2 and at least ten samples are taken in each of the other experiments. Our timing experiments are reported with 95% confidence intervals. Our speed ups are reported as the ratio of the means of the relevant measurements. Spinning time and access latency related experiments were conducted with Intel V-Tune XE 2017.

Table 1. Hardware details of the test machines.

Machine name	Machine A	Machine B
CPU Model	Xeon L7555	Xeon E5-2697 v2
Sockets	4	2
Cores/Socket	8	12
LLC/Socket	18 MB	30 MB
Mem. Contr./Socket	1	1
QPI Band./Link	5.86GT/s	8GT/s
Hyperthr.	Deactivated	Deactivated
Prefetchers	Active	Active
Linux Kernel	4.4.36	3.10.0

Table 2. Benchmark application details. The letter s to c and numbers 64 to 8192 indicate standard input sizes.

App.	Stencil type	Source	Memory consumption
Srad v1	Jacobi	Rod	16 MB
Srad v2	Jacobi	Rod	122 MB
Hotspot	Jacobi	Rod	64: 10 MB; 128: 12 MB; 256: 11 MB; 512: 15 MB; 1024: 19 MB; 2048: 54 MB; 4096: 202 MB; 8192: 800 MB
MG	Multigrid	NPB	S: 10 MB; A: 619 MB; B: 620 MB; C: 4,736 MB
FT	Butterfly D&C	NPB	S: 21 MB; A: 450 MB; B: 1,760 MB; C: 6,897 MB

6   Evaluation

6.1   Stencil Aware Page Placement

To assess the performance of *Stencil Aware* PP, we compare it in Fig. 6 against two state of the art PP schemes available on Linux: *First-Touch* and *Interleaved* PP. In most cases, Stencil Aware PP either matches or improves performance over state of the art PP schemes. Large speed ups over First-Touch PP without pinning can be observed for very small problem sizes i.e. mg with problem size s and hotspot with problem sizes 64 to 512. A maximum speed up of 12x has been achieved with the hotspot benchmark on machine A.

Results with small problem sizes and the standard PP schemes show that pinning significantly benefits performance. Stencil Aware PP still improves performance by up to 2x over First-Touch PP with pinning, and pinning has a very small, and in some cases no influence on performance for larger problem sizes. In only a small number of cases do the standard schemes with pinning perform slightly better. For example, the standard PP schemes perform better than Stencil Aware PP when we measure the total execution time with hotspot 64, 128 and 256 on machine A. However, Stencil Aware PP performs better in these cases when we measure the execution time spent in the stencil iterations. This indicates that Stencil Aware PP still improves the performance of the stencil computations but that the overhead of the page placement outweighs the performance benefits of Stencil Aware PP in these few instances. In summary, our results show that Stencil Aware PP is a viable alternative to the current built-in schemes of Linux and should be used instead.

6.2   Performance Degradation Through NUMA Balancing

To assess the impact of automatic NUMA Balancing (from now referred to as "*LinuxNUMA*") we compare Stencil Aware PP without LinuxNUMA against all PP schemes with LinuxNUMA in Fig. 7. Most of the applications and schemes perform worse with LinuxNUMA than Stencil Aware PP without LinuxNUMA. In the few cases where LinuxNUMA is beneficial the differences are small (max:

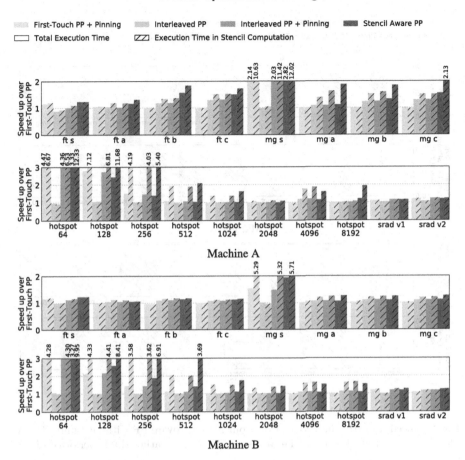

Fig. 6. Speed ups over standard implementations without pinning and the standard Linux First-Touch PP scheme with the total execution time and the execution time spent in the stencil iterations.

0.09x) and present on only one machine, or the PP schemes already perform slightly better than our scheme even without LinuxNUMA (see hotspot with input size 4096 and 8192 in Fig. 6.1) and continue to do so with LinuxNUMA. It is important to note that LinuxNUMA degrades the performance of Stencil Aware PP in all cases, by up to 0.27x with mg and input c on machine A. Thus, in addition to using Stencil Aware PP, LinuxNUMA should be deactivated for stencil computations (for example, in stencil skeleton libraries).

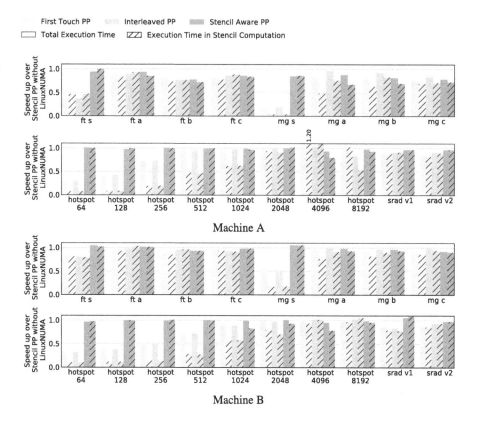

Fig. 7. Speed up with LinuxNUMA over our Stencil Aware PP without LinuxNUMA. Most speed ups are below 1.0 i.e. are slow downs indicating the superiority of our scheme.

6.3 Bad Work Distribution and Stencil Aware Work Distribution

The uneven idle time effect discussed in Sect. 4 is present to varying degrees across our benchmark suite and machines. The expected variation in idle times occurs with the srad v2 benchmark on Machine A and B as shown in Fig. 8. Adjacent cores in Fig. 8 share data and cores that share data with a remote NUMA node, like core 7 and 8 on machine A have the expected, consistently lower spinning times which indicate that they are slowed down by remote memory accesses as discussed in Sect. 4. The expected variations are also visible for the NAS-PB mg benchmark on Machine A with input size a and b. However, the idle time differences are very small and statistically insignificant.

In contrast, the effect is not visible in other cases for the following reasons. For the NAS-PB ft benchmark implementation the stencil has a 2D neighborhood and the input buffer is 3D. The computation is parallelized over the third dimension of the input buffer and, therefore, the cores do not share data, and so the idle time imbalance is not present. Meanwhile, the data set of srad v1 fits

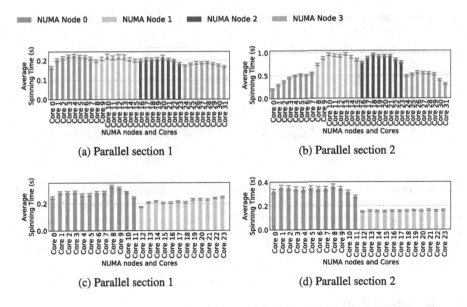

Fig. 8. Uneven idle times with srad v2 on Machine A (a + b) and B (c + d).

into the combined LLCs which causes the latency differences between local and remote memory accesses to the LLCs to be very small and so the variations of the idle times become too small to report.

6.4   NUMA and Stencil Aware Work Distribution

We compare our work distribution scheme with a range of alternatives, all of which are extensions of our basic pinned, Stencil Aware PP scheme as introduced in Sect. 4. These are created by selecting different OpenMP schedules for the stencil iterations. The best work distribution for our scheme was determined experimentally. Figure 9 shows execution times with OpenMP's built-in schedules and with our stencil aware work distribution. *"Static"* corresponds to our basic stencil aware PP scheme from Sect. 4. Our new *stencil aware work distribution* scheme achieves improved performance of up to 1.1x for srad v2. In contrast, none of the standard OpenMP schedules can mitigate the negative effects of the uneven idle time distribution. This shows that our scheme addresses the work imbalance caused by variable NUMA memory latencies. To make this applicable within a generic stencil scheme it would be important to predict the stencil instances for which an improvement is achievable.

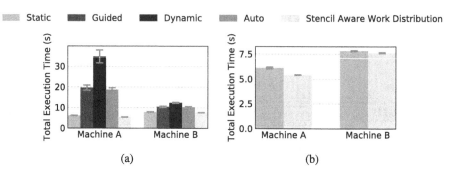

Fig. 9. Execution times of srad v2 with OpenMP schedules and with our NUMA and stencil aware work distribution (a). A direct comparison of the best OpenMP schedule with the stencil aware work distribution (b). *Static, guided, dynamic* and *auto* are OpenMP schedules. *"Static"* corresponds to our basic stencil aware PP scheme from Sect. 4. The stencil aware work distribution reflects the uneven idle times discussed in Sect. 6.3.

7   Related Work

We first review state of the art page placement schemes, then NUMA stencil optimizations and, lastly, work on NUMA aware schedulers and work distribution.

Carrefour reduces congestion on interconnects and memory controllers via page collocation, replication and interleaving [14]. It has to monitor memory accesses to inform the usage of these techniques and cannot, like our approach, leverage information about the structure of a computation that is available prior to execution.

Mechanisms for automatic thread and page migration have been developed for the Linux kernel [3,15–17]. These mechanisms monitor memory accesses and, therefore, cannot act until sufficient data is collected. This monitoring based approach can result in pathological behavior such as page [18,19] and task bouncing [3,20]. Our scheme can find an optimal task and page placements before a computation starts.

Stencil aware memory management for NUMA systems has been mentioned in side notes [21–24]. To the best of our knowledge we are the first to report an in-depth analysis of stencil aware memory management for NUMA systems with a broad range of stencil types and problem sizes.

Pilla et al. present a NUMA-Aware scheduler [25]. The scheduler considers the communication between concurrently executing threads and collocates them on NUMA nodes to minimize communication across CPU boundaries. This approach suffers from similar problems as other monitoring based approaches (see above). Chen and Olivier et al. present work stealing for NUMA systems [26,27]. Their approach reschedules work at run time in case work was not distributed equally. Our approach distributes work equally before a computation starts by taking the memory system of the target system and stencil specific memory access patterns into account.

8   Conclusion and Future Work

We argue that NUMA optimizations should be embedded in skeleton implementations by utilizing implicit knowledge encoded in them. We present a case study with stencil computations. We evaluate a stencil aware page placement (PP) scheme that exploits the regular and predictable stencil memory access patterns. We then investigate two further optimizations that build on Stencil Aware PP. Firstly, we show that automatic NUMA Balancing, an advanced optimization technique in the Linux kernel, degrades the performance of stencil computations when Stencil Aware PP is used. Secondly, we investigate a novel stencil and NUMA aware work distribution scheme. Stencil Aware PP improves the performance of applications by up to 12x over standard PP schemes if they are not combined with pinning and 2x if they are combined with pinning. Furthermore, stencil aware PP never degrades performance. NUMA Balancing degrades the performance of stencil applications by up to 0.27x if stencil aware PP is used and should be deactivated. Finally, we show that the performance of some stencil computations can be further improved by up to 1.1x with our stencil aware work distribution. Future work includes a heuristic that predicts whether the new stencil aware work distribution scheme will be beneficial. We plan to investigate a model for our NUMA and stencil aware work distribution that is based on parameters of a given stencil computation and target NUMA architecture. Furthermore, we will consider the fact that, in multiprogrammed scenarios, the proposed deactivation of LinuxNUMA has an impact on other applications that run on the system. Finally, we will investigate NUMA optimizations for further skeletons.

Acknowledgments. Thanks to Tom Deakin and Simon McIntosh-Smith from the University of Bristol for giving us access to their machines. Grants EPSRC EP/L01503X/1 for the University of Edinburgh School of Informatics Centre for Doctoral Training in Pervasive Parallelism as well as EPSRC EP/P010946/1 and EPSRC EP/P022642/1 supported this work.

References

1. Talbot, S.A.M., Kelly, P.H.J.: High performance computing systems and applications. In: Schaeffer, J. (ed.) Stable Performance for CC-NUMA Using First-Touch Page Placement and Reactive Proxies. SECS, vol. 478, pp. 251–266. Springer, Boston (1998). https://doi.org/10.1007/978-1-4615-5611-4_26
2. McCurdy, C., Vetter, J.: Memphis: finding and fixing NUMA-related performance problems on multi-core platforms. In: Proceedings of ISPASS (2010)
3. van Riel, R., Chegu, V.: Automatic NUMA balancing. In: Red Hat Summit (2014)
4. Gaud, F., et al.: Challenges of memory management on modern NUMA system. Queue **13**(8), 70 (2015)
5. Cole, M.: Bringing skeletons out of the closet: a pragmatic manifesto for skeletal parallel programming. Parallel Comput. **30**(3), 389–406 (2004)
6. González-Vélez, H., Leyton, M.: A survey of algorithmic skeleton frameworks: high-level structured parallel programming enablers. Softw. Pract. Exp. **40**(12), 1135–1160 (2010)

7. Enmyren, J., Kessler, C.W.: SkePU: a multi-backend skeleton programming library for multi-GPU systems. In: Proceedings of HLPP (2010)
8. Ribeiro, C.P., Mehaut, J.F., Carissimi, A., Castro, M., Fernandes, L.G.: Memory affinity for hierarchical shared memory multiprocessors. In: Proceedings of ICS (2009)
9. Yang, R., Antony, J., Rendell, A., Robson, D., Strazdins, P.: Profiling directed NUMA optimization on Linux systems: a case study of the Gaussian computational chemistry code. In: Proceedings of IPDPS (2011)
10. Bircsak, J., et al.: Extending OpenMP for NUMA machines. In: Proceedings of ICS (2000)
11. Broquedis, F., Furmento, N., Goglin, B., Wacrenier, P.A., Namyst, R.: Forest-GOMP: an efficient OpenMP environment for NUMA architectures. Int. J. Parallel Program. **38**(5), 418–439 (2010)
12. Che, S., et al.: Rodinia: a benchmark suite for heterogeneous computing. In: Proceedings of IISWC (2009)
13. Baily, D., et al.: The NAS parallel benchmarks. Technical report RNR-94-007, NASA Ames Research Center (1994)
14. Dashti, M., et al.: Traffic management: a holistic approach to memory placement on NUMA systems. In: ACM SIGPLAN Notices, vol. 48. ACM (2013)
15. Corbet, J.: AutoNUMA: the other approach to NUMA scheduling, March 2012. https://lwn.net/Articles/488709/
16. Corbet, J.: Toward better NUMA scheduling, March 2012. https://lwn.net/Articles/486858/
17. Gorman, M.: Foundation for automatic NUMA balancing, November 2012. https://lwn.net/Articles/523065/
18. Bolosky, W., Fitzgerald, R., Scott, M.: Simple but effective techniques for NUMA memory management. ACM SIGOPS Operat. Syst. Rev. **23**(5), 19–31 (1989)
19. Gaud, F., Lepers, B., Decouchant, J., Fuston, J., Fedorova, A., Quéma, V.: Large pages may be harmful on NUMA systems. In: Proceedings of USENIX ATC (2014)
20. Gorman, M.: Automatic NUMA balancing V4, November 2012. https://lwn.net/Articles/526097/
21. Christen, M., Schenk, O., Burkhart, H.: PATUS: a code generation and autotuning framework for parallel iterative stencil computations on modern microarchitectures. In: Proceedings of IPDPS (2011)
22. Kamil, S., Chan, C., Oliker, L., Shalf, J., Williams, S.: An auto-tuning framework for parallel multicore stencil computations. In: Proceedings of IPDPS (2010)
23. Shaheen, M., Strzodka, R.: NUMA aware iterative stencil computations on many-core systems. In: Proceedings of IPDPS (2012)
24. Lin, P.-H., Yi, Q., Quinlan, D., Liao, C., Yan, Y.: Automatically optimizing stencil computations on many-core NUMA architectures. In: Ding, C., Criswell, J., Wu, P. (eds.) LCPC 2016. LNCS, vol. 10136, pp. 137–152. Springer, Cham (2017). https://doi.org/10.1007/978-3-319-52709-3_12
25. Pilla, L.L., et al.: Improving parallel system performance with a NUMA-aware load balancer. Technical report TR-JLPC-11-02, INRIA-Illinois Joint Laboratory on Petascale Computing (2011)
26. Chen, Q., Guo, M., Guan, H.: LAWS: locality-aware work-stealing for multi-socket multi-core architectures. In: Proceedings of the International Conference on Supercomputing (2014)
27. Olivier, S.L., Porterfield, A.K., Wheeler, K.B., Spiegel, M., Prins, J.F.: OpenMP task scheduling strategies for multicore NUMA systems. IJHPCA **26**(2), 110–124 (2012)

Improving System Turnaround Time with Intel CAT by Identifying LLC Critical Applications

Lucia Pons[✉], Vicent Selfa, Julio Sahuquillo, Salvador Petit, and Julio Pons

Department of Computer Engineering, Universitat Politècnica de València,
Valencia, Spain
lupones@inf.upv.es

Abstract. Resource sharing is a major concern in current multicore processors. Among the shared system resources, the Last Level Cache (LLC) is one of the most critical, since destructive interference between applications accessing it implies more off-chip accesses to main memory, which incur long latencies that can severely impact the overall system performance. To help alleviate this issue, current processors implement huge LLCs, but even so, inter-application interference can harm the performance of a subset of the running applications when executing multiprogram workloads. For this reason, recent Intel processors feature *Cache Allocation Technologies* (CAT) to partition the cache and assign subsets of cache ways to groups of applications. This paper proposes the *Critical-Aware* (CA) LLC partitioning approach, which leverages CAT and improves the performance of multiprogram workloads, by identifying and protecting the applications whose performance is more damaged by LLC sharing. Experimental results show that CA improves turnaround time on average by 15%, and up to 40% compared to a baseline system without partitioning.

1 Introduction

Recent processors implement huge Last Level Caches (LLC) and prefetching mechanisms to hide long main memory access latencies. LLC caches are typically shared among all applications running in the cores. The LLC is sized according to the processor core count, and typically takes a few MBs (e.g. 1 to 4) per core, resulting in an overall cache capacity in the order of tens of MBs. This capacity is even higher in processors using 3D stacking technologies [1].

Cache sharing yields important problems to the system from a performance perspective. These problems appear due to inter-application interferences at the shared cache, making the system become unpredictable. As a consequence, issues like system throughput [2–4], and fairness [5–8] have been addressed in previous research.

Most research work on cache sharing during the last decade has been developed using simulators because hardware in commercial processors did not support it. Fortunately, some processors manufacturers like Intel and ARM have

© Springer International Publishing AG, part of Springer Nature 2018
M. Aldinucci et al. (Eds.): Euro-Par 2018, LNCS 11014, pp. 603–615, 2018.
https://doi.org/10.1007/978-3-319-96983-1_43

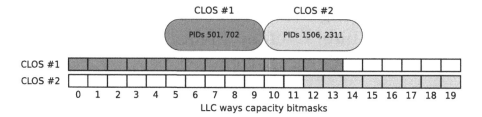

Fig. 1. Intel CAT example with PIDs associated to two CLOSes.

recently deployed technologies that allow distributing LLC cache ways among co-running applications. For instance, Intel has deployed *Cache Allocation Technology* (CAT) which is being delivered in some recent processors.

These technologies provide a hardware-software interface, which allows the software to take decisions about the cache distribution. This means that a cache sharing approach can be more elaborated than if it was entirely implemented in hardware.

The main focus of this paper is to reduce the **turnaround time** of a set of applications running concurrently (mix). This time is defined as the elapsed time between the mix's execution start and the instant the last application of the mix finishes. Turnaround time is especially important in batch based systems, since improving this performance metric allows the system to transit to a low power state and helps energy savings. Eyerman and Eeckhout [9] claim that program turnaround time in general-purpose systems and interactive environments should be considered one of the primary performance criteria.

In this work we characterize the LLC behavior of applications in isolated execution, and their dynamic behavior when they are executed with other co-runners. This study revealed that some applications, *namely critical*, should be protected (i.e. exposed to less inter-application interference) by assigning them exclusive cache ways. On the contrary, other applications, *namely non-critical*, present *fewer* space requirements, hence suffering less from inter-application interference.

Based on this characterization study we propose the Critical-Aware (CA) algorithm, a simple and low-overhead LLC partitioning approach, which is the main contribution of this work. The fact that it is simple and has a minimum cost, is key to adapt to different execution phases, as fast and frequent decisions are needed to be taken. CA approach, by design, divides the cache in two partitions (one for critical and one for non-critical applications) and dynamically assigns or removes ways to each group, allowing some degree of way sharing between them. Experimental results show that CA improves turnaround time by up to 40% and system unfairness over 55%, compared to execution under a baseline system without partitioning.

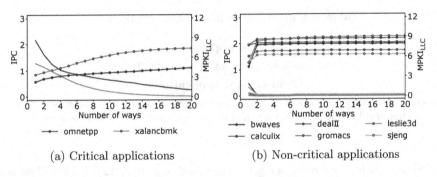

(a) Critical applications   (b) Non-critical applications

Fig. 2. Example of behavior of critical and non-critical applications in a workload. Legend: marked lines (with circles) represent IPC and solid lines $MPKI_{LLC}$.

2 Intel Cache Allocation Technology

Intel Cache Allocation Technology allows assigning a given amount of LLC cache ways to a set of applications. This technology is available in limited models of processors of the Xeon E5 2600 v3 family and in all processors of the Xeon E5 v4 family. CAT allocates PIDs (Processors Identifiers) or logical cores to Classes Of Service (CLOSes). In the most recent processors, the maximum number of CLOSes is 16. For each CLOS, the user has to specify (i) the subset of ways that can be written, and (ii) which applications or logical cores belong to the CLOS. The cache ways that can be written by the applications belonging to a CLOS are defined with a *capacity bitmask* (CBM). Cache ways are not necessarily private to a CLOS, as they can be shared with other CLOSes by overlapping the CBMs.

Figure 1 shows an example for a possible CAT configuration using 2 CLOSes and a cache with 20 ways. In this example, we assign PIDs to the CLOSes instead of logical cores, a feature available starting with Linux 4.10. Note that CLOS #0 is special, in the sense that is the one used by default by applications that have not been assigned to a particular CLOS. Also note that due to hardware limitations, the ways assigned to a given CLOS have to be consecutive.

3 Application Characterization

In order to design the partitioning algorithm, we performed a characterization of the applications of the SPEC2006 [10] benchmark suite from the LLC perspective, illustrating the relationship between cache space and overall performance. To this end, we executed each application with a cache space from 1 to 20 ways. After analyzing the results, we concluded that applications can be divided in two main categories, according to the impact that the cache space has on their performance: cache critical applications and non-cache critical applications. The non-cache critical applications do not show significant performance gains as they have more cache space for a number of ways greater than one. On the other hand, cache critical applications experience important performance gains as the number of ways increases. However, these performance gains diminish as the number

Table 1. Categorization of SPEC2006 applications.

Critical applications
omnetpp, soplex, sphinx3, xalancbmk, lbm, mcf

Non-critical applications
astar, bwaves, bzip2, cactusADM, calculix,dealII, gamess, gobmk, gromacs, h264ref, hmmer, leslie3d, libquantum, namd, povray, sjeng, tonto, wrf, zeusmp

of assigned cache ways reaches a given threshold (e.g. 10 or 12). Table 1 classifies the studied applications in cache critical and non-cache critical.

Figure 2 illustrates both behaviors, showing how the Instructions Per Cycle, IPC, (dotted line, Y axis scale on the left) and the LLC Misses Per Kilo Instructions, $MPKI_{LLC}$, (plain line, Y axis scale on the right) change as the number of ways increases for eight applications running alone. Figure 2a and b show the results for critical and non-critical applications, respectively. Notice that both IPC and the $MPKI_{LLC}$ are almost constant for non-cache critical applications, varying only when just one way is available. The reason of this divergent behavior with one way is that this configuration behaves like a direct-mapped cache, which presents a high number of conflict misses. Notice also that the $MPKI_{LLC}$ in these applications is always below 0.5. In contrast, critical applications, like omnetpp and xalancbmk exhibit a much higher $MPKI_{LLC}$ that decreases with the number of assigned cache ways, which results in IPC improvements.

We also found that the huge LLC space (20 MB) in our experimental platform, is completely occupied, or close to being so, by any of the studied applications when running in isolation, regardless being cache critical or not. This is due to the huge working set that studied applications use considering the entire execution. Results in Fig. 2b, however, show that the *live working set* of non-critical applications for a specific interval of time fits in two cache ways.

This analysis has yielded key observations that are the pillars on which CA relies: (i) assigning two cache ways to non-critical applications suffices for performance, (ii) non-critical applications should have a limited cache space; otherwise, they will occupy precious cache space that, on the one hand will not result in individual performance gains, and on the other hand, will prevent critical applications from using it, indirectly harming their performance, and (iii) critical applications need to be protected by assigning them a significant fraction of the cache ways to preserve their performance. To provide further insights into these claims we performed a dynamic analysis, discussed below.

Dynamic Characterization. To study the impact of sharing the cache with other co-runners in multicore execution, we characterized a large set of randomly generated mixes. For illustrative purposes, we used mix #23, composed of the eight previously studied applications, when running together in a baseline system without partitioning.

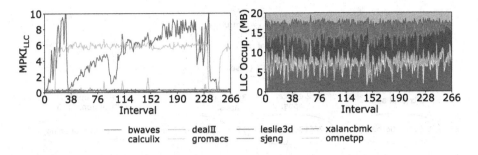

Fig. 3. LLC dynamic occupancy and MPKI$_{LLC}$ in mix #23 without partitioning.

To check if a non-partitioning scheme meets the demands of individual applications, we analyzed the LLC occupancy per application and its MPKI$_{LLC}$. It can be observed in Fig. 3 that non-critical applications like bwaves occupy almost all the time between five and seven ways (which represents between one quarter and one third of the total cache space) in spite of, as shown in the static analysis, barely needing two cache ways to achieve its maximum performance. On the contrary, xalancbmk which has been identified as a critical application, presents a much lower cache occupancy than some of the non-critical ones. As a result, its MPKI$_{LLC}$ severely rises (Fig. 3), turning into important IPC drops.

This example supports our three claims mentioned above, which are the basis of which the CA approach relies.

4 The Critical-Aware Partitioning Approach

This section presents the Critical-Aware Partitioning Approach (CA). The general idea behind our proposal is to dynamically determine which applications present a cache critical behavior and divide the LLC into two partitions, one larger for the cache critical applications and the other, smaller, for the rest of applications. Since not all the cache critical applications show the *same criticality*, CA tries to further refine the partitions, dynamically readjusting their size, until the number of applications showing critical behavior changes, and the process is restarted. CA consists of three main phases: cache warm-up and application classification, partition allocation, and dynamic readjusting of cache ways, which are discussed next.

4.1 Cache Warm-Up and Application Classification

The first step in this phase is the cache warm-up phase (e.g. 10 intervals of 0.5 s), at the beginning of the execution, where no data is collected and therefore no action is taken. After that, the algorithm enters the reset state, in which, using the hardware counters mem_load_uops_retired.l3_miss and instructions, the MPKI$_{LLC}$ for all the applications is computed.

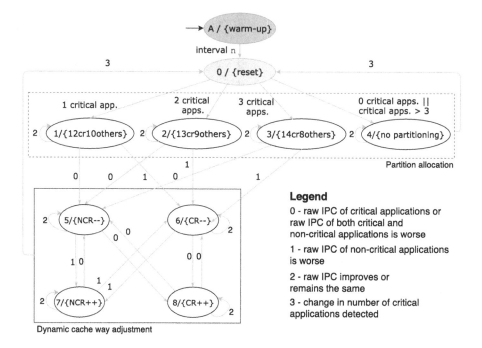

Fig. 4. State diagram of CA algorithm. Acronyms: NCR stands for the number of ways assigned to the CLOS with non-critical applications and CR stands for the number of ways assigned to the CLOS with critical applications. (Color figure online)

As concluded in Sect. 3, critical applications experience a much higher $MPKI_{LLC}$ than non-critical ones. Therefore, considering that there are less critical than non-critical applications (less than 25% in the SPEC2006 suite), it is expected that critical applications are outliers, with respect to the general $MPKI_{LLC}$ trend. So, following this rationale, the algorithm computes the rolling mean of the $MPKI_{LLC}$ for each application, and then, using the Miller's criterion [11], all the applications with a $MPKI_{LLC}$ greater than three standard deviations from the average of the total rolling $MPKI_{LLC}$, are classified as critical. We have also tested other methods to detect outliers, like the Median Absolute Deviation (MAD) [12], but the former approach achieved better results for our purposes.

4.2 Partition Allocation

After the applications have been classified, the algorithm creates two partitions, whose sizes depend on the number of critical applications detected, and assigns applications to one or another, depending on their criticality. This stage is marked in red in Fig. 4. The used partition layouts were empirically determined based on a depth and thorough study of static configurations, evaluating application mixes with different numbers of critical applications, listed in Table 2.

Table 2. Initial cache mask configurations.

Configuration name	# of critical appl.	CLOS 1 ways	CLOS 2 ways
12cr10others	1	12	10
13cr9others	2	13	9
14cr8others	3	14	8
no_partitioning	0 or more than 3	20	20

These partitioning layouts are based on the fact that non-critical applications need an average of 2 cache ways to sustain their performance. The next step of the algorithm (*Dynamic cache way adjustment* box in Fig. 4) is devoted to fine-tune the partitions, iteratively varying their size. While CA could use this mechanism right from the start to dynamically converge to the best configuration, predefined configurations (*Partition Allocation* box in Fig. 4) are used as a starting point to speed up convergence towards it.

Selfa *et al.* [5] proved that a design with CLOSes having a fraction of the cache ways shared with other CLOSes results in a better cache utilization. CA takes this claim into account and grants the CLOS hosting the critical applications a high number of exclusive cache ways, and a small fraction of shared ways. The more critical applications detected, the more cache ways are assigned to its CLOS, except for the workload mixes where a majority or no critical applications are detected. In these cases, the cache configuration remains untouched (all the applications have 20 ways), as limiting the space of a dominant number of critical applications and placing them together does not improve performance.

4.3 Dynamic Adjusting of Partitions

Since there is not an optimal cache configuration that perfectly suits all the application mixes, CA readjusts the initial configuration dynamically, depending on its response to the changes performed. To check how good a change in the actual partitioning is, CA needs to estimate what would have been the performance if such a change was not made. A simple approach is to assume that the IPC in the next measured interval will remain similar as in the previous one. This provided us estimates with around 4% Mean Square Error. Other methods, like using an Exponentially Weighted Moving Average and ARIMA models were also evaluated, but the reduction in the prediction error did not compensate the increase in complexity.

The dynamic adjusting (*Dynamic cache way adjustment* box in Fig. 4) has 4 states, labeled 5, 6, 7 and 8. States 5 and 8 decrease and increase, respectively, the number of ways of the partition of non-critical applications. On the other hand, states 6 and 7 decrease and increase, respectively, the number of ways of the partition that has the critical applications mapped. Transitions can happen due to four reasons, numbered as they appear in the figure:

0. The raw IPC of critical applications or the raw IPC of both groups is worse than the estimated IPC.
1. The raw IPC of non-critical applications is worse than the estimated IPC.
2. The raw IPC improves the estimated IPC. This causes a transition to the same state, and no action is taken for 5 intervals.
3. The number of critical applications has changed. We perform a reset in the partitioning, and depending on the number of critical applications detected, a new partitioning layout will be applied.

In the case where the raw IPC is worse than the prediction, a deeper study of the IPC is carried out to analyze where exactly is the source of performance loss. When the raw IPC of either non-critical or critical applications is lower than estimated, then a shared cache way becomes exclusive to the CLOS holding the affected applications. In case the total IPC of both CLOSes is worse than estimated, the same actions are taken as if only the raw IPC of the critical applications was worse. Giving more cache space to critical applications will result in a higher increase in performance than if it is given to the non-critical applications (see Sect. 3). If any action taken results in a performance loss of the other CLOS, the action is reverted, i.e. the exclusive way is transformed back into a shared way.

Since applications have a non-uniform behavior during their execution, the number of applications detected as outliers can vary considerably along the execution, which can result in a high number of *resets* (i.e. transiting to the *reset* state), and consequently, in a reduction of the system throughput. To deal with this fact, if in a given interval an application is not detected as an outlier but it has been critical during more than 50% of the execution time, it is again considered as critical.

5   Experimental Framework

The experiments have been conducted in a machine with an Intel Xeon E5-2620 v4 processor, with 8 SMT cores running at 2.20 GHz. It has a 20-way LLC of size 20 MB (1 MB/way) that supports CAT, having available 16 CLOSes. Only CLOS #1 and #2 were used in the experiments. We deliberately skipped CLOS #0 since it is the default CLOS, as explained in Sect. 2, and using it affects *all* the processes in the system, including the kernel processes.

To conduct the experiments, we have developed a framework that measures performance using a library based on *Linux perf* [13], and partitions the cache using the primitives provided by the Linux kernel. The results presented in this paper have been obtained using a vanilla Linux 4.11. Our framework samples the performance counters every half a second. The information gathered is used to guide the partitioning policy. When no partitioning is applied, the overhead of collecting data is around 1%. With our proposal, which collects data and executes the partitioning algorithm, the overhead is 1.3%. This means that the overhead caused by the execution of CA is minimal.

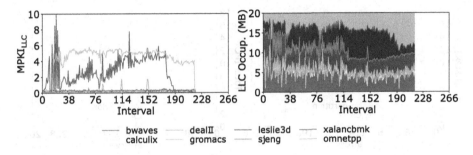

Fig. 5. LLC dynamic occupancy and MPKI$_{LLC}$ in mix #23 with CA algorithm.

The workload mixes were randomly generated using 25 applications from the SPEC2006 [10] benchmark suite. To guide their design, we used the insights presented in Sect. 3, which showed that the number of critical applications is much lower than the number of non-critical ones. Taking this observation into account, we generated 34 application mixes, each one with 8 applications, with the applications randomly selected from the categories shown in Table 1. We generated 17 mixes (mixes 1 to 17) with 1 critical application, 10 mixes (mixes 18 to 27) with 2 critical applications, and 7 mixes (mixes 29 to 34) with 3 critical applications.

The experimental methodology followed was to execute each workload until all the applications completed the same number of instructions they execute when running alone for 60 s. When an application reached this limit, and it is not the last one to reach such limit, it is restarted, but only the results of the first run were considered. Each experiment was repeated 3 times, and the average was derived.

6   Evaluation

This section evaluates the performance and fairness of the CA approach, against a baseline system where no partitioning is done, referred to as *No partition*; but first, we illustrate how CA achieves its objectives through a case study.

6.1   LLC Dynamic Occupancy and MPKI with the CA Approach

This section illustrates how the proposal properly distributes the cache space, by assigning it according to the type of application. For this purpose, we use the same mix example (i.e. mix #23) as in Sect. 3.

Figure 5 shows how the LLC occupancy and MPKI$_{LLC}$ of the 8 benchmarks of mix #23 evolves along time under the CA approach. Compared to non-partitioned system (see Fig. 3), it can be observed that non-critical applications (e.g. bwaves) are allowed to use less space, while critical applications

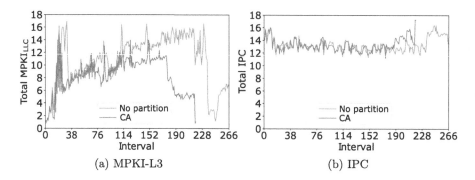

Fig. 6. CA vs Linux: Dynamic cumulative MPKI$_{LLC}$ and raw IPC in mix #23.

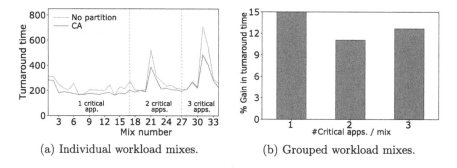

Fig. 7. Turnaround time of CA vs Linux.

(e.g. `xalancbmk`) are assigned more cache space, which confirms that CA properly addresses the design objectives. Notice that both compared figures have the same number of intervals (X axis), however, the mix execution ends, under CA, around interval 205, which means that the gain in turnaround time is about 22%. This is achieved by significantly reducing the MPKI$_{LLC}$, clearly appreciated by comparing the results of each individual application applying CA (see Fig. 5) with those achieved with Linux reference system (see Fig. 3). Under Linux, critical applications like `xalancbmk` suffer a high MPKI$_{LLC}$, exceeding 6 around half of the execution time.

The previous observations can also be appreciated by presenting the aggregated MPKI$_{LLC}$ and IPC values of all the benchmarks that make up the mix, for both the reference system and CA. This can be seen in Fig. 6. As can be observed, the aggregated MPKI$_{LLC}$ is much better with CA than with a non-partitioned system, which translates into ending the execution much before, hence improving system throughput. Regarding raw IPC, it can be appreciated that CA achieves similar or slightly better (around intervals 190 to 210) raw IPC than the baseline system.

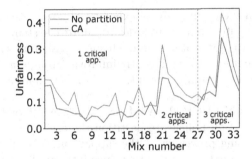

Fig. 8. Comparison of average unfairness value of the workload mixes.

6.2 Performance and Fairness

Performance has been analyzed in terms of turnaround time, which is the main focus of the CA approach. Figure 7 shows the turnaround times (in intervals of half a second) of both CA and the reference system across the 34 studied mixes. As observed, CA reduces the turnaround time of the mixes that have only one critical application (mixes 1 to 17), on average, by 15%. For mixes with two critical applications (mixes 18 to 27) the reduction is by around 11.5% and for mixes with 3 critical applications (mixes 28 to 24) it decreased 13.5%. Note that for some of the mixes, the turnround time is reduced by more than 40%.

This turnaround time reductions are achieved by allowing slower applications (i.e. critical) to run faster and by slightly slowing down non-critical applications. As a result, the execution time of fast and slow applications becomes closer, hence improving system fairness. A comparison of unfairness values for each workload using both policies is presented in Fig. 8. Unfairness is calculated as the standard deviation across all progresses of each individual application over the average progress, which in turn is calculated as the the total time when executing alone over the total time taken in multiprogram execution [14]. CA reduces unfairness, on average, by more than 55%, being this value even larger on mixes with one critical application, which is the most common case. In these mixes the percentage gain rises to 75%.

7   Related Work

Heracles [15] and Dirigent [16] focus on improving the performance of latency sensitive applications, determined *a priori*, by ensuring the other *batch* applications do not interfere with them. While in this work we also use the concept of *critical application*, we determine them dynamically, by measuring their cache behavior. Ginseng [17] partitions the LLC into isolated partitions using a marked-driven auction system. It is focused in environments like the cloud, where each guest can bid based on the amount of resources it wants to use. Selfa *et al.* [5] cluster applications using the k-means algorithm and distribute cache ways between the groups, giving exponentially more space to the applications suffering more interferences, in order to improve system fairness. El-Sayed *et al.* [4] also group applications into clusters, assigning them to different CLOSes. While it manages to significantly improve throughput in selected workloads, it uses a detailed profiling, resulting in a much more complex algorithm than CA.

Some approaches like UCP [2], ASM [18], Vantage [19] or PriSM [3] modify the eviction and insertion policies to partition the cache, hence they cannot be implemented in existing processors. Other approaches like the filter cache [20], split the cache in different structures to reduce inter-application interferences.

8   Conclusions

Recent cache partitioning approaches implemented in commercial processors have been shown to be effective addressing fairness and throughput.

This paper has characterized the static and dynamic cache behavior when multiple applications compete among them for cache space, finding that some applications need few ways to achieve their maximum performance while some others require a higher number of ways. Therefore, they should be protected to avoid performance losses, by allocating them in a separate cache partition with a greater amount of cache space.

Based on this study, we have proposed CA, a simple and effective cache partitioning approach that significantly improves the turnaround time of workload mixes. Experimental results show that CA improves turnaround time up to 40% and system unfairness over 55%, compared to a baseline system without partitioning.

Acknowledgment. This work was supported by the Spanish Ministerio de Economía y Competitividad (MINECO) and Plan E funds, under grants TIN2015-66972-C5-1-R and TIN2017-92139-EXP. It was also supported by the ExaNest project, with funds from the European Union Horizon 2020 project, with grant agreement No 671553.

References

1. Sodani, A., et al.: Knights landing: second-generation intel xeon phi product. IEEE Micro **36**(2), 34–46 (2016)
2. Qureshi, M.K., Patt, Y.N.: Utility-based cache partitioning: a low-overhead, high-performance, runtime mechanism to partition shared caches. In: Proceedings of MICRO, pp. 423–432 (2006)
3. Manikantan, R., Rajan, K., Govindarajan, R.: Probabilistic shared cache management (PriSM). In: Proceedings of the 39th Annual International Symposium on Computer Architecture (ISCA), pp. 428–439 (2012)
4. El-Sayed, N., Mukkara, A., Tsai, P.A., Kasture, H., Ma, X., Sanchez, D.: Kpart: a hybrid cache partitioning-sharing technique for commodity multicores. In: Proceedings of HPCA (2018)

5. Selfa, V., Sahuquillo, J., Eeckhout, L., Petit, S., Gómez, M.E.: Application clustering policies to address system fairness with intel's cache allocation technology. In: Proceedings of PACT, pp. 194–205 (2017)

6. Feliu, J., Sahuquillo, J., Petit, S., Duato, J.: Addressing fairness in SMT multicores with a progress-aware scheduler. In: Proceedings of IPDPS, pp. 187–196 (2015)

7. Van Craeynest, K., Akram, S., Heirman, W., Jaleel, A., Eeckhout, L.: Fairness-aware scheduling on single-ISA heterogeneous multi-cores. In: Proceedings of PACT, pp. 177–188 (2013)

8. Wu, C., Li, J., Xu, D., Yew, P.C., Li, J., Wang, Z.: FPS: a fair-progress process scheduling policy on shared-memory multiprocessors. J. Trans. Parallel Distrib. Syst. **26**(2), 444–454 (2015)

9. Eyerman, S., Eeckhout, L.: System-level performance metrics for multiprogram workloads. IEEE Micro **28**(3), 42–53 (2008)

10. Henning, J.L.: SPEC CPU2006 benchmark descriptions. Comput. Archit. News **34**(4), 1–17 (2006)

11. Miller, J.: Short report: reaction time analysis with outlier exclusion: bias varies with sample size. J. Exp. Psychol. **43**(4), 907–912 (1991)

12. Leys, C., Ley, C., Klein, O., Bernard, P., Licata, L.: Detecting outliers: do not use standard deviation around the mean, use absolute deviation around the median. J. Exp. Soc. Psychol. **49**(4), 764–766 (2013)

13. Gleixner, T., Molnar, I.: Performance counters for Linux (2009)

14. Van Craeynest, K., Akram, S., Heirman, W., Jaleel, A., Eeckhout, L.: Fairness-aware scheduling on single-ISA heterogeneous multi-cores. In: Proceedings of the 22nd International Conference on Parallel Architectures and Compilation Techniques. PACT 2013, Piscataway, NJ, USA, pp. 177–188. IEEE Press (2013)

15. Lo, D., Cheng, L., Govindaraju, R., Ranganathan, P., Kozyrakis, C.: Heracles: improving resource efficiency at scale. In: Proceedings of ISCA, pp. 450–462 (2015)

16. Zhu, H., Erez, M.: Dirigent: enforcing QoS for latency-critical tasks on shared multicore systems. In: Proceedings of ASPLOS, pp. 33–47 (2016)

17. Funaro, L., Ben-Yehuda, O.A., Schuster, A.: Ginseng: market-driven LLC allocation. In: Proceedings of USENIX, pp. 295–308 (2016)

18. Subramanian, L., Seshadri, V., Ghosh, A., Khan, S., Mutlu, O.: The application slowdown model: quantifying and controlling the impact of inter-application interference at shared caches and main memory. In: Proceedings of MICRO, pp. 62–75 (2015)

19. Sanchez, D., Kozyrakis, C.: Vantage: scalable and efficient fine-grain cache partitioning. In: Proceedings of ISCA, pp. 57–68 (2011)

20. Sahuquillo, J., Pont, A.: The filter cache: a run-time cache management approach1. In: 25th EUROMICRO 1999 Conference (1999)

Dynamic Placement of Progress Thread for Overlapping MPI Non-blocking Collectives on Manycore Processor

Alexandre Denis[1], Julien Jaeger[2], Emmanuel Jeannot[1], Marc Pérache[2], and Hugo Taboada[1,2(✉)]

[1] Inria, LaBRI, Univ. Bordeaux, CNRS, Bordeaux-INP, Bordeaux, France
{alexandre.denis,emmanuel.jeannot,hugo.taboada}@inria.fr
[2] CEA, DAM, DIF, 91297 Arpajon, France
{julien.jaeger,marc.perache}@cea.fr

Abstract. To amortize the cost of MPI collective operations, non-blocking collectives have been proposed so as to allow communications to be overlapped with computation. Unfortunately, collective communications are more CPU-hungry than point-to-point communications and running them in a communication thread on a dedicated CPU core makes them slow. On the other hand, running collective communications on the application cores leads to no overlap. To address these issues, we propose an algorithm for tree-based collective operations that splits the tree between communication cores and application cores. To get the best of both worlds, the algorithm runs the short but heavy part of the tree on application cores, and the long but narrow part of the tree on one or several communication cores, so as to get a trade-off between overlap and absolute performance. We provide a model to study and predict its behavior and to tune its parameters. We implemented it in the MPC framework, which is a thread-based MPI implementation. We have run benchmarks on manycore processors such as the KNL and Skylake and get good results for both performance and overlap.

1 Introduction

MPI is the standard interface for communications in HPC applications. It is used by applications for inter-node (i.e. network) and intra-node (processes on the same node) communications. The cost of communications is one of the main obstacles to get a good speedup for parallel applications. To amortize the cost of MPI communications, application programmers try to overlap communications with computation by using non-blocking communication primitives, and let them progress in background while keeping the CPU busy with computation.

Initially the non-blocking communications were only available for point-to-point communications. The extension of the non-blocking communications to collective operations (i.e. primitives that involve more than two nodes, such as broadcast, reduce, scatter, gather, ...) is an addition of the latest major MPI

M. Aldinucci et al. (Eds.): Euro-Par 2018, LNCS 11014, pp. 616–627, 2018.
https://doi.org/10.1007/978-3-319-96983-1_44

version [1]. It opens the door to communication/computation overlap for collective operations too. However, collective communications are more CPU-hungry than point-to-point communications, and are therefore it is harder to make them progress in background.

In this paper, we tackle the problem of overlapping communication and computation for non-blocking collectives on manycore processors. We study the case of MPI tasks spread on a manycore processor, with one task per core, and how to improve overlap with cores dedicated to communications. We explore the trade-off between executing collective communication on dedicated CPU cores versus using application cores. We restrict ourselves to the case of tree-based collective operations (broadcast, reduce, scatter, gather, allreduce) because they are the one where this trade-off has the most impact on the performance as we are able to tune it dynamically.

In short, this paper makes the following contributions:

- we propose an *algorithm* that splits the tree of the collective operation, running parts of the tree on cores dedicated to communication, and parts of the tree on the application core;
- we propose a *model* for the above algorithm, so as to demonstrate the improvement of global performance when overlapping communication and computations, and to tune its parameters;
- we *implemented* the algorithm in the MPC MPI implementation [2].

The rest of the paper is organized as follows. Section 2 presents related works about communication/computation overlap in general, and for collective communication in particular. Section 3 presents our split-tree algorithm for tree-based collective communications. In Sect. 4, we present a model of the algorithm and how to tune it for optimal performance. Section 5 describes how the algorithm is implemented in the MPC software. Section 6 reports experimental results, and Sect. 7 concludes.

2   Related Works

The topic of communication progression has already been studied for some aspects in the literature. Several strategies do exist for background progression of point-to-point communications, such as offloading the communication to hardware [3,4] and let the hardware do the progression; use of a thread [5] or process [6] dedicated to communication progression; opportunistic scheduling of communication tasks [7,8].

MPI non-blocking collective communications are more difficult to make progress in the background, since not only the data transfer but the collective algorithm too needs to progress, which makes it harder to rely on hardware. There is specific work [9] for hardware-assisted progression on Blue Gene, or offloading shared memory collectives to a kernel module [10] (although authors only address performance of blocking collectives, not progression of non-blocking collectives). The reference NBC implementation [11] relies on a progression thread, with some tricks [12] to improve overlap on InfiniBand. This approach is quite different from ours since it leads to one progression thread per MPI task, while our approach runs multiple MPI ranks in the same process and the algorithm for the collectives is shared across all MPI ranks in the same process.

3   A Split-Tree Algorithm for MPI Collective Operations

In this Section, we propose a split tree algorithm for MPI collective communications which improves communication/computation overlap.

In this paper, we focus on intra-node communications on a manycore machine, with one MPI task per core. To obtain a good overlap for communications and computation, they have to run in parallel. On a manycore machine, the straightforward way to get background progression of communication is to dedicate some cores to communications, thus some cores host an MPI rank, we call them *application cores*; the remaining cores (one or several) host communication progression threads, we call them *communication cores*.

However, collective communication algorithms involve a huge amount of point-to-point communications, and thus a lot of communication tasks. When communication cores perform all communications on behalf of all application cores, the algorithm is *folded* and communications from a given step of the collective algorithm may be serialized. As a consequence, when folded on few communication cores, collective communications get much slower than when executed as a blocking call on all application cores simultaneously.

There are multiple topologies for collective communications. We restrict ourselves to *tree-based* algorithms (reduce, broadcast, gather, scatter, allreduce). The time steps of such a tree-based collective is depicted in Fig. 1: each level of the tree is a step in the algorithm, from the root to the leaves. The rank of MPI tasks participating to each step is represented in the vertices. The left child of a vertex is the same MPI task; only the right child involves a communication. When represented as time steps of the algorithm, it is a binary tree, although when considering the data flow by deduplicating vertices which are the same task, the algorithm is really a binomial tree.

On such tree-based algorithms, we observe that the amount of work is very unbalanced in time and space. On the example depicted in Fig. 1 for 16 MPI tasks, there are 15 communication tasks and the algorithm needs 4 steps. If

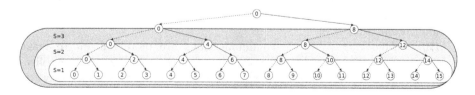

Fig. 1. Communication tree for a broadcast collective with 16 MPI tasks. S is the number of steps (tree levels) running on application cores. Plain edges are communications. Vertices are the MPI tasks.

we fold these communications on a single communication core, it would need 15 steps which is 4 times slower. Since half of the work is in the last step, represented as $S = 1$ with levels numbered from the leaves, we can trade some performance against some overlap by executing different parts of the tree on different cores. If only the upper part of the tree is executed on the communication cores, and the last step $S = 1$ is executed on the application cores, then the total is twice as fast as running everything on communication cores, while only a single step cannot be overlapped with computation.

Our proposed algorithm is a generalization of this principle for a *trade-off between communication performance and overlap*: split the communication tree with the upper part running on communication cores, so as to have full overlap, and the lower part running on all application cores. Let S the number of steps (tree levels) running on application cores. $S = 0$ is equivalent to running all the communication on communication cores. The algorithm runs S steps of the tree on application cores as depicted in Fig. 1. When $S = 1$, the algorithm runs the short but heavy part of the tree on application cores whereas the long but narrow part of the tree is running on one or several communication cores. All the communications running on application cores cannot be overlapped by computation because they are running on the same cores. However, this part of the tree is the heaviest and running these communications on few communication cores would jeopardize communication performance. The part of the tree running on communication cores benefits of total overlapping of its communications.

If S is increased, the algorithm loses a bit of its ability of being overlapped but can increase its absolute performance depending on the communication/computation ratio. We have to get a trade-off between overlap and absolute performance.

4   Modeling and Tuning

In this Section, we propose a performance model of the algorithm described in Sect. 3, so as to show its relevance and to tune its S parameter.

Model for Collective Operations. Let N_{proc} the total number of cores, and N the number of cores for the application (i.e. number of MPI ranks), then the number of dedicated cores for communication is $P(N) = N_{proc} - N$.

We consider collective operations as binomial trees only. The proposed model could be easily extended to N-nomial trees if needed. It applies to operations such as: reduce, broadcast, gather, scatter; scan and alltoall, not based on a tree topology, are out of scope. We model communication cost as linear, neglecting latency and cache effects. We take as unit the point-to-point transfer time of one buffer of the size of the considered collective operation. We study first operations with a constant buffer size across the whole tree (reduce, broadcast). We will extend it to variable-buffer size operations (scatter, gather) in a second step.

The height of the tree[1] is $H(N) = \lceil \log_2(N) \rceil$. In the case of a blocking operation where communication is performed simultaneously by all application cores, we get the following execution time:

$$T_{blocking}(N) = H(N) = \lceil \log_2(N) \rceil \tag{1}$$

Let $C(N)$ the computation time on N nodes. To model computation and communication overlap, we consider the application programmer tried to reach perfect overlap and sized computation to have the same duration on all cores as the blocking collective operation, i.e. $C(N_{proc}) = T_{blocking}(N_{proc})$. If we assume computation scales linearly, we have the following time for computation on N nodes:

$$C(N) = \frac{N}{N_{proc}} \times C(N_{proc}) \tag{2}$$

Model for the Proposed Algorithm. We now model the split tree algorithm itself. As defined in Sect. 3, S is the number of steps running on application cores; the time to run these steps is the depth of the sub-trees, namely S, unless the tree height is smaller than S. The algorithm schedules operations from the upper $H(N) - S$ levels on communication cores, folded on $P(N)$ cores. Let $R(N) = N - 2^{\lfloor \log_2(N) \rfloor}$ the number of leaves that are not on the largest complete binary sub-tree of the tree. Let $F(N, i)$ the number of communications for N MPI tasks in the level i:

$$F(N, i) = 2^{\lfloor \log_2(N) \rfloor - (H(N) - i + 1)} + \left\lfloor \frac{R(N) + 2^{(H(N) - i)}}{2^{(H(N) - i + 1)}} \right\rfloor \tag{3}$$

Since each level of the tree contains $F(N, i)$ communications for level i numbered from 1 for the root, it takes a time of $\lceil F(N, i)/P(N) \rceil$ once folded on $P(N)$ communication cores, assuming each level is run in sequence because of communication dependencies. As a result, the time for a non-blocking collective with split steps algorithm is Eq. 4 as below:

$$T_{non-blocking}(S, N) = \underbrace{\min(S, H(N))}_{\text{last } S \text{ steps from leafs}} + \underbrace{\sum_{i=1}^{\max(0, H(N) - S)} \left\lceil \frac{F(N, i)}{P(N)} \right\rceil}_{\text{upper levels of tree, up to } S} \tag{4}$$

With communication and computation overlap with the same collective operation, given that the part running on application cores cannot be overlapped and the part running on communication cores is fully overlapped, we get the result in Eq. 5 as time for overlapped computation and non-blocking collective with split tree:

---

[1] We use a binomial tree where the N MPI tasks are leaves. In case of a binary tree, we will have N vertices and $H(N) = \lceil \log_2(N + 1) \rceil - 1$.

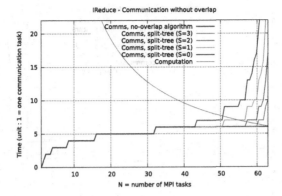

Fig. 2. Model of communication cost for operations with constant-size buffer (broadcast, reduce) on 64 cores.

$$T_{overlapped}(S, N) = \underbrace{\min(S, H(N))}_{\text{non-overlapable comms}} + \max\left(C(N), \underbrace{\sum_{i=1}^{\max(0, H(N)-S)} \left\lceil \frac{F(N, i)}{P(N)} \right\rceil}_{\text{overlapable communications}} \right)$$

(5)

The graph $C(N)$, $T_{blocking}$, and $T_{non-blocking}(N, S)$ for increasing values for S and $N_{proc} = 64$ is depicted in Fig. 2. We observe that for large values of N (i.e. small number of communication cores), the communication is huge for $S = 0$ (all communication on communication cores). The cost decreases when S increases.

Figure 3 represents the total time of computation overlapped with communications when using blocking communications (computation and communication run in sequence) and when using non-blocking communications with split tree algorithm. We observe that increasing values for S increases the cost for small values of N (reduces overlap), but this cost is amortized for large values of N where the total time is dominated by the cost of the communication folded on few communication cores.

Discussion and Tuning. From observation of Fig. 3, the absolute minimum time is reached for $S = 0$ and $N = 51$. However, it means that 13 cores are dedicated to communications, which may not be desirable for the user since it would degrade performance of parts of the application without communication. With 7 cores dedicated to communications ($N = 57$), the optimal is $S = 1$; for 4 cores dedicated to communication ($N = 60$), the optimal is $S = 2$; and finally $S = 3$ for $N = 62$ (2 communication cores).

As a general case, for a given value of N, it is enough to compute the predicted performance with the model for a few values of S to find the optimal value. However finding N for the best overall performance depends on application scalability and communication/computation ratio and is out of scope for this paper. We can extend the proposed model for collective operations where

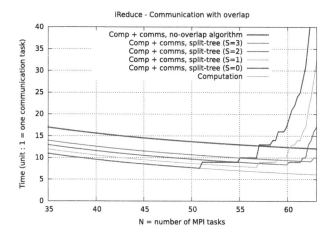

Fig. 3. Model of communication/computation overlap for operations constant-size buffer (broadcast, reduce) on 64 cores.

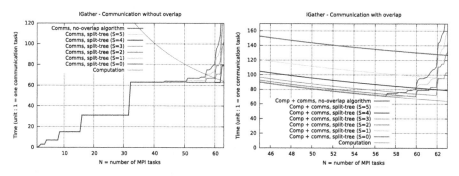

Fig. 4. Model of communication cost (left) and communication/computation overlap (right) for operations with increasing buffer size (scatter, gather) on 64 cores.

not all tree edges have the same weight, such as scatter and gather; when going from leaves to root, data size doubles at each level of the tree. If we modify the model for such operations, we get the graphs for communication cost and overlapped time as depicted in Fig. 4, which exhibits a behavior similar to the previous one.

5   Implementation

In this Section, we present the implementation of the algorithm in MPC [2], our thread based MPI implementation.

In MPC, MPI tasks are implemented with threads. MPC also implements POSIX threads and an OpenMP runtime system. MPC has its own scheduler allowing a fine-grained scheduling of all these threads. Thus, we bypass the system scheduler. MPC uses a tuned version of libNBC [11] to implement MPI 3

Non-Blocking Collectives. One progress thread is created for each MPI task. These threads can be bound through different algorithms. In the default behavior used in our experiments, MPI tasks are bound with a scatter policy and progress threads are bound to the closest idle cores.

In this implementation, a MPI non-blocking collective is decomposed in MPI point-to-point non-blocking calls fulfilling the collective algorithm. When a MPI non-blocking collective is called, each MPI task creates a *schedule* containing requests for the point-to point non-blocking calls corresponding to its part of the collective algorithm, and attach it to its associated progress thread. Thus, the progress threads handle the communication described by the schedules while MPI tasks continue to execute computation.

To implement our algorithms, we define the parameter S to be the number of steps (tree levels) that we want to run on application cores. For *all-to-one* algorithms (reduce, gather), we run the S steps on MPI tasks using MPI point-to-point blocking communication before creating the NBC schedule of $H(N) - S$ steps. Then, we attach it to its associated progress thread. Thus, the first part of the algorithm is running on application cores whereas the last part is running on the cores dedicated to the progress threads. For *one-to-all* algorithms (broadcast, scatter), we define the requests of $H(N) - S$ steps and create the NBC schedule first. We attach it in its associated progress thread. Then we implement the S steps in the MPI_Wait function executed by the MPI tasks. Hence, the first part is running on the cores dedicated to the progress threads whereas the last part is running on application cores.

6   Experimental Results

In this Section, we present experimental results of our algorithm implemented within MPC.

We implemented our own micro-benchmarking tool to evaluate the performance of our algorithm. This tool works similarly to the Intel MPI Benchmarks [13] but with fixed problem size allowing us to have the same computation workload for different number of MPI tasks. We arbitrary set the buffer size to 2 MB and sized the computation workload to reach perfect overlap Then, we reduce the number of MPI tasks while keeping the same global computation workload. Thus, when we have less MPI tasks, the duration of computation increases and more idle cores are available for progress threads. This contributes to decreasing the time of communications and maximize the overlap. When all cores are used by the MPI tasks, they are no cores left for progress threads. In this case, the algorithm is the same as for the blocking call. Thus we do not show these points in the following performance figures.

We ran our benchmark on two different manycore architectures: a 1.4 GHz Intel Xeon Phi Knights Landing with 64 cores (KNL) and a 2.7 GHz bi-socket Xeon Platinum Skylake with a total of 48 cores (SKL).

Comparing Split-Tree Algorithm to Default Setup. In our first experiments, we tested the interest of the split-tree algorithm. As described in Sect. 5, MPC already provides progress threads for communication collectives. The progress threads are gathered on the available cores. This mapping brings good performances when the number of available cores is high. However, performances collapse when too many progress threads are gathered on the same core. The blue lines labeled "Comp + comms, split-tree (S=0)" show this behavior on KNL for collective Ibcast (Fig. 5) and for collective Ireduce on KNL and Skylake (Fig. 6). The label "Comp + comms, split-tree (S=0)" means that no level of the communication tree is done on the MPI tasks, thus all communications are realized on the progress threads.

Thanks to the split tree algorithm, we were able to balance more efficiently communications between the MPI tasks and the progress threads. The orange line labeled "Comp + comms, split-tree (S=1)" (resp. purple line labeled "Comp + comms, split-tree (S=2)" and green line labeled "Comp + comms, split-tree (S=3)") shows the performance of the same algorithms when 1 (resp. 2 and 3) levels of the communication tree remains on the MPI tasks. If enough cores are available to correctly handle the progress threads, the split-tree version is less performant. However, when the number of available cores is shrinking, the split-tree version is more stable. For each additional level attached to the MPI tasks, the sudden performance drop is observed with fewer available cores, until S=3 allows to maintain better performances than the blocking call even in the least favorable case (only one core available for all progress threads). Hence, it is possible to select the best split-tree value S depending on the algorithm and the number of cores hosting progress threads.

Comparing Performance Results to Model. To help select the number of tree levels to leave on the MPI tasks, we proposed a model in Sect. 4. The model projection for Ireduce collective on 64 cores is shown in Fig. 3. Comparing this projection to the result of Ireduce on the 64 cores KNL displayed in Fig. 6, we can see that the model is really close to the results.

Moreover, the values for switching from a value S in the split-tree to the next one are the same between the prediction and the measured performance. This allows us to select the correct number of levels to leave on the MPI tasks by implementing this model in the MPI runtime system.

Comparing MPI Implementations. We also compare our algorithm with other MPI implementation such as Intel-MPI and OpenMPI. We ran OpenMPI and Intel-MPI tests with the same compute workload as for our previous experiments. We compare these results to our split-tree algorithm with the S value chosen accordingly to our model. Hence, when the model predicts that an S value is better than another one, this value is automatically applied. For example, on KNL, we switch from S=0 to S=1 for 52 MPI tasks, from S=1 to S=2 for 58 MPI tasks, and from S=2 to S=3 for 62 MPI tasks.

The results for all tested MPI implementation, including our MPC model-based results, are depicted in Fig. 7 for MPI_Ireduce.

We observe that our split-tree algorithm, with the selection of the number of levels left on the MPI tasks based on our model (MPC model-based – green),

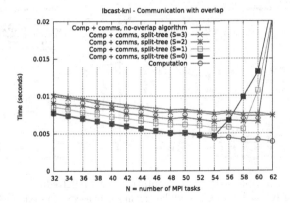

Fig. 5. Result of split-tree algorithm with different values of S, for MPI_Ibcast with constant-size buffer of 2 MB on 64 cores (KNL). (Color figure online)

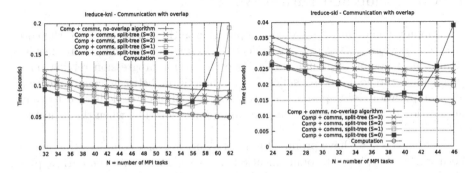

Fig. 6. Result of split-tree algorithm with different values of S, for MPI_Ireduce with constant-size buffer of 2 MB on KNL (left) and Skylake (right) processors. (Color figure online)

performs well on KNL and Skylake. On KNL, MPC model-based (green lines) is always better than OpenMPI (purple) and IntelMPI (royalblue). To be fair, we activated for IntelMPI the flags allowing asynchronous progression (*I_MPI_ASYNC_PROGRESS* and and *I_MPI_ASYNC_PROGRESS_PIN*), but these flags reduced the performances (skyblue and blue lines) instead of improving them. On Skylake, OpenMPI performs better than on KNL. However, except for last number of MPI tasks, MPC model-based managed to have better performance thanks to the split-tree algorithm.

Very interestingly, we also see that in this case, the best performance is obtained with 50 cores for the KNL and 38 cores for the SKL, meaning that the best trade-off is far from using all the available cores.

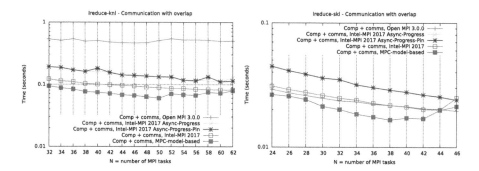

Fig. 7. Result of multiple MPI implementation for MPI_Ireduce with constant-size buffer of 2 MB on KNL (left) and Skylake (right) processors (Y-axis in log scale).

7   Conclusion and Future Work

Overlapping communications with computation is the key to amortize the cost of communications, especially for collective communications which are heavier than point-to-point communications. Approaches for progression relying on a progression thread per task suffer from competition between communication and computation, and approaches relying on a pool of cores dedicated to communication exhibit a slowdown in pure communication time when the collective is folded on few cores.

In this paper, we have proposed a novel algorithm that combines the best of both worlds. It splits the communication tree so as to execute the narrow part of the tree, representing most of its depth, on dedicated communication cores; this part may be fully overlapped with computation. It places the widest part of the tree, which represents a small part of its depth but a large part of the total work, on all applications cores to benefit from parallelism.

We have modeled the algorithm to demonstrate its relevance and to tune its parameter. We have implemented the algorithm in the MPC software and evaluated its performance on manycore processors (Intel KNL and Skylake). Thanks to the excellent accuracy of the model we are able to almost always find the best trade-off between using dedicated CPU cores or application cores and hence exceed the performance of state-of-the-art competitors. Moreover, it is important to notice that our solution is not bound to the MPC runtime system but can be implemented in any MPI library featuring progress threads for communication.

As future work, we plan to extend the approach of our algorithm to inter-node communications, which have a different behavior than intra-node communications considered in this paper. Moreover, we also plan to extend auto-tuning to choose the number of MPI tasks (parameter N) to optimize the overall performance and not only sections with non-blocking collectives.

References

1. MPI Forum: MPI: A Message-Passing Interface Standard Version 3.0, September 2012
2. Pérache, M., Jourdren, H., Namyst, R.: MPC: a unified parallel runtime for clusters of NUMA machines. In: Luque, E., Margalef, T., Benítez, D. (eds.) Euro-Par 2008. LNCS, vol. 5168, pp. 78–88. Springer, Heidelberg (2008). https://doi.org/10.1007/978-3-540-85451-7_9
3. Sur, S., Jin, H., Chai, L., Panda, D.: RDMA read based rendezvous protocol for MPI over InfiniBand: design alternatives and benefits. In: Proceedings of the Eleventh ACM SIGPLAN Symposium on Principles and Practice of Parallel Programming, pp. 32–39. ACM, New York (2006)
4. Rashti, M.J., Afsahi, A.: Improving communication progress and overlap in MPI rendezvous protocol over RDMA-enabled interconnects. In: 2008 22nd International Symposium on High Performance Computing Systems and Applications. HPCS 2008, pp. 95–101. IEEE (2008)
5. Hoefler, T., Lumsdaine, A.: Message progression in parallel computing - to thread or not to thread? In: Proceedings of the 2008 IEEE International Conference on Cluster Computing. IEEE Computer Society, October 2008
6. Lai, P., Balaji, P., Thakur, R., Panda, D.: ProOnE: a general purpose protocol onload engine for multi- and many-core architectures. Comput. Sci. Res. Dev. **23**, 133–142 (2009)
7. Denis, A.: pioman: a pthread-based Multithreaded Communication Engine. In: Euromicro International Conference on Parallel, Distributed and Network-based Processing, Turku, Finland, March 2015
8. Si, M., Peña, A., Balaji, P., Takagi, M., Ishikawa, Y.: MT-MPI: multithreaded MPI for many-core environments. In: Proceedings of the International Conference on Supercomputing, June 2014
9. Almási, G., et al.: Optimization of MPI collective communication on BlueGene/L systems. In: Proceedings of the 19th Annual International Conference on Supercomputing. ICS 2005, pp. 253–262. ACM, New York (2005)
10. Ma, T., Bosilca, G., Bouteiller, A., Goglin, B., Squyres, J.M., Dongarra, J.J.: Kernel assisted collective intra-node MPI communication among multi-core and many-core CPUs. In: IEEE (eds.) 40th International Conference on Parallel Processing (ICPP-2011), Taipei, Taiwan, September 2011
11. Hoefler, T., Lumsdaine, A., Rehm, W.: Implementation and performance analysis of non-blocking collective operations for MPI. In: Proceedings of the 2007 International Conference on High Performance Computing, Networking, Storage and Analysis, SC07. IEEE Computer Society/ACM, November 2007
12. Hoefler, T., Lumsdaine, A.: Optimizing non-blocking collective operations for InfiniBand. In: Proceedings of the 22nd IEEE International Parallel & Distributed Processing Symposium, CAC 2008 Workshop, April 2008
13. IMB-NBC benchmarks. https://software.intel.com/fr-fr/node/561946. Accessed 10 May 2018

Efficient Load Balancing Techniques for Graph Traversal Applications on GPUs

Federico Busato$^{(\boxtimes)}$ and Nicola Bombieri

Department of Computer Science, University of Verona, Verona, Italy
{federico.busato,nicola.bombieri}@univr.it

Abstract. Efficiently implementing a load balancing technique in graph traversal applications for GPUs is a critical task. It is a key feature of GPU applications as it can sensibly impact on the overall application performance. Different strategies have been proposed to deal with such an issue. Nevertheless, the efficiency of each of them strongly depends on the graph characteristics and no one is the best solution for any graph. This paper presents three different balancing techniques and how they have been implemented to fully exploit the GPU architecture. It also proposes a set of support strategies that can be modularly applied to the main balancing techniques to better address the graph characteristics. The paper presents an analysis and a comparison of the three techniques and support strategies with the best solutions at the state of the art over a large dataset of representative graphs. The analysis allows statically identifying, given graph characteristics and for each of the proposed techniques, the best combination of supports, and that such a solution is more efficient than the techniques at the state of the art.

1 Introduction

Graph traversal refers to the process of visiting (i.e., checking or updating) vertices in a graph and is a core feature in many graph algorithms (e.g., BFS, SSSP, STCON). The high variability of graph characteristics over multiple dimensions such as, size, diameter, and degree distribution, makes the parallel implementation of graph traversal for GPUs a very challenging task.

Load balancing is a key aspect to face when implementing parallel graph traversal algorithms as it can strongly affect the performance of the overall application. Different solutions have been proposed to efficiently deal with such an issue during graph traversal on GPUs [9–11,17,18,21]. Although they provide good results for specific graph characteristics, no one of them is flexible enough to be considered the most efficient for any input dataset. This makes each of these solutions, and in turn the higher level algorithm in which they are included, not efficient in several circumstances (in some cases, less efficient than the sequential implementation [16]).

This paper presents three different load balancing techniques for graph traversal applications on GPUs and, in particular, the key details of their architecture-oriented implementations. The paper also presents a set of features, which we

© Springer International Publishing AG, part of Springer Nature 2018
M. Aldinucci et al. (Eds.): Euro-Par 2018, LNCS 11014, pp. 628–641, 2018.
https://doi.org/10.1007/978-3-319-96983-1_45

call *support strategies*, which can be statically selected and modularly applied to the main balancing techniques to better address the graph characteristics.

The paper presents the results obtained by applying the different techniques to implement a common graph traversal algorithm (i.e., BFS) and how they impact on the overall performance. The analysis, which has been conducted on a large set of representative real-world and synthetic graphs, allows understanding the correlation between graph characteristics and load balancing configurations. The paper also shows how the performance of existing and widespread BFS implementations (*Gunrock* [21], *B40C* [18], and *BFS-4K* [3]) have been improved by substituting the original load balancing strategy with those presented in this paper, with and without the support strategies. The results show that the proposed solutions allow the BFS implementations to reach throughput up to 11,800 MTEPS on single GPU device, with speedups from 1x to 12.7x w.r.t. the original implementations.

The paper is organized as follows. Section 2 presents the background and related work. Section 3 presents the key details of the proposed balancing techniques and support strategies. Section 4 presents the experimental results, while Sect. 5 is devoted to the concluding remarks.

2   Background and Related Work

Different solutions for GPUs have been proposed in the last decade to improve load balancing aspects and accelerate graph traversal applications. They can be organized in three classes depending on the high-level strategy adopted to map GPU threads to graph vertices/edges.

Vertex-Based Mapping. Harish et al. [9] presented the first balancing solutions for BFS and SSSP applications, which target vertex parallelism to inspect every vertex in a graph at each *frontier* iteration [5]. Hong et al. [10] improved the previous approach by exploiting SIMD features of GPU architectures targeting irregular workloads for different graph applications (BFS, SSSP, and STCON). Jia et al. [11] evaluated and compared load balancing for vertex and edge parallelism to accelerate graph traversal in the context of centrality metrics (betweenness, graph, stress, and closeness). McLaughlin et al. [17] focused on the same techniques to accelerate betweenness centrality (BC) computation. All these balancing approaches do not require to maintain additional data structures, they involve very simple implementations but, on the other hand, they perform quadratic work. This makes the parallel implementations asymptotically slower than the sequential implementations. More recent research focused on efficient algorithms for linear-work graph traversal. Luo et al. [16] presented the first work-efficient BFS implementation based on single thread vertex-based mapping. Busato et al. proposed an advanced technique for BFS [3] and SSSP [4], which exploits tunable thread group size for vertex-based mapping and dynamic parallelism to process high-degree vertices.

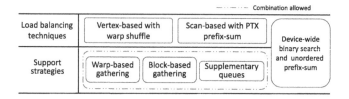

Fig. 1. Overview of the load balancing techniques and support strategies.

Differently from all the approaches of this class, our first solution implements an optimized vertex-based mapping for linear-work graph traversal which relies on warp shuffle instructions and fully exploits coalesced memory accesses.

Scan-Based Mapping. Merrill et al. [18] presented a high-performance solution (B40C) which relies on a scan-based thread mapping for low-degree vertices and two additional techniques to handle mid-degree vertices at warp and block-level. Wang et al. [21] presented an optimized and flexible GPU graph library (Gunrock) that provides a high-level abstraction to reduce the developing effort of graph primitive programming (Pagerank, SSSP, BC, etc.). The Gunrock library relies on the same thread mapping strategy adopted in B40C.

Differently from these approaches, our second solution includes an efficient scan-based technique that fully exploits the GPU shared memory and implements a low-latency PTX prefix- sum.

Binary Search Mapping. Bisson et al. [2] presented a BFS solution for distributed multi-node GPU platforms, which exploits a binary search algorithm to achieve perfect load balancing among all device threads. Khorasani et al. [12] presented a warp-based binary search strategy for BFS, SSSP, and PageRank. Davidson et al. [6] described and evaluated a merge-path search strategy[1] [8] at different thread hierarchy levels (i.e., warp, block, and device) in the context of SSSP. Gunrock also implements a device-wide merge-path search as an alternative load balancing technique.

Our third solution rely on a deeply revisited device-wide binary search mapping, which exploits three different and significant optimizations.

Differently from all the approaches in literature, we propose a set of strategies that can be modularly combined to support and improve any of the balancing technique.

3   Load Balancing Techniques and Support Strategies

Figure 1 shows an overview of the main load balancing techniques considered and optimized in this work and the corresponding support strategies. The three main techniques (i.e., *vertex-based mapping with warp shuffle*, *scan-based mapping with PTX prefix-sum*, and mapping based on *device-wide binary search and unordered*

---

[1] Merge-path search can be represented as a 2D binary search.

prefix-sum) can be implemented in a mutual exclusive way in any graph traversal application to partition the workload and to map work items to the GPU threads. The support strategies can be applied singularly or combined to the selected load balancing technique.

3.1   The Vertex-Based Mapping with Warp Shuffle

The *vertex-based* technique partitions the workload by directly mapping groups of threads to the edges of each frontier vertex. The left-most side of Fig. 2 shows an example of the standard approach, in which the 8 threads of a thread group access to the vertex V_1 identifier in parallel and, then, each thread calculates the corresponding edge to be processed. Then, in sequence, the whole thread group moves to the other frontier vertices. The thread group size is set depending on the average degree of the graphs (smaller warp sizes for graphs with lower average degrees). Nevertheless, in case of large thread group sizes, it may lead to many non-coalesced memory accesses during the frontier loading (8 accesses in the example), which in turn cause a strong loss of performance.

We propose an optimized version of such a vertex-based technique that combines *warp shuffle* instructions to the direct thread-to-edge mapping. The right-most side of Fig. 2 shows the strategy main idea. Each thread accesses to a different frontier vertex and broadcasts the vertex identifier to the threads through warp shuffle. This increases memory coalescing at the cost of a minimum overhead involved by the warp-shuffle instructions. As an example, the memory accesses for the frontier loading in Fig. 2(b) are reduced to 1 coalesced access.

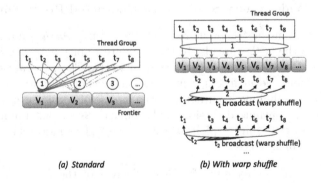

Fig. 2. Vertex-based mapping.

3.2   The Scan-Based Mapping with PTX Prefix-Sum

The *scan-based* load balancing technique is an alternative of the vertex-based mapping. Instead of directly mapping threads to edges, each thread organizes the own edge offsets in shared memory through scan operations. The proposed

Algorithm 1. OPTIMIZED WARP-LEVEL BINARY SEARCH

Input: Sequence of values represented by the variable val
            of each thread; value to search: searched
Output: lower bound of searched

```
1: low = 0;
2: #pragma unroll
3: for ( i = 1;  i ≤ LOG₂(WARPSIZE);  i++ ) do
4:     pos = low + (WARPSIZE ≫ i); //≫: compile time evaluated
5:     if (searched ≥ __shfl(val, pos)) then
6:         low = pos;
7: end
8: return low;
```

solution implements such scan operations at *warp-level* through an optimized prefix-sum[2]. Since such a procedure involves a large number of condition statements, which cause thread divergence, the proposed solution combines intrinsic *warp shuffle* instructions and *PTX instructions* [20] to implement *branch predication* (i.e., <if(predicate) instruction> C statements are replaced with <@predicate instruction> PTX instructions.

The proposed solution, thanks to the prefix sum result, allows exploiting the whole shared memory during the *frontier* propagation phase. It also adopts a warp-synchronous paradigm [19] to avoid any explicit synchronization.

A further optimization consists of a rewriting of loop iterations to exploit instruction-level parallelism (ILP). This is possible since the size of the shared memory is known at compile-time and each warp thread visits the same number of edges (except for the last iteration). The loops have been reorganized and unrolled to eliminate branches and iteration dependencies.

3.3 Device-Wide Binary Search with Unordered Prefix-Sum

The third load balancing technique relies on the *binary search* primitive to map the workload to the GPU threads. In the standard implementation, it provides the best load balancing in case of very irregular workloads (i.e., graphs with high standard deviation). Nevertheless, it involves a significant computation overhead, which makes the technique itself not suitable in case of regular workloads.

We propose an optimized version of the binary search that minimizes such an overhead and that fully exploits the GPU shared memory. The algorithm consists of three main steps:

(1) It computes the prefix-sum of the out-degrees of the frontier vertices. It executes an *optimized binary search* to equally partition the workload over the thread hierarchy, i.e., at warp, block, and device-wide level.
(2) It stores and reorganizes the edge offsets in shared memory.
(3) It processes the shared memory elements in parallel.

---

[2] Given an input sequence $a_1, a_2, \ldots, a_n$ the *prefix-sum* procedure computes the output as $a_1, (a_1 + a_2), \ldots, (a_1 + \ldots + a_n)$.

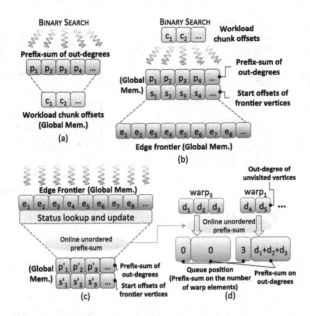

Fig. 3. Overview of the device-wide binary search.

The implementation strategy of the first step and, in particular, of the binary search over the thread hierarchy, is the key of the proposed technique performance. Algorithm 1 shows the pseudo-code of the proposed binary search *at warp-level*. The algorithm implements a variant of the standard procedure called *uniform binary search* [13], which relies on a lookup table. In our case, such a lookup table is implicit since the size of our input is a power of two. Thanks to the organization of the frontier information into shared memory, the binary search allows the following operations on the edge offsets to be performed through coalesced memory accesses. As for the *scan-based* technique, we implemented this technique by adopting the warp-synchronous paradigm to avoid barriers among warps of the same block.

The binary search *at block level* is similarly implemented to guarantee load balancing among threads of the same block.

The *device-wide* binary search guarantees equal workload among all threads of the GPU device. Given the prefix-sum of the out-degrees and the edge offsets of the frontier vertices, such a search consists of three main phases:

(A) A first kernel computes the binary search over the whole workload to uniformly partition the frontier edges among the grid blocks. Figure 3(a) shows an example, where p_i are the prefix-sum elements and c_i are the equally sized chunks of elements. The size of a workload chunk (i.e., the number of edges per chunk) is equal to the available shared memory per block.

(B) A second kernel applies a block-level load partition by following the steps of the binary search. Each block identifies the corresponding workload chunk

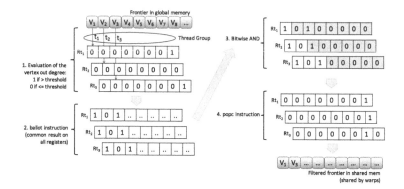

Fig. 4. The 4-instructions binary prefix-sum

by using the offsets calculated by the first kernel. This step generates the neighbour frontier starting from the edge offsets (Fig. 3(b)).

(C) A third kernel generates all the information necessary to build the new frontier (Fig. 3(c)). The kernel procedure executes the status lookup and update of the frontier elements, it removes previously visited vertices, and it computes an *online unordered prefix-sum*. In this particular case, the online procedure computes the prefix-sum of the out-degrees and of the number of warp elements at the same time. This allows avoiding double memory accesses to compute the prefix-sum offline through a specialized kernel procedure, which must load and store the degrees of the frontier vertices. The two informations are merged into a single value through the 64-bit `atomicAdd` instruction. We implemented a *second optimization* to discard vertices with out-degree equal to zero (for directed graphs) and equal to one (for undirected graphs) since they never contribute to the new frontier generation. Such an optimization is particularly useful in case of power-law graphs since they present a high number of *leaf* vertices (up to 20% in some instances).

The basic implementation of the device-wide binary search sets the workload chunk size proportional to the available shared memory per block. It is suitable for large frontiers, but it involves inactive threads in case of small frontiers. We implemented such a technique with a *third optimization*, which allows dynamically configuring the workload chunk size as follows:

$$\min \left\{ \begin{array}{l} \left\lceil \dfrac{sum\,of\,out-degrees}{\#resident\,threads} \right\rceil \cdot block\_size \\ shared\_mem\_per\_block \end{array} \right.$$

The device-wide binary search is an atomic strategy. Because of its radically embedded structure, it cannot be combined with any support techniques.

3.4   Load Balancing Support Strategies

The first support strategy is *warp-based gathering*, which aims at identifying heavy frontier vertices (i.e., vertices with out degree greater than a threshold) and, instead of mapping them to threads by following the main load balancing technique, it maps each of them to a whole warp of threads. It relies on a low latency *binary prefix-sum*, which is implemented by four hardware-implemented instructions (see Fig. 4). Each warp thread saves the predicate result about the vertex out degree (1 if degree > threshold, 0 otherwise) in the own register. Each register value (boolean 0 or 1) is then saved on the register bit corresponding to the thread id, in each thread register with a `ballot` instruction. After this step, all the registers of the same warp threads contain the same 32 bit value. It then computes the bitwise **and** between the register value and the thread id lower mask (e.g., the lower mask of thread 3 is 111). Such a lower mask is efficiently obtained by reading a special register via a single PTX instruction. Finally, each thread counts the number of true values of the non-masked bits with the `popc` instruction and updates the corresponding register.

The result is a *filtered* prefix sum that gives information about all vertices of the frontier that must be processed by whole warps of threads (V_1 and V_3 in the example of Fig. 4) instead of using the adopted basic mapping technique. The filtered prefix sum is stored in shared memory and, thus, it is shared by whole warps of threads, thus minimizing memory accesses. The vertices in the filtered prefix sum are processed by warps and, then, the remaining vertices of the original frontier are processed with the basic mapping approach (scan-based or vertex-based mapping).

The threshold corresponds to the *warp size* (32 for the NVIDIA GPU devices adopted in this work) to fully exploit the parallelism at warp level.

The second support strategy is *block-based gathering*, which is similar to the warp-based one (with a threshold set to the *thread block size*), but with a substantial difference in the prefix-sum implementation. The block-level gathering relies on an *unordered* binary prefix-sum, which does not guarantee a strict ordering of the output while maintaining monotonic increasing values in the resulting sequence[3]. The parallel implementation of such an algorithm at block-level can take advantage of loose ordering to accelerate the computation. The unordered prefix-sum applies the same procedure of ordered variant at warp level but relies on *atomic operations* among different warps. In particular, each warp atomically updates a single value in shared memory for block-wide computation with the total sum of its values and getting back the previously stored value. Thanks to the *hardware-implemented* atomic operations in modern GPU architectures (i.e., from NVIDIA Maxwell on) the unordered binary prefix-sum allows achieving performance better than the conventional ordered scan-then-fan algorithm [22].

The third support strategy is *supplementary queues*, which is applied in graphs with maximum degree greater than half of the available device threads (e.g., 16,384 on the GeForce 980 GTX).

---

[3] A possible output of the unordered prefix-sum is $a_3, (a_3+a_5), (a_3+a_5+a_1), \ldots, (a_1 + \ldots + a_n)$.

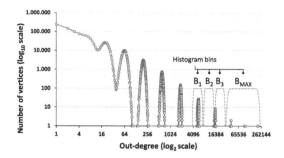

Fig. 5. Example of supplementary queues applied to the kron_g500-logn21 graph.

It aims at organizing the high degree vertices (vertices with out degree $>$ $threshold_{SQ}$) of the frontier in different *bins*. Each bin holds vertices with sizes of the same (approximate) power of two (see the example of Fig. 5). In particular, the i-th bin holds vertices with out-degree in the range $[2^{(b+i)}, 2^{(b+i+1)}]$, where 2^b identifies the base size, and b can be tuned by the user. Such a classification allows running a single kernel for the different bins, properly configured for the bin characteristics. In our tests, the total number of grid threads has been set equal to the lower bound of the bin ($2^{(b+i)}$) times the number of bin elements. This is motivated by the fact that the worst case involves at most two memory accesses among elements in consecutive queues. Finally, the bound value of the last bin is limited to the maximum number of resident device threads, since no more parallelism is possible for greater values.

$threshold_{SQ} = \frac{total\_device\_threads}{2}$ guarantees that at least half threads of the device are active when this technique is applied and, as confirmed by the experimental results, it avoids underutilization of threads and useless overhead.

4 Experimental Results

We conducted the analysis and the performance evaluation on a dataset of 19 graphs, which includes both real-world and synthetic graphs from different application domains. Table 1 presents the graphs and their characteristics in terms of structure (directed/undirected), number of vertices (V, in millions), edges (E, in millions), average degree, standard deviation, Gini coefficient, maximum degree, and average eccentricity (or BFS depth).

The graphs have been selected to be representative of a wide range of characteristics, including size, diameter, degree distribution (from regular to power-law). The graphs have been selected from the University of Florida Sparse Matrix Collection [7], the 10th DIMACS Challenge [1], and the SNAP dataset [15].

We ran the experiments on a NVIDIA GeForce GTX 980 device with CUDA Toolkit 7.5, AMD Phenom II X6 1055 T 3 GHz host processor, Ubuntu 14.04 O.S., and clang 3.6.2 host compiler with the -O3 flag. We ran all tests 100 times from random sources to obtain the average execution time t_{avg}. The traversal

Table 1. Graph dataset.

Graph	Category	U/D	V (M)	E (M)	Avg. degree	Std. deviation	Gini coeff.	Max degree	Avg. eccentricity
asia_osm	Road Network	U	12.0	25.4	2.1	0.5	0.08	9	36, 626.7
europe_osm	Road Network	U	50.9	108.1	2.1	0.5	0.09	13	19, 738.2
USA-road-d.USA	Road Network	U	23.9	58.3	2.4	0.9	0.21	9	6, 418.6
hugebubbles-00020	Num. simulation	U	21.2	63.6	3.0	0.0	0.00	3	6, 205.9
rgg_n_2_23_s0	Random Geometric	U	8.4	127.0	15.1	3.9	0.14	40	1, 715.7
delaunay_n24	Structural	U	16.8	100.7	6.0	1.3	0.12	26	1, 588.3
channel-500 × 100x100	Num. simulation	U	4.8	85.4	17.8	1.0	0.01	18	381.6
ldoor	Structural	U	1.0	47.5	49.9	11.9	0.13	78	161.4
nlpkkt160	Num. simulation	U	8.3	237.9	28.5	2.7	0.02	29	145.2
audikw_1	Structural	U	0.9	78.6	83.3	42.4	0.23	346	61.8
circuit5M	Circuit simulation	D	5.6	59.5	10.7	772.6	0.52	1,290,501	58.0
FullChip	Circuit simulation	D	3.0	26.6	8.9	23.1	0.35	2,312,481	38.3
cage15	DNA electrophoresis	D	5.2	99.2	19.2	5.7	0.17	47	37.3
indochina-2004	Social Network	D	7.4	194.1	26.2	215.8	0.74	6,985	31.0
soc-LiveJournal1	Social Network	D	4.8	69.0	14.2	36.1	0.72	20,293	14.3
soc-pokec-relationships	Social Network	U	1.6	61.2	37.5	59.5	0.62	20,518	10.2
er-fact1.5-scale23	Erdös-Rényi	U	8.4	200.6	23.9	4.9	0.12	53	7.8
hollywood-2009	Social Network	U	1.1	115.0	100.9	271.9	0.73	11,469	7.6
kron_g500-logn21	Kronecker	U	2.1	182.1	86.8	680.1	0.92	213,906	5.1

throughput is computed as E/t_{avg} for all tools and is expressed in MTEPS (million traversed edges per second).

To evaluate the efficiency of the proposed techniques, we measured how the performance of the best and most representative BFS implementations for GPUs at state of the art (*Gunrock* [21], *BFS-4K* [3], and *B40C* [18]) have been improved by substituting the original load balancing implementations with those presented in this paper. Figure 6 shows the results.

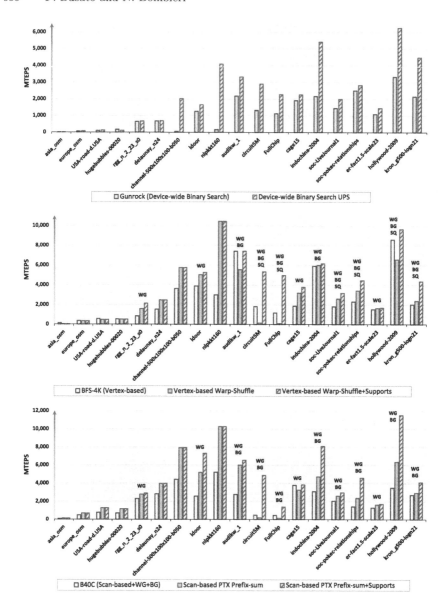

Fig. 6. Performance comparison: Gunrock (upper-side), BFS-4K (middle-side), B40C (bottom-side). WG= warp-based gathering, BG= block-based gathering, SQ= supplementary queues.

The upper side plot compares the performance of the original *Gunrock*, whose load balancing is set on a *device-wide binary search*, with the corresponding version in which we implemented the proposed device-wide binary search with unordered prefix-sum (UPS). As explained in Sect. 3.3, it was not possible to apply any support strategy due to the radically embedded structure of this load

Table 2. Configuration table.

Load balancing support	Rules
Warp-based gathering	max. degree > Warp size,
Block-based gathering	max. degree > Block size,
Supplementary queues	max. degree > Half device threads

balancing technique. However, the results show that applying only the proposed balancing technique allowed us to improve the BFS performance in all graphs, with speedups from $1x$ to $12.7x$.

Figure 6 - middle-side - compares the results of *BFS-4K*, which in the original version implements a direct vertex-based mapping strategy, with the corresponding version with *warp-shuffle*. First with no support strategies applied, and then with the supports applied in graphs satisfying the characteristics reported in Table 2. We observed that the performance of the proposed optimized technique are substantially higher than the standard implementation in most cases. In graphs with very irregular degree distribution, the original *BFS-4K* is better as it takes advantage of additional load balancing techniques, such as dynamic parallelism, to alleviate the workload unbalancing. However, the proposed strategy properly combined with the load balancing support strategies selectively enabled depending on the graph characteristics (reported on the top of the bar), provides the best results in all graphs (from $1x$ to $4.2x$, and $0.9x$ in a single case).

Finally, the bottom-side plot compares the results of the original *B40C* implementation, which relies on a scan-based mapping strategy, with the corresponding version based on *PTX prefix-sum*, without and with the proposed supports. It is important to note that the original tool also implements a support (which is always enabled) comparable to the warp- and block-level gathering proposed in this work. The results show that, thanks to the highly optimized prefix-sum and the instruction-level parallelism technique, the proposed load balancing technique (with no supports) provides performance almost always better and up to two times faster than the original *B40C* implementation. The throughput is further improved by enabling the proposed support techniques (right-most bar of the plot), thus providing speedups from $1x$ to $9.7x$. Such supporting techniques significantly contribute to the graph traversal performance thanks to their new algorithms based on binary prefix-sum, which, differently from the standard version implemented in B40C, it allows avoiding sequential iterations over high-degree vertices.

5 Conclusions

This paper presented three load balancing techniques for graph traversal applications on GPUs and the most important details of their architecture-oriented implementations. The paper presented a set support strategies that can be statically selected and modularly applied to the main balancing techniques to better address the different graph characteristics. Experimental results have been presented to show how the performance of existing and widespread BFS implementations have been improved by substituting the original load balancing strategy with those presented in this paper, with and without the support strategies.

References

1. Bader, D.A., Meyerhenke, H., Sanders, P., Wagner, D.: Graph partitioning and graph clustering, 10th DIMACS implementation challenge workshop. Contemporary Mathematics 588 (2013)
2. Bisson, M., Bernaschi, M., Mastrostefano, E.: Parallel distributed breadth first search on the Kepler architecture. IEEE Trans. Parallel Distrib. Syst. **27**(7), 2091–2102 (2015)
3. Busato, F., Bombieri, N.: BFS-4K: an efficient implementation of BFS for Kepler GPU architectures. IEEE Trans. Parallel Distrib. Syst. **26**(7), 1826–1838 (2015)
4. Busato, F., Bombieri, N.: An efficient implementation of the Bellman-Ford algorithm for Kepler GPU architectures. IEEE Trans. Parallel Distrib. Syst. **27**(8), 2222–2233 (2016)
5. Cormen, T., Leiserson, C., Rivest, R., Stein, C.: Introduction to Algorithms. MIT Press, Cambridge (2009)
6. Davidson, A., Baxter, S., Garland, M., Owens, J.D.: Work-efficient parallel GPU methods for single-source shortest paths. In: Proceedings of IEEE IPDPS, pp. 349–359 (2014)
7. Davis, T.A., Hu, Y.: The University of Florida sparse matrix collection. ACM Trans. Math. Softw. **38**(1), 1 (2011)
8. Green, O., McColl, R., Bader, D.A.: GPU merge path: a GPU merging algorithm. In: Proceedings of ACM SC, pp. 331–340 (2012)
9. Harish, P., Narayanan, P.: Accelerating large graph algorithms on the GPU using CUDA. In: Proceedings of IEEE HiPC, pp. 197–208 (2007)
10. Hong, S., Kim, S.K., Oguntebi, T., Olukotun, K.: Accelerating CUDA graph algorithms at maximum warp. In: Proceedings of ACM PPoPP, pp. 267–276 (2011)
11. Jia, Y., Lu, V., Hoberock, J., Garland, M., Hart, J.C.: Edge v. node parallelism for graph centrality metrics. In: GPU Computing Gems 2, pp. 15–30 (2011)
12. Khorasani, F., Rowe, B., Gupta, R., Bhuyan, L.N.: Eliminating intra-warp load imbalance in irregular nested patterns via collaborative task engagement. In: Proceedings of IEEE Parallel and Distributed Processing Symposium, pp. 524–533 (2016)
13. Knuth, D.E.: The Art of Computer Programming, vol. 3. Pearson Education, London (1997)
14. Kunegis, J., Preusse, J.: Fairness on the web: alternatives to the power law. In: Proceedings of ACM WebSci, pp. 175–184 (2012)
15. Leskovec, J., et al.: Stanford network analysis project (2010). http://snap.stanford.edu
16. Luo, L., Wong, M., Hwu, W.M.: An effective GPU implementation of breadth-first search. In: Proceedings of ACM/IEEE DAC, pp. 52–55 (2010)
17. McLaughlin, A., Bader, D.A.: Scalable and high performance betweenness centrality on the GPU. In: Proceedings of the IEEE International Conference for High Performance Computing, Networking, Storage and Analysis, pp. 572–583 (2014)

18. Merrill, D., Garland, M., Grimshaw, A.: Scalable GPU graph traversal. In: Proceedings of ACM PPoPP, pp. 117–128 (2012)
19. NVidia Corporation: Kepler Tuning Guide (2014). http://docs.nvidia.com/cuda/kepler-tuning-guide/index.html
20. NVidia Corporation: Parallel Thread Execution ISA (2014). http://docs.nvidia.com/cuda/parallel-thread-execution/index.html
21. Wang, Y., Davidson, A., Pan, Y., Wu, Y., Riffel, A., Owens, J.D.: Gunrock: a high-performance graph processing library on the GPU. In: Proceedings of ACM PPoPP, pp. 265–266 (2016)
22. Wilt, N.: The CUDA Handbook: A Comprehensive Guide to GPU Programming. Pearson Education, London (2013)

Energy Efficient Stencil Computations on the Low-Power Manycore MPPA-256 Processor

Emmanuel Podestá Jr., Bruno Marques do Nascimento,
and Márcio Castro[(✉)] [iD]

Graduate Program in Computer Science (PPGCC),
Federal University of Santa Catarina (UFSC), Florianópolis, SC, Brazil
{emmanuel.podesta,bruno.mn}@grad.ufsc.br, marcio.castro@ufsc.br

Abstract. A new class of highly-parallel low-power manycore chips that cope with energy constraints have been unveiled. Sunway's SW26010 and Kalray's MPPA-256 are examples of them, featuring more than two hundred cores in a single low-power chip. Although they may present better energy efficiency than general-purpose multicore processors, architectural characteristics such as their limited amount of distributed on-chip memory make the development of efficient scientific parallel applications a challenging task. In this paper we propose and evaluate a new backend of PSkel, a framework that provides a single high-level abstraction for stencil programming on CPUs and GPUs, for the low-power manycore MPPA-256 processor. This relieves programmers of the burden of explicitly dealing with communications and the hybrid underlying programming model of MPPA-256. Our results showed that the energy consumption of stencil applications running on MPPA-256 is up to 7.34x and 4.71x lower than on an Intel Xeon E5 multicore and NVIDIA Tesla K40 GPU, respectively.

Keywords: MPPA-256 · Manycore · PSkel · Energy efficiency

1 Introduction

High Performance Computing (HPC) platforms have been evaluated based almost exclusively on their raw processing speed. However, their energy efficiency have become as important as raw performance. Because of that, a new class of highly-parallel low-power manycore chips that cope with energy constraints was unveiled. Sunway's SW26010 [6] and Kalray's MPPA-256 [5] are examples of

The authors would like to thank CAPES and CNPq for funding this research. This work was also supported by STIC-AmSud/CAPES scientific cooperation program under EnergySFE research project grant No. 99999.007556/2015-02. Finally, a special thank to Jean-François Méhaut (LIG/CNRS) for giving access to the MPPA-256 platform to the authors.

M. Aldinucci et al. (Eds.): Euro-Par 2018, LNCS 11014, pp. 642–655, 2018.
https://doi.org/10.1007/978-3-319-96983-1_46

such processors, providing more than two hundred low-power autonomous cores that can be exploited through both data and task parallelism.

Although low-power manycores may present better energy efficiency than general-purpose multicore processors [5], their particular architectural characteristics make the development of efficient scientific parallel applications a very challenging task [2,18]. Processing cores with non-coherent caches are usually distributed in a clustered architecture that features a hybrid programming model. On the one hand, cores in the same cluster share a limited amount of directly addressable memory. On the other hand, distinct clusters must communicate through the Network-on-Chip (NoC) in a distributed fashion. For that reason, communication costs between cores may vary significantly, depending on the location of the communicating cores on the NoC.

One possible approach to ease the development of parallel applications for low-power manycores is through the use of skeletons [3]. Skeletons allow programmers to focus on designing algorithms rather than worrying about synchronization issues and task scheduling, which are transparently handled by the skeleton framework, thereby speeding up application development and debugging. Among several existing patterns of parallel skeletons (*e.g.*, map, reduce, pipeline and scan), the stencil pattern has been used in applications of many important fields, such as quantum physics, weather forecasting and digital image processing [8]. The stencil pattern operates on n-dimensional data structures, using an input data value and its neighbors to compute the corresponding output data element. This process is repeated for every input data value in the n-dimensional data structure.

Indeed, many frameworks have been proposed to ease the development of parallel stencil computations on multicores and Graphics Processing Units (GPUs) such as PSkel [11], SkePU [16] and SkelCL [15]. In particular, PSkel is a stencil framework that provides a single high-level abstraction for stencil programming on heterogeneous CPU-GPU systems, while allowing automatic data partition, assignment and computation to both CPU and GPU. In this paper, we present the design, implementation and evaluation of a new back-end of PSkel for the low-power manycore MPPA-256 processor (PSkel-MPPA). The same high-level, low overhead and intuitive PSkel code that already ran transparently on GPUs and multicores is extended to run also on the MPPA-256 architecture. This relieves programmers of the burden of explicitly dealing with NoC communications, the hybrid underlying programming model and the absence of cache coherence on MPPA-256. Our solution uses a trapezoidal tiling technique to reduce the number of communications and synchronization barriers on MPPA-256, which improves considerably the overall performance. Our results show that the energy consumption of stencil applications on MPPA-256 is up to 7.34x and 4.71x lower than on an Intel Xeon E5 multicore and NVIDIA Tesla K40 GPU, respectively, while presenting competitive performance.

The remainder of this paper is organized as follows. Section 2 presents an overview of MPPA-256 and PSkel. Next, Sect. 3 describes our proposal (PSkel-MPPA) as well as its implementation details. Then, Sect. 4 presents the results

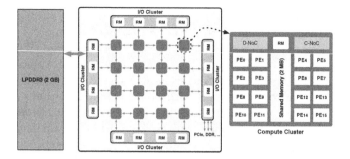

Fig. 1. Overview of the low-power MPPA-256 manycore processor.

obtained with PSkel-MPPA, comparing them against reference implementations of PSkel for multicores and GPUs. Section 5 discusses related work. Finally, Sect. 6 concludes this paper.

2   Background

2.1   MPPA-256

MPPA-256 is a single-chip low-power manycore processor developed by Kalray that integrates 256 user cores and 32 system cores in 28 nm CMOS technology running at 400 MHz. These cores are distributed across 16 compute clusters and 4 Input/Output (I/O) clusters that communicate through data and control NoCs. The board used in this paper has one of the I/O clusters connected to an external Low-Power Double Data Rate 3 (LPDDR3) of 2 GB. Figure 1 shows an architectural overview of the MPPA-256 processor. Overall, each compute cluster has the following components:

- 16 cores called Processing Elements (PEs), which are dedicated to run user threads (one thread per PE) in non-interruptible and non-preemptible mode. Each PE has private 2-way associative 32 kB instruction and data caches;
- a Resource Manager (RM), which is responsible for running the operating system and managing communications;
- a low-latency shared memory of 2 MB, which enables a high bandwidth and throughput between PEs within the same compute cluster; and
- two NoC controllers, one for data and other for control.

The processor features a distributed memory model. Compute clusters and the I/O clusters have their own address spaces. Applications must use two parallel programming libraries to exploit all processor resources: a thread library (Pthread or OpenMP) and a proprietary library called Asynchronous Operations Application Programming Interface (Async API). The former is used to parallelize computations in computing clusters via shared memory. The latter follows a distributed memory model, and it must be used for cluster-cluster and cluster-I/O communications through the NoC.

Async API is based on one-sided communications between the compute clusters' local memory and LPDDR3. The main concepts behind Async API are *execution domains*, *segments* and `put`/`get` operations. The execution domain represents a set of cores sharing a local memory, being isolated from other execution domains. Considering the MPPA-256 distributed memory model, an execution domain corresponds to a compute cluster or to an I/O cluster. Memory that is not directly accessible from the cores of an execution domain can be structured into segments, which correspond to the entire or part of the local memory of cores located in another execution domain. Each segment has a *unique signature*, which is specified when the segment is created in an execution domain through the `mppa_async_segment_create()` function. Then, other execution domains can reference a previously created segment by passing its unique signature the function `mppa_async_segment_clone()`. Once segments are created and referenced by different execution domains, one should use put/get operations to read data from a remote segment into the local memory (`get` operation) or to write local data to the remote segment (`put` operation). Different flavors of these operations are available in Async API, allowing contiguous or spaced data transfers (*e.g.*, `mppa_async_put()` and `mppa_async_get_spaced()`) as well as 2D block transfers (`mppa_async_sget_block2d()`), which is useful for transferring 2D data blocks.

The execution flow of an MPPA-256 application is the following. The main process (called *master process*) runs on an RM of the I/O cluster connected to the LPDDR3 and is responsible for allocating the input data in its local memory (LPDDR3) and spawning *worker processes* (one for each compute cluster) by calling the `mppa_power_base_spawn()` function. The necessary data segments should be created by the master process so it can exchange data with the compute clusters. Finally, the master process should wait all worker processes to finish by calling the `mppa_power_base_waitpid()` function. Each worker process should make references to remote segments allocated in the LPDDR3 to exchange data during the execution and may create up to 16 threads using Pthreads or OpenMP (one thread for each PE) to perform computations in parallel. Each PE has its own private cache memory without any automatic coherence mechanism among the remaining PEs cache memories. Although this improves the cache performance, it requires the developer to explicitly flush data when needed.

2.2 Stencil Pattern and PSkel

The stencil computational pattern operates on n-dimensional data structures and uses a sliding window (*a.k.a* mask) that scans the entire input data set and produces output data using a user-defined stencil kernel function. The mask size corresponds to a specific number of neighbors of each element of the input data. The stencil application repeats that process on every element of the input data. Stencil applications can be iterative, which means that the output data produced after an iteration t is used as the input for an iteration $t+1$.

```
 1 __parallel__ void stencilKernel(Array2D<float> A, Array2D<float> B,
 2                       struct Arguments args, int x, int y) {
 3   B(x,y) = args.alpha*(A(x,y+1)+A(x,y-1)+A(x+1,y)+A(x-1,y)+args.beta);
 4 }
 5
 6 void jacobi(float *A, float *B, int M, int N, float alpha, float beta,
 7            int timesteps) {
 8   Array2D<float> input(A,M,N);
 9   Array2D<float> output(B,M,N);
10   struct Arguments args(alpha, beta);
11   Stencil2D<Array2D<float>, struct Arguments> stencil(input,output,args);
12   stencil.runIterativeGPU(timesteps);
13 }
```

Fig. 2. Simplified example of a PSkel stencil code.

PSkel is a framework for high-level programming stencil computations, based on the concept of parallel skeletons, which offers parallel execution support on CPUs and GPUs [11]. PSkel offers a single programming interface, decoupled from the runtime back-ends, that releases the programmer from the responsibility of writing boiler-plate code for parallel stencil computation. Instead, the programmer is responsible for implementing a stencil kernel describing solely the computation, while the framework translates the abstractions described into low-level parallel C++ code. Synchronization, memory management and data transfers are transparently handled by the framework.

Figure 2 shows an example of the Jacobi method for solving matrix equations [4] written in PSkel. The PSkel Application Programming Interface (API) provides templates for manipulating input and output data via template classes for n-dimensional arrays, called Array, Array2D (Fig. 2, lines 8–9) and Array3D. These abstractions provide methods that encapsulate the data management procedures, such as memory allocation, memory copy and data transfer (e.g., communication between CPU and GPU). Moreover, it provides abstractions for specifying the stencil kernel and to manage the stencil execution. The stencil kernel (prototype function stencilKernel()) is the application specific method that describes the computation that will be performed on each entry of the input array and its neighbors (Fig. 2, lines 1–4). The stencilKernel() prototype function must be implemented by the user of the PSkel. Finally, the API provides a set of classes for managing the whole execution of the user-defined number of iterations of the stencil kernel over the input and output data, such as Stencil, Stencil2D (Fig. 2, line 11) and Stencil3D.

In the given example, the stencilKernel() function will be executed on the GPU. The runIterativeGPU() method hides from the user all the CUDA code needed to correctly execute the specified stencil kernel on the GPU.

3   PSkel-MPPA

As previously discussed in Sect. 2.2, PSkel currently supports the execution of stencil applications on CPUs and GPUs. In this paper, we propose a new back-end of PSkel for the low-power manycore MPPA-256 processor, which differs significantly from the CPU and GPU ones due to the intrinsic characteristics of MPPA-256 discussed in Sect. 2.1, such as: (i) limited amount of on-chip memory; (ii) clustered architecture with NoC constraints; (iii) processing cores with non-coherent caches; and (iv) proprietary low-level communication API.

The new back-end, named PSkel-MPPA, supports 2D stencils (Stencil2D class in PSkel) and adopts the master-worker model. The master process is executed in the I/O cluster connected to the LPDDR3 memory, in which the input and output data (Array2D objects) are allocated, whereas the worker processes are executed on the compute clusters (one worker process per compute cluster) to perform the stencil computation in parallel. Given the memory limitation inside compute clusters (2 MB), the input Array2D is partitioned into *tiles* of fixed user-defined size to be sent to them. When tiling stencil computations, neighborhood dependencies inherent to the stencil parallel pattern must be considered before partitioning the input data.

We used the trapezoidal tiling technique to handle neighborhood dependencies in PSkel-MPPA, resulting in redundant data and computation per tile [13]. We use a formal definition to illustrate this technique. Let A be a 2D data matrix, with dimensions $\dim(A) = (w, h)$, where w and h are, respectively, its width and height. Using tiles of dimensions (w', h') yields $\lceil \frac{w}{w'} \rceil \lceil \frac{h}{h'} \rceil$ possible tiles of A. Let $A_{i,j}$ be one such tile, where $0 \leq i < \lceil \frac{w}{w'} \rceil$ and $0 \leq j < \lceil \frac{h}{h'} \rceil$. $A_{i,j}$ has offset (iw', jh') relative to the top left corner of A and $\dim(A_{i,j}) = (\min\{w', w - iw'\}, \min\{h', h - jh'\})$. The offset is an indexing displacement required for accessing the elements of the tile.

Figure 3 shows a graphical view of this technique. A logical tile (inner solid line) is contained in a 2D data matrix (outer dashed line) with vertical and horizontal offsets given by jh' and iw'. If t iterations of a stencil application should be executed, it is possible to compute t' consecutive iterations on $A_{i,j}$ ($t' \in [1, t]$) without the need of any data exchange between adjacent tiles (*a.k.a* inner iterations). To do so, the logical tile ($A_{i,j}$) must be enlarged with a ghost zone (area between the inner solid line and the outer solid line), which is comprised of a halo region (the area between the inner solid line and the inner dashed line). Let r be the most distant displacement required for the neighborhood defined by the stencil mask. The area of range r comprising the neighborhood is denominated *halo region*. The number of adjacent halo regions that compose the ghost zone is proportional to t'. Thus, the enlarged tile $A_{i,j}^*$ has offsets $(\max\{iw' - rt', 0\}, \max\{jh' - rt', 0\})$ relative to A. Thus, sizing the ghost zones poses a trade-off between the cost of redundant computations and the reduction in communication and synchronizations on the NoC when processing iterative stencil computations on MPPA-256.

The execution flow of PSkel-MPPA follows the one described in Sect. 2.1. During the initialization phase, the master process running on the I/O cluster allocates the input and output data in the LPDDR3, and creates a specific segment for each one of them. Next, it calculates the number of enlarged tiles that will be produced as well as their dimensions based on: (i) user-defined parameters, such as the input data and logical tile dimensions, the number of compute

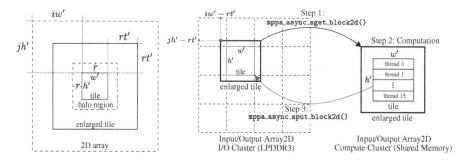

Fig. 3. 2D tiling [13].   **Fig. 4.** Communications with `block2d`.

clusters and the number of inner iterations; and (ii) stencil kernel parameters, such as the mask size. Then, it spawns up to 16 worker processes (one for each compute cluster) and informs each worker process about the number of enlarged tiles produced, their dimensions and the subset of tiles it should compute later on. Finally, the master process waits for all workers to finish. Each worker process, on the other hand, allocates data to store the input and output enlarged tiles in the compute cluster local memory and clones both input and output remote segments that were already created by the master process to make data transfers further on. The initialization phase in both master and worker processes is encapsulated in the `Stencil2D` class.

The computation phase consists of the execution of the stencil kernel by the worker processes. The following three main steps are performed to compute each tile assigned to a worker process: (1) the enlarged tile is extracted from the input data allocated in LPDDR3 and transferred to compute cluster local memory to be processed; (2) t' iterations of the stencil kernel (inner iterations) are executed by the worker process over the enlarged tile; and (3) the resulting logical tile is transferred back from the compute cluster local memory to its corresponding position in the LPDDR3. Once all tiles assigned to each worker process were successfully computed, all worker processes must synchronize at a global barrier, since the data computed during t' iterations will be needed by the others in the following iteration to solve neighborhood dependencies. We used the `mppa_rpc_barrier_all()` function for this purpose. The whole procedure described before is then repeated until the total number of iterations defined by the user (t) is reached. The aforementioned steps are depicted in Fig. 4 and they are described in more detail below:

Step 1. Based on the information given by the master process during the spawn procedure, the worker process is capable of calculating the coordinates of each enlarged tile assigned to it with respect to the input data allocated in the LPDDR3 ($iw' - rt'$ and $jh' - rt'$ coordinates) without any other intervention from the master process. The `mppa_async_sget_block2d()` function takes such information and the block size as input parameters and it transfers the enlarged tile to be processed by the worker process from the input remote segment into the compute cluster local memory through the NoC.

Step 2. The worker process computes t' iterations of the user-defined stencil kernel over the enlarged tile. In each t' iteration, the computation is parallelized by means of an OpenMP parallel region. The parallel region creates up to 16 threads (one for each PE). Each PE is responsible for executing the stencil kernel on a subset of the enlarged tile cells.

Step 3. After the stencil kernel computation, the resulting logical tile is transferred back to the LPDDR3. The `mppa_async_sput_block2d()` function is used for this purpose, allowing the logical tile to be extracted from the enlarged tile in the compute cluster local memory and transferred to its corresponding position in the output remote segment.

Fortunately, all complex tasks related to the tiling technique, NoC communications and adaptations discussed in this section are hidden from the developers, since they were included in the back-end of PSkel. This means that current applications developed with the PSkel framework can run seamlessly on MPPA-256 without any source code modifications.

4 Experimental Evaluation

4.1 Platforms, Applications and Inputs

We evaluate the performance and energy consumption of the proposed solution (PSkel-MPPA) against reference multicore and GPU implementations available in PSkel. Energy measurements were collected from power and energy sensors available on MPPA-256, which include all clusters, memory (on-chip memory and LPDDR3) and NoCs. The reference implementations of PSkel for CPUs and GPUs were executed on the platforms described bellow. Compilation was done using GCC 5.4 (MPPA-256 and CPU) and NVCC version 8.0 (GPU) with the flags -O3 (all platforms), -march=native -mtune=native -ftree-vectorize (CPU and GPU) and -arch=sm_35 (GPU).

- **Xeon E5**: a desktop server featuring an Intel Xeon E5-2640 v4 (Broadwell) processor with 10 physical cores running at 2.4 GHz and 64 GB of RAM. Energy measurements on this platform are based on Intel's Running Average Power Limit (RAPL) interface, which considers the power consumption of hardware components through hardware counters. We used this approach to obtain the energy consumption of the CPU (PACKAGE_ENERGY) and DRAM (DRAM_ENERGY).
- **Tesla K40**: a NVIDIA Tesla K40c graphics board featuring 2880 CUDA parallel-processing cores with a base clock of 745 MHz and 12 GB of GDDR5 GPU memory. Energy measurements on this platform were obtained from NVIDIA Management Library (NVML). We used the NVML to gather the power usage for the GPU and its associated circuitry (e.g., internal memory).

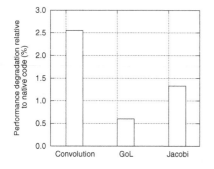

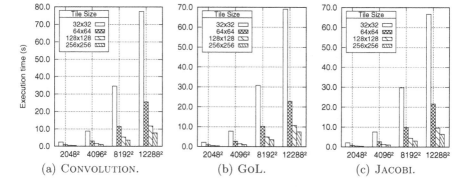

Fig. 5. Performance degradation of PSkel-MPPA (in percentage) relative to hand-optimized code for MPPA-256.

Fig. 6. Empirical study to find the best value for t'. The best trade-off is achieved with $t' = 10$.

Fig. 7. Impact of tile size on the performance of the stencil applications.

(a) CONVOLUTION.   (b) GOL.   (c) JACOBI.

We carried out several experiments with three stencil applications[1] implemented in PSkel: (i) CONVOLUTION, which implements a classical convolution method used in signal and image processing; (ii) GOL, which is a cellular automaton implementing Conway's Game of Life; and (iii) JACOBI, which is an iterative method for solving matrix equations [4]. We also considered four input data sizes (2048×2048, 4096×4096, 8192×8192 and 12288×12288) to evaluate the performance of the aforementioned PSkel applications on MPPA-256, Xeon E5 and Tesla K40. Moreover, we evaluated the performance impacts of using different tile sizes (32×32, 64×64, 128×128 and 256×256) on MPPA-256, since input/output data sizes do not fit into compute clusters memory (2 MB). The maximum input/output and tile sizes were chosen carefully to fill MPPA-256 memories (2 GB of LPDDR3 and 2 MB of local memory in compute clusters). Finally, we fixed the number of iterations for each application to $t = 100$ in all experiments. All results represent averages of 20 runs with a maximum standard deviation of less than 1%.

---

[1] A detailed description about these PSkel applications is not presented in this paper due to space constraints but can be found in [11,12].

4.2   Overhead of PSkel

We first analyze the overhead introduced by our new back-end of PSkel (PSkel-MPPA). Figure 5 shows the performance degradation of all three stencil applications implemented with PSkel-MPPA compared to hand-optimized ones implemented without PSkel abstractions. As it can be observed, the performance degradation introduced by PSkel-MPPA is minimal when compared to MPPA-256 native stencil code (less then 2.6%).

4.3   Sizing the Ghost Zone

In our solution, the trapezoidal tiling technique allows us to easily fine tune the size of the ghost zone with the t' parameter. Indeed, this is an important feature to exploit the low amount of on-chip memory and to make a better use of the NoC available in low-power manycores. Thus, we carried out an empirical study with the aforementioned applications to determine the best value for this parameter. Figure 6 shows the performance gains when varying t' from 2 to 16 (performance gains are relative to $t' = 1$). As we mentioned earlier, sizing the ghost zone poses a trade-off between the cost of redundant computations and the reduction in communication and synchronizations on the NoC. Our empirical study shows that the best trade-off is achieved when $t' = 10$ (performance obtained with $t' > 16$ varied around 4 and were omitted from the figure). Because of that, all results presented in next sections were carried out with $t' = 10$.

4.4   Tile Size vs. Performance

In this section, we analyze the impact of the tile size on the performance of PSkel applications on MPPA-256. Figure 7 shows the performance of the stencil applications when varying the input data size and the tile size. Overall, we observed an average increase in the execution time of the applications between 2x and 3.3x as we double the input size. This behavior is expected since more communications and synchronizations must be performed for larger data inputs.

Moreover, we observed that the performance of the applications is greatly improved as we increase the tile size, regardless of the input size. The main reason for that is twofold. On the one hand, the number of put/get operations and synchronizations between the I/O and compute clusters on the NoC is greatly reduced as we increase the tile size. This allows for bigger data transfers per put/get operation, improving the NoC throughput. On the other hand, bigger tiles mean higher parallelism inside compute clusters (*i.e.*, OpenMP threads will have more work to compute), reducing the overhead imposed by OpenMP parallel regions. When varying the tile size from 32×32 to 64×64, we observed improvements of up to 3x on all applications. The performance gains increase to at least 6.9x and 10.3x when varying the tile size from 32×32 to 128×128 and from 32×32 to 256×256, respectively.

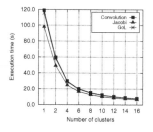

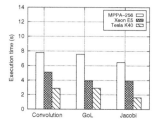

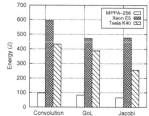

Fig. 8. Scalability. **Fig. 9.** Performance and energy comparison.

4.5 Scalability Analysis

Next, we analyze the scalability of PSkel-MPPA. Figure 8 shows the execution time of each application on MPPA-256 when varying the number of compute clusters from 1 to 16. For this experiment, we used input data and tiles of size 12288 × 12288 and 256 × 256, respectively. As it can be noticed, all stencil applications present a similar behavior and have their execution times reduced as we increase the number of compute clusters. Overall, we observed a speedup gain of 15.3x with 16 compute clusters over the execution with a single compute cluster. This means that our solution is able to exploit all computing resources and the NoC of MPPA-256.

4.6 Comparison with CPU and GPU: Performance vs. Energy

Finally, we compare the execution time and energy consumption achieved by PSkel-MPPA against reference implementations of PSkel for CPU and GPU. In these experiments, we used input data of size 12288 × 12288. Based on the best performance achieved on Fig. 7, we used tiles of size 256 × 256 on MPPA-256. To make a fair comparison, we used the best tiling optimizations for Xeon E5 and Tesla K40 that were available in the multicore and GPU back-ends of PSkel, respectively. Figure 9 presents the results obtained with all stencil applications.

Overall, PSkel-MPPA achieves competitive execution times compared to the CPU and GPU counterparts. As expected, the best performance was achieved on the GPU, since it has much more processing power than the other processors. The execution times of CONVOLUTION, GoL and JACOBI on MPPA-256 were 1.52x, 1.93x and 1.67x higher than on CPU, respectively. On the other hand, the execution times of CONVOLUTION, GoL and JACOBI on MPPA-256 were 2.72x, 2.61x and 4.04x higher than on GPU, respectively.

PSkel-MPPA achieved the best results with respect to the energy consumption on all applications. The main reason is that MPPA-256 offers a high parallelism and yet has a low power consumption. As we showed in Sect. 4.3, the trapezoidal tiling technique implemented in PSkel-MPPA was extremely important to achieve such energy improvements. We observed that the energy consumption on MPPA-256 was up to 7.34x and 4.71x lower than on the CPU and GPU, respectively.

5 Related Work

Due to the importance of parallel skeletons, and specifically the stencil parallel pattern, many recent efforts in research sought to improve the performance and broaden the support of skeletons on manycore processors. *Buono et al.* [1] ported a framework based on parallel skeletons, called FastFlow, to the manycore processor TilePro64. The TILEPro64 has 64 identical processing cores interconnected by a mesh of network-on-chip. Similarly, *Thorarensen et al.* [16] presented a new back-end of the SkePU framework for the low-power manycore Myriad2. It features a heterogeneous architecture, targeting power constrained devices and mainly computer vision applications. *Lutz et al.* [9] used tiling techniques in stencil computations on multi-GPU environments by using the GPU memories collectively. Similarly, *Gysi et al.* [7] propose a framework for automatic tiling optimizations of stencil computations on CPU-GPU hybrid systems.

Recent works studied the performance and/or the energy efficiency of low-power manycore processors. *Totoni et al.* [17] compared the power and performance of Intel's Single-Chip Cloud Computer (SCC) to other types of CPUs and GPUs. Although they showed that there is no single solution that always achieves the best trade-off between power and performance, the results suggest that manycores are an opportunity for the future. *Morari et al.* [10] proposed an optimized implementation of radix sort for the Tilera TILEPro64 manycore processor. The results showed that their solution for TILEPro64 provides much better energy efficiency than an general-purpose multicore processor (Intel Xeon W5590) and comparable energy efficiency with respect to a GPU NVIDIA Tesla C2070. *Souza et al.* [14] proposed a benchmark suite to evaluate MPPA-256 manycore processor. The benchmark offers diverse applications regarding parallel patterns, job types, communication intensity and task load strategies, suitable for a broad understanding of performance and energy consumption of MPPA-256 and upcoming manycores. *Francesquini et al.* [5] evaluated three different classes of applications (CPU-bound, memory-bound and mixed) using highly-parallel platforms such as MPPA-256 and a 24-node, 192-core NUMA platform. They showed that manycore architectures can be very competitive, even if the application is irregular in nature. Using the Adapteva's Epiphany-IV low-power manycore, *Varghese et al.* [18] described how a stencil-based solution to the anisotropic heat equation using a two-dimensional grid was developed. This manycore has a low power budged (2 W) and has 64 processing cores. Similar to MPPA-256, Epiphany-IV has a very limited amount of local memory available to each core and no automatic prefetching mechanism exists.

To the best of our knowledge, PSkel-MPPA is the first complete implementation of a parallel stencil framework on MPPA-256. Our solution relieves programmers of the burden of explicitly dealing with NoC communications, the hybrid underlying programming model and the absence of cache coherence on MPPA-256. The trapezoidal tiling technique allows developers to fine tune the trade-off between the cost of redundant computations and the reduction in communication and synchronizations on the NoC when processing iterative stencil computations on MPPA-256.

6   Conclusion

Low-power manycores have emerged as a building block for constructing energy-efficient HPC platforms. However, the development of efficient parallel applications is very challenging on these processors because developers must deal with hybrid programming models, limited amount of directly addressable memory and NoC constraints. In this paper, we propose to ease the development of stencil applications on the low-power MPPA-256 manycore processor by means of parallel skeletons. More precisely, we proposed a new back-end of the PSkel stencil framework for MPPA-256 named PSkel-MPPA, providing a single high-level abstraction for stencil programming on CPUs, GPUs and MPPA-256. Our solution relieves programmers of the burden of explicitly dealing with communications and the hybrid underlying programming model of MPPA-256.

The trapezoidal tiling technique adopted in our solution was essencial to exploit the low-power MPPA-256 manycore processor, improving the performance of our solution. Our results showed that PSkel-MPPA achieved the best results with respect to the energy consumption on all applications, being up to 7.34x and 4.71x more energy efficient than on the CPU and GPU considered in this study, respectively. Moreover, PSkel-MPPA achieved competitive performance on MPPA-256 in comparison to the CPU and GPU reference implementations. The GPU achieved the best performance, since it has much more processing power than the other processors.

As future works, we intend to extend our support in PSkel-MPPA for 3D stencils. In this case, it would be necessary to consider a prefetching scheme to overlap communications with computations. Moreover, we intend to compare our results on MPPA-256 against low-power ARM processors, which may also include a low-power GPU. Finally, we intend to provide similar abstractions for dealing with other kinds of skeletons.

References

1. Buono, D., Danelutto, M., Lametti, S., Torquati, M.: Parallel patterns for general purpose many-core. In: 2013 21st Euromicro International Conference on Parallel, Distributed, and Network-Based Processing, pp. 131–139 (2013). https://doi.org/10.1109/PDP.2013.27
2. Castro, M., Francesquini, E., Dupros, F., Aochi, H., Navaux, P.O., Méhaut, J.F.: Seismic wave propagation simulations on low-power and performance-centric many-cores. Parallel Comput. **54**, 108–120 (2016). https://doi.org/10.1016/j.parco.2016.01.011
3. Cole, M.: Bringing skeletons out of the closet: a pragmatic manifesto for skeletal parallel programming. Parallel Comput. **30**(3), 389–406 (2004)
4. Demmel, J.W.: Applied Numerical Linear Algebra. SIAM, Philadelphia (1997)
5. Francesquini, E., et al.: On the energy efficiency and performance of irregular applications on multicore, NUMA and manycore platforms. J. Parallel Distrib. Comput. **76**, 32–48 (2014). https://doi.org/10.1016/j.jpdc.2014.11.002
6. Fu, H., et al.: The sunway taihulight supercomputer: system and applications. Sci. China Inf. Sci. **59**(7), 1–16 (2016). https://doi.org/10.1007/s11432-016-5588-7

7. Gysi, T., Grosser, T., Hoefler, T.: MODESTO: data-centric analytic optimization of complex stencil programs on heterogeneous architectures. In: International Conference on Supercomputing (ICS), pp. 177–186. ACM, Irvine (2015)

8. Holewinski, J., Pouchet, L.N., Sadayappan, P.: High-performance code generation for stencil computations on GPU architectures. In: International Conference on Supercomputing (ICS), pp. 311–320. ACM, Venice (2012)

9. Lutz, T., Fensch, C., Cole, M.: PARTANS: an autotuning framework for stencil computation on multi-GPU systems. ACM Trans. Archit. Code Optim. 9(4), 59:1–59:24 (2013)

10. Morari, A., Tumeo, A., Villa, O., Secchi, S., Valero, M.: Efficient sorting on the Tilera manycore architecture. In: International Symposium on Computer Architecture and High Performance Computing (SBAC-PAD), pp. 171–178. IEEE Computer Society, New York (2012)

11. Pereira, A.D., Ramos, L., Góes, L.F.W.: PSkel: a stencil programming framework for CPU-GPU systems. Concurr. Comput.: Pract. Exp. 27(17), 4938–4953 (2015)

12. Pereira, A.D., Rocha, R.C.O., Castro, M., Goes, L.F.W., Dantas, M.A.R.: Extending OpenACC for efficient stencil code generation and execution by skeleton frameworks. In: International Conference on High Performance Computing and Simulation (HPCS), pp. 719–726. IEEE Computer Society, Genoa (2017). https://doi.org/10.1109/HPCS.2017.110

13. Rocha, R.C.O., Pereira, A.D., Ramos, L., Ges, L.F.W.: TOAST: automatic tiling for iterative stencil computations on GPUs. Concurr. Comput.: Pract. Exp. 29(8), 1–13 (2017). https://doi.org/10.1002/cpe.4053

14. Souza, M.A., et al.: CAP bench: a benchmark suite for performance and energy evaluation of low-power many-core processors. Concurr. Comput.: Pract. Exp. 29, e3892 (2016). https://doi.org/10.1002/cpe.3892

15. Steuwer, M., Kegel, P., Gorlatch, S.: SkelCL - a portable skeleton library for high-level GPU programming. In: IEEE International Symposium on Parallel and Distributed Processing Workshops (IPDPSW), pp. 1176–1182. IEEE Computer Society, Shanghai (2011)

16. Thorarensen, S., Cuello, R., Kessler, C., Li, L., Barry, B.: Efficient execution of SkePU skeleton programs on the low-power multicore processor Myriad2. In: Euromicro International Conference on Parallel, Distributed, and Network-Based Processing (PDP), pp. 398–402 (2016). https://doi.org/10.1109/PDP.2016.123

17. Totoni, E., Behzad, B., Ghike, S., Torrellas, J.: Comparing the power and performance of intel's SCC to state-of-the-art CPUs and GPUs. In: IEEE International Symposium on Performance Analysis of Systems and Software (ISPASS), pp. 78–87. IEEE Computer Society, New Brunswick (2012). https://doi.org/10.1109/ISPASS.2012.6189208

18. Varghese, A., Edwards, B., Mitra, G., Rendell, A.P.: Programming the adapteva epiphany 64-core network-on-chip coprocessor. In: International Parallel Distributed Processing Symposium Workshops (IPDPSW), pp. 984–992. IEEE Computer Society, Phoenix (2014)

Theory and Algorithms for Parallel Computation and Networking

High-Quality Shared-Memory Graph Partitioning

Yaroslav Akhremtsev[1][(✉)], Peter Sanders[1], and Christian Schulz[2]

[1] Karlsruhe Institute of Technology (KIT), Karlsruhe, Germany
{yaroslav.akhremtsev,peter.sanders}@kit.edu
[2] University of Vienna, Vienna, Austria
christian.schulz@univie.ac.at

Abstract. Partitioning graphs into blocks of roughly equal size such that few edges run between blocks is a frequently needed operation in processing graphs. Recently, size, variety, and structural complexity of these networks has grown dramatically. Unfortunately, previous approaches to parallel graph partitioning have problems in this context since they often show a negative trade-off between speed and quality. We present an approach to multi-level shared-memory parallel graph partitioning that guarantees balanced solutions, shows high speed-ups for a variety of large graphs and yields very good quality independently of the number of cores used. For example, on 31 cores, our algorithm partitions our largest test instance into 16 blocks cutting *less than half* the number of edges than our main competitor when both algorithms are given the same amount of time. Important ingredients include parallel label propagation, parallel initial partitioning, a simple yet effective approach to parallel localized local search, and cache-aware hash tables.

1 Introduction

Partitioning a graph into k blocks of similar size such that few edges are cut is a fundamental problem with many applications. For example, it often arises when processing a single graph on k processors.

The graph partitioning problem is NP-hard. Thus, to solve the graph partitioning problem in practice, one needs to use heuristics. A very common approach to partition a graph is the multi-level graph partitioning (MGP) approach. The main idea is to contract the graph in the *coarsening* phase until it is small enough to be partitioned by more sophisticated but slower algorithms in the *initial partitioning* phase. Afterwards, in the *uncoarsening/local search* phase, the quality of the partition is improved on every level of the computed hierarchy using a local improvement algorithm.

There is a need for shared-memory parallel graph partitioning algorithms that efficiently utilize all cores of a machine. This is due to the well-known fact that CPU technology increasingly provides more cores with relatively low clock rates

---

This is the short version of the technical report [2].

© Springer International Publishing AG, part of Springer Nature 2018
M. Aldinucci et al. (Eds.): Euro-Par 2018, LNCS 11014, pp. 659–671, 2018.
https://doi.org/10.1007/978-3-319-96983-1_47

in the last years since these are cheaper to produce and run. Moreover, shared-memory parallel algorithms implemented without message-passing libraries (e.g. MPI) usually give better speed-ups and running times than its MPI-based counterparts. Shared-memory parallel graph partitioning algorithms can in turn also be used as a component of a distributed graph partitioner, which distributes parts of a graph to nodes of a compute cluster and then employs a shared-memory parallel graph partitioning algorithm to partition the corresponding part of the graph on a node level.

Contribution: We present a high-quality shared-memory parallel multi-level graph partitioning algorithm that parallelizes all of the three MGP phases – coarsening, initial partitioning and refinement – using C++14 multi-threading. Our approach uses a parallel label propagation algorithm that is able to shrink large complex networks fast during coarsening. Our parallelization of localized local search [10] is able to obtain high-quality solutions and guarantee balanced partitions despite performing most of the work in mostly independent local searches of individual threads. Using *cache-aware hash tables* we limit memory consumption and improve locality. Our approach scales comparatively better than other parallel partitioners and has considerably higher quality which does not degrade with increasing number of processors.

After presenting preliminaries and related work in Sect. 2, we explain details of the multi-level graph partitioning approach and the algorithms that we parallelize in Sect. 3. Section 4 presents our approach to parallelization of the multi-level graph partitioning phases. Extensive experiments are presented in Sect. 5.

2   Preliminaries

2.1   Basic Concepts

Let $G = (V = \{0, \ldots, n-1\}, E)$ be an undirected graph, where $n = |V|$ and $m = |E|$. We consider positive, real-valued edge and vertex weight functions ω and c extending them to sets, e.g., $\omega(M) := \sum_{x \in M} \omega(x)$. $N(v) := \{u : \{v, u\} \in E\}$ denotes the neighbors of v. The degree of a vertex v is $d(v) := |N(v)|$. Δ is the maximum vertex degree. A vertex is a *boundary vertex* if it is incident to a vertex in a different block. We are looking for disjoint *blocks* of vertices $V_1, \ldots, V_k$ that partition V; i.e., $V_1 \cup \cdots \cup V_k = V$. The *balancing constraint* demands that all blocks have weight $c(V_i) \leq (1 + \epsilon) \lceil \frac{c(V)}{k} \rceil =: L_{\max}$ for some imbalance parameter ϵ. We call a block V_i *overloaded* if its weight exceeds $L_{\max}$. The objective is to minimize the total *cut* $\omega(E \cap \bigcup_{i<j} V_i \times V_j)$. We define the gain of a vertex as the maximum decrease in cut size when moving it to a different block. We denote the number of processing elements (PEs) as p.

A clustering is also a partition of the vertices. However, k is usually not given in advance and the balance constraint is removed. A size-constrained clustering constrains the size of the blocks of a clustering by a given upper bound U.

An abstract view of the partitioned graph is the *quotient graph*, in which vertices represent blocks and edges are induced by connectivity between blocks.

The *weighted* version of the quotient graph has vertex weights which are set to the weight of the corresponding block and edge weights that are equal to the weight of the edges that run between the respective blocks.

In general, our input graphs G have unit edge weights and vertex weights. However, even those will be translated into weighted problems in the course of the multi-level algorithm. In order to avoid a tedious notation, G will denote the current state of the graph before and after a (un)contraction in the multi-level scheme throughout this paper.

We analyze algorithms using the concept of total *work* (the time spent by one processor) and *span*; i.e., the time spent using an unlimited number of PEs.

2.2 Related Work

There has been intensive research on graph partitioning so that we refer the reader to the full version of the paper and a recent overview [2,4]. Here, we focus on issues closely related to our main contributions. All general-purpose methods that are able to obtain good partitions for large real-world graphs are based on the multi-level principle. Well-known software packages based on this approach include Jostle, KaHIP, Metis and Scotch.

Probably the fastest available distributed memory parallel code is the parallel version of Metis, ParMetis [5]. This parallelization has problems maintaining the balance of the blocks since at any particular time, it is difficult to say how many vertices are assigned to a particular block. In addition, ParMetis only uses very simple greedy local search algorithms that do not yield high-quality solutions. Mt-Metis by LaSalle and Karypis [6,7] is a shared-memory parallel version of the ParMetis graph partitioning framework. LaSalle and Karypis use a hill-climbing technique during refinement. The local search method is a simplification of k-way multi-try local search [10] in order to make it fast. The idea is to find a set of vertices (hill) whose move to another block is beneficial and then to move this set accordingly. However, it is possible that several PEs move the same vertex. To handle this, each vertex is assigned a PE, which can move it exclusively. Other PEs use a message queue to send a request to move this vertex.

Meyerhenke et al. [9] propose ParHIP, to partition large complex networks on distributed memory parallel machines using *label propagation*. The resulting system is more scalable and achieves higher quality than state-of-the-art systems like ParMetis or PT-Scotch. There are other parallel graph partitioners: PT-Scotch, KaPPa, and PDiBaP. See details in the full version of the paper [2].

3 Multi-level Graph Partitioning

We now give an in-depth description of the three main phases of a multi-level graph partitioning algorithm: coarsening, initial partitioning and uncoarsening/local search. In particular, we give a description of the sequential algorithms that we parallelize in the following sections. Our starting point here is the KaHIP framework [10]. For the development of the parallel algorithm, we add the k-way multi-try local search scheme which gives higher quality, and improve it to perform less work than the original sequential version.

Coarsening. To create a new level of a graph hierarchy, we compute a clustering and build a coarse graph G'. Each original cluster corresponds to a single vertex in G'. The weight of this vertex is set to the sum of the weights of all vertices (in the finer graph) in the cluster. There is an edge between two vertices of G' if the corresponding clusters are connected by at least one edge. The weight of this edge is set to the sum of all edges (in the finer graph) that connect these clusters. The hierarchy created in this recursive manner is then used by the partitioner. Note that a partition of the coarse graph corresponds to a partition of the finer graph with the same cut and balance. We now describe the clustering algorithm that we parallelize.

Clustering. We denote the set of all clusters as C and the cluster ID of a vertex v as $C[v]$. In our framework, we use the label propagation algorithm by Meyerhenke et al. [8] that creates clusters with constrained size. The size constrained label propagation algorithm works in iterations; i.e., the algorithm is repeated ℓ times (ℓ is a tuning parameter). Initially, each vertex is in its own cluster ($C[v] = v$) and all vertices are put into a queue Q in increasing order of their degrees. During each iteration, the algorithm iterates over all vertices in Q. A neighboring cluster $\mathcal{C}$ of a vertex v is called *eligible* if $\mathcal{C}$ will not become overloaded once v is moved to $\mathcal{C}$. When a vertex v is visited, it is moved to the eligible cluster $\mathcal{C}$ that maximizes $\omega(\{(v, u) \mid u \in N(v) \cap \mathcal{C}\})$. If a vertex changes its cluster then all its neighbors are added to a queue Q' for the next iteration. At the end of an iteration, Q and Q' are swapped, and the algorithm proceeds with the next iteration. The sequential running time of one iteration of the algorithm is $\mathcal{O}(m + n)$.

Initial Partitioning. After we have built the coarsest graph G', we partition it into k blocks using the algorithms from KaHIP [10]. To get a better solution, the graph G' is partitioned into k blocks I times and the best solution is returned.

Uncoarsening/Local Search. After initial partitioning, a local search algorithm is applied on each level of the multi-level hierarchy to decrease the cut size. There are a variety of local search algorithms: size-constraint label propagation, Fiduccia-Mattheyses k-way local search (FM), max-flow min-cut based local search, k-way multi-try local search (MLS) [10] .... Sequential versions of KaHIP use combinations of those. Since k-way local search is P-complete, we use a combination of the size-constrained label propagation algorithm and MLS. MLS achieves higher quality than FM [10] and decomposes the optimization into many small local searches which is a good basis for parallelization.

We now describe MLS that performs a k-way local searches around a single boundary vertices. This gives better chances of finding a nontrivial improvements [10]. The algorithm is organized in a nested loop of global and local iterations. In the beginning of a global iteration, we put *all* boundary vertices into a todo list T. Initially, all vertices are unmarked. Afterwards, the algorithm repeatedly chooses and removes a random vertex $v \in T$. If v is not marked then it performs a k-way local search around v. It marks v and $N(v)$ and inserts them into the priority queue PQ using gain values as keys. Next, the algorithm extracts a vertex w with the maximum key in the PQ. If the corresponding move of w does not produce an overloaded block then it performs the move and inserts all unmarked neighbors of w into the PQ. The algorithm stops when the priority queue is empty or an adaptive stopping rule decides to stop. In the end, the best partition that has been seen during the process is reconstructed. In one local iteration, this is repeated until the todo list is empty. Afterwards, the algorithm reinserts moved vertices into T in a random order. If the achieved gain improvement is larger than a certain percentage (currently 10 %) of the total improvement during the current global iteration, it continues to perform moves around the vertices currently in the todo list (next local iteration). This allows to further decrease the cut size without significant impact to the running time. When improvements fall below this threshold, the next global iteration is started that initializes the todo list with all boundary vertices. After a fixed number of global iterations (currently 3), the MLS algorithm stops. Our experiments show that 3 global iterations is a fair trade-off between the running time and quality of the partition. This nested loop of local and global iterations is an improvement over the original MLS search from [10] since they allow for a better control of the running time of the algorithm.

The running time of one local iteration is $\mathcal{O}(n + \sum_{v \in V} d(v)^2)$. Because each vertex can be moved only once during a local iteration and we update the gains of its neighbors using a bucket heap. Since we update the gain of a vertex at most $d(v)$ times, the $d(v)^2$ term is the total cost to update the gain of a vertex v. Note, that this is an upper bound for the worst case, usually local search stops significantly earlier due the stopping rule or an empty priority queue.

4 Parallel Multi-level Graph Partitioning

Profiling the sequential algorithm shows that each of the components of the multi-level scheme has a significant contribution to the overall algorithm. Our general approach is to avoid bottlenecks as well as performing independent work as much as possible.

4.1 Coarsening: Parallel Size-Constraint Label Propagation

To parallelize the size-constraint label propagation algorithm, we adapt a clustering technique by Staudt and Meyerhenke [12]. First, we sort the vertices in increasing order of their degrees using a parallel sorting Algorithm [3]. Then we form work packets of vertices and put them into a concurrent queue. We constraint each packet to contain vertices with a total number of at most $\sqrt{m}$ neighbors. Additionally, we have an empty queue Q' that stores packets for the next iteration. During an iteration, each PE tries to extract a packet from the queue Q. It chooses a new cluster for each vertex in the currently processed packet. A vertex is then moved if the cluster size is still feasible to take on the weight of the vertex. Cluster sizes are updated atomically using a compare and swap instruction. This is important to guarantee that the size constraint is not violated. Neighbors of moved vertices are inserted into a packet for the next iteration. If the sum of vertex degrees in that packet exceeds the work bound $\sqrt{m}$ then this packet is inserted into queue Q' and a new packet is created for subsequent vertices. When the queue Q is empty, the main PE exchanges Q and Q' and we proceed with the next iteration. One iteration of the algorithm can be done with $\mathcal{O}(n + m)$ work and $\mathcal{O}(\frac{n+m}{p})$ span.

Coarsening: Parallel Contraction

The contraction algorithm takes a graph $G = (V, E)$ as well as a clustering C and constructs a coarse graph $G' = (V', E')$. The contraction process consists of three phases: the remapping of cluster IDs to a consecutive set of IDs, edge weight accumulation, and the construction of the coarse graph. The remapping of cluster IDs assigns new IDs in the range $[0, |V'| - 1]$ to the clusters by calculating a prefix sum on an array that contains ones in the positions equal to the current cluster IDs. This phase can be done in $\mathcal{O}(n)$ work. Sequentially, the edge weight accumulation step calculates weights of edges in E' using hashing. For each cut edge $(v, u) \in E$, we insert a pair $(C[v], C[u])$ into a hash table and accumulate weights for the pair if it is already contained in the table. Due to hashing cut edges, the expected work of this phase is $\mathcal{O}(|E'| + m)$. To construct the coarse graph, we iterate over all edges E' contained in the hash table. This takes $\mathcal{O}(|V'| + |E'|)$ work. Hence, the total expected work to compute the coarse graph is $\mathcal{O}(m + n + |E'|)$.

The parallel contraction algorithm works as follows. First, we remap the cluster IDs using parallel prefix sums. Edge weights are accumulated by iterating over the edges of the original graph in parallel. This uses a concurrent hash table. The third phase is performed sequentially in the current implementation since profiling indicates that it is so fast that it is not a bottleneck.

4.2   Initial Partitioning

To improve the quality of the resulting partitioning of the coarsest graph $G' = (V', E')$, we partition it into k blocks $\max(p, I)$ times instead of I times. Each PE creates a copy of the coarsest graph and runs KaHIP sequentially on it using a random seed. Assume that one partitioning can be done in T time. Then $\max(p, I)$ partitions can be built with $\mathcal{O}(\max(p, I) \cdot T + p \cdot (|E'| + |V'|))$ work and $\mathcal{O}(\frac{\max(p, I) \cdot T}{p} + |E'| + |V'|)$ span.

4.3   Uncoarsening/Local Search

Our parallel algorithm first uses size-constraint parallel label propagation to improve the current partition and afterwards applies our parallel MLS. The idea is that label propagation is easy to parallelize and will do all the easy improvements. Subsequent MLS will then invest considerable work to find nontrivial improvements. In this combination, only few nodes actually need be moved globally which makes it easier to parallelize MLS scalably. When using the label propagation algorithm to improve a partition, we set the upper bound U to L_{max}.

Parallel MLS works in a nested loop of local and global iterations as in the sequential version. Initialization of a global iteration uses a simplified parallel shuffling algorithm where each PE shuffles the nodes it considers into a local bucket and then the queue is made up of these buckets in random order. During a local iteration, each PE extracts vertices from a producer queue Q. Afterwards, it performs *local* moves around it; that is, global block IDs and the sizes of the blocks remain *unchanged*. When the producer queue Q is empty, the algorithm applies the best found sequences of moves to the global data structures and proceeds with the next local iteration.

Performing Moves. Each PE performs moves in the function `PerformMoves`. Starting from a single boundary vertex, each PE performs *local* moves of vertices to find a sequence of moves that decreases the cut. That is, moves do not affect the current global partition – they are stored in the local memory of the PE performing them. To perform a move, a PE chooses a vertex with maximum gain and marks it so that other PEs cannot move it. Then, we update the sizes of the affected blocks and save the move. During the course of the algorithm, we store the sequence of moves yielding the best cut. We stop if there are no moves to perform or the adaptive stopping rule signals the algorithm to stop. When a PE finished, the sequences of moves yielding the smallest cut is returned.

In order to improve scalability, only the array for marking moved vertices is global. Note that within a local iteration, only bits in this array are set (using compare and swap instruction) and they are never unset. Hence, the marking operation can be seen as priority update operation (see Shun et al. [11]) and thus causes only little contention. The algorithm keeps a local array of block sizes, a local priority queue, and a local hash table storing changed block IDs of vertices. Note that since the local hash table is small, it often fits into cache which is crucial for parallelization due to memory bandwidth limits. When the call of `PerformMoves` finishes and the thread executing it notices that the queue Q is empty, it sets a global variable to signal the other threads to finish the current call of the function `PerformMoves`. This way, isolated very long MLS searches cannot lead to bad load balance.

Let each PE process a set of edges $\mathcal{E}$ and a set of vertices $\mathcal{V}$. Since a vertex can be moved only by one PE and moving it requires to compute gain for its neighbors, the span of the function `PerformMoves` is $\mathcal{O}(\sum_{v\in\mathcal{V}}\sum_{u\in N(v)} d(u) + |\mathcal{V}|) = \mathcal{O}(\sum_{v\in\mathcal{V}} d^2(v) + |\mathcal{V}|)$ since the gain of a vertex v is updated at most $d(v)$ times.

Applying Moves. Let M_i denote the set of sequences of moves performed by PE i. We apply moves sequentially in the following order $M_1, M_2, \ldots, M_p$. We can not apply the moves directly in parallel since a move done by one PE may affect a move done by another PE and the cut size may even increase. To prevent this, we recalculate the gain of each move in a given sequence and apply the subsequence of moves that gives the best cut. Finally, we insert all moved vertices into the queue Q. Let M be the set of all moved vertices during this procedure. The overall running time is then given by $\mathcal{O}(\sum_{v \in M} d(v))$. Note that our initial partitioning algorithm generates balanced solutions. Since moves are applied sequentially our parallel local search algorithm maintains balanced solutions.

4.4   Differences to Mt-Metis

We now discuss differences between our algorithm and Mt-Metis. In the coarsening phase, we use a cluster contraction while Metis is using a matching-based scheme. Our approach is especially well suited for networks that have a pronounced and hierarchical cluster structure. The general initial partitioning scheme is similar in both algorithms. However, the employed sequential techniques differ because different sequential tools (KaHIP and Metis) are used to partition the coarsest graphs. In terms of local search, unlike Mt-Metis, our approach guarantees that the updated partition is balanced if the input partition is balanced and that the cut can only decrease or stay the same. The hill-climbing technique, however, may increase the cut of the input partition or may compute an imbalanced partition even if the input partition is balanced. Our algorithm has these guarantees since each PE performs moves of vertices locally in parallel. When all PEs finish, one PE globally applies the best sequences of local moves computed by all PEs. Usually, the number of applied moves is significantly smaller than the number of local moves performed by all PEs, especially on large graphs. Thus, the main work is still made in parallel. Additionally, we introduce a cache-aware hash table that we use to store local changes of block IDs made by each PE. This hash table is more compact than an array and takes the locality of data into account.

4.5   Further Optimization

In this section, we list further optimization techniques that we use to achieve better speed-ups and overall speed. More precisely, we use cache-aligned arrays to mitigate the problem of false-sharing, the TBB scalable allocator [1] for concurrent memory allocations and pin threads to cores to avoid rescheduling overheads. Additionally, we use a cache-aware hash table that is described in the full version of the paper [2]. In contrast to usual hash tables, this hash table allows us to exploit locality of data and hence to reduce the overall running time of the algorithm.

5 Experiments

We implemented our algorithm Mt-KaHIP (Multi-threaded KaHIP) within the KaHIP [10] framework using C++ and the C++14 multi-threading library. We plan to make our program available in the framework. All binaries are built using g++-5.2.0 with the -O3 flag and 64-bit index data types. We run our experiments on two machines. Machine A is an Intel Xeon E5-2683v2 (2 sockets, 16 cores with Hyper-Threading, 64 threads) running at 2.1 GHz with 512 GB RAM. Machine B is an Intel Xeon E5-2650v2 (2 sockets, 8 cores with Hyper-Threading, 32 threads) running at 2.6 GHz with 128 GB RAM.

We compare ourselves to Mt-Metis 0.6.0 using the default configuration with hill-climbing being enabled (*Mt-Metis*) as well as sequential KaHIP 2.0 using the fast social configuration (*KaHIP*) and ParHIP 2.0 [9] using the fast social configuration (*ParHIP*). According to LaSalle and Karypis [6] Mt-Metis has better speed-ups and running times compared to ParMetis and Pt-Scotch. At the same time, it yields similar solution quality. Hence, we do not perform experiments with ParMetis and Pt-Scotch. Our algorithm consumes 44.3% less memory than Mt-Metis on the largest graph from our benchmark set for $p = 31$ on machine A. For more details, we refer the reader to [2].

Our default value of allowed imbalance is 3%. We call a solution imbalanced if at least one block exceeds this amount. We perform ten repetitions for every algorithm using different random seeds for initialization and report the arithmetic average of computed cut size and running time on a per instance (graph and number of blocks k) basis. If at least one repetition returns an imbalanced partition of an instance then we mark this instance imbalanced. Our experiments focus on the cases $k \in \{16, 64\}$ and $p \in \{1, 16, 31\}$ to save running time.

We use performance plots to present quality comparisons and scatter plots to present the speed-up and the running time comparisons. A curve in a performance plot for algorithm X is obtained as follows: For each instance (graph and k), we calculate the normalized value $1 - \frac{best}{cut}$, where best is the best cut obtained by any of the considered algorithms and cut is the cut of algorithm X. These values are then sorted. Thus, the result of the best algorithm is in the bottom of the plot. We set the value for the instance above 1 if an algorithm builds an imbalanced partition. Hence, it is in the top of the plot.

Any multi-level algorithm has a considerable number of tuning parameters. We adopt parameters from the coarsening and initial partitioning phases of KaHIP. Mt-KaHIP uses 10 and 25 label propagation iterations during coarsening and refinement, respectively, partitions a coarse graph $\max(p, 4)$ times in initial partitioning and uses 3 global iterations of parallel MLS in the refinement phase.

Instances. We evaluate all algorithms on a benchmark of 24 large graphs and for $k \in \{16, 64\}$. This collection consist of different kinds of graphs: numeric simulations, complex networks (focused on social networks and web graphs), and random graphs (*random geometric graphs, delaunay graphs,* and *random* *hyperbolic graphs*). Details of the benchmark can be found in the full version of the paper [2].

5.1   Quality Comparison

In this section, we compare our algorithm against competing state-of-the-art algorithms in terms of quality. The performance plot in Fig. 1 shows the results of our experiments performed on machine A for all of our benchmark graphs.

Our algorithm gives the best overall quality, usually producing the overall best cut. Even in the small fraction of instances where other algorithms are best, our algorithm is at most 7% off. The overall solution quality does not heavily depend on the number of PEs used. Indeed, more PEs give slightly higher partitioning quality. The original fast social configuration of KaHIP as well as ParHIP produce worse quality than Mt-KaHIP, since parallel MLS significantly improves solution quality. Mt-Metis with $p = 1$ has worse quality than our algorithm on almost all instances. For Mt-Metis this is expected since it is considerably faster than our algorithm. However, Mt-Metis also suffers from deteriorating quality and many imbalanced partitions as the number of PEs goes up. This can also be seen from the geometric means of the cut sizes over all instances, including the imbalanced solutions.

For our algorithm they are 727.2K, 713.4K and 710.8K for $p = 1, 16, 31$, respectively. For Mt-Metis they are 819.8K, 873.1K and 874.8K for $p = 1, 16, 31$, respectively. For ParHIP they are 809.9K, 809.4K and 809.71K for $p = 1, 16, 31$, respectively, and for KaHIP it is 766.2K. For $p = 31$, the geometric mean cut size of Mt-KaHIP is 18.7% smaller than that of Mt-Metis, 12.2% smaller than that of ParHIP and 7.2% smaller than that of KaHIP.

Additionally, we compare the effectiveness of our algorithm Mt-KaHIP against competitors. We give the faster algorithm the same amount of

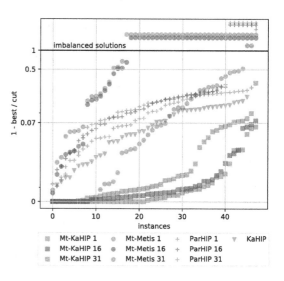

Fig. 1. Performance plot for the cut size. The number behind the algorithm name denotes the number of threads.

time as the slower algorithm for additional repetitions that can lead to improved solutions. The detailed description of these experiments is in the full version of the paper [2]. Still in 80.4% of the tests Mt-KaHIP has better quality than Mt-Metis. In the worst-case, Mt-KaHIP has a 5.5% larger cut than Mt-Metis. In 96.5% of the tests, Mt-KaHIP has better quality than ParHIP. In the worst-case,

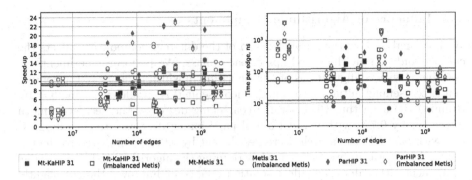

Fig. 2. From left to right for $p = 31$: (a) full speed-up, (b) full running time per edge in nanoseconds. Horizontal lines are harmonic and geometric means.

Mt-KaHIP has a 5.4% larger cut than ParHIP. In 98.9% of the tests, Mt-KaHIP has better quality than KaHIP. In the worst-case, Mt-KaHIP has a 3.5% larger cut than KaHIP.

5.2 Speed-Up and Running Time Comparison

In this section, we compare the speed-ups and the running times of our algorithm against competitors. We calculate a relative speed-up of an algorithm as a ratio between its running time and its running time with $p = 1$. Figure 2 show scatter plots with speed-ups and time per edge for a full algorithm execution on machine A. We calculate the geometric and harmonic means *only* for instances that were partitioned in ten repetitions *without imbalance*. Note that among the top 20 speed-ups of Mt-Metis 60% correspond to imbalanced instances (*Mt-Metis 31 imbalanced*) thus we believe it is fair to exclude them.

The harmonic mean full speed-up of our algorithm, Mt-Metis and ParHIP for $p = 31$ are $9.1, 11.1$ and 9.5, respectively. The harmonic mean local search speed-up of our algorithm, Mt-Metis and ParHIP are $13.5, 6.7$ and 7.5, respectively. Our full speed-ups are comparable to that of Mt-Metis but our local search speed-ups are significantly better than that of Mt-Metis. The geometric mean full time per edge of our algorithm, Mt-Metis and ParHIP are 52.3 nanoseconds (ns), 12.4 [ns] and 121.9 [ns], respectively. The geometric mean local search time per edge of our algorithm, Mt-Metis and ParHIP are 3.5 [ns], 2.1 [ns] and 16.8 [ns], respectively. Note that with increasing number of edges, our algorithm has comparable time per edge to Mt-Metis. Superior speed-ups of parallel MLS are due to minimized interactions between PEs and using cache-aware hash tables locally. Although on average, our algorithm is slower than Mt-Metis, we consider this as a fair trade off between the quality and the running time. We also dominate ParHIP in terms of quality and running times.

5.3 Influence of Algorithmic Components

We now analyze how the parallelization of the different components affects the cut size and present the speed-ups of each phase. We perform experiments on machine B with configurations of our algorithm in which *only one* of the components (coarsening, initial partitioning, uncoarsening) is parallelized using $p = 16$. Running the algorithm with parallel coarsening decreases the geometric mean of the cut by 0.7%, with parallel initial partitioning decreases the cut by 2.3% and with parallel local search decreases the cut by 0.02%. Compared to the full sequential algorithm, we conclude that running the algorithm with any parallel component either does not affect solution quality or improves the cut slightly on average. The parallelization of initial partitioning gives better cuts since it computes more initial partitions than the sequential version.

To show that the parallelization of each phase is important, we consider instances where one of the phases runs significantly longer than other phases in the experiments on machine A using $p = 31$. The *coarsening phase* may take up to 91% of the running time and its parallelization gives a speed-up of 13.6 for 31 threads and a full speed-up of 12.4. The *initial partitioning phase* may take up to 40% of the running time and its parallelization gives a speed-up of 6.1 and the overall speed-up is 7.4. The *uncoarsening phase* may take up to 57% of the running time and its parallelization gives a speed-up of 13.0 and the overall speed-up is 9.1. The harmonic mean speed-ups of the coarsening phase, the initial partitioning phase and the uncoarsening phase for $p = 31$ are 10.6, 2.0 and 8.6, respectively.

6   Conclusion and Future Work

We presented a shared-memory parallel graph partitioner that is able to partition graphs with very good quality as well as guaranteed balance which also shows good speed-up on a variety of large graphs. Previous approaches show a negative trade-off between quality and speed. The important parts of our algorithm are parallel label propagation, a simple yet effective approach to parallel MLS, parallel initial partitioning, and cache-aware hash tables. Considering the good results of our algorithm, we want to further improve it and release its implementation. An interesting problem is how to apply moves in Sect. 4.3 in parallel whose solution will increase the performance of parallel MLS.

References

1. Intel threading building blocks. https://www.threadingbuildingblocks.org/
2. Akhremtsev, Y., Sanders, P., Schulz, C.: High-quality shared-memory graph partitioning. CoRR abs/1710.08231 (2017)
3. Axtmann, M., Witt, S., Ferizovic, D., Sanders, P.: In-place parallel super scalar samplesort (IPSSSSo). In: Proceedings of the 25th ESA, pp. 9:1–9:14 (2017)

4. Buluç, A., Meyerhenke, H., Safro, I., Sanders, P., Schulz, C.: Recent advances in graph partitioning. In: Kliemann, L., Sanders, P. (eds.) Algorithm Engineering. LNCS, vol. 9220, pp. 117–158. Springer, Cham (2016). https://doi.org/10.1007/978-3-319-49487-6_4

5. Karypis, G., Kumar, V.: Parallel multilevel k-way partitioning scheme for irregular graphs. In: Proceedings of the ACM/IEEE Conference on Supercomputing (1996)

6. LaSalle, D., Karypis, G.: Multi-threaded graph partitioning. In: Proceedings of the 27th IPDPS, pp. 225–236 (2013)

7. LaSalle, D., Karypis, G.: A parallel hill-climbing refinement algorithm for graph partitioning. In: Proceedings of the 45th ICPP, pp. 236–241 (2016)

8. Meyerhenke, H., Sanders, P., Schulz, C.: Partitioning complex networks via size-constrained clustering. In: Gudmundsson, J., Katajainen, J. (eds.) SEA 2014. LNCS, vol. 8504, pp. 351–363. Springer, Cham (2014). https://doi.org/10.1007/978-3-319-07959-2_30

9. Meyerhenke, H., Sanders, P., Schulz, C.: Parallel graph partitioning for complex networks. In: IEEE Transactions on Parallel and Distributed Systems, pp. 2625–2638 (2017)

10. Sanders, P., Schulz, C.: Engineering multilevel graph partitioning algorithms. In: Demetrescu, C., Halldórsson, M.M. (eds.) ESA 2011. LNCS, vol. 6942, pp. 469–480. Springer, Heidelberg (2011). https://doi.org/10.1007/978-3-642-23719-5_40

11. Shun, J., Blelloch, G.E., Fineman, J.T., Gibbons, P.B.: Reducing contention through priority updates. In: Proceedings of the 25th SPAA, pp. 152–163 (2013)

12. Staudt, C.L., Meyerhenke, H.: Engineering parallel algorithms for community detection in massive networks. IEEE Trans. Parallel Distrib. Syst. **27**(1), 171–184 (2016)

Design Principles for Sparse Matrix Multiplication on the GPU

Carl Yang[1,2]($\boxtimes$) (iD), Aydın Buluç[2,3] (iD), and John D. Owens[1,2] (iD)

[1] University of California, Davis, CA 95616, USA
ctcyang@ece.ucdavis.edu
[2] Lawrence Berkeley National Laboratory,
Berkeley, CA 94720, USA
[3] University of California, Berkeley,
CA 94720, USA

Abstract. We implement two novel algorithms for sparse-matrix dense-matrix multiplication (SpMM) on the GPU. Our algorithms expect the sparse input in the popular compressed-sparse-row (CSR) format and thus do not require expensive format conversion. While previous SpMM work concentrates on thread-level parallelism, we additionally focus on latency hiding with instruction-level parallelism and load-balancing. We show, both theoretically and experimentally, that the proposed SpMM is a better fit for the GPU than previous approaches. We identify a key memory access pattern that allows efficient access into both input and output matrices that is crucial to getting excellent performance on SpMM. By combining these two ingredients—(i) merge-based load-balancing and (ii) row-major coalesced memory access—we demonstrate a 4.1× peak speedup and a 31.7% geomean speedup over state-of-the-art SpMM implementations on real-world datasets.

Keywords: Sparse matrix multiplication · Parallel · GPU

1 Introduction

Many algorithms in machine learning, data analysis, and graph analysis can be organized such that the bulk of the computation is structured as sparse matrix-dense matrix multiplication (SpMM). Examples include inference on pruned neural networks [1], graph centrality calculations [2], all-pairs shortest paths [3], iterative solvers with multiple righthand sides [4], blocked eigensolvers such as Blocked Lanczos [5] or Locally Optimal Block Preconditioned Conjugate Gradient (LOBPCG) [6], sparse matrix precision estimation [7], multi-scale spectral graph decomposition [8], non-negative matrix factorization [9], and tomographic reconstruction [10]. SpMM is also one of the possible instantiations of the most prevalent GraphBLAS primitive, namely the matrix-matrix multiplication operation on a semiring (GrB_mxm) [11], depending on the sparsity of operands.

M. Aldinucci et al. (Eds.): Euro-Par 2018, LNCS 11014, pp. 672–687, 2018.
https://doi.org/10.1007/978-3-319-96983-1_48

Given an m-by-k sparse matrix $\mathbf{A}$ and a k-by-n dense matrix $\mathbf{B}$, SpMM computes an m-by-n dense matrix $\mathbf{C} = \mathbf{AB}$. We assume $n \ll m$ and $n \gg k$, that is to say, SpMM is multiplying a sparse matrix with a tall-skinny dense matrix. We choose the most common sparse matrix format—compressed sparse row (CSR)—because we avoid the substantial cost of matrix conversion. However, CSR results in a challenging problem on the GPU, because the sparse row can vary significantly in how many nonzeroes there are. We combine recent advances from the related problem of sparse matrix-dense vector multiplication (SpMV) [12–14] and a key memory access pattern we identify as critical to SpMM performance in order to propose and implement two SpMM algorithms that demonstrate superior performance to state-of-the-art specialized matrix formats and vendor-supplied CSR SpMM implementations.

Our main contributions in this paper are:

1. We generalize two main classes of SpMV algorithms—(1) row splitting and (2) merge-based—for the SpMM problem and implement them on the GPU.
2. We introduce a simple heuristic that selects between the two kernels with an accuracy of 99.3% compared to optimal.
3. Using our multi-algorithm and heuristic, we achieve a geomean speed-up of 31.7% and up to a maximum of 4.1x speed-up over state-of-the-art SpMM implementations over 157 datasets from the SuiteSparse Matrix Collection [15].

2 Background and Preliminaries

2.1 GPUs

Modern GPUs are throughput-oriented manycore processors that rely on large-scale multithreading to attain high computational throughput and hide memory access time. The latest generation of NVIDIA GPUs have up to 80 "streaming multiprocessors" (SMs), each with up to hundreds of arithmetic logic units (ALUs). GPU programs are called *kernels*, which run a large number of threads in parallel in a single-program, multiple-data (SPMD) fashion.

The underlying hardware runs an instruction on each SM on each clock cycle on a *warp* of 32 threads in lockstep. The largest parallel unit that can be synchronized within a GPU kernel is called a *cooperative thread array* (CTA), which is composed of warps. For problems that require irregular data access, a successful GPU implementation needs to (1) ensure coalesced memory access to external memory and efficiently use the memory hierarchy, (2) minimize thread *divergence* within a warp, and (3) maintain high *occupancy*, which is a measure of how many threads are available to run on the implementation on the GPU.

2.2 Sparse Matrix Formats and SpMM

An $m \times n$ matrix is often called *sparse* if its number of nonzeroes nnz is small enough compared to $\mathcal{O}(mn)$ such that it makes sense to take advantage of sparsity. The compressed sparse row (CSR) format stores only the *column indices* and *values* of nonzeroes within a row. The start and end of each row are then stored in terms of the column indices and value in a *row offsets* (or *row pointers*) array. Hence, CSR only requires $m + 2nnz$ memory for storage. We say a dense matrix is in *row-major order* when successive elements in the same row are contiguous in memory. Similarly, we say it is in *column-major order* when successive elements in the same column are contiguous in memory.

Similarly to sparse matrix-dense vector multiplication (SpMV), a desire to achieve good performance on SpMM has inspired innovation in matrix storage formatting [16–18]. These custom formats and encodings take advantage of the matrix structure and underlying machine architecture. Even only counting GPU processors, there exist more than sixty specialized SpMV algorithms and sparse matrix formats [19].

The vendor-shipped library cuSPARSE library provides two functions csrmm and csrmm2 for SpMM on CSR-format input matrices [20]. The former expects a column-major input dense matrix and generates column-major output, while the latter expects row-major input and generates column-major output. Among many efforts to define and characterize alternate matrix formats for SpMM are a variant of ELLPACK called ELLPACK-R [16] and a variant of Sliced ELLPACK called SELL-P [17]. Hong et al. performs dynamic load-balancing by separating the sparse matrix into heavy and light rows. The heavy rows are processed by CSR and the light rows by doubly compressed sparse row (DCSR) in order to take advantage of tiling [21].

However, there is a real cost to deviating from the standard CSR encoding. Firstly, the rest of the computation pipeline will need to convert from CSR to another format to run SpMM and convert back. This process may take longer than the SpMM operation itself. Secondly, the pipeline will need to reserve valuable memory to store multiple copies of the same matrix—one in CSR format, another in the format used for SpMM.

3 Design Principles

In this section, we discuss two design principles that every irregular problem on the GPU must follow for good performance. Ideally, we attain *full utilization* of the GPU hardware, where a ready warp can be run on every cycle, all computational units are doing useful work on every cycle, and all memory accesses are coalesced. Our principles for reaching this goal are (1) effective latency-hiding through a combination of thread- and instruction-level parallelism (TLP and ILP) and (2) efficient load-balancing. Then we will look at state-of-the-art SpMM implementations to understand their inefficiencies.

3.1 Latency Hiding with TLP and ILP

Memory operations to a GPU's main memory take hundreds of clock cycles. The GPU's primary technique for hiding the cost of these long-latency operations is through thread-level parallelism (TLP). Effective use of TLP requires that the programmer give the GPU enough work so that when a GPU warp of threads issues a memory request, the GPU scheduler puts that warp to sleep and another ready warp becomes active. If enough warps are resident on the GPU (if we have enough TLP), switching between warps can completely hide the cost of a long-latency operation. We quantify the amount of TLP in a program as *occupancy*, the ratio of available (issued) warps to the maximum number of warps that can be supported by the GPU. Higher occupancy yields better latency-hiding ability, which allows us to approach full utilization.

Another latency-hiding strategy is exploiting instruction-level parallelism (ILP) and its ability to take advantage of overlapping the latency of multiple memory operations within a single thread. Because the GPU's memory system is deeply pipelined, a thread can potentially issue multiple independent long-latency operations before becoming inactive, and those multiple operations will collectively incur roughly the same latency as a single operation. While this yields a significant performance advantage, it relies on the programmer exposing independent memory operations to the hardware. We can achieve this goal by assigning multiple independent tasks to the same thread ("thread coarsening").

GPUs have a fixed number of registers. TLP requires many resident warps, each of which requires registers. ILP increases the work per thread, so each thread requires more registers. Thus TLP and ILP are in opposition, and attaining full utilization requires carefully balancing both techniques. While TLP is commonly used across all of GPU computing, ILP is a less explored area, with prior work limited to dense linear algebra [22] and microcode optimization [23].

3.2   Load-Balancing

We now turn to the problem of ensuring that all computational units are doing useful work on every cycle, and that the memory accesses from those warps are coalesced to ensure peak memory performance. In the context of SpMV and SpMM, this "load-balancing" problem has two aspects:

1. Load imbalance *across* warps. Some CTAs or warps may be assigned less work than others, which may lead to these less-loaded computation units being idle while the more loaded ones continue to do useful work. In this paper, we term this "Type 1" load imbalance.
2. Load imbalance *within* a warp, in two ways, which we collectively call "Type 2" load imbalance. (a) Some warps may not have enough work to occupy all 32 threads in the warp. In this case, thread processors are idle, and we lose performance. (b) Some warps may assign different tasks to different threads. In this case, SIMD execution within a thread means that some threads are idle while other threads are running; moreover, the divergence in execution across the warp means memory accesses across the entire warp are unlikely to be coalesced.

For irregular matrices, we claim that SpMV and SpMM are fundamentally load-balancing problems on the GPU. As evidence, Fig. 1 shows load imbalance

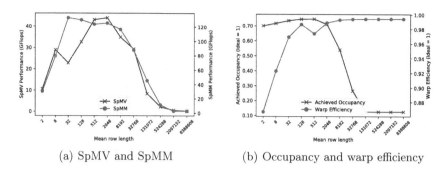

(a) SpMV and SpMM   (b) Occupancy and warp efficiency

Fig. 1. Synthetic benchmark showing NVIDIA cuSPARSE SpMV and SpMM performance as a function of matrix dimensions on a Tesla K40c, and SpMM's achieved occupancy and warp efficiency (inverse of divergence).

in a vendor-supplied implementation from a synthetic benchmark. The experimental setup is described in Sect. 5. The right side of the x-axis represents Type 1 load imbalance, where long matrix rows are not divided enough, resulting in some computation resources on the GPU remaining idle while others are overburdened. The left size of the x-axis represents Type 2 load imbalance where too many computational resources are allocated to each row, so some remain idle.

4   Parallelizations of CSR SpMM

This section reviews three existing parallelizations of SpMV through the lens of the design principles from Sect. 3. While our implementations of SpMM share some characteristics with SpMV parallelizations, we also faced several different design decisions for SpMM, which we discuss below. The three SpMV variants are illustrated in Fig. 2 and summarized here:

1. Row split [24]: Assigns an equal number of rows to each processor.
2. Merge based: Performs two-phase decomposition—the first kernel divides work evenly amongst CTAs, then the second kernel processes the work.
   (a) Nonzero split [12,13]: Assign an equal number of nonzeroes per processor. Then do a 1-D (1-dimensional) binary search on *row offsets* to determine at which row to start.
   (b) Merge path [14]: Assign an equal number of {nonzeroes and rows} per processor. This is done by doing a 2-D binary search (i.e., on the diagonal line in Fig. 2(c)) over *row offsets* and *nonzero indices* of matrix **A**.

While row split focuses primarily on ILP and TLP, nonzero split and merge path focus on load-balancing as well. We consider nonzero split and merge path to be *explicit load-balancing* methods, because they rearrange the distribution of work such that each thread must perform T independent instructions; if $T > 1$, then explicit load-balancing creates ILP where there was previously little or none. Thus load-balance is closely linked with ILP, because if each thread is

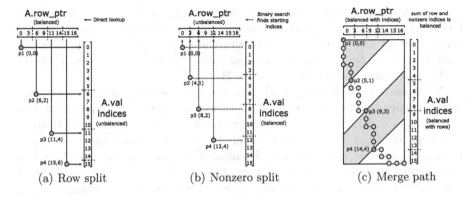

(a) Row split　　　　　　(b) Nonzero split　　　　　　(c) Merge path

Fig. 2. The three parallelizations for CSR SpMV and SpMM on matrix **A**. The orange markers indicate segment start for each processor ($P = 4$). (Color figure online)

guaranteed $T > 1$ units of independent work (ILP), then each thread is doing the same amount of work (i.e., is load-balanced).

We contend that nonzero split and merge path despite having different structure possess similar performance characteristics. The binary search being done in 2-D (i.e. on the diagonal line in Fig. 2(c)) as opposed to 1-D is equivalent to making an implicit assumption that a write to **C** has the same cost as a memory read from **A** and **B**. As Merrill and Garland point out, this solves the pathological case of matrices that have infinitely many empty rows. However, the merge path is more challenging to implement, so we decide to extend the Baxter's nonzero split concept [12] to SpMM under the moniker "merge-based SpMM".

4.1 Algorithm I: Row-Splitting SpMM

Row split aims to assign each row to a different thread, warp, or CTA. Figure 3(a) shows the warp assignment version. The typical SpMV row split is only the leftmost column of matrix **B** with orange cells replaced by green cells. This gives SpMV 1 independent instruction and uncoalesced, random accesses into the vector. Although row-split is a well-known method for SpMV [24], we encountered three important design decisions when extending it to SpMM:

1. Granularity: Should each row be assigned to a thread, warp, or CTA?
2. Memory access pattern: How should work be divided in fetching **B**? What is the impact on ILP and TLP?
3. Shared memory: Can shared memory be used for performance gain?

1. Granularity. We assigned each row to a warp compared to the alternatives of assigning a thread and a CTA per row. This leads to the simplest design out of the three options, since it gives us coalesced memory accesses into **B**. For matrices with few nonzeroes per row, the thread-per-matrix-row work assignment may be more efficient. This is borne out by Fig. 4.

2. Memory Access Pattern. This design decision had the greatest impact on performance. To our knowledge, this is the first time in literature this novel memory access strategy has been described. Our thread layout is shown in Fig. 3(c). For SpMM, we have two approaches we could take: each thread is responsible for loading a column or a row of the matrix **B**.

We discovered the first approach is better, because the memory accesses into **B** are independent and can be done in a coalesced manner (provided that **B** is in row-major order). In contrast, memory accesses into a column-major **B** would be independent but uncoalesced. Compared to the SpMV case, each thread now has 32 independent instructions and coalesced memory accesses into **B**, which significantly amortizes the cost of memory accesses compared to accessing a single vector. However, since we are forcing threads to pass a dummy column index if they are out of bounds within a row, the effective number of independent instructions and coalesced memory accesses is sensitive to row lengths that do not divide 32. For example, if the row length is 33, then we will be doing 64 independent instructions and coalesced memory accesses into **B**. Whether or not they divide 32 does not matter for very long rows, because the cost is amortized

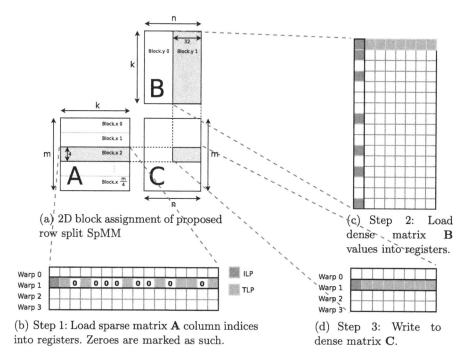

(a) 2D block assignment of proposed row split SpMM

(c) Step 2: Load dense matrix **B** values into registers.

(b) Step 1: Load sparse matrix **A** column indices into registers. Zeroes are marked as such.

(d) Step 3: Write to dense matrix **C**.

Fig. 3. (a) shows the tiling scheme we use. (b), (c), (d) represent the yellow blocks from (a). Row split SpMM ILP (orange) and TLP (green) are shown using warp 1 with 8 threads per warp. In practice, we use 32 threads per warp and 4 warps per GPU cooperative thread array (CTA). Matrix **A** is sparse in CSR format. Matrices **B** and **C** are both dense in row-major format. (Color figure online)

by efficiently processing batches of 32. However, we would expect row split to be negatively impacted by Type 2 load imbalances. The summary of this ILP analysis is shown in Table 1.

3. Shared Memory. The key component required is a round of 32 broadcasts (using the "shuffle" warp intrinsic __shfl) by each thread to inform all other threads in the warp which **B** row ought to be collectively loaded by the entire warp. This is required or otherwise each thread would be responsible for loading its own row, which would result in uncoalesced access. We could have also implemented this using shared memory, but since all threads are within a single warp, there is no disadvantage to preferring warp intrinsics. That they are within a single warp is a consequence of our decision to assign each row to a warp rather than a CTA.

Table 1. This table shows the number of independent instructions per GPU thread for SpMV and SpMM with default value shown in brackets, as well as the register usage and the extra number of memory accesses with respect to the row-split algorithm. T is the number of work items per thread (typically specified as a tuning parameter to the algorithm). L is the number of nonzeroes modulus 32 in the row of **A** that we are computing. B is the CTA size. Typical values for T in SpMV and SpMM are 7 and 1 respectively, while a typical value for B is 128. T cannot be set arbitrarily high, because high register usage causes lower occupancy. **A**.nnz is the number of nonzeroes in the sparse matrix **A**. **B**.$ncols$ is the number of columns of the dense matrix **B**.

	SpMV		SpMM	
Operation	Row-split	Merge-based	Row-split	Merge-based
Read **A**.col_ind and **A**.val	1	$T(7)$	1	$T(1)$
Read **x**/Read **B**	1	$T(7)$	$0 < L \leq 32$	$32T(32)$
Write **y**/Write **C**	1	$T(7)$	1	$32T(32)$
Register usage	2	$2T(14)$	64	$64T(64)$
Memory access overhead	0	$\frac{\mathbf{A}.nnz}{B \times T}$	0	$\frac{\mathbf{B}.ncols \times \mathbf{A}.nnz}{B \times T}$
		$\left(\frac{\mathbf{A}.nnz}{896}\right)$		$(2\mathbf{A}.nnz)$

4.2 Algorithm II: Merge-Based SpMM

The essence of merge-based algorithms is to explicitly and evenly distribute the nonzeroes across parallel processors. It does so by doing a two-phase decomposition: In the first phase (PARTITIONSPMM), it divides the work between threads so that T work is assigned per thread, and based on this assignment deduces the starting indices of each CTA. Once coordinated thusly, work is done in the second phase. In theory, this approach should eliminate both Type 1 and Type 2 load imbalances, and performs well in recent SpMV implementations [14]. We made the following design decisions when generalizing this technique to SpMM:

1. Memory access pattern. For fetching **B**, we adapt the memory access pattern that was successful in row-splitting. However, here, we must first apply the first phase (i.e., PARTITIONSPMM, Line 2 of Algorithm 1) to tell us the rows each CTA ought to look at if we want an equal number of nonzeroes per CTA. Then, we can apply the broadcast technique to retrieve **B** values using coalesced accesses.

2. Register usage. Since we opted for the coalesced memory access pattern explained in the row-splitting section, we require $32\times$ the number of registers in order to store the values. Due to this limitation, the number of independent instructions per thread T is limited to 1, so we see no further latency-hiding gain from ILP over that of row-split.

3. Memory access overhead. There are two sources of memory access overhead compared to the row-splitting algorithm: (1) the additional GPU kernel that determines the starting rows for each block (Line 2), and (2) the write of the carry-out to global memory for matrix rows of **C** that cross CTA boundaries (Line 24). Since the user is unable to synchronize CTAs in CUDA, this is the only way the user can pass information from one CTA to another. The first source of additional memory accesses is less of a problem for SpMM compared to SpMV, because they are amortized by the increased work. The second source, however, scales with the number of **B** columns. Thus we face a trade-off between having more efficient memory access pattern (assign 32 columns per CTA so memory access is coalesced), and having less memory access overhead (assign 4 columns per CTA so T can be set higher resulting in fewer CTA boundaries that need to be crossed). The first approach resulted in better performance.

5   Experimental Results

5.1   Experimental Setup

We ran all experiments in this paper on a Linux workstation with $2\times$ 3.50 GHz Intel 4-core E5-2637 v2 Xeon CPUs, 256 GB of main memory, and an NVIDIA K40c GPU with 12 GB on-board memory. The GPU programs were compiled with NVIDIA's nvcc compiler (version 8.0.44). The C code was compiled using gcc 4.9.3. All results ignore transfer time (from disk-to-memory and CPU-to-GPU). The merge path operation is from the Modern GPU library [12]. The version of cuSPARSE used was 8.0. The code generated during the current study are available in the figshare repository [1] and GitHub repository[2] [25].

The 157 datasets mentioned in the previous section represent a random sample from the SuiteSparse sparse matrix collection. The topology of the datasets varies from small-degree large-diameter (road network) to scale-free. In the microbenchmark Fig. 1(a), dense matrices (varying from 2 rows with 8.3M

---

[1] https://doi.org/10.6084/m9.figshare.6378764.

[2] https://github.com/owensgroup/merge-spmm.

Algorithm 1. The merge-based SpMM algorithm.

Input: Sparse matrix in CSR $\mathbf{A} \in \mathbb{R}^{m \times k}$ and dense matrix $\mathbf{B} \in \mathbb{R}^{k \times n}$.
Output: $\mathbf{C} \in \mathbb{R}^{m \times n}$ such that $\mathbf{C} \leftarrow \mathbf{AB}$.
 1: **procedure** SPMMMERGE($\mathbf{A}, \mathbf{B}$)
 2:     limits[] $\leftarrow$ PARTITIONSPMM($\mathbf{A}$, blockDim.x) ▷ **Phase 1:** Divide work and run binary-search
 3:     **for** each CTA i **in parallel do**   ▷ **Phase 2:** Do computation
 4:         num_rows $\leftarrow$ limits[$i + 1$] $-$ limits[i]
 5:         shared.csr $\leftarrow$ GLOBALTOSHARED($\mathbf{A}$.row_ptr $+$ limits[i], num_rows) ▷ Read $\mathbf{A}$ and store to shared memory
 6:         end $\leftarrow$ min(blockDim.x, $\mathbf{A}$.nnz - blockIdx.x $\times$ blockDim.x)
 7:         **if** row_ind $<$ end **then**
 8:             col_ind $\leftarrow$ $\mathbf{A}$.col_ind[row_ind]   ▷ Read $\mathbf{A}$ if matrix not finished
 9:             valA $\leftarrow$ $\mathbf{A}$.values[row_ind]
10:         **else**
11:             col_ind $\leftarrow$ 0   ▷ Otherwise do nothing
12:             valA $\leftarrow$ 0
13:         **end if**
14:         **for** each thread j **in parallel do**
15:             **for** $j = 0, 1, \ldots, 31$ **do**   ▷ Unroll this loop
16:                 new_ind[j] $\leftarrow$ Broadcast(col_ind, j)   ▷ Each thread broadcasts
17:                 new_val[j] $\leftarrow$ Broadcast(valA, j)   ▷ col_ind and valA
18:                 valB[j] $\leftarrow$ $\mathbf{B}$[col_ind][j] $\times$ new_val[j]   ▷ Read $\mathbf{B}$
19:             **end for**
20:         **end for**
21:         terms $\leftarrow$ PREPARESPMM(shared.csr)   ▷ Flatten CSR-to-COO
22:         carryout[i] $\leftarrow$ REDUCETOGLOBALSPMM($\mathbf{C}$, valB, valB) ▷ Compute partial of $\mathbf{C}$ and save carry-outs
23:     **end for**
24:     FIXCARRYOUT($\mathbf{C}$, limits, carryout) ▷ Carry-out fix-up (rows spanning across blocks)
25:     **return** $\mathbf{C}$
26: **end procedure**

---

nonzeroes per row to 8.3M rows with 2 nonzeroes per row) used in the micro-benchmark are generated to be nonzero, and converted to CSR sparse matrix storage. We then multiply the matrix by a dense vector and a dense matrix with 64 columns using the vendor-supplied SpMV and SpMM implementations respectively.

5.2 Algorithm I: Row-Split

Figure 5(a) shows the performance of our row split implementation on 10 SuiteSparse datasets with long matrix rows (62.5 nonzeroes per row on average). We obtain a geomean speed-up of 30.8% over the next fastest implementation and 39% peak improvement.

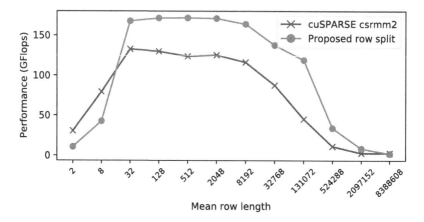

Fig. 4. The performance of our proposed SpMM row split kernel vs. NVIDIA cuS-PARSE's SpMM as a function of aspect ratio on a Tesla K40c.

We suspect our performance drop to the left in Fig. 4 comes from the sensitivity to parameter L on row lengths that are significantly less than 32. This causes divergence and uncoalesced memory accesses. On the right hand side, we do much better than cuSPARSE. We believe this is due to the additional occupancy that we can get from superior ILP, which is better at hiding latency. Using the profiler, we noted a 102% improvement in executed instructions per cycle for the matrix sized 128-by-131072.

We also tried loading in the transpose configuration, where each thread performs a texture load, and loads a different row of the dense matrix. Then, the threads could perform a shuffle reduce, which is a common pattern in GPU programming. However, we observed that this resulted in poorer performance than the vendor-supplied library on average. We suspect the reason for this is there was too much contention amongst different threads for the very limited texture cache resource.

We tried variants that generate the output in column-major order, because this is what cuSPARSE csrmm and csrmm2 produces as output. However, we found that doing such a transpose in the write to global memory causes at most a loss of 3–4 GFlops in performance. The results track Fig. 5(a) very closely. Another reason for our performance improvement comes from our use of the shuffle broadcast technique, where we have all 32 threads take turns in broadcasting their values to other threads. This saved shared memory (both in capacity and throughput) which could be put to use elsewhere.

5.3   Algorithm II: Merge-Based

Figure 5(b) shows the performance of our merge-based SpMM kernel on 10 SuiteSparse datasets with short matrix rows (7.92 nonzeroes on average). We obtain a geomean speed-up of 53% over cuSPARSE csrmm2 and 237% peak

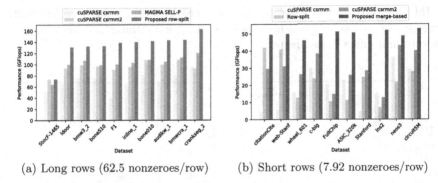

(a) Long rows (62.5 nonzeroes/row)   (b) Short rows (7.92 nonzeroes/row)

Fig. 5. Performance comparison between the proposed ILP-centric row split kernel and other state-of-the-art kernels on matrices with *long* and *short* row lengths on Tesla K40c using single-precision floating-point. cuSPARSE csrmm and csrmm2 are from a vendor-supplied library [20]. MAGMA SELL-P is by Anzt, Tomov, and Dongarra [17].

improvement. We think the biggest reason that merge path is doing better than the other methods is because it handles Type 2 load imbalances much better. Other methods inevitably encounter warp efficiency degradation due to the divergence caused by short rows, as shown in Fig. 1(b). However, merge path can handle these short rows very well by simply allocating more rows to a CTA if the rows are short.

Another interesting observation to make is that the merge path performance in Fig. 5(b) all tend to be lower than their row split equivalents. This means that merge path has more overhead than row split, so it is only worth it to perfectly load-balance matrices when it is profitable to do so (Sect. 5.4). While Merrill and Garland found their merge-based solution was better than row split on SpMV [14], ours did not perform as well on SpMM, as explained in the next paragraph.

As Table 1 shows, merge path's advantage in SpMV comes from being able to obtain T times more ILP per thread than row split, but it enjoys no such advantage in SpMM, where row splitting gets as much ILP as there are nonzeroes in the sparse matrix row as long as row split can afford to pay the register cost. This can be seen in Fig. 3(a). While merge path has the opportunity to obtain T times more ILP, we discovered that we need to keep $T = 1$ in order to keep the register count manageable. In typical merge path SpMV implementations, T can be as high as 7. The ILP advantage merge-based had in SpMV is not so assured.

5.4 Heuristic

By comparing the speed-up of row split and merge-based to the fastest vendor-supplied SpMM on 157 SuiteSparse sparse matrix collection datasets [15] (see Fig. 6(a)), we show that the two proposed algorithms achieve speed-ups over the

SpMM state-of-the-art in separate regions on the spectrum of matrix irregularity. However, the geomean speed-up is only a 13.2% gain and 21.5% slowdown for row split and merge-based respectively.

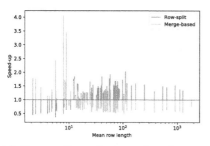

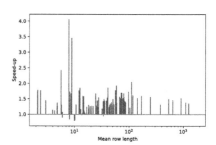

(a) Row split and merge-based separately vs. cuSPARSE csrmm2.

(b) Combined row split and merge-based
vs. cuSPARSE csrmm2.

Fig. 6. Performance comparison between proposed row split kernel, proposed merge-based kernel, and cuSPARSE csrmm2 on 195 non-trivial datasets from the SuiteSparse sparse matrix collection [15].

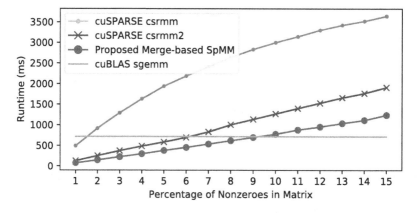

Fig. 7. Runtime as a function of the percentage of nonzeroes in the sparse matrix on Tesla K40c using single-precision floating-point. cuSPARSE csrmm, csrmm2 are sparse-dense matrix multiplication functions from a vendor-supplied library [20]. cuBLAS sgemm is a dense-dense matrix multiplication function from a vendor-shipped library.

Therefore, we propose a heuristic for switching between them using an inexpensive $O(1)$ calculation $d = \frac{nnz}{n}$. Our heuristic is simply computing the average row length for the matrix, and using this value to decide whether to use merge-based or row split. To pinpoint the transition point, we examine Fig. 6(a). For our heuristic, we decide that we will use merge-based on datasets whose mean row length is less than 9.35, and row split otherwise.

Using this heuristic, we obtain an overall 31.7% geomean speed-up, and up to a peak of 4.1×, over the vendor-supplied library cuSPARSE csrmm2. Over cuS-PARSE csrmm, we obtain a 2.69× geomean speed-up and 22.4× peak speed-up. The result is shown in Fig. 6. Using this heuristic as a binary classifier, we get 99.3% accuracy vs. an oracle that perfectly chooses the fastest implementation.

6   Conclusion and Future Work

In this paper we implement two promising algorithms for computing sparse matrix dense matrix multiplication on the GPU. Our results using SpMM show considerable performance improvement over the vendor-supplied SpMM on a wide spectrum of graphs. One of the keys to our high performance is our memory-access strategy that allows coalesced access into all 3 matrices (see Fig. 3(a)).

In Fig. 7, we generate a $100,000 \times 100,000$ random matrix by making a fixed percentage of elements in each row nonzero by sampling indices between 1 and 100,000 without replacement. Our experiments indicate that when multiplying a sparse matrix randomly generated thusly with a tall-skinny dense matrix of size $100,000 \times 64$, our proposed merge-based SpMM is faster than a dense matrix-dense matrix (GEMM) multiplication when less than 9% of the sparse matrix is filled.

Greiner and Jacob have proven theoretically [26] that as the number of nonzeroes per row exceeds some hardware threshold, namely $\frac{m}{M}$ where m is the number of rows in the sparse matrix and M is the size of the fast memory of the device, tiling will become more efficient than the access pattern described in this paper (i.e. going across the sparse matrix and selecting nonzeroes in the dense matrix). Indeed, they claim that tiling both the sparse matrix $\mathbf{A}$ and $\mathbf{B}$ in a manner akin to tiling dense matrix-matrix multiplication is optimal. In future work, it would be interesting to find out whether doing this tiling will extend SpMM's effectiveness range beyond 9% sparsity.

Our codes only use the popular CSR data structure, hence avoiding the penalty of sparse matrix format conversions. There are legitimate reasons for considering other formats. For example, certain iterative algorithms require multiplication of a sparse matrix (SpMM) as well as its transpose (SpMM_T) within the same code. Compressed Sparse Blocks (CSB) [27] is a format that is specifically designed for this task and it has already been utilized for SpMM and SpMM_T [18] in CPUs. However, achieving high performance with CSB on irregular matrices requires an efficient load balancer and it is not clear whether GPUs are suitable for this task.

An interesting future direction for research is designing a library around load-balancing techniques such as merge path. While merge path is already present in two libraries–Modern GPU and CUB [12,28]—they are not designed as layers separated from computation. Similarly in our code, computation and load-balancing are very tightly knit. It would be interesting to discover how to abstract out the load balancing from the computation. Ideally, the user would have to identify the quantities that are desirable for load balancing separately from the computation. Then the load-balancing library would handle the rest making load-balanced GPU kernels much easier to write. The impact of our improved SpMM kernels on application codes is also worth investigating in the future. In particular, we expect a co-design approach to provide more pronounced performance benefits to applications compared to drop-down kernel replacement.

Acknowledgments. We appreciate the funding support from the National Science Foundation (Award # CCF-1629657), the DARPA XDATA program (US Army award W911QX-12-C-0059), and the DARPA HIVE program. For HIVE support, this material is based on research sponsored by Air Force Research Lab (AFRL) and the Defense Advanced Research Projects Agency (DARPA) under agreement number FA8650-18-2-7836. The U.S. Government is authorized to reproduce and distribute reprints for Governmental purposes notwithstanding any copyright notation thereon. The views and conclusions contained herein are those of the authors and should not be interpreted as necessarily representing the official policies or endorsements, either expressed or implied, of Air Force Research Lab (AFRL) and the Defense Advanced Research Projects Agency (DARPA) or the U.S. Government.

This manuscript has been authored by an author at Lawrence Berkeley National Laboratory under Contract No. DE-AC02-05CH11231 with the U.S. Department of Energy. The U.S. Government retains, and the publisher, by accepting the article for publication, acknowledges, that the U.S. Government retains a non-exclusive, paid-up, irrevocable, world-wide license to publish or reproduce the published form of this manuscript, or allow others to do so, for U.S. Government purposes.

This research was supported in part by the Applied Mathematics program of the DOE Office of Advanced Scientific Computing Research under Contract No. DE-AC02-05CH11231, and in part the Exascale Computing Project (17-SC-20-SC), a collaborative effort of the U.S. Department of Energy Office of Science and the National Nuclear Security Administration.

References

1. Han, S., Mao, H., Dally, W.J.: Deep compression: compressing deep neural networks with pruning, trained quantization and huffman coding. In: International Conference on Learning Representations (ICLR) (2016)
2. Sarıyüce, A.E., Saule, E., Kaya, K., Çatalyürek, Ü.V.: Regularizing graph centrality computations. J. Parallel Distrib. Comput. **76**, 106–119 (2015)
3. Tiskin, A.: All-pairs shortest paths computation in the BSP model. In: Orejas, F., Spirakis, P.G., van Leeuwen, J. (eds.) ICALP 2001. LNCS, vol. 2076, pp. 178–189. Springer, Heidelberg (2001). https://doi.org/10.1007/3-540-48224-5_15
4. Simoncini, V., Gallopoulos, E.: An iterative method for nonsymmetric systems with multiple right-hand sides. SIAM J. Sci. Comput. **16**(4), 917–933 (1995)
5. Bai, Z., Demmel, J., Dongarra, J., Ruhe, A., van der Vorst, H.: Templates for the Solution of Algebraic Eigenvalue Problems: A Practical Guide. SIAM, Philadelphia (2000)
6. Knyazev, A.V.: Toward the optimal preconditioned eigensolver: locally optimal block preconditioned conjugate gradient method. SIAM SISC **23**(2), 517–541 (2001)
7. Wang, H., Banerjee, A., Hsieh, C.J., Ravikumar, P.K., Dhillon, I.S.: Large scale distributed sparse precision estimation. In: NIPS, pp. 584–592 (2013)

8. Si, S., Shin, D., Dhillon, I.S., Parlett, B.N.: Multi-scale spectral decomposition of massive graphs. In: NIPS, pp. 2798–2806 (2014)
9. Kannan, R., Ballard, G., Park, H.: A high-performance parallel algorithm for non-negative matrix factorization. In: ACM SIGPLAN, vol. 51. ACM (2016)
10. Vazquez, F., Garzon, E.M., Fernandez, J.J.: A matrix approach to tomographic reconstruction and its implementation on GPUs. J. Struct. Biol. **170**(1), 146–151 (2010)
11. Buluç, A., Mattson, T., McMillan, S., Moreira, J., Yang, C.: Design of the Graph-BLAS API for C. In: IEEE Workshop on Graph Algorithm Building Blocks, IPDPSW (2017)
12. Baxter, S.: Modern GPU library (2015). http://nvlabs.github.io/moderngpu/
13. Dalton, S., Olson, L., Bell, N.: Optimizing sparse matrix-matrix multiplication for the GPU. ACM TOMS **41**(4), 25 (2015)
14. Merrill, D., Garland, M.: Merge-based parallel sparse matrix-vector multiplication. In: Supercomputing 2016, pp. 678–689. IEEE, November 2016
15. Davis, T.A., Hu, Y.: The University of Florida sparse matrix collection. ACM TOMS **38**(1), 1 (2011)
16. Ortega, G., Vázquez, F., García, I., Garzón, E.M.: FastSpMM: an efficient library for sparse matrix matrix product on GPUs. Computer **57**(7), 968–979 (2014)
17. Anzt, H., Tomov, S., Dongarra, J.: Accelerating the LOBPCG method on GPUs using a blocked sparse matrix vector product. In: Proceedings of the Symposium on High Performance Computing, pp. 75–82 (2015)
18. Aktulga, H.M., Buluç, A., Williams, S., Yang, C.: Optimizing sparse matrix-multiple vectors multiplication for nuclear configuration interaction calculations. In: Proceedings of the IPDPS. IEEE Computer Society (2014)
19. Filippone, S., Cardellini, V., Barbieri, D., Fanfarillo, A.: Sparse matrix-vector multiplication on GPGPUs. ACM TOMS **43**(4), 30 (2017)
20. Naumov, M., Chien, L.S., Vandermersch, P., Kapasi, U.: CUSPARSE library: a set of basic linear algebra subroutines for sparse matrices. In: GTC (2010)
21. Hong, C., et al.: Efficient sparse-matrix multi-vector product on GPUs. In: Proceedings of the 27th International Symposium on High-Performance Parallel and Distributed Computing. HPDC 2018, pp. 66–79. ACM, New York (2018)
22. Volkov, V., Demmel, J.W.: Benchmarking GPUs to tune dense linear algebra. In: Supercomputing 2008, pp. 31:1–31:11, November 2008
23. Jablin, J.A., Jablin, T.B., Mutlu, O., Herlihy, M.: Warp-aware trace scheduling for GPUs. In: ACM PACT 2014, pp. 163–174 (2014)
24. Bell, N., Garland, M.: Implementing sparse matrix-vector multiplication on throughput-oriented processors. In: Supercomputing 2009, pp. 18:1–18:11, November 2009
25. Yang, C., Buluc, A., Owens, J.D.: Supporting data for design principles for sparse matrix multiplication on the GPU paper at euro-par 2018 (2018). https://doi.org/10.6084/m9.figshare.6378764
26. Greiner, G., Jacob, R.: The I/O complexity of sparse matrix dense matrix multiplication. In: López-Ortiz, A. (ed.) LATIN 2010. LNCS, vol. 6034, pp. 143–156. Springer, Heidelberg (2010). https://doi.org/10.1007/978-3-642-12200-2_14
27. Buluç, A., Fineman, J.T., Frigo, M., Gilbert, J.R., Leiserson, C.E.: Parallel sparse matrix-vector and matrix-transpose-vector multiplication using compressed sparse blocks. In: Proceedings of SPAA (2009)
28. Merrill, D.: CUB library (2015). http://nvlabs.github.io/cub

Distributed Graph Clustering Using Modularity and Map Equation

Michael Hamann, Ben Strasser, Dorothea Wagner, and Tim Zeitz[✉]

Institute of Theoretical Informatics, Karlsruhe Institute of Technology,
Karlsruhe, Germany
{michael.hamann,dorothea.wagner,tim.zeitz}@kit.edu,
academia@ben-strasser.net

Abstract. We study large-scale, distributed graph clustering. Given an undirected graph, our objective is to partition the nodes into disjoint sets called clusters. A cluster should contain many internal edges while being sparsely connected to other clusters. In the context of a social network, a cluster could be a group of friends. Modularity and map equation are established formalizations of this internally-dense-externally-sparse principle. We present two versions of a simple distributed algorithm to optimize both measures. They are based on Thrill, a distributed big data processing framework that implements an extended MapReduce model. The algorithms for the two measures, DSLM-Mod and DSLM-Map, differ only slightly. Adapting them for similar quality measures is straight-forward. We conduct an extensive experimental study on real-world graphs and on synthetic benchmark graphs with up to 68 billion edges. Our algorithms are fast while detecting clusterings similar to those detected by other sequential, parallel and distributed clustering algorithms. Compared to the distributed GossipMap algorithm, DSLM-Map needs less memory, is up to an order of magnitude faster and achieves better quality.

1 Introduction

Graph clustering is a well researched topic [8,10] and has many applications, such as community detection in social networks where users can be modeled as nodes and friendships as edges between them. These graphs can be huge and may not fit into the main memory of a single machine. We therefore study distributed extensions of established single machine clustering algorithms. This enables us to efficiently compute clusterings in huge graphs.

We consider the problem of clustering a graph into disjoint clusters. While there is no universally accepted definition of a good clustering, it is commonly accepted that clusters should be internally densely and externally sparsely connected. Our algorithms optimize two established quality measures that formalize this concept: modularity [19] and map equation [21]. Other community detection formalizations have been considered. For example, EgoLP [7] is a distributed algorithm to find overlapping clusters.

This work was partially supported by the DFG under grants WA654/19-2 and WA654/22-2. The authors acknowledge support by the state of Baden-Württemberg through bwHPC.

© Springer International Publishing AG, part of Springer Nature 2018
M. Aldinucci et al. (Eds.): Euro-Par 2018, LNCS 11014, pp. 688–702, 2018.
https://doi.org/10.1007/978-3-319-96983-1_49

1.1 Related Work

Existing distributed approaches follow one of two approaches.

The first is to partition the graph into a subgraph per machine. Each subgraph is then clustered independently on one machine. Then, all nodes of each cluster are merged summing up weights of parallel edges. The resulting coarser graph is clustered on a single machine. This assumes the coarsened graph fits in the memory of a single machine. In [25], for the partitioning, the input node ID range is chunked into equally sized parts. This can work well, but is problematic if input node IDs do not reflect the graph structure. In [23], the input graph is partitioned using the non-distributed, parallel graph partitioning algorithm ParMETIS [14]. While this is independent of node IDs, it requires that the graph fits into the memory of one machine for the partitioning.

The second approach consists of distributing the clustering algorithm itself. Using MPI, [20] have introduced a distributed extension of the Louvain algorithm [5]. Similarly, [18] have presented an algorithm that uses the GraphX framework. Another algorithm named GossipMap is presented in [3] which uses the GraphLab framework. Our algorithms also use this second approach.

All of these related algorithms heuristically optimize modularity except GossipMap, which optimizes the map equation.

1.2 Contribution

We propose two distributed graph clustering algorithms, DSLM-Mod and DSLM-Map, that optimize modularity and map equation, respectively. Our algorithms are the first graph clustering algorithms based on Thrill [4], a distributed big data processing framework written in C++ that implements an extended MapReduce model. Our algorithms are easy to extend for optimizing different density-based quality measures. To evaluate the clustering quality, we compare against ground truth communities on synthetic LFR [16] graph clustering benchmark graphs with up to 68 billion edges. Even for these graphs, 32 hosts of a compute cluster are enough. Our results show that our algorithms scale well and DSLM-Map is better at recovering the ground truth than the sequential Infomap algorithm [21]. On real-world graphs, our algorithms perform similarly to non-distributed baseline algorithms in terms of the quality of the detected clusterings and stability between different runs. We evaluate both similarities and quality scores, as for quality scores small changes can result in vastly different clusterings [11].

Similar to most related work, we make implicit assumptions on the structure of the graph. We assume that all edges incident to nodes in a single cluster fit into the memory of a single compute node. In practice, this is only a limitation when a graph has huge clusters. In many scenarios like social networks or web graphs, this is no limitation as cluster sizes are not that huge. Our algorithms can be modified to avoid these restrictions, but this would increase running times.

Outline. In the following we introduce our notation and present the quality measures we optimize. We also give a brief introduction to Thrill. In Sect. 3, we present our algorithms. In Sect. 4 we present our experimental results. We conclude in Sect. 5.

2   Preliminaries

Conceptually, our algorithms work on undirected graphs. However, we represent all graphs $G = (V, E, \omega)$ as symmetric, directed, weighted graphs of $|V| = n$ nodes and $|E| = m$ edges. The pair $(u, v) \in E$ represents the edge from u to v. Unless stated otherwise, there are no multi-edges. We describe our algorithms for weighted graphs. As our input graphs are unweighted, we set $\omega(u, v) = 1$ for every edge $(u, v) \in E$.

A cluster C is a node subset. A clustering $\mathcal{C}$ is a set of clusters such that each node is part of exactly one cluster.

The *weighted degree* $\deg(x)$ of a node x is the sum over the weights of all outgoing edges (x, y) of x. The weight of loop edges is counted twice. The volume $\text{vol}(C)$ of a set of nodes C is the sum of their weighted degrees. The cut $\text{cut}(C, D)$ between two sets of nodes C, D is the sum of the weights of all edges (x, y) such that $x \in C$ and $y \in D$. As a simplification, we write $\text{cut}(v, C)$ for $\text{cut}(\{v\}, C)$, $\text{cut}(C) := \text{cut}(C, V \setminus C)$ for the cut between C and the rest of the graph.

Many approaches exist to formalize the quality of a clustering. In this work, we study two popular ones: modularity [19] and map equation [21]. The modularity of a clustering $\mathcal{C}$ is defined as

$$\mathcal{Q}(\mathcal{C}) := \sum_{C \in \mathcal{C}} \frac{\text{vol}(C) - \text{cut}(C)}{\text{vol}(V)} - \sum_{C \in \mathcal{C}} \frac{\text{vol}(C)^2}{\text{vol}(V)^2}.$$

Higher modularity values indicate better clusterings. However, sometimes higher modularity values can also be achieved by merging small but actually clearly distinct clusters. This effect is called resolution limit [9]. For the map equation, this effect is much weaker [15]. Clusterings are better when they have a lower map equation score. To simplify its definition, we set $\text{plogp}(x) := x \log x$. The definition is

$$L(\mathcal{C}) := \text{plogp} \left(\sum_{C \in \mathcal{C}} \frac{\text{cut}(C)}{\text{vol}(V)} \right) - 2 \sum_{C \in \mathcal{C}} \text{plogp} \left(\frac{\text{cut}(C)}{\text{vol}(V)} \right)$$
$$+ \sum_{C \in \mathcal{C}} \text{plogp} \left(\frac{\text{cut}(C) + \text{vol}(C)}{\text{vol}(V)} \right) - \sum_{v \in V} \text{plogp} \left(\frac{\deg(v)}{\text{vol}(V)} \right).$$

The last term is independent of the clustering and therefore does not affect the optimization. Thus, we omit it in our algorithms. Optimizing modularity is NP-hard [6] but it can be optimized heuristically in practice [5]. Only heuristic map equation optimization algorithms are known to us [21].

To compare clusterings, either with ground truth communities or with a clustering calculated using a different algorithm, we use the *adjusted rand index* (ARI) [13]. The maximum value of 1 indicates that both clusterings are equal. ARI is normalized such that when one of the two clusterings is random, its expected value is 0. It can also be negative.

2.1   Thrill

Thrill [4] is a distributed C++ big data processing framework. It can distribute the program execution over multiple machines and threads within a machine. Each thread is called *worker*. Every worker executes the same program.

If there is not enough main memory available, Thrill can use local storage such as an SSD as external memory to store parts of the processed data.

Data is maintained in distributed immutable arrays (DIA). Distributed Thrill operations are applied to the DIAs. For example, Thrill contains a *sort* operation, whose input is a DIA and whose output is a new sorted DIA. Similarly, the *zip* operation combines two DIAs of the same length into one DIA where each element is a pair of the two original elements.

Thrill also supports DIAs with elements of non-uniform size, as long as each element fits into the memory of a worker. This allows elements to be arrays.

Apart from zip and sort, we use the following operations: The *map* operation applies a function to each element of a DIA. The return values are the elements of the new DIA. *Flatmap* is similar, but the function may emit 0, 1, or more elements. This is similar to the map operation in the original MapReduce model.

A DIA can be *aggregated* by a key component. All elements with the same key are combined and put into an array. This is similar to the reduce operation in the original MapReduce model. An aggregation is much more efficient if the keys are consecutive integers. In that case, the result is also automatically sorted by the keys. We use this optimized variant for all aggregations that are based on node IDs.

3   Algorithm

The basis of our algorithm is the Louvain algorithm [5], a fast algorithm for modularity optimization that delivers high-quality results. The original Infomap algorithm proposed for optimizing the map equation [21] is based on the same scheme, but introduces additional steps to improve the quality.

Initially, every node is in its own cluster. This is called a singleton clustering.

In the local moving phase, the Louvain algorithm works in rounds. In each round, it iterates in a random order over all nodes v. For every v, it considers v's current cluster and all clusters C such that there is an edge from v to a node of C. For all these clusters, the difference in quality score $\Delta_{v,C}$ if v was to be moved into C is computed. If an improvement is possible, v is moved into a cluster with maximal $\Delta_{v,C}$, resolving ties uniformly at random. The local moving phase stops when no node is moved in a round or a maximum number of rounds is reached.

After the local moving phase, the contraction phase starts. All nodes inside a cluster are merged into a single node. The weights of all edges from a cluster C to D are summed up and added as an edge from the node representing C to the node representing D. All edge weights within a cluster are summed up and added as a loop edge. The contraction does not change the quality score. On the contracted graph, the algorithm is applied recursively. It terminates when the contraction phase is entered and the clustering is still the singleton clustering.

3.1 Distributed Synchronous Local Moving (DSLM)

In local moving, the i-th move depends on the clustering after the first $i-1$ moves are executed. This data dependency makes the parallelization difficult. We therefore split a round into sub-rounds. Every node picks a random sub-round in which it is *active*. In the i-th sub-round, all active nodes are moved synchronously and in parallel with respect to the clustering after the $(i-1)$-th sub-round. For the first sub-round, this is with respect to the initial clustering. We call this scheme *synchronous local moving*. For our *distributed* synchronous local moving, a global hash function h maps a tuple of a node ID v, the number of completed rounds and a global seed onto the sub-round r_v in which v is active. Figure 1 illustrates the data flow of our algorithm.

We represent a graph and its clustering as two DIAs. They have length n and are stored sorted by their first item, the node ID v. The graph DIA stores triples $(v, \langle u_i \rangle, \langle w_i \rangle)$, where $\langle u_i \rangle$ and $\langle w_i \rangle$ are equally-sized arrays. For every i, there is an edge (v, u_i) with weight w_i. The clustering DIA of pairs (v, C) stores for every node v its cluster ID C.

In DSLM, a sub-round is composed of a bidding and a compare step. In the bidding step, the clusters place bids for active nodes. In the compare step, every active node compares its bids and becomes part of the cluster with the best bid.

To allow a node v to compute the change in modularity or map equation when joining the neighboring cluster C, each bid contains: (a) volume $\text{vol}(C \setminus v)$, (b) cut weight $\text{cut}(v, C \setminus v)$ between $C \setminus v$ and v, and (c) cut weight $\text{cut}(C)$ between C and the remaining graph.

The bidding step starts by zipping the clustering DIA and graph DIA and aggregating this zipped DIA by cluster ID. The result is a DIA with one large element per cluster C. Each element contains all nodes in the cluster C and the neighborhoods of these nodes. This allows us to compute the measures (a), (b), and (c) using a non-distributed algorithm inside a worker. Using a flatmap, our algorithm emits for every cluster C bids for all active nodes inside C and adjacent to C. It can determine which nodes are active as the hash function h is globally known. The generated bid DIA consists of quintuples $(C, v, \text{vol}(C \setminus v), \text{cut}(v, C \setminus v), \text{cut}(C \setminus v))$. Each quintuple is a bid of cluster C for active node v.

The compare step aggregates the bid DIA by node v. After the aggregation, the result is zipped with the graph DIA to obtain the nodes' degree and loop edge weight. In a map operation, we use this information to compute for every active node the best bid and return the according cluster. We retrieve the old cluster ID for non-active nodes by zipping with the original clustering DIA. This yields the updated clustering DIA, which is the input of the next sub-round.

Implementation Details and Optimizations. If modularity is optimized, our algorithm can be improved in two ways. First, we can omit $\text{cut}(C \setminus v)$ as it is only needed for the map equation. Second, we can compare bids without knowing the current cluster. This allows us to use a pairwise reduction instead of one that first waits for all elements. As we still need the node's degree, each worker stores the degree of the nodes that are reduced on that worker in a plain array. This is possible because we know on which worker each node will end up.

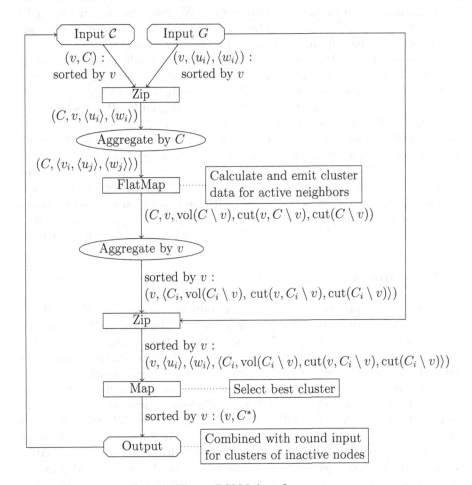

Fig. 1. DSLM data flow

3.2 Distributed Contraction and Unpacking

The contraction is performed in three steps: (a) obtain consecutive cluster IDs, (b) replace all node IDs by the cluster IDs, and (c) combine multi-edges.

We first zip the graph and clustering DIAs and aggregate them by cluster ID. To get consecutive cluster IDs, we replace them with the element positions. From the result, which contains tuples $(C, \langle v_i, \langle u_j \rangle, \langle w_j \rangle \rangle)$, we derive two DIAs.

The first DIA is a new clustering DIA with consecutive cluster IDs. To obtain it, we first drop the neighborhood information. We store this intermediate DIA $(C, \langle v_i \rangle)$ for the unpacking phase. Then, we expand it into pairs (v_i, C) of node and cluster ID using a flatmap operation and sort by node IDs.

The second DIA is the contracted graph DIA. To obtain it, we first emit a triple (C_u, v, w) for every node v that is a neighbor of a node in C_u in a flatmap operation. The weight w is the sum of all edge weights from nodes in C_u to v. We aggregate this DIA by v, zip it with the new clustering DIA and replace v by v's cluster ID C_v. We then aggregate by C_v to obtain pairs $(C_v, \langle C_{u,i}, w_i \rangle)$ containing the neighboring clusters $C_{u,i}$ for every C_v. Finally, we sum up the weights w_i for the same neighboring cluster for every cluster C_v in a map operation.

To unpack the clustering calculated in a level, we zip the clustering DIA (v, C_v) with the intermediate clustering DIA $(v, \langle v_i \rangle)$ of a cluster v and its nodes $\langle v_i \rangle$ from the previous contraction phase. A flatmap operation assigns the cluster ID C_v of the contracted node to all original nodes $u \in \langle v_i \rangle$, resulting in a clustering DIA (u, C_u). After sorting it by node, it is returned to the next level.

4 Experiments

In this section, we present an experimental evaluation of our algorithm DSLM[1]. The source code of our implementation is publicly available on GitHub[2]. We first describe our experimental setup. Then, we present weak scaling experiments to evaluate the running time, compare the quality on LFR benchmark graphs [16] and evaluate the performance on established real-world benchmark data.

All running time experiments were performed on a compute cluster. Each compute node has two 14-core Intel Xeon E5-2660 v4 processors (Broadwell) with a default frequency of 2 GHz, 128 GiB RAM and 480 GiB SSD. They are connected by an InfiniBand 4X FDR Interconnect. We use the TCP back-end of Thrill due to problems with the combination of multithreading and OpenMPI. We use Thrill's default parameters, except for the block size, which determines the size of data packages sent between the hosts. Preliminary experiments found that a block size of 128 KiB instead of the default 2 MiB yields the best results.

For our algorithms, we use four sub-rounds as suggested in a preliminary study [24]. Using less results in problems with the convergence. Using more does

---

[1] This paper only covers parts of our experiments. Under https://github.com/kit-algo/distributed_clustering_thrill_evaluation you can find additional analyses, links to our raw data and information on how to explore our data on your own.

[2] https://github.com/kit-algo/distributed_clustering_thrill.

not significantly improve quality but increases running time. In each local moving phase, we perform at most eight rounds. All experiments were performed with 16 threads per host. More threads do not improve the running times much further. Preliminary experiments indicate that the performance is RAM bound.

Apart from DSLM-Mod and DSLM-Map that optimize modularity and map equation, we also evaluate a variant DSLM-Mod w/o Cont. that stops after the first local moving phase. This significantly decreases the running time and surprisingly also improves the quality on synthetic instances. We evaluate this behavior in more detail in Sect. 4.2.

For modularity, we compare against our own implementation of the sequential Louvain algorithm [5] and the shared-memory parallel PLM [22]. For map equation, we compare against the sequential Infomap [21], the shared-memory parallel RelaxMap [2] and the distributed GossipMap [3] implementations.

In a preprocessing step, we remove degree zero nodes, make the ID space consecutive and randomize the node order. This ensures that our algorithms are independent of input order and improves load balancing.

All experiments were repeated 10 times with different random seeds. We report averaged results and standard deviation where possible as error bars.

During the experiments, the meltdown and spectre vulnerabilities became public and performance impacting patches were applied to the machines. Rerunning some experiments showed a slowdown of up to 1.6 for runs with 32 hosts but no significant slowdown for runs with a single host. We did not have the resources to rerun all experiments. Also, we expect the performance of the machines to change further in the future. Patches with less impact (Retpoline) are available but have not been rolled out yet. More vulnerabilities have been discovered in the meantime and it is unclear if fixes for them will have further performance implications[3]. At the point of initial patch distribution, most distributed algorithm runs were already done. About half of the GossipMap runs on the real world graphs were performed afterwards and are excluded from the running time reports. All runs for non-distributed algorithms were performed with patches applied, as their performance should not have been affected significantly.

Synthetic Instance Generation. Our synthetic test data is generated using the established LFR benchmark generation scheme [16]. To generate graphs of up to 512 million nodes and 67.6 billion (undirected) edges in a reasonable time, we use the external memory LFR generator implementation of [12].

LFR benchmark graphs feature a ground truth clustering. Node degrees and cluster sizes are drawn from power law distributions. The mixing parameter μ determines the fraction of edges that are between different clusters. For details, we refer the reader to the original description [16]. We set a minimum degree of 50 and a maximum degree of 10 000 with a power law exponent of 2. This leads to an average degree of approximately 264. For the communities, we set 50 as minimum and 12 000 as maximum size with a power law exponent of 1. Unless otherwise noted, we set the mixing parameter μ to 0.4.

---

[3] https://securityaffairs.co/wordpress/72158/hacking/spectre-ng-vulnerabilities.html.

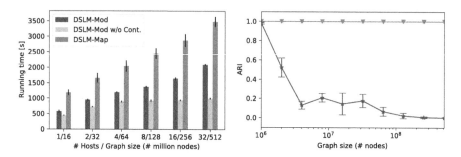

Fig. 2. Weak scaling: running time of our distributed algorithms and ARI with ground truth. The DSLM-Mod w/o Cont. ARI line is hidden by the DSLM-Map line.

4.1 Weak Scaling

For the weak scaling experiments, we use LFR graphs with 16, 32, 64, 128, 256 and 512 million nodes. We cluster them on 1, 2, 4, 8, 16, and 32 hosts respectively. The left part of Fig. 2 shows the running time of our algorithms. Our algorithms utilize almost the entire available RAM. GossipMap is less memory-efficient and was unable to cluster the graphs in these configurations and crashed.

With a linear time algorithm and perfect scaling, we would expect that the running time remains constant as we increase graph size and the number of nodes. For the variant of DSLM-Mod w/o Cont., the running time actually does not increase much. The running time of the full DSLM-Mod and DSLM-Map algorithms increases approximately linearly though as the number of hosts is scaled exponentially. The reason for this is that LFR graphs get very dense during contraction and thus in particular larger graphs still have a significant amount of edges after the contraction. Also, DSLM-Map is approximately a factor of two slower than DSLM-Mod. This is expected as the optimizations described at the end of Sect. 3.1 are not applicable to DSLM-Map.

4.2 Quality

First, we evaluate the quality of the clusterings obtained in the weak scaling experiment. The right part of Fig. 2 depicts the similarities of the clusterings found by our algorithms and the ground truth. From the plot, we observe that DSLM-Map finds a clustering very close to the ground truth. DSLM-Mod w/o Cont. achieves similar results. Unfortunately, DSLM-Mod fails to find a clustering similar to the ground truth on the larger instances. This shows that after the contraction, clusters are merged that should not be merged. To verify if the worse results of DSLM-Mod are due to the resolution limit, we started a sequential Louvain algorithm on a graph where we contracted the ground truth. This algorithm indeed merges clusters, showing that the resolution limit is relevant here. However, the thereby detected clusters are much more similar to the ground truth than those detected by DSLM-Mod and even the ground truth alone has higher modularity scores than those found by DSLM-Mod.

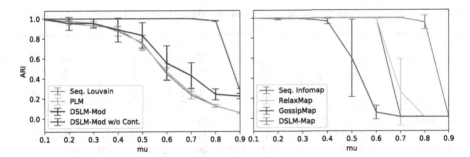

Fig. 3. Adjusted rand index with ground truth for $\mu \in [0.1, 0.9]$.

We also use smaller LFR graphs with 1M nodes and varying mixing parameter to compare the quality of the communities found by all compared algorithms. Figure 3 shows the adjusted rand index of the detected clusterings with the ground truth. DSLM-Mod w/o Cont. and DSLM-Map outperform all other algorithms by a significant margin. On average, DSLM-Mod still outperforms the other modularity-optimizing algorithms. For all values of μ, the ground truth has a higher modularity score than the clustering found by the modularity-optimizing algorithms. Merging clusters of the ground truth again improves the modularity score but leads to clusterings that still have an ARI of above 0.99 for $\mu < 0.9$. With the algorithms optimizing map equation, the situation is similar. For $\mu < 0.8$, the ground truth, which DSLM-Map consistently finds, has a better map equation score than the clusterings found by all other algorithms. For $\mu \geq 0.8$, a singleton clustering yields a better map equation score than the ground truth clustering. GossipMap finds neither good map equation scores nor the ground truth for $\mu > 0.4$.

Overall, for these LFR benchmark graphs, DSLM seems to be superior to sequential local moving. Examining sequential local moving algorithms, we noticed that high-degree nodes attract many nodes in the first local moving round. After a few nodes join their cluster, many others follow. In contrast to that, with DLSM, 25% of the nodes can join the cluster of another node before any cluster sizes come into play. Apparently, this avoids such accumulation effects.

4.3 Real-World Graphs

To assess whether our results on LFR benchmark graphs are also true for real-world graphs, we performed experiments on a set of different real-world graphs. From the Stanford Large Network Dataset Collection [17], we include three social networks (com-LiveJournal, com-Orkut and com-Friendster). From the 10th DIMACS Implementation challenge [1], we include two web graphs where nodes represent URLs and edges links between them (uk-2002 and uk-2007-05).

We clustered these graphs both with the sequential baseline algorithms and our distributed algorithms. Table 1 depicts the sizes of the graphs, the number

Table 1. Average running time in seconds of the algorithms on the real-world graphs.

	# Nodes	# Edges	# Hosts	Louvain	PLM	DSLM-Mod	DSLM-Mod w/o Cont.	Infomap	RelaxMap	GossipMap	DSLM-Map
LiveJournal	4M	34M	8	99	25	31	14	1329	163	372	49
Orkut	3M	117M	8	170	53	47	34	2405	415	700	84
uk-2002	18M	261M	8	572	142	46	22	6656	240	682	52
Friendster	66M	1806M	16	6002	1755	1047	742	oom	oom	13743	1161
uk-2007-05	105M	3302M	16	7993	2520	151	106	oom	oom	4211	214

of hosts we used for the distributed algorithms and the running times in seconds. RelaxMap and GossipMap use the directed version of the map equation that includes a PageRank approximation as preprocessing step. To allow for a fair comparison, we only report the running time of the actual clustering step after this preprocessing. As three GossipMap runs on uk-2007-05 crashed, there are less samples. Unfortunately, both the original Infomap implementation and RelaxMap were not able to cluster all instances. On the two largest graphs, 128 GB of RAM were not enough memory (oom).

With 8 or 16 hosts, our distributed algorithms are almost always faster than the sequential and shared-memory parallel algorithms. Note that due to the randomized node order, PLM is slower in our experiments than reported in [22]. DSLM-Map with 8 hosts is more than a factor of 5, for uk-2002 even a factor of 20 faster than RelaxMap and also a factor of 10 faster than GossipMap. DSLM-Mod is faster than DSLM-Map, but the difference is less pronounced than in the weak scaling experiments. This shows the advantage of our algorithmic scheme in combination with the efficient Thrill framework.

Table 2. Average modularity/undirected map equation scores obtained by the respective algorithms.

	Louvain	PLM	DSLM-Mod	DSLM-Mod w/o Cont.	Infomap	Directed Infomap	RelaxMap	GossipMap	DSLM-Map
LiveJournal	0.752	**0.752**	0.749	0.591	**9.899**	9.900	9.943	9.963	9.981
Orkut	0.664	**0.666**	0.658	0.524	11.826	**11.825**	11.849	11.979	11.896
uk-2002	**0.990**	0.990	0.990	0.879	6.458	**6.458**	6.476	6.550	6.468
Friendster	0.622	**0.627**	0.616	0.553	oom	oom	oom	16.271	**14.785**
uk-2007-05	0.996	**0.996**	0.996	0.919	oom	oom	oom	9.034	**8.057**

Table 2 shows the average modularity and map equation scores obtained by the algorithms. We observe that PLM on average finds the best modularity scores with a minor exception on uk-2002 where Louvain finds better values. DSLM-Mod performs slightly worse, DSLM-Mod w/o Cont. significantly worse. This shows that DSLM-Mod w/o Cont., which performed really well on the LFR benchmark graphs, is unsuited for real-world graphs.

The best map equation scores are found by the Infomap algorithm where it finished the computation. Since RelaxMap and GossipMap use the directed map equation, we also include the directed Infomap algorithm to evaluate if using the directed map equations leads to different results. Surprisingly, in some cases Infomap optimizing the directed map equation finds better clusterings with respect to the undirected map equation than the undirected Infomap, though the differences are very small. On the two smallest graphs, RelaxMap finds better clusterings than the distributed algorithms. On uk-2002, RelaxMap is outperformed by DSLM-Map. DSLM-Map finds better clusterings than GossipMap on all graphs except for LiveJournal, on the two largest graphs by a significant margin. Since modularity and map equation feature counterintuitive behavior like the resolution limit, quality scores on their own can be misleading. We therefore also compare the obtained clusterings in terms of ARI.

Table 3. Average similarities in terms of ARI with best clustering found according to the respective quality score. Underlined entries indicate the algorithm which found the clustering with the best score.

	Louvain	PLM	DSLM-Mod	DSLM-Mod w/o Cont.	Infomap	Directed Infomap	RelaxMap	GossipMap	DSLM-Map
LiveJournal	0.571	0.639	0.600	0.179	0.976	0.973	0.376	0.784	0.769
Orkut	0.632	0.625	0.659	0.220	0.919	0.925	0.807	0.491	0.819
uk-2002	0.730	0.724	0.674	0.047	0.986	0.985	0.928	0.698	0.970
Friendster	0.640	0.623	0.569	0.361	oom	oom	oom	0.013	0.748
uk-2007-05	0.873	0.877	0.816	0.279	oom	oom	oom	0.132	0.986

Among all algorithms that optimize the same quality score, we determine for each graph the detected clustering with best score. We use these best clusterings as baselines to which we compare all other detected clusterings that were detected optimizing the same quality measure. Table 3 shows the average similarity in terms of adjusted rand index and highlights which algorithm detected the used baseline clustering. In most cases, this is the sequential baseline.

For modularity, this is in contrast to the results from Table 2 where on average, PLM outperforms Louvain for most graphs. Only on Friendster and uk-2002, the modularity-optimizing algorithm that found the best clustering also has the highest average quality scores. We observe that the modularity-optimizing algorithms do not consistently find the same clustering. Clusterings may vary vastly depending on the random seed. Further, on social networks the adjusted rand indices are smaller than on web graphs. This is probably due to web graphs having a more pronounced community structure. DSLM-Mod produces clusterings that are less similar, but still much more similar than DSLM-Mod w/o Cont., which produces vastly different clusterings. This confirms our observation from Table 2. Omitting the contraction significantly decreases the quality of clusterings on real world graphs.

Infomap is in general much more stable than Louvain with an adjusted rand index close to 1. DSLM-Map produces very similar clusterings on uk-2002. On the LiveJournal and Orkut graphs, the clusterings are slightly less similar. Quite interestingly, the parallel RelaxMap and the distributed GossipMap algorithms produce significantly different clusterings in particular for the two social networks. As the results of the directed Infomap algorithm shows, this is not due to optimizing the directed map equation. We conclude that RelaxMap and GossipMap indeed fail to find similar clusterings reliably.

5   Conclusion

We have introduced two distributed graph clustering algorithms, DSLM-Mod and DSLM-Map, that optimize modularity and map equation, respectively. They are based on the Thrill framework. In an extensive experimental evaluation, we have shown that on LFR benchmark graphs, DSLM-Map achieves excellent results, even better than the sequential Infomap algorithm. For DSLM-Mod, we also evaluate a variant without contraction which has great performance on LFR benchmark graphs. The full DSLM-Mod algorithm with contraction fails to recover the ground truth on LFR benchmark graphs – similar to the sequential Louvain algorithm – but significantly outperforms the variant without contraction on real-world graphs. On real-world graphs, both distributed algorithms find clusterings only slightly different than the sequential algorithms. Compared to GossipMap, the state-of-the-art distributed algorithm for optimizing map equation, DSLM-Map is up to an order of magnitude faster while detecting clusterings that have similar or better map equation scores and are more similar to the clustering with the best map equation score.

In the first local moving phase, synchronous local moving seems to be superior to sequential local moving. Further research is needed to see if this is a phenomenon particular to the LFR graphs we studied or if synchronous local moving could be a way to avoid local maxima when optimizing such quality functions. After the contraction, more careful local moving strategies should be developed though to avoid the problems we see in particular on LFR graphs. Therefore, further research on different local moving strategies seems to be a promising direction.

References

1. Bader, D.A., Meyerhenke, H., Sanders, P., Schulz, C., Kappes, A., Wagner, D.: Benchmarking for graph clustering and partitioning. In: Rokne, J., Alhajj, R. (eds.) Encyclopedia of Social Network Analysis and Mining, pp. 73–82. Springer, Heidelberg (2013). https://doi.org/10.1007/978-1-4614-6170-8
2. Bae, S., Halperin, D., West, J.D., Rosvall, M., Howe, B.: Scalable and efficient flow-based community detection for large-scale graph analysis. ACM Trans. Knowl. Disc. Data **11**(3), 32:1–32:30 (2017)
3. Bae, S., Howe, B.: GossipMap: a distributed community detection algorithm for billion-edge directed graphs. In: Proceedings of the International Conference for High Performance Computing, Networking, Storage and Analysis, pp. 27:1–27:12. ACM Press (2015)
4. Bingmann, T., et al.: Thrill: high-performance algorithmic distributed batch data processing with C++. Technical report, arXiv arXiv:1608.05634 (2016)
5. Blondel, V., Guillaume, J.L., Lambiotte, R., Lefebvre, E.: Fast unfolding of communities in large networks. J. Stat. Mech. Theory Exp. **2008**(10) (2008)
6. Brandes, U., et al.: On modularity clustering. IEEE Trans. Knowl. Data Eng. **20**(2), 172–188 (2008)
7. Buzun, N., et al.: EgoLP: fast and distributed community detection in billion-node social networks. In: Proceedings of the 2014 IEEE International Conference on Data Mining Workshops, pp. 533–540. IEEE Computer Society (2014)
8. Fortunato, S.: Community detection in graphs. Phys. Rep. **486**(3–5), 75–174 (2010)
9. Fortunato, S., Barthélemy, M.: Resolution limit in community detection. Proc. Natl. Acad. Sci. U.S.A. **104**(1), 36–41 (2007)
10. Fortunato, S., Hric, D.: Community detection in networks: a user guide. Phys. Rep. **659**, 1–44 (2016)
11. Good, B.H., de Montjoye, Y.A., Clauset, A.: Performance of modularity maximization in practical contexts. Phys. Rev. E **81**, 046106 (2010)
12. Hamann, M., Meyer, U., Penschuck, M., Wagner, D.: I/O-efficient generation of massive graphs following the LFR benchmark. In: Proceedings of the 19th Meeting on Algorithm Engineering and Experiments (ALENEX 2017). SIAM (2017)
13. Hubert, L., Arabie, P.: Comparing partitions. J. Classif. **2**(1), 193–218 (1985)
14. Karypis, G., Kumar, V.: A parallel algorithm for multilevel graph partitioning and sparse matrix ordering. J. Parallel Distrib. Comput. **48**, 71–95 (1998)
15. Kawamoto, T., Rosvall, M.: Estimating the resolution limit of the map equation in community detection. Phys. Rev. E **91**, 012809 (2015)
16. Lancichinetti, A., Fortunato, S., Radicchi, F.: Benchmark graphs for testing community detection algorithms. Phys. Rev. E **78**(4), 046110 (2008)
17. Leskovec, J., Krevl, A.: SNAP datasets: stanford large network dataset collection, June 2014. http://snap.stanford.edu/data
18. Ling, X., Yang, J., Wang, D., Chen, J., Li, L.: Fast community detection in large weighted networks using graphx in the cloud. In: 18th IEEE International Conference on High Performance Computing and Communications, pp. 1–8. IEEE (2016)
19. Newman, M.E.J., Girvan, M.: Finding and evaluating community structure in networks. Phys. Rev. E **69**(026113), 1–16 (2004)
20. Que, X., Checconi, F., Petrini, F., Gunnels, J.A.: Scalable community detection with the louvain algorithm. In: 29th International Parallel and Distributed Processing Symposium (IPDPS 2015), pp. 28–37. IEEE Computer Society (2015)

21. Rosvall, M., Axelsson, D., Bergstrom, C.T.: The map equation. The Eur. Phys. J. Spec. Top. **178**(1), 13–23 (2009)
22. Staudt, C., Meyerhenke, H.: Engineering parallel algorithms for community detection in massive networks. IEEE Trans. Parallel Distrib. Syst. **27**(1), 171–184 (2016)
23. Wickramaarachchi, C., Frincu, M., Small, P., Prasanna, V.K.: Fast parallel algorithm for unfolding of communities in large graphs. In: Proceedings of the 2014 IEEE High Performance Extreme Computing Conference, pp. 1–6. IEEE (2014)
24. Zeitz, T.: Engineering distributed graph clustering using MapReduce. Master's thesis, Karlsruhe Institute of Technology (2017)
25. Zeng, J., Yu, H.: A study of graph partitioning schemes for parallel graph community detection. Parallel Comput. **58**, 131–139 (2016)

Improved Distributed Algorithm for Graph Truss Decomposition

Venkatesan T. Chakaravarthy[1]([⊠]), Aashish Goyal[2], Prakash Murali[3], Shivmaran S. Pandian[1], and Yogish Sabharwal[1]

[1] IBM Research, Bangalore, India
{vechakra,shivmaran,ysabharwal}@in.ibm.com
[2] Indian Institute of Technology - Delhi, New Delhi, India
aashishgoyal01@gmail.com
[3] Princeton University, Princeton, USA
pmurali@cs.princeton.edu

Abstract. The truss decomposition provides a popular model for discovering cohesive communities in a given network (graph). The problem has been well studied in sequential, shared memory and MapReduce settings. We study the problem on distributed memory systems. Our work builds on two prior algorithms. The first algorithm is optimized in terms of the computational load and communication volume, but it involves a large number of iterations, leading to high load imbalance and synchronization costs. The second algorithm significantly reduces the number of iterations, but at the cost of increasing the load and the volume. We design an algorithm that offers a tradeoff between the two extremes, with the number of iterations being close to that of the second algorithm and load/volume being close to that of the first. We develop an efficient distributed (MPI) implementation based on the new algorithm. We present an experimental evaluation on large real-world graphs. The evaluation shows that the new algorithm outperforms the two prior algorithms on large system sizes with the performance gain ranging up to 2x.

1 Introduction

Discovering cohesive subgraphs or communities in a given graph is an important problem arising in diverse domains ranging from social networks to biological processes. Different models have been proposed for this purpose, among which the truss decomposition [1] is a prominent model. Apart from ensuring that the entities (vertices) in the subgraph are strongly connected among one another, the model also focuses on the strength of the connections (edges). The model is based on the intuition that the edge between two vertices can be considered strong, if they share many common neighboring entities, or alternatively, the edges are included in many triangles. For instance, in a social network, we can say that more common friends two people have, the stronger is their connection.

Given a graph G and an integer k, the k-truss is defined as the largest subgraph, in which every edge is included in at least $(k-2)$ triangles within the

© Springer International Publishing AG, part of Springer Nature 2018
M. Aldinucci et al. (Eds.): Euro-Par 2018, LNCS 11014, pp. 703–717, 2018.
https://doi.org/10.1007/978-3-319-96983-1_50

subgraph. The model provides a hierarchical decomposition of the graph. The whole graph G is the 2-truss, and for $k \geq 3$, the k-truss is contained within the $(k-1)$-truss. For an edge e, the truss number $\tau(e)$ is defined as the largest k such that e belongs to the k-truss. The *truss decomposition problem* is to compute the truss numbers of all the edges.

The truss decomposition model is useful in applications such as community detection [2], visualization of large networks [3], and discovering cohesive structures containing a given set of entities [4]. The truss decomposition model builds on the prior k-core formulation [5] and the recently proposed nucleus decomposition [6] generalizes both the concepts by considering higher order cliques in place of triangles. Given the utility of the model, the truss computation is included as part of the recently proposed Graph Challenge benchmark effort (https://graphchallenge.mit.edu/).

Cohen [1] introduced the truss decomposition model and presented a polynomial time algorithm for constructing the decomposition. Building on the above work, Wang and Cheng [7] described an I/O efficient implementation. Rossi [8], Smith et al. [9], Kabir and Madduri [10,11] and Voegele et al. [12] proposed algorithms for the shared memory and GPU settings. Green et al. evaluated truss computation under GPU setting [13]. Zhang and Parthasarathy [14] independently described the model and used it as a preprocessing step for finding cliques and other dense structures. Chen et al. [15], Cohen [16] and Shao et al. [17] studied the problem on MapReduce setting.

Shared memory systems and GPUs have limitations in terms of the number of cores and/or memory availability, leading to impediments in enhancing the performance further. For instance, on a popular social network graph named `friendster` (1.8 billion edges, 4.2 billion triangles), the execution time achieved in shared memory setting (with 24 cores) is about 25 min [10]. Prior work has also considered MapReduce framework [16], but the execution times are significantly higher, due to framework overheads. Our aim is to achieve execution times of about one minute on graphs of the above size. Towards that goal, we study the problem on distributed memory systems using MPI.

We build on two prior procedures (which we adapt to the MPI setting) and study the problem from an algorithmic perspective. The first procedure, due to Cohen [1], lies at the heart of most prior implementations. While the algorithm is optimized in terms of the computational load, it takes a large number of iteration to converge. In a distributed setting the slow convergence leads to high synchronization costs and load imbalance. Working within the MapReduce framework, Chen et al. [15] proposed an algorithm which takes much lesser number of iterations, at the cost of increased computational load. We denote the two algorithms as MinTruss and PropTruss, respectively. Our main contribution is a new algorithm that offers a tradeoff between the prior algorithms in terms of the two fundamental metrics of number of iterations and load.

Truss computation is performed in two steps: a first phase that enumerates triangles and a second phase that computes the truss numbers of the edges. Triangle enumeration is a well-studied problem and efficient algorithms have been developed (e.g., [18]). We focus on the second phase of truss computation. The second phase is iterative. In each iteration, we need to find the triangles incident on some of the edges. The prior work considers two different implementation settings. The first setting (e.g., [15,17]) explicitly stores the list of triangles enumerated in the first phase and reuses the list in the second phase, whereas the second (e.g., [8,10]) does not store the list of triangles and recomputes. The first setting has higher memory usage due to the presence of large number of triangles, but it facilitates efficient implementation of the second phase. Our implementation is based on the setting of explicitly storing the triangles. In contrast to shared memory systems, we can afford to store the list of triangles, as sufficient memory is available under the distributed memory setting.

Our Contributions

- We propose a new algorithm, denoted Hybrid, that offers a tradeoff between the prior algorithms on the two performance metrics: iterations close to PropTruss and load close to MinTruss. We present an efficient distributed memory (MPI) implementation based on the above algorithm.
- We present an experimental evaluation involving large real-world graphs (having up to 4 billion triangles). The results show that PropTruss performs the best in terms of the number of iterations. Relative to PropTruss, Hybrid is higher by at most 16x factor, whereas MinTruss is as high as 76x. In terms of load, MinTruss performs the best. Relative to MinTruss, Hybrid is higher by at most 2.3x factor, whereas PropTruss is as high as 17x.
- In terms of the execution time (truss number computation), Hybrid achieves better performance on large system sizes. On the largest system size in our study (512 MPI ranks), it outperforms MinTruss and PropTruss by up to 2x and 3.4x factors, respectively. Over the different benchmark graphs, it outperforms the best of the prior algorithms by a factor of up to 2x. The implementation is able to solve graphs having more than billion edges and 4 billion triangles in about a minute.

2   Preliminaries

Let $G = (V, E)$ be an undirected graph. A triple of vertices u, v and w is said to form a triangle, if $\langle u, v \rangle$, $\langle u, w \rangle$ and $\langle v, w \rangle$ are edges in G. We denote the triangle as $\Delta(u, v, w)$. The three edges are said to be *incident* on the triangle and vice versa. Two edges e and e' are called *neighbors*, if they are incident on a common triangle. Let $\gamma(G)$ denote the number triangles in G and for an edge e, let $\gamma(e)$ denote the number of triangles incident on e.

By a *subgraph*, we refer to a graph $H = (V', E')$ such that $V' \subseteq V$ and $E' \subseteq (V' \times V') \cap E$; we denote this as $H \subseteq G$. The size of a subgraph H is measured by the number of edges in it. For a subgraph H and an edge e found in H, the *support of e within H*, denoted $\text{supp}_H(e)$, is defined as the number of triangles in H incident on e. For an integer $k \geq 2$, the *k-truss* of G is defined as the largest subgraph $H \subseteq G$ such that every edge e in H has $\text{supp}_H(e) \geq k - 2$ (the k-truss may not be connected). The k-truss of a graph is unique.

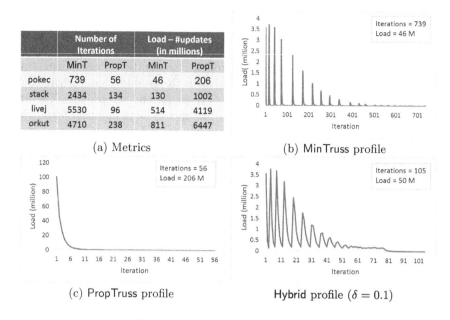

(a) Metrics

(b) MinTruss profile

(c) PropTruss profile

Hybrid profile ($\delta = 0.1$)

Fig. 1. Analysis of prior algorithms

Let κ be the largest value such that the κ-truss is non-empty. The 2-truss is simply the whole graph G. The k-trusses, for $k \geq 2$, form a hierarchical decomposition: $G =$ 2-truss $\supseteq$ 3-truss $\supseteq$ 4-truss $\supseteq \cdots \supseteq \kappa$-truss. For an edge e, the *truss number of e*, denoted $\tau(e)$, is defined as the largest value k such that e is found in the k-truss. Given a graph G, the truss decomposition problem is to construct the hierarchical decomposition; equivalently, the goal is to compute the truss number $\tau(e)$ for all the edges.

3   Prior Algorithms

In this section, we present an outline of the two prior algorithms MinTruss [1] and PropTruss [15]. Both the algorithms involve a preprocessing phase, where they compute the $\mathsf{supp}_G(e)$ for all the edges via enumerating triangles of the input graph G. Triangle enumeration is a well-studied problem and efficient techniques have been developed (e.g., [18]). We describe the algorithms assuming that the supports have already been computed. For the clarity of exposition, we present the algorithms at a conceptual level, deferring distributed aspects and other implementations details to Sect. 5. A brief discussion on the preprocessing procedure can also be found in the same section.

Algorithm MinTruss: For each edge e, the algorithm maintains an upperbound $\widehat{\tau}(e)$ on the true truss number $\tau(e)$; it is initialized as $\widehat{\tau}(e) = \mathsf{supp}_G(e) + 2$. The algorithm marks all edges as *not settled* and proceeds iteratively. In each iteration, among the edges not settled, select the edges with the least truss value and declare them to be settled. We then update the truss values of their neighbors in the following manner. Let $e = \langle u, v \rangle$ be a selected edge. For each triangle $\Delta(u, v, w)$ incident on e, if both $\langle u, w \rangle$ and $\langle v, w \rangle$ are not settled already, then decrement the truss values $\widehat{\tau}(u, w)$ and $\widehat{\tau}(v, w)$ by one. Proceed in the above manner till all the edges are settled.

Intuitively, imagine that the settled edges are deleted from the graph. The deletion of an edge e destroys the triangles incident on it. When a triangle is destroyed, the other two edges lose the support of the triangle. So, we decrement their truss values, provided e is the first edge to be deleted among the three edges. We can show that for each edge e, the truss value $\widehat{\tau}(e)$ gets decremented monotonically and becomes the true truss number $\tau(e)$ before termination.

Algorithm PropTruss: In each iteration of the MinTruss algorithm, only the neighbors of the edges with the least truss value get updated. As a result, the algorithm incurs a large number of iterations and converges slowly. Chen et al. [15] proposed an algorithm that exhibits better parallelism by taking much lesser number of iterations. We denote the algorithm as PropTruss. We rephrase and present a sketch of the algorithm.

The core idea is to select every edge e whose truss value changed in the prior iteration and propagate its new truss value to its neighbors. Since edges having various truss values propagate simultaneously, the update operation becomes more intricate, as against the simple decrement operation under the MinTruss algorithm. For a triangle $\Delta(u, v, w)$, define the truss number of the triangle as $\tau(u, v, w) = \min\{\tau(u, v), \tau(u, w), \tau(v, w)\}$. The new update operation is based on the following proposition. The truss numbers can be seen as stationary solutions satisfying the condition given by the proposition.

Proposition 1. *For any edge* $e = \langle u, v \rangle$, *we have that*

$$\tau(e) = \max\{j \ : \ |\{\Delta(u, v, x) \ : \ \tau(u, v, x) \ge j\}| \ge j - 2\}$$

For each triangle $\Delta(u, v, w)$, the algorithm maintains an upperbound $\widehat{\tau}(u, v, w) \ge \min\{\widehat{\tau}(u, v), \widehat{\tau}(u, w), \widehat{\tau}(v, w)\}$. These are initialized to ∞. We ensure that for any edge $e = \langle u, v \rangle$, a condition analogous to the proposition is true throughout the execution of the algorithm:

$$\widehat{\tau}(e) = \max\{j \ : \ |\{\Delta(u, v, x) \ : \ \widehat{\tau}(u, v, x) \ge j\}| \ge j - 2\} \tag{1}$$

The PropTruss algorithm can be summarized as follows. In each iteration, consider all the edges $e = \langle u, v \rangle$ whose truss value changed in the prior iteration. For each triangle $\Delta(u, v, w)$ incident on e, if $\widehat{\tau}(e) < \widehat{\tau}(u, v, w)$, then we update the truss value of the triangle to $\widehat{\tau}(e)$. As a result, the truss values of the edges $\langle u, w \rangle$ and $\langle v, w \rangle$ may no longer satisfy condition (1). So, for both the edges, we recompute the right hand side and update their truss values accordingly. We proceed in this manner, until a stable solution is reached, wherein the truss value of none of the edges changes. In the first iteration, all the edges get selected and perform the above propagate operation.

Comparison of MinTruss **and** PropTruss: We compare the algorithms using two fundamental metrics: (i) number of iterations; (ii) *load* - the total number of updates (one update is counted whenever an edge changes the truss value of a triangle and propagates to the other two edges of the triangle). In a distributed setting, higher number of iterations leads to higher synchronization cost and load imbalance. The second metric determines the computational load and the communication volume.

The PropTruss algorithm is superior on the first metric, because edges from multiple truss levels propagate their truss value simultaneously leading to faster convergence. On the other hand, the MinTruss algorithm is better in terms of load. The reason is that any edge e propagates its truss value only once during the entire execution (when its truss value $\hat{\tau}(e)$ settles to the true truss number $\tau(e)$), whereas the same edge may propagate multiple times under PropTruss.

Figure 1(a) illustrates the above tradeoff by providing the two metrics on four sample graphs drawn from our experimental evaluation (properties are graphs can be found in Sect. 6). We can see that PropTruss involves significantly lesser number of iterations, but MinTruss is superior on load.

4   Algorithm **Hybrid**

In this section, we present a new algorithm, denoted Hybrid, that strikes a tradeoff between the two prior algorithms. It aims at achieving load close to MinTruss and the number of iterations close to PropTruss.

The new algorithm is motivated from an analysis of prior algorithms in terms of their load profiles, a plot that shows the load incurred in each iteration of the algorithm. As an illustration, Fig. 1(b) and (c) provide the load profiles of the two algorithms on the **pokec** graph. We can see that PropTruss incurs the maximum load in the first iteration and the load monotonically decreases until the algorithm converges. On the other hand, in the case of MinTruss, the iterations are grouped into many blocks; within each block the load is maximum in the initial iteration and then decreases monotonically. Each block corresponds a truss value k and all the edges with the truss number $\tau(e) = k$ settle in the successive iterations of the block. While the MinTruss algorithm involves a large number of iterations, most of the iterations incur very little load. The core idea behind the Hybrid algorithm is to eliminate the low-load iterations, without compromising much on the overall load incurred.

Algorithm Hybrid: Like the prior algorithms, we maintain an upperbound $\hat{\tau}(e)$ on the true truss number $\tau(e)$, for all edges e, and initialize it to $\mathsf{supp}_G(e)+2$. Let $k_{\min}$ and $k_{\max}$ denote the minimum and the maximum truss value $\hat{\tau}(e)$ among all the edges e. We imagine that each truss value is a bucket and each edge e resides in the bucket corresponding to its truss value $\hat{\tau}(e)$. As the algorithm proceeds, whenever $\hat{\tau}(e)$ decreases, we visualize that the edge moves from its current bucket to a lower bucket. We maintain a set of edges called the *active set*, denoted Act. The edges in the set would propagate their truss values in each iteration. The edges belonging to the active set are drawn from a window of

Pre-processing: Compute $\text{supp}_G(e)$ for all edges.
Initialization:
For each triangle $\Delta(u, v, w)$, set $\hat{\tau}(u, v, w) \leftarrow \infty$
For all $e = \langle u, v \rangle \in E$
  Set $\hat{\tau}(e) \leftarrow \text{supp}_G(e) + 2$.
  Set $g_e \leftarrow \hat{\tau}(e) - 2$ and for $0 \leq j < \hat{\tau}(e)$, set $h_e(j) \leftarrow 0$
Truss Computation:
$k_{\min} \leftarrow \min\{\hat{\tau}(e) : e \in E\}$ and $k_{\max} \leftarrow \max\{\hat{\tau}(e) : e \in E\}$
Window $W \leftarrow [k_{\min}, k_{\min}]$
$\text{Act} \leftarrow \{e : \hat{\tau}(e) \in W\}$ /* Active set */
$\gamma_{\max} \leftarrow 0$
Loop   /* Iterations */
  if($\text{Act} = \emptyset$ and $W = [k_{\min}, k_{\max}]$) then **terminate.**
  Execute procedure *Window-Expansion.*
  For each $e = \langle u, v \rangle \in \text{Act}$
    For each triangle $\Delta(u, v, w)$ with $\hat{\tau}(e) < \hat{\tau}(u, v, w)$
      $\text{val}_{\text{old}} \leftarrow \hat{\tau}(u, v, w)$ and $\hat{\tau}(u, v, w) \leftarrow \hat{\tau}(e)$ and $\text{val}_{\text{new}} \leftarrow \hat{\tau}(u, v, w)$
      Update($\langle u, w \rangle, \text{val}_{\text{old}}, \text{val}_{\text{new}}$) and Update($\langle v, w \rangle, \text{val}_{\text{old}}, \text{val}_{\text{new}}$)
  $\text{Act} \leftarrow \{e : \hat{\tau}(e) \in W$ and $\hat{\tau}(e)$ changed in the current iteration$\}$
  Let $\gamma(\text{Act}) = \sum_{e \in \text{Act}} \gamma(e)$, where $\gamma(e)$ is the number of triangles on e
  $\gamma_{\max} \leftarrow \max\{\gamma_{\max}, \gamma(\text{Act})\}$.
Procedure *Window-Expansion:*
Let k be the last bucket in W.
while($(\gamma(\text{Act}) \leq \delta \cdot \gamma_{\max})$ and $(k \neq k_{\max})$)
    $W = [k_{\min}, k + 1]$ and $\text{Act} \leftarrow \text{Act} \cup \{e : \hat{\tau}(e) = k + 1\}$ and $k \leftarrow k + 1$
Procedure Update($e', \text{val}_{\text{old}}, \text{val}_{\text{new}}$)
  Case 1 [$\text{val}_{\text{old}} \geq \hat{\tau}(e')$ and $\text{val}_{\text{new}} \geq \hat{\tau}(e')$]: do nothing.
  Case 2 [$\text{val}_{\text{old}} \geq \hat{\tau}(e')$ and $\text{val}_{\text{new}} < \hat{\tau}(e')$]: Decr. $g_{e'}$; incr. $h_{e'}(\text{val}_{\text{new}})$
  Case 3 [$\text{val}_{\text{old}} < \hat{\tau}(e')$ and $\text{val}_{\text{new}} < \hat{\tau}(e')$]: Decr. $h_{e'}(\text{val}_{\text{old}})$; incr. $h_{e'}(\text{val}_{\text{new}})$
  if($g_{e'} < \hat{\tau}(e') - 2$) then decr. $\hat{\tau}(e')$ and $g_{e'} \leftarrow g_{e'} + h_{e'}(\hat{\tau}(e'))$.

Fig. 2. Algorithm Hybrid

buckets, denoted W. To start with, the window consists of only the bucket $k_{\min}$, i.e., $W = [k_{\min}, k_{\min}]$. In each iteration, we construct the active set by including all edges e such that $\hat{\tau}(e)$ changed in the prior iteration and e belongs to one of the buckets in the window.

In the next and the crucial step, we use an appropriate heuristic to estimate whether the current active set would result in the load being too low. In this case, we expand the window by including the next bucket, and add all the edges in the bucket to the active set. We repeat the above process until the heuristic determines that the load would be sufficiently high.

We proceed in the above manner until all the buckets have been added and the window becomes the complete range $[k_{\min}, k_{\max}]$. At this stage, we continue with the iterations until the active set becomes empty; namely, the truss value does not change for any of the edges. A pseudocode for Hybrid is given in Fig. 2.

Window Expansion Heuristic: We develop a heuristic for window expansion by estimating the load to be incurred on the current active set Act. Let $e = \langle u, v \rangle$ be an edge in Act. For each triangle $\Delta(u, v, w)$ incident on e, we update the two neighboring edges provided $\widehat{\tau}(u, v) < \widehat{\tau}(u, v, w)$; let $\widetilde{\gamma}(e)$ denote the number of such triangles. The exact load under Act is the sum of $\widetilde{\gamma}(e)$ for all edges $e \in$ Act. Unfortunately, $\widetilde{\gamma}(e)$ changes dynamically and its computation requires an expensive scan of the triangles incident on e. We avoid the scan by using the upperbound $\gamma(e)$ (the number of triangles incident on e). In contrast to $\widetilde{\gamma}(e)$, the quantity $\gamma(e)$ is static and can be computed as part of the preprocessing stage. Define $\gamma(\text{Act}) = \sum_{e \in \text{Act}} \gamma(e)$. We take $\gamma(\text{Act})$ as an estimate on the load incurred by the set Act.

We determine if the above estimate is high enough by comparing against the maximum number of triangles encountered in the prior iterations. Meaning, let Act_j denote the active set in a prior iteration j and let $\gamma(\text{Act}_j)$ denote aggregate number of triangles incident on the edges in Act_j. We keep track of the quantity $\gamma_{\max} = \max_j \gamma(\text{Act}_j)$. The heuristic estimates that the load on Act would be low, if the ratio of $\gamma(\text{Act})$ to $\gamma_{\max}$ is below a threshold δ. In this case, we expand the window by including the next bucket. The process is repeated until the estimate on the load becomes sufficiently high. In the above procedure, δ is a tunable parameter. Pseudocode for the procedure can be found in Fig. 2.

Update Operation: As in the case of the PropTruss algorithm, our update operation is also based on Proposition 1. Recall that in the PropTruss algorithm, whenever an edge $e = \langle u, v \rangle$ updates the truss value $\widehat{\tau}(u, v, w)$ for a triangle $\Delta(u, v, w)$, the truss values are recomputed for the other two edges $\langle u, w \rangle$ and $\langle v, w \rangle$ via evaluating the right hand side of condition (1). We develop a more efficient method that avoids the expensive recomputation by maintaining suitable histograms, as described below.

Consider any edge $e = \langle u, v \rangle$. We group the triangles incident on e based on their truss values and maintain a histogram consisting of two components, $h_e(\cdot)$ and g_e. For $j < \widehat{\tau}(e)$, $h_e(j)$ stores the number of triangles with truss value exactly j, whereas g_e keeps track of the number of triangles with the truss values at least $\widehat{\tau}(e)$. Namely:

$$\forall j < \widehat{\tau}(e): \quad h_e(j) = |\{\Delta(u, v, x) : \widehat{\tau}(u, v, x) = j\}| \tag{2}$$

$$\text{and} \quad g_e = |\{\Delta(u, v, x) : \widehat{\tau}(u, v, x) \geq \widehat{\tau}(e)\}| \tag{3}$$

For each triangle $\Delta(u, v, w)$, we initialize $\widehat{\tau}(u, v, w) = \infty$. For each edge e, the histogram is initialized as $g_e = \widehat{\tau}(e) - 2$ and for all $j < \widehat{\tau}(e)$, $h_e(j) = 0$.

The iterations are executed as follows. Consider each edge $\langle u, v \rangle$ found in the active set. For each triangle $\Delta(u, v, w)$ incident on e, if $\widehat{\tau}(e) < \widehat{\tau}(u, v, w)$, we update $\widehat{\tau}(u, v, w) = \widehat{\tau}(e)$. Let val_{old} denote the value of $\widehat{\tau}(u, v, w)$ before the update was performed and val_{new} be the new value $(= \widehat{\tau}(e))$. We update the histogram and $\widehat{\tau}(\cdot)$ value for the other two edges $\langle u, w \rangle$ and $\langle v, w \rangle$ in such a manner that the conditions (1), (2) and (3) continue to be satisfied.

Let e' be one of other two edges. Before the update, the triangle is counted as part of $g(e')$, if $\text{val}_{\text{old}} \geq \hat{\tau}(e')$ and as part of $h_{e'}(\text{val}_{\text{old}})$, if $\text{val}_{\text{old}} < \hat{\tau}(e')$. Similarly, after the update the triangle is counted as part of $g(e')$, if $\text{val}_{\text{new}} \geq \hat{\tau}(e')$ and as part of $h_{e'}(\text{val}_{\text{new}})$, if $\text{val}_{\text{new}} < \hat{\tau}(e')$. Thus, based on the value of val_{old} and val_{new}, we adjust (increment/decrement) $g(e')$, $h_{e'}(\text{val}_{\text{old}})$ and $h_{e'}(\text{val}_{\text{new}})$; see Fig. 2. We then decrement $\hat{\tau}(e')$, if $g_{e'} < \hat{\tau}(e') - 2$. Furthermore, in this case, $h_{e'}(\hat{\tau}(e'))$ must now be counted as part of $g_{e'}$ and we add $h_{e'}(\hat{\tau}(e'))$ to $g_{e'}$. Our implementation of PropTruss also uses the above histogram strategy.

Discussion: The two prior algorithms can be realized by modifying the window expansion heuristic: PropTruss via initializing the window to include all the buckets; MinTruss via expanding the window with the next bucket only when the active set becomes empty. By tuning the parameter δ, we get a spectrum of algorithms offering tradeoff between the two extremes. On one hand, restricting the active set to a window of buckets leads to lesser load than PropTruss. On the other hand, ensuring that the load is high enough in each iteration leads to faster convergence and lesser number of iterations than MinTruss. We can prove the following tradeoff for any value of $\delta \in [0, 1]$:

$$\text{Number of iterations : PropTruss} \leq \text{Hybrid} \leq \text{MinTruss}$$

$$\text{Load : MinTruss} \leq \text{Hybrid} \leq \text{PropTruss}$$

Figure 1(c) shows the load profile for the pokec graph with $\delta = 0.1$. We can see that the number of iterations is close to PropTruss and the load is close to MinTruss. The profile also exhibits a blocked behavior, but the load in any iteration is sufficiently high.

At a high level, computing the truss decomposition shares similarities with the single source shortest path problem (SSSP). Similar to truss computation, prior algorithms for SSSP maintain an upperbound on the shortest distances which get iteratively refined. Here, we can draw parallels between edges and the truss numbers on one hand, and the vertices and the shortest distances on the other. Viewed from this perspective, the MinTruss and the PropTruss algorithms are analogous to the well-known Dijkstra's and the Bellman-Ford algorithms, respectively. The Hybrid algorithm is inspired by the Δ-stepping algorithm [19].

5 Distributed Implementation

Graph Distribution: We distribute the input graph $G = (V, E)$ among the processors (MPI ranks) using a degree-based ordering proposed in prior work in the context of efficient triangle counting (e.g., [18]). For a vertex u, let $\deg(u)$ denote its degree. Arrange the vertices in the increasing order of degrees, breaking ties via lexicographic identifiers. Namely, we say that $u \prec v$, if either $\deg(u) < \deg(v)$, or $\deg(u) = \deg(v)$ and $\text{id}(u) < \text{id}(v)$. Let $\deg_+(u)$ be the number of neighbors of u with $v \succ u$.

We assign each vertex u to a processor chosen uniformly at random, called the owner of u. We also assign ownership for each edge $e = \langle u, v \rangle$: assign e to the owner of u, if $u \prec v$, and to the owner of v, if $v \prec u$. Let $V(p)$ and $E(p)$ denote the set of vertices and edges owned by a processor p.

For a processor p, let $\gamma(p)$ denote the aggregate number of triangles incident on the edges owned by p, i.e., $\gamma(p) = \sum_{e \in E(p)} \gamma(e)$. The quantity $\gamma(p)$ is an indicator of the number of updates performed by the processor during the truss computation. We can derive a bound on $\gamma(p)$ follows. For each vertex $u \in V(p)$, the processor owns $\deg_+(u)$ edges incident on u; each of these edges can be incident on at most $\deg(u)$ triangles. Hence, $\gamma(p)$ is at most $\sum_{u \in V(p)} \deg(u)\deg_+(u)$. Intuitively, if u is a low-degree vertex, then $\deg_+(u)$ is also low, whereas if u is a high-degree vertex, then it cannot have too many neighbors succeeding it in the ordering and so, $\deg_+(u)$ is again low. As a result, the above distribution helps in achieving good load balance.

Preprocessing - Triangle Enumeration: All the three algorithms involve a preprocessing stage of computing the support of the edges, via triangle enumeration. For this purpose, we adopt an efficient strategy proposed in prior work (e.g., [18]). We say that a pair of edges $\langle u, v \rangle$ and $\langle u, w \rangle$ is a *monotone wedge*, $v \succ u$ and $w \succ u$. The strategy is to enumerate all the monotone wedges $\langle u, v \rangle$ and $\langle u, w \rangle$ and test whether $\langle v, w \rangle$ is also an edge. The advantage with this approach is that the number of wedges considered is only $\sum_{u \in V} \deg_+^2(u)$.

In our distributed implementation, each processor p builds a hash table over edges $E(p)$ owned by it. For each vertex $u \in V(p)$, the processor p enumerates all monotone wedges $\langle u, v \rangle$ and $\langle u, w \rangle$, and sends the triple (u, v, w) to the processor owning v, say q. Using its hash table, the processor q checks if the pair $\langle v, w \rangle$ is an edge in G and if so, the triangle $\Delta(u, v, w)$ has been discovered. In this case, q increments $\mathsf{supp}_G(v, w)$ and sends the triple (u, v, w) back to p, upon receiving which p increments both $\mathsf{supp}_G(u, v)$ and $\mathsf{supp}_G(u, w)$. In the above process, for each edge e, its owner stores the list of triangles incident on e.

Truss Computation: The algorithms are implemented under the bulk synchronous parallel model. For each edge $e = \langle u, v \rangle$, the owner of e maintains $\widehat{\tau}(e)$, histogram $h_e(\cdot)$ and g_e. In addition, for each triangle $\Delta(u, v, w)$ incident on e, the processor also stores a local copy of $\widehat{\tau}(u, v, w)$. In each iteration, for each edge $e = \langle u, v \rangle \in \mathsf{Act}$, the owner of e propagates the new truss value $\widehat{\tau}(e)$, as follows. For each triangle $\Delta(u, v, w)$ with $\widehat{\tau}(e) < \widehat{\tau}(u, v, w)$, p sends update messages to the owners of the edges $\langle u, w \rangle$ and $\langle v, w \rangle$, wherein the message consists of the identification of the triangle $\Delta(u, v, w)$, as well as the new value of $\widehat{\tau}(u, v, w)$. The messages are exchanged using the $MPI\_Alltoallv$ primitive. Each processor executes the update procedure on the received messages, updating the edge truss values, histograms, as well as the local copies of the triangle truss values. The buckets and the active sets are stored in a distributed manner: each processor p maintains the buckets and active sets restricted to the edges owned by it.

6   Experimental Evaluation

Experimental Setup: The experiments were conducted on a cluster of Power-8 nodes (20 physical cores, $512\,\mathrm{GB}$ memory, $4\,\mathrm{GHz}$) connected via InfiniBand in

Graphs	n	m	Δ	κ
pokec	1.6	31	34	29
stackoverflow	2.6	36	114	79
livejournal	4.8	69	292	362
orkut	3.1	117	633	78
flickr	2.3	33	841	297

Graphs	n	m	Δ	κ
gplus	0.11	14	1076	418
uk-2002	18.5	298	4607	944
hollywood-2009	1.14	114	4918	2209
friendster	65.6	1806	4244	129

Fig. 3. Graph properties: number of vertices (n), edges (m) and triangles (Δ), all in millions. The maximum truss number κ is also shown.

	Iterations			Normalized load			Normalized max-load		
	MinT	Hybrid	PropT	MinT	Hybrid	PropT	MinT	Hybrid	PropT
stack	2434	471	134	1.1	1.4	8.8	13.3	7.5	16.9
livej	5530	600	96	1.8	4.1	14.1	83.9	37.7	25.9
orkut	4710	523	238	1.3	1.5	10.2	5.0	3.1	12.2
flickr	10188	2739	178	1.2	2.5	19.2	77.5	45.9	42.8
gplus	13574	3597	222	1.2	2.7	21.5	114.3	75.9	90.3
uk	35080	4407	4404	2.0	2.4	6.5	13.8	6.9	8.8
hollywood	12629	1657	165	2.6	2.8	7.0	30.0	17.2	14.6
friendster	7430	706	706	1.2	1.5	7.4	1.7	1.6	7.6

Fig. 4. Basic metrics

a fat-tree topology. We launch 16 MPI ranks per node, each mapped to a core. We use 2 to 32 nodes, leading to a total of 32 to 512 MPI ranks.

The dataset consists of eight representative real-world graphs obtained from the SNAP repository[1], the Koblenz network collection[2] and the University of SuiteSparse Matrix Collection[3]; the uk-2002 and hollywood-2009 graphs are based on the prior work [20]. Four of the graphs are medium-sized with more than 100 million triangles, and the other four are large graphs with more than billion triangles. Figure 3 shows the properties of the graphs, including the small pokec graph used as a case study in earlier discussion (the graphs are sorted by the number of triangles).

Prior work has presented efficient shared memory implementations for truss computation [10,13]. These are based on the MinTruss algorithm and provide optimizations for the above setting. Our objective is to study the two extremes of MinTruss and PropTruss, and the effect of the tradeoff offered by Hybrid under distributed memory setting. Towards the objective, our experimental evaluation focuses on the three algorithms.

Recall that Hybrid offers a tradeoff between MinTruss and PropTruss, controlled by δ. We experimented with different values of the parameter on different graphs and system sizes, and found that setting $\delta = 0.1$ offers the best tradeoff. All the experiments discussed below use the above setting of the parameter.

Basic Metrics: We first evaluate the algorithms on the two basic metrics: number of iterations and load (number of updates). We normalize the load by $\gamma(G)$, the number of triangles in the graph. An ideal value for normalized load

---

[1] http://snap.stanford.edu/data.

[2] http://konect.uni-koblenz.de/.

[3] https://sparse.tamu.edu/.

is one unit, which is attained when an algorithm performs only a single update per triangle.

The results, shown in Fig. 4, confirm our earlier analysis (Sect. 3). We can see that MinTruss incurs a large number of iterations, whereas PropTruss takes much lesser number of iterations, with the reduction being as high as 76x (on hollywood). The above trend is reversed on the metric of load. The MinTruss algorithm performs the best with near-ideal load, whereas the quantity is as high as 22 units for PropTruss. The Hybrid algorithm strikes a balance between the two algorithms. In terms of the number of iterations, relative to PropTruss, Hybrid is higher by at most 16x factor (whereas MinTruss is as high as 76x). In terms of load, relative to MinTruss, Hybrid is higher by at most 2.3x factor (whereas PropTruss is as high as 17x).

Another metric of importance is the max-load, which quantifies the load balance characteristics. We compute the max-load by finding the maximum load among the processors in each iteration and summing up across all the iterations. An ideal value of the metric is $\gamma(G)/P$, where P is the number of processors; We normalize the max-load by this quantity. Figure 4 presents the normalized max-load at $P = 512$ (the largest system size in our study). In spite of achieving near-ideal load, the MinTruss algorithm incurs the highest max-load in most cases. The reason is that the load gets spread over the large number of iterations, leading to load imbalance. The PropTruss and the Hybrid algorithms involve lesser number of iterations and perform comparatively better.

stack	PreP	MinT	Hybrid	PropT		livej	PreP	MinT	Hybrid	PropT		orkut	PreP	MinT	Hybrid	PropT		flickr	PreP	MinT	Hybrid	PropT
32	10.5	4.7	5.7	28.3		32	18.3	22.1	30.9	94.5		32	64.5	30.9	39.5	235		32	55.4	69.7	96.9	562.6
64	5.0	2.6	2.8	12.6		64	8.9	15.5	16.7	43.3		64	31.2	14.7	17.9	105		64	26.5	49.7	54.93	256
128	2.4	1.7	1.5	6.2		128	4.2	12.5	10.4	20.9		128	15.2	7.5	8.4	46.9		128	12.8	39.4	35.11	123
256	1.1	1.3	1.0	3.2		256	1.9	10.9	7.0	10.6		256	7.5	4.8	4.3	21.4		256	6.29	35.1	25.3	60.6
512	0.6	1.4	0.7	2.0		512	0.9	10.8	5.3	5.9		512	3.4	3.4	2.4	10.3		512	3.3	33.2	20.8	34.7

gplus	PreP	MinT	Hybrid	PropT		uk	PreP	MinT	Hybrid	PropT		hollyw	PreP	MinT	Hybrid	PropT		friend	PreP	MinT	Hybrid	PropT
32	77.8	119	164	990		32	344.2	266	309	599		32	335	416	428	1081		32	1219	359	453	1246
64	44.3	93.4	110	575.0		64	165	151	161.2	341		64	167	272.3	255.5	507		64	584	148	187	653
128	25.5	78.1	78.6	350.3		128	78.2	91.2	85.1	175		128	85.8	179	153.8	272		128	266	70.2	88.6	343
256	16	70.5	64.8	226.3		256	38	61.3	48.9	93.2		256	48.6	132.8	101.5	166		256	130	33.9	41.5	162
512	8.74	65.6	50.0	118.2		512	17.5	46.8	28.4	44.9		512	24.3	100.9	67.5	86.5		512	62.7	17.5	19.2	71.5

Fig. 5. Execution time (seconds) on the benchmark graphs on ranks from 32 to 512. The best running times are highlighted.

Truss Computation: Execution Time: We next evaluate the truss computation time of the algorithms on different systems sizes (32 to 512 ranks). The results are shown in Fig. 5 (the running times are for a single run of the algorithms). The best execution time is highlighted for each configuration. The figure also includes the preprocessing time (triangle enumeration), which is common for all the algorithms.

We can observe that the MinTruss algorithm performs the best on small system sizes. However, as the system size increases, the algorithm suffers from

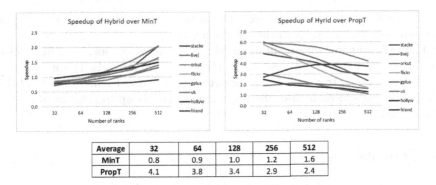

Average	32	64	128	256	512
MinT	0.8	0.9	1.0	1.2	1.6
PropT	4.1	3.8	3.4	2.9	2.4

Fig. 6. Speedup of Hybrid over MinTruss and PropTruss. The average speedup on the eight graphs at different ranks are also shown.

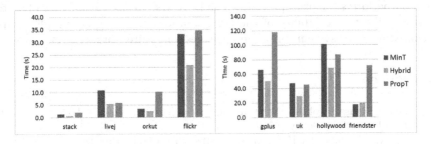

Fig. 7. Truss computation time(s) at 512 ranks

synchronization costs and load imbalance arising out of the large number of iterations, resulting in degradation of the performance. Except friendster, the Hybrid algorithm outperforms both the prior algorithms on larger systems sizes.

The friendster graph is one of the largest in terms of the number of triangles. However, the maximum truss number κ is comparatively smaller leading to lesser number of iterations for MinTruss. Consequently, the synchronization cost and load imbalance are lesser, and so, MinTruss outperforms Hybrid on all the system sizes in the study. We expect Hybrid to outperform MinTruss at system sizes larger than 512 ranks.

Figure 6 provides the speedup of Hybrid over MinTruss and PropTruss on the different graphs, as the number of ranks is varied from 32 to 512. The speedup is measured as a ratio of the running time of the competing algorithm (MinTruss or PropTruss) to that of Hybrid. The figure also provides the average speedup over the eight benchmark graphs across 32 to 512 ranks. With respect to MinTruss, the speedup is less than one on small systems sizes (since MinTruss is superior). On the largest system size of 512, Hybrid outperforms MinTruss, with the speedup ranging up to 2x with the average being 1.6x. With respect to PropTruss, Hybrid achieves better speedup at smaller ranks. As the number of ranks increases, the speedup decreases because of increase in synchronization cost and load imbalance under Hybrid. Nevertheless, we see that on the largest system size of 512, the speedup is up to 4.2x with the average being 2.4x.

Figure 7 compares the execution times on the largest system size of 512 ranks. We can see that Hybrid outperforms MinTruss and PropTruss by factors of up to 2x (on `stackoverflow`) and 4x (on `orkut`), respectively. Taking the best of the prior algorithms in each case, the performance gain is up to a factor of 2x (on `stackoverflow`).

7   Conclusions

We presented a new distributed algorithm for truss decomposition that offers a tradeoff between two prior procedures in terms of the metrics of number of iterations and the number updates. Our experimental study shows that the algorithm outperforms the prior procedures on large system sizes by a factor of up to 2x. Improving the scalability of the algorithm and exploring Hybrid algorithm on shared memory systems are useful avenues for future work.

References

1. Cohen, J.: Trusses: cohesive subgraphs for social network analysis. Technical report, National Security Agency (2008)
2. Saito, K., Yamada, T., Kazama, K.: Extracting communities from complex networks by the k-dense method. IEICE Trans. Fundam. Electron. Commun. Comput. Sci. **91**(11), 3304–3311 (2008)
3. Alvarez-Hamelin, J., Dall'Asta, L., Barrat, A., Vespignani, A.: Large scale networks fingerprinting and visualization using the k-core decomposition. In: NIPS (2005)
4. Huang, X., Lakshmanan, L., Yu, J., Cheng, H.: Approximate closest community search in networks. Proc. VLDB Endow. **9**(4), 276–287 (2015)
5. Seidman, S.: Network structure and minimum degree. Soc. Netw. **5**(3), 269–287 (1983)
6. Sariyuce, A., Seshadhri, C., Pinar, A., Catalyurek, U.: Finding the hierarchy of dense subgraphs using nucleus decompositions. In: WWW (2015)
7. Wang, J., Cheng, J.: Truss decomposition in massive networks. Proc. VLDB Endow. **5**(9), 812–823 (2012)
8. Rossi, R.A.: Fast triangle core decomposition for mining large graphs. In: Tseng, V.S., Ho, T.B., Zhou, Z.-H., Chen, A.L.P., Kao, H.-Y. (eds.) PAKDD 2014. LNCS (LNAI), vol. 8443, pp. 310–322. Springer, Cham (2014). https://doi.org/10.1007/978-3-319-06608-0_26
9. Smith, S., Liu, X., Ahmed, N., Tom, A., Petrini, F., Karypis, G.: Truss decompositions on shared-memory parallel systems. In: HPEC (2017)
10. Kabir, H., Madduri, K.: Shared-memory graph truss decomposition. In: HiPC (2017)
11. Kabir, H., Madduri, K.: Parallel k-truss decomposition on multicore systems. In: HPEC (2017)
12. Voegele, C., Lu, Y., Pai, S., Pingali, K.: Parallel triangle counting and k-truss identification using graph-centric methods. In: HPEC (2017)
13. Green, O., et al.: Quickly finding a truss in a haystack. In: HPEC (2017)

14. Zhang, Y., Parthasarathy, S.: Extracting analyzing and visualizing triangle k-core motifs within networks. In: ICDE (2012)
15. Chen, P., Chou, C., Chen, M.: Distributed algorithms for k-truss decomposition. In: IEEE International Conference on Big Data (2014)
16. Cohen, J.: Graph twiddling in a MapReduce world. Comput. Sci. Eng. 11(4), 29–41 (2009)
17. Shao, Y., Chen, L., Cui, B.: Efficient cohesive subgraphs detection in parallel. In: SIGMOD (2014)
18. Kolda, T., Pinar, A., Plantenga, T., Seshadhri, C., Task, C.: Counting triangles in massive graphs with MapReduce. SIAM J. Sci. Comput. 36(5), S48–S77 (2014)
19. Meyer, U., Sandersr, P.: Δ-stepping: a parallelizable shortest path algorithm. J. Algorithms 49(1), 114–152 (2003)
20. Boldi, P., Vigna, S.: The webgraph framework i: compression techniques. In: WWW (2004)

Parallel Numerical Methods and Applications

Exploiting Data Sparsity for Large-Scale Matrix Computations

Kadir Akbudak[1], Hatem Ltaief[1], Aleksandr Mikhalev[1(✉)],
Ali Charara[1], Aniello Esposito[2], and David Keyes[1]

[1] Extreme Computing Research Center,
Division of Computer, Electrical,
and Mathematical Sciences and Engineering,
King Abdullah University of Science
and Technology, Thuwal Jeddah 23955,
Kingdom of Saudi Arabia
{kadir.akbudak,hatem.ltaief,
aleksandr.mikhalev,ali.charara,david.keyes}@kaust.edu.sa
[2] Cray EMEA Research Lab, Bristol, UK
esposito@cray.com

Abstract. Exploiting data sparsity in dense matrices is an algorithmic bridge between architectures that are increasingly memory-austere on a per-core basis and extreme-scale applications. In this work, we leverage the Hierarchical matrix Computations on Manycore Architectures (HiCMA) library in order to tackle this challenging problem by achieving significant reductions in time to solution and memory footprint, while preserving a specified accuracy requirement of the application. We have extended HiCMA to provide a high-performance implementation on distributed-memory systems of one of the most widely used matrix factorization in large-scale scientific applications, i.e., the Cholesky factorization. It employs the tile low-rank data format to compress the dense data-sparse off-diagonal tiles of the matrix. It then decomposes the matrix computations into interdependent tasks and relies on the dynamic runtime system StarPU for asynchronous out-of-order scheduling, while allowing high user productivity. Performance comparisons and memory footprint on matrix dimensions up to eleven million show a performance gain and memory saving of more than an order of magnitude for both metrics on thousands of cores, against state-of-the-art open-source and vendor optimized numerical libraries. This represents an important milestone in enabling large-scale matrix computations toward solving big data problems in geospatial statistics for climate/weather forecasting applications.

1 Introduction

State-of-the-art dense linear algebra libraries are confronting memory capacity limits and/or are not able to produce solutions in reasonable times, when performing dense computations (e.g., matrix factorizations and solutions) on large

M. Aldinucci et al. (Eds.): Euro-Par 2018, LNCS 11014, pp. 721–734, 2018.
https://doi.org/10.1007/978-3-319-96983-1_51

matrix of size n, with n in the billions. The current trend of hardware over-provisioning in terms of floating-point units (e.g., with wide SIMD implementations) and the increase of memory capacity (e.g., with new fast non-volatile memory layer) are not sufficient to cope with the emergence of big data problems involving dense matrices due to the prohibitive cubic algorithmic complexity $O(n^3)$ and the expensive quadratic memory footprint $O(n^2)$. To overcome both challenges, matrix approximations may be considered as an effective remedy, as long as the numerical fidelity of the original problem is preserved.

This paper introduces the Hierarchical matrix Computations on Manycore Architectures (HiCMA) library, which exploits the data sparsity structure of dense matrices on shared and shared to distributed-memory systems. In particular, the class of covariance-based matrices emerges from various scientific big data applications in environmental applications, including geospatial statistics for climate/weather forecasting [29,30]. Under such an apparently dense matrix representation lies a family of sparse representations. HiCMA currently employs a tile low-rank (TLR) data format, which leverages the data descriptor behind the traditional dense/plain tile format [1,2,13]. The idea consists in compressing the off-diagonal tiles, and retaining the most significant singular values with their associated singular vectors up to an application-dependent accuracy threshold. HiCMA can then perform matrix operations on these compressed tiles. A dynamic runtime system StarPU [10] orchestrates the various computational tasks representing the nodes of a directed acyclic graph, and asynchronously schedules them on the available processing units in an out-of-order fashion, while carefully tracking their data dependencies. This systematic approach enhances the productivity for the library development, while facilitating the code deployment from shared to distributed-memory systems [4].

We assess the numerical robustness and parallel performance of HiCMA using two matrix kernels. The first one is a synthetic matrix kernel, and has been inspired from wave-based frequency domain matrix equation problems. It gives a useful flexibility, since it permits to generate customized matrices with various rank sizes and accuracy thresholds. This flexibility can be employed to avoid stressing the solver infrastructure. The second kernel corresponds to a realistic application coming from the family of parametrizable Matérn covariance function [22], and represents the state-of-the-art in modeling geostatistics and spatial statistics [16]. The resulting covariance matrices for both aforementioned kernels are symmetric and positive-definite. The Cholesky factorization is the core operation when solving linear systems of equations for the former or calculating the matrix determinant for the latter. The Cholesky factorization reduces a symmetric positive-definite matrix into lower or upper triangular form and is usually used as a pre-processing step toward solving dense linear system of equations. Thanks to the resulting low arithmetic intensity of the numerical kernels, HiCMA is able to translate the original dense compute-bound application into a data-sparse communication-bound on distributed-memory systems. While time to solution is significantly reduced, the bottlenecks are shifted and data traffic reduction may rapidly become central in strong scaling mode of operation, as usually observed for sparse computations.

We report performance comparisons and memory footprint on matrix dimensions up to eleven million and 16,000 cores. We show a gain of more than an order of magnitude for both metrics against state-of-the-art open-source and vendor optimized numerical libraries, when applicable. In these experiments, we employ a threshold which preserves the specific accuracy requirement of the application while removing the irrelevant information data from the matrix. We also provide a comprehensive profiling and tracing results to identify current performance bottlenecks in HiCMA. Last but not least, we show preliminary power profiling results to study the impact of the numerical accuracy on the overall energy consumption. The energy consumption stands as a new critical metric to monitor and optimize, especially when solving big data problems in geospatial statistics for climate/weather forecasting applications.

The remainder of the paper is organized as follows. Section 2 provides a bibliography in hierarchical low-rank matrix computations and our research contributions. Section 3 introduces and describes the HiCMA software infrastructure for solving large-scale data-sparse problems. Section 4 defines the kernels for synthetic matrix generations and real world applications from climate/weather forecasting applications based on a geospatial statistics approach. Section 5 gives implementation details of the tile low-rank Cholesky, which relies on the StarPU dynamic runtime system. Section 6 presents the results and a comprehensive performance analysis. It compares our implementation against existing state-of-the-art implementations on distributed-memory system. We conclude in Sect. 7.

2 Related Work

Discovered around two decades ago [17–19,21,31], hierarchical low-rank matrix approximations are currently a leading algorithmic trend in the scientific community to solve large-scale data-sparse problems. Based on recursive formulations, they exploit the data sparsity of the matrix by compressing the low-rank off-diagonal blocks using an adequate data storage format such as HODLR [6,9], $\mathcal{H}$ [20], HSS [5,27] and $\mathcal{H}^2$ [12]. The aforementioned data compression formats are characterized by linear and log linear upper bounds for their algorithmic complexities. The resulting low arithmetic intensity of the kernel in addition to the recursive formulation impede their parallel performance. They turn out to be difficult to implement, and not amenable to effectively map on manycore shared and distributed-memory systems, due to their fork-join paradigm.

More recently, with the emergence of asynchronous task-based programming models, these hierarchical low-rank matrix approximations algorithms have been revisited by flattening their recursions and exposing them to task-based runtime systems such as Intel Threading Building Blocks (Intel TBB) [24] and OpenMP [4]. While these dynamic runtimes permit to mitigate the overhead from the bus bandwidth saturation on single shared-memory nodes, they do not support distributed-memory systems. Moreover, the authors in [14] have also demonstrated the importance of flattening the recursion during the compression of $\mathcal{H}^2$-matrices, when targeting massively parallel GPU accelerators. Since memory is a scarce resource on the GPU, porting the $\mathcal{H}^2$-matrix approximation kernel to multiple GPUs appears mandatory but seems to be a very tedious exercise, due to the complex handmade memory management across GPUs.

Another data compression format has been introduced [7], i.e., the block low-rank data format, which is a subset of the $\mathcal{H}$-matrix class of data-sparse approximation. It consists of splitting the dense matrix into blocks and to perform low-rank matrix computations, while compressing the final results on-the-fly. Although distributed-memory systems do not appear as a hostile environment anymore with this new format in the context of sparse direct solvers [8], there may be still two main limitations: the lack of a systematic approach to schedule the computational tasks onto resources and the high memory footprint, since the matrix is not compressed initially, but rather gets compressed as the computation goes.

This paper introduces the HiCMA library, the first implementation of task-based tile low-rank Cholesky factorization on distributed-memory systems. Compared to the initial implementation on shared-memory environment [4] based on OpenMP, this paper uses instead the StarPU [10] dynamic runtime system to asynchronously schedule computational tasks across interconnected remote nodes. This highly productive association of task-based programming model with dynamic runtime systems permits to tackle in a systematic way advanced hardware systems by abstracting their complexity from the numerical library developers. This separation of concerns between hardware and software facilitates in solving large-scale simulations and allows porting HiCMA onto large resources and large problems sizes, i.e., $16,000$ cores and 11 million, respectively. We have also conducted performance and power profiling analysis to provide further insights when scheduling this new class of algorithms for hierarchical low-rank matrix computations. The HiCMA software library[1] has been released and is freely available for public download under the open-source modified BSD license.

3   The HiCMA Software Library

The HiCMA software library provides a high-performance implementation of the Cholesky factorization for symmetric positive-definite matrices with a data sparse structure. A complete list of HiCMA features can be found at https://github.com/ecrc/hicma. HiCMA is rooted in tile algorithms for dense linear algebra [2], which split the matrix into dense tiles. HiCMA leverages the tile data descriptor in order to support the new tile low-rank (TLR) compression format. While this data descriptor is paramount to expose parallelism, it is also critical for the data management in distributed-memory environment [1,13]. HiCMA adopts a flattened algorithmic design to bring to the fore the task parallelism, as opposed to plain recursive approach, which has constituted the basis for performance of previous $\mathcal{H}$-matrix libraries [18,19,21].

---

[1] https://github.com/ecrc/hicma.

Once the matrix has been divided into tiles, HiCMA relies on the STARS-H library [2], a high performance $\mathcal{H}$-matrix market, to generate and compress each tile independently. This allows to create the TLR matrix in compressed format, without having a global dense representation, and therefore, opens opportunities to solve large-scale applications, thanks to a low memory footprint. This may eventually become cumbersome even for sparse solvers [7], when dealing with high dimensional problems, since the global intermediate dense matrices are explicitly generated. Figure 3(b) in [4] sketches the TLR matrix after compressing on-the-fly each tile with a specific application-dependent fixed accuracy. This may result into low-rank tiles with non-uniform ranks to maintain the overall expected accuracy. Although the scope of HiCMA described in this paper focuses on dense covariance-based scientific applications, it may have a broader impact. Indeed, as previously mentioned, it can also service sparse direct solvers, i.e., supernodal [23,28] and multifrontal numerical methods [8,26], during the low-rank Schur complement calculations on the fronts/supernodes, which are the crux of sparse computations. Furthermore, the fixed rank feature of HiCMA, as shown in Fig. 3(a) in [4], allows to generate TLR matrices with uniform ranks across all low-rank tiles. This rough approximations may be of high interest for speeding up sparse preconditioners (e.g., incomplete Cholesky/LU factorizations) during iterative solvers, since important *a priori* assumptions can be made to optimize and improve parallel performance.

4   Definition of Matrix Kernels

The matrix kernel is a function that generates matrix entries, i.e., $A_{ij} = f(x_i, y_j)$, from two sets $\{x_i\}$ and $\{y_j\}$. Typically, the matrix kernel function $f(x, y)$ calculates the interaction between two objects x and y, using a distance-based formulation. Although some matrix kernels may lead to sparse matrices, we investigate matrix kernels that translate into dense matrices.

Synthetic Matrix Kernel. The first matrix kernel is a synthetic one, inspired from the core matrix kernel of wave-based matrix equations, as in electrodynamics, electromagnetic and acoustic applications. The matrix kernel can be defined as $f(x, y) = \frac{\sin(\lambda r(x,y))}{r(x,y)}$, where λ is a wave number and $r(x, y)$ is an Euclidian distance between x and y. In fact, this corresponds to the imaginary part of a fundamental solution $\frac{e^{i\lambda r}}{r}$ of the Helmholtz equation. This modified function is very convenient, since the wave number has a direct impact of the rank distribution on the TLR matrix. This permits to test the numerical robustness of HiCMA with a large number of rank configurations. Figures 1(a)-(d) depict the rank distribution for various wave numbers λ on a matrix of size 2500×2500 with an accuracy threshold set to 10^{-9}. It shows a homogeneity among rank sizes of the off-diagonal tiles for a given λ, while it displays rank growth as λ increases.

---

[2] https://github.com/ecrc/stars-h.

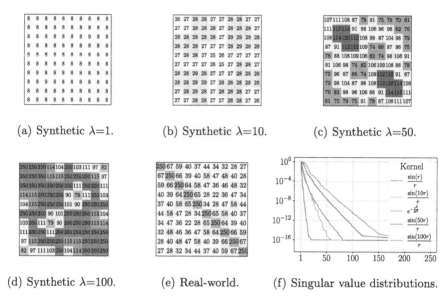

(a) Synthetic λ=1. (b) Synthetic λ=10. (c) Synthetic λ=50.

(d) Synthetic λ=100. (e) Real-world. (f) Singular value distributions.

Fig. 1. Rank distributions for the synthetic matrix kernel with different wave numbers λ and acc=10^{-9} (a)-(d). Rank distributions the spatial statistics applications with acc=10^{-8} (e). Distribution of normalized singular values for both matrix kernels on the bottom-left off-diagonal tile (f). Matrix size $N = 2500$.

Matérn Matrix Kernel for Covariance Problems. The Matérn matrix kernel is at the core of spatial statistics and is used as the state-of-the-art model to drive climate/weather forecasting applications [22]. We have implemented the square exponential variant of this Matérn matrix kernel to demonstrate the effectiveness of our TLR approach for solving real world applications. The square exponential kernel can be defined as $f(r) = e^{-\frac{r^2}{2l^2}}$, where r is a distance between spatial points and l is a correlation length. For the experiments presented in the paper, we set the correlation length to 0.1. The resulting TLR covariance matrix is then used to evaluate the maximum likelihood function during an optimization and iterative procedure, as explained in [4]. Each iteration requires the calculation of the matrix determinant involving the Cholesky factorization, which is the most time-consuming phase. Figure 1(e) shows the rank distributions on a matrix of size 2500×2500 with tile size 250 for the square exponential kernel. The ranks are not too disparate for the corresponding accuracy of 10^{-8}.

The singular value distributions for the tile located at the bottom-left of the TLR matrix generated from each type of matrix kernels is depicted in Fig. 1(f). Their distributions highlight an exponential decay, and therefore, reveal the data sparsity structure of such matrices. It is also clear that, given these rank heatmaps, data compression formats with weak admissibility conditions (i.e., HODLR and HSS) may not be appropriate for this application, due to nested dissection, which operates only for diagonal super tiles. The off-diagonal super tiles may then engender excessive larger ranks after compression, which may eventually have a negative impact on performance and memory footprint.

5 Implementation Details

This section provides insights into two main ingredients for porting the HiCMA library to distributed-memory systems: the data descriptor and the StarPU dynamic runtime system.

The Data Descriptor. The data descriptor defines the backbone of HiCMA, as it dictates how the data management takes place across the distributed-memory computational nodes. Originally developed for ScaLAPACK [11] and inspired later DPLASMA's [13], the descriptor draws how the data is scattered among processing units following the classical two-dimensional block cyclic distribution to ensure load balancing between nodes. HiCMA leverages this single descriptor for dense matrices and creates three descriptors to carry on computations over the compressed bases of each tile, calculated by using the randomized SVD compression algorithm from the STARS-H library. These bases, i.e., U and V, are of sizes nb-by-k and k-by-nb, respectively, with nb the tile size and k the tile rank. The first descriptor stitches the rectangular bases U and V^T of each tile together. Since k is not known *a priori*, we define a maximum rank ($maxrk$), which can be tuned for memory footprint as well as performance. The second descriptor contains the actual ranks of each tile after compression and gets updated during the computation accordingly. The last descriptor store information about the dense diagonal tiles. The main challenge with these descriptors is that they enforce each data structure they inherently describe to be homogeneous across all tiles. While the rank and dense diagonal tiles descriptors are obviously important to maintain for numerical correctness, the descriptor for the off-diagonal tiles has a direct impact on the overall communication volume. Therefore, tuning the $maxrk$ parameter is mandatory. However, dense data-sparse matrices with a large disparity in the ranks of the off-diagonal tiles may encounter performance bottlenecks, due to excessive remote data transfers. One possible remedy is to implement a fine-grained descriptor for each single tile, as explained in [25].

The StarPU Dynamic Runtime System. The StarPU dynamic runtime system [10] maps a sequential task-based application onto a complex underlying parallel shared and/or distributed-memory systems. This allows endusers to focus on getting correctness from their sequential implementations and leave the challenging part of porting their codes to parallel environment to the runtime. The pseudo-code for the task-based TLR Cholesky factorizations is presented in Algorithm 1. We refer readers to [4] for the full description of the sequential kernels. The Insert_Task API encapsulates the task, its parameters with their data directions, i.e., read and/or write (STARPU_R, STARPU_W and STARPU_RW). Not only does StarPU execute its tasks asynchronously within

Algorithm 1. `hicma_dpotrf` (HicmaLower, D, U, V, N, nb, rank, acc)

```
p = N / nb
for k = 1 to p do
    StarPU_Insert_Task(hcore_dpotrf, HicmaLower, STARPU_R, D(k), rank, acc)
    for i = k+1 to p do
        StarPU_Insert_Task(hcore_dtrsm, STARPU_RW, V(i,k), STARPU_R, D(k,k))
    end for
    for j = k+1 to p do
        StarPU_Insert_Task(hcore_dsyrk, STARPU_RW, D(j), STARPU_R, U(j,k), STARPU_R, V(j,k))
        for i = j+1 to p do
            StarPU_Insert_Task(hcore_dgemm, STARPU_R, U(i,k), V(i,k), STARPU_R, U(j,k), STARPU_R, V(j,k),
            STARPU_RW, U(i,j), STARPU_RW, V(i,j), rank, acc)
        end for
    end for
end for
```

each node in an out-of-order fashion, but it also performs remote non-blocking point-to-point MPI communications to mitigate the data movement overhead by overlapping it with computations.

6   Performance Results

Our experiments have been conducted on two Cray systems. The first one, codenamed *Shaheen-2*, is a Cray XC40 system with the Cray Aries network interconnect, which implements a Dragonfly network topology. It has 6174 compute nodes, each with two-socket 16-core Intel Haswell running at 2.30 GHz and 128 GB of DDR3 main memory. The second system, codenamed *Cray-SKL*, has roughly 300 nodes with mixed stock keeping units (SKUs) The majority of nodes has at least two-socket 20-core Intel Skylake and at least 192GB of DDR4 memory, where the base frequency of the different SKUs varies between 2.1 GHz and 2.4 GHz. HiCMA and StarPU have been compiled with Intel compiler suites v16.3.3.210 and v17.0.4.196 on *Shaheen-2* and *Cray-SKL*, respectively. Calculations have been performed in double precision arithmetic and the best performance after three runs is reported.

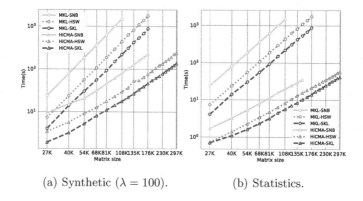

(a) Synthetic ($\lambda = 100$).   (b) Statistics.

Fig. 2. Time to solution of Intel MKL's dense `dpotrf` and `hicma_dpotrf` for both matrix kernels on Sandy Bridge, Haswell, and Skylake shared-memory systems.

Figure 2 shows the performance of the dense and TLR Cholesky factorizations from Intel MKL and HiCMA Cholesky factorizations, respectively, on shared-memory systems. We compare against various Intel chip generations, i.e., Sandy Bridge, Haswell and Skylake, for both matrix kernels. Not only can HiCMA solve larger problems than Intel MKL and with a much lower slope when scaling up, the obtained performance gain is also between one and two orders of magnitude for the synthetic and the square exponential matrix kernels, respectively.

Figure 3 shows the memory footprint for various accuracy thresholds of dense (calculated) and TLR (measured) Cholesky factorizations on a million covariance matrix size from the synthetic and real world application matrix kernel, as introduced in Sect. 4. As seen in the figure, the TLR-based compression scheme exhibits more than an order of magnitude memory footprint saving with respect to naive dense Cholesky factorization from ScaLAPACK for both matrix kernels. We refer the readers to [4] for the TLR algorithmic complexity study. Furthermore, the geospatial statistics matrix kernel can not support high accuracy thresholds, since the overall matrix looses its positive definiteness. However, the fixed accuracy of 10^{-8} is used for the latter matrix kernel, as required by the original application.

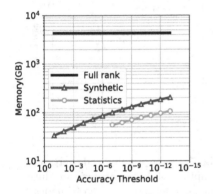

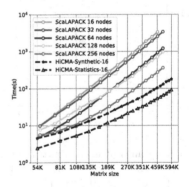

Fig. 3. Memory footprint of ScaLAPACK and hicma_dpotrf on 1M matrix size.

Fig. 4. Runtimes of ScaLAPACK's pdpotrf and hicma_dpotrf on *Shaheen-2*. Synthetic $\lambda = 100$.

Figure 4 shows performance comparisons of HiCMA against Intel ScaLAPACK for the TLR and dense Cholesky factorization on *Shaheen-2* distributed-memory system using both matrix kernels (including generation and compression). Since ScaLAPACK performs brute force computations, it is agnostic to the matrix kernel applications. HiCMA outperforms ScaLAPACK by using only 16 nodes as opposed to 256 nodes, up to half a million matrix size.

Figure 5 shows the time breakdown spent in generation and compression versus computation for HiCMA and ScaLAPACK Cholesky factorization on both

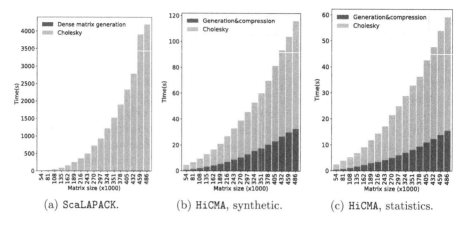

(a) ScaLAPACK.   (b) HiCMA, synthetic.   (c) HiCMA, statistics.

Fig. 5. Time breakdown of ScaLAPACK's pdpotrf and hicma_dpotrf on *Shaheen-2* for both matrix kernels. $\lambda = 100$ for the synthetic application.

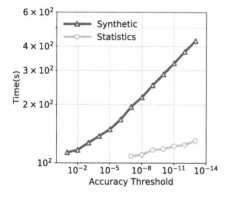

Fig. 6. Runtimes of hicma_dpotrf for different accuracy thresholds on 64 nodes of *Shaheen-2*. Matrix size $n = 1M$ and $nb = 2700$. Synthetic $\lambda = 200$.

Fig. 7. Power profiling and energy consumption of hicma_dpotrf for different accuracy thresholds on 64 nodes of *Cray-SKL*. Matrix size $n = 1M$ and $nb = 2700$. Synthetic $\lambda = 200$.

matrix kernels. The cost of generating the dense matrix for ScaLAPACK is negligible compared to the computational time. However, the time to generate and compress is noticeable for HiCMA and counts around 25% of the elapsed time, on matrix sizes up to half a million.

Figure 6 highlights the performance impact of various accuracy thresholds for both matrix kernels. The curves have expected trends, although varying accuracy threshold does not seem to impact the performance of the square exponential matrix kernel. This is due to *maxrk*, which stays relatively the same across the accuracy thresholds.

Figure 7 show some preliminary results of power profiling and energy consumption for HiCMA TLR Cholesky factorization with various accuracy thresholds on both matrix kernels using Perftools from *Cray-SKL*. The energy consumption saving is commensurate to the performance gain in time. The recorded power offset of HiCMA compared to running HPL corresponds the under-utilized CPUs, due to low arithmetic intensity kernels.

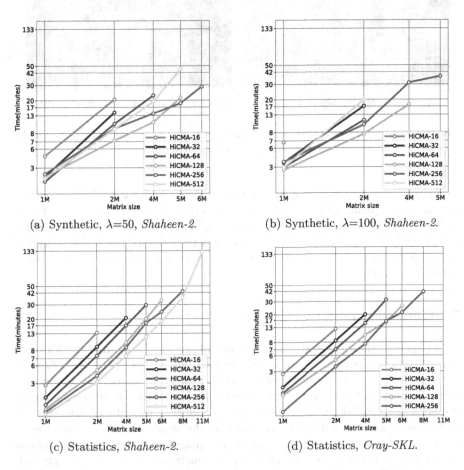

(a) Synthetic, $\lambda=50$, *Shaheen-2*.

(b) Synthetic, $\lambda=100$, *Shaheen-2*.

(c) Statistics, *Shaheen-2*.

(d) Statistics, *Cray-SKL*.

Fig. 8. Elapsed time of hicma_dpotrf for larger matrices (up to 11 million) for both matrix kernels on *Shaheen-2* and *Cray-SKL*.

Figure 8 depicts the strong scaling of HiCMA on both systems for the two matrix kernels. The synthetic matrix kernel is indeed important since it permits to show the performance bottleneck of the HiCMA's data descriptor supporting homogeneous ranks for large-scale problem sizes. Due to a large disparity of the ranks, *maxrk* has to be set to the actual maximum rank for all low-rank tiles, which engenders excessive data movement. The computation is, however, only applied on the eligible data. For the square exponential matrix kernel, the obtained scalability is decent on both systems, considering the low arithmetic intensity of the kernels.

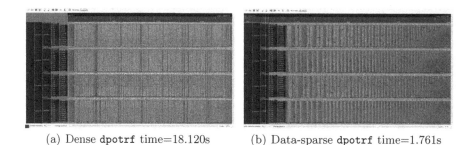

(a) Dense `dpotrf` time=18.120s   (b) Data-sparse `dpotrf` time=1.761s

Fig. 9. Execution traces of Chameleon's `dpotrf` (a) and `hicma_dpotrf` (b) on 4 nodes of *Shaheen-2* with a matrix size of 54K. (Color figure online)

Figure 9 presents the execution traces of dense and TLR Cholesky factorizations, as implemented in task-based `Chameleon` [1] and `HiCMA`, respectively. These traces highlight the CPU idle time (red color) in `HiCMA`, since `StarPU` is not able to compensate the data movement overhead with the tasks' computations (green color). Nevertheless, there is an order of magnitude in performance between both libraries.

7   Conclusion

This paper introduces the `HiCMA` numerical library on distributed-memory systems. `HiCMA` implements a task-based tile low-rank algorithm for the Cholesky factorization. It relies on the `StarPU` dynamic runtime system to asynchronously schedule computational and communication tasks. `HiCMA` outperforms state-of-the-art dense Cholesky implementations by more than an order of magnitude in performance and saves memory footprint by the same ratio while still preserving the specific accuracy requirement of the application. The numerical robustness and high performance of `HiCMA` are demonstrated at scale using synthetic and real world matrix kernels. In particular, `HiCMA` stands as a pathfinder for approximating and effectively solving geospatial statistics applications. Future work includes using a more flexible data descriptor to better handle situations with disparate ranks, porting `HiCMA` to hardware accelerators, introducing batch processing [15] and integrating `HiCMA` into existing sparse direct solvers for the Schur complement calculations.

Data Availability Statement and Acknowledgments. The datasets and code generated during and analysed during the current study are available in the figshare repository: https://doi.org/10.6084/m9.figshare.6388202 [3] The authors would like to thank the StarPU team at INRIA, France. This work has been partially funded by the Intel Parallel Computing Center Award. For computer time, this research used the resources from KAUST Supercomputing Laboratory for *Shaheen-2* core hours allocation.

References

1. Agullo, E., et al.: Achieving high performance on supercomputers with a sequential task-based programming model. In: IEEE TPDS (2017)
2. Agullo, E., et al.: Numerical linear algebra on emerging architectures: the PLASMA and MAGMA projects. J. Phys.: Conf. Ser. **180**, 12–37 (2009)
3. Akbudak, K., Ltaief, H., Mikhalev, A., Charara, A., Esposito, A., Keyes, D.: HiCMA (Hierarchical Computations on Manycore Architectures) library. Presented in Euro-Par 2018 paper. Figshare. Code (2018). https://doi.org/10.6084/m9.figshare.6388202
4. Akbudak, K., Ltaief, H., Mikhalev, A., Keyes, D.: Tile low rank cholesky factorization for climate/weather modeling applications on manycore architectures. In: Kunkel, J.M., Yokota, R., Balaji, P., Keyes, D. (eds.) ISC 2017. LNCS, vol. 10266, pp. 22–40. Springer, Cham (2017). https://doi.org/10.1007/978-3-319-58667-0_2
5. Ambikasaran, S., Darve, E.: An $\mathcal{O}(N \log N)$ fast direct solver for partial HSS matrices. J. Sci. Comput. **57**(3), 477–501 (2013)
6. Ambikasaran, S., Foreman-Mackey, D., Greengard, L., Hogg, D.W., O'Neil, M.: Fast direct methods for Gaussian processes. IEEE Trans. Pattern Anal. Mach. Intell. **38**(2), 252–265 (2016)
7. Amestoy, P., Ashcraft, C., Boiteau, O., Buttari, A., L'Excellent, J.Y., Weisbecker, C.: Improving multifrontal methods by means of block low-rank representations. SIAM J. Sci. Comput. **37**(3), A1451–A1474 (2015)
8. Amestoy, P.R., Duff, I.S., L'Excellent, J.Y.: Multifrontal parallel distributed symmetric and unsymmetric solvers. Comput. Methods Appl. Mech. Eng. **184**(2), 501–520 (2000)
9. Aminfar, A., Ambikasaran, S., Darve, E.: A fast block low-rank dense solver with applications to finite-element matrices. J. Comput. Phys. **304**, 170–188 (2016)
10. Augonnet, C., Thibault, S., Namyst, R., Wacrenier, P.A.: StarPU: a unified platform for task scheduling on heterogeneous multicore architectures. Concurr. Comput.: Pract. Exp. **23**(2), 187–198 (2011)
11. Blackford, L.S., et al.: ScaLAPACK Users' Guide. SIAM, Philadelphia (1997)
12. Börm, S.: Efficient Numerical Methods for Non-local Operators: $\mathcal{H}^2$-Matrix Compression, Algorithms and analysis. EMS Tracts in Mathematics, vol. 14. European Mathematical Society (2010)
13. Bosilca, G., et al.: Flexible development of dense linear algebra algorithms on massively parallel architectures with DPLASMA. In: IPDPS Workshops, pp. 1432–1441. IEEE (2011)
14. Boukaram, W.H., Turkiyyah, G., Ltaief, H., Keyes, D.E.: Batched QR and SVD algorithms on GPUs with applications in hierarchical matrix compression. Parallel Comput. **74**, 19–33 (2017)
15. Charara, A., Keyes, D.E., Ltaief, H.: Tile Low-Rank GEMM Using Batched Operations on GPUs. In: Aldinucci, M., et al. (eds.) Euro-Par 2018. LNCS, vol. 11014, pp. xx–yy. Springer, Cham (2018)
16. Chiles, J.P., Delfiner, P.: Geostatistics: Modeling Spatial Uncertainty, vol. 497. Wiley, Hoboken (2009)

17. Hackbusch, W.: A sparse matrix arithmetic based on $\mathcal{H}$-matrices. part i: introduction to $\mathcal{H}$-matrices. Computing **62**(2), 89–108 (1999)
18. Hackbusch, W., Börm, S.: Data-sparse approximation by adaptive $\mathcal{H}^2$-matrices. Computing **69**(1), 1–35 (2002)
19. Hackbusch, W., Khoromskij, B., Sauter, S.: On H^2-matrices. In: Bungartz, H.J., Hoppe, R., Zenger, C. (eds.) Lectures on Applied Mathematics, pp. 9–29. Springer, Heidelberg (2000). https://doi.org/10.1007/978-3-642-59709-1_2
20. Hackbusch, W.: Hierarchical matrices: Algorithms and analysis, vol. 49. Springer, Heidelberg (2015). https://doi.org/10.1007/978-3-662-47324-5
21. Hackbusch, W., Börm, S., Grasedyck, L.: HLib 1.4 (1999–2012), Max-Planck-Institut, Leipzig
22. Handcock, M.S., Stein, M.L.: A Bayesian analysis of kriging. Technometrics **35**, 403–410 (1993)
23. Hénon, P., Ramet, P., Roman, J.: Pastix: a high-performance parallel direct solver for sparse symmetric positive definite systems. ParCo **28**(2), 301–321 (2002)
24. Kriemann, R.: $\mathcal{H}$-LU factorization on many-core systems. Comput. Vis. Sci. **16**(3), 105–117 (2013)
25. Kurzak, J., et al.: Designing slate: software for linear algebra targeting exascale. SLATE Working Notes 3, ICL-UT-17-06, University of Tennessee (10–2017 2017)
26. Li, X.S., Demmel, J.W.: SuperLU_DIST: a scalable distributed-memory sparse direct solver for unsymmetric linear systems. ACM TOMS **29**, 110–140 (2003)
27. Rouet, F.H., Li, X.S., Ghysels, P., Napov, A.: A distributed-memory package for dense hierarchically semi-separable matrix computations using randomization. ACM TOMS **42**(4), 27:1–27:35 (2016)
28. SuiteSparse: A suite of sparse matrix software (2017). http://faculty.cse.tamu.edu/davis/SuiteSparse/
29. Sun, Y., Li, B., Genton, M.G.: Geostatistics for large datasets. In: Porcu, M., Montero, J.M., Schlather, M. (eds.) Space-Time Processes and Challenges Related to Environmental Problems. Lecture Notes in Statistics, vol. 207, pp. 55–77. Springer, Heidelberg (2012). https://doi.org/10.1007/978-3-642-17086-7_3
30. Sun, Y., Stein, M.L.: Statistically and computationally efficient estimating equations for large spatial datasets. J. Comput. Graph. Stat. **25**(1), 187–208 (2016)
31. Tyrtyshnikov, E.E.: Mosaic-skeleton approximations. Calcolo **33**(1), 47–57 (1996)

Hybrid Parallelization and Performance Optimization of the FLEUR Code: New Possibilities for All-Electron Density Functional Theory

Uliana Alekseeva[✉], Gregor Michalicek, Daniel Wortmann, and Stefan Blügel

Institute for Advanced Simulation and Peter Grünberg Institut,
Forschungszentrum Jülich and JARA, 52425 Jülich, Germany
{u.alekseeva,g.michalicek,d.wortmanm,s.bluegel}@fz-juelich.de
http://www.fz-juelich.de/pgi

Abstract. A hybrid MPI+OpenMP parallelization strategy has been implemented into the density functional theory code FLEUR. Based on the full-potential linearized augmented plane-wave (FLAPW) method, FLEUR is a well-established all-electron code specialized on the simulation of materials properties of crystalline bulk solids and surfaces with significant electronic and magnetic complexity. Developed in over 30 years the Fortran implementation included two layers of MPI-based distributed memory parallelization that serves as a reference for our work. The revised code version shows superior performance, improved scalability and thereby opens the path to exploit current and future high performance computing architectures efficiently. Multiple threads per MPI process can be utilized by interfacing with optimized linear algebra subroutines from the BLAS and LAPACK libraries as well as in code sections with explicit OpenMP statements. We demonstrate that the additional multithreading helps to avoid the communication induced scalability limit of the pure-MPI version and simultaneously boosts the single node-performance on current multi-core systems. This enables FLEUR calculations for unit cells with over 1000 atoms to simulate extended defects, surfaces and disordered solids.

Keywords: DFT · FLAPW · Hybrid parallelization

1 Introduction

Over the last decades density functional theory (DFT) calculations [10] have become an indispensable tool for the simulation of material properties and the prediction of new materials showing novel functionality. The increasing computational resources together with algorithmic advances and methodological developments make the calculation of more and more properties for more and more complex materials feasible. Due to the large variety of properties, physical effects and

© Springer International Publishing AG, part of Springer Nature 2018
M. Aldinucci et al. (Eds.): Euro-Par 2018, LNCS 11014, pp. 735–748, 2018.
https://doi.org/10.1007/978-3-319-96983-1_52

the difference in the computational challenges that arise, many established DFT-codes have been developed [4] that typically implement different algorithms.

The increase in computational resources, however, also comes with a change of the hardware architectures. Decades ago a typical mainframe computer featured a small number of computational cores and parallelism utilized few of these single-core nodes with distributed memory. Nowadays HPC machines typically are cluster systems consisting of many shared memory nodes connected through a communication network and featuring several multi-core CPUs each. The additional parallelization layers in such architectures together with the larger but also shared memory capacity on each node entail the requirement to adapt the software parallelization strategies.

We perform this adaption for the FLEUR [2] code developed at the Research Center Jülich. This is a full-potential linearized augmented-plane-wave (FLAPW) [5, 11, 18, 19] implementation of DFT. Being an all-electron code FLEUR is employable to perform highly precise simulations for solids, surfaces and molecular systems consisting of arbitrary compositions of chemical elements and it has its particular strength in the simulation of magnetism and relativistic effects.

To utilize modern hierarchical architectures efficiently, a "hierarchical", hybrid parallelization is implemented, i.e. the distributed memory paradigm (MPI) and a multi-threaded shared memory paradigm are combined. The aim of the new hybrid parallelization scheme presented here is not only to make the intra-node CPU usage effective, but also to enable simulations of big unit cells using many nodes. To achieve this, the "top-down" approach [17] was applied, i.e. for a given test case, first the efficiency of MPI parallelization was investigated and improved when needed, then multi-threading was added, either as calls to external multi-threaded libraries or as direct implementation of OpenMP pragmas. We show that we obtained significant performance and scalability enhancements pushing the limit of applicability of the code to simulations with over 1000 atoms.

While we implemented many improvements throughout the code, we will concentrate the discussion on the setup of the matrices and the subsequent matrix diagonalization. The latter part can efficiently be solved using standard libraries for dense generalized eigenvalue problems. The first of these two most time consuming parts of the code other authors also discussed before in detail [14, 16]. While we agree with those works in the aspect of stressing the benefit of using standard matrix operations, we use a significantly different algorithm exploiting in addition the analytic properties of the problem and thereby reducing the number of computations needed. We tested our approach against simpler schemes and found it to show superior performance and scaling.

In the next chapter we introduce the FLAPW algorithm. In Sect. 3 we discuss the parallelization and optimization performed to achieve the benchmark results presented in Sect. 4, Sect. 5 concludes the paper.

2 Density Functional Theory and the FLAPW Method

According to density functional theory [9,12], the total energy of a system of interacting atoms and electrons is a functional of its electron density $n(\boldsymbol{r})$. Hence, the Hamiltonian (the energy operator) of the system

$$\hat{H}[n(\boldsymbol{r})] = \hat{T} + V_{\text{eff}}[n(\boldsymbol{r})], \tag{1}$$

which is the sum of the kinetic energy operator $\hat{T}$ and the effective potential V_{eff}, depends directly on the electron density. The electron density can be expressed in terms of N_{occ} occupied single-particle orbitals $\psi_\nu(\boldsymbol{r})$:

$$n(\boldsymbol{r}) = \sum_{\nu}^{N_{\text{occ}}} |\psi_\nu(\boldsymbol{r})|^2, \tag{2}$$

where ν labels the states. The single-particle orbitals $\psi_\nu(\boldsymbol{r})$ are the solutions of the Kohn-Sham equations, an eigenvalue problem with eigenvalues ϵ_ν:

$$\hat{H}[n(\boldsymbol{r})]\psi_\nu(\boldsymbol{r}) = \epsilon_\nu \psi_\nu(\boldsymbol{r}). \tag{3}$$

Since the Hamiltonian in the equation depends on its solution, this is a self-consistency problem which has to be solved iteratively: starting with an initial guess the ground-state density is therefore obtained in an iterative scheme that produces a new density in each iteration. The new input density is obtained by a mixing procedure from the old input density, the output density, and optionally further densities related to earlier iterations of this self-consistency cycle. The final ground-state density is self-consistent with respect to this procedure.

We solve the Kohn-Sham equations for crystalline solids described by a unit cell with a finite number of atoms, which is repeated indefinitely in all three spatial dimensions to fill up the whole space. For such solids the Hamiltonian matrix can be block-diagonalized and each block provides an independent eigenvalue problem. Each block is indexed by the so called Bloch vector $\boldsymbol{k}$, hence in the following the matrices, their eigenvalues and eigenvectors feature an extra $\boldsymbol{k}$-index [7].

2.1 FLAPW Method

A common approach to solving Eq. (3) is to expand the wave functions in terms of a set of basis functions $\{\phi_{\boldsymbol{k}}^{G}\}$ as

$$\psi_{\nu,\boldsymbol{k}}(\boldsymbol{r}) = \sum_{G} c_{\nu,\boldsymbol{k}}^{G} \phi_{\boldsymbol{k}}^{G}(\boldsymbol{r}). \tag{4}$$

By this the Hamiltonian becomes a Hermitian matrix and the eigenvalue problem is solved by a matrix diagonalization. Equation (3) becomes the generalized eigenvalue problem

$$\sum_{G'} H_{G,G'}^{k} c_{\nu,k}^{G'} = \epsilon_{\nu,k} \sum_{G'} S_{G,G'}^{k} c_{\nu,k}^{G'}, \tag{5}$$

where

$$H_{G,G'}^k = \int (\phi_k^G)^* \hat{H} \phi_k^{G'} dr \quad \text{and} \quad S_{G,G'}^k = \int (\phi_k^G)^* \phi_k^{G'} dr \quad (6)$$

are the Hamiltonian matrix and the overlap matrix.

In the all-electron full-potential linearized augmented-plane-wave method (FLAPW) [5,11,18,19] the basis functions are linearized augmented-plane-waves (LAPWs) which are based on a partitioning of space into non-overlapping but nearly touching muffin-tin (MT) spheres centered at each atom and an interstitial region (INT) in between the spheres. Formally a LAPW is given by

$$\phi_k^G(r) = \begin{cases} \frac{1}{\sqrt{\Omega}} e^{i(k+G)r} & \text{in INT} \\ \sum_\alpha \sum_L^{l_{max}^\alpha} \sum_p a_{L,\alpha}^{k,G,p} u_{l,\alpha}^p(r_\alpha) Y_L(\hat{r}_\alpha) & \text{in MT}_\alpha \end{cases}, \quad (7)$$

where G is a reciprocal lattice vector used to index the LAPW, Ω is the volume of the unit cell, and $r_\alpha = r - \tau_\alpha$ is the position vector relative to atom α at τ_α. The MT part of the function is a linear combination of radial functions $u_{l,\alpha}^p$ times spherical harmonics Y_L, where $p \in \{0,1\}$ is an index to select one of the radial functions. The coefficients $a_{L,\alpha}^{k,G,p}$ are determined by matching the MT part of the LAPW in value and slope to the plane wave in the interstitial region. The set of LAPW basis functions is defined by the reciprocal plane wave cutoff parameter $K_{max} = |K|_{max} = |k + G|_{max}$ and its MT representation is bounded by the angular momentum cutoffs l_{max}^α for the sum over the composite index $L = (l,m)$. Typically one needs about 100 basis functions per atom and an l_{max}^α between 8 and 12 to obtain converged FLAPW results.

Besides the basis functions, the representations of the density and the potential are FLAPW specific and their constructions are important parts of an FLAPW program. However, the runtime of an FLAPW calculation is typically strongly dominated by the setup and solving of the generalized eigenvalue problem. In the following we therefore focus on the computation of the Hamiltonian and overlap matrices.

2.2   Hamiltonian and Overlap Matrices

After integrating (Eq. 6) over the LAPWs (Eq. 7), the Hamiltonian and overlap matrices are given as sums over the MT contributions from each atom and the INT contribution as

$$H_{G,G'}^k = H_{G,G'}^{k,INT} + \sum_\alpha H_{G,G'}^{k,MT_\alpha} = H_{G,G'}^{k,INT} + \sum_\alpha H_{G,G'}^{k,\alpha,sph} + H_{G,G'}^{k,\alpha,nsph} \quad (8)$$

and

$$S_{G,G'}^k = S_{G,G'}^{k,INT} + \sum_\alpha S_{G,G'}^{k,\alpha}, \quad (9)$$

where we also distinguish for each MT sphere between the spherical contributions to the Hamiltonian matrix $H_{G,G'}^{k,\alpha,sph}$ and those due to the non-spherical part of the potential $H_{G,G'}^{k,\alpha,nsph}$.

Since an interstitial LAPW is a plane wave the calculation of the related matrix contributions is fast. Its time requirements only scale quadratically with the system size. We discuss the more challenging MT setup.

The MT contributions to the Hamiltonian are given as

$$H_{G,G'}^{k,\alpha} = \sum_{L,L'} \sum_{p,p'} \left(a_{L,\alpha}^{k,G,p} \right)^* t_{L,L'}^{\alpha,p,p'} a_{L',\alpha}^{k,G',p'} \tag{10}$$

in which $t_{L,L'}^{\alpha,p,p'}$ denotes the local Hamiltonian matrix for the respective atom in the basis of the radial functions times spherical harmonics. The calculation of $H_{G,G'}^{k,\alpha}$ is computationally expensive and in comparision to a simple implementation we use several measures to reduce these computational demands.

The first of these makes use of analytical calculations that can be performed for the spherical contributions, by making use of the addition theorem for spherical harmonics [6]. One obtains

$$\begin{aligned} H_{G,G'}^{k,\alpha,\mathrm{sph}} &= \sum_{L} \sum_{\sigma} \left(a_{L,\alpha}^{k,G,\sigma} \right)^* \sum_{\sigma'} t_{L,L}^{\alpha,\sigma,\sigma'} a_{L,\alpha}^{k,G',\sigma'} \\ &= \sum_{l=0}^{l_{\max}^{\alpha}} \frac{2l+1}{4\pi} P_l \left(\frac{KK'}{|KK'|} \right) \left[\sum_{\sigma} \left(a_{l,\alpha}^{k,G,\sigma} \right)^* \sum_{\sigma'} t_{l,l}^{\alpha,\sigma,\sigma'} a_{l,\alpha}^{k,G',\sigma'} \right] \end{aligned} \tag{11}$$

in which P_l denotes the Legendre polynomial of degree l. An analogous expression is obtained for the MT contributions to the overlap matrix $S_{G,G'}^{k,\alpha}$ which is computed as a byproduct. Note that the analytic m summation reduces the computational demands for these matrix elements by a factor of about 10.

The remaining Hamiltonian matrix contributions due to the non-spherical part of the potential are

$$H_{G,G'}^{k,\alpha,\mathrm{nsph}} = \sum_{L} \sum_{\sigma} \left(a_{L,\alpha}^{k,G,\sigma} \right)^* \left(\sum_{L' \neq L} \sum_{\sigma'} t_{L,L'}^{\alpha,\sigma,\sigma'} a_{L',\alpha}^{k,G',\sigma'} \right). \tag{12}$$

The last measure to reduce the required computational effort is based on the realization that in comparison to Eq. (11), Eq. (12) has lower demands with respect to the cutoff of the L sums. Therefore in practice one uses a new cutoff $l_{\mathrm{nsph}}^{\alpha} \approx \min(8, l_{\max}^{\alpha} - 2)$ for the L and L' sums in this equation. This provides another reduction of the time requirements for these calculations by 30 to 50%. However, calculating the non-spherical contributions remains the most time-consuming step in the setup of the matrices.

2.3   Scaling and Time Requirements

Of course, the computational demands of the different steps of an FLAPW calculation feature different scaling behaviors with respect to the system size defined by the number of atoms N_{at}. Table 1 shows these different behaviors depending

Table 1. Scaling of the most time-consuming parts of an FLAPW self-consistency iteration

Computational task	Scaling vs. numerical parameters	Scaling vs. system size
Potential generation	$\mathcal{O}\left(\sum_{\alpha}(l_{\max}^{\alpha}+1)^2 N_G + N_G \log(N_G)\right)$	$\mathcal{O}\left(N_{\mathrm{at}}^2\right)$
Matrix setup	$\mathcal{O}\left(N_k \sum_{\alpha}(l_{\max}^{\alpha}+1)^2 N_G{}^2\right)$	$\mathcal{O}\left(N_{\mathrm{at}}^3\right)$
Diagonalization	$\mathcal{O}\left(N_k N_G{}^3\right)$	$\mathcal{O}\left(N_{\mathrm{at}}^3\right)$
Charge density generation	$\mathcal{O}\left(N_k \sum_{\alpha}(l_{\max}^{\alpha}+1)^2 N_G N_{\mathrm{occ}}\right)$	$\mathcal{O}\left(N_{\mathrm{at}}^3\right)$

on N_{at} but also more explicitly on the number of LAPW basis functions N_G, the angular momentum cutoff $l_{\max}^{\alpha}$, the number of $\boldsymbol{k}$-points N_k, and the number of occupied eigenstates N_{occ} (see sum over ν in Eq. (2)).

All of these parameters are system-dependent but only N_G and N_{occ} are proportional to the number of atoms, while $l_{\max}^{\alpha}$ is independent of N_{at} and N_k is reciprocal to N_{at} in each direction but at least 1. Overall this implies a cubical scaling of the time requirements with respect to the number of atoms.

Typical time requirements for the different steps in a single iteration of the self-consistency loop are shown in Table 2. The run time dominance of the matrix setup and the diagonalization step are clearly visible for all problem sizes. For larger numbers of atoms this dominance becomes even more pronounced.

Table 2. Run time measurements of the FLEUR code (MaX Release 2.0) for three test unit cells: NaCl (64 atoms), AuAg (108 atoms) and CuAg (256 atoms). All simulations are performed on the CLAIX computing cluster with one $\boldsymbol{k}$-point, for one self-consistency iteration. The measurements are provided in seconds (left side) as well as relative percentage values (right side).

Test system	NaCl		AuAg		CuAg	
Number of atoms	64		108		256	
Potential generation	3.5	12.5%	12.4	3.9%	47.2	4.8%
Matrix setup	8.1	29.0%	127.7	40.4%	455.2	46.3%
Diagonalization	10.6	38.2%	145.5	46.0%	384.2	39.1%
New charge density generation	2.9	10.4%	22.5	7.1%	78.6	8.0%
Total time	27.8	100%	316.3	100%	982.4	100%

3   Parallelization and Optimization

Since different parts of the code have different algorithms and scaling behaviour, there is no single parallelization strategy which is applicable to the whole code.

Figure 1(left) summarizes how the computational load is distributed for each section of the code on every parallelization level. There are two layers of MPI parallelization for the most time-consuming parts, matrix setup, the diagonalization and for the new charge density generation part. To make the code suitable for modern HPC architectures with their hierarchical structure of parallelism, it has been extended with multi-threading and SIMD parallelization schemes.

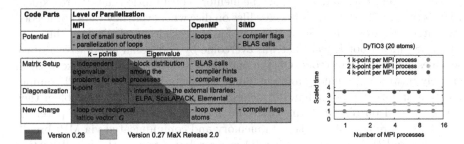

Code Parts	Level of Parallelization		
	MPI	OpenMP	SIMD
Potential	- a lot of small subroutines - parallelization of loops	- loops	- compiler flags - BLAS calls
	k – points	Eigenvalue	
Matrix Setup	- independent eigenvalue problems for each k-point	- block distribution among the processes	- BLAS calls - compiler hints - compiler flags
Diagonalization		- interfaces to the external libraries: ELPA, ScaLAPACK, Elemental	
New Charge	- loop over reciprocal lattice vector G	- loop over atoms	- compiler flags

■ Version 0.26   ▨ Version 0.27 MaX Release 2.0

Fig. 1. *Left Side:* The schematic summary of parallelization strategies used for different parts of the code. *Right Side:* Week scaling over *k*-points for test unit cell DyTiO3. The number of *k*-points is proportional to the number of MPI processes. The red points show the run times for calculations with 1, 2, 4, 6, 8, and 12 *k*-points distributed over 1, 2, 4, 6, 8, and 12 MPI processes correspondingly. The green and blue points show the run times for test cases with 2 and 4 *k*-points per MPI process. Run time is scaled to the run time of the test case with 1 *k*-point on 1 node (94 s for one self-consistency iteration). The horizontal lines are theoretical predictions. Simulations are done on the RWTH Bull Cluster, one MPI process per node. (Color figure online)

3.1 MPI Parallelization

The MPI parallelization relies on two levels of parallelism. On the first level, the different *k*-points for which the Kohn-Sham Eq. (3) have to be solved are distributed. As these are independent problems only the final results of the diagonalization has to be communicated and hence this parallelization is extremely efficient with nearly ideal scaling. Figure 1(right) demonstrates and confirms this perfect weak scaling. While this level of parallelization is very efficient in terms of distributing the computational load, it has two shortcomings. First, in large systems the number of *k*-points to be considered is small and hence this parallelization is very limited. Second, as the diagonalization part of the code corresponds to peak memory usage, the *k*-point parallelization does not reduce memory requirements per node.

The second level of MPI parallelization implements the distribution of the matrices and hence additionally distributes the computation of the matrix setup, the diagonalization and some critical parts of the charge generation routines. We will discuss details of the distributed matrix setup of the new version in the next section. The distributed memory parallelization was very performant at the time of its implementation [8], it worked excellent for machines like the CRAY T3E (512 CPUs).

The new code version (FLEUR version 0.27 MaX Release 2.0) reported in this work extends the existing MPI parallelization into further code parts and hence pushes the scalability limit as set by Amdahl's law. The old optimization (FLEUR version 0.26) for a small memory footprint also affected the quadratically scaling storage of the eigenvectors and the linearly scaling storage of the potential and the density. To reduce the memory consumption these were sequentially written to Fortran direct access files on disc whenever they were not needed and later read from disc again. However for large scale parallelization this approach becomes a bottleneck that was overcome by additional alternative storage schemes for the eigenvectors. On the one hand it is now possible to keep them entirely in working memory and communicate them by one-sided MPI communication and on the other hand if memory consumption still is a problem they can be stored on disc in terms of HDF5 files with parallel IO. The potential and density are now always kept in memory and communicated via MPI broadcasts. Overall the reduction of disc IO measurably increases the parallelization scalability.

3.2   Hybrid Parallelization and Optimized Matrix Setup

One of the main optimization targets was the matrix setup. In the old version, it was heavily optimized to reduce memory footprint. For example, several matrix-matrix multiplications were unrolled to enable the calculation of matrix elements on the fly without storing the whole matrix. In all of the matrix setup routines the second level of MPI parallelization utilizes a cyclic row distribution [1] of the matrices. This ensures good load-balancing and effective re-use of calculated quantities. The interstitial contribution can be easily calculated, does not take much time and allows for a straightforward MPI and an additional OpenMP parallelization over the matrix rows. It scales almost perfectly due to the independence of the computations and the absence of communication.

As discussed above, the matrix setup in the MT spheres is the most computationally relevant part of the matrix setup. In the old (version 0.26) implementation of FLEUR, spherical contributions to the H and S matrices and non-spherical contribution to the H matrix were calculated in a single subroutine which contained more than 1500 lines of code. This coarse-grained modularity of the code is beneficial if the heavy reduction of the memory footprint is aspired. Nowadays modularity in routines in which the main computational effort is performed by the lowest kernels is more advantageous. It is less error-prone and improves readability and maintainability of the code. Besides that, in case these low kernels perform some common mathematical operation such as linear algebra operations or Fourier transforms, external libraries can be used which are usually highly optimized for a given hardware. Hence, the first step was to increase the modularity of the code. The huge initial subroutine was split to several smaller ones.

The most important code split reflected the separation of the spherical and non-spherical contributions. In the routines for the spherical MT contribution the parallelization over the basis vectors on the MPI-level shows close to ideal scaling. To further distribute the computations in this code section, a layer of OpenMP parallelization over the atoms of the system has been added.

The non-spherical contributions to the Hamiltonian are now calculated by first explicitly constructing the matrices $A_\alpha^k = [a_{L,\alpha}^{k,G,\sigma}]$ and $T_\alpha = [t_{L,L'}^{\alpha,\sigma,\sigma'}]$ such that the sums over L, L', σ, σ' can now be performed as matrix multiplications. Hence the algorithm in this part basically consists of the construction of the A-matrices, a first matrix-matrix multiplication

$$C_\alpha^k = T_\alpha * A_\alpha^k \tag{13}$$

and a second multiplication

$$H_\alpha^{k,\mathrm{nsph}} = \left(A_\alpha^k\right)^H * C_\alpha^k. \tag{14}$$

These two different matrix computations scale significantly different with system size. The first is an $\mathcal{O}\left((l_{\max}^\alpha + 1)^4 N_G\right)$ operation, the second scales as $\mathcal{O}\left((l_{\max}^\alpha + 1)^2 N_G^2\right)$ and hence is most relevant for large systems. As the first of these matrix multiplications has to be performed on all MPI-ranks, it is simply mapped onto a standard matrix-matrix multiplication that enables us to exploit highly optimized BLAS-3 libraries for this operation.

For the second matrix multiplication, the MPI-distribution over rows and the property of the Hamiltonian should be considered. The algorithm we implemented here is a trade-off of the two contradictory conditions. On the one hand, it is determined by the fact that the final matrix is Hermitian and only one half of it has to be calculated and stored. On the other hand, we wish to use again optimized, vendor supplied BLAS3 (matrix-matrix multiply) routines to increase the efficiency. $H_\alpha^{k,\mathrm{nsph}}$ is distributed between MPI processes in cyclic row distribution: if there are M processes, the line i of the matrix can be found on the process with the number $mod(i, M)$. That means, each MPI process possess data from a rectangular matrix with size $(N_G/M) \times N_G$. Note that line i only has i elements. The matrix is stored as a packed storage vector. To be able to use BLAS3 routines, the matrix $H_\alpha^{k,\mathrm{nsph}}$ is divided into blocks (Fig. 2). Each block is calculated as matrix-matrix multiplication, then the values from the block are copied to the packed storage vector. Here we had to find a trade-off between a small block-size that exploits the fact that the final result is Hermitian most effectively, and a larger block-size that leads to better performance of the matrix-matrix multiplication. We found a value of about 64–128 most suitable on the machines we considered. As a final point we should stress, that our scheme has the important advantage that all operations performed in the matrix setup are local for each MPI-process. No communication is required as the MPI-distributed matrix elements are obtained independently for each process.

Besides the matrix-setup the second time consuming part is the diagonalization of the matrices. Here we rely on standard libraries. The old code

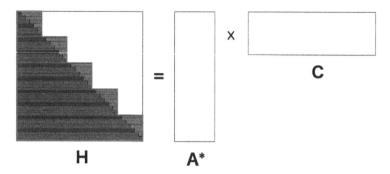

Fig. 2. Example of parallel data layout distributed between 3 MPI processes (red, yellow and green). Matrix **H** is distributed among MPI processes in line-wise fashion, so that each MPI process has data from a rectangular matrix with size $(N_G/M) \times N_G$. To be able to use BLAS3 routines, the matrix $H_\alpha^{k,\mathrm{nsph}}$ is divided into blocks (pink). Each block is calculated as matrix-matrix multiplication, then the values from the block are copied to the packed storage vector. (Color figure online)

implemented an interface to the ScaLAPACK [1] for this purpose. To obtain reasonable performance this requires a redistribution of the matrix from the simple row cyclic scheme used in the matrix setup to a two-dimensional block-cyclic scheme. While this imposes a communication overhead in theory, such a redistribution turns out to be fast enough that it does not impose a relevant restriction in practice. We furthermore implemented additional interfaces to external hybrid-parallel libraries (ELPA [13], Elemental [15]). It turns out that the ELPA library outperforms ScaLAPACK significantly and also has the additional benefit of delivering much more consistent performance for different levels of MPI and OpenMP parallelism resulting in different processor grids.

With substantial parallelization, also other parts of the code start to play substantial roles: for example, the potential generation could not be left sequential any more. In the other parts of the code either the usage of multi-threaded libraries or the explicit implementation of OpenMP pragmas provided the needed scaling on top of the existing MPI parallelization.

4   Benchmarks

We demonstrate the performance and scalability of the code by showing some exemplary cases. As we have already shown that the additional k-point parallelization leads to ideal scaling behaviour we restrict the presentation to calculations using a single k-point, in realistic simulations one would have an additional parallelization allowing to use a factor 3–20 (depending on system size) more computational cores effectively. In addition we only consider a single iteration. As the code usually has to perform approximately 20–50 iterations sequentially, the total runtime would increase accordingly.

4.1 Computational Environment

We have parallelized and optimized the FLEUR code for typical architectures found in HPC today: compute clusters with several levels of parallelism: internode with distributed memory, intra-node with shared memory and SIMD inside the core. The concrete specifications of the compute clusters used for the performance evaluations in this work are given in Table 3.

Table 3. Hardware systems used to perform the benchmark calculations.

	CPU	Cores per node	Node performance	Memory	Mem. bandwidth
RWTH Bull Cluster	Intel X5675	12	147 GFlops	24 GB	40 GB/s
CLAIX	Intel E5-2650v4	24	840 GFlops	128 GB	120 GB/s

4.2 Efficient Usage of a Single Node

To investigate the behaviour of FLEUR on a single node we use a small test case: NaCl with 64 atoms. The intranode scaling of the whole code and its main parts are shown in Fig. 3. Only parts of the code whose running time is more than 1% of the total time are considered. We see that the most time-consuming parts are the matrix setup and the diagonalization. The potential generation and the new charge generation do not contribute much to the run time on one core, but as we try to distribute the workload among all cores on this node, their negative influence on the overall efficiency becomes more important.

Most significant in these plots is the limited scalability of the matrix setup in the old, MPI only version. Here we can see that the MPI parallelization shows scalability limits as soon as the workload per MPI process becomes too small. This is not a communication based bottleneck as the matrix setup is local, but a limitation induced by the underlying algorithm with its complex loop structure being heavy on memory access tasks. The new version shows significant improvements not only on the scaling but also on the sequential runtime. This leads to a difference in wall-clock time for the utilization of a full node between the old version requiring 198 s versus 97 s for the new version. Tests on Intel Knights Landing processors (Xeon Phi 7210) showed comparable results indicating performance portability of the new implementation.

4.3 Internode Hybrid Scaling

To investigate the full scaling of the hybrid code we studied two setups (Fig. 4): A smaller system on the RWTH Bull Cluster and a larger system on the more

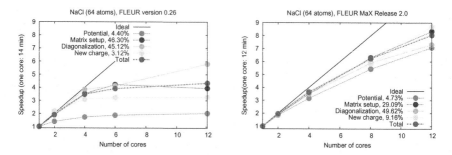

Fig. 3. Intranode scaling of the FLEUR code in total (red) as well as of its most relevant parts (time requirements are given as percentage of the total runtime for a single core (14 min/12 min)), before (MPI-only version 0.26, left side) and after (hybrid version MaX Release 2.0, right side) optimization. For the optimized version: up to 4 cores - only MPI processes, on 8 und 12 cores - hybrid parallelization. The simulations were performed on the RWTH Bull Cluster. (Color figure online)

modern CLAIX machine. Here we not only compared to the pure MPI parallelization of the older code version but we also studied the effect of shifting resources between the MPI- and the multithreaded parallelization. In all cases we utilized all cores of the node, but with a different number of MPI ranks per node and a resulting change in mutlithreading. Both systems on both machines show similar behavior. While the pure MPI parallelization is still efficient for small numbers of MPI-ranks, it becomes less favorable with increasing parallelization. Notably, in an intermediate range of parallelization there is little difference between the two approaches demonstrating that both implementations have a similar efficiency.

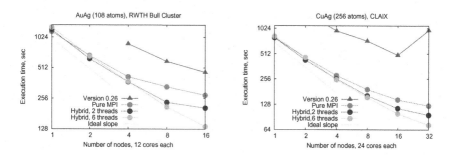

Fig. 4. Internode scaling of the FLEUR code, before (MPI-only version 0.26) and after (hybrid version MaX Release 2.0) optimization. For the hybrid version different hybrid setups are shown: pure MPI, i.e. 1 thread per MPI process (green), 2 threads per MPI process (blue) and 6 threads per MPI process (magenta). (Color figure online)

As a final test we also show (Fig. 5) that the new version of the code enables the simulation of significantly larger setups utilizing stronger parallelization.

Here we stress that the hybrid approach also is required as a pure MPI parallelization over 24 ranks per node will fail for larger setups due to memory constraints.

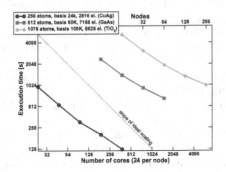

Fig. 5. Comparison of the scaling of the FLEUR code for three systems with different number of atoms, basis functions and electrons. The smallest system is the one discussed in Fig. 4, the largest system contains more than 1000 atoms. Due to the higher computational demand, the scaling for the larger systems extends to more nodes. (MaX Release 2.0, CLAIX compute cluster)

5 Conclusions

We demonstrated that the hybrid MPI+OpenMP parallelization of the large legacy DFT code FLEUR enables the efficient use of modern computer architectures to perform simulations of large unit-cells. The two most performance relevant parts, the matrix setup and the matrix diagonalization show improved scaling and performance by implementing interfaces to optimized standard libraries and by implementing an additional layer of OpenMP parallelization on top of the MPI parallelization. The possibility to shift computational resources between these different parallelization approaches not only shows the effectiveness of the hybrid scheme but also enables the adaptation to different hardware.

The new FLEUR version is able to treat setups with more than 1000 atoms. While this limit imposes an important milestone in itself, this also paves the way for the investigation of effects in heterogeneous multilayer structures, reconstructed surfaces, adsorbates on surfaces, defects and extended defects in solids, complex magnetic superstructures or simply large bulk superstructures.

Acknowledgments. This work has been supported by a JARA-HPC seed-fund project and by the MaX Center of Excellence [3] funded by the EU through the H2020-EINFRA-2015-1 project: GA 676598. The authors gratefully acknowledge the computing time granted by the JARA-HPC Vergabegremium on the RWTH supercomputer.

References

1. ScaLAPACK users' guide (1997). http://www.netlib.org/scalapack/slug
2. The Jülich FLEUR project (2018). http://www.flapw.de
3. MaX Centre of Excellence - Materials Design at the Exascale (2018). http://www.max-centre.eu
4. Psi-k: software codes (2018). http://psi-k.net/software
5. Andersen, O.K.: Linear methods in band theory. Phys. Rev. B **12**, 3060–3083 (1975)
6. Arfken, G.: The Addition Theorem for Spherical Harmonics, pp. 693–695. Academic Press, Orlando (1985)
7. Ashcroft, N.W., Mermin, N.D.: Solid State Physics. Holt, Rinehart and Winston, New York (1976)
8. Blügel, S., Bihlmayer, G.: Full-potential linearized augmented planewave method. In: Grotendorst, J., Blüel, S., Marx, D. (eds.) Computational Nanoscience: Do It Yourself! NIC Series. vol. 31, pp. 85–129. John von Neumann Institute for Computing, Jülich (2006)
9. Hohenberg, P., Kohn, W.: Inhomogeneous electron gas. Phys. Rev. **136**, B864–B871 (1964)
10. Jones, R.O.: Density functional theory: its origins, rise to prominence, and future. Rev. Mod. Phys. **8**, 897–923 (2015)
11. Koelling, D.D., Arbman, G.O.: Use of energy derivative of the radial solution in an augmented plane wave method: application to copper. J. Phys. F: Metal Phys. **5**, 2041–2054 (1975)
12. Kohn, W., Sham, L.: Self-consistent equations including exchange and correlation effects. Phys. Rev. **140**, A1133–A1138 (1965)
13. Marek, A., et al.: The ELPA library: scalable parallel eigenvalue solutions for electronic structure theory and computational science. J. Phys.: Condens. Matter **26**, 213201 (2014)
14. Napoli, E.D., et al.: High-performance generation of the hamiltonian and overlap matrices in FLAPW methods. Comput. Phys. Commun. **211**, 61–72 (2017)
15. Poulson, J., et al.: Elemental: a new framework for distributed memory dense matrix computations. ACM Trans. Math. Soft. **39**, 1–24 (2013)
16. Solca, R., et al.: Efficient implementation of quantum materials simulations on distributed CPU-GPU systems. In: Proceedings of the International Conference for High Performance Computing, Networking, Storage and Analysis, Texas, pp. 1–12 (2015)
17. Supalov, A., Semin, A., Klemm, M., Dahnken, C.: Optimizing HPC Applications with Intel Cluster Tools. Apress Media, Berkely (2014)
18. Weinert, M., Wimmer, E., Freeman, A.: Total-energy all-electron density functional method for bulk solids and surfaces. Phys. Rev. B **26**, 4571–4578 (1982)
19. Wimmer, E., Krakauer, H., Weinert, M., Freeman, A.J.: Full-potential self-consistent linearized-augmented-plane-wave method for calculating the electronic-structure of molecules and surfaces - O2 molecule. Phys. Rev. B **24**, 864–875 (1981)

Efficient Strict-Binning Particle-in-Cell Algorithm for Multi-core SIMD Processors

Yann Barsamian[1,2]([✉]) [iD], Arthur Charguéraud[1,2] [iD],
Sever A. Hirstoaga[2,3], and Michel Mehrenberger[2,3] [iD]

[1] Université de Strasbourg, CNRS, ICube UMR 7357,
Strasbourg, France
ybarsamian@unistra.fr
[2] Inria, Nancy, France
{arthur.chargueraud,sever.hirstoaga}@inria.fr
[3] Université de Strasbourg,
CNRS, IRMA UMR 7501, Strasbourg, France
mehrenbe@math.unistra.fr

Abstract. Particle-in-Cell (PIC) codes are widely used for plasma simulations. On recent multi-core hardware, performance of these codes is often limited by memory bandwidth. We describe a multi-core PIC algorithm that achieves close-to-minimal number of memory transfers with the main memory, while at the same time exploiting SIMD instructions for numerical computations and exhibiting a high degree of OpenMP-level parallelism. Our algorithm keeps particles sorted by cell at every time step, and represents particles from a same cell using a linked list of fixed-capacity arrays, called chunks. Chunks support either sequential or atomic insertions, the latter being used to handle fast-moving particles. To validate our code, called Pic-Vert, we consider a 3d electrostatic Landau-damping simulation as well as a 2d3v transverse instability of magnetized electron holes. Performance results on a 24-core Intel Skylake hardware confirm the effectiveness of our algorithm, in particular its high throughput and its ability to cope with fast moving particles.

Keywords: Particle-in-Cell · Plasma physics · Multi-core
SIMD architecture · Shared memory · Chunks · Strict binning
Magnetized electron holes

1 Introduction

The Particle-in-Cell (PIC) method enables large-scale simulations of plasma physics. PIC simulations are, for example, key to the design of ITER fusion reactor, and they also apply to other domains, e.g., astrophysics. As of 2018, PIC simulations accommodate at the order of 10^{13} particles, involving the hundreds of thousands of cores available on the world's top super-computers.

© Springer International Publishing AG, part of Springer Nature 2018
M. Aldinucci et al. (Eds.): Euro-Par 2018, LNCS 11014, pp. 749–763, 2018.
https://doi.org/10.1007/978-3-319-96983-1_53

To reach such a scale, state-of-the-art PIC codes exploit parallelism available at three levels: inter-node parallelism using, e.g., MPI; shared-memory multi-threading using, e.g., OpenMP, and register-level parallelism using SIMD instructions. A number of implementations also leverage GPUs or MICs. Implementations include EMSES [17], GTC-P [20], ORB5 [12], OSIRIS [8], PICADOR [19], PIConGPU [5], PSC [10], VPIC [4].

A recent paper [20] studied GTC-P performances in details, and points out that: *"metrics such as flop/s or percentage-of-peak are less relevant for the predominantly memory-bound gyrokinetic PIC methods."* The authors then present a model able to predict execution time as a function of data transfers. Most predominant is the intra-node operations on the shared memory (60% to 80% of the execution time). Their cost is decomposed between in-cache accesses, contiguous accesses, and random accesses—the latter being the most costly. This study shows that, to improve the performance of multi-core (intra-node) processing in PIC simulations, we must decrease the amount of costly memory accesses. Of course, we must do so by preserving the OpenMP-level parallelism as well as the crucial use of SIMD instructions.

The *strict-binning* approach to implementing the PIC method enables significant reduction in the number of random accesses and cache misses [1,7,17,21]: at every time step, particles that fall in the same cell are stored together. Doing so brings two main benefits. First, the electric field values can be read only once per cell, avoiding numerous cache misses and allowing SIMD computations when updating particle velocities. Second, the representation saves the need to store a cell index for each particle, thereby saving memory loads and stores.

A central challenge with the strict-binning approach is the representation of the dynamically-sized bins storing the particles. A state-of-the-art proposal by Nakashima et al. [17] organizes particles in a big array, ordering them according to their cell index, and leaving variable-size *gaps* between the groups of particles associated with each cell. Yet, this approach suffers from two important limitations. First, as particles move, maintaining the variable-size gaps requires costly operations for shifting particles. Second, the algorithm, which uses a coloring scheme [13] to avoid data races when processing the cells in parallel, does not handle well *fast-moving particles* (particles moving more than a couple cells away at a given time step): it resorts to sequential processing for these particles.

These two limitations are exacerbated when the percentage of *crossing particles* (particles changing cells at each time step) increases, to the point of possibly becoming a major bottleneck. For example, in a parallel execution using 64 cores, having as little as 0.5% of fast-moving particles can result in a 32% slowdown on the total execution time due to the sequential processing of these particles.[1]

We propose an algorithm implementing strict-binning for the PIC method that addresses the aforementioned limitations, while still supporting efficient OpenMP/SIMD parallelization of all critical loops. Our algorithm leverages the use of *chunk bags*, i.e. linked lists of fixed-capacity arrays, to achieve SIMD-

---

[1] Let t denote the single-core execution time. Assume 0.5% of sequential execution, and 99.5% using 64 cores. The parallel execution time is: $0.005t + 0.995t/64 = 1.32t/64$.

friendly storage of particles with limited memory overheads. These chunk bags are furthermore devised to support atomic push operations, which are used to handle fast-moving particles within the main parallel loop. Our algorithm minimizes the amount of memory transfers: at each time step, each particle gets read from and written to memory exactly once. In particular, no further move or reordering is ever required, regardless of the percentage of fast-moving particles.

This algorithm is efficient provided that the average number of particles per cell exceeds a couple hundreds. Although laser-driven particle acceleration simulations can use as few as 30 particles per cell [5], large-scale, high-precision simulations may involve hundreds to thousands of particles per cell [4,10,21].

Through the rest of this paper, we describe our algorithm, comment on its theoretical properties (space usage, parallelization of critical loops, amount of memory transfers), discuss performance results (bandwidth usage, impact of fast-moving particles), numerical results (simulation of Landau-damping and of transverse instability of magnetized electron holes), and related work.

Parameters

N: number of particles.

nbCells $= X \cdot Y \cdot Z$: size of the grid.

Δt: duration of a time step.

Variables

particles[0..N − 1]: set of particles, with position x_p and velocity v_p.

$\rho[0..X][0..Y][0..Z]$: charge density.

$E[0..X][0..Y][0..Z]$: electric field.

Algorithm

Foreach time step

  Set all cells of ρ to 0

  Foreach particle

    Interpolate E to x_p Stored in E_p

    Update velocity $v_p \mathrel{+}= \frac{q}{m} E_p \Delta t$

    Update position $x_p \mathrel{+}= v_p \Delta t$

    Accumulate charge from x_p on ρ

  Compute E from ρ Poisson solver

Fig. 1. High-level description of the Particle-in-Cell (PIC) method.

2   An Efficient, Strict-Binning, Multicore PIC Algorithm

Figure 1 describes the PIC method, applied to the resolution of the Vlasov-Poisson system, which models the time evolution of the distribution function of charged particles in a plasma. Following the Cloud-in-Cell model [3, Sect. 2.6.], we interpolate the electric field and accumulate the charges linearly from/to the eight corners of the grid cell where each particle lies. The Poisson solver takes less than 5% of the execution time, we thus focus our attention on the particle loop.

Our implementation performs all computations in double precision, with the exception of positions, which are stored using the "index plus offset" representation [4, III.E.], whereby the position of a particle is described relative to the corner of the cell containing the particle, using 3 `float` values, yielding sufficient precision. In the strict binning approach, the index of the containing cell is implicit. Thus, each particle admits a 36-byte representation.

Particles are stored in fixed-capacity arrays (*chunks*, e.g., [1]). Several chunks might be needed to store all the particles contained in a same cell. Each cell is thus described by a linked list of chunks (a *chunk bag*). The number of particles in a chunk, denoted by K thereafter, should enable efficient vectorization (K is a multiple of 16 for 512-bit registers), and at the same time be large enough to tame the cost of following a pointer from a chunk to the next (e.g., 128 or 256).

Benchmarking on the hardware considered reveals that the structure of arrays (SoA) layout, which enables better vectorization, improves performance compared with the array of structures (AoS) layout. The memory layout we use for the particles is summarized on the next page. (Arrays should be aligned.)

```
struct chunk { struct chunk* next; int size; // 0 <= size <= K
               float  dx[K], dy[K], dz[K];
               double vx[K], vy[K], vz[K]; } chunk;
struct { chunk* front, back; } bag; // linked list of chunks
```

The chunk bag data structure supports $O(1)$ insertion of a particle (adding a fresh chunk if needed), $O(1)$ merge of two bags thanks to the *back* field (note that chunk compaction is not needed), and $O(n)$ iteration over the contents, all with excellent constant factors. Furthermore, unlike chunks introduced by prior work [1], our chunk bags are devised to support a thread-safe atomic insertion operation. Atomic insertions are central to the handling of fast-moving particles. Atomic insertion uses a fetch-and-add instruction to reserve a slot in the chunk for the particle. If a thread attempts to reserve the one-past-the-end slot, it acquires responsibility to extend the bag with a fresh chunk, in which case it sets the *next* pointer of the fresh chunk to the current *front* pointer of the bag, and sets the *front* pointer of the bag to the address of the fresh chunk.

When processing a chunk of particles, the algorithm first updates velocities and positions, then migrates the particles to different chunks, depending on the cell associated with their new position. Once all particles from the chunk are processed, the chunk is stored into a (per-core) free list, so as to be subsequently reused to extend a bag whose last chunk becomes full. Our algorithm preserves the following invariant: at the beginning of a time step, all the particles are stored in at most $\lceil N/K \rceil + 2 \cdot$ nbCells chunks, where N denotes the total number of particles, and K denotes the number of particles per chunk.

To dispatch particles according to their target cells, we associate two bags with each cell: a *private bag*, accessed at most by one thread at a time; and a *shared bag*, accessed concurrently, to handle fast-moving particles. To initialize these two bags, we need an additional $2 \cdot$ nbCells empty chunks. In total, we need $\lceil N/K \rceil + 4 \cdot$ nbCells chunks. We have proved that this number of chunk suffices at any point of a simulation, regardless of how particles move. Thus, the space used by our algorithm, in addition to the minimal amount of memory needed to represent the particles, grows in proportion with $4K \cdot$ nbCells $\cdot$ sizeof(particle).[2]

---

[2] In practice, we allocate a dozen extra chunks per core, giving some slack and avoiding dynamic load balancing of free chunks. Note that it is very unlikely for these chunks to ever be needed, because cores free chunks at a faster rate than they fill chunks.

In order to maximize the number of insertions into private bags while preserving a high degree of OpenMP parallelism, we follow the coloring scheme proposed by Kong et al. [13], and generalized from 2d to 3d by Nakashima et al. [17]. The idea is to fill the space with *tiles*, of size $2 \times 2 \times 2$ (or more), in a regular manner. Tiles are colored using 8 different colors in such a way that two adjacent tiles have distinct colors. At each of the 8 color phases, $\frac{1}{8}$ of the tiles are processed, in parallel by nbCores threads.[3] Because cells processed in parallel by distinct threads are at least 2 cells away from each other, all the particles that move, at a given time step, no more than one cell away (no more than half a tile away, in general) can be pushed into private bags, in a thread-safe manner.

The pseudo-code of our algorithm appears in Fig. 2. Particles from a same cell are processed sequentially by a same thread. To benefit from SIMD performance, we split the loop over each chunk. (If one chunk does not fit into L1 cache, additional splitting is needed.) First, our code updates velocities (line 12). Second, it computes the new positions (line 14), introducing an auxiliary array for storing the new cell indices. Third, it sequentially pushes each particle into the chunk associated with its target cell. If the target cell lies in the current tile, or lies in the closer half of an immediate neighboring tile, a non-atomic insertion is performed on a private bag (line 19). Otherwise, an atomic insertion is performed on a shared bag (line 21). Note that the boolean condition involved can be evaluated using a simple arithmetic test.

Once all the particles are processed, the algorithm merges, for each cell, its private bag with its shared bag (line 26). No chunk compaction is performed at this point; as a result, the bag associated with one cell may contain up to 2 non-full chunks. Thus, there are at most $\lceil N/K \rceil + 2 \cdot$ nbCells nonempty chunks at the beginning of the next time step. It follows that at least $2 \cdot$ nbCells empty chunks must have been freed during the current time step. This number corresponds exactly to the number of chunks needed to initialize the private and the shared bags for the next time step. Our algorithm performs this initialization efficiently in parallel (using a prefix sum array, based on the sizes of the per-core free lists).

We next describe the treatment of the charge density and the electric field (ρ and E). When processing particles from one cell, the algorithm first reads from memory the values of the electric field on the 8 corners of that cell (line 9). Importantly, thanks to the strict-binning approach, this data needs only be loaded once from memory. As particles are processed and moved to their target cells, the charge of each particle is accumulated (line 22) into the array ρNext, which, at the end of the time step, is used to update E for the next iteration. We exploit a recently-proposed, ingenious technique allowing to accumulate the charge on the 8 corners using SIMD instructions [22]. Concretely, the array ρNext involves some amount of redundancy: for each cell, 8 values are stored adjacently in memory, describing the charge on the 8 corners of that cell. At the end of a time step,

---

[3] For a $2 \times 2 \times 2$ tiling, at the i-th coloring phase, the algorithm processes cells whose coordinates satisfy: $((x/2) \bmod 2) + 2 \cdot ((y/2) \bmod 2) + 4 \cdot ((z/2) \bmod 2) = i$. Using larger tiles is possible but greatly reduces the number of tiles processed in parallel.

```
1   bag particles[0..nbCells−1]; // Particles by cell, at current time step
2   bag particlesNextPrivate[0..nbCells−1], particlesNextShared[0..nbCells−1];
3   double ρ[0..X][0..Y][0..Z], E[0..X][0..Y][0..Z];
4   double ρNext[0..nbCores−1][0..nbCells−1][0..7]; // 8 corners per cell
5   Foreach time step
6     Foreach color in [0..7] // 8 coloring phases
7       Parallel Foreach tile of that color // OpenMP parallel
8         Foreach cell idCell in that tile
9           Read E[x][y][z], foreach (x, y, z) among the 8 corners of cell idCell
10          Foreach chunk in particles[idCell]
11            Foreach particle in that chunk // SIMD vectorized
12              Update particle velocity
13            Foreach particle in that chunk // SIMD vectorized
14              Update particle position
15              Compute idCellNext, the index of the cell containing the particle
16            Foreach particle in that chunk
17              If the particle moves inside its tile
18              Or it moves to the closer half of a neighbor tile
19                Add the particle into particlesNextPrivate[idCellNext]
20              Else
21                Atomically add the particle into particlesNextShared[idCellNext]
22              Add its charge into ρNext[thisCoreId][idCellNext][..] // SIMD
23            Put a pointer to that chunk into the freelist of the current core
24    Parallel Foreach idCell in [0..nbCells−1] // OpenMP parallel
25      Set particles[idCell] to particlesNextPrivate[idCell]
26      Merge particlesNextShared[idCell] into particles[idCell]
27      Set particlesNextPrivate[idCell] to empty, using an empty chunk
28      Set particlesNextShared[idCell] to empty, using an empty chunk
29    Parallel Foreach (x, y, z) in [0..X]x[0..Y]x[0..Z] // OpenMP parallel, collapsed
30      Foreach of the 8 pairs (idCell,i) such that (x,y,z) is i−th corner of idCell
31        Foreach idCore in [0..nbCores−1]
32          ρ[x][y][z] += ρNext[idCore][idCell][i]
33          ρNext[idCore][idCell][i] = 0
34    Compute E from ρ using a Poisson solver and set ρ to 0 // FFTW + OpenMP
```

Fig. 2. Our parallel algorithm for the PIC method on multicore architectures.

the charge at a grid point is computed by summing the values associated with the 8 cells that have this grid point as one of their corners (line 32).

We considered two different possibilities for updating ρNext. The first possibility is to decompose ρNext into a *private* array and a *shared* array, just like we do for bags of particles. In this approach, only the deposit of the charge of fast-moving particles triggers atomic operations; for all others particles, we can use SIMD operations. The second possibility is to decompose ρNext into nbCores arrays. In this approach, each core has exclusive access to its charge array, so all accesses use SIMD operations. The downside is a slight increase in the memory footprint, and in the time needed to sum up the values. However, under our assumption of a reasonably large number of particles per cell, these additional costs are tiny in front of the gains. Thus, we opted for the latter approach.

Under the assumption of (at least) hundreds of particles per cell in average, the operations for manipulating chunks (following pointers, pushing/popping in free lists) and for manipulating per-cell information are all well amortized. Overall, our algorithm is not far from optimal in terms of memory transfers.

Optimization When Particles Move at Most One Cell per Time Step. For simulations whose physical parameters ensure that movement is restricted to immediate neighboring cells (e.g., [4,10]), we can optimize our algorithm by removing the shared bags altogether. In this case, we require only $\lceil N/K \rceil +$ $2 \cdot$ nbCells + nbCores chunks, and do not need any atomic insertion operation. Likewise, ρNext can be stored in a single array (indexed by cells and by corners).

3   Performance Results

To assess correctness and performance of our code, which is called Pic-Vert, we considered two classical test cases: a 3d Landau-damping simulation and a 2d3v electron hole simulation. Section 4 presents details on these experiments, and argues that the numerical results produced by our simulation match the expected results. In the remaining of this section, we discuss performance results.

Experimental hardware is an Intel Xeon Platinum 8160 @ 2.1 GHz (Skylake), with 96 GB of RAM, 6 memory channels, and 24 cores. Our C code was compiled using Intel C Compiler 17.0.4, and the FFTW3 library [9] for the Poisson solver.

The algorithm depends on two parameters. First, we use tiles of size 2 x 2 x 2 for the coloring. Tiles of size 4 x 4 x 4 lead to similarly good performances. Using larger tiles degrades performance. Second, we use K = 256 for the chunk capacity. Larger values of K increase the space usage and do not reduce the execution time. Smaller values of K increase the execution time overheads: +12% for K = 128, and +52% for K = 64. Note that, for K = 256, the memory "slack", which is equal to $4 \cdot$ nbCells $\cdot$ sizeof(chunk), represents in the Landau-damping simulation only 13% of the amount of memory strictly required for representing the particles.

Achieved Throughput. For the end-user of a simulation, the metric that matters is the number of particles processed per second. The Pic-Vert code achieves:

- 740 million particles per second (30.8 m/s/core) in the 3d Landau-damping simulation, where 31% of the particles change cell at each iteration;
- 910 million particles per second (37.9 m/s/core) in the 2d3v electron hole simulation, where 32% of the particles change cell at each iteration.

Analysis in the Roofline Performance Model. As argued in Sect. 2, our algorithm performs not far from the minimal number of memory operations— a key feature for PIC simulations hit by the memory bandwidth bottleneck.

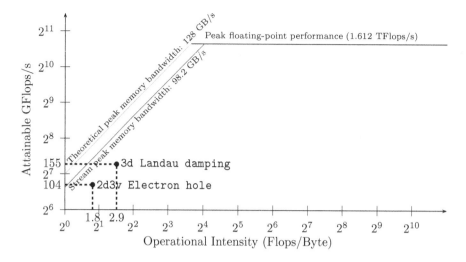

Fig. 3. Analysis of performances in the roofline model.

With this property in mind, it is interesting to compare the memory band-width achieved by our algorithm against the capacity of the hardware. Consider the Landau-damping simulation. The memory bandwidth achieved is 53.6 GB/s.[4] The *theoretical peak* advertised by the manufacturer is 127.99 GB/s. The Stream benchmark [15], which aims at evaluating the *practical peak* using a few microbenchmark programs, and which is commonly used as a baseline, provides the measure 98.2 GB/s. Our algorithm thus achieves 42% of the theoretical peak and 55% of the practical peak bandwidth. Reaching higher percentage in a PIC simulation appears to be very challenging.

Our algorithm is memory bound. In general, an algorithm may be *compute bound* (i.e. limited by the number of floating-point operations per second) or *memory bound* (i.e. limited by the number of bytes per second transfered from main memory) depending on its *operational intensity*, defined as the number of operations performed divided by the number of bytes moved from or to the main memory. We computed the operational intensity of the 3d code by counting the number of floating point operations per particle (79 operations in single-precision and 65 in double-precision, which leads to 209 operations when normalized to single-precision), and counting the number of bytes used to represent a particle (36 bytes, plus 0.25 byte to account for chunk headers). We thus derive that our

---

[4] The bandwidth is obtained by multiplying the size of a particle (36 bytes, plus $\frac{64}{K}$ bytes to account for chunk headers) by the number of particle processed per second (740 million), and by a factor 2 (one read plus one write). It would be very interesting to compare with other algorithms. Unfortunately, such numbers are rarely advertised, and comparisons are often hazardous due to differences in hardware, in particle representation (e.g., `float` vs `double`), in numerical schemes, etc.

3d code has an operational intensity equal to $209/(2 \cdot 36.25) \approx 2.9$. Similarly, we computed the operation intensity for the 2d3v code to be $114/(2 \cdot 32.25) \approx 1.8$.

Figure 3 represents the bounds on computation and memory bandwidth, in a chart showing the operational intensity on the x-axis, and the computation performance on the y-axis [23]. Note that both axes are log-scale. The computation bound is an horizontal line, at 1,612 GFlops/s (billion floating-point operations per second), a figure provided by the hardware manufacturer. The theoretical and practical memory bounds (bytes/s) are diagonal lines, because the bound in performance (flop/s) is equal to the operational intensity (flop/byte) multiplied by the memory bandwidth (bytes/s). Each diagonal line meets the horizontal line at the point of break-even between memory bound and compute bound.

Efficient Processing of Fast-Moving Particles. In addition to being memory efficient, our algorithm also benefits from another key feature not found in prior strict-binning algorithms: fast-moving particles are handled efficiently within the main parallel loop. For a particle moving more than half a tile away, we require only one extra atomic operation. Moreover, the contention associated with this atomic operation is relatively limited. Indeed, for two atomic operations to be issued on the same memory cell at the "same time" (i.e., close enough in time for a race on the cache line to occur), it must be the case that two particles taken from two distinct tiles spaced away by at least one full tile are moving towards the same cell of a third tile, at the "same time". Thus, the performance of our algorithm should be relatively independent form the heat.

To empirically evaluate the impact of fast-moving particles, we consider a simulation in which we artificially varied the initial distribution of particle velocities. To that end, we manually tuned these distributions in such a way as to obtain several test cases with increasing number of fast-moving particles.[5] Each test case is reflected by a column from Table 1. More specifically, the three first rows show the percentage of particles that move away from 1, 2 or 3 cells from their current grid cell at each time step (no particle move further away).

Table 1. Impact on performance of increasing the percentage of fast particles.

Particles that move 1 cell away	8.0%	8.0%	8.0%	8.0%	8.0%	8.0%	8.0%
Particles that move 2 cells away	0	0.7%	1.9%	3.1%	4.3%	5.6%	4.4%
Particles that move 3 cells away	0	0	0	0	0	0.2%	1.4%
Particles pushed atomically (line 21)	0.0%	0.4%	1.0%	1.6%	2.2%	3.1%	3.7%
Slowdown w.r.t. first column	0	0.0%	0.9%	3.8%	4.4%	4.2%	7.0%

By instrumenting the code, we measured the number of push operations that trigger an atomic write (line 21 from Fig. 2). These numbers, relative to the total

---

[5] Particle velocities in the experiment of Table 1 follow the sum of two Gaussian distributions, like in the bump-on-tail instability. Details may be found in [2].

number of particles, appear in the fourth line of the table: they vary from 0% to 3.7%. The last row of Table 1 gives the corresponding slowdown on the total execution time. Figures show that even when the percentage of particles whose move require an atomic operation is as high as 3.7%, the cost of processing these fast moving particles remains fairly limited: +7.0%. In comparison, any alternative algorithm that sequentially processes 3.7% of the particles in a 24-core execution would suffer at least from a +85% slowdown (recall Sect. 1).

Scaling. Although inter-node parallelism is orthogonal to the focus of the present paper, we used particle decomposition to scale our algorithm on 128 Skylake sockets (each with 24 cores, 12.3 TB of RAM in total), using one MPI process per socket. We simulated Landau-damping with 256 billion particles, achieving a throughput of 89.6 billion particles per second: 123x speedup w.r.t. one socket.

4   Numerical Results

3d3v Landau-Damping. We consider a classical Landau-damping test case [3, 11], simulating 2 billion particles on a $64 \times 64 \times 64$ grid, for 500 time steps. We use the same parameters as in [18]: time step of 0.05, periodic boundary conditions on spatial domain $\Omega = [0, 22]^3$ and initial distribution function:

$$f_0(x, y, z, \mathbf{v}) = \frac{1}{(2\pi)^{3/2}} e^{-|\mathbf{v}|^2/2} L(x)L(y)L(z) \quad \text{with } L(w) = 1 + 0.05\cos(\pi w/11).$$

Figure 4 represents the evolution of electric energy. It shows that the decay slope in our simulation is in accordance with the theoretical value $\gamma = -0.008466$ obtained from the dispersion analysis.

2d3v Electron Hole. We consider a more complex test case proposed by Muschietti et al. [16]. We simulate 64 billion particles on a 512×512 grid (on

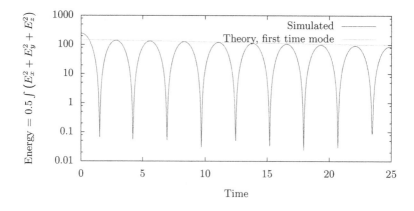

Fig. 4. Time evolution of electric energy in the Landau damping simulation.

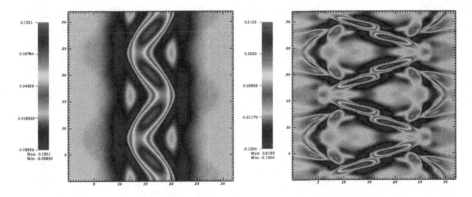

Fig. 5. Time evolution of $\rho(t, x, y)$ in the electron hole simulation, at $t = 20$ and $t = 40$.

32 Skylake sockets). Time step is 0.1 and spatial domain is $[0, L]^2$, with $L = 32$. The initial function is $f(x, y, v) = F_1(v_1^2 - 2\phi(x, y))e^{-50(v_2^2 + v_3^2)}$ with potential $\phi(x, y) = e^{-0.5\left((x - L/2)/\Delta_\parallel - 0.3\cos(0.39y)\right)^2}$, with $\Delta_\parallel = 3$ and F_1 defined as:

$$F_1(w) = \begin{cases} \frac{\sqrt{-w}}{\pi \Delta_\parallel^2}\left(1 + 2\ln(\frac{\psi}{-2w})\right) + \frac{6 + (\sqrt{2} + \sqrt{-w})(1-w)\sqrt{-w}}{\pi(\sqrt{2} + \sqrt{-w})(4 - 2w + w^2)}, & \text{for } -2\psi \leq w < 0, \\ \frac{6\sqrt{2}}{\pi(8 + w^3)}, & \text{for } w > 0. \end{cases}$$

The external magnetic field is aligned with x and has amplitude $B_0 = 0.2$.

Figure 5 shows the charge density $\rho(t, x, y) = 1 - \int f(t, x, y, v)dv$, on the left at time $t = 20$, and on the right at time $t = 40$. These results are qualitatively similar to those from Muschietti et al. [16].

In addition, we studied the convergence of the simulation with respect to the number of particles and to the grid size. To that end, we compare, for different settings of these two parameters, the time evolution of a quantity representative of the instability.[6] Results appear in Fig. 6. They show that using a small 32×32 grid with 200 million particles as considered by Muschietti et al. exhibits the correct qualitative behavior up to $t = 50$, but diverges beyond this point.

For a quick simulation, it appears preferable to use a 64×64 grid with only 20 million particles, as it gives quantitatively accurate results up to $t = 50$. For longer simulations, our results show that using a 128×128 or a 256×256 grid with 200 million particles suffices to give accurate results up to $t = 100$. Indeed, the two corresponding curves are close to that of our large-scale simulation, which uses a 512×512 grid with 64 billion particles (the top-most curve at $t = 100$).

---

[6] This quantity, which we call "y part of electric field norm", is defined as half of the square root of the electric energy $\int (E_x^2 + E_y^2)$ minus the part of that energy corresponding to the modes in x (here, the first 20 modes).

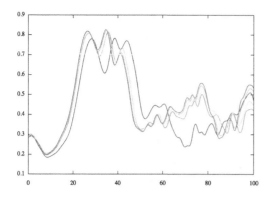

200 million particles, 32x32 cells ——————
200 million particles, 64x64 cells ——————
20 million particles, 64x64 cells ——————
200 million particles, 128x128 cells ··········
200 million particles, 256x256 cells
64 billion particles, 512x512 cells ——————

Fig. 6. Time evolution of the y part of electric field norm in the electron hole simulation, for different values of the number of particles and of the grid size.

5 Technical Comparison to Related Work

We organize the discussion of related work by focusing on three main criteria: strict or non-strict binning, representation of particles, and treatment of data races arising when two threads push data onto a same target cell.

To ensure efficient accesses to the electric field and charge arrays, locality is essential in PIC simulations. In numerous algorithms, particles are stored in an array and ordered by their cell index. Yet, because particles move in the grid, their locality in the array decreases at each time step. Thus, reordering operations must be performed: either at every time step, to maximize locality (e.g., [12]), or at some lower frequency, reducing locality but mitigating the cost of re-sorting (e.g., [4,10]). Depending on the option, performances suffer either from numerous costly random accesses or from suboptimal locality.

Rather than sorting, other algorithms rely on *coarse-grained binning* [5,19, 20,22]. Particles are organized in super-cells (of size, e.g., 10 x 10 x 10), and a dynamically-sized data structure is used to represent particles from a same super-cell. For example, *attribute tiles* [5] have been used to store particles on GPU using doubly linked lists of fixed-capacity arrays. Unlike with our chunks, particles in an attribute tile are processed in place. If a particle moves to a different super-cell, it is migrated to a transfer buffer, and its slot is marked as a *hole* in an auxiliary bitmap. Subsequently, holes are filled with particles incoming from neighboring super-cells. Remaining holes, if any, are filled using particles taken from the end of the attribute tile. In contrast, in our algorithm, particles are directly moved to their target bin—they get moved exactly once per time step.

While *strict binning* overcomes several of the aforementioned limitations, it is nontrivial to implement efficiently. Representing each cell by a single fixed-capacity array [6,21] is space inefficient, and falls short outside of specific scenarios where uniform particle density can be assumed. Linked lists [11, Sect. 8.4.] lead to tremendous overheads both in terms of space (to represent list cells) and time (to follow indirections). Vectors, a.k.a. resizable arrays, suffer from a prohibitive 2x space overhead and involve costly resize operations.

Packed Memory Arrays (PMAs) [7] have been proposed as a specialized data structure for keeping particles sorted by their cell index. This data structure stores particles in a large array that also contains a fraction of unused cells, called *gaps* (a.k.a. *holes*). The width of the gaps may increase or decrease as particles move cells. When a gap closes, rebalancing operations involving backward or forward shifting of the particles must be performed to restore balanced gaps.

Nakashima et al. [17] propose a data structure that we view as a parallelism-friendly version of PMAs. To tame the frequency of rebalancing operations, the authors introduce thread-local *overflow buffers*. However, as the authors acknowledge [17, III.D.], these buffers come at the cost of increased complexity in the code, of additional space usage, and of slower processing of the overflow buffers, on which SIMD operations do not apply.

In Nakashima et al.'s work [17], most data races are eliminated thanks to the use of a 8-color scheme [13], which we also use. For the remaining data races, which are associated with fast-moving particles, their algorithm processes them in a separate sequential loop, which induces a major sequential bottleneck as soon as the percentage of fast-moving particles exceeds a fraction of a percent. In contrast, we are able to integrate the processing of these particles within the main parallel loop, using an atomic operation.

Furthermore, unlike prior work exploiting PMAs, our approach relies on a general-purpose bag representation, based on chunks. We only customize the bag implementation to accommodate SoA layout. Our data structure does not involve any shifting of data nor any overflow buffer. This has two main benefits. First, we save numerous memory operations. Second, the performance of our algorithm is robust to an increase in the percentage of fast-moving particles.

6   Future Work

In this work, we focused on multicore and SIMD parallelism. In future work, it would be great to extend our algorithm with a layer of domain decomposition, using MPI communications. We speculate that chunks could be used as buffers for emission and reception of particles reaching the cells at the frontier of a domain. These chunks could then be merged, at the end of the time step, with the locally-processed chunks. The flexibility offered by chunks might be helpful for dealing with dynamically-sized domains. Furthermore, it would be interesting to adapt our algorithm to target architectures with larger number of cores, such as GPUs or MICs. We think that the organization in chunks could help addressing the issue of load balancing, which is critical on these architectures (e.g., [14]).

Data Availability Statement. The datasets and code generated during and/or analyzed during the current study are available in the figshare repository [2].

Acknowledgments. We would like to thank the anonymous reviewers for their valuable suggestions and comments. This work has been carried out within the framework of the EUROfusion Consortium and has received funding from the Euratom Research and Training Program 2014–2018 under Grant Agreement No. 633053. Simulations were run on the EUROfusion Marconi supercomputer, in the context of the Selavlas project led by K. Kormann. The views and opinions expressed herein do not necessarily reflect those of the European Commission.

References

1. Barsamian, Y., Charguéraud, A., Ketterlin, A.: A space and bandwidth efficient multicore algorithm for the particle-in-cell method. In: Wyrzykowski, R., Dongarra, J., Deelman, E., Karczewski, K. (eds.) PPAM 2017. LNCS, vol. 10777, pp. 133–144. Springer, Cham (2018). https://doi.org/10.1007/978-3-319-78024-5_13

2. Barsamian, Y., Charguéraud, A., Hirstoaga, S.A., Mehrenberger, M.: Software artifacts for Euro-Par 2018 paper: "Efficient Strict-Binning Particle-in-Cell Algorithm forMulti-Core SIMD Processors". In: Figshare (2018). https://doi.org/10.6084/m9.figshare.6391796

3. Birdsall, C.K., Langdon, A.B.: Plasma Physics via Computer Simulation. McGraw-Hill, New York (1985)

4. Bowers, K.J., Albright, B.J., Yin, L., Bergen, B., Kwan, T.J.T.: Ultrahigh performance three-dimensional electromagnetic relativistic kinetic plasma simulation. Phys. Plasmas **15**(5), 055703 (2008). https://doi.org/10.1063/1.2840133

5. Bussmann, M., Burau, H., Cowan, T.E., Debus, A., Huebl, A., Juckeland, G., Kluge, T., Nagel, W.E., Pausch, R., Schmitt, F., Schramm, U., Schuchart, J., Widera, R.: Radiative signatures of the relativistic Kelvin-Helmholtz instability. In: International Conference on High Performance Computing, Networking, Storage and Analysis (SC), pp. 5:1–5:12 (2013). https://doi.org/10.1145/2503210.2504564

6. Decyk, V.K., Singh, T.V.: Particle-in-Cell algorithms for emerging computer architectures. Comput. Phys. Commun. **185**(3), 708–719 (2014). https://doi.org/10.1016/j.cpc.2013.10.013

7. Durand, M., Raffin, B., Faure, F.: A packed memory array to keep moving particles sorted. In: Workshop on Virtual Reality Interaction and Physical Simulation (VRIPHYS) (2012). https://doi.org/10.2312/PE/vriphys/vriphys12/069-077

8. Fonseca, R.A., Vieira, J., Fiuza, F., Davidson, A., Tsung, F.S., Mori, W.B., Silva, L.O.: Exploiting multi-scale parallelism for large scale numerical modelling of laser wakefield accelerators. Plasma Phys. Control. Fusion **55**(12), 124011 (2013). https://doi.org/10.1088/0741-3335/55/12/124011

9. Frigo, M., Johnson, S.G.: The design and implementation of FFTW3. Proc. IEEE **93**(2), 216–231 (2005). https://doi.org/10.1109/JPROC.2004.840301. http://www.fftw.org

10. Germaschewski, K., Fox, W., Abbott, S., Ahmadi, N., Maynard, K., Wang, L., Ruhl, H., Bhattacharjee, A.: The plasma simulation code: a modern particle-in-cell code with patch-based load-balancing. J. Comput. Phys. **318**, 305–326 (2016). https://doi.org/10.1016/j.jcp.2016.05.013

11. Hockney, R.W., Eastwood, J.W.: Computer Simulation Using Particles. Institute of Physics, Philadelphia (1988). https://doi.org/10.1201/9781439822050

12. Jocksch, A., Hariri, F., Tran, T.-M., Brunner, S., Gheller, C., Villard, L.: A bucket sort algorithm for the particle-in-cell method on manycore architectures. In: Wyrzykowski, R., Deelman, E., Dongarra, J., Karczewski, K., Kitowski, J., Wiatr, K. (eds.) PPAM 2015. LNCS, vol. 9573, pp. 43–52. Springer, Cham (2016). https://doi.org/10.1007/978-3-319-32149-3_5

13. Kong, X., Huang, M.C., Ren, C., Decyk, V.K.: Particle-in-cell simulations with charge-conserving current deposition on graphic processing units. J. Comput. Phys. **230**(4), 1676–1685 (2011). https://doi.org/10.1016/j.jcp.2010.11.032

14. Larin, A., Bastrakov, S., Bashinov, A., Efimenko, E., Surmin, I., Gonoskov, A., Meyerov, I.: Load balancing for particle-in-cell plasma simulation on multi-core systems. In: 12th Internationall Conference Parallel Processing and Applied Mathematics (PPAM), pp. 145–155 (2018). https://doi.org/10.1007/978-3-319-78024-5_14

15. McCalpin, J.D.: Memory bandwidth and machine balance in current high performance computers. In: IEEE Technical Committee on Computer Architecture Newsletter (TCCA), pp. 19–25 (1995). https://www.cs.virginia.edu/stream/

16. Muschietti, L., Roth, I., Carlson, C.W., Ergun, R.E.: Transverse instability of magnetized electron holes. Phys. Rev. Lett. **85**(1), 94–97 (2000). https://doi.org/10.1103/PhysRevLett.85.94

17. Nakashima, H., Summura, Y., Kikura, K., Miyake, Y.: Large scale manycore-aware PIC simulation with efficient particle binning. In: IEEE International Parallel and Distributed Processing Symposium (IPDPS), pp. 202–212 (2017). https://doi.org/10.1109/IPDPS.2017.65

18. Ricketson, L.F., Cerfon, A.J.: Sparse grid techniques for particle-in-cell schemes. Plasma Phys. Control. Fusion **59**(2), 024002 (2017). https://doi.org/10.1088/1361-6587/59/2/024002

19. Surmin, I., Bastrakov, S., Matveev, Z., Efimenko, E., Gonoskov, A., Meyerov, I.: Co-design of a particle-in-cell plasma simulation code for Intel Xeon Phi: a first look at knights landing. In: Carretero, J., et al. (eds.) ICA3PP 2016. LNCS, vol. 10049, pp. 319–329. Springer, Cham (2016). https://doi.org/10.1007/978-3-319-49956-7_25

20. Tang, W., Wang, B., Ethier, S., Kwasniewski, G., Hoefler, T., Ibrahim, K.Z., Madduri, K., Williams, S., Oliker, L., Rosales-Fernandez, C., Williams, T.: Extreme scale plasma turbulence simulations on top supercomputers world-wide. In: International Conference for High Performance Computing, Networking, Storage and Analysis (SC), pp. 502–513 (2016). https://doi.org/10.1109/SC.2016.42

21. Tskhakaya, D., Schneider, R.: Optimization of PIC codes by improved memory management. J. Comput. Phys. **225**(1), 829–839 (2007). https://doi.org/10.1016/j.jcp.2007.01.002

22. Vincenti, H., Lobet, M., Lehe, R., Sasanka, R., Vay, J.-L.: An efficient and portable SIMD algorithm for charge/current deposition in particle-in-cell codes. Comput. Phys. Commun. **210**, 145–154 (2016). https://doi.org/10.1016/j.cpc.2016.08.023

23. Williams, S., Waterman, A., Patterson, D.: Roofline: an insightful visual performance model for multicore architectures. Commun. ACM **52**(4), 65–76 (2009). https://doi.org/10.1145/1498765.1498785

Task-Based Programming on Emerging Parallel Architectures for Finite-Differences Seismic Numerical Kernel

Salli Moustafa[1(✉)], Wilfried Kirschenmann[1],
Fabrice Dupros[2], and Hideo Aochi[2]

[1] ANEO, Boulogne-Billancourt, France
{s.moustafa,w.kirschenmann}@aneo.fr
[2] BRGM, Orléans, France
{f.dupros,h.aochi}@brgm.fr

Abstract. In recent years, heterogeneous hardware have generalized in almost all supercomputer nodes, requiring a profound shift on the way numerical applications are implemented. This paper, illustrates the design and implementation of a seismic wave propagation simulator, based on the finite-differences numerical scheme, and specifically tailored for such massively parallel hardware infrastructures. The application data-flow is built on top of PaRSEC, a generic task-based runtime system. The numerical kernels, designed for maximizing data reuse can efficiently leverage large SIMD units available in modern CPU cores. A strong scalability study on a cluster of Intel KNL processors illustrates the application performances.

Keywords: High-performance computing
C++ generic programming · SIMD · Task-based runtime system
PaRSEC · Seismic wave propagation

1 Introduction

Since the advent of multicore processor at the beginning of 2000's, the compute power is not more driven by the clock frequency [1], but instead, by the number of functional units into multi/many-core processors featuring large SIMD units or in accelerators such as GPUs. The combination of these computing devices lead to highly heterogeneous hardware infrastructures. Hence, maximizing application performance on such systems is a major challenge [2–4]. Indeed, for coping with these systems, application developers use to mix several programming paradigms, following the now classical MPI+X approach. MPI manages communication through the network interconnect and is completed by OpenMP, Intel TBB, CUDA or OpenCL for addressing each node.

Task-based approach coupled with a generic runtime system is an emerging programming paradigm that greatly improves programmer productivity, leaving

© Springer International Publishing AG, part of Springer Nature 2018
M. Aldinucci et al. (Eds.): Euro-Par 2018, LNCS 11014, pp. 764–777, 2018.
https://doi.org/10.1007/978-3-319-96983-1_54

him to focus on the algorithm and computational kernels implementation. From this perspective, building high-performance codes require fine-tuned kernels. As the main bottleneck on modern platforms is the memory bandwidth [5], those kernels must ensure a good data locality. In addition, the kernels have to leverage the SIMD units available on modern processors. To achieve both performances and portability across various architectures, the kernel must use generic high-level concepts (like a DSL[1]) encapsulating these specific optimizations [6].

In this work, we conducted a study on the above mentioned challenges through the linear seismic wave propagation problem. Seismic wave propagation from an earthquake in the Earth has been always numerical challenge, because of its dimension, resolution and medium complexity with respect to the geo-scientific knowledge and engineering requirements (e.g. [7,8]). Basic problem is well formulated in the framework of elasto-dynamic equations and linear elasticity. Finite difference method has been applied since 1970-80's (e.g. [9]), suitable for structural discretization of continuous medium. In particular, the *4th* order approximation in space on staggered grids is the most popular option because of its efficiency and stability (e.g. [10,11]).

As reported in several recent research papers (e.g. [12,13]), explicit parallel elastodynamics application usually exhibits very good weak and strong scaling up to several tens of thousands of cores. Significant works have been made to extend this parallel results on heterogeneous and low-power processor (e.g. [14,15]). For instance the efforts to benefits from modern architecture with large vector unit is described in [16] where the use of explicit intrinsics appears mandatory to squeeze the maximum performance out of the underlying architecture.

One major contributions of this paper is the design and implementation of a fully task-based model for the seismic wave propagation into the SeWaS application [17]. To the best of our knowledge, this is the first end-to-end task-based implementation of the seismic wave model including the time-step dependency and efficient vectorization. We validate our results with the ONDES3D [18] production code. We consider Intel KNL manycore platforms for our experiments because of the complexity of such architecture and its capability to deliver both high memory bandwidth level and high peak floating point performance thanks to its AVX-512 units.

This paper is organized as follows. Section 2 provides the numerical background on seismic wave propagation. The task-based algorithm is described in Sect. 3 and its implementation in Sect. 4. Finally, we discuss the parallel performances in Sects. 5 and 6 concludes this paper.

2 Numerical Background and Classical Implementation

2.1 Numerical Scheme

Let us recall that elasto-dynamic equations allow for evaluating the three components of the velocity (V_x, V_y, V_z) and stress field $(\sigma_{xx}, \sigma_{yy}, \sigma_{zz}, \sigma_{xy}, \sigma_{xz}, \sigma_{yz})$

---

[1] Domain Specific Language.

Table 1. Notations used to define tasks.

Parameter	Definition	Possible values
d_s	Spatial discretization step (km)	> 0
(l_x, l_y, l_z)	Size of the global domain (km)	$(> 0, > 0, > 0)$
(n_x, n_y, n_z)	Total number of grid points	$(l_x/ds, l_y/ds, l_z/ds)$
T_{max}	Duration of the simulation (s)	> 0
dt	Time step (s)	> 0
N_t	Number of time-steps	$2 * T_{max}/dt$
(c_x, c_y, c_z)	Number of grid points per tile	$(> 0, > 0, > 0)$
(n_{xx}, n_{yy}, n_{zz})	Total number of tiles per axis	$(n_x/c_x, n_y/c_y, n_z/c_z)$
t	Time-step index	$\{1, \cdots, N_t - 1\}$
l	Location of the halo within a tile	$\{0, \cdots, 5\}$
d	Velocity component	$\{0, 1, 2\}$
s	Stress field component	$\{0, \cdots, 5\}$
(ii, jj, kk)	Coordinates of a tile	$[\![0, n_{xx} - 1]\!] \times [\![0, n_{yy} - 1]\!] \times [\![0, n_{zz} - 1]\!]$
(i, j, k)	Coordinates of a cell within a tile	$[\![0, n_x - 1]\!] \times [\![0, n_y - 1]\!] \times [\![0, n_z - 1]\!]$

of the seismic wave. Fully discretized forms of these quantities as given in [10]. For instance, the discretized form of V_x is given in (1).

$$V_x^{t+\frac{1}{2}}(i+\frac{1}{2}, j, k) = V_x^{t-\frac{1}{2}}(i+\frac{1}{2}, j, k) + (D_x\sigma_{xx} + D_y\sigma_{xy} + D_z\sigma_{xz})^t(i+\frac{1}{2}, j, k) \quad (1)$$

D_x is the $4th$ order central finite difference operator defined in (2).

$$D_x f(x, y, z) = c_1 * f(x + \Delta_1, y, z) + c_2 * f(x - \Delta_2, y, z)$$
$$+ c_3 * f(x + \Delta_3, y, z) + c_4 * f(x - \Delta_4, y, z), \quad (2)$$

where c_i and Δ_i, $i = 1, \cdots, 4$, are constant numerical coefficients depending on the discretization scheme. D_y and D_z are defined similarly. We considered this numerical scheme as a basis for building our seismic wave simulator for modern architectures. In particular, we designed a novel task-based implementation of the seismic wave propagation and implemented generic performance-portable numerical kernels.

2.2   Standard Implementation

In the remaining of the paper, we assume the notations defined in Table 1. The general algorithm describing the seismic wave propagation is given in Algorithm 1. The model takes as input the velocities of the compression and shear waves, V_p and V_s, defined for every layer contained within the computational domain; the density ρ and the seismic sources. Given the inputs, the algorithm iterates over all time-steps and successively computes the velocity components (Line 7) and stress field components (Line 10) for every spatial grid point.

Algorithm 1. Linear seismic wave propagation

In : V_p, V_s, ρ, sources
Out: Global Velocity and Stress of the seismic wave
1 **for** $t \in \{0, 2, \cdots, N_t - 2\}$ **do**
2   **for** $i \in \{0, \cdots, n_x - 1\}$ **do**
3   **for** $j \in \{0, \cdots, n_y - 1\}$ **do**
4   **for** $k \in \{0, \cdots, n_z - 1\}$ **do**
5   ▷ *Compute V_x, V_y and V_z*
6   **for** $d \in \{x, y, z\}$ **do**
7   ComputeVelocity(d, t, i, j, k);
8   ▷ *Compute S_{xx}, S_{yy}, S_{zz}, S_{xy}, S_{xz} and S_{yz}*
9   **for** $s \in \{xx, yy, zz, xy, xz, yz\}$ **do**
10   ComputeStress($s, t + 1, i, j, k$);

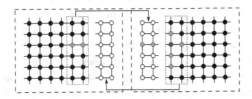

Fig. 1. Stencil for V_x computation (2D) and halo exchange between subdomains. Each subdomain, delimited by dashed boxes, is enlarged with the additional points for containing the halo. Computing the velocity at the blue colored grid point requires computing the stress fields at the red colored grid points. (Color figure online)

The velocity and the stress fields are evaluated at grid points separated by half of the discretization step. This is coming from the implementation of the staggered grid described for instance in [9]. Velocity computation at time step t depends on some computed values of the stress field at time step $t - 1$, as shown in (1). These dependencies represent the *stencil* for the computation of the velocity and are illustrated in Fig. 1. Similarly, the computation of the stress field depends on some previously values of the velocity. Nevertheless, computing the different velocity components are independent and the same for all the stress field components. Hence, each of the loops at Line 6 and Line 9 can be evaluated in parallel.

The parallelization of this algorithm on this distributed memory computers has been extensively studied, relying mainly on MPI and OpenMP. Typically, the time-step loop (Line 1) is considered as sequential and the parallelization is achieved by regularly splitting the spatial domain among all the workers. Each MPI process will handle $(n_x/P) \times (n_y/Q)$ cells, where P and Q are the total number of MPI processes along the x and y axes. Within each MPI process, a team of OpenMP threads is spawned to perform the computations on the local cells. At the end of each time-step, each MPI process exchanges its boundaries with neighboring processes as depicted in Fig. 1. For instance, a classical implementation is described in [18]. However, there are three main concerns with this approach: explicit synchronization required when exchanging the halo at the end of each time-step; serialization of the time-step loop and the lack of explicit vectorization.

3   A Fully Task-Based Model of the Linear Seismic Kernel

We considered the Algorithm 1 as a basis, and we made several optimizations on it, with the goal of making it scalable at high core count: we redesigned the algorithm into a fully task-based version including the time-step loop. Throughout this process, we considered different constraints: scalability, communication overlap, data locality, and vectorization efficiency.

Scalability: A task is an independent unit of work that will be processed by a thread. For instance, the computation of the x component of the velocity (rest. stress field) at time t and on the cell (i, j, k) is a task. To scale at high-core count, the algorithm must expose a large number of such tasks that can be processed concurrently. To that end, we need to define dependencies that are going to be used by a runtime system. It will schedule the tasks as soon as they become ready among all available computing resources. An important point to note is that the runtime system introduces some scheduling overhead due to calculations required for selecting the task to execute. To enhance the scalability of our model, by minimizing the former overhead, we partitioned the global domain into a set of 3D *tiles* defined by a contiguous collection of cells, on which the tasks are going to work, rather than on a single cell. In the following, we will omit the prefix 3D when referring to a tile, and we will use the index (ii, jj, kk) for its coordinates. Due to the nature of the stencil computation scheme, each tile will be enlarged to contain the halo retrieved from neighboring tiles, as in Fig. 1.

Instead of performing the extraction and update of the halo, we add two new tasks dedicated to these actions: ExtractVelocityHalo and UpdateVelocity with the advantage of increasing the amount of available parallelism. This is required to maximize the parallel efficiency on modern distributed computing platforms. In summary, our task-based algorithm contains six types of tasks:

1. ComputeVelocity(d, t, ii, jj, kk) computes the d component of the velocity on tile (ii, jj, kk) at time-step t. It depends on UpdateStress$(s, t - 1, ii, jj, kk)$.
2. ExtractVelocityHalo(d, t, ii, jj, kk) first extracts all the boundaries of the d-component of the velocity on the tile (ii, jj, kk). The extracted boundaries are placed in temporary buffers and sent to the UpdateVelocity tasks on neighboring tiles. It depends on ComputeVelocity(t, d, ii, jj, kk).
3. UpdateVelocity(d, t, ii, jj, kk) receives the velocity halo from neighbouring ExtractVelocityHalo tasks and update the tile (ii, jj, kk). It depends on ExtractVelocityHalo(d, t, ii, jj, kk).
4. ComputeStress(s, t, ii, jj, kk) defined similarly as ComputeVelocity.

Algorithm 2. Task-based algorithm for the seismic wave propagation

---

In : V_p, V_s, ρ
Out: Global Velocity and Stress of the seismic wave

```
1  forall t ∈ {0, 2, · · · , Nt − 2} do
2  |   ▷ Compute Vx, Vy and Vz
3  |   forall d ∈ {x, y, z} do
4  |   |   forall ii ∈ {0, · · · , nxx − 1} do
5  |   |   |   forall jj ∈ {0, · · · , nyy − 1} do
6  |   |   |   |   forall kk ∈ {0, · · · , nzz − 1} do
7  |   |   |   |   |   ComputeVelocity(d, t, ii, jj, kk);
8  |   |   |   |   |   ExtractVelocityHalo(d, t, ii, jj, kk);
9  |   |   |   |   |   UpdateVelocity(d, t, ii, jj, kk);

10 |   ▷ Compute Sxx, Syy, Szz, Sxy, Sxz and Syz
11 |   forall s ∈ {xx, yy, zz, xy, xz, yz} do
12 |   |   forall ii ∈ {0, · · · , nxx − 1} do
13 |   |   |   forall jj ∈ {0, · · · , nyy − 1} do
14 |   |   |   |   forall kk ∈ {0, · · · , nzz − 1} do
15 |   |   |   |   |   ComputeStress(s, t + 1, ii, jj, kk);
16 |   |   |   |   |   ExtractStressHalo(s, t + 1, ii, jj, kk);
17 |   |   |   |   |   UpdateStress(s, t + 1, ii, jj, kk);
```

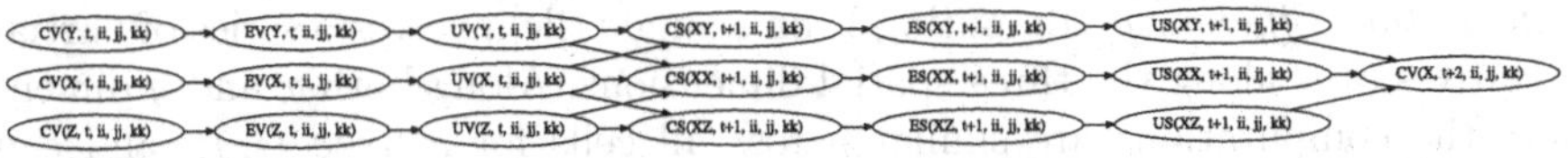

Fig. 2. Data-flow for the task-based linear seismic wave model (case of V_x computation). CV, EV and UV designate ComputeVelocity, ExtractVelocityHalo and UpdateVelocity. A similar definition holds for CS, ES and US.

5. ExtractStressHalo(s, t, ii, jj, kk) defined similarly as ExtractVelocityHalo.
6. UpdateStress(s, t, ii, jj, kk) defined similarly as UpdateVelocity.

The fully task-based version of the linear seismic wave propagation is presented in Algorithm 2. In Fig. 2, we give the data-flow corresponding to this algorithm. On the same tile, and for a fixed d and t, the tasks ComputeVelocity, ExtractVelocityHalo and UpdateVelocity are serialized. As we will see in Sect. 5, combining the time-step loop with the spatial cells when defining tasks allows overlapping computations of different time-steps, hence reducing the execution time.

Communication Overlap: by delegating extraction and update of the halo per tile to dedicated tasks, we enforce the potential of overlapping communications with computations. Indeed, once a ComputeVelocity task is completed, we can start extracting and sending its boundaries to UpdateVelocity tasks associated to neighboring tiles, while another ComputeVelocity task is in progress.

Data Locality: to maximize cached data reuse, we considered a hierarchical representation of the manipulated data structures, typically V and S, as following:

- $V(x|y|z)(ii, jj, kk)(i, j, k)$
- $S(xx|yy|zz|xy|xz|yz)(ii, jj, kk)(i, j, k)$

$V(x)$ is a column-major 3D tensor whose elements are 3D tiles. Each 3D tile, $V(x)(ii, jj, kk)$, is stored as a row-major 2D tensor whose elements are 1D arrays of floating point values, oriented according the z-axis. The tile object implements an `operator()` (`const int i, const int j`) for extracting the z-vector indexed by i and j. The velocities are block-wise computed, where each block is a z-vector of coordinates (i, j) within the considered tile. Prior computations, each thread will load a z-vector of their respective tiles into the L1 cache of the core on which it is bound. Hence, with an appropriate tile size, for all (i_0, j_0) and (i_1, j_1), the z-vectors $V(x)(ii, jj, kk)(i_0, j_0)$ and $V(x)(ii + 1, jj, kk)(i_1, j_1)$ will never be on the same cache line. Consequently, the proposed approach minimizes the probability of *false-sharing* during execution. Moreover, by appropriately adjusting the tile size, all its data can fit into cache, hence increasing the arithmetic intensity of the computation, required for a better vectorization efficiency.

Vectorization Efficiency: computing V on a single tile involves a series of partial derivatives of S along the three spatial dimensions. Along both x and y dimensions, the computations are similar across all cells for a fixed (i, j), and can thus be performed in parallel. To leverage this fine-grained parallelism, the data layout has been designed so that each tile is a 2D grid of 1D vectors along the z-axis. For instance, $V(x)(ii, jj, kk)(i, j)$ is a 1D vector, eventually padded with additional cells to match the SIMD width on the target architecture. This strategy allows us for explicitly computing the derivatives using SIMD instructions. The same analysis holds for the computation of S.

4   A Hierarchical Implementation Tailored for Modern Architectures

4.1   Implementation on Top of PaRSEC

Emergence of Task Scheduling Engines: The past years have witnessed the emergence of generic task-based runtime systems [19–21]. These systems were introduced to cope with the application development issues arising since the advent of massively parallel and heterogeneous computing. Such a system offers a unified view of the underlying hardware and let the developer focus on the algorithm, described as Directed Acyclic Graph (DAG) of tasks. The runtime system will then manage all data transfers and synchronizations between computing devices

Listing 1.1. ComputeVelocity task in the JDF language.

```
1   ComputeVelocity(d, t, ii, jj, kk)
2   d   = 0 .. dim-1
3   t   = 2 .. nt-2 .. 2
4   /* ii, jj, kk from 0 to nxx-1, nyy-1, nzz-1 */
5
6   : ddesc(ii, jj, kk)
7
8   CTL SxxH<- ( d==X            && t > 2) ? SxxH UpdateStress(XX, t-1, ii, jj, kk)
9   CTL SxyH<- ((d==X || d==Y) && t > 2) ? SxyH UpdateStress(XY, t-1, ii, jj, kk)
10  CTL SxzH<- ((d==X || d==Z) && t > 2) ? SxzH UpdateStress(XZ, t-1, ii, jj, kk)
11
12  BODY
13  {
14    computeVelocity(d, t, ii, jj, kk);
15  }
16  END
```

(CPUs/GPUs/MICs) and the scheduling of tasks among available computing resources. Hence, these frameworks allow for the separation of major concerns in HPC: design of the algorithm, creating a data distribution and developing computational kernels.

While the general principle of the runtime systems is similar for all, two major tendencies exist and differ according to the DAG of tasks construction: Parametrized Task Graph (PTG) [22] and Dynamic Task Graph (DTG) models [23]. In the PTG approach, the DAG is constructed as a problem size independent symbolic representation of the algorithm and can thus be generated at compile time. Hence, the instantiation of new tasks is performed during execution through a closed formula depending on the task parameters. Such an approach is implemented by the PARSEC [21] framework, offering a specific annotation-based language, the Job Data Flow (JDF), for describing the DAG of tasks according to their INPUT and OUTPUT data. Conversely, with the DTG approach, the DAG of tasks is fully constructed and kept in memory, which the runtime system is going to explore during execution for discovering and scheduling ready tasks. Thus, the DAG memory occupation grows with the problem size. Nevertheless, DTG frameworks (e.g. STARSS [19] and STARPU [20]) usually allow to customize a window of visible tasks for avoiding the full generation of the DAG of tasks at runtime. An appropriate window size can therefore help reducing the memory footprint with a minimal performance penalty. Given the regular pattern of the spatial mesh we considered in this study, we choose to implement our data flow on top of the PTG-based framework PARSEC.

Implementation: Building an application on top of PARSEC requires to define the algorithm data-flow using the JDF language and a data distribution that will be used by the runtime system for tasks placement on the target architecture. The Listing 1.1 shows a simplified version of the JDF implementation of the ComputeVelocity task. There are four main parts in the task description.

1. The execution space (Line 2 to Line 4) is defined by a valid range, for each of the task parameters, determining the total number of similar tasks.

Listing 1.2. UpdateStress task in the JDF language.

```
1   UpdateStress(s, t, ii, jj, kk)
2   s = 0 .. nsc-1
3   t  = 1 .. nt-3 .. 2
4   /* ii, jj, kk from 0 to nxx-1, nyy-1, nzz-1 */
5
6   : ddesc(ii, jj, kk)
7
8   READ SLeft   <- (ii>0 && t>1)      ? SRight ExtractStressH(s, t, ii-1, jj, kk)
9   READ SRight  <- (ii<nxx-1 && t>1)  ? SLeft  ExtractStressH(s, t, ii+1, jj, kk)
10
11  CTL  SxxH    -> (s==XX && t>1)     ? SxxH ComputeVelocity(X, t+1, ii, jj, kk)
12  CTL  SxyH    -> (s==XY && t>1)     ? SxyH ComputeVelocity(X, t+1, ii, jj, kk)
13  CTL  SxzH    -> (s==XZ && t>1)     ? SxzH ComputeVelocity(X, t+1, ii, jj, kk)
14
15  BODY
16  {
17    updateStress(LEFT,  s, t, ii, jj, kk, SLeft);
18    updateStress(RIGHT, s, t, ii, jj, kk, SRight);
19  }
20  END
```

2. The parallel partitioning (Line 6) is a symbolic reference to a data element that is going to be used by the runtime system to execute the task according to the owner compute rule. Basically, the task will be scheduled on the node where the data element is located.

3. Task data-flow (Line 8 to Line 10) defines the input and output dependencies of the task, eventually conditioned by a C-style ternary operator. Here, the keyword CTL (Control flow) is used as a counter by the runtime system (not a real data transfer). For instance, computing V_x requires the reception of three controls: Line 8, Line 9 and Line 10, notifying the completion of UpdateStress task on respectively xx, xy and xz components of the stress field. In Listing 1.2, we can see the matching control flows sent by UpdateStress task at Line 11, Line 12 and Line 13. Also, UpdateStress has an input data dependency as indicated on Line 11. This line specifies that UpdateStress will create a temporary read-only (READ keyword) buffer SLeft where an output data SRight sent by ExtractStressH will be stored.

4. The task body between BODY and END keywords contains the code executed by the task. Here, the body is given at Line 14 as a function call to our implementation of the velocity computation on a single tile.

This JDF is complemented with a data distribution implementation, through two PARSEC provided functions, evaluated by all processes: data_of and rank_of. The former returns the pointer to the actual data described by ddesc(ii, jj, kk) and the latter returns the rank of the MPI process holding that data. The combination of the JDF and the data distribution will be used by PARSEC to schedule and execute tasks, according to the provided computational kernels.

Listing 1.3. Computation of V_x on a single tile.

```
1   for (int i=iStart; i<iEnd; i++){
2     for (int j=jStart; j<jEnd; j++){
3       vX(i,j) +=(fdo_.apply<SWS::X>(sigmaXX, i, j)
4           + fdo_.apply<SWS::Y>(sigmaXY, i, j)
5           + fdo_.apply<SWS::Z>(sigmaXZ, i, j))*dt*bx(i,j);
6     }
7   }
```

Table 2. Characteristics of TestA and TestB benchmarks.

	T_{max}	dt	N_t	l_x	l_y	l_z	ds	n_x	n_y	n_z
TestA	1.6	0.008	200	20	20	10	0.1	200	200	100
TestB	20	0.2	2000	650	1000	50	0.5	1300	2000	100

4.2 Building Generic Optimized Computational Kernels

To build the kernels, we considered three metrics: expressivity, performance and performance portability across various architectures. In the following, we demonstrate how our implementation managed to maximize these metrics.

Expressivity: We adopted the C++ language that allows for building complex and meaningful expressions, close to the mathematical formulations used in an algorithm. Let us consider the V_x computation as given in Listing 1.3. The code shows a tile traversal in the (x, y) plane. For each position (i, j), velocities of all cells along the z axis are computed at Line 3, according to block-wise evaluations. fdo_ is an object of type **CentralFDOperator**, a class implementing the $4th$ order central finite-differences scheme through the member function **apply**, templated with the derived direction. We can notice the similarity between expression on Line 3 with the numerical formulation of V_x as shown in (1).

Performance and Performance Portability: Using Expression Templates to build our containers on top of the generic C++ Eigen library [24] avoids the creation of temporary 1D vectors for each call to the **apply()** method on Line 3 of Listing 1.3. In addition, Eigen supports explicit vectorization with various SIMD extensions, including SSE2, AVX2, AVX-512, and ARM NEON allowing the application to be portable across a large number of architectures.

5 Experiments

We conducted strong scalability studies on the Frioul supercomputer from GEN-CI/CINES[2], based on Intel KNL 7250, comprising 68 cores running at 1.4 GHz. There is 16 GB of MCDRAM on-chip memory per node and 192 GB of DDR4 off-chip memory. The computing nodes are interconnected through an InfiniBand

---

[2] https://www.cines.fr/le-supercalculateur-frioul/.

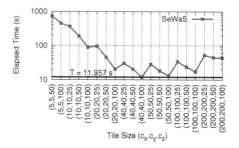

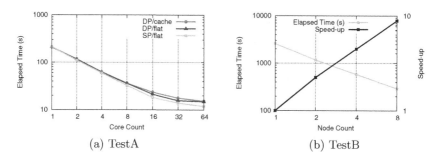

Fig. 3. Evaluation of the best tile size running TestA in single precision.

(a) TestA   (b) TestB

Fig. 4. SeWaS strong scaling. The left curve shows the single-node performance using TestA. It compares the performances of single and double precisions for both KNL configurations (cache and flat modes). The right curve shows the multi-node performance using TestB where all nodes are configured on flat mode.

EDR fabric, providing a theoretical bandwidth of 100 Gb/s. All the experiments have been carried out using two test cases: TestA and TestB (see Table 2). The former is a small test case and the latter, representing a real earthquake, is larger. In the following, both SeWaS and ONDES3D applications are compiled using Intel compiler version 18.0.1 and Intel MPI version 5.1.3.

5.1 Tuning Single Node Performances

As mentioned in Sect. 3, the performances of the application is strongly dependent of the tile size. To evaluate the best size, we considered the TestA benchmark and compared the computation time of SeWaS for different configurations of (c_x, c_y, c_z) on a single 64-cores node. The results are presented in Fig. 3. For the considered test case, the absolute discrepancy compared to the double precision results is an order of 10^{-4} which is acceptable for the purposes of our experiments.

We found that the best computation time (11.957 s) is obtained with a tile of size $(40, 40, 100)$. For this size, the total number of tasks is 67500, that is 1054 tasks per thread. We can also notice that for a fixed c_x and c_y, the best computation time is obtained when using c_z is 100. This result is justified by the fact the computations are vectorized along the z axis, and thus the performances

Table 3. Illustration of time-steps overlapping.

T_{max} (s)	1	2	4	8	16	20
N_t	100	200	400	800	1600	2000
Computation time (s)	108.3	117.6	136.7	175.4	252.6	291.5

tend to be better when c_z is large enough to fit the SIMD units. In the following, all the presented results were obtained using the determined best tile size.

Figure 4a presents a single-node strong scalability study of SeWaS using TestA benchmark. It shows that the run with flat mode is slightly faster than with cache mode.

In double precision, SeWaS computation time on 64 cores is 14.9 s, whereas ONDES3D takes 56.9 s. This difference is due to the explicit vectorization used in SeWaS and a better data locality. Even if ONDES3D is a more generalistic application and does implement other features that are not present in SeWaS, such as absorbing boundary condition, we expect that this comparison will give to the reader an order of magnitude of how SeWaS compares to ONDES3D. In the following, all results are obtained in single precision and using the flat mode.

5.2 Distributed Memory Scaling

We consider the TestB benchmark. This test case contains 1300 cells along the x dimension. As it is not divisible by 40, we will be using the $(50, 50, 100)$ tile size whose performance are very close.

Strong Scaling: The Fig. 4b presents SeWaS strong scaling using TestB benchmark on 8 nodes. The benchmark runs in 2589.7 s on a single node, and 291.8 s using 8 nodes, corresponding to a speed-up of 8.8. The super linear scalability observed is due to the fact the computation on a single node requires around 40 GB of memory which is larger than the size of the on-chip MCDRAM. Indeed, on a single node, 24 GB of data will be allocated in DDR4. Starting from 4 nodes, all data can fit in the MCDRAM, and thus the performances are improved.

Impact of Time-Steps Overlapping: We conducted an experiment to study the behavior of computations overlap for successive time-steps in SeWaS. We measured the computation time for several values of T_{max} from 2 s to 20 s. The results are presented in Table 3. We observe that the computation time increases with T_{max}, following a linear trend experimentally determined as:

$$\text{Computation Time} \approx T_{init} + 9.7 * T_{max},$$

where $T_{init} \approx 98.6$ s is the time spent to initialize the computations. Let us first consider the core simulation time, that is computation time without the initialization. We notice that the ratio of the core simulation time between $T_{max} = 20$ s and $T_{max} = 2$ s is 7.8 representing an overlap ratio of 22%. This is a remarkable result as it shows a high overlapping rate for the computations of different time-steps. A preliminary experiment showed that the initialization can be fully parallelized allowing to mitigate its impact on the computation time.

6   Conclusion

In this paper, we presented the design and implementation of SeWaS, a linear seismic wave propagation code, adapted for modern computing platforms. We studied the main challenges related to the development of efficient and scalable computation code on these platforms. A fully task-based model has been designed and its implementation combines the state-of-the-art frameworks and libraries PaRSEC and Eigen. Performance studies conducted on a cluster of Intel KNL processors showed that the application exhibits a good strong scalability up to 8 nodes. The proposed approach demonstrated a clear path toward code modernization required to take advantage of computing power brought by current and coming Exascale systems. In the future, we will extend our computational kernels for GPUs to cope with highly heterogeneous systems.

Data Availability Statement and Acknowledgments. The datasets generated during and/or analyzed during the current study are available in the Figshare repository: https://doi.org/10.6084/m9.figshare.6387743. We would like to thank GENCI and CINES for providing us computing facilities to perform our experiments.

References

1. Ross, P.E.: Why CPU frequency stalled. IEEE Spectr. **45**(4), 72 (2008)
2. Moustafa, S., Faverge, M., Plagne, L., Ramet, P.: 3D cartesian transport sweep for massively parallel architectures with PaRSEC. In: IEEE International Parallel and Distributed Processing Symposium (IPDPS), pp. 581–590. IEEE (2015)
3. Taylor, R.A., Jeong, J., White, M., Arnold, J.G.: Code modernization and modularization of APEX and SWAT watershed simulation models. Int. J. Agric. Biol. Eng. **8**(3), 81–94 (2015)
4. Jundt, A., Tiwari, A., Ward Jr, W.A., Campbell, R., Carrington, L.: Optimizing codes on the Xeon Phi: a case-study with LAMMPS. In: Proceedings of the 2015 XSEDE Conference: Scientific Advancements Enabled by Enhanced Cyberinfrastructure, p. 28. ACM (2015)
5. McKee, S.A.: Reflections on the memory wall. In: Proceedings of the 1st Conference on Computing Frontiers, p. 162. ACM (2004)
6. Kirschenmann, W., Plagne, L., Vialle, S.: Multi-target C++ implementation of parallel skeletons. In: Proceedings of the 8th Workshop on Parallel/High-Performance Object-Oriented Scientific Computing, p. 7. ACM (2009)
7. Furumura, T., Chen, L.: Large scale parallel simulation and visualization of 3D seismic wavefield using the Earth Simulator. Comput. Model. Eng. Sci. **6**, 153–168 (2004)
8. Aochi, H., Ulrich, T., Ducellier, A., Dupros, F., Michea, D.: Finite difference simulations of seismic wave propagation for understanding earthquake physics and predicting ground motions: advances and challenges. J. Phys: Conf. Ser. **454**, 012010 (2013)

9. Virieux, J., Madariaga, R.: Dynamic faulting studied by a finite difference method. Bull. Seismol. Soc. Am. **72**(2), 345–369 (1982)
10. Graves, R.W.: Simulating seismic wave propagation in 3D elastic media using staggered-grid finite differences. Bull. Seismol. Soc. Am. **86**(4), 1091–1106 (1996)
11. Kristek, J., Moczo, P.: Seismic-wave propagation in viscoelastic media with material discontinuities: a 3D fourth-order staggered-grid finite-difference modeling. Bull. Seismol. Soc. Am. **93**(5), 2273–2280 (2003)
12. Roten, D., et al.: High-frequency nonlinear earthquake simulations on petascale heterogeneous supercomputers. In: Proceedings of the International Conference for High Performance Computing, Networking, Storage and Analysis, SC 2016, Salt Lake City, UT, USA, 13–18 November 2016, pp. 957–968 (2016)
13. Breuer, A., Heinecke, A., Bader, M.: Petascale local time stepping for the ADER-DG finite element method. In: 2016 IEEE International Parallel and Distributed Processing Symposium, IPDPS 2016, Chicago, IL, USA, 23–27 May 2016, pp. 854–863 (2016)
14. Göddeke, D., Komatitsch, D., Geveler, M., Ribbrock, D., Rajovic, N., Puzovic, N., Ramírez, A.: Energy efficiency vs. performance of the numerical solution of PDEs: an application study on a low-power ARM-based cluster. J. Comput. Phys. **237**, 132–150 (2013)
15. Castro, M., Francesquini, E., Dupros, F., Aochi, H., Navaux, P.O.A., Méhaut, J.: Seismic wave propagation simulations on low-power and performance-centric manycores. Parallel Comput. **54**, 108–120 (2016)
16. Sornet, G., Dupros, F., Jubertie, S.: A multi-level optimization strategy to improve the performance of stencil computation. Procedia Comput. Sci. **108**, 1083–1092 (2017)
17. Moustafa, S., Kirschenmann, W., Dupros, F., Aochi, H.: Code and input data for SeWaS: Seismic Wave Simulator: Euro-par 2018 artifact. figshare. Code (2018). https://doi.org/10.6084/m9.figshare.6387743
18. Dupros, F., Aochi, H., Ducellier, A., Komatitsch, D., Roman, J.: Exploiting intensive multithreading for the efficient simulation of 3D seismic wave propagation. In: 11th IEEE International Conference on Computational Science and Engineering, CSE 2008, pp. 253–260. IEEE (2008)
19. Planas, J., Badia, R.M., Ayguadé, E., Labarta, J.: Hierarchical task-based programming with StarSs. Int. J. High Perform. Comput. Appl. **23**(3), 284–299 (2009)
20. Augonnet, C., Thibault, S., Namyst, R., Wacrenier, P.A.: StarPU: a unified platform for task scheduling on heterogeneous multicore architectures. Concur. Comput.: Pract. Exp. **23**(2), 187–198 (2011)
21. Bosilca, G., Bouteiller, A., Danalis, A., Herault, T., Lemarinier, P., Dongarra, J.: DAGuE: a generic distributed DAG engine for high performance computing. Parallel Comput. **38**(1), 37–51 (2012)
22. Danalis, A., Bosilca, G., Bouteiller, A., Herault, T., Dongarra, J.: PTG: an abstraction for unhindered parallelism. In: Proceedings of the Fourth International Workshop on Domain-Specific Languages and High-Level Frameworks for High Performance Computing, pp. 21–30. IEEE Press (2014)
23. Advea, V., Sakellariou, R.: Compiler synthesis of task graphs for parallel program performance prediction. In: Midkiff, S.P., et al. (eds.) LCPC 2000. LNCS, vol. 2017, pp. 208–226. Springer, Heidelberg (2001). https://doi.org/10.1007/3-540-45574-4_14
24. Guennebaud, G., Jacob, B., et al.: Eigen v3 (2010). http://eigen.tuxfamily.org

Accelerator Computing for Advanced Applications

CEML: a Coordinated Runtime System for Efficient Machine Learning on Heterogeneous Computing Systems

Jihoon Hyun, Jinsu Park, Kyu Yeun Kim, Seongdae Yu, and Woongki Baek[✉]

School of ECE, UNIST, Ulsan, Republic of Korea
{jhyun0812,jinsupark,kyuyeunk,sd3392,wbaek}@unist.ac.kr

Abstract. Heterogeneous computing is rapidly emerging as a promising solution for efficient machine learning. Despite the extensive prior works, system software support for efficient machine learning still remains unexplored in the context of heterogeneous computing. To bridge this gap, we propose CEML, a coordinated runtime system for efficient machine learning on heterogeneous computing systems. CEML dynamically analyzes the performance and power characteristics of the target machine-learning application and robustly adapts the system state to enhance its efficiency on heterogeneous computing systems. Our quantitative evaluation demonstrates that CEML significantly improves the efficiency of machine-learning applications on a full heterogeneous computing system.

1 Introduction

Heterogeneous computing is a promising solution for efficient machine learning [7]. Heterogeneous computing systems can effectively improve the efficiency of the target machine-learning application by concurrently executing its operations across the heterogeneous computing devices that exhibit different performance and power characteristics.

Prior works have extensively investigated the system software [4,7,9] and architectural support [5,6,10,16] for efficient machine learning. While insightful, the prior works have limitations in that they lack the runtime support for controlling all the heterogeneous computing devices in a coordinated manner [4,7,9] and/or require intrusive hardware modifications, making it difficult to apply them to existing commodity computer systems [5,6,10,16].

To bridge this gap, this work proposes CEML, a coordinated runtime system for efficient machine learning. CEML dynamically analyzes the performance and power characteristics of the target machine-learning application and generates the accurate performance and power estimators without requiring any per-application offline profiling. Guided by its performance and power estimators, CEML robustly finds the efficient system state and accordingly configures the underlying heterogeneous computing system to significantly improve the efficiency of the target application.

© Springer International Publishing AG, part of Springer Nature 2018
M. Aldinucci et al. (Eds.): Euro-Par 2018, LNCS 11014, pp. 781–795, 2018.
https://doi.org/10.1007/978-3-319-96983-1_55

Specifically, this paper makes the following contributions:

– We propose CEML, a coordinated runtime system for efficient machine learning on heterogeneous computing systems. CEML consists of the estimators that accurately estimate the performance and power consumption of the target machine-learning application for a system state of interest. The runtime manager of CEML explores the system state space, determines the efficient system state, and runs the target application with the efficient system state to significantly improve its efficiency in terms of the user-specified optimization metric (e.g., energy optimization, performance maximization under the power limit). To the best of our knowledge, CEML is the first runtime system that holistically controls all the heterogeneous computing devices for efficient machine learning.
– We implement a prototype of CEML. Since the CEML prototype is implemented as a user-level runtime system, it requires no modification to the underlying OS kernel or GPU device driver. The CEML prototype implements two search algorithms (i.e., the local and exhaustive search algorithms), each of which explores the system state space with different coverage and runtime overheads.
– We quantify the effectiveness of CEML using various machine-learning applications on a full heterogeneous computing system. Through quantitative evaluation, we demonstrate that CEML consumes significantly less energy (e.g., 30.8% less on average) than the baseline version that uses the maximum device frequencies, which is a commonly-used configuration in heterogeneous computing. We also show that the energy efficiency of CEML is comparable with the static best version, which requires extensive offline profiling across the applications.

2   Background and Motivation

2.1   Heterogeneous Computing

A heterogeneous computing system comprises multiple computing devices that show functional and performance/power heterogeneity. Heterogeneous computing devices exhibit the functional heterogeneity in the sense that they implement different instruction-set architectures and the performance/power heterogeneity in that they have different performance and power characteristics.

In this work, we assume that the underlying heterogeneous computing system is equipped with a single-chip heterogeneous application processor that consists of a multi-core CPU and a multi/many-core GPU. We also assume that the CPU and GPU communicate through the main memory. This architectural configuration is widely used in various computing domains including the embedded computing domain [1,2].

We assume that the CPU, GPU, and memory in the underlying heterogeneous computing system provide N_{f_C}, N_{f_G}, and N_{f_M} voltage and frequency (V/F) levels. The V/F level of each device can be dynamically controlled in software, similarly to commodity embedded systems [1]. A *system state* is defined as a tuple of the device frequencies (i.e., (f_C, f_G, f_M)). The *system state space* is then defined as the set of all the possible system states.

2.2 The TensorFlow Machine-Learning System

TensorFlow is a widely-used machine-learning system [4]. TensorFlow allows for programmers to express their machine-learning algorithms as dataflow graphs. A *dataflow graph* mainly consists of tensors and operations. *Tensors* are multi-dimensional arrays, whose elements have one of the basic primitive data types such as `int32` or `float32`. An *operation* takes zero or more input tensors and produces zero or more output tensors [4].

When all the input tensors for an operation are produced, the operation becomes ready to be executed. The TensorFlow scheduler schedules the operation on one of the computing devices in the underlying heterogeneous computing system. The scheduling decision is made based on various factors such as the computational complexity of the operation, the utilization of each computing device, and the scheduling hint provided by the programmer [4]. Independent operations can be executed across the computing devices in a concurrent manner. One of the main design goals of the TensorFlow scheduler is to maximize the utilization of all the computing devices by concurrently executing as many independent operations as possible across the computing devices.

In this work, we focus on the efficiency optimization of the training phase of machine-learning applications. In each *training epoch* (or epoch), a machine-learning application iterates all the training data to train its model. In each *training step* (or step), the machine-learning application processes a batch of the training data. For instance, if 20,000 images are used as the training data and a batch size of 10 is used, an epoch consists of 2,000 steps.

We assume that the target machine-learning application is implemented as a TensorFlow application. While we evaluate the effectiveness of CEML using TensorFlow, we believe that the design of CEML is sufficiently generic to be readily applicable to other widely-used machine-learning platforms such as Caffe [9].

We have implemented a user-level, low-overhead API similar to the Application Heartbeats API [8] and instrumented each of the evaluated benchmarks (Sect. 3) with the API to make it generate a heartbeat every time it finishes a predefined number of steps. CEML employs the heartbeat data to dynamically track the current performance of the target machine-learning application.

2.3 Need for Coordinated Runtime Support

Machine-learning applications exhibit widely different performance and power characteristics on heterogeneous computing systems. To illustrate this, Figs. 1 and 2 show the performance and power characteristics of the seven machine-learning benchmarks (i.e., CF, IN, LR, MN, RB, VP, and WD) on the target heterogeneous computing system evaluated in this work (see Sect. 3 for details). We observe the following data trends.

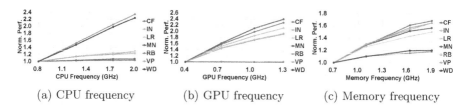

(a) CPU frequency   (b) GPU frequency   (c) Memory frequency

Fig. 1. Performance characteristics of the machine-learning applications

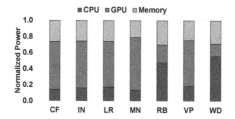

Fig. 2. Power characteristics at the maximum device frequencies

First, the performance sensitivity of each benchmark is widely different to device frequencies. For instance, the performance of CF is highly sensitive to the GPU frequency but insensitive to the CPU frequency, whereas the performance of WD is highly sensitive to the CPU frequency but insensitive to the GPU frequency.

Second, the power consumption of each device in the heterogeneous computing is widely different across the evaluated benchmarks. For example, the GPU consumes significantly more power than the other devices with CF. In contrast, with WD, the CPU is the device that consumes the highest power among the three devices (i.e., CPU, GPU, and memory).

These data trends show that static approaches require the offline performance and power profile data for every application to achieve high efficiency, which is nearly infeasible. To summarize, this case study clearly demonstrates the need for a coordinated runtime system that efficiently analyzes the performance and power characteristics of the target machine-learning application at runtime, robustly generates the accurate performance and power estimation models, and effectively manages all the devices in the underlying heterogeneous computing system to significantly enhance the overall efficiency without extensive per-application offline profiling.

3   Experimental Methodology

For all the experiments performed in this work, we use a full heterogeneous computing system, the NVIDIA Jetson TX2 embedded development board [1]. In this work, we employ the dual-core Denver processor based on the ARMv8-A architecture and the 256-core NVIDIA Pascal GPU equipped in the heterogeneous

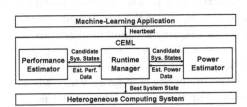

Fig. 3. Overall architecture of CEML

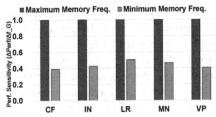

Fig. 4. Performance interaction between GPU and memory

computing system. The evaluated frequency ranges of the CPU, GPU, and memory are 0.81–2 GHz, 0.42–1.3 GHz, and 0.67–1.87 GHz, respectively. The heterogeneous computing system includes sensors, each of which periodically samples the power consumption of the CPU, GPU, or memory. We use the sensor data to generate the power estimation model of CEML and measure the power consumption of the target machine-learning application. The heterogeneous computing system is installed with Ubuntu 16.04 and Linux kernel 4.4.38.

We use seven machine-learning benchmarks (i.e., CIFAR-10 (CF), ImageNet (IN), Learning to Remember Rare Events (LR), MNIST (MN), REBAR (RB), Video Prediction (VP), and Wide & Deep (WD)), which are available in the official TensorFlow code repository [3]. We configure CF, IN, LR, MN, RB, VP, and WD to run 4000, 2000, 1000, 30000, 10136, 1000, and 32550 training steps, respectively.

4 Design and Implementation

CEML comprises the three main components – (1) the performance estimator, (2) the power estimator, and (3) the runtime manager. Figure 3 illustrates the overall architecture of CEML.

The main design principles applied to CEML are as follows. First, CEML controls the V/F level of each device in the underlying heterogeneous computing system in a coordinated manner to significantly improve the efficiency of the target machine-learning application. Second, CEML is designed as a versatile system in that it can support various optimization scenarios (e.g., energy optimization, performance maximization under the power limit). Third, CEML eliminates the need for per-application offline profiling. Fourth, the online profiling and adaptation functionalities of CEML are designed and implemented in a lightweight manner to minimize the potential runtime overheads.

4.1 Performance Estimator

The *performance estimator* estimates the performance of the target machine-learning application for a system state of interest. Specifically, the performance of the target machine-learning application is defined as the *training steps performed per second*.

We first investigate the performance sensitivity of various machine-learning applications to device frequencies to guide the design of the performance estimator. As shown in Fig. 1, the performance of machine-learning applications is (largely) linearly proportional to the frequency of each device when the frequencies of other devices are fixed (at the maximum frequency), which is intuitive.

Further, the performance sensitivity to the frequency of a device varies when the frequencies of the other devices change. For instance, as shown in Fig. 4, the performance of the GPU-intensive benchmarks becomes less sensitive to the GPU frequency with the decreasing memory frequency because the memory gradually becomes the overall performance bottleneck as its frequency decreases. This indicates that there is performance interaction between devices.

Based on the aforementioned observations, the performance estimator employs Eq. 1 to estimate the performance of the target application for a system state of interest (i.e., (f_C, f_G, f_M)). Equation 1 has a linear term for each device frequency to model the linear relationship between the performance and the device frequency. Equation 1 also has an interaction term for each device pair (e.g., $\alpha_{C,G}$ for f_C and f_G) to model the performance interaction between the pair of devices.

$$
\begin{aligned}
Perf = {} & \alpha_C \cdot f_C + \alpha_G \cdot f_G + \alpha_M \cdot f_M + \alpha_{C,G} \cdot f_C \cdot f_G + \\
& \alpha_{G,M} \cdot f_G \cdot f_M + \alpha_{M,C} \cdot f_M \cdot f_C + \beta
\end{aligned}
\tag{1}
$$

To compute the coefficients in Eq. 1, seven performance data samples are required because there are seven unknown coefficients. Each performance data sample is collected with a different system state. Section 4.3 discusses how CEML collects the performance data samples to generate the performance estimation model at runtime.

4.2   Power Estimator

The *power estimator* estimates the power consumption of the target machine-learning application for a system state of interest. In line with prior works, the power estimator assumes that the power consumption of each device is proportional to the device utilization because it is simple and accurate [14,17].

Specifically, CEML employs Eq. 2 to estimate the power consumption of the device D (i.e., CPU, GPU, or memory) when the device frequency is set to f_D. We experimentally determine the regression coefficients (i.e., ϵ_{D,f_D} and ζ_{D,f_D}) for each device based on the offline profiling using the stress benchmarks that we have developed. Each of the stress benchmarks is designed and implemented to stress the CPU, GPU, or memory.

$$
P_{D,f_D} = \epsilon_{D,f_D} \cdot U_D + \zeta_{D,f_D}
\tag{2}
$$

To estimate the power consumption of the target machine-learning application for a system state of interest, the power estimator estimates the utilization of each device. We first investigate the device utilization sensitivity to the device frequencies. Our experimental results show the following data trends.

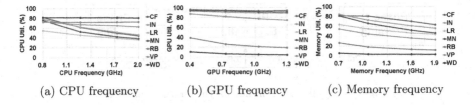

(a) CPU frequency   (b) GPU frequency   (c) Memory frequency

Fig. 5. Device utilization sensitivity to its frequency

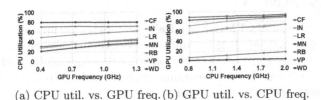

(a) CPU util. vs. GPU freq. (b) GPU util. vs. CPU freq.

Fig. 6. Device utilization sensitivity to the other device frequency

First, as shown in Fig. 5, the utilization of each device is (largely) linearly proportional to the device frequency when the frequencies of the other devices are fixed (at the maximum frequency). This is mainly because the device stays active for a shorter (or longer) time duration at higher (or lower) frequency by processing the assigned work faster (or slower).

Second, as shown in Fig. 6, the utilization of each device is (largely) linearly proportional to the frequency of the frequencies of the other devices. When the other devices run faster (or slower), they produce more (or less) data to be processed by the device per unit time, making its utilization higher (or lower).

We now discuss how the power estimator estimates the utilization of each device. For instance, the power estimator uses Eq. 3 to estimate the CPU utilization for a system state of interest (i.e., (f_C, f_G, f_M)).[1] In Eq. 3, the first-order and interaction terms are used to model the individual effect of each device and the interaction between devices, respectively.

$$U_C = \gamma_{C,C} \cdot f_C + \gamma_{C,G} \cdot f_G + \gamma_{C,M} \cdot f_M + \gamma_{C,CG} \cdot f_C \cdot f_G +$$
$$\gamma_{C,GM} \cdot f_G \cdot f_M + \gamma_{C,MC} \cdot f_M \cdot f_C + \delta_C \qquad (3)$$

To compute the coefficients in Eq. 3, seven utilization data samples are required because there are seven unknown coefficients. Section 4.3 discusses how CEML collects the utilization data samples to generate the power estimation model at runtime. Finally, the power estimator estimates the total power consumption of the underlying heterogeneous computing system by summing the estimated power consumption of all the devices (i.e., $P = P_C + P_G + P_M$).

---

[1] While omitted, the power estimator employs the equations similar to Eq. 3 to estimate the GPU and memory utilization.

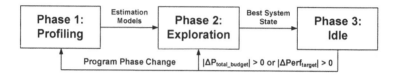

Fig. 7. Overall execution flow of the runtime manager

4.3 Runtime Manager

The *runtime manager* of CEML dynamically profiles the performance and power consumption data samples. It then builds the performance and power estimation models and determines the efficient system state that significantly enhances the efficiency of the target machine-learning application by exploring the system state space based on the estimation models.

The runtime manager mainly comprises the three phases – (1) profiling, (2) exploration, and (3) idle phases. Figure 7 shows its overall execution flow.

During the *profiling phase*, the runtime manager executes a small portion of the total training steps of the target machine-learning application with the following seven system states that cover a wide range of the device frequencies (in GHz) – (2, 1.3, 1.87), (1.42, 0.83, 0.67), (1.42, 0.42, 1.33), (0.81, 0.83, 1.33), (0.81, 0.42, 1.06), (0.81, 0.62, 0.67), and (1.11, 0.42, 0.67). Specifically, the runtime manager starts with the initial system state. When the runtime manager collects N heartbeats[2] generated by the target application, it stores the performance and utilization data, configures the system with the next one among the seven system states, and repeats the data collection process. When the performance and utilization data is collected with all the seven system states, the runtime manager proceeds with the exploration phase.

During the *exploration phase*, the runtime manager constructs the performance and power estimation models using the data collected during the profiling phase. Specifically, it computes all the coefficients in Eqs. 1 and 3 using the efficient equation solver that we have developed.

The runtime manager then explores the system state space to determine the system state, which is estimated to significantly improve the efficiency[3] of the target machine-learning application. We propose two search algorithms, each of which explores the system state space with different coverage and runtime overheads.

The first algorithm is the exhaustive search algorithm shown in Algorithm 1. It explores all the feasible system states in an exhaustive manner and selects

---

[2] In this work, N heartbeats contain the performance and utilization data collected during the execution of 1% of the total training steps for each benchmark.

[3] We use the generic term "efficiency" because CEML can be extended to perform optimizations using the metrics (e.g., energy-delay product) other than energy (i.e., $\frac{Power}{Performance}$ (Joules per training step)) by customizing the estimateScore function in Algorithms 1 and 2.

Algorithm 1. The exhaustive search function

```
 1: procedure EXPLOREWITHEXHAUSTIVESEARCH
 2:      bestState ← getInitialState()
 3:      bestScore ← estimateScore(bestState)
 4:      for fC ∈ FC
 5:          for fG ∈ FG
 6:              for fM ∈ FM
 7:                  cState ← (fC, fG, fM)
 8:                  cScore ← estimateScore(cState)
 9:                  if cScore > bestScore ∧ checkConstraint(cState)
10:                      bestState ← cState
11:                      bestScore ← cScore
12:                  end if
13:              end for
14:          end for
15:      end for
16:      setSystemState(bestState)
17: end procedure
```

---

the best system state, which is estimated to maximize the efficiency of the target machine-learning application without violating the user-specified constraint[4] such as the total power budget (Line 9). The time complexity of the exhaustive search algorithm is $O(N_{f_C} \cdot N_{f_G} \cdot N_{f_M})$.

While the time complexity of the exhaustive search algorithm is rather high, it may be still practically used for commodity heterogeneous computing systems. For example, the system state parameters of the heterogeneous computing system evaluated in this work are $N_{f_C} = 9$, $N_{f_G} = 10$, and $N_{f_M} = 6$. In this case, the total number of the candidate system states is 540, which can be explored in 176.4 microseconds (on average) on the evaluated heterogeneous computing system.

Since the exhaustive search algorithm has high time complexity, we also propose a local search algorithm that explores the system state space using a variant of the hill-climbing algorithm (Algorithm 2). Specifically, the local search algorithm starts with the initial system state. It estimates the efficiency of all the neighbor system states and selects the system state, which is estimated to achieve the maximum efficiency without violating the user-specified constraint (Line 5).[5] If the best neighbor state is estimated to be more efficient than the current state, it selects the best neighbor state as the next system state to

---

[4] We assume that there are one or more system states (in the system state space) that satisfy the user-specified constraint. The getInitialState function returns one of such system states.

[5] If there is no neighbor state that satisfies the user-specified constraint, the getBestNeighborState function returns invalidState. If the input parameter is set to invalidState, the estimateScore function returns the minimum score.

Algorithm 2. The local search function

```
 1: procedure EXPLOREWITHLOCALSEARCH
 2:     bestState ← getInitialState()
 3:     bestScore ← estimateScore(bestState)
 4:     while true
 5:         cState ← getBestNeighborState(bestState)
 6:         cScore ← estimateScore(cState)
 7:         if cScore > bestScore
 8:             bestState ← cState
 9:             bestScore ← cScore
10:         else
11:             break
12:         end if
13:     end while
14:     setSystemState(bestState)
15: end procedure
```

transition and continues the search process (Lines 7–9). Otherwise, it terminates the search process (Line 11).

Once the best system state is selected by the search algorithm, the runtime manager accordingly configures the system to significantly enhance the efficiency of the target machine-learning application (Line 16 in Algorithm 1 and Line 14 in Algorithm 2). The runtime manager then transitions into the idle phase.

During the *idle phase*, CEML keeps monitoring the target machine-learning application to detect its phase changes without performing any adaptation activities. Specifically, CEML periodically collects the heartbeats from the target application and computes the differences between consecutive data samples to detect a program phase change. When detecting a program phase change, CEML terminates the idle phase and re-triggers the adaptation process to determine a new efficient system state.

Further, CEML keeps monitoring the underlying system to detect any change in the total power budget or performance target. When detecting a change, CEML immediately triggers the re-adaptation process to discover an efficient system state for the new constraint.

5   Evaluation

We quantify the effectiveness of CEML. Specifically, we aim to investigate the following – (1) the estimation accuracy, (2) the energy efficiency, (3) the effectiveness of re-adaptation, and (4) the performance overheads.

We first investigate the accuracy of the performance and power estimators of CEML. To quantify the accuracy of the estimators, we generate 25 test datasets for each benchmark by executing each benchmark with 25 different system states and compute the average estimation error across all the test datasets.

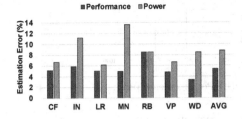

Fig. 8. Accuracy of the estimators   Fig. 9. Energy consumption

Figure 8 shows the average performance and power estimation errors. We observe that the performance and power estimators achieve high estimation accuracy. Specifically, the average estimation errors of the performance and power estimators are 5.4% and 8.8% across all the benchmarks. The use of the first-order and interaction terms in the performance and power estimators effectively models the linear and interactive effects of each device in the underlying heterogeneous computing system, achieving high estimation accuracy.

We now investigate the effectiveness of CEML in terms of energy consumption (i.e., Joules per training step). We evaluate four versions for each benchmark. The baseline version executes each benchmark at the maximum device frequencies. The static best version selects the best frequency of each device based on the extensive offline experiments (i.e., 32 system states for each benchmark). The CEML-L and CEML-E versions are managed by CEML using the local and exhaustive search algorithms, respectively.

Figure 9 shows the energy consumption of each version of the benchmarks, normalized to the baseline version. The rightmost bar shows the geometric mean of each version.

First, the CEML versions significantly reduce the energy consumption across all the evaluated machine-learning benchmarks. For instance, CEML-E consumes 30.8% less energy (on average) than the baseline version. The baseline version achieves low energy efficiency because it executes the target machine-learning application at the maximum device frequencies without considering the performance and power characteristics of the target machine-learning application. In contrast, CEML robustly finds the efficient system state based on its performance and power estimators and accordingly configures the system, consuming significantly less energy than the baseline version.

Second, the CEML versions achieve the energy efficiency similar to the static best version. For instance, the energy consumption of CEML-E is 2.9% higher (on average) than the static best version. The CEML versions consume slightly more energy than the static best version because it executes the target machine-learning application with suboptimal system states during the profiling phase (e.g., RB) and finds a slightly less efficient system state due to the estimation errors with some of the evaluated benchmarks (e.g., IN and LR). Nevertheless, our experimental results demonstrate the effectiveness of CEML in that the CEML

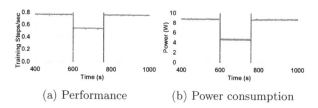

(a) Performance   (b) Power consumption

Fig. 10. Effectiveness of re-adaptation

versions achieve the energy efficiency comparable with the static best version without requiring any extensive per-application offline profiling.

Third, CEML-E achieves slightly higher energy efficiency than the CEML-L (i.e., 2.6% on average). This is mainly because the local search algorithm of CEML-L may converge to a less efficient state (e.g., MN). However, CEML-L achieves the energy efficiency comparable with CEML-E across all the evaluated benchmarks, demonstrating the potential for CEML-L in that its local search algorithm has significantly lower average-case time complexity than the exhaustive search algorithm of CEML-E.

To investigate the effectiveness of the re-adaptation functionality of CEML, we design a case study in which the total power budget allocated to the underlying heterogeneous computing system changes during the execution of the LR benchmark with CEML. In this case study, CEML is configured to maximize the performance of LR while satisfying the power constraint.

Figure 10 shows the runtime behavior of CEML. Initially, the benchmark runs with a high power budget. Since the power budget is sufficient, CEML runs the benchmark at the maximum device frequencies while satisfying the power constraint. At $t = 600.1$, the total power budget changes to a low power budget. CEML robustly detects the total power budget change and adapts to the new system state that is efficient (i.e., similar performance to the static best version) for the low power budget, guided by its performance and power estimators. At $t = 760.1$, the total power budget changes back to the high power budget. Again, CEML robustly detects the total power budget change and accordingly performs adaptations to find the efficient system state for the new total power budget.

Finally, we quantify the performance overheads of CEML. Our experimental results demonstrate that CEML incurs insignificant performance overheads. Specifically, the CPU utilization of CEML is 1.0% on average, which is low. In addition, the system state exploration times with the CEML-L and CEML-E versions are 7.2 and 176.4 microseconds on average, which are insignificant.

In summary, our quantitative evaluation shows that CEML is effective in the sense that it consumes significantly less energy than the baseline version, achieves the energy efficiency similar to the static best version, robustly adapts to the external events such as total power budget changes, and incurs small performance overheads.

6   Related Work

Prior works have extensively investigated the architectural and system software techniques to improve the efficiency of heterogeneous computing systems [11–15,17]. While insightful, the prior works manage a subset of heterogeneous computing devices (i.e., CPU [11,13,17], CPU and GPU [12,14], GPU and memory [15]) with multithreaded and gaming workloads.

Our work significantly differs in that it investigates the performance and power characteristics of machine-learning applications with various device frequencies, presents the accurate performance and power estimators, proposes a coordinated runtime system that robustly controls all the devices (i.e., CPU, GPU, memory) in the underlying heterogeneous computing system, and demonstrates the effectiveness of CEML using a full heterogeneous computing system.

Prior works have proposed the system software support for efficient machine learning [4,7,9]. The prior works mainly focus on the design and implementation of parallel and distributed programming platforms for machine learning with support for task scheduling [4,7,9]. In contrast, our work investigates the coordinated runtime support that robustly manages the hardware resources in heterogeneous computing systems for efficient machine learning.

Prior works have investigated the design and implementation of hardware accelerators for machine learning [5,6,10,16]. While effective, the prior works cannot be directly applied to existing commodity systems because they require intrusive hardware modifications. Our work differs in that CEML is designed and implemented as a coordinated runtime system to enable efficient machine learning on commodity heterogeneous computing systems. When the hardware accelerators for machine learning become widely available in upcoming commodity systems, coordinated runtime systems such as CEML can be effectively used to robustly manage a variety of heterogeneous computing devices including the hardware accelerators.

7   Conclusions

In this paper, we propose CEML, a coordinated runtime system for efficient machine-learning on heterogeneous computing systems. CEML dynamically analyzes the performance and power characteristics of the target machine-learning application and adapts the system state to enhance its efficiency on heterogeneous computing systems. Our experimental results demonstrate that CEML consumes significantly less energy than the baseline version that employs the maximum device frequencies and achieves the energy efficiency comparable with the static best version that requires extensive per-application offline profiling. As future work, we plan to apply and extend our proposed techniques for efficient machine learning in heterogeneous distributed computing environments.

Acknowledgements. This research was partly supported by the National Research Foundation of Korea (NRF-2016M3C4A7952587, PF Class Heterogeneous High Performance Computer Development), Basic Science Research Program through the National

Research Foundation of Korea (NRF-2018R1C1B6005961), and Institute for Information & Communications Technology Promotion (IITP) grant funded by the Korea government (MSIP) (No. R0190-16-2012, High Performance Big Data Analytics Platform Performance Acceleration Technologies Development).

References

1. http://www.nvidia.com/object/embedded-systems-dev-kits-modules.html
2. http://www.samsung.com/semiconductor/products/exynos-solution/application-processor/EXYNOS-5-OCTA-5422
3. https://github.com/tensorflow/models
4. Abadi, M., et al.: TensorFlow: a system for large-scale machine learning. In: 12th USENIX Symposium on Operating Systems Design and Implementation (OSDI 2016) (2016)
5. Chen, Y.-H., Emer, J., Sze, V.: Eyeriss: a spatial architecture for energy-efficient dataflow for convolutional neural networks. In: Proceedings of the 43rd International Symposium on Computer Architecture (2016)
6. Han, S., et al.: EIE: efficient inference engine on compressed deep neural network. In: Proceedings of the 43rd International Symposium on Computer Architecture (2016)
7. Hauswald, J., et al.: DjiNN and Tonic: DNN as a service and its implications for future warehouse scale computers. In: Proceedings of the 42nd Annual International Symposium on Computer Architecture (2015)
8. Hoffmann, H., Eastep, J., Santambrogio, M.D., Miller, J.E., Agarwal, A.: Application heartbeats: a generic interface for specifying program performance and goals in autonomous computing environments. In: Proceedings of the 7th International Conference on Autonomic Computing (2010)
9. Jia, Y., et al.: Caffe: convolutional architecture for fast feature embedding. In: Proceedings of the 22nd ACM International Conference on Multimedia (2014)
10. Jouppi, N.P., et al.: In-datacenter performance analysis of a tensor processing unit. In: Proceedings of the 44th Annual International Symposium on Computer Architecture (2017)
11. Muthukaruppan, T.S., Pricopi, M., Venkataramani, V., Mitra, T., Vishin, S.: Hierarchical power management for asymmetric multi-core in dark silicon era. In: Proceedings of the 50th Annual Design Automation Conference (2013)
12. Park, J., Baek, W.: RCHC: a holistic runtime system for concurrent heterogeneous computing. In: 2016 45th International Conference on Parallel Processing (ICPP) (2016)
13. Park, J., Baek, W.: HAP: a heterogeneity-conscious runtime system for adaptive pipeline parallelism. In: Dutot, P.-F., Trystram, D. (eds.) Euro-Par 2016. LNCS, vol. 9833, pp. 518–530. Springer, Cham (2016). https://doi.org/10.1007/978-3-319-43659-3_38
14. Pathania, A., Irimiea, A.E., Prakash, A., Mitra, T.: Power-performance modelling of mobile gaming workloads on heterogeneous MPSoCs. In: Proceedings of the 52nd Annual Design Automation Conference (2015)
15. Sethia, A., Mahlke, S.: Equalizer: dynamic tuning of GPU resources for efficient execution. In: Proceedings of the 47th Annual IEEE/ACM International Symposium on Microarchitecture (2014)

16. Song, L., Wang, Y., Han, Y., Zhao, X., Liu, B., Li, X.: C-brain: a deep learning accelerator that tames the diversity of CNNs through adaptive data-level parallelization. In: Proceedings of the 53rd Annual Design Automation Conference (2016)
17. Yun, J., Park, J., Baek, W.: HARS: a heterogeneity-aware runtime system for self-adaptive multithreaded applications. In: Proceedings of the 52nd Annual Design Automation Conference (2015)

Stream Processing on Hybrid CPU/Intel® Xeon Phi™ Systems

Paulo Ferrão, Hélder Marques, and Hervé Paulino$^{(\boxtimes)}$ (ID)

NOVA Laboratory for Computer Science and Informatics,
Departamento de Informática, Faculdade de Ciências e Tecnologia,
Universidade Nova de Lisboa, 2829-516 Caparica, Portugal
{p.ferrao,hd.marques}@campus.fct.unl.pt,
herve.paulino@fct.unl.pt

Abstract. Stream processing is currently central to handle large volumes of data generated at high rates. However, the efficient processing of such quantity of data demands massively parallel hardware. The usual approach is to rely on clusters of multi-processors, where network communication may become a bottleneck. Some work has also been done in the GPU computing field. Yet, the GPUs' programming complexity and the existence of synchronization-related overheads, when the streaming graph scales, have hampered the integration of GPUs in the Big Data streaming frameworks. In this paper we explore the unique characteristics of the Intel Xeon Phi processor to develop a stream processing framework for hybrid CPU/Intel Xeon Phi systems. We built atop the Intel Threading Building Blocks library and the Marrow algorithmic skeleton framework to offer an easily programmable high performance system. Our experimental results show that offloading the computationally heavy nodes of a streaming graph to the Xeon Phi may earn considerable speed-ups. Furthermore, additional gains may be obtained by sharing the processing load between the CPU(s) and the Xeon Phi processor(s).

Keywords: Stream processing · Parallel computing · Intel Xeon Phi
Algorithmic skeletons

1 Introduction

Stream processing is currently paramount to handle large volumes of data that are generated at high rates and, thus, must be processed swiftly. To accomplish such endeavour, stream processing systems require massively parallel hardware. The most common approach is to resort to distributed computing on clusters, typically virtual clusters running in some computation cloud. Popular distributed stream processing frameworks include Spark Streaming [17], Flink Streaming [4] and Storm [2]. In such systems, computing resource scaling implies more nodes. However, as the data processing stages are spread among this increasing number

This work was partially supported by NOVA LINCS (Ref. UID/CEC/04516/2013).

of nodes, communication latency becomes a bottleneck when large amounts of data have to be communicated across the network.

Accelerators are a rather economic way to boost the computing power of individual nodes, and, with that, reduce a cluster's dimension and, consequently, mitigate network communication. Accordingly, there has been some work on the use of Graphics Processing Units (GPUs) [11,15,16,18]. There are, however, some limitations that have to be considered: 1. code written for the CPU is usually not portable to the GPU; in fact, the GPU programming model differs considerably from the one of conventional CPUs, requiring knowledge of parallel programming and even computer architecture, and 2. GPUs do not support global synchronization, the scope of thread synchronization is restricted to thread blocks (or work-groups, using the OpenCL nomenclature). Consequently, a global barrier may only be performed by handing control back to the host, which means that applying a sequence of stages upon a set of data implies a kernel execution per stage. There has been some work on kernel fusion [7,13] to reduce the number of global barriers. However, applicability is still limited.

In this paper, we propose to explore the unique characteristics of the Intel Xeon Phi co-processor to provide a high performance stream processing framework that leverages on hybrid CPU(s)/Intel Xeon Phi nodes. The most well known of these characteristics is Intel's Many Integrated Core (MIC) architecture, which combines many Intel x86 cores, and hence may be programmed with standard C, C++ or FORTRAN. Therefore, code developed for the CPU may run almost unmodified on the Xeon Phi. One other advantage (specially over GPUs) is that it supports global barriers. Therefore, a streaming graph may run entirely on the Xeon Phi, without requiring control transfers to the host.

Our approach is to build upon the widely used Intel Threading Building Blocks (TBB) library [12], namely on its Flow Graph interface [9]. Being a C++ template library, TBB Flow Graph (TBB FG) already provides the means for programming computations that run exclusively on the Xeon Phi, via the native execution mode. There is, however, no support for hybrid CPU/Xeon Phi execution, where part(s) of the graph run on the host and others run on one (or more) Xeon Phi processors, and with that leverage the best each type of processor has to offer. The contributions of our work are thus:

1. *Marrow Streaming*, a framework that enables the use of the TBB FG interface to process streams on hybrid CPU/Xeon Phi nodes (Sect. 2).
2. The use of the Marrow algorithmic skeleton framework [1,10] to transparently manage all host ⇆ Xeon Phi communication, and to simplify the programming of the data processing nodes, ensuring vectorization on both the Xeon Phi and the host's CPUs by design (Sect. 2).
3. The characterization of the computations (graphs) whose execution may be boosted by the use of hybrid CPU/Xeon Phi systems (Sect. 3).

2 The Marrow Streaming Framework

Intel's SDK for the Xeon Phi enables the execution of TBB FG computations natively on the co-processor (Fig. 1a), where flow graphs are launched and exe-

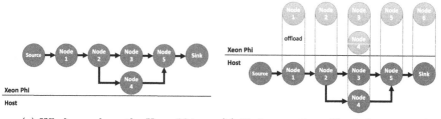

(a) Whole graph on the Xeon Phi   (b) Node execution offloaded one at a time

Fig. 1. Currently possible graph execution models

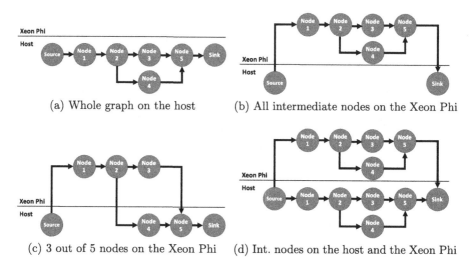

(a) Whole graph on the host   (b) All intermediate nodes on the Xeon Phi

(c) 3 out of 5 nodes on the Xeon Phi   (d) Int. nodes on the host and the Xeon Phi

Fig. 2. Graph configuration examples with Marrow Streaming

cute on the Xeon Phi with no communication with the host. It also enables
the offloading of one node at a time (Fig. 1b), resulting in an execution model
with control transfers between the host and the co-processor, similarly to what
is possible to implement on GPUs (due to the absence of global barriers). It is,
however, not possible to deploy graphs with nodes running on the CPU and on
a MIC card (Xeon Phi). Moreover, data transfers must be explicitly managed
and only occur at the beginning or end of an offload operation.

   The Marrow Streaming framework exports the same set of operations as
TBB FG, but with a significant difference: nodes in the data-flow graph may
be placed either on the host (be it single or multi-CPU) or on one (or more)
MIC cards, such as an Xeon Phi processor. The motivation is to allow for the
offload of sub-graphs, rather than single nodes. The host may execute the nodes
that perform input/output operations and interface with distributed stream processing systems, while some, or all, of the remaining nodes execute on the MIC
cards. Figure 2 illustrates several possible configurations for the execution of a

```
using namespace marrow;
using namespace marrow::streaming;
typedef std::tuple< vector<int>*, vector<int>* > out_tuple;

graph g;
source_node<vector<int>*> source (g, source_f())
function_node<vector<int>*, vector<int>*, MIC> node1 (g, unlimited, f1());
function_node<vector<int>*, vector<int>*, MIC> node2 (g, unlimited, f2());
function_node<vector<int>*, vector<int>*, MIC> node3 (g, unlimited, f3());
function_node<vector<int>*, vector<int>*> node4 (g, unlimited, f4());
join<out_tuple> node5 (g, f5());
function_node<out_tuple, vector<int>*> sink (g, unlimited, sink_f());

make_edge(source, node1);
make_edge(node1, node2);
make_edge(node2, node3);
make_edge(node2, node4);
make_edge(node3, input_port<0>(node5));
make_edge(node4, input_port<1>(node5));
make_edge(node5, sink);
```

Listing 1. Implementation of the example of Fig. 2c

graph with a single source, a single sink and five intermediate nodes, in a system with a single Xeon Phi. To be noted that on Fig. 2d the graph's intermediate nodes are deployed on both the host and the Xeon Phi. The source node must then split the stream among both sub-graphs—by using a push strategy with a round-robin policy or have both *Nodes 1* pull the data—and, with that, leverage the processing power of both host and co-processor.

2.1   Programming Model

The programming model extends the one of TBB FG with the node location indication $\in$ {Host, MICi}, where i denotes the number of the MIC processor: MIC0 may also be referred to as simply MIC. Graphs are, hence, represented by instances of a TBB-equivalent `graph` class, upon which many kinds of nodes may be attached to. Prominent examples are:

source_node that generates a stream of data items of the given data-type;
function_node that applies a computation to an input stream, producing an output stream that is broadcast to all of the node's successors;
split_node that applies a computation to a input stream of tuples, producing an output stream for each element of the tuple;
join_node that joins multiple input streams into a single stream of tuples, composed of one element from each input stream.

Listing 1 illustrates how the example from Fig. 2d may be programmed, when assuming a stream of integer vectors. As intended, the code is very close to the equivalent implementation in TBB FG, differing from the latter in just three details:

(a) the use of the `marrow::streaming` name space, rather than the original `tbb::flow`, to commute between implementations.

(b) the explicit indication that nodes 1, 2 and 3 are to the executed on the Xeon Phi (MIC) co-processor. Note that, by default, nodes execute on the host, making the code for example in Fig. 2a the same for `marrow::streaming` and `tbb::flow`.

(c) the use of container `marrow::vector`, which automatically manages all data transfers between the host and the Xeon Phi.

Host ⇆ Xeon Phi Communication: The addressing spaces of the host and of a Xeon Phi co-processor are disjoint, which implies transferring data to and from the co-processor, when needed. Marrow provides its own versions of the C++ STL's `array` and `vector` containers. These versions allow for the creation of clones of themselves, either on the same or on another addressing space, namely on GPUs and/or the Xeon Phi. Updates to the original container and its clones are done automatically without programmer intervention, rendering all host ⇆ Xeon Phi communication transparent.

Lastly, the construction of the graph's edges is left unchanged from TBB. The use of C++ templates deduces specifications of the `make_edge` function for all possible scenarios in {Host, MIC0, ..., MICn} × {Host, MIC0, ..., MICn}.

Node Behavior Implementation: The procedure for node behavior implementation in Marrow Streaming is identical to the one for TBB FG, i.e. indiscriminate code supplied as a C++ functor. However, good performance on the Xeon Phi is tightly bound to the ability to explore the vectorization capabilities of each individual core. As a result, the use of the co-processor is specially advantageous when running nodes that perform multiple data-independent operations, such as many operations over vectors.

The programmer must then reason about which kind of nodes to place on the co-processor, and the vectorization properties of a particular node's code. In this section we will focus on the second of these concerns, leaving the first for future work discussion (Sect. 5).

A mandatory requirement for vectorization is data alignment. This is automatically handled by Marrow's `array` and `vector` container implementations, but must be explicitly handled when using other data structures. Additionally, in TBB, values are passed by copy from node to node. Thus, the use of pointers[1] is recommended when passing large objects along the stream. This raises a new problem for code vectorization, because it may not be easy to guarantee that memory accesses do not overlap. The usual approach is to aid the compiler by qualifying pointers with the **restrict** keyword (or equivalent), whenever the memory accessible from a given pointer may only be accessed by that same pointer in the current scope.

In order to remove these concerns from the programmer's mind, we have built upon previous knowledge on skeletal programming, acquired in the development of the Marrow framework [10,14]. Accordingly, we devised a MIC-directed implementation of some of Marrow's skeletons, namely *map*, *reduce* and *loop*. *Map* and

---

[1] References are not fully supported.

reduce were designed to be data-independent and, hence, have been vectorized by design. With regard to *loop*, no restrictions are imposed on the code of its body. Hence, all behaviors are allowed, including not vectorizable ones. Nevertheless, if the loop's body is programmed only by combining Marrow skeletons, these build on the concept of *expression template* to generate a compile time abstract syntax tree that may be analysed for data-dependency detection, and provide useful hints to the programmer. This is, however, ongoing work.

Listing 2 showcases the use of Marrow skeletons to implement the behavior of a node, concretely of node 1 from Listing 1. The map skeleton applies functor `clean_filter` that zeros (in place) all values below a given threshold.

```
template <typename T, typename U> struct clean_filter {
  void operator() (T& result, const U& threshold) const {
    if (result < threshold) result = 0;
  }
};

struct f1 {
  marrow::vector<int>* operator() (marrow::vector<int>* v) {
    marrow:map<clean_filter<int>>() (*v, 10);
    return v;
  }
};
```

Listing 2. A simple filter implementation in Marrow

2.2 Execution Model

A graph spread across the host and Xeon Phi co-processors is internally supported by multiple TBB FG sub-graphs, denoted, respectively, by $graph_{host}$ and $graph_{mic_i}$, where i is the number of the MIC card. Naturally, nodes to execute on the host are attached to $graph_{host}$, while the others are attached to the respective $graph_{mic}$.

Given that the whole graph is built on the host (see Listing 1), to attach nodes to a $graph_{mic}$ we have to offload the creation and the connection of the nodes to the target MIC processor. So, rather than offloading the execution of the nodes as in Fig. 1b, we offload the construction of the graph and, once the graph is built, its edges behave as plain TBB FG edges. To achieve this goal, some offload blocks need to refer to graphs and nodes created on previous offload operations. However, the compiler-generated address translation mechanism that enables the access of data, allocated in the host, inside offload blocks is only valid while such block executes. This clashes with our need. To bypass the restriction we take advantage of the fact that address translation is not performed for void pointers[2]. Hence, building an edge between two nodes located on a MIC takes the nodes' surrogates on the host, retrieves the address of the original node on the target MIC, and offloads the edge construction to that same MIC card.

Lastly, given that the co-processor version of the Xeon Phi is currently available as an add-on PCIe card, edges that (on the original graph) connect nodes

---

[2] We acquired this information from experience. To the best of our knowledge it is not reported.

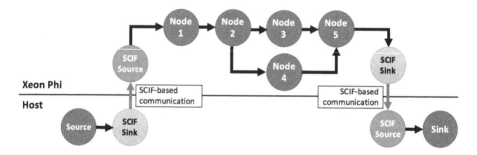

Fig. 3. Wormholes that connect graphs running on the host and on the Xeon Phi

running on different locations require communication over the PCIe bus. To that end, we resort to the Symmetric Communication InterFace (SCIF): a library included in the Intel Manycore Platform Software Stack (MPSS) [8] to provide a socket-like API for communicating with Xeon Phi cards over such bus.

To seamlessly combine SCIF-based communication with TBB FG, we developed a wormhole that transfers a data stream between graphs. This wormhole is created and deployed automatically when function make_edge is called to connect two nodes running on different locations. The wormhole is supported by a pair interconnected nodes, named *Entry* and *Exit*, being that (as expected) data send to the wormhole's entry end disappears from the current graph, surfacing at wormhole's exit. *Entry* is implemented as a TBB FG function_node that sends the incoming data stream to a pre-established SCIF communication socket. Conversely, *Exit* is a TBB FG source_node that reads the stream from such socket and writes it to the edge that connects the node to the rest of the graph. Hence, calling make_edge upon two nodes n_1 and n_2 – running on the aforementioned different locations – connects n_1 to the wormhole's *Entry* node, and the associated *Exit* node to n_2. Figure 3 illustrates the procedure applied to the graph of Fig. 2b.

Communicating Marrow Containers: Marrow containers allocate, and manage, data residing on the addressing space of the location where they were created. When they are first sent through a wormhole to another location, a clone is then created there (i.e. the necessary memory is allocated on the new location and the current contents of the container copied). Subsequent transmissions over wormholes cause the contents of the host and Xeon Phi clones to be updated. Looking once again to Fig. 3, the sending of a container created on the host through the wormhole that connects node *Source* to *Node 1*, causes a clone to be created on the Xeon Phi. In turn, the sending of a container through the wormhole that connects *Node 5* to the *Sink* node, may result in one of the following two behaviors: (a) if the container was created on the host and its contents have been modified on the Xeon Phi, the modified contents are copied to the host; (b) if, on the other hand, the vector was created on the Xeon Phi,

Table 1. Benchmark configuration parameters

Parameter	Experimented values	Impact
Where is the graph executed	Host (Fig. 2a); MIC0 (Fig. 2b); Both (Fig. 2d)	
Number of images (vectors) to process	4; 60; 120	Inter-core parallelism
The images' size	720p (3.3 MB); 1080p (7.6 MB); 1440p (13.2 MB)	Communication and Vectorization
Number of intermediate nodes	10; 40; 80	Inter-core parallelism
Operation applied by each node	Integer (addition); Floating-point (power)	Type of computation to each vector element
Number of operations applied per node	50; 100; 400	Vectorization

by one of the nodes running there, a clone must then be created on the host. When a container goes out of scope, all clones are automatically deleted.

3 Experimental Results

The goal of our evaluation is to characterize the scenarios where it is beneficial to use hybrid CPU/Xeon Phi nodes to process a data-flow graph, and quantify such gains.

Benchmark: We implemented a synthetic benchmark that deploys a graph with a single source, a single sink and a parametrizable number of intermediate nodes. The latter apply the same computation, a given number of times, to a stream of marrow::vectors, which in this case contain images in Portable Gray Map (PGM) format. This benchmark is highly customizable through the parameters presented in Table 1. The nodes are configured to use the TBB FG unlimited concurrency strategy, meaning that any node activation may spawn a new task.

Setup: Experiments have been performed on a machine with an Intel Xeon E5-2603 CPU (quad-core, hyper-threading, 1.80 GHz, 15 GB RAM, 10 MB Cache) and one Intel Xeon Phi 5110P (60 cores, 1.05 GHz, 8 GB GDDR5 2.5 GHz RAM, 30 MB L2 cache). The source code was compiled with Intel Composer version 17.0.1, and run with MPSS driver version 3.6.1-1.

All reported measurements are the mean of 20 experiments, and account the time elapsed between the instant the first image is received by the *Source* node, and the instant the last one is processed by the *Sink* node.

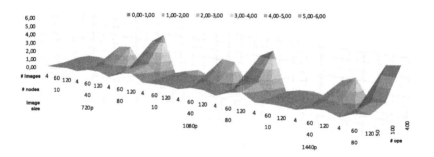

Fig. 4. Speed-up of MIC0 versus Host: Integer

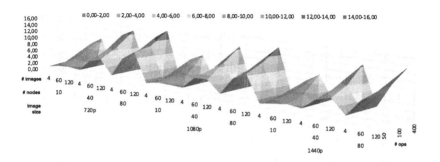

Fig. 5. Speed-up of MIC0 versus Host: Floating-point

Speedup FP			# nops		
image size	# nodes	# images	50	100	400
720p	10	4	1,04	1,38	1,81
		60	1,75	2,96	7,13
		120	2,00	2,80	9,10
	40	4	1,62	1,80	1,94
		60	4,80	7,41	11,28
		120	5,91	8,81	13,00
	80	4	1,75	1,89	1,91
		60	7,33	9,08	12,11
		120	9,63	10,76	14,49
1080p	10	4	1,17	1,42	1,83
		60	1,96	3,04	6,99
		120	1,88	3,65	8,62
	40	4	1,68	1,85	1,93
		60	5,09	6,29	9,09
		120	5,15	8,94	12,80
	80	4	1,84	1,92	1,94
		60	6,66	8,21	9,49
		120	8,46	10,73	14,13
1440p	10	4	1,05	1,46	1,84
		60	1,63	3,07	5,81
		120	2,16	3,64	8,11
	40	4	1,66	1,78	1,95
		60	4,66	6,29	8,10
		120	5,77	8,06	12,61
	80	4	1,86	1,90	1,93
		60	6,47	7,57	8,49
		120	8,85	10,40	13,48

Fig. 6. Speed-up of MIC0 versus Host: Floating-point

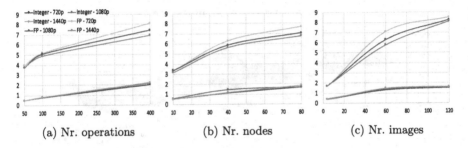

(a) Nr. operations   (b) Nr. nodes   (c) Nr. images

Fig. 7. Speed-up - Parameter sensitivity analysis. The values represent the average of the results for all configurations with the parameter under analysis fixed.

Xeon Phi (MIC0) Versus Host: For this first experiment we executed the Host and MIC0 benchmark configurations over all possible values for the remainder parameters. The results, depicted on Figs. 4 and 5, show that the gains are much higher when floating-point operations are into play. In fact, for integer processing, speed-ups are only observed in scenarios with either: (a) 40, or more, computationally heavy (400 operations per image pixel) intermediate nodes – with speed-ups attaining ≈4 for 60 images and ≈5 for 120 images, for all configurations, or (b) 80 nodes executing 100 operations – with speed-ups reaching up to 3.11 for 60 images and 3.22 for 120. The less work generating configurations do not take enough advantage of the Xeon Phi's parallel hardware to compensate the PCIe communication overhead and the higher computing power of the CPU's cores. This is mostly observable in the 4 image configurations, with a bottom speed-up of 0.2 (slow-down of ≈5).

On the other hand, all floating-point configurations yield positive speed-ups from 1.04 to 14.49 (Figs. 5 and 6). From 40 nodes upward, all configurations achieve a speed-up of, at least, ≈5. This renders the Xeon Phi particularly interesting for floating-point heavy stream applications.

Conducting a parameter sensitivity analysis, we conclude that both inter- and intra-core parallelism are important to attain the reported speed-ups. Regarding the first, thread-level parallelism is necessary to make use of Xeon Phi's many cores. In this context, increasing either, or both, the number of graph nodes (Fig. 7b) and the number of data items (images) to process (Fig. 7c) increases the number of concurrent tasks[3], and hence boost parallelism. The results do not significantly differ for both parameters, since the side-effects are the same: more node activations. However, given that the number of nodes is application-dependent, having a steady flow of images becomes essential to obtain the necessary volume of core-level parallelism, and also to mask the overhead of PCIe communication by overlapping it with computation on the Xeon Phi.

Regarding intra-core parallelism, granularity, bound firstly to the number of operations executed per node and secondly to the size of the images, is key for leveraging the vectorization capabilities of the Xeon Phi. The chart of Fig. 7a

---

[3] Due to the use of the unlimited concurrency strategy.

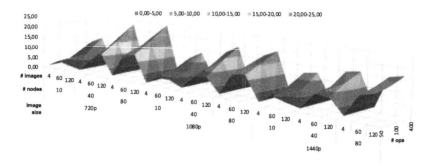

Fig. 8. Speed-up of both (Host + MIC0) versus Host

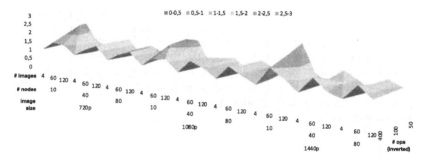

Fig. 9. Speed-up of both (Host + MIC0)versus MIC0

Speed-up / Image size	# nodes	# images	# ops 50	100	400	Average
720p	10	4	1,35	1,12	1,05	1,17
		60	2,34	1,67	1,53	1,85
		120	1,43	2,50	1,48	1,80
	40	4	1,07	1,00	1,01	1,03
		60	1,46	1,56	1,40	1,47
		120	1,81	1,81	1,71	1,78
	80	4	1,05	1,03	1,04	1,04
		60	1,62	1,58	1,42	1,54
		120	1,36	1,70	1,66	1,57
1080p	10	4	1,10	1,20	1,05	1,12
		60	2,29	2,13	1,51	1,98
		120	2,30	1,72	1,59	1,87
	40	4	1,08	1,04	1,02	1,05
		60	1,51	1,74	1,72	1,65
		120	1,64	1,60	1,47	1,57
	80	4	1,04	1,03	1,02	1,03
		60	1,73	1,70	1,76	1,73
		120	1,43	1,47	1,37	1,42
1440p	10	4	1,45	1,17	1,05	1,22
		60	2,94	2,45	2,02	2,47
		120	1,47	2,05	1,56	1,69
	40	4	1,13	1,09	1,02	1,08
		60	1,88	1,62	1,85	1,78
		120	1,48	1,58	1,26	1,44
	80	4	1,04	1,05	1,04	1,05
		60	1,75	1,73	1,83	1,77
		120	1,43	1,35	1,24	1,34

Fig. 10. Speed-up of both (Host + MIC0) versus MIC0

shows that speed-up increases considerable and consistently with the number of operations. In opposition, analysing the 3 charts, we conclude that the impact of image size is negative. This happens because, although boosting granularity, bigger image sizes also implies more communication from/to the host to/from the Xeon Phi, and more inter-graph-node communication in the Xeon Phi (via shared memory and the L2 cache).

Collaborative Graph Execution: In this second experiment, we want to assess if there are considerable gains in sharing the load between the Xeon Phi and the host by duplicating the graph on both processors (the Both version), when compared with placing all intermediate nodes on the Xeon Phi (the MIC0 version). We confine the discussion to the floating-point benchmark, being that the conclusions for the integer counterpart are generally the same. Figure 8 illustrates the speed-up against the host-only execution. The values range from 1.41 for configuration ⟨720p images, 10 intermediate nodes, 4 images, 50 operations⟩ to 24.09 for configuration ⟨720p images, 80 intermediate nodes, 120 images, 400 operations⟩. These results represent a boost relatively to the MIC0 version. In fact, we observed this speed-up boost for all configurations, as depicted in Figs. 9 and 10.

As expected, these gains are minimal for the 4 image configurations, given that the execution on both locations is pretty much on a par (see Fig. 10). Regarding the others, the CPU is more effective when the number of nodes is small. With the increase of thread parallelism, the CPU's four cores are not able to sustain the same throughput level, and hence the percentage of the work they are capable to process decreases.

Discussion: Offloading computationally heavy nodes of a dataflow graph to the Xeon Phi, while keeping the I/O bound nodes in the CPU, may yield considerable speed-ups. In the proposed framework, these gains are particularly noticeable for floating operations, for which we consistently observed speed-ups close to 10. Equivalent gains were also observed when increasing the load, i.e., the number of items flowing in the graph.

The Both configuration is particularly useful when the load is high, but the combined computational weight of the nodes to execute on both types of processors is not. In such settings, the latency of processing individual data items on the CPU and on the Xeon Phi is closer, and so, the CPU's contribution has more impact. For many of such configurations we obtained speed-ups of 20 against the host-only execution. This latency gap (between the execution on both processors) is, in fact, inversely proportional to the usefulness of processing data items on the CPU. So, as the gap increases, the ideal configuration will likely be to duplicate only part of the graph, which raises the challenge of knowing which sub-graph(s) to duplicate. Automating such decisions is not trivial and may require profiling and code inspection.

4 Related Work

As mentioned in the beginning of Sect. 2, to the best of our knowledge, there is no system that distributed nodes of a data-flow graphs among the host and

Xeon Phi co-processors. There are nonetheless other relevant works that take advantage of hybrid CPU/Xeon Phi systems.

HyPhi [5] is task-based library that also extends Intel TBB with the purpose of executing tasks on hybrid CPU/Xeon Phi systems. The purpose and applicability of this work is different from ours: it is a batch processing system that offers operations such as hybrid parallel loops and hybrid map/reduce, which are closer to Marrow's original skeletons than to the contributions of this paper. As in our work, communication (in this case thread synchronization) within a running hybrid computation is accomplished through the SCIF library.

StarPU [3] is a library for task scheduling and data management on heterogeneous systems, including the CPUs and the Intel Xeon Phi. It is work at a much lower-level than ours that also operates at a much finer grain. They offload tasks to the Xeon Phi, while we offload data-flow graphs.

MAGMA [6] is linear algebra library that leverages hybrid CPU/Xeon Phi execution. It provides MIC-accelerated implementations of Cholesky, QR and LU factorizations by executing some operations (trailing matrix update) on the Xeon Phi and others (panel factorization) on the CPU.

5   Conclusion and Future Work

We proposed a solution to efficiently run TBB FG computations on hybrid CPU/Xeon Phi systems, with minor modifications to the source code. To deviate the data flow to the Xeon Phi and back to the host, the programmer simply has to augment his program with the indication of which nodes to run on the co-processor(s). To collaboratively use both the host and the co-processor, the programmer has to precede the sub-graphs to run on both locations with a node that splits the stream among them, and succeed it with a node that gathers the results. Both nodes are straightforward to implement in TBB FG, and future work will address its automatic generation via a new specification of the make_edge function.

The experimental results show that for some loads it is possible to obtain high speed-ups (close to 15) by offloading a (sub)graph to the Xeon Phi, and close to 25 when using both the host and the co-processor to process the (sub)graph. Given these promising results, future work will focus on (a) the use of heuristics for automating the placing of the nodes, removing from the programmer's mind the burden of reasoning about which nodes to place where, (b) the interface with Apache Spark or Storm to enable the seamless integration of the Xeon Phi in distributed stream processing systems, and (c) the application to real-life scenarios.

References

1. Alexandre, F., Marqués, R., Paulino, H.: On the support of task-parallel algorithmic skeletons for multi-GPU computing. In: Symposium on Applied Computing, SAC 2014, Gyeongju, Republic of Korea, 24–28 March 2014, pp. 880–885. ACM (2014)
2. Apache Software Foundation.: Apache Storm. https://storm.apache.org. Accessed Feb 2018
3. Augonnet, C., Thibault, S., Namyst, R., Wacrenier, P.-A.: STARPU: a unified platform for task scheduling on heterogeneous multicore architectures. In: Sips, H., Epema, D., Lin, H.-X. (eds.) Euro-Par 2009. LNCS, vol. 5704, pp. 863–874. Springer, Heidelberg (2009). https://doi.org/10.1007/978-3-642-03869-3_80
4. Carbone, P., Katsifodimos, A., Ewen, S., Markl, V., Haridi, S., Tzoumas, K.: Apache flink™: stream and batch processing in a single engine. IEEE Data Eng. Bull. **38**(4), 28–38 (2015)
5. Dokulil, J., Bajrovic, E., Benkner, S., Sandrieser, M., Bachmayer, B.: HyPHI - task based hybrid execution C++ library for the Intel Xeon Phi coprocessor. In: 2013 42nd International Conference on Parallel Processing (ICPP), pp. 280–289 (2013)
6. Dongarra, J.J., et al.: HPC programming on Intel many-integrated-core hardware with MAGMA port to Xeon Phi. Sci. Program. **2015**, 502593:1–502593:11 (2015)
7. Huynh, H.P., Hagiescu, A., Wong, W., Goh, R.S.M.: Scalable framework for mapping streaming applications onto multi-GPU systems. In: 17th Symposium on Principles and Practice of Parallel Programming, PPOPP 2012, pp. 1–10. ACM (2012)
8. Intel® Corporation: Manycore Platform Software Stack (Intel® MPSS). https://software.intel.com/en-us/articles/intel-manycore-platform-software-stack-mpss. Accessed Feb 2018
9. Intel® Corporation: Intel® Threading Building Blocks – tutorial: Flow graph. https://www.threadingbuildingblocks.org/tutorial-intel-tbb-flow-graph. Accessed Feb 2018
10. Marques, R., Paulino, H., Alexandre, F., Medeiros, P.D.: Algorithmic skeleton framework for the orchestration of GPU computations. In: Wolf, F., Mohr, B., an Mey, D. (eds.) Euro-Par 2013. LNCS, vol. 8097, pp. 874–885. Springer, Heidelberg (2013). https://doi.org/10.1007/978-3-642-40047-6_86
11. Pinnecke, M., Broneske, D., Saake, G.: Toward GPU accelerated data stream processing. In: Proceedings of the 27th GI-Workshop Grundlagen von Datenbanken, vol. 1366, pp. 78–83. CEUR-WS.org (2015)
12. Reinders, J.: Intel Threading Building Blocks, 1st edn. O'Reilly & Associates Inc., Sebastopol (2007)
13. Sato, S., Iwasaki, H.: A skeletal parallel framework with fusion optimizer for GPGPU programming. In: Hu, Z. (ed.) APLAS 2009. LNCS, vol. 5904, pp. 79–94. Springer, Heidelberg (2009). https://doi.org/10.1007/978-3-642-10672-9_8
14. Soldado, F., Alexandre, F., Paulino, H.: Execution of compound multi-kernel opencl computations in multi-CPU/multi-GPU environments. Concurr. Comput.: Pract. Exp. **28**(3), 768–787 (2016)
15. Udupa, A., Govindarajan, R., Thazhuthaveetil, M.J.: Software pipelined execution of stream programs on GPUs. In: The Seventh International Symposium on Code Generation and Optimization, CGO 2009, pp. 200–209. IEEE Computer Society (2009)
16. Verner, U., Schuster, A., Silberstein, M., Mendelson, A.: Scheduling processing of real-time data streams on heterogeneous multi-GPU systems. In: The 5th Annual International Systems and Storage Conference, SYSTOR 2012, p. 7. ACM (2012)

17. Zaharia, M., Das, T., Li, H., Hunter, T., Shenker, S., Stoica, I.: Discretized streams: fault-tolerant streaming computation at scale. In: ACM SIGOPS 24th Symposium on Operating Systems Principles, SOSP 2013, pp. 423–438. ACM (2013)
18. Zhang, Y., Mueller, F.: GStream: a general-purpose data streaming framework on GPU clusters. In: International Conference on Parallel Processing, ICPP 2011, pp. 245–254. IEEE Computer Society (2011)

Tile Low-Rank GEMM Using Batched Operations on GPUs

Ali Charara$^{(\boxtimes)}$ (iD), David Keyes (iD),
and Hatem Ltaief (iD)

Extreme Computing Research Center, Division of Computer, Electrical,
and Mathematical Sciences and Engineering, King Abdullah University of Science
and Technology, Thuwal Jeddah 23955, Kingdom of Saudi Arabia
{Ali.Charara,David.Keyes,Hatem.Ltaief}@kaust.edu.sa

Abstract. Dense General Matrix-Matrix (GEMM) multiplication is a core operation of the Basic Linear Algebra Subroutines (BLAS) library, and therefore, often resides at the bottom of the traditional software stack for many scientific applications. In fact, chip manufacturers give a special attention to the GEMM kernel implementation since this is exactly where most of the high-performance software libraries extract hardware performance. With the emergence of big data applications involving large data-sparse, hierarchically low-rank matrices, the off-diagonal tiles can be compressed to reduce the algorithmic complexity and the memory footprint. The resulting tile low-rank (TLR) data format is composed of small data structures, which retain the most significant information for each tile. However, to operate on low-rank tiles, a new GEMM operation and its corresponding API have to be designed on GPUs so that the data sparsity structure of the matrix can be exploited while leveraging the underlying TLR compression format. The main idea consists of aggregating all operations into a single kernel launch to compensate for their low arithmetic intensities and to mitigate the data transfer overhead on GPUs. The new TLR-GEMM kernel outperforms the cuBLAS dense batched GEMM by more than an order of magnitude and creates new opportunities for TLR advanced algorithms.

Keywords: Hierarchical low-rank matrix computations
Matrix multiplication - GEMM · High performance computing
GPU Computing · KBLAS

1 Introduction

With the convergence of the third and fourth paradigms (i.e., simulation and big data), large-scale scientific applications, such as climate/weather forecasting [31], require a profound redesign to reduce the memory footprint as well as the overall algorithmic complexity. When considering multi-dimensional problems, with a large number of unknowns, n, the resulting covariance matrix may

© Springer International Publishing AG, part of Springer Nature 2018
M. Aldinucci et al. (Eds.): Euro-Par 2018, LNCS 11014, pp. 811–825, 2018.
https://doi.org/10.1007/978-3-319-96983-1_57

render its structure fully dense. To overcome the curse of dimensionality without violating the fidelity of the physical model, application developers rely on approximation methods, which drastically reduce the constraints on the memory footprint and the algorithmic complexity. For instance, hierarchical matrices or $\mathscr{H}$-matrices have been recently resurrected for high-performance computing [29,32] as a potential algorithmic solution to tackle the aforementioned challenge. Because of their inherent recursive formulations, they are not amenable to massively parallel hardware systems such as GPUs.

We have designed, investigated, and implemented, on x86 shared-memory systems within the HiCMA library, an approximation method that exploits the natural data sparsity of the off-diagonal tiles while exposing parallelism to the fore [8]. Based on the tile low-rank (TLR) data format, the off-diagonal tiles of a dense covariance matrix are compressed up to a specific accuracy threshold, without compromising the model fidelity. The resulting data structure, much smaller than the original dense tiles, represents the new building blocks to pursue the matrix computations. Since main memory is a scarce resource on GPUs, TLR should enable solving even larger GPU-resident problems and eventually fall back to out-of-core algorithms. Although this TLR scenario may look utterly GPU friendly and more compliant, there are still some lingering performance bottlenecks. Indeed, decomposing an off-diagonal low-rank matrix problem into tasks may lead to a computational mismatch between the granularity of the task and the computational power of the underlying hardware. In particular, heavily multi-threaded accelerators such as NVIDIA GPUs need to maintain high occupancy and would require developers to move away from the current model, where tasks occupy all hardware computing elements, and, instead, simultaneously execute multiple smaller tasks, each spanning across a subset of hardware resources. This mode of operation, called *batched execution* [19], executes many smaller operations in parallel to make efficient use of the hardware and its instruction-level parallelism. To our knowledge, this work introduces the first TLR general matrix-matrix multiplication (TLR-GEMM) operating on data sparse matrix structures using GPU hardware accelerators. Our research contribution lies at the intersection of two concurrent and independent efforts happening in the scientific community: $\mathscr{H}$-matrix and batched operations for BLAS/LAPACK. Our TLR-GEMM leverages the current batched execution kernels in BLAS and LAPACK to support the matrix-matrix multiplication operation, which is perhaps one of the most important operations for high-performance numerical libraries, in TLR data format. In this paper, we focus on compressing data-sparse matrices and operating on them with uniform rank sub-blocks. Non-uniform rank compression and operation is a subject under investigation and beyond the scope of this paper. Our TLR-GEMM implementation is available in the open source KBLAS library maintained at https://github.com/ecrc/kblas-gpu.

The remainder of the paper is organized as follows: Sect. 2 presents related work and details our research contributions; Sect. 3 recalls the batched linear algebra community effort and gives a general overview of the hierarchical low-rank matrix approximation; Sect. 4 introduces the new TLR-GEMM and its variants; the implementation details of the various TLR–GEMM kernels are given in Sect. 5; Sect. 6 assesses the accuracy and performance of TLR–GEMM on the latest NVIDIA GPU hardware generation and compares it to the state-of-the-art high-performance batched dense GEMM, as implemented in [2]; we conclude in Sect. 7.

2   Related Work

The general matrix-matrix multiplication (GEMM) operation is the primitive kernel for a large spectrum of scientific applications and numerical libraries. GEMM has been optimized on various hardware vendors for large matrix sizes and constitutes the basic reference for Level-3 BLAS [18] operations and their usage in dense linear algebra algorithms. With the need to solve multicomponent partial differential equations, the resulting sparse matrix may have a dense block structure. The block size is relatively small and corresponds to the number of degrees of freedom per mesh element. The blocks are usually stored in a compressed block column/row data format. Matrix computations are then performed on these independent blocks by means of batched operations. For instance, batched dense matrix-vector multiplication is employed in sparse iterative solvers for reservoir simulations [6], while batched dense LAPACK factorizations [15] are required in sparse direct solvers for the Poisson equation using cyclic reduction [17]. Moreover, with the emergence of artificial intelligence, batched dense GEMM of even smaller sizes are needed in tensor contractions [4,5,33] and in deep learning frameworks [3,27,28]. To facilitate the adoption of all these efforts, a new standard has been proposed to homogenize the various batched API [19]. While the literature is rich in leveraging batched executions for dense and sparse linear algebra operations on x86 and hardware accelerators [4–6,14,15,19], this trend has faced challenges and has not penetrated data-sparse applications yet, involving large hierarchically low-rank matrices (i.e., $\mathscr{H}$-matrices). In fact, there are three points to consider when designing batched operations for $\mathscr{H}$-matrices. First, there should be an efficient batched compression operation for $\mathscr{H}$-matrices on x86 and on hardware accelerators. Second, the inherent recursive formulation of $\mathscr{H}$-matrix resulting from nested dissections should be replaced, since it is not compliant with batched operations. Third, strong support is eventually required to handle batched matrix operations on the data-sparse compressed format, such as $\mathscr{H}^2$, Hierarchically Semi-Separable representation (HSS), and the Hierarchical Off-Diagonal Low-Rank (HODLR) matrix. More recently, a block/tile low-rank (TLR) compressed format has been introduced on x86 [8,11], which further exposes parallelism by flattening the recursion trees. The TLR data format may engender new opportunities and challenges for batched matrix compression and operation kernels on advanced SIMD architectures. Moreover, an effective implementation of the randomized SVD [26] for $\mathscr{H}^2$ matrix compression has been ported to hardware accelerators [14]. The aforementioned three bottlenecks may now be relieved to deploy TLR matrix computations on GPUs.

3   Background

Batched Dense Linear Algebra. GPUs are massively parallel devices optimized for high SIMD throughput. Numerical kernels with low arithmetic intensity may still take advantage of the high memory bandwidth, provided they operate on large data structures to saturate the bus bandwidth. When operating on relatively small workloads on GPUs, the GPU overheads are twofold: (1) the overhead of moving the data from the CPU to the GPU memory through the thin PCIe pipe may be not worthwhile, and (2) the overhead of launching the kernels is not compensated by the low computation complexity. High-performance frameworks for batched operations [1,2,15] attempt to overcome both challenges by stitching together multiple operations occurring on independent data structures. This batched mode of execution increases hardware occupancy to attain higher sustained peak bandwidth while launching a single kernel to remove the kernel launch overheads all together. Figure 1(a) sketches batched operations of small dense GEMM operations $C + = A \times B$. Following the same community effort for the legacy BLAS, a community call for standardizing the batched API [19] has been initiated, gathering hardware vendors and researchers. This standardization effort enhances software development productivity, while the batched API gains maturity in the scientific community.

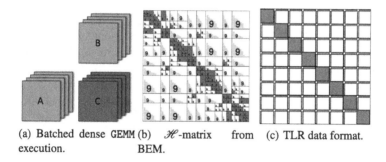

(a) Batched dense GEMM execution.   (b) $\mathcal{H}$-matrix from BEM.   (c) TLR data format.

Fig. 1. Consolidating batched operations and $\mathcal{H}$-matrix through TLR data format. (Color figure online)

Hierarchical Low-Rank Matrix Computations. The hierarchically low-rank matrix, or $\mathcal{H}$-matrix [21,23–25,34] is a low-rank block approximation of a dense (sub)matrix, whose off-diagonal blocks may be each represented by an outer product of rectangular bases obtained from compression, e.g., via orthogonal transformations with singular value decomposition. An $\mathcal{H}$-matrix captures the most significant singular values and their corresponding singular vectors up to an application-dependent accuracy threshold for each block. Figure 1(b) highlights the structure of an $\mathcal{H}$-matrix resulting from a boundary element method. Each off-diagonal green block has been approximated to a similar rank up to 9. The red blocks are dense blocks and are mostly located around the diagonal structure of the matrix. This data sparse structure may be exposed by performing nested dissection after proper reordering and partitioning. This recursive formulation allows traversing low-rank off-diagonal blocks and compressing them using an adequate data storage format such as $\mathscr{H}$ [29], Hierarchical Off-Diagonal Low-Rank (HODLR) [12], $\mathscr{H}$ [22], Hierarchically Semi-Separable representation (HSS) [10,32], and $\mathscr{H}^2$ [13]. All these data compression formats belong to the family of $\mathscr{H}$-matrices and can be differentiated by the type of their bases i.e., nested (HSS and $\mathscr{H}^2$) or non-nested ($\mathscr{H}$ and HODLR), in addition to the type of admissibility conditions, i.e., strong ($\mathscr{H}$ and $\mathscr{H}^2$) or weak (HODLR and HSS). Each of these compression data formats exhibits different algorithmic complexities and memory footprint theoretical upper-bounds. The tile low-rank (TLR) [8,11] data format is another case of the $\mathscr{H}$ data format with non-nested bases and strong admissibility conditions. The matrix is logically split into tiles, similar to the tile algorithms from the PLASMA library [7]. The off-diagonal tiles may then be compressed using the rank-revealing QR once the whole dense matrix has been generated [11] or *on-the-fly* using the randomized singular value decomposition [26] while performing the matrix computations [8]. Figure 1(c) shows an illustration of such a TLR matrix composed of an 8 × 8 logical tile. Owing to its simplicity, TLR permits flattening the inherent recursive formulation. Although TLR may not provide such optimal theoretical bounds as for the nested-basis data formats, regarding algorithmic complexities and memory footprint, it is very amenable to advanced performance implementations and optimizations.

The main objective of this paper is to consolidate the three messages conveyed by the sketches of Fig. 1, i.e., batched operations (including matrix compression and computations), $\mathscr{H}$-matrix applications and TLR data format. This consolidation is the crux of the TLR–GEMM implementation on GPUs.

4   Design of Tile Low-Rank GEMM Kernels

This section describes the design of the TLR–GEMM kernel and identifies its variants using a bottom-up approach: from the single GEMM kernel operating on low-rank data format to the corresponding batched operations, and then all the way up to the actual TLR–GEMM driver.

Low-Rank Data Format. Low-rank approximation consists of compressing a dense matrix X of dimensions m-rows and n-columns and representing it as the product of two tall and skinny matrices, such that $X = X_u \times X_v^T$, with X_u and X_v of dimensions (m-rows, k-columns) and (n-rows, k-columns), respectively, and k the rank of X. The choice for the compression algorithms is typically Rank-Revealing QR (RRQR), adaptive cross-approximation (ACA), or (randomized) singular value decomposition (SVD), etc. The randomized Jacobi-based SVD [26] maps well on SIMD architectures because it does not involve pivoting nor element sweeping, as in the RRQR and ACA methods, respectively. It is perhaps the most optimized compression algorithm on GPUs, as implemented in [14].

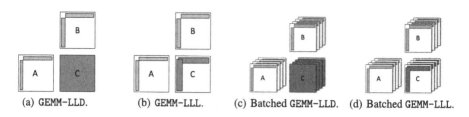

| (a) GEMM-LLD. | (b) GEMM-LLL. | (c) Batched GEMM-LLD. | (d) Batched GEMM-LLL. |

Fig. 2. Illustrating single and batched low-rank GEMM variants.

Low-Rank GEMM Variants. We identify four possible variants, based on the input data format of the involved matrices A, B, and C. We use the following notation: GEMM$-T_A T_B T_C$ is the GEMM kernel for a given input type (Dense or Low-rank) for the matrices A, B, and C. The variants are as follows: (1) either of A or B in low-rank format, C in dense format: GEMM-DLD, or GEMM-LDD, (2) either of A or B in low-rank format, C in low-rank format: GEMM-DLL, or GEMM-LDL, (3) A and B in low-rank format, C in dense format: GEMM-LLD, as illustrated in Fig. 2(a), and, (4) A, B and C in low-rank format: GEMM-LLL, as illustrated in Fig. 2(b). We focus solely on the last two variants in this paper, i.e., GEMM-LLD and GEMM-LLL, since they are the bases for supporting the Schur complement calculation and for matrix factorization, in the context of sparse direct solvers [11] and data-sparse matrix solvers [8], respectively. In fact, the other possible variants, i.e., when both A and B are in dense format and C in dense (GEMM-DDD) or in low-rank format (GEMM-DDL), are not considered because the first is the actual legacy GEMM operation, and the second is more expensive than regular GEMM in terms of flops.

Batched Low-Rank GEMM. We can then derive the batched low-rank GEMM routines from their corresponding single low-rank GEMM routines. The new batched low-rank GEMM kernels are now defined as single kernels, i.e., Batched-GEMM-LLD and Batched-GEMM-LLL, which simultaneously execute independent GEMM-LLD and GEMM-LLL operations, as demonstrated in Fig. 2(c) and (d), respectively. This batched kernel is used as a building block for the main driver performing the TLR-GEMM on large TLR matrices, as described in the following paragraph.

TLR-GEMM (driver). In the driver of the TLR-GEMM operation, the data-sparse matrices A, B, and C are subdivided into a grid of tiles, where each tile may individually be compressed into low-rank data form, as illustrated in Fig. 3. Indeed, Fig. 3(a) and (b) represent the TLR-GEMM operation, when T_C is tile dense or tile low-rank, respectively. In a standard GEMM operation, each tile of the matrix C is updated by an inner-product composed of a sequence of pair-wise GEMM operations of its corresponding row of tiles from matrix A and column of tiles from matrix B. However, when dealing with TLR data format, since the workload of each low-rank tile is too small to saturate a modern GPU with sufficient work, concurrent processing of these independent low-rank tiles inner-products is necessary to increase the GPU occupancy. To overcome this challenge, we need to process these inner-product low-rank GEMM calls in a batched mode.

However, available batched GEMM routines assume the batched operation is a primitive CUDA kernel rather than a sequence of calls; thus, we re-formulate the set of inner-products into a set of successive outer-products by means of loop re-ordering. Each outer-product is a call to batched GEMM-LLD or GEMM-LLL routine which updates all tiles of matrix C in parallel. This process is repeated nt times, nt being the number of tiles in a row of matrix A or a column of matrix B, as illustrated in Fig. 3 for both variants of TLR-GEMM.

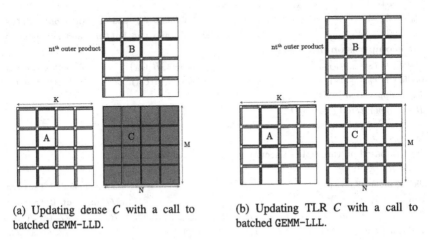

(a) Updating dense C with a call to batched GEMM-LLD.

(b) Updating TLR C with a call to batched GEMM-LLL.

Fig. 3. Processing TLR-GEMM as a series of nt outer-products using batched GEMM-LLD or GEMM-LLL kernels.

5   Implementation Details

Update Dense C: GEMM-LLD. This operation is performed as a sequence of three small GEMM calls. Assuming matrices C and A are of m-rows, C and B of n-columns, A and B of k-columns and k-rows respectively, and A and B are of ranks r_a, and r_b, respectively, the operation $C = \alpha A \times B + \beta C$ is equivalent to $C = \alpha A_u \times A_v^T \times B_u \times B_v^T + \beta C$.

Update Low-Rank C: GEMM-LLL. We describe the second variant of the low-rank GEMM operation when updating C in low-rank format, as outlined in the corresponding Algorithm 1. In fact, this algorithm corresponds to the randomized SVD, as described in [26]. We assume the non-transpose case for both matrices A and B. The matrix-matrix multiplication $C = \alpha A \times B + \beta C$ involves two sub-stages, where matrices A, B, and C are represented by their low-rank format $(A_u, A_v), (B_u, B_v)$, and (C_u, C_v), respectively. The first stage consists of the multiplication of low-rank matrices A and B, as shown in steps $2 - 3$ of Algorithm 1. The second stage highlights the final addition of the intermediate matrix with the low-rank matrix C, as demonstrated in steps $4 - 6$. This second stage produces low-rank $\dot{C} = \dot{C}_u \times \dot{C}_v$ with bloated rank $\dot{r}_c$. As such,

---

Algorithm 1. GEMM-LLL$(m, n, k, \alpha, A_u, A_v, r_a, B_u, B_v, r_b, \beta, C_u, C_v, r_c, W_a, W_b)$.

Input: A_u, A_v, B_u, B_v, C_u, and C_v are $m \times r_a$, $k \times r_a$, $k \times r_b$, $n \times r_b$, $m \times r_c$, and $n \times r_c$ matrices, respectively. W_a and W_b are workspaces of size $r_a \times r_b$ and $r_a \times n$ respectively.

1 Setup work-space buffer.;
2 //**Multiply** A and B;
3 GEMM$(Trans, noTrans, r_a, r_b, k, \alpha, A_v, B_u, 0, W_a)$: $W_a \leftarrow \alpha A_v^T \times B_u$;
4 GEMM$(noTrans, Trans, r_a, n, r_b, 1, W_a, B_v, 0, W_b)$: $W_b \leftarrow W_a \times B_v^T$;
5 //**Add to** C $\dot{r}_c \leftarrow r_c + r_a$;
6 $\dot{C}_u \leftarrow C_u | A_u$;   // Concat C_u and A_u into one buffer
7 $\dot{C}_v \leftarrow \beta(C_v | W_b)$;   // Concat C_v and W_b into one buffer, and scale by β
8 //**Recompression of** $\dot{C}_u$ and $\dot{C}_v$;
9 GEQRF$(m, \dot{r}_c, \dot{C}_u, \tau_u)$: $\ddot{C}_u \leftarrow QR(\dot{C}_u)$;   // factorize $\dot{C}_u$
10 GEQRF$(n, \dot{r}_c, \dot{C}_v, \tau_v)$: $\ddot{C}_v \leftarrow QR(\dot{C}_v)$;   // factorize $\dot{C}_v$
11 $R_u = $ *upper triangular of* $\ddot{C}_u$;
12 $R_v = $ *upper triangular of* $\ddot{C}_v$;
13 GEMM$(noTrans, Trans, \dot{r}_c, \dot{r}_c, \dot{r}_c, 1, R_u, R_v, 0, R)$: $R = R_u \times R_v^T$;
14 GESVD$(\dot{r}_c, \dot{r}_c, R, S, \dot{R}_u, \dot{R}_v)$;
15 Pick $\ddot{r}_c$ based on threshold of accuracy or maximum rank.;
16 Scale $\dot{R}_v$ by S;
17 ORGQR$(m, \dot{r}_c, \ddot{C}_u, \tau_u)$;   // extract Q factors
18 ORGQR$(n, \dot{r}_c, \ddot{C}_v, \tau_v)$;   // extract Q factors
19 GEMM$(noTrans, noTrans, m, \ddot{r}_c, \dot{r}_c, 1, \ddot{C}_u, \dot{R}_u, 0, C_u)$: $C_u = \dot{C}_u \times \ddot{R}_u$;   // final C_u
20 GEMM$(noTrans, noTrans, n, \ddot{r}_c, \dot{r}_c, 1, \ddot{C}_v, \dot{R}_v, 0, C_v)$: $C_v = \dot{C}_v \times \ddot{R}_v$;   // final C_v
21 **return**;

---

low-rank matrix addition, as described by Grasedyck [20], requires a process of recompression based on QR factorization to restore a minimal rank for the product matrix as well as the orthogonality of its components. This recompression is achieved by reforming the product $\dot{C}_u \times \dot{C}_v$ in terms of its SVD representation, i.e., its singular values and their corresponding right and left singular vectors. By factorizing $\dot{C}_u = Q_u \times R_u$, and $\dot{C}_v = Q_v \times R_v$, we can then represent $\dot{C} = Q_u \times R_u \times (Q_v \times R_v)^T = Q_u \times (R_u \times R_v^T) \times Q_v^T$, as the SVD of $\dot{C}$. Recompressing the result of the tiny product $R_u \times R_v^T$ using SVD or ACA, enables restoration of the rank of $\dot{C}$ to a minimum value based on a predetermined fixed accuracy threshold or fixed rank truncation. This process of re-compression is described in steps 7–18 of Algorithm 1. The implementation of this variant leverages the randomized SVD on GPUs from [14], in the context of matrix compression for H^2 data format, to the TLR data format.

Batched Low-Rank GEMM. For batching the two GEMM-LLD and GEMM-LLL variants, the challenges are quite different. Batched GEMM-LLD is straightforward to implement on GPUs (and even on x86), due to existing fast batched GEMM implementations on small sizes [2,27]. The task is far more complex for GEMM-LLL, since the recompression involves numerical kernels (GEQRF, ORGQR and GESVD), which are not as regular as standard GEMMs, e.g., in terms of memory accesses.

The support from vendor numerical libraries for batched versions of these routines is limited with poorly performing or simply inexistent implementations. We have further leveraged the batched GEQRF and ORGQR from [14] and integrated this into the batched GEMM-LLL. For the batched GESVD on the tiny $k \times k$ matrix, there are two options. The first is again based on the randomized SVD itself, while the second uses a novel ACA implementation on GPUs. Although ACA may require an expensive element sweeping procedure, this overhead is mitigated by the small matrix size. The resulting algorithm for batched low-rank is very similar to Algorithm 1, except that each call is now performed in a batched mode of execution.

TLR-GEMM (driver). Putting all previous standard and batched kernels together, we present TLR-GEMM on GPUs. We leverage the batched low-rank GEMM and operate on TLR matrices. This modular approach allows assessing the performance of each component, while enhancing software development productivity. The algorithm for TLR-GEMM driver consists of a single loop of nt successive outer-products, each corresponding to a batched GEMM-LLD or GEMM-LLL call, as depicted in Fig. 3. Compared to a GEMM operation on matrices with non-TLR data formats (involving recursion and tree traversals), TLR proves to be a simple yet effective approach, especially when considering hardware accelerators. For the algorithmic complexity of each variant, it is obvious that TLR-GEMM based on GEMM-LLL is more expensive than the one based on GEMM-LLD, because of the recompression stage.

6   Experimental Results

The benchmarking system is a two-socket 20-core Intel Broadwell running at 2.20 GHz with 512 GB of main memory, equipped with an NVIDIA GPU Volta V100 with 16 GB of main memory and PCIe 16x. We use a data-sparse matrix kernel (i.e., Hilbert) with singular values following an exponential decay. In fact, such decay in singular values is frequently observed in many matrix kernels in covariance-based scientific applications, such as climate/weather forecasting simulations [9]. All calculations are performed in double precision arithmetics. The reported performance numbers are compared to cuBLAS batched dense GEMM. Figure 4 illustrates the singular value distribution and the numerical accuracy assessment. The singular values of the Hilbert matrix kernel exponentially decay, as seen in Fig. 4(a). Approximately the first 30 are the most significant, while the remainder are close to machine precision and can be safely ignored. Figure 4(b) demonstrates the numerical robustness of the single GEMM-LLD and GEMM-LLL kernel variants using the same Hilbert matrix operator. GEMM-LLD approaches expected accuracy for rank smaller than GEMM-LLL, due to the rounding errors introduced by the additional floating-point operations from the recompression stage. Otherwise, both variants show correctness when truncating at ranks close to the accuracy threshold shown in Fig. 4(a).

Figure 5 highlights the speedups of batched GEMM-LLD and GEMM-LLL, against cuBLAS batch dense GEMM considering various ranks and a fixed batch size of

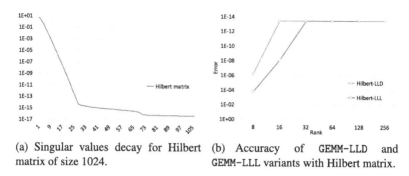

(a) Singular values decay for Hilbert matrix of size 1024.

(b) Accuracy of GEMM-LLD and GEMM-LLL variants with Hilbert matrix.

Fig. 4. Singular value distribution and accuracy assessment of the Hilbert matrix kernel.

1000. Figure 5(a) and (b) illustrate the speedups of batched GEMM-LLD with and without compression overhead, respectively. Similarly, Fig. 5(c) and (d) illustrate the speedups of batched GEMM-LLL with and without compression overhead, respectively. Obviously, compression may turn out to be an expensive operation, which may slow down the the performance of batched GEMM-LLD (Fig. 5(a)) and batched GEMM-LLL (Fig. 5(c)); however, this overhead is usually occurring once, since the compressed form of the corresponding matrices may be used repeatedly (see TLR-GEMM in Fig. 5(b) and (d)). The speedups recorded for batched GEMM-LLD are higher than those for GEMM-LLL, when comparing to the cuBLAS batch dense GEMM, because of the recompression step. While speedups are obtained for all ranks for batched GEMM-LLD (Fig. 5(b)), batched GEMM-LLL (Fig. 5(d)) records speedups only for relatively small rank sizes. Although the Hilbert matrix kernel has an exponential singular value decay, we also assess performance for larger ranks. These extra flops, although unnecessary, allow stretching of the batched kernels and observing when the crossover point occurs. For instance, in Fig. 5(b), the batched GEMM-LLD with rank 128 runs out of memory, due to the dense storage of the matrix C, while still outperforming the cuBLAS batch dense GEMM. In Fig. 5(d), the batched GEMM-LLL with rank 128 runs out of memory, due to the temporary memory space required by the recompression stage, while not being able to outperform the cuBLAS batch dense GEMM.

Figure 6 shows the speedups for batched GEMM-LLD and GEMM-LLL, with varying batch count, against cuBLAS batch dense GEMM, when using the ranks at which numerical accuracy is reached from Fig. 4(b), i.e., 16 and 32, respectively. The performance speedup increase as the batch count rises reveals how the device becomes overwhelmed due to high occupancy.

Figure 7 presents the elapsed time of TLR-GEMM based on batched GEMM-LLD, named TLR-GEMM-LLD (Fig. 7(a) and (b)), and based on batched GEMM-LLL, named TLR-GEMM-LLL (Fig. 7(c) and (d)), considering various ranks, against cuBLAS dense GEMM. TLR-GEMM-LLD (solid line plots) outperforms cuBLAS dense GEMM (double line plot) by more than an order of magnitude when A and B are already compressed, as shown in Fig. 7(a). When the matrices A and B are

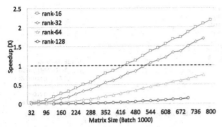

(a) GEMM-LLD: updating dense C with compression overhead.

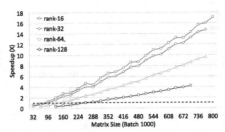

(b) GEMM-LLD: updating dense C without compression overhead.

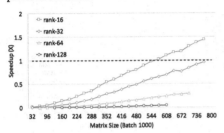

(c) GEMM-LLL: updating low-rank C with compression overhead.

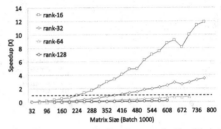

(d) GEMM-LLL: updating low-rank C without compression overhead.

Fig. 5. Speedups of batched GEMM-LLD and GEMM-LLL against batched dense cuBLAS GEMM, with batch size 1000.

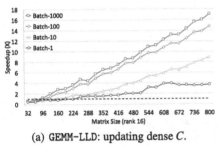

(a) GEMM-LLD: updating dense C.

(b) GEMM-LLL: updating low-rank C.

Fig. 6. Speedups of batched GEMM-LLD and GEMM-LLL against batched dense cuBLAS GEMM, with varying batch count, while fixing ranks to 16 and 32, respectively.

not compressed, the performance speedup slightly drops to eightfold, as seen in Fig. 7(b). Indeed, the expensive compression of matrices A and B is only performed once, followed by successive outer-products, in the form of batched GEMM-LLD calls. This allows to mitigate the compression overhead, discussed earlier in the section. TLR-GEMM-LLL (solid line plots) outperforms cuBLAS dense GEMM (double line plot) by more than an order of magnitude when A and B are already compressed, as shown in Fig. 7(c). When the matrices A and B are not compressed, the performance speedup remains almost the same, since

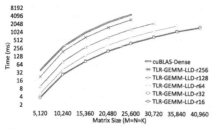

(a) TLR-GEMM-LLD with input matrices A and B already compressed.

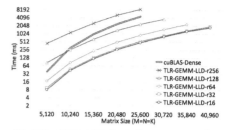

(b) TLR-GEMM-LLD including compression of input matrices A and B.

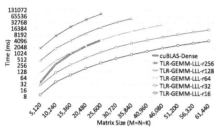

(c) TLR-GEMM-LLL with matrices A, B and C already compressed.

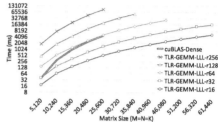

(d) TLR-GEMM-LLL including compression of matrices A, B and C.

Fig. 7. Elapsed time of TLR-GEMM-LLD and TLR-GEMM-LLL with various ranks.

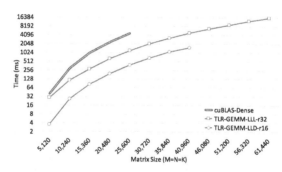

Fig. 8. Elapsed time of TLR-GEMM-LLD and TLR-GEMM-LLL with rank 16 and 32, respectively, with tile size 1024, compared to elapsed time of cuBLAS dense GEMM.

the (re)compression is the most time consuming part of the batched GEMM-LLL operations (Fig. 7(d)).

Figure 8 highlights the performance enhancements when using the Hilbert matrix kernel to perform TLR-GEMM with appropriate ranks for GEMM-LLD and GEMM-LLL, 16 and 32, respectively. Although the number of floating-point operations varies, the objective is to achieve the expected numerical accuracy. TLR-GEMM-LLD and TLR-GEMM-LLL kernels (solid line plots) score a speedup of more than an order of magnitude and fourfold, respectively, against cuBLAS dense GEMM (double line plot).

7   Conclusions and Future Work

This paper presents a novel batched tile low-rank (TLR) GEMM kernel on GPUs, which is a core operation of large-scale data sparse applications. Results demonstrate the numerical robustness and manifold performance speedups against cuBLAS batched dense GEMM on the latest NVIDIA V100 GPU generation. This work represents a pathfinder toward enabling advanced hierarchical matrix computations on GPUs. Moreover, owing to its simplicity and modularity, the TLR data format may facilitate the port to multiple GPUs of batched low-rank matrix operations. Future work includes supporting non-uniform ranks for compression and operations to further reduce the memory footprint and flop count cost, in addition to supporting the other BLAS routines. We would like also to integrate the TLR compression and the TLR-GEMM operation in the Multi-Object Adaptive Optics application [30] in the context of computational astronomy and assess its real-time performance impact.

Data Availability Statement and Acknowledgments. The datasets and code generated during and/or analysed during the current study are available in the figshare repository: https://doi.org/10.6084/m9.figshare.6387623 [16]. We would like to acknowledge Paris Observatory (LESIA, France) for giving us remote access to their Volta-based system, sponsored through a grant from project #671662 (Green Flash), funded by European Commission under program H2020-EU.1.2.2 coordinated in H2020-FETHPC-2014.

References

1. Matrix Algebra on GPU and Multicore Architectures. Innovative Computing Laboratory, University of Tennessee. http://icl.cs.utk.edu/magma/
2. The NVIDIA CUDA Basic Linear Algebra Subroutines (CUBLAS). http://developer.nvidia.com/cublas
3. Abadi, M., Agarwal, A., Barham, P., Brevdo, E., et al.: TensorFlow: large-scale machine learning on heterogeneous distributed systems. arXiv preprint arXiv:1603.04467 (2016)
4. Abdelfattah, A., et al.: High-performance tensor contractions for GPUs. Procedia Comput. Sci. **80**, 108–118 (2016). International Conference on Computational Science 2016, ICCS 2016, San Diego, California, USA, 6–8 June 2016
5. Abdelfattah, A., Haidar, A., Tomov, S., Dongarra, J.: Performance, design, and autotuning of batched GEMM for GPUs. In: Kunkel, J.M., Balaji, P., Dongarra, J. (eds.) ISC High Performance 2016. LNCS, vol. 9697, pp. 21–38. Springer, Cham (2016). https://doi.org/10.1007/978-3-319-41321-1_2
6. Abdelfattah, A., Ltaief, H., Keyes, D.E., Dongarra, J.J.: Performance optimization of sparse matrix-vector multiplication for multi-component PDE-based applications using GPUs. Concurr. Comput.: Pract. Exp. **28**(12), 3447–3465 (2016)
7. Agullo, E., et al.: Numerical linear algebra on emerging architectures: the PLASMA and MAGMA projects. J. Phys: Conf. Ser. **180**(1), 012037 (2009)
8. Akbudak, K., Ltaief, H., Mikhalev, A., Keyes, D.: Tile low rank cholesky factorization for climate/weather modeling applications on manycore architectures. In: Kunkel, J.M., Yokota, R., Balaji, P., Keyes, D. (eds.) ISC 2017. LNCS, vol. 10266, pp. 22–40. Springer, Cham (2017). https://doi.org/10.1007/978-3-319-58667-0_2

9. Akbudak, K., Ltaief, H., Mikhalev, A., Charara, A., Keyes, D.: Exploiting data sparsity for large-scale matrix computations. In: Aldinucci, M., et al. (eds.) Euro-Par 2018. LNCS, vol. 11014, pp. xx–yy. Springer, Cham (2018)
10. Ambikasaran, S., Darve, E.: An $\mathcal{O}(N \log N)$ fast direct solver for partial hierarchically semiseparable matrices. J. Sci. Comput. **57**(3), 477–501 (2013)
11. Amestoy, P.R., Ashcraft, C., Boiteau, O., Buttari, A., L'Excellent, J.Y., Weisbecker, C.: Improving multifrontal methods by means of block low-rank representations. SIAM J. Sci. Comput. **37**(3), A1451–A1474 (2015). https://doi.org/10.1137/120903476
12. Aminfar, A., Darve, E.: A fast sparse solver for Finite-Element matrices. arXiv:1403.5337 [cs.NA], pp. 1–25 (2014)
13. Börm, S.: Efficient numerical methods for non-local operators: $\mathcal{H}^2$-Matrix compression, algorithms and analysis. EMS Tracts in Mathematics, vol. 14. European Mathematical Society (2010)
14. Boukaram, W.H., Turkiyyah, G., Ltaief, H., Keyes, D.E.: Batched QR and SVD algorithms on GPUs with applications in hierarchical matrix compression. Parallel Comput. **74**, 19–33 (2017)
15. Charara, A., Keyes, D., Ltaief, H.: Batched triangular dense linear algebra kernels for very small matrix sizes on GPUs. ACM Trans. Math. Softw. (2017, submitted). (under review, http://hdl.handle.net/10754/622975)
16. Charara, A., Keyes, D., Ltaief, H.: Software artifact for Euro-Par 2018: Tile Low-Rank GEMM Using Batched Operations on GPUs. figshare. Code. (2018). https://doi.org/10.6084/m9.figshare.6387623
17. Chávez, G., Turkiyyah, G., Zampini, S., Ltaief, H., Keyes, D.: Accelerated cyclic reduction: a distributed-memory fast solver for structured linear systems. Parallel Comput. **74**, 65–83 (2017)
18. Dongarra, J., Du Croz, J., Hammarling, S., Hanson, R.J.: An extended set of Fortran basic linear algebra subprograms. ACM Trans. Math. Softw. **14**, 1–17 (1988)
19. Dongarra, J., et al.: A proposed API for batched basic linear algebra subprograms. Mims preprint, University of Manchester (2016). http://eprints.maths.manchester.ac.uk/id/eprint/2464
20. Grasedyck, L., Hackbusch, W.: Construction and arithmetics of $\mathcal{H}$-matrices. Computing **70**(4), 295–334 (2003). https://doi.org/10.1007/s00607-003-0019-1
21. Hackbusch, W.: A sparse matrix arithmetic based on $\mathcal{H}$-matrices. part i: introduction to $\mathcal{H}$-matrices. Computing **62**(2), 89–108 (1999). https://doi.org/10.1007/s006070050015
22. Hackbusch, W.: Hierarchical Matrices: Algorithms and Analysis. Springer Series in Computational Mathematics, vol. 49. Springer, Heidelberg (2015). https://doi.org/10.1007/978-3-662-47324-5
23. Hackbusch, W., Börm, S.: Data-sparse approximation by adaptive $\mathcal{H}^2$-matrices. Computing **69**(1), 1–35 (2002). https://doi.org/10.1007/s00607-002-1450-4
24. Hackbusch, W., Börm, S., Grasedyck, L.: HLib 1.4. Max-Planck-Institut, Leipzig (2012)
25. Hackbusch, W., Khoromskij, B., Sauter, S.: On $\mathcal{H}^2$-matrices. In: Bungartz, H.J., Hoppe, R.H.W., Zenger, C. (eds.) Lectures on Applied Mathematics, pp. 9–29. Springer, Heidelberg (2000). https://doi.org/10.1007/978-3-642-59709-1_2
26. Halko, N., Martinsson, P.G., Tropp, J.A.: Finding structure with randomness: probabilistic algorithms for constructing approximate matrix decompositions. SIAM Rev. **53**(2), 217–288 (2011). https://doi.org/10.1137/090771806

27. Heinecke, A., Henry, G., Hutchinson, M., Pabst, H.: LIBXSMM: accelerating small matrix multiplications by runtime code generation. In: 0001, J.W., Pancake, C.M. (eds.) Proceedings of the International Conference for High Performance Computing, Networking, Storage and Analysis, SC 2016, Salt Lake City, UT, USA, 13–18 November 2016, p. 84. ACM (2016)

28. Kim, K., et al.: Designing vector-friendly compact BLAS and LAPACK kernels. In: Proceedings of the International Conference for High Performance Computing, Networking, Storage and Analysis, SC 2017, pp. 55:1–55:12. ACM, New York (2017). https://doi.org/10.1145/3126908.3126941

29. Kriemann, R.: LU factorization on many-core systems. Comput. Vis. Sci. **16**(3), 105–117 (2013). https://doi.org/10.1007/s00791-014-0226-7

30. Ltaief, H., et al.: Real-time massively distributed multi-object adaptive optics simulations for the european extremely large telescope. In: 2018 IEEE International Parallel and Distributed Processing Symposium (IPDPS), accepted, May 2018

31. North, G.R., Wang, J., Genton, M.G.: Correlation models for temperature fields. J. Clim. **24**, 5850–5862 (2011)

32. Rouet, F.H., Li, X.S., Ghysels, P., Napov, A.: A distributed-memory package for dense hierarchically semi-separable matrix computations using randomization. ACM Trans. Math. Softw. **42**(4), 27:1–27:35 (2016)

33. Shi, Y., Niranjan, U.N., Anandkumar, A., Cecka, C.: Tensor contractions with extended BLAS kernels on CPU and GPU. In: HiPC, pp. 193–202. IEEE Computer Society (2016)

34. Tyrtyshnikov, E.: Mosaic-skeleton approximations. Calcolo **33**(1), 47–57 (1996)

Correction to: Early Termination of Failed HPC Jobs Through Machine and Deep Learning

Michał Zasadziński, Victor Muntés-Mulero, Marc Solé,
David Carrera, and Thomas Ludwig

Correction to:
**Chapter "Early Termination of Failed HPC Jobs Through
Machine and Deep Learning" in: M. Aldinucci et al. (Eds.):**
Euro-Par 2018: Parallel Processing, **LNCS 11014,**
https://doi.org/10.1007/978-3-319-96983-1_12

In the original version of the paper, in page 168, section 4.1, the sentence starting "(…) that has 10% of jobs (samples), and the test set with 10% of jobs. (…)" was inadvertently published with an error. It has been corrected to "(…) that has 10% of jobs (samples), and the test set with 20% of jobs. (…)".

The updated online version of this chapter can be found at
https://doi.org/10.1007/978-3-319-96983-1_12

Author Index

Printed in the United States
By Bookmasters